# The Eerdmans Critical Commentary

David Noel Freedman, *General Editor*

Astrid B. Beck, *Associate Editor*

The Eerdmans Critical Commentary offers the best of contemporary Old and New Testament scholarship, seeking to give modern readers clear insight into the biblical text, including its background, its interpretation, and its application.

Contributors to the ECC series are among the foremost authorities in biblical scholarship worldwide. Representing a broad range of confessional backgrounds, authors are charged to remain sensitive to the original meaning of the text and to bring alive its relevance for today. Each volume includes the author's own translation, critical notes, and commentary on literary, historical, cultural, and theological aspects of the text.

Accessible to serious general readers and scholars alike, these commentaries reflect the contributions of recent textual, philological, literary, historical, and archaeological inquiry, benefiting as well from newer methodological approaches. ECC volumes are "critical" in terms of their detailed, systematic explanation of the biblical text. Although exposition is based on the original and cognate languages, English translations provide complete access to the discussion and interpretation of these primary sources.

# *The First and Second Letters to* TIMOTHY

*A New Translation*
*with*
*Notes and Commentary*

JEROME D. QUINN
WILLIAM C. WACKER

WILLIAM B. EERDMANS PUBLISHING COMPANY
GRAND RAPIDS, MICHIGAN / CAMBRIDGE, U.K.

NIHIL OBSTAT:
Rev. Frederick J. Campbell
March 5, 1995

IMPRIMATUR:
†John R. Roach, D.D.
March 8, 1995

The *Imprimatur* states simply that the material contained in a book has been read, and that nothing contrary to Catholic doctrinal or moral teaching has been found in it.


255 Jefferson Ave. S.E., Grand Rapids, Michigan 49503 /
P.O. Box 163, Cambridge CB3 9PU U.K.


Printed in the United States of America

05 04 03 02 01 00 7 6 5 4 3 2 1

**Library of Congress Cataloging-in-Publication Data**

ISBN 0-8028-2443-9

*To the memory of*
*my teacher and friend*
*Msgr. Jerome D. Quinn*

# Contents



## NOTES AND COMMENTS ON THE FIRST LETTER TO TIMOTHY

## NOTES AND COMMENTS ON THE SECOND LETTER TO TIMOTHY

# Preface

I first met Msgr. Jerome Quinn at the St. Paul Seminary during my brief time as a seminarian. About ten years later, in 1983, I was a part-time instructor at the then College of St. Thomas. The theology faculty of the College and faculty of the Seminary met several times, and we renewed our acquaintance. That next summer he offered to help me prepare for an exam in Sacred Scripture before the Pontifical Biblical Commission in Rome. From that point until his death in the fall of 1988 I had the privilege of being his student and friend. It was out of my respect for his work and my love for him as a mentor, along with great feelings of inadequacy, that I accepted the task of bringing his *magnum opus* to completion.

He was quite aware of his failing health, and when I visited him in the summer of 1988, just before he was completely incapacitated, he told me he would soon die. At that time his goal was to finish his reworking of the commentary on First Timothy through 4:5; in his opinion this was the central axis of the PE — "Pastoral Epistles" (see his Introduction to First Timothy). He had already shipped off to the copy editor the commentary on Titus (hereafter AB *Titus*) along with the five excursuses in that volume. Moreover, the introduction to Titus was intended to serve as the introduction to the whole PE. It goes without saying that he would have liked to have finished his work, but it is a small comfort, to me at least, to know that he completed the portions of his work that he deemed most important.

Indeed, that was as far as he was able to go. On Good Friday, in the spring of 1989, I accepted the invitation to complete his work, but I had no idea of what was in store. As his last student, I had many opportunities to converse with him about the commentary, and I thought I knew, as much as anyone, how much work was ahead. I was mistaken. I was somewhat surprised with the state of the manuscript that I inherited. Fr. Quinn had drafted his commentary as a continuous narrative without any hint of what he would put in the NOTES or COMMENT sections. Apparently, his system was to separate the text into these components as he rewrote and updated the draft. When he died, there were over 1,442 pages of triple-spaced manuscript that had to be reworked into the final version — this on 1 Tim 4:6 through the end of Second Timothy. These pages contained copious editorial remarks — many in his hand and some from Michael Patrick O'Connor, who had edited the first draft — but never was there any hint of how he would have divided the manuscript. Further, the draft contained an early version of his translation, and that had to be brought up to date as well.

The NOTES sections from 1 Tim 4:6 through the end of Second Timothy were composed by me. Most of the scholarship and research, as well as the actual wording, is from Fr. Quinn's original draft, but my work was too extensive to indicate clearly in any practical way what is his and what is mine (except for translations from the original language, which I have noted). The COMMENT sections are for the most part his actual words, but again, the changes that had to be made were too numerous to acknowledge in any practical manner. Even if Fr. Quinn is not correct about the authorship of the PE, I, at any rate, understand what it means to write in another's name and have some firsthand experience with using source material!

In the time between his death and the completion of his manuscript, research has progressed. If he had had the opportunity, the reader can be confident that Fr. Quinn would have included the latest findings. He had read everything that was even remotely connected with the PE, their historical background, philology, and so on, and he incorporated those studies (as of 1988) in the manuscript up to 1 Tim 4:5 and to a lesser extent in what followed. Since I have had to fit my work on the commentary in with my other responsibilities as headmaster, teacher, husband, and father, and because of the enormous amount of work that had to be done, I have not undertaken in any systematic way a revision or an updating of Fr. Quinn's work. As it stands, it is a gold mine of scholarship and insight into the PE, their author/redactor, the community that preserved them, and the world of which they were a part. So I ask his colleagues and friends kindly to overlook the imperfections that must inevitably accompany a work whose author died *in medias res.*

One of the casualties of his untimely death is the absence of the "full-dress bibliography" that in AB *Titus* he promised would appear in the present volume. I have rather followed his lead and supplied a Bibliographic Key for this volume, and have included most of the bibliography from AB *Titus* in the present volume. It should be noted that this volume was intended to be read with the volume on Titus. Further, Fr. Quinn explained his method, to which I have tried to remain faithful, in the preface to that volume, which we have reprinted with permission in this volume.

The careful reader will also note that I have made about eight relatively minor changes in the translation of First and Second Timothy that was published in AB *Titus.* Most are small matters designed to clarify the text or to supply words that had been inadvertently left out. The only change of any substance is to be found at 2 Tim 3:6, where Fr. Quinn had the opponents of the gospel trying to worm their way into the homes of "the little ladies." The Greek term is intended to be pejorative, but I thought the English idiom "little ladies" would offend for the wrong reasons, so I have supplied "idle women" as a more fitting translation.

As in Phil Boelter's preface to AB *Titus,* a few other notes are in order.

1. Translations of biblical passages are Msgr. Quinn's unless otherwise noted.
2. Citations of biblical manuscripts follow the system used in the twenty-sixth edition of the Nestle-Aland *Novum Testamentum Graece.*
3. Most citations of classical authors refer to the Loeb Classical Library editions. Only the exceptions are noted, with editions, if known, cited in the body of the commentary.

All authors acknowledge the bittersweet burden of thanking those whose assistance made their work possible. The sweetness comes in expressing heartfelt gratitude for the support that is needed, the bitterness comes in the sure knowledge that no matter how careful, they will forget someone who justly deserves acknowledgment. In the first place, Fr. Quinn and I were spared numerous embarrassments and the work was greatly enhanced by the editing of David Noel Freedman. His encouragement and his patience along with that of his assistant, Dr. Astrid Beck, were invaluable to me as I labored over these last several years. I must also mention the support and patience of the Doubleday Religion Department. Thanks also goes to John R. Huddlestun for his valuable assistance in tracking down difficult references.

I am grateful to the typists who entered the manuscript on to the computer, especially my mother-in-law, Dolores Grevious, who gave up her precious vacation to type for me. I must also thank Michael Kueber, my colleague at Trinity School, who spent his entire summer with me in the John Ireland Library, checking references and helping to ensure accuracy. To the staff of the John Ireland Library, where Fr. Quinn had done all of his original research, I also owe a great debt of thanks. I cannot fail to mention the support of my colleagues and students at Trinity School at Greenlawn in South Bend, Indiana, where I was the headmaster for the first two years of this project, and at Trinity School at River Ridge in Bloomington, Minnesota, where I am currently the headmaster. Without their support and without the encouragement of the president of Trinity Schools, Dr. Kerry Koller, I could not have done this work.

Finally, and as Fr. Quinn said in his preface, "with some trepidation," I too thank my friends and family who have prayed for me and supported me through this time. My parents have opened their home for me on many occasions to provide a quiet space, and my children have lived through my absences, even when I was physically present. They have come to think of "the book," as they call it, as almost another member of the family — one whom they are glad to say is about to move out.

In this litany of thanksgiving, I have saved the place of honor for my loving wife, Adella. She more than any other has sacrificed to bring this commentary to completion. Not one of those 1,442 pages of manuscript had been entered on computer when I took the assignment; she entered most of them. She has also been tireless in entering corrections, and her careful work has spared me numerous mistakes. In addition to this practical assistance, she has worked her own part-time job and cared for our home and children. She has been unfailing in her encouragement, and she has lightened my burden the whole way. In thanks I can only echo the words of Proverbs 31: "A good wife who can find? She is far more precious than jewels. The heart of her husband trusts in her, and he will have no lack of gain."

Having acknowledged all the invaluable help I have received along the way, it is also evident to me that I must assume responsibility for the final product. Clearly, Fr. Quinn will, and should, get the praise for this great work, and I will get the blame for the mistakes, which after all are mine; it is a burden that I bear gladly for this great man. However, I would be remiss if I did not add that writing in another's persona with an accompanying anonymity, as Fr. Quinn has suggested happened here in the PE, has definite advantages.

Those who knew Fr. Quinn are aware that he suffered enormously throughout the last years of his life. His illness often allowed him only two or three hours of work each day. This was a double burden because he so loved his work. I have thought of him often during these last several years and have desired to make the extraordinary fruit of his labor available to all. With the end in sight, I can say that his effort was not in vain. Now he can say with Paul:

> I have contended in the fine contest. I have run the whole track. I have kept faith. Whatever happens there lies in store for me the crown of the upright life with which the upright Judge, the Lord, will recompense me on that Day — and not only me but all who have their hearts set on his revelation. (2 Tim 4:7-8)

William C. Wacker
*Headmaster*
Trinity School at River Ridge
Bloomington, Minnesota

## A FURTHER NOTE

This work was originally conceived as the companion volume of *Titus* in the Anchor Bible commentary series, which was published shortly after Msgr. Quinn's death. In order to help this volume "stand alone" as much as possible, the "Introduction to the Pastoral Epistles" and the "New Translation of 1 and 2 Timothy" that are found in AB *Titus* have been reprinted with Doubleday's permission. There are also very many references to the Notes, Comments, and Excursuses in AB *Titus.* Where it was possible I have, with the wonderful help of Eerdmans' staff, included some of the relevant information from that volume. I have tried to smooth out the lumps, but the reader will still find it very helpful to have access to the first volume since it is referenced continually. Finally, I am very grateful to Eerdmans for publishing the work of this great scholar and for helping to make it a much better book. I am especially grateful to Astrid Beck, who did not give up hope and saw this project through to the end.

William C. Wacker
*April 10, 1999*

# *Principal Abbreviations*

| | |
|---|---|
| AB | Anchor Bible |
| ACW | Ancient Christian Writers |
| AGJU | Arbeiten zur Geschichte des antiken Jundentums und des Urchristentums |
| AnBib | Analecta biblica of PBI |
| *ANRW* | *Aufstieg und Niedergang der Römischen Welt* |
| Ap. Frs. | Apostolic Fathers |
| AzT | Arbeiten zum Theologie |
| BAGD | W. Bauer, W. F. Arndt, F. W. Gingrich, and F. W. Danker, *Greek-English Lexicon of the NT* (2nd ed.; Chicago: University of Chicago, 1979) |
| *BAT* | *Biblical Archaeology Today: Proceedings of the International Congress on Biblical Archaeology, April 1984,* Jerusalem. *IES* (1985, "An Unpublished Halakhic Letter from Qumran," E. Qimron and J. Strugnell) |
| BDB | F. Brown, S. R. Driver, and C. A. Briggs, *The New Brown, Driver, and Briggs Hebrew and English Lexicon of the Old Testament* (London: Oxford University Press, 1907) |
| BDF | F. Blass, A. Debrunner, and R. W. Funk, *A Greek Grammar of the New Testament and Other Early Christian Literature* (E.T. with revision by R. W. Funk; Chicago: University of Chicago, 1961) |
| *BGU* | *Berliner griechische Urkunden* |
| *BJRL* | *Bulletin of the John Rylands (University) Library (of Manchester)* |
| BSGRT | Bibliotheca scriptorum graecorum et romanorum teubneriana |
| CAC | Corpus apologetarum christianorurn saeculi secundi (ed. J. Otto) |

| | |
|---|---|
| CC | Corpus Christianorum |
| *CIG* | *Corpus inscriptionum graecarum* |
| *CII* | *Corpus inscriptionum iudaïcarum* |
| *CIL* | *Corpus inscriptionum latinorum* |
| CSEL | Corpus scriptorum ecclesiasticorum latinorum |
| *DACL* | *Dictionnaire d'archéologie chrétienne et de liturgie* (15 vols.; Paris: Letouzey et Ané, 1910) |
| *DBS* | *Supplément au Dictionnaire de la Bible* |
| D-C | M. Dibelius and H. Conzelmann, *Die Pastoralbriefe* (HNT 13; Tübingen: Mohr, 1966). E.T. *The Pastoral Epistles* (Hermeneia; E.T. by P. Buttolph and Y. Yarbro; Philadelphia: Fortress, 1972) |
| *DELG* | P. Chantraine, *Dictionnaire étymologique de la langue grecque: historie des mots* (Paris: Klinksieck, 1968-1980) |
| DJD | Discoveries in the Judean Desert (of Jordan) (Oxford: Clarendon) |
| DS | *Enchiridion symbolorum, definitionum et declarationum de rebus fidei et morum* (ed. H. Denzinger and A. Schönmetzer, 36th ed., Freiburg in Breisgau: Herder, 1965 |
| E.T. | English translation |
| FRLANT | Forsuchungen zur Religion und Literatur des Alten und Neuen Testaments |
| *GNT*$^{3corr}$ | *Greek New Testament* of UBS (3rd ed., corrected; ed. K. Aland et al.) |
| HNT | Handbuch zum NT |
| HNTC | Harper's New Testament Commentary |
| H-R | E. Hatch and H. A. Redpath, *A Concordance to the LXX and the Other Greek Versions of the OT* (3 vols.; Grand Rapids: Baker, 1983, reprint of 1897 ed.) |
| ICC | International Critical Commentary |
| *IDB* | G. A. Buttrick, ed., *Interpreter's Dictionary of the Bible* (Nashville: Abingdon, 1962) |
| *IDBSup* | *IDB Supplementary Volume* (Nashville: Abingdon, 1976) |
| IG | Inscriptiones Graecae |
| *JBL* | *Journal of Biblical Literature* |
| *JJS* | *Journal of Jewish Studies* |
| *JR* | *Journal of Roman Studies* |
| *JSOT* | *Journal for the Study of the Old Testament* |
| *JTS* | *Journal of Theological Studies* |
| LCL | Loeb Classical Library |
| LP | E. Lobel and D. Page, eds., *Poetarum lesbiorum fragmenta* (Oxford: Clarendon, 1955) |

| | |
|---|---|
| LSJ | Henry George Liddell, Robert Scott, and H. S. Jones, *A Greek-English Lexicon* (9th ed., with Supplement, by E. Barber; Oxford: Clarendon, 1940, 1968) |
| LXX | Septuagint |
| *MAMA* | W. M. Chalder, W. H. Buckler, et al., *Monumenta Asiae Minoris Antiqua,* Manchester, I-VIII; 1928-62 |
| MM | James H. Moulton and George Milligan, *The Vocabulary of the Greek NT* (Grand Rapids: Wm. B. Eerdmans Publishing Co., 1930; reprint, 1972) |
| MT | Masoretic Text |
| NAB | New American Bible, successor to Confraternity Version |
| NCBC | New Century Bible Commentary |
| NCCHS | R. C. Fuller et al., eds., *A New Catholic Commentary on Holy Scripture* (London: Nelson, 1969) |
| NEB | New English Bible |
| *NHL* | *Nag Hammadi Library* (ed. J. M. Robinson; New York: Harper & Row, 1977) |
| *NOAB* | *New Oxford Annotated Bible* |
| *NovT* | *Novum Testamentum* |
| *NovTSup* | *Supplements to NovT* |
| NT | New Testament/Neue Testament/Nouveau Testament |
| NTD | Das Neue Testament Deutsch |
| *NTG*[26corr] | *Novum Testamentum Graece* (ed. K. Aland et al.; Stuttgart: Deutsche Bibelgesellschaft, 1983) |
| *NTS* | *New Testament Studies* |
| *OCD* | *Oxford Classical Dictionary* (ed. Max Carey; Oxford: Clarendon, 1949) |
| *OGIS* | *Orientis graeci inscriptiones selectae* (2nd ed.; ed. Wilhelm Dittenberger) |
| OL | Old Latin |
| *OLD* | *Oxford Latin Dictionary* |
| OT | Old Testament/Alten Testament/Ancien Testament |
| OxyP | Oxyrhynchus Papyri |
| PBI | Pontifical Biblical Institute (Rome) |
| PE | the Pastoral Epistles; Titus, 1-2 Timothy |
| *PG* | *Patrologia graeca* (ed. J. Migne) |
| *PL* | *Patrologia latina* (ed. J. Migne) |
| PSI | Pubblicazioni della Società Italiana: Papiri greci e latini |
| *RAC* | *Reallexikon für Antike und Christentum* (ed. T. Klausner) |
| *RB* | *Revue Biblique* |

| | |
|---|---|
| *RGG* | *Die Religion in Geschichte und Gegenwart* (3rd ed., ed. K. Galling; Tübingen: Mohr [Siebeck], 1957-65) |
| *RevQ* | *Revue de Qumran* |
| RSV | Revised Standard Version |
| SBL | Society of Biblical Literature |
| SBLDS | SBL Dissertation Series |
| SBLMS | SBL Monograph Series |
| SBLSBS | SBL Sources from Biblical Studies |
| SBT | Studies in Biblical Theology |
| SC | Sources chrétiennes |
| SCBO | Scriptorum classicorum bibliotheca Oxoniensis |
| SCM | Student Christian Movement |
| SCS | Septuagintal and Cognate Studies |
| *SEG* | *Supplementum Epigraphicum Graecum* (G. Daux et al.; Amsterdam: J. C. Gieben, 1984) |
| *SFG* | *Synopsis of the Four Gospels,* ed. Kurt Aland (2nd ed.; reprint, Stuttgart: UBS, 1972) |
| *SJT* | *Scottish Journal of Theology* |
| *TDNT* | *Theological Dictionary of the NT* (E.T. by G. W. Bromiley of *Theologisches Wörterbuch zum NT,* ed. G. Kittel and G. Friedrich; 10 vols.; Grand Rapids: Wm. B. Eerdmans Publishing Co., 1964-1976) |
| *TDOT* | S. Steingrimsson, *Theological Dictionary of the Old Testament* (E.T. of *Theologisches Wörterbuch zum Alten Testament,* ed. G. J. Botterweck and H. Ringgren, 5 vols. to date; Grand Rapids: Wm. B. Eerdmans Publishing Co., 1979-1986) |
| *TGF* | *Tragicorum Graecorum fragmenta* (ed. A. Nauck; Leipzig: Teubner, 1889; reprint, Snell; Hildesheim: Olms, 1964) |
| Theod. | Theodotion's Greek Translation of the OT |
| THKNT | Theologischer Handkommentar zum NT |
| TSMAO | Typologie des sources du Moyen Âge occidental |
| TU | Texte und Untersuchungen |
| *TWAT* | original of *TDOT* |
| *TWNT* | original of *TDNT* |
| UBS | United Bible Societies |
| *VD* | *Verbum domini* |
| *VL* | *Vetus Latina* (ed. H. Frede) |
| *VTSupp* | *Vetus Testamentum Supplement* |
| WH | Westcott and Hort, United Bible Society |

# *Other Abbreviations*

| | |
|---|---|
| *1 Clem.* | Clement of Rome, *Ep. to Corinthians* |
| *Ag. Ap.* | Josephus, *Against Apion* |
| al. | alii = other MSS |
| *Ant.* | Josephus, *Antiquities* |
| Apoc. | Apocalypse |
| app. crit. | apparatus criticus |
| Aq. | Aquila |
| *bis* | two occurrences |
| cod. | codex |
| d. | died |
| E | English version numbering |
| ed. | editor, edited by |
| ep. | epistle, *epistola* |
| lit. | literally |
| *k.t.l.* | *kai ta loipa,* and the rest |
| LXX | Septuagint |
| *m.* | *Mishna* (tractate named) |
| MS(S) | manuscript(s) |
| MT | Masoretic Text |
| n.s. | new series (any language) |
| NT | New Testament |
| opp. | opposed (to) |
| or. | *oratio,* oration |
| OT | Old Testament |
| OxyP | Oxyrhynchus Papyrus |

| | |
|---|---|
| pap. | papyrus |
| repr. | reprinted |
| rev. | revised |
| serm. | *sermo*, sermon |
| Sym | Symmachus |
| *T.* | *Testament (of)* |
| Tg. | Targum |
| trans. | translator, translated by |
| *v.l.* | *varia lectio*, variant reading |
| Vg | Vulgata, Vulgate |
| VL | Vetus Latina, Old Latin |

**Writings of Ignatius of Antioch**

| | |
|---|---|
| Ign. *Eph.* | *Ep. to the Ephesians* |
| Ign. *Magn.* | *Ep. to the Magnesians* |
| Ign. *Phld.* | *Ep. to the Philadelphians* |
| Ign. *Pol.* | *Ep. to Polycarp* |
| Ign. *Rom.* | *Ep. to the Romans* |
| Ign. *Smyrn.* | *Ep. to the Smyrnaeans* |
| Ign. *Trall.* | *Ep. to the Trallians* |

**Writings of Philo of Alexandria**

| | |
|---|---|
| *Abr.* | *Abrahamo* |
| *Aet.* | *Aeternitate mundi* |
| *Agric.* | *Agricultura* |
| *Cher.* | *Cherubim* |
| *Conf.* | *Confusione linguarum* |
| *Congr.* | *Congressu quaerendae eruditionis causa* |
| *Dec.* | *Decalogo* |
| *Det.* | *Quod deterius potiori insidiari solet* |
| *Ebr.* | *Ebrietate* |
| *Flacc.* | *In Flaccum* |
| *Fug.* | *Fuga et inventione* |
| *Gig.* | *Gigantibus* |
| *Jos.* | *Josepho* |
| *Leg. ad Gai.* | *Legatio ad Gaium* |
| *Leg. alleg.* | *Legum allegoriarum liber* |
| *Mig. Abr.* | *Migrations Abrahami* |
| *Mos.* | *Vita Mosis* |
| *Mut.* | *Mutatione nominum* |
| *Omn. prob. lib.* | *Quod omnis probus liber sit* |

| | |
|---|---|
| *Op. mund.* | *Opificio mundi* |
| *Plant.* | *Plantatione* |
| *Post.* | *Posteritate Caini* |
| *Praem.* | *Praemiis et poenis* |
| *Quis her.* | *Quis rerum divinarum heres* |
| *Quod Deus imm.* | *Quod Deus immutabilis sit* |
| *Sacr.* | *Sacrificiis Abelis et Caini* |
| *Sobr.* | *Sobrietate* |
| *Som.* | *Somniis* |
| *Virt.* | *Virtutibus* |
| *Spec. leg.* | *Specialibus legibus* |
| *Vita cont.* | *Vita contemplativa* |

**Dead Sea Scrolls and Related Texts**

| | |
|---|---|
| CD | Cairo (Genizah text of the) Damascus Document |
| Mur | Wadi Murabbaʿat texts |
| p | Pesher (commentary) |
| Q | Qumran |
| QL | Qumran Literature |
| 1Q, 2Q, etc. | Numbered caves of Qumran, yielding written materials; followed by abbreviation of biblical or nonbiblical work |
| 1QapGen | *Genesis Apocryphon* of Cave 1 |
| 1QH | *Hôdāyôt (Thanksgiving Psalms)* from Cave 1 |
| 1QpHab | *Pesher on Habbakuk* from Cave 1 |
| 1QM | *Milḥāmāh (War Scroll)* from Cave 1 |
| 1QS | *Serek hayyaḥad (Rule of the Community, Manual of Discipline)* from Cave 1 |
| 1QSa | Appendix A *(Rule of the Congregation)* to 1QS |
| 4QEn | Enoch texts from Cave 4 |
| 11QtgJob | Targum of Job from Cave 11 |

The numbering of chapters and verses in the OT follows that of the Hebrew MT. This is especially to be noted when reference is made to the Psalter. Even if the discussion concerns the Greek form of a psalm in the LXX, the numbering still follows the Hebrew text. In case of doubt, one can always consult the NAB, which uses the numbering of the Hebrew OT.

# *Bibliographic Key*


Aalen, "Formula"

Aalen, S. "A Rabbinic Formula I Cor. 14,34," *Studia Evangelica* II and III, papers presented to the Second International Congress on New Testament Studies held at Christ's Church, Oxford, 1961, ed. F. L. Cross (1964), pp. 513-525.

Aland, *Konkordanz*

Aland, K., *Vollständige Konkordanz zum griechischen Neuen Testament* (3 vols.; Berlin: de Gruyter, 1978-1983).

Aland, *Repertorium*

———. *Repertorium der griechischen christlichen Papyri: biblische Papyri* (Patristische Texte und Studien 18; Berlin: de Gruyter, 1976).

———. *Synopsis of the Four Gospels* (New York: UBS, 1964). *SFG* in Principal Abbreviations.

Albright, *Analogy*

Albright, W. F. *Archaeology, Historical Analogy, and Early Biblical Tradition* (Baton Rouge: Louisiana State University Press, 1966).

Albright, *ARI*

———. *Archaeology and the Religion of Israel* (Garden City, N.Y.: Doubleday, 1969).

Albright, "Retrospect"

———. "Retrospect and Prospect in New Testament Archaeology," in *The Teacher's Yoke: Studies in Memory of Henry Trantham* (ed. E. J. Vardaman and J. L. Garrett, Jr.; Waco, Tex.: Baylor University Press, 1964), pp. 27-41.

Albright, *Yahweh*

———. *Yahweh and the Gods of Canaan: A Historical Analysis of Two Contrasting Faiths* (Garden City, N.Y.: Doubleday, 1968).

Allan, "In Christ"

Allan, John A. "In Christ Formula in the Pastoral Epistles," *NTS* 10 (1963): 115-121.

Allmen, *PTM*

Allmen, Jean-Jacques von. *Pauline Teaching on Marriage* (E.T. from the French; New York: Morehouse-Barlow, 1963).

Altaner, *Patrology*

Altaner, Berthold. *Patrologia: Orba Compuesta en Alemán* (Madrid: Espasa-Calpe, 1949).

Ambroggi, *Le Epistole Pastorali*

Ambroggi, P. De. *Le Epistole Pastorali di S. Paolo a Timoteo e a Tito* (Turin: Marietti, 1964).

Andersen and Freedman, AB *Hosea*

Andersen, Francis I., and David Noel Freedman. *Hosea* (AB 24; Garden City, N.Y.: Doubleday, 1980).

Andrieu, "Fragments"

Andrieu, M., and P. Collomp. "Fragments sur papyrus de l'anaphore de Saint Marc," *R. Sci. Relig.* 8 (1928): 489-515.

Arnim, *SVF*

Arnim, Hans F. A. von. *Stoicorum veterum fragmenta collegit Joannes ab Arnim* . . . (4 vols.; Leipzig: Teubner, 1903-1924; reprint, Dubuque, Iowa: Brown Reprint, n.d.).

Audet, "Bénédiction"

Audet, J. P. "Esquisse historique du genre littéraire de la 'Bénédiction' Juive et de l' 'Eucharistie' Chrétienne," *RB* 65 (1958): 371-399.

Audet, *Didache*

*La Didache: Instructions des Apôtres* (Études bibliques; Paris: Gabalda, 1958).

Aune, "Magic"

Aune, David E. "Magic in Early Christianity," in *ANRW* II.23/2 (ed. H. Temporini and W. Haase; Berlin: de Gruyter, 1980), pp. 1507-1557.

Aune, *Prophecy*

———. *Prophecy in Earliest Christianity* (Grand Rapids: Wm. B. Eerdmans Publishing Co., 1983).

Balch, *Code*

Balch, D. L. *Let Wives Be Submissive: The Domestic Code in I Peter* (SBLMS 26; Chico, Calif.: Scholars Press, 1981).

Bammel, "Galater"

Bammel, Ernst. "Galater 1:23," *Zeitschrift für die neutestamentliche Wissenschaft* 59, nos. 1-2 (1968): 108-112.

Bammel, "Rom 13"
Bammel, Ernst, and C. F. D. Moule, eds. *Jesus and the Politics of His Day* (Cambridge: University Press, 1984), pp. 365-383.

Barclay, "Papyri"
Barclay, William. "New Testament Papyri," in *New Testament in Historical and Contemporary Perspective* (ed. H. Anderson and W. Barclay; Oxford: Blackwell, 1965), pp. 57-81.

Barnes, *Tertullian*
Barnes, Timothy D. *Tertullian: A Historical and Literary Study* (Oxford: Clarendon, 1971).

Barr, *Words for Time*
Barr, James. *Biblical Words for Time* (SBT 33, 2nd ser.; Naperville, Ill.: Allenson, 1962).

Barrett, *Adam*
Barrett, C. K. *From First Adam to Last: A Study in Pauline Theology* (London: Adam & Charles Black, 1962).

Barrett, *NT Essays*
———. *New Testament Essays* (London: SPCK, 1972).

Barrett, *Pastoral Epistles*
———. *The Pastoral Epistles* (Oxford: Clarendon, 1963).

Barrett, "*Pseudapostoloi*"
———. "*Pseudapostoloi* (2 Cor 11:13)," in *Mélanges biblique en hommage au R. P. Béda Rigaux* (ed. A. Descamps and A. de Halleux; Gembloux: Duculot, 1970), pp. 377-396.

Barrett, *Signs*
———. *The Signs of an Apostle* (the Cato Lecture, 1969; London: Epworth, 1970).

Barrett, "Titus"
———. "Titus," in *Neotestamentica et Semitica: Studies in Honor of Matthew Black* (ed. E. E. Ellis and M. Wilcox; Edinburgh: Clark, 1969), pp. 1-14.

Bartchy, *Slavery*
Bartchy, S. S. *Mallon Chresai: First-Century Slavery and the Interpretation of 1 Corinthians 7:21* (SBLDS 11; Missoula: University of Montana, 1973).

Barth, AB *Eph*
Barth, Marcus. *Ephesians* (AB 34, 34A; Garden City, N.Y.: Doubleday, 1974).

Barth, "Traditions"
———. "Traditions in Ephesians," *NovTSup* 30 (1984): 3-25.

Barthélemy and Rickenbacher, *KHS*
Barthélemy, D., and O. Rickenbacher, *Konkordanz zum hebräischen Sirach; mit syrischen-hebräischen Index* (Göttingen: Vandenhoeck & Ruprecht, 1973).

Bauer, *Rechtgläubigkeit/Orthodoxy*

Bauer, W. *Rechtgläubigkeit und Ketzerei im ältesten Christentum* (Beiträge zur historischen Theologie 10; Tübingen: Mohr, 1934). E.T. *Orthodoxy and Heresy in Earliest Christianity* (ed. R. A. Kraft and G. Krodel; Philadelphia: Fortress, 1971).

Bauer, W., W. F. Arndt, and F. W. Gingrich. *A Greek-English Lexicon of the New Testament and Other Early Christian Literature* (E.T. and adaptation of W. Bauer's 4th revised and augmented edition, Chicago: University of Chicago, 1957). The 2nd ed. (1979) is a rev. and augmented E.T. of Bauer's 5th ed. of 1958, by F. Gingrich and F. W. Danker.

Baumstark, *Liturgy*

Baumstark, Anton. *Comparative Liturgy* (English ed. by F. L. Cross; Westminster, Md.: Newman Press, 1958).

Beasley-Murray, *Bapt. NT*

Beasley-Murray, G. R. *Baptism in the New Testament* (Exeter: Paternoster, 1962).

Beneden, *Aux Origines*

Beneden, Pierre van. *Aux Origines d'une terminologie sacramentelle: Ordo, Ordinaire, Ordinatio dans la littérature chrétienne avant 313* (Louvain: Spicilegium Sacrum Lovaniense, 1974).

Benko, "Criticism"

Benko, Stephen. "Pagan Criticism of Christianity during the First Two Centuries A.D.," in *ANRW* II.23/2 (ed. H. Temporini and W. Haase; Berlin: de Gruyter, 1980), pp. 1055-1118.

Benko and O'Rourke, *Catacombs*

Benko, Stephen, and John J. O'Rourke, eds. *The Catacombs and the Colosseum: The Roman Empire as the Setting of Primitive Christianity* (Valley Forge, Pa.: Judson Press, 1971).

Berge, "Savior"

Berge, Paul. "Our Great God and Savior," unpublished thesis, Union Theological Seminary, Richmond, Va., 1973 (copyright 1974).

Berger, *Sacred Canopy*

Berger, Peter. *The Sacred Canopy: Elements of a Sociological Theory of Religion* (Garden City, N.Y.: Doubleday, 1967).

Berger and Luckmann, *Social Construction*

Berger, Peter, and Thomas Luckmann. *The Social Construction of Reality: A Treatise in the Sociology of Knowledge* (Garden City, N.Y.: Doubleday, 1966).

Bernard, *Pastoral*

Bernard, J. H. *The Pastoral Epistles* (Cambridge: University Press, 1899; Thornapple reprint from Grand Rapids: Baker, 1980).

Best, "Gentiles"
Best, Ernest. "The Revelation to Evangelize the Gentiles," *JTS* 35 (1984): 1-30.
Betz, *Gal.*
Betz, Hans Dieter. *Galatians* (Hermeneia; Philadelphia: Fortress, 1977).
Betz, *GMP*
———. *The Greek Magical Papyri in Translation, Including Demotic Spells* (Chicago: University of Chicago Press, 1986).
Bevenot, "Clement of Rome"
Bevenot, Maurice. "Clement of Rome in Irenaeus's Succession-List," *JTS* 17 (1966): 98-107.
Beyer, *Texte*
Beyer, Klaus. *Die Aramäischen Texte vom Toten Meer* (Göttingen: Vandenhoeck & Ruprecht, 1984).
*Bib. Pat.*
*Biblia Patristica* (ed. J. Allenbach et al.; Paris: Editions du centre national de la recherche scientifique, 1975-).
*Biblical Archaeology Today: Proceedings of the International Congress on Biblical Archaeology* of April 1984, in Jerusalem. See *BAT* in Principal Abbreviations.
Bieber, *Theater*
Bieber, Margarete. *The History of the Greek and Roman Theater* (2nd ed.; Princeton, N.J.: University Press, 1961).
Bisbee, "Acts of Justin"
Bisbee, Gary A. "The Acts of Justin Martyr: A Form-Critical Study," *The Second Century* 3 (1983): 129-157.
Black, *Apoc. Henochi*
Black, Matthew. *Apocalypsis Henochi Graece* (Leiden: Brill, 1970).
Black, *Aramaic Approach*
———. *An Aramaic Approach to the Gospels and Acts* (Oxford: Clarendon, 1946).
Black, *Enoch*
———. *The Book of Enoch* (Leiden: Brill, 1985).
Blass, F., A. Debrunner, and R. W. Funk. *A Greek Grammar of the New Testament and Other Early Christian Literature.* See BDF in Principal Abbreviations.
Böhlig and Wisse, *G Egypt*
Böhlig, A., and F. Wisse, eds. *The Gospel of the Egyptians* (Grand Rapids: Wm. B. Eerdmans Publishing Co., 1975).
Boismard, *Hymnes*
Boismard, M.-E. *Quatre hymnes baptismales dans la première Épître de Pierre* (Paris: Cerf, 1961).

Bömer, *Religion der Sklaven*

Bömer, Franz. *Untersuchungen über die Religion der Sklaven in Griechenland und Rom* (4 vols.; Mainz: Akademie der Wissenschaften und der Literatur, 1958-1963).

Bonner, *Education*

Bonner, Stanley F. *Education in Ancient Rome: From the Elder Cato to the Younger Pliny* (Berkeley: University of California Press, 1977).

Boring, *Sayings*

Boring, M. Eugene. *Sayings of the Risen Jesus: Christian Prophecy in the Synoptic Tradition* (New York: Cambridge University Press, 1982).

Bornkamm, *Early Christian Experience*

Bornkamm, Günther. *Early Christian Experience* (New York: Harper & Row, 1969).

Bornkamm, *Paul*

———. *Paul* (E.T. by D. M. G. Stalker; New York: Harper & Row, 1971).

Boswell, *Homosexuality*

Boswell, John. *Christianity, Social Tolerance, and Homosexuality: Gay People in Western Europe from the Beginning of the Christian Era to the Fourteenth Century* (Chicago: University of Chicago Press, 1980).

Botterweck, G. J., and Helmer Ringgren. *Theological Dictionary of the Old Testament* (9 vols. thus far; ET of *TWAT* by J. T. Willis et al.; Grand Rapids: Wm. B. Eerdmans Publishing Co., 1974-1986). See *TDOT, TWAT* in Principal Abbreviations.

Bourguet, *Painting*

Bourguet, Pierre M. du. *Early Christian Painting* (E.T. by Simon Watson Taylor; New York: Viking Press, 1966).

Bousset, *Kyrios*

Bousset, Wilhelm. *Kyrios Christos* (E.T. by John Steely; Nashville: Abingdon, 1970).

Bradshaw, *Canons Hipp.*

Bradshaw, Paul, ed. *The Canons of Hippolytus* (E.T. by C. Bebawi; Bramcote, Notts.: Grove Books, 1987).

Bratcher, *Translator*

Bratcher, R. G. *A Translator's Guide to Paul's Letters to Timothy and to Titus* (New York and London: UBS, 1983).

Brilliant, *Art*

Brilliant, Richard. *Arts of the Ancient Greeks* (New York: McGraw-Hill, 1973).

Bromiley, Geoffrey W., E.T. and ed. *Theological Dictionary of the New Testament* (10 vols.; ed. G. Kittel and G. Friedrich; Grand Rapids: Wm. B. Eerdmans Publishing Co., 1964-1976). See *TDNT, TWNT* in Principal Abbreviations.

Brooten, *Leaders*

Brooten, Bernadette J. *Women Leaders in the Ancient Synagogue: Inscriptional Evidence and Background Issues* (Chico, Calif.: Scholars Press, 1982).

R. Brown, AB *JN*

Brown, R. E. *The Gospel according to John* (2 vols.; AB 29, 29a; Garden City, N.Y.: Doubleday, 1966).

R. Brown, *Birth*

———. *The Birth of the Messiah: A Commentary on the Infancy Narratives in Matthew and Luke* (Garden City, N.Y.: Doubleday, 1977).

R. Brown, "*Episkope*"

———. From "*Episkope* and *Episkopos:* The New Testament Evidence," *Theological Studies* 41 (1980): 322-338, in *The Critical Meaning of the Bible* (New York: Paulist, 1981).

R. Brown, *Epistles*

———. *The Epistles of John* (AB 30; Garden City, N.Y.: Doubleday, 1982).

R. Brown, *Meaning*

———. *The Critical Meaning of the Bible* (New York: Paulist, 1981).

R. Brown, *Semitic*

———. *The Semitic Background of the Term "Mystery" in the New Testament* (Philadelphia: Fortress, 1968).

R. Brown and Meier, *Antioch/Rome*

Brown, R. E., and J. P. Meier. *Antioch and Rome: New Testament Cradles of Catholic Christianity* (Ramsey, N.J.: Paulist, 1983).

S. Brown, *AP*

Brown, Schuyler. *Apostasy and Perseverance in the Theology of Luke* (Rome: PBI, 1969).

Brownlee, *Qumran*

Brownlee, W. H. *The Meaning of the Qumran Scrolls for the Bible* (New York: Oxford University Press, 1964).

Brox, *Pastoralbriefe*

Brox, N. *Die Pastoralbriefe* (Regensburger Neues Testament 7; Regensburg: Pustet, 1969).

Bruce, "Tacitus"

Bruce, F. F. "Tacitus on Jewish History," *Journal of Semitic Studies* 29 (1984): 33-44.

Bruns, *Canones*

Bruns, H. T. *Canones Apostolorum et Conciliorum Saeculorum* (Berolini: G. Reimeri, 1893).

Buck, *Indoesyn*

Buck, C. D. *A Dictionary of Selected Synonyms in the Principal Indo-European Languages* (Chicago: University of Chicago, 1949).

Bultmann, *Primitive Christianity*
Bultmann, R. *Primitive Christianity in Its Contemporary Setting* (Cleveland: World, 1956).
Bultmann, *Th. NT*
———. *Theology of the New Testament* (2 vols.; London: SCM; New York: Scribners, 1955).
Burnett, "Philo"
Burnett, F. "Philo on Immortality: A Thematic Study of Philo's Concept of *Palingenesia*," *Catholic Biblical Quarterly* 46 (1984): 447-470.
Cadbury, *Acts*
Cadbury, H. J. *The Book of Acts in History* (London: Black, 1955).
Cadbury, "Erastus of Corinth"
———. "Erastus of Corinth," *JBL* 50 (1931): 42-58.
Calder, *MAMA*
Calder, W. M. *Monumenta Asiae Minoris Antiqua* (London: Longman, Green, 1928-1962).
Callan, "Midrash"
Callan, Terrance. "Pauline Midrash: The Exegetical Background of Gal 3:19b," *JBL* 99 (1980): 549-567.
Campbell, *Greek Lyric*
Campbell, D. A. *Greek Lyric* (LCL; Cambridge: Harvard University Press, 1982).
Campenhausen, "Polycarp"
Campenhausen, Hans von. *Polycarp von Smyrna und die Pastoralbriefe* (Heidelberg, 1951, as reprinted in *Aus der Frühzeit des Christentums: Studien zur Kirchengeschichte des ersten und zweiten Jahrhunderts* [Tübingen: Mohr, 1963], pp. 197-252).
Campenhausen, *Tradition*
———. *Tradition and Life in the Church* (Philadelphia: Fortress, 1968).
Carcopino, *Cicero*
Carcopino, J. *Cicero: The Secrets of His Correspondence* (E.T. by E. O. Lorimer, 2 vols.; London: Routledge and Kegan Paul, 1951; reprint, New York: Greenwood, 1969).
Carcopino, *Rome*
———. *Daily Life in Ancient Rome* (E.T. by H. T. Rowell; New York: Penguin, 1956).
Carmignac, "La notion d'eschatologie"
Carmignac, Jean. "La notion d'eschatologie dans la Bible et à Qumran," *RevQ* 7 (December 1969): 17-31.
Carr, *Angels*
Carr, W. *Angels and Principalities: The Background, Meaning, and Development*

*of the Pauline Phrase "hai archai kai hai exousiai"* (Cambridge: University Press, 1981).

Casson, *Ancient Comedy*

Casson, Lionel. *Masters of Ancient Comedy* (New York: Macmillan, 1960).

Cavallin, *Life*

Cavallin, H. C. C. *Life after Death: Paul's Argument for the Resurrection of the Dead in 1 Cor 15* (Lund: Gleerup, 1974).

Cazelles, "L'Anaphore"

Cazelles, Henri. "L'anaphore et l'Ancient Testament," in *Eucharisties d'Orient et d'Occident* I (Paris: Cerf, 1970), pp. 11-21.

Cerfaux, *Christian*

Cerfaux, Lucien. *The Christian in the Theology of St. Paul* (London: Chapman, 1967).

Chadwick, *Chr. Thgt.*

Chadwick, H. *Early Christian Thought and the Classical Tradition: Studies in Justin, Clement, and Origen* (New York: Oxford University Press, 1966).

Chadwick, *Contra Celsum*

———. *Contra Celsum* (New York: Cambridge University Press, 1980).

Chadwick, "Gewissen"

———. "Gewissen," *RAC* 10.1025-1107.

Chadwick, *Sentences*

———. *The Sentences of Sextus: A Contribution to the History of Early Christian Ethics* (Cambridge: University Press, 1959).

Chantraine, *DELG*

Chantraine, Pierre. *Dictionnaire étymologique de la langue grecque: histoire des mots.* See *DELG* in Principal Abbreviations.

Charles, *AP*

Charles, R. H., ed. *Apocrypha and Pseudepigrapha of the Old Testament in English: With Introduction and Critical and Explanatory Notes to the Several Books* (2 vols.; Oxford: Clarendon, 1913).

Charles, *Enoch*

———. *The Book of Enoch* (Oxford: Clarendon, 1893).

Charlesworth, *Concordance*

Charlesworth, J. H. *Graphic Concordance to the Dead Sea Scrolls* (Louisville: John Knox Press, 1991).

Charlesworth, *OT Pseud.*

———, ed. *The Old Testament Pseudepigrapha* (2 vols.; Garden City, N.Y.: Doubleday, 1983/1985).

Charlesworth, *Pseud.*

Charlesworth, J. H. *The Pseudepigrapha and Modern Research with a Supplement* (Missoula, Mont.: Scholars Press, 1976).

Clark, "*Spes*"

Clark, M. E. "*Spes* in the Early Imperial Cult," *Numen* 30 (1983): 80-105.

Cohen, "Timothy"

Cohen, Shaye J. D. "Was Timothy Jewish (Acts 16:1-3)? Patristic Exegesis, Rabbinic Law, and Matrilineal Descent," *JBL* 105, no. 2 (1986): 251-268.

J. J. Collins, *Athens*

Collins, J. J. *Between Athens and Jerusalem: Jewish Identity in the Hellenistic Diaspora* (New York: Crossroad, 1983).

J. J. Collins and Nickelsburg, *Ideal Figures*

Collins, J. J., and G. W. E. Nickelsburg, eds. *Ideal Figures in Ancient Judaism: Profiles and Paradigms* (Missoula, Mont.: Scholars Press, 1980).

R. F. Collins, "Image of Paul"

Collins, Raymond F. "Image of Paul in the Pastorals," *Laval theologique et philosophique* 31 (1975): 147-173.

R. F. Collins, *Letters*

———. *Letters That Paul Did Not Write* (Wilmington, Del.: Michael Glazier, 1988).

Condon, "Calling"

Condon, Kevin. "*Klēsis* — Call and Calling," *Irish Biblical Studies* 6 (1984): 71-84.

Constable, *Letters*

Constable, Giles. *Letters and Letter Collections* (TSMAO 17; Turnhout: Brepols, 1976).

Conybeare, *Rit. Armenorum*

Conybeare, Frederick Cornwallis. *Rituale Armenorum* (Oxford: Clarendon, 1905).

Conzelmann, *1 Cor.*

Conzelmann, H. *First Corinthians* (Hermeneia; Philadelphia: Fortress, 1975).

Cook, *Troad*

Cook, J. M. *The Troad: An Archaeological and Topographical Study* (Oxford: Clarendon, 1973)

Coppens, "L'Élu"

Coppens, J. "L'Élu et les élus dans les écritures saintes et les écrits de Qumrân," *Ephemerides theologicae lovanienses* 57 (1981): 120-124.

Coppens, "L'Imposition"

———. "L'Imposition des Mains dans les Actes des Apôtres," in *Les Actes des Apôtres* (ed. J. Kremer; Gembloux: Duculot, 1979).

Coppens, *L'Imposition des Mains*

———. *L'Imposition des Mains et les Rites Connexes dans le Nouveau Testament et dans L'Église Ancienne* (Paris: Gabalda, 1925).

Corbett, *Marriage*

Corbett, Percy E. *The Roman Law of Marriage* (Oxford: Clarendon, 1930; reprint, 1969).

Corriveau, *Liturgy*

Corriveau, R. *The Liturgy of Life: A Study of the Ethical Thought of Saint Paul in His Letters to the Early Christian Communities* (Brussels: Desclée, 1970).

Cramer, *Catena*

Cramer, John A. *Catenae Graecorum Patrum in Novum Testamentum* (Hildesheim: G. Olms, 1967).

Cranfield, *Rom.*

Cranfield, C. E. B. *A Critical and Exegetical Commentary on the Epistle to the Romans* (ICC 32; 2 vols.; Edinburgh: Clark, 1975/1979).

Cremer, *BW*

Cremer, H. J. *Biblisch-theologisches Wörterbuch des Neutestamentlichen Griechisch* (Gotha: L. Klotz, 1923).

Cross, *Cyril*

Cyril, St., Bishop of Jerusalem. St. Cyril of Jerusalem's Lectures on the Christian Sacraments: *Pro Catechesis and the Five Mystagogical Catechesis* (ed. F. L. Cross; Crestwood, N.Y.: St. Vladimir's Press, 1986).

Crouch, *Haustafel*

Crouch, J. E. *The Origin and Intention of the Colossian Haustafel* (FRLANT 109; Göttingen: Vandenhoeck & Ruprecht, 1972).

Crum, *CD*

Crum, W. E. *A Coptic Dictionary* (Oxford: Clarendon, 1962).

Cullman, *Peter*

———. *Peter: Disciple, Apostle, Martyr* (2nd rev. expanded ed.; E.T. by Floyd B. Filson; Philadelphia: Westminster Press, 1962).

Cullman, *Worship*

———. *Early Christian Worship* (London: SCM, 1953).

Cullmann, *Christ and Time*

Cullmann, O. *Christ and Time: The Primitive Christian Conception of Time and History* (3rd ed.; E.T. by Floyd B. Filson; Philadelphia: Westminster Press, 1964).

Cullmann, *Christology*

———. *The Christology of the New Testament* (London: SCM, 1959).

Culpepper, *School*

Culpepper, R. A. *The Johannine School: An Evaluation of the Johannine-School Hypothesis Based on an Investigation of the Nature of Ancient Schools* (Missoula, Mont.: Scholars Press, 1975).

Cuming, "Anaphora"

Cuming, Geoffrey. "The Anaphora of St. Mark," *Le Muséon* 95 (1982): 115-129.

Cuming, "Early Anaphoras"

———. "Four Very Early Anaphoras," *Worship* 58 (1984): 168-172.

Cuming, *Essays*

———, ed. *Essays on Hippolytus* (Grove Liturgical Study 15; Bramcote, Notts.: Grove Books, 1978).

Cuming, "Eychēs"

———. "DI' EYCHĒS LOGOU," *JTS* 31 (1980): 80-82.

Cuming, *Hippolytus*

———. *Hippolytus: A Text for Students* (Grove Liturgical Study 8; Bramcote, Notts.: Grove Books, 1976)

Cumont, *ORRP*

Cumont, Franz. *Oriental Religions in Roman Paganism* (from E.T. of 1911 ed.; New York: Dover, 1956).

Dagens, "Velatio"

Dagens, Claude. "A propos du cubiculum de la 'velatio,'" *Revista di Archeologia cristiana* 47 (1971): 119-129.

Dahl, "One God"

Dahl, Nils. "The One God of Jews and Gentiles (Rom 3:29-30)," in *Studies in Paul* (Minneapolis: Augsburg, 1977), pp. 178-191.

Dahl, "Particularity"

———. "Particularity of the Pauline Epistles as a Problem in the Ancient Church," in *Neotestamentica et Patristica; eine Freundsgabe O. Cullmann* (ed. W. C. van Unnik et al.; Leiden: Brill, 1962), pp. 261-271.

Dahood, AB *Psalms*

Dahood, M. *Psalms II* (AB 17; Garden City, N.Y.: Doubleday, 1968).

Dalton, *CPS*

Dalton, William. *Christ's Proclamation to the Spirits: A Study of 1 Peter 3:18–4:6* (Rome: PBI, 1965).

C. Daniel, "Faux prophètes"

Daniel, Constantin. "'Faux prophètes': surnom des Esseniens dans le sermon sur la Montagne," *RevQ* 7 (December 1969): 45-79.

S. Daniel, *Le vocabulaire*

Daniel, Suzanne. *Le vocabulaire du culte dans la septante* (Paris: Klincksieck, 1966).

Danker, "Menander and the NT"

Danker, F. W. "Menander and the New Testament," *NTS* 10 (1964): 365-368.

Daube, *Rabbinic Judaism*

Daube, David. *The New Testament and Rabbinic Judaism* (New York: Arno Press, 1973).

Daube, "They Know Not"

———. "'For They Know Not What They Do' Lk 23,34." *Studia Patristica* IV (ed. F. L. Cross; Berlin: Akademie-Verlag, 1961).

D. Davies, "Position"

Davies, David F. "The Position of Adverbs in Luke," in *Studies in New Testament Language and Text* (ed. J. Elliott; Leiden: Brill, 1976), pp. 106-121.

P. Davies, *Damascus Document*

Davies, Phillip. *The Damascus Covenant: An Interpretation of the "Damascus Document"* (Sheffield: JSOT, 1983).

Deer, "*Hina*"

Deer, D. S. "Still More about the Imperatival *Hina*," *The Bible Translator* 30 (1979): 148.

Deichgräber, *Gotteshymnus*

Deichgräber, Reinhard. *Gotteshymnus und Christushymnus in der frühen Christenheit* (Göttingen: Vandenhoeck & Ruprecht, 1967).

Deissmann, *B ST*

Deissmann, G. Adolf. *Bible Studies: Contributions, Chiefly from Papyri and Inscriptions, to the History of the Language, the Literature, and the Religion of Hellenistic Judaism and Primitive Christianity* (2nd ed.; E.T. by A. Grieve; Edinburgh: Clark, 1909).

Deissmann, *LAE*

———. *Light from the Ancient East; The New Testament Illustrated by Recently Discovered Texts of the Greco-Roman World* (2nd ed.; E.T. by L. Strachan; London: Hodder & Stoughton, 1911; New York: G. H. Doran, 1927).

Deissmann, *Paul*

———. *Paul: A Study in Social and Religious History* (E.T. by W. E. Wilson; New York: Harper & Row, 1957, from 1927 ed.).

Delling, *Worship*

Delling, G. *Worship in the New Testament* (E.T. by Percy Scott; Philadelphia: Westminster Press, 1962).

Derrett, "Palingenesia"

Derrett, J. D. M. "*Palingenesia* (Matthew 19.28)," *Journal for the Study of the New Testament* 20 (1984): 51-58.

Descamps, *Les Justes*

Descamps, Albert. *Les Justes et la Justice dans les évangiles et le christianisme primitif: hormis a doctrine proprement paulinienne* (Louvain: Publications Universitaires de Louvain, 1950).

Dibelius, *James*

Dibelius, M. *James* (Hermeneia; E.T. by Michael A. Williams, revised by Heinrich Greeven, ed. Helmut Koester; Philadelphia: Fortress, 1976).

Dibelius, M., and H. Conzelmann. *Die Pastoralbriefe.* E.T. *The Pastoral Epistles.* See D-C in Principal Abbreviations.

Diels, *Vorsokratiker*

Diels, Herman, and W. Kranz, eds. *Fragmente der Vorsokratiker* (Zürich: Weidmann, 1966).

Di Lella, *Dan*

Di Lella, A. A., and L. F. Hartman. *The Book of Daniel* (AB 23; Garden City, N.Y.: Doubleday, 1978).

Di Lella, *Sir.*

Di Lella, A. A., and P. W. Skehan. *The Wisdom of Ben Sira* (AB 39; Garden City, N.Y.: Doubleday, 1987).

Dittenberger, *Syll.*

Dittenberger, A. *Sylloge Inscriptionum Graecarum* (4 vols.; reprint, Hildesheim: G. Olms, 1986; orig., 1915-1924).

Dockx, *Chronologies*

Dockx, S. *Chronologies neotestamentaires et vie de l'Église primitive: recherches exégetiques* (Gembloux: Duculot, 1976).

Dodd, *Acc. Scr.*

Dodd, Charles H. *According to the Scriptures: The Substructure of New Testament Theology* (New York: Scribners, 1953).

Dodd, *Bible and Greeks*

———. *The Bible and the Greeks* (London: Hodder & Stoughton, 1964).

Dodd, *More NT*

———. *More New Testament Studies* (Manchester: University Press, 1968).

Donelson, *Pseudepig.*

Donelson, Lewis R. *Pseudepigraphy and Ethical Argument in the PE* (Tübingen: Mohr, 1986).

Donfried, "Paul"

Donfried, K. "Paul and Judaism," *Interpretation* 38 (July 1984): 242-253.

Donfried, *Setting*

———. *The Setting of Second Clement in Early Christianity* (*NovTSup* 38; Leiden: Brill, 1974).

Dornier, *Pastorales*

Dornier, Pierre. *Les Épitres Pastorales* (Paris: Gabalda, 1969).

Dover, *Homosexuality*

Dover, Kenneth J. *Greek Homosexuality* (New York: Vintage Books, 1978).

Dover, *Morality*

———. *Greek Popular Morality in the Time of Plato and Aristotle* (Berkeley: University of California, 1974).

Dumézil, *ARR*

Dumézil, Georges. *Archaic Roman Religion with an Appendix on the Religion of the Etruscans* (2 vols.; Chicago: University of Chicago Press, 1970).

Dunbabin, "Invida"

Dunbabin, K. "Invida rumpantur pectora . . . ," *Jahrbuch für Antike und Christentum* 26 (1983), pp. 7-37, pls. 1-8.

Dupont, "Emmaus"

Dupont, Jacques. "Le disciples d'Emmaus (Lk 24:13-35)," in *La pâque du Christ mystère de salut* (ed. Martin Benzerath; Paris: Cerf, 1982), pp. 167-195.

Dupont, *Gnosis*

———. *Gnosis: la connaissance religieuse dans les Épîtres de Saint Paul* (Louvain: E. Nauwelaerts; Paris: Gabalda, 1949).

Dupont, "La Rencontre"

———. "La Rencontre entre Christianisme et hellénisme dans le discours à l'Aréopage (Actes 17,22-31)," in *Fede e cultura/Foi et culture* (Turin: Elle de Ci, 1981).

Dupont, *Sources*

———. *The Sources of Acts* (New York: Herder and Herder, 1964).

Dupont, *Syn Christōi*

———. *Syn Christōi: L'union avec le Christ suivant saint Paul* (Paris: Desclée, 1952).

Dupont, *Synoptiques*

———. *Études sur les Évangiles synoptiques* (Leuven, Belgium: Leuven University Press, 1985).

Dupont-Sommer, *EWQ*

Dupont-Sommer, A. *The Essene Writings from Qumran* (E.T. by G. Vermes; Cleveland: World, 1962).

Durham, *Voc. Men.*

Durham, Donald B. *Vocabulary of Menander* (Amsterdam: Aakkert, 1969, reprint of 1913).

Easton, *Pastoral Epistles*

Easton, B. S. *The Pastoral Epistles* (New York: Scribners, 1947).

Edwards and Wild, *Sentences*

Edwards, Richard A., and Robert A. Wild. *The Sentences of Sextus* (Chico, Calif.: Scholars Press, 1981).

Ehrhardt, *Framework*

Ehrhardt, Arnold. *Framework of the New Testament Stories* (Cambridge: Harvard University Press, 1964).

J. H. Elliott, *Home*

Elliott, John Hall. *A Home for the Homeless: A Sociological Exegesis of 1 Peter; Its Situation and Strategy* (Philadelphia: Fortress, 1981).

J. K. Elliott, *Greek Text*

Elliott, James Keith. *The Greek Text of the Epistles to Timothy and Titus* (Salt Lake City: University of Utah, 1968).

Ellis, *Paul's Use of OT*

Ellis, E. E. *Paul's Use of the Old Testament* (Grand Rapids: Baker, 1957).

Ellis, *Prophecy*

———. *Prophecy and Hermeneutic in Early Christianity* (Grand Rapids: Wm. B. Eerdmans Publishing Co., 1978).

Ellis, "Wives"

———. "The Silenced Wives of Corinth: 1 Cor 14:34-35," in *New Testament Textual Criticism* (ed. E. Epp and G. Fee; Oxford: Clarendon, 1981), pp. 213-220.

Ernout and Meillet, *DELL*

Ernout, Alfred, and Antoine Meillet. *Dictionnaire étymologique de la langue latine* (2 vols.; 3rd ed.; Paris: Klincksieck, 1951).

Evans, *Tertullian*

Evans, Ernest. *Tertullian's Homily on Baptism* (London: SPCK, 1964).

Fahey, *Cyprian and the Bible*

Fahey, Michael Andrew. *Cyprian and the Bible: A Study in Third-Century Exegesis* (Tübingen: Mohr, 1971).

Falconer, *PE*

Falconer, Robert A. *The Pastoral Epistles* (Oxford: Clarendon, 1937).

Farnedi, *Matrimonio*

Farnedi, Giustino. *La celebrazione cristiana del matrimonio: simboli e testi* (Rome: Pontificio Ateneo S. Anselmo, 1986).

Fears, "Virtues"

Fears, J. Rufus. "The Cult of Virtues and Roman Imperial Ideology," in *ANRW* II.7/2 (1981), pp. 887-948.

Fee, *Timothy*

Fee, G. D. *1 and 2 Timothy, Titus* (Good News Commentary; San Francisco: Harper & Row, 1984).

E. Ferguson, "Laying on of Hands"

Ferguson, Everett. "Laying on of Hands: Its Significance in Ordination," *JTS* 26 (1975): 1-12.

J. Ferguson, *Values*

Ferguson, John. *Moral Values in the Ancient World* (London: Methuen, 1958).

Fiensy, *Prayers*

Fiensy, David A. *Prayers Alleged to Be Jewish: An Examination of the Constitutiones Apostolorum* (Chico, Calif.: Scholars Press, 1985).

Fiore, *Function*

Fiore, Benjamin. *The Function of Personal Example in the Socratic and Pastoral Epistles* (AnBib 105; Rome: PBI, 1986).

Fischer, *Concordantiae*

Fischer, Bonifatius. *Novae concordantiae bibliorum sacrorum iuxta vulgatam versionem critice editam* (5 vols.; Stuttgart: Frommann-Holzboog, 1977).

Fishwick, "Ruler Worship"

Fishwick, Duncan. "The Development of Provincial Worship in the Western Roman Empire," in *ANRW* II.16/2 (ed. H. Temporini and W. Haase; Berlin: de Gruyter, 1978), pp. 1201-1253.

Fitzmyer, AB *Lk*

Fitzmyer, Joseph A. *The Gospel according to Luke* (2 vols.; AB 28, 28a; Garden City, N.Y.: Doubleday, 1981-1985).

Fitzmyer, *Advance*

———. *To Advance the Gospel: New Testament Studies* (New York: Crossroad, 1981).

Fitzmyer, *Aramean*

———. *A Wandering Aramean: Collected Aramaic Essays* (Missoula, Mont.: Scholars, 1979).

Fitzmyer, "Divorce"

———. "Divorce among First-Century Palestinian Jews" (H. L. Ginsburg vol. of *Eretz Israel,* 14; Jerusalem: Israel Exploration Society, 1978), pp. 103-110, 193.

Fitzmyer, *ESBNT*

———. *Essays on the Semitic Background of the New Testament* (London: Chapman, 1971).

Fitzmyer, *Gen. Apoc.*

———. *The Genesis Apocryphon of Qumran Cave I: A Commentary* (Rome: Biblical Institute, 1971)

Fitzmyer, "Kyrios"

———. "Kyrios," in *Exegetisches Wörterbuch zum Neuen Testament* (3 vols.; ed. H. Balz and G. Schneider; Stuttgart: Kohlhammer, 1978-), 2.811-819.

Fitzmyer, "Office of Teaching"

———. "The Office of Teaching in the Christian Church according to the New Testament," in *Lutheran Catholics Dialogue VI: Teaching Authority and*

*Infallibility in the Church* (ed. Paul C. Empie, T. Austin Murphy, and Joseph A. Burgess; Minneapolis: Augsburg, 1980), pp. 186-212.

Foakes Jackson and Lake, *Beginnings*

Foakes Jackson, F. J., and Kirsopp Lake. *The Beginnings of Christianity, Part I: The Acts of the Apostles* (5 vols.; Grand Rapids: Baker, 1922).

Ford, AB *Rev*

Ford, J. Massyngberde. *Revelation* (AB 38; Garden City, N.Y.: Doubleday, 1975).

Forkman, *Limits*

Forkman, Göran. *The Limits of the Religious Community* (Lund: Gleerup, 1972).

Frede, *VL*

Frede, Josef Hermann. *Vetus Latina* (vol. 25; Freiburg: Herder, 1979). See *VL* in Principal Abbreviations.

Freeman, *Ancilla*

Freeman, Kathleen. *Ancilla to the Pre-Socratic Philosophers* (Cambridge: Harvard University Press, 1948).

Friberg and Friberg, *Analytical GNT*

Friberg, Barbara, and Timothy Friberg, eds. *Analytical Greek NT: Greek Text Analysis* (Grand Rapids: Baker, 1981).

Friedman, *Marriage*

Friedman, Mordechai. *Jewish Marriage in Palestine: A Cairo Geniza Study* (New York: Jewish Theological Seminary of America, 1980).

Friedrich, *Aphrodite*

Friedrich, P. *The Meaning of Aphrodite* (Chicago: University of Chicago Press, 1978).

Fuller, "Elders"

Fuller, R. H. "Of Elders and Triads in 1 Timothy 5:19-25," *NTS* 29 (1983): 258-263.

Fuller, *Foundations*

———. *The Foundations of New Testament Christology* (New York: Scribner's, 1965).

F. X. Funk, *Constitutiones*

Funk, Francis X. *Didascalia et Constitutiones Apostolorum* (2 vols.; Tubingae: H. Laupp, 1901).

R. Funk, *Language*

Funk, Robert W. *Language, Hermeneutic, and Word of God* (New York: Harper & Row, 1966).

R. Funk, "Parousia"

———. "The Apostolic Parousia: Form and Significance," in *Christian History and Interpretation: Studies Presented to John Knox* (ed. W. R. Farmer, C. F. D.

Moule, and R. R. Niebuhr; Cambridge: University Press, 1967), pp. 249-268.

Furneaux, *Annals*

Furneaux, Henry. *Annals of Tacitus* (Oxford: Clarendon, 1965).

Furnish, AB *2 Cor*

Furnish, Victor Paul. *II Corinthians* (AB 32A; Garden City, N.Y.: Doubleday, 1984).

Galtier, "La réconciliation"

Galtier, P. "La réconciliation des pécheures dans la première épître Timothée," *Recherches de science religieuse* 39 (1951): 317-320.

Gärtner, *Gospel of Thomas*

Gärtner, Bertil. *Theology of the Gospel of Thomas* (E.T. by Eric Sharpe; London: Collins, 1961).

Gärtner, *Temple*

———. *The Temple and the Community in Qumran and the New Testament* (Cambridge: Cambridge University Press, 1965).

Gaster, *DSS*

Gaster, T. H. *The Dead Sea Scriptures, in English Translation with Introduction and Notes* (3rd ed. used unless 2nd or 1st is noted; Garden City, N.Y.: Doubleday, 1956, 1964, 1976).

Gaston, *Stone*

Gaston, Lloyd. *No Stone on Another: Studies in the Significance of the Fall of Jerusalem in the Synoptic Gospels* (Leiden: Brill, 1970).

Gealy, *IB*

Gealy, F. D. *The Pastoral Epistles,* in *Interpreter's Bible* (Nashville: Abingdon, 1955).

Geertz, *Religion*

Geertz, Clifford. *The Religion of Java* (Glencoe, Ill.: Free Press, 1960).

Gelston, "Euches"

Gelston, A. "Di' Euches Logou," *JTS* 33 (1982): 172-175.

Gennep, *Rites*

Gennep, Arnold van. *The Rites of Passage* (E.T. by Monika Vizedom and Gabrielle Caffee; Chicago: University of Chicago Press, 1960).

Gerhardsson, *Memory*

Gerhardsson, Birger. *Memory and Manuscript: Oral Tradition and Written Transmission in Rabbinic Judaism and Early Christianity* (E.T. by Eric Sharpe; Uppsala: C. W. K. Gleerup, 1961).

Gernet, *Anthropology*

Gernet, L. *The Anthropology of Ancient Greece* (E.T. from the French of 1968 by J. Hamilton and B. Nagy; Baltimore: Johns Hopkins, 1981).

Gibb and Kramers, *SEI*

Gibb, H. A. R., and J. H. Kramers, eds. *Shorter Encyclopedia of Islam* (Leiden: Brill, 1953).

Giblin, "Monotheistic"

Giblin, Charles H. "Three Monotheistic Texts in Paul (1 Cor 8:1-13, Gal 3:15-29, Rom 3:27-31)," *Catholic Biblical Quarterly* 37 (1975): 527-547.

Giblin, *Threat*

———. *The Threat to Faith: An Exegetical and Theological Re-examination of 2 Thessalonians 2* (AnBib 31; Rome: PB1, 1967).

Giverson, *Apocryphon*

Giverson, S. *Apocryphon Johannis* (Copenhagen: Munksgaard, 1963).

Goldstein, AB *1 Macc, 2 Macc*

Goldstein, Jonathan A. *1 Maccabees* (AB 41; Garden City, N.Y.: Doubleday, 1976); *2 Maccabees* (AB 41a; Garden City, N.Y.: Doubleday, 1983).

Gomme and Sandbach, *Commentary*

Gomme, Arnold W., and Francis Henry Sandbach. *Menander: A Commentary* (London: Oxford University Press, 1973).

Good, *Sheep*

Good, Robert M. *The Sheep in His Pasture: A Study of the Hebrew Noun 'Am(m) and Its Semitic Cognates* (Chico, Calif.: Scholars Press, 1983).

Goodenough, *Symbols*

Goodenough, E. R. *Jewish Symbols in the Greco-Roman Period* (New York: Pantheon, 1953).

Goodspeed, *Index*

Goodspeed, E. J. *Index apologeticus sive clavis Iustini martyris operum* (Leipzig: J. Ninrich, 1969; reprint of 1912 ed.).

Goppelt, *Typos*

Goppelt, Leonhard. *Typos: The Typological Interpretation of the Old Testament in the New* (E.T. by Donald H. Madvig; Grand Rapids: Wm. B. Eerdmans Publishing Co., 1982, from the German of 1939 and 1965).

A. Gordon, *Epigraphy*

Gordon, Arthur Ernest. *Illustrated Introduction to Latin Epigraphy* (Berkeley: University of California, 1983).

C. Gordon, *Ugaritic Textbook*

Gordon, Cyrus H. *Ugaritic Textbook* (Analecta Orientalia 38; Rome: PBI, 1965).

Grant, *Pompeii*

Grant, Michael. *The Art and Life of Pompeii and Herculaneum* (New York: Newsweek, 1979).

Grant and Freedman, *Secret Sayings*

Grant, R. M., and D. N. Freedman. *The Secret Sayings of Jesus* (London: Collins, 1960).

Grayston, "Hand"

Grayston, Kenneth. "The Significance of the Word *Hand* in the New Testament," in *Mélanges biblique en hommage au R. P. Béda Rigaux* (ed. A. Descamps and A. de Halleux; Gembloux: Duculot, 1970), pp. 479-488.

Grayston, "Meaning of *parakaleo*"

———. "A Problem of Translation: The Meaning of *parakaleo, paraklesis* in the NT," *Scripture Bulletin* 11 (1980): 27-31.

Grayston, "Not Ashamed"

———. "Not Ashamed of the Gospel . . . ," in *Studia Evangelica: Papers Presented to the Second International Congress on New Testament Studies* 1961, vol. 2 (ed. F. L. Cross; Berlin: Akademie-Verlag, 1964), pp. 569-573.

Greenberg, *Prayer*

Greenberg, Moshe. *Biblical Prose Prayer: A Window to the Popular Religion of Ancient Israel* (Los Angeles: University of California, 1983).

Griffiths, "Isis"

Griffiths, J. Gwyn. "Isis and *Agape*," *Classical Philology* 80 (1985): 139-141.

Gryson, *Women*

Gryson, Roger. *The Ministry of Women in the Early Church* (E.T. by Jean LaPorte and Mary Louise Hall; Collegeville, Minn.: Liturgical Press, 1976).

Guelich, *Sermon*

Guelich, Robert. *The Sermon on the Mount: A Foundation for Understanding* (Waco, Tex.: Word, 1982).

Guillaumount, *Gospel according to Thomas*

Guillaumount, A., H.-Ch. Puech, G. Quispel, W. Till, and Yassah ʿabd Al Masīh. *The Gospel according to Thomas: Coptic Text Established and Translated* (New York: Harper & Brothers, 1959).

Gundry, "Hymn"

Gundry, Robert H. "The Form, Meaning and Background of the Hymn Quoted in 1 Timothy 3:16," in *Apostolic History and Gospel* (ed. W. Gasque and R. Martin; Grand Rapids: Wm. B. Eerdmans Publishing Co., 1970), pp. 203-222.

Guthrie, *Pastoral Epistles*

Guthrie, D. *The Pastoral Epistles: An Introduction and Commentary* (Tyndale New Testament Commentaries 14; Grand Rapids: Wm. B. Eerdmans Publishing Co., 1957).

Haelst, *Catalogue*

Haelst, Joseph van. *Catalogue des papyrus littéraires juifs et chrétiens* (Paris: Publications de la Sorbonne, 1976).

Haenchen, *Acts*

Haenchen, Ernst. *The Acts of the Apostles: A Commentary* (E.T. by Bernhard Noble and Gerald Shinn; Oxford: Blackwell, 1971).

Haft, "Cretan Lies"

Haft, Adele J. "Odysseus, Idomeneus and Meriones: The Cretan Lies of *Odyssey* 13–19," *The Classical Journal* 79 (April-May 1984): 289-306.

Hagner, *Use*

Hagner, Donald A. *The Use of the Old and New Testaments in Clement of Rome* (*NovTSup* 34; Leiden: Brill, 1973).

Hahn, "One God"

Hahn, Ferdinand. "The Confession of the One God in the New Testament," *Horizons in Biblical Theology* 2 (1980): 69-84.

D. Hall, "Fellow Workers"

Hall, D. R. "Fellow Workers with the Gospel," *Expository Times* 85 (1974): 119-120.

S. Hall, "Easter"

Hall, Stuart George. "The Origins of Easter," in *Studia Patristica* 15 (1984), pp. 554-567.

S. Hall, *Melito*

———, ed. *Melito of Sardis on Pascha and Fragments: Texts and Translations* (Oxford: Clarendon, 1979).

Hallevy, "Man of God"

Hallevy, Raphael. "Man of God," *Journal of Near Eastern Studies* 17 (1958): 237-244.

Hamman, "La Prière"

Hamman, A. "La Prière chrétienne et la Prière païenne, formes et différence," in *ANRW* II.23/2 (ed. H. Temporini and W. Haase; Berlin: de Gruyter, 1980), pp. 1190-1247.

Hammond, *Epirus*

Hammond, N. G. L. *Epirus* (Oxford: Clarendon, 1967).

Handley, *Dyskolos*

Handley, Eric W., ed. *Dyskolos* (Cambridge: Harvard University Press, 1965).

Hanfmann, *Sardis*

Hanfmann, George M. *Sardis from Prehistoric to Roman Times* (Cambridge: Harvard University Press, 1983).

Hanhart et al., Göttingen LXX

Hanhart, Robert, et al., eds. *Septuaginta: Vetus Testamentum Graecum* (19+ vols. available; Göttingen: Vandenhoeck & Ruprecht, 1983).

A. T. Hanson, "Domestication"

Hanson, Anthony Tyrell. "The Domestication of Paul: A Study in the Development of Early Christian Theology," *BJRL* 63 (1981): 402-418.

A. T. Hanson, *PE*

———. *The Pastoral Epistles* (NCBC; Grand Rapids: Wm. B. Eerdmans Publishing Co., 1982).

A. T. Hanson, *SPTT*

———. *Studies in Paul's Technique and Theology* (London: SPCK, 1974).

A. T. Hanson, *Studies*

———. *Studies in the Pastoral Epistles* (London: SPCK, 1968).

R. P. C. Hanson, "Interpolation"

Hanson, R. P. C. "Interpolation in the 'Western' Texts of Acts," *NTS* 12 (1966): 211-230.

Harnack, *Mission*

Harnack, A. *The Mission and Expansion of Christianity in the First Three Centuries* (E.T. by J. Moffatt; New York: Harper, 1968; reprinted from 1908 orig.).

J. R. Harris, *Psalms*

Harris, J. Rendel. *The Odes and Psalms of Solomon: Published from the Syriac Version* (2nd ed.; Cambridge: University Press, 1911).

J. R. Harris, "Tobit and the NT"

———. "Tobit and the New Testament," *Expository Times* 41 (1930): 315-319.

M. Harris, "Titus 2:13"

Harris, Murray J. "Titus 2:13 and the Deity of Christ," in *Pauline Studies: Essays Presented to F. F. Bruce on His 70th Birthday* (ed. Donald A. Hagner and Murray J. Harris; Grand Rapids: Wm. B. Eerdmans Publishing Co., 1980), pp. 262-277.

Harrison, *Paulines*

Harrison, Percy N. *Paulines and Pastorals* (London: Villiers Publications, 1964).

Harrison, *Problem*

———. *The Problem of the Pastoral Epistles* (Oxford: Humphrey Milford, Oxford University Press, 1921).

Harvey, "The Workman"

Harvey, A. E. "'The Workman Is Worthy of His Hire': Fortunes of a Proverb in the Early Church," *Novum Testamentum* 24, no. 3 (1982): 209-221.

Hasler, *Timotheus*

Hasler, Victor August. *Die Briefe an Timotheus und Titus: Pastoralbriefe* (Zürcher Bibelkommentar 12; Zürich: Theologischer, 1978).

Hatch, Edwin, and Henry A. Redpath. *A Concordance to the LXX and the Other Greek Versions of the OT.* See H-R in Principal Abbreviations.

Hay, *Glory*

Hay, David M. *Glory at the Right Hand: Psalm 110 in Early Christianity* (Nashville: Abingdon Press, 1973).

Heal, "Canterbury"

Heal, Felicity. "The Archbishops of Canterbury and the Practice of Hospitality," *Journal of Ecclesiastical History* 33 (1982): 544-563.

Heinemann, *Prayer*

Heinemann, Joseph. *Prayer in the Talmud Forms and Patterns* (New York: De Gruyter, 1977).

Hemer, "Name of Paul"

Hemer, Colin J. "The Name of Paul," *Tyndale Bulletin* 36 (1985): 179-183.

Hengel, *Atonement*

Hengel, Martin. *The Atonement: The Origins of the Doctrine in the New Testament* (E.T. by John Bowden; Philadelphia: Fortress, 1981).

Hengel, *BJP*

———. *Between Jesus and Paul: Studies in the Earliest History of Christianity* (E.T. by John Bowden; London: SCM, 1983).

Hengel, *Charismatic*

———. *The Charismatic Leader and His Followers* (E.T. by James Grieg; New York: Crossroad, 1981).

Hengel, *Hellenism*

———. *Judaism and Hellenism: Studies in Their Encounter in Palestine during the Early Hellenistic Period* (2 vols.; E.T. by John Bowden; Philadelphia: Fortress, 1974).

Hengel, *PREC*

———. *Property and Riches in the Early Church* (Philadelphia: Fortress, 1974).

Hengel, "Proseuche"

———. "Proseuche und Synagoge: jüdische Gemeinde, Gotteshaus und Gottesdienst in der Diaspora und in Palästina," in *Tradition und Glaube: das frühe Christentum (in seiner Umwelt)* (ed. G. Jeremias; Göttingen: Vandenhoeck & Ruprecht, 1971), pp. 157-184.

Hengel, *Son*

———. *Son of God: The Origin of Christology and the History of Jewish-Hellenistic Religion* (1st Amer. ed.; Philadelphia: Fortress, 1967).

Hengel, *Zeloten*

———. *Die Zeloten: Untersuchungen zur jüdischen freiheits Bewegung in der Zeit von Herodes I. bis 70 n. Chr.* (AGJU 1; Leiden: Brill, 1961, 2nd ed. 1976; E.T. from Edinburgh: T. Clark, 1988).

Hennecke and Schneemelcher, *NT Apoc.*

Hennecke, Edgar, and Wilhelm Schneemelcher. *New Testament Apocrypha* (E.T. by A. Higgins; ed. R. McL. Wilson; 2 vols.; Philadelphia: Westminster Press, 1963-1965).

Héring, *1 Cor*

Héring, Jean. *The First Epistle of Saint Paul to the Corinthians* (London: Epworth Press, 1962).

Hill, "False Prophets"

Hill, David. "False Prophets and Charismatic: Structure and Interpretation in Matthew 7:15, 23," *Biblica* 57 (1976): 327-348.

Hill, *Greek Words*

———. *Greek Words and Hebrew Meanings: Studies in the Semantics of Soteriological Terms* (London: Cambridge University Press, 1967).

Hinson, "Essene Influence"

Hinson, E. "Evidence of Essene Influence in Roman Christianity: An Inquiry," in *Studia Patristica,* ed. E. A. Livingston; 17 (1982), pp. 697-701.

Hitchcock, "Latinity"

Hitchcock, F. R. M. "Latinity of the Pastorals," *Expository Times* 39 (1927-1928): 347-352.

Hobart, *Medical Language*

Hobart, William K. *The Medical Language of St. Luke: A Proof from Internal Evidence that "The Gospel of Luke" and "The Acts of the Apostles" Were Written by the Same Person, and That the Writer Was a Medical Man* (Dublin: Hodges, Figgis, 1882; reprint, Grand Rapids: Baker, 1954).

Holtz, *Pb*

Holtz, G. *Die Pastoralbriefe* (THKNT 13; Berlin: Evangelische, 1965-1972).

Hommes, "Women"

Hommes, N. J. "Let Women Be Silent in Church," *Calvin Theological Journal* 4 (1969): 5-22.

Hopkins, *Conquerors*

Hopkins, Keith. *Conquerors and Slaves* (Cambridge: Cambridge University Press, 1978).

Horbury, "False Prophecy"

Horbury, W. "1 Thess 2:3 . . . ," *JTS* 33 (1982): 492-507.

G. Horsley, *NDIEC*

Horsley, G. H. R. *New Documents Illustrating Early Christianity* (4 vols.; North Ryde, Australia: Macquarie University, 1981-1987).

R. Horsley, "Zealots"

Horsley, Richard A. "The Zealots: Their Origin, Relationships, and Importance in the Jewish Revolt," *NovT* 28 (April 1986): 159-192.

R. Horsley and Hanson, *Bandits*

Horsley, Richard A., and John S. Hanson. *Bandits, Prophets, and Messiahs: Popular Movements in the Time of Jesus* (Minneapolis: Winston, 1985).

Hort, *Ecclesia*

Hort, F. J. A. *The Christian Ecclesia: A Course of Lectures on the Early History and Early Conceptions of the Ecclesia and One Sermon* (London: Macmillan, 1914).

Hort, *James*

———. *The Epistle of Saint James* (London: Macmillan, 1909).

Houlden, *Pastoral Epistles*

Houlden, James L. *The Pastoral Epistles: I and II Timothy, Titus* (New York: Penguin Books, 1976).

Hultgren, "Persecutions"

Hultgren, Arland J. "Paul's Pre-Christian Persecutions of the Church: Their Purpose, Locale, and Nature," *JBL* 95 (1976): 97-111.

Huxley, *Greek Epic*

Huxley, George Leonard. *Greek Epic Poetry from Eumelos to Panyassis* (London: Faber and Faber, 1969).

Isaksson, *Marriage*

Isaksson, Abel. *Marriage and Ministry in the New Temple: A Study with Special Reference to Mt 19:3-12 and 1 Cor. 6:3-16* (E.T. by Neil Tomkinson; Lund: Gleerup, 1965).

Jaeger, *Paideia*

Jaeger, Werner W. *Paideia: The Ideals of Greek Culture* (3 vols.; New York: Oxford University Press, 1945).

Jaekel, *Sententiae*

Jaekel, Siegfried. *Menandri sententiae: comparatio Menandri et Philistionis* (BSGRT; Leipzig: Teubner, 1964).

Jalabert and Mouterde,

Jalabert, L., and R. Mouterde. *Inscriptions grecques et latines de la Syrie* (3 vols.; Paris: Geuthner, 1950).

Janzen, "'ASRE"

Janzen, Waldemar. "'ASRE in the OT," *Harvard Theological Review* 58 (1965): 215-226.

Jasper, *Prayers*

Jasper, R. C. D., and G. J. Cuming, eds. *Prayers of the Eucharist: Early and Reformed* (London: Collins, 1975).

Jastrow, *Dictionary*

Jastrow, Marcus. *A Dictionary of the Targumim, The Talmud Gabli and Yerushalmi, and the Midrashic Literature* (New York: Pardes, 1950).

Jaubert, "Image"

Jaubert, A. "L'image de la colonne (1 Timothée 3,15)," in *Studiorum Paulinorum Congressus Internationalis Catholicus II, Analecta Biblica* 17-18 (1963), pp. 101-108.

Jeremias, *Parables*

Jeremias, Joachim. *The Parables of Jesus* (E.T. by S. H. Hooke; London: SCM, 1954).

Jeremias, *Prayers*

———. *The Prayers of Jesus* (Philadelphia: Fortress, 1978).

Jeremias, "*Presbyterion*"

———. "*Presbyterion* ausserchistlich bezeugt," *Zeitschrift für die neutestamentliche Wissenschaft* 48 (1957): 127-132.

Jeremias, *Sayings*

———. *Unknown Sayings of Jesus* (E.T. by Reginald Fuller; London: SPCK, 1958).

Jeremias and Strobel, *NTD*

Jeremias, Joachim, and A. Strobel. *Die Briefe an Timotheus und Titus; Der Brief an die Hebräer* (NTD; Göttingen: Vandenhoeck & Ruprecht, 1975).

Jervell, *Paul*

Jervell, Jacob. *The Unknown Paul: Essays on Luke-Acts and Early Christian History* (Minneapolis: Augsburg, 1984).

Jervell, "Traditions"

———. "The Problem of Traditions in Acts," in *Luke and the People of God* (Minneapolis: Augsburg, 1972), pp. 19-40.

Jewett, *Anthropological Terms*

Jewett, Robert. *Paul's Anthropological Terms: A Study of Their Use in Conflict Settings* (Leiden: Brill, 1971).

Jewett, "Conscience"

———. "Conscience," *IDBSup* (Nashville: Abingdon, 1976), pp. 173-174.

Johnson, "*Topos*"

Johnson, Luke Timothy. "James 3:13–4:10 and the *Topos peri Phthonou*," *NovT* 25 (October 1983): 327-347.

Johnson, *Writings*

———. *The Writings of the New Testament: An Interpretation* (Philadelphia: Fortress, 1986).

Johnston, "*Kosmos*"

Johnston, George. "*Oikoumene* and *Kosmos* in the New Testament," *NTS* 10 (1964): 352-360.

Jones, "Imperial Cult"

Jones, D. L. "Christianity and the Roman Imperial Cult," in *ANRW* II.23/2 (ed. H. Temporini and W. Haase; Berlin: de Gruyter, 1980), pp. 1023-1054.

Jonge, *T. 12 Patr.*

Jonge, M. de. *The Testaments of the Twelve Patriarchs: Critical Edition of the Greek Text* (with cooperation of H. W. Hollandes et al.; Leiden: Brill, 1978).

Jongeling et al., *Aramaic Texts*

Jongeling, B., C. J. Labuschagne, and A. S. van der Woude. *Aramaic Texts from Qumran* (Leiden: Brill, 1976).

Jungmann, *Mass*

Jungmann, Josef A. *The Mass of the Roman Rite* (New York: Bruzinger, vol. 1, 1951, vol. 2, 1955).

Karris, "Polemic"

Karris, R. "The Background and Significance of the Polemic of the Pastoral Epistles," *JBL* 92 (1973): 549-564.

Käsemann, *Essais*

Käsemann, Ernst. *Essais Exégétiques* (Neuchâtel: Delachaux & Niestlé, 1972).

Käsemann, *Festschrift*

———. "Das Fomular einer neutestamentlichen Ordinationsparänese," in *Neutestamentliche Studien für Rudolf Bultmann* (ed. W. Eltester; Berlin: Töpelmann, 1957).

Käsemann, *Freedom*

———. *Jesus Means Freedom* (Philadelphia: Fortress, 1970).

Käsemann, *Questions*

———. *New Testament Questions of Today* (E.T. by W. J. Montague; Philadelphia: Fortress, 1969).

Käsemann, *Rom.*

———. *Commentary on Romans* (E.T. by Geoffrey W. Bromiley; Grand Rapids: Wm. B. Eerdmans Publishing Co., 1980).

Katsouris, *Tragedy*

Katsouris, A. G. *Linguistic and Stylistic Characterization: Tragedy and Menander* (Dodone, Supplement 5; Joannina: University Press, 1975).

Kearns, *NCCHS*

Kearns, Conleth, Old Testament ed. *A New Catholic Commentary on Holy Scripture* (London: Nelson, 1969).

Kelly, *Commentary*

Kelly, J. N. D. *A Commentary on the Pastoral Epistles: I Timothy, II Timothy, Titus* (Black's New Testament Commentaries; London: A. Black, 1963).

Kelly, *Creeds*

———. *Early Christian Creeds* (3rd ed.; New York: Longman, 1972).

Kenny, *Stylometric*

Kenny, Anthony. *A Stylometric Study of the NT* (Oxford: Clarendon, 1986).

Keresztes, "Imperial Government"

Keresztes, Paul. "The Imperial Government and the Christian Church," in *ANRW* II.23/1 (Berlin: de Gruyter, 1979), pp. 247-315.

Kilpatrick, "1 Tim 5:22"
Kilpatrick, G. D. "1 Tim 5:22 and Tertullian *De Baptismo* 18:1," *JTS* 16 (1965): 127-128.
Kilpatrick, "Possessive"
———. "The Possessive Pronouns in the NT," *JTS* 42 (1941): 184-186.
Kim, *Recommendation*
Kim, Chan-Hie. *Form and Structure of the Familiar Greek Letter of Recommendation* (SBLDS 4; Missoula, Mont.: Scholars Press, 1972).
Kittel, *Hymns*
Kittel, Bonnie. *The Hymns of Qumran* (SBLDS 50; Chico, Calif.: Scholars Press, 1981).
Klauser, "Akklamation"
Klauser, T. "Akklamation," *RAC* 1 (1950), pp. 216-233.
Knibb, *Enoch*
Knibb, M. *Ethiopic Book of Enoch* (Oxford: Clarendon, 1976).
Knight, "*Authenteō*"
Knight, George W. "*AUTHENTEŌ* in Reference to Women in 1 Timothy 2:12," *NTS* 30 (1984): 143-157.
Knight, *Sayings*
———. *The Faithful Sayings in the PE* (Grand Rapids: Baker, 1979 [Kok, 1968]).
Koester, *HLEC*
Koester, Helmut. *History and Literature of Early Christianity* (Hermeneia; Foundations and Facets, 2 vols.; Philadelphia: Fortress, 1982).
Korn, *PEIRASMOS*
Korn, J. H. *PEIRASMOS: die Versuchung des Gläubigen in der griechischen Bibel* (Stuttgart, 1937).
Kosmala, "Three Nets"
Kosmala, H. "The Three Nets of Belial," *Annual of the Swedish Theological Institute* (Leiden: Brill, 1965), IV, 91-113.
Kraable, *ANRW*
Kraable, A. Thomas. "The Diaspora Synagogue: Archaeological and Epigraphic Evidence Since Sukenik," in *ANRW* II/19.1 (Berlin: de Gruyter, 1979).
Kraable, "*Hypsistos*"
———. "*Hypsistos* and the Synagogue at Sardis," *Greek Roman and Byzantine Studies* 10 (1969): 81-93.
Kraft, *Clavis*
Kraft, Henricus. *Clavis patrum apostolicorum* (Munich: Kösel, 1963).
Kramer, *Christ*
Kramer, Werner. *Christ, Lord Son of God* (London: SCM, 1966).

Krause, *Essays NH*

Krause, Martin, ed. *Essays on the Nag Hammadi Texts: In Honor of Pahor Labib* (Leiden: Brill, 1975).

Kretschmar, "Glaube"

Kretschmar, Georg. "Der paulinische Glaube in der Pastoralbriefen," in *Glaube in NT: Studien zu Ehren von Hermann Binder anlässlich seines 70 Geburtstags* (ed. F. Hahn and H. Klein; Neukirchen-Vluyn: Neukirchener, 1982), pp. 115-140.

Kuhn, "Epheserbrief"

Kuhn, K. G. "Der Epheserbrief im Licht der Qumrantext," *NTS* 7 (1961): 334-346.

Kuhn, *Konkordanz*

———. *Konkordanz zu den Qumrantexten* (Göttingen: Vandenhoeck & Ruprecht, 1960).

Kuhn, *Scrolls*

———. "The Lord's Supper and the Common Meal at Qumran," in *The Scrolls and the New Testament* (ed. K. Stendahl; New York: Harper & Row, 1957).

Lacey, "One Lord"

Lacey, D. de. "One Lord in Pauline Christology (Gal 3:16; 2 Thess 1:8-16; 1 Cor 8:6)," in *Christ the Lord: Studies in Christology Presented to Donald Guthrie* (ed. H. Rowdon; Downers Grove, Ill.: InterVarsity Press, 1982), pp. 191-203.

Lampe, *PGL*

Lampe, Geoffrey W. H. *Patristic Greek Lexicon* (Oxford: Clarendon, 1961).

LaPorte, *Philon*

LaPorte, Jean. *La doctrine eucharistique chez Philon d'Alexandrie*, E.T. *Eucharistia in Philo* (New York: E. Mellen Press, 1983).

Lash, "Hymn-Hunting"

Lash, C. J. "Fashionable Sports: Hymn-Hunting in I Peter," in *Studia Evangelica, Vol. VII: Papers Presented to the Fifth International Congress on Biblical Studies,*" held at Oxford, 1973 (ed. E. A. Livingstone, TU 126; Berlin: Akademie, 1982), pp. 293-297.

A. R. C. Leaney, *RQM*

Leaney, A. R. C. *The Rule of Qumran and Its Meaning* (London: SCM, 1966).

R. Leaney, "*Nomikos*"

Leaney, Robert. "*Nomikos* in Luke's Gospel," *JTS* (1951): 166-167.

Le Deaut, *Nuit*

LeDeaut, Roger. *La Nuit paschale: essai sur la signification de la Pâque juive a partir du Targum d'Exode xii,42* (Rome: PBI, 1963).

Ledogar, *Acknowledgment*

Ledogar, Robert J. *Acknowledgment: Praise-Verbs in the Early Greek Anaphora* (Rome: Herder, 1968).

E. K. Lee, "Words"

Lee, E. K. "Words Denoting 'Pattern' in the New Testament," *NTS* 8 (1962): 166-173.

G. Lee, "Epimenides"

Lee, G. M. "Epimenides in the Epistle to Titus (I 12)," *NovT* 22 (1980): 96.

Légasse, "Prière"

Légasse, Simon. "La prière pour le chefs d'état antécédents judaïques témoins chrétiens du premier siècle," *NovT* 29 (1987): 236-253.

Leipoldt, *Frau*

Leipoldt, Johannes. *Die Frau in der antiken Welt und im Urchristentum* (Gütersloh: Gütersloher Verlagshaus G. Mohn, 1962).

Leivestad, "Meekness"

Leivestad, Ragnar. "The Meekness and Gentleness of Christ," *NTS* 12 (1965-1966): 156-164.

Lemaire, *MOE*

Lemaire, Andre. *Les ministères aux origines de l'Église* (Paris: Cerf, 1971).

LeSaint, *Tertullian*

LeSaint, William P. *Tertullian: Treatises on Penance: On Penitence and on Purity* (ACW 28; Westminster, Md.: Newman, 1959).

Lestapis, *L'Énigme*

Lestapis, Stanislas de. *L'Énigme des Pastorales de Saint Paul* (Paris: Gabalda, 1976).

Levi, *Pausanias*

Levi, Peter. *Pausanias: Guide to Greece* (2 vols.; New York: Penguin, 1979).

Lewis, "Women"

Lewis, Robert M. "The 'Women' of I Timothy 3:11," *Bibliotheca Sacra* 136 (April-June 1979): 167-175.

Liddell, Henry George, Robert Scott, and H. S. Jones. *A Greek-English Lexicon* (9th ed., with Supplement, by E. Barber). See LSJ in Principal Abbreviations.

Lieu, "Greeting"

Lieu, Judith. "'Grace to You and Peace': The Apostolic Greeting," *BJRL* 68 (1985): 161-178.

Lifshitz, *Donateurs*

Lifshitz, Baruch. *Donateurs et fondateurs dans les synagogues juives* (Paris: Gabalda, 1967).

Lightfoot, *AF*

Lightfoot J. B. *The Apostolic Fathers: Part I: S. Clement of Rome* (London: Macmillan, 1890).

Lightman and Zeisel, "Univira"

Lightman, Marjorie, and William Zeisel. "Univira: An Example of Continuity and Change in Roman Society," *Church History* 46 (1977): 19-32.

Ligier, "Last Supper"

Ligier, L. "From the Last Supper to the Eucharist," in *The New Liturgy* (ed. L. Sheppard; London: Darton, 1970).

Ligier, "Origins"

———. "The Origins of the Eucharistic Prayer from the Last Supper to the Eucharist," *Studies Liturgica* 9 (1973): 176-185.

Loader, "Sonship"

Loader, William R. G. "Apocalyptic Model of Sonship: Its Origin and Development in New Testament Tradition," *JBL* (1978): 525-554.

Lock, *Commentary*

Lock, W. *A Critical and Exegetical Commentary on the Pastoral Epistles (I and II Timothy and Titus)* (ICC; Edinburgh: Clark, 1924).

Lohse, *Col*

Lohse, Eduard. *Colossians and Philemon* (Hermeneia; E.T. by William R. Poehlmann and Robert J. Karris; Philadelphia: Fortress, 1971).

Lohse, "Episkopos"

———. "Episkopos in den Pastoralbriefen," in *Kirche und Bibel* (O. Böcher et al.; Zürich: Schöningh, 1979), pp. 225-232.

Longenecker, *Christology*

Longenecker, Richard N. *The Christology of Early Jewish Christianity* (London: SCM, 1970).

Lucchesi, "Precedents"

Lucchesi, E. "Precedents," *JTS* 28 (October 1977): 537-540.

Luck, *Arcana*

Luck, George. *Arcana Mundi* (Baltimore: Johns Hopkins, 1985).

Lührmann, *Glaube*

Lührmann, Dieter. *Glaube im Frühen Christentum* (Gütersloh: Mohr, 1976).

Luther, *Lectures on Titus*

Luther, Martin. *Luther's Works,* vol. 29, *Lectures on Titus, Philemon, and Hebrews* (St. Louis: Concordia, 1968), p. 57. The German edition is *D. Martin Luthers Werke* (Kritische Gesamtausgabe: Weimar edition, 1883ff.).

Lys, "Connotations"

Lys, Daniel. "L'arrière-plan et les connotationes vétérotestamentaires de *sarx* et de *sōma,*" *Vetus Testamentum* 36, no. 2 (1986): 161-204.

MacCary, "Old Men"

MacCary, W. Thomas. "Menander's Old Men," in *Transactions and Proceedings of the American Philological Association,* vol. 102 (ed. John Joseph Keaney; published for the Association by the Press of Case Western Reserve University, 1971), pp. 303-325.

Macho, *Neophyti*

Macho, A. Diez. *Neophyti 1 Targum Palestinense. MS de la Biblioteca Vaticana* (5 vols.; Madrid: Consejo Superior de Investigaciones Científicas, 1968, 1971, 1974, 1978).

MacRae, "Heaven"

MacRae, George W. "Whom Heaven Must Receive until the Time," *Interpretation* 27 (1973): 151-165.

Magie, *Roman Rule*

Magie, David. *Roman Rule in Asia Minor: To the End of the Third Century after Christ* (Princeton, N.J.: Princeton University, 1950).

Makaronas, "Via Egnatia"

Makaronas, Charles. "Via Egnatia and Thessalonike," in *Studies Presented to David M. Robinson on His Seventieth Birthday* (ed. Geo. E. Mylonas; St. Louis: Washington University, 1951), pp. 380-388.

Malherbe, *Cynic Epistles*

Malherbe, Abraham J. *The Cynic Epistles* (SBLSBS 12; Missoula, Mont.: Scholars Press, 1977).

Malherbe, "Inhospitality"

———. "The Inhospitality of Diotrephes," in *God's Christ of His People: Studies in Honor of Nils A. Dahl* (ed. Jacob Jervell and Wayne Meeks; Oslo: Universitetsforlaget, 1977), pp. 222-232; reprinted in his *Social Aspects* (2nd ed.).

Malherbe, "Medical Imagery"

———. "Medical Imagery in the PE," in *Texts and Testaments: Critical Essays on the Bible and Early Church Fathers* (ed. W. Eugene March; San Antonio: Trinity University Press, 1980), pp. 19-35.

Malherbe, *Social Aspects*

———. *Social Aspects of Early Christianity* (2nd ed., enlarged; Philadelphia: Fortress, 1983).

Malherbe, "Theorists"

———. "Ancient Epistolary Theorists," *Ohio Journal of Religious Studies* 15 (1977): 3-77.

Malherbe and Ferguson, *Gregory Moses*

Gregory of Nyssa, St. *Vita Mosis.* Introduction, translation, and notes by Everett Ferguson and Abraham Malherbe (New Haven, Conn.: Yale Divinity School, 1975).

Mandelbaum, "Alcohol"

Mandelbaum, D. G. "Alcohol and Culture," *Current Anthropology* 6 (1965): 281-293; reprinted in *Cross-Cultural Studies of Behavior,* ed. I. A. Issa and W. Dennis (New York: Holt, Rinehart and Winston, 1970), pp. 528-547.

Mansoor, *Hymns*

Mansoor, Menahem. *The Thanksgiving Hymns* (Grand Rapids: Wm. B. Eerdmans Publishing Co., 1961).

Marrou, *Education*

Marrou, Henri I. *A History of Education in Antiquity* (E.T. by George Lamb; New York: Sheed and Ward, 1956).

Marrow, "*Parrhesia*"

Marrow, Stanley B. "*Parrhesia* and the New Testament," *Catholic Biblical Quarterly* 44 (1982): 431-442.

I. Marshall, *Luke*

Marshall, I. Howard. *The Gospel of Luke* (Exeter: Paternoster, 1978).

P. Marshall, "Hybrists"

Marshall, Peter. "Hybrists Not Gnostics in Corinth," *Seminar Papers: SBL* 23 (Chico, Calif.: Scholars Press, 1984), pp. 275-287.

P. Marshall, "Review"

———. "Review of S. G. Wilson *Lk PE,*" *Journal for the Study of the New Testament* 10 (1981): 69-74.

Martimort, *Deaconesses*

Martimort, Aime Georges. *Deaconesses: An Historical Study* (E.T. by K. D. Whitehead; San Francisco: Ignatius Press, 1986).

Martin, *Carmen*

Martin, Ralph P. *Carmen Christi: Philippians 2:5-11 in Recent Interpretation and in the Setting of Early Christian Worship* (London: Cambridge University Press, 1967).

Martin, "N.T. Hymns"

———. "Some Reflections on New Testament Hymns," in *Christ the Lord: Studies in Christology Presented to Donald Guthrie* (ed. Harold Rowdon; Leicester: Inter-Varsity Press, 1982), pp. 37-39.

McCasland, "The Black One"

McCasland, Selby V. "The Black One," in *Early Christian Origins: Studies in Honor of H. R. Willoughby* (ed. A. Wikgren; Chicago: Quadrangle, 1961), pp. 77-80.

McEleney, "Vice Lists"

McEleney, Neil J. "The Vice Lists of the Pastoral Epistles," *Catholic Biblical Quarterly* 36 (1974): 203-219.

McNamara, *NTPT*

McNamara, Martin. *The New Testament and the Palestinian Targum to the Pentateuch* (Rome: PBI, 1966).

McNamara, *Targum*

———. *Targum and Testament* (Shannon, Ireland: Irish University, 1972).

Meeks, *Urban*

Meeks, Wayne. *The First Urban Christians: The Social World of the Apostle Paul* (New Haven, Conn.: Yale, 1983).

Meershoek, *Latin Biblique*

Meershock, C. Q. A. *Le Latin Biblique d'Après Saint Jérôme* (Nijmegen and Utrecht: Dekker and Van de Vegt, 1966).

Meier, "*Presbyteros*"

Meier, John P. "*Presbyteros* in the Pastoral Epistles," *Catholic Biblical Quarterly* 35 (1973): 323-345.

Meijer, "Philosophers"

Meijer, P. "Philosophers, Intellectuals, and Religion in Hellas," in *Faith, Hope, and Worship: Aspects of Religious Mentality in the Ancient World* (ed. H. S. Versnel, Studies in Greek and Roman Religion 2; Leiden: Brill, 1981), pp. 216-263.

Meillet, *DELL*

Meillet, A. *Dictionnaire étymologique de la langua latine, historie des mots* (Paris: Klincksieck, 1959).

Meineke, *FPCN*

Meineke, Augustus. *Fragmenta Poetarum Comoediae Novae* (Berlin: Reimer, 1841).

Menxel, *Elpis*

Menxel, François van. *Elpis, espoir, espérance: Études sémantiques et théologiques de l'espérance dans l'Hellenisme et le Judaisme avant le Nouveau Testament* (Frankfurt am Main and New York: Peter Lang, 1983).

Merk, "Glaube"

Merk, Otto. "Glaube und Tat in der Pastoralbriefen," *Zeitschrift für die neutestamentliche Wissenschaft* 66 (1975): 91-102.

B. Metzger, *Canon*

Metzger, Bruce M. *The Canon of the NT: Its Origin, Development, and Significance* (Oxford: Clarendon, 1987).

B. Metzger, "Early Fragment"

———. "A Hitherto Neglected Early Fragment of the Epistle to Titus," *NovT* 1 (1956): 149-150.

B. Metzger, *TCGNT*

———. *Textual Commentary on the Greek NT* (New York: UBS, 1975).

W. Metzger, *Christushymnus*

Metzger, Wolfgang. *Der Christushymnus 1 Timotheus 3, 16; Fragment einer Homologie der paulinischen Gemeinden* (AzT 62; Stuttgart: Calwer, 1979).

W. Metzger, *Die letzte Reise*

———. *Die letzte Reise des Apostels Paulus. Beobachtungen und Erwagungen zu weinen Itinerar nach Pastoralbriefen* (AzT 59; Stuttgart: Calwer, 1976).

Meyer, *Mithras*

Meyer, Marvin W. "*The Mithras Liturgy*" (edition with E.T. in Greaco-Roman Religion Series 2; Missoula, Mont.: Scholars Press, 1976).

Milgrom, AB *Lev 1–16*

Milgrom, Jacob. *Leviticus 1–16* (AB 3; New York: Doubleday, 1991).

Milik, *Enoch*

Milik, Joseph T. *The Books of Enoch: Aramaic Fragments of Qumran Cave 4* (Oxford: Clarendon, 1976).

Milik, "Melki-sedeq"

———. "Melki-sedeq et Melki-rěsa' dans les anciens écrits juifs et chrétiens," *JJS* 23 (1972): 95-144.

Miller, "Eros"

Miller, Stella G. "Eros and the Arms of Achilles," *American Journal of Archaeology* 90 (1986): 159-170.

Minear, "Apoc. Adj."

Minear, P. S. "An Apocalyptic Adjective," *NovT* 12 (1970): 218-222.

Minear, "Note on Luke"

———. "A Note on Luke 17:7-10," *JBL* 93 (1974): 82-87.

Mohrmann, "Epiphania"

Mohrmann, Christine. "Epiphania," in *Études sur le latin des Chrétiens* (4 vols.; Rome: Edizione d'Istoria e Letteratura, 1958-1977), 1.245-275.

Mohrmann, *Études*. Same as above.

Momigliano, *Quarto Contributo*

Momigliano, Arnaldo. "Time in Ancient Historiography," in *Quarto Contributo Alla Storia degli Studi Classici e del Mondo Antico* (Rome: Edizioni di Storia, 1969), pp. 13-41.

Mommsen, *Provinces*

Mommsen, Theodor. *The Provinces of the Roman Empire: From Caesar to Diocletian* (E.T. by William P. Dickson; 2 vols.; Chicago: Ares, 1974, reprint of 1909 ed.).

Monsengwo, *Nomos*

Monsengwo, Pasinya L. *La notion de Nomos dans le pentateuque* (Rome: PBI, 1973).

C. A. Moore, AB *Dan, add.*

Moore, Carey A. *Daniel, Esther, and Jeremiah: The Additions* (AB 44; Garden City, N.Y.: Doubleday, 1977).

G. F. Moore, "Fate and Free Will"

Moore, G. F. "Fate and Free Will in the Jewish Philosophies according to Josephus," *Harvard Theological Review* 22 (1929): 371-389.

Morgenthaler, *Die lukanische Geschichtsschreibung*

Morgenthaler, R. *Die lukanische Geschichtsschreibung als Zeugnis* (2 vols.; Zürich: Zwingli, 1949).

Morton, *Concordance*

Morton, A. Q., S. Michaelson, and J. D. Thompson. *A Critical Concordance to the PE* (Wooster, Ohio: Biblical Research Associates, 1982).

Mott, "Benevolence"

Mott, Stephen Charles. "The Power of Giving and Receiving: Reciprocity in Hellenistic Benevolence," in *Current Issues in Biblical and Patristic Interpretation: Studies in Honor of Merrill C. Tenney* (ed. Gerald F. Hawthorne; Grand Rapids: Wm. B. Eerdmans Publishing Co., 1975), pp. 60-72.

Mott, "Deliverance"

———. "The Greek Benefactor and Deliverance from Moral Distress," unpublished 1972 Ph.D. thesis; see *Harvard Theological Review* 65 (1972): 601 for summary.

Mott, "Ethics"

———. "Greek Ethics and Christian Conversion: The Philonic Background of Titus 2:10-14 and 3:3-7," *NovT* (1978): 22-48.

Moule, *Birth*

Moule, C. F. D. *Birth of the NT* (3rd ed., rev. and rewritten; HNTC; San Francisco: Harper & Row, 1982).

Moule, *Essays*

———. *Essays in NT Interpretation* (Cambridge: University Press, 1982).

Moule, *Idiom*

———. *Idiom Book of NT Greek* (Cambridge: University Press, 1959).

Moulton, *Grammar*

Moulton, James H. *Grammar of NT Greek* (2 vols.; Edinburgh: Clark, 1908-1919).

Mullins, "Benediction"

Mullins, Terence Y. "Benediction as a NT Form," *Andrews University Seminary Studies* 15 (1977): 59-64.

Munck, "Discourse d'adieu"

Munck, Johannes. "Discourse d'adieu dans le Nouveau Testament et dans littérature biblique," in *Aux Sources de la littérature biblique* (Fest.

M. Goguel; ed. O. Cullmann; Neuchâtel: Delachaux & Niestlé, 1950), pp. 155-170.

Munck, *PSM*

———. *Paul and the Salvation of Mankind* (London: SCM, 1959).

Murphy-O'Connor, "Angels"

Murphy-O'Connor, J. "Redactional Angels in 1 Tim 3:16," *RB* 91 (1984): 178-187.

Murphy-O'Connor, "1 Cor., VIII, 6"

———. "1 Cor., VIII, 6: Cosmology and Soteriology," *RB* 85 (1978): 253-267.

Murphy-O'Connor, *PQ*

———. *Paul and Qumran* (ed. J. Murphy-O'Connor; Chicago: Priory Press, 1968).

Mussier, *Dio Chrys*

Mussier, G. *Dio Chrysostom and the New Testament, Parallels* . . . (Leiden: Brill, 1972).

Musurillo, *Acts*

Musurillo, Herbert A. *The Acts of the Christian Martyrs* (Oxford: Clarendon, 1972).

Musurillo, *Pagan Martyrs*

———, ed. *The Acts of the Pagan Martyrs* (Oxford: Clarendon, 1954).

Muszynski, *Fundament aus Qumran*

Muszynski, Henry K. *Fundament, Bild, und Metaphor in den Handschriften aus Qumran* (AnBib 61; Rome: PBl, 1975).

Nautin, "Rituel"

Nautin, Pierre. "Le rituel de mariage et la formation des sacramentaires 'léonien' et 'gélasien,'" *Ephemerides Liturgicae* 98 (1984): 425-457.

Neufeld, *Confessions*

Neufeld, Vernon. *Earliest Christian Confessions* (Grand Rapids: Wm. B. Eerdmans Publishing Co., 1963).

Nickelsburg, *Ideal Figures*

Nickelsburg, George W., and J. J. Collins, eds. *Ideal Figures in Ancient Judaism: Profiles and Paradigms* (SCS 12; Chico, Calif.: Scholars Press, 1980).

Nock, *Conversion*

Nock, A. D. *Conversion: The Old and the New in Religion from Alexander the Great to Augustine of Hippo* (Oxford: Clarendon, 1993).

Nock, *EGC*

———. *Early Gentile Christianity and Its Hellenistic Background* (New York: Harper Torchbooks, 1964).

Nock, *ERAW*

———. *Essays on Religion and the Ancient World* (ed. Zephaniah Stewart; 2 vols.; Cambridge: Harvard University Press, 1972).

Nolland, "Grace"

Nolland, John. "Grace as Power," *NovT* 28 (January 1986): 26-31.

Nordheim, *Das Testament*

Nordheim, E. von. *Die Lehre der Alten: I. Das Testament als Litteraturgattung im Judentum der hellenistisch-römischen Zeit* (Arbeiten zur Literatur und Geschichte des hellenistischen Judentums 13; Leiden: Brill, 1980).

O'Brien, "Thanksgiving"

O'Brien, P. T. "Thanksgiving and the Gospel in Paul," *NTS* 21 (1974): 144-145.

O'Callaghan, "Cueva 7"

O'Callaghan, Jose. "Los papiros griegos de la cueva 7 de Qumrân," *JBL* 95 (1976): 459.

O'Connor, *Verse*

O'Connor, Michael Patrick. *Hebrew Verse Structure* (Winona Lake, Ind.: Eisenbrauns, 1980).

Oke, "Doxology"

Oke, C. Clare. "Doxology Not to God but to Christ [1 Timothy 1:17]," *Expository Times* 67 (1956): 367-368.

Oldfather, "Menander"

Oldfather, W. R., and W. L. Daly. "A Quotation from Menander in the Pastoral Epistles," *Classical Philology* 38 (1943): 202-204.

Olley, *Righteousness*

Olley, John W. *"Righteousness" in the Septuagint of Isaiah: A Contextual Study* (SBL Septuagint and Cognate Studies Series; Missoula, Mont.: Scholars Press, 1979).

O'Malley, *Tertullian*

O'Malley, T. P. *Tertullian and the Bible* (Nijmegen: Dekker, 1976).

Ong, *Presence*

Ong, Walter J. *The Presence of the Word: Some Prolegomena for Cultural and Religious History* (New Haven, Conn.: Yale University Press, 1967).

Oulton, *Alexandrian*

Oulton, John E. L., and Henry Chadwick. *Alexandrian Christianity* (vol. 2 of the Library of Christian Classics; Philadelphia: Westminster Press, 1954).

Owens, "*Kalon*"

Owens, J. "The *Kalon* in Aristotle's Ethics," in *Studies in Aristotle* (ed. Dominic J. O'Meara, Studies in Philosophy and the History of Philosophy 9; Washington, D.C.: Catholic University of America, 1981), pp. 261-277.

Pagels, "Adam"

Pagels, Elaine. "Adam, Eve, and the Serpent," *Commonweal* 115 (1988): 570-571.

Palmer, *RRRE*

Palmer, Robert E. A. *Roman Religion and Roman Empire* (Philadelphia: University of Pennsylvania, 1974).

Pardee, *Handbook*

Pardee, Dennis. *Handbook of Ancient Hebrew Letters: A Study Edition* (with a chapter on Tannaitic letter fragments by S. David Sperling; with the collaboration of J. David Whitehead and Paul E. Dion; Chico, Calif.: Scholars Press, 1982).

Pardee, "Overview"

———. "An Overview of Ancient Hebrew Epistotography," *JBL* 97 (1978): 321-346.

Pardee, *RevQ*

———. "A Restudy of the Commentary on Psalm 37 from Qumran Cave 4," *RevQ* 8 (1973): 163-194.

Parry, *Pastoral Epistles*

Parry, R. St. John. *The Pastoral Epistles* (Cambridge: University Press, 1920).

Penella, *Apollonius*

Penella, Robert J. *The Letters of Apollonius of Tyana* (Lugduni Batavorum; Leiden: Brill, 1979).

Penna, "Configurazione"

Penna, Romano. "Configurazione Giudeo-Cristiana della chiesa de Roma nel I secolo," *Lateranum* 50 (1984): 101-113.

Penna, "Juifs/Ebrei"

———. "Les Juifs à Rome au temps de l'apôtre Paul," *NTS* 28 (1982): 321-347; corrected and enlarged in "Gli Ebrei a Roma al tempo dell'Apostolo Paole," *Lateranum* 50 (1983): 101-113.

Perdue, "Parenesis"

Perdue, Leo G. "Parenesis and the Epistle of James," *Zeitschrift für neutestamentliche Wissenschaft* 72 (1981): 241-256.

Petrolini, "Valenza *Kairos*"

Petrolini, Enrica. "Valenza filosofica dell'antico termine *Kairos*," *Sapienza* 30 (1977): 346-362.

Pfitzner, *Agon*

Pfitzner, Victor C. *Paul and the Agon Motif* (Leiden: Brill, 1967).

Pfitzner, *PAM*

———. *Paul and the Agōn Motif: Traditional Athletic Imagery in the Pauline Literature* (*NovTSup* 16; Leiden: Brill, 1967).

Plumpe, *Mater*

Plumpe, Joseph. *Mater Ecclesia* (Washington, D.C.: Catholic University of America, 1943).

Porter, "Adjectival Attributive"

Porter, Stanley E. "The Adjectival Attributive Genitive in the NT: A Grammatical Study," *Trinity Journal* 4 (spring 1983): 3-17.

Potterie, "Mari"

Potterie, Ignace. "Mari d'une seule femme: Le Sens théologique d'une formule paulinienne," in *Paul de Tarse: Apôtre du Notre Temps* (Rome: Abbaye de S. Paul, 1979), pp. 619-638.

Potterie, "Truth"

———. "Truth," in *Dictionary of Biblical Theology* (ed. Xavier Leon-Dufour, 2nd ed.; New York: Seabury, 1973), pp. 618-621.

Potterie, *Ver. S. Jn*

———. La Vérité dans Saint Jean (2 vols.; Rome: PBI, 1977).

Preisigke, *Namenbuch*

Preisigke, Friedrich. *Namenbuch* (Heidelberg: Gelbstverlag, 1922).

Preisigke, *Wörterbuch*

———. *Wörterbuch der griechischen papyrusurkunden* . . . (Berlin: Grete Preisigke Grohzig, 1927).

Price, *Rituals*

Price, S. R. F. *Rituals and Power* (Cambridge: University Press, 1984).

Prior, *Paul*

Prior, Michael Patrick. *Paul the Letter-Writer and the Second Letter to Timothy* (*Journal for the Study of the New Testament* supplement series; Sheffield: Sheffield Academic Press, 1989).

Pritchard, *ANEP*

Pritchard, James. *The Ancient NE in Pictures* (Princeton, N.J.: Princeton University Press, 1954).

Purvis, "Paleography"

Purvis, James D. "The Paleography of the Samaritan Inscription from Thessalonica," *American Schools of Oriental Research Bulletin* 221 (1976): 121-123.

Quasten, *Music*

Quasten, Johannes. *Music and Worship in Pagan and Christian Antiquity* (E.T. by Boniface Ramsey; Washington, D.C.: National Association of Pastoral Musicians, 1983).

Quasten, *Patrology*

———. *Patrology* (3 vols.; Utrecht, Holland: Spectrum, 1950).

Quimron and Strugnell, "Halakhic Letter"

Quimron, E., and J. Strugnell. "An Unpublished Halakhic Letter from Qumran," in *BAT,* pp. 400-407.

Quinn, "Ap. Ministry"

Quinn, Jerome D. "Apostolic Ministry and Apostolic Prayer," *Catholic Biblical Quarterly* 33 (1971): 479-91.

Quinn, "Captivity"

———. "Paul's Last Captivity," *Studia Biblica* 3 (1978) (ed. E. A. Livingstone; Sheffield: JSOT, 1980), pp. 289-299.

Quinn, "Holy Spirit"

———. "The Holy Spirit in the Pastoral Epistles," in *Sin, Salvation, and the Spirit: Commemorating the Fiftieth Year of the Liturgical Press* (ed. D. Durken; Collegeville, Minn.: Liturgical, 1979), pp. 345-368.

Quinn, "Jesus as Savior"

———. "Jesus as Savior and Only Mediator (1 Tim 2:3-6): Linguistic Paradigms of Acculturation," in *Fede e Cultura/Foi et culture* (Turin: Elle di Ci, 1981), pp. 249-260.

Quinn, *AB Titus*

———. *The Letter to Titus* (AB 35; New York: Doubleday, 1990).

Quinn, "Ministry"

———. "Ministry in the New Testament," in *Biblical Studies in Contemporary Thought* (Somerville, Mass.: Grerno, Hadden, 1975), pp. 130-160.

Quinn, "Ordination"

———. "Ordination in the Pastoral Epistles," *Communio International Catholic Review* 8 (1981): 358-369.

Quinn, "$P^{46}$"

———. "$P^{46}$ — the Pauline Canon?" *Catholic Biblical Quarterly* 36 (1974): 379-385.

Quinn, "Parenesis/Settings"

———. "Parenesis and the Pastoral Epistles," in *Semeia*, forthcoming; the first part is a revision of H. Cazelles, *Mélanges, De la Tôrah au Messie* (ed. J. Doré, P. Grelot, and M. Carrez; Paris: Desclée, 1981), pp. 495-501.

Quinn, *Perspectives*

———. "The Last Volume of Luke: The Relation of Luke-Acts and the PE," in *Perspectives on Luke-Acts* (ed. C. Talbert; Macon, Ga.: Mercer, 1978), pp. 62-75.

Quinn, "Propitiation"

———. "Propitiation," in *Lutherans and Catholics in Dialogue III: The Eucharist as Sacrifice* (1967), pp. 37-44.

Quinn, "Seven Times"

———. "Seven Times He Wore Chains (*I Clem.* 5.6)," *JBL* 97 (1978): 574-576.

Quinn, "Terminology"

———. "On the Terminology for Faith, Truth, Teaching, and the Spirit in the PE: A Summary," in *Teaching Authority and Infallibility in the Church: Lu-*

*therans and Catholics in Dialqgue VI* (ed. P. Empie, T. A. Murphy, and J. A. Burgess; Minneapolis: Augsburg, 1980), pp. 232-237.

Rad, *Hexateuch*

Rad, Gerhard von. *The Problem of the Hexateuch and Other Essays* (E.T. by E. W. Trueman Dicken; Edinburgh: Oliver & Boyd, 1966).

Rahlfs, *Sept.*

Rahlfs, Alfred, ed. *Septuaginta* (5th ed.; Stuttgart: Württembergische Bibelanstalt, 1952).

Rahmani, *Testamentum*

Rahmani, Ignatius Ephraem II. *Testamentum Domini Nostri* (Moguntiae: Kirchenheim, 1899; reprint, Georg Olms, 1968).

Rahner, "*Theos* in NT"

Rahner, Karl. "*Theos* in the New Testament," in *Theological Investigations* (Baltimore: Helicon, 1961), pp. 79-148.

Räisänen, "Werkgerechtigkeit"

Räisänen, Heikki. "Werkgerechtigkeit eine frükatholische Lehre?" *Studia Theologica* 37 (1983): 79-99.

Reicke, "Chronologie"

Reicke, Bo. "Chronologie der Pastoralbriefe," *Theologische Literaturzeitung* 101 (1976): 81-93.

Reicke, *Luke*

———. *The Gospel of Luke* (Richmond, Va.: John Knox Press, 1962).

Reitzenstein, *Mystery-Religions*

Reitzenstein, Richard. *Hellenistic Mystery-Religions: Their Basic Ideas and Significance* (E.T. by John E. Steely; Pittsburgh: Pickwick Press, 1978).

Renehan, *Notes*

Renehan, Robert. *Greek Lexicographical Notes: A Critical Supplement to the Greek-English Lexicon of LSJ* (Göttingen: Vandenhoeck & Ruprecht, 1975).

Renehan, "Quotations"

———. "Classical Greek Quotations in the NT," in *The Heritage of the Early Church* (ed. David Neiman and Margaret Schatkin; Orientalia Christiana Analecta 195; Rome: Pontificale Institutum Studiorum Orientalium, 1973), pp. 17-45.

Renehan, *Text. Crit.*

———. *Greek Textual Criticism: A Reader* (Cambridge: Harvard University Press, 1969).

Rengstorf, "Traces"

Rengstorf, Karl H. "Old and New Testament Traces of a Formula of the Judean Royal Ritual," *NovT* 5 (1962): 229-244.

Reumann, "Covenant"

Reumann, John N. P. "Oikonomia = 'Covenant': Terms for Heilsgeschichte in Early Christian Usage," *NovT* 3 (1959): 282-292.

Reumann, "Ethical Accommodation"

———. "Oikonomia as 'Ethical Accommodation' in the Fathers, and Its Pagan Backgrounds," in *Studia Patristica* III (ed. F. L. Cross [Texte und Untersuchungen zur Geschichte der altchristlichen Literatur 78]; Berlin: Akademie-Verlag, 1961).

Reumann, "Heilsgeschichte"

———. "Heilsgeschichte in Luke: Some Remarks on Its Background and Comparison with Paul," in *Studia Evangelica* 4 (1968).

Reumann, "Jesus the Steward"

———. "'Jesus the Steward': An Overlooked Theme in Christology," in *Studia Evangelica* 512 (ed. F. L. Cross; Texte und Untersuchungen 103; Berlin: Akademie Verlag, 1968), pp. 21-29.

Reumann, "Oikonomia"

———. "Oikonomia — Terms in Paul in Comparison with Lucan Heilsgeschichte," *NTS* 13 (1966-1967): 147-167.

Reumann, *Righteousness*

———. *"Righteousness" in the NT,* with responses by Joseph A. Fitzmyer and Jerome D. Quinn (Philadelphia: Fortress, 1982).

Reumann, "Stewards"

———. "Stewards of God: Pre-Christian Religious Application of Oikonomos in Greek," *JBL* 77 (1958): 339-349.

Reumann, "Use of *Oikonomia*"

———. "The Use of *Oikonomia* and Related Terms in Greek Sources to about A.D. 100 as a Background for Patristic Applications," *Ekklesiastikos Pharos* (Addis Ababa: 60 [3-4, 1978]), Part I (1978), 482-579; Part II (1979), 563-603; Part II (1980), 368-430; Part II (1981), 591-617; Part II (1982), 115-140.

Riesenfeld, "*Arneisthai*"

Riesenfeld, H. "The Meaning of the Verb *Arneisthai*," in *Coniectanea Neotestamentica* (Lund: Gleerup, 1947), pp. 207-219.

Rigaux, *Letters*

Rigaux, Beda. *The Letters of St. Paul: Modern Studies* (ed. S. Yonick; Chicago: Franciscan Herald Press, 1968).

Ringgren, *Faith*

Ringgren, Helmer. *The Faith of Qumran: Theology of the Dead Sea Scrolls* (E.T. by Emilie T. Sander; Philadelphia: Fortress, 1963).

Roberts, *Codex*

Roberts, Colin H. *The Codex*, in *Proceedings of the British Academy* 40 (1954), pp. 169-204.

Roberts, *Manuscript*

———. *Manuscript, Society, and Belief in Early Christian Egypt* (London: Oxford University Press, 1979).

Roberts, "P. Yale I"

———. "P. Yale I and the Early Christian Book," in *American Studies in Papyrology*, vol. 1, *Essays in Honor of C. Bradford Welles* (New Haven, Conn.: American Society of Papyrologists, 1967), pp. 25-28.

Roberts and Skeat, *Birth*

Roberts, Colin H., and Theodore Cressey Skeat. *The Birth of the Codex* (London: Oxford University Press for the British Academy, 1983).

J. A. Robinson, *Texts*

Robinson, J. Armitage. *Texts and Studies* (Cambridge: University Press, 1891; Krause, 1967).

J. M. Robinson, "Historicality"

Robinson, James M. "The Historicality of Biblical Language," in *The Old Testament and Christian Faith* (ed. B. W. Anderson; New York: Harper & Row, 1963), pp. 124-158.

J. M. Robinson, "Hodayot-formel"

———. "Die Hodayot-formel in Gebet und Hymnus der Frühchristentums," in *Apophoreta: Festschrift für Ernst Haenchen zu seinem 70 Geburtstag* (ed. W. Eltester; Berlin: Toepelmann, 1964), pp. 194-235.

J. M. Robinson, *NHL*

———, ed. *The Nag Hammadi Library* (San Francisco: Harper & Row, 1977).

Romaniuk, "L'Origine . . . Pour Nous"

Romaniuk, Kazimierz. "L'Origine des Formules Pauliniennes 'Le Christ c'est Livré pour nous,' 'Le Christ nous a aimés et c'est livré pour nous,'" *NovT* 5 (1962): 55-76.

Rordorf, *Sunday*

Rordorf, Willy. *Sunday: The History of the Day of Rest and Worship in the Earliest Centuries of the Christian Church* (E.T. by A. A. K. Graham; Philadelphia: Westminster Press, 1968).

Rossi, *Column*

Rossi, Lino. *Trajan's Column and the Dacian Wars* (E.T. revised by J. M. C. Toynbee; Ithaca, N.Y.: Cornell University Press, 1971).

Sachot, "Salut"

Sachot, M. "Pour une étude de la notion de salut chez les Pères Apostoliques," *Recherches de science religieuse* 51 (1977): 54-70.

Sampley, *Two/One*

Sampley, J. Paul. *And the Two Shall Become One Flesh: A Study of Traditions in Ephesians 5:21-33* (Cambridge: University Press, 1971).

Sandbach, *Menandri*

Sandbach, Francis Henry. *Menandri Reliquiae selectae* (Oxford: Clarendon, 1972).

Sandmel, "Myths"

Sandmel, Samuel. "Myths, Genealogies, and Jewish Myths and the Writing of the Gospels," in *Two Living Traditions: Essays on Religion and the Bible* (Detroit: Wayne State University Press, 1972), pp. 158-165.

Sass, "*Doulos*"

Sass, G. "Zur Bedeutung von *doulos* bei Paulus," *Zeitschrift für neutestamentliche Wissenschaft* 40 (1941): 24-32.

Schadewaldt, "Humanitas Romana"

Schadewaldt, Werner von. "Humanitas Romana," in *ANRW* I.4 (ed. Hildegard Temporini; Berlin: de Gruyter, 1973), pp. 43-62.

Schalit, *Concordance*

Schalit, A. *A Complete Concordance to Flavius Josephus: Supplement* (Leiden: Brill, 1973-).

Schenk, "Forschung"

Schenk, W. "Die Pastoralbriefe (I und II Tim. und Tit.) in der neueren Forschung (1945-1985)," in *ANRW* II.25/4 (ed. W. Haas; Berlin: de Gruyter, 1988).

Schiffman, "Non-Jews"

Schiffman, Lawrence H. "Legislation Concerning Relations with Non-Jews in the *Zadokite Fragments* and in Tannaitic Literature," *RevQ* 11, no. 43 (December 1983): 379-389.

Schiffman, "Testimony"

———. "The Qumran Law of Testimony," *RevQ* 8 (December 1975): 603-612.

Schlier, *Galater*

Schlier, Heinrich. *Der Brief an die Galater* (Göttingen: Vandenhoeck, 1965 [1949]).

Schmidt, "Interpolation"

Schmidt, Daryl. "1 Thess 2:13-16: Linguistic Evidence for Interpolation," *JBL* 102 (1983): 269-279.

Schnackenburg, "Apostles Before"

Schnackenburg, Rudolf. "Apostles before and during Paul's Time," in *Apostolic History and the Gospel* (E.T. by M. Kwiran and W. Gasque; ed. W. Gasque; Grand Rapids: Wm. B. Eerdmans Publishing Co., 1970), pp. 287-303.

Schnackenburg, *God's Rule*

———. *God's Rule and Kingdom* (New York: Herder and Herder, 1968).

Schoder, *Hellas*

Schoder, Raymond V. *Wings over Hellas: Ancient Greece from the Air* (New York: Oxford University Press, 1974).

Schoedel, *Ignatius*

Schoedel, William R. *Ignatius of Antioch: A Commentary on the Letters of Ignatius of Antioch* (ed. Helmut Koester; Philadelphia: Fortress, 1985).

Schoonheim, "*Huperēphanos*"

Schoonheim, P. L. "Der alttestamentliche Boden der Vokable *huperēphanos* Lukas 1:51," *NovT* 8 (1966): 235-246.

Schramm, *Fest/Festival*

Schramm, Tim, and Otto Eckert. *Fest und Freude* (Stuttgart: Kohlhammer, 1977); E.T. by James L. Blenins, *Festival and Joy in the NT* (Nashville: Abingdon, 1980).

Schubert, *Form*

Schubert, Paul. *Form and Function of the Pauline Thanksgivings* (Berlin: A. Töpelman, 1939).

Schürer, *HJP*

Schürer, E. *History of the Jewish People in the Age of Jesus Christ* (2nd ed.; Edinburgh: Clark, 1973-1986).

Schweizer, "Creeds"

Schweizer, Eduard. "Two New Testament Creeds Compared," in *Current Issues in New Testament Interpretation* (ed. W. Klassen; London: SCM, 1962).

Schweizer, *Lordship*

———. *Lordship and Discipleship: Studies in Biblical Theology* (London: SCM, 1960).

Scott, *Pastoral Epistles*

Scott, E. F. *The Pastoral Epistles* (London: Hodder & Stoughton, 1936).

Scroggs, *Homosexuality*

Scroggs, Robin. *The New Testament and Homosexuality* (Philadelphia: Fortress, 1993).

Selwyn, *1 Pet*

Selwyn, Edward G. *The First Epistle of Saint Peter* (London: Macmillan, 1961).

Sherwin-White, *RSRL*

Sherwin-White, A. N. *Roman Society and Roman Law in the New Testament* (Oxford: Clarendon, 1963).

Silk, *Imagery*

Silk, M. S. *Interaction in Poetic Imagery* (Cambridge: University Press, 1974).

Simpson, *Pastoral Epistles*

Simpson, E. K. *The Pastoral Epistles: The Greek Text with Introduction and Commentary* (Grand Rapids: Wm. B. Eerdmans Publishing Co., 1954).

Skeat, "On 2 Tim 4:13"

Skeat, T. C. "Especially the Parchments: A Note on 2 Timothy 4:13," *JTS* 30 (1979): 173-177.

Skeat, "Vaticanus"

———. "The Codex Vaticanus in the Fifteenth Century," *JTS* 35 (October 1984): 454-465.

Smallwood, *Jews*

Smallwood, E. Mary. *The Jews under Roman Rule from Pompey to Diocletian* (Leiden: Brill, 1976).

Snyder, *Pacem*

Snyder, Graydon F. *Ante Pacem: Archaeological Evidence of Church Life before Constantine* (Macon, Ga.: Mercer University Press, 1985).

Sophocles, *Greek Lexicon*

Sophocles, E. A. *Greek Lexicon of the Roman and Byzantine Periods* (2 vols.; New York: Frederick Ungar Publishing, 1957).

Spicq, *Agape*

Spicq, Ceslaus. *Agape dans le NT/Agape in the New Testament* (E.T. by Marie A. McNamara and Mary H. Richter, 3 vols.; St. Louis: B. Herder, 1963-1966).

Spicq, *"Aretē"*

———. "Note de lexicographie: *ARETĒ*," *RB* 89 (1982): 161-176.

Spicq, *EP*

———. *Les Épîtres Pastorales* (Paris: Gabalda, 1969).

Spicq, "1 Tim 5:23"

———. "1 Tim 5:23," in *L'Évangile hier et aujourd'hui* (Paris: Labor et Fides, 1968), pp. 143-150.

Spicq, *Lexic./Supp. Lexic.*

———. *Notes de Lexicographie Néotestamentaire* (2 vols. and Supplement: Göttingen: Vandenhoeck & Ruprecht, 1982).

Spicq, "Pèlerine"

———. "Pèlerine et vêtements (A propos de II Tim IV, 13 et Act XX, 33)," in *Mélanges Eugène Tisserant* by P. Hennequin et al. (Vatican City: Biblioteca Apostolica Vaticana, 1964), pp. 384-391.

Spicq, "*Philostorgos*"

———. "*Philostorgos:* a propos de Rom. 12:10," *RB* 62 (1955): 497-510.

Spicq, *Prolégomènes*

———. *Agape Prolégomènes a une étude de théologie néo-testamentaire* (Leiden: Brill, 1955).

Spicq, "Religion"

———. "Religion (vertu de). Nouveau Testament," in *Dictionnaire de la Bible, Supplément,* vol. 10 (Paris: Letouzey & Ane, 1987), pp. 223-228.

Spinks, "Anaphora"

Spinks, B. "A Complete Anaphora? A Note on Strasbourg Gr. 254," *Heythrop Journal* 25 (1984): 51-59.

Spinks, "Anaphoral Evolution"

———. "Beware the Liturgical Horses! An English Interjection on Anaphoral Evolution," *Worship* 59 (1985): 211-219.

Staden, "Hairesis"

Staden, Heinrich von. "Hairesis and Heresy: The Case of the *Hairesis Ioctrikoci*," in *Jewish and Christian Self-Definition* (ed. Ben E. Meyer and E. P. Sanders, vol. 3; Philadelphia: Fortress, 1980), pp. 76-100.

Stanley, *Church*

Stanley, David M. *The Apostolic Church in the New Testament* (Westminster, Md.: Newman Press, 1965).

Stanley, *Resurrection*

———. *Christ's Resurrection in Pauline Soteriology* (Rome: PBI, 1961).

Stenger, *Christushymnus*

Stenger, W. *Der Christushymnus I Tim 3,16: Eine Strukturanalytische Untersuchung* (Regensburger Studien zur Theologie 6; Frankfort: Peter Lang, 1977).

Stern, *Authors on Jews*

Stern, Menahen, ed. *Greek and Latin Authors on Jews and Judaism* (3 vols.; Jerusalem: Israel Academy of Sciences and Humanities, 1974).

Stevenson, *Nuptial*

Stevenson, Kenneth W. *Nuptial Blessing: A Study of Christian Marriage Rites* (New York: Oxford University Press, 1983).

Stillwell, *PECS*

Stillwell, Richard, ed. *Princeton Encyclopedia of Classical Sites* (Princeton, N.J.: Princeton University, 1976).

Stowers, *Letter Writing*

Stowers, Stanley K. *Letter Writing in Greco-Roman Antiquity* (Library of Early Christianity 5; ed. W. A. Meeks; Philadelphia: Westminster Press, 1986).

Strack and Billerbeck

Strack, Hermann, and Paul Billerbeck. *Kommentar zum Neuen Testament aus Talmud und Midrasch* (6 vols.; Munich: Beck, 1922-1961).

Strange, *1 Tim 3:16*

Strange, J. F. *Critical and Exegetical Study of 1 Timothy 3:16* (Madison, N.J.: Drew University, 1970).

Strobel, "Schreiben des Lukas?"

Strobel, A. "Schreiben des Lukas? Zum sprachlichen Problem der Pastoralbriefe," *NTS* 15 (1969): 191-210.

Strugnell, "Notes"

Strugnell, John. "Notes en marge du Volume V," *Römische Quartalschrift für christliche Altertumskunde und Kirchengeschichte* 1 (1970): 163-276.

Stuiber, "Eulogia"

Stuiber, A. "Eulogia," *RAC* (1966), 6.904-920.

Sudhaus

Sudhaus, Siegfried. *Philodemi: Volumina Rhetorica* (2 vols. and Supplement; Leipzig: Teubner, 1892).

Sutcliffe, "Hatred"

Sutcliffe, Edmund. "Hatred at Qumran," *RevQ* 2 (1960): 345-355.

Swete, *Theodore*

Swete, Henry B., ed. *Epistolas B. Pauli comentarii, the Latin version with the Greek Fragments . . .* (2 vols.; Cambridge: University Press, 1880).

Swift, "War"

Swift, L. J. "War and the Christian Conscience, I: The Early Years," in *ANRW* II.25/1 (1979), pp. 835-868.

Talley, "Eucharistic Prayer"

Talley, Thomas J. "The Eucharistic Prayer of the Ancient Church according to Recent Research: Results and Reflections," *Studia Liturgica* 11 (1976): 138-158.

Talley, "From *Berakah*"

———. "From *Berakah* to *Eucharistia:* A Reopening Question," *Worship* 50 (1976): 115-137.

Talley, "Tradition"

———. "The Eucharistic Prayer: Tradition and Development," in *Liturgy Reshaped* (ed. K. Stevenson; London: SPCK, 1982), pp. 48-64.

Testuz, *Bodmer X-XII*

Testuz, M. *Papyrus Bodmer X-XII.XII: Fragment d'un hymne liturgique* (Cologny-Genève: Bibliotheca Bodmeriana, 1959).

Theissen, *Setting*

Theissen, G. *The Social Setting of Early Christianity: Essays on Corinth* (E.T. with an introduction by J. H. Schotz; Philadelphia: Fortress, 1982).

Therrien, *Discernement*

Therrien, Gerard. *Le Discernement dans les écrits pauliniens* (Paris: J. Gabalda, 1973).

Thiede, "7Q"

Thiede, Carsten Peter. "7Q: ein Rückkehr zu den neutestamentlichen Papyrusfragmenten in der siebten Höhle von Qumran," *Biblica* 65 (1984).

Thompson, *Origin*

Thompson, Thomas L. *The Origin Tradition of Ancient Israel,* vol. 1, *The Liter-*

*ary Formation of Genesis and Exodus 1–23* (*JSOT* Supplement 55; Sheffield: Sheffield Academy Press, 1987).

Throckmorton, "*Sōzein*"

Throckmorton, B. N. "*Sōzein, sōtēria* in Luke-Acts," in *Studia Evangelica: Papers Presented to the Fourth International Congress on NT Studies Held at Oxford, 1969* (ed. Elizabeth A. Livingstone, vol. 6; Berlin: Akademie, 1973), pp. 515-526.

Towner, "Eschatology"

Towner, P. H. "The Present Age in the Eschatology of the Pastoral Epistles," *NTS* 32 (1986): 427-448.

Trites, *NT Concept of Witness*

Trites, Allison A. *The New Testament Concept of Witness* (Cambridge: University Press, 1977).

Tuckett, "Paul"

Tuckett, C. M. "Paul and the Synoptic Mission Discourse," *Ephemerides Theologicae Lovanienses* 60 (1984), 4.376-381.

E. Turner, *Typology*

Turner, Eric G. *The Typology of the Early Codex* (Philadelphia: University of Pennsylvania Press, 1977).

N. Turner, *Grammar*

Turner, Nigel, ed. *A Grammar of NT Greek,* vols. 3 and 4 (ed. James Hope Moulton; Edinburgh: Clark, 1963-1976).

N. Turner, *Insights*

———. *Grammatical Insights into NT Greek* (Edinburgh: Clark, 1965).

N. Turner, "NT Vocab."

———. "New Testament Vocabulary," *NovT* 16 (April 1974): 149-160.

N. Turner, *Words*

———. *Christian Words* (Nashville: Nelson, 1981).

V. Turner, *Forest*

Turner, Victor Witter. *The Forest of Symbols; Aspects of Ndembu Ritual* (Ithaca, N.Y.: Cornell University Press, 1967).

V. Turner, *Ritual*

———. *From Ritual to Theatre: The Human Seriousness of Play* (New York: Performing Arts Journal Publications; Baltimore: Johns Hopkins University Press, 1982).

Unnik, "Background"

Unnik, W. C. van. "'Worthy Is the Lamb': The Background of Apoc 5," in *Mélanges biblique en hommage au R. P. Béda Rigaux* (ed. A. Descamps and A. de Halleux; Gembloux: Duculot, 1970), pp. 445-461.

Unnik, "Kirchenordungnen"

———. *RGG* (1959), 3.1496-1497.

Unnik, *Sparsa*

———. *Sparsa Collecta, the Collected Essays of W. C. van Unnik* (3 vols.; Leiden: Brill, 1973-1983).

Unnik, *Tarsus*

———. *Tarsus or Jerusalem: The City of Paul's Youth* (E.T. by George Ogg; London: Epworth, 1962; reprinted in his *Sparsa* 1.259-320).

Van Der Horst

Van Der Horst, P. W. *The Sentences of Pseudo-Phocylides* (Leiden: Brill, 1978).

Vaux, *Israel*

Vaux, Roland de. *Ancient Israel* (E.T. by John McHugh; New York: McGraw-Hill, 1961).

Vaux, *SOTS*

———. *Studies in Old Testament Sacrifices* (Cardiff: University of Wales Press, 1964).

Vermes, *Discovery*

Vermes, Geza. *Discovery in the Judean Desert* (New York: Desclée Co., 1956).

Vermes, *DSS*

———. *The Dead Sea Scrolls in English* (Baltimore: Penguin, 1962).

Vermes, "Impact"

———. "Impact of the Dead Sea Scrolls on the Study of the New Testament," *JJS* 27 (1976): 107-116.

Vermeulen, "*EPIPHANEIA*"

Vermeulen, A. J. "*EPIPHANEIA*," in *Graecitas et Latinitas Christianorum Primaeva* (ed. C. Mohrmann et al.; *Supplementa fasciculus I;* Nijmegen: Dekker and Van de Vegt, 1964).

Verner, *Household*

Verner, David C. *The Household of God: The Social World of the PE* (SBLDS 71; Chico, Calif.: Scholars Press, 1983).

Vielhauer, *Geschichte*

Vielhauer, Philipp. *Geschichte der Urchristlichen Literatur* (Berlin: de Gruyter, 1975).

Vliet, *Testimony*

Vliet, H. van. *No Single Testimony: A Study on the Adoption of the Law of Deuteronomy 19:15 Par. into the NT* (Utrecht: Drukkerij, 1958).

Vogel, *Column*

Vogel, Lise. *The Column of Antonius Pius* (Cambridge: Harvard University Press, 1973).

Vogt, "Peace among Men"

Vogt, E. "Peace among Men of God's Good Pleasure," in K. Stendahl, *Scrolls and the New Testament* (New York: Harper, 1957), pp. 114-117.

Volkmann, *Res Gestae*
Volkmann, Hans. *Res Gestae Divi Augusti: Das Monumentum Ancyranum* (Berlin: Walter de Gruyter, 1969).

Vouaux, *Pierre*
Vouaux, Leon. *Les Actes de Pierre* (Paris: Letouzey, 1922).

Wallace, "Adjective"
Wallace, Daniel B. "The Relation of Adjective to Noun in Anarthous Constructions in the NT," *NovT* 26 (April 1984): 128-167.

Walsh, "*Spes*"
Walsh, P. G. "*Spes Romana, Spes Christiana,*" *Prudentia* 6 (1974): 33-42.

Walton, *Polyglotta*
Walton, Brian. *Biblia Sacra Polyglotta* . . . (London: Thomas Roycroft, 1965).

Walzer, *Galen*
Walzer, Richard. *Galen on Jews and Christians* (London: Oxford University Press, 1949).

Ward-Perkins, *Pompeii*
Ward-Perkins, J. *Pompeii* AD *79* (New York: Knopf, 1978).

B. Weiss, *Handbuch*
Weiss, Bernhard. *Kritisch exegetisches Handbuch über die Briefe Pauli und Timotheus und Titus* (Göttingen: Vandenhoeck und Ruprecht, 1986).

H. Weiss, "*Pagani*"
Weiss, Harold. "The *Pagani* among the Contemporaries of the First Christians," *JBL* 86 (1967): 42-52.

Welles, *Correspondence*
Welles, Charles Bradford. *Royal Correspondence in the Hellenistic Period* (Chicago: Ares, 1974; reprinted from 1934).

C. Westermann, *Blessing*
Westermann, Claus. *Blessing in the Bible and the Life of the Church* (E.T. by Keith Crim; Philadelphia: Fortress, 1978).

C. Westermann, *Genesis*
———. *The Genesis Accounts of Creation* (trans. with an introduction by Norman E. Wagner; Philadelphia: Fortress, 1964).

C. Westermann, *Praise*
———. *Praise and Lament in the Psalms* (E.T. by Keith R. Crim and Richard N. Soulen; Atlanta: John Knox Press, 1981).

W. Westermann, *Slave*
Westermann, William L. *The Slave Systems of Greek and Roman Antiquity* (Philadelphia: American Philosophical Society, 1955).

Whiston, *Josephus*
Whiston, William. *The Works of Flavius Josephus* (Hartford, Conn.: S. S. Scranton, 1912).

Whitaker, "Baptism"

Whitaker, Charles. "Baptism," in *Hippolytus* (ed. G. Cumming; Bramcote, Notts.: Grove, 1978), pp. 52-60.

Whitaker, "Formula"

———. "The History of the Baptismal Formula," *Journal of Ecclesiastical History* 16 (1965): 1-12.

White, *Body*

White, John L. *The Body of the Greek Letter: The Form and Function of the Body of the Greek Letter in the Non-Literary Papyri and in Paul the Apostle* (Missoula: University of Montana, 1972).

White, "Epistolary"

White, John L. "NT Epistolary Literature in the Framework of Ancient Epistolography," in *ANRW* II.25/2 (ed. Wolfgang Haase and Hildegard Temporini; Berlin: de Gruyter, 1984), pp. 1730-1756.

Whittaker, *Tatian*

Whittaker, Molly, ed. and trans. *Oratio ad Graecos and Fragments* (Oxford: Clarendon, 1982).

Wiedemann, *Slavery*

Wiedemann, T. *Greek and Roman Slavery* (Baltimore: Johns Hopkins University Press, 1981).

Wiesenberg, "Liturgical Term"

Wiesenberg, E. J. "Liturgical Term *melekh ha-ʿolam*," *JJS* 15 (1964): 1-56.

Wikgren, "Problems"

Wikgren, Allen. "Some Problems in Jude 5," in *Studies in the History and Text of the New Testament: In Honor of Kenneth Willis Clark* (ed. B. L. Daniels and M. J. Suggs; Studies and Documents 29; Salt Lake City: University of Utah, 1967), pp. 147-152.

Wilcox, *Semitisms*

Wilcox, Max. *The Semitisms of Acts* (Oxford: Clarendon, 1965).

Wilken, *Christians*

Wilken, Robert L. *The Christians as the Romans Saw Them* (New Haven, Conn.: Yale University Press, 1984).

R. Wilson, "Sōtēria"

Wilson, R. M. "Sōtēria," *SJT* 6 (1953): 406-416.

S. Wilson, *Lk PE*

Wilson, Stephen G. *Luke and the PE* (London: SPCK, 1979).

Wink, *Powers*

Wink, Walter, *Naming the Powers: The Language of Power in the New Testament* (Philadelphia: Fortress, 1984).

Winston, AB *Wisd.*

Winston, David. *The Wisdom of Solomon* (AB 43; Garden City, N.Y.: Doubleday, 1979).

Wolff, *Hos.*

Wolff, Hans Walter. *Hosea* (Hermeneia; E.T. by Gary Stansell; Philadelphia: Fortress, 1974).

Wolfson, *Philo*

Wolfson, Henry A. *Philo: Foundations of Religious Philosophy in Judaism, Christianity, and Islam* (2 vols.; Cambridge: Harvard, 1948).

Wordsworth and White, *NTL*

Wordsworth, J., and H. White. *Novum Testamentum Latine, Secundum Editionem Sancti Hieronymi ad Codicum Manuscriptorum Fidem Recensuerent* (Oxonii, Clarendoniano, 1955).

A. Wright, *Midrash*

Wright, Addison. *The Literary Genre Midrash* (Staten Island, N.Y.: Alba House, 1967).

D. F. Wright, "Clement"

Wright, D. F. "Clement and the Roman Succession in Irenaeus," *JTS* 18 (1967): 144-154.

D. F. Wright, "Homosexuals"

———. "Homosexuals or Prostitutes: The Meaning of *arsenokoitai*," *Vigiliae Christianae* 38 (1984): 125-153.

Yadin, "Symbols"

Yadin, Yigael. "Symbols of Deities at Zinjirli, Carthage and Hazor," in *Near Eastern Archaeology in the 20th Century* (ed. J. A. Sanders; Garden City, N.Y.: Doubleday, 1970), pp. 199-232.

Yadin, *Temple*

———. *The Temple Scroll* (3 vols.; Jerusalem: Israel Exploration Society, 1983).

Yadin, *War*

———, ed. *The Scroll of the War of the Sons of Light against the Sons of Darkness* (E.T. by Batya and Chaim Rabin; New York: Oxford University Press, 1962).

Zerwick, *Analysis*

Zerwick, Max, and Mary Grosvenor. *A Grammatical Analysis of the Greek New Testament* (Rome: Biblical Institute Press, 1981).

Ziesler, *Righteousness*

Ziesler, J. A. *The Meaning of Righteousness in Paul: A Linguistic and Theological Enquiry* (Cambridge: University Press, 1972).

Zimmer, "Lügner"

Zimmer, C. "Die Lügner-Antinomie in Titus 1,12," *Linguistica Biblica* 59 (1987): 79-99.

Zuntz, *Text*

Zuntz, Günther. *The Text of the Epistles: A Disquisition upon the Corpus Paulinum* (The Schweich Lectures of the British Academy, 1946; London: Published for British Academy by Oxford University, 1953).

# *Introduction to the Pastoral Epistles*

## NOMENCLATURE

Thirteen letters in the NT have been transmitted under the name of the apostle Paul. The pair "To Timothy" are the main concern of this commentary. Several centuries have passed since German NT studies began to call the letters to Timothy and Titus "the Pastoral Epistles," that term implying that a certain theological as well as literary unity is proper to them. The eighteenth-century phrase had its precedent already in Thomas Aquinas, who had characterized First Timothy as "a rule, so to speak, for pastors" (see Fiore, *Function,* p. 3 n. 7, and Thomas Aquinas, *Commentaria* 2.184D; *Super I Epistolam ad Timotheum, lectio ii in 1:3;* Turin: Marietti, 1929).

The letters to Timothy and Titus are, like Philemon, addressed to individuals, and their individuality as letters ought not to be overlooked (see Johnson, *Writings,* p. 389). The PE are "Pastoral" in a way that Philemon is not; that is, these three letters are concerned with "shepherding" the church of the living God. Already around the turn of the second century the Muratorian Fragment (lines 60-63) justified their position in the Christian canon because of their contribution to ecclesial discipline in the church universal, a case made in the name of Paul the apostle (see B. Metzger, *Canon,* p. 196). In the last analysis they are concerned with what believers do. The PE certainly are exercised at every turn about what Christians believe (and what their neighbors believe about them); but these letters emphatically have no time for speculative thinking or theoretical research, and they little appreciate Christians who pursue such activities (Titus 3:9; 1 Tim 1:4; 2 Tim 2:14; 3:7; regularly the data and arguments for the assertions of this INTRODUCTION about the PE are found in the NOTES and COMMENTS on the texts cited). These letters are "Pastoral" because they are *practical* — in other words, they are ordered to a Christian *praxis,* to the activities of believers.

## DOCUMENTS AND DATA

The varied hypotheses about the origin and purpose of the PE have been extrapolated from the facts about the tangible documents of which the original text remains extant in Greek. A review of the concrete and observable phenomena of that text will precede a survey of those matters which are inferred with more or less certainty from the observable data. The text of the PE is the first, basic reality to be analyzed; then the literary form in which this text has been composed and transmitted; third, the literary and nonliterary materials that the author incorporated into this form. Finally, the data referred to by the PE will be surveyed to glean some of the information that they give about the secular and ecclesial milieus that once packaged these compositions. From that vantage one can then review, in the next main section of this Introduction, the varied hypotheses about and reconstructions of the origin and purpose of the PE. The final section precedes a translation of 1 and 2 Timothy, which in turn is followed by the NOTES and COMMENTS.

The Greek text of the PE, like the rest of the NT, has been transmitted in numerous ancient codices, that is to say, on leaves of papyrus or parchment bound together into what we call a "book." But before 100 C.E. practically all Hellenistic literary compositions were copied on rolls (Roberts and Skeat, *Birth;* see 2 Tim 4:13; Skeat, "On 2 Tim 4:13"). It was in Rome in the latter part of the first Christian century that secular authors began to experiment with the codex for literary compositions (though Julius Caesar may have used a codex notebook before this time for his letters to the Roman Senate [Suetonius, *Iulius* 1.56.6]). The innovation was attractive to late first-century Christians, again probably those in Rome, and by the end of that century Christians (in distinction from their Jewish and pagan contemporaries) had transferred their sacred literature, the LXX Greek OT and the compositions that came to be called the NT, from the rolls on which they had been copied originally into codices or books. The very earliest scraps of Christian documents, including a papyrus page of the Letter to Titus, are already in "book" form. This innovation gave a visible identity to the Christian writings; it was also in every sense a pastoral, that is, practical, measure that met a need in the second-century churches: for the codex was an efficient way of gathering several compositions under one cover for easy consultation in public reading or private study.

From the earliest papyrus, all of the manuscripts of the PE are in codex form. Yet the Greek text of the PE was originally composed, in all probability, on one or more rolls (depending on whether the letters were originally written together as a collection or were composed and dispatched separately). The reconstruction of any intervening process has its repercussions for every hypothesis about the origin and purpose of these letters. Certain features of the process can be discerned in the arrangement of the compositions within the extant NT codices; thus the Gospels and Acts are always separate from the epistolary literature, and within the latter a Pauline collection, dating from about the year 100 (Zuntz, *Text,* p. 279; see pp. 216-283), can be distinguished from a collection of seven other epistles (or eight if Hebrews is included). Within these epistolary collections the length of an individual letter appears generally to have determined its place within the collection (thus, among the Paulines, Romans first and Philemon last; see *VL* 24[2].290-303). The PE appear to mark a new beginning within the extant Pauline codices, for First Timothy is notably longer than Second Thessalonians. Probably this point marks the seam where two second-century collections of Pauline letters were joined, a collection of letters to churches (at times including Hebrews, as in $P^{46}$ and the archetype of B) and a smaller collection of Pauline letters addressed to individuals (also arranged in almost all extant codices with the longest first and Philemon, the shortest, last; see Quinn, "$P^{46}$"; Roberts, *Manuscript,* pp. 60, 62). An alternate and perhaps even earlier order, attested in the Muratorian Fragment and the fourth-century Latin commentary on the Paulines called Ambrosiaster, reads Titus before First and Second Timothy.

The Greek text of the PE (*NTG*$^{26corr}$ and *GNT*$^{3corr}$) has been transmitted in many manuscript codices since the fourth century (see especially S, A, C, D), and $P^{32}$ may be as early as 200 (Aland, *Repertorium,* p. 253; Haelst, *Catalogue,* p. 189, §534; E. Turner, *Typology,* p. 147). The absence of the PE from B still provokes questions (Skeat, "Vaticanus," pp. 464-465). J. K. Elliott, in *Greek Text,* has studied every significant variant in the PE with a variety of principles for textual criticism. The PE are alluded to or cited by many ancient Christian writers, and for the second Christian century alone *Biblia Patristica,* 1.507-518, offers about 450 references. In the mid–second century Marcion refused the PE a place in his canon, according to Tertullian (*Adversus Marcionem* 5.21). Tatian rejected Timothy while retaining Titus, according to Jerome (*PL* 26.556; cited also in Whittaker, *Tatian,* pp. 82-83). But Polycarp almost certainly quoted the letters to Timothy in his *Phil.* 4.1, perhaps as early as 120 C.E. Whether Ignatius and *First Clement* knew the text of the PE is more problematic but seems on the whole more likely now than it did a generation ago (Spicq, *EP,* pp. 162-163; Hagner, *Use,* pp. 236-237; Quinn, "Seven Times").

The language of the PE (their actual vocabulary, syntax, and style) has a certain homogeneity throughout the small corpus. These letters somehow sound different from the rest of the Paulines, including the other "private" letter to Philemon (see the tables assembled and revised by Harrison, *Problem* and *Paulines*). As A. D. Nock (*ERAW* 1.342-343) noted, "it is clear that as we pass from the Pauline Epistles to the Pastorals . . . there is an approximation to the phraseology of the world around, a lessening of the feeling of isolation, and an increase in intelligibility to the ordinary contemporary man, had he happened upon these books." Roughly one-third of the words in the PE (names of persons and places aside) do not appear in the other Paulines; almost one-fifth do not appear elsewhere in the NT (though the overwhelming majority of them do appear in Greek documents that predate 50 C.E., including Philo and the LXX). The language of the PE has notable resemblances to that of Luke-Acts (Strobel, "Schreiben des Lukas?"; Quinn, *Perspectives;* S. Wilson, *Lk PE;* P. Marshall, "Review"; Moule, *Birth,* pp. 264-265, 281-282; *Essays,* pp. 113-132). Moreover, in their narrow compass the PE coin about half a dozen terms (N. Turner, "NT Vocab.," pp. 149-150) and use some terms in a quite unusual sense (thus *themelios* in 1 Tim 6:19). Granted the ineradicable exuberance of ancient Greek and that no author then had an unabridged dictionary to consult, such coinages are not only "spontaneous and unconscious creations." They also "may represent an attempt to convey ideas which seemed to need new expressions" as well as devices for "stylistic emphasis or dramatic effect" (Nock, *ERAW* 2.642-643).

Computer analyses of linguistic data from the PE have become available (Aland, *Konkordanz;* Friberg and Friberg, *Analytical GNT;* Morton, *Concordance;* Kenny, *Stylometric,* with further bibliography). It becomes feasible with their aid to analyze in precise detail the use and distribution of the Greek particles and the length of the words and sentences in the compositions before us. Earlier and more narrowly based studies appeared to confirm that the PE were quite homogeneous internally and different from the rest of the Paulines. Anthony Kenny in his recent and more broadly based study finds scarcely any significant difference between the PE and the rest of the Paulines, Titus alone excepted. He sees "no reason to reject the hypothesis that twelve of the Pauline Epistles are the work of a single, unusually versatile author" (*Stylometric,* p. 100). The relatively limited word pool in the individual letters (not to mention the limitations imposed by our lack of precise knowledge of the processes of composition and authorship in the ancient world) restricts the certitude of the inferences that can be drawn from stylometric data (N. Turner, *Grammar,* pp. 102-104).

The large number of terms that are peculiar to the PE in biblical Greek already alert the reader to their affinities with the more literary traditions in Hellenistic Greek. Their vocabulary generally is less biblical (i.e., Septuagintal) than Paul's, though there are notable contacts with sapiential and other ethical compositions of Hellenistic Judaism (e.g., Fourth Maccabees; *Testaments of the Twelve Patriarchs*). One hears some language typical of the popular Epicurean, Cynic, and Stoic philosophers (e.g., Philodemus of Gadara; Epictetus; see N. Turner, *Grammar*, p. 102). The language of the Greek drama (staged everywhere in the Hellenistic world for the public at large) — particularly the tragedies of Euripides and the comedies of Menander — had its effect on ordinary people and their speech. Philo has a still moving description of the enthusiastic standing ovation that he saw given in response to Euripides' encomium of freedom in a performance of the *Auge*, a tragedy now lost (*Quod omn. prob.* 141). With a language thus formed the PE sought to address such people.

The fifty-five proper nouns and adjectives of the PE belong to the total working vocabulary of the author: some of them are unique to these letters (thus "Jewish" in Titus 1:14); some occur otherwise only in the other Paulines ("Luke" in 2 Tim 4:11 and Col 4:14; Philem 24); still others are found elsewhere only in the Lukan corpus (thus "Crete" in Titus 1:5 [see 1:12]; "Antioch," "Iconium," and "Lystra" in 2 Tim 3:11; and the double name "Pontius Pilate" in 1 Tim 6:13). Other cities and places are mentioned too: Nicopolis in Titus 3:12; Ephesus in 1 Tim 1:3; 2 Tim 1:18; 4:12; Rome in 2 Tim 1:17; Thessalonika in 2 Tim 4:10; Troas in 2 Tim 4:13; Corinth and Miletus in 2 Tim 4:20; in addition, the areas or provinces of Macedonia (1 Tim 1:3), of Asia (2 Tim 1:15), of Galatia or Gaul, and of Dalmatia (2 Tim 4:10). Together they suggest the geographical world presupposed by this correspondence. Of the personal names none occurs more often than that of Jesus, and thus the christological concerns of these compositions are telegraphed.

Particularly in two areas the vocabulary of the PE already reflects specialized patterns of use. The first falls in the area of Christian conduct or ethics, and the terminology is that for distinguishing good from bad acts (Donelson, *Pseudepig.*, pp. 171-183). The second area (and it intersects with the first) is that of particular Christian ministries and the vocabulary for designating those who shoulder specific roles in the service of the body of believers, a vocabulary still notably uncultic (see Johnson, *Writings*, p. 385). In both areas the PE share some of their emerging technical vocabulary with other first-century Christian documents (such as the terminological clusters around faith and love or apostle and presbyter). Other terminology is almost unique to the PE (*chera,* the term for widow; the clusters of words built around *sōphrōn* [sensible] and *eusebēs* [godly]).

The second major consideration about the language of the PE is their syntax; i.e., the way in which the words are ordered into sentences, their patterns in the use of coordinating and subordinating particles (note computer analyses mentioned above), their characteristic ways of employing the Greek moods and tenses (thus the optative, a mood rarely used in the NT, almost certainly appears several times in Second Timothy [e.g., 1:16, 18]). The influences of the LXX, of Hellenistic Judaism, and of Latin surface regularly. A striking and hardly appreciated syntactical phenomenon in the PE is the periodic breakdown of syntax, ranging from inordinately rough, abrupt transitions (thus Titus 2:6-8; 1 Tim 3:1a-b), through inexplicable shifts in the inflection of verbs (1 Tim 2:15), to sentence fragments that are without a verb or object to weld their endless phrases together (thus Titus 1:1-4; 1 Tim 1:3-7). All of this belongs to the individual character of the PE as Greek compositions.

With the question of the style in which the PE are written one is beyond issues of vocabulary and syntax as such and at the utmost verge of the data about their language (see N. Turner, *Grammar*, pp. 101-105, 172). When their text is read aloud in Greek, the author's use of sound to accent his thought is often notable. The reader hears alliteration, assonance, rhyme, paronomasia, polysyndeton (for abundant expressiveness), asyndeton (for a vivid, impassioned effect, adding a certain brilliance to epistolary style; see BDF §460 and 1 Tim 1:8-10). Poetic citations ornament the composition (Titus 1:12; 1 Tim 3:16; 2 Tim 2:11-13), and the prose has at times distinctly poetic rhythmic structure, particularly when prayers are alluded to or cited (thus 1 Tim 1:12-17). A predilection for unusual, even unique terminology has already been observed. By and large, the style of the PE is Hellenistic (note the compound words) rather than Hebraic and lacks the energetic versatility that characterizes other parts of the Pauline epistolary. The PE read in a calm, slow, colorless, monotonous fashion. Their tone is sententious, stern, didactic, sober, stiff, domesticated, with an occasional striving by means of unusual terminology for literary effect and an atmosphere of erudition. Their style is by and large parenetic, that is, the author urges his points rather than argues them (Quinn, "Parenesis/Settings").

The PE stand before us both in the form of three individual "letters" and as part of a small group of Pauline letters that were addressed to individuals (including, besides the PE, only Philemon). These in turn stand in the NT after a larger collection or epistolary of Pauline letters to Christian congregations or churches. In the current order of the NT collection, still another eight letters follow the Pauline collection. The epistolary constitutes about one-third of the NT.

Compositions in epistolary form represent the oldest surviving Christian literature, though the form (unlike that of the Gospel genre) was a borrowing from the contemporary, first-century world, where the letter already had a long and instructive history in Roman, Hellenistic, and Semitic cultures. The epistolary form was relatively little used for literary composition (in contrast to everyday communication) in Palestinian Judaism, though one must note 4QEn$^{g}$

and the "polemic-halakic letter" of 4Q 394-399 (MMT), edited by Qimron and Strugnell ("Halakhic Letter"). The authors call attention to the similar character of some Pauline letters. First Timothy comes to mind. Still, the popularity of the letter form in Greek-speaking Judaism appears in the epistolary compositions cited in LXX Esther, Baruch, and Maccabees, not to mention *Enoch,* the *Epistle of Aristeas,* and the *Apocalypse of Baruch.*

Current studies of epistolary theory in the ancient rhetoricians (Malherbe, *Cynic Epistles;* "Theorists," *Social Aspects,* pp. 13-17, 57-58, 101-107; White, "Epistolary," pp. 1730-1756; Stowers, *Letter Writing*), not to mention the innumerable texts that the ancient world called "letters" or "epistles," are making it clearer what the early Christians expected when they read or heard a composition in an epistolary form. They did not look for a technical, scientific treatise; and letters were felt to be a limited, even an inadequate substitute for personal, face-to-face communication (see 1 Tim 3:14; 4:13). Spontaneity and confidentiality were not considered to belong to the essence of an ancient letter (though evidently sometimes these characteristics occur). Still, the ancient reader probably made the distinction immediately between personal, private letters and those which were intended to be read by anyone who was interested in picking them up (not unlike the distinction between first- and second-class mail in the United States). A letter was received as a gift, a sign of personal, individual attention and care for the recipient, a part of a conversation between friends. In a letter the recipient expected to see the character of the sender, "an icon of the soul"; and thus in ancient rhetorical schools letters were written as exercises in characterization of famous persons, mythical or historical (see Ovid, *Heroides*). Just as the ancient author of a history composed the kind of speech that a certain person would and could have given (sometimes using sources, sometimes not), so a letter or letters could be written to depict the personality and character of a philosopher or statesman or literary figure (see Malherbe, *Cynic Epistles;* and Horace, *Epistles,* passim).

When ancient Christians began to read a letter "To Titus" or "To Timothy," they expected in virtue of the epistolary form to hear (or overhear) a Pauline conversation in writing, to receive an icon of the apostle's soul and a convincing characterization that conveyed his heartfelt personal care as well as his teaching, directives, and requests. The readers expected all of this whether the letter was originally a piece of private correspondence originating before the apostle's death, or a "characterization" composed after his martyrdom, or a combination of the two (i.e., an originally private correspondence got up for publication in an expanded form).

As noted above, the PE have not come down to us simply as separate letters. They are proposed (perhaps with Philemon) as letters to individuals, an epistolary collection, already distinct from the collection of Pauline letters to churches in the second century, when they were being read in the order Titus–First Timothy–Second Timothy. The opening of the Letter to Titus (1:1-4), which is out of all proportion to the letter that follows, is an internal indication that it headed such a collection (see Quinn, *Perspectives,* pp. 63-64, 72).

A letter collection is itself a literary genre that enjoyed a limited popularity in Greek philosophical circles but came into its own in Roman political life (see Carcopino, *Cicero* 1.4-37) and only later among poets and philosophers. Thus collections of "letters" by persons as diverse as Cicero, Augustus, Horace, Ovid, Seneca, and Pliny were published (or, in Augustus's case, available in the archives; see Suetonius, *Augustus* 2.71, 76; *Claudius* 5.4), whether in prose or poetry, whether on personal or literary matters, whether on political or philosophical (i.e., ethical) questions, whether edited by themselves while they were still alive or published by others after their deaths. The premise of all such collections is that there are letters worth saving for the education, instruction, and enjoyment of the next generation, for individuals and groups to whom they were not originally addressed. The actual authors or their admirers assembled such collections because they were convinced of the enduring importance of the one who wrote the letters and the importance and permanent interest of the matters that had been discussed in the individual epistolary "conversations."

The epistolary genre was used not only for letters, separate or in freestanding collections, but also for letters in other genres of composition. Sometimes a letter or an epistolary collection was prefixed to another work (thus the seven letters that open Revelation, the pair that open Second Maccabees, and perhaps the "Edict" from Cyrus at the beginning of Ezra); sometimes they are given within the composition (as is the correspondence with the exiles in Jer 29; 1 Macc 10:22-45; 12:5-23; the LXX Esther 3:13[a-g]; 8:12[a-x] [RSV 13:1-7; 16:1-24]; Acts 15:23-29; 23:25-30); sometimes they are added at the end (examples in Quinn, *Perspectives,* pp. 68-69; see the LXX Esther 10:3[l] [RSV 11:1]; additions to Justin, *Apology* 1.69-71). The appearance of compositions in the epistolary form within a larger work of instructive history signaled the genuineness, the credibility, and the authority of what was going to be or had been narrated. A cluster of letters intensified these impressions. From another point of view letters within a narrative served to satisfy with edifying biographical notices the questions in a community about outstanding and yet controversial personalities whose past teaching and acts were still appreciated.

Accordingly, the PE were opened and read as a collection in the second century, and perhaps even in the first (regardless of whether the letters also had an individual preexistence). The collection offered an authoritative message from the past, a message from a significant personality, a message containing (at least in the judgment of the collectors) observations and instructions the significance of which was meant to transcend the setting presupposed in their text. The collected letters thus come as a "prophecy" from the past to a new generation (see Pliny citing M. Cato's letter to his son in *Naturalis historia* 7.51.171; 29.7.14; Ovid occasionally describes his elegiac letters *Ex Ponto* as containing prophecies). The original addressees of such correspondence tend to sink below the historical horizon, while the author (genuine or putative) remains the polestar around which a new public revolves. Thus Titus and Timothy in the PE are less actual historical individuals than paradigmatic persons, models with which the new public is expected to identify (Fiore, *Function;* see also Nickelsburg, *Ideal Figures*). "The essence of the epistolary genre, both in antiquity and the Middle Ages, was not whether the letter was actually sent but whether it performed a representative function" (Constable, *Letters,* p. 13). The PE incontrovertibly aim to *represent* Paul as herald, apostle, teacher (1 Tim 2:7; 2 Tim 1:11), instructing and directing the men who shared his apostolate. These men in turn, as Paul's true children (cf. Titus 1:4 with 2:15; see 1 Tim 1:2) and his heirs, transmit the apostle's doctrine and directives to "God's house, which is the church of the living God" (1 Tim 3:15). They also see to it that this household has managers (see Titus 1:7), presbyters as well as bishops with their deacons, whose lives and teaching represent Paul (note also the "faithful men" of 2 Tim 2:1-2).

Other recent studies have more closely specified the parenetic — in other words, hortatory — character of the PE as the ancient world understood parenesis (Perdue, "Parenesis"), namely, as traditional ethical exhortation, universally applicable to individual persons, addressed to an audience that is paradigmatic and typical rather than genuinely individual and historical, and often an admonition that does not envision or admit contradiction (Quinn, "Parenesis/Settings"). Such letters expect not answers but action from the recipients. The epistolary form of Second Timothy has attracted special attention because it has many characteristics of the testamentary genre in the ancient world (Nordheim, *Das Testament*). Paul becomes the illustrious, dying patriarch, leaving his goods, his wisdom, and his wealth to his children who carry on his name, his plan, his hopes. The dead man's parenesis is endowed with a prophetic thrust, weight, and authority as the last words of a very important person. The *topos* is a commonplace in the OT, as the testament or last will of Jacob (Gen 49), of Moses (Deut 33), of Joshua (Josh 23–24), and of David (2 Sam 23:1-6 [or 7]) illustrate. The Johannine speech of Jesus at the last supper shows the adaptable tenacity of the rhetorical figure (Aristotle, *Rhetoric* 1.2.21 [1358a14]; 2.22.10–23.30; and see Philodemus, *Volumina rhetorica* 1.226).

At every turn in the PE there appear quotations of and allusions to compositions that served as sources for this parenetic epistolary. Greek versions of the OT are quoted (1 Tim 5:18a) as well as an oracular line from a pagan poet

(Titus 1:12); there is a saying in 1 Tim 5:18b which Luke 10:7 places on Jesus' lips. An allusion to an apocryphal composition about Jannes and Jambres appears in 2 Tim 3:8 (see Charlesworth, *OT Pseud.* 2.427-442). There are citations of archaic Christian hymns (1 Tim 3:16; 2 Tim 2:11-13; see W. Metzger, *Christushymnus;* Stenger, *Christushymnus;* Quinn, "Holy Spirit," pp. 353-355) and prophecies (1 Tim 1:18; 4:1; Quinn, "Holy Spirit," pp. 346-347, 356-360), and possibly some short dispatches that originated at the end of Paul's life (thus Titus 1:1, 4-5; 3:12-15; 2 Tim 1:1-2, 15-18; 4:9-15). Although the case has been argued (A. T. Hanson, "Domestication"), there is no convincing evidence that the PE quote from the other Pauline letters, unless perhaps Romans.

If the foregoing compositions were already in relatively fixed texts, there appear to be sources cited in the PE that were in more plastic forms, relatively open to redactional activity. Such are the Christian domestic codes *(Haustafeln)* of Titus 2:2-10 (see Sampley, *Two/One,* pp. 18-30; Verner, *Household,* pp. 13-25, 83-111; Donelson, *Pseudepig.*, pp. 171-183) and 1 Tim 5:1-2 (to be read with 6:1-2). Similarly, there are more than a few lists that specify good and bad ethical qualities as well as bad and good persons (e.g., Titus 1:6-10; 1 Tim 1:9-10; 2 Tim 3:2-5). The lists of bad qualities appear to use more archaic, catechetical materials that aim to identify the Christian in contrast to the unbeliever; the lists of virtuous qualities are not addressed to the whole believing community but to particular classes or orders of believers. Relatively specific conduct is demanded, often with an apologetic if not a missionary goal. Also among the more plastic materials cited by the PE are those which contain directives for the Christian life, particularly for those who engage in liturgical worship, materials that we classify as church orders. They occupy 1 Tim 2–3 and 5:3-25. The former, perhaps from a congregation of predominantly Gentile origin, begins with directives for the public prayer of the church; then it treats the liturgical conduct of men and women (with an added note on the role of the Christian wife in public teaching, 1 Tim 2:11–3:1a); and finally it turns (1 Tim 3:1b-13) to the qualifications and regulations for the specific ministries of men (bishop, deacons) and women (a group without title who parallel the deacons in 1 Tim 3:11). Sacral language is conspicuously absent in describing any of these persons. The other church order of First Timothy, perhaps from a house church of predominantly Jewish origin, is enclosed within a household code (5:1-2; 6:1-2) and deals with widows (1 Tim 5:3-15) and presbyters.

Prayers abound in the PE. The briefest are in the opening and closing epistolary blessings (twofold in 2 Tim 4:22; there was originally perhaps no blessing in 1 Tim 6:21b [note the way Irenaeus, *Adversus haereses* 3.3.3 (SC 211.34), cites the correspondence with Timothy]). Other prayers appear too, brief and spontaneous (thus 2 Tim 1:16-17) as well as long and solemn (thus 1 Tim 1:12-17; 2 Tim 1:3-14). Flexible as these compositions are, they often appear to contain traditional elements and to move formulaically from an opening address to the body of the prayer, which then concludes in a doxology. Another type of prayer that verges on the creedal is the acclamation form preserved in 1 Tim 2:5-6 (Quinn, "Jesus as Savior," pp. 253-257).

Of the materials cited or redacted by the author of the PE, the most difficult to bring into precise focus are those which may be characterized as ecclesial parenesis (as distinct from the epistolary parenesis noted above). An authoritative teaching office seems to be presumed which articulates Pauline apostolic doctrine through creed, cult, and catechesis, and it is to be received in faith. Compositions of various types, cited under the rubric *pistos ho logos,* "this is the Christian message meant to be believed" (indicated with an asterisk among the following references), also figure in this kind of parenesis (Knight, *Sayings*).

Creedal formulas in the PE are relatively rare, brief, and closely identified with Paul's gospel and his prayer (1 Tim 1:15*; 2 Tim 2:8). The parenesis characteristic of the public worship of believers, the sacramental cult in the widest sense, including liturgical orations and homilies, appears frequently in the PE. See Titus 2:4-5 for a citation from a marriage charge; 2:11-14 for a baptismal confession; 3:4-7* for a didactic baptismal oration; 1 Tim 2:13-15* for another citation from a marriage homily; and 1 Tim 6:11-16 for an ordination charge. The previously noted hymn of 2 Tim 2:11-13* could have been used in a baptismal liturgy. Various types of ethical catechesis also appear to draw on previously existing materials and redact them in an authoritative way for a particular purpose. Thus Titus 2:7 adapts the household code with the qualities it demands of believers of various ages and classes to make it apply to the apostolic minister himself; in 1 Tim 4:8* the teaching on godliness is particularly applied to the figure of Timothy; in 1 Tim 6:6-10 and 17-19, the wealthy believers are the object of what seems to be partially traditional exhortation.

After surveying the text of the PE, their literary form, and the previous compositions on which they drew, one broaches the methodologically delicate task of disengaging from these materials a sketch of the world, geographical and social, to which the PE refer. The places and the persons, named and unnamed, that figure explicitly in the text suggest materials for a societal profile of ecclesial life as the PE conceive it, that is to say, the ways in which believers are to relate to their God, to one another, and to those who do not share their faith.

Titus and First Timothy profess to come from Paul en route to Macedonia and Nicopolis in northwest Greece; Second Timothy comes from Rome (Quinn, "Captivity"). The island of Crete is the destination for Titus; the metropolis of Asia Minor, Ephesus, for the correspondence with Timothy. In the whole correspondence a total of perhaps fifteen places and areas are mentioned that are found from modern Italy and France through former Yugoslavia and Greece into central Turkey. Within this theater of action one encounters almost forty persons by name, a few of whom belong to OT traditions (Adam and Eve, Moses, Jannes and Jambres, David). Jesus Christ, God, the Spirit, angels, and the devil are discussed below. In the "present" that the PE presuppose, Paul and more than a dozen of his current and past co-workers, along with some members of the churches, are explicitly named; more surprisingly, some opponents of the apostle and his mission are also noted by name (1 Tim 1:20; 2 Tim 1:15; 2:17; 4:14). Beyond these names the reader gets a glimpse of other "brothers," the "faithful" of the Christian generation being addressed (1 Tim 4:6; 6:2; 2 Tim 4:21; 1 Tim 4:3, 10, 12), as well as unfaithful and unnamed opponents of the Pauline teaching, some of whom are Jewish Christians (Titus 1:10, 14-16; 1 Tim 1:3-7; etc.). A secular society, its rules, and even its rulers are in the author's peripheral vision (see Titus 1:12; 3:1; 1 Tim 1:9; 2:1-2; 6:15), and he senses their pressure on and scrutiny of Christian marriages and ministries (Titus 2:5, 8; 1 Tim 3:7), even of the conduct of Christian slaves (1 Tim 6:1).

A social description of the ecclesial communities presupposed by the PE indicates a clearly stratified social structure within them, a structure that the author generally perceives (on the model of the extended family in the Hellenistic and Roman world) as the household of the living God (1 Tim 3:15; Verner, *Household*), in other words, as the family to which God as Father gives life. Within that extended family (which need not be numerically large) are old and young; male and female; free and slave; married and single (including the widowed); parents and children; rich and poor; Jewish and pagan, all who have accepted faith in Christ and worship the one God through him. The faith and the worship it engenders are the keys for understanding the life of the church as the PE present it.

The adage has it, "The rule for praying is the rule for believing." The rule of faith in the PE is rooted in the liturgical acclamation and confession of the one and only God of Israel, "who wills that all human beings be saved" (see 1 Tim 2:3-7; Quinn, "Jesus as Savior"). God is seldom called Father in the PE (only in the opening blessing of each letter), and Jesus is never called the Son.

Still, what specifies the articulation of the faith in the PE and differentiates it from normative forms of Judaism is its attitude to Jesus, "risen from the dead, from the line of David" (2 Tim 2:8), who receives (as God does) the titles "our savior" and "Lord" (thus Titus 1:3-4; 1 Tim 1:2; 6:15; 2 Tim 1:18). He can be addressed directly in prayer (1 Tim 1:12; 2 Tim 1:18). In Titus 2:13 he is, almost certainly, "our great God" (M. Harris, "Titus 2:13"). As previously observed, no name occurs more often in the PE (thirty-two times) than Jesus Christ or Christ Jesus (Christ alone in 1 Tim 5:11).

From this faith in "the Man, Christ Jesus, who gave himself as a ransom for all" (1 Tim 2:5-6) derives the vision of the church's mission in the PE and their intense concern for prayers by believers for the unbelieving society around them (1 Tim 2:1-2; 4:10). In this setting of ecclesial prayer and mission a doctrine about the Holy Spirit has begun to take shape (Quinn, "Holy Spirit"). The Spirit appears to be involved in the words of prophecy (1 Tim 1-18; 4:1, 14), in the transmission of the words of apostolic teaching (2 Tim 1:14), and especially in the inspiration of the sacred written words of all Scripture (2 Tim 3:15-16). Yet the only person to receive the title "prophet" is the pagan poet Epimenides (Titus 1:12). The liturgical actions of what we call baptism and ordination are more or less explicitly linked with the Spirit (Titus 3:5; 2 Tim 1:6-7; Reumann, *Righteousness*, pp. 234-235, 237-238 [J. Quinn]). Fragmentary citations of compositions that may have emanated from liturgies of marriage, reconciliation (2 Tim 2:25-26), and possibly even the eucharist (1 Tim 2:1; 4:4-5; A. T. Hanson, *Studies*, pp. 97-109), though they contain no reference to the Spirit, witness to the inclusive ecclesial vision that inspired the liturgical texts cited by the PE.

This ecclesial vision of the PE includes an eschatological aspect, which is also revealed by the Spirit; these days are the last days (1 Tim 4:1; 2 Tim 3:1). The prayers of these letters set one's hope on life eternal, which has begun in this last age (Titus 1:2; 2:12; 1 Tim 4:8) but will reach its consummation on "that Day" (2 Tim 1:12, 18; 4:8) when Jesus appears in glory (Titus 2:13; 1 Tim 6:14) as judge of "the living and the dead" (2 Tim 4:1). Paul prays for the Lord's mercy on that judgment day upon a fellow Christian, apparently deceased, who had been kind to him (2 Tim 1:16-18; see 4:19); he leaves a still living coppersmith called Alexander to the Lord to be judged according to his works, which are bad (2 Tim 4:14-15). Belief in the final judgment is closely linked to that in the final resurrection (cf. Titus 3:5 with 2 Tim 2:17-19), though the PE do not emphasize the latter as such. Eternal life will consist in living with Christ, sharing his reign (2 Tim 2:10-12), and thus receiving "the crown of the upright life" (2 Tim 4:8) from him.

The PE have passing references to the angelic orders (1 Tim 3:16 may refer to the apostolic "messengers" of the resurrection). "The elect angels" of 1 Tim 5:21, loyal to God, stand in contrast to spirits and demons that inspire false doctrines (1 Tim 4:1). The devil or Satan is perceived as implicated in certain activities for which believers face condemnation (1 Tim 1:20; 3:6-7; 5:15; 2 Tim 2:26).

This rule for faith expresses itself in the order for public worship that the PE presume. A strong sense of community pervades the correspondence (first-person plural pronouns are frequent), and the directives about assemblies for worship emphasize the groups involved. Thus the men are distinguished from the women in 1 Tim 2:8-10; the wives from women in general in verses 11-15. Various groups of ministers can be discerned (see below). The place for worship is not described. One infers from the parenesis addressed to well-to-do believers (1 Tim 6:6-10, 17-19) that the wealthy man or woman, married or widowed, offered his or her house for the liturgical assemblies and perhaps hospitality to itinerant apostolic ministers as well as to some indigent Christians (Titus 3:13-14; 1 Tim 5:10, 16; 2 Tim 1:18; 4:13, 19). Such a "house church" might be limited to one (extended) family; it could scarcely accommodate an assembly of more than a few dozen persons for worship. As numbers increased, more homes would be the sites for separate assemblies. It is conceivable that a group of believers who were wholly of Jewish origin might have retained their own Jewish place of liturgical assembly, a larger home or a small building *(proseuchē),* for their Jewish prayer, which was now in the process of becoming identifiably Christian.

If the place for worship, as the PE envision it, is elusive, the setting in time is irrecoverable. There is no evidence for the hour of the day or the day of the week favored by these congregations for their public worship, though the silence could be taken as willingness to tolerate worship on the Sabbath (because other Jewish practices are explicitly criticized). "The widow proper . . . stays on night and day in entreaties and prayers" (1 Tim 5:5), a turn of phrase that suggests the Jewish way of reckoning the day from sunset to sunset. A hint at a ritual order for worship in 1 Tim 4:13 evinces no concern that it be observed by all congregations. The only ceremonial observance that the PE proffer as specific to their (Pauline) practice is that a wife does not teach or direct her husband in the liturgical assemblies (1 Tim 2:12).

The practical, day-to-day conduct of all believers is, for the PE, an integral part of their faith and worship, to such an extent that "the rule for praying" is the rule for action. The faith that expresses itself publicly in worship to God also expresses itself publicly in "fine works," *erga kala,* by which is meant not simply good deeds (*agatha;* 1 Tim 2:10) but visibly and attractively good actions (Titus 2:7, 14; 3:8, 14; etc.). From these actions unbelievers can get a glimpse of the power of the gospel and its grace, delivering from bad acts (Titus 2:11-12; 3:3-7), enabling believers to take their share in the suffering and death of Jesus (2 Tim 1:8; 2:11-12) and "to live in a sensible, honest, godly way in this present age." As there is a strong accent on the community in worship in the PE, so there is a corresponding emphasis on the exemplary conduct of the baptized as "a people of his [God's] very own, enthusiastic for fine deeds" (Titus 2:14) and on the conduct of people in various groups or classes or orders within the body of the faithful. The household codes urge certain types of action upon various age groups, both according to their sex and according to their legal status as slave or free (thus Titus 2:2-10; cf. 1 Tim 5:1-2; 6:1-2). Similarly, the conduct of the aspirants to the presbyteral, diaconal, and widow's ministries is prescribed with a view to the group or order to which they will pertain. In contrast, the qualifications for the candidate for bishop are always in the singular and envision him as an individual (1 Tim 3:1b-7 and perhaps Titus 1:6-9). Yet even he is in his class a typical figure, as are the Paul, the Titus, and the Timothy of this correspondence (2 Tim 3:10-11; Titus 2:7-8; 1 Tim 1:16; 4:12).

Ethical conduct is urged on believers (whether addressed as individuals or as members of the orders or classes of persons within the community) as an essential part of their missionary witness to the ambient Hellenistic world. Ethical questions attracted popular interest in that society, and philosophers lectured about moral issues on the streets and in the baths. The ancient Greek drama had a powerful popular influence often overlooked in this regard: the plays, particularly those of Euripides and Menander, kept ethical debates constantly before the eyes of the populace. Thus when the PE observe "that law is not laid down for an upright person" (1 Tim 1:9), they are speaking not only the language of the Greek philosophical tradition but also that of the Greek New Comedy (Reumann, *Righteousness*, p. 236 [J. Quinn]; see the Index of Ancient Authors under Menander). The list of vicious persons that follows (1 Tim 1:9-10) reminds the reader not only of the Decalogue but also of the acts that destroy the characters in Greek tragedy.

Finally, for the PE, "the rule for praying" is the rule for leadership. The approach of these letters to the conduct of apostolic ministers is typological. It is significant that, in this typology, persons (in the fullest sense of that term, which designates not only what an individual is but also what he has done) precede what we call "office" or "function." Paul is a "model of" and a "model for those who are going to believe in him [i.e. Jesus] for eternal life" (1 Tim 1:16; see 2 Tim 1:13). His individual teaching, his experience of the will of Christ, and his sufferings, his way of living define what it means to be an apostle. He does not fit an *a priori* abstract definition of an apostle; he personally defines what the term signals. As Paul is the apostle for the PE, so he is the teacher with one coherent teaching about how the believer lives according to the word of God. In contrast, the PE hear the plurals "teachers" and "teachings" (2 Tim 4:3; 1 Tim 4:1) in a bad sense (Quinn, "Terminology," p. 235). Paul also functions as a prophet without being named as such, as he builds up, exhorts, and consoles his correspondents (see 1 Cor 14:3). Still, there is no evidence that the author of the PE remembered (much less tried to perpetuate) a tripartite local leadership called apostles, prophets, and teachers (1 Cor 12:28).

Titus and Timothy are in a true sense Paul's "children" (see Titus 1:4; 1 Tim 1:2, 18; etc.), and the dying patriarch directs his last will and testament to the latter as his heir. He who, by Paul's choice (and that choice appears to be the all-important factor), shared Paul's ministry during the apostle's life will continue to do so after Paul's death. For the PE Titus and Timothy are paradigmatic persons who furnish the pattern (Titus 2:7; 1 Tim 4:12) of what the continuing Pauline apostolate is and does. They are models of Paul and models for believers as they are designated to carry on the apostle's work, carry out his commands, imitate his sufferings, teach his gospel and practice it themselves, preside at the liturgy, receive material support for their ministerial work, and choose other men who will in their turn share their apostolic ministry (see Titus 1:5; 1 Tim 1:3-6, 18-19; 4:12-16; 6:11-14; 2 Tim 1:6-14; 2:1-8; 3:10-17; 4:2-5).

Even the opponents envisioned by the PE (Karris, "Polemic") have a typological character, for to the extent that they are "anti-Paul" they are also "anti-Christ" (2 Tim 4:14); to the extent that their doctrines are opposed by the Holy Spirit they belong to unholy demons (1 Tim 4:1-2). The designation of some of the opposition by name in the PE (1 Tim 1:20; 2 Tim 1:15; 2:17; 4:14) — an unusual phenomenon in ancient Jewish and Christian polemic, which regularly demurred at granting that limited acknowledgment of existence to opponents (see Ign. *Smyrn.* 5.3) — underscores their typological function. The Pauline cadre of ministers and their teaching contrast sharply with the mob of competitors who have been making inroads on the house churches, perhaps particularly through wealthy patronesses (see Titus 1:11; 2 Tim 3:6-7) who shared their strong Jewish interests in "myths and endless genealogies" (cf. 1 Tim 1:4 with Titus 1:14; 3:9) as well as their quite un-Jewish rejection of marriage (1 Tim 4:3). Interest in emancipation from the constraints of domestic life seems to have played its part (see Titus 2:3-5; 1 Tim 2:11-15; 5:13-14). The key contention, however, of the opponents is "that the resurrection has already occurred" (2 Tim 2:18), a collapsed eschatology in which the future resurrection of all believers has been simply identified with Jesus' resurrection. A form of this oversimplified eschatology had already been bruited about Corinth in the mid-fifties (1 Cor 15:12).

Behind the figures of Paul, Titus, and Timothy in the PE stand the unnamed leaders of the churches, leaders whose prerequisite qualities, particularly in verifiably good conduct, are spelled out in lists of vices and virtues. Presumably the congregation participates in verifying such conduct and presenting suitable candidates to Titus and Timothy, who, in virtue of the apostle's order, designate them for a Pauline ministry as they once were themselves designated (see Titus 1:5; 1 Tim 5:22; 2 Tim 1:6; 2:2). Prophetic oracles appear to have been traditional in the liturgical action surrounding some appointments (1 Tim 1:18; 4:14). Those appointed lead the worship of the community, teach, care for the temporalities, provide for the needy (see Titus 1:7-9; 1 Tim 3:2-10, 12-13; 5:17). Unmarried women (1 Tim 3:11) and widows (1 Tim 5:3-16) have their own qualifications to collaborate in some of these ministries. From the two church orders in First Timothy the names of four groups or classes of ecclesial ministers appear (a representative of each in the Roman church may be sending a greeting in 2 Tim 4:21). A hint at the archaic Jewish

Christian origins of the ministers called "widows" and "presbyters" is that they are expected to receive financial support from believers, whereas the sources for the income of "bishop" and "deacons" are ignored (though they are not to be money-minded [1 Tim 3:3, 8; Titus 1:7] like the teachers who belong to the opposition [Titus 1:11]; see Theissen, *Setting,* pp. 27-67).

Titus envisions the establishment of Pauline ministers on Crete, perhaps combining the titles "presbyter" and "bishop" in order to designate them (no deacons or widows are mentioned). They are God's stewards (see Titus 1:7) for communities that appear to be small, independent house churches, dispersed throughout the many towns of the island (but not in the rural areas as such; Titus 1:5). If their members were of predominantly Jewish origin, with strong Jewish ties and interests, the enticements of anti-Pauline teachers "from the circumcision" (Titus 1:10) with consequent controversies about the function of the Mosaic Law in Christian life become understandable (Titus 3:9; see 3:13). Perhaps one should think of these congregations as typologically as one does "Titus" and the "presbyter-bishop." They represent in this construction the more archaic, Jewish Christian congregations of the Christian movement being updated according to a Pauline model.

First Timothy envisions its text being read in a large metropolitan center, Ephesus (1 Tim 1:3). Apparently a significant number of the congregations are of predominantly Gentile origin, for Paul in the first church order in this letter (2:1–3:13) is emphatically "the Gentiles' teacher in faith and truth" (1 Tim 2:7; contrast 2 Tim 1:11). A bishop with deacons and women assistants presides over a house church with this background. The Qumran *mebaqqer,* "overseer," and his assistants offer a possible explanation of the quarter of the Jewish community in Palestine that gave rise to the Christian titles of bishop and deacon and their original functions. By contrast, the second church order of First Timothy (5:1–6:2) envisions house churches of predominantly Jewish origin, in which the registered widows and ordained presbyters, who constitute a presbyteral body, a "presbytery" (1 Tim 4:14), are the key ministers. The abuses that have arisen in these orders and the set procedures for dealing with them give the impression that the Jewish Christian house churches have been in existence somewhat longer than the predominantly Gentile congregations (though these, too, have their members of long standing; see 1 Tim 3:6). Again, like Crete with a congregation in each large town, Ephesus may be understood typologically: but it is any large, Greek-speaking metropolis of the latter first century in which more or less established congregations of Jewish and Gentile Christians live close to one another. First Timothy proposes a Pauline symbiosis for the different ways in which these groups of believers receive their guidance from those who direct their worship and works of charity.

## HYPOTHESES TO EXPLAIN THE DATA

The PE, even in translation, differ notably from the other ten letters of the Pauline collection in the NT in their vocabulary and style, in their subject matter, in the development of their thought, in the settings presupposed. The other Paulines appear to be earlier, some of them much earlier, than the PE. If, however, the PE are approached from the very end of the first and beginning of the second centuries, from the ecclesial world of Clement, of Ignatius and Polycarp, of Hermas, the same documents appear to be very close indeed to the other Pauline letters (thus the commentaries of Barrett versus Kelly; but contrast Brox with Jeremias).

The PE tend to resist questions about their background and origin, about when they were composed, and by whom; from what place they were sent, to whom, and where. The historical-critical method gives these questions an urgency for present-day commentators that was not always present. All scholars of the PE draw inferences from practically the same concrete data in and about the letters, analyzing the linguistic, historico-sociological, and theological components of the correspondence. Yet these data have provoked the most dramatically different hypotheses to explain the origin and purpose of the PE.

The preceding overview of materials about the text, genre, and contents of the PE was arranged in a roughly descending order of the historical accessibility and certainty of the data. Now, in the light of these varied materials one can review the hypotheses that modern students of the PE construct to answer questions about the origin and purpose of these letters. Basically, these questions are five: Who was the author of the PE? When were they written? From what place were they dispatched? To whom and where were they sent? The answers to these questions have their part to play in understanding the purpose of the PE; why were they written?

"Who wrote the PE?" If one answers simply from what the text of the letters says, Paul is as much the author of them as he is of the other ten letters that begin with his name (thus the commentaries of Bernard, Guthrie, Spicq, and many more). Yet the language of this correspondence is notably different from that of the rest of the Paulines. On this basis, some have proposed that these letters were actually written by a member of the Pauline entourage and dispatched under Paul's authority at various times in the fifties and early sixties of the first Christian century (thus, in various forms, Jeremias, Kelly, Holtz, and Fee; see also the special studies by Dockx, *Chronologies;* Lestapis, *L'Énigme;* Reicke, "Chronologie"; W. Metzger, *Die letzte Reise;* and Prior, *Paul*). When an interest in gathering the apostle's correspondence began at the end of the first century, the PE were copied in a codex of Paul's letters to individuals along with Philemon, a letter with considerable similarities to other Pauline texts and a few to the PE. On this construction Paul is author of the PE because they were authorized by the apostle during his own ministry.

Other students of the PE submit that this hypothesis does not adequately account for the church orders and domestic codes cited in Titus and First Timothy or for the ministerial orders discussed in the correspondence (not to mention the differences of language). Such phenomena seem to presume that a generation of Christian development and reflection has intervened between Paul's time and that of the PE.

The ancient conception of authorship was rather wider than ours. Even the epistolary genre and particularly the genre of the letter collection were not always taken as written by the person whose name stood at the head of these compositions. If the origin of the PE before the death of Paul is in fact indefensible, then it is conceivable that the letters were written in the second (70-100 C.E.) or even the third (100-130 C.E.) Christian generation.

Hypotheses have been advanced for each time frame. Walter Bauer (*Orthodoxy*, pp. 222-224) has even argued that the PE were written as a riposte to Marcion (see also F. Gealy, *Interpreter's Bible* 11.358-360). Helmut Koester (*HLEC* 2.305, 308) probably also sides with him. A date in the early second century and the third Christian generation is proposed (or presupposed) in the commentaries of Easton, Barrett, Dibelius and Conzelmann (D-C), Hanson, and Hultgren. A similar dating is found in other works from Harrison, *Problem*, through Campenhausen, "Polycarp," to Donelson, *Pseudepig.* There is a tendency to favor an origin at the turn of the first Christian century. The ecclesial ministries envisioned by the PE, described without sacral imagery, appear less clearly organized and rather less developed than those in *First Clement* and second-century Christian documents. Moreover, at least some, perhaps all (see Zuntz, *Text*, p. 279), of the other Pauline letters had been collected and were for the first time being cited as such by the authors in this third generation (beginning with *First Clement* in 96 C.E.). If the PE originated in the second century, it is striking that they, intent on transmitting the Pauline heritage, do not quote the apostle's own words. At most one reads in several places two or three words running that appear to be slogans from a Pauline tradition; none of these slogans is a proper citation of one of his letters. Thus Titus 1:15 has "For the clean, all things are clean"; this is cited as if it were a proverb already in Rom 14:20.

The years from about 70 to 100 C.E. offer a time frame that allows for post-Pauline ecclesial developments as well as some linkage with the Paul of history and his apostolate (including perhaps short dispatches that he had sent to his co-workers); thus W. Lock (*Commentary*, p. xxii, "between 60 and 90 is probable"; see Falconer, *PE*). This commentary favors 80-85 for the letters as we have them.

Some authors have been impressed by the linguistic and theological links between the PE and Luke-Acts. The NOTES and COMMENTS that follow call particular attention to the parallels in the Lukan corpus, so that the reader may judge for himself whether these links might reflect two different authors, both drawing on common first- and/or second-generation traditions; or, it may be — depending on the date assigned to Luke-Acts — whether the author of the PE had access to Luke-Acts or vice versa. Some scholars have hypothesized that one author was responsible for both Luke-Acts and the PE. Some moderns suggest that the author of Luke-Acts was Paul's amanuensis for the PE (Lock, *Commentary,* p. xxix; Moule, *Essays,* pp. 113-132; *Birth,* pp. 281-282; Strobel, "Schreiben des Lukas?"); another argues that they are quite separate compositions of the same author, written well into the second Christian generation (S. Wilson, *Lk PE,* with P. Marshall, "Review"); another has submitted that the PE were written by the author of Luke-Acts as the "third roll," intended to be read after the two volumes of Luke-Acts as an epistolary appendix that carried the narrative up to Paul's death (Quinn, *Perspectives*).

Those positing an author for the PE in the second Christian generation point to a variety of data. The emphatic apologia for Paul offered by the PE fits the decades immediately after his execution. The apostle had died as a Roman citizen subject to Roman law. There was an understandable tendency among believers, due to the shame of his end as a criminal, to play down the person of the apostle, his ministry, and his teaching (which had been controversial in the first place). Whoever wrote the PE wants to counter that tendency. Moreover, for the PE, Jewish Christianity is still a live option. House churches are still being established for Jewish Christians and are growing. Their relation with the Pauline apostolate and doctrine must still be worked out in practice. By the end of the first century, however, large-scale conversion from Judaism had dwindled and Jewish Christian house churches were withering on the vine.

Still, if this correspondence was composed in the second Christian generation, why are there three letters? One might have sufficed. The genre of letter collections suggests the answer. Various churches in the second generation knew they had received letters from Paul. This correspondence as a whole was yet to be collected (Dahl, "Particularity"; B. Metzger, *Canon,* pp. 257-261). The PE as a collection would have been received and read not as individual letters from the Paul of history but as a "characterization" of the great apostle and his teaching for the new generation.

The original order of the letters within the collection is probably that in which Titus leads off, followed by First Timothy and then Second Timothy. The elaborate, sixty-six-word epistolary prologue of Titus 1:1-4 sounds like a preface to the collection, not only to the short letter that follows. At the same time, First and Second Timothy complement each other, and a final position for the epistolary testament of Second Timothy is evidently appropriate (Quinn, *Per-*

*spectives,* pp. 63-64). Titus does more in its initial position than introduce on a small scale the themes that First Timothy then expands at length. The house churches envisioned by Titus take first place in this collection not because they are small and relatively isolated but because they are predominantly Jewish Christian. The Pauline proclamation of the gospel in the previous generation had been "to everyone who believes"; but that universal proclamation involved a divinely willed priority, "to the Jew first and also to the Greek" (Rom 1:16 [RSV]; see 2:9-10). The PE preserve this priority in their positioning of Titus before First Timothy (where the house churches appear to be of predominantly pagan origin and Paul is explicitly "the Gentiles' teacher" [1 Tim 2:7]).

Where were the PE composed? Titus and First Timothy profess to have been sent while the apostle was on a journey that extended from the island of Crete past Ephesus, with Macedonia and eventually Nicopolis in Epirus as his goal; Second Timothy claims a Roman setting. If the letters originated as a collection in the second Christian generation, the data admit of several reconstructions. Some have proposed that Asia Minor and specifically Ephesus, the destination proposed by the text of the PE for the correspondence with Timothy, were actually the letters' place of origin (most recently, the commentaries by Hanson and Hultgren). On this hypothesis an Ephesian leader with a deep attachment to the Pauline apostolate of the previous generation wrote the PE in the name of Paul to the Ephesian Christians. It is significant that, in this reconstruction, the author of the correspondence proposes that this collection comes not only from Paul but from Rome.

It is also possible that the PE actually derive from the Roman church, where an author composed the collection to rehabilitate the apostle martyred in that city of which he was legally a citizen and to propose him as a teacher for the urban churches of the whole central Mediterranean area, whether the congregations be Jewish or pagan in origin. This proposal emphasizes the elements in the PE that reflect the archaic, Jewish Christian organization of the Roman church, its Greek language, and its interests as they are documented from Romans and Acts through *First Clement* and Hermas (see R. Brown and Meier, *Antioch/Rome;* Penna, "Juifs/Ebrei" and "Configurazione"). The Pauline apostolate had been an urban mission, not a rural one (Meeks, *Urban,* pp. 9-50). The roads that he had traversed all led to the *Urbs* of late antiquity, the city of Rome, its influence palpable in every other city of the empire. If the imperial *Urbs* had executed Paul, the Roman Christians were determined to keep his apostolate alive. It is appropriate on this hypothesis that Rome was the place in which letter collections had become popular and the codex had its origin.

To whom were the PE sent and to what destination(s)? Possible answers were implicit in the preceding discussion. Now they can be marshaled explicitly. According to the hypothesis of the origin of the PE before Paul's martyrdom, the Titus whom we know from Galatians and Second Corinthians and the Timothy whom we encounter in the rest of the Paulines as well as in Acts are the recipients of these letters, on the island of Crete and in Ephesus, respectively.

If the PE appeared after Paul's death, not only Titus and Timothy but also the places to which the letters are addressed may have a typical or representative function. Thus the many small congregations on "Crete" seem to be conceived of as comparatively new Jewish Christian churches, and accordingly "Titus" transmits and represents what Paul has to contribute to the organization and formation of such congregations. In First Timothy, Paul is emphatically "a herald and apostle — it is a fact though it sounds incredible — the Gentiles' teacher in faith and truth" (2:7). In this perspective, "Ephesus" stands for the result of the great Pauline mission in the metropolis of Asia Minor; some of these metropolitan congregations have a majority of members who are of pagan origin, others are predominantly Jewish Christian house churches; "Timothy, his [Paul's] true child in faith" (1:2), visibly joins these groups of congregations within a large urban center with the Pauline family of churches. In the Pauline last will and testament of Second Timothy, the addressee is heir to the apostolic inheritance, the "deposit" (1:11-12) of Paul's teaching as well as his mission to "all of the pagans" (4:17). One might hazard that the Christian congregations in Rome, whether of Jewish or of pagan origin, were the actual models for the paradigmatic congregations of the PE.

## THE PURPOSE OF THE PE

Why were the PE written? Although one would have to nuance the purpose differently according to each hypothesis submitted above, whether one or all of these letters originated at the end of the first Christian generation or at the beginning of the second generation they aim at providing continuity in the apostolic and ecclesial mission of bringing *all* persons, Jew and Gentile, slave and free, male and female, old and young to faith in and worship of Jesus. They emphasize the links of Christians with their past, with the Scriptures of the OT, with Jewish ethics and family practices, with the Pauline apostolate and its teaching, with the ambient Hellenistic and Roman culture from which they all came. The letters also emphasize the links among Christians and the symbiotic unity that ought to characterize believers here and now. They not only score divisive persons but also positively urge a common Pauline faith and worship, a Pauline ethic, and Christian ministries that accord with Pauline precedents. The PE further intend to prepare Christians for the future, a future that in fact found the "catholic church" and the catholic canon of Scripture pitted against the gnostics and the followers of Marcion. But the PE have their eye on a present Christian continuity with another future. "'Godliness is useful for everything, because it contains the promise of a life that is now and that is going to be.' This is the Christian message, meant to be believed and worth welcoming wholeheartedly" (1 Tim 4:8-9).

# *To Timothy (1 Tim)*

## I. AN APOSTLE'S GREETING (1:1-2)

*1 [1]Paul, apostle of Christ Jesus, at the order of God, our savior, and of Christ Jesus,*
*our hope, [2]writes this to Timothy, his true child in faith. Grace, mercy, peace from*
*God the Father and Christ Jesus, our Lord.*

## II. THE APOSTOLIC COMMISSION TO TIMOTHY: PART ONE (1:3–3:13)

### II.A. Apostolic Commands (1:3-20)

#### II.A.1. HETERODOXY (1:3-7)

*1 [3]It was at my explicit encouragement while I was en route to Macedonia that*
*you, Timothy, stayed on in Ephesus. My purpose was that you charge certain peo-*
*ple not to propound strange teachings, [4]not to dote on tales and endless genealogies*
*that can only proffer lucubrations instead of God's own plan that one receives in*
*faith. [5]The goal of your charge and mine is, rather, charity arising from a clean*
*heart and from a clear conscience and from a faith unfeigned. [6]Some people, once*
*they have deviated from these, have slipped off into mere chattering. [7]They want to*
*be "rabbis" but they have no idea either of what they are saying or of the things*
*that they insist on.*

## II.A.2. ORTHODOXY (1:8-17)

### *II.A.2.a. Paul on Law (1:8-11)*

*1 [8]Fine as we know the Law is, there is still the question of one's using it lawfully.*
*[9]That involves knowing that law is not laid down for an upright person; rather, it is for lawless and refractory persons,*

*for godless people and sinners,*
*for the unholy and profane,*
*for patricides and matricides,*
*for murderers,*
*[10]for the incestuous,*
*for homosexuals,*
*for slave traders,*
*for liars,*
*for perjurers;*

*— and anything else that stands opposed to the wholesome instruction [11]that accords with the gospel I was entrusted with, the good news of the glory of the blessed God.*

### *II.A.2.b. Paul at Prayer (1:12-17)*

*1 [12]I give thanks to Christ Jesus, our Lord,*

*who put his strength in me*
*because he regarded me as trustworthy*
*and placed me in his ministry,*
*[13]a man who was formerly*
*a blasphemer*
*and a persecutor*
*and insanely arrogant.*
*But mercy found me out*
*because I did not know what I was doing*
*in my unbelief.*
*[14]Still the grace of our Lord superabounded*
*along with that faith and charity,*
*which come from union with Christ Jesus.*
*[15]The Christian message,*
*meant to be believed*

*and worth welcoming wholeheartedly,*
*is "Christ Jesus came into the world to save sinners."*
*Among them I have first place.*
[16]*But for this very reason mercy found me out*
*so that Christ Jesus could evidence patience to the utmost,*
*using me as a model of those who are going to believe in him for eternal life.*
[17]*So to the king of eternity,*
*the immortal, invisible, only God,*
*are the honor and glory for all eternity.*
*Amen.*

### II.A.3. TIMOTHY'S TASK (1:18-20)

*1 [18]This is the charge I am setting out before you, Timothy, my child, a charge that*
*accords with the prophecies that conducted us to you in the first place. They were*
*given to help you campaign the fine campaign, [19]with faithfulness and a clear con-*
*science. Certain people, once they spurned their conscience, went on to shipwreck*
*in their faith. [20]Among their number were Hymenaeus and Alexander, whom I*
*handed over to Satan to teach them a lesson for having insulted God.*

## II.B. Apostolic Exhortations (2:1–3:13)

### II.B.1. PRAYER AND WORSHIP (2:1–3:1A)

#### *II.B.1.a. For Whom and Why (2:1-7)*

*2 [1]Now I urge, first of all, that entreaties, prayers, intercessions, thanksgivings be*
*made for all human beings, [2]for kings and all in high station. Our purpose is to*
*spend a tranquil and quiet existence in an altogether godly and reverent way. [3]This*
*is an excellent thing and welcome in the eyes of our savior God, [4]who wants all hu-*
*man beings to be saved and to come to full knowledge of the truth, [5]which amounts*
*to this:*

*God is one;*
*one also is the mediator of God and human beings;*
*the Man,*
*Christ Jesus,*

*[6]who gave himself as a ransom for all;*
*the testimony to this has occurred in due time.*

*[7]For that testimony I was appointed a herald and apostle — it is a fact though it sounds incredible — the Gentiles' teacher in faith and truth.*

### *II.B.1.b. By Whom and How (2:8–3:1a)*

*2 [8]Now my wish is that the men take part in the prayer "in every place" of worship,*
*that they lift up hands that are holy, that they be without wrath and resentment.*
*[9]Similarly, I also wish the women to make themselves attractive in a becom-*
*ing costume, with sensible discretion. Their beauty is not in their coiffure and gold*
*ornaments, or in their pearls or extravagant clothing, [10]but it comes through their*
*excellent deeds — that suits women who are professing real godliness.*
*[11]Let a married woman quietly learn in the assemblies for worship and quite*
*obediently. [12]Moreover, I do not allow a wife to teach in the public worship and to*
*boss her husband. That is learning "quietly." [13]The reasons for my directive are*
*that God fashioned Adam first, then Eve; [14]and furthermore that Adam was not*
*fooled [by the serpent] but his wife was made a fool of and she turned to sin. [15]"A*
*person will be saved rearing children, provided they persevere in faithfulness and*
*charity and a sensible holiness." 3 [1a]That is the Christian message, meant to be be-*
*lieved.*

## II.B.2. ON THE MINISTERS (3:1B-13)

### *II.B.2.a. The Bishop (3:1b-7)*

*3 [1b]If anybody aspires to the episcopate, he sets his heart on fine work. [2]Thus a*
*bishop has to be*

*irreproachable,*
*a husband to one wife,*
*temperate,*
*sensible,*
*urbane,*
*one who likes guests,*
*a skilled teacher*
*[3]not a drinker,*
*not a bully,*
*but gentle,*

*not argumentative,*
*not one who likes money.*

*[4]He is to be outstanding in his direction of his own home, with children who are obedient and quite reverent. [5](For if anybody does not know how to direct his own home, how will he take care of God's church?) [6]He must not be a neophyte lest, inflated with vanity, he fall under the devil's condemnation. [7]But he must enjoy also a fine recommendation from outsiders, lest he fall into disgrace and a snare of the devil.*

### *II.B.2.b. The Deacons and Women Ministers (3:8-13)*

*3 [8]Similarly, deacons have to be*

*serious persons,*
*not retailing gossip,*
*not addicted to heavy drinking,*
*not money-minded,*

*[9]but persons who hold the mystery of the faith with a clean conscience. [10]Let them first be put to the test; then let those who are unimpeachable serve as deacons. [11](Similarly, the women who are ministers have to be*

*serious persons;*
*not devils at gossip;*
*temperate;*
*believers in every sense.)*

*[12]Deacons are to be husbands of one wife, outstanding in the direction of their own children and homes. [13]For men who give outstanding diaconal service gain a fine standing for themselves and a right to speak out for the faith that is theirs in Christ Jesus.*

## III. A PIECE IN PAUSE (3:14–4:5)

### III.A. Pauline Introduction (3:14-15)

*3 [14]I am putting these matters in writing for you, Timothy, though I still hope to come to you before long. [15]Still, if I do delay, this letter will let you know how a person has to behave in God's house, which is the church of the living God. [There you, Timothy, are] a pillar and pedestal for the truth.*

## III.B. Hymn (3:16)

*3 16And great is the mystery of godliness. There is no denying it!*

*. . . He who was revealed in human flesh,*
*Was made victorious in the Spirit:*
*He who was seen by God's messengers,*
*Was heralded to the pagans:*
*He who was received in faith, in the world,*
*Was taken up in glory.*

## III.C. Prophecy (4:1-5)

### III.C.1. ORACLE (4:1)

*4 1Here is the Spirit expressly declaring, "In these latter times some people, who dote on seductive spirits and demonic doctrines, will apostatize from the faith."*

### III.C.2. INTERPRETATION OF ORACLE (4:2-5)

#### *III.C.2.a. Doctrines of Opponents (4:2-3)*

*2These lying frauds, with their cauterized consciences, 3interdict marriage and demand abstinence from foods, things that God created for believers and persons who have recognized the truth, to share in thankfully.*

#### *III.C.2.b. Refutation from Scripture (4:4-5)*

*4For everything in God's creation is fine and none is despicable when received with thanksgiving. 5Every one of them is hallowed by God's word in Scripture and intercessory prayer.*

# IV. THE APOSTOLIC COMMISSION TO TIMOTHY: PART TWO (4:6–6:21A)

## IV.A. As Apostolic Teacher (4:6-16)

### IV.A.1. PERSONALLY (4:6-10)

*4 [6]When you suggest matters such as the preceding to your brothers, Timothy, you will be a fine minister of Christ Jesus, yourself nourished on the words of the faith and of that fine instruction with which you are quite familiar. [7]Have nothing to do with profane old wives' tales. Train for action that aims at godliness. [8]"Whereas physical exercise is useful for a little, godliness is useful for everything, because it contains the promise of a life that is now and that is going to be." [9]This is the Christian message, meant to be believed and worth welcoming wholeheartedly. [10]Ultimately this promise is the reason for our job and our contest, that we have fixed our hope on the living God, savior of all, particularly of believers.*

### IV.A.2. FOR THE FAITHFUL (4:11-14)

*4 [11]These are the matters, Timothy, to charge and to teach. [12]No one is to disdain you for your youth. Rather keep on being a pattern for believers —*

> *in word,*
> *in behavior,*
> *in charity,*
> *in faithfulness,*
> *in purity.*

*[13]Until I arrive, concentrate on your public reading of the Scriptures, on your preaching, on your instruction. [14]Neglect not that gracious gift within you, the one given to you under prophetic direction, with an imposition of the hands of the presbytery.*

### IV.A.3. SUMMARY EXHORTATION (4:15-16)

*4 [15]Let these matters be your study. Be absorbed in them, so that your progress can be perceived by all. [16]Pay attention to yourself and to your instruction. Persevere in these activities; for, if you do this, you will save both yourself and the persons listening to you.*

## IV.B. As Apostolic Supervisor (5:1–6:2)

### IV.B.1. DOMESTIC CODE: PART ONE (5:1-2)

*5 [1]Never scold an elderly man but keep encouraging him as if he were your own father. Encourage young men as if they were your own brothers; [2]older women as mothers; young women as if your own sisters, in complete purity.*

### IV.B.2. THE ORDER OF WIDOWS (5:3-16)

*5 [3]Honor the claims of widows who deserve that title.*

*[4]Thus, in the case of a widow who has children or grandchildren, they should be the first to learn the meaning of reverence for one's own home and of giving recompense to their forebears. For this is a welcome thing in the eyes of God [the Father].*

*[5](The case is otherwise with the widow proper, one who is a completely destitute woman who has fixed her hope in God and stays on night and day in entreaties and prayers. [6]A widow indulging herself voluptuously has died while still living. [7]And charge them on these matters, so that they will be irreproachable.)*

*[8]In the case of a man who does not provide for his own people and particularly his immediate family, he has disowned the faith and is worse than an unbeliever.*

*[9]Follow these rules for enrolling a widow on the official roster: she must have lived no less than sixty years; she must have been a wife to one husband; [10]she must have public attestation of fine deeds. Thus,*

*did she rear children?*
*did she welcome guests?*
*did she wash traveling Christians' feet?*
*did she come to the help of the oppressed?*
*did she set out to do every excellent deed possible?*

*[11]On the other hand, have nothing to do with the younger widows. The reason is that they want to remarry whenever they feel attractions that are incompatible with their commitment to Christ. [12]They stand condemned because they broke their previous pledge to him, [13]not to mention that, at the same time, they also learn how to be lazy while circulating from house to home, and not just lazy but gossips as well, saying what they have no right to say. [14]Now my wish is that younger widows remarry, rear children, run their homes, offer no pretext for reviling to the adversary, [15]for some of them have already slipped off after Satan.*

*[16]In the case of a woman who is a believer and who welcomes widows into her home, let her continue to come to their help and the local church not be burdened but free to help the widows proper.*

## IV.B.3. THE ORDER OF PRESBYTERS (5:17-25)

*5 [17]The presbyters who have given outstanding direction deserve to get double pay, particularly those whose jobs are preaching and instruction; [18]for the Scripture says, "You shall not tie shut the mouth of the ox that is threshing grain," and "The workman is deserving of his wage."*

*[19]Do not give a hearing, Timothy, to a charge against a presbyter, unless the evidence comes from two or three witnesses. [20]Those who are sinning you are to refute while all of the presbyters look on, to put fear of wrongdoing into the rest of them.*

*[21]As God [the Father] and Christ Jesus and the elect angels look on, I adjure you, Timothy, to keep these directives without prejudice, that is, not doing anything out of partisanship.*

*[22]Be in no hurry, Timothy, to impose hands on anyone.*

*Incur no responsibility for the sins of others.*
*Keep yourself chaste.*

*[23]Drink only water no longer, but take wine, moderately, for your bad stomach and your frequent bouts with illness.*

*[24]The sins of some people are obvious enough, escorting them to judgment; others trail their sins behind them.*

*[25]Similarly also, fine deeds are obvious, and those that are not obvious cannot stay hidden always.*

## IV.B.4. DOMESTIC CODE: PART TWO (6:1-2)

*6 [1]Those Christians who are bound in slavery are to regard their masters as deserving all esteem. Thus God's name and the instruction will not be defamed. [2]Moreover, slaves that have masters who are believers are not to disdain them. After all, they are brothers. Instead they are to be even better slaves because they have masters who practice kindness as men who are believers and beloved.*

*These are things, Timothy, for you to teach and encourage.*

# IV.C. In Relation to Problems (6:3-21a)

## IV.C.1. THE HETERODOX (6:3-5)

*6 [3]In the case of a man who propounds strange teachings and has no recourse to the wholesome sayings that come from our Lord, Jesus Christ, or to the godly instruction, [4]one can only conclude that he has become a conceited ignoramus with a morbid craving for speculation and quibbling about terminology. These in turn produce —*

*jealousy,*
*controversy,*
*vituperations,*
*vicious insinuations,*
*5the incessant bickerings of men*
*whose minds are a shambles and*
*who have been robbed of the truth;*
*they think godliness is a means*
*for gain.*

## IV.C.2. RICHES: PART ONE (6:6-10)

*6 6No question of it. Godliness brings gain, great gain — for someone contented*
*with what he has. 7The reason is that we brought nothing into the world; as a re-*
*sult we cannot take anything out of it. 8So then if we have keep and covering, with*
*them we shall be content. 9Those, however, who want to be wealthy topple into a*
*temptation and a trap and multiple lusts, senseless and injurious, the kind that en-*
*gulf people in utterly ruinous destruction. 10The root that lies under all evils is the*
*love of money. Certain persons who have craved it have strayed off from the faith*
*and have skewered themselves with multiple tortures.*

## IV.C.3. AN ORDINATION CHARGE (6:11-16)

*6 11You, O man of God, must shun these things. Instead pursue —*

*upright conduct,*
*godliness,*
*faithfulness,*
*charity,*
*steadfastness,*
*gentleness.*

*12Contend in the fine contest, the contest in the arena of faith. Lay hold on eternal*
*life. You were called into that life and for it you made that fine profession before the*
*eyes of many witnesses. 13Before the eyes of the God who keeps all things alive and*
*of Christ Jesus who publicly attested to the fine profession before Pontius Pilate, I*
*charge you 14to keep the apostolic command beyond blemish, beyond reproach,*

*until the revelation of our Lord, Jesus Christ. [15]That revelation God will make in due time, he who is*

*the blessed and only suzerain;*
*the king of those who act as kings*
*and lord of those who act as lords;*
*[16]the only one who possesses immortality,*
*who inhabits inaccessible light;*
*the one whom no human being ever saw*
*or can see*
*to whom belong honor*
*and might eternal.*
*Amen.*

## IV.C.4. RICHES: PART TWO (6:17-19)

6 *[17]Timothy, charge the wealthy of the present age —*

*not to be snobbish,*
*to have set their hope not on precarious wealth,*
*but on the God who lavishly provides*
*everything for our satisfaction;*
*[18]charge them to do good;*
*to become wealthy in fine deeds;*
*to be munificent,*
*sharing all around,*
*[19]making their deposits in an*
*excellent fund for the future,*
*so that they can lay hold*
*on the life which deserves*
*that name.*

## V. CLOSING SUMMARY (6:20-21A)

6 *[20]O Timothy, keep what has been deposited with you. Keep your distance from the profane drivel and dialectic of so-called knowledge. [21a]Some, who profess to have this at their disposal, have in fact deviated in their faith.*

## VI. FINAL PRAYER (6:21B)

*6 $^{21b}$Grace be with you all.*

# *To Timothy (2 Tim)*

## I. AN APOSTLE'S GREETING (1:1-2)

*1 [1]Paul, apostle of Christ Jesus, by the will of God and for the sake of the promise of
life that is in Christ Jesus, [2]writes this to his dear child, Timothy. Grace, mercy,
peace from God the Father and Christ Jesus, our Lord.*

## II. THANKSGIVING PRAYER (1:3-14)

### II.A. The Past (1:3-5)

*1 [3]I give thanks to the God whom I, like my forebears, worship with a clean con-
science, as I make unceasing mention of you in my entreaties, night and day. [4]When I
remember your tears, I yearn to see you and so to have my fill of joy. [5]I have a re-
minder of your unfeigned faith, the very same as that which first dwelt in your
grandmother, Lois, and in your mother, Eunice, and in you too, I am convinced.*

### II.B. The Present (1:6-12)

*1 [6]So I, with good reason, remind you, Timothy, to rekindle that gracious gift of God
the Father, which is within you through the imposition of these hands of mine; [7]for
God gave us not a dastard spirit but one of dynamic strength and of charity and of
discretion. [8]May you not be ashamed about the testimony to our Lord or about me,*

*his prisoner. Instead, along with me take your share of suffering for the gospel, as God gives the strength, [9]the God who saved us and called us for a holy life. That saving call did not correspond to our deeds. It corresponded with his own design, his own grace, given us in Christ Jesus from all eternity. [10]That gracious design, however, has now been made clear through the revelation of our savior, Christ Jesus. He broke the power of death. He made life and immortality shine forth through the gospel, [11]for which I in turn was appointed herald and apostle and teacher. [12]Thus I, with good reason too, am undergoing these afflictions; but I am not ashamed of them, for I know the one in whom I have put my faith and I am convinced that he has the power to keep for that Day what has been deposited with me.*

### II.C. The Future (1:13-14)

*1 [13]With that faith and charity which are yours in Christ Jesus, stick to the model of the wholesome words that you heard from me. [14]Keep that fine deposit, Timothy, through the Holy Spirit who dwells in us.*

## III. PERSONAL NOTE ONE (1:15-18)

*1 [15]You know this, of course, that all in the province of Asia — to name only Phygelus and Hermogenes — abandoned me. [16]May the Lord, however, grant mercy to the family of Onesiphorus, for time and again he revived my spirits and was unashamed about this manacle on me. [17]Instead, when he came to Rome he hunted for me right away and he found [me]. [18]So may the Lord grant him to find — indeed, he will find mercy from the Lord on that Day. And you know well enough how many services he provided in Ephesus.*

## IV. TESTAMENT OF PAUL (2:1–4:8)

### IV.A. The Legator (2:1-13)

*2 [1]Now, my child, find strength in that grace which is in Christ Jesus; [2]and those things that you heard from me, through many witnesses, set out for trustworthy men, the kind who will also be competent to teach others. [3]As a fine soldier of Christ Jesus take your share of suffering along with me. [4]No one on active duty in the military gets involved in the business of civilian life. He avoids this to please the man who called him to arms. [5]Moreover, take the case of a man who competes in the public games: he does not get the winner's crown if he does not compete accord-*

*ing to the rules. [6]Or again: the farmer on the job ought to be the first to have his share of the crops. [7]Consider what I am saying here, Timothy; for in every way the Lord will grant you insight.*

*[8]Keep in mind Jesus Christ,*

*risen from the dead,*
*from the line of David.*

*That corresponds to my gospel [9]for which I am being wronged, put into chains as though a wrongdoer — but the word of God has not been chained. [10]For this very reason, that is, for the sake of the elect, I am submitting to everything. My purpose is that they too reach the salvation which is in Christ Jesus with eternal glory.*

*[11]The Christian message, meant to be believed, is this:*

*". . . for if we shared in his death,*
*we shall share in his life.*
*[12]If we submit now,*
*we shall share in his reign.*
*If we ever disown him,*
*he is the one who will disown us.*
*[13]If we are faithless,*
*he is the one who stays faithful,*
*for he cannot possibly disown himself."*

## IV.B. The Challengers Challenged (2:14–3:9)

### IV.B.1. THE ERRORS (2:14-26)

*2 [14]Bring these matters to mind, Timothy, I adjure you, as God looks on. Shun quibbling over words — good for nothing except the utter ruin of the listeners. [15]Do your best to make yourself a fit offering to God, a workman who has no reason for shame, one who clears the way for the message of the truth. [16]Steer clear, however, of "profane drivel," for it progresses ever more deeply into godlessness [17]and its message spreads like gangrene. Take Hymenaeus and Philetus as examples. [18]It is men like those who have deviated in the truth when they say that the resurrection has already occurred, and so they overturn some people's faith.*

*[19]God's solid foundation stands, nevertheless, bearing this seal:*

*"The Lord knows those who are his,"*
*and*
*"Let everyone who names the Lord's name abandon wickedness."*

*[20]Still in any great house there are not only the utensils of gold and silver but also
wooden ones and earthenware, for noble and ignoble purposes. [21]So if a person will
only purge himself of that drivel, he will be a utensil for a noble purpose —*

*hallowed,*
*useful to the master,*
*ready for any excellent deed.*

*[22]Shun juvenile desires. Rather, pursue*

*upright conduct,*
*faithfulness,*
*charity,*
*peace,*

*in company with those who invoke the Lord from a clean heart. [23]Steer clear, how-
ever, of foolish and undisciplined researches; as you are well aware, they breed only
wranglings. [24]The Lord's slave ought not to wrangle. Instead, he has to be*

*gentle with all,*
*a skilled teacher,*
*forbearing,*

*[25]considerate in correcting the unmanageable, just in case God may grant
them a change of heart that will lead back into full knowledge of the truth. [26]Then
their heads would clear and they would find their way "out of the snare of the devil
in which he has been keeping them alive" and into the will of God himself.*

## IV.B.2. THE ERRING (3:1-9)

*3 [1]Realize this, however, that in the last days rough times will be at hand; [2]for then
people will be*

*intent on themselves,*
*intent on money,*
*pretentious,*
*arrogant,*
*blaspheming;*
*to those who bore them,*
  *undutiful,*
  *ungrateful,*
  *irreligious,*
  *[3]unaffectionate,*

*irreconcilable;*
*devils at gossip,*
*uncontrolled,*
*uncouth,*
*uncaring about goodness;*
4 *renegade,*
*reckless,*
*conceited,*
*intent on pleasure*
*rather than intent on God.*

5 *These people hold onto the appearance of godliness but they have repudiated its*
*dynamic. Keep people like that at a distance too.* 6 *For from their ranks come those*
*who are worming their way into homes to captivate the little ladies,*

*loaded with sins*
*and driven by diverse cravings,*
7 *ever learning*
*and never turning to full knowledge*
*of the truth.*

8 *Just as once Jannes and Jambres defied Moses, so too these numbskulled counterfeit-*
*ers of the faith are defying the truth,* 9 *but they will not progress far. Their own stupid-*
*ity is going to become just as obvious to everyone as the stupidity of those two.*

## IV.C. The Legatee (3:10–4:8)

### IV.C.1. PAUL'S LIFE (3:10-13)

3 10 *You, however, Timothy, were quite familiar*

*with the instruction,*
*with the approach to living,*
*with the design,*
*with the faithfulness,*
*with the patience,*
*with the charity,*
*with the steadfastness*

*that were mine,* 11 *along with the persecutions, with the sufferings, such as hap-*
*pened to me in Pisidian Antioch, in Iconium, in Lystra. What persecutions I bore!*
*Still, from all of them the Lord delivered me.* 12 *Moreover, all who want to live in a*

godly way in Christ Jesus will be persecuted. [13]However, vicious people and charla-
tans will progress — from bad to worse, deluding and deluded.

## IV.C.2. TIMOTHY'S IMITATION OF PAUL (3:14–4:4)

3 [14]You, however, Timothy, persevere in the things you learned and became sure of.
You are well aware of the people you learned from [15]and that from your tenderest
years you have known the sacred letters which have the power to make you astute
in attaining salvation through faith which comes from union with Christ Jesus.
[16]All the Scripture is inspired by God and useful

for instruction,
for censuring,
for straightening people out,
for giving training in upright conduct,

[17]so that the man of God may be complete, that is, completely equipped for every
excellent deed.

4 [1]As God the Father looks on, and Christ Jesus who is going to judge the liv-
ing and dead, I adjure you, Timothy, while bearing witness to his revelation and
his kingdom:

[2]herald the message;
stand on the alert, when convenient,
when inconvenient;
refute;
reprove;
encourage —

with the utmost patience in the task of teaching. [3]For there will come a time when
they will not put up with this wholesome instruction. Instead, they will load them-
selves with teachers who answer their craving to get relief for their itchy ears. [4]Fur-
thermore, as they turn a deaf ear to the truth, they will slip off after tales.

### IV.C.3. Paul's Death (4:5-8)

4 [5]You, however, Timothy,

keep calm, in every sense;
accept being wronged;

do the work of one who announces the gospel;
carry out fully the ministry that is yours.

[6]For now my own blood is to spill as a wine-offering. The time set for my embarkation has come. [7]I have contended in the fine contest. I have run the whole track. I have kept faith. [8]Whatever happens there lies in store for me the crown of the upright life with which the upright judge, the Lord, will recompense me on that Day — and of course not only me but all who have their hearts set on his revelation.

## V. PERSONAL NOTE TWO (4:9-21)

### V.A. News for Timothy (4:9-15)

4 [9]Do your best to come here soon; [10]for Demas, his heart set on this present world, left me helpless and set out for Thessalonika. Crescens has gone to Gaul; Titus, to Dalmatia. [11]Only Luke is with me now. Pick up Mark and bring him along with you, for he can be helpful to me in my ministry. [12]I have appointed Tychicus to go to Ephesus.

[13]When you come, bring along that cape which I left behind in Troas at Carpus's home — and bring the books, too, particularly the notebooks. [14]There in Troas Alexander, the coppersmith, brought many false charges against me. (The Lord will give him the recompense that corresponds to his deeds.) [15]Watch out for him yourself now, because his defiance of our words was frenzied.

### V.B. Paul at Law (4:16-18)

4 [16]At my first appearance in court no one was on my side; instead, all left me helpless. (May it not be held against them!) [17]Still the Lord stood by me and put his strength in me, so that through me the proclamation would be carried out fully, or, in other words, so that all the pagans would listen to it, and I was delivered "from the lion's mouth." [18]The Lord will deliver me from every one of these vicious attacks and he will save me for his kingdom, in heaven. To him, the glory for all eternity. Amen.

### V.C. Pauline Greetings to Ephesus (4:19-21a)

4 [19]Greet Prisca and Aquila and the family of Onesiphorus. [20]Erastus stayed on in Corinth. I had to leave Trophimus behind in Miletus when he fell ill. [21a]Do your best to come here before winter.

## V.D. Roman Greetings (4:21b)

4 [21b]*Eubulus sends along greetings to you, Timothy, as do Pudens and Linus and Claudia and all our brothers.*

## VI. FINAL PRAYERS (4:22)

4 [22]*The Lord be with your spirit, Timothy. Grace be with you all.*

# Notes and Comments on the First Letter to Timothy

# Outline of First Timothy

I. An Apostle's Greeting (1:1-2)
II. The Apostolic Commission to Timothy: Part I (1:3–3:13)
  A. Apostolic Commands (1:3-20)
    1. Heterodoxy (1:3-7)
    2. Orthodoxy (1:8-17)
      a. Paul on Law (1:8-11)
      b. Paul at Prayer (1:12-17)
    3. Timothy's Task (1:18-20)
  B. Apostolic Exhortations (2:1–3:13)
    1. Prayer and Worship (2:1–3:1a)
      a. For Whom and Why (2:1-7)
      b. By Whom and How (2:8–3:1a)
        1. By Men (2:8)
        2. By Women (2:9–3:1a)
    2. On the Ministers (3:1b-13)
      a. The Bishop (3:1b-7)
      b. The Deacons and Women Ministers (3:8-13)
III. A Piece in Pause (3:14–4:5)
  A. Pauline Introduction (3:14-15)
  B. Hymn (3:16)
  C. Prophecy (4:1-5)
    1. Oracle (4:1)
    2. Interpretation of Oracle (4:2-5)
      a. Doctrines of Opponents (4:2-3)
      b. Refutation from Scripture (4:4-5)
IV. The Apostolic Commission to Timothy: Part II (4:6–6:19)
  A. As Apostolic Teacher (4:6-16)
    1. Personally (4:6-10)
    2. For the Faithful (4:11-14)
    3. Summary Exhortation (4:15-16)
  B. As Apostolic Supervisor of the Orders in the Church (5:1–6:2)
    1. Domestic Code: Part I (5:1-2)
    2. The Order of Widows (5:3-16)
    3. The Order of Presbyters (5:17-25)
    4. Domestic Code: Part II (6:1-2)
  C. In Relation to Problems (6:3-19)
    1. The Heterodox (6:3-5)

2. Riches: Part I (6:6-10)
3. An Ordination Charge (6:11-16)
4. Riches: Part II (6:17-19)

V. Closing Summary (6:20-21a)

VI. Final Prayer (6:21b)

# Introduction to First Timothy

The second part of the collection of letters that we call the PE has the form of an epistolary diptych directed to Timothy. What we title First Timothy constitutes an epistolary commission for this Pauline co-worker; what we call Second Timothy is an epistolary testament to Timothy in the name of the apostle.

As the letter to Titus had the cities of Crete and Jewish Christians principally in view, First Timothy is concerned with the metropolis of Ephesus and Christian converts that come mainly from paganism. The letter opens with a brief apostolic greeting and blessing for Timothy, another of Paul's true children in Christian belief.

The body of the following composition turns on a central axis of prophetic texts, hymnic and oracular, which are proposed and interpreted for Timothy by Paul for the benefit of the church, conceived of as God's household (3:14–4:5). Around this axis, apostolic commissions for Timothy are arranged, 1 Tim 1:3–3:13 preceding, 4:6–6:21a following.

The former Pauline commission opens with the singular address to Timothy (1:3) in a series of apostolic commands about Judaizing heterodoxies in applying the Law among the converts from paganism. These errors have occasioned the decision to put Timothy in charge at Ephesus (1:3-7). The true Pauline teaching about the function of the Law is complemented by the apostle's thanksgiving prayer to the risen Jesus for his conversion and vocation (1:12-17). This section of commands closes with an emphatic repetition of the singular address to Timothy in the charge of 1:18-20. Then the figure of Timothy sinks out of view as Paul delivers a series of apostolic exhortations on the public worship of believers (2:1–3:1a) and the ministers who serve them (3:1b-13). The section on public worship employs an already traditional Christian order for community prayer which opens with a description of the universal scope of Christian liturgical prayer and the reasons, practical as well as theological, for this catholic inclusiveness (2:1-7). Then the church order turns to the praying community as such, dealing first with the dispositions appropriate for the men in the assembly, then for the women (2:8-10). Public teaching by a married woman in the liturgical assembly poses a special problem because of her prior commitment to her husband and children. The order proposes a solution grounded on the liturgical charge which a bride heard in her Christian marriage (2:11–3:1a).

Finally, the order turns to the qualifications and dispositions required in those who minister to the liturgical assembly. The ministerial offices have the Pauline titles of bishop and deacon. In the first place, the ideal bishop is described with a catalogue of the virtues to be sought in him and the vices that disqualify a candidate (3:1b-7). Second, the order submits catalogues of the qualities to be investigated in another cadre of ministers, male and female. The former are titled deacons; the latter receive no formal title (3:8-13).

The lengthy church order concludes at the central axis, previously noted (3:14–4:5). At this point Timothy again appears, as Paul, in the first person, addresses him. This singular address, relatively rare in the preceding apostolic commission, dominates the development of the second commission, which occupies the last half of First Timothy.

The second commission is divided into three sections. It may presuppose metropolitan house churches with stronger Jewish ties than the former commission. The first section addresses Timothy personally as a Pauline teacher, faithful to the apostolic instruction that he has received, putting it into practice for his own sake and for the sake of his fellow Christians to whom he reads out the OT and whom he teaches in the assembly for public worship. For this task he has received a charism through a presbyterial laying on of hands (4:6-16).

In the following section of the commission Timothy appears as an apostolic supervisor of the orders of the church. A domestic code is used to frame this section (5:1-2 and 6:1-2). The implication is that the household was conceived of as the primary unit in the local church and that this was to be Timothy's primary concern. The orders of presbyters and widows suggest a more Jewish structuring of the congregations envisioned in this section than earlier. Timothy's supervision of an order of widows is described in terms of an already traditional church order (5:3-16). His relationship to an order of presbyters is delineated next, again using traditional materials (5:17-25).

The third and final section of the Pauline commission, after a brief polemic against heterodox opponents (6:3-5), turns to the problems which wealth occasions among believers (6:6-10, 17-19). In the middle of this exposition appears a traditional ordination charge that serves here to hearten the apostolic co-worker as he deals with the rich and thus the powerful and influential members of the Christian congregation (6:11-16).

First Timothy closes with a summary warning to avoid speculative adventures and to adhere to the content of the preceding apostolic commissions (6:20-21a).

The blessing prayer which closes many manuscripts of First Timothy (6:21b) may not be part of the original composition.

# To Timothy (1 Tim)

## I. AN APOSTLE'S GREETING (1:1-2)

*1 [1]Paul, apostle of Christ Jesus, at the order of God, our savior, and of Christ Jesus, our hope, [2]writes this to Timothy, his true child in faith. Grace, mercy, peace from God the Father and Christ Jesus, our Lord.*

### ♦ NOTES

1:1-2. For *at the order,* Sinaiticus reads *kat' epaggelian,* "according to the promise," thus editing out the non-Attic *epitagēn* with a phrase that occurs in this position in the greeting of 2 Tim 1:1 (J. K. Elliott, *Greek Text,* p. 15).

Almost all the terminology of this greeting prayer has been reviewed in the Notes to Titus 1:1-4 in AB *Titus,* with further cross references. For *mercy* see Titus 3:5. The name *Timothy* (a pagan name meaning "one who honors god") appears here for the first of four times in the PE (see the vocative address in 1:18 and 6:20, as well the greeting of 2 Tim 1:2). His Jewish mother, Eunice, and grandmother, Lois, are singled out for praise in 2 Tim 1:5 (see 2 Tim 3:14-15). The same Timothy figures as one of Paul's closest co-workers in eight of the other Pauline letters, where his name appears thirteen times. The Acts describes his induction into and participation in the Pauline mission in 16:1; 17:14-15; 18:5; 19:22; 20:4. Hebrews 13:23 apparently refers to the same person. No one by this name appears in Ap. Frs., and the only appearance of the name in the LXX is in the Maccabean literature, where the person (if indeed it is one individual) called Timothy is a pagan general and enemy of the Jews (see Josephus, *Ant.* 12.329, 330, 337, 339, 341, 343, and Goldstein, AB *1 Macc,* pp. 296-297, and *2 Macc,* pp. 339-340). Though common enough in the Hellenistic world, the name does not appear to have been popular among Jewish people (thus, *CII* does not have a verifiable occurrence).

In this greeting, the term *Lord, kyrios,* appears for the first time in the PE. Apart from Titus and the Johannine Epistles, every book of the NT employs *kyrios* for a total of 719 occurrences, of which 22 are in this Timothy correspondence. The other Paulines have 253; Luke-Acts, 211 (in contrast to the 80 in Matthew, 18 in Mark, and 53 in John; see Fitzmyer, "Kyrios," 2.811, and AB *Lk,* pp. 200-204, as well as Spicq, *Supp. Lexic.,* pp. 415-425, and Lacey, "One Lord," pp. 191-203, for the history and meaning of *kyrios* as a title for Jesus and for the

God of Israel). The question remains moot whether copies of the LXX for Jews and antedating the Christian era used *kyrios* for the name of Yahweh, though Jewish authors appear to have read *kyrios* as a version of the tetragrammaton on occasion (see Josephus, *Ant.* 13.68 [Isa 19:19]; 20.90; *Ep. Arist.* 155 [Deut 7:18]; and Philo in Fitzmyer, *Aramean,* pp. 121-122, 139 n. 51). Palestinian Jews were using the Hebrew *'adonay* and the Aramaic *mare'* for Yahweh without further qualification for more than a century (and perhaps much more) before the birth of Jesus, and it appears probable that it was the first-generation Palestinian Jewish Christians who began to use these terms and the Greek *kyrios* of Jesus as well as Yahweh (see Fitzmyer, *Advance,* pp. 221-223; see Lacey, "One Lord," p. 194). Unquestionably the usage was firmly in possession by the time the earliest Christian documents appeared, and it remained so throughout the NT and Ap. Frs.

Five out of six uses of *kyrios* in First Timothy are in the phrase *kyrios hēmōn, our Lord,* which explicitly designates *Christ Jesus* or Jesus Christ here as well as in 1:12; 6:3, 14, and surely refers to Jesus in 1:14. When the doxology of 1 Tim 6:15 uses *kyrios* without *hēmōn* of the God "who is the blessed and only suzerain, the king of those who act as kings and lord of those who act as lords," the reference is to the one God of Israel. The textual variants in 1 Tim 5:5 and 2 Tim 2:14 can be disregarded for the present survey. Though Second Timothy uses *kyrios* sixteen times, the phrase *our Lord* appears only twice, referring explicitly to Jesus in the greeting of 1:2 and implicitly in 1:8. In Ap. Frs. also, *our Lord* refers to Jesus, particularly in *First Clement* (see *inscr.;* 20.11; 42.3; 44.1; 49.6; 50.7; 65.2).

## ♦ COMMENT

First Timothy (as we title it) now opens the second part of the epistolary collection which we call the PE. This document is intended to be read in tandem with Second Timothy, as the lack of a closing affectionate greeting (contrast Titus 3:15 and 2 Tim 4:19, 21) and the probable omission of the final blessing in 6:21b signal. The similar though not identical greeting in 2 Tim 1:1-2 reinforces the impression that these two epistles are intended to be read as two parts of a single whole.

The opening greeting and blessing in First Timothy are far briefer than in Titus 1:1-4, though this composition is fully twice as long. As has been observed, the greeting to Titus served to introduce also the whole collection. At this point, the greeting to Timothy uses the vocabulary of Titus, every word (except *Timothy* and *Lord*) having figured, even conspicuously, in the argument of the previous epistle. Thus a smooth transition, leaving a strong impression of continuity between the letters, has been forged. The lack of a thanksgiving prayer immediately after the greeting also reminds one of the preceding epistle.

The form of the greeting blessing in the PE differs from the other Paulines on two counts: (1) it contains only a wish for a blessing and the divine source of the blessing and omits the recipient of the wish, thus precluding the use of a second-person singular, which would have implied the correspondence was simply between two individuals and not between the apostle and the whole congregation of believers, addressed as they are in 6:21b: "Grace be with you all"; and (2) the title "Father" for God is employed only in the greeting blessing and not elsewhere in the epistle. These differences make it difficult to sustain the case that the greetings of the PE are directly cited from earlier Pauline letters. There is certainly an influential memory of how the apostle expressed himself when he wrote to believers. Even the adoption of the epistolary form for an authoritative communication is probably due to the fact that Paul was remembered as having invested that form with his authority when he introduced it into his apostolate (see White, "Epistolary," pp. 1739-1741, 1751-1752). The coincidences in form and in phraseology that do exist between the greetings of the PE and those of the other Paulines are not close enough or extensive enough to demand positing citations from a collection of Pauline correspondence. The resemblances and the differences are more explicable in terms of a Christian community that had a living memory of the Pauline apostolate and perhaps one Pauline letter, such as Romans, which they read and upon which they reflected.

1:1. *Paul, apostle of Christ Jesus, at the order of God, our savior, and of Christ Jesus, our hope.* The personal name of Paul is here followed by an identification of the extrinsic basis of his authority that differs just enough from the heading of Titus to remind one, literarily, that this letter will have a somewhat different character and purpose. The very Jewish title "slave of God" has been dropped; now *Paul* is *apostle of Christ Jesus,* not "of Jesus Christ" (see J. K. Elliott, *Greek Text,* pp. 199-201, on the textual variants).

The five Greek terms that are now translated as *at the order of God, our savior* are all but identical with a phrase in Titus 1:3. The slight variants appear to be dictated stylistically because of a phrase that is not found in the greeting of Titus, a phrase which asserts that the command which constituted *Paul* as an *apostle of Christ Jesus* was emphatically an *order . . . of Christ Jesus, our hope.* If the description of Paul's apostolic office in the greeting to Titus (and especially in Titus 1:3) witnesses to the Jewish Christian orientation of that letter, then this addition prepares the way for an exposition that will emphasize Paul's apostolate to the pagans. Already in Rom 15:8-9, 12-13, the Jewish Christians are to perceive in Christ God's truthfulness (*alētheias;* cf. *epignōsis alētheias* in Titus 1:1), whereas the pagans praise the mercy of God toward them, a mercy which gave them hope in Christ. Thus the blessing that opens both sections of this correspondence with Timothy includes *mercy,* a leitmotiv which will resound below in Paul's thanksgiving prayer for the mercy that he received (1:13-16), and in the description of "our savior God, who wills that all human beings be saved" and who appointed Paul "a herald and apostle, . . . the Gentiles' teacher in faith and truth" (2:3-7; cf. 4:10). The universal, saving will of God and his Christ takes shape in *the order* which effects the Pauline mission to the nations. In the OL versions, the phrase presented by *at the order* is translated with *secundum imperium,* a pregnant theological usage of a Roman constitutional and legal term (see also Vg 1 Tim 6:16; Titus 1:3; 2:15; and Vg Luke 3:1, where *imperii* translates "the fifteenth year *of the rule* of Tiberius Caesar").

The will and command which created the apostle are linked to *Christ Jesus, our hope,* a defense formula describing the content of the Pauline proclamation to the community *(our)* of believers. The "hope of life eternal" (Titus 1:2; 3:7), "the blessed hope revealed in the glory of Jesus Christ, our great God and savior" (Titus 2:13), is the hope which the risen Jesus gives for the final resurrection of the people whom God has rescued. The Paul of the Letter to the Colossians describes the content of the proclamation to the Gentiles as "the riches of the glory of this mystery which is Christ in you, the hope of glory" (1:27). The conceptualization is not far from that of the PE. The risen and glorified Jesus is the hope of final resurrection and glory for believers. The central task of the apostle is to proclaim that hope, to summon all human beings to put their faith in the hope which God has given them.

2. Paul *writes this to Timothy, his true child in faith,* lit. "Paul . . . to Timothy, true child in faith." The address varies somewhat from Titus 1:4, where the addressee was Paul's "true child, for the faith all share." The phrase here echoes the immediately preceding *en pistei* of Titus 3:15 and prepares the reader for 1:4. The sense is precisely equivalent to "in Christ" (not to "Christian," *pace* Bultmann, *Th. NT* 2.184) in the other Paulines and can hardly be distinguished in meaning from *en pistei* in Gal 2:20 (see Betz, *Gal.,* pp. 124-125) and James 2:5 (see also James 1:6 and Dibelius, *James,* p. 138). Ignatius offers a daring definition of the phrase when he urges the Trallians to renew themselves "in faith *(en pistei),* which is the flesh of the Lord" (8.1; somewhat differently in Ign. *Magn.* 1.1; 6.1). Though the simple phrase *en pistei* occurs often enough in the PE (*en pistei/apistiai* occurs ten times in the PE) to make one suspect that it may have been formulaic in the congregation that produced this correspondence, it is by no means common in the rest of the NT or Ap. Frs. Apart from the passages cited above, the anarthrous *en pistei* appears only in conjunction with other words and phrases (thus 2 Cor 8:7; 2 Thess 2:13; Ign. *Smyrn. inscr.;* Polycarp, *Phil.* 9.2).

In this greeting Timothy is Paul's legitimate son in Christ, but he has, like

Titus, a particular relation to Paul that is rooted in their sharing in the Pauline apostolate itself. This relationship is distinct from that produced by faith in Paul's proclamation of the gospel and subsequent conversion (a relationship which Paul also compared to a father begetting children, as in 1 Cor 4:15 and Philem 10). However, in the PE Timothy's conversion is not attributed to Paul's preaching as such, though his familiarity with Paul's activity in his Lycaonian homeland is explicitly noted (2 Tim 3:10-11). This correspondence presumes that he was reared as a Jew and then as a Christian by his mother and grandmother (2 Tim 1:5; 3:14-15), a notice that appears to supplement the tradition about Timothy transmitted in Acts 16:1-3 (*pace* Cohen, "Timothy," pp. 267-268), where his father was a pagan (perhaps deceased) and his mother a Jewish Christian, probably in Lystra or its environs. There is not a word about Timothy (or his mother for that matter) having been converted precisely during the previous visits to Lystra (Acts 14:6, 21). Yet he appears to have had some standing among Christians in the locality by the time Paul and Barnabas appeared again. Acts remembers his having received circumcision from Paul himself, not as part of Christian initiation but as a requisite for sharing in Paul's apostolate among Jews. Yet Acts never explicitly describes Timothy as proclaiming the gospel or teaching the new congregations alongside Paul (as, e.g., Silas does).

Timothy appears at the side of Paul from the first letters of the apostle's European mission (1 Thess 1:1; 2 Thess 1:1; 2 Cor 1:1; Phil 1:1; Col 1:1; Philem 1), a trusted liaison (1 Thess 3:2, 6; see Acts 17:14-15; 18:5) who proclaims the gospel with Paul (2 Cor 1:19), "my co-worker" (Rom 16:21), "doing the Lord's work just as I am" (1 Cor 16:10). The work of the Lord, i.e. the apostolate, is a differentiated activity and the image that Paul used to clarify it emerges several times. In 1 Cor 4:17, after urging the Corinthians to imitate him, he writes, "For that reason I sent you Timothy, my beloved child *(teknon)*, faithful in the Lord, to remind you of my ways in Christ Jesus, just as I teach them everywhere in every church." In Phil 2:19-20, 22, Paul writes: "I hope in the Lord Jesus to send Timothy to you soon . . . I have no one like him, who will be genuinely concerned for your welfare . . . Timothy's worth you know, how he has served *(edouleusen)* with me in the gospel as a child with his father *(hōs patri teknon)*."

The father/child paradigm is the master image in the PE for analyzing the relationship between Paul and his co-worker–successors, an image which simultaneously suggests the intimate continuity as well as the profound, incommunicable difference between the man whom Christ and God the Father charge with the apostolic office in the strict sense and those persons who come to share in that office in a less immediate fashion. In this correspondence with Timothy, he is not addressed as Paul's "brother," which would imply equality in the relationship in question (see the conventions of Aramaic epistolography noted by Fitzmyer, *Aramean*, pp. 190-191, 221). He is Paul's *true child* because he has received and transmits the Pauline preaching and teaching and, in fact, the apostle's whole way of life (see 2 Tim 3:10-11, 14). The Timothy of the PE certainly has a role that resembles that in the other Paulines. He is a spokesman and liaison for Paul, who charges him to teach what the apostle taught about the Christian way of life (see 2 Tim 1:13; 2:2). He is, as is noted above, repeatedly described in this apostolic role as Paul's *child.* He is "the Lord's slave" (2 Tim 2:24; see Titus 1:1), which reminds one to a certain extent of the description of him and Paul as "slaves of Christ Jesus" in Phil 1:1 (cf. Rom 1:1). He does "the work *(ergon)* of one who announces the gospel" (2 Tim 4:5). He is in all but the name itself the apostle's "co-worker *(synergos),*" and that omission reminds the reader that the verbal coincidences in the descriptions of Timothy in the PE and the other Pauline notices about him are not so pervasive or so striking that they demonstrate that the author of the PE consulted and quoted a collection of the previous Pauline correspondence. It looks as if the traditions about Timothy recorded in Acts were being supplemented here from an independent tradition in a congregation which remembered how the Paul of history and his apostolic entourage regarded themselves. If the PE derive from another author than the person who wrote Luke-Acts, then the tradition of Luke-Acts is being supplemented, if not corrected. In any case, in the light of the references to the Lycaonian mission and the necessity of Christian suffering in 2 Tim 3:11-12 as well as the references to Timothy's family, it is very probable that the author of the PE knew at least the traditions about Timothy which appear in Acts, if not the text itself. If both Luke-Acts and the PE derive from the same author, then he has reserved certain traditions about Timothy for this correspondence, where they would illustrate more forcibly how the Pauline apostolate continued in the apostle's *true child.*

The opening blessing of this letter recurs verbatim in 2 Tim 1:2. The asyndetic triad of anarthrous nouns, *grace, mercy, peace,* conveys a certain intensity. The parallel phrase in 2 John 3 supplies a verb in the future indicative (rather than the present subjunctive or optative), and such would have been the mood of the verb here if the singular address had appeared (see Titus 1:4). *Eleos* opens the triadic blessing, "May there abound for you mercy and peace and love," in Jude 2. A Hellenistic Jewish background for this mention of *mercy* is suggested by its appearance in the opening blessing of the letter of Baruch: "Mercy and peace be with you" (*2 Apoc. Bar.* 78.2). The conditional blessing that concludes the letter to the Galatians, "Peace upon them and mercy, and upon the Israel of God" (6:16), quite unique in Paul's undisputed letters, appears to have precedents in the benedictions of Jewish synagogue worship (see Betz, *Gal.*, pp. 320-322). Since the extant Hebrew and Aramaic letters do not use the equivalent of *mercy* in their initial greetings, this epistolary usage appears to have originated among Jews (whether Christian or not) who spoke Greek. The LXX offers a few examples of the coupling of *charis kai eleos* which may have served as precedents for the epistolary usage. Thus the Wisdom of Solomon writes, "Grace and mercy are for his chosen and a gracious visitation for his holy ones" (3:9; 4:15; *s.v.l.,* see Winston, AB *Wisd.,* pp. 129, 143). The turn of phrase in Tob 7:12 (v. 11 in Hanhart et al., Göttingen LXX, p. 124) where Sinaiticus has the Lord "make mercy and peace upon you" sounds more Jewish. In Ap. Frs. only Polycarp *(Phil.)* opens his letter with "May mercy and peace abound for you . . ." *(inscr.),* but Ign. *Smyrn.* 12.2, in a closing blessing, writes, "Grace to you, mercy, peace, endurance forever."

The gifts of *grace, mercy, peace* which are the object of the apostolic prayer are to come *from God the Father and Christ Jesus, our Lord.* The binary schema reflects a creedal statement of the specifically Christian faith in which the prayer is offered. In Titus 1:3-4 God was both "our savior" and "Father" (never "our Father"); here he is again *our savior* and then simply *Father.* In Titus 1:4 *Christ Jesus* was also titled "our savior." Here and in 2 Tim 1:2 that title gives way to *our Lord,* a phrase that always applies to Jesus in First Timothy (as was noted above, God is simply Lord, *kyrios,* in 1 Tim 6:15). While in First Timothy only God is called "savior" (1:1; 2:3; 4:10), only in 2 Tim 1:10 does that title again refer to Jesus. This pattern suggests that the author of this correspondence intended to develop, particularly in First Timothy, a Christology about Jesus as *our Lord,* i.e. the Lord of the church, the master at whose disposal believers stood. This teaching would stand in contrast to the Christology proposed by Titus which develops around the title "savior" and derives from the name of Jesus himself, which "defines" the terms *savior* and *salvation,* in whom God's salvation is personified. This very archaic Jewish Christian way of explaining the identity of Jesus and the nature of his mission is not repudiated but presumed in the approach to Jesus as *kyrios* in the correspondence with Timothy.

In Second Timothy it is more difficult to determine the referent of *Lord.* In 2 Tim 1:2, 8, "our Lord" surely refers to Jesus whereas the anarthrous *kyrios* in the OT citations in 2 Tim 2:19, "'The Lord knows those who are his,' and 'Let everyone who names the Lord's name abandon wickedness,'" can be heard as the proper name of the God of Israel (see Quell, *TDNT* 3.1059, who calls attention also to the inconsistency of the LXX in the use of the article with *kyrios*). Similarly, the description of Timothy with an anarthrous *kyrios* as "the Lord's slave" in 2 Tim 2:24 would designate his relation to God (as he is "man of God" in 1 Tim 6:11; 2 Tim 3:17, and Paul is "slave of God" in Titus 1:1). On the other hand, the articular *ho kyrios* of 2 Tim 1:16, 18, "May the Lord grant mercy," is an appellative title for Jesus and stands in contrast to the anarthrous *kyrios* in the latter half of 1:18 which appears to name the God of the OT. All of the remaining uses of "the Lord" in Second Timothy are articular (2:7, 22; 3:11; 4:8,

14, 17, 18, 22) and in various degrees of probability refer to Jesus. If First Timothy submits a Christology of *our Lord,* it appears fair to say that Second Timothy proposes one of Jesus under the title of "the Lord."

Two currents run beneath the *kyrios* Christology in the letters to Timothy, one secular, one Jewish and Christian. In the Hellenistic world *kyrios* designated a person who had power, authority, mastery over other persons or things (on this and what follows see Spicq, *Supp. Lexic.,* pp. 415-425). They were at the disposal of the *kyrios,* though he may not have had absolute possession of them (which was specific to the *despotēs;* see Titus 2:9). The *kyrios* had the right to give orders to other individuals, particularly his slaves, his clients, and the members of his family. The *kyrios* was "the head of the household *(oikias)*" (cf. Menander, *Dysc.* 72-73, 97-98, with Mark 13:35, *SFG* §294). From Pindar on, the gods were *kyrioi;* and heads of state, both men and women, in Ptolemaic Egypt were *hoi kyrioi theoi megisthoi* [*sic*], "very great lord gods." Augustus in his lifetime is styled "Caesar, emperor, god and lord," and Nero is "lord of all the world." Acts 25:26 has Festus speak of Nero as *kyrios* (see Jones, "Imperial Cult," pp. 1030-1031). Plutarch has Cassius disclaim divinity when he says to the Rhodians, "I am neither king or lord *(kyrios)* but the chastiser and slayer of a lord and king [i.e. one of those who assassinated the deified Julius Caesar]" (*Brutus* 30.3). The confession of Jesus as "our Lord" in the PE contrasts the conviction of the community of Christian believers with the usage of Roman and Hellenistic groups around them. They have their "lords," human and divine; the Christians have a Lord, human and divine, of their own.

This confession of the PE has earlier Jewish and then Christian antecedents. The title *kyrios* for the God of Israel, though perhaps not written as such in Jewish copies of the LXX, was not unpopular in Jewish religious works composed in Greek (see Lacey, "One Lord," pp. 194-195, for this and much of the following). Philo employs the term often as a name for God which is to be distinguished from *theos.* He regularly hears *kyrios* as suggesting the divine power and authority to govern as a king who brings dreadful punishments and injuries upon the evil who defy his laws. Fools make him prove that he is Lord. Furthermore, "No one created is truly *kyrios* even though he be invested with a rule from pole to pole" (*Mut.* 22-23, LCL modified; see 15-24 and *Leg. alleg.* 1.95-96; *Plant.* 86–89; *Som.* 1.163; *Abr.* 124). A similar connotation can be heard in the great doxology of 1 Tim 6:15 and in the second anarthrous *kyrios* in the prayer of 2 Tim 1:18 as well as in the allusion to Korah's rebellion (see LXX Num 16:5) in 2 Tim 2:19, all cited above. In contrast, Philo hears the name *theos* as suggesting the divine benefactions and gracious power. This systematization coincides with that of earlier Palestinian Judaism, which had taken Yahweh as a name suggesting punishment and *'elohim,* mercy. Later Palestinian Jewish reflection reversed the field and parted company with Philo (Wolfson, *Philo* 1.223-225).

The texts of the PE which exhibit the anarthrous *kyrios* appear in materials already traditional (versions of the OT, prayers, a ministerial title) which are more or less nuanced with the older Palestinian and Philonic understanding of *kyrios* as designating God as possessing power to rule, to judge, and to punish the wicked. A specifically Christian tradition surfaces when Jesus is called "our Lord" and "the Lord." The former title, as is noted above, proposes Jesus as Lord of the church and contrasts him in this function with the lords, divine and human, at whose disposal other groups of men and women stood. This title is already taken for granted in the earliest Pauline correspondence (1 Thess 1:3; 2:19; 3:11; and passim) as well as in other NT traditions (thus Heb 7:14; 13:20; James 2:1; Jude 4; etc.). The first person plural, *our*, identifying those who used the title with the person who was so named, serves already to neutralize the suggestion of terrible punishment with which the name *kyrios* was invested in contemporary OT interpretation, while retaining the core meaning of a ruler who commanded obedience (thus 1 Tim 6:3, 14).

When Second Timothy speaks of Jesus as "the Lord," *ho kyrios*, one hears again a very archaic appellative title for Jesus risen and expected to return in glory as judge (2 Tim 1:16, 18; 4:8, 14, 18; cf. the *maranatha* of 1 Cor 16:22 with the "Come, Lord Jesus" of Rev 22:20; see Fitzmyer, *Aramean*, pp. 123-130). Thus exalted, Jesus receives "the name which is above every name," a name that had been used of the one God of Israel. Jesus is "Lord" (Phil 2:9, 11) over all persons, seen and unseen, and the invocation or acclamation of Jesus as the Lord identifies the Christian assembly (see 2 Tim 2:22). It is Jesus' possession of the name of the one and only God of Israel that led Paul, in 1 Cor 8:6, to declare that there is "one Lord, Jesus Christ," just as, in the confession of Israel and the church, "For us there is one God, the Father" (see Lacey, "One Lord," pp. 199-202). On this line of reasoning, all human *kyrioi*, all the *kyrioi* of the pagan pantheon and the Roman imperium, are emptied of power in any ultimate sense before Jesus Christ as *ho kyrios*. The phrase *our Lord* left some room for the reality of other lords. All ambiguity vanishes with "the Lord" conceived of as "the one Lord."

With Kramer, *Christ*, pp. 169-173, one must note that Paul most often employs forms of the *kyrios* title in his treatments of ecclesial or personal conduct, conduct mandated here and now by the Lord and of which he in the end is judge. The title adds authority and urgency to such moral directives, which are as inclusive as his universal dominion over all persons and things. Furthermore, Paul sees an intrinsic link between the confession of Jesus as Lord and all of Christian conduct. *Lex orandi, lex agendi*, "the rule for prayer is the rule for acting." The Pauline cachet appears on the usage of the PE (e.g., 1 Tim 1:12, 14; 6:2b-3, 14; 2 Tim 1:8; 2:7, 22), and it is particularly notable that the phrase *our Lord* which opens this correspondence with Timothy appears in a prayer of blessing, for a setting of personal or public Pauline prayer frames every later occurrence of this phrase (1:12, 14; 6:14; 2 Tim 1:2, 8) except in 6:3.

## II. THE APOSTOLIC COMMISSION TO TIMOTHY: PART I (1:3–3:13)

### II. A. Apostolic Commands (1:3-20)

#### II.A.1. HETERODOXY (1:3-7)

*1 [3]It was at my explicit encouragement while I was en route to Macedonia that you, Timothy, stayed on in Ephesus. My purpose was that you charge certain people not to propound strange teachings, [4]not to dote on tales and endless genealogies that can only proffer lucubrations instead of God's own plan that one receives in faith. [5]The goal of your charge and mine is, rather, charity arising from a clean heart and from a clear conscience and from a faith unfeigned. [6]Some people, once they have deviated from these, have slipped off into mere chattering. [7]They want to be "rabbis" but they have no idea either of what they are saying or of the things that they insist on.*

#### ♦ NOTES

1:3. *It was at my explicit encouragement.* The Greek sentence which sprawls at least through verse 4 and perhaps through verse 7 opens with the particle *kathōs,* spurned by the Atticists but common enough in koine Greek, secular as well as Jewish. The phrase here is lit. "Just as I exhorted you," and it apparently is to be understood as if it were preceded by "Do" or "Act." In OxyP 1299.9 a parallel construction appears when the writer says, "Just as I gave orders about the *lōbin* [*sic*] of the knives and about the pepper" (MM *s.v.;* BAGD *s.v.*). The PE do not otherwise use this particle, which appears 181 times elsewhere in the NT. Half of these occurrences are in the other Paulines (Philemon excepted); there are 28 uses in Luke-Acts. As for *parekalesa,* represented by *at my encouragement,* see Titus 1:9.

*while I was en route to Macedonia.* Lit. "When setting out," *poreuomenos,* from a verb that reappears in this correspondence in 2 Tim 4:10, "Demas . . . left me helpless and set out for Thessalonika" (also in Macedonia). The lion's share, 89 out of the 152 other NT uses of this term, are in Luke-Acts. Particularly notable is Acts 20:1, in which Paul, after the riot in Ephesus, "sent for the disciples and when he had exhorted them *(parakalesas)*, he embraced them and departed, setting out for Macedonia *(poreuesthai eis Makedonian)*." The verb is not particularly characteristic of Paul, appearing only in Rom 15:24-25 and 1 Cor 10:27; 16:4, 6. In Ap. Frs. there are uses of the verb with *eis*, including setting out for a region (Syria, in Ign. *Pol.* 7.2; 8.2) or a city (Cumae, in Hermas, *Vis.* 1.1.3; 2.1.1). For the literal as well as the enriched Hebraic sense of *poreuesthai* in the LXX and in Philo, see Hauck and Schulz, *TDNT* 6.570-573.

*that you, Timothy, stayed on in Ephesus.* See the Introduction on the world of the PE for *Macedonia* (only here in the PE) and *Ephesus* (also in 2 Tim 1:18; 4:12). *Stayed on* represents the aorist infinitive of *prosmenein*, a verb unattested otherwise in the Paulines but reappearing with an ethical nuance in 5:5 of "the widow proper, one . . . who stays on night and day in entreaties and prayers." Three of the five other NT uses are in Acts, where there is a similar oscillation between an ethical emphasis (Acts 11:23; 13:43) and a material one (18:18; see Mark 8:2 = Matt 15:32). The verb does not appear in Ap. Frs. and appears only twice in the LXX, where Wis 3:9 has "The faithful will stay on with him in charity," but see 3 Macc 7:17, "The fleet waited for them" (see Tob 2:2 in S / Hanhart et al., Göttingen LXX, p. 72, and Judg 3:25 in A). For the coupling of *poreuesthai* with *prosmenein* see Menander, *Epitr.* 537-538 (Koerte; Sandbach, *Menandri*, pp. 857-858) and *Perikeir.* 108-109 (Koerte; Sandbach, *Menandri*, pp. 298-299).

*My purpose was that you charge certain people.* A new sentence here translates a Greek *hina* clause as meaning *purpose*, but it also could be taken with imperative force (BDF §387.3). *Paraggellein, charge,* and the cognate noun, *paraggelia*, occur in the PE only in First Timothy (4:11; 5:7; 6:13, 17; the noun in vv. 5 and 18 below). The verb appears in the imperative (or its equivalent) four out of five times in First Timothy; it appears seven times in the remaining Paulines (First Corinthians; First and Second Thessalonians); fifteen out of the twenty remaining NT occurrences are in Luke-Acts. *First Clement* writes not only of God commanding (27.2) but also of the Corinthian church charging Christian wives to fulfill their domestic responsibilities (1.3; see Ign. *Pol.* 5.1, the only other use of the verb in Ap. Frs.). Regularly in the almost two dozen LXX uses of the verb the context is that of a commander of the military giving orders to his people or his army (thus LXX Josh 6:7; Jth 7:1; 3 Macc 1:1; see O. Schmitz, *TDNT* 5.762-763, on this and Philo, whose usage resembles the NT more than the LXX). See Spicq, *Lexic.*, pp. 647-649, for the secular texts.

*certain people.* A form of the plural indefinite pronoun which will reappear in First Timothy half a dozen times (see vv. 6, 19; 4:1; 5:15, 24 [adj.]; 6:10, 21; in Second Timothy only in 2:18), always in a bad sense (also at times in Paul, e.g., in Rom 3:3, 8; 1 Cor 4:18; Gal 1:7; 2:12, as well as in Luke 18:9; Acts 15:1; 19:9).

*not to propound strange teachings.* Lit. "to teach another doctrine," *heterodidaskalein* (BDF §115.1), a neologism repeated in 6:3 but undocumented previously in secular or LXX Greek or elsewhere in the NT. Ignatius, *Pol.* 3.1, writes of "those who appear to be plausible" *(hoi dokountes axiopistoi)* that are "teaching strange doctrines." Dionysius of Alexandria uses the verb of those who were teaching other than what his predecessor had taught (*ap.* Eusebius, *Church History* 7.7.4; see the *heterodidaskaloi* of 3.32.8). Origen writes of "erroneous teachings" as *heterodidaskaliai* (*In Johannem* 13.50; *PG* 14.493).

4. *not to dote on tales and endless genealogies.* For *to dote on tales* see Titus 1:14; for *genealogies,* Titus 3:9. Since these nouns occur separately in Titus, their appearance here is probably not a hendiadys and consequently only *genealogies* are qualified as *endless* or "boundless," *aperantois,* an adjective undocumented in the papyri (see Spicq, *Lexic.,* p. 122) and appearing only here in the NT but used in LXX Job 36:26 of the number of years of God, as well as in 3 Macc 2:9 of "the endless and immeasurable earth." Similarly, in the only use of the word in Ap. Frs., *First Clement* writes of "the ocean endless for human beings" (20.8). In Josephus, *Ant.* 17.131, a deadlocked confrontation is "endless." Philo once uses the term of "unbounded generosity" (*Abr.* 110) as well as of "the worthless man whose life is one long restlessness [as he] haunts market-places, theatres, law-courts, council-halls, assemblies, and every group and gathering of persons; his tongue he loosens for unmeasured, endless, indiscriminate talk, bringing chaos and confusion into everything, mixing true with false, fit with unfit, public with private, holy with profane, sensible with absurd . . ." (*Abr.* 20; LCL modified). In *Congr.* 53 he scores the skeptics as "word-mongers and word-hunters who neither wish nor practise to cure their life. . . . They act as though happiness depended on the endless and fruitless hypercriticism of nouns and verbs, instead of . . . establishing character . . ." (LCL modified). In *Aet.* 102 he mentions the Stoic hypothesis of "an infinite void" outside of the universe which receives an "endless flow" from the cosmos. Timon of Philus, according to Athenaeus, *Deipnosophistai* 1.22, satirized the philosophers who occupied positions in the Museum of Alexandria as "well-fed pedants endlessly *(apeirita)* contending in the birdcage of the Muses." On the Roman scene the Stoic Philodemus of Gadara writes of the *logos aperantos,* an argument that is not demonstrative and so unable to produce a conclusion (*De Ira,* p. 97, §49.23-24). Cicero sighs in his country retreat about the "endless chatter," *aperantologia,* of a local bore.

*that can only proffer lucubrations.* Lit. "such as by their very nature *(haitines)* offer occasion for *(parechousin)* speculations *(ekzētēseis)*." For *haitines . . . parechousin,* see Titus 1:11; 2:7. *Zētēseis,* cognate to the quite unusual *ekzētēseis* here, occurred in Titus 3:9. *Lucubrations* as a translation is meant to convey the effect of a term, still undocumented in secular Greek and otherwise unattested in the NT, the LXX, or Ap. Frs. (though the verb, with the meaning "to seek out, search for," appears, e.g., in Sir 39:1, Luke 11:50-51, and Acts 15:17 [citing LXX Amos 9:12] as well as in Rom 3:11 [citing LXX Ps 13:2]).

*instead of God's own plan that one receives in faith.* Lit. "rather than *(mallon ē)* God's own order *(oikonomian)* which [is] in faith." For *mallon ē*, which will appear again in 2 Tim 3:4 (cf. 6:2 for *alla mallon*), see BDF §185.2 and Acts 4:19; 5:29; 20:35.

*Oikonomian* is the reading of a great number of major witnesses (to which the sixth-century parchment leaf published by K. Treu can now be added; see G. Horsley, *NDIEC* 2.137, and Haelst, *Catalogue* §531). The Latin version of Theodore of Mopsuestia represents this with *dispensatio* (Swete, *Theodore* 2.69, 73). However, the Western texts of D* and D$^c$ have *oikodomē* and *oikodomia* (i.e. "edification"), which apparently stood in texts translated into Latin as early as the middle of the second century (see Frede, *VL* 25.398-400), not to mention those translated into the Syriac. The reading is too weakly and narrowly attested (*pace* J. K. Elliott, *Greek Text*, p. 19) to enter the text, though its witness to second-century exegesis of this verse is notable.

*Oikonomia,* only here in the PE, appears eight times otherwise in the NT but only in Luke (16:2-4) and three of the Paulines (see commentary). For these texts and those that follow as well as the literature, see Spicq, *Lexic.,* pp. 606-613, and Reumann, "Stewards," pp. 339-349; "Covenant," pp. 282-292; "Ethical Accommodation," pp. 370-379, "Jesus the Steward," pp. 21-29; "Oikonomia," pp. 147-167; "Heilsgeschichte," pp. 86-115; "Use of *Oikonomia*," I, pp. 482-579; "Use of *Oikonomia*," II 1979, pp. 563-603; "Use of *Oikonomia*," II 1980, pp. 368-430; "Use of *Oikonomia*," II 1981, pp. 591-617; "Use of *Oikonomia*," II 1982, pp. 115-140. In Ap. Frs. only Ignatius employs the term, and he only when he writes to the Ephesian congregation. He compares the local bishop to the one whom the master of the household *(oikodespotēs)* dispatches for household management (*oikonomian;* 6.1); then in 18.2 he declares, "For our God, Jesus the Christ, was conceived by Mary according to God's plan *(kat' oikonomian theou)*." In 20.1 he sketches out a second treatise that he would like to dispatch to the Ephesians, "concerning the plan *(oikonomias)* for the new man Jesus Christ, about the faith which is his and about the clarity which is his, about his passion and about his resurrection" (see also Justin, *Trypho* 30.3; 45.4; *PG* 6.540, 572-573, and Aristides, *Apology* 15; J. A. Robinson, *Texts* 1.110). In the LXX *oikonomia* is used only to translate Isa 22:19, 21, about the transfer of the office of King Hezekiah's arrogant palace manager, Shebna, to a worthy servant. The archangel, Michael, tells the reluctant Abraham in *Testament of Abraham B,* 7.17, "Now, therefore, Abraham, make a will (governing) the things of your household and concerning your sons, for you have heard completely the arrangement for you *(tēn oikonomian sou)*."

*that one receives in faith.* For the anarthrous prepositional attributive phrase, see BDF §272.

5. *The goal of your charge and mine is, rather.* Lit. "The end, however, of the charge is," *to de telos tēs paraggelias estin.* The weakly adversative *de* is represented by *rather. Your . . . and mine* do not appear in the Greek but emphasize the link with *my purpose was that you charge* in verse 3. *Telos, goal,* occurs otherwise in the NT thirty-nine times, with thirteen appearances in the other Paulines and four in Luke. The noun originally meant an achievement or a carrying out, and its "dynamic character" refracts into a wide variety of meanings (G. Delling, *TDNT* 8.49, 54) in ancient Greek literature, not to mention Jewish and Christian compositions, meanings that range from cessation and termination to fulfillment and completion. The usage here in Timothy resembles that in Rom 6:21, 22; 10:4, and in 1 Pet 1:9; it does not particularly resemble that in Luke, even 22:37. *Telos* appears in some of Ap. Frs., but the closest parallel to this passage in the PE is in Ign. *Eph.* 14.1, where the Antiochene bishop describes faith and charity as the beginning and end *(telos)* of life *(zōēs),* "for the beginning is faith and the end is charity *(telos de agapē)* . . ." (cf. *Barn.* 1.6). The end is differentiated in *Magn.* 5.1, when Ignatius observes, "Since therefore activities have an end *(telos)* and two options are available, that is, death and life *(hē zōē),* each person also is going to go to his own place." LXX Job 23:3 seems to be the closest that the Greek Bible comes to this differentiated understanding of *telos,* which appears in the version of the teaching about the "Two Ways" in the *Testaments of the Twelve Patriarchs.* "God has granted two ways to the sons of men, two mind-sets, two lines of action, two models, and two goals *(telē)*. . . . The two ways are good and evil" (*T. Asher* 1.3, 5; see 1.9; 2.1, 4 on *telos* as the aim or outcome of human activities). "For the ultimate end [lit. 'the ends'] of human beings displays their righteousness. . . . For when the evil soul departs, it is harassed by the evil spirit. . . . But if anyone is peaceful with joy he comes to know the angel of peace and enters eternal life" (*T. Asher* 6.4-5).

*Charge, paraggelia,* reappears in verse 18 and otherwise in the NT only in 1 Thess 4:2 (plural) and Acts 5:28; 16:24. In Ap. Frs. only *1 Clem.* 42.3 uses the noun in the plural to describe the commands which the apostles (Peter and Paul?) had received from Christ to entrust the gospel "to us" (42.1, the Roman and Corinthian churches?). The LXX does not use this noun, which, like *paraggellein,* often suggests in secular Greek usage an order with a certain content passed on from a military leader through his subordinates to those who are expected to listen and obey (thus Xenophon, *Hellenica* 2.1.4; Polybius, *Histories* 6.27.1; cf. the use of *paraggellein/paraggelma* in Onosander, *Strategos* 25.1-2). For Aristotle the noun could mean a set of rules or precepts for ethical conduct (*NE* 2.2.4; 1104a 7; in fact unavailable for every particular circumstance of each human life), and for Diodorus Siculus the rules that guide the literary form taken by an author are *paraggelia . . . logikē* (26.1; see Philodemus of Gadara, *Volumina Rhetorica* 1.78). An Egyptian guild of Zeus the highest, in the middle of the first century B.C.E., directed all its members to be present "at all command *(paraggelias)* occasions" prescribed by the leadership (Nock, *ERAW* 1.414; G. Horsley, *NDIEC* 1.28).

*charity arising from a clean heart. Charity, agapē,* appeared in Titus 2:2, but the other 9 occurrences in the PE are in this correspondence with Timothy: see verse 14; 2:15; 4:12; 6:11; 2 Tim 1:7, 13; 2:22; 3:10. The other Paulines have 65 out of the remaining 106 NT uses of *agapē,* but relatively few explicitly mention "the love of God" (Rom 5:5; 8:39; 2 Cor 13:13; 2 Thess 3:5), and even in these the genitive sometimes signifies God's love for us rather than our love for God. The noun is found only once in Luke ("you . . . neglect justice and the love of God," 11:42), not at all in Acts (as it is not found in Mark and James). Among Ap. Frs. *First Clement* and Ignatius frequently use *agape,* but not often of love for God (as in *1 Clem.* 49.2, 5 and Ign. *Magn.* 1.1 and perhaps *Phld.* 1.1).

In the LXX *agapē* appears principally in the Song of Songs and wisdom writings and usually implies sexual love, even when used figuratively (thus LXX Jer 2:2 of Israel's bridal love for Yahweh; Wis 6:17-18 in the context of love of wisdom personified as a woman). By the time of Aristeas, the sexual connotation is absent when godliness *(eusebeia)* is described as "the foremost beauty; its power *(dynaton)* is love *(agapē)* and this is God's gift" (229). In *Pss. Sol.* 18.3 the Lord is addressed, saying, "Your love *(agapē)* is for the seed of Abraham, the sons of Israel." In the *Testaments of the Twelve Patriarchs* there is scarcely a trace of the Septuagintal connotation of the noun (perhaps in *T. Benjamin* 8.2), and once "the love of the Lord" is mentioned (*T. Gad* 5.2; perhaps in the disturbed text of *T. Benjamin* 3.5, "For he is helped by the love of Lord, which he has towards his neighbor"). Both surviving uses of *agapē* in Philo speak of love toward God, in contrast with fear (*Quod Deus imm.* 69; *Quaestiones in Exod. 23:27a,* as in R. Marcus, LCL, *Philo Supplement* 2.60, 247).

Whereas the noun, *agapē,* appears only 20 times in the LXX, the verb, *agapan,* occurs 268 times (often with the suggestion of preference, reverence, and loyalty; see 2 Tim 4:8 for further details). The proportion of occurrences is just the opposite of that in the PE, where the noun is five times more frequent than the verb (Spicq, *Agape,* 2.384 n. 2; *Prolégomènes,* p. 72; for his most recent review of the subject and further literature, see *Lexic.,* pp. 15-30). A tendency that had begun in the earlier Paulines (as Spicq has observed) has become prominent in the PE. The dynamic of the verb *agapan* has been nominalized, objectified.

*arising from a clean heart.* Lit. "from a clean heart," *ek katharas kardias,* a phrase which recurs at the end of the parenesis of 2 Tim 2:22, "Pursue upright conduct, faithfulness, charity, peace, in company with those who invoke the

Lord from a clean heart." The precise phrase appears elsewhere in the NT only in 1 Pet 1:22 *s.v.l.* (see B. Metzger, *TCGNT*, pp. 688-689) and never in Ap. Frs. or the LXX. Various forms of *kathara kardia* are found in Matt 5:8; in *1 Clem.* 18.10 (LXX Ps 50:10); *2 Clem.* 11.1 (with *en*); *Barn.* 15.1, 6 *(bis);* and as many as ten times in Hermas, who favors the phrase with *en* and who appears to emphasize the worship-service of God in *Sim.* 5.1.5; 6.3.6, 7.6; 8.3.8; 8.6.2. Ignatius and Polycarp do not use the phrase at all.

The LXX, for all its uses of *katharos* and *kardia,* never joins these terms with *ek,* and other forms of the phrase are rare: see LXX Gen 20:5-6 with *en;* Job 11:13; 33:3 *(s.v.l.);* Pss 23:4 *(katharos tēi kardiai)* and 50:10. The usage of the Psalms is in a context of the prerequisites for authentic worship of Yahweh. In *T. Naphtali* 3.1 the dying patriarch admonishes his sons to avoid greed and "empty phrases, because those who are silent in purity of heart *(en katharotēti kardias)* will be able to hold fast God's will. . . ."

In Sextus, *Sententiae* 46b, there appears the saying "The best altar for God is a heart clean *(kardia kathara)* and sinless," which can be compared to the Pythagorean maxim 119, "God has no better place to make his home on earth than a clean soul" (*psychēs katharas;* see Chadwick, *Sentences,* pp. 16-17, 94, 166; Edwards and Wild, *Sentences,* pp. 20-21).

For *clean, kathara,* see Titus 1:15. *Kardia,* "heart," appears 155 times in the NT outside of the repeated phrase of the PE, with 50 uses in the other Paulines, especially Romans and Second Corinthians (see Jewett, *Anthropological Terms,* pp. 305-333, for the literature and his case for Paul's usage in the undisputed letters as "uniformly within the Judaic tradition," p. 448). There are 43 uses of *kardia* in Luke-Acts. In the latter Peter, speaking of the God who knows the heart (*kardiognōstēs;* cf. Acts 1:24 of the Lord), reminds the Jerusalem assembly of the baptism of the pagan Cornelius and his household whose "hearts [God] cleansed by faith (*tēi pistei katharisas tas kardias autōn;* Acts 15:8-9)." The many appearances of *kardia* in Ap. Frs., particularly in Hermas, are by and large firmly within the Septuagintal tradition, which, as Jewett has noted, 726 times translated the Hebrew root *lb/lbb/lbh* with *kardia* (only 6 times with *nous*). When one comes to the books that may not have had a Semitic original (thus the Maccabean literature, Wisdom, Judith), the use of *kardia* with its Hebraic sense drops notably. This cutback corresponds to a similar drop in the usage of *kardia* in a figurative sense in contemporary Hellenistic literature, including Philo and Josephus (see BAGD *s.v.*). The phenomenon appears to be a philological echo of a developing Greek medico-philosophical debate about the heart as a physical organ only and not the seat of the human will and intelligence (see Jewett, *Anthropological Terms,* pp. 308-309). Still, Lucretius can affirm that human understanding, *consilium,* i.e. intelligence and the mind, *animum mentemque,* "inhere in their place in the middle region of the breast, *media regione in pectoris haeret*" (*De rerum natura* 3.139-140).

*from a clear conscience and from a faith unfeigned.* For the lit. "good (*agathos*) conscience," which will reappear in 1:19, see Titus 1:15. *Faith unfeigned* is the object of one of several prepositional phrases with *pistis* found in the PE. The commonest of these, *peri tēn pistin,* is used pejoratively of those who have shipwrecked (1 Tim 1:19), missed the point in (6:21; cf. 1:6), and counterfeited (2 Tim 3:8) their faith. The context is similar for the only use of *apo tēs pisteōs* in 1 Tim 6:10, where it refers to those who "have strayed off from the faith" for love of money. *Faith unfeigned* reappears in 2 Tim 1:5, and *anypokritos,* "unfeigned," occurs otherwise in the NT in Rom 12:9, 2 Cor 6:6 of charity, and 1 Pet 1:22 of brotherly love. James 3:17 thus describes the "wisdom from above." Only the adverb appears in Ap. Frs. (*2 Clem.* 12.3), and the LXX uses the adjective only in Wis 5:18, of "undissembling" judgment, and in 18:15 of the Lord's "irrevocable" order to slay every Egyptian firstborn male. The term is unattested in the papyri and in secular Greek before the first Christian century (Spicq, *Lexic.,* pp. 105-107, and *Supp. Lexic.,* pp. 656-657), but its link with the Greek terminology for drama, in which the actor or comedian is *hypokritēs,* still nuances its meaning (for the ps.-Demetrius, *De elocutione* 194, "What is unemotional is essentially undramatic [*anypokriton*]"). However, already in Philo, *Quaestiones in Gen 3.29* (R. Marcus, LCL, *Philo Supplement* 1.217 and 2.210), the adjective describes a way of living that is sincere.

6. *Some people, once they have deviated from these. Deviated* is lit. not having touched the target (cf. *stochein,* "to aim, shoot at," with *stochos,* "target, a brick pillar"), a term peculiar in the NT to this correspondence with Timothy (6:21; 2 Tim 2:18). In Ap. Frs. it appears in *Did.* 15.3 in a curious sense, "Let no one speak to anyone doing amiss (*astochounti;* Lampe, *PGL s.v.,* suggests 'erring') against another," and in *2 Clem.* 17.7, where "those who have done amiss" are parallel to those who have "denied (*arnēsamenous*) Jesus." In the LXX only Sirach uses the verb: in 7:19 of disregarding "a wise and good wife" and in 8:9 of disregarding "the discourse of aged men." Josephus always uses the verb to refer to some kind of missing of the mark: thus *War* 2.159 says of the Essenes, "seldom, if ever, do they miss in their predictions"; in 4.116 he writes of the "disappointed resentment" of Titus and in 5.61 of flying arrows missing him (note the adjectival phrase of the "unerring fire [*bolas . . . ouk astochous*]" by the Zealots from the Temple). Chrysostom nicely captured this nuance when he noted that Paul "put it elegantly when he said *astochēsantes,* because it requires technical skill to shoot straight and not miss the target" (*Homily 2 in 1 Tim; PG* 62.509).

*have slipped off into mere chattering.* The second aorist passive of *ektrēpein* is used in a middle sense, lit. "have turned themselves away." The widows' ordo in 5:15 mentions younger widows who "have already slipped off after Satan," and in the closing summary of this letter, in 6:20, this verb means "keep your distance from profane drivel *(kenophōnias)*. . . ." In 2 Tim 4:4, Timothy is warned about those who "will slip off after tales *(epi tous mythous)*." The only other NT occurrence is in Heb 12:13, where the word may have the medical sense of "dislocated, put out of joint" (see BAGD *s.v.*). Ignatius (*Magn.* 11.1) uses the verb when speaking of the birth, suffering, and resurrection "truly and certainly done by Jesus Christ, our hope (see 1 Tim 1:1), from which God grant that none of you turn yourselves aside *(ektrapēnai)*." Justin in his *Dialogue with Trypho* 8.2 (*PG* 6.492) writes of never spurning the Savior's words which "have in themselves such tremendous majesty that they can instill fear into those who have slipped off *(ektrepomenous)* the straight road."

The LXX employs *ektrepein* only of Yahweh, who "turns deep darkness into the morning" (Amos 5:8), but the speaker in *Ode of Solomon* 11.9 says, "I turned myself *(exetrapēn)* from empty things *(mataiōn)* to God most high."

*Mere chattering* represents *mataiologia,* found only here in the NT and not at all in the LXX. Polycarp exhorts the Philippians to "put aside empty (*kenen;* pleonasm?) chatter and the error of many" (*Phil.* 2.1). See Titus 1:10 and 3:9 for the spouters of nonsense *(mataiologoi)* and activities that are fruitless *(mataia)*. There are no secular authors certainly before the first Christian century who use *mataiologia,* but it appears in Plutarch, *Moralia* 6F-7A, when he warns against allowing young people to give extempore speeches which issue in "extreme chattering *(mataiologias tēs eschatēs aition)*." Vettius Valens liked the word (see W. Kroll, pp. 150, 257, 301; MM *s.v.*), and there is one occurrence in the second-century-C.E.(?) Epicurean Diogenianus. The term reappears in Christian authors only after Nicea, and then rarely (see Athanasius, *De incarnatione* 3.1, *PG* 25.101, and *Epistula ad Epictetum* 1, *PG* 26.1049; Theodoret of Cyrrhus, *In Gen. Quest.* 15, *PG* 80.96, as he critiques horoscopes).

7. *They want to be "rabbis."* Lit. "wishing *(thelontes)* to be law-teachers *(nomodidaskaloi)*," i.e. intending this purpose but flying in the face of the facts (see 2 Pet 3:5). *Thelein* reappears in various forms in 2:4; 5:11; 2 Tim 3:12, and 205 times otherwise in the NT, including 42 times in the other Paulines and 43 times in Luke-Acts. The verb appears often in Ap. Frs. and comparatively less often in the LXX.

*Nomodidaskalos* is used otherwise in the NT only in Luke 5:17 (coupled with the Pharisees and perhaps equivalent to the scribes; see Schürer, *HJP* 2.324-325) and Acts 5:34 (of Gamaliel, the Pharisee; see Fitzmyer, AB *Lk,* p. 581). There is no secular use of the word, and it does not appear in Ap. Frs., the LXX, Philo, or Josephus. Late in the second century, Irenaeus (or the gnostic document which he is paraphrasing) designates the "teachers *(didaskaloi)*" in whose midst the young Jesus sat (Luke 2:46) as *nomodidaskaloi* (*Adversus haereses* 1.3.2; *PG* 7.469). Clement of Alexandria (*Strom.* 7.3; *PG* 9.417B; cf.

656D) and Origen (*In Johannem* 28.20; *PG* 14.724B) continue to apply the term to the official teachers of Judaism. Eusebius, *De laudibus Constantini* 17 (*PG* 20.1433), calls Jesus' apostles "legislators and teachers of the law *(nomothetas kai nomodidaskalous)* for the human world." About the middle of the fifth century C.E. a man with the Semitic name Samoe is "priest and *sophodidaskalos* ['wise teacher' or 'teacher of wisdom']" and the principal religious personage in the great Sardis synagogue. His title probably means what "rabbi" then meant in Judaism (see John 1:38 and A. T. Kraable in Hanfmann, *Sardis,* pp. 183, 184, 189).

*but they have no idea either of what they are saying or of the things that they insist on.* The opening phrase represents *mē noountes,* lit. "not knowing," from *noein,* which will appear again in 2 Tim 2:7 and a dozen times otherwise in the NT. The other Pauline uses are in Rom 1:20, of God's unseen characteristics being known through what he has made (see Heb 11:3), and Eph 3:4, 20. Luke-Acts do not use this verb. In Ap. Frs. *noein* appears more frequently, particularly in Hermas, who also very frequently employs the negative form (cf. *Sim.* 5.4.2 with *Barn.* 17.2). Of the three dozen LXX appearances of the verb, see especially Isa 32:6, "The foolish speaks foolish things and his heart knows empty things *(mataia noēsei)* . . . ," and Wis 4:14, 17, "The masses see this and do not understand *(kai mē noēsantes)* . . . for they will see the wise man's end and will not understand *(ou noueōusin)* what the Lord purposed for him . . ." (Winston, AB *Wisd.,* p. 136).

*either of what they are saying or of the things that they insist on.* See BDF §293.5 on relative as well as interrogative clauses after verbs of knowing. On *saying,* see *legein* in Titus 2:8. For *diabebaiountai,* "they insist on," see Titus 3:8.

## ♦ COMMENT

1:3. The Greek syntax of this whole section is an anacoluthon in which "utter chaos" has been produced "by interminable insertions and appended clauses" (BDF §467). This phenomenon is by no means unheard of in the openings of Greek letters. It already has appeared in the PE in the opening of Titus 1:1-4; it is an almost regular feature of the Ignatian epistolary (thus Ign. *Eph.* 1.1; *Magn.* 2.1; *Rom.* 1.1; *Phld.* 1.1; and perhaps *Smyrn.* 1.1). The rest of the Paulines too on occasion offer impenetrable anacolutha (thus Gal 2:4-6; for other examples see BDF §467). Even the author of Acts 24:5-8 lets the thread of thought snap in the speech of Tertullus.

The literary form of Titus as well as First Timothy resembles that of the administrative correspondence of Hellenistic and Roman society, i.e. the epistolary communication of authoritative directives at a distance. The ruler's correspondence *(epistolē)* is his command (*entolē;* Spicq, *EP,* pp. 34-36). There is, moreover, no lack of evidence that this section has been artfully crafted as an opening for the body of this epistle. The first clause, with its introductory *kathōs* and its delicate reference to an antecedent command, followed by its summary of the negative and positive objects of the previous instruction as well as by an implied confidence in Timothy (which becomes explicit in 1:18-19), is a variation on the "compliance statement" that regularly introduces the body of certain kinds of ancient letters (see White, *Body,* pp. 41-42).

The tattoo of *p* sounds that began in 1 Tim 1:1-2 becomes insistent in verses 3-5, adding urgency to the words used and reinforcing the impression of strong feelings at work, which the anacoluthon too suggests. The terminology in its turn stakes out the development of this section as well as of the letter as a whole. Thus *paraggeilēis/paraggelias* in verses 3 and 5 look forward to the closing of the whole first section on apostolic commands in 1:18; the verb then introduces the second part of the apostolic commission for Timothy in 4:11, crops up in the middle of it in 5:7, and recurs as the commission concludes in 6:13, 17. Similarly, the mention of faith in verses 4-5 recalls its occurrence in the apostle's greeting in verse 2 and prepares for its appearance in the prayer of 1:14 and at the conclusion of these apostolic commands in 1:19 (not to mention its use in every succeeding chapter of both letters to Timothy).

Similarly, words and concepts of this section crop up again in the closing summary of 1 Tim 6:20-21a *(ektrepein, tines . . . astochein, kenophōnia, k.t.l.).* Even the placing of Timothy in Ephesus in 1:3 corresponds with the summoning of him from that city that is implied as the second part of this correspondence closes (2 Tim 4:9, 12).

In the commentary on Titus a case was submitted that a previous Pauline letter of recommendation had been recycled into the letter as it stands. It is also conceivable that fragments of a memorandum from Paul to Timothy in the mid-sixties of the first Christian century have been built into the opening greeting of First Timothy and the introduction to the apostolic commission in 1:3a. Splinters from the original dispatch may appear below in 3:14-15 and 4:13. The old materials have been incorporated with little concern that they appear erratic in the new structure. Perhaps the author of the PE as the collection now stands wanted to authenticate his procedure by prefixing a quotation from the apostle himself and thought that the anacoluthon of 1:3-7 was a small price to pay. The original dispatch may have constituted a letter patent that contained the Pauline empowerment and directives for his co-worker, orders that consequently opened rather solemnly with "Just as I exhorted you to stay on in Ephesus." The first person singular and the following singular address place all that follows in the framework of the relationship between Paul and his lieutenant, a relationship in which Paul articulates the orders and Timothy listens.

3-4. *It was at my explicit encouragement while I was en route to Macedonia that you, Timothy, stayed on in Ephesus. My purpose was that you charge certain people not to propound strange teachings, not to dote on tales and endless genealogies that can only proffer lucubrations instead of God's own plan that one receives in faith.*

The text as it stands and the hypothetical dispatch conceive of Paul as en route in the direction of Macedonia and northern Greece, whereas Timothy is relatively fixed in the metropolis of Asia Minor, Ephesus, which, as was observed above, serves as a frame and background for both of the letters to Timothy. If in fact the PE are to be read in their ancient sequence and if there are previous epistolary materials in the collection as it now stands, then it is possible that the original Pauline dispatches that surface at points in the PE were the spin-off of a journey of the Pauline entourage that had touched on Crete and then made its way up the coast of Asia Minor, past Ephesus and the Troad, intending eventually to visit the Christian churches of Macedonia and, perhaps after a stop in Corinth, to go on to Epirus and winter in Nicopolis (see Titus 3:12). In fact the trip never got beyond Troas, where Paul's final missionary journey (as the PE propose it) came to an abrupt halt with the arrest of the apostle (see 2 Tim 4:13). There followed the final Roman imprisonment, which produced the last poignant dispatch to Timothy with which the author of the PE concluded his Pauline epistolary testament that we call Second Timothy.

The *stay* of Timothy in Ephesus had been at Paul's urging, and the form of the verb implies that it is for the occasion and thus not permanent. This too may signal the presence of an old dispatch which presumed that when Paul's co-worker was left in a given place, it was only for a time and for a given task. Then he was expected to return to the apostolic entourage (see Titus 1:5; 3:12). The Western text of D had Timothy "wait," *perimeinai,* in Ephesus for Paul (see the Western reading at Acts 10:24 as well as the text of Acts 1:4). The effect of this adjustment of the text is to distance the apostle himself from Ephesus and to forestall interpreting *poreuomenos,* "while I was en route," in terms of Ephesus as the *terminus a quo* of the journey (it is notable that 2 Tim 4:10 makes the *terminus a quo* explicit). The D text may be making certain that Paul's prophecy in Acts 20:25, that the Ephesians would not see him again, is not contradicted by inferring from the *prosmeinai* directed here at Timothy that Paul had been in Ephesus but did not remain. In any case, the *poreuomenos* at this point specifies unambiguously only the *terminus ad quem* of the apostle's journey, *Macedonia.*

Surely it would be reasonable to infer, from the point of view of the PE, that Paul and his entourage had passed through Ephesus itself, left Timothy there, handed Hymenaeus and Alexander over to Satan (1:20), and then proceeded to northern Greece with an assurance that they would soon come back to Ephesus (1 Tim 3:14; 4:13). Paul might be entrusting Timothy (in 2 Tim 1:18) to the good offices that he saw Onesiphorus give Paul in Ephesus on this visit. Still it is by no means clear that Paul was the recipient of those services. Sometimes he did pass severe judgments at a distance (see 1 Cor 5:3-5). *Poreuomenos* need only mean "en route," and *prosmeinai,* "made a stay," was very early on understood to mean "wait," and could in the usage of the PE mean "to be constant." Thus any critical reconstruction of the setting and events which the PE take for granted must not depend on Paul's having been present in or absent from Ephesus just before this letter was written. Either alternative is hypothetical and becomes acceptable or not in the light of other data.

It is possible that the author of the PE wanted to leave moot the question of whether Paul had been in Ephesus on the journey that produced this letter. He certainly wanted the readers of this part of his epistolary to envision the metropolis of Ephesus, fourth-largest city of the Roman Empire, as the *mise-en-scène* for this Pauline intervention. First Corinthians contains the only undisputed references to this city in the rest of the Paulines (1 Cor 15:32; 16:8; see the *v.l.* of Eph 1:1). Ignatius (*Eph.* 12.2) makes the somewhat surprising observation that Paul mentions the church in Ephesus "in every letter *(en pasē epistolēi).*" Yet that may only mean that the Pauline collection which Ignatius used included First (and Second?) Corinthians, First and Second Timothy, and an edition of Ephesians which contained the city name in the first verse. The author of Luke-Acts mentions the city eight times and uses the adjective *Ephesios* five times in Acts 18–21. The importance of the city for Christians as well as in the province of Asia Minor is attested by Rev 1:11; 2:1, where Ephesus leads off the seven cities of Asia to which the scroll of seven letters is addressed.

The reason for the Pauline directive to Timothy to *stay on in Ephesus* is explained in terms of the faith that he and *his true child* share. The apostolic concern for faith appears at every turn in this whole chapter with its various uses of the **pist-* root (see vv. 2, 4-5, 11-16, 19 *bis*). The concern is first expressed negatively. Timothy is *to charge certain people not to propound strange teachings.* The indefinite pronoun, *tisin,* may imply not only a number of unreliable and dubious individuals but a comparatively large number. Thus in 1 Cor 10:7-8, "some" refers to the 23,000 who perished for their sin. In Ign. *Phld.* 2.2, the "many specious wolves" become "certain people *(tines)*" in 7.1; 8.2. Here in the PE the author envisions these people as exercising some sort of leadership in teaching the Christians in the metropolis. They appear to have an impressive command of Jewish traditions and literature which they proposed as authoritative direction for their Christian followers. They probably had Jewish origins, habits, and interests (see v. 7). For the author of this correspondence their teachings were anomalous and deviant, because they did not follow "the wholesome instruction" (see v. 10 and Titus 1:9) of Paul, i.e. his method of interpreting the OT and working out the relationship of Christian believers, particularly those of pagan origin, to the Jewish traditions.

The strange teachings of these people are not necessarily in contradiction to that of Paul (and consequently false); they are, however, different from Paul in content and method (and consequently pointless if not suspect). Already in classical Greek *hetero-* is compounded with forms of *doxa,* "opinion," to designate opinions that are in some respect lacking (see Plato, *Theaetetus* 190E, *heterodoxein,* and 193D, *heterodoxia*). Philo uses *heterodoxein* of conflicting cosmological opinions (*Quis Her.* 247), and Josephus, *War* 2.129-130, when he describes the Essene midday assembly, notes that the *heterodoxoi* (i.e. those who do not yet share the opinions of the sectaries) cannot be present. In a Qumran Hymn those who teach people to observe another liturgical calendar and to interpret the Scriptures in a way that differs from that of the Teacher of Righteousness are "lying prophets, men by error seduced" (1QH 4.16; Gaster, *DSS*).

Ignatius took up *heterodoxein* (*Smyrn.* 6.2) to describe those whose docetic teaching is scored at every turn in the Smyrnean letter. In Ign. *Magn.* 8.1 *heterodoxia* is explicitly linked with hoary, useless myths (see Titus 3:9) which are apparently of Jewish origin. Yet the specific criteria which Ignatius had for sorting out what kind of Jewish traditions were innocent are not readily recoverable. The controversies among Christians later in the second century (see S. Hall, "Easter," pp. 554-567) about the date for celebrating Easter indicate the potential for internal conflict in matters that appear indifferent to the academic observer.

To these erring leaders the Pauline commands come through Timothy as through the lieutenant of a general. In the PE First Timothy is preeminently the letter of commands *(paraggellein, paraggelia).* Only Paul and Timothy give orders, and the latter is commanded to command. Thus the Pauline authority is exercised not only in giving a charge to another (see 1 Tim 6:13) but also in communicating his authority and demanding its exercise by others. In this letter the apostolic orders concern teaching and instruction as well as the Christian's way of acting (see 1 Tim 5:7; 6:13-14, 17-19). In 1 Tim 4:11 the command refers in a positive way to teaching the preceding materials, whereas in the present context the *strange teachings* are to terminate. The narrative in Acts about the commands (4:18; 5:28, 40) of the Sanhedrin forbidding the apostolic teaching about Jesus illustrates that not all teaching is self-evident or persuasive and all authority to command is not self-authenticating, much less universally acceptable. What Acts portrayed as occurring from one viewpoint in the story of the first-generation Jewish church vis-à-vis the synagogue, the PE portray from another point of view as they depict the Pauline intervention in the doctrinal clashes between groups of believers.

The negative phrase *not to propound strange teachings,* at the end of verse 3, is in tandem with another negative phrase that takes up the language of a similar parenesis for Jewish Christians in Titus. The practitioners of the new (i.e. non-Pauline) hermeneutic *dote on tales and endless genealogies that can only proffer lucubrations.* The terminology here is a conflation of that in Titus 1:14; 3:9, and one reasonably infers, particularly in the light of verse 7 below, that the materials alluded to are still typically Jewish and Jewish Christian stories and edifying vignettes, based upon the OT and even upon the ministry of Jesus. Certainly the author of the PE knew something about the story of Jannes and Jambres (see 2 Tim 3:8). One can only speculate whether such works as *Jubilees, Life of Adam and Eve,* the ps.-Philo, Biblical Antiquities, and their congeners (see Charlesworth, *OT Pseud.* 2.35-142; 249-377) were actually the object of the contempt expressed here.

The vignettes in question are stigmatized as *endless,* "the kind of thing which is bound to happen in genealogies," as Theodore of Mopsuestia drily notes (Swete, *Theodore* 2.73). Because they are *endless* they are pointless. Perhaps John 20:30-31; 21:25 bear witness to a similar, though less strident, reaction to the pullulation of traditions about Jesus. It is instructive that the members of the guild of Zeus the highest, when being admonished about factions at their meetings, are forbidden "to enter into one another's pedigrees *(genealogēsein)* at the banquet or to abuse one another at the banquet or to chatter *(lalesein)* . . ." (G. Horsley, *NDIEC* 1.28-29, §5).

*Tales and endless genealogies* by their very nature (*haitines;* see the use of this term of Jewish Christian troublemakers in Titus 1:11) issue only in speculations. The "foolish speculations," *mōras zētēseis,* of Titus 3:9 are here designated with the neologism *lucubrations, ekzētēseis,* which, like the unique *heterodidaskalein* of verse 3, conveys exactly that nuance of frenetic, barely intelligible activity which flutters like a moth at the penumbra of Christian life.

These *lucubrations* are then contrasted with *God's own plan that one receives in faith,* a plan that *tales and endless genealogies* do not furnish. But what does *God's own plan, oikonomia theou,* mean? Already in the second century some Western texts (including that cited by Irenaeus, *Adversus haereses* 1, Preface; *PG* 7.437; Harvey 1.2) interpreted the divine *plan* as referring to God's "building up" of Christians in their faith. The reason for this reinterpretation of *oikonomia* is that the term had a shady sense as well as a good one (see Reumann, "Ethical Accommodation," pp. 370-379). The management of a household requires discretion, shrewdness, even what outsiders perceive as sharp practices. *Oikonomia,* in the rhetorical terminology of the second Christian century, had already for centuries designated a literary arrangement of events, not in their natural (i.e. chronological) order, but in an artificial order more persuasive to the listener. Moreover, in areas of human conduct *oikonomia* can designate actions that superficially appear to have one intention but are really devices of expediency working out a hidden purpose. This last usage has ethical ambiguities; thus when pagan philosophers said "that man should imitate the divine economy, they seek to inculcate virtues like dependability, order, or unity." Yet, as J. Reumann has put it (p. 377), "If . . . the economy of God portrays the deity winking at shady practices or playing a part in them himself, then the way is open for his followers to justify similar breaches of conduct for themselves, still imitating the divine example; this is exactly what could happen in patristic ethical application of the idea of a divine economy, and, it would seem, did." The substitution of *oikodomē* at this point in the Western texts was intended to preclude the shady sense of *oikonomia. God's plan* involves no sharp practices, no rhetorical flimflam, no hypocrisy, for he is "the God who is without deceit" (Titus 1:2).

Another aspect of this concern with the meaning of *God's plan* appears in Clement of Alexandria as he appeals to the divine *oikonomia* in his discussion of the way in which God teaches his people the conduct that he desires. However, *oikonomia* does not clearly design the training or instruction of persons (e.g., *Paed.* 1.8.64; O. Stählin 1.128; *Strom.* 1.24.160; O. Stählin 2.101; moreover, this meaning is not found in Lampe, *PGL s.v.*). Even in a passage regularly cited (*Paed.* 1.8.69-70; O. Stählin 1.130), Clement is saying that the divine plan which explicitly threatens horrific punishments contains a loving call to conversion as God "gently shows alongside of the threatening plan *(para tēn oikonomian tēs apeilēs)* his love for human beings." God's plans are not here synonymous with education or training in the concrete, human order, though they are evidently not unrelated to such discipline.

The meaning of *oikonomia theou,* "God's plan," for the PE, is closer at hand than Clement of Alexandria. Already at Titus 1:7 and below in 1 Tim 3:4-5, 15, Christian believers are conceived of as members of God's household, his *oikos* or *oikia,* "God's house which is the church of the living God." The parable of the "great house" in 1 Tim 2:20 is grounded on the same concept. The model to which all this terminology is related is the human home or family, as the ancient world perceived it (see Titus 1:11 on *oikos,* as well as 1 Tim 3:12; 5:4; 2 Tim 1:16, 18, and *oikia* in 1 Tim 5:13; 2 Tim 3:6). The household is the primary theater for all human relationships; so is the church for the relationships between God and his people.

Though the *oikonom-* terminology was used rarely by the LXX in translating Hebrew biblical texts (see Reumann, "Oikonomia," pp. 150-153 on this, and pp. 153-166 on Luke and Paul, as well as his "Heilsgeschichte," pp. 94-115), the terminology had become more common in Jewish literature of the Hellenistic period for describing God's rule over the universe (thus Wis 8:1, 14; 15:1; *Ep. Arist.* 254 [all *dioikein*]; and Philo and Josephus [see Reumann, "Oikonomia," p. 152 nn. 5 and 6, and p. 154 n. 2]). In the Hellenistic world generally these terms for household management had come to mean not only the political management of the city-state and the world but also the divine "ordering and administration of the universe" (Reumann, "Oikonomia," p. 150). Thus Menander has one of his characters describe human nature *(anthrōpon)* as "very weak by nature though it administers *(oikonomeitai)* the most important affairs" (Koerte 740.13-14/531K; Sandbach, *Menandri,* p. 323). When Epictetus the Cynic was asked how he conceived his task as a philosopher, he began his reply by stating that one did not start such a work without God, "For in a well-ordered house *(oikiai kalōs oikoumenei)* no one comes along and says to himself, 'I ought to be manager of this household *(oikonomon).*' Or if he does, the master *(kyrios),* when he turns around and sees the fellow giving orders in a high and mighty fashion, drags him out and gives him a dressing down; so it goes also in this great city (i.e. the universe); for here also there is a Master of the house *(oikodespotēs)* who assigns each and every thing its place," from the sun and stars to human heroes and fools (Epictetus 3.22.1-8).

In the NT the figurative use of the *oikonom-* language is predominantly Pauline. The apostle conceived his own commission to preach the gospel as an *oikonomia* that God had entrusted to him (1 Cor 9:17) as one of the "*oikonomoi* of the mysteries of God" (1 Cor 4:1). The conjunction of *oikonom-* terms with mention of the "mystery" is regular in the Paulines. It reappears in altered form in the references to conduct "in God's house *(oikoi)*" as well as in the following acclamation of "the mystery of godliness" in 1 Tim 3:15-16.

Paul's personal, apostolic commission and authority as an *oikonomos,* with a certain office of management, *oikonomia,* flow from and participate in God's own *oikonomia* as the letters to the Colossians and Ephesians conceive it. God himself is never *oikonomos* in the NT because the term suggests servile status, but in the Captivity Letters Paul explicitly attributes to him an *oikonomia.* So the apostle, in writing of his sufferings for Christ's body, the church, says of the latter, "Of which I became a minister *(diakonos)* according to the plan of God *(kata tēn oikonomian tou theou)* which was given to me for you, to make the word of God known fully, the mystery *(to mystērion)* hidden for ages and generations but now made manifest to his saints" (Col 1:25-26). Here, as in Eph 1:10 (where the context of prayer is to be noted); 3:2, 9-10, *oikonomia* refers to God's plan of action for executing his purpose with respect to humankind and indeed all creation. This practical plan and process of administration (whether of God or of his apostle) is not to be confused with God's plan as such, i.e. the mystery, still incompletely grasped, of his will and purpose (see Reumann, "Oikonomia," pp. 165-166).

The author of Luke-Acts is the only other NT author to employ the *oikonom-* cluster of terms (see Reumann, "Oikonomia," pp. 153-155, and

"Heilsgeschichte," pp. 86-115 on what follows). In Luke 12:42, in the parabolic parenesis for ecclesial leaders, the first requisite for an *oikonomos* is that he be "trustworthy," *pistos,* as in 1 Cor 4:2 (see Titus 1:7). In the parable about the dishonest manager (Luke 16:1-8), the sharp practices of his administration *(oikonomian)* have some redeeming aspects from which "the children of light" could learn. The ambiguous connotation of *oikonomia* in Hellenistic society is evident here, but it must be admitted that neither passage sheds direct light on God's plan for history as Luke narrated it. However, as J. Reumann has submitted, Hellenistic historians, including Josephus, liked to posit an overarching, divine plan for human history, and Luke, when he set out on the path of his Christian predecessors "to compile an orderly account of the events that have come to fulfillment among us" (Luke 1:1), may have been open to the position of the Hellenistic historiographers as well as to that of the OT itself on a divine plan, i.e. an *oikonomia,* in the history of salvation. In the LXX particularly, Reumann suggests, Luke found the literary precedents for understanding God's plan in terms of the covenant with his people, now a new covenant articulated in the kerygmatic summaries of Acts, worked out in the lives of believers according to the apostolic teaching *(didachē),* sanctioned ultimately by the return of Jesus in glory as judge.

Thus without exploiting the *oikonom-* terminology, Luke seeks to describe God's plan in history for the salvation of his people through Jesus and through those whom Jesus has sent. Paul, proceeding in the opposite direction, actually uses the *oikonom-* cluster of words to describe himself as one sent by Jesus and God and as having a task to perform in the process by which God is ushering in the consummation of the ages. History, properly speaking, is the story of persons whose words and decisions have influenced the lives of their contemporaries and succeeding generations. Salvation history, at least as Paul conceives it, gathers around a series of persons who more or less clearly focus, in what they say and do, God's own purpose and plan for men and women. In Barrett's summary, "Paul sees history gathering at nodal points, and crystallizing upon outstanding figures — men who are notable in themselves as individual persons, but even more notable as representative figures" (*Adam,* p. 5). Luke appears to be concerned with the series as such, the trajectory as well as the individual points on the line.

The PE resemble Paul, who has, with Timothy and Titus, become a representative figure in whose words and acts the divine plan for Christians is working itself out. Just as Titus was to "proffer" himself "as a pattern for fine deeds" in Titus 2:7, so here in 1 Tim 1:4 *tales and endless genealogies* do not *proffer God's own plan* for the conduct of his household, as Paul and Timothy do. For the PE, *God's own plan,* while it is explicitly *God's,* has been entrusted to human beings. As an *oikonomia* it is no longer simply *God's* or simply human, though it belongs primarily and always to the former, who calls to account those managers who have abused their trust. The juridical links of the *oikonom-* cluster are notable (Spicq, *Lexic.*, p. 613). Since in both the Pauline and Lukan traditions the *oikonomos* is to be *pistos*, i.e. one to be trusted or believed in, it is distinctly possible that the emphatic *tēn en pistēi*, "that one receives in faith" (see 2 Tim 3:15), means that the master plan here is one grasped by faith and worthy of trust, quite the opposite of myths and *genealogies*.

5. *The goal of your charge and mine is, rather, charity arising from a clean heart and from a clear conscience and from a faith unfeigned. God's* master *plan*, which human beings appropriate by *faith*, has its goal and thus its fulfillment (*symplērōma*, Chrysostom, *PG* 62.509, citing Rom 10:4) in *charity* rather than in pseudo-theological researches. The apostolic *charge*, at this point defined in one term, *charity*, expands to occupy the rest of this chapter (see 1:18). Paul had once reminded the Thessalonian Christians of "what *paraggelias* we [i.e. Paul, Silvanus, and Timothy] gave through the Lord Jesus" on how "to live and to please God" (1 Thess 4:1-2). A similar ethico-moral program begins to unfold at this point in First Timothy, and the *paraggel-* terminology suggests here, as it does in other secular, Jewish, and Christian texts, not only authority transmitting a traditional, set content but also obedient conduct in response. Already in the opening of this letter, as in the opening of Titus, a chain of command that transmits the will and orders of the commander runs from God the Father and Jesus Christ through Paul the apostle to Timothy or to Titus and thence to particular congregations of believers. As First Timothy continues, this paradigm of transmission keeps surfacing; thus the relation of the risen Jesus to Paul dominates 1:12-16, which is framed by sections which define the apostle's relation to Timothy (1:3, 18), who in his turn is to transmit the Pauline charge to others (1:3; 4:11-16; 6:2, 20).

The harvest of the apostolic work of Paul and Timothy is described in Semitic fashion with the one word *charity*, which is in turn modified by three phrases, bound to one another with a polysyndetic *kai* and each in its turn further qualified. Is it love for God or for neighbor or for both together that is meant by *charity* here? The answer begins in the first adjectival phrase attached to this term, *charity arising from a clean heart*. When 2 Tim 2:22 employs the same phrase, it is to describe those who call upon Christ Jesus in faith and prayer. Moreover, the adjective *clean*, *kathara*, in the PE is clearly linked with Israel's worship and here with its radically interior character (note also the following *clear* and *unfeigned*), for *heart*, *kardia*, in these letters is equivalent to *nous*, "a way of thinking," which in turn is a synonym of and a locus for conscience (see Titus 1:15). In *1 Clem.* 41.1; 45.7, a "clear/clean conscience" is explicitly linked with Christian worship (see also the citation from Irenaeus below). Similarly in 2 Tim 1:3, Paul's worship of the one God of Israel takes place "with a clean conscience," *en katharai syneidēsei,* and the deacons are to "hold the mystery of the faith with a clean conscience," *en katharai syneidēsei,* in 1 Tim 3:9. Philo as well had noted that the worshipper who lays his hands on a sacrificial victim ought to be able to proclaim "from a pure conscience *(ek katharou tou syneidotos)*" that he has taken no bribes, has not profited from violence, has not murdered, etc. (*Spec. leg.* 1.203). From such data one infers that *charity arising from a clean heart and from a clear conscience and from a faith unfeigned* refers primarily to love for the one God of Israel, a love which the *Shema*ʿ of Deut 6:4-5 described as "with your (sg.) whole heart and your whole soul and your whole strength," with the triple parallel for supreme emphasis.

The Pauline charge here has its root in Israel's greatest confession-commandment and in Jesus' making that command his own. Nothing takes precedence over the total, undivided love for God which has its privileged expression in the worship-prayer of believers (see the church order of 1 Tim 2; Spicq, *Prolégomènes,* pp. 95, 119; Quinn, "Ap. Ministry," pp. 481-482). The description of worship as *charity arising from a clean heart and from a clear conscience* would not be lost on unbelievers. From Cicero through Seneca Latin spoke also of a good or bad conscience *(bona/mala conscientia),* but it did not often use the phrase equivalent to *a clean heart.* Still Ennius says, "This is freedom — conducting oneself with a heart pure and firm *(pectus purum et firmum)*" (Warmington, LCL 1.332, line 310; cf. Periander's reply to the question, "What is freedom?": "A good conscience" [*agathē syneidēsis;* Stobaeus, *Ekl.* 3.25.12]; Persius, *Satura* 2.74 on a "soft heart," *incoctum* [lit. "uncooked"] *pectus*). Later there is a striking passage in Minucius Felix in which Octavius explains why Christians do not have temples and altars by asking, "Is not the mind a better place of dedication? our inmost heart *(intimo pectore)* of consecration? . . . the acceptable victim is a good disposition *(animus)* and a pure mind *(pura mens)* and an incorrupt judgment *(sincera sententia).*" He concludes by saying, "These are our sacrifices, these the rites sacred to God" (*Octavius* 32.2-3; see also Irenaeus, *Adversus haereses* 4.18.3; *PG* 7.1026, "So sacrifices do not make people holy; for God has no need of sacrifice. But the conscience [*conscientia*] of him who offers, when it is pure [*pura*], makes the sacrifice holy," and Chrysostom, *In Matthaeum* 50, *PG* 58.508, on the ministry to the freezing, thinly clad poor which "does not require altar cloths but a pure soul [*psychēs katharas*]).

The three phrases here in First Timothy, like those in the *Shema*ʿ, are substantially synonymous (see Spicq, *Agape* 2.388-389), yet each lends its nuance to the understanding of the love for God which involves the *heart,* i.e. the whole internal, affective life; the *conscience,* i.e. the human power of discerning good and evil actions with regard to God and neighbor; and *faith,* i.e. the wholehearted acceptance of the revelation of God's will which has occurred in Christ

Jesus. The *charity arising . . . from faith* coincides conceptually to a large extent with Paul's description of "faith working through charity," *pistis di' agapēs energoumenē* (Gal 5:6). Faith is the taproot through which the love for God draws its nourishment.

Each of the three nouns which describe the internal origin of charity is emphatically qualified by an adjective that reinforces the frail link between what human beings do and what they think. The author leaves no room for driving wedges between the external manifestations of love for God and the internal Christian life from which they proceed. Thus the *heart* must be *clean,* dedicated solely to the one God and his Christ (see "To cleanse for himself a people of his very own" in Titus 2:14). The *conscience* must be *clear,* i.e. "good," *agathē,* leveling no reproach about the deeds of the worshipper's life. The *faith* must be *unfeigned,* not simulated but a genuine adherence to the whole revelation proclaimed by Paul (note the semantic dissonance in *oikonomia* and Spicq, *Supp. Lexic.,* p. 657). Not only a Christian's prayer and good acts but even his faith could be merely playacting; hence the ferocity of the censure below of "people who dote on seductive spirits and demonic doctrines . . . lying frauds *(en hypokrisei pseudologōn)*" (1 Tim 4:1-2).

At this point one can compare and contrast the uses of *agapē* in the rest of this correspondence with what has been observed above (see Spicq, *Agape* 2.406-422, on what follows). In all the other instances in the PE where *charity* is mentioned, it appears either coupled with faith (1 Tim 1:14; 2 Tim 1:13) or as an item in a longer list. In the former cases it designates primarily the love for God. However, in the long lists of 1 Tim 4:12 (where for the only time in the PE charity precedes *pistis*); 6:11; and 2 Tim 2:22; 3:10, the emphasis falls on acts of love of neighbor that visibly identify the apostolic minister. A decision about the emphasis is difficult in the three-member lists that remain. In Titus 2:2, where the older men are exhorted to be "robust in faithfulness, in charity, in steadfastness," the primary meaning may well be the love and worship of God. Similarly in 1 Tim 2:15 Christian wives (and their children) are to "persevere in faithfulness and charity and sensible holiness." In this passage, the only one in the Pauline corpus where women are explicitly the subject of charity, the emphasis appears to fall on love for God. The case may be otherwise in 2 Tim 1:7, the only passage in the PE where charity is mentioned without a mention of faith. There Timothy and Paul have received from God "a spirit . . . of dynamic strength and of charity and of discretion." The connection with the apostolic ministers, as in the longer lists noted above, as well as the absence of *pistis,* seems to bring love of neighbor into focus at this point.

In summary, for the PE (as for the Hebrew Scriptures and the teaching of Jesus) love for God is the primary and indispensable human response to revelation. That love, which is rooted in Christian faith and issues in Christian worship, is distinguishable but not really separable from love of neighbor. Thus in Justin's description of the second-century Roman Sunday eucharist, the reading from the Scriptures is followed by the leader's urging those who have heard the revelation to imitate these fine things *(tēs ton kalon touton mimēseōs)*. Then the thanksgiving to God is followed not only by distributing the bread and wine to those present but also by sending help from the well-to-do believers through the leader of the assembly for worship to the destitute, to the sick, to prisoners, to travelers, and to other needy Christians (*Apology* 1.67; *PG* 6.429). The rule for worship embodied the rule for action; *lex orandi lex agendi.*

6-7. *Some people, once they have deviated from these, have slipped off into mere chattering. They want to be "rabbis" but they have no idea either of what they are saying or of the things that they insist on.* With these verses the involuted Greek returns to the heterodox teachers of verses 3-4 (note the correspondence of *heterodidaskalein, to propound strange teachings,* with the *nomodidaskaloi, "rabbis,"* in v. 6, as well as the *mē . . . mēde* in 3-4 with the emphatic *mē . . . mēte . . . mēte* in v. 7). There is not a word at this point of a general apostasy of these people from the Christian faith, much less from the God of Israel (the focus sharpens in vv. 19-20). They have missed the point of the radically internal character of the origins of *charity.* By ignoring the *heart,* the *conscience,* and *faith,* they have emptied the love of God of genuine meaning. They have taken a wrong turn, and what they point to as the way of Christian prayer and worship is actually a dead-end street. Their directions are only verbiage (see Titus 1:10; 3:9). The *mere chattering* here corresponds in the closing summary of this letter to "the profane drivel," *tas bebēlous kenophōnias,* to which Timothy is to give a wide berth (1 Tim 6:20; see 2 Tim 2:16).

These heterodox teachers want to be *"rabbis," nomodidaskaloi.* The reader infers that they desire to impose publicly and authoritatively a given interpretation and application of the Scriptures of Israel (see Titus 1:9 on *didaskalia* as well as 2:1, 7, 10; and 3:9, 13 on *nomikos*). The translation *"rabbis"* suggests the irony of the Greek term in its context here, for it implies that the teachers who would like this honorary title, probably themselves of Jewish Christian origin, want to be numbered not with the former Pharisee, Paul, whose teaching and interpretation of the OT this correspondence transmits, but with the prestigious, current teachers of their Jewish countrymen who were at best neutral with regard to Jesus and surely not believers (see Schürer, *HJP* 2.325-326, on the origin and early history of the use of the title *rabbi*).

Moreover, there is a gap between what these teachers want to be and what actually happens as a result of their teaching, a gap which the continuing exercise of their limited perception will not enable them to bridge. When later in this correspondence Timothy is enjoined to "consider" (*noei;* 2 Tim 2:7) what

Paul is saying, he is promised that "in every way the Lord will grant . . . insight" for the continuing exercise of his intelligence upon and his comprehension of the parabolic exhortation that has immediately preceded. The heterodox here have no such promise and thus are unable to grasp either the meaning of the words that they say (see *ho legō* in 2 Tim 2:7) or the realities to which their confident speaking refers (see Titus 3:8).

The thick fabric of verbal and conceptual parallels of the description here in Timothy with the passages in Titus cited above suggests to the reader that these self-appointed *"rabbis,"* who pit their teaching against that of Paul (note v. 11) and Paul's co-workers, are in fact Jewish Christians whose aberrations are rooted in their Jewish background. The reference to ignorance of the meaning of words may refer not only to the words they speak but also to the written words which they cite (note again that in 2 Tim 2:7 *lego* refers to what has just been written; see also Mark 13:14; Matt 24:15 in *SFG* §290). If that is the case, then one probably ought to infer that various cultic aspects of Jewish life, derived more or less directly from the Torah, were being imposed on Christians (Jewish and otherwise) who did not want to adopt them but still did not know how to counter the authority of the scriptural word as propounded by these teachers (see the use of "Do you not know . . . [*ou noeite*]" in Mark 7:18; Matt 15:17, *SFG* §150, in the context of dietary and purificatory rules). Perhaps *mere chattering* stigmatizes also an ignorant etymologizing that the Torah itself appeared to warrant (Gen 3:19-20).

If Paul and Timothy are representative figures for this correspondence and their teaching is proposed in what the author of the PE considers its typical form, then one could infer that the Jewish Christian teachers pilloried here and their doctrinal interests are also set out in representative and typical fashion. This would not mean that they and their teachings were only scarecrows set up for this author's garden any more than Paul and his entourage and their teaching were figments of a religious imagination. For the questions about the nature and identity of Paul's opponents as the PE conceive them, see Spicq, *DBS* 7.30-44; Karris, "Polemic," pp. 549-564; Ellis, *Prophecy*, pp. 80-128; and the Introduction.

## II.A.2. ORTHODOXY (1:8-17)

### *II.A.2.a. Paul on Law (1:8-11)*

*1 [8]Fine as we know the Law is, there is still the question of one's using it lawfully. [9]That involves knowing that law is not laid down for an upright person; rather it is for lawless and refractory persons,*

*for godless people and sinners,*
*for the unholy and profane,*
*for patricides and matricides,*
*for murderers,*
10 *for the incestuous,*
*for homosexuals,*
*for slave traders,*
*for liars,*
*for perjurers;*

*— and anything else that stands opposed to the wholesome instruction* 11 *that accords with the gospel I was entrusted with, the good news of the glory of the blessed God.*

## ♦ NOTES

1:8. *Fine as we know the Law is.* Lit. "We know that the Law *(ho nomos)* is attractive *(kalos).*" On *kalos* in comparison with *agathos* see Titus 1:16; 2:7. *We know, oidamen,* has appeared in impersonal forms in Titus 1:16; 3:11 (see v. 9 here as well as 2 Tim 2:23; 3:14). The personal usage in 3:5 (indefinite), 15, and 2 Tim 1:12, 15; 3:15 is closer to this verse.

*The Law, ho nomos,* reappears in the following verse but not elsewhere in the PE. Out of the 193 other NT occurrences, 119 are in the other Paulines, and 106 of these appear in Romans and Galatians. Luke-Acts have 27 uses where Mark has none.

In Ap. Frs. *nomos* appears in a suspect reading in *1 Clem.* 1.3, but Ignatius does use the term, once of a deacon, subject to the presbytery as to "the law of Christ" *(Magn.* 2.1 *s.v.l.);* once of "the law of Moses" (*Smyrn.* 5.1), which, along with the prophets and the gospel and the sufferings of rank-and-file Christians, does not convince certain other Christians of the reality of Jesus' passion and resurrection. Ignatius's reading of *nomcs* once in a bad sense in *Magn.* 8.1 (a passage that coincides otherwise with the PE) declares, "For if until this moment we live according to the Jewish law *(nomon ioudaikon* or *ioudaismon),* we confess that we have not obtained grace." With Schoedel, *Ignatius,* p. 119 n. 7, this weakly supported reading ought to be rejected. The author of *Barnabas* resembles Ignatius when he says, speaking of the OT laws for sacrificial worship, that God "abolished these things that the new law *(ho kainos nomos)* of our Lord Jesus Christ which is without the yoke of necessity might not have a man-made oblation" (2.6). A little later, when citing the prophetic critique of Jewish fasts, he adds that God "made a revelation about all these matters beforehand to us, lest we be shipwrecked by becoming converts to the law of those people" (3.6). In Hermas there are many more references to the law (principally in *Sim.* 1 and 8).

The LXX employs *nomos* 228 (229) times, using it as the equivalent of the Hebrew *torah* 192 times, though occasionally using it also for *dabar,* "word," *ḥoq,* and *ḥuqqah,* "prescription, statute" (see Monsengwo, *Nomos,* pp. 55-57). In each of the *Testaments of the Twelve Patriarchs, nomos* appears at least once, for a total of 38 times. The reference is usually to the law of the Lord (15 times) or the law of God (10 times), but it may mean simply custom or ritual, as in the reference in *T. Simeon* 9.1 to *ho nomos tou penthous,* "the custom of/ritual for mourning." On the lips of Potiphar's wife when she says to Joseph that she will murder her husband and take Joseph as her spouse *nomoi,* "by law," the meaning is equivalent to *nomimos,* "legally" (*T. Joseph* 5.1; see the variants).

*there is still the question of one's using it lawfully.* Lit. "if anyone use *(chrētai)* it lawfully *(nomimōs)*." For *ean tis* see Titus 1:6. The adverbial *nomimōs* (which takes up the preceding *nomos*) occurs again in 2 Tim 2:5 of an athlete competing according to the rules, but not otherwise in the NT or Ap. Frs. In the LXX this term appears only on the lips of the aged Eleazar in 4 Macc 6:18 as he rejects the advice of those who are urging him to simulate violating the Torah by citing his having lived for the truth onto an advanced age and having rightly *(nomimōs)* kept a good reputation *(doxan)* for this.

The verb *chrasthai,* "using," here has wine as its object in 1 Tim 5:23. As in Attic Greek, it takes the dative when the object is a thing (a couple of manuscripts have the accusative). The present subjunctive here has been read as an aorist, *chresētai,* by A, P, 1245, 2344 as well as by Clement of Alexandria, *Strom.* 1.27 (O. Stählin, 2.108). It was the tendency of koine and the scribes to change present non-indicatives into aorists (see J. K. Elliott, *Greek Text,* p. 21). The ten other NT appearances of *chrasthai* are in the Corinthian correspondence (1 Cor 7:21, 31; 9:12, 15; 2 Cor 1:17; 3:12; 13:10) and in Acts 27:3, 17, but none of these speaks of *using* the Law. In Ap. Frs. this verb appears in *1 Clem.* 37.5; *2 Clem.* 6.5, as well in Ignatius (quoted at 5:23), but only Hermas writes of "using the law that is yours" (i.e. as a Christian; *Sim.* 1.6) in contrast to "using the laws *(nomois)*" of the secular city in which the author dwells (*Sim.* 1.3, 4). Although the LXX uses *chrasthai* about sixty times, the verb has *nomos* (in the plural) as its object only in Esther 8:11 (see 12$^{s}$), where the decree of Artaxerxes is quoted as saying that the king allowed the Jews "to use their own laws *(nomois)*," and also in 2 Macc 11:31, where the letter of Lysias permits "the Jews to use their own foods (see 1 Tim 5:23) and laws *(nomois)*."

9. *That involves knowing that law is not laid down for an upright person.* See the preceding verse on *that involves knowing that law,* noting here that the demonstrative *touto* is used (as in 2 Tim 1:15) to prepare for the *hoti* clause (BDF §290.1).

See Titus 1:8 for *upright, dikaios,* as an adjective and Titus 3:5, 7 for the cluster of **(a-)dik-* terminology.

*Is laid down,* from *keisthai,* occurs two dozen times in the NT but only here with *nomos.* Out of the half dozen uses in the Third Gospel, the sense closest to that here occurs in Simeon's prophecy, "Behold, this [child] is set *(keitai)* for the fall and rising of many in Israel and for a sign of contradiction" (Luke 2:34). Paul uses this verb four times. Notable is 1 Thess 3:3, where, speaking of the sufferings of his converts, he writes, "For you yourselves know that *(oidate hoti)* we are destined *(keimetha)* for this." Similarly, in Phil 1:16, describing those who proclaim Christ, he writes that there are those who do it "out of love, knowing that *(eidotes hoti)* I am destined *(keimai)* for the defense *(eis apologian)* of the gospel." In Ap. Frs. forms of *keisthai* begin to appear in *Barnabas* (7.11 *v.l.* and 12.7 are about OT types of Jesus' passion; 17.2 about teaching "set out" in parables), and they are regular in Hermas. In his *Man.* 6.1.1, speaking of the first command *(entolē)* "to maintain faith and fear and self-control" and how it works, his mentor explains that there are two ways of working and ". . . they are laid down *(keintai)* for righteous *(epi dikaioi)* and unrighteous."

Out of more than two dozen LXX uses of *keisthai,* there is none with *nomos,* although 2 Macc 4:11 writes of "the royal favors laid down for the Jews *(ta keimena tois Ioudaiois).*" In LXX Isa 9:3 "the yoke laid *(keimenos)* upon them (*ep' auton,* i.e. the people of Galilee)" is that of exile, captivity, and slavery, which suggests why there was a reluctance to speak of the Law being laid down for Israel. Still, Philo can use the phrase with no hesitation when he writes, "So also a law is laid down *(nomos keitai),* 'Righteously pursue that which is righteous *(dikaios to dikaion diōkein;* LXX Deut 16:20 with *diōxei),*' so that we should go after righteousness and all virtue by means of the deeds which have some relation to these virtues and not by the deeds that are contrary to them" (*Det.* 18).

In a fragment which may come from Menander, a girl appeals to her father, saying, "The law is laid down for a man as well as a woman *(est' andri kai gynaiki keimenos nomos)*" (Papyrus Didot 1.14; Sandbach, *Menandri,* p. 329).

*rather it is for lawless and refractory persons. Rather* represents the weakly adversative *de* (but perhaps the Attic *te,* meaning "and so," which is characteristic of Luke-Acts, should be read here with F G 33 1319 2344; see BDF §443). See Titus 2:14 on the use of *anomos,* "lawless," and 1:6, 10 on the *refractory, anypotaktoi.*

*for godless people and sinners.* For *asebēs,* "godless," see Excursus III, "*Eusebeia* and Its Cognates in the PE," in AB *Titus,* adding at this point that the phrase *godless and sinners* occurs in the plural only here in biblical Greek, though 1 Pet 4:18 cites the singular form from LXX Prov 11:31: "If the righteous man *(dikaios)* is hardly saved, where will the ungodly person and sinner *(ho de asebēs kai hamartōlos)* appear?" Jude 15 writes of "ungodly sinners *(hamartōloi asebeis),*" citing *Enoch* 1.9. The Ap. Frs. never employ any form of the phrase, though *Barn.* 10.10; 11.7 cite LXX Ps 1:1, 5, where the ungodly and the sinners occur in parallel members of the pôem (see also LXX Ps 57:11; Sir 12:6; 41:5; as well as *T. Judah* 25.5).

*First Clement* uses *asebēs* a few times (3.4; 59.4 *v.l.*), citing it from LXX Psalms in 14.5; 18.13, and Proverbs in 57.7. *Second Clement* 18.1 and *Barn.* 10.5 with their references to the judgment on the ungodly can be compared with *T. Zebulun* 10.3, "But the Lord shall bring down eternal fire on the ungodly and will destroy them to all generations."

*Sinners, hamartōloi,* recurs in the saying cited in verse 15 below and forty-five times otherwise in the NT, usually in the plural, as here in the PE. The four other Pauline uses are confined to Romans and Galatians. Though there are eighteen uses in Luke, there is none in Acts. In Ap. Frs. *First Clement* employs the word only in his citations of the LXX (8.2; 22.8; 35.7; 56.5, and cf. *Barn.* 10.10; 11.7). The use in *2 Clem.* 2.4, "I came not to call the righteous but sinners" (also in *Barn.* 5.9), resembles that in verse 15 below. Barnabas also writes of "sinners and the evil (*poneroi;* 4.2)," of sinners crucifying Jesus (8.2 *bis*), and the "error of sinners" who think Jesus is only son of David and not Son of God (12.10). For the usage of Hermas as well as of the LXX, see 1:15.

*for the unholy and profane. Anosios,* "unholy," appears in 2 Tim 3:2 but not otherwise in the NT. In Ap. Frs. only *First Clement* uses it (1.1) of the "abominable and unholy revolt" in the Corinthian church; 6.2 of the "terrible and unholy punishments" inflicted on Roman women martyrs; and 45.4 of righteous persons being imprisoned "by the unholy." In LXX Ezek 22:9, in a catalogue of sins that has reminded commentators of Lev 18–20, *anosia,* "unholy things," translates the Hebrew *zimmah,* "lewdness" (see S. Steingrimsson, *TDOT* 4.90). Wis 12:4 has a similar use of the term for the "unholy rites" of the Canaanites. The only other uses of *anosios* are in the Maccabean literature, always of pagan persecutors or their plans to subvert the religion of Israel (2 Macc 7:34; 8:32; 3 Macc 2:2 [with *bebēlos*]; 5:7; 4 Macc 12:11; see the adverb in 3 Macc 1:21 and LXX Esther 8:12$^{g}$). Josephus describes Joab's murder of Amasa as "an ungodly deed and unholy *(asebēs ergon . . . kai . . . anosion)*" (*Ant.* 7.284). Philo uses a variation on the phrase here in the PE when he is speaking of blasphemy and exclaims, "Away with profane and unholy *(bebēlon kai anosion)* thoughts!" (*Mos.* 2.199).

*Profane, bebēlos,* occurs below in 4:7; 6:20, and 2 Tim 2:16. The only other NT use is in Heb 12:16, where the Jewish Christians of that church are admonished "that no one be immoral *(pornos)* or profane like Esau, who sold his birthright for a single meal." The Ap. Frs. do not use the word, but it appears almost a dozen times in the LXX. Notable for this passage in First Timothy is LXX

Lev 10:10, describing the function of the sons of Aaron "to distinguish between the holy and the profane (*ton hagion kai ton bebēlon* [see also Exod 22:26])." In the variant reading in LXX Ezek 4:14 as well as 1 Kgdms 21:5-6, the word is used in a context of food laws and such matters.

*for patricides and matricides.* These words are quite unknown in the rest of the NT, the LXX, and Ap. Frs. They first appear in Greek drama: *matricides* in Aeschylus, *Eumenides* 153, 210; *patricides* in Aristophanes, *Frogs* 274-275 (with *perjurers*); *Clouds* 911, 1327 (where the suggestion of striking, *typtein,* draws out the etymology of this compound from *patēr* and *alo(i)an,* "to thrash one's father" [see MM *s.v.;* for the Attic spelling, BDF §26; 35.2; 119.2]). Plato once speaks playfully of criticism of an earlier philosopher as a *patricide* (*Sophist* 241D-242A) and seriously of the punishments of those "who dare to lay hands on father or mother or grandparents" and then specifically of the matricide (*Laws* 9.880E-881A). Once he uses the phrase *patricides and matricides* (*Phaedo* 114A). Lysias *(Against Theomnestus I)* 10.8 uses the phrase in the singular and with the meaning "father-thrasher or mother-thrasher." Josephus (*Ant.* 16.356) uses *patricides* when he cites a letter from Augustus to Herod as the latter sought imperial indulgence for the execution of plotting sons. Marcus Aurelius writes contemptuously of "the pleasures of highwaymen, catamites, *patricides,* tyrants" (6.34).

*for murderers. Androphonoi,* lit. "homicides," appears only here in the NT and Ap. Frs. The LXX uses the term once, along with *blasphemer,* to characterize Antiochus Epiphanes (2 Macc 9:28; see the use of the verb in 4 Macc 9:15). See Philo on murderers in *Spec. leg.* 3.83-91, 118 (infanticide). The "gray-haired viper," Knemon, in Menander's *Dysc.* 480-481, calls visitors "murderous beasts *(androphona theri'[a]).*"

10. *for the incestuous.* Lit. "fornicators," *pornoi,* a term which appears only here in the PE and nine times otherwise in the NT, usually, as here, in lists of vices (see 1 Cor 5:9-11; 6:9-10; Eph 5:3-5; Rev 21:8; 22:15). The other uses are in Heb 12:16 (cited above) and 13:4 (where the *pornoi* are paired with adulterers). In Ap. Frs. only Polycarp uses the word as he appeals to the text of 1 Cor 6:9 in advising the young Christian men at Philippi that "neither fornicators *(pornoi)* nor effeminates *(malakoi)* nor homosexual men *(arsenokoitai)* will inherit the kingdom of God" (*Phil.* 5.3).

In the LXX only Sir 23:16-17 (and perhaps 18 *s.v.l.*) writes of the *anthrōpos pornos,* "the man impure in the body of his flesh" and "all bread [i.e. all flesh] is sweet for the impure man." Finally, "the man turning aside from his [marriage] bed" may also be branded as a *pornos.* Thus the term in the biblical tradition was understood generically of a man (the feminine *pornē* designates the harlot) engaging in forbidden sexual conduct, alone or with others, whether married or unmarried.

In secular Greek the catamite (Aristophanes, *Plutus* 155; Xenophon, *Memorabilia* 1.6.13; Demosthenes 22.73; see Dover, *Homosexuality,* pp. 20, 146) or sodomite (Demosthenes, *Epistle* 4.11) was a *pornos.* Classical Greek usage also heard the term as a cognate of *pernanai,* "to sell" (see Chantraine, *DELG, s.v. pernēmi*), perhaps because young men and women were purchased in the slave markets for their sexual services. Dionysius of Halicarnassus comments bitterly about slaves in his day "who have amassed wealth from robbery and burglary and *porneias* and every other foul means" and then straightway buy their freedom and Roman citizenship (*Antiquities* 4.24.4). In the Hellenistic koine the **porn-* cluster can designate whatever erotic behavior that a given author considered contemptible (see Dover, *Homosexuality,* pp. 17, 20), and so this usage coincides with the biblical one described above.

*for homosexuals. Arsenokoitai,* lit. "men who lie with males," appears for the first time in Greek in the vice list of 1 Cor 6:9, where it is preceded by "adulterers and effeminate men *(malakoi)*" and followed by "thieves." Here in First Timothy, the only other NT use of the noun, it is preceded by the *pornoi* and followed by the "slave traders" (kidnappers). Polycarp, *Phil.* 5.3, noted above, picks up the term along with the others in the list in First Corinthians. Though the term *arsenokoitai* does not appear in the LXX, it seems to have been coined using the terminology of LXX Lev 18:22, "And with a male *(arsenos)* you shall not go to bed *(koimēthēsēi koitēn)* [as if with a] woman, for this is an abominable thing," and 20:13, "And any man who goes to bed with a male *(koimēthēi meta arsenos koitēn)* [as if with a] woman, both have done an abominable thing; let them be put to death, they are guilty" (see Scroggs, *Homosexuality,* pp. 85-86, 106-107). There is little to be said lexically for confining the meaning of *arsenokoitai* to "male prostitutes" or "call-boys" (see D. F. Wright, "Homosexuals," pp. 125-153, with its critique of Boswell, *Homosexuality,* and his review of Scroggs, *Homosexuality,* in *SJT* 38 [1985]: 118-120). The noun apparently was not used widely, except in quotations of 1 Cor 6:9 and this passage of First Timothy (thus Irenaeus, *Adversus haereses* 4.27.4; 5.11.1, *PG* 7.1060, 1150, where only the Latin, *masculorum concubitores,* is extant; see Frede, *VL* 25.408-412, for more Latin examples). There is a notable occurrence of *arsenokoitēs* in the third-century *Acts of John* 36.6-7 (*CC, series apocryphorum,* 1.189; see 2.459-460), where that apostle is portrayed as preaching in the theater at Ephesus to the people of the city. In a catalogue of the vicious who are to receive punishment after death, the homosexual is listed after the swindler *(apostereteēs)* and before the thief *(kleptēs).* Verbal forms of *arsenokoit-* appear in *Sibylline Oracle* 2.73 (in a list of evil acts to be avoided) as well as in (pseudo- ?) Origen, *Exposition on Prov.* 7.12 (*PG* 17.181B), and in Eusebius, *Demonstratio Evangelica* 1.6.23 (*PG* 22.65C).

*for slave traders.* The *andrapodistēs,* from *andrapodon,* "a prisoner of war sold as a slave" (as in 3 Macc 7:5; see Chantraine, *DELG*, p. 87). The word is not documented elsewhere in the NT, Ap. Frs., or the LXX. However, it was a term of opprobrium in the writers of comedy (see Aristophanes, *Knights* 1030; *Plutus* 521; and Menander, *Sikyonios* 272), and Plato, in a list of those who violate justice, notes "temple-robbers and *andrapodistai* and burglars and swindlers and thieves" (*Republic* 344B). Philo thought of the kidnapper as synonymous with the slave trader: "The *andrapodistēs* is also a kind of thief who steals the best of all things which have come to be on earth. . . . And so everyone who is inspired with zeal for virtue is harsh in his wrath and quite implacable in regard to *andrapodistai*, who for the sake of the most unjust profit dare to reduce to slavery those who are not only born free but share the same nature as themselves" (*Spec. leg.* 4.13-14). In retelling the story of Joseph he has Reuben cry out in frustration to the other sons of Jacob, "A fine business you have started! Let us divide the profits! We are competitors with slave traders *(andrapodistōn)* for the prize for wickedness" (*Jos.* 18). Here it is clear that the merchants who purchased Joseph are *andrapodistai* even though they did not steal him by force.

*for liars. Pseustai* appears in the citation from Epimenides in Titus 1:12 and eight times in the NT outside of the PE. In the other Paulines it occurs only in Rom 3:4: "Let God be true, though every man be a liar" (citing LXX Ps 115:2). The other NT uses of the noun are in John and First John. In Ap. Frs. *pseustēs* appears in the complex lists of *Did.* 3, which include "My child, do not be a liar, since lying leads to theft, nor a money-lover nor vain-glorious, for from all these things thefts are conceived" (33). Hermas speaks of the deadly luxuries as those of "the adulterer and the drunkard and the slanderer and the liar and the covetous and the robber" (*Sim.* 6.5.5).

In the LXX Sirach speaks of "a rich man who is a *liar*" (15:8; cf. Prov 19:22 *s.v.l.*) and of the *liars* who never think of wisdom, i.e. the Law. Considering the blanket statement of LXX Ps 115:2, cited above, it is notable that *liars* are rather rarely mentioned.

*for perjurers.* The *epiorkoi* do not appear elsewhere in the NT or Ap. Frs., though *Did.* 2.3 employs the corresponding verb in citing Exod 20:16 (as does Matt 5:33; LXX translates with *ou pseudomartyrēseis*). The commandment "You shall not take the name of Yahweh, your God, in vain . . ." (Exod 20:7; Deut 5:11) may have been understood as including perjury (see Lev 19:11-12). The LXX only once writes of the *epiorkos* in describing how every thief and perjurer is going to be exterminated in the land of Judah (Zech 5:3; see 8:17, "Do not love a false oath"). *T. Asher* 2.6 uses the cognate verb when it teaches, "He who cheats his neighbor provokes God's wrath; he who swears falsely *(epiorkei)* before the Most High, and yet has mercy on the poor, disregards the Lord who uttered the Law's commands."

Aristophanes coupled *perjurers* with *patricides,* as was noted above. Menander wrote, "By this it is proved that of the gods Eros has the most power: because of him people swear falsely *(epiorkousi)* by the other gods" (Koerte 383/449K).

*and anything else that stands opposed to the wholesome instruction.* Lit. "and anything *(ei ti)* other *(heteron),*" a phrase that does not recur precisely in this form in the NT (though see Rom 13:9), Ap. Frs., or the LXX (cf. *hetera toiauta legōn,* 2 Macc 2:3). Perhaps it is a Latinism, *et si quid est aliud.* See 2 Tim 2:2 for the only other appearance of *heteros* in the PE, in the phrase "the kind who will also be competent to teach others *(heterous).*"

For *wholesome instruction* see Titus 1:9.

*Stands opposed, antikeitai,* recurs in participial form in 1 Tim 5:14 to mean an "adversary," perhaps even Satan (see *1 Clem.* 51.1 for the only use in Ap. Frs. and the predominantly participial usage of the LXX). In the rest of the Paulines the word designates the persons opposing Paul (1 Cor 16:9) or the Philippian Christians (Phil 1:28), as well as the Antichrist (2 Thess 2:4) and the flesh opposing the spirit (Gal 5:17). Otherwise in the NT the term appears only in the Third Gospel of the enemies of Jesus (Luke 13:17) and the opponents of Jesus' disciples (Luke 21:15).

11. *that accords with the gospel I was entrusted with, the good news of the glory of the blessed God.* Lit. "According to the gospel of the glory of the blessed God with which I was entrusted." For *I was entrusted with* see Titus 1:3; for *glory* and *blessed,* Titus 2:13.

This is the first appearance of the *euaggeli-* terminology in the PE; *gospel* will reappear in 2 Tim 1:8, 10; 2:8, and "the work of one who announces the gospel *(euaggelistēs)*" in 2 Tim 4:5. *Euaggelion* appears seventy-two times otherwise in the NT, principally in the other Paulines (fifty-six times, standing in contrast to twenty-one uses of *euaggelizesthai*). Whereas Mark uses the noun eight times, it does not appear at all in the Third Gospel and only twice in Acts (see Fitzmyer, AB *Lk,* pp. 148-149, on Luke's use of the verb *euaggelizesthai*).

In Ap. Frs. *First Clement* employs *euaggelion* when he describes what Paul wrote to the Corinthians "at the beginning of the *gospel*" (47.2), i.e. when the apostle began to preach about Christ in that city or perhaps at the beginning of First Corinthians itself (see Spicq, *Supp. Lexic.,* p. 305 n. 3). *Second Clement* cites a saying of Jesus as being "in the *gospel*" (8.5) and quotes a logion that partially coincides with Luke 16:10 (see 19:17 and Donfried, *Setting,* pp. 72-73). Ignatius writes of the *gospel* eight times, but only in two of his letters: *Phld.* 5.1-2; 8.2; 9.2 and *Smyrn.* 5.1; 7.2. In the last citation he speaks of ". . . the *gospel* in which the passion *(to pathos)* has been revealed *(dedēlōtai)* to us and the resurrection has been consummated *(teteleiōtai).*" *Didache* 8.2; 11.3; 15.3-4 use *euaggelion* of Jesus' directions for prayer and action. *Barnabas* is notable for linking *euaggelion* to the preaching of the (twelve) apostles (5.9; 8.3).

*Euaggelion* appears scarcely three times in the LXX and always in the plural (2 Kgdms 4:10; and perhaps 18:22, 25, with *euaggelizein* and *euaggelia* half a dozen times in the context). Paul used LXX Isa 52:7 as the capstone of his argument for authorized preachers of Jesus when he wrote, "How beautiful are the feet of those who announce good news *(euaggelizomenōn agatha)*" of salvation and the rule of God. "But they [who heard] have not all obeyed *tōi euaggeliōi*" (Rom 10:15-16). Here one sees how the Christian term *gospel* as well as its content (the death and rising of Jesus) was understood to be "according to the Scriptures" (cf. 1 Cor 15:1 with 3-4). See Spicq, *Supp. Lexic.*, pp. 296-306, for further materials and the literature, as well as O. Schilling, *TDOT* 2.313-316, on the Hebrew root *bśr,* which the LXX translates with the *euaggeli-* terminology.

## ♦ COMMENT

1:8-9a. *Fine as we know the Law is, there is still the question of one's using it lawfully. That involves knowing that law is not laid down for an upright person.* The repeated *m* sounds of the Greek of verse 7 are now threaded through these verses, emphasizing the connection between the *nomodidaskaloi,* the "rabbis," of that verse and the authentic explanation of the law at this point, a connection that is further reinforced with the repetition of *nomos* as well as the use of *nomimōs* and *anomois* as verse 9b begins calling the roll of the vicious whom the Law identifies.

In contrast to the specious knowledge of the would-be teachers (the adversative *de* is represented by the inverted structure of the translation), *we know,* i.e. Paul and Timothy, the apostle and his co-worker, have a sure and definitive grasp of what the *nomos* is. Those who listen to this apostolic correspondence, who "overhear" this briefing, are expected to identify with the Pauline interpretation of the OT that is about to be given and so include themselves in the first person plural (contrast the first person plural objects in Titus 2:12). Thus what on the face of it is apostolic instruction becomes ecclesial. Timothy, as the recipient of Paul's authentic teaching, has the specific responsibility of transmitting this apostolic instruction within the local ecclesial setting which this letter presumes, i.e. house churches of the second Christian generation and of predominantly Gentile origin in an urban environment (see Introduction).

The basic affirmation of the Pauline teaching is that *the Law is fine,* that is, an attractive and beautiful reality. It is an assertion with which the Jewish Christian opposition envisaged here would have to agree. The Torah and, by the same token, "all the Scripture," "the sacred letters" (2 Tim 3:15-16), like the creation of which they are part (1 Tim 4:4), are manifestly pleasing and attractively good. Already for the Paul of Rom 7:12-16 the law is holy, it has an origin from the Spirit *(pneumatikos),* it is a fine thing *(kalos),* and its commandment is holy and righteous *(dikaia)* and an excellent thing *(agatha).* The tradition transmitted by the PE has condensed the Pauline teaching about the law into the single adjective *kalos.*

Yet, like the rest of creation, the Law can be misused as a tool "in the workshop of sin" (Käsemann, *Rom.,* p. 205; see p. 198). Hence the clause *there is still the question of one's using it lawfully,* introduced by the Septuagintal *ean tis,* has the form typical of the casuistic laws of the LXX (see Knight, *Sayings,* p. 55; also 2 Tim 2:5, 21), and it conditions the basic principle about the Law as a fine thing in a way that is reminiscent of Rom 7:7: "What shall we say then? That the Law is sin? Not by any means! Yet, if it had not been for the Law, I should not have known sin." Still, to say that the Law itself is subject to law *(nomimōs)* is not an obviously Pauline way of putting the matter. As often occurs in the PE, *nomimōs* has been chosen as much for its sound in the wordplay on *nomōs* in this passage as for its meaning. The rhetoric and the conceptualization have more than a little in common with 1 Cor 9:20, 22: "To the Jews I became as one under the Law — though not being myself under the Law — that I might win those under the Law. . . . I have become all things to all men, that I might by all means save some." So Paul is the one who knows how to use the Law lawfully (see 2 Tim 3:16). He recognizes that it functions differently for Jew and Gentile, as he puts it in Rom 3:19: "Now we know that whatever the Law says, it speaks to those who are under the Law. . . ." So the Jewish Christian can use the Law for what it can give while not expecting what it cannot bestow; with due allowances, something similar can be said to the convert from paganism. Still, in the last analysis, as Rom 3:20 continues, ". . . no human flesh will be made righteous in his [God's] sight from the works of the Law. For full knowledge of sin comes through the Law" (cf. 1:17 with 3:28). It is that Pauline teaching which this passage in First Timothy seeks to probe and rearticulate.

Is there an anterior principle, universal in character, that enables a believer, whether Jewish or Gentile in origin, to make legitimate use of the Law? How can a Christian be "a friend of the Law" (*amicus legis,* Ambrosiaster on Rom 2:12 [*PL* 17.67])? On the presupposition, this passage responds, that the believer recognizes for whose sake *law is laid down* (the passive form suggests the principle applies to the divine lawgiver of the Torah as well as to the legislation of human rulers; the generalizing character of 1:9a is suggested by the anarthrous nouns). Law is not meant for an upright person, including those made upright by God's grace (see Titus 3:7). Even God's law is for the lawless as his grace is for the upright. Thus Clement of Alexandria, explaining why he has said that "both the law and gospel are the energy *(energeia)* of the one Lord who is 'the power and wisdom of God,'" cites 1 Tim 1:7-8 to nail down his point (*Strom.* 1.27 [O. Stählin 2.108]; cf. 7.2 [O. Stählin 3.8]).

These verses of First Timothy reminded Clement of the teaching of the Greek philosophers about law. He cites the saying of Heraclitus, "They would not have known the name of Justice *(Dikē)*, if these things [i.e. the opposite] had no existence" (*Strom.* 4.3 [O. Stählin 2.252]). He adds (from an unknown source), "Socrates says that law was not produced for the sake of the good *(nomon heneka agathon ouk an genesthai)*." Stobaeus (9.15 [ed. C. Wachsmuth 3.349]; Jaekel, *Sententiae,* Pap. xvii [p. 20]) cites Antiphanes (fourth-third century B.C.E.) to the same effect: "The one who does no wrong needs no law *(ho mēden adikon oudenos deitai nomou)*."

The relation of *nomos* to nature, chance, and human life and virtue was an ongoing theme in Greek drama. Thus Menander submits in principle, "Laws are very fine things *(kalon hoi nomoi sphodr' eisin);* but one who looks too sharply at the laws *(nomous)* is shown up as a pettifogger" (Koerte 545/635K). Again, "What is good *(to kalōs echōn)* is better even, I guess, than law *(nomou)*" (Koerte 231/265K; cf. Jaekel, *Sententiae, Monostichoi* 382). Chance *(Tychē)* "does not use laws *(chrētai nomois)* by which to decide things" (Koerte 295/355K). "Righteous *(dikaios)* as you may be, in some way you use law *(chrēsei nomoi)*" (Koerte 495/772K). In competition with nature, laws come off second best. The old nurse, Sophrona, in *Epitr.* 1123 (Sandbach, *Menandri;* Koerte 765), solemnly declaims Euripides to the effect that "Nature *(hē physis)*, to whom laws *(nomon)* do not matter, willed it" (see the elegant parody on the same tragic line cited in Aristotle, *NE* 1152 a 23). The slave's counsel to his younger master in Koerte 740/531K amounts to saying that if "you are a human being *(anthrōpos ei)*" and "are very weak by nature *(asthenestaton gar on physei)*," then you must live "under just the same laws *(epi tois autois nomois)*" as your fellow creatures. Another fragment distinguishes the hardships that nature imposes on human beings from the ills that they bring on themselves, i.e. "worries, conceits, ambitions, laws *(nomoi)*" (Koerte 620.12/534K). Generally *nomos* suggests that which puts a limit on what a person wants, and an arbitrary one at that as far as the individual is concerned. Nature's laws are irksome enough; human laws are worse. Behind this impatience with law, the writer of comedy can discern and satirize human selfishness.

Other sayings from Greek comedy, if not from Menander, illustrate proverbial views about law in the Hellenistic world. "It is not possible to learn the laws of nature." "All things come to be and are judged by law." "Without law nothing fine *(kalon)* comes to be in life." "A prudent man must follow the laws in all respects." "Following laws is a great glory for mortals." Moreover, "The law is a strong thing if it has the rule." "A law which has been kept is nothing but a law *(nomos phylachtheis ouden estin ē nomos);* when it has not been kept, it is both law and public executioner *(dēmios).*" "Having feared the law, you will not be disturbed by the law." "Do not suffer under the law first and so learn; before you suffer at all, anticipate it by fear" (Jaekel, *Sententiae, Monostichoi* 746, 513, 538, 527, 537, 368; *Comp.* 2.144-148/700, 701K).

First-century Latin circles also took up the thought that laws were not for those who were already good. Ovid described that golden age when humankind "used to keep faith and right conduct without law *(sine lege fidem rectumque colebat)*" (*Metamorphoses* 1.89-90). Later Tacitus notes the eruption of evils that have brought it about that human beings "have preferred laws *(leges maluerunt)*" (*Annales* 3.26).

A passage in *Enoch* may presume the same problematic for the origin of law, when Enoch is described as saying, "I was born the seventh during the first week, during which time judgment [*or* justice] and righteousness continued to endure. After me there shall arise in the second week great and evil things. . . . After it [the flood] is ended, injustice shall become greater, and he [God or Noah] shall make a law for the sinners" (93.3-4; Charlesworth, *Pseud.* 1.74; the text has been transmitted only in Ethiopic [Knibb, *Enoch* 1.349; E.T., 2.223-224] and has not been found at Qumran). This view about who needs the law appears in other words in Philo, *Leg. alleg.* 1.93-94, and perhaps in LXX Esther 5:1f (see the still later form in Vulgate Esther 15:13).

So the PE qualify the principle that the Law is a fine thing by setting it within current Hellenistic and Roman and even Jewish explanations about the purpose of law in general. Paul himself had taught, "now it is evident that no man is justified before God by the Law, for he that through faith is righteous *(ho dikaios)* shall live" (Gal 3:11; cf. 2:16). The PE set out to rearticulate that Pauline teaching. The Pauline gospel is retained and reaffirmed with the emphatically placed *dikaioi* of 1 Tim 1:9. For the upright person (and that means for the believer whom God alone has justified), the law as such — whether Jewish or Roman — has no power to make upright and to sanctify. Thus the PE at this juncture deliberately initiate a dialogue between the Pauline gospel and certain views circulating among those who had not yet believed. The principle adduced at this point in verse 9a is another example of the methods used by the believers of the second Christian generation to prepare themselves to address the ambient cultures and to invite them to the faith. It is instructive that Irenaeus applies 1 Tim 1:9a to the patriarchs of Israel (*Adversus haereses* 4.16.3; cf. his *Demonstration of the Apostolic Preaching* §35).

Granted *that law is not laid down for an upright person,* the Christian believer is not an antinomian, any more than he is a liar or a murderer (1:9b). He does not reject all laws, divine and human, as the pagans charged was the case with both Jews (LXX Esther 3:13d [RSV 13:4]) and Christians (Tacitus, *Annales* 15.44). The point at stake here is that the law is "superfluous" (*superflua,* three times in Swete, *Theodore* 2.76-78) for the believer who in virtue of faith in Christ already does and more than does what laws can only command. For Diognetus, Christians "obey the established laws and surpass them in their own lives" (5.10). In the Latin tradition, Augustine put it thus: "He who fulfills the law is not under the law but with the law *(qui enim legem implet, non est sub lege, sed cum lege)*" (*In Ioannem* 3.2; *Corpus Christianorum, series latina* 36.21).

9b. *rather it is for lawless and refractory persons, for godless people and sinners, for the unholy and profane, for patricides and matricides, for murderers.* The wordplay on forms of *nomos* in 9a contrasts rhetorically as well as conceptually (note *de*) with the *anomois,* the *lawless* who open the catalogue that extends through the following verse. The shift from the generic singular *for an upright person* in 9a to the fourteen plurals of 9b-10 suggests rhetorically that the upright are in fact a small flock in comparison with those for whom laws are meant.

This is the first of the ethical lists in the Timothy correspondence, and the meaning of its individual terms is qualified by the several principles of arrangement which run through the catalogue. One notes immediately that the first eight terms are paired with a conjunctive *kai.* An assonance with an initial *alpha,* eight times repeated (and not always privative; thus chosen not with an eye to sense so much as with an ear for sound), extends almost to the end of the catalogue. The ending in *-ois/-ais* for thirteen words suggests a rhyme scheme.

The four pairs with which the list begins, followed by six single terms, imply that the author of the list as it stands wanted to compose something or to redact a previously existing list in a form that would clearly suggest a decalogue, i.e. the Ten Commandments as the Law par excellence (see McEleney, "Vice Lists," pp. 204-210, for the literature and some of the observations here). The polysyndetic pairs at the beginning of this list make it clear what the author is about; the shift to asyndeton for the last six items here is not because the rhetorical device had become burdensome but because it had fulfilled its purpose of signaling the specific "decalogic" form and viewpoint for the list (BDF §460.2). It is quite conceivable that the fourteen individual items here had a previous existence in one or even several vice catalogues (perhaps two lists of seven; see the pair of six-item lists in Titus 1:7-8). There is very little similarity of the vocabulary with the Lukan corpus; there are more coincidences with the vocabulary of the other Paulines (but even those regularly go back to pre-Pauline materials). On the whole the terminology appears only in the PE, and most of that in this list alone in the NT. The redactor's hand, if it can be detected at all, may be responsible for the polysyndetic *kai* joining the first four pairs and thus making a decalogue from the received items. Perhaps the opening pairs of terms, with the adversative *de* and their coincidences, few as they are, with Lukan and Pauline language, are the adhesive by which the catalogue was attached at this point in the composition of First Timothy. A further trace of the redactor's viewpoint may be evidenced as the quartet of paired terms ends and the sestet of single terms begins, for by this means the decalogue is divided into two parts that correspond to the "two tables of the testimony, tables of stone, written with the finger of God" (Exod 31:18; see 24:12; 32:15-16, 19; 34:1, 28; Deut 9:10-11, 15, 17; 10:1-5). Since the biblical text did not indicate which of the divine commands went on which tablet, there was room for speculation (particularly since the wording of the individual commandments, the divisions between them, and the order among them varied in the text [cf. Exod 20:2-17 with Deut 5:6-21] and its tradition [cf. LXX B with A and F; Nash papyrus]). In Philo and Josephus the commandment about supporting parents was considered the fifth (*Dec.* 50-51; *Ant.* 3.90-91), and Philo viewed it as marking the end of the first tablet and the enactments, he speculated, about human relations with God (as contrasted with one's fellow human beings). Some such speculative principle may have dictated the division of the list here in Timothy after the mention of *patricides* and *matricides.*

That particular pair of criminal characters highlights two characteristics, specific to this list. First, it is a catalogue of vicious persons, not a list of vices as such; second, these dissolute persons are guilty of the most abominable sins. Yet it is inaccurate to assert that only grave or extraordinary sins are noted (there are small lies, and illicit sexual activities are scarcely unusual). Still there is no gainsaying that the general effect of the catalogue is to fill the reader with awe at the human capacity for vice. Was there a setting in the ancient world within which one regularly encountered such vicious people as are listed here? If one cast about for an adjective that would do justice to this catalogue, one could do worse than say that as a whole and in its parts it is dramatic. These evil people, larger than life, belong on the stage, and the ancient Greek drama, particularly the tragedy, was peopled with characters that illustrate why laws, human and divine, are laid down and why retribution overtakes them.

The venerable trilogy of Aeschylus, the *Agamemnon, Libationbearers,* and *Eumenides,* turned around monstrous murder and matricide, which became the occasion for the Athenian legal system, under the aegis of the goddess Athena. The patricide and incest of Sophocles' *Oedipus Rex* rivet the attention of vast audiences to this day. There is no lack of *perjurers* or *liars* in Euripides *(Hippolytus* 612; *Iphigeneia at Aulis* and *Iphigeneia in Taurica)* or in Sophocles *(Philoctetes; Trachiniae).* The human spoils of war, populations and individuals reduced to slavery, figure in Euripides' *Hecuba, Daughters of Troy,* and *Andromache.* In *Cyclops* (581-584) the one-eyed giant reveals that he is homosexual, and Euripides' lost tragedy, *Chrysippus,* was based on the myth of the homosexual rape of the title character by Laius, father of Oedipus. A lost tetralogy by Aeschylus began with a tragedy called *Laios,* but there is no surviving evidence that the rape of Chrysippus figured in it. There is scarcely any question, however, that Aeschylus portrayed Achilles as sexually involved with Patroclus in the trilogy that began with the *Myrmidons* (see H. Lloyd-Jones, LCL fragments 64-66 [Nauck, *TGF,* pp. 135-137]; Plato, *Symposium* 179E-18OA; Dover, *Homosexuality,* p. 197; Miller, "Eros," pp. 165-166). Murderers of every stripe walked the ancient Greek stage. The heroine of Sophocles' *Antigone* is legally murdered by Creon for her passionate devotion to the "unwritten and unchangeable laws of the gods" (see esp. 449-470).

The tragedies themselves characterize one or another of the *dramatis personae* as *lawless* (see Sophocles' *Oedipus Colonus* 142 disclaiming this perception of himself; Euripides, *Bacchae* 995, has the chorus describe Pentheus as "atheistic, *lawless,* wicked [*atheon, anomon, adikon*]") or *godless* (thus Oedipus of himself in Sophocles, *Oedipus Rex* 1382, 1441) or *unholy* (Teiresias of Oedipus in the same tragedy, 353; see Aeschylus, *Seven against Thebes* 611) or *profane* (Sophocles, fragment 154; Euripides, fragment 648). If there is no instance of the term used here for *sinners,* it is because *hamartōloi* was a very rare word. In its earliest appearance in Aristophanes, *Thesmophoriazusae* 1111, it is used barbarously to describe an "old rascal" (*amartolē* [*sic*] *gerōn;* see *TDNT* 1.317-318). Similarly the term *refractory, anypotaktoi,* began to appear in Greek only after 200 B.C.E., but Aeschylus's *Prometheus Bound* personifies all that is meant by insubordination. Wrongdoers, deliberate and otherwise, as well as the rebellious abound in Greek tragedy, as do the ungodly, the impure, and the profane.

The "dramatic decalogue" submitted here becomes more plausible when one recalls that Alexandrian Jewish authors were acquainted with the myths and the poets of the Greeks (see Hengel, *Hellenism* 1.69, 109; 2.52 n. 139) and that one of them wrote a tragedy based on the LXX version of the Moses story, the *Exagōgē* of Ezekiel the Tragedian (about 200 B.C.E.). The Euripidean language has been noted in the surviving fragments, and the drama did not emphasize the giving of the Law as such or the national privileges of Israel (see J. J. Collins, *Athens,* pp. 207-211). The list here in Timothy has similar characteristics as it seeks to separate the question of salvation for all persons from questions about Israel and the Law.

As the inner development of this decalogue is traced more closely, one notes that the *lawless,* which lead off the catalogue and link up verbally with *law* in verse 9a, are people who are "uncontrolled by any law" (Dodd, *More NT,* p. 135 n. 2). They have received no authoritative guidance, no revealed command from God, and by that very fact they end by opposing revelation. The *refractory* are understood here as Jewish Christians (see Titus 1:6, 10), and thus can here be paired with the *lawless;* i.e. those who have no revelation paired with those who balk at God's guidance in any case. With *godless people and sinners* the vocabulary of the sapiential tradition in the LXX escalates the polemic. The appearance of *hamartōlois,* "sinners," with its aspirate alpha in the midst of the alpha-privatives of this part of the catalogue, might signal a redactor's hand, at this point ruffling the smooth coincidences of sound and sense, to make certain that this dramatic language would be understood "biblically." As with the preceding *lawless* and *godless* (see Titus 2:12), the term *sinners* meant at times, in Jewish speech, not only non-Jews (see Gal 2:15, 17; also cf. Luke 24:7 with Mark 14:41) but also Jews who did not obey the Law (see Luke 5:30, 32; 6:32-34). The phrase here couples the ideologically *godless* with *sinners,* i.e. those "practical" or amateur atheists who, regardless of their pagan or Jewish origin, deny the revelation that they profess to have received by the way they live.

There is a mounting irony in this solemn roll call of those for whom law and the Law are intended; for *law is laid down* for those who refuse it. In other words, law, human or divine, reveals those who systematically and practically reject authoritative guidance, even God's. This irony is intensified because the polemic aims at Jewish Christians who are seeking to exalt and extol the very Law which had revealed that all human beings, including themselves, were pitted against their God. Their misapprehension of the Law had actually numbered them among the *lawless and refractory,* the *godless people and sinners* for whom they had contempt.

The third pair of vicious characters, *the unholy and profane,* opens with another alpha-privative, *anosiois,* followed by *bebēlois.* The terms suggest persons of utter moral turpitude complemented with total ritual unfitness for the public worship of the God of Israel. Law keeps such people as far as possible from the sanctuary. If the Decalogue influenced the content of the catalogue at this point, the commandment about observing the Sabbath may be the positive counterpart of the negative formulation here. In this connection one notes, with Rordorf, *Sunday,* p. 106, "that whenever we come across the use of the decalogue within the Christian Church, the sabbath commandment is always missing."

The *patricides and matricides* in this version correspond to Greek terms whose three concluding syllables rhyme. Is this pair to be heard as the climax of the preceding pairs or as the solemn opening of the single-member list that follows? It is surely more than a coincidence that parricides are violating the commandment "Honor your father and mother that it may be well with you and that you may be a long time in the good land which the Lord, your God, will give you" (LXX Exod 20:12) and that the persons listed from this point on have some correlation with the following commands of the Decalogue. Formally, this pair goes with the polysyndetic pairs that preceded it, whereas the rhymes in *-ois* and *-ais* look forward as well as backward. Perhaps the transition looks both ways deliberately. The worst of crimes against another human being, parricide, concludes a list that looked particularly to one's being in total revolt against God. Simultaneously the *patricides and matricides* lead off a list that referred to abuses of one's neighbor forbidden by the Decalogue.

*Murderers,* which introduces the single-item part of this list, occurs in relatively the same position as do the commandments "You shall not murder (LXX Exod 20:13, *ou phoneuseis*) . . . commit adultery . . . steal" in the MT, in the LXX of A and F, and in Mark 10:19 (*SFG* §254; B puts the command forbidding adultery in first place among these three, as do Rom 13:9 and Luke 18:20; see Fitzmyer, AB *Lk,* pp. 1, 199). Thus the catechesis here presumes a Palestinian tradition of the Hebrew text of the Decalogue that the MT adopted (not the tradition represented by the Nash papyrus). If Mark can be pressed for a hint, a Greek version of this tradition was in use in Jewish Christian house churches in Rome already in the first Christian generation.

10a. *for the incestuous, for homosexuals, for slave traders, for liars, for perjurers.* With the mention of *the incestuous* and *homosexuals* the catalogue turns from *murderers* and the actions forbidden by the commandment "You shall not murder" to persons who engage in sexual activities that are prohibited by "You shall not commit adultery" (LXX Exod 20:13; *ou moicheuseis*). However, adulterers are not explicitly mentioned here (as they are in the Pharisee's prayer in Luke 18:11 with its mention of "robbers, evildoers, adulterers [*harpages, adikoi, moichoi*]"). The *pornoi* here could, in Hellenistic Greek usage, designate persons who engaged in any sexual activity outlawed by (in this case) the Jewish tradition. Interpreted thus, the usage in the tradition taken up here in First Timothy is in continuity with the Pauline teaching on *porneia* that leads off the catalogue of "the works of the flesh" in Gal 5:19 as well as his placing the *pornoi* at the head of the list of those who "will not inherit the kingdom of God" (1 Cor 6:9-10; see Eph 5:5). At the redactional level this traditional generic meaning was probably meant to be heard as *incestuous.* In the first Christian generation Paul was calling it *porneia* (1 Cor 5:1) for a man to marry his stepmother (and so within a degree of kinship forbidden by Lev 18:8, not to mention Roman law; see Conzelmann, *1 Cor.,* pp. 95-96, for the ancient texts). Such an incestuous man was preeminently a *pornos* (1 Cor 5:9-11), and thus the apostle has put a point on the more generic terminology of the catechetical lists known to him and his churches as authoritative (note the phrase "Or do you not know . . ." in 1 Cor 6:9). A Christian man who has "married" his stepmother is living in incest, not in marriage, however much some Corinthian believers are prepared to accept it as such. The Pauline application of Israel's Law to conduct within a Christian congregation (though without actually citing Leviticus) raises precisely the question that this passage in First Timothy is addressing. The Law does not bind the Christian, but the authority and direction of the apostle do.

The memory of such apostolic enforcement of the Levitical marriage legislation upon converts from paganism certainly appears to lie behind the apostolic letter from the Jerusalem church (Acts 15:20, 29; see 21:25), which asks such converts to observe certain parts of the Torah that forbid eating offerings to idols, *porneia,* eating things strangled, and eating blood (as in Lev 17–18, though the LXX does not use *porn-* terminology there). Entrance into marriages forbidden by the Law also seems to lie behind the description of Esau as *pornos* in Heb 12:6 (apparently a contemptuous reference to his "marriages" with native Canaanite women; cf. Gen 26:34 with 27:46; 28:1, 6-9). The reference in Heb 13:4 to God judging *pornous . . . kai moichous* would then mean those who violate the law by entering forbidden, i.e. incestuous, marriages as well as by committing adultery.

The Pauline and other NT usage, as well as the dramatic character of the list itself, have led to the translation of *pornoi* as *the incestuous* (lexically, the *pornoi* could be homosexuals in the terminology of this era). If this specification of the *pornoi* as those engaged in a particularly objectionable form of heterosexual activity holds, then the following term, *arsenokoitai,* "homosexuals," can be appropriately paired with it. Yet it must be admitted that the text itself gives no hint, beyond writing the terms one after the other, that the redactor meant for the reader to differentiate sexually the abuses indulged in by these people any more than he intended to make a morally significant point out of the sexual differentiation between the homicidal acts committed by *patricides and matricides* (which are explicitly paired by *kai*).

Homosexual practices were a regular phenomenon in Greek culture and in the Hellenistic Roman world. They can be documented in the literature, philosophy, and art (see Dover, *Morality,* pp. 213-216; *Homosexuality,* passim). Homosexuality ordinarily expressed itself in sexual relationships between grown men and adolescent boys. They were publicly tolerated and regulated legally (see Dover, *Homosexuality,* pp. 19-39), though there was an ongoing uneasiness about such practices too. Thus about 100 B.C.E. a sanctuary in Lydian Philadelphia had among the conditions for entry to worship that "a man . . . is not to seduce a boy *(paida)* or a maiden *(parthenon)* or to counsel another to do this" (Dittenberger, *Syll.* 3.117.26-31, no. 985; see Nock, *Conversion,* pp. 216-218, for a version and comments).

If some pagans considered homosexuality aberrant (see Plato, *Symposium* 182A-C; *Laws* 8.836C-E; Plutarch, *Erotikos* 751B-752B, 768E-F, 769B, 770B-C), there is not a single text in the Jewish tradition, biblical or otherwise, from Lev 18:22 through Philo, *Spec. leg.* 3.37-42, that expresses less than total rejection of all homosexual practices, including pederasty (see J. J. Collins, *Athens,* pp. 142-144, 148-149, 151-152, 186; Scroggs, *Homosexuality,* pp. 85-97, for further references, with D. F. Wright's critique of the latter in *SJT* 38 [1985]:

119-120). It is notable, even surprising in the light of the preceding sexual distinction of patricides, that the *arsenokoitai* are not explicitly distinguished from the *malakoi* (i.e. the active homosexual partners from the passive), as is the case in the list of the vicious in 1 Cor 6:9. Unless the *pornoi* here in First Timothy are the catamites (and that is lexically possible), the *malakoi* have been edited out of the source (Pauline or pre-Pauline) that is being used. The reason is that the *arsenokoitai* are now understood to be all homosexuals, active or passive, old or young. On this understanding, the *malakoi* could have been omitted from the source for the sake of the decalogue format without cutting back on the meaning of the Levitical law which probably was the original linguistic matrix for this Jewish and Jewish Christian neologism. If Paul himself coined the term *arsenokoitai* and inserted it into the list of the vicious in First Corinthians, it was because the *malakoi* could be legalistically understood as if only passive homosexual partners would not inherit the kingdom. The Levitically inspired *arsenokoitai* would end such cavils. The Pauline moral teaching on homosexuals is thus in continuity with and "according to the Scriptures," though not explicitly citing Leviticus, a pattern already seen in Paul's teaching on incestuous relationships. Such a method of assimilating and applying the Torah to the moral life of the Christian believer was not original with Paul, who was not the first one to cite a verse of Leviticus to explain that love of God involved the love of neighbor as oneself (Rom 13:9-10; Mark 12:31 [*SFG* §282] quoting Lev 19:18).

With the *slave traders* one encounters a dramatic example of those who violate the commandment "You shall not steal" (LXX *ou klepseis,* Exod 20:14) in a particularly heinous fashion; i.e. those who "steal" or kidnap human beings to sell them into slavery (see Deut 24:7; Rev 18:13; *CD* 12:10-11 forbids the sale of Jewish household slaves). Dio Chrysostom, in his discourse on slavery (15.25), notes that perhaps the oldest method of getting slaves was by taking a prisoner of war or kidnapping. In a generation that had witnessed whole cities of Jewish men, women, and children auctioned off in the slave markets of the Roman world in a kind of genocide that can be compared only to the Nazi Holocaust, there must have been few Jewish Christians who had not had one of their own flesh and blood involved in the catastrophe of the Palestinian revolt. For many the *slave traders* of this list would have been the men who had bought and sold members of their family. Josephus uses the verb *andrapodizein* for the Jewish prisoners taken in that war and previously (*War* 1.28; 2.68; 3.62; 7.208; *Ant.* 14.120; 17.289). The Law was for such slave dealers, not for Christians.

It may be significant that the earliest Latin versions of this list heard *andrapodistai* as *plagiarii/plagiatoribus,* i.e. kidnappers (see Frede, *VL* 25.413; G. Horsley, *NDIEC,* p. 50, §12), as in Seneca's listing of *avaros, cimumscriptores, latrones, plagiarios,* "misers, frauds, thieves, kidnappers," in *Dialogues* 9.8.4 *(De* *tranquillitate animi).* In a recently discovered letter of Augustine (Epistle 24*; CSEL 83 [1981]), the bishop of Hippo in North Africa appeals to the drastic penalties levied by a constitution of the emperor Honorius upon those who kidnapped free people and sold them into slavery. Augustine's express contempt for Christians who plied this trade, when he saw them within the walls of his church, is preserved in his sermon on Ps 127:11 (CC 40.1875).

With the *liars* and *perjurers* (as with *incestuous* and *homosexuals*) one may again have two groups of people who violate in different ways the same commandment ("You shall not make a false testimony [*pseudomartyrēseis . . . martyrian pseudē*] against your neighbor," LXX Exod 20:16). It is human beings who lie and not God ("who is without deceit," Titus 1:2). So the Law is for liars, not for God's children who speak the truth.

The *perjurers* are those who lie under oath, calling the true God as witness to an untruth, the very worst kind of lying because it attempts to make God a liar (on the Johannine theology about this see R. Brown, *Epistles,* pp. 212, 351, 533, 590). From the perspective of Wis 14:27-29, idolaters are the people who "prophesy lies *(pseudē),* or live unrighteously, or readily perjure themselves *(epiorkousin).* Placing their trust in lifeless idols, they expect no punishment when swearing falsely" (Winston, AB *Wisd.,* p. 270; see "perjury," *epiorkia,* in the horrendous list of pagan sinners in 14:25). The closing speech of Castor in Euripides' *Electra* 1349-1356, contrasting those who "love holiness and justice" with those who "act wickedly" and are "perjurers," bears comparison with this Alexandrian Jewish exposition.

The list here in First Timothy stops short of citing the commandments of the Decalogue that extend God's domain into the hearts and minds of human beings, i.e. the forbidding of unchaste desires and greed. Possibly they have not been mentioned of set purpose, for it is the external aspects of the Law from which the author-redactor wished to argue at this point. On this view the Law is concerned with the verifiable and evidential aspects of human conduct which it could illuminate with its cold, searching beam but which it could not penetrate, much less heal. The commandments which start to probe the human heart, even though in a negative fashion (see Rom 7:7-12), would take the edge off the argument here. Hence this "decalogue" trails off, with syntactical vagueness, into the generic phrase of verse 10b.

10b-11. *and anything else that stands opposed to the wholesome instruction that accords with the gospel I was entrusted with, the good news of the glory of the blessed God.* At the end of the long catalogue of the "works of the flesh" in Gal 5 the apostle observes, "and things like these" (5:21), as if to say there would be no end to listing the forms that evil takes in human conduct. A similar phrase appears at the end of a partial citation from the decalogue in Rom 13:9, and seemingly for the same reason. The *wholesome teaching* is the Pauline interpretation of the OT, and here it means the way in which Paul was conceived of as interpreting the Law, specifically the Decalogue, for those who had believed in Jesus. The interpretation corresponds in turn *with the* Pauline *gospel of the glory of the blessed God.*

On this initial mention of *the good news* it is solemnly qualified with sonorous, pleonastic phrases whose cadences are liturgical, whose genitival form sounds Semitic. First, *the gospel* is *of the glory.* The latter term can be understood adjectivally (i.e. as meaning "the glorious gospel") or objectively (as meaning "the gospel about the glory"). In the former interpretation the emphasis is upon the lustrous or luminous or visibly shining character of the gospel. In the latter, *the glory* almost means the risen Jesus himself. However, although the possibility that "glory" could be a designation for Jesus himself has been debated in various forms since early in this century, these arguments have not proved convincing; Jesus is called "God" in very few NT passages, and in none is he clearly designated "the glory of God" (see Notes on 2 Tim 1:10 below, on how Christ Jesus "made life and immortality shine forth through the gospel"; also 2 Cor 4:4, 6, and Furnish, AB *2 Cor,* pp. 221-225).

*The blessed God* is the Father of the Christ who is his *glory.* As was already observed in Titus 2:13, *blessed* suggests the language of liturgical acclamation but the application of the term to God is peculiar to First Timothy. However, the LXX and Ap. Frs. call men and women through whom God spoke and acted *blessed;* thus Moses (*1 Clem.* 43.1), the apostle Paul (*1 Clem.* 47.1; Polycarp, *Phil.* 3.2), and Judith (*1 Clem.* 55.4). The distance between God and the persons whom he has blessed is not great, and so here a tradition of prayer goes beyond previous biblical usage and calls the giver of blessings *blessed.* Such a usage could contain an implicit corrective and criticism of the cult of the Roman emperor who was venerated as *Felicitas Augusti* (see Spicq, *EP,* pp. 337-338, 573; *Supp. Lexic.,* p. 444). If this is the case, then here and in 6:15-16 the language of the Christian faith and its public worship has entered upon a collision course that is destined to shatter the self-image of imperial Rome and the ritual language with which it constructed its power (see Price, *Rituals,* pp. 234-248). The one God and Father is the only God, Lord, and Ruler (6:15) and thus the only really *blessed* one. As *makarios* already suggests, he is the only immortal one and so the only one who bestows immortality, "the blessed hope" (Titus 2:13) of eternal life which he possesses. He is accordingly the blessed one as no imperial Caesar was or could be.

*The gospel I was entrusted with* is, in the view of the correspondence with Timothy, *the good news* precisely as proclaimed and taught by Paul. Paul had seen the glory of the risen Jesus on the road to Damascus, had believed, and had shared out what God had *entrusted to* him. He is, so to speak, a secretary in charge of the correspondence in the imperial household that belongs to "the blessed and only suzerain, the king of those who act as kings and lord of those who act as lords" (6:15; see Deissmann, *LAE,* p. 379). It is Paul's way of presenting the gospel that is at stake here. In Greek this sentence ends with a sharply emphatic *egō* that takes the reader back to the first person singular of verse 3. The phrase *I was entrusted with* occurred in Titus 1:3, the majestic apostolic exordium to the PE. There the antecedent for the phrase was Paul's kerygma, the proclamation or preaching, i.e. the process itself of communicating the fact of God's victory and its effects to those who had not yet heard about it. Here in First Timothy the term *gospel* includes that audience, but it extends also to those who have believed in Jesus and have been baptized. *The wholesome instruction that accords with the gospel* is the Pauline interpretation and application of the OT to the lives and conduct of those who have accepted the kerygma (which is also "according to the Scriptures"). Thus, for the PE, the *gospel* includes the continuing, postbaptismal formation of the believing congregation by the apostle and those who share his apostolic task; indeed, central to this whole correspondence is carrying on and sustaining an authoritative, undeniably Pauline instruction in churches of the second Christian generation.

The PE do not conceive of Christians as outgrowing the content of the kerygma that was originally proclaimed to them for their belief. Thus 2 Tim 2:8 exhorts Timothy to "keep in mind Jesus Christ, risen from the dead, from the line of David. That corresponds to my gospel." The believer can never transcend or put behind him that encounter with the risen Jesus which the kerygma transmitted, with its invitation to accept eternal life and to continue proclaiming it to others. As the Corinthians were firmly brought back to the gospel about the Christ who was raised from dead, a gospel that they had believed in when Paul, Timothy, and Silvanus first proclaimed it to them in their unbelief (see 1 Cor 15:1-11; 2 Cor 1:19), so here the central reality of the gospel is the Christ, i.e. the anointed son of David, whom God has raised from the dead. The man who carries on the apostle's work can never forget that.

The *gospel* in these letters to Timothy is firmly linked with the apostolic work and the apostolic suffering (see 2 Tim 1:8-12) as the death of Jesus and his resurrection into eternal life continue in the lives of his apostles as well as in their words (see 1 Cor 1:22; 4:9-13; 2 Cor 4:7-12). Indeed, the apostle's life is, in a sense, his *gospel* which refutes and discredits his opponents. That is why the positive part of the exhortation with which this letter now continues (1:12-17) englobes its orthodox teaching in the life of Paul and particularly in his thanksgiving prayer (his "eucharist") for the gift and grace that had alone made him what he was (see 1 Cor 15:10; 2 Cor 12:9). More critical and more fundamental even than Paul's theology (1:8-11) was Paul's experience as a Jew, as a Christian, as an apostle, an experience that crystallizes now in his apostolic prayer.

### *II.A.2.b. Paul at Prayer (1:12-17)*

*1[12] I give thanks to Christ Jesus, our Lord,*
*who put his strength in me*
*because he regarded me as trustworthy*
*and placed me in his ministry,*
*[13] a man who was formerly*
*a blasphemer and a persecutor and insanely arrogant.*
*But mercy found me out*
*because I did not know what I was doing*
*in my unbelief.*
*[14] Still the grace of our Lord superabounded*
*along with that faith and charity,*
*which come from union with Christ Jesus.*
*[15] The Christian message,*
*meant to be believed*
*and worth welcoming wholeheartedly,*
*is "Christ Jesus came into the world to save sinners."*
*Among them I have first place.*
*[16] But for this very reason mercy found me out,*
*so that Christ Jesus could evidence patience to the utmost,*
*using me as a model of those who are going to believe*
*in him for eternal life.*
*[17] So to the king of eternity,*
*the immortal, invisible, only God,*
*are the honor and glory for all eternity.*
*Amen.*

## ♦ NOTES

1:12. *I give thanks to Christ Jesus, our Lord.* A substantial number of witnesses, mostly Western and Byzantine, insert *kai,* "and," at the beginning of this verse, thus tying what follows tightly with the preceding. The shorter and somewhat abrupt reading of S A F G P 33 is preferable (*pace* J. K. Elliott, *Greek Text,* p. 207).

The bound phrase *charin echein,* to "give thanks," recurs in 2 Tim 1:3 but not otherwise in the Paulines, which opt for forms of *eucharistein* (see Rom 1:8; 1 Cor 1:4; Phil 1:3; Col 1:3). The phrase does appear in Luke 17:9, "Does he thank *(mē echei charin)* the servant because he did what was commanded?" The usage in Acts 2:47, describing the primitive Jerusalem church as "praising God and having favor *(echontes charin)* with the people," has a different sense, comparable to *charin heuriskein* in Luke 1:30 and Acts 7:46 (see Philem 7, *charan . . . pollēn eschon kai paraklēsin,* "I had much joy and comfort"). Elsewhere in the NT only Heb 12:28 uses the phrase, again in a worship setting: "Therefore, let us be grateful *(echōmen charin)* for receiving a kingdom that cannot be shaken and thus let us offer to God acceptable worship with reverence and awe." This meaning does not appear in Ap. Frs., and in the LXX it appears only in 2 Macc 3:33, citing a visionary message to Heliodorus which says, "Be very grateful *(pollas . . . charitas eche)* to Onias the high priest. . . ." For the *koinē* usage see Spicq, *Lexic.,* pp. 963-966. Euripides has his *Iphigeneia in Taurica,* as priestess of Artemis, cry out in her brother's behalf to their homeland, "I give thanks *(charin echo)* for his life, I give thanks *(charin echo)* for his rearing" (847). Latin used the same idiom, as appears when Cicero declaims against Catiline, before the statue of Jupiter Stator, "Great thanks must be given to the immortal gods . . . *(Magna dis immortalibus habenda est . . . gratia)*" for deliverance from this pest (see also Caesar, *Bellum civile* 3.73.3; Ovid, *Tristia* 5.9.12; Quintilian, *Institutio* 5.10.121).

*Christ Jesus, our Lord.* See 1:1-2.

*who put his strength in me.* The aorist, *endynamōsanti me,* of a host of strong witnesses (see *GNT*[3corr] *ad loc.* for full citation), outweighs the present tense of S 33 etc. which probably derives from the influence of Phil 4:13 (B. Metzger, *TCGNT,* p. 639 contra J. K. Elliott, *Greek Text,* pp. 24-25).

The verb *endynamoun* is undocumented in secular Greek before the first Christian century, and its seven NT uses are in the Pauline corpus and Acts. It appears below in 2 Tim 2:1; 4:17. In the former passage, "Now, my child, *find strength* in that grace which is in Christ Jesus," Timothy, as a co-worker who shares the apostle's responsibility, is the subject addressed, and the grace *(charis)* mentioned can hardly be understood apart from "that gracious gift *(charisma)* of God the Father" and the spirit "of dynamic strength *(dynameōs)*" mentioned in 2 Tim 1:6-7. As Second Timothy closes, the description of Paul's trial says, "Still the Lord (*ho kyrios,* the risen Jesus) stood by me and *put his strength* in me, so that through me the proclamation would be carried out fully, or, in other words, so that all the pagans would listen to it" (4:17). In Phil 4:13, as Paul wrote from straitened circumstances to his generous Philippian converts, he said, "I can do all things in him who strengthens me *(endynamounti me),*" and there the present tense underscores the constant aid that the Lord gives to his apostle. Ephesians 6:10 (after its *Haustafel*), with an imperative address that is reminiscent of 2 Tim 2:1, says, "Finally, be strong *(endynamousthe)* in the Lord and in the strength of his might." In Rom 4:20 Paul says of Abraham, "He was strengthened *(enedynamōthē)* in his faith as he gave glory to

God." Outside of the Paulines, only Acts 9:22 uses this verb, as the author summarizes the result of Paul's conversion, baptism, and Damascus preaching by saying, "But Saul kept increasing all the more in strength *(enedynamouto)* and he confused the Jews living in Damascus with his teaching that Jesus was the Christ."

In Ap. Frs. this term appears to describe how women became strong by the grace of God (*1 Clem.* 55.3), and Ignatius writes that "the perfect man [Jesus] gives me strength" (*Smyrn.* 4.2). Of the uses in Hermas, the most notable speak of "the Lord giving strength" to keep the commandments that have been received (*Man.* 12.6.4) and of the prophet "strengthened by the Spirit" to grasp the revelation bestowed on him (*Sim.* 9.1.2). In the LXX there are three uses of *endynamoun:* in Judg 6:34 and 1 Chron 12:19 *s.v.l.* the spirit of the Lord is its subject; in LXX Ps 51:9 a man "grew powerful" in empty wealth.

*because he regarded me as trustworthy.* The common Greek particle *hoti,* "because," appears almost 1,300 times in the NT and 20 times in the PE (the single appearances in Titus 3:11 and 3 John 12 are the lowest counts in the NT documents). The causal meaning makes its first appearance here in the PE. It will recur in the following verse, in 4:4, 10; 5:12; 6:2, 7, and finally in 2 Tim 1:16. Thus 40 percent of the usage in the PE is causal, compared with about 31 percent in Luke-Acts and about 22 percent in the rest of the Paulines.

*Pistos,* "trustworthy," occurs seventeen times in the PE and sixty-seven times in the NT, with sixteen of those usages falling in the other Paulines. As used in the PE, it refers to both the body of believers in Christ or groups within that body and to an individual believer, as here of Paul. The verb *hēgeisthai* appears twenty-eight times in the NT, often in the participial form, which means "leaders." It will reappear below in 6:1, "Those Christians who are bound in slavery are to *regard* their masters as deserving all esteem." There are nine occurrences in the rest of the Paulines. Acts 26:2 has Paul use the verb in the sense that it has in this letter to Timothy, when he says to Agrippa, "I regard myself as blessed *(makarion)* that I am going to make my defense today before you. . . ." Though the verb occurs regularly in Ap. Frs., the sense that it has here appears less often. Ignatius, *Smyrn.* 8.1, directs, "Let that be regarded as a valid eucharist which is by a bishop or by one whom he appoints"; *2 Clem.* 5.6 describes Christians as those who "conduct themselves with holiness and righteousness and who regard these worldly things as alien to us and do not lust after them."

*and placed me in his ministry.* The verb *tithēnai,* "place," appears 100 times in the NT, relatively seldom in the Pauline corpus and there usually for God's action. In the PE it will recur in 2:7 and 2 Tim 1:11, both times in the identical passive phrase, of Paul asserting, "For that [testimony/gospel] I was appointed [i.e. by God and Christ] a herald and apostle." The significance of these so-called divine passive forms becomes clear from the use of the active in 1 Cor

12:28 (see also 12:18): "And God has placed *(etheto)* in the church first apostles, second prophets, third teachers. . . ." Similarly, Acts 1:7 has Jesus speak of "the times or seasons that the Father has constituted *(ho pater etheto)* by his own authority";. and Acts 20:28 has Paul speak of the Holy Spirit having "placed *(etheto)* bishops" as shepherds in the Lord's flock (see LXX 4 Kgdms 11:18, "And the priest placed overseers [*ethēken . . . episkopous*] at the Lord's house," and 1 Macc 10:65, "The king . . . made him general [*etheto auton stratēgon*] and provincial governor"). Of the uses in Ap. Frs. the general principle adduced by *1 Clem.* 38.1 is significant in connection with Pauline usage: "Therefore, let our whole body be kept safe in Christ Jesus and let each person be subject to his neighbor, just as it has been established by his charism *(etethē en tōi charismati autou).*"

*in his ministry.* Lit. "for service," *eis diakonian.* The *diakon-* cluster of terms is confined to the letters to Timothy within the PE. *Diakonia* recurs in 2 Tim 4:5, 11, and thirty-one times elsewhere in the NT. Except for Heb 1:14 (of angels sent "for service") and Rev 2:19 (in a list of the good works of the church at Thyatira), all the other occurrences are in the Paulines and Luke-Acts. For the *diakonos,* see 1 Tim 3:8, 12; 4:6; for the verb *diakonein,* 1 Tim 3:10, 13; 2 Tim 1:18.

In Ap. Frs. *1 Clem.* 40.5, using the priestly terminology of the OT, says, "On the Levites are imposed their proper ministries *(diakoniai).*" Ignatius writes of Magnesian deacons "entrusted with the service *(diakonia)* of Jesus Christ" (*Magn.* 6.1). The bishop of Philadelphia "obtained the ministry *(diakonian)* which relates to the community, not from himself or through human beings or for vain glory but by *(en)* love of God the Father and the Lord, Jesus Christ" (*Phld.* 1.1). Of the deacon messenger from that congregation to the one in Antioch, Ignatius writes, "Blessed by *(en)* Jesus Christ be the one who shall be found worthy of such a ministry *(diakonias)*" (*Phld.* 10.2). Again of a messenger deacon, Burrhus, "He is an exemplar of God's ministry (*exemplarion theou diakonias* [note the Latinism])" (*Smyrn.* 12.1). Hermas favors the *diakon-* cluster, most notably in *Sim.* 9.26.2, as he writes of "the *diakonoi* who ministered *(diakonēsantes)* badly and devoured the lives of widows and orphans and acquired wealth from the ministry *(diakonias)* that they received for ministering *(diakonēsai)*. . . . If they convert and holily fulfill their ministry *(diakonia),* they will be able to live."

The LXX seldom employs the *diakon-* terminology. *Diakonia* occurs only in 1 Macc 11:58 and then in an unusual sense, of the utensils used at table (as in "silver service" in English; see Athenaeus, *Deipnosophistai* 5.208B, apparently of kitchenware). The noun appears as a variant in Esther 6:3, 5 in A. Philo employs the *diakon-* terminology comparatively seldom; Josephus uses it with some regularity, and *diakonia* is used in describing Hannah's promise to dedicate the future Samuel "to the service of God" in the Shilo sanctuary as well as Solomon's transfer of "all the vessels for the service of the sacrifices to God" into the new temple in Jerusalem (*Ant.* 5.344; 8.101).

13. *a man who was formerly a blasphemer. A man who was* represents the participial *onta,* on which see BDF §413.3.

*Formerly* translates the Hellenistic *to proteron* (corrected in an Attic direction by some Western and Byzantine witnesses), which appears in Gal 4:13 as well as in John 6:62; 9:8. Forms of *proteros* occur seven times otherwise in the NT. In Ap. Frs. (apart from *2 Clem.* 13.1, who writes of "former sins") Hermas is the only one who uses *proteros,* including *to proteron.* The LXX employs forms of *proteros* regularly (see *to proteron* in Gen 13:3; 28:19). The one occurrence in the *Testaments of the Twelve Patriarchs* is in *T. Levi* 8.1: "There I again saw the vision as formerly *(hōsper to proteron).*"

*A blasphemer, blasphēmon,* appears again for the abusive or contemptuous in the prophetic catalogue of the vicious in 2 Tim 3:2 (for the cluster see Titus 2:5). Otherwise in the NT, only 2 Pet 2:11, speaking of "insulting judgment," and Acts 6:11 use this term. In the latter passage, false witnesses against Stephen, the leader of the Seven, say, "We have heard him speak blasphemous words *(rhēmata blasphēma)* against God and Moses," i.e. "against this holy place [the Jerusalem temple and its worship] and the Law [the Torah]" (7:13). In Ap. Frs. only Hermas writes of "blasphemers," whom he numbers with apostates, hypocrites, and traitors (*Sim.* 9.18.3; 9.19.1 and 3). The LXX uses *blasphēmos* half a dozen times, notably in 2 Macc 9:28 of Antiochus as "the murderer and blasphemer" (see 10:4, 38 of "blasphemous and barbarous nations" and the fate of blasphemers; also Wis 1:6; Sir 3:16; Isa 66:3).

*and a persecutor, diōktēs,* a noun otherwise unattested in the NT and the LXX and unknown to Philo and Josephus as well as to secular Greek, though "the persecutors of the good" appear in the list of vicious who are on the "Way of Death/of the Black One" in *Did.* 5.2; *Barn.* 20.2. However, the compound *ergodiōktēs,* "taskmaster," was in secular Greek in the middle of the third century B.C.E. (see MM, p. 166) and in the LXX (Exod 3:7; 5:6, 10, 13, etc.). Philo takes up the compound (*Quis Her.* 255) and comments on the aptness of its origin (*Mos.* 1.37). For the verb, *diōkein,* which is used in both a good and a bad sense (including Paul's persecuting the church), see 1 Tim 6:11.

*and insanely arrogant, hybristēs,* otherwise in the NT only in the catalogue of vicious pagans in Rom 1:30, though the cognates occur more often. The Ap. Frs. do not employ this noun and seldom use *hybris* (*1 Clem.* 59.3; Hermas, *Man.* 8.10; *Sim.* 9.11.8) and *hybrizein* (*2 Clem.* 14.4; Hermas, *Sim.* 6.3.4). On the other hand, the LXX had used *hybristēs* as many as ten times, particularly in sapiential books, where it translates the Hebrew *rwm* (Prov 6:17) or *ge'/ge'eh* (Job 40:11; Prov 15:25; 16:19); see also LXX Prov 27:13; Sir 8:11 *(lys);* 35:21

(*zdwn;* RSV 32:18). As early as Homer, *Iliad* 13.633, this is how Menelaus characterizes all Trojan men, as he lodges his complaint with Zeus for showing them graciousness. The connotations of the term are heard very clearly when Euripides speaks of bulls as *hybristai,* i.e. restive, violently aggressive, wanton, and unruly (*Bacchae* 743). Its Greek ethical antithesis is *sophrosynē,* an attitude of sane balance (for a sketch of classical Greek usage of the *hybris* cluster of words, see P. Marshall, "Hybrists," pp. 276-279; Chantraine, *DELG,* p. 1150).

*But mercy found me out.* Lit. "mercy was had on me," *ēleēthēn,* a divine passive repeated in verse 16. Of the remaining twenty-seven NT uses of this verb, ten occur in the other Paulines. Though Luke 16:24; 17:13; 18:38-39 use the active form of the verb (the latter two passages in an address to Jesus), the passive does not appear in Luke-Acts.

In Ap. Frs., Polycarp, *Phil.* 2.3, and *1 Clem.* 13.2 cite as a saying of the Lord Jesus (not found in so many words in the Gospels, but see LXX Prov 17:5): "Be merciful so that you may obtain mercy *(eleēthēte).*" *First Clement* takes up the verb in 18.2 as he cites the opening of LXX Ps 50:3. In 56.16 he describes God as a "kind father" who "disciplines *(paideuei)* so that we may obtain mercy *(eleēthēnai)* through his holy discipline *(paideias)*"; and in the great prayer of 59.4, one of the petitions to God is, "Have mercy on the humble." In all of these passages God is the explicit or implicit subject of *eleein.* In *2 Clem.* 1.7 it is Jesus who "has had mercy *(ēleēsen)* on us and saved us in his pity." Ignatius likes to address a given church as "having obtained mercy" (*inscr.* for *Rom., Phld., Smyrn.;* cf. *Eph.* 12.1). In *Rom.* 9.2, in a turn of phrase that reminds one of First Timothy, he writes ". . . but I have obtained mercy *(all' ēleēmai)* to be someone, if I attain to God." To the Philadelphians he writes, "But your prayer will make me perfect for God, so that I may attain the lot in which I obtained mercy *(ēleēthēn)*" (5.1). In all these passages the implicit subject appears to be God. In Hermas, *Vis.* 1.3.2, it is the Lord (Jesus?). *Didache* 5.2 and *Barn.* 20.2, in their lists of the vicious on the Way of Death, mention those who do not have mercy on the poor man (cf. *Barn.* 3.5, citing a non-LXX form of Isa 58:10).

Though the LXX frequently uses *eleein* with God as subject, there is no occurrence of the phrase *but mercy found me out.* The use of the passive, *ēleēmenē,* however, for the name of "your [pl.] sister" in LXX Hos 2:3 is notable (see Andersen and Freedman, AB *Hosea,* pp. 212-213). Spicq, *Supp. Lexic.,* pp. 250-258, adds that this terminology for mercy is seldom found in secular inscriptions and papyri because feelings of pity for those who suffer deserved punishments were regarded with suspicion as a manifestation of weakness. Thus Aristotle observes that "pity has for its object one who does not merit his misfortune" (*Poetics* 13; 1453 a 4; see the longer explanation in his *Rhetoric* 2.8; 1385 b-1386 b).

*because I did not know what I was doing in my unbelief.* The phrase *I did not know* is lit. "unknowing," *agnoōn,* a circumstantial participle (BDF §417) characterizing an ongoing internal state (Moule, *Idiom,* p. 101). There are twenty-one other NT uses of *agnoein* outside of this one occurrence in the PE, with fifteen of them in the Paulines and three in Luke-Acts. Ignatius, *Second Clement,* and Hermas, among Ap. Frs., use *agnoein* and its cognates a few times. Ignatius writes of the Docetists, "There are some who ignorantly *(agnoountes)* deny him [Jesus in the flesh]; but rather they were denied by him, since they are legal advocates of death rather than of the truth" (*Smyrn.* 5.1).

In the LXX the Wisdom of Solomon favors *agnoein,* but the passages in the Torah about sins of ignorance ought not to be overlooked (LXX Lev 4:13; 5:18; and Aaron's cry on seeing the leprous Miriam, Num 12:11). In *T. Judah* 12.5 the dying patriarch remembers his sin with Tamar, whom he wanted to kill when she conceived, "because I did not understand what she did *(agnoōn de ho epoiēsen).*" In 19.3-4, after confessing his greed, he says, "But the God of my fathers, who is compassionate and merciful, pardoned me because I acted in ignorance *(en agnoiai epoiēsa).* The prince of error blinded me, and I was ignorant *(ēgnoēsa)* as a human being and as flesh I was corrupted by sins — until I learned of my own weakness after supposing myself to be invincible."

For *what I was doing, epoiēsa,* see Titus 3:5. The use of this verb to summarize Paul's activities as a persecutor is parallel with Acts 26:10 ("A thing which I also did in Jerusalem," *ho kai epoiēsa en Hierosolymois*); it is not used thus in the rest of the Paulines, and hereafter in the PE it refers to the action of one who is already a Christian.

*In my unbelief, en apistiai,* marks the only occurrence of *apistia* in the PE, and its use is anarthrous, as opposed to the four other Pauline usages (Rom 3:3; 4:20; 11:20, 23). The Ap. Frs. use *apistia* three times. Ignatius submits as a principle, "They who are fleshly are unable to do spiritual things, nor can the spiritual do fleshly things, just as the faith cannot do the things that pertain to unbelief *(ta tēs apistias),* nor unbelief *(apistia)* do the things that pertain to the faith" (*Eph.* 8.2). *Second Clement* 19.2 teaches, "Sometimes when we do evil things we do not know it *(ou ginōskomen)* because of the double-mindedness and unbelief *(tēn dipsychian kai apistian)* that dwell in our breasts." In Hermas, *Sim.* 9.15.3, *Apistia* is personified as a woman in black clothing with hair loose and shoulders bare. There is one use of *apistia* in the LXX, in the list of the vices of idolatrous pagans in Wis 14:25 (see the reading of A for 4 Macc 12:3).

14. *Still the grace of our Lord superabounded along with that faith and charity, which come from union with Christ Jesus.* For *the grace,* see Titus 1:4; 2:11; 3:7; for *of our Lord,* 1:2 above; for *faith and charity,* Titus 2:2 and 1:5 above.

The verb *hyperpleonazein,* translated by *superabounded,* is a neologism, unattested in secular Greek or the LXX before the first Christian century. One must wait to meet the verb again for Hermas and *Man.* 5.20.5 (of vicious spirits crowding a human vessel to overflowing). The prefix *hyper-* (as in the English *superpower*) adds superlative force to the verb here. The PE seldom use *hyper-* compounds (see 2:2 for *hyperochē;* 2 Tim 3:2 for *hyperēphanos*). In this they resemble the Lukan writings rather than Paul, who favored such compounds (see Furnish, AB *2 Cor,* pp. 205, 489-490).

15. *The Christian message, meant to be believed and worth welcoming wholeheartedly, is.* A handful of Western witnesses read *humanus sermo* at this point, as if they read a Greek text which had *anthrōpinos ho logos* (see 3:1[a]), i.e. "The word or message is humane or popular" (see Frede, *VL* 25.420-422; B. Metzger, *TCGNT,* pp. 639-640). J. K. Elliott, *Greek Text,* pp. 27-28, sides with some previous critics who have opted for *anthrōpinos* as the original text here. Since there is not a single Greek witness to this reading at this point, the relatively few Western Latin witnesses are very unlikely to transmit the original text.

See Titus 3:8a on *pistos ho logos,* here expanded with *and worth welcoming wholeheartedly, kai pasēs apodochēs axios,* lit. "and worthy of all welcome." *Axios* appears forty-one times in the NT, and half the Pauline uses are here in First Timothy, in 4:9 where this phrase recurs, as well as in 5:18; 6:1 (but not elsewhere in the PE). Luke-Acts employ *axios* fifteen times. The term appears in Ap. Frs., especially Ignatius and Hermas, but without a notable parallel to the usage here. Similarly the LXX hardly offers a parallel, though one of seven martyred sons speaks of "things worthy of astonishment that have occurred" and their mother is called "worthy of good memory *(mnēmēs agathēs axia)*" (2 Macc 7:18, 20).

*Apodochē,* "welcoming," which recurs in 4:9, is not attested otherwise in the LXX, the NT, or Ap. Frs. (on the cognate *apodektos,* see 2:3 and 5:4). Though the term has not been found in the papyri, it appears in forms of this phrase in inscriptions (where forms of *axios* regularly follow *apodochē,* as here) and in late koine literary works, secular as well as Jewish (Thucydides 4.81.2 contains, however, the earliest use of the term). Thus the man who was intent on God and goodness was for Philo "worthy of approval *(apodochēs axios)*" (*Fug.* 129; *Praem.* 13). Diogenes Laertius called Strato, the physicist and philosopher, "a man worthy of much approval *(pollēs tēs apodochēs axios)*" (*Lives* 5.64). See the further materials in Spicq, *Lexic.,* pp. 132-133; Knight, *Sayings,* pp. 22-30.

*Wholeheartedly* is a translation of an intensive *pas,* "all." The adjective could be heard in an extensive sense (i.e. as "worthy of universal acceptance" or approval by all believers), but the parallel phrase at 6:1, "deserving all esteem," as well as the use of *pas* in similar phrases in Titus 2:10, 15; 3:2, and 1 Tim 2:2, 11, etc., make the elative sense most likely (see the "great approval from the crowd" in *Ep. Arist.* 308). Similar formulas in the inscriptions also appear to be heard superlatively. On the parallel usage in Acts 24:3, see Knight, *Sayings,* p. 27.

*"Christ Jesus came into the world to save sinners."* The quotation marks represent the Greek *hoti recitativum* (in contrast to the causal uses that have just preceded; see BDF §397.5; 470.1). On the order of *Christ Jesus,* see Titus 1:1, 4. For *ēlthen,* "came," used only here of Christ in the PE, see Titus 3:12. The whole phrase *came into the world, eis ton kosmon,* which recurs in its mundane sense in 6:7, is a flash from the Johannine heaven (see John 1:9; 3:19; 9:39 ["this world"]; 11:27; 12:46; 16:28; 18:37). *Kosmos,* "world," also appears in the hymnic fragment quoted in 3:16. Of the 183 NT appearances of *kosmos* outside of the PE, over 100 occur in the Johannine literature and 44 in the other Paulines, although only of sin is it said that it "came into the world *(eis ton kosmon eisēlthen)*" (Rom 5:12). *First Clement* 3.4 writes of "the unrighteous and godless hatred *(zēlon)* by which also 'death came *(eisēlthen)* into the world,'" quoting Wis 2:24 (cf. 14:14). He also uses the mundane sense of the phrase when he says, "Let us take into account, brothers, of what material we were made, who we are, and with what nature we came into the world *(eisēlthamen eis ton kosmon),* from what kind of a dark grave he brought us into the world *(eisēgagen eis ton kosmon),* he who formed and created us, who prepared his benefits before we were born" (38.3). Though the LXX as well as Ap. Frs. use the term *kosmos* on other occasions, the only forms of the phrase "to come into the world" are those cited. The *Testaments of the Twelve Patriarchs* use variations on the phrase "Savior of the world" (see *T. Levi* 10.2; 14.2; 17.2; *T. Benjamin* 3.8), but not the phrase here in First Timothy.

In the phrase *to save sinners,* the verb *sōizein* appears 7 times in the PE, 22 times in the other Paulines, and 106 times in the NT. In the PE the subject of the verb, the actor, is God the Father, although here (and in 2 Tim 4:18), because of his relationship with the Father, Jesus takes on that role (see also the Notes on *hamartōloi* in 1:9 above). At this point it is important to note that, although *hamartōlos* is hardly found in secular Greek, it is frequent enough in the LXX, and sixty-eight out of ninety-four occurrences are in the Psalms (see Knight, *Sayings,* p. 42). There the person who lives by the revelation of the God of Israel is contrasted with *sinners* who do not (LXX Ps 1:1, 5). Often the worshipper begs to receive cleansing from his *hamartia/-ai* (see LXX Ps 50:4-5, 7, 11), but in no instance in the LXX, unlike the NT (see Comment), does a worshipper call himself an *hamartōlos.* In Ap. Frs., in *Man.* 4.2.3, the first grounds for Hermas's questioning are "because I am a sinner *(hoti hamartōlos eimi).*" Later he writes of "the pagans and the sinners" where the *ethnē* are those who do not recognize the one who created them and the *hamartōloi* are those who have sinned but have not repented (*Sim.* 4.4). In the *T. Benjamin,* after observing that "the sinless one will die for the sake of impious men" (3.8), the dying patriarch urges imitation of the good man who "is merciful to all, even though they may be sinners *(hamartōloi)*" (4.2).

*Among them I have first place.* Lit. "of whom the first *(prōtos)* am I," with an emphatic *egō* ending the Greek sentence. The adjectival *prōtos* appears in the following verse as well as in 2:13; 5:12; and 2 Tim 4:16. The adverbial form is used in 2:1 (governing the genitive); 3:10; 5:4, and 2 Tim 1:5; 2:6. There are 147 adjectival and adverbial uses otherwise in the NT. There are only 7 adjectival uses in the other Paulines, none followed by the genitive (contrast the usage of Luke-Acts, where there are 21 occurrences, among which half a dozen govern the genitive, e.g., Acts 16:12; 28:17). The term is used frequently in Ap. Frs. and the LXX. The most notable parallel is an antithetical one, i.e. those passages in the LXX Isaiah where the translators have Yahweh declare that he is the first God (41:4): "I am the first and I am after these things; besides me there is no god. Who is as I am?" (44:6), and especially 48:12: "I am first *(egō eimi prōtos)* and I am for eternity," and 43:25-26: "I am I am, the one who blots out your [sg.] crimes and I shall not remember [them]; but you are to recall [them] and we shall have a trial. You are to be first *(prōtos)* to tell your crimes, in order that you may be justified *(dikaiōthēis)*."

16. *But for this very reason mercy found me out.* See verse 13 for *but mercy found me out. Dia touto,* "for this very reason," recurs in 2 Tim 2:10, and in the Paulines otherwise nineteen times. There are only five uses of the phrase in Luke-Acts.

*so that Christ Jesus could evidence patience to the utmost.* Lit. "so that in me first Christ Jesus might show *(endeixētai)* all patience *(tēn hapasan makrothymian)*." See Titus 2:10 on *endeiknysthai.* This is the only use of *hapas* in the PE, and its sense of *the utmost* or "perfect" (Aquinas, *ad loc.*, has *perfectam*) is unparalleled in the NT (see BDF §275.3, 7; Spicq, *EP*, p. 345, on the daring use of the article here as in Gal 5:14; Acts 20:18; P Tebt 1.567 [late second century B.C.E. as cited in MM, p. 54]). Literary texts tend to favor *hapas* after a consonant for "considerations of euphony" (MM), and that tendency would adequately account for the form at this point in Timothy, though the PE, like Luke-Acts, do not demur to use *pas* after a consonant. In 2 Tim 4:2 the phrase *en pasēi makrothymiai,* "with the utmost patience," appears, and occurring in Acts 4:29 is *meta parrēsias pasēs,* "with the utmost freedom" (see also 5:23; 23:1).

Luke-Acts have twenty-three out of the other thirty-three NT uses of *hapas,* whereas the other Paulines have only one textually sure use (Eph 6:13, which is anarthrous). In Ap. Frs. forms of *hapas* seem to be characteristic of formulaic phrases in *Did.* 3.2, 3, 4, 5, 6 *(ek gar toutōn hapantōn);* and 5.2 *(apo toutōn hapantōn),* as well as in *First Clement* ("the ruler of all things," 8.2; 20.11; 33.2; 52.1, or "the creator of all things," 26.1; 59.2).

*Patience, makrothymia,* occurs again in 2 Tim 3:10 (of Paul) and 4:2 (of Timothy). It appears eleven times otherwise in the NT, of which seven are in the rest of the Paulines (not at all in the Gospels or Acts). Among Ap. Frs., *First*

*Clement* and Hermas favor *makrothymia* and its cognates. However, only Ign. *Eph.* 11.1 speaks of "the patience of God" (as in 1 Pet 3:20), though Hermas employs the adjective *makrothymos* when he says, "The Lord being patient wills that those be saved who received the baptismal calling through his Son" (*Sim.* 8.11.1; see also *Barn.* 3.6, where God is simply "the Patient One").

*Makrothymia,* lit. "long in temper *or* endurance," begins to appear about Menander's time in secular Greek, where it suggests accepting the inevitable. "Since you are a human being *(anthrōpos)* never ask from the gods an existence without pain but ask for great endurance *(makrothymian).* If you want to feel absolutely no pain, you're going to have to be a god or else straightway a corpse. Assuage ills by regarding the ills of others" (549K; Jaekel, *Sententiae, Comp.* 2.201-205 [p. 113]). The noun appears only five times in the LXX and (unlike the cognates) never of God, perhaps because of its connotation in secular usage. In *Ep. Arist.* 188 the Egyptian king is told that he will best safeguard his rule "by imitating the constant gentleness *(epieikes)* of God; for by exercising patience *(makrothymiai)* and dealing with those who deserve punishment more gently than they merit, you will turn them from evil and bring them to repentance *(eis metanoian).*" Though Philo does not use *makrothymia,* Josephus places the term on the lips of Titus as the latter incites his troops by pointing out "the patience *(makrothymia)* of the Jews and the tenacity with which they suffer adversity" (*War* 6.37). Still, the noun is not applied to God, and this remains the case in the *Testaments of the Twelve Patriarchs,* though *T. Gad* 4.7 does speak of "the spirit of love in patience *(en makrothymiai)* that works together with the law of God for the salvation of human beings."

*using me as a model of those who are going to believe in him for eternal life.* Lit. "for a model *(hypotypōsin)* of those who are going *(mellontōn)* to believe upon him *(pisteuein ep' autōi)* unto eternal life." *Hypotypōsis, model,* reappears in 2 Tim 1:13, there referring to Paul's words in his apostolic teaching as here it refers to his apostolic life. There is no other occurrence in the NT, Ap. Frs., or the LXX, though the one use in Philo, *Abr.* 71, is quite parallel to the sense here: "Great things are often known by their *hypotypōsei* as shown in smaller things and by looking at them the observer finds the scope of his vision infinitely enlarged" (see Galen in MM). The word begins to appear in secular Greek only in the first century B.C.E.; thus Strabo speaks once of the sketch or outline of his *Geography* (2.5.18). Quintilian describes a figure of speech called ocular or vivid illustration, adding that "Others give the name of *hypotypōsis* to any representation of things which is so expressed in words that it seems to be seen rather than heard" (*Institutio* 9.2.40).

The phrase *of those who are going to believe, tōn mellontōn pisteuein,* appears also in *1 Clem.* 42.4 (see also Hermas, *Man.* 4.3.3 *bis; Sim.* 9.30.3). The verb *mellein* recurs in the PE in 4:8; 6:19; and 2 Tim 4:1 with an eschatological resonance (see Excursus IV, "The Terminology for Life in the PE," in AB *Titus*). The verb appears 105 times otherwise in the NT, with 10 in the other Paulines (half in Romans) and 46 in Luke-Acts. The Ap. Frs. use *mellein* frequently and with eschatological connotations. Notable in connection with this passage is *Barn.* 5.9, "When he [the Lord] picked out his apostles who were going *(mellontas)* to proclaim his gospel, he chose those who were wicked above measure [lit. beyond all sin], to show that he did not come to call the righteous but sinners *(hamartolous).*" There are more than 40 uses of *mellein* in the LXX, with most of them in the latest books and half in the Maccabean literature.

*Mellontōn* takes the present infinitive as it usually does in the NT (84 times, BAGD), in this instance, *pisteuein ep' autōi.* Occurrences of *pisteuein, to believe,* number 6 in the PE, 48 in the other Paulines, 241 in the NT, with 48 in Luke-Acts. The present tense suggests "expectant confidence" and readiness to believe (R. Bultmann in *TDNT* 6.211, 214). Only here in the PE does *pisteuein* govern *ep' autōi,* a construction that is by no means common in the NT. Thus in the Lukan corpus only Luke 24:25 writes, ". . . to believe in all *(pisteuein epi pasin)* that the prophets had said," whereas *pisteuein epi* followed by the accusative appears in Acts 9:42; 11:17; 16:31; 22:19. In the rest of the Paulines there are only two instances, Rom 9:33 and 10:11 (not 4:18), but on both occasions the phrase in the dative appears in the citation of LXX Isa 28:16 (a text also cited by 1 Pet 2:6; otherwise in the LXX the construction with *pisteuein epi* is with the accusative, and that only in Wis 12:2). The *T. Dan* 5.13 has, "The one who believes in him *(ho pisteuon ep' autōi)* will reign in truth in the heavens." *First Clement* 34.4 writes that the Lord "exhorts us who believe in him *(pisteuontas . . . ep' autōi)* from the whole heart, not to be lazy. . . ." The meaning of the phrase with the dative is equivalent to *pisteuein epi* (or *eis*) with the accusative, common enough in the Paulines (Rom 4:5, 24; 10:14; Gal 2:16; Phil 1:29) and in Acts, as is noted above (see BDF §187.6; Moule, *Idiom,* p. 50).

*Eternal life, zōē aiōnios,* occurs five times in the Paulines and forty-three times in the NT (five occurrences in Luke-Acts), and in its four usages in the PE is the privileged phrase for designating life in its specifically Christian sense. Its use here appears to derive from the sacramental catechesis of Titus 3:4-8a.

17. *So to the king of eternity.* Though *king, basileus,* appears 115 times in the NT, it is infrequently applied to God as it is here and in 6:15, where he is "the king of those who act as kings" (see Matt 5:35; Rev 15:3). When Jesus is called *king,* it is with full knowledge that the title was politically a ticking bomb (see Luke 19:38; 23:2-3, 37-38; Acts 17:7).

*Basileus* refers to secular rulers in 2:2 (as it does in its one use in the other Paulines, 2 Cor 11:32, of the ethnarch "of Aretas, the king"). Luke uses the term for Herod the Great (Luke 1:5), for the ancient kings of the people of God (10:24, where Matt 13:17 has "righteous men"; see *SFG* §181), for a parabolic reference to the cost of conflicts between kings (14:31), for "the kings of the gentiles who lord it over them" (22:25) as well as "the kings of the earth . . . and the rulers" from LXX Ps 2:2, whom the praying congregation of Acts 4:26 identifies with Herod Antipas and Pontius Pilate. In Acts 7:10, 18 the pharaoh is "king of Egypt" and his successor, "another king." In Acts 9:15 the newly converted Saul is described by Jesus as "a chosen instrument of mine to carry my name before the gentiles and kings (*basileōn;* see Luke 21:12) and the sons of Israel." Herod Agrippa I is designated as king in Acts 12:1, 20 (as is Herod Agrippa II throughout Acts 25 and 26), where it is notable that the Roman emperor is *sebastos,* "Augustus" (25:21, 25; see 27:1), or *Kaisar,* "Caesar" (Acts 25, passim). In Acts 13:21-22 Saul and David receive the title *king* from Paul.

The usage of *First Clement* resembles that of Luke-Acts. Regularly forms of *basileus* designate pagan and Israelite kings (4.10, 13; 12.2, 4; 32.2; 55.1), once even the emperor (37.3). In the great concluding prayer of the letter, however, God is addressed, as here in the PE, as "king of the ages," *basileu tōn aiōnōn* (61.2). The single appearance of *basileus* in Hermas is when he speaks of "mercy from the great king" (*para tou basileōs tou megalou; Vis.* 3.9.8, with a title found in LXX Pss 46:3; 47:3; 94:3). *Didache* 14.3 cites "for I am the great king *(basileus megas),* says the Lord," from LXX Mal 1:14. Though *Barnabas* twice uses the term of secular kings in alluding to LXX Dan 7:8, 24 and LXX Isa 45:1, he once uses *basileus* of God in adducing LXX Isa 33:17, "You shall see the king with glory" (11.5).

In contrast to the usage of the early Christian documents, Palestinian Judaism and the Hebrew Bible (thus Isa 6:5; 33:22) as well as the LXX and the Alexandrian Jewish tradition apparently had little scruple about applying the term *king* to the God of Israel (see LXX Pss 5:3; 73:12; 83:4 with the citations above, as well as those in Spicq, *Supp. Lexic.*, pp. 88-98). Though the *Testaments of the Twelve Patriarchs* regularly use forms of *basileus* for pagan kings as well as those of Israel, it is only *T. Benjamin* 10.7 that writes of God as "the king of the heavens" before whom the patriarchs and their progeny will prostrate themselves at the final resurrection. Notable also is Philo, *Mig. Abr.* 146: "For it is better to walk in the middle of the road, the really 'Royal Road' [see Num 20:17] which God, the great and only king *(ho megas kai monos basileus theos),* laid out as a very attractive place to stay for souls that love virtue."

*the king of eternity.* Lit. "the king of the ages *(tōn aiōnōn).*" The phrase appears in important MSS of the great "prayer of rejoicing" in the LXX Tobit, commanding praise for "the king of the ages" (13:7, 11; see Hanhart et al., Göttingen LXX, pp. 168-171), but nowhere else in the Greek Bible. There are Hebrew and Aramaic precedents for the title in the MT of Jer 10:10 as well as in the solemn oath of 1QapGen 2.4, 7, "by the king of all ages," *bmlk kwl ʿ[lmym]* (cf. Fitzmyer, *Gen. Apoc.*, pp. 52-53, 84, with the prayer of 1QapGen 21.2 calling upon "the Lord of the ages," *mrh ʿlmyʾ*, pp. 66-67, 144). A fragmentary phrase from an Apocalypse of Lamech, "before the Lord of the age," *qwdm mrh ʿlmʾ*, appears in 1Q 20.2.5 (DJD 1.87). The Greek *Enoch* 9.4 may describe God not only as "Lord of lords and God of gods" but also as "King of ages," and it surely has its hero say in 12.3, "And I, Enoch, began to bless the Lord of majesty and the King of the ages *(tōi basilei tōn aiōnōn)*" (the original Aramaic is missing at these points; see Milik, *Enoch*, pp. 171-172, 190, 345, 348, suggesting *mlk ʿlmyʾ*).

For *aiōn*, here *of eternity* and below in this verse *for all eternity*, lit. "for the ages of ages," see Titus 1:2; 2:12, and Excursus IV, "The Terminology for Life in the PE," in AB *Titus*.

*the immortal, invisible, only God. Immortal, aphthartos,* lit. "incorruptible." Although *aphtharsia* (2 Tim 1:10) and its cognates cluster in the Petrine and Pauline letters in the NT, only here does the noun occur in the PE, their lone use of the adjective "immortal, incorruptible" being in this doxology for a divine attribute. Six out of the other seven NT uses of the adjective do not apply to God and are in Romans and First Corinthians, in Second Peter, and in the shorter ending of Mark, about "the holy and immortal proclamation of eternal salvation." Similarly Ap. Frs. and the LXX do not describe God as *aphthartos*, whereas Philo does so in *Quod Deus imm.* 26 ("the immortal and blessed [*makarios*] One"), *Mos.* 171 ("the immortal and uncreated One"), and *Sacr.* 63, 101 ("the Passover of the uncreated and immortal One," "the uncreated and immortal and unchangeable and holy and solely blessed [*monou makariou*] God"). Josephus takes to task the Epicureans for refusing to believe "that all things are directed by a blessed and immortal being *(hypo tēs makarias kai aphthartou . . . ousias)*" (*Ant.* 10.278; see 3.88 of God's voice).

*Invisible, aoratos,* appears three times otherwise in the NT. Romans 1:20 uses the term of the unseen things that pertain to God, saying, "Ever since the creation of the world his *aorata*, namely his everlasting power and deity, have been clearly perceived in the things that have been made." In the great hymn of Colossians, Christ is "the image of the invisible God," "for in him all things were created, in heaven and on earth, things visible and invisible *(ta aorata)*." The latter are then specified in terms of the angelic ministers (1:15-16; see Ign. *Trall.* 5.2; *Rom.* 5.3; *Smyrn.* 6.1). Hebrews 11:27 uses this word when describing Moses, "unafraid of the anger of the king *(basileōs)*, for he endured as seeing him who is invisible" (*ton . . . aoraton*, i.e. God as king or possibly the Christ of v. 26).

*Aoratos* appears more frequently in Ap. Frs., particularly in Ignatius, who applies the term as noted above and to both the Father (*Magn.* 3.2) and the Son (*Pol.* 3.2), as well as to insight into the things of God (*Pol.* 2.2). *Barnabas* 11.4 cites the word from LXX Isa 45:3 (of the treasures God has hidden for Cyrus).

Hermas writes of "the invisible power of the Master" (*Vis.* 3.3.5; see the *v.l.* at 1.3.4). A notable parallel occurs in *2 Clem.* 20.5, where the doxology is "to the only, invisible God *(tōi monōi theōi aoratōi)*" (see *Diogn.* 7.2).

Whereas the early Christian documents evince no hesitation about describing God as *aoratos,* the same cannot be said of the LXX, where its three uses are never of God (see above as well as LXX Gen 1:2 of the earth as "unseen" [= *tohu*] when God creates and 2 Macc 9:5 of "the incurable and unseen blow" with which God struck Antiochus Epiphanes). Similarly, the *Testaments of the Twelve Patriarchs* use the adjective only of "wars visible and invisible" (*T. Reuben* 6.12) and of "invisible spirits" (*T. Levi* 4.1).

Josephus only once (out of eight uses of *aoratos*) applies the term to God, and then indirectly, when he describes the human soul *(psychē)* as "remaining, like God himself, invisible from human eyes" (*War* 7.345-346; in 347-348 the soul is also *aphtharton* and possesses *athanasia,* "immortality"). Philo frequently applies *aoratos* to God (thus *Leg. alleg.* 290, 310, 318; further references in Spicq, *EP,* p. 347, and W. Michaelis, *TDNT* 5.368-370), and he repeatedly links this invisibility with the covenant command that the God of Israel is to have no man-made image for his worship.

This God is *the only God,* using *monos* as in the doxology at 6:15 (the one other use in the PE is for Luke in 2 Tim 4:11). There are dozens of occurrences of this adjective in the NT, but it is otherwise applied to God only in the doxologies of Rom 16:27 and Jude 25 (cf. v. 4 and Rev 15:4 as well as Luke 5:21 and John 5:44; 17:3). There is a similar pattern in the usage of Ap. Frs., where the doxological prayers of *1 Clem.* 43.6; 59.3-4; and *2 Clem.* 20.5 (cited above) are especially worthy of note (see also *1 Clem.* 61.3; Ign. *Eph.* 9.2; Hermas, *Sim.* 5.7.3).

In the LXX *monos* is used of God (or the Lord) over a dozen times, usually in contexts of prayer and confession (see 1 Kgdms 7:3-4; Esther 4:17[1]; LXX Ps 85:10; Isa 37:16, 20; Dan 3:45; 2 Macc 1:24-25 ["who are the only king"]; 7:37; 4 Macc 5:24). Only in *T. Joseph* 6.5 do the *Testaments of the Twelve Patriarchs* apply *monos* to God, in the phrase "to the Lord alone."

*are the honor and glory for all eternity. Amen.* On *glory, doxa,* see Titus 2:13. *For all eternity* is lit. "for the ages of the ages," *eis tous aiōnas tōn aiōnōn,* which was analyzed at the beginning of this verse.

*Honor, timē,* occurs in a doxology with *kratos aiōnion,* "might eternal," in 6:16. The "double pay" of 5:17 represents *diplēs timēs* (see *1 Clem.* 1.3; 55.2); the masters in 6:1 deserve "all esteem," *pasēs timēs,* which includes courteous consideration. In 2 Tim 2:20-21 *timē* appears in an unusual adjectival phrase describing a vessel "for a noble purpose," *eis timēn* (see the Notes on this passage for Rom 9:21 and Ignatius), whose use or function makes it "honorable," i.e. an object of admiring attention, or dishonorable, i.e. *eis atimian,* an object of disgusted abhorrence. *Timē* appears thirty-five times otherwise in the NT. A dozen of these are in the other Paulines (six in Romans), a half dozen in Acts (none doxological). The term is heard doxologically when coupled with *doxa* (as here) or with similar words.

The phrases *honor and glory,* as here, and *glory and honor* appear (sometimes within a longer list) in the NT. Only in 2 Pet 1:17 does *honor and glory* recur, however, as the author describes Jesus receiving *timē kai doxa* from God in the transfiguration. The reference is surely to the clothing "glistening, intensely white" (see Mark 9:3; *SFG* §161) which Peter saw on that occasion, and the phrase is linked with the references to royal apparel to be noted below. In Rev 5:12-13 the phrase appears in longer lists (along with *plouton,* "wealth") which are part of the acclaimations offered to the Lamb.

Hebrews 2:7, 9 applies the variant order of the phrase *glory and honor* to Jesus when the author cites LXX Ps 8:6, answering its question, "What is man?" by saying, "With glory and honor you crowned him." Paul takes this form of the phrase up in a different context in Rom 2:7, of human beings seeking for "glory and honor and immortality," and then at 2:10 of "glory and honor and peace for every one who does good." Elsewhere in the NT, First Peter writes of authentic faith redounding "to praise and glory and honor at the revelation of Jesus Christ" (1:7). Revelation 4:9 describes the worship of the living creatures as giving "glory and honor and thanksgiving" to the enthroned and living God, and at 4:11 their song is quoted as "Worthy are you, our Lord and God, to receive glory and honor and power *(dynamin).*" The individual terms recur in the list of seven contained in the doxology to God and to the Lamb in 7:12. Only at Rev 21:26 does the phrase again stand alone and not as part of a longer list. At that point, through the gates of the new Jerusalem, the seer beholds the kings of the earth who "bring into it the glory and honor of the nations." The reference is to the precious metals, jewels, and fabrics treasured by human beings.

Only Hermas among Ap. Frs. writes of the "exceeding honor and great glory" which the celibate have "with the Lord" (*Man.* 4.4.2), but the variant order of the phrase *glory and honor* appears in contexts of prayer in *1 Clem.* 45.8; 61.1, 2 (where "authority" is added; see 64.1 for "glory and majesty, might [*kratos*] and honor" and 65.2 for "glory, honor, might and majesty, an eternal throne").

In the LXX *timē* appears several times with *doxa.* In LXX Pss 28:1 and 95:7 the phrase appears in the form "Bring glory and praise to the Lord," an acclamation which has a cultic setting. In both contexts the rich vestments of the liturgy are noted. The link with precious clothing appears also in the devastating irony of LXX Job 40:10 where the Lord challenges Job, "Clothe yourself, too, with glory and honor" (see 37:22). The Spartan letter to Simon, the high priest, and to the elders, priests, and people, declares that the Greeks had heard of their "glory and honor" (1 Macc 14:21), and the reference seems to be to the splendor of the cult over which Simon presided in the theocracy that he headed. In 2 Macc 5:16 the phrase certainly refers to the precious, sacred vessels of the Jerusalem temple and its other offerings that Antiochus Epiphanes confiscated (see 5:21; 9:16).

In the preceding instances the LXX authors wrote *doxa kai timē;* only twice does the LXX employ *timē kai doxa.* In LXX Exod 28:2 the Lord directs Moses: ". . . you shall make holy garments for Aaron, your brother, for honor and glory"; then in LXX Dan 2:37, when Daniel begins his interpretation of Nebuchadnezzar's dream, he says, "You, O King, the king of kings, to whom the God of heaven has given the rule and the kingdom and the might and the honor and the glory, . . . you are the head of gold." This language reminds one of the crown of glory and honor in Ps 8:5 and that golden headpiece which is the apparel proper to a king.

Philo regularly uses variants on *doxa kai timē* in a pejorative sense when he lists "wealth and glory and honors and offices and all such things" (*Det.* 33; see 122; *Cher.* 117; *Post.* 112, 117; *Gig.* 15). Josephus in his few uses of the phrase never attributes glory and honor to God, but the phrase appears always in contexts that suggest royal wealth and splendor (see *Ant.* 6.200; 10.266 [*timē te kai doxa*]; 11.217 [cf. 254]; 12.118).

A transliterated Hebrew *amēn* (as in LXX 1 Chron 16:36; 2 Esd 15:13; 18:6 [= MT Neh 5:13; 8:6]) is suffixed to the preceding doxology. No other Semitic word appears so often in the NT (130 times). In the PE it will recur at the end of the doxologies of 6:16 and 2 Tim 4:18. In Ap. Frs. *amēn* is common in the doxologies of *First Clement* (32.4; 38.4; 43.6, 45.7, 8 *s.v.l.;* 50.7; 58.2; 61.3; 64.1; 65.2). Otherwise it is certainly attested only in the doxology of *2 Clem.* 20.5 and the conclusion of the great eucharistic prayer of *Did.* 10.6. In the LXX *amēn* appears scarcely 5 times outside of the instances noted above (1 Esd 9:47 *s.v.l.;* Tob 8:8; 14:15 *s.v.l.;* 3 Macc 7:23; and in the concluding doxology of 4 Macc 18:24). Even in the MT *'amen* appears only a couple of dozen times, of which half are in Deut 27:15-26 (see A. Jepsen, *TDOT* 1.320-323).

## ♦ COMMENT

1:12-13. *I give thanks to Christ Jesus, our Lord, who put his strength in me because he regarded me as trustworthy and placed me in his ministry, a man who was formerly a blasphemer and a persecutor and insanely arrogant. But mercy found me out because I did not know what I was doing in my unbelief.* Beginning with these verses and extending through verse 17, a thanksgiving prayer is heard on Paul's lips. The mention of "the gospel I was entrusted with" at the end of the preceding section reminds one of a characteristic Pauline note in the context of his thanksgiving prayers in the earlier letters (see O'Brien, "Thanksgiving," pp. 148-152). The opening Greek sentence, with its often repeated *m* and *n* sounds, is addressed directly to *Christ Jesus* as *Lord,* thanking him for Paul's conversion and apostolate. It extends through verse 14. The body of the prayer consists of a second sentence, occupying verses 15-16. This opens with the formal citation of *the Christian message* in 15a, followed by its application to Paul. Then the reason for this application (v. 16; *dia touto . . . hina*) to the past event of Paul's conversion is discerned in the use that *Christ Jesus* is going to make of that event in bringing the invitation to faith to all humankind. The conclusion of the prayer occupies a third sentence (v. 17) containing a great doxology to God as *king.*

The appearance of a thanksgiving prayer at this point in the PE is surprising on several counts. The Letter to Titus had no such prayer at all; here in First Timothy it appears dislocated, from the point of view of the normal positioning of the thanksgiving prayer in the ancient epistolary genre as well as in other letters of Paul. When the other Paulines use a thanksgiving prayer, it occurs immediately after the opening address and greeting (the positioning it has below in 2 Tim 1:3-14). Perhaps each of the letters in this collection is thus being formally differentiated from its neighbors. If Pauline memoranda of two decades previous do lie behind the PE and if Titus was originally a familiar letter of recommendation (whose traditional structure does not include a thanksgiving; see Titus 3:12), then the author of Titus as we have it respected the form of the note that he had used to frame his text. The previous epistolary material that has found a place in Second Timothy is formally of a different structure from Titus and seems to have emerged from circumstances that resemble the ones which surrounded the writing of other Pauline letters (see the thanksgiving in Philem 4-7). The conventional positioning of the epistolary thanksgiving in Second Timothy appears to corroborate this view. First Timothy resembles Titus insofar as most of the text does not use previous epistolary materials. Yet the text is directed to a different member of the Pauline entourage and through him to different congregations of believers. The "dislocated" epistolary thanksgiving thus serves to remind the reader of the special character of this central letter among the PE.

A closer look at the language of the prayer shows that there is hardly any literary attempt to link up the words of this prayer with those used previously by the apostle in such contexts. Though the texts turn about the concept of thanksgiving, only the PE use the expression *charin echein;* though the use of the causal *hoti* in verse 12 is typical of one of the Pauline forms of the thanksgiving prayer (Schubert, *Form,* pp. 179-183, on Type 1b in the more impersonal, formal epistles), all of the other Pauline thanksgivings (including the one in Second Timothy) are addressed to God the Father, not *Christ Jesus, our Lord,* as here. The Pauline thanksgivings in general have proved upon further analysis to be more Jewish and liturgical than one would have suspected from P. Schubert's emphatic concentration upon their Hellenistic and epistolary character (see J. M. Robinson, "Historicality," p. 149 n. 29; "Hodayot-formel," pp. 201-213; Rigaux, *Letters,* pp. 120-122). The opening phrase of gratitude takes one back to the opening phrases in ancient Jewish daily prayers (see Baumstark, *Liturgy,* p. 64), and the ultimately biblical roots of its form have been uncovered by J. P. Audet, "Bénédiction," pp. 375-393 (note the careful critique of Ledogar, *Acknowledgment,* pp. 121-124, 165-166), as he discusses the pattern taken by "those spontaneous expressions of adoration and awe uttered by individuals who face some miraculous, marvelous occurrence in which the presence of God is experienced" (Heinemann, *Prayer,* p. 82, see p. 238; and Greenberg, *Prayer,* pp. 30-37). The most archaic pattern does not demand set words, but it does consist of two recognizable elements: a relatively fixed proclamatory opening or introduction addressed to God, including titles affixed to his name; then a content clause rehearsing the particulars and circumstances of the wonderful divine acts which the grateful worshipper has witnessed on his behalf (this statement of motive becomes the "anamnesis" in the later development of the form). A law court setting appears to be presupposed by the pattern of the oldest Jewish prayers of thanksgiving, for such prayers were simultaneously prayers of acknowledgment of guilt and confession of sins as well as of an obligation to gratitude and praise (see Heinemann, *Prayer,* pp. 196, 206). Though Schubert is correct in noting that the Pauline thanksgiving had a critical function in introducing a given letter whose occasion and content it announced (*Form,* pp. 26-27), the Jewish elements in the form considerably enriched its meaning.

Thus here in First Timothy the form of the thanksgiving prayer enables the reader to see the missionary purpose and contents of the epistle from the perspective of the risen Jesus' conversion of and apostolic mission for Paul. The Jewish and biblical pattern of thankful proclamation of the divine name puts the name of Jesus in place of God's name in the relatively fixed opening of the prayer, then the basis for this grateful acknowledgment is declared to be the miraculous, historical intervention in the sinful existence of Paul of this Christ, risen from the dead and Lord of the church. Even the traces of the old law court setting can be traced in the apologia for the divine mercy based on Paul's former ignorance, and that setting in turn reminds one that the prayer stands in the text as "a statement about God rather than a speech made to him" and thus is meant to be a grateful public testimony to the grace of the Pauline conversion and apostolate, a witness meant "for the greater glory of God" (Greenberg, *Prayer,* p. 32).

The quotation of *the Christian message, meant to be believed,* in verse 15 is parallel to the formulaic introduction of explicit quotations from the OT in the liturgical prayers of the synagogue (Baumstark, *Liturgy,* pp. 64-65; see "Hellenistic Synagogal Prayers" from about 150 C.E. and thereafter, culled from *Apostolic Constitutions* 7 and 8 in Charlesworth, *OT Pseud.* 2.677-697). *The message* itself is cited almost as if it were a prophetic text that had found its fulfillment in Paul and all those whom his apostolate would touch (see Audet, "Bénédiction," pp. 385-386 n. 2, remarking that the citation of prophetic promises is part of the climate appropriate to a thanksgiving prayer). Granted Audet's distinction of the thanksgiving properly speaking from the prayer that accompanies it, one may be encountering here a further development of such a prayer, in which an eschatological thrust has been built into the anamnesis, a thrust that includes, as here (v. 16), the community's hope for that *eternal life* which the risen Jesus has revealed to them through the Pauline gospel (see Audet, "Bénédiction," pp. 395-396).

In Audet's analysis of thanksgivings he detected in the later development of the form a third literary element, the doxology or eulogy which served to frame the anamnesis by returning to a note of praise on the theme which the opening benediction had introduced. This form appears to have influenced the earliest Jewish Christian liturgical thanksgivings (with reservations noted in the Comment on 2:1), but it was not the line of development taken in later Jewish prayers (see Heinemann, *Prayer,* pp. 85-86). The closing sentence of the thanksgiving in First Timothy (v. 17) constitutes formally the doxological inclusion that Audet has described. Certain turns of phrase, moreover, are precisely those of pre-Christian Jewish synagogue usage (thus, *for all eternity;* see Baumstark, *Liturgy,* p. 11). The one God of Israel is now addressed as king, just as the initial thanksgiving had expressed gratitude to Jesus as Lord.

As one reviews the generous development of the three formal elements in this thanksgiving prayer in First Timothy, one recognizes, with Audet ("Bénédiction," p. 379), not only the form of a liturgical (as distinguished from an individual) prayer for grateful blessing but also a distinct hymnic character in the rather elaborately articulated composition, a character about which much more will be said on 3:16. This is not to say that 1 Tim 1:12-17 ever was part of a liturgy or sung as a hymn; it is to submit that the liturgical and hymnic practices of a first-century Jewish Christian congregation influenced the composition of this passage.

With the qualifications which the form of a thanksgiving prayer implies, a closer analysis of the content of verses 12-14 becomes feasible. Both the form and the language indicate that the text would have been heard as a proclamation of gratitude for a particular, historical divine wonder worked by the risen Jesus, the conversion and apostolate of Paul. If Paul himself did not pen the text, where did the author of this prayer obtain his data? Otherwise in the NT Paul himself refers a few times to his conversion experience; Acts, a generation later, recounts the story three times. Similarly, there are references in Paul's letters to the Corinthians, to the Galatians, and to the Philippians as well as in Acts to his persecution of Christians before his conversion (see Hultgren, "Persecutions," pp. 97-111, for this and some of the following). It is notable that Paul himself does not use the phrase *who put his strength in me* for his conversion experience whereas Luke does use a form of it in describing the results of that encounter. As Hultgren has shown, Paul and Acts are in basic agreement when they describe Paul's activities as a persecutor as beginning in Judea and as directed against Jews who believed in and proclaimed a crucified and risen Messiah. Paul's concept of persecution, however, is rather milder than that of Acts, which suggests a legalized and systematic violence and bloodshed: "Saul still snorting out murderous threats against the Lord's disciples" (Acts 9:1).

The circumstantial, schematic contrast of the one *who was formerly a blasphemer and a persecutor and insanely arrogant* with what resulted from the intervention of the risen Lord's power ought to be read, as the almost hymnic prayer form indicates (see the prayer of Paul in *Acts of Peter,* chap. 2 [Vouaux, *Pierre,* p. 240; Hennecke and Schneemelcher, *NT Apoc.* 2.281]), as a poetic confession of gratitude from the biblical tradition, which puts the Lord's choice into the sharpest possible contrast with the whole previous existence of the subject. The form alone would dictate some circumspection in disengaging the events of Paul's life, whether as a Jew or as a Christian, from the rhetorical contrasts used here. A thanksgiving prayer is not an autobiographical note or a psychological case report. The author (if he is not the apostle) is not embroidering the Pauline notices of a generation previous with terms which those notices did not employ; he is not even taking up in systematic fashion the language of the notices of Acts; he is adopting the heightened concept of persecution that was current in the second Christian generation and expressing it solemnly (note the polysyndeton) in progressively broader, black brush strokes, which move from insulting words through judicial harassment to the whole internal attitude or stance of overbearing insolence from which the words and acts had issued. All serve to highlight the dazzling intervention of divine mercy that turned Paul into an apostle, an intervention that has been condensed into the single point of the participial *who put his strength in me,* with its reference to the power of the risen Jesus which the Paul of history was convinced sustained him always and on every occasion in his apostolic ministry.

From that powerful personal intervention and encounter proceeded the ministry of the apostle Paul. It was the very reason that the Lord Jesus *regarded me as trustworthy and placed me in his ministry.* The Greek stylistic trick of subordinating the principal action (*themenos* here) to a verb that expresses one aspect of that action *(hēgēsato)* throws the emphasis upon the free will, initiative, and choice of the risen Lord. "The grace *(charis)* of our Lord" (v. 14), including the *charis* of *his ministry*, was unearned, unsought, even undesired by Paul. Yet this most unlikely and unlikable man the Lord considered *as trustworthy*, as one to whom he was going to entrust his gospel (see v. 11), who is to be believed, who transmits "the Christian message meant to be believed" (v. 15). Thus the faithful Lord (see 2 Tim 2:13) has created a faithful apostle with a faithful message (see Titus 1:9) which his co-workers are in their turn to entrust to faithful men (see 2 Tim 2:2) who are to teach others. God entrusts his gospel (v. 11) to those whom he has made *trustworthy;* their own merits or demerits do not determine the Lord's choice.

With the phrase *placed me in his ministry*, the verb implies the divine institution of the Pauline apostolate which is described as a *ministry*, a term which is programmatic for the letters to Timothy, whose central concern is the origin, functions, and goals of ministries in the churches and the way in which they relate to the apostolic ministry, particularly that of Paul. Since there is no question that for the PE Paul is emphatically an apostle (see 1:1; Titus 1:1-3), it is notable that at this point where the conversion-vocation encounter is being gratefully acknowledged (and formally the occasion and content of the following correspondence are being telegraphed), Paul's appointment is called one for a *ministry*, and only at 2:7 is it specified as the appointment of "a herald and apostle." In the PE *ministry, diakonia*, is the generic term for fulfilling a ministerial task, official or not. Thus it is in 2 Tim 4:5, in the exhortation to Timothy: "Keep calm, in every sense; accept being wronged; do the work of one who announces the gospel; carry out fully the ministry *(tēn diakonian)* that is yours." Here the definite article as well as the parallel with performing the task of an evangelist indicates that Timothy's *ministry* is conceived of as both related to and yet distinct from that to which Paul had been appointed. When 2 Tim 4:11 (which might belong to a Pauline dispatch from the sixties of the first Christian century) tells Timothy, "Pick up Mark and bring him along with you, for he can be helpful to me in my *ministry*," the final phrase is identical with 1 Tim 1:12 and probably refers to Paul's own apostolic ministry in which Mark is to collaborate (for another possible sense, see the commentary there).

Because for the correspondence with Timothy *ministry* is both apostolic and capable of being shared with others, it is not surprising to read of Timothy in 4:6, "When you suggest matters such as the preceding to your brothers, Timothy, you will be a fine minister *(diakonos)* of Christ Jesus, yourself nourished on the words of the faith and of that fine instruction with which you are quite familiar." More intriguing is the fact that the noun *diakonos* also designates men who along with (and apparently subordinate to) the bishop have a recognized function for and office in the church (see 3:8, 12). The verb *diakonein*, "give diaconal service," designates the activities of these *diakonoi* in 3:10, 13. In that context it is difficult to isolate what specific activities are meant. However, when the verb is used of the services of Epaphroditus to Timothy (and the church) in Ephesus (2 Tim 1:18), it seems to mean the material ministrations and human care for other Christians (the apostle, his co-worker, the members of the congregation).

Epaphroditus probably was never a *diakonos* in the technical sense in which the PE use that term, but it seems probable that these later *diakonoi* (and their women counterparts, as well as the widows) had become the official administrators of the charity of the churches. This appears to be borne out by the way in which Luke-Acts (which never use the term *diakonos*) describe *diakonia* and use the verb *diakonein*. In the Third Gospel the first three uses of the verb (Luke 4:39; 8:3; 10:40) and the only use of the noun (10:40) refer to the ministrations of women to Jesus and his followers in matters of meals and money. In Luke 12:37 the returning master (i.e. Jesus the judge) girds himself, seats the servants who have watched for him, and waits on *(diakonēsei)* them at table. In the parable of Luke 17:8 the servant at the end of his day's work is still to gird himself, prepare a meal, and serve food and drink to his master. In Jesus' sayings on leadership at his last meal with the Twelve, the apparent contradiction in Luke 22:26-27 is resolved as the disciples are taught that they are all to wait on one another, to minister to one another, as Jesus had waited on them and provided for their food and drink. On these passages, see Fitzmyer, AB *Lk*, pp. 549, 696-698, 892-894, 988, 1146, 1417-1418.

In Acts the first *diakonia* to be mentioned — and it is emphatically identified as "*this* service" — is the *diakonia* of apostleship (*apostolēs;* Acts 1:17, 25) into which a qualified man (note the *andron* of 1:21) can be inducted and thus be "enrolled with the eleven apostles" (1:26). In Acts 6:1-2, 4 the noun and verb are applied to the daily distribution of food at table to the Christian widows (see 1 Tim 5:9-16), a *diakonia* that the Twelve judge is not to be theirs but ought to be entrusted to another body of seven men (note again *andras* in 6:3). The Twelve are said to have called their *diakonia* (and apostolate) "service of the word *(logou)*" of God, which may refer not only to their proclamation to unbelievers that Jesus was the Christ, according to the Scriptures, but also to their interpretation and explanation of these Scriptures to baptized believers (Gerhardsson, *Memory,* pp. 222-225, 240-245, 330-332). They serve the Scriptures to people who are hungry for the word as their collaborators are to serve food and drink to the helpless poor, whatever their national origin. In Acts 11:29; 12:25 the noun *diakonia* refers to the famine-relief collection that Paul and Barnabas brought to the Jerusalem church. After the verb is used to refer to Timothy and Erastus as among Paul's assistants (Acts 19:22), the noun appears on Paul's lips as he describes "the ministry *(tēn diakonian)* which I received from our Lord Jesus, to testify to the gospel of the grace of God" (Acts 20:24; see 20:32, on "the word of his grace"). When Acts 21:19 narrates Paul's report to the Jerusalem church of all "that God had done among the gentiles through his ministry *(dia tēs diakonias autou),*" the noun appears for the last time in this work, in which Paul has had not only a *diakonia* like that envisioned for the Seven in bringing material aid to the hungry but also a *ministry* and apostolate like that which had fallen to the Twelve. Their "ministry of the word" is practically equivalent to a ministry which witnesses to "the gospel of the grace of God" to pagans. In Acts 14:3-4 the Lord's "witnessing to the word of his grace" among the new converts from paganism is also the context where Paul and Barnabas are first called "apostles" by Acts (see Haenchen, *Acts,* p. 420, who has pointed out that the language of the passage is, with reason, parallel to the description of the twelve Jerusalem apostles in Acts 5:12). The usage of the PE coincides substantially with Luke-Acts in the use of *diakonia* and *diakonein;* an advance beyond Luke-Acts appears in the introduction of the *diakonos* in the letters to Timothy.

Not too much ought to be made of the coincidence, however, for the rest of the Paulines also use *diakonia* of Paul's apostolate to the pagans (Rom 11:13), of his ministry of material relief to the Jerusalem church (Rom 15:25 [verb], 31), and of a variety of specialized works for the church (Rom 12:7; 1 Cor 12:5; 16:15; see also Eph 4:12; Col 4:17). For the dozen uses of the noun, *diakonia,* and three of the verbs in Second Corinthians, see Furnish, AB *2 Cor,* pp. 202, 204, with his further references there.

*But mercy found out* a Paul whose outrageous insolence is depicted as dominating his whole previous existence. He was *hybristēs,* and the term recalls the cluster of words that defined the tragic flaw which the Greek world understood as utterly sinful and ultimately totally destructive of a human being (recall the devastating irony of Creon's condemnation of Antigone's *hybris* in Sophocles, *Antigone* 480-485). The LXX considered *hybristēs* an apt translation for prophetic and sapiential passages that scored the insolent and overbearing. The Pauline uses of the cognates (1 Thess 2:2; 2 Cor 12:10) seem somewhat tamer with their allusions to the legal persecutions and insults which he and his colleagues underwent, "the insolence of office and the spurns that patient merit of the unworthy takes." The usage of the cluster in Luke-Acts shows occasionally some flashes of the violence, even murderous violence, that *hybristēs* has here in First Timothy (see Luke 18:32; Acts 14:5). The translation here has added *insanely* to *arrogant* because the Greek term suggests an almost pathological outrage, akin to madness (thus the insolence of Sophocles; *Ajax* [762-778] issues in an episode of madly mistaken butchery, for which he is branded a *hybristēs* [1088; cf. 1081]). Paul's self-description in Acts 26:11, "Enraged beyond measure at them I persecuted them," includes even women (Acts 9:1;

22:4) in his almost pathological fury. In the starkest possible contrast to this ruthless, merciless human existence (note the adversative *alla*) stands the forgiving pity of God or the Lord, who hides, so to speak, behind the merciful action designated by the passive verb (see in the Paulines in Rom 11:30-31 [contrast 32]; 1 Cor 7:25; 2 Cor 4:1 [see Furnish, AB *2 Cor*, p. 217]). *But mercy found me out* has a Pauline ring about it, and certainly not a Lukan resonance except insofar as *eleos* and *ēleēson* belonged to his language of prayer.

This thanksgiving prayer now poses the first of two reasons for the divine mercy given to Paul: *because I did not know what I was doing in my unbelief;* a second appears in verse 16, *But for this very reason mercy found me out, so that Christ Jesus could evidence patience to the utmost, using me as a model of those who are going to believe in him for eternal life.* The first is more psychological and juridical, the latter more teleological and christological. The former focuses upon the limitations and inadequacy, the inherent frailty, of human judgments, plans, goals, and their execution. The latter turns to the plan and judgment and goal of God which, in Christ, envelops and transforms those who oppose him. The former makes no attempt to justify the actions (see Titus 3:5) but makes a case for the mercy that they have received on the basis of their proceeding from an ignorant person who did them *in unbelief, en apistiai,* a phrase that is equivalent to the Jewish Christian unbelievers, *apistoi,* of Titus 1:15 (see also 1 Tim 5:8). Romans 3:3 applies *apistia* (as well as the verb) to Jews who have not believed God's oracles (in contrast to Abraham, Rom 4:20; see 11:20, 23). This use would coincide substantially with the intent here, where Paul is described as a Jew but one who had not yet accepted God's final revelation and thus is still able to describe himself as *in unbelief* with respect to Jesus.

If Paul before his meeting with the risen Lord belonged to an Israel that was in unbelief, it was because he personally *did not know what [he] was doing.* Just as being *en apistiai* is the opposite of being *en pistēi,* so being *agnoōn* is the opposite of having an *epignōsis alētheias,* "full knowledge of the truth." In the PE truth is usually opposed by both intellectual and moral error, with (mis-)conduct and (mis-)understanding in a symbiotic relationship with each other (see also the contrast in 2 Cor 6:9). This concern over a lack of knowledge is not alien to Paul, who has a stock phrase about not wanting his readers to be ignorant of a given matter (see Rom 1:13, etc.), and this at times verges on the point at stake here. Thus Rom 2:4: "Do you not know that God's kindness is meant to lead you to a change of heart *(metanoian)*?" At Rom 10:3 Paul's fellow Jews, "not knowing *(agnoountes)* of the righteousness that comes from God and seeking to establish their own, did not submit to God's righteousness." The kind of nonrecognition that this verb implies is vividly illustrated in Gal 1:22 as Paul notes that still some time after his conversion his presence was "not known *(agnooumenos)* to the churches of Christ in Judea." When Paul offers a palliative for the crime of those who crucified Jesus, he uses a variation on this failure to recognize the one who was present in Jesus; "none of the rulers *(archontōn)* of this age understood *(egnōken)* this [the secret and hidden wisdom of God], for if they had known *(egnōsan),* they would not have crucified the Lord of glory" (1 Cor 2:8).

An explicit and systematic interest in the theme of excusing ignorance appears in Luke-Acts (see Daube, "They Know Not," pp. 58-70, for this and what follows). The disciples are not the only ones who do not "understand *(ēgnooun)*" the saying on the passion of Jesus in Luke 9:45 (note the additions from Mark 9:32). In fact Luke 12:47-48 (*SFG* §203; see Fitzmyer, AB *Lk,* p. 992, for the Qumran references) is the only Gospel pericope transmitting a teaching of Jesus on the difference in punishment for the ignorant wrongdoer versus the deliberate. The textually doubtful prayer of Jesus for his executioners, "Father, forgive them; they do not know what they are doing" (Luke 23:34; see Fitzmyer, AB *Lk,* pp. 1503-1504), is transposed into a different key in the kerygma of Acts 3:17, which has Peter say concerning the role of his fellow Israelites in the death of Jesus: "And now, brothers, I know that you acted in ignorance *(kata agnoian),* as did also your rulers." At Acts 13:26-27 the same teaching is placed on Paul's lips as he describes how the Jews of Jerusalem "did not know *(agnoēsantes)*" this "word of salvation" that their God had sent them and so sought Jesus' death. In Acts 14:16 the canvas widens somewhat as the apostles Paul and Barnabas are depicted as saying to the pagans of Lystra that the living God "in past generations . . . allowed all the nations to walk in their own ways," and the meaning of that statement is more clearly articulated in the Areopagus address, which takes its point of departure from the Athenian altar inscribed "To (an) unknown god *(agnōstōi theōi)*" and has Paul say, "What you therefore worship without knowing *(agnoountes)* it, I proclaim to you" (Acts 17:23). The review of the attempts of pagans to reach and represent this God is then summarized with: "The times of ignorance *(tēs agnoias)* God overlooked, but now he commands all human beings everywhere to repent *(metanoein)*" (Acts 17:30; see Dupont, "La Rencontre," pp. 275-277). Thus *agnoia,* like *apistia,* designates the state of any person, Jew or pagan, who has not recognized the identity of Jesus of Nazareth. The latter term tends to emphasize the culpability of the failure; the former, to soften and excuse the rejection as a relatively inculpable failure to grasp the identity of Jesus, due to lack of information or of understanding. The Paul who says in Acts 26:10, "I myself was convinced that I ought to do many things in opposing the name of Jesus of Nazareth," is in identifiable continuity with the Paul who says in the course of his prayer here, *I did not know what I was doing in my unbelief.*

14. *Still the grace of our Lord superabounded along with that faith and charity which come from union with Christ Jesus.* In Greek this verse completes the first

sentence of the thanksgiving prayer. The superlative force of the neologism *superabounded,* and its emphatic position, serve to accent the new and incomparable *grace* of Jesus that entered Paul's life on the day of his conversion and vocation. Though Paul favored *hyper-* compounds, he used a different verb when he wrote in Rom 5:20 that "where sin increased, grace *(hē charis)* overflowed (*hypereperisseusen;* see 2 Cor 7:4)." Still he alone in the NT (except for 2 Pet 1:8) uses *pleonazein* (see 1 Thess 3:12, with *perisseusai;* 2 Thess 1:3; Rom 5:20; 6:1; 2 Cor 4:15; 8:15 [LXX Exod 16:18]; Phil 4:17). Because the individual terms in this passage are typically Pauline, it is all the more striking that the words are combined in a slightly non-Pauline way. Thus, as Spicq has noted, nowhere else in the NT does *charis* come from "our Lord" except here and at 2 Tim 1:8-9 (the absolute use of "our Lord" is found otherwise in the NT only at Heb 7:14).

The phrase *with (meta) faith and charity* is unknown to the rest of the Paulines or to Luke-Acts, though Eph 6:23 in its closing blessing prays for "love with *(meta)* faith from God the Father and the Lord Jesus Christ." Again the terms individually are Pauline enough (and Lukan), but their use here with *meta* appears unique in the NT. The pairing of faith and love at this point contrasts with their use in the triad of Titus 2:2 and the still longer lists of 1 Tim 1:4; 2:15; 6:11; etc. It resembles most closely the *en pistēi kai agapēi tēi en Christōi Iēsou,* "With that faith and charity which are yours in Christ Jesus," of 2 Tim 1:13. The sense would be rather clearer if one could certainly say that *meta pisteōs* here is equivalent to *en pistēi* of 2 Tim 1:13 (a usage which the PE favor; see Titus 1:1). Yet the final phrase of this verse, *tēs en Christōi Iēsou,* is certainly adding that qualification to *agapēs* and possibly to *pisteōs* as well, thus indicating that *meta* in relation to *agapēs* was not synonymous with *en.* In other words, *en pistēi* for the PE was practically synonymous with "in Christ"; *en agapēi* was not, and required the explanatory phrase. When *meta* replaced *en,* the same distinction was felt and the same qualification was attached to the latter term in the formula, *with faith and charity.*

Though "faith and love" appear as a pair and in that order early in the Paulines (1 Thess 3:6; 5:8; even Gal 5:6), yet the order is not constant (Philem 5; Eph 6:23 cited above) and the terms are embellished theologically as individual items (Eph 1:15; 3:17-18). Hereafter in the PE the phrase *faith and charity* appears only in the great thanksgiving prayer opening 2 Tim 1:13. At this point the phrase is hardly a fixed formula. Ignatius uses it as if it had become so for him (see *Eph.* 1.1; 14.1; *Magn.* 1.2; 13.1; *Smyrn. inscr.;* 6.1; and Schoedel, *Ignatius,* pp. 24-26). Yet it is only *2 Clem.* 15.2 who writes of a person speaking and hearing *meta pisteōs kai agapēs.* All the linguistic evidence indicates that the use of the preposition here is a deliberately different usage; the precise point of it remains elusive. It was not meant to emphasize that the *agapē* here refers to love for God (as it surely does). The following phrase seems to do that.

The phrase *which come from union with Christ Jesus,* lit. "that which [is] in Christ Jesus," is noticeably infrequent in the PE compared with the rest of the Paulines (see Allan, "In Christ," pp. 115-121, with whose study this paragraph is taking issue). Even within the PE it does not appear at all in Titus; of the nine occurrences in the letters to Timothy, only one more is in First Timothy. The phrase modifies "in faith" at 1 Tim 3:13. At 2 Tim 3:15 it modifies "through faith"; at 2 Tim 1:1 it describes Christ's "life" in believers (see Gal 2:20); at 2:13, "love"; at 2:1, "grace"; at 2:10, "salvation." The phrase occurs alone in 2 Tim 1:9 and 3:12 (for the use of "to live," *zēn,* see Gal 2:20). Is the phrase no more than a cipher for indicating that Christ is "the source of faith, love, godly living," and the rest (Allan, p. 117)? The PE are a relatively small epistolary collection in comparison with the remainder of the Paulines, with a notably narrower range of interests and concerns than the latter. It is not surprising that the phrase *in Christ* appears *less* frequently and even with less range of meaning. On the face of it, the frequent use of the phrase in connection with persons in the rest of the Paulines is quite different from the usage in the letters to Timothy, where the phrase never directly modifies persons. The contrast is specious, however, for faith, love, grace, salvation, life, and godly living are, for these letters, not abstractions denoting impersonal realities that exist apart from God and believers. All are personal qualities, proceeding from persons, inhering in persons, and the one set phrase of the PE serves thus to draw out various aspects of meaning from the different forms of the *in Christ* phrase in the Pauline tradition. Arguments from the Pauline mysticism connoted by the *in Christ* language, not to mention those from the depth of feeling conveyed in the language, are difficult to define and control objectively (see A. Oepke, *TDNT* 2.541-543; W. Grundmann, *TDNT* 9.550 n. 366; BAGD, *s.v. en* §5). Once one admits that the thanksgiving prayer here conveys a certain depth of feeling and that 2 Tim 1:9 does in fact posit the kind of relationship with Christ that Paul often adverted to, it seems arbitrary to exclude one or another of these qualities in the remaining passages, when the context and this author's usage are compatible with such admittedly soft concepts.

15. *The Christian message, meant to be believed and worth welcoming wholeheartedly, is "Christ Jesus came into the world to save sinners." Among them I have first place.* The body of the thanksgiving prayer begins at this point. The mention of faith and the name of *Christ Jesus* in the previous verse serve as hinges connecting the whole preceding account of the conversion-vocation of the apostle in his historical encounter with the risen Jesus to an authoritative doctrinal summary of what that intervention implies. The thought moves from the act of Christ to the word of Christ, from what he did to what he taught (see Acts 1:1, describing the *logon* of the Third Gospel as being about all the matters which Jesus "began to do and to teach"; note the perception of Jesus as "a

prophet mighty in deed and word," Luke 24:19). The act and the word are complementary and mutually illuminating, though the verbal articulation of the revelation follows the act of Christ and the gratitude expressed for it. Both act and word call for faith; *with faith and charity* in verse 14, *the Christian message (logos) meant to be believed (pistos)* here (see Titus 3:8 for the way in which *pistos* puts the materials cited into the ambit of faith). At this point as well as in 4:9 *the message meant to be believed* is further qualified as *worth welcoming wholeheartedly,* a phrase unique to the PE in biblical and early Christian Greek. Though Luke-Acts, which favor the *apo-* compounds as do the PE, alone in the NT use *apodechesthai* (Luke 8:40; 9:11; Acts 18:27; etc.), not too much ought to be made of the fact literarily. However, the basic sense here is the one that appears in all the uses of the compound, of accepting or receiving with a connotation of friendly or appreciative welcome (see Knight, *Sayings,* pp. 22-23). The description of those who were baptized after having "accepted [Peter's] word *(apodexamenoi ton logon)*" (Acts 2:41) offers a notable parallel to the meaning of this phrase about *the Christian message worth welcoming wholeheartedly.* Here the accent falls on the thorough and deep personal acceptance of an objective teaching that one was also obliged to believe *(pistos).* Even the formulaic character of this introduction prepares the listener for the already traditional and authoritative character of the text that is about to be cited.

*Christ Jesus came into the world to save sinners.* Not only does the full naming of Jesus lend solemnity to the saying, but there also may be a conscious allusion to the meaning of the name *Jesus,* "salvation," a meaning which this saying begins to unpack. *Jesus* was a common personal name in Judaism, meaning "to save or rescue," until the second century C.E., but it had begun to recede from consciousness in the Greek-speaking world of this time. Thus it was considered necessary to preserve the sense of the name, that this is the one through whom God brought salvation. The theologoumenon does not as such speak to the question of an existence of Jesus previous to his earthly life, for the phrase *came into the world* does not necessarily raise that question (thus "we brought nothing into the world" in 6:7 and *1 Clem.* 38.3 in Notes). Yet in the light of the conspicuous parallels to this language in the Johannine tradition, it was open to an interpretation involving preexistence. The whole thrust of the phrase is toward the goal of Jesus' coming, and that *terminus ad quem* is called *the world, ton kosmon. Didache* 16.8, "The world shall see the Lord's coming on the clouds of the sky," is a reminder that the Lord's coming into the world is originally an apocalyptic vision of the end of human history that has been transferred into the *beginning* of Jesus' earthly life. To emphasize that more than the physical earth is meant is not to deny that this planet is indeed the "theater" (Knight, *Sayings,* p. 41) and proper locus of the work of Jesus. As in the Johannine tradition, however, it is the world as the society of human beings that is meant here, and specifically a society of persons alienated from their God and from one another. To come *into the world* is not only to be enmeshed in human flesh but to be caught within the web of human sin.

The purpose of this entry into the society of fallen human beings is *to save sinners.* In Greek the transposition of the infinitive here and its object draws attention to each term in the formula (see Knight, *Sayings,* p. 45). Moreover, the positioning of *hamartōlous,* "sinners," immediately after *kosmon* implies the aspect of *the world* that is being accented, whereas the final *sōsai* introduces the once-for-all act of God intervening in human history. The term *sinners* here includes all human beings, pagan and Jewish alike, for Paul the Jew is immediately placed in their number. The universal inclusiveness of the term corresponds to the extension of the divine plan which is the subject of this saying and anticipates the principal point of the church order (see 2:3-4 and the use of *apodekton* there) which follows this prayer. The source being cited here certainly intended the universal sense for *sinners,* and basically the same point is made in the acclamation formula cited in 2:3-4. The author of the PE has no qualms about placing that sense on the lips of Paul. Accordingly, however, the sense of *sinners* in this *message meant to be believed* is somewhat different from the only other use of the word in the PE, at 1:9 above, where it refers to people who live in a way that contradicts the revelation that they have received.

As to the root from which this *Christian message meant to be believed* grew, the piety of the OT, especially as expressed in the Psalms, may well have prompted the originally Jewish Christian teaching that eventually condensed into this theologoumenon. Thus in the Lukan parable of the Pharisee and the publican, it is on the lips of the latter, praying in terms reminiscent of the thought of LXX Ps 50:3, "O God, have pity on me," that one finds added the appositional phrase "sinner that I am *(tōi hamartōlōi)*" (Luke 18:13; Fitzmyer, AB *Lk,* p. 1188). With that phrase one has crossed the boundary between the society of good people who have their faults to enter the country of sinners. In Luke's view a good prayer not only confesses sins; it admits frankly that a person comes, even to prayer (perhaps especially to prayer), as a sinner, one who has resisted and spurned revelation. If the parable in fact goes back to Jesus (Jeremias, *Parables,* pp. 139-144), it is part and parcel of a teaching attributed to him by the synoptic tradition (see Mark 2:17 and par.; *SFG* §44, noting that Luke adds *eis metanoian,* "to repentance"). In any case, Luke found this teaching consonant with his understanding of Jesus' mission (see Luke 7:34, 37-39; 15:1-2, 7, 10; 19:7; etc.). The prayer here in the PE, placed on the lips of Paul, cites a positive theological formulation of what the Lukan parable presupposes, that in God's eyes all are sinners, all need repentance, and (in Käsemann's phrase) none more than those who are "just."

So when the *Christian message meant to be believed* has been cited, Paul, the converted Pharisee (Acts 23:6; 26:5; Phil 3:5), confesses like the tax collector of the Lukan parable that he is to be numbered with sinners, *among them I have first place.* His thanksgiving prayer is the antitype of that of the Lukan Pharisee (note the *eucharistō* of Luke 18:11). Simon Peter was the first in Luke's Gospel (5:8) to call himself "a sinful man," *anēr hamartōlos;* now the last use of this term in the PE is a self-designation by Paul. The superlative *first, prōtos,* here as in verse 16, ought to be interpreted through the prayer genre within which it is used. The word has its effect and its resonance in suggesting the profound emotion that the apostle feels at the transition in his personal existence effected by his encounter with the risen Jesus. The prayer form also dictates the interpretation of the very emphatic Greek, which reads literally, "Of whom the first am I *(eimi egō).*" The apostle in prayer does not admit, "I *was* the first of sinners." He says, "I am," as though still poised in that dazzling, overwhelming moment of his conversion-vocation, a moment which gave him an unforgettable and ever present revelation of his own sinfulness in the same instant that it revealed the even greater mercy of God. The *message meant to be believed,* with its objective and formal articulation of God's saving plan, has in this sentence shaded off into the personal thanksgiving prayer of Paul, who in a unique encounter had experienced that *Christ Jesus came into the world to save sinners.*

16. *But for this very reason mercy found me out, so that Christ Jesus could evidence patience to the utmost, using me as a model of those who are going to believe in him for eternal life.* As in verse 13 above, the mention of the personal sinfulness of Paul at the end of verse 15 occasions immediately a probing for the reason why. Thus again the prayer takes up *mercy found me out* from verse 13, strengthening the phrase at this point with *but for this very reason,* as a more christological and a more teleological problematic is offered for understanding the mercy lavished on the apostle-to-be. *The Christian message* cited in verse 15 furnishes the base from which the divine purpose is explored, taking up the elative *first* of the previous self-description and incorporating it into the phrase, *so that Christ Jesus could evidence patience to the utmost, using me,* lit. "in me first." The *en* of "in me first" has an instrumental and even exemplary sense (Moule, *Idiom,* p. 77) which colors the meaning of *prōtos* as it prepares for *pros hypotypōsin,* "as a model." It is notable that in 1 Tim 2:13 where *God fashioned Adam first,* both the literary form and the argument take a quite different tack on "primacy" in sin. In the prayer here this self-designated "first" of sinners received mercy, so that *Christ Jesus* might reveal how all-inclusive was his merciful *patience* in saving human beings. Paul perceives himself as instrumental to the person and purpose of *Christ Jesus,* who has willed to reveal in the conversion-vocation of the apostle the full extent of divine forbearance. The aorist of the verb translated here as "could evidence" highlights the manifestation in time and place of a merciful patience emanating from another order.

The previous uses of this non-Lukan verb in Titus for a slave's manifestation of complete loyalty or a Jewish Christian émigré's gentle consideration remind the reader that this text is treating of verifiable personal acts in this world of flesh and blood, of time and space. Through his dealing with this historical individual, Paul, *Christ Jesus* demonstrates the full extent of his *patience.*

*To the utmost* represents the articular *tēn hapasan* in Greek, which implies that even Jesus could have shown no more *patience* toward his bitter enemy. The patient forbearance of Christ (2 Pet 3:15) is that of God himself, waiting for the opportune time to bestow his grace (Rom 2:24; 9:22). In the rest of the Paulines this noun usually describes one among several qualities to be found in Paul, his co-workers, and Christians in general (see 2 Cor 6:6; Gal 5:22; Eph 4:2; Col 1:11; 3:12). The cluster of *makrothym-* terminology is not large in the NT, and seldom do the terms refer to God (see the verb in Luke 18:7 with Fitzmyer, AB *Lk,* p. 1180; the parable in Matt 18:26, 29, implying a complementary, inner relationship between the patience of God and of human beings; 1 Pet 3:20 on "the patience of God in Noah's days"). The precedents for the pattern in which the NT uses this cluster appear in the LXX, which also uses a variation that may be the source of the usage that begins to appear in some NT and later documents, with particular associations with the Roman church. The LXX about twenty times uses an adjectival *makrothymos,* "long-suffering, very patient" (only the adverb appears in the NT, in Acts 26:3). Well over half the time this adjective is used of the God of Israel, and on eight occasions it appears in a formulaic confessional phrase, *makrothymos kai polyeleos* (see LXX Exod 34:6; Num 14:18; etc., and the variation in Wis 15:1), which in turn translates the Hebrew *'erek 'appayim werab hesed,* "slow to anger and abundant in mercy." From this venerable confessional description of Yahweh in the covenant faith of Israel could have come the NT opening to the *makrothym-* cluster of terms for addressing God and Christ, perhaps especially in the Jewish Christian house churches of Rome. Perhaps the remembrance of the creedal *polyeleos* lies behind the repeated *ēleēthēn* of verses 13 and 16, as *makrothymos* lies behind *makrothymia* here.

Paul is the prime exhibit in the evidence which proves the *patience* of *Christ Jesus;* Paul's life and his teaching are Christ's brief for his own mercy and guidance. This prayer now characterizes the mission given to the converted apostle as a *model,* a vivid sketch (see Eusebius, *Church History* 5.1.23, of the martyr deacon Sanctus, of Vienne), and an outline that will be filled in by generations of believers to come (see the verb in Aristotle, *NE* 1.7.17; 1098 a 21: "Let this account then serve to outline the treatment of the good; for surely one ought to make a sketch [*hyptyposai*] / and then to write it up fully"; E. K. Lee, "Words," pp. 166-173). From this sketch they will learn what is meant by putting one's faith in Christ *for eternal life.* The reference to *those who are going to believe* shifts the emphasis of the prayer from the actual lifetime of Paul to the future believers whom his apostolate will affect and the eschatological age to come which is in continuity with both. The perspective is here consistent with that in Luke-Acts. While coming to terms with the delayed parousia (notably through an appeal to the divine *patience, makrothymia,* as do Second Peter and *First Clement*), the text here addresses second-generation Christians as if they were the last or should so regard themselves.

17. *So to the king of eternity, the immortal, invisible, only God, are the honor and glory for all eternity. Amen.* The third literary element in this thanksgiving prayer, the doxology or eulogy, begins at this point. In Greek, as in the version here, *eternal* in verse 16 serves as the hinge term fastening the preceding citation and its application to the opening address *to the king of eternity* here. The doxology itself opens and closes with the thrice-repeated Greek *aiōnōn/aiōnas.* The formal links with the two preceding sections of this prayer triptych are closer than those arising from content. *Christ Jesus* and Paul are indisputably the axis on which the preceding sections turn. The solemn doxology turns abruptly to the one God of Israel — so abruptly that Oke, "Doxology," pp. 367-368, has argued that this doxology is in fact addressed to Christ, noting particularly the anarthrous *theōi* (but see 2:5) and a way in which the attributes adduced could in fact be understood of Jesus. Still, the epithet *invisible* as applied to Jesus poses a substantive difficulty for this hypothesis, particularly when one recalls that in the doxology of 6:15-16 "the king of those who act as kings" is clearly distinguished from "our Lord, Jesus Christ."

The abrupt shift from thanksgiving to Christ Jesus to a doxology for the God of Israel accents the Jewish character of this final element in the prayer. Moule, *Essays,* pp. 171, 180-182, has noted and discussed the reluctance of the first-century Christians to call Christ *basileus,* a reluctance not shared by their Jewish countrymen with respect to their God. However, the whole phrase here, *the king of eternity,* may be rooted in popular rather than formally liturgical Jewish prayers (where the mention of the kingship of God came in the blessing rather than in the eulogy; popular prayers were not so strictly controlled; see Heinemann, *Prayer,* pp. 157, 160, 178). Blessings addressing God as *melek ʿolam* seem to appear in public, synagogue worship about 100 C.E. (Heinemann, *Prayer,* pp. 94-97, who senses a protest against emperor worship; however, see Wiesenberg, "Liturgical Term," pp. 1-56, for his history of this phrase and its meanings). The syncretistic Jewish blessing of a ring to be used as an amulet exemplifies another aspect of this popular piety. In that text the rhetorical questions of the body of the oration receive the answer, "One God immortal; Begetter of all things, you make them grow, assign souls to all, and rule all things, King and Lord of aeons, before whom mountains and plains tremble, as well as the flow of springs and rivers, the glens of the earth, and the spirits, and [all things] that are" (*PG* 2.71-76 [Pap. xii. 202-267]; E.T. modified from Goodenough, *Symbols* 2.293, and Betz, *GMP*, p. 163). The one who prays perceives himself in this prayer as in the doxology of First Timothy, standing in this world before the divine king who rules both temporal and atemporal orders (the *aiōnes*). The Jewish character of the opening phrase has its complement in the phrase immediately following.

*The immortal, invisible, only God,* with its solemn roll of epithets, climaxing in the anarthrous *theōi* (C. Oke), sounds Hellenistic in its cadences (note the four final *ōis*) as well as in its description of God's nature rather than his character or purpose (see E. Stauffer, *TDNT* 3.112). The terminology is not particularly Septuagintal, but its occasional links with the Jewish communities of Alexandria and Rome and the Roman Christian communities ought not to be overlooked. *Immortal* represents a Hellenistic recasting of the Hebraic confessional description of God as "living" in a manner and in an order unavailable to the mortal addressing him (see 6:13, 16, "the God who keeps all things alive . . . the only one who possesses immortality"; and Excursus IV, "The Terminology for Life in the PE," in AB *Titus*). *Invisible* summarizes in a manner congenial to Greek ears that central concern of Israel which permitted no representation of Yahweh with a visible, man-made image. The same note sounds again in the doxology of 6:16 to "the one whom no human being ever saw nor can see." It is intriguing, in the light of the Johannine resonances of verse 15, to note that the Johannine corpus is particularly concerned about God as unseen (thus John 1:18; 5:37; 6:46; 1 John 4:12, 20). However, the key to the meaning of the adjective here is to be seen in its aligning the worship that is being offered with the covenant faith of Israel. As the Greek translated by *immortal* was related to Israel's faith in the God who is living and living always, so *invisible* directs prayer and praise to no man-made image but to an unseen and unseeable God.

The final adjective in the triad is the climactic one. *The immortal, invisible* God is the *only God.* With this the central confession of the faith of Israel in one God is articulated. The Deuteronomic *Shema*ʿ (Deut 6:4) and the first covenant commandment (Exod 20:3; Deut 5:7) are given with *monoi* an emphatically exclusive sense that was typical of the prayer tradition of Israel and of intertestamental Judaism. The *lex credendi* has indeed established the *lex orandi.* The link between this use of *only, monos,* and the traditional monotheistic creed of Israel becomes quite explicit below at 2:5 (see also Rom 3:30; 1 Cor 8:4-6; Eph 4:6). Though the language does correlate with Hellenistic interests and concerns, it is just as striking that at every turn its concerns also lead back into Judaism, particularly the worship of Judaism. If the words are those of Hellenism, the tune is that of Jewish Hellenism, which in its turn transmitted the heritage of Palestinian forebears who spoke Semitic languages. If this observation is correct, it is unlikely that such prayer formulae as one encounters at this point in the PE, with their venerable Jewish antecedents, were originally composed for polemical use against the worship of the Roman emperors (though one cannot rule that out as a side effect which the author of the PE would have willingly tolerated).

To this divine king, undying, unseen, unique, *are the honor and glory for all eternity.* In doxologies the verb (as here in Greek) is regularly omitted. It is difficult to determine whether the author intended an indicative sense (as opted for in the version here) or a subjunctive. A subjunctive or optative sense appears in later forms of doxological prayer, but the more primitive texts appear regularly to have (or to imply) the indicative (see the ancient understanding of the *gloria Patri et Filio* etc. ["Glory is to the Father and to the Son . . ."] as well as the *est* in the conclusion of eucharistic prayers in the West; Jungmann, *Mass* 1.328 n. 41; 2.265-266). This is the case with other liturgical prayer formulae also (see 2 Tim 4:22; Unnik, *Sparsa* 3.362-391). The doxology is pronounced with a certitude and conviction that transcend the possible and hoped-for. It demands the indicative. God will have his glory. Human beings cannot ultimately foil him, as the whole preceding thanksgiving has illustrated.

To this divine king *are the honor and glory.* As this doxology and that of 6:15-16 apply the Danielic royal style to God (cf. LXX Dan 2:37 with 47), so the royal apparel of *honor and glory* belongs uniquely to him. The splendid vestments and vessels of human worship and praise in this life are only reflections of the splendor of the king whom they honor.

The doxology closes, as it began, with reference to *eternity,* now in the liturgical conclusion that orients all the preceding elements in the direction of public prayer to which a congregational response is expected. The form of the conclusion here, *eis tous aiōnas tọ̄n aiōnōn,* reappears in the doxology of 2 Tim 4:18 and on at least two other occasions in Pauline doxologies (Gal 1:5; Phil 4:20; perhaps Rom 16:27). This solemn, expansive form (characteristic of liturgical conclusions) contrasts with the shorter *eis tous aiōnas/eis tōn aiōna* of Rom 1:25; 9:5; 11:36; 16:27; etc., which do not appear in the PE. Some synagogue prayers, and perhaps especially prayers that were used in the Temple worship, once concluded with these formulae which meantime have vanished, though they survive in Christian liturgical prayers, ancient and modern (Baumstark, *Liturgy,* p. 11; Heinemann, *Prayer,* pp. 134-137; Charlesworth, *OT Pseud.* 2.671-686). It may be more than coincidental that doxological prayers and formulae gradually disappeared in Jewish worship after the destruction of the Temple; they remained part of Jewish Christian worship (and thus among Christians generally), where a new conception of priesthood and Temple was developing. They may have been less congenial to the synagogue for that very reason (see Heinemann, *Prayer,* pp. 64, 83 n. 9, 89 n. 18, 135-137, 284-285, on doxological prayers in the OT and later Judaism).

Elsewhere in the NT this sonorous, solemn formula appears in Heb 13:21; 1 Pet 4:11; perhaps 5:11; and at least a dozen times in Revelation. The effect of the repetition of *aiōnes* is (as Spicq has noted) that of a superlative of duration. The mode of affirming the ultimate duration of which the human mind can conceive in the sphere of time is quite Hebraic and reminds one that the phrase "holy of holies" is a superlative for that which is ultimately and transcendently holy in "the holy place," i.e. in the Temple. Thus, too, "king of kings" and "lord of lords" designate one who is king and lord in a qualitatively unique way, i.e. one who rules other rulers as they rule their own subjects. The generic character of the praise in the archaic Christian doxologies (in contrast to the "specific praise clause" of the old Jewish eulogies or liturgical blessing; see Heinemann, *Prayer,* p. 137) makes any precision in isolating the author's intention problematic. Still, it is suggestive to recall, in fixing the meaning of *aiōnes,* the Pauline antithesis of 2 Cor 4:18: "We do not focus our attention on the things that are seen, but on the things that are not seen; for the things that are seen are temporary, whereas the things that are not seen are eternal *(aiōnia)*" (Furnish, AB *2 Cor,* p. 252; see p. 263). The unseen king of this world is not transient as this world (or age) is. He outlasts all worlds, all ages. Thus the solemn phrase becomes "forever and ever," or, in the version here, *for all eternity.*

The Hebrew *Amēn* concludes this doxology, as is customary in this form of prayer in the NT. The response here implies that the thanksgiving prayer is conceived of as public, as delivered orally before the assembly of the people of God, for their affirmation in faith. In the Pauline letters *Amēn* always appears after the solemn, expansive conclusion (see also Eph 3:21). It occurs also after forms of the short conclusion (see 1 Tim 6:16; 2 Tim 4:18). The *Amēn,* like the *pistos ho logos* formula of the PE, places the words cited in the order of faith, as communicating and expressing the revealed reality of God and his Christ and as eliciting belief in those realities. The *Amēn* is undoubtedly of more archaic origin than the *pistos ho logos* formula, but that does not necessarily mean that the thanksgiving prayer or the doxology is of similar antiquity and origin. The persistent use of this brief Hebrew response to Christian prayers even to this day is a witness not only to its extraordinary durability but also to its quite detachable character in relation to the composition to which it is suffixed. The OT usage of *'amen* implies (as H. Schlier has noted in *TDNT* 1.335-336) that the speaker is accepting a divinely willed task, taking his place in the doxological worship of Yahweh, and finally confirming that he stands under a divine curse or blessing as he does this. Believing Jews identified closely with the blessings and curses solemnly pronounced by their priestly leaders in the name of the God of Israel. The doubled *'amen* response to the rite for the entry into the covenant at Qumran (as understood by the sectaries) illustrates vividly this attitude (1QS 1.20; 2.10, 18). One hazards the suggestion that a prayer such as this one in the PE is conceived of as offered by Paul as part of the priestly task of his apostolate (see Rom 15:16) and that it receives accordingly the *Amen* that Israel gave to the benedictions and doxologies of its priests.

## II.A.3. TIMOTHY'S TASK (1:18-20)

*1 [18]This is the charge I am setting out before you, Timothy, my child, a charge that accords with the prophecies that conducted us to you in the first place. They were given to help you campaign the fine campaign, [19]with faithfulness and a clear conscience. Certain people, once they spurned their conscience, went on to shipwreck in their faith. [20]Among their number were Hymenaeus and Alexander, whom I handed over to Satan to teach them a lesson for their insulting God.*

### ♦ NOTES

1:18. *This is the charge I am setting out before you, Timothy, my child.* For *Timothy* and *child* see verse 1; for *charge,* verse 3. The verb *paratithenai,* lit. "to place before or beside," reappears in 2 Tim 2:2 and seventeen times otherwise in the NT, with only one other Pauline use (1 Cor 10:27, of food "set before" men at table). The verb occurs nine times in the Lukan corpus (versus twice in Matthew and four times in Mark), and regularly of setting out food and drink (Luke 9:16; 10:8; 11:6; Acts 16:34). The last words of Jesus from the cross, "Father, into your hands I entrust *(paratithemai)* my spirit" (Luke 23:46), quote almost exactly LXX Ps 30:6 (see 1 Pet 4:19 and Fitzmyer, AB *Lk,* p. 1519). In Acts 14:23 Paul and Barnabas committed *(parathento)* to the Lord, in a service of prayer of fasting, the presbyters whom they had appointed; and in Acts 20:32 Paul tells the Ephesian presbyter bishops, "And now I entrust *(paratithemai)* you to God *(s.v.l.)* and to the word of his grace which is able . . . to give you the inheritance among all those who are sanctified." The usage in Acts 17:3 is similar to that in the PE, as Luke describes Paul arguing from the Scriptures in the Thessalonian synagogue, "opening up and setting out *(paratithemenos)* that Christ had to suffer and to rise from the dead. . . ." A logion of Jesus cited in Luke 12:48 concludes with a proverb: "(From the one) to whom they entrust *(parathento)* much, of him they will demand more." Again the sense coincides with that in the PE. Ignatius, among Ap. Frs., uses this verb of setting out the food of "heavenly things" on which immature believers could choke (*Trall.* 5.1; see 6.1 and contrast *Mart. Pol.* 7.2, which writes of setting out ordinary food). In Hermas, *Sim.* 9.10.6, *paradidonai* and *paratithenai* are both used of committing a person to the care of others.

*Paratithenai* appears forty-two times in the LXX, generally of serving food. However, LXX Exod 19:7 and Deut 4:44 describe Moses *setting out* the words of the Law to the elders *(presbyterous)* and all Israel. The verb also describes depositing money for safekeeping with another (see LXX Lev 5:23; Tob 1:14; 4:1, 20; 5:3 [S]). In Tob 10:12 (Göttingen; v. 13 in Rahlfs) a daughter is "entrusted as a trust" to the man she marries (see *T. Joseph* 13.3 of Joseph and C. Maurer, *TDNT* 8.162-163).

For the secular usage, see MM *s.v.*, and especially Menander, Koerte 133 and 451.5 (146, 518K).

*a charge that accords with the prophecies that conducted us to you in the first place.* Lit. "in accord with the prophecies *(prophēteias)* made long ago over you." The phrase *kata tas prophēteias* does not appear again in biblical Greek or Ap. Frs. In the PE *prophēteia* reappears (again in the plural?) only in 4:14 (see Titus 1:12 for *prophētēs*). Of the seventeen other NT occurrences, seven are in the other Paulines (pl. in 1 Thess 5:20; 1 Cor 13:8) and seven in Revelation. In the Gospel traditions and Acts only Matt 13:14 uses the term, with reference to a passage of Isaiah (see also 2 Pet 1:20-21 and Aune, *Prophecy*, p. 198). Such usage became regular in Ap. Frs. (*1 Clem.* 12.8 of Rahab; Ign. *Smyrn.* 5.1 of the OT prophecies generally; *Barn.* 13.4 of Jacob). Only Hermas takes up the predominant NT usage, and then of a man "accepting payments for his prophecy" (*Man.* 11.12). The LXX employs *prophēteia* no more than fifteen times, and almost half of these are in Sirach, who regularly uses the term of oral and written oracles produced in the distant past. Against this background it is striking to read in his description of Wisdom, "I will again pour out teaching *(didaskalian)* like prophecy and leave it to all future generations" (24:33). In *T. Levi* 8.2 a priestly garment is "the apron *(ephoud)* for prophecy"; *T. Benjamin* 3.8 offers "a heavenly prophecy" whose text is itself problematic.

The verb *proagein*, represented by *conducted in the first place* in the version above, recurs in 1 Tim 5:24 (where the direct object is understood, as it is here). Of the twenty other NT uses, five are in Luke-Acts, none in Paul. The term emphasizes either a temporal or local "coming/going before" (see BDF §150, 208), though this nice verbal distinction is difficult to apply in reality (see the temporal usage in Polybius 18.8.1). The temporal emphasis has been opted for by BDF and BAGD in the PE (thus here, "the prophecies made long ago"). This usage in turn has led to taking *epi se* as introducing the one by reason of whom the prophecies once occurred (BAGD, p. 289, III.1.b.ζ). Yet the verb was heard basically as one designating local movement in leading and escorting another (cf. Plato, *Phaedrus* 227C with 228B; Menander, *Dysc.* 906, 910; *Sam.* 690-691, 725 [F. Sandbach]; *Kitharistes* 50), and Luke always takes it thus (Luke 18:39; Acts 12:6 *s.v.l.;* 16:30; 17:5; 25:26). Similarly Ign. *Rom.* 9.3 writes of fellow believers who "went before me from city to city." Polycarp describes "love of

God and Christ and of neighbor going before or escorting" the faith of the Philippian church (*Phil.* 3.3; contrast *Mart. Pol.* 1.1). Of more than a dozen uses of *proagein* in the LXX, the most notable parallel to this passage in First Timothy is in 2 Macc 10:1: "Now Maccabaeus and his followers, the Lord leading them on *(proagontos),* recovered the temple and the city" (RSV).

*They were given to help you campaign the fine campaign.* Lit. "So that you may campaign in them *(en autais)* the fine *(kalēn)* campaign." The inner accusative phrase, *strateuesthai strateian,* is quite Greek (see BAGD, *s.v. strateia,* for examples; for a Latin example see Horace, *Epodes* 1.23-24) and appears also in 4 Macc 9:24, as the youthful martyr exhorts his brothers, "Fight a holy and honorable fight *(strateian strateuesthai)* on behalf of godliness . . ."; Philo exploits the same phrase when he says of Moses that ". . . having fought the fight in the cause of virtue, he has no rest from battles . . ." (*Leg. alleg.* 3.14). Of the individual terms in the phrase, *strateia* appears elsewhere in the NT only in 2 Cor 10:3-4, where Paul writes that he and his co-workers do not carry on a fight *(strateuometha)* as the world understands it, "for the weapons of our warfare *(hopla tēs strateias)* are not of this world but empowered for God . . ." (see Furnish, AB *2 Cor,* p. 457). In Ap. Frs. the noun appears only in the form *stratia,* of Pharaoh's "army" in the Exodus narratives (*1 Clem.* 51.5). This is practically always the meaning of the term in the LXX (except 4 Macc 9:24, cited above; see the variant reading in 16:14).

The verb *strateuesthai* recurs in 2 Tim 2:4. In the other Paulines it appears only in the Corinthian correspondence, 2 Cor 10:3 just cited, and 1 Cor 9:7. In the latter passage the apostle, justifying the material support received by apostolic ministers, takes three examples to make his point, leading off with, "Who serves as a soldier *(strateuetai)* at his own expense?" In James 4:1 and 1 Pet 2:11 the verb describes the onslaught of human passions and implies a somewhat different view of the enemy than one would infer from the Pauline usage (see O. Bauernfeind, *TDNT* 7.712). Only once in the NT does this term describe "men on military duty," *strateuomenoi* (Luke 3:14; see Fitzmyer, AB *Lk,* p. 470).

In Ap. Frs. the author of *1 Clem.* 37.1-2 exhorts his fellow Christians: "Let us then campaign *(strateusometha),* brothers, following his [Christ's] faultless commands. Let us consider those who are on military duty *(tous strateuomenous),* with what good order, habitual readiness and submissiveness they perform their commands." Ignatius urges a congregation, "Be pleasing to him in whose ranks you do military duty *(strateuesthe),* from whom you receive your pay . . ." (*Pol.* 6.2). When Polycarp writes to Philippi that "Every lust campaigns *(strateuetai)* against the Spirit . . ." (*Phil.* 5.3), the usage puts one in mind of 1 Pet 2:11. Outside the passage of Fourth Maccabees cited above, there appears to be no precedent for the Christian usage in the few appearances of this verb in the LXX. For further examples in Philo and in secular literature, particularly Epictetus, see D-C, p. 33; Pfitzner, *PAM,* pp. 42-43.

19. *with faithfulness and a clear conscience.* Lit. "Having *or* keeping [the?] faith and a good conscience." *Pistis,* here *faithfulness,* appears 33 times in the PE, 109 times in the Paulines, and 243 times in the NT, with 26 occurrences in Luke-Acts. As here, it is frequently the object of the verb (never the subject in the PE), and in the latter part of this verse appears in a prepositional phrase, *peri tēn pistin,* used pejoratively of those who have shipwrecked their faith. The addition of the article *tēn* in P may be a harmonization with *tēn pistin* that follows in this verse (see J. K. Elliott, *Greek Text,* p. 32). For the phrase *a clear conscience,* see verse 5; Titus 1:15; Wallace, "Adjective," pp. 152, 155.

*Certain people, once they spurned their conscience, went on to shipwreck in their faith.* Lit. "Having rejected which, some suffered shipwreck in respect to the faith." For *some people, tines,* see verses 3 and 6. *Spurned, apōsamenoi,* an aorist participle for an action that is coincident with the main verb, derives from *apōthein,* which appears elsewhere in the Paulines only in Rom 11:1-2 (citing LXX Ps 93:14): "God (LXX: the Lord) has not rejected his people." Otherwise in the NT the verb is used only in the Lukan speeches of Acts 7:27, 39 (describing the way Israelites repudiated Moses) and of 13:46 (describing the Jewish rejection of "the word of God" as Paul and Barnabas had proclaimed it in the synagogue of Pisidian Antioch). In Ap. Frs. only *Barn.* 4.13 employs the verb, of the devil forcing sinful Christians out of the kingdom of the Lord (see v. 20 below). The LXX regularly uses this verb of God's abandoning Israel. A few times, but significantly, the prophetic tradition has Yahweh referring to his being spurned, as when he announces, "Because you [the priests of Israel] abandoned knowledge (*epignosin;* i.e. of revelation), I will abandon you" (LXX Hos 4:6); or predicting punishment for Judah "on account of their rejecting the law of the Lord" (LXX Amos 2:4); or charging, "They rejected my law" (LXX Jer 6:19; see 23:17 on "those who reject the word of the Lord"). In *T. Asher* 1.8 one reads, "But if the mind is disposed toward evil, all of its deeds are wicked; thrusting aside *(apō thoumenos)* the good, it accepts the evil and is overmastered by Beliar . . ." (i.e. the devil). In *T. Joseph* 2.5 God, unlike earthly creatures, is not thrust aside *(apōthetai).*

*went on to shipwreck. Nauagein* appears once more in the NT, and then literally of Paul himself in 2 Cor 11:25. Neither Ap. Frs. nor the LXX uses the term. The figurative usage here appeared among philosophers as early as Theophrastus, whose will (according to Diogenes Laertius 5.55) described a certain man who "had made shipwreck of his own affairs," and in the late first century B.C.E. Philodemus of Gadara, in Rome, writes of a person who burdens himself beyond reason "and not even when he undergoes total shipwreck *(nauagon en hapasi)* stops this madness" (*Peri kakion,* p. 33, line 33). The popular philosophers of the first and second Christian centuries used the figure (see D-C, p. 33 n. 12, for the texts of Cebes, Lucian, and Galen). Thus Plutarch noted, "Most drinking-parties, without proper guidance [for the games, humor, and the like] suffer shipwreck *(nauagei)*" (*Quaestiones conviviales* 1.4.622B). In the Jewish tradition Philo has an exuberant development of the metaphor describing human beings "who if we but catch a puff of the air of prosperity shake in every timber and let the breeze blow fresh and clear, and then with a strong steady wind to swell our canvas speed on to the enjoyments of the passions, and never do we draw in the loose and slack license of our lusts until we strike the rocks and shipwreck *(nauagēsomen)* the whole boat of the soul" (*Mut.* 215, LCL modified; see *Som.* 2.147; *Leg. alleg.* 371).

20. *Among their number were Hymenaeus and Alexander.* Lit. "Of whom is [thus 2 Tim 1:15; 2:17 also] Hymenaeus and Alexander." The name *Hymenaeus* recurs in 2 Tim 2:17 along with a person called Philetus as examples of "those who have deviated in the truth" about the resurrection. The name is not documented otherwise in the NT, Ap. Frs., or the LXX. The Greeks and Romans invoked the god of marriage under that name (or Hymen), but they rarely named their children after him (no example in Preisigke, *Namenbuch,* but see the last entry in the second- or first-century-B.C.E. list of rulers on Tenos in the Aegean, *SEG* 14.553.II.52). Jewish people did not use the name at all.

The name *Alexander* appears again in 2 Tim 4:14, borne by a man explicitly identified as "the coppersmith," residing in Troas. Acts 4:6 notes a Jew of the high-priestly house named Alexander as well as another Jew in Ephesus (Acts 19:33). Otherwise in the NT only Mark 15:21 writes of an Alexander, this time one of the sons of Simon of Cyrene. The name does not appear in Ap. Frs., but in the LXX First Maccabees writes of Alexander the Great as well as Alexander Balas. The Maccabean ruler Alexander Jannaeus (103-76 B.C.E.) used this as his Greek name; the second element is apparently an equivalent for the Hebrew name *yhwntn* on a coin which contains both names (see Goldstein, AB *2 Macc,* pp. 77-78). By the first Christian century the name had become common among Jewish men (see Schalit, *Concordance, s.v.*), notably in Rome (*CII* 84[?], 85, 92, 140, 370, 501).

*whom I handed over to Satan. Paradidonai* appears only in this quasi-formulaic expression in the PE, though 118 times otherwise in the NT, with 18 in the other Paulines, including a close parallel to this phrase in 1 Cor 5:5. The legal usage of Matt 18:34 is notable. Luke-Acts share 30 occurrences between them (note the juridical phrases in Luke 24:20 and the *v.l.* of Acts 28:16). In Ap. Frs. the expression "to deliver to death" is regular in *Barnabas* (of Israel delivered to death because of sins in 12.2, 5) and in Hermas (see *Man.* 12.1.2-3 [evil desire which does this is "the daughter of the devil" in 12.2.2]; *Sim.* 6.5.4; 9.23.5). Instruction *(paideia)* through affliction and the agency of an angel are associated in *Sim.* 6.3.6; 7.1-2, 5. Of the many uses of *paradidonai* in the LXX, there is not a precise parallel to the passage here, though one is reminded of the

LXX Job 2:6, "But the Lord said to the devil *(tōi diabolōi),* 'Behold, I hand him over *(paradidōmi)* to you,'" and of the psalmists' prayers about deliverance into enemy hands, to wild beasts, to death (LXX Pss 40:3; 73:19; 117:18). The many occurrences in legal contexts about possession (see LXX Num 32:4; Deut 1:8, 21) or punishment (LXX Deut 19:12, about handing over the murderer to one who takes blood vengeance) are notable.

*Satan* is transliterated from the Greek *Satanas,* which was in its turn transliterated from the Aramaic *śaṭana'* as in 4Q TLevi ar[a] 1.17. Hebrew *śaṭan* is transliterated *satan/satanan* in 3 Kgdms 11:14 and Sir 21:27. The transliteration from Aramaic appears three dozen times in the NT but in the PE only here and in 5:15 (of certain young widows who "have slipped off after Satan"). In the other Paulines *Satanas* occurs eight times of an enemy who afflicts the apostle (2 Cor 12:7; anarthrous), opposes his mission (2 Cor 2:11; 11:14; 1 Thess 2:18); tempts believers (1 Cor 7:5); and chastises others (1 Cor 5:5). Still the *Satanas* is bound for final defeat after he has deceived the people who refuse to believe (2 Thess 2:9-12; Rom 16:20).

The Lukan tradition uses *Satanas* for the evil one who opposes the apostles (Luke 22:31), taking possession of one (Luke 22:3; anarthrous). Jesus is both opposed to and more powerful than the *Satanas* (Luke 11:18-22), and has in fact beheld him plummeting down to defeat (Luke 10:18). Yet Satan has still the power to afflict the people of God — a "daughter of Abraham" — with physical infirmity (Luke 13:16) and to bring sinful Christian believers to death (Acts 5:3, where Peter, like Paul in First Corinthians, lets Satan have those whose hearts he had filled, and they die). In Acts 26:18 Paul is described as summarizing the purpose of his apostolate to the pagans as "to open their eyes, that they may turn from darkness to light and from the power of Satan to God." The Markan interpretation of the sower parable has *ho satanas* coming to pick up the seed sown on the path; Luke explicitly interprets the Markan name as *ho diabolos,* "the devil" (Mark 4:15; Luke 8:12). The regular use of the article with Satan in the NT indicates a unique being whose title is to be taken practically as a personal name (see BDF §254.1).

In Ap. Frs. Ignatius sees "the powers of Satan" routed by the unity of the assemblies of believers (*Eph.* 13.1). In a series of denunciations of false teachings that Polycarp pens to the Philippian church, the apex is reached with one who perverts "the oracles *(ta logia)* of the Lord" for his own lusts. For such a man there is neither resurrection (*anastasin;* see 2 Tim 2:18) nor judgment; he is the "first-born of Satan" (*Pol.* 7.1). *Barnabas* 18.1 states that "angels of Satan" preside over one of the two ways "of teaching *(didachēs)* and of power."

In the two occurrences of *satan* and *satanas* in the LXX (cited above), the term refers to human adversaries. Similarly, in the scroll of morning prayers from Qumran (4QDibHam), in a passage describing the blessings that God has given his people in Jerusalem, the text says, "Nor was an adversary *(stn)* there nor misfortune, but only peace and blessing" (4Q 504.1-2.iv.12-13; DJD 7.144; Gaster, *DSS* modified). *Stn* has appeared three times in fragmentary contexts in 1QH f4.6; f45.3; 1QSb 1.8, though the use with *kwl* surely means from "adversaries" understood in a generic sense and not from a person conceived of as the adversary par excellence. The 4QFlor (4Q 174.9; DJD 5.53), alleged by J. Allegro to contain a phrase reminiscent of 1 Tim 1:20, ought to be corrected from Strugnell, "Notes," p. 221.

On the other hand, in the *Testaments of the Twelve Patriarchs* the *satanas* is always a spiritual enemy. Thus *T. Dan* 3.6 writes of the spirit of anger, it "always moves with falsehood at the right hand of Satan, in order that such deeds may be done through savagery and deception"; in 5.6 sinners are told, "Your prince is Satan"; and in 6.1 the dying patriarch says, "And now, my children, be on guard against Satan and his spirits." The *T. Gad* 4.7 teaches, "For among all human beings the spirit of hatred works by Satan through human frailty for the death of mankind." Finally, *T. Asher* 6.4 writes, "The ultimate ends of human beings display their righteousness, since they recognize what belongs to the angels of God and of Satan."

*to teach them a lesson for their insulting God.* Lit. "So that they might be taught *(paideuthōsin)* not to blaspheme *(blasphēmein).*" On *paideuein* see Titus 2:12; on *blasphēmein,* Titus 2:5; 3:2.

## ♦ COMMENT

Formally this short section on Timothy's task looks back to the opening of the apostolic commission to Timothy and its commands (1:3-7, which from a purely grammatical point of view could be read as the protasis of an apodosis that finally appears at 1:18). The intervening materials are enclosed within these compositional parentheses (a similar relation obtains between Titus 1:16 and 2:15). *This charge* of 1:18 echoes the cognate verb of 1:3 and noun of 1:5, and the demonstrative emphatically specifies that passage. The triple use of the singular address (not heard since v. 3), the repetition of Timothy's name (from v. 1), of the phrase *a clear conscience* (see v. 5), and of the terms for *faith* (see vv. 4-5), all serve the same formal function of linking verses 18-20 with verses 3-7. On the other hand, the frequent *t(h)* sounds of verse 18 put it into sharp contrast with the many *m* and *n* sounds of the preceding doxology while signaling the return to the framework for the apostolic commands left behind at verse 7.

1:18. *This is the charge I am setting out before you, Timothy, my child, a charge that accords with the prophecies that conducted us to you in the first place.* The heterodox Jewish Christian teachings that have been scored in verses 3-7 throw into relief not only the authentic Pauline interpretation of the Old Testament (vv. 8-11) but also the apostolic experience of Paul himself as crystallized in his thanksgiving prayer (vv. 12-17). All of that is framed within the apostolic *charge* to which Paul is now depicted as returning, in order to commit that *charge* (in his own person) "to Timothy, his true child in faith" (v. 2), to whom this whole letter is addressed. The father-to-son (and heir) model for expressing the relationship of the apostle to his co-worker, as well as the first and second person singular construction, emphasizes the intimate and personal character of *setting out the charge,* in which the active initiative of the apostle in communicating it is complemented by the basically passive attitude of the co-worker who accepts it as a soldier does the commands of his general and as a pupil the teaching of his mentor. The Pauline teaching is the content of *the charge,* which is served, like wholesome food, by the apostle-father to his co-worker–son (cf. *hypotithemenos . . . entrephomenos* in 1 Tim 4:6 with 2 Tim 2:2). The verb translated *setting out* is cognate with the nominal *parathēkē,* "what has been deposited," a noun peculiar to the PE in the NT (see 1 Tim 6:20), which turns the doctrinal process of *setting out the charge* into a noun (as the Pauline *paradidonai,* "to transmit," became the nominal *paradosis,* "tradition").

*a charge that accords with the prophecies that conducted us to you in the first place.* The Pauline commission to Timothy in the epistolary present is now justified by an appeal to a unique past event which supports the present action. Paul's initiative is not simply his own and thus arbitrary. It *accords with the prophecies.* Just as the gospel which Paul and the other apostles proclaimed is accredited emphatically as "according to the Scriptures" (in the unique phrase of 1 Cor 15:3-4), so the unique *kata tas prophēteias* here accredits the minister of that gospel. Paul shares his apostolic work with his *child,* but not without the express guidance of the Spirit through *the prophecies.* The scenario adverted to here almost certainly ought to be read in conjunction with 4:13-14: "Until I arrive, concentrate on your public reading of the Scriptures, on your preaching, on your instruction. Do not neglect that gracious gift within you *(tou en soi charismatos),* the one given to you under prophetic direction *(dia prophēteias),* with an imposition of the hands of the presbytery." The gift of God (of the Holy Spirit) which came to Timothy in a setting of liturgical worship and ritual (which later generations would call ordination) has been authenticated or vouched for by that same Spirit through one or more of those who had received the charism of prophecy. Though it is possible to understand the aorist participial phrase *(that conducted us . . .)* complexively of discrete prophetic interventions on quite separate occasions long ago (with a consequent emphasis on the permanent, once-for-all character of the designation), the phrase probably should be taken to refer to several prophetic oracles delivered by as many persons in a Christian assembly for worship within which the apostle is conceived as announcing generically his need for a man to share his work. In this connection it is helpful to recall the Pauline treatment of prophecy and his directions for the Corinthian prophets (1 Cor 12–14). In 1 Cor 14:37-38 the apostle addresses the real possibility of the local prophets disagreeing with the apostle's letter. To that Paul only says: "If anyone thinks that he is a prophet or spiritual [i.e. guided by the Spirit], he should acknowledge that what I am writing you is a command of the Lord. If anyone does not recognize this, he is not recognized [i.e. as a genuine prophet inspired by God]." Thus prophetic teaching and apostolic teaching are to corroborate each other, but if they do not, the apostolic order takes precedence over what only appears to be prophetic. The passages cited in First Timothy have not a trace of public prophetic disagreement with Paul's decision. The local presbyters seem to preside in the setting proposed here (though there is no hint where the community is). Those who deliver *the prophecies,* however, are not named, even generically (e.g., as prophets). Perhaps it is not an "order" of prophets that is envisioned but a prophetic inspiration coming transiently to one or another member of the assembly (see the scenario for the liturgy proposed below).

In any case the oracles, apparently oral, pointed specifically to Timothy *(to you, epi se)* and led the assembly, including Paul, to him. The precise sense of *epi se* is as vexed as that of the verb to which it stands in function. The phrase is not in the genitive as in 6:13, *epi Pontiou Pilatou* (see Acts 25:26 where Festus remarks, "I have brought him [i.e. Paul] before you [*eph' hymōn*] and especially before you [*epi sou*], King Agrippa . . ."). *Epi* with the accusative is also used of bringing someone to another person, particularly for some kind of public, legal action (see BAGD, p. 288, III.1.a.γ). Here in the PE a different nuance appears, for the prophecies have not brought Paul and the presbytery to Timothy as to a judge. The prophetic interventions in the liturgical setting presupposed here have made Timothy the center of attention in the whole assembly (see the use of *ep' autōn* in Mark 5:21; Matt 27:27). The use of *eis* after *proagein* in this setting of worship would too strongly accent local movement (see 5:24 and Acts 17:5: "They kept seeking to bring them [Paul, Silas, Timothy] out to the people [*proagagein eis ton dēmon*]"). The prophetic oracles which direct the eyes and hearts of the worshipping assembly to Timothy *(epi se)* remind one that the Spirit of prophecy is "the Holy Spirit that he poured out lavishly on us *(eph' hēmas)*" in Titus 3:5b-6a (see *epi* with the accusative in Acts 1:8; 2:17; 10:45).

Can the liturgical scenario envisaged by this passage and probably by 4:13-14 be further reconstructed? A notable parallel appears in Acts 13:1-3, describing a first-generation Christian liturgical assembly in Syrian Antioch. Five leaders of that church, who are called "prophets and teachers" (including Paul), receive, while they are engaged in public prayer and fasting, an oracle from the

Holy Spirit: "Set apart [plural] for me Barnabas and Saul for the work *(eis to ergon)* to which I have called them." Formally the oracle appears closest to a common Greek type called prescriptive, a "one-part oracular response [that] tells the inquirer what course of action he is to take" (Aune, *Prophecy,* pp. 57-58, with examples; see p. 266). A less pronounced but still recognizable relationship exists with those unsolicited legitimation oracles, which Aune has classified as recognition oracles (pp. 266, 68-70, 140-141). Granted the parallel, Timothy is reminded here of similar prophetic directions that were given in a past assembly for public worship when he started to share Paul's ministry. If the local church of Antioch could send Paul and Barnabas on their great mission into Asia Minor, then perhaps one has precedent for proposing that the recently founded church of Lystra and its presbyters (see Acts 14:23) offered Timothy for the Pauline mission (Acts 16:1-3). There is nothing in 1 Tim 1:18 that would exclude the Spirit's having spoken through the apostle himself on this occasion as well as through other members of the assembly, including the presiding presbyters (Acts makes a point of Paul's initiative as well as the good report of Timothy's fellow believers in the local churches). In fact, the Paul of history could invoke, as occasion demanded, revelation which he had received for a given course of action (Gal 2:2).

At the beginning of the second Christian century, in Philadelphia in Asia Minor, the Christian community assembled for worship with the soon-to-be-martyred Ignatius, bishop of Antioch (for this and what follows see Aune, *Prophecy,* pp. 291-293). Recalling the occasion a few weeks later as he wrote back to them from Troas, Ignatius described the way he had participated in the assembly: "I cried out while in your midst, I kept speaking in a great voice, the voice of God, 'Heed the bishop and the presbytery and deacons.' Still there were those who suspected me of saying these words because I had advance news about the division of some people. But he for whom I am in chains is my witness that I knew nothing from human flesh. But the Spirit made the proclamation, saying things like this, 'Without the bishop do nothing. Keep your flesh as God's temple. Set your hearts on unity. Flee divisions. Be imitators of Jesus Christ as he also is of his Father'" (*Phld.* 7.1-2). The prophetic interventions in this liturgical service have affinities formally with 1 Thess 5:15-22. Ignatius describes himself as excited by the impulse of the Spirit "who tests hidden things" (cf. 1 Cor 14:24-25), loudly repeating his oracle (note the imperfect *elaloun*), which is brief, poetic, "oracular parenesis . . . with no eschatological emphasis." His own oracle was the more credible in its content because it was accompanied by five others, apparently from members (and leaders) of the local church, who seconded his message while adding others. If the following sections of the *Letter to the Philadelphians* refer to the same liturgical setting, one would infer that readings from the Old Testament had also occurred (perhaps about its priesthood) which were expounded and applied by the visiting bishop in terms of the death and rising of Jesus. Perhaps the prophecies then expressed the Spirit's approbation, through the community, of the explanations offered (and the overwhelming agreement of these prophetic interventions goaded the opposition to open confrontation). A setting that resembles those in Acts and Ignatius appears to be presupposed in 1 Tim 1:18 and 4:13-14.

*The prophecies that conducted us to you in the first place* are conceived of as still remembered, still full of power, still bestowing energy (see 4:14 and perhaps 2 Tim 1:6-7; E. Cothenet, *DBS* 8.1313). The Paul of the PE is *setting out the charge before Timothy* with an eye to them, for it is *a charge that accords with the prophecies.* The unique phrase may still contain a clue as to how the prescriptive oracles were expressed, for it leads into the following sentence.

18b-19a. *They were given to help you campaign the fine campaign, with faithfulness and a clear conscience.* In the Greek text the purpose of the preceding prophecies is "so that *(hina)* you may campaign in them *(en autais)* the fine campaign, having *(echōn)* faithfulness and good conscience." The language of the latter phrase (19a) is so typical of the PE generally that it appears to be an explanatory gloss added to the previous clause which in its turn appears to explain the unusual phrase about *the prophecies that conducted us to you in the first place.* Similarly, *en autais* (with its ambivalent meaning, oscillating among the instrumental, temporal, and the local nuances) emphatically links the phrase being quoted with the prophetic intervention of the past. On this reconstruction the author of the PE submitted that at least one of the prescriptive oracles addressed Timothy with the words "Campaign the campaign." The author of the PE has made the phrase his own by adding an adjective that he particularly prizes, *fine,* here *kalēn,* with its unmistakable emphasis on visible excellence (as in the *kalos agon,* "the fine contest" of 6:12 and 2 Tim 4:7). The Paul of 2 Tim 2:3-4 (certainly talking the language of this passage of First Timothy and perhaps expounding on this oracle) can urge Timothy himself: "As a fine soldier *(kalos stratiōtēs)* of Christ Jesus take your share of suffering along with me. No one on active duty in the military *(strateuomenos)* gets involved in the business of civilian life. He avoids this to please the man who called him to arms." In this connection it is notable that the archaic ordination charge which is incorporated into 6:11-16 opens by addressing the ordinand with "O man of God" (see 2 Tim 3:17 also), which seems to be a prophetic title, and urging him, "Contend in the fine contest," which is reminiscent of the oracle here in 1:18. On other occasions First Timothy cites the products of prophetic interventions (thus the oracle of 4:1 and perhaps the hymn of 3:16).

The content of the brief, prescriptive oracle that has been isolated here in 1:18 is more eschatological than might appear on a superficial reading, for this is an imperative from the Spirit to enter the holy war, the great final but ongoing *campaign* of God and his anointed against the forces of evil (note the present tense). The Pauline tradition, as far back as it can be traced (see Giblin, *Threat,* pp. 89-109, on 2 Thess 2:8-10; the divinely given panoply, including the sword of the Spirit, in Eph 6:10-20), and that of the PE (see Titus 2:14) and Ap. Frs. conceive of all of the baptized as engaged in a holy war. Paul himself applied the OT terminology of the holy war to apostolic ministers (note that Archippus's ministry in Col 4:17 is that of "our fellow soldier" in Philem 2) and (with no little irony) to the battle he and his colleagues were waging against the specious wisdom and theology of Corinthian Christian opponents. The author of the PE similarly has Paul charging his lieutenant to quell doctrinal insurrection among the troops in Ephesus and justifying that with an appeal to a prophetic utterance that committed Timothy to this kind of leadership *in the first place* (see Pfitzner, *PAM,* pp. 167-168).

Several aspects of the OT ideology for the holy war are suggested by this oracle and later developments in the context (see Vaux, *Israel,* pp. 258-267, on what follows). It is difficult to overemphasize the most primitive and basic Israelite concept of the holy war as a war that Yahweh, and he only, fought for the life and existence of his people. It was not conceived of originally as a war for spreading Yahwistic faith. Yahweh himself initiated and directed the war, often through prophetic oracles (see Judg 4; 1 Kings 20, 22). To him all the spoils and captives were consecrated (*herem;* the LXX regularly translated this with forms of *anathēma;* see N. Lohfink, *TDOT* 5.180-199). Yahweh could declare war on members of his own people when their actions and beliefs deserved it (thus on the tribe of Benjamin for the heinous crime of Judg 20; on a city which apostatized from Yahweh to other gods, Deut 13:13-18). The war demanded from its participants complete faith in God for victory and observance of a special ritual purity in the course of the campaign.

The continuing fascination of the complex concept of the holy war is documented at Qumran by 1QM, the scroll containing the scenario for the war of the sons of light against the sons of darkness (fragments of other copies of the work indicate its relative popularity among the people at Qumran; see 4Q 491-496: DJD 7.12-68). The primitive ideology lived on. Thus when the priest exhorts the assembled troops, he begins his discourse with an appeal based on Deut 20:2-4: "Hear, O Israel, you are drawing near this day of battle. . . . Fear not . . . for your God is marching with you to do battle for you against your foemen to save you." Then the subordinate officers take up the exhortation, adding, "[To none] but you belong the [issues of] war. . . . Yours is the battle; from you comes the power, and it is not ours. It is not our strength nor the might of our hands that achieves this valor, but it comes through your strength and through your great, valorous might." After citing Balaam's prophecy about the star from Jacob (Num 24:17-19), the exhortation appeals to the writings of the

OT prophets, saying, "Moreover, by the hand of your anointed, the men who had vision of things foreordained, you have related to us the warlike triumphs of your hands — how you waged battle against our foes and caused the troops of Belial, the seven vain nations, to fall by the hand of the poor people whom you redeemed by wondrous might [and set] in [safe]ty and peace" (1QM 10.3-4; 11.1, 4-5, 8-9; E.T. of Gaster, *DSS,* p. 413, modified). A liturgy with the high priest surrounded by priests and Levites precedes the climactic encounter with the army of Belial. In the course of this ceremony a specially delegated priest goes up to the assembled sons of light and walks up and down their ranks exhorting them in terms that bring to mind the prophetic oracle cited in 1 Tim 1:18. Thus, "Be strong and stout-hearted and acquit yourselves as men of valor. . . . Be courageous and be strong for God's battle" (1QM 15.8, 12; E.T. of Gaster, *DSS,* p. 419, modified). At every turn this rule for the eschatological holy war presumes total trusting faith in God and total observance of the Law as it explicitly imposes a series of special requisites for the ritual purity of the troops and their camp (1QM 7.3-7; 10.1; see Yadin, *War,* pp. 4-5). The demand for *faithfulness and a clear conscience* in 1 Tim 1:19 transposes these attitudes into a Christian key, but the old tune is still audible.

The eschatological atmosphere and OT precedents for this prophetic liturgy ought not to be taken to mean that ordinary people would find the language about life as a warfare exotic or incongruous. Quite the contrary. In the last couple of centuries B.C.E. (and not only then), "the Roman state was almost continually at war" (Hopkins, *Conquerors,* p. 25; see through p. 37 for what follows, as well as E. Badian's review in *JRS* 72 [1982]: 166). The staggering effects of this phenomenon on the whole of Hellenistic society and its mentality are still being sorted out. It was no philosophical commonplace for Seneca to write *Atqui vivere, Lucili, militare est,* "And still, Lucilius, living is military campaigning" (Letters 46.5), though Philostratus has Nilus say to Apollonius, "I have been campaigning until now together with the naked sages, and I joined myself with some ranks of their light-armed soldiers or slingers, but now I mean to put on heavy armor and it is your shield that will ornament me" (*Vita* 6.16). Horace (*Carmina* 3.26.1-8) and Ovid (*Amores* 1.9.1-46) might romanticize sexual love as warfare (with no lack of mythical precedent), but bloody, brutal, continuous warfare, straining in preparation for it and mopping up after it, had occupied the hands and the minds of the Romans and everyone whose lives they touched for centuries. The author of the PE had reason to touch up the old oracle to Timothy by noting that this was *the fine campaign,* not (for instance) the horrendous one that torched Palestine and Jerusalem between 66 and 70 C.E.

In 1:5 the Pauline *charge* is to issue in *charity arising . . . from a clear conscience and from a faith unfeigned* among the believers to whom Timothy ministers. So now in 1:19 Timothy's personal *faithfulness and clear conscience* are singled out as his own response to the Pauline teaching as well as to the prescription given by the prophetic Spirit to *campaign the fine campaign* with the apostle. At 3:9 "persons who hold *(echontas)* the mystery of the faith with a clean *(katharai)* conscience" are deacons. The uncommon phrase *echōn pistin* seems more Lukan (cf. Luke 17:6 with par., *SFG* §231; Acts 14:9) than Pauline (Rom 14:22; 1 Cor 13:2). The only other appearances of the phrase in the NT, in James 2:1, 18, remind one, with their Jewish Christian resonances, of the PE. However, one ought not to place too much emphasis on the phrase (thus Spicq). Its appearance may have been dictated more by the fact that *conscience* has no appropriate verbal form than that *pisteuein* would not have been a strong enough verb for the activity that the author of the PE wanted to designate.

19b. *Certain people, once they spurned their conscience, went on to shipwreck in their faith.* In 1:3-4 the heterodox teachers were mentioned before conscience and faith. Here in 1:19, after mentioning *faithfulness and a clear conscience,* the text turns to the erring Christian teachers. First they are characterized as *certain people, tines,* which, as was already noted at 1:3, may be a discreet way of saying "many." Then it is specified that they repudiated (the aorist would imply a specific past occasion) the kind of *clear conscience* that Timothy cultivates. If anti-Pauline Jewish Christian (or at least Judaizing Christian) opponents are envisioned here (see 1:3-4, 6-7), this passage coordinates with Acts 7:27, 39; 13:46 (see Notes above). A certain progression appears from the Jewish rejection of Moses in the OT to Jewish rejection of Jesus as the Christ as preached by Paul and finally to the rejection by Christians (Jewish in origin or not) of Paul's teaching about and application of the Law.

The internal, moral collapse of repudiating conscience is here submitted as the reason for *shipwreck in faith.* What Timothy has and keeps *(echōn),* others have lost. Whereas 1:5-6 had described the heterodox as swerving or lurching off "from a clean heart and from a clear conscience and from a faith unfeigned," this passage asserts the internal nexus between sinful acts (i.e. actions contrary to conscience) and loss of faith, an attitude rooted in the sapiential traditions of the OT (see, e.g., Spicq, *EP,* pp. 220-223, on Sirach in the PE) in which what a human being does and thinks (or believes) is warp and woof of the same cloth. The author of the PE, in typically OT fashion, gives action a priority in this symbiotic relationship.

It is an occupational hazard of the theologian, who is bound to think about such matters, to impose his problematic on life itself. Thought is not always (and does not always have to be) prior to all action. The pastoral character of this correspondence is illustrated by this practice of appealing to life as the author observes it, including Christian life, where people often act and then justify themselves. In this approach the reasons or the evidence that may (or may not) motivate a particular individual's conduct commands less attention. The PE articulate their teaching and direction in a way that differs from the Pauline letters to the churches, for the PE are directed to individuals who are committed without qualification to Paul's gospel. The recipients of most of the letters to churches are, for one reason or another, not so committed, and thus evidence must be gleaned from the ideas and terminology of the actual opponents (or the uninformed or the unconvinced) to prove that Paul's preaching and teaching are indeed the gospel of Christ. The PE do not argue with opponents because they are not written to opponents. They do not demonstrate that apostates have first been immoral because the author has simply observed that often enough a sinful life precedes loss of faith. He is aware that loss of faith, too, can issue in immorality. There is sin that does not issue in loss of faith, as there is a loss of faith that does not necessarily spawn other sins. The author of the PE has chosen to express his mind (and Paul's mind as he understood it) on some of these situations; he has not expressed it systematically on all of them. He is in fact a pastor attempting to confront actual problems, not a speculative theologian systematically uncovering, analyzing, and ordering all the possibilities.

The apostates are figuratively described as having been shipwrecked (again the aorist for a specific past event). What travel by air is still for many persons today, travel by sea was for many in antiquity — the utterly unnerving experience of being separated from practically certain death by a frail vessel in an unpredictable but basically hostile environment into which human beings ought not to have ventured in the first place (see the forty lines of elegant trepidation wrung out of Horace in *Carmina* 1.3).

The *shipwreck* has occurred lit. "in respect to *(peri)* the faith." On the half dozen uses of *peri* with the accusative in the PE, see Titus 2:7 and Moule, *Idiom,* p. 62. The personal and subjective belief of the immoral heterodox has finally snapped and come apart.

20. *Among their number were Hymenaeus and Alexander, whom I handed over to Satan to teach them a lesson for their insulting God.* Here for the first time in the PE two opponents are actually named, a practice which continues in 2 Tim 1:15 (Phygelos and Hermogenes); 2:17 (Hymenaeus and Philetus); and 4:14 (Alexander the coppersmith). The unusual name *Hymenaeus* probably designates the same person in both First and Second Timothy, and one infers that the un-Pauline (or anti-Pauline) doctrine about the resurrection denounced there has played its part on a past occasion in provoking the official Pauline act that the aorist verb here expresses with *I handed over to Satan.* A slightly variant form of the phrase appears in 1 Cor 5:5 when Paul is prescribing what ought to be done about the Corinthian Christian man who had married within a degree of kinship that the Mosaic Law interdicted (see Lev 18:6-8;

Deut 22:30; 27:20). Because of such "impurity," *porneia* (1 Cor 5:1; see the *pornoi* in 1 Tim 1:10), Paul avers that he has pronounced judgment already and he directs, "When you are assembled, and my spirit is present, with the power of our Lord Jesus, hand over this man to Satan *(paradounai . . . tōi Satanai)* for the destruction of the flesh, that *(hina)* his spirit may be saved in the day of the Lord." Just how the community participated in the act that Paul himself was going to perform from afar is uncertain (and, as Reitzenstein notes, the unclarity probably intentional; see his *Mystery-Religions,* p. 462). The brief description of the action proposed appears almost formulaic, with its variants on *paradidonai* plus *tōi Satanai* plus a purpose clause (with *hina*). Nothing precisely parallel appears in the other Pauline uses of *paradidonai* nor elsewhere in the PE. Rather than literary dependence of the latter upon First Corinthians, these verbal coincidences between the letters sound like quotations or allusions to a formulaic expression of which Paul was aware in the mid-fifties of the first century and which the author of the PE still heard in the mid-eighties.

The formula, "to hand over to Satan," resembles the wording in considerably later manuscripts for magical spells. Thus the third-century-C.E. *PG* iv. 1227-1264 submits a formula for exorcism, addressed to the God of Israel, Jesus, the Holy Spirit, and others, which closes with "Come out, daimon, since I bind you with unbreakable adamantine fetters, and I deliver you *(paradidōmi se)* into the black chaos in perdition" (E.T. from Betz, *GMP,* p. 62; see MM, p. 483, for the text). The fourth-century C.E. *PGM* v. 334-335 contains a magical rite for a dispatch to the powers of the netherworld (a *defixio*), to be tucked away in a hole made in "the grave of someone untimely dead," preferably under a waning moon. The message is, "Spirit of the dead, who[ever] you are, I give over NN to you *(paradidōmi soi),* so that *(hopōs)* he may not do NN thing" (E.T. by M. Smith from Betz, *GMP,* p. 106; see MM, p. 483, for the text ["NN" refers to the person or thing to be mentioned at this point]). The lateness of the texts and the parasitic character of magical language (in relation to other formally accepted systems of law, and medicine, not to mention the religious language of the orthodox strata in Judaism and Christianity) make one hesitant about positing an otherwise unattested magical source for this quasi-formulaic phrase in the Pauline corpus.

A more likely possibility is that this usage belonged to traditional legal, juridical discourse, particularly about capital punishment. There is a papyrus circular dating 198-199 C.E. in which a Roman prefect made known his intention of prosecuting magicians and diviners throughout Egypt to the limit of the law (the basic edict from Augustus in 11 C.E. is given *apud* Dio Cassius 56.25.5; see also Hopkins, *Conquerors,* pp. 231-242). He writes, "But if anyone is discovered sticking to this undertaking [magic arts], let him be sure that he will be handed over for capital punishment *(tēi escha[t]ēi timōrai paradothēsetai)*" (G.

Horsley, *NDIEC*, pp. 47-48, §12). Jewish and Christian texts often have this nuance also in their use of *paradidonai.* On this hypothesis the use of the phrase by Paul and the later use in magical texts both show the influence of a traditional legal formula for capital punishment.

There is no denying the cultivation of magical practices, divination, and witchcraft in the Hellenistic and Roman worlds. Ephesus was proverbial for these interests, even among Jews, as Luke remembers (see Acts 19:11-20 with its Jewish exorcists and books of magic). Acts, moreover, recalls not only an encounter of Peter in Samaria with a professional magician named Simon (8:9-11, 18-24), but also the fact that the Pauline mission began on Cyprus with a furious confrontation with an itinerant "magician, a Jewish false prophet named Bar Jesus." At Paul's adjuration this "son of the devil" goes blind on the spot (Acts 13:6-11; see Nock, *ERAW* 1.308-330). The PE, similarly, pit Paul, his apostolate, and his teaching against the practitioners of magic (see 2 Tim 3:8, 13). Still it must be granted from the strictly anthropological viewpoint and "within a structural-functional framework" (Aune, "Magic," p. 1510; see the whole article for much of the following) that "religion" and "magic" do not designate mutually exclusive or intrinsically contradictory realities. There are elements in religious life that the anthropologist calls magical (without any adverse value judgment), and there are elements in magic that he similarly speaks of as religious. The social scientist has no criterion within his discipline for isolating the essential distinction between incantation and prayer, between magical and religious (or sacramental) ritual, between magic and miracle. The anthropologist, observing the competition between Moses and Pharaoh's magicians, must forgo ultimate questions and be content to define magic "as that form of religious deviance whereby individual or social goals are sought by means alternate to those normally sanctioned by the dominant religious institution" (Aune, "Magic," p. 1515; note the papyrus cited above). Moses and Aaron were deviant outsiders to the religion of Pharaoh and the Egyptian court; the Egyptian magicians were deviant in the eyes of Israel. The exorcisms and healings of Jesus evoked similar responses from some of his Jewish contemporaries and later from pagans who heard about them.

Paul was himself convinced and expected his correspondents to believe that God had worked signs and wonders through his ministry (see Rom 15:18-19; 2 Cor 12:12). He apparently anticipated that his directive in the Spirit to the Corinthian church to deliver to Satan the man who had married his stepmother would lead to the physical death of the offender. Paul insists that the ultimate purpose of this "reverse exorcism" is not vindictive or totally destructive but "so that his spirit may be saved . . ." (1 Cor 5:5), and thus he tries to forestall a charge that he himself is above morality, unconcerned with sin and forgiveness, and free to indulge hateful cruelty, all of which were taken for granted in many of the ancient traditions for magic (thus Theocritus, *Idyl* 2; Horace, *Epode* 5; Virgil, *Aeneid* 4.450-705; see Luck, *Arcana,* pp. 5, 17, with the texts cited on pp. 68-75, 79-84). In the same letter Paul later drives home his point about the abuses at the Lord's Supper by noting, "That is why many of you are weak and ill and some have died" (1 Cor 11:30). For Paul, all that ends in death began in sin. One cannot break the set or take only part of the package. But that principle belongs to revelation and Christian faith, not to empirical science. The application of the principle is not univocal, as one can see in Paul's repeated prayers to be delivered from his own bouts with an illness inflicted by "an angel of Satan" (2 Cor 12:7; see Furnish, AB *2 Cor,* pp. 528-530, 546-550; Aune, "Magic," p. 1549). The apostle's discernment comes not from any observable difference in the phenomena themselves, whether extraordinary or not, but from the (prophetic) Spirit that enables him to distinguish God's work from Satan's. In this connection it is instructive to recall how the extraordinary works of a messianic prophet serve as divine legitimation for such a role in millennial movements, which are, from the sociologist's point of view, "a collective form of deviant behavior" (Aune, "Magic," p. 1527; see p. 1539). Granted the millennial character of the earliest Christian movement in which Jesus' messianic role is vindicated by his healings and exorcisms, the ultimately christological purpose of even a handing over to Satan becomes more intelligible.

The Paul of First Timothy mitigates somewhat the judgment transmitted to the Corinthian Christians, for now the handing over *to Satan* is *to teach a lesson* to *Hymenaeus and Alexander.* Satan functions here as a pedagogue, putting his rod to the back not of schoolboys but of adult, influential Christian teachers who will not otherwise stop acting and teaching in a way that is an insult to God and his apostolic spokesman (see 2 Tim 2:26). The emphasis is upon the sufferings and chastisements that characterized elementary education in the ancient world. The handing over *to Satan* here envisions something less than the penalty of physical death for their rebellious and insulting verbal mockery of God's gifts in Paul, his apostolate, and his teaching. They are not declared *herem* in a holy war, but they are to learn through physical afflictions to stop their opposition. The writer and his readers would have anticipated such punishments as weakness, illness, and the breakdown of the sense faculties. Even Euripides has the hero of his *Orestes* wasted and sickened, mentally as well as physically, by his matricide. When asked what has brought this about, he replies, "The conscience *(hē syneidēsis),* for I am conscious *(synoida)* of having done terrible things" (396). The blinding of Bar Jesus in Acts answers expectant questions about condign punishment on the part of Christian readers. Apocryphal books later featured for the opponents of God's spokesmen such calamities as dumbness (*Acts of Peter* 2.15 [Vercel.]), a fatal ulcer (Book of Jannes and Jambres [Charlesworth, *OT Pseud.* 2.438]), and death by snakebite (*Acts of John*

86) or a lion (*Acts of Thomas* 8). The individual illustrations are not as important as the basic attitude which they illustrate. The punishments are not inflicted by Christians or even by pagans; they come through the nature human beings share and of which they are part. Satan can indeed administer such punishments, but even when an apostle turns his opponents over to Satan, the case is ultimately being turned over to the God who directs this superhuman adversary.

## II.B. Apostolic Exhortations (2:1–3:13)

### II.B.1. PRAYER AND WORSHIP (2:1–3:1A)

#### *II.B.1.a. For Whom and Why (2:1-7)*

*2 [1]Now I urge, first of all, that entreaties, prayers, intercessions, thanksgivings be made for all human beings, [2]for kings and all in high station. Our purpose is to spend a tranquil and quiet existence in an altogether godly and reverent way. [3]This is an excellent thing and welcome in the eyes of our savior God, [4]who wants all human beings to be saved and to come to full knowledge of the truth, [5]which amounts to this:*

*God is one;*
*One also is the mediator of God and human beings;*
*the Man,*
*Christ Jesus,*
*[6]who gave himself as a ransom for all;*
*The testimony to this has occurred in due time.*

*[7]For that testimony I was appointed a herald and apostle — it is a fact though it sounds incredible — the Gentiles' teacher in faith and truth.*

### ♦ NOTES

2:1. *Now I urge, first of all. Now, oun,* appears for the first time here in the PE and below at 2:8; 3:2; 5:14 (all traditional materials), as well as in 2 Tim 1:8; 2:1, 21. With almost five hundred other NT uses, the complete absence of the particle in Titus as well as First and Second John and Jude is notable. Ap. Frs. never employ the term either, but it is common enough in the LXX and in the *Testaments of the Twelve Patriarchs.*

For *parakalō,* "urge," see Titus 1:9. For the adverbial *first* see 1 Tim 1:15. This is the only time in the NT that the term governs *pantōn,* "all" (reinforcing the superlative *prōton*), but *Did.* 5.1 as well as Hermas, *Man.* 1.1 and *Sim.* 5.3.6 and 9.12.1, use this phrase. In Hermas, *Vis.* 2.4.1, the church "was created first of all," *pantōn prōtē ektisthē.*

*that entreaties, prayers, intercessions, thanksgivings be made for all human beings.* For *be made, poieisthai,* see Titus 3:5; for *for (hyper) all human beings,* Titus 2:11, 14; 3:2.

*Entreaties* translates the plural *deēseis,* which recurs in the ordo for widows at 5:5 of their constant "entreaties and prayers," and then in 2 Tim 1:3 of Paul's "unceasing mention" of Timothy "in my entreaties, night and day." Of the fifteen other NT uses, Luke 2:37 uses the plural of the old widow Anna's constant *entreaties* in the temple court, and 5:33 says of the Pharisees and the followers of the Baptist that "they make entreaties" (with *poiein,* as here in First Timothy). In Luke 1:13 Zechariah's *entreaty* for a son has been heard (see *T. Simeon* 2.2, the unique use of *deēsis* in the *Testaments of the Twelve Patriarchs*). The other Gospels and Acts do not use *deēsis,* but the rest of the Paulines use the word of the apostle's own prayer as well as that of his churches (see Rom 10:1; 2 Cor 1:11; 9:14; Eph 6:18 *bis* with *proseuchai;* Phil 1:4 *bis* with *poioumenos,* 19; 4:6 with *proseuchē*). In Heb 5:7 Jesus "offered entreaties and supplications" just before his death (perhaps at Gethsemane). When James 5:16 uses *deēsis* in teaching that "The entreaty of a righteous man has great power in its effects," he illustrates his point with the example of the prophet Elijah. First Peter 3:12, citing LXX Ps 33:16, reads, "For the eyes of the Lord are upon the righteous and his ears are open to their entreaty." Among Ap. Frs., *1 Clem.* 22.6 cites the same passage and 59.2 uses *deēsin . . . poioumenoi* when the author says, "We shall make eager entreaty and supplication that the Creator of all things may guard unhurt the number of his elect. . . ." Ignatius, *Magn.* 7.1, urges: "Let there be in common one prayer, one entreaty, one mind, one hope in love, in the joy which is without fault. . . ." Polycarp, *Phil.* 7.2, writes of "begging the all-seeing God with entreaties." *Barnabas* 12.7 writes of those who expected an *entreaty* by Moses. Hermas, *Vis.* 3.10.7, hears the reproach, "Why do you constantly beg for revelations in your entreaty?"

*Deēsis* appears in the LXX almost eighty times. Psalms contains almost thirty of these uses. Those in the Solomonic prayer at the dedication of the Jerusalem temple are noteworthy (3 Kgdms 8:28, 30, 38, 45, 49 *s.v.l.,* 52; 9:3; see LXX 2 Chron 6:19-40). The plural appears in the LXX only in the great prayer of Daniel (9:17; see Theod. 9:3, 17) and in the epistolary prayer opening 2 Macc 1:5.

*Prayers* represents the anarthrous plural from *proseuchē,* which will recur with *deēsis* in 5:5 (in articular form and with *kai*). There are thirty-five other uses of the term in the NT, of which a dozen are in the other Paulines (seven are plural) and a dozen in Luke-Acts. The word is not common in the Gospel tradition. Luke 19:46 shares it with the other synoptics (*SFG* §273) in citing LXX Isa 56:7 about the temple being "a house of prayer." Otherwise in the Gospels (outside of Luke) the term appears only in the saying of Jesus about the one way in which a certain demon can be cast out (Matt 17:21; Mark 9:29: *SFG* §163). The Lukan tradition uses *proseuchē* of Jesus' own prayer (Luke 6:12; 22:45) as well as, in Acts, of the prayer of the Christian community (1:14; 2:42 [pl.]; 12:5), of the community prayer as a special responsibility of the Twelve (6:4), of the public prayer of Judaism in the Temple (3:1), of the Jewish prayer observed by Cornelius and his household (10:4 [pl.], 31), and of an area in which Jewish people gathered to pray at Philippi (16:13, 16). For the other NT uses of *proseuchē,* see James 5:17; 1 Pet 3:7; 4:7 (both pl.); Rev 5:8; 8:3, 4 (all pl.).

There are over two dozen uses of *proseuchē* in Ap. Frs., and twenty of these are in Ignatius (see *Magn.* 7.1 above and Schoedel, *Ignatius,* pp. 55-56). The plural appears only in his *Eph.* 10.2; *Magn.* 14.1; *Trall.* 13.1; and *Pol.* 1.3. For the occurrences outside of Ignatius, see *2 Clem.* 2.2 (pl.); 16.4 *bis; Did.* 4.14; and Hermas, *Vis.* 2.1.3.

In the LXX *proseuchē* appears somewhat over a hundred times, with most of the uses in the Psalms and the prayer of Solomon cited above at *deēsis.* However, only four of these uses are certainly in the plural: Dan 9:18, 20, of the prophet's prayers; Tob 12:15, of "the seven holy angels who present the prayers of the saints and enter into the presence of the glory of the Holy One"; and 1 Macc 12:11, citing the letter of the Jewish high priest to the Spartans, in which he writes, "Throughout the years we have unfailingly made mention of you, on our festivals and on the other appropriate occasions in connection with the sacrifices we offer, as well as in our prayers, inasmuch as it is right and proper thus to make mention of brothers" (Goldstein, AB *1 Macc*). The *Testaments of the Twelve Patriarchs* use only the singular (*T. Levi* 4.2; *T. Naphtali* 8.8; *T. Joseph* 4.8; 10.1). Josephus, *War* 5.388, writes of hands raised in prayers, but in his few other uses of the word he means a building or an open place for prayer (*Ant.* 14.258; *Vita* 277, 280, 293; *Apion* 2.10). Philo uses *proseuchē* only in *Ad Gaium* and *In Flaccum* and always with the meaning of a place for Jewish prayer (thus also the Jewish inscriptions; see *CII* 1.662, 682, 683, 690, 726, 884; Lifshitz, *Donateurs* §3, 11, 86, 92, 94, 99; see Hengel, "Proseuche," pp. 157-184; Schürer, *HJP* 2.425-426). In non-Jewish Greek the term is uncommon; for the papyri and inscriptions see MM and BAGD *s.v.* In Latin, Juvenal's drunken bully taunts his victim with *"In qua te quaero proseucha?"* "In what prayer-place shall I find you?" (*Satires* 3.296).

*Intercessions,* from *enteuxis,* recurs in 4:5 (in the singular) but not elsewhere in the NT. In *1 Clem.* 63.2 the emissaries of the Roman church who bear the letter are to be witnesses between the Roman and Corinthian congregations of what has occurred as a result of the plea of the Roman church to make peace "according to the intercession for peace and concord which we have made *(kata tēn enteuxin . . . epoiēsametha)* in this letter" (see *2 Clem.* 19.1). Hermas uses *enteuxis* more than a dozen times (never in the plural). The sole LXX use is in 2 Macc 4:8, where the sense of a face-to-face encounter or an audience with the king (as well as the petition in that setting) coincide (note the cognate noun at 3 Macc 6:40 and verb at Wis 8:21, where it introduces the great prayer for wisdom in the next chapter).

*Thanksgivings, eucharistias,* recurs twice in 4:3-4, in the phrase *meta eucharistias,* "thankfully/with thanksgiving," but not elsewhere in the PE. There are a dozen other NT occurrences, nine of them in the other Paulines (note the only other use of the plural in 2 Cor 9:12 and *meta eucharistias* in Phil 4:6). In 1 Cor 14:16, with its question, "If you bless with the Spirit how can anyone in the position of him with gifts say 'Amen' to your thanksgiving *(epi tēi sēi eucharistiai)* when he does not know what you are saying?" the *eucharistia* is a public, spontaneous prayer of gratitude in the Christian liturgy at Corinth in the middle of the first century (see Conzelmann, *1 Cor.,* pp. 238-239). The Gospel tradition does not speak of *eucharistia,* but the term appears once in Acts 24:3 when Tertullus opens his address to Felix with the phrase *meta pasēs eucharistias.* The two other NT uses are in Rev 4:9 and 7:12, in a description and then a quotation of the hymnic, doxological worship given to God and the Lamb.

By the time of the Ap. Frs., a technical sense is emerging for *eucharistia,* which now designates, at times, what a later age calls the sacrament of the eucharist. Thus Ign. *Smyrn.* 7.1, "They abstain from eucharist and prayer *(eucharistias kai proseuchēs)* because they do not confess that the eucharist *(tēn eucharistian)* is the flesh of our savior Jesus Christ who suffered for our sins . . . ," has the technical sense (see 8.1 and *Phld.* 4.1). The usage in Ign. *Eph.* 13.1, where he writes, "Be eager, then, to meet more often for thanksgiving *(eis eucharistian theou)* and glory to God," may be understood more generically (Schoedel, *Ignatius,* p. 74; but see H. Conzelmann, *TDNT* 9.414-415). *Didache* 9.1, 5 use the word only of the sacramental thanksgiving.

Three out of four LXX uses of *eucharistia* refer to gratitude to fellow humans (LXX Esther 8:12d; Sir 37:11; 2 Macc 2:27), but Wis 16:28 employs the term of prayer to God before dawn. In *T. Issachar* 5.3 his sons are to work the land, "offering gifts gratefully *(met' eucharistias)* to the Lord." In secular Greek the term is common enough in inscriptions (see MM *s.v.* and H. Conzelmann, *TDNT* 9.407) but almost unheard of in papyri (a copy of a letter in P Lond 3.1178.25 from the emperor Claudius conveys his "gratitude" for games held in his honor). An ancient Greek couplet, perhaps from Menander, said, "Show gratitude *(eucharistian poiei)* rather to someone who is absent, for showing it to someone who is present is too much strain" (Jaekel, *Sententiae, Comp.* 2.87-88 [p. 106]; 693K). Polybius describes the Carthaginians after a victory over the Romans as exulting "in gratitude to god" *(dia te tēs pros ton theon eucharistias)* and cheerful parties (*Histories* 1.36.1). See Ledogar, *Acknowledgment*, pp. 90-106, 125-132, 150-155, on the uses of the *eucharist-* cluster.

2. *for kings and all in high station.* See 1:17 on *basileus,* "king." *High station, hyperochē,* lit. "projection" or "prominence," appears elsewhere in the NT only in a phrase in 1 Cor 2:1, where Paul writes, ". . . I did not come proclaiming to you the testimony [*s.v.l.*] of God in lofty words *(kath' hyperochēn logou)* or wisdom." The same faintly pejorative phrase recurs in *1 Clem.* 57.2. The LXX once employs *hyperochē* with this nuance (2 Macc 13:6; see the *lect. dub.* in 1 Kgdms 2:3), but otherwise the word refers to physical height (LXX Jer 52:22 of a pillar) or prominent position in a good sense (2 Macc 3:11; 6:23; 15:13). See MM *s.v.* for the titles of honor, "excellency," or "eminence."

*Our purpose is to spend a tranquil and quiet existence in an altogether godly and reverent way.* On *to spend an existence,* lit. "so that we may lead a life," *hina . . . bion diagōmen:* the phrase *bion diagōmen* is not otherwise documented in the LXX, the NT, or the Ap. Frs., although Josephus uses it six times. When *bios* is used in the other NT texts, it is qualified only by *pas* or *holos,* but here, possibly due to the materialistic connotations of *bios* alone, the phrase "tranquil and quiet" (also used only here) defines it. The petition here is for blessing on the work of world leaders, who, by discharging their duties properly, can provide a "tranquil and quiet existence" for the people under their charge (see also Titus 3:3). In Ap. Frs. the author of *1 Clem.* 62.1 declares that the document just written contains matter "most helpful for a virtuous existence *(enareton bion).*" The use of the adjective may be dictated by the fact that in Christian writing, *bios* alone did not have acceptable ethical overtones. Thus in *2 Clem.* 1.6 the *bios* of the unconverted is simply *thanatos,* "death," and in 20.2 the present *bios* offers gymnastic exercise. When Ignatius in *Phld.* 11.1 describes a certain Rheus as a man who has "renounced life *(tōi biōi)*" to follow the condemned bishop of Antioch, his meaning is close to that which predominates in early Christian documents. More difficult to classify are his *Eph.* 9.2, where he seems to imply that believers have another *bios* with God (alluding to a proverb? see Schoedel, *Ignatius,* p. 68 n. 28), and *Rom.* 7.3. See MM, *s.vv. bios, diagō,* and *zōē,* for papyri and inscriptions.

Regarding *in an altogether godly and reverent way, en pasēi eusebeiai kai semnotēti,* this marks one of ten uses of *eusebia,* "godliness," in the PE (fifteen in the NT); *semnotēs,* "reverent," occurs three times in the PE (none in the rest of the NT) (see also Titus 1:1; 2:7, and MM, p. 572.

*Tranquil, ēremos,* appears only here in the NT, not at all in Ap. Frs., and only in a variant reading in LXX Esther 3:13b.

*Quiet, hēsychios,* appears once more in the NT, in 1 Pet 3:4 of the "quiet disposition *(pneumatos)*" of good women (see the noun *hēsychia* in 1 Tim 2:11-12). The one LXX occurrence is in Isa 66:2, where the adjective alone translates the Hebrew *neke ruaḥ,* "contrite in spirit." The author of *1 Clem.* 13.4 cites the LXX form. The list of virtues in *Did.* 3.8 and *Barn.* 19.4 may also allude to it. Although Hermas uses the term in lists of virtues (*Man.* 5.2.3; 6.2.2; 8.10; 11.8; three out of four times with *praüs,* "gentle," in the context), the Isaian connection is not apparent. Josephus wrote of Hyrcanus as one who "much preferred a quiet existence" *(bion hēsychion mallon ēgapēkōs, Ant.* 13.407; see *Ant.* 8.263 of Rehoboam).

Variations on *to spend a tranquil and quiet existence* in Josephus are notable. Thus, *Ant.* 1.42 describes "the blissful *(makarion)* existence" promised by the serpent of Eden; 2.185 refers to Joseph's brothers spending their existence as shepherds; 3.88 has Moses say that his hearers will spend a happy *(eudaimona)* existence if they follow the commandments; in 9.215 the description of the reign of Jeroboam II of Israel concludes by noting that he spent his existence in "complete prosperity *(meta pasēs eudaimonias)*"; at 10.45 Manasseh, after his repentance, is said to have spent "the rest of his existence in such a way as to be accounted a blessed *(makaristos)* and enviable *(zēlōtēs)* man after the time when he began to show piety *(eusebein)* toward God."

3. *This is an excellent thing and welcome in the eyes of our savior God.* For *excellent, kalon,* see Titus 2:7; regarding *our savior God,* the personal title *sōtēr* occurs ten times in the PE, as opposed to only twice in the rest of the Paulines and four times in Luke-Acts.

*Welcome in the eyes, apodekton enōpion,* is a phrase that recurs of God in 5:4. *Apodektos* (cognate with *apodochē* in 1:15) does not appear otherwise in the NT or in Ap. Frs. or the LXX. When accented on the antepenult (as here), the meaning is "pleasing"; when accented on the final syllable (as in *Diogn.* 8.3), the meaning is "acceptable" (see LSJ, BAGD, and MM *s.v.* for the few secular Greek examples). Other phrases with *enōpion* recur half a dozen times in the letters to Timothy: of God (and Christ) in 1 Tim 5:21; 6:13; 2 Tim 2:14; 4:1; of human beings in 1 Tim 5:20 and 6:12. There are eighty-six other NT uses. Of the nine uses in the other Paulines, only Rom 12:17 and 2 Cor 8:21b use it of human beings. Of the remaining NT occurrences, thirty-five are in Luke-Acts and thirty-five in Revelation.

In Ap. Frs. *enōpion* refers to human beings (*Barn.* 4.11; *1 Clem.* 18.3, citing LXX Ps 50:5; *2 Clem.* 3.2) as well as to God (thus *1 Clem.* 7.3; 18.4, citing LXX Pss 50:6; 21:1; etc.). Two passages are notable for the parallel they give to the thought in 1 Tim 2:3. In *1 Clem.* 60.2 (cf. 61.2), with its psalmic petition, one reads, "Guide our steps to walk in holiness of heart to do fine *(ta kala)* and pleasing things before you (see LXX Deut 12:25, 28; 13:19; 21:9) and before our rulers *(enōpion tōn archontōn hēmōn).*" The last phrase recalls the context of this passage in First Timothy with its reference to what is *kalon* in the sight of this world's kings as well as the king of this world. Polycarp, *Phil.* 6.1, in urging presbyters to care for the abandoned poor, tells these ministers to provide "for that which is an ever fine thing *(tou kalou)* before God and human beings," perhaps paraphrasing LXX Prov 3:4 (note also Rom 12:17; 2 Cor 8:21 [of Paul's collection for the Jerusalem poor]). *Enōpion* appears frequently in the LXX, especially in the Psalms and the four Books of Kings, as well as in the *Testaments of the Twelve Patriarchs.*

4. *who wants all human beings to be saved and to come to full knowledge of the truth.* For *wants, thelei,* see 1:7; for *all human beings,* see Titus 2:11, 14; *to be saved, sōthēnai,* marks the only occurrence in the PE where the subject of *thelein* is God, although the usage is somewhat common in Luke-Acts and the other Paulines; for *to come,* see Titus 3:12; regarding *to full knowledge of the truth, alētheia* occurs fourteen times in the PE, where generally the usage comports with that of the other Paulines (thirty-three uses), i.e. truth being the revelation of the divine world and its claims, not knowledge in its generic sense; fifteen of the twenty NT uses of *epignōsis* fall in the Pauline epistolary, and the four occurrences in the PE of *epignōsis* are with *alētheias* and are governed by *eis* or *kata.*

5. *which amounts to this: God is one; one also is the mediator of God and human beings; the Man, Christ Jesus. Which amounts to this, gar,* is equivalent to *de,* meaning "indeed, to be sure," and expressing continuation/connection (see BAGD *s.v.* §4).

For *God,* see Titus 1:1; for *one,* Titus 1:6; 3:10; for *human beings, anthrōpoi/the Man* (lit. [a] man), *anthrōpos,* Titus 2:11, and Comment below; for *Christ Jesus,* Titus 1:1, 4.

*The mediator* is *mesitēs,* which recurs in the Paulines in Gal 3:19-20. There the apostle has described the law *(ho nomos)* as "ordained through angels by the hand of a mediator *(en cheiri mesitou).*" He then abruptly observes, "Now a mediator *(ho de mesitēs)* is not of one *(henos ouk estin),* but God is one *(ho de theos heis estin),*" but his meaning is elusive (see Betz, *Gal.,* pp. 161, 170-173). The only other NT uses of *mesitēs* apply the term directly to Jesus as mediator of a new covenant in Heb 8:6; 9:15; 12:24 (note the association with death and shedding of blood in the latter references; the cognate verb is linked with an oath in 6:17). *Mesitēs* does not appear in Ap. Frs.

The LXX Job 9:32-33 has the protagonist wish that God were "a human being like me *(anthrōpos kat' eme)*" and that "our mediator [i.e. arbitrator] and examiner *(ho mesitēs hēmōn kai elegchōn)*" existed. The Greek *elegchōn* translates here (as elsewhere) the Hebrew *mokiaḥ;* the *mesitēs hēmōn* corresponds with the Hebrew *beyneynu* (lit. "between us"; *pace* A. T. Hanson, *Studies,* p. 58).

The MT of Job 16:20 and 33:23 employs the Hebrew *meliṣ,* which refers to an umpire, but the LXX does not render these texts with *mesitēs.* The phrase employed at this point in the PE appears in the description of the archangel Michael in *T. Dan* 6.2, which reads: "Draw near to God and to the angel who intercedes for you, for he is a mediator between God and human beings *(houtos esti mesitēs theou kai anthrōpōn)* for the peace of Israel. He shall stand up against the kingdom of the enemy" (see Charlesworth, *OT Pseud.* 1.810 and 927, 929, for E.T. of the Latin references to Moses as mediator of the covenant in *The Testament [Assumption] of Moses* 1.14; 3.12).

*Mesitēs* begins to appear in Hellenistic Greek literary works. It is not found as often in the papyri and only rarely in inscriptions. Polybius, *Histories* 28.17.8, uses the term of the Rhodians as "mediators," i.e. peacemakers between warring nations. Josephus, *Ant.* 16.24, describes Herod as "mediator" for those who wanted benefits from Agrippa; his use of the term in the sense of "guarantor" in *Ant.* 4.133 is similar to its meaning "witness" in the papyri (see Spicq, *Lexic.,* pp. 549-552).

6. *who gave himself as a ransom for all; the testimony to this has occurred in due time.* For *who gave himself for, ho dous edoken . . . hyper,* see Titus 2:14; for *in due time,* see Titus 1:3. *Ransom, antilytron,* does not appear elsewhere in the NT, Ap. Frs., or the LXX. It has yet to be found in a secular text predating 100 C.E. and is rare thereafter (see BAGD *s.v.* and Spicq, *Supp. Lexic.,* p. 431 n. 3).

*The testimony, to martyrion,* recurs in 2 Tim 1:8. Of seventeen other NT uses (regularly in the phrase *eis martyrion,* "for a proof" or "evidence"), five are in Luke-Acts and three in the other Paulines. In Ap. Frs. *martyrion* is used only in set phrases by *First Clement,* Ignatius, and *Barnabas,* but Polycarp uses the articular *to martyrion* when he writes, "Whoever does not confess the testimony of the cross belongs to the devil" (*Phil.* 7.1). The LXX uses the word many times in the set phrase "the tent of testimony," but the only parallel to the passage here in the PE is the verbally similar oracle of LXX Zeph 3:8: "For this reason wait for me, says the Lord, for the day of my rising *(anastaseōs mou),* for a proof *(eis martyrion).*"

7. *For that testimony I was appointed a herald and apostle — it is a fact though it sounds incredible — the Gentiles' teacher in faith and truth.* For *I was appointed, etethēn,* see 1:12; for *apostle,* see Titus 1:1; *in faith* marks one of ten instances in the PE of the anarthrous prepositional phrase *en pistei,* here, as elsewhere in the PE, having a "qualitative force" (Moulton, *Grammar* 1.82); *alētheiai, truth,* used fourteen times in the PE, is here the second component of the hendiadys begun with *pistei* and underlines the revelation offered for belief.

*It is a fact though it sounds incredible* paraphrases the Greek, which reads literally, "I speak (*legō;* see Titus 2:8) the truth, I do not lie *(pseudomai).*" The short reading adopted here is that of $S^c$, A, D*, G, P, Ψ, as well as Old Latin and other Western texts. A longer reading has "I speak the truth in Christ," which brings this text into harmony with that of Rom 9:1 (thus S*, D$^c$, H, K, perhaps 33, etc.; see B. Metzger, *TCGNT*, p. 639). *Ou pseudomai,* "I do not lie," is an expression found only in the Paulines in the NT (Rom 9:1; 2 Cor 11:31; Gal 1:20). An imperatival form of the phrase appears in Col 3:9 (see James 3:14). Luke employs the verb in his Ananias and Sapphira story (Acts 5:3-4). There are four other NT uses, including that of Heb 6:18 of the matters in which God cannot lie (see Titus 1:2). In Ap. Frs. *pseudomai* appears in the citation of the LXX Ps 77:36 in *1 Clem.* 15.4 and in the allusion to Heb 6:18 in 27.2. Hermas, *Man.* 3.2, writes that those who lie reject the Lord. Of almost three dozen uses of the verb in the LXX, the *ou pseusomai* of Job 6:28; 27:11 is notable, as well as the address to the Law in 4 Macc 5:34, *ou pseusomai se . . . ,* "I shall not be false to you, O Law that trained me," which recalls the *ou pseusesthe* in the paraphrase of the Decalogue in LXX Lev 19:11. In the only occurrence of the verb in the *Testaments of the Twelve Patriarchs,* Joseph is accused of lying (*T. Joseph* 13.9). For secular examples of the parenthetical exclamation, see Plutarch, *De communibus notitiis* 1059 A 1, and Lucian's paradoxical play on the phrase, "At any rate I shall tell the truth *(alētheusō)* this one time when I say that I am lying *(pseudomai)*" (*Vera historia* 1.4).

*A herald, kēryx,* will appear in this same phrase in 2 Tim 1:11. In the rest of the NT this term is used only of Noah as "a herald of righteousness" in 2 Pet 2:5. The single instance of its use in Ap. Frs. is in the great encomium of Paul, "who became a herald both in the east and in the west" in *1 Clem.* 5.6.

In LXX Gen 41:43 *kēryx* designates the herald who preceded Joseph, Pharaoh's viceroy. Sirach 20:15 ironically describes a voluble fool as one who "opens his mouth like a herald," and LXX Dan 3:4 uses this noun of the herald who proclaimed Nebuchadnezzar's order to worship the golden image, under penalty of death. The only other LXX use is in 4 Macc 6:4, where the herald cries out to the aged Eleazar, "Obey the orders of the king." The meaning favored by all of these passages coincides with the secular Greek usage, whereby *kēryx* regularly means the man officially designated to make announcements to an assembly (see also *Mart. Pol.* 12.1-2). The term appears in religious contexts, too; thus Epictetus writes that a herald figured in the Greek Mysteries (see also Xenophon, *Hellenica* 2.4.20) and that the Cynic philosopher is "the herald of the gods" *(theōn kēryx).*

At this point, the usage for the **kēr-* cluster of terms, begun at the appearance of *kērygma* in Titus 1:3, can be completed. The rest of the Paulines use this noun in 1 Cor 1:21; 2:4; 15:14, as well as in Rom 16:25, always of the apostolic proclamation of Paul and of others. The Q saying of Luke 11:32/Matt 12:41 (*SFG* §119) uses *kērygma* of Jonah's prophetic announcement of judgment to the Gentiles (one of the four uses in the LXX is in Jon 3:2 [see also 2 Chron

30:5; 1 Esd 9:3; Prov 9:3]). In Ap. Frs. *kērygma* appears only in *Barn.* 12.6, of Moses calling the people to the bronze serpent, and in Hermas, *Sim.* 8.3.2, of the proclamation of "God's son to the ends of the earth" (see 1 Tim 3:16); *Sim.* 9.15.4 of the "forty prophets and teachers of the proclamation of the Son of God"; and *Sim.* 11.16.5 of the "apostles and teachers" who after their own death "gave the seal of the proclamation to those who had fallen asleep before them."

Whereas the nominal forms of the **kēr-* root are relatively infrequent, the same cannot be said for the verb *kēryssein,* which, though it appears in the PE only in 1 Tim 3:16 and 2 Tim 4:2, occurs seventeen times otherwise in the Paulines. Luke-Acts have seventeen occurrences between them, in comparison with Mark's fourteen and Matthew's nine (the Johannine corpus has a single use in Rev 5:2). Including 1 Pet 3:19, there is a total of sixty-one uses of *kēryssein* in the NT, twice the number in the LXX, though it is notable that no single LXX book uses the verb more often than Jonah (1:2; 3:2, 4, 5, 7).

*Kēryssein* appears eighteen times in Ap. Frs., again rather frequently in comparison with their use of nominal forms from the **kēr-* cluster. Of the half dozen uses in *First Clement,* those at 7.6 and 9.4 have Noah as subject and the one at 7.7 has Jonah. On the other hand, in 17.1 the OT prophets are "proclaiming the coming of Christ." In the famous chapter 42 the apostles who are from Christ go out into the world, "with the full assurance that the Holy Spirit gives, announcing the gospel that the kingdom of God is coming. So proclaiming *(kēryssontes)* this in city and country, they appointed the first fruits [of their mission], testing these with regard to the Spirit, to be bishops and deacons of the believers to come." Here for the only time in *First Clement* the verb is used of the apostolic proclamation and closely linked with the Holy Spirit in a way that is reminiscent of the unique use of the verb in Ign. *Phld.* 7.2, where the author asserts that his public charge in the course of the liturgy to pay attention to the local hierarchy was not due to coaching in advance, "but the Spirit kept proclaiming *(ekēryssen)* and saying this, 'Do nothing without the bishop. Love unity. . . .'"

*the Gentiles' teacher, didaskalos ethnōn.* The author of *Diognetus* uses the phrase of himself (11.1). *Didaskalos* appears fifty-nine times in the NT. The three uses in the PE — reserved, when in the singular (here and in 2 Tim 1:11; see 2 Tim 4:3 for the lone, negative plural usage), for the one teacher the PE revere, Paul — contrast with the four in the other Paulines. The only use of the singular there is in the ironic address to the Jew in Rom 2:20 as "teacher of the young"; otherwise the plural appears, referring to a group of Christian ministers who are distinct from apostles and prophets (1 Cor 12:28-29) as well as from evangelists and pastors (Eph 4:11). In the Gospel tradition Jesus is the one most often addressed as or implied to be *teacher.* Luke expands the Markan practice in this respect. Even when the plural is used for the Jewish teachers in the Temple in Luke 2:46, and the singular twice in the traditional material in Luke 6:40, the implication is that Jesus really is the *teacher.* When for the only time *didaskalos* appears in Acts (13:1), Paul is numbered among the Christian "prophets and teachers" at Antioch.

In Ap. Frs., for Ignatius Jesus is "the one teacher" (*Eph.* 15.1) and "the only teacher" for whom the prophets looked (*Magn.* 9.1-2). *Didache* 13.2 submits rules for a "true teacher," and "the ministry *(leitourgian)*" of prophets and teachers appears in 15.1-2. *Barnabas* 1.8; 4.9 are insistent that the author is not writing as a teacher. Of the half dozen uses in Hermas (all pl.), *Vis.* 3.5.1 interprets the stones as "the apostles and bishops and teachers and deacons." *Similitudes* 9.15.4 writes of "forty apostles and teachers of the proclamation *(kērygmatos)* of the Son of God"; 9.16.5, of "the apostles and teachers who proclaimed *(kēryxantes)* the name of the Son of God"; 9.19.2, of "hypocrites and teachers of wickedness"; and 9.25.2, of "apostles and teachers who proclaimed *(kēryxantes)* to the whole world and taught reverently and purely the word of the Lord."

*Didaskalos* appears only twice in the LXX, in Esther 6:1 (to describe the functionary who reads to the king) and 2 Macc 1:10 (of a pagan priest). Philo and Josephus were more ready to use the term than the Greek biblical tradition. Not only human beings but also nature and its law (*Quis Her.* 182; *Agric.* 66), the universe (*Spec. leg.* 1.41), the Torah (*Post.* 80), and the God of Israel himself can be called *teacher* (*Sacr.* 65; *Quis Her.* 19, 102; *Congr.* 114; *Mos.* 1.80). There are also teachers of bad deeds (*Post.* 54; *Spec. leg.* 1.56), of sins (*Quis Her.* 295), of incontinence (*Som.* 2.202), of slackness and luxury (*Spec. leg.* 2.99). In this bad sense, the term practically means "instigator," a sense which Josephus, too, has in *War* 7.442, 444; *Ant.* 1.61. Josephus uses *didaskalos* for Moses in *Ant.* 3.49 (see *Apion* 2.145) and possibly for Jesus in 18.63 *s.v.l.*

*Gentiles', ethnōn,* recurs in the hymnic fragment in 3:16, "Was heralded to the pagans," and then in 2 Tim 4:17, "Still the Lord stood by me and put his strength in me, so that through me the proclamation would be carried out fully, or, in other words, so that all *(panta)* the pagans would listen to it. . . ." There are 159 other NT occurrences of *ethnos,* 54 in the other Paulines (over half in Romans) and 56 in Luke-Acts. The plural appears most frequently and means all the (unbelieving) nations in contrast to Israel; in the singular it may refer to Israel or to a pagan nation. The emphatic *panta ta ethnē* of 2 Tim 4:17 appears twenty times otherwise in the NT; five times in Luke-Acts (including the citation of LXX Amos 9:12 in Acts 15:17) and otherwise in the Paulines only in Gal 3:8 (citing LXX Gen 12:3) and Romans (three times, including the citation of LXX Ps 116:1 in 15:11).

There are over 40 uses of *ethnos* in Ap. Frs., almost all of them in the plural and over a dozen times in quotations, especially in *First Clement* (who, with Hermas, uses the term more than all of the other Ap. Frs. combined). The uses with *hapanta/panta* in *1 Clem.* 59.4 and Hermas, *Sim.* 9.17.4, are parallel to 2 Tim 4:17.

For a survey of the hundreds of LXX uses of *ethnos,* see G. Bertram, *TDNT* 2.364-369, and now, for the Hebrew *goy* which this term regularly translates, R. Clements and G. Botterweck, *TDOT* 2.426-433. All of the 40 uses of *ethnos* in the *Testaments of the Twelve Patriarchs* are in the plural, and forms of *panta ta ethnē* appear fourteen times. The *Testament of Levi* has the largest number of references to the *ethnē;* in *Reuben* and *Gad* the term is not found.

## ♦ COMMENT

The second section of the apostolic commission to Timothy, Part I, entitled "Apostolic Exhortations," begins at this point. The transition is marked negatively by the disappearance throughout this whole section (2:1–3:13) of the explicit, singular address to Timothy, and positively by solemn Pauline exhortations which envision as recipients the whole community of believers and their ministers.

Behind these epistolary exhortations several sources may be discerned. There are resemblances to those early patristic manuals recording ecclesial codes of moral conduct as well as directives for liturgical and private worship and guidelines for organizing congregations of believers and their interrelations. These enchiridia, because of their common interests and contents, have been called church orders and include such venerable documents as the *Didache,* the *Apostolic Tradition* of Hippolytus, the *Didascalia,* the *Apostolic Church Order,* the *Apostolic Constitutions* (including the *Eighty-Five Apostolic Canons*), *The Testament of Our Lord Jesus Christ,* and the *Canones Hippolyti* (Altaner, *Patrology,* pp. 54-61; also see Quasten, *Patrology* 1.30, and Unnik, "Kirchenordnungen" 3.1496-1497). A notable characteristic of these compositions is their citation of and allusions to one another as well as their culling of materials from the then current life and liturgy of the congregations which produced them or for which they were edited. In a word, church orders are from every aspect traditional documents.

To classify the exhortations of 1 Tim 2:1–3:13 as a church order is already to hypothesize that there stands behind this section of the letter a traditional source which antedates all the extant compositions that patrologists have classified as church orders. The chapters in question appear to be too short to have constituted an independent, freestanding work, but, considering the techniques used by the author of the PE elsewhere in his composition, there is no compelling reason for him to cite the whole traditional composition here. Some sections he may well have chosen to cite later (see below, "The Apostolic Commission to Timothy: Part II [4:6–6:19]," especially 5:1–6:2, 11-16); some he may have omitted. If, in fact, the first church order is being cited here, one readily understands why this innovation of the church which produced it can use the stamp of Pauline approval and authority. One concludes from the proliferation in the genre in the following generations that that church order and the Pauline imprimatur had no small clout. Perhaps it was some such "pattern of teaching" that Paul himself had gone out of his way to acknowledge in the Roman house churches (Rom 6:17; 16:17; see Cranfield, *Rom.* 1.323-325; 2.798; Käsemann, *Rom.*, pp. 180-182, who hesitantly suggests the baptismal creed of the Roman congregations). Thus the church order cited here could represent one (or a combination of several) such composition from the Roman church of the first Christian generation. This would go far toward explaining an expectation of its ready acceptance as enjoying Pauline approval when it was transmitted to other areas that the apostle and his co-workers had visited. In any case, the powerful, formative influence of the PE among believers from the second century on is illustrated.

Since even this first church order contains materials that are already themselves traditional, the present chapters of First Timothy are going to offer liturgical compositions, such as acclamations and parenetic charges, as well as lists of virtues and vices and titles for ecclesial ministries which give fragmentary but precious glimpses of the life and worship of first-generation (Roman?) Christians. These will be analyzed as they are encountered in the Comments below.

2:1-2. *Now I urge, first of all, that entreaties, prayers, intercessions, thanksgivings be made for all human beings, for kings and all in high station. Our purpose is to spend a tranquil and quiet existence in an altogether godly and reverent way.*

The opening Greek *parakalō*, "I urge," echoes, as it shifts to the present tense, the aorist *parekalesa* of 1:3 that had been directed to Timothy. The shift in tense suggests that one is moving from *ad hoc* guidance to Timothy (and through him to the believers of Ephesus) to materials that are of permanent significance for all. The past has served as preface to the present, and Paul continues to teach across time as his correspondence once allowed him to bridge geographical distance. The resonance is perhaps reinforced by the postpositive *oun*, "now," which can suggest in historical narrative that one is taking up again matters that had been broached previously (see BAGD *s.v.*). In letters of recommendation (Kim, *Recommendation*, p. 61) the transitional *oun* signals formally that the background has ended and that a request for a favor for a third party is about to begin. Hebrew and Aramaic letters regularly fashioned the transition between *praescriptio* and the body of the letter with *wʿt,* "and now" (see Pardee, "Overview," p. 339, and the many examples indexed under *ʿnh₃ / ʿt* in Pardee, *Handbook,* p. 228). The phrase first of all is, with variations, a regular formula also for opening the body of ancient Greek letters (see White, *Body,* p. 35, for an example with *pro pantōn*).

In this perspective the Pauline thanksgiving prayer of 1:12-17, the centerpiece of the preceding section, has set the precedents for the directives about prayer and worship by all believers that occupy 2:1–3:1a. At each major step thus far in this correspondence the apostle has offered a prayer for his addressees (see Titus 1:4; 3:15; 1 Tim 1:2). This primacy for prayer flows from the primacy of love for God (see 1:5), and thus the first injunction of the apostle for the ongoing life and public worship of the churches bases itself upon their confession of faith in the one God and the one mediator who redeemed all (see 2:5-6). The changes are rung upon various aspects of universality throughout 2:1–3:1a, where forms of *pas* are heard eight times in the first eleven verses. Prayer is to be offered *for all human beings, all in high station,* because the one God wants to save "all human beings" (2:4), because one mediator "gave himself as a ransom for all" (2:6). Paul in turn has an apostolic mission for the nations, without exception (cf. 2:7 with 2 Tim 4:17); men and women alike have their roles in worship "in every place" (2:8).

The four plural nouns, *entreaties, prayers, intercessions, thanksgivings,* all designate aspects of the activity of worship, and their meanings partially coincide. Their asyndetic construction here as well as their coincidences in sense demand that all be taken closely together, almost as if hyphenated to one another, thus accenting the complexity of the single, simple, probably eucharistic (see Kelly, *Commentary,* p. 60) reality that they denote. Their relation to the infinitive *poieisthai* is somewhat vexed, because this verb could be taken as a Greek middle or a passive. If *poieisthai* is understood as a middle, then one must posit either an indefinite subject or an implicit reference to Timothy back in 1:18; moreover, at least in the phrase *deēsin poieisthai* (Luke 5:33; Phil 1:4; see also Rom 1:9; Heb 13:18-19), the idiomatic formula places the object before this verb (see also the examples from the papyri in MM, p. 137). However, in 1 Tim 2:1 *deēseis* leads off four asyndetic nouns that follow the infinitive, signaling thus that they are the subjects of a passive *poieisthai.*

*Deēseis,* "entreaties," is a strong word, emphasizing the specific, concrete needs of the petitioners. The plural here and in the following terms implies a gathering of believers, a liturgical setting, as well as the continual, repeated activity which the present tense of the infinitive also highlights. The PE do not use the verb *deisthai,* though Paul employs it of his prayer (Rom 1:10; 1 Thess 3:10) and Luke uses it fifteen times (of prayer, e.g., in Luke 10:2 [Q; *SFG* §177]; Acts 4:31). There is no parallel in secular Greek for the characteristically Jewish and then Christian theme of constant prayer, "night and day" (Hamman, "La Prière," p. 1195).

The more generic *prayers, proseuchai,* are in tandem here (as on occasion in the LXX) with *entreaties,* whose scope they broaden. Luke never pairs them with anything else except alms (Acts 10:4). They are one of the quartet of activities ascribed to the first Christians in Jerusalem (Acts 2:42). The usage at this point in the PE is not characteristic of either Luke or the other Pauline letters, though there are resemblances to both. Perhaps both were influenced by already traditional liturgical expressions. In this connection, for the only use of the cognate verb *proseuchesthai* in the PE, see 2:8.

*Intercessions, enteuxeis,* reminds the reader of papyri in which this word describes requests made to kings, rulers, or their administrative agents, personally or (more regularly) through a written petition. The latter consisted in a statement of the petitioner's case, the actual request *(deomai oun sou),* and an expression of gratitude in advance (see Spicq, *Lexic.,* pp. 246-249; *EP,* p. 357). When one recalls that the thanksgiving prayer of the previous chapter ended with a doxology of God as "king" (1:17) and that the *entreaties* here will be specified as *for kings and all in high station,* the appropriateness of the juridical and even royal connotations of *enteuxeis* in this list becomes evident. The *entreaties* of Christians are to mediate between their secular rulers and the king of kings (see 6:15).

Finally, climactically, these prayers are *thanksgivings,* public expressions, verbally or in actions, of grateful, internal feelings about a gift *(charis)* that has been received (thus Ledogar, *Acknowledgment,* p. 92). There is no hard evidence for moving the meaning on the semantic trajectory to the sacramental action and elements, a sense that the word has assumed in the *Didache* and Ignatius (see Hamman, "La Prière," pp. 1197-1198). When the OL versions were made, *eucharistias* was still translated *(gratiarum actiones/ -em),* not transliterated (as it would have been if it were understood sacramentally). Even this translation is more literal than one might suspect, for Greek-speaking Jews and Christians already heard *eucharistia* and its cognates with the added meaning "to praise," and enriched with sacrificial overtones (see Stuiber, "Eulogia" 6.904-920; Meershoek, *Latin Biblique,* pp. 78-79; but qualified with Ledogar, *Acknowledgment,* pp. 91-98, 119-121, 124; Cazelles, "L'Anaphore" 1.11-21; LaPorte, *Philon,* pp. 62-140, 257-259 [E.T. pp. 37-97; 179-181]). Moreover, all concede that one cannot read back the developed characteristics of sacramental eucharistic prayers of later ages into the Christian assemblies that celebrated the Lord's Supper in the late first and early second centuries. If the Strasbourg papyrus (PGr. 254) does indeed represent a very archaic form of a sacramental eucharistic prayer that had second-century roots (175-200 has been hazarded), then the pattern which its authors had in mind consisted "of thanksgiving for creation, offering, intercession, and doxology" (Cuming, "Anaphora," p. 121; see the whole study, pp. 115-129, and his "Early Anaphoras," pp. 168-172; for the text of Gr. 254 see Andrieu, "Fragments," pp. 489-515; E.T. in Jasper, *Prayers,* p. 43).

There is an even older Jewish (and Jewish Christian) schema behind this order, i.e. the thanksgiving, anamnesis, doxology outline already documented in the Comment on 1:12-17. At this point one can venture, with the cautions added by Spinks ("Anaphora," pp. 51-55; "Anaphoral Evolution," pp. 211-219), a hypothesis about the *thanksgivings* mentioned here in the PE. The benedictions of synagogue worship occurred in a series, with certain repetitions of the basic pattern; even more pertinently, from the viewpoint being developed here, the most ancient form of the Jewish table prayers after meals, the *birkat ha-mazon,* consisted of a series of three blessing prayers (E.T. in Jasper, *Prayers,* pp. 9-10; see Talley, "From *Berakah,*" pp. 120-124, and "Tradition," pp. 48-52; further material in Ligier, "Last Supper," pp. 113-150, and "Origins," pp. 176-185). Perhaps as early as 70 C.E. each concluded with a sentence beginning, "Blessed are you, O Lord, . . ." but only the last in the series received the response "Amen." The first opened with the address of blessing, too; the second began with "We give thanks to you, O Lord, our God. . . ." The third was a prayer for the Lord's mercy on Jerusalem, a supplication that he remember (in the Hebraic sense) his people, city, and temple. The content and concern of the first prayer are the gifts of creation (see 1 Tim 4:3-4); of the second, the redemption of his people; of the third, the restoration and security of Jerusalem. Against this background, it is possible to envision Jewish Christians (of Rome?), after participating in the regular synagogue services, assembling for their specifically Christian worship in their own house churches. There they used their three Jewish table prayers as models for *thanksgivings* in their Christian assemblies for "the breaking of bread and the prayers" (see Acts 2:42). The plural *eucharistiai* would then be taken of the series of *birkat ha-mazon* (as the singular would refer to only the first one in 1 Tim 4:3-4), which accompanied the Lord's Supper with the bread and cup that proclaimed his death until his final coming (see 1 Cor 11:20-26). Already in Philo the plural *eucharistiai* regularly means thanksgiving offerings or sacrifices (see LaPorte, *Philon,* pp. 62-63 [E.T. p. 37]), and the nuance would be appropriate in this setting also. Perhaps this most archaic (Roman) Christian terminology is still being recalled by Justin when he explains to the Jewish Trypho how "the eucharist of the bread and cup" fulfills the prophecy of Mal 1:11 (which is cited in Strasbourg Papyrus Gr. 254; see 1 Tim 2:8), for he writes of this within the context of "prayers and thanksgivings" (twice in *Trypho* 117; see 41/*PG* 6.745, 749; see 564) and "praises and thanksgivings" (*Trypho* 118; *PG* 6.749). When Justin describes the Roman Sunday eucharist, the core event occurs when "bread and wine and water are brought up, and the president offers prayers in like manner and thanksgivings *(euchas homoios kai eucharistias)* to the best of his ability, and the people assent saying the Amen . . ." (*Dialogue* 67; see "when he has finished the prayers and thanksgiving [*tas euchas kai eucharistian*]" in 65; *PG* 6.429, see 428). In the light of this development Augustine's application of the language here to the celebration of the eucharist in his day looks quite discerning (see his *Epistle* 149.16; CSEL 44.362).

Granted this hypothesis about the meaning of *thanksgivings,* the immediately preceding *intercessions* comes into focus as a specifically Christian feature of the basically Jewish table prayers used for the *eucharistiae.* Again the Strasbourg PGr. 254 devotes a substantial portion of its short text to prayers of intercession for the church and "for all of the peoples *(laōn)* and all of your flocks." In Jewish Christian assemblies the characteristically Christian *intercessions* could well have been added to the third meal prayer, after the beseeching of God's mercy on his people, Israel; his city, Jerusalem; his temple on Zion; "and the great and holy houses over which your name is invoked" (one is reminded of Irenaeus's enigmatic observation that heretical Jewish Christian Ebionites of his day "persevere in these customs [*consuetudinibus*] which accord with the law and in a Jewish style [*iudaico charactere*] of life, so that they even adore Jerusalem as if it were God's house [*uti et Hierosolymam adorent, quasi domus sit Dei*]," *Adversus haereses* 1.26.2; SC 264.346).

The author of the PE singles out the first of the specifically Christian *intercessions* by beginning with the one *for all human beings,* taking for granted that the already traditional petition for the people of God has preceded. The phrase has a Pauline resonance about it, reminding one of the closing directives in 1 Thess 5:15-17: ". . . seek in every circumstance to do good to one another and to all *(eis pantas),* in every circumstance rejoice, pray unceasingly, give thanks at every turn, for this is God's will in Christ Jesus for you." But Paul never explicitly tells believers to pray for all men and women. Thus the directive in 1 Tim 2:1 is an innovation, and in 2:4, 6 it is justified by envisioning the prayer of Christians as an extension and manifestation of God's saving will for humankind as that will has been revealed in the redemptive death of Christ Jesus "for all, *hyper pantōn.*" The explicit opening of Christian public prayer to include all human beings seems to be alluded to in the great prayer cited in *1 Clem.* 60.4: "Give harmony and peace to us and to all inhabitants of the earth." Later Ignatius of Antioch, on his way to death in a Roman arena, embroiders a Pauline phrase to urge, "Now 'pray unceasingly' for other people *(hyper tōn allōn de anthrōpōn),* for there is in them hope of repentance, that they may find God" (*Eph.* 10.1; see Tertullian, *De oratione* 3.4 [CC 1.259]), and in *Pol.* 1.2 he urges his brother bishop "to exhort all *(pantas)* that they may be saved."

The inclusive universality envisioned in the preceding verse is now in verse 2 specified in terms of *kings and all in high station.* The state is the paradigm for public, human associations beyond the family unit. The people who sit at the controls of states are singled out as objects of the peculiarly Christian enterprise of prayer because God's will is to save all human beings not only and simply as individuals but also as united in ultra-familial organizations for their common good. Not only human beings but also their societies need the divine healing and rescue. Earlier guidance for Christian conduct vis-à-vis the state and its officers had appeared in Paul (Rom 13:1-7), in the Petrine traditions (gathered in 1 Pet 2:13-17), and in the PE in Titus 3:1-2 (all linked in one fashion or another with the city of Rome). As Bammel has suggested for the matter in Rom 13:1-7 ("Rom 13," pp. 372-375), Paul seems to be exploiting a traditional Jewish intercession for the Roman officials (see Ezra 6:10; Bar 1:11-12; Jer 29:7 [LXX 36:7]; 1 Macc 7:33; see Philo, *Flacc.* 49; Schürer, *HJP* 2.310-312) that was already in use among Jewish Christians in the West (if not in Rome itself). Yet here in this church order of the PE, for the first time one encounters the prescription that Christian believers pray for their pagan governors (for further Jewish texts, biblical and other, see the excursus, "Prayer for Pagan Authority," in D-C, pp. 37-39). *First Clement* takes such prayer for granted as he cites, perhaps from a Roman liturgy: ". . . grant that we may be obedient to your almighty and glorious name, and to our rulers and governors *(archousin kai hēgoumenois)* on earth [an astonishing collocation; see Légasse, "Prière," pp. 236-253]. Master, you have given the authority of rule *(tēn exousian tēs basileias)* to them through your excellent and inexpressible might, that we may recognize the glory and honor given them by you, and may be subject to them, resisting your will in nothing. And to them, Lord, give health, peace, harmony, stability that they may administer the government which you gave them without offence. For you, heavenly Master, king of eternity *(tōn aiōnōn),* gave to the sons of men glory and honor and authority over the things which are on earth. Direct their counsels, O Lord, according to that which is fine and pleasing in your sight, that they may administer in a godly way with peace and gentleness the authority given them by you, and may find your mercy" (60.4–61.2). The practice is still commended by Polycarp (extant in Latin): "Pray for all the saints. Pray also for rulers [*regibus* may include the emperor] and for potentates, and leaders, and 'for those who persecute you and hate you'" (*Phil.* 12.3). In his old age in the days immediately before his martyrdom, his *Acts* portray him staying at a small estate in the suburbs of Smyrna; "day and night he did little else but pray for everyone (*peri pantōn;* cf. Ign. *Pol.* 1.2, cited above) and for all the churches scattered throughout the world, as he was indeed accustomed to do" (*Mart. Pol.* 5; Musurillo, *Acts,* pp. 6-7; in the West, see Tertullian, *Apology* 31-32; CC 1.142-143). Athenagoras closes his *Legatio* by noting for the emperor that "We [Christians] pray for your government, so that you may, as is most right, succeed to rulership as child to his father, and that your government will receive increase and addition, all people becoming subject to your sway. And this also is to our advantage, 'that we may spend a tranquil and quiet existence,' and may ourselves perform readily all things that have been commanded" (*Legatio* 37; *PG* 6.972; see also Theophilus of Antioch, *Ad Autolycum* 3.14; *PG* 6.1141). Though the intercessions in Strasbourg PGr. 254 begin to become fragmentary at just this point, they seem to have contained a very old petition asking that the ruler(s) "of the land" entertain (?) "peaceful dispositions towards us and towards your holy name"; similarly, the military, the governors, the councils.

Some have proposed that the plural *kings* at this point in the PE refers to the imperial co-rulers from 137 C.E. onward. This theory appears to put too fine a point on the broad Hellenistic usage of *basileis,* which extended even to leaders and patrons in the nonpolitical order. The usage here is of a piece with that of Luke-Acts, in which the term refers to the many petty, crowned heads of state that were under the Roman imperium as well as its Caesar (who could be included in the title; see Spicq, *EP,* p. 359; *Supp. Lexic.,* p. 97, for citations). Frequently when used in the plural, *basileis* has at least one other term joined after it. In this passage an expansive phrase describes *all in high station.* The whole spectrum of government officials, municipal, royal, imperial, can be included in the phrase, whose widest application is emphasized by *pantōn, all* (see Spicq, *EP,* pp. 359-360, for the inscriptions and papyri; Diogenes Laertius, *Lives* 6.78 writes of the *hyperechontes,* the "influential men" of Corinth). The terminology has been chosen with an ear for sound as well as an eye to sense, for *all,* recurring now for the third time, sounds like a refrain as this church order develops (see vv. 4, 6, 8, 11). The unusual noun *hyperochēi,* translated "high station," offers a variation on the *hyper* that has just occurred twice as well as on the ten-times-repeated alliterative *p* sound that has punctuated this sentence from its beginning in 2:1. A similar linking together by sound seems to have dictated the *onton,* whose final *-nton* has occurred at regular intervals three times (not to mention the final *-on* of three other terms).

The remainder of verse 2, *our purpose is to spend a tranquil and quiet existence in an altogether godly and reverent way,* is in Greek a result clause introduced by *hina,* which is synonymous with *hopōs* (in fact, this is precisely the way in which Athenagoras above cites these words, with *hopōs* and the optative; see Spicq, *EP,* p. 360, and D-C, p. 38). The balanced, formal, and probably Hellenistic character of the phraseology of the clause (see the inscriptions cited in MM and BAGD *s.vv.*) bears little if any resemblance to the language of the rest of the NT, and it is not clear how closely it is to be taken with the preceding petition. It looks as if Athenagoras understood it as shading off into an injunction for the reader (D-C), an injunction which even one who did not share the

Christian faith could understand and appreciate. The version here favors this nuance. Rulers are to understand that the public prayers of Christians for the officers of the state are not part of a program that aims at taking over political leadership by bringing about the conversion of secular leaders to faith in Christ and the Christian way of life. Failing that, they are not implicitly threatening revolt, sedition, and treason against those who do not share their beliefs (see Titus 2:14-15; 3:1-3). Their well-being as Christians does not depend on Christian rulers. The purposes of God, including his will "that all human beings be saved," do not preclude loyalty and obedience to the purposes of civil authorities for the common good of human beings in this earthly existence (the book of Revelation does not share, to say the least, this relatively optimistic view of the Roman Empire). The muddled charges of Celsus on the subject of a Christian emperor appear to catch what was in the air in the second century, though it had no documentary foundation (see Chadwick, *Contra Celsum* 8.71, pp. 506-507). Christian reluctance to serve in the Roman army as well as their refusal to participate in what they perceived as the worship of the emperor may have excited these suspicions (see Chadwick, *Contra Celsum* 8.68-69, 73, pp. 505-506, and Swift, "War," p. 845).

As *existence* had been characterized as *tranquil and quiet,* so now *to spend* is qualified with the adverbial doublet *en pasēi eusebeiai kai semnotēti,* here translated as *in an altogether godly and reverent way.* Only here in the NT is *eusebeia,* "godliness," qualified with *pas,* which reminds one that the PE know a *eusebeia* that is only apparent and merely external as well as one that has *dynamis,* a "dynamic" from the Holy Spirit (cf. 2 Tim 3:5 with 1:7). "All godliness" here accents the Christian sense of this term, for the secular terminology of the immediate context would, at first blush, lead the reader to understand the term simply in its Hellenistic, pagan sense. *Semnotēs,* "reverence," is etymologically cognate *(seb-/sem-)* with *eusebeia,* and the pairing of both with a single adjective underlines their complementary character. Note the difference when Josephus writes, "Inquire of these [witnesses] then what sort of life I led *(tina tropon ebiōsa),* whether I have acted in a political capacity here with all reverence and all virtue *(meta pasēs semnotētos kai pasēs aretēs)*" (*Life* 258). *Semnotēs* was above urged on Titus (2:7) as it here applies to the attitude and action of the community of believers taken as a whole, with perhaps an eye to their fulfilling their divinely given roles in the community (note the first person plural and *1 Clem.* 41.1). In 1 Tim 3:4 the bishop's children are to be obedient, lit. "with all reverence," *meta pasēs semnotētos.* This is the only other use of the noun in the NT; the use with *pas* may indicate a characteristic turn of phrase in the church order being used in both chapters. The context of its use in Titus leads one to suspect the influence of the same source on the language there. The usage of the **seb-/sem-* cluster here may be contrasted with the more vigorous apocalyptic critique which a Jewish baptist sect recorded around 80 C.E. in *Sibylline Oracle* 4 (see lines 26, 35, 42-45, 112, 117, 136, 152, 156, 167, 170-171, 184, 187, 190; E.T. in Charlesworth, *O.T. Pseud.* 1.384-389).

3-4. *This is an excellent thing and welcome in the eyes of our savior God, who wants all human beings to be saved and to come to full knowledge of the truth. This,* i.e. the whole complex of prayer activity just mentioned (not simply the immediately preceding clause about *a quiet existence* [*pace* Holtz, *Pb,* p. 59]), is characterized as *kalon, an excellent thing,* i.e. an action visibly attractive in the eyes of one's contemporaries (the term qualifies the "fine deeds" of Titus 2:7, 14). Contemporary paganism knew how to insert the rapier edge of satire between what public prayers professed and what hearts privately cherished (see Horace, *Epistles* 1.16.59-62; Persius, *Satura* 2.3-16 and passim thereafter); thus a further, expansive, resonant phrase here, *welcome in the eyes of our savior God,* complements the meaning of *kalon.* In Greek the unusual *apodektos,* "welcome," sounds solemnly juridical. Its meaning here may be illuminated from its cognate, *dektos,* "acceptable," which occurs five times in the NT. Paul uses it at 2 Cor 6:2 (citing LXX Isa 49:8) for the phrase "At an acceptable time *(kairoi dektoi)* I have listened to you . . ." and at Phil 4:18 for "a sacrifice acceptable *(dektēn)* and pleasing to God," i.e. the alms that his Philippian converts have sent to him. Luke uses forms of *dektos* three times, in Luke 4:19 (citing LXX Isa 61:2 of "a year acceptable to the Lord") and 24 (of a prophet not being "acceptable in his own country"), and then in the narrative about Cornelius, whose prayers and alms are well known and of whom Peter says, "In truth, I perceive that God shows no partiality but in every nation any one who fears him and does right things is acceptable to him" (Acts 10:34-35). The Septuagintal link of this cluster of *dektos* words with the sacrificial worship of Israel is notable, and, when LXX Prov 10:24 writes, "The desire of the just man is acceptable [to God]," the concern is to seal the unity between the internal and external aspects of public prayer, a concern not unlike that in this church order.

In line with the preceding observations, the phrase *enōpion theou,* "in the eyes of God," and variants on it appear regularly in contexts of prayer and sacrifice (see Luke 1:15, 17, 19, 75-76; Acts 10:31, 33). The shorter form of the phrase, whether anarthrous or not (as in 5:4 and 2 Tim 2:14), is probably the more primitive. A liturgical origin and character may explain its liability to expansion (with *our savior* here and with references to God as giving life and to Christ Jesus, the angels [see also Luke 12:9; 15:10], and judgment in 5:21; 6:13; and 2 Tim 4:1). The legal or juridical nuance which comes to the fore in a context of judgment is not alien to the situation for prayer, since coming before God in prayer involves coming before him for his judgment about the prayer and the person who offers it. The petition to the king demands that one come with honesty and sincerity, facing him openly without flinching. Thus *enōpion theou* suggests the oath by which a person bares his heart and his intentions before God as well as his earthly judges. The court of heaven as well as of this world is called to witness this. The face-to-face meaning also leads to the term's being understood as meaning "in person" as contrasted with "in writing" (see the papyri cited in MM, *s.v. enōpion*). The image of the law courts and their requirements may have much to do with the emphasis upon visibly fine deeds, involving such acts as almsgiving, in many of the contexts in which *enōpion theou* appears. The Christian brings the verifiable evidence of his good works before the judgment seat of God and his fellow men. Thus, on July 17, 180, one of the Scillitan Christians, soon to be executed, says to his judge, "I have not stolen; and on any purchase I pay the tax, for I acknowledge my lord *(domnum* [*sic*] *meum),* who is the emperor of kings and of all nations" (*Acts of the Scillitan Martyrs,* §6: Musurillo, *Acts,* pp. 86-87).

The ground and motive proposed for the apostolic priority given here to the public Christian prayer (see Acts 6:4 and Quinn, "Ap. Ministry," pp. 487-488) *for all human beings* are a theologoumenon that is based on the mention of *our savior God* as verse 3 concludes. As has been noted before, when the PE describe God, the Father, or Jesus as literally "savior of us," *hēmōn,* the first person plural (otherwise in the NT with *sōtēr* only in Jude 25) emphasizes the present believing community, identifiably Pauline and thus apostolic. An exclusivist interpretation of *hēmōn* is precluded by the emphatic juxtaposition of the gracious will of *our savior* with *all human beings* (similarly in Titus 2:11-14). The community of believers has become the visible, tangible revelation of the *savior God, who wants all human beings to be saved and to come to full knowledge of the truth.* The passive *to be saved, sōthēnai,* not only avoids making God subject of the verb but also helps prepare for the question, "By whom does the savior God save?" Yet the saving act proceeds from the person of the *savior* God, and it precedes that human response that he also wants and which is described as *to come to full knowledge of the truth.* As Jesus came *(ēlthen)* into the world *(eis ton kosmon)* to save *(sōsai)* sinners (see 1:15), so in complementary fashion, human beings are to come to full knowledge of the truth. This phraseology, which had originated in Jewish sapiential and apocalyptic circles, now with kerygmatic and parenetic overtones designates conversion to Christ. For the PE *the truth* is Christ Jesus as Paul has witnessed to him (cf. 2:7 with Titus 1:1). *Full knowledge* of the Christ, the goal of that witness, is the discovery and recognition of Jesus, with the concomitant total commitment of faith and life to him (see Irenaeus, *Adversus haereses* 4.33.7-8; SC 100.818-821, on what constitutes "true knowledge").

The theologoumenon here in the PE presumes the problematic that is sketched here from Excursus V, "The PE on Salvation," in AB *Titus* (see also Quinn, "Jesus as Savior," pp. 250-253, an essay that is being cited throughout this section of the Comment). A very archaic Jewish Christian, even Palestinian theology of the name Jesus, understood as meaning "savior," is being used to probe and illuminate the meaning of what happened in his life and death and rising. God's salvation had been "personified" in Jesus of Nazareth, whose healing ministry, e.g., revealed that his name was no mere word. Furthermore, the healing (salvation) that he gave to those who asked him was not just for visible, physical diseases but extended to unseen sins. These aspects of the salvation that he brought were not simply contiguous but were coordinated and complementary. Thus what people saw and heard Jesus doing was a parable and paradigm of that saving act of God which they could not sense. The two are related, not by any natural, intrinsic bond between illness and evil, but by the deliberate word and act of Jesus, who revealed the one by means of the other. Visible healing became a window through which men and women saw that hidden, inner world where God saves by forgiveness.

For the PE the already traditional coordination of physical healing and health with salvation has been reorchestrated in a new key because of the concentration on the internal, moral character of the salvation bestowed through Jesus. Healthy instruction, health in faith, wholesome preaching, and healthy words are in this correspondence the sign and paradigm of the inner, moral deliverance effected by the baptismal renewal in God's grace (see Titus 3:4-8). Human deeds, attractive and good *(kala, agatha),* are now perceived as the complement of sound teaching, whereas vicious conduct complements gangrenous teaching (cf. 2 Tim 2:16-18 with 3:1-9).

Against this background for the theologoumenon of 2:3b-4, the function of the citation which follows becomes clear.

5-6. *which amounts to this: God is one; one also is the mediator of God and human beings; the Man, Christ Jesus, who gave himself as a ransom for all; the testimony to this has occurred in due time.* The abrupt, evocative clauses, densely written without verbs, are not characteristic of the style of the PE in general or of the hypothetical church order that has been posited as a source for these chapters. Their form, moreover, is not simply that of a creed or confession of faith; it is rather to be identified as an acclamation (Spicq, *EP,* p. 366) on the part of a congregation at worship, i.e. an originally more or less spontaneous response, filled with faith and reverence and gratitude for the stupendous benefits that these believers had experienced from the regal, divine power at work in their midst (thus Murphy-O'Connor, "1 Cor., VIII, 6," pp. 256-257; see Klauser, "Akklamation," pp. 216-233, for the secular, Jewish, and Christian uses of the form, with the literature cited there; Vielhauer, *Geschichte,* pp. 32-35). The typical acclamation, pagan (as in Acts 19:28, "Great [is] Artemis of the Ephesians") or Christian (as in 1 Cor 12:3, "Jesus [is] Lord"), had one brief member. As in a blessing or doxology, a verb does not appear. The initial position for the attributive adjective gives it an elative nuance. Formally, that applies not only to "great" of an Isis or an Artemis, but to "one" of "Zeus Sarapis" or the God of Israel. The worshippers mean, in their enthusiastic response to benefits, that they perceive themselves as having received, "As far as we are concerned you alone are god" (see Josh 24:15-24; 1 Cor 8:6: "But for us one God [is] the Father"). The acclamation *God is one* in Israel is, however, more than an enthusiastic elative, for it occurs within the long traditional public worship of a people whose essential, indispensable confession of the revelation in which they believed was articulated through the *Shema*ʿ, which began with Deut 6:4, "Hear, O Israel: Yahweh our God, Yahweh is one" (see Hahn, "One God," pp. 69-72, for this and what follows; also Schürer, *HJP* 2.454-455). In the worship setting (as contrasted with the context in Deuteronomy) this great confession was heard as referring to Yahweh as creator of the universe (see Heinemann, *Prayer,* pp. 31, 33, 230), a reference that is explicit in 1 Cor 8:6 and presupposed for the argument of Rom 3:29-30 (see Dahl, "One God," pp. 178-191, for material here and below on the latter passage). In one of the comparatively few passages where the OT speaks of "one God" (as contrasted with "one Yahweh/ Lord"), LXX Mal 2:10 asks: "Did not one God *(theos heis)* create you? Is there not one Father *(patēr heis)* of all of you?" It sounds as if, centuries before Paul, an already traditional double acclamation could be adduced as an irrefutable presupposition in the prophetic parenesis for the people of God (see also the parenesis for the Jewish Christians in James 2:19). Mark's Gospel still keeps very close to the text of the *Shema*ʿ when citing (for Roman Christians?) Jesus' answer to the question, "What is the first commandment of all?" (Mark 12:28-30). When Paul has opened the case for his gospel for the Roman Jewish Christians, he presumes this long traditional attitude toward and understanding of the *Shema*ʿ. If the one God created all, then he wants to save all.

If in fact a Roman church order lies in the background of these chapters of First Timothy, some of these acclamations may have come from that liturgical tradition. On the hypothesis about the form of the *thanksgivings* of 2:1, *heis theos,* "God is one," could have been an acclamation after the first of the *birkat ha-mazon,* blessing "the Lord, our God, king of the universe" for nourishing all his creatures. In that case, the author of the church order or of the PE seems to have understood this first acclamation in terms of the first part of the theologoumenon just cited, i.e. *God our savior* is the *one God* who has created everything. The second, much more complex acclamation, *One also is the mediator . . . a ransom for all,* undergirds the preceding *who wants all human beings to be saved.* Finally, *the testimony to this has occurred in due time* seems to complement *to come to full knowledge of the truth.*

Formally the second acclamation, *one also is the mediator . . . ,* is not simply joined in tandem with the previous *God is one.* A carefully developed triadic parallelism binds together in a classic Hebrew pattern the first five stichs (in the arrangement above). Key terms, *one* and *God,* are repeated from the first to the second stich, and then another term, *anthrōpos,* is introduced in the second stich and repeated in the third (in this version becoming *human beings/the Man;* see Ps 29:5-6 and Albright, *Yahweh,* pp. 1-46, on the archetypes for this kind of versification). The form and the content of these lines point to an origin in a very archaic Jewish Christian milieu in which the *Shemaʿ* was being complemented with public confession of faith in Jesus as savior (see James 2:19). Again, on the hypothesis proposed for the *thanksgivings* in 2:1, that they are the three *birkat ha-mazon* of a (Roman?) Jewish Christian meeting to eat the Lord's Supper, then this double acclamation could have followed the second prayer in the series, the thanksgiving for God's redemptive interventions in history to give his people a covenant, a land, a law, to which the faithful would now add the new covenant in Jesus' blood. In this setting the double acclamation would take up the one used for the previous prayer about creation and would expand it in terms of the culmination of the redemption. The repeated *one* with its *also* would emphatically give to Jesus the worship that Israel gives to Yahweh alone.

The designation of Jesus as *the one mediator of God and human beings* has its parallels in the Letter to the Hebrews (where Jesus as mediator contributes to the explanation of his unique priesthood and sacrifice), but in the Paulines only this passage in the PE calls Jesus *mediator.* The unique LXX use of *mesitēs* in Job 9:33 may have furnished the biblical precedent for the use of *mesitēs* in this acclamation. The passage may have functioned as if it were an entry in a dictionary for justifying one's usage. There is no evidence that the OT passage itself generated the concept that is being articulated here. The only Pauline uses of *mesitēs,* in Gal 3:19-20, appear to be reacting against the OT and Jewish Greek conception of Moses as mediator par excellence between God and his people and to be extolling the "immediatorship" of Jesus (Giblin, "Monotheistic," pp. 537-543; see Callan, "Midrash," p. 555). This negative critique of Mosaic mediatorship does not exclude the possibility that Christ is *mesitēs,* even for Paul, any more than Paul's criticism of "the law of Moses" forbids his writing of "the law of Christ" (Gal 6:2). Yet the apostle does not, in fact, call Jesus *mesitēs.* The term apparently was not immediately or irresistibly attractive in the LXX tradition or in the Pauline one, for all the acceptance that it had in Philo (citations in A. Oepke, *TDNT* 4.617-618) and Jewish apocryphal literature.

The originators of the acclamation *One also is the mediator of God and human beings* swam against the currents of both Septuagintal and Pauline terminology. The term *mesitēs* looks as if it were favored for describing the priestly work of Jesus in at least one Jewish Christian tradition where the Letter to the

Hebrews originated. The whole phrase may have had a pre-Christian Jewish existence in the *Testament of Dan* (see Notes), where the emphasis on prayer belongs at the hard core of the mediator's work (as the OT conceived it), along with the complementary task of bringing God's guiding words to human beings. The passage in the *Testament of Dan* looks as if it had been spawned by Jewish speculation on angels as mediators, with the presupposition that a genuine mediator could not belong to either of the sides that was being reconciled. In this problematic, neither God nor man could be *mediator of God and human beings,* but only an angel (A. T. Hanson, *Studies,* pp. 57, 61). This acclamation adopts the phrase while it denies the presupposition of this speculation. The *one mediator of God and human beings* is *the Man, Christ Jesus.* Origen appears already to be defending Christians against misunderstandings of their notion of mediatorship when he replied to Celsus, "We have to send up every petition, prayer, intercession, and thanksgiving to the supreme God through the high-priest of all angels, the living and divine Logos" (Chadwick, *Contra Celsum* 5.4; p. 266).

All speculation about the nonhuman nature of the mediator is emphatically set aside when an individual human being, *the Man, anthrōpos, Christ Jesus,* is acclaimed as the *one mediator.* The version here (with Jeremias and Strobel, *NTD,* p. 20; *TDNT* 1.143, 366; 6.544; see C. Colpe, *TDNT* 8.404-405, 470) takes the anarthrous *anthrōpos* as a more literate Greek equivalent of the Semitic *ho huios tou anthrōpou* and a very archaic self-designation for Jesus (thus, "The Son of Man did not come to be ministered to but to minister and to give [*dounai*] his life as ransom [*lytron*] for many [*anti pollōn*]," Mark 10:45). In this acclamation, as in the hymn in Phil 2:7 (not to mention LXX Ps 8:5 cited in Heb 2:6 of Jesus), the anarthrous *anthrōpos* title (see BDF §252, 257.3, and Martin, *Carmen,* pp. 209-211) represents substantially the Aramaic *bar naša',* "son of man," which designated Jesus as an individual but in his representative function on behalf of all human beings. He as an individual displaces Moses, for the latter was Yahweh's mediator with the people of Israel (see Philo as cited above) whereas Jesus is *the one mediator of God and human beings* in general, acting for the *savior God, who wants all human beings to he saved* when he *gave himself as a ransom for all (hyper pantōn).* The repetition in Greek of *anthrōpon/anthrōpos* emphatically places Jesus as mediator in the order of and on the side of human beings precisely as mortal, i.e. bound for death. As God he is not mediator, and it is noteworthy that this acclamation does not explicitly refer to Jesus' divine preexistence any more than the Letter to the Hebrews links Jesus' mediation directly with his personal preexistence as Son. He is mediator as *Jesus,* i.e. with the name that means *savior.* It is as mortal *Man* that he has become the *one mediator* for humankind in a given moment of human history.

As mediator Jesus brings God's word to people in their own language.

Thus the Hebrew *meliṣ* in Gen 42:23 means the "interpreter" between Joseph and his brothers, and the word becomes, in the LXX, *hermēneutēs.* It is in that sense that *meliṣ* appears in 1QH 2.13-14, 31; 4.7, 9; 6.13(?), 19; and 18.11. The hymnist is "an interpreter of knowledge of deep mysteries" (T. Gaster modified) and a controversial figure for other "interpreters" "of misguidance," "of lies," "of deceit." 1QH 18.11-12 is striking, as the hymnist prays that God will stay by his people and this community for whom the hymnist himself is an interpreter *(wlmlyṣ)* of God's commands to those who are dust like himself *(l ʿpr kmwny).* With this biblical and intertestamental concept of the *meliṣ* as *mediator* in the sense of the human interpreter who "translates" God's words and commands for his people, this acclamation in the PE is in agreement with its emphasis on the humanity of *the one mediator between God and human beings.* Unlike Qumran, First Timothy asserts that all mankind (not just the chosen people) have *one mediator* who is made from the same dust as Adam and who speaks not only their language but God's language. He is thus *mediator* precisely as *the Man* who speaks for God to man (revelation) and to God for man (prayer and intercession).

Yet the linguistic influence of the Jewish tradition ought to be seen as part of a broader pattern of assimilation and adaptation. The language from the Hellenistic social and economic world has also been borrowed to express what was effected when *Christ Jesus gave himself.* The early Latin West heard and understood the *mesitēs* of the PE as the Latin *sequester,* the person to whom disputed property was entrusted while the case was being litigated *(OLD s.v.;* Frede, *VL* 25.448, notes also *mediator* and *arbiter).* When Tertullian cited 1 Tim 2:5, Jesus is once *mediator* (*De carne* 15.1), three times *sequester Dei et hominum* (*De resurrectione mortuorum* 51.2; 63.1; *Adversus Praxeam* 27.15). The Vulgate Deut 5:5 has Moses, bringing the covenant revelation to God's people, say *Ego sequester et medius fui inter Dominum et vos,* "I was the trustee and middleman between the Lord and you." The perils of such acculturation increase with time, to the point where the model of the modern mediator in labor disputes is quite misleading for an interpretation of *mesitēs.*

The acclamation itself defines and describes *the one mediator* in three gradually lengthening stichs: he had originally designated himself as *the Man;* he was in the apostolic preaching called *Christ Jesus,* i.e. the messiah-savior; he is the center of the worship of the church as the one *who gave himself as a ransom for all.* If the initial *anthrōpos* linked mediatorship with a new Adam and representative Man, the closing climactic affirmation focuses that mediatorship into the once-for-all, obedient death of Jesus on the cross (note the aorist participle and the resemblances to Heb 2:9; 10:5-14). The terminology of the *mesitēs* has something novel about it, but it is because of its link with the central scandal of the kerygma, Christ crucified, who above all on the cross was seen as *the one mediator of God and human beings.* The terminology used in this expansive climax of the second acclamation is reminiscent of the saying of Jesus in Mark 10:45 and Matt 20:28 (cited above). It also recalls the report of Jesus' words over the bread and cup on the night he was betrayed (cf. 1 Cor 11:24-25 with Mark 14:22-24). Another reworking of that language appeared in the creedal confession of Titus 2:14 (not to mention the *hyper pantōn* of Rom 8:32; 2 Cor 5:14-15). The most Semitic turns of phrase are preserved in Mark (see J. Jeremias, *TDNT* 6.543-544), but all three traditions share the language about Jesus freely giving *(dounai)* himself, which probably reflects the gesture as well as the word of Jesus at the supper before his passion, a gesture which continued in the liturgical repetition of that meal. The act, heavy with meaning, is then explained in the sacrificial problematic which the phrase *for all, hyper, pantōn,* suggests, a problematic that is rooted in a very archaic, Palestinian use of the prophecy about the suffering servant of Yahweh, "who makes his soul an offering for sin *('ašam)*" in Isa 53:10 (see D. Kellerman, *TDOT* 1.435, who also notes that the precise meaning of *'ašam* had been lost in Hellenistic Jewish Greek). As the oldest Palestinian liturgy (including its teaching of the Lord's sayings) was rendered in Greek, *lytron* and its various cognates made their appearance in Christian texts (see J. Jeremias, *TDNT* 5.711; Hill, *Greek Words,* pp. 66-81, with qualifications; for the extensive secular and pagan usage of *lytron,* see G. Horsley, *NDIEC* 2.90 [§58]; 3.72-75 [§46]). One hears in the innovative *antilytron* of the liturgical acclamation cited by the church order here in the Pastorals what this Jewish Christian congregation thought the Isaian *'ašam* ought to mean. Whether it actually ever meant that is another question (to which Barrett answered negatively, *NT Essays,* p. 20, with further literature cited there). Perhaps they coined the word by taking the first two words of the phrase *lytron anti pollōn,* recorded in Mark 10:45, to form the new noun, emphasizing the substitutionary character of Jesus' crucifixion (see Moule, *Idiom,* p. 64, and Josephus, *Ant.* 14.107, for *anti* meaning taking the place of another person or thing). When Eusebius was explaining Isa 53:6-7 (*PG* 24.457), coming to the phrase "And the Lord turned him over *(paredōken)* for our sins," he noted that this occurred "so that he might become our substitute and ransom *(antipsychon kai antilytron hēmōn).* For thus he became the Lamb of God, taking away and cleansing the world's sin." The Barberini Euchologium, written down in the eighth century, has several prayers for Christian sacrifices of animals. In the course of the first one, a petition reads, "Multiply also their irrational herds, for whose sake they offer to you the ransom *(to antilytron)* of the exchange of this animal; let its fat become a sacrifice as though of incense acceptable before your holy glory . . ." (Conybeare, *Rit. Armenorum,* p. 413). With appropriate caution, one surmises that the emphatic, expansive neologism *antilytron* belongs to a second-generation (Roman?) Jewish Christian attempt to render an already traditional liturgical acclamation from Aramaic-speaking Christian forebears.

The all-inclusive universality of the effect of Jesus' death has been articulated in terms of an act of emancipation by *ransom.* The ransom for this liberation is nothing other than Jesus himself. The huge slave population of the Hellenistic, Roman world, a population replenished regularly from prisoners of war, thus has become a parable of the whole of humankind, a huge, enslaved society for which Jesus paid the ransom on the cross. Yet this slavery had been not political, economic, or social but moral and ethical. The freedom purchased has been from human sin and evil. The crucified *mediator* both reveals the enormity of that evil and unites the prayers of sinners for freedom to his intercession from the cross.

The third member of the acclamation as it stands in 2:6b, *The testimony to this has occurred in due time,* appears to have been attached by the author of the PE to round out the composition that he has been citing from his source. The sentence is densely elliptical and has eluded definitive explanation. Understanding *the testimony* as an appositive with *who gave himself,* and thus with a primary reference to God's witnessing to humankind concerning his saving will (thus the variants of 1 Cor 1:6; 2:1), appears to be crabbed and uncivil Greek as well as pointlessly repetitive in thought, qualities not unheard of in the PE but hardly to be summarily invoked. Rather, *the testimony* is the apostolic witness. That is certainly the sense of the word in 2 Tim 1:8, its only other use in the PE, where it means Paul's witnessing to the Lord by his own suffering (see Acts 4:33; 2 Thess 1:10). Though one cannot separate absolutely the apostolic witness from God's witness and that of God's Spirit (a fact which makes sense out of inserting this elliptical note at just this point), the primary meaning here is the witness which the apostles give to all people by their proclamation of and their suffering for the crucified *mediator of God and human beings.*

The varied character which this *testimony* assumes in various times and places before different audiences is signaled by the articular *to martyrion* instead of *hen martyrion,* "one testimony," which might have been expected after the confession of *one God* and *one mediator.* In this connection, it is instructive to note that the Arabic *shahada* designates the central profession of Islamic faith, "There is no God but God, Muhammad is the Prophet of God," and then its meaning extends to include the testimony or witness that a person gives by fighting annd dying for Islam (see Gibb and Kramers, *SEI,* p. 515). The *due time,* lit. "their appropriate seasons," for this apostolic *testimony* to the *one God* and his *one mediator* is not to be understood of the OT times or the stages of salvation history but rather of the seasons that God has himself set for the apostolic proclamation, "i.e. the time when persons have become suitably disposed toward the faith" (Clement of Alexandria, a fragment of *Hypotyposeis* 7 cited by

Eusebius, *PG* 9.747). The same phrase for *due time* appeared in the great description of the apostolic mission in Titus 1:3, where it belongs to the redactor's analysis. It seems to pertain to the redactional level here in 1 Tim 2:6, and for much the same reason: the clarification of the function of the apostolate. The phrase, however, was not created by the author of the PE; he exploited the closing verses of the ordination parenesis of 1 Tim 6:14-15. This already traditional liturgical charge concludes by exhorting a typological Timothy who stands for the ordination candidate, "to keep the apostolic command beyond blemish, beyond reproach, until the revelation *(epiphaneias)* of our Lord, Jesus Christ. That revelation *(hen)* God will make in due time, he who is the blessed and only suzerain. . . ." The old and very popular doxology in this influential rite is the most probable source for the phrase *in due time* in Titus and in 1 Tim 2:6. The type of liturgical charge being cited corroborates the link that the author of the PE discerns between the continuing apostolic mission and the present age, the "now," enclosed by the life, death, and rising of Jesus and his ultimate appearance in glory as judge. Already in the archaic ordination parenesis the *due time* is emphatically the time of the eschatological "revelation of our Lord, Jesus Christ" and a time, not necessarily remote, when his ministers must give an accounting for their task (see Towner, "Eschatology," pp. 439, 441-442). Their continuing apostolic witness is the tangible sign of God's continuing desire that *all human beings be saved and come to full knowledge of the truth.*

7. *For that testimony I was appointed a herald and apostle — it is a fact though it sounds incredible — the Gentiles' teacher in faith and truth.* With the return of the first person singular (see 2:1) in this verse, the generic theologoumenon that concluded the previous verse becomes specific. The Pauline apostolate, his kerygma to unbelievers and his further teaching of baptized converts from paganism, telescopes out of the preceding summary which had served as a commentary and conclusion on the liturgical acclamations. Now it links Paul personally with the apostolic witness. God has *appointed* him (with the almost technical sense that appeared in 1:12, with the Greek passive representing the usual reverent periphrastic). The emphatic *egō* suggests not Paul *alone* but Paul as well as, i.e. with the same title as, the other apostles (see 1 Cor 15:8-10) has received a "ministry" (1:12) from the risen Jesus, and this *diakonia* is described at this point with the phrase *a herald and apostle.* After an exclamatory interjection an expansive, appositive phrase, quite in the style of the PE, appears: *the Gentiles' teacher in faith and truth* (see the modifications, verbal and stylistic, at 2 Tim 1:11, which transform the whole into a polysyndetic triad whose climax appears in *teacher*). In both passages the critical significance of the *teacher* and the consequent apostolic, indeed specifically Pauline, teaching come to the fore. Paul is not the only *apostle* for these letters; he is not the only *teacher* (both terms are always anarthrous in the PE); yet it is precisely the Pau-

line apostleship and teaching that the PE strive to preserve, communicate, and justify. If one may so put it, Paul is the apostle among apostles, the teacher among teachers.

In the first phrase describing his ministry Paul is *a herald and apostle,* a hendiadys in which each term complements and illuminates the other. The *kērygma,* "proclamation," which was the central content in the apostle's task in Titus 1:3 (see 2 Tim 4:17), now is personalized as the *apostle* becomes *kēryx.* Perhaps the archaic usage of the prophetic hymn cited in 1 Tim 3:16, confessing Christ as ". . . seen by God's messengers, . . . heralded to the pagans *(ekērychthē en ethnesin),*" gives the precedents for applying this unusual turn of phrase to Paul. At 2 Tim 4:2, the only other use of the verb *kēryssein* in the PE, Paul solemnly charges his co-worker, "Herald *(kēryxon)* the message." There one notes a sharing out and passing on of the task of the apostolic proclamation, or, as it is put in 2 Tim 4:5, "Do the work of one who announces the gospel; carry out fully the ministry that is yours."

Thus for the PE, Paul is the herald-apostle, or apostolic herald, entrusted with the *kērygma* for which he in turn commissions others. If the herald by definition is one who brings news of what has happened to those who have not yet heard it, the apostolic herald is the man who has been commissioned by the risen Jesus to proclaim the good news of what he has done to those who have not yet believed and been baptized. The exclamatory interjection, *it is a fact though it sounds incredible,* separates the herald-apostle title from the title *the Gentiles' teacher in faith and truth.* Grammatically the exclamation could be taken of the preceding phrase or of the following (see Best, "Gentiles," pp. 25-26) or of both. If it applies to the apostolic herald, it reflects that astonishment at the conversion and vocation of the apostle which has appeared already in the great thanksgiving of 1:12-17, an astonishment which took a more sinister form among those believers who controverted the fact of his apostleship. If the exclamation applies to the title *the Gentiles' teacher,* then it becomes the strongest possible affirmation of the legitimacy of the inclusive scope of an apostleship which is itself beyond denial. The manner of speaking here placed on Paul's lips, even the terminology of the expression, is Pauline enough. One recalls the appeal to the witness *(martyrion)* of the conscience of Paul, Timothy, and Silvanus on the integrity of their apostolic conduct in 2 Cor 1:12 (see also 11:31; 12:6, as well as Gal 1:20). The whole phrase at this point in 1 Tim 2:7 is found, with an addition, in Rom 9:1: "I speak the truth in Christ, I do not lie." The variations of expression may represent a Pauline trick of speech, a recollection of the way in which he deliberately varied phrases that were, at least to some extent, part of the oral discourse of his day. If this correspondence originated in a church in which Romans was read out publicly, one cannot dismiss the possibility that the remembered text reinforced the memory of how the apostle had expressed himself.

The alternative object for the astonishment and an equally convincing reason for the apostle's assertion of truthfulness is the fact that he indeed is *the Gentiles' teacher in faith and truth.* On this interpretation he is undeniably the man sent by the risen Jesus to bring the gospel to pagans (as distinguished from those sent to the Jews). But the further question remains. Who will provide direction and formation to those who have believed and been baptized as they seek to live out their baptismal commitment, practically as well as theologically? There is a profound sense in which God and his Christ will provide this. There is another sense which, from the first Christian generation, seemed at worst contradictory and incredible and at best a risky business. Christians would have to teach and guide their fellow Christians. Paul is depicted here as insisting that the God who *appointed* human beings apostles had appointed human beings teachers and, in his case at least, an authoritative Jewish Christian *teacher for the Gentiles* who had believed the gospel which he proclaimed to them. This divinely sanctioned magisterial aspect of Paul's apostolate is not a speculative matter for this correspondence with Timothy. The Letter to Titus did not advert to Gentiles, converted or not, for it was exercised about the problems of Jewish Christian churches. The correspondence with Timothy is explicitly concerned with the *ethnē,* whether still unbelievers as in 3:16 and 2 Tim 4:17 or those who have presumably, as in the present text, believed and been baptized. These Gentile Christians are being misled, in the view of First Timothy particularly, by Christian pseudo-"rabbis" who "propound strange teachings" (1:3, 7) and "demonic doctrines" (4:1). To this pack of "teachers" with their questionable credentials (2 Tim 4:3), Paul, divinely appointed *the Gentiles' teacher,* stands opposed. He remains their guide and leader after baptism, lest anyone object that their further formation belonged to other, less controversial apostles (as they saw the situation).

The Pauline formation is summarily described as *in faith and truth.* The Greek hendiadys with *en* (R. Bultmann, *TDNT* 1.243) could be read as though the particle were *eis* (thus Spicq, *EP,* p. 371), or adverbially (as in the prayer of *1 Clem.* 60.4; the phrase is not found otherwise in the NT or Ap. Frs.). On the former interpretation, Paul is *teacher* of the *faith and truth* to pagans who have not yet believed (note the description of him as *apostle* in Titus 1:1: "for the faith of God's elect and for full and godly knowledge of the truth"). Yet this does not appear to be the meaning of *didaskalos* in the NT, although the distinction between proclaiming to an unbeliever and teaching a believer seems to be disappearing in Hermas and *Diognetus.* The adverbial interpretation, which would take the phrase to mean that Paul is a herald-apostle who teaches the pagans faithfully and truly, labors under the same difficulty. Hence the present version takes the phrase adjectivally, and so as equivalent to *the Gentiles' teacher,* trustworthy and sincere (see Rev 3:14, "The Amen, the faithful and true witness, says these things . . .").

### *II.B.1.b. By Whom and How (2:8–3:1a)*

#### *II.B.1.b.1. By Men (2:8)*

#### *II.B.1.b.2. By Women (2:9–3:1a)*

2 [8]*Now my wish is that the men take part in the prayer "in every place" of worship, that they lift up hands that are holy, that they be without wrath and resentment.*

[9]*Similarly, I also wish the women to make themselves attractive in a becoming costume, with sensible discretion. Their beauty is not in their coiffure and gold ornaments, or in their pearls or extravagant clothing,* [10]*but it comes through their excellent deeds — that suits women who are professing real godliness.*

[11]*Let a married woman quietly learn in the assemblies for worship and quite obediently.* [12]*Moreover, I do not allow a wife to teach in the public worship and to boss her husband. That is learning "quietly."* [13]*The reasons for my directive are that God fashioned Adam first, then Eve;* [14]*and furthermore that Adam was not fooled [by the serpent] but his wife was made a fool of and she turned to sin.* [15]*"A person will be saved rearing children, provided they persevere in faithfulness and charity and a sensible holiness."* 3 [1a]*That is the Christian message, meant to be believed.*

## ♦ NOTES

2:8. *Now my wish is that the men take part in the prayer "in every place."* Lit. "I wish *(boulomai)* therefore *(oun)* the men *(tous androus)* to pray *(proseuchesthai)*." For *boulomai,* see Titus 3:8; for *oun,* 2:1 above; for *anēr,* Titus 1:6; 2:5. *Proseuchesthai* appears only here in the PE, but eighty-five times elsewhere in the NT, of which eighteen are in the rest of the Paulines and thirty-five are divided between Luke and Acts. The appearance of the verb in Ap. Frs. is not particularly frequent; see *Did.* 1.3; 2.7; 8.2-3, as well as Hermas, *Vis.* 1.1.3-4, 9; 2.1.2; 3.1.6; 5.1; *Sim.* 9.11.7 with its reference to praying without ceasing. Ignatius is more notable as he urges prayer for all human beings (*Eph.* 10.1, cited in the comments on 2:1 above), "for *(hyper)* the church that is in Syria" (*Eph.* 21.2), for Ignatius himself (*Trall.* 12.3), and even for the heretical teachers (*Smyrn.* 4.1). Of more than a hundred LXX uses of the verb, 2 Chron 6:26, 32, with its reference to praying "toward this place (*eis ton topon touton,* i.e. the Temple)," ought to be noted in connection with *"in every place"* which follows here. *Proseuchesthai* occurs seven times in the *Testaments of the Twelve Patriarchs,* once of Joseph begging his father to pray the Lord not to take account of the wrong that his brothers had inflicted on him (*T. Benjamin* 3.6).

*"in every place" of worship. Of worship* does not appear in Greek. The quo-

tation marks around *"in every place," en panti topōi,* signal the citation of these words from LXX Mal 1:11, though the phrase appears fifteen times otherwise in the LXX (in contexts of worship in Exod 20:24; Num 18:31; Deut 12:13; LXX Ps 102:22). Among the ninety-four NT uses of *topos,* the term appears in the PE only at this point, in an expression which also appears in contexts of prayer in 1 Thess 1:8; 1 Cor 1:2; 2 Cor 2:14, but not elsewhere in the NT (though Luke-Acts use *topos* thirty-seven times, and though the argument of Stephen in Acts turns on *topos,* the one that comes closest to the expression here in the PE is the *eis panta topon* of Luke 4:37). The Ap. Frs. frequently employ *topos,* but *en panti topōi* is rare. A negative form of the phrase appears in *1 Clem.* 41.2, describing the sacrifices of the Jerusalem temple (see also 54.3, which may refer to every congregation [*pas topos*] receiving the self-exiled lover of peace; 62.2 is irrelevant to this discussion). The most striking parallel to the phrase here in the PE appears in *Did.* 14.1-3, which will be discussed in the Comment below.

*that they lift up hands that are holy.* Lit. "lifting up *(epairontas)* holy *(hosious)* hands *(cheiras).*" *Epairein* appears only here in the PE and eighteen times otherwise in the NT. The sense is quite different in the other Pauline uses (2 Cor 10:5; 11:20), but some of the eleven appearances in Luke-Acts (with such predicates as *heads, eyes,* and *voice*) resemble this use in the PE, including Luke 24:50 of the risen Jesus, who, in parting from his disciples, "lifting up his hands *(eparas tas cheiras autou),* blessed them." The context of prayer for this phrase (found only in the PE and Luke in the NT and Ap. Frs.) as well as various positions presumed for the hands ought to be noted. The verb *epairein* appears in *First Clement* (in a bad sense four out of five times) and Hermas, *Vis.* 3.2.4 (neutral sense), but not otherwise in Ap. Frs.

The precedents for the phrase to *lift up hands* appear in the LXX where *epairein tas cheiras* can refer to prayer (thus Exod 17:11 of Moses; LXX 2 Esd 18:6 [Neh 8:6] of all the people, responding "Amen, Amen" to Ezra's blessing while "lifting up their hands"; LXX Ps 133:2, a directive to the priests, "Lift up your hands to the Holy Place and bless Yahweh"; and Sir 50:20 [see 48:20] of Simon the high priest who "lifted up his hands over the whole congregation of the sons of Israel to pronounce the blessing of the Lord with his lips and to glory in his name"). The same phrase can refer also to raising violent or destructive hands against someone or something (thus 3 Kgdms 11:27; LXX Ps 73:3; Sir 46:2). *Epairein* occurs only in the middle voice in the *Testaments of the Twelve Patriarchs* and always in a bad sense of self-exaltation. The context makes it clear how the gesture is to be understood, and this may be one of the reasons for speaking of *hands that are holy (hosious)* here in First Timothy, since *wrath and resentment* are explicitly mentioned. Neither the LXX or Ap. Frs. or the *Testaments of the Twelve Patriarchs* employ the phrase *cheires hosioi,* though forms of it are found in Greek tragedy (thus Aeschylus, *Choephoroi* 378, of hands that are not holy, *cheres ouch hosiai,* praying for vengeance; Sophocles, *Oedipus Colonus* 470, on making a water libation with hands that are holy, *di' hosion cheiron*). There is scarcely any evidence for this formula that predates the PE (the examples in D-C are of the second Christian century or later), and it was certainly not a meaningless stereotype, constantly repeated in Jewish and Christian Greek. If a very early church order in fact lies behind this passage in First Timothy, then that source and this citation of it are the first evidence for the Christian use of the phrase *lift up hands that are holy,* which must have had an air of novelty about it at that point in Christian history.

For the adjective *holy, hosios,* see Titus 1:8; its antonym, *anosios,* appeared in 1 Tim 1:9. The noun, *cheir, hand,* is a favorite one in the biblical traditions, occurring 178 times in the NT and perhaps ten times that often in the LXX. In the 3 other appearances of the term in the PE, all in the correspondence with Timothy, it is linked with the gesture of imposing hands (1 Tim 4:14; 5:22; 2 Tim 1:6). There are only 13 uses of *cheir* in the rest of the Paulines, and of these only 5 are in the plural. None notably coincides with usage in the PE. The Gospel tradition favors the term (Luke-Acts have 72 occurrences), as do Ap. Frs. (except Ignatius, who does not employ it). The *Testaments of the Twelve Patriarchs* also favor the word.

*without wrath and resentment, chōris orgēs kai dialogismou.* The particle *chōris,* documented forty-one times in the NT, which will appear in another formulaic phrase in 5:21, is not otherwise used in the PE. Whereas the particle is more characteristic of the rest of the Paulines (fourteen times), it appears in the Lukan corpus only in Luke 6:49. Among Ap. Frs. only Ignatius and Hermas use the word. It is relatively infrequent in the LXX and not found in the *Testaments of the Twelve Patriarchs.*

*Orgē,* "wrath," appears thirty-five times otherwise in the NT but only here in the PE. In the Paulines (eighteen times) and in the Gospel tradition (except Mark 3:5), the term ordinarily refers to the eschatological *wrath* of God (including Luke 3:7; 21:23). In the Paulines, only in Col 3:8 and Eph 4:31, as listed in second place in a list of five or six vices, does *orgē* mean human *wrath* (as in James 1:19-20). The reference to human wrath becomes more frequent in Ap. Frs. (*1 Clem.* 13.1; 39.7, citing LXX Job 5:2; 63.2; Ign. *Eph.* 10.2; *Phld.* 8.1; Polybius, *Phil.* 6.1, in a list; *Did.* 3.2; 15.3; Hermas, *Man.* 5.2.4), though references to the wrath of God continue (*1 Clem.* 50.4, citing LXX Isa 26:20; Ign. *Eph.* 11.1; Hermas, *Vis.* 3.6.1; 4.2.6; *Man.* 12.4.1). In the LXX *orgē* designates the divine wrath about two hundred times versus human anger (as in 2 Macc 4:25, 40) about fifty times (thus O. Grether and J. Fichtner, *TDNT* 5.409 n. 194). The *Testaments of the Twelve Patriarchs* censure human *orgē* (thus *T. Simeon* 4.8; see 2.11), but the lengthiest critique of it comes under the title of *thymos* throughout the *Testament of Dan.*

*Dialogismos* appears fourteen times in the NT, where its meaning is usually "reasoning" and then "dispute, argument" (always in a bad sense when it appears in the Gospel traditions, including six times in Luke, as well as in the four Pauline uses outside of this unique instance in the PE and in James 2:4). The plural of S^c^, F, G, H, 33, etc. harmonizes with the generally plural usage of this term in the NT (but note Luke 9:46-47). *Resentment* is the version here because of the preceding epexegetic *kai* as well as the striking parallel in Phil 2:14, where the apostle urges his converts, "Do all things without murmuring or argument *(chōris goggysmōn kai dialogismōn)*." There the audible grumbling and disputations correspond with the internal *wrath and resentment* in the citation here in the PE. The one use of *dialogismos* in Ap. Frs. is in *1 Clem.* 21.3, where the author observes that no human thoughts or "reasonings that we make" escape the Lord's notice. Most of about a score of Septuagintal uses appear in Psalms and Sirach, among which Sir 40:2, rehearsing the miseries of humankind, observes "their *dialogismous (resentments?)* and fear of heart, their anxious foreboding of the day that ends it all." In *T. Judah* 14.3 "impure schemings" for sexual satisfaction are scored.

9. *Similarly, I also wish the women to make themselves attractive.* For *similarly, hōsautōs,* see Titus 2:3. *Also, kai* (single brackets for a disputed reading in *GNT*$^{3\text{corr}}$, Nestle$^{26}$), is not found in S, A, H, P, 33, 81, 1175, and a few other witnesses. Still the scribe of S in the PE tended to omit *kai,* and the phrase sounded more elegant without it. Hence the original is probably transmitted by S$^{c}$, D, F, G, and others (thus J. K. Elliott, *Greek Text,* pp. 207-208). *I wish* has been supplied in the version from the preceding verse. See Titus 1:6 for *the women, gynaikas,* here an anarthrous plural, though J. K. Elliott, *Greek Text,* p. 39, has some reservations because of the articular reading in D$^{bc}$, K, L, H, Ψ, 69, 108, and T.R.; however, the usage of the lists below (esp. 3:11) and in Titus 2:2-3 tips the balance of probabilities in favor of an anarthrous original at this point too. The addition does suggest that the *kai* was not as helpful as had been expected. See Titus 2:10 for the verb *kosmein* used here with *heautas* in the phrase translated *to make themselves attractive.*

*in a becoming costume, en katastolēi kosmiōi.* The *kosmiōi* of S*, A, D$^{c}$, L, P, 69, 1908 was Atticized into *kosmiāi* in 323, 547, 2401, 2412. The adverbial *kosmiōs* of S$^{c}$, D*, F, G, H, 33, 1739 is another attempt to confine the meaning of *katastolē* somewhat too rigorously to its supposedly classical limits ("quiet demeanor, restraint"; see *Ep. Arist.* 284, 285). *Katastolē* appears only here in the NT and Ap. Frs., but there is one occurrence in the LXX, where the one anointed by the Spirit of the Lord bestows on the mourners in Sion a "costume of glory *(katastolēn doxēs)* instead of a spirit of apathy" (LXX Isa 61:3). Josephus, *War* 2.126, in his description of the Essenes, writes that their "costume and bodily appearance *(katastolē de kai schēma sōmatos)* are like that of youngsters disciplined fearsomely." *Kosmios,* "becoming," recurs in the list of virtues below at 3:2 but not otherwise in the NT or Ap. Frs. The LXX Eccles 12:9 uses *kosmion* of the orderly way in which the preacher Qohelet tracks down parables. In Hellenistic Greek the term regularly occurs with forms of *aidōs* and *sōphrosynē* (as here), suggesting "a decent sort" of person (as in Menander, *Sam.* 18, 273, 344; *Georgos* 42 [F. Sandbach; see MacCary, "Old Men," pp. 309-310, for *Aspis* 538]; more at Comment on 3:2 and Spicq, *Lexic.,* p. 442).

*with sensible discretion.* Lit. "with modesty *(meta aidous)* and self-control *(sōphrosynē)*." *Aidōs* does not occur otherwise in the NT or Ap. Frs., though the LXX uses it at 3 Macc 1:19 (in connection with the proper dress for women) and 4:5. The term appears in a principle that *T. Judah* 14.7 cites for the one who drinks wine: "So long as he is decent *(aidō),* he may drink." *Sōphrosynē* will reappear with the particle *meta* in verse 15 below (forming an *inclusio* around this instruction for women). Otherwise in the NT only Acts 26:25 uses this noun, of Paul's speaking "words of truth and of self-control." Josephus uses *aidōs* almost four dozen times, yet never with *sōphrosynē,* and only in his *War* 2.351 does the phrase *meta aidous* appear, in Agrippa's speech about those who maltreated the Jews "in secret and with a feeling of shame."

In Ap. Frs. *sōphrosynē* appears in *1 Clem.* 62.2 and in 64.1 in lists of virtues. Ignatius, *Eph.* 10.3, prays that his readers "remain in all purity and self-control in Jesus Christ, both in the flesh and in the Spirit." In the letter from Artaxerxes in LXX Esther 3:13$^{e}$, the villain Haman is commended for his *sōphrosynē;* in Wis 8:7 righteousness "teaches self-control and prudence" and other virtues. The "self-control and abundantly good conduct" of the murdered Onias excite the pity of Antiochus in 2 Macc 4:37. The cluster of uses of *sōphrosynē* in 4 Macc 1:3, 6, 18, 30-31; 5:23 constitutes a little apologetic treatise on self-control and the Law. This was an old title for the *Testament of Joseph,* and self-control, manifested in sexual continence, explicitly figures in 4.1-2; 6.7; 9.2-3; 10.2-3, regularly with other virtues. Generally, the *sōphron-* cluster in the PE, which always appears in lists or codes, is used to illustrate the nexus between the health given by salvation and the internal moral character that ensues from such healing (see the cognate terms in Titus 1:8; 2:2, 4, 5-6, 12).

The Greek *aidōs* and *sōphrosynē,* particularly when applied to women, suggest reverent modesty and chastity. Philo spoke of the public meetings of the Therapeutae on every seventh day, in a "common sanctuary *(semneion),*" which was divided in such a way that men and women could both hear the speaker for the day without seeing one another. Of this practice he remarked, "The modesty *(aidō)* becoming to the female sex is preserved" thus, for in the context he had considered noteworthy this gathering of both men and women for the characteristic religious observance of this Jewish sect (*Vita. cont.* 33).

When he describes and explains the midwives of Exod 1:15, he links blushing with "modesty and discretion *(aidō kai sōphrosynēn)*" (*Quis Her.* 128), and he uses the same phrase for Lady Learning, who has "the glorious beauty, inviolate, undefiled, and truly virginal, of her modesty and self-control," which scholars wish to contemplate (*Congr.* 124). In his *Mut.* 217 this phrase and the verb correspond with 1 Tim 2:9, as the author, commenting on the presence of an older person, says that this "gives to the youth the adornment of modesty and self-control" (see also *Spec. leg.* 3.51). Philo's *Flacc.* 89 describes the Jewish women of Alexandria "who for modesty's sake *(di' aidō)* avoided the sight of men, even of their closest relations" (see 28, where King Agrippa's nighttime entry into Alexandria to avoid fanfare and publicity is characterized as "with such modesty," *meta toautēs aidous*). Josephus, *War* 2.465, describing the corpses left by the Syrian pogrom, mentions "poor women stripped of the last covering of modesty, *ep' aidō*."

*Their beauty is not in their coiffure. Their beauty is* takes up the thought of *to make themselves attractive* in what is a single, long sentence in Greek. *Coiffure* translates a plural *plegma*, unattested elsewhere in the NT, Ap. Frs., and the LXX, but Aquila and Theodotion use the term as the equivalent of the Hebrew "a diadem *(ṣpyrh)* of beauty" (Isa 28:5 in the Göttingen LXX, 14.216). The reference is to a woven chaplet or coronet or wreath on the head. Thus Euripides, *Ion* 1393, uses the plural for the sacred fillets or chaplets kept for the hero. In secular Greek generally the word suggests that which is woven or wicker work (see Plato, *Laws* 734E; *Timaeus* 79D; *Greek Anthology* 7.24.2). Philo uses the word seldom, in the singular in *Ebr.* 101 and *Som.* 1.204, 206, but in the plural as he describes the high priest's robes whose lower edges were decorated "with golden pomegranates and flowery intertwinings" (*Mos.* 2.111). Josephus uses *plegma* little more than Philo, though he favors it in his description of the basket in which the infant Moses is set adrift (*Ant.* 2.220, 221 [once pl.], 224; other uses in 2.246 [pl.] and 12.72, 79).

*and gold ornaments.* Lit. "and with gold," using the diminutive *chrysion* that included pure gold coins and jewelry (thus A F[*] G H I P Ψ 33, 81 etc.; purist scribes tended to eliminate diminutives, which would explain the reading with *chrysos* [see 2 Tim 2:20] of S, D, and most other manuscripts; J. K. Elliott, *Greek Text,* p. 41). In the rest of the Paulines there is no sure occurrence of *chrysion* (*v.l.* 1 Cor 3:12), but of the eleven other NT uses it means gold coins in Acts 3:26; 20:33. In 1 Pet 1:7, 18, faith is more precious than refined gold and the ransom for believers is the blood of Christ rather than perishable gold; 1 Pet 3:3, of women's ornaments, will be treated in the Comment. In Heb 9:4 the ark of the old covenant is completely covered with gold (see LXX Exod 25:10-11; 38:2). The book of Revelation offers some striking parallels and contrasts with the usage here in First Timothy; in 3:18 the Laodiceans are urged to buy pure gold from Christ. The ornaments of the great harlot-city of 17:4 and 18:16 contrast with those of the city of new Jerusalem, the bride of the lamb, which is altogether, even its street [*sic*], of pure, clear gold (cf. 20:9 with 21:18, 21). In Ap. Frs. only Hermas, *Vis.* 4.3.4 *(bis)*, uses *chrysion* in describing the process of purification for those who have fled the world. Later, in *Mart. Pol.* 18.2, the burned bones of the old bishop Polycarp are kept as more precious than gold. Though there are many uses of *chrysion* in the LXX, the reference to "the ornament of a wig of gold" at the end of the catalogue of luxurious feminine ornaments in Isa 3:24 (not in MT) offers some parallel to the list here in First Timothy. Among the uses in the *Testaments of the Twelve Patriarchs,* the most notable is a variant reading in *T. Judah* 13.5, where Anan's father "decked her in gold *(chrysōi/chrysiōi)* and pearls and made her pour out wine for us in a feast." The longer text of the Greek *Enoch* 8.1 (substantially transmitted in Aramaic in 4Q En$^{b}$ l.ii. 26, 27$^{a}$, 27 [see Milik, *Enoch*, p. 167]) has Asael teaching men to make armor and weapons for war and showing them the metals in the earth "and gold *(to chrysion)* and how to work them and make them ornaments for women . . . ," as well as to produce mascara, gems, and dyes.

*or in their pearls, margaritais,* a noun whose nine NT uses are concentrated otherwise in Matthew's special parabolic material (Matt 7:6; 13:45-46) and in Revelation in contexts that already have been noted above about the harlot-city (Rev 17:4; 18:12, 16) and the bride of the lamb, the new Jerusalem (21:21, *bis*). In the passage about the harlot-city, the mention of pearl(s) occurs in lists that mention gold *(chrysion, chryson)* and precious stones as part of the exotic cargoes brought by the merchants of the world. The passages also note purple and scarlet, fine linen and silk clothing, in addition to such treasures (see *extravagant clothing* here in the PE). In Ap. Frs. *pearls* are mentioned only in Ign. *Eph.* 11.2, where the prisoner-bishop admonishes the Ephesian believers, "Let nothing seem attractive to you without him [Christ]; for in him I wear chains around as the pearls of the Spirit *(tous pneumatikous margaritas)* in which may it be my privilege to rise again by your prayer." The LXX does not write of *pearls; T. Judah* 13.5 was cited above. For the lore about *pearls* and their value among the ancients, see the elder Pliny, *NH* 9.104-124, and Athenaeus, *Deipnosophistai* 3.93A-F, 94A-B. The term *margarita* seems to have come from the East and Alexander's conquests (perhaps from old Persian, which may have borrowed it too [from Sanskrit?]; see Chantraine, *DELG*, p. 666). The term was a Jewish name in Rome (*CII* 136, 373).

*Extravagant clothing, himatismōi polytelei,* is an unusual phrase. The noun *himatismos* appears only four times otherwise in the NT, once in John 19:24 (citing LXX Ps 21:19 of Jesus' seamless tunic; see *Barn.* 6.6) and otherwise only in the Lukan writings (Luke 7:25, "those who are in splendid *clothing* are in royal courts"; Luke 9:29, at Jesus' transfiguration "his *clothing* became dazzling white"; Acts 20:33, Paul avers that he has "not set his heart on anyone's silver or gold or *clothes*"). *Didache* 13.7 notes, among the firstfruits that an authentic prophet or teacher may receive from a congregation, "silver coin and *clothing.*" Hermas's half dozen uses of *himatismos* (thus of the old woman "clothed in shining *clothing*" in *Vis.* 1.2.2) witness to attire that is in some way unusual. The linking with gold and/or silver is also a Septuagintal usage (see LXX Exod 3:22; 11:2; 12:35; 3 Kgdms 10:25; 1 Macc 11:24).

*Extravagant* or "very costly" translates *polytelēs,* which appears in a similar context in 1 Pet 3:4 to describe what is very precious before God. The only other NT use is of the costly perfume poured over Jesus' head by an unnamed woman (Mark 14:3). *Barnabas* 6.2, quoting LXX Isa 28:16 on the "very costly cornerstone" laid in Sion, uses *polytelēs,* as does Hermas, *Sim.* 1.1, of "very costly establishments and buildings and vain dwellings." The LXX regularly uses this word of precious stones (thus Sir 45:11 of the jewels set on Aaron's vestment). The *T. Judah* 26.3 closes with the dying patriarch's admonition, "Do not bury me in very costly garb *(polytelei esthēti).*"

10. *but it comes through their excellent deeds — that suits women who are professing real godliness.* In Greek a single sentence that began in verse 9 (or even 8) concludes here. *Through their excellent deeds,* "by means of good works," represents *di' ergōn agathōn,* discussed at Titus 1:16 (see 2:7, 14). See Titus 2:1 for *that suits, ho prepei,* and Titus 1:6 for *women.* The verb translated here as *professing* is a form of *epaggelein,* which is analyzed in Titus 1:2.

A cognate of *eusebeia, theosebeia, real godliness,* is found only here in the NT and only once in Ap. Frs., in *2 Clem.* 20.4, where a life of instant satisfactions without faith and waiting is described as "commerce and not *real godliness.*" The LXX uses *theosebeia* in translating "fear of God/of the Lord" (Gen 20:11; Job 28:28). Sirach 1:24 says, "*Real godliness* is an abomination to the sinner," and Bar 5:4 promises Jerusalem that she will be called "the glory of *real godliness.*" The remaining four LXX occurrences are in Fourth Maccabees. The noun was not especially common in secular Greek. It is first documented in Xenophon, *Anabasis* 2.6.26, in a short list; Plato, *Epinomis* 985C, 990A, uses the word for an authentic divine worship; Plutarch, *Moralia* 15.160 §67 (LCL), in a fragment of his comments on Hesiod, *Works and Days* 465 ("Pray then to chthonian Zeus and holy Demeter"), writes, "These are also dogmas of *real godliness,* inclining people as they begin their works to invocations of the gods who watch over these works and have the power to perfect them." Philo (who uses the term nine times, once even in the plural, *Quis Her.* 60) calls *theosebeia* "the finest possession" (*Fug.* 150), "the perfect good" (*Congr.* 130), "the greatest of the virtues," symbolized by the tree of life in paradise (*Op. Mund.* 154). For the wise man it is "an impregnable wall" (*Virt.* 186). When listed with one or more other virtues, it appears in last place (*Mos.* 1.303; *Spec. leg.* 4.134, 170).

11. *Let a married woman quietly learn in the assemblies for worship.* For *gynē* as *married woman* see Titus 1:6; for *learn,* Titus 3:14. *Quietly* translates *en hēsychiai,* a phrase taken up again in verse 12. The noun (but not the phrase) reappears in Acts 22:2 and 2 Thess 3:12. In the latter passage Paul instructs the busybodies "to do their work with quietness *(meta hēsychias),*" where the phrase envisions not spreading exciting rumors but not complete silence. In like manner, in the passage from Acts when Paul addresses the excited Jerusalem crowd in Aramaic, they became "more quiet *(mallon . . . hēsychian).*" The *hēsychia* of Christ and God in Ign. *Eph.* 15.2; 19.1 (with *en*), though it is of another order, is not unrelated to the kind of "silence" being enjoined here. The same observation would apply to the one other use of the noun in Ap. Frs., in Hermas, *Man.* 5.2.6, where "the gentle spirit" wants to make its dwelling "with meekness and quietness" *(meta praotētos kai hēsychias).* The LXX uses this noun a dozen times. Only twice can it be understood of complete silence (LXX Job 34:29; Prov 11:12), and in 1 Macc 9:58 the unique occurrence of the phrase *en hēsychiai* describes men who are living quietly (not silently). In *T. Asher* 7.3 *en hēsychiai (s.v.l.)* qualifies "crushing the dragon's head in the water," and in a list of contrasted virtues and vices in *T. Benjamin* 6.5, *hēsychia* is opposed to strife. See Spicq, *Lexic.,* pp. 358-364, for a survey of Jewish and Hellenistic usage which illustrates that this noun and its cognates do not necessarily designate absolute silence or ceasing from all activity.

*and quite obediently.* Lit. "in all obedience," *en pasēi hypotagēi.* The phrase appears without *pasēi* in 3:4, where the list of virtues describes the relation of a bishop-elect's children to the bishop-elect (note the *tekna . . . anypotakta* of Titus 1:6). Otherwise in the NT *hypotagē* appears only in the Pauline epistolary, in Gal 2:5 (of the submission to false brethren which Paul did not give) and in 2 Cor 9:13 (of following Paul's directives for the collection for the poor of the Jerusalem church). In Ap. Frs., *1 Clem.* 1.3 notes *ho kanon tēs hypotagēs,* "the rule of obedience" of wife to husband, and 37.5 describes the mutual subordination of the members of the body in a single *hypotagē;* Ign. *Eph.* 2.2 uses the noun to describe the relation of the members of the Ephesian church to bishop and presbytery. The term is not certainly attested in the LXX or the *Testaments of the Twelve Patriarchs,* and apparently first appeared in Hellenistic Greek in the first century B.C.E. in Dionysius of Halicarnassus 3.66.3, where it describes the voluntary Sabine submission to King Tarquinius of Rome.

12. *Moreover, I do not allow a wife to teach in the public worship.* For *a wife,* see Titus 1:6; *to teach,* Titus 1:11 (*in the public worship* is not in the Greek). *I do not allow, ouk epitrepō,* with a verb is found only here in the PE but seventeen times otherwise in the NT. The two other occurrences in the Paulines are in First Corinthians. As the letter closes, the apostle expresses the hope to stay with his Corinthian converts for a time "if the Lord permits *(ho kyrios*

*epitrepsēi)*" (1 Cor 16:7). In 14:34, in a passage whose authenticity has been unduly suspect (see B. Metzger, *TCGNT*, pp. 565-566; Ellis, "Wives," pp. 213-220), Paul avers that in the liturgical assemblies Christian wives "are not permitted [the passive presumes God as subject] to speak [i.e. to teach], but they should be subordinate just as the law also says" *(ou gar epitrepetai autais lalein alla hypotassesthōsan . . .).* The verse will be discussed in its context in the Comment. Only in Heb 6:3 in the NT is God explicitly the subject of *epitrepein;* otherwise Moses or Pilate or Jesus himself is subject. In Luke-Acts it is not only Jesus who is the expressed or implied subject but, in Acts, the public authority of Rome and its representatives (see Acts 21:39, 40; 26:1 [contrast this passive with that in 1 Cor 14:34]; 27:3; 28:16).

*Epitrepein* appears also in the domestic code that underlies *1 Clem.* 1.3, in a command imposed on young men as distinguished from the instruction for women. In *Did.* 10.7 this verb introduces a directive for the way in which the prophets are to give thanks (or offer the eucharist) in the order proposed there for the sacramental action (*Did.* 9.1–10.7, which Audet, *Didache,* pp. 372-433, regards as pertaining to the first stage of the composition of the work). In Ign. *Eph.* 10.1 and *Smyrn.* 8.1 *epitrepein* designates actions that ought to pertain to the Christian worship assemblies (though this is not the case in Ign. *Rom.* 6.3; Polycarp, *Phil.* 3.1; or Hermas). Among the eight LXX uses of the verb, most refer to a royal, and once even to a divine, appointment (thus LXX Esther 9:14; Wis 19:2; 1 Macc 15:6; 4 Macc 4:17-18; 5:26).

*and to boss her husband.* For *husband,* lit. "man," *andros,* see Titus 1:6. *To boss, authentein,* appears only here in the NT, Ap. Frs., and the LXX. The handful of secular Greek uses, conveniently assembled for study in Knight, "*Authenteō,*" pp. 143-157, include only three that predate the PE (or their source at this point). One is a first-century-B.C.E. Alexandrian note on the text of Aeschylus, *Eumenides* 42, where the scholiast (or compiler) explains Orestes' "hands dripping with blood" as vividly presenting by this means one who has just now "murdered" *(euthentēkota)* his own mother. Some kind of euphemism seems to be involved in this usage, perhaps a resemblance to the Greek *thenein,* "to strike" (see Chantraine, *DELG*, pp. 138-139; note the American slang phrase "hit man," meaning a professional murderer, from a use of *hit* with the meaning *kill, rob*). In any case, in contemporary Greek documents *authentein* was understood to mean ruling or acting with full authority and jurisdiction. Thus a fragmentary text of Philodemus of Gadara, *Rhetorica* 2, p. 133, lines 14-15, speaks of those who are at odds "with rulers acting with full authority" *(syn authent[ou]sin an[axin]),* and a papyrus dating from 27/26 B.C.E. contains a letter wherein the author describes how he had obtained the compliance of the reluctant manager of a ferrying service. The key sentence reads, "When I had leaned on him [lit. 'exercised full jurisdiction in regard to him,' *Kamou authentekotas pros auton*], he consented to provide for Calatytis the boatman, for the full fare, within the hour" (*BGU* 4.1208.37-42). The sparse documentation for the succeeding centuries suggests that *authentein* did not often appear in secular compositions that were composed with an eye to survival. The reason is probably given in a couple of old grammatical notes (see Hommes, "Women," pp. 16-19). One observes that whereas Attic says *autodikēn/-ein*, Hellenistic Greek has *authentēn/-ein*, i.e. *authentein*, "to boss," which is the vulgar equivalent of to have independent jurisdiction or to be a law unto oneself (thus Moeris, second-century-C.E. Attic grammarian). Much later the medieval Thomas Magister urges his students to say *autodikein, ouk authentein koinoteron gar* "for the latter is too vulgar." *Authentein* evidently grated on an educated Greek ear for more than a millennium. Except in a couple of astrological texts, it regularly appears in a context that suggests that the complete authority in question is not altogether warranted (a nuance which on this reading is present in the texts marshaled by Knight, "*Authenteō*," pp. 146-148). The English *to boss* in this version intends to convey some of the effect of the inelegant Greek at this point, suggesting something questionable in the activity without either condemning it in advance (as *to domineer* would do) or taking a quite neutral stance (as *to have authority* might suggest).

*that is learning "quietly."* Lit. "but to be in quietness," repeating *en hēsychiai* from verse 11 *q.v.*

13. *The reasons for my directive are that God fashioned Adam first, then Eve.* Lit. "For Adam was first formed *(prōtos eplasthē)*, then *(eita)* Eve." On *first*, see 1:15. *Eita* recurs in 3:10 (where an adverbial *prōton* precedes it too) but not otherwise in the PE. There are thirteen other NT uses of the particle, one in Luke 8:12 in the interpretation of the sower parable. In the rest of the Paulines, *eita* appears only in First Corinthians, twice in the citation of the source in 15:5, 7, and once more in 15:24, in all of which a temporal succession is being described. Ignatius does not use the particle at all, but it is regularly encountered otherwise in Ap. Frs. It appears fewer than two dozen times in the LXX, with most uses in the LXX Job. *Eita* appears in the *Testaments of the Twelve Patriarchs* twice: in *T. Dan* 4.2, with *prōton*, and in *T. Naphtali* 2.8.

*Fashioned* with *God* supplied as subject in this version represents the passive *eplasthē*, from *plassein*, whose only other use in the NT is in Rom 9:20: "But who are you, O man, talking back to God? Will that which is fashioned say to the fashioner (*tōi plasanti;* LXX Isa 29:16), 'Why did you make me thus?'" In Ap. Frs. *1 Clem.* 33.4; 38.3 use the verb *plassein* of the creation of human beings, and 16.2 (LXX Isa 53:11) of forming the understanding of the Servant of the Lord. *Barnabas* 2.10 similarly has a reference to God's fashioning the human heart, and then 19.2 refers to him as the fashioner of creation. Of over four dozen appearances of *plassein* in the LXX, the most influential upon later Jewish and Christian usage appear to be those in the narrative of the fashioning of "the man" *(eplasen ho theos ton anthrōpon)* in Gen 2:7 (cf. 2:8, 15, and 19 [of the wild animals]). Notable, too, are the passages about the Maccabean martyrs whose mother in 2 Macc 7:23 says to her sons, "Therefore the creator of the world who fashioned *(ho plasas)* the beginning of man *(anthrōpou genesin)* and brought about the beginning of all things will in his mercy give life and breath back to you." These are the men who in 4 Macc 13:20 are described as a fraternity in which each of them dwelt the same length of time in his mother's womb and "was fashioned *(plasthentes)* during the same period of time, and growing from the same blood and through the same life, they were brought to the light of day." Menander has some infamous railing against Prometheus which reads, "O you right reverend gods, he was the one who fashioned women *(gynaikas eplasen)*, a foul lot, I think, hateful to all the gods" (Koerte 718.4-5; 535.4-5K).

*Adam,* as a name here and in the verse following, has been transliterated from the Hebrew *'adam,* which is both a true generic substantive (as in the anarthrous English *man*) and a name (F. Maass, *TDOT* 1.75). Five out of the seven remaining NT uses appear in Rom 5:14 (twice, with *parabasis* as here in the PE) and 1 Cor 15:22, 45 (twice, citing LXX Gen 2:7, adding *prōtos* to *anthrōpos* as well as inserting the name *Adam*). In the Gospels the name *Adam* occurs only in the Lukan genealogy (3:38), in which he is "Adam who is of God." As J. Fitzmyer has noted: "Here, as in much of intertestamental literature, Adam's 'sin' is forgotten and his 'glory' as the first-formed is extolled. Luke even enhances his status by calling him 'son of God'" (AB *Lk,* p. 504). In Jude 14 the name *Adam* serves as a calendrical marker for the first in a series of human generations. The name appears in Ap. Frs. only in *1 Clem.* 6.3 (where he is "our father"); 29.2 (of the "sons of Adam," citing LXX Deut 32:8); 50.3 (representing the first human generation); and in *Barn.* 6.9 ("For the fashioning of Adam [*hē plasis tou Adam*] took place from the surface of the earth," alluding to Gen 2:7). *Adam* begins to appear as a name abruptly in LXX Gen 2:16 and, after a couple dozen appearances, ceases to be employed regularly after LXX Gen 5:5 (Deuteronomy has been noted above; *Adam* begins the genealogy of LXX 1 Chron 1:1; Tob 8:6 will be cited in the Comment; Sir 33:10 alludes to Adam's creation from dust; 40:1 uses the phrase "sons of Adam"; and 49:16 avers that Adam is honored "above every living thing in creation"). In the Christian interpolation in *T. Simeon* 6.5, when God will be manifest on earth as a man, "By himself he will save Adam." In *T. Levi* 18.10 the eschatological priest "shall open the gates of paradise; he shall remove the sword that has threatened since Adam, and he will grant the saints to eat of the tree of life."

*Eve, Heua,* is a transliteration of the Hebrew *hawwah* (see A. Kapelrud, *TDOT* 4.257). Its one other appearance in the NT is in 2 Cor 11:3 (see Notes and Comment on v. 14). In Ap. Frs. only *Barn.* 12.5 uses the name in his explanation of the episode about the serpents during the exodus: "For the Lord made every serpent bite them and they were dying, for the transgression *(he parabasis)* took place through the serpent in Eve *(en Heuai)*." The name makes its appearance in the LXX only in Gen 4:1, 25 (thus long after *Adam*). It recurs in Tob 8.6 in the course of the marriage prayer to be cited in the Comment.

14. *and furthermore that Adam was not fooled [by the serpent] but his wife was made a fool of. Adam* as in verse 13; *wife* as in Titus 1:6. *Fooled/made a fool of* represent the cognate verbs *apatan/exapatan.* The former appears otherwise in the NT only in Eph 5:6 (of deception with empty words; see *T. Naphtali* 3.1) and James 1:26 (of deceiving oneself about unbridled speech), and in Ap. Frs. only in Hermas (seven times). In the almost three dozen LXX uses of *apatan,* the woman uses this verb about the serpent in LXX Gen 3:13 (see *T. Zebulun* 9.7). Another notable occurrence is in LXX Susanna 56 (of the effect of Susanna's beauty; see *T. Judah* 11.2; 12.3; 13.3).

*Exapatan,* the emphatic, compounded form of *apatan,* is found only here in the PE and five times, only in the Paulines, in the rest of the NT. Thus 2 Thess 2:3 urges those frightened by exact predictions of the coming of Jesus in glory, "Let no one make a fool of you in any way." The same verb appears in the warning to the wise men of Corinth: "Let no one make a fool of himself" (1 Cor 3:18; see 19 for *panourgia*). After a description of those who openly oppose the apostolic teaching, Rom 16:18 says, "For such people do not serve our Lord Christ but their own belly [see Phil 3:19], and by fair and flattering words they make fools of the hearts of the simple-minded *(akakōn)*." The connotation of leading astray the guileless and naive is everywhere present, and that is the nuance that the verb has at Rom 7:11, where in the dramatic retelling of the Genesis account of the fall of Adam, the apostle can say in the person of the first man, "For sin, finding opportunity in the commandment, made a fool of me and by it killed me." The passage can scarcely be separated from 2 Cor 11:3, where Paul sees himself as the father of the Corinthian church, which in its turn is conceived of as the bride that he has betrothed to Christ, her "one husband (*heni andri* [see Titus 1:6])." He explains or rather refracts his own anxiety and concern through the Genesis account of the fall, saying, "But I am afraid that as the serpent deceived Eve *(ho ophis exēpatēsen Heuan)* by his cunning *(en tēi panourgiai)*, your thoughts will be led astray from a sincere and pure devotion to Christ." The thought of Eve as naive and guileless in her fatal dialogue with the serpent is certainly at the fore here, as is the emphasis upon the craftiness of the serpent.

*Exapatan* appears only twice in Ap. Frs., in the Ignatian epistolary. Writing of heretical teachers, Ign. *Eph.* 8.1 says, "Let no one therefore make fools of you; and indeed you have not been made fools of but belong wholly to God." Then, in *Rom.* 6.2, he asks that church, "Do not give to the world one who desires to belong to God and do not make a fool of him with material things." In the LXX *exapatan* is used only of Pharaoh trying to make a fool of Moses by reneging on his promise to let Israel go to sacrifice in the desert (LXX Exod 8:25; see Theodotion's Susanna 56).

*and she turned to sin.* Lit. "and she became *(gegonen)* in transgression *(en parabasei).*" See Titus 3:7 for the verb, here a second perfect. It is used with *en* in 4:12 as well as in 2 Tim 1:17; 3:11, meaning to have entered into a given situation, condition, or state (Spicq, *EP,* pp. 381-382). The perfect could imply the continuing or lasting effect of the action upon the subject (BDF §342). The precise phrase *en parabasei* is unique to this place in the PE, appearing nowhere else in the NT, Ap. Frs., or the LXX. The noun *parabasis* occurs half a dozen times in the NT outside of this passage in the PE. Hebrews 2:2 parallels *parabasis* with *parakoē* ("disobedience") in connection with the Law; 9:15 uses the plural in describing the sins committed under the former covenant. The remainder of the uses are Pauline; those in Gal 3:19; Rom 2:23; 4:15 link *parabasis* with breaking the Law, and that in Rom 5:14 with "those whose sins were not like the *parabasis* of Adam. . . ." In *Barn.* 12.5 (partially cited above at *Heua*) the fatal bite of the desert serpents is meant to remind Israel that "because of their *parabasis* they will be turned over to mortal affliction." The only other textually certain use is in Hermas, *Vis.* 2.3.1, of the sins of the prophet's family. In the LXX *parabasis* is used four times (4 Kgdms 2:24 [*s.v.l.* A]; LXX Ps 100:3; Wis 14:31; 2 Macc 15:10 [of the violation of oaths]). In the *Testaments of the Twelve Patriarchs* Levi asserts, "See, I am free of responsibility for any of your godlessness and *parabasis* which you may commit unto the finish of the ages" (*T. Levi* 10.2). Judah urges, "But if you wish to live prudently, abstain completely from drinking in order that you might not sin by uttering immoderate words, by fighting, by slander, by the *parabasis* of God's commands, then you shall not die in your prime" (*T. Judah* 16.3).

15–3:1a. *"A person will he saved rearing children, provided they persevere in faithfulness and charity and a sensible holiness." A wife* does not appear in the Greek; (he/she) *will be saved,* one of seven uses of the verb *sōizein* in the PE, is here in the passive (*dia* regularly occurs with the passive of *sōizein* in the NT, thus explicitly raising the question of instrumentality); *sensible* [*holiness*] marks another occurrence of *sōphro(n)-* terminology, always appearing in lists and codes, this one with two other virtues, in the PE (see also 1 Tim 2:9); *in faithfulness* is one of ten instances in the PE of the anarthrous prepositional phrase *en pistēi/apistiai;* for *charity,* see Titus 2:2; 1 Tim 1:5.

*rearing children.* Lit. "through the bearing of a child," *dia tēs teknogonias.* This noun does not appear otherwise in the NT, Ap. Frs., or the LXX, and Lampe, *PGL,* records no instance of it, though it does appear in Methodius of Olympus, *Symposium* 2.1, along with the cognate *teknogonein* (SC 95.68). It is rare in secular Greek texts. Aristotle uses it in the plural of multiple childbearings (*Hist. Anim.* 7.1.8; 582a 28). The cognate verb, *teknogonein,* appears in 5:14, the church order for widows, but nowhere else in the NT, Ap. Frs., or the LXX, and a few times in the Greek Fathers (see Lampe, *PGL s.v.*). It is hardly found in secular Greek, though the *Greek Anthology* 9.22.4 has it in an epigram of Philippus of Thessalonica about a pregnant heifer chosen for sacrifice but "sent back free to the herd to bear her young one *(teknogonein)*" when labor pains started. Common as the noun *teknon* is in biblical Greek (see Titus 1:4), it is all the more notable that First Timothy is the only NT document to employ the compound forms just noted, as well as *teknotrophein* (which is unattested in Ap. Frs. or the LXX) in 5:10 in the church order for widows.

*provided they persevere.* Lit. "provided that they remain," *ean meinōsin.* This particle with the present subjunctive is in standard sequence with the future of the apodosis (see BDF §371.4; 373.1), and ought to mean "that which under certain circumstances is expected from an existing general or concrete standpoint in the present." The Hebrew *ki* can similarly introduce a clause. *Menein* (118 times in the NT, 67 of which are in John and First and Second John; see R. Brown, *Epistles,* pp. 259-261, 339-340) appears only here in First Timothy and 3 times more in 2 Tim 2:13 (another *message meant to be believed*); 3:14 (where Timothy is urged, "Persevere in [*en*] the things you learned and became sure of"); and 4:20 (where it has its physical sense of staying in [*en*] a place). That physical sense is the only one which appears in the 20 uses of *menein* in Luke-Acts. In the remaining Paulines, *menein* appears 13 times, with 11 in the Corinthian letters. In 1 Cor 7:20, 24 Paul writes of persevering in *(en)* the calling which came with conversion (see Condon, "Calling," pp. 71-84); in 2 Cor 3:11 he writes of how much that which "remains in *(en)* glory" surpasses that which is ephemeral. In Ap. Frs. some of Ignatius's usage is notable; thus the conclusion to the exhortation to prayer in Ign. *Eph.* 10.3 is "that you may persevere in complete purity and self-control *(en pasēi hagneiai kai sōphrosynēi)* in Jesus Christ, both in the flesh and in the Spirit *(pneumatikos)*." When he writes to Polycarp about encouraging married couples, he adds, "If any one can persevere in purity *(en hagneiai menein)* for the honoring of the Lord's flesh, let such a person persevere without boasting *(en akauchēsiai)*" (Ign. *Pol.* 5.2; see 6.2). *Barnabas* 2.3 (see 21.4) writes of fear, hope, patience, and self-control "holily *(hagnōs)* persevering in the Lord's affairs" while "wisdom, insight, understanding, and knowledge rejoice with them." *Didache* 11.5; 12.2 refer to a physical stay. Because of the figurative rhetoric of Hermas, several of his uses have more than a physical sense (thus the uses with *en* in *Vis.* 3.2.9; *Sim.* 9.13.9). Though the LXX uses *menein* often enough, it appears only half a dozen times with *en.* Of these latter, LXX Eccles 7:15 notes "the godless persevering in his evil"; 2 Macc 8:1 describes those who had kept the faith of Israel as "people who had persevered in Judaism."

*in . . . a sensible holiness.* Lit. "in holiness *(hagiasmōi)* with self-control *(meta sōphrosynēs* [see v. 9])." *Hagiasmos* (ten times in the NT) occurs only here in the PE and seven times in the rest of the Paulines as well as in Heb 12:14 and 1 Pet 1:2 (whose *en hagiasmōi pneumatos* is also in 2 Thess 2:13). The usage in 1 Thess 4:3, 4, 7 (the latter pair with *en*) is particularly pertinent because it appears in the apostolic instructions about sexual purity in Christian marriage. There *hagiasmos,* "the will of God," is to abstain from unchastity. *Holiness* is synonymous with honor, *timē,* and the opposite of uncleanness, *akatharsia* (see Rom 6:19, 22). A connection with the Holy Spirit occurs in the context in 1 Thess 4:8 (2 Thess 2:13 has already been noted). In 1 Cor 1:30 it is Christ crucified "whom God made our wisdom, our righteousness and *holiness* and redemption." In Ap. Frs. only *First Clement* uses *hagiasmos* in 30.1 of performing all things that pertain to *holiness* and avoiding such things as slander, various lustful acts, and pride; in 35.2, among the astonishing and blessed gifts of God is "self-control *(egkrateia) in holiness.*" The author may be citing a source in both instances. *Hagiasmos* appears infrequently in the LXX (about eight times), almost always with the sense or the suggestion of complete consecration or dedication (LXX Judg 17:3 in A; Amos 2:11 [of Nazarites in MT]; Ezek 45:4 of the area set aside for the future temple; Sir 7:31 of a sacrifice [but not so obvious in 17:10 of God's "name of *holiness*"]; 2 Macc 2:17; 14:36 [see Goldstein, AB *2 Macc,* pp. 188, 491]; 3 Macc 2:18 of the temple consecrated to God). In *T. Levi* 18.7 "a spirit of understanding and *holiness*" is prophesied for the eschatological priest; *T. Benjamin* 10.11 urges his children to "live in *holiness* in accord with the Lord's commands," and the emphasis upon the result of ethical conduct is unusual if in fact the text is of non-Christian origin.

3:1a. *That is the Christian message, meant to be believed.* On the phrase, see Titus 3:8a. Important Latin versions as well as D* read *humanus/anthrōpinos,* which would mean "a human *or* popular message" for *pistos,* here translated *meant to be believed.* A very early slip of the scribal pen, however it is to be justified, lies behind the reading (see B. Metzger, *TCGNT,* p. 640). The reading appears to presume that verse 1a is read with what follows about the episcopate. Perhaps the variant originated in a reading of this section which separated verse 2:15 completely from the following chapter. Still, even in the ancient Christian world Chrysostom (Homily 9 on First Timothy; *PG* 62.546) read *pistos ho logos* with 2:15. For the literature and older editions of the text, see Knight, *Sayings,* pp. 50-54, though since he has written, the critical tide has turned and Nestle$^{26corr}$ as well as *GNT*$^{3corr}$ reads the text with the division adopted here.

## ♦ COMMENT

2:8 *Now my wish is that the men take part in the prayer "in every place" of worship, that they lift up hands that are holy, that they be without wrath and resent-*

*ment.* The recurrence of the first person singular with the particle *oun* marks the second division within the apostolic exhortations that began in 2:1 with the same pattern, though *boulomai oun* here is stronger than *parakalō oun* there. Paul's wish is virtually a command for the church, and that command is to *take part in the prayer.* The previous section articulated the goal and reason for public prayer; this section now turns to the questions of by whom and how Christian prayer is to be offered. The previous section emphatically urged the prayer of the church for all people; now it is to be by all believers, and the distinction between the sexes is employed to show that Christian men and women alike are equally bound by the apostolic directive.

*The men* are addressed first, with no distinction in this articular plural form between the married and the unmarried. One verse of the text is devoted to them, whereas *the women* (v. 9) receive a much lengthier series of directives in which distinctions are made and explanations given (2:10–3:la). One reason may be the relative novelty of this equality of the sexes in Christian public worship vis-à-vis the practices in much contemporary religious worship, Jewish or pagan. In this connection, the inscription about the conduct of men and women being initiated into the Mysteries in southern Greece (Dit., *Syll* 2.461-473, §653; E.T. in Goodenough, *Symbols* 9.136) ought to be noted; two requisites are noted for the men, but many for the women. Like social innovations before and since, common worship by men and women was subject to misinterpretation and misuse, and as a consequence more detailed guidance for the women is required to implement the new style in prayer.

If a Jewish Christian church order, with its worship assemblies in house churches, is the source behind the text here in the PE, one can divine another reason why this passage deals explicitly and first of all with the Christian men, for they were *the* worshippers in the Jewish tradition, the only ones bound by the Torah on worship. Men came to the synagogue to learn, women to listen (see Str-B 3.468-469). Men formed the *minyan* for worship, though women certainly attended synagogue services along with them (Brooten, *Leaders,* p. 130; note also the Court of Women in the Jerusalem Temple precinct). Already bound by centuries of Jewish tradition on the worship proper to the one God (see 2:5 above on the *Shema*ʿ), the directives for Jewish Christian men remain brief and emphasize what should be characteristic of the Jewish *Christian.* If the redactor's hand appears anywhere in this verse, it is in the telegraphic *in every place,* which has, for all practical purposes, so trimmed the citation of the OT that it has become a directive for all believing men, whatever their religious antecedents. The prayer of Christian men is prescribed under three headings, perhaps part of the archaic church order hypothesized as a source for 1 Tim 2–3. First, the men's prayer is to be offered *"in every place";* second, it requires them to *lift up hands that are holy;* third, their assembly for prayer is to *be without wrath and resentment.*

The first heading, *en panti topōi,* takes up once more the theme of universality that has pervaded the whole exposition thus far, and its motivation becomes clear when the quotation of the source is traced. The instruction of *Did.* 14.1-3 on the Sunday liturgy at the turn of the first Christian century furnishes an entry into the explanation of "*in every place*" in 1 Tim 2 and in the archaic church order upon which it is drawing. The passage in the *Didache* belongs to the "second stage" of the development of the composition (according to Audet, *Didache,* pp. 458-464), a stage in which legal order and canonical order are emerging concerns. Those concerns coincide with those of 1 Tim 2 and the hypothetical church order upon which it is based. The coincidence becomes verbally explicit with the phrase *en panti topōi,* for reasons that will be seen below. Both 1 Tim 2 and the *Didache* are at this point exercised about the public prayer of Christians. The *Didache* is, moreover, quite explicit that its concern here is the sacramental eucharist offered on Sundays. Both documents are concerned about an undefiled purity of the offering; both are concerned that there be no anger and quarreling brought in one's heart to the liturgical prayer. The reason for these directives finds the two documents coinciding verbally, *Did.* 14.3 stating at some length what 1 Tim 2:8 communicates with laconic density. "For this is that which was spoken by the Lord, 'In every place *(en panti topōi)* and time [not in MT] offer me a pure sacrifice, for I am a great king,' says the Lord, 'and my name is wonderful among the pagans.'" The text is a periphrastic conflation of the LXX Mal 1:11, 14, and it looks as if it were used as a base for reflection upon and guidance in the practice of Christian worship even in the first Christian generation, for Paul seems to allude to the same context (Mal 1:7, 12; Audet, *Didache,* p. 460) in advising the Corinthian believers on the radical incompatibility of the Christian eucharistic liturgy with pagan sacrifices (see the conclusions of Dodd, *Acc. Scr.,* pp. 126-138, about the method that may have been used). In all three passages one encounters the somewhat free and flexible use of a scriptural passage that reminds one of liturgical rather than strictly academic practice. In the Strasbourg PGr 254, the first completely extant sentence of this archaic eucharistic prayer addresses the Father, saying, "You made everything through your wisdom, your true light, your Son, our Lord and Savior Jesus Christ, through whom with him and the Holy Spirit we give thanks *(eucharistountes)* to you and offer this reasonable and bloodless service, which all the nations offer you, from sunrise to sunset, from south to north, (for) your name is great among all the nations, and in every place *(en panti topōi)* incense is offered to your holy name and a pure sacrifice" (Jasper, *Prayers,* p. 38, modified). Irenaeus cites this prophetic oracle in his striking references to the eucharistic bread and cup in *Adversus haereses* 4.17.5-6 (SC 100.590-594). If this allusion to the prophecy of Malachi was already a feature in the thanksgiving prayers at the celebration of the Lord's Supper around 70 C.E. in Roman

Jewish Christian house churches, then the citation of "*in every place*" at this point in the directives for the Christian men becomes a shorthand reference for such a eucharistic assembly which is "according to the Scriptures" and so ought to be attended by all believers.

The prophetic text has been pressed into service for a principle governing the liturgical action which it accompanies and justifies, and that principle in turn becomes the rule for the conduct of the members of the congregation. Uniformity in worship and discipline was a pressing concern for Paul, whether in liturgy, ethics, apologetics, or other matters (see, e.g., 1 Cor 4:17; 7:17; 14:26-40; etc.). It is notable that the stronger and more direct the exercise of the apostolic (or at least Pauline) authority, the less direct and extensive the use of Scripture. The very brief and allusive *in every place* at this point in 1 Tim 2:8 may represent the redactor's curtailing, in order to exalt the Pauline authority of the directives that begin here, of the citation of a venerable *testimonium* from Scripture or an already well-known thanksgiving prayer. On the other hand, there is a reluctance in the PE to sever these and the other directives completely from the OT and from liturgical practice, for the congregations remembered that the apostolic preaching, teaching, and prayers were "according to the Scriptures." The fact that the Pauline correspondence itself is not cited here indicates that, even if one or another letter was known to the author of the PE and/or his source, that letter was not yet received as "Scripture" and on a par with the books of the OT (by the time 2 Pet 3:16 was written, this was no longer the case).

The *topos* in the phrase *in every place* could well have been heard as meaning the house church as "the place" where Christians gathered for their liturgy. On rare occasions the LXX translates the Hebrew *bayt,* "house," with *topos* (1 Kgdms 24:23; 3 Kgdms 8:42 [temple]; 2 Chron 6:32 [temple]; LXX Ps 118:54; and note the citation of LXX Isa 66:1 in *Barn.* 16.2, where *oikon* [temple] is parallel to *topos*). *Topos* means a site for worship, a holy place, in LXX Zeph 2:11: "Every one [of the pagan gods] bows down to Yahweh from his place *(ek tou topou autou* [i.e. from his cult site; MT, *mqwm*]) on every island of the peoples" (see O'Connor, *Verse,* p. 253). In the Stobi inscription made around 200 C.E., the synagogue is *toi hagioi topoi,* "the holy place," made out of preexisting buildings *(oikous)* that belonged to a private individual and his family (*CII* §694; see pp. 76-77; for the use of *topos* as a religious center for the Jews in Sardis, see Kraable, *ANRW* 2.19.1, 484). In this understanding, the Christian use of *topos* here coincides partially with the meaning of *oikos* below in 3:4, 5, 12, and especially 15. The emphasis upon universality in the *panti* of the prophetic and eucharistic texts and in the context here in the PE urgently directs men to join every liturgical assembly. Any impression that Christian prayer must take place in groups for men only (as in Mithraism) or women only (as among the Maenads and some Isis cults) is excluded.

After prescribing that the Christian men are to be found in every assembly for public prayer, the next directive turns to their external conduct and demeanor, *that they lift up hands that are holy. First Clement* 29.1 has a similar development of thought but not the same words, as the author writes, "Let us then approach him [God] in holiness *(en hosiotēti)* of soul, raising pure and unstained hands *(hagnas kai amiantous cheiras airontes)* to him, loving our kind and merciful Father" (see 2.3 also). Variant biblical formulas using various Greek verbs to describe the position of the hands (stretched out, spread out, raised) appear in LXX 3 Kgdms 8:22, 54; LXX Ps 27:2; 62:5; Isa 1:15; Lam 2:19. In Israelite tradition (and that of the Near East generally) the hands might be outstretched while one was kneeling or standing (see Vaux, *Israel*, pp. 458-459), though prayer while standing seems to have been the usual style. Bodily stance could change, too, in the course of the prayer, to express visibly and physically the internal dispositions that people brought to worship. Some gestures (prostration, kneeling, and bowing until the head touched the earth), accenting intensity as well as abasement, came from ancient court ceremonial into liturgy and were not particularly congenial to the Greek world (cf. Aeschylus, *Persians* 242, of the Greeks, with 584-590 of the Persians).

Is it possible to visualize more clearly the lifted hands of this passage in the PE? Virgil has his *pius Aeneas* say, in response to a night vision, *tendoque supinas/ad caelum cum voce manus*, "and I stretch my upturned hands out to the sky with a word of prayer" (*Aeneid* 3.176-177; see Seneca, *Naturales questiones* 3. praef. 14, "What is important? . . . To lift pure hands to the sky"). His posture, standing with arms raised and hands spread open to heaven, is that of *pietas*, as personified and represented in Roman art, whether sculptured or numismatic (see Hamman, "La Prière," pp. 1212-1215, for this and what follows). The *Orante* in Roman art is conventionally a standing female figure, veiled and clad in a woman's tunic. When a tradition of Christian painting begins to appear at the beginning of the third Christian century (Bourguet, *Painting*, p. 35), this convention is adopted and becomes the most frequently depicted representation in pre-Constantinian Christian art (see Snyder, *Pacem*, pp. 19-20, for the literature as well as the observations here). Because of the conventional character of the *Orante* symbol, it cannot be firmly linked as such with the sex of the one thus represented; it certainly suggested to the Roman viewer the highly esteemed virtue of *pietas (eusebia);* and finally it glorified *pietas* as a familial virtue, the root of the peace and security that one found in the house church on earth and with Christ in heaven.

The Christians perceived the position of their uplifted hands as distinguishable from the way in which their non-Christian neighbors raised their hands in prayer. Numerous stelae of pagan religious origin from the second millennium down through the days of Punic Carthage show praying arms with open hands extended vertically and in parallel (see Yadin, "Symbols," pp. 218-222). The first-century-B.C.E. Rhenia stele, with its prayer for vengeance on a murdered Jewish woman, shows upright arms with open hands (palms facing the one who reads the inscription; see Deissmann, *LAE*, fig. 64; *CII* §725). If this is not an accommodation to a non-Jewish artisan's catalogue of standard designs (see Calder, *MAMA* 1.§294, 399 [pp. 156, 208], for curses thus illustrated and other illustrations in 7.§165 [p. 34] and p. xxxv), it may indicate a contemporary Jewish posture for prayer. At least it suggests that there was no religious scruple about that stance among the Jews who commissioned this inscription. In the praise of the Jews in *Sibylline Oracle* 3.591-593, the Egyptian Jewish poet says, ". . . at dawn they lift up holy arms toward heaven, from their beds, always sanctifying their flesh [*al. lect.* hands] with water" (E.T. from Charlesworth, *OT Pseud.* 1.375). For the various positions of the arms of the Jewish priest in blessing, see Schürer, *HJP* 2.453 n. 137.

Early on, the Christians were looking for scriptural precedents for the position of their arms in prayer, a position which visibly represented the cross. Sometime around the turn of the first century the Jewish Christian hymnbook called the *Odes of Solomon* describes the believer at prayer, saying: "I extended my hands and hallowed my Lord; for the expansion of my hands is his sign. And my extension is the upright cross. Hallelujah" (E.T. of *Odes of Solomon* 27 by Charlesworth, *OT Pseud.* 2.759; see also 42.1-3, 2.770). *Barnabas* has: "The Spirit speaks to the heart of Moses to make a representation of the cross, and of him who should suffer, . . . Moses therefore placed one shield upon another in the midst of the fight, and standing *(statheis)* there raised above them all kept stretching out his hands *(exeteinen tas cheiras)*, and so Israel kept conquering" (12.2). Justin develops the same symbolism (*Dialogue with Trypho* 90.1). Tertullian, *De oratione* 14, says of Christians, "We not only lift up our hands but open them out; when we have modeled the Lord's passion, then praying, we give praise to Christ the Lord" (see 17.1; *De baptismo* 20.5; *Adversus Marcionem* 3.18; *Adversus Iudaeos* 10.10). *De oratione* concludes in 39.4 with an evocation of all creatures at prayer in which Tertullian asserts, "Indeed, the birds too, rising up, are borne aloft to the sky, and they open their wings instead of hands into a cross and sing something that seems to be a prayer." The typically Christian posture at prayer was thus visibly different and remained so (see Minucius Felix, *Octavius* 29.8). The believer did not raise his arms and hands straight up as did his contemporaries. The *Orante* was refashioned into a symbol of the Crucified.

Another archaic Christian symbolism linked to the cross is that of the tree of life whose branches extend to all people with God's salvation. This universalism is close to the surface of the passages from the *Odes of Solomon* cited above. Irenaeus, in his discussion of the tree of knowledge and the cross in his *Demonstration of the Apostolic Preaching* 34, wrote, "And because he is himself the Word of God almighty, who in his invisible form pervades us universally in the whole world, and encompasses both its length and breadth and height and depth . . . the Son of God was also crucified in these, imprinted in the form of a cross on the universe" (E.T. by J. P. Smith in the ACW series, no. 16; see Irenaeus, *Adversus haereses* 5.17.4; SC 153.232-234). The Christian at prayer with arms outstretched makes visible God's wish to save *in every place* and time. In this line of interpretation, just as the previous prescription here in the PE for *the men* required all believing men to be present for a public worship that was occurring *in every place* and for all people, so this second directive is concerned with a visible stance that reminds those who do not yet believe of *the mediator of God and human beings . . . who gave himself as a ransom for all* on the cross.

As its rarity in secular and biblical texts shows, *hands that are holy, hosious,* is no stereotyped phrase. The phrase resembles a somewhat commoner, though scarcely formulaic, expression, *katharos tas cheiras,* "with clean hands," and its variations, found in secular as well as biblical texts (thus Job 9:30; 17:9; further citations in J. Bergman, *TDOT* 5.396; C. Spicq; and D-C). That form of expression applies to an external, ritual cleanliness as well as to an internal moral quality (see 1 Tim 1:5). *Hosios,* however, is the term for a personal, moral quality and is not applied to a material object as such (Spicq, *EP,* pp. 373-374; see the inscriptions collected by Nock, *ERAW* 2.850-851).

A late Jewish context for the *hands that are holy* may be detected in the Qumran community. There, of the instructor of the community it is said, "He shall judge each man according to his spirit *(krwḥw)* and shall cause each man to approach according to the purity of his hands *(kbwr kpyw)*" (1QS 9.15). The final phrase has not appeared anywhere else at Qumran, and one notes that the man's purity is paralleled with his spirit, recalling the description of the final judgment in 1QS 4.20-21: "Then God will cleanse *(ybrr)* by his truth all the works of every man, and will purify *(zqq)* for himself the bodily fabric of every man, to banish every spirit *(kwl rwḥ)* of perversity from his members, and purify him of all wicked deeds by the spirit of holiness *(brwḥ qwdš);* and he will cause the spirit of truth *(rwḥ 'mt)* to gush forth upon him like lustral water." Thus the spirit/purity of the member of the Qumran sect is to be understood in terms of the eschatological divine gift of cleansing and purification through the spirit, whose activity is in turn compared to that of waters of purification (see 1QS 3.4, 9 in context). The way in which this teaching and its terminology were articulated in the prayer of the community is vividly illustrated by 1QH 16.9-12, where the hymnist, addressing God, says:

> Yours, yours is righteousness.
> For you have made ever[y spirit]

[With its strength] 10and understanding;
For it is you who have allotted the spirit *(rwḥ)* of the just.
And I have chosen to cleanse my hands *(lhbr kpy)* according
to your will,
And the soul of your servant has l[oath]ed every 11work of perversity.
And I know that none is righteous except for you;
For I have appeased your face
Because of the spirit *(brwḥ)* which you have put [in me]
To accomplish 12your [f]avors toward [your] servant for[ever]
By cleansing me by your holy spirit *(brwḥ qwdšk)*. . . .
(A. Dupont-Sommer, *EWQ,* p. 248, modified)

The instructor (*mskyl,* 1QS 12) of the community can proceed in his judgments about a member only from "the work of his hands" (1QS 9.22, 23), which should in turn correspond with that member's determination to carry out the revealed will of God. Such works lead the instructor to decide that the member's internal and external dispositions (spirit and purity of hands) allow him to advance in the community. These dispositions in their turn are understood to be the eschatological gift of God's spirit. On the other hand, the member of the community who prays (as in the hymn cited above) begins from his belief in the gift of the cleansing spirit that God has bestowed upon him, which was the goal of the previous inquiry. That spirit enabled him to cleanse his hands, i.e. to put his hands to doing the works that God wills. These works are the love of God and keeping his commandments, i.e. the work of worship and that of avoiding evil in relation to one's fellow men (see 1QH 16.13-18). The same road runs from Athens to Thebes or Thebes to Athens; all the difference lies in the direction one travels.

It is an open question whether the Jewish Christian church order being redacted here in 1 Tim 2:8 had *hosious cheirous* or the more biblical *katharous cheirous* (as in James 4:8). If it had the latter, then the author of the PE changed its adjective to *hosious,* the adjective that Acts preferred when citing biblical texts to apply to the risen Jesus (see the use of LXX Ps 15:10 in Acts 2:27 and 13:35; LXX Isa 55:3 in 13:34). Christian men are to raise their hands in the liturgical worship, probably the celebration of the Lord's Supper, as their Lord had raised his wounded hands in blessing and prayer over his disciples (cf. Luke 24:50 with v. 39). Cyril of Jerusalem, in his *Mystagogical Catechesis* 2.5 *ad fin.,* says: "Christ received the nails in his undefiled hands and feet in contrast to the Christian's receiving salvation through the baptismal immersion into Christ's passion and death. The Christian raises pure hands in prayer because the wounded and pure hands of his Lord have first blessed and prayed over him" (E.T. in Cross, *Cyril,* pp. 20, 61). The blessing of the laity in Serapion (d. 362),

*Euchologium* 6.1, begins, "May the living and pure hand *(kathara cheir)*, the hand of the only-born [Son] which has endured all evils and kept all things holy and secure, be stretched out over the heads of this people" (text in F. X. Funk, *Constitutiones* 2.164). Further patristic materials on the hand outstretched in prayer are in Lampe, *PGL s.v.*

The third and final prescription for the public prayer of Christian men is that they offer it *without wrath or resentment*, the very opposite of raising clenched fists in anger and disagreement. The dialogical character of significant parts of ancient Christian worship, not to mention the varied social backgrounds represented within the relatively small assemblies in the house churches, gave participants a chance to verbalize hurts and fears which other participants took (and may have been intended to take) as personal criticisms. To forestall such a liturgical debacle, this final requisite for public worship by Christian men presses to its ultimate consequence the previous prescription to *lift up hands that are holy*, for human hands suggest the full and total commitment of the person, "wholly directed towards God" (Grayston, "Hand," p. 482). Hence there follows this most internal, and, of the three, probably the most characteristically Christian, directive, with its implication of unqualified forgiveness (see Matt 5:21-26, 43-46; 6:14-15; Mark 11:25; Gal 5:13-15, 20; *Did.* 14.2; 15.3-4; Irenaeus, *Adversus haereses* 4.18.1).

*Without wrath and resentment* is lit. "without anger and quarreling," and *kai dialogismou* is practically epexegetic, ensuring that *wrath* will not be taken of the divine, eschatological wrath but of human anger (the catalogue context ensures the same in Colossians and Ephesians). *Dialogismos* means the internal, unseen questioning that goes on in a person's heart *(kardia)* into which only Jesus can peer (see Luke 9:46-47 for the singular; plural in 2:35; 5:22; 6:8; 24:38). Paul in Rom 1:21 uses the plural of the pagans' futile reasonings about God, in 14:1 about disputes among Christians; in 1 Cor 3:20 the term figures in the citation of LXX Ps 93:11 about the Lord knowing the questionings of people ("of the wise," as Paul cites it). The usage of First Timothy reminds one of Luke. Probably it figured also in the source being cited, particularly when one takes into account the parenesis of James 2:4, describing conduct odious in a Jewish Christian assembly for worship (*synagogē* in James 2:2), as well as the spirited, hyperbolic polemic of 4:1, which reaches its climax in "Cleanse your hands, you sinners, and purify your hearts, you men of double mind" (4:8). The book of Enoch transfers a similar concern into apocalyptic figures when, describing the worst of the fallen angels, it says, "Asael taught men to make swords of iron and breastplates of bronze and every weapon for war" (8.1; E.T. from Black, *Enoch*, p. 28; see p. 127). The remainder of the verse, cited above in Notes to 1 Tim 2:9, blames him for showing men the precious metals with which they make jewelry for women.

The concern that anger and quarreling be ironed out of community life and prayer was not uniquely Christian, as both the Qumran Rule and the Damascus Document illustrate. Still, the parallel addition in 1QS 10.20-21, where the ideal sectary speaks, betrays a notably narrowed horizon, reminiscent of Matt 5:43; for the Rule reads, "I will bear no rancor *(lw' 'ṭwr b'p)* against them that turn from transgression but will have no pity on all who depart from the Way" (slightly modified E.T. from Vermes, *DSS,* p. 91; see 1QS 9.16 and A. R. C. Leaney, *RQM,* pp. 234-235, 249). A similar concern for intramural peace and mildness appears in 1QS 7.8-9, which reads, "And whoever bears malice *(yṭwr)* toward his fellow unjustly *(lw' bmšpṭ)* shall be punished for six months [one year]; and likewise for whoever takes revenge for any reason whatever" (E.T. from Dupont-Sommer, *EWQ,* p. 88). The more elaborate provisions of CD 9.2-8, based on Lev 19:18 and its forbidding taking revenge or bearing malice against fellow Israelites, twice note violations that occur "in the heat of anger."

9-10. *Similarly, I also wish the women to make themselves attractive in a becoming costume, with sensible discretion. Their beauty is not in their coiffure and gold ornaments, or in their pearls or extravagant clothing, but it comes through their excellent deeds — that suits women who are professing real godliness.* The remainder of this chapter expounds guidelines for Christian women. The *gynaikes* of this long sentence are balanced with the repeated references to the *gynē* of verses 11-15; the *sōphrosynē* of verse 9 recurs to form an inclusion with verse 15. The opening *similarly* (which may go back to the source; see Titus 2:3) . . . *also* puts them on par with the men just addressed. Thus Christian women are to pray in precisely the way that the men have just been directed to and are subject to the same apostolic order.

The innovative and liberating character of this directive is not to be understood in the light of such passages of the Greek tradition as Aristotle's *Pol.* 1.2.12; 1254b ("The male also is by nature superior, and the female inferior; so the former rules and the latter is ruled; this principle necessarily applies to all human beings"). This directive of the PE is to be understood in relation to the ancient Jewish traditions about the relation of women to the Torah, an attitude which was to be articulated in the (often misunderstood) rabbinic thanksgiving for not having been born a woman. In context, that is a thanksgiving for being asked to keep every command of Yahweh, every prescription of the Torah, especially those pertaining to worship. Women were not bound by the latter, because of the laws on ritual cleanliness from menstrual blood, as well as the demands of domestic life. Slaves and children were similarly not bound to Israel's public prayer (*Ber.* 3.3). As the Pauline tradition perceived it, the legislation about ritual cleanliness in the Torah would no longer bind Jewish Christian women in public worship. Accordingly, they as much as the men were obliged to participate in the Christian liturgy, to raise their holy hands in prayer (the adjective *hosious* as the equivalent of *katharous* would have a special resonance in this context), to quench personal anger and quarrelsomeness.

Because the command for women to assume this role in worship was novel in the light of normal Jewish practice, the directives of the OT had to be further supplemented. The Hebrew Bible in Gen 2 "is unique among the creation myths of the whole of the Ancient Near East in its appreciation of the meaning of woman, i.e. that human existence is a partnership of man and woman" (C. Westermann, *Genesis* 1.232), and the Hebrew Scriptures had explicitly brought women along with men into the covenant with Yahweh (Deut 29:10-13; Neh 8:2-3, 6 [cited above]) and increasingly were concerned with protecting their human rights (cf. Exod 29:17 MT with LXX; Deut 5:21, both MT and LXX). In its Greek form this was the Scripture of Jewish Christians, and they probed it for guidance about the course on which they had embarked.

With the *kai,* "also," here, there is an echo of a very early (if not original) and inelegant attempt by the redactor of the Jewish Christian church order to make clear that the preceding verse was to be understood of Christian *women also.* The insertion of the article *tas* before *gynaikas* in some MSS was a further attempt to clarify the meaning by making *the women* completely parallel to *the men* above. The addition is a further indication that the *kai* was not as helpful as had been expected. In its favor, however, rhetorically, is the fact that it fits the pattern of repeated *k* sounds which characterize the opening of verse 9 and this new subject.

The special directives for women answer a characteristic question upon being invited to appear in a public gathering: "What shall I wear?" This question raises an antecedent one about the meaning of clothing in human society. The answer of this church order implicitly shifts that question into another sphere. Clothing is external; the answer deals primarily with that which is internal. If one must give directives for external appearance, then these directions are going to run counter to what human beings might expect. The Christian assembly for prayer is in some sense an assembly of the poor; that fact dictates what a believer who is not poor does not wear.

As the verb *kosmein,* "to add luster," was used in the household code of Titus 2:10 of the way in which the conduct of slaves adorns the apostolic teaching, so in the list of virtues here the verb describes the way in which Christian women *make themselves attractive.* As in the previous instance, the term is well on the way to being used figuratively, here of *katastolē,* "costume," which is ultimately understood in terms of internal disposition and observable conduct, a meaning documented in Epictetus 2.10.15; 2.21.11 as well as the Priene inscription from about 120 B.C.E. and the papyrus of 88 B.C.E. cited in MM, p. 333, and D-C, pp. 45-46. The term embraces a person's whole deportment, clothing, lifestyle, habits, all the external signals of interior disposition that a human being employs. Clothing is parabolic of the person who, as the ancient world perceived it, was refracted through what he wore and how he wore it (see Spicq, *EP*, p. 375). This "social significance" of clothing sounds strange in the modern West, where clothing is "an individual phenomenon" (C. Westermann, *Genesis* 1.251). The *costume* here is qualified as *becoming, kosmios* (cognate with *kosmein*).

The modifying phrase, *with sensible discretion,* lit. "with modesty and self-control," defines the preceding *becoming costume* in the way that *their excellent deeds* in the following verse specifies (with a rhetorical variation of the preposition) what is to take the place of an expensive wardrobe. "Modesty and self-control" are parallel with the preceding noun-plus-adjective of *in a becoming costume. Aidōs,* "modesty," links clothing to a sense of modesty, and *sōphrosynē,* "self-control," further defines that which is *becoming* in terms of prudent balance (see 3:2 below).

The language in these phrases, unprecedented in the early Christian literature, suggests an archaic Jewish Christian source that antedated the PE, a source that here is notably Hellenistic and even secular in its terminology and conceptualization. Thus Euripides (*Cresphontes, TGF* §457) and Aristotle (*Rhetoric* 2.6.18; 1384a, *ad fin.*) allude to a Greek proverb about the eyes as the home of modesty. One surmises that, since there were no appropriate Jewish guidelines for women at public prayer, those Jewish Christians who fashioned this church order used their own liturgical and catechetical materials when appropriate and that they combined these with ethical terminology and directives from the contemporary Jewish and secular scene as contributing to the Christian mission to all men and women.

The internal apparel of virtue is next contrasted with expensive bodily adornments in a rhetorical pattern that is amply documented in biblical and other Jewish literature. Such lists begin with the head and face, then turn to the neck and the limbs, and finally speak of the textiles used to cover the rest of the body. Texts as diverse as Eccles 12:1-8; Cant 5:10-16; and 4Q 184 (DJD 5.82; E.T. in Gaster, *DSS*, pp. 497-498) illustrate the pattern which here in Timothy starts with the hair and its arrangement; then turns to the necklaces, pendants, bracelets, and rings for neck and limbs; and finally refers to expensive clothing for the rest of the body.

The opening phrase about *their coiffure and (kai) gold ornaments* is followed by the repeated disjunctive *ē* in the rest of the list. At first reading, the *kai* seems awkward and confusing and is conceivably left over from a combination of two different lists. Perhaps it is meant to suggest that the *plegmata* of the hair and the *chrysion* are to be understood together, i.e. of gold thread intertwined in the braids or even of a golden hair net (see 2 Sam 1:24 for clothing with threads [?] of gold). Another redaction of the source that lies behind this passage in First Timothy appears in 1 Pet 3:3-4, where, in its guidelines for married women in general, one reads, "Let not yours be the outward adorning with braiding *(emplokēs)* of hair and *(kai)* decoration with the putting on of gold ornaments *(chrysion)* or *(ē)* of wearing fine clothing *(himatiōn)*. . . ." If the language of First Peter gives any indication, the conjunctive/disjunctive coordination belonged to the source, as did a series of cognate terms, including the *hypotassomenai* of 1 Pet 3:1, which would correspond to *en pasēi hypotagēi* of 1 Tim 2:11 (see Selwyn, *1 Pet,* pp. 432-435; Balch, *Code,* pp. 97-99). Perhaps the source referred, as does First Peter, to married women as a class (not to women in general). The author of the PE has here redacted the materials with an eye to women in general, married or not. At verse 11 the directives turn to married women alone (1 Tim 5:3-16 contains the directives for single women, i.e. widows).

The "decoration with putting on of gold ornaments" in 1 Pet 3:3 seems to have understood the source as speaking of wearing things made out of gold, possibly in or on the hair (threads or nets), possibly earrings, necklaces, pendants, bracelets (see the illustrations in Ward-Perkins, *Pompeii,* pp. 32, 132-133, and the mosaic portrait on p. 138, though its coiffure is simple; Grant, *Pompeii,* pp. 75, 82-83, 115-116). The source probably had the difficult singular form attested here in First Timothy, with an ambiguity that would embrace any ostentatious use of that precious metal. Martial 2.29.9-10; 8.33.22 writes of the *splenia,* the patches of gold leaf that some Roman men and women used to cover facial blemishes. In another illustration of conspicuous consumption, Josephus, *Ant.* 8.185, describes Solomon's tall, handsome cavalrymen as dusting their shoulder-length hair every day "with gold dust *(psēgma . . . chrysou),* so that their heads sparkled as the gleam of the gold *(chrysou)* was reflected by the sun." The historian is probably reading back this barbaric splendor into the Solomonic age from something that he had heard of, even witnessed, in his own day. For the regulation of women's finery in the Mysteries, see Goodenough, *Symbols* 9.136-137, and in a *kalathos* procession, Nock, *ERAW* 2.851.

The mention of *gold ornaments* leads naturally enough in the list here to jewels, specifically *pearls.* If the *gold ornaments* referred specifically to those for the hair, the *pearls* may have suggested earrings (Pliny, *NH* 9.110; 114, where finger rings are also noted; 117, which also suggests necklaces [Athenaeus, *Deipnosophistai* 3.93a]; 121). The Hellenistic world, including the Asiatic, valued pearls very highly, the bigger the better (though they had nothing to match the fourteen-pound, football-sized Pearl of Allah, the largest in the world). Martial 8.81 is a merciless caricature of a Roman matron's devotion to her pearls (see also Suetonius 1.50.2 on Julius Caesar's affair with Servilia and her daughter; Juvenal, *Satire* 6.458-459, 495-503, on jewels and coiffure; Seneca, *ad Helviam* 16.3-4, praising one who had avoided such ostentation).

The *extravagant clothing* that is in tandem with *pearls* here may summarize the source, which not only was used in a catechetical form to teach the virtues for Christian wives (thus 1 Pet 3:4 contrasts expensive clothing with the hidden Christian heart and its precious treasures of the Spirit) but also was refracted apocalyptically to become a judgment on the vices of pagan Rome. Similarly, in the second century the *Sentences of Sextus* teach that "self-control *(sōphrosynē)* ought to be considered the ornament *(kosmos)* for a faithful wife" (§235; see 237; Chadwick, *Sentences,* p. 38), whereas *Apocalypse of Peter* 7 (Ethiopic), in its lurid sketch of the punishments of hell, depicts a pair of women; "they are hung up by their neck and by their hair and are cast into the Pit. These are they who plaited their hair, not to create beauty, but to turn to fornication, and that they might ensnare the souls of men to destruction" (E.T. from Hennecke and Schneemelcher, *NT Apoc.* 2.673; see also *T. Reuben* 5).

Roman writers, such as Pliny and Martial and Juvenal, were as ruthless as Hebrew prophets in satirizing their rich women's insatiable appetite for jewelry and other finery. The critique here in the PE accordingly need not have been perceived as a bitter, sectarian jeremiad, utterly at odds with all that was best and most appreciated in Roman society at large. It would be heard rather as one further voice in a respectable literary tradition whose ethical concerns were not altogether alien from those of the new religious practices of the Christians. Plutarch's graceful letter-essay to a prospective bride and groom, to which there will be occasion to refer again in reconstructing a setting for the materials here in the PE, quotes Crates the Stoic to the effect that "decoration *(kosmos)* is that which decorates, and that which decorates a wife is that which makes her more decorous. Neither gold does this nor emerald nor purple dye but whatever betokens seriousness, good behavior, modesty *(aidous)*" (*Moralia* 2.141E, §26, LCL). At the beginning of the fifth century, Paulinus of Nola wrote an epithalamium that attractively exploited these themes for a young cleric and his bride (*Carmen* 25; CSEL 30.238-245). Thus, "The holy wife of a bishop's son, the spouse of a boy already consecrated, must receive as dowry the light of life. She must reject garments tricked with gold or purple, for the shining grace of God is her golden garment. She must spurn also necklaces adorned with motley jewels, so that she herself may be a notable jewel for the Lord God, for no weight of loathsome avarice must oppress a neck dedicated to bearing the yoke of Christ the Lord. Rather, her adornment designed to please must depend on an inward grooming, and her mind must be decked with the dowry that brings salvation. She must not long to squander her income vainly on costly jewels or silken wraps; instead, her soul must be adorned with the virtues of chastity so that she may be a precious asset and not a liability to her husband" (25.41-54; E.T. by P. C. Walsh, *Paulinus,* ACW 40.246-247; see Bourguet, *Painting,* p. 25, pl. 80, for a fourth-century fresco of a Christian matron flaunting her wealth while "pretending to be an *orans*").

Verse 10 begins *but (all') it [their beauty] comes through their excellent deeds* — , though the Greek keeps that for the climactic conclusion of this lengthy sentence, placing an almost parenthetical *that suits women who are professing real godliness* immediately after *all'*. As in 1 Pet 3:4, the adversative *all'*, like the preceding *kai . . . ē . . . ē . . .* , appears to reflect the common source. In any case, in the liturgical assembly the *excellent deeds* that adorn the hearts of Christian women are their real finery. Perhaps *agatha* is used here to emphasize this internal, unseen, ethical goodness which contrasts with the visible, aesthetic beauty, the *kala*, of *coiffure, gold ornaments, pearls*, and *extravagant clothing*. However, the usage of Acts 9:36 should be noted also, where *excellent deeds* means needlework in making clothing for the poor.

The parenthetical *ho prepei*, "that suits," reminds one of the opening of the household code that began in Titus 2:1. The relation of the latter to the church order that is being posited as a source here is not immediately apparent. One surmises that the liturgical source was the older and that it was exploited in later catechetical materials for the apostolic teaching, the *didaskalia*, that it was considered to contain. Thus in *Barn.* 4.9 there are two uses of the verb, the former of which appears to be from a source that the *didaskalos* author is citing. Here in 1 Tim 2:9 the apostolic command for the adornment of women, single or married, is advanced as fitting and suitable, i.e. corresponding to the reason for their participation in Christian public prayer. Good works befit persons *who are professing real godliness, theosebeia*. That unusual last term designates much that *eusebeia*, "godliness," signifies elsewhere in the PE. In fact, it is probably the influential and authoritative character of the source that dictates the retention of *theosebeia* at this point. The relative reluctance of the biblical tradition and the earliest Christian documents to use the word doubtless has something to do with its use for the reverent worship due the pagan gods. Still, the terminology was not utterly abhorrent, as the citations above and inscriptions illustrate (a Jewish Agrippa in Rome is *theosebes, CII* §500, and see §748 for the Miletus theater inscription; also Lifshitz, *Donateurs* §17, 18, 28, 30, and p. 89 of his Prolegomenon to *CII* §731e). Though Christ Jesus is not named at this point, the reader cannot assume that the source was Jewish but not Jewish Christian. The context of the church order (see 2:5) argues for the latter. This is not to say that Jewish Christian liturgists and catechists did not have some Jewish models in mind. The context of *real godliness* here in the PE surely draws the meaning of *theosebeia* into the ethical sphere. Some sort of articulated, intelligible content is implied with *professing* (note the use with *gnosin* in 6:21) as well as with its relation to the use of *eusebeia* in the PE. Participation in the Christian liturgy, with its readings and their application to Christian life, involves both an intellectual and a moral response to revelation and God's word. *Theosebeia* functions as a bridge-word between profession and *excellent deeds*.

In later Christian usage *theosebeia* is practically synonymous with the religion specific to the Christians, in contrast to not only the pagans but the Jews (see *Diogn.* 1; 3.3; 4.5-6; 6.4).

11. *Let a married woman quietly learn in the assemblies for worship and quite obediently.* The previous two verses spoke of *women* in the plural. Verses 11-15 turn upon *gynē,* three times in the singular. In the PE the singular *gynē* appears in a set phrase, "a man of one woman" or "woman of one man" (thus Titus 1:6; 1 Tim 3:2, 12; 5:9). This phrase always refers to *a married woman,* i.e. a wife, and in it *anēr* means a husband. An archaic Christian marriage formula may lie behind it. The plural *women* of verses 9-10 applies the directives of verse 8 to all Christian women, whether married or not. The singular *gynē* of verses 9-11 is meant to narrow the exposition to *a married woman,* a wife (see Hommes, "Women," p. 13; Ellis, "Wives," pp. 216-217).

The initial directive of this verse is consistent with the analysis above, for it is a command, *Let a married woman quietly learn (in the assemblies for worship) and quite obediently.* The phrases in parentheses here are not in the Greek but are implied by the church order which is posited as a source. The imperative mood of the verb is a distinct intensification of the *boulomai,* "my wish is that," which governs verses 8-9. *Hypotagē,* in the phrase *quite obediently,* is the nominal cognate of the standard verbal expression *gynaikes hypotassomenai tois idiois andrasin* ("Wives are to be subordinate to their husbands," 1 Pet 3:1; see Col 3:18; Eph 5:21-22), reworked somewhat at Titus 2:5, where young prospective wives are the subject of the same phrase. The reason for the redactional shift here in the PE is clear if this writer wanted his use of the plural to refer to all women, married or not. One would infer that the source read substantially as does 1 Pet 3:1 and that the redactor's hand appears in the nominal phrase *en pasēi hypotagēi.* The use of *pasēi* with the sense of *complete* or *perfect* is surely typical of the PE. The redactor may have picked up *en hypotagēi* from 3:4 below, adding at this point his characteristic *pasēi,* which gives the obedience in question its widest possible extension. It is not simply that of wife to husband but here of *a married woman* to the leadership of the Christian liturgical assemblies.

The command that Paul gives is to *learn,* and in both letters to Timothy the verb appears in contexts that deal with women. Thus in the instructions about the order of widows in 1 Tim 5:4, 13, the children of a widowed mother are to learn how to take care of her, and the young widows are said to learn bad habits of idleness and the like. In 2 Tim 3:6-7, "the idle women" are victimized because they are "ever learning and never turning to full knowledge of the truth." In contrast, Timothy is told: ". . . persevere in the things you learned and became sure of. You are well aware of the people you learned from and that from your tenderest years you have known the sacred letters . . ." (2 Tim 3:14-

15). The reference here to Timothy's teachers extends to the teachers of his childhood, his Jewish Christian grandmother and mother, Lois and Eunice, who have been explicitly mentioned at 2 Tim 1:5.

As in Titus 3:14, the learning here is presumably of a practical character, learning what to do rather than simply what to think. The reference is not to the speculative analysis of the classroom, but to the exhortation to action given the congregation assembled for the worship, the application of the OT Scriptures, after they had been publicly read out, to the lives of those who had listened (contrast the Jewish tradition, cited in the Comment on 2:8, from Str-B 3.468-469). The PE evidently envision Christian women learning and teaching in their home. At this point the correspondence is attempting to find a working solution to the problem that arises in their worship assemblies, a problem that arises precisely because a woman may be married and her Christian husband is bound, as she is, to attend this assembly for public prayer. How can a wife both be subject to her husband and give him authoritative, practical directives?

This passage of First Timothy proposes a line of conduct that forestalls a public confrontation. *Let a married woman quietly learn, en hēsychiai.* The phrase is repeated in the following verse, where the general principle enunciated here crystallizes into a concrete, specific directive. *En hēsychiai* is surely adverbial here, and the noun itself is cognate with the adjective above describing the "quiet and tranquil existence" that all believers want to lead (2:2; see 1 Pet 3:4 of women). The phrase is equivalent to the adverb *hēsychōs,* which in its occurrence in *1 Clem.* 44.3 describes the way in which the leaders of the Corinthian congregation had "led the worship *(leitourgēsantes)* . . . peaceably *(hēsychōs).*" Complete silence is certainly not being envisioned in that passage. When Aristotle cites Sophocles' apothegm, "Silence *(hē sigē)* befits women" (see *Ajax* 293; *Pol.* 1.13.8; 1260a), he is not articulating what the author of the PE or his source had in mind for *hēsychia.* A better parallel would be the fragmentary Alexandrian commentary on Sappho which described her (perhaps in contrast to Alcaeus) as a woman "who quietly *(ep' hēsychias)* trained the girls from the best families, not only from the locality but also from Ionia . . ." (Campbell, *Greek Lyric,* pp. 202-203, §214B, who translates the phrase in question as "in peace and quiet," i.e. without interference, as in Aristophanes, *Wasps* 1517).

The general rule is thus that the *married woman* is peaceably and without aggressive public confrontation to learn to accept guidance *quite obediently in the assemblies for worship.* A similar principle is given in *1 Clem.* 57.2 to the refractory men who are creating divisions in the Corinthian Christian liturgies: "Learn to be submissive *(mathete hypotassesthai),* putting aside the boastful and haughty self-confidence of your tongue. . . ." One infers that the excesses of a "liberation" movement were an embarrassment to the congregation that *First Clement* is addressing and that a kind of irritable questioning erupted often in the prayer assemblies, a kind which did not expect an answer (see the usage of *hēsychiazein* in Luke 14:3; 23:56; Acts 11:18; 21:14, as well as in 1 Thess 4:11). The same principle is laid down here in the PE for *a married woman.* She, too, is to desist from such aggressive confrontations that were in some way provoked by her own home life and could contribute to the destruction of her marriage while disrupting the minds and homes of others as well as the worship of the church. In the mind of the PE the Christian liturgy is no family court.

12. *Moreover, I do not allow a wife to teach in the public worship and to boss her husband. That is learning "quietly."* The relative quiet of verse 11 at one point now escalates to complete silence. A *wife* is not *to teach in the public worship. Moreover* corresponds to an adversative *de* in Greek, which puts some slight contrast between this directive and the preceding, qualifying one part of what has been said rather than negatively reworking the whole. The repeated *"quietly,"* introduced by the strongly adversative *all'* in Greek, means that the peaceful participation of *a wife* in the liturgy excludes the function of teaching, *didaskein,* which further involves apostolic authentication (see Titus 1:9). The way in which the PE conceive the transmission and authentication of the function of teaching can be seen in 4:11 and 6:2 (of Timothy) below and in 2 Tim 2:2 (of faithful men to whom Timothy commits Paul's teaching). Apostolic authorization is explicitly denied to Christian wives, in the churches to which the PE are directed, on the authority of the apostle Paul: *I do not allow a wife to teach. . . .*" In 1 Cor 14:33-35 the apostle prescribed a rather more drastic procedure for what he understood to be a more drastic problem in the Corinthian liturgy: "As in all the churches of the saints, the married women *(hai gynaikes)* should keep silence *(sigatōsan)* in the church assemblies . . . [see Notes]. If there is something they want to learn *(mathein),* let them ask their husbands *(andras)* at home. For it is shameful for a wife to speak *(lalein)* in a church assembly." Here, as in the PE, the directive deals with Christian wives in public worship, but complete silence is enjoined upon them. *Lalein* here refers to an individual proclaiming to or publicly informing a group (see 1 Cor 2:6-7; 14:2; Titus 2:1, 15) and is materially equivalent to *didaskein.* It appears not to refer to prayers, hymns, confessions, and the like, which all the people present spoke or sang together.

The directive of 1 Tim 2:12 is notably more liberal by comparison, for the attribution of the command to Paul leaves open the possibility that other usages that at least claimed to be apostolic were known. Perhaps, as Ellis, "Wives," pp. 214-215, has suggested, the Jewish Christian practice was already part of a normative catechesis when First Corinthians was penned, and Paul inserted 1 Cor 14:34-35 from a source that he knew when he sent off the final draft of that letter (p. 219; see Aalen, "Formula," pp. 513-525, on the possibility of a liturgical source from Hebrew- and Aramaic-speaking Judaism for the technical vocabulary of permission and directive at this point). The language of the source may have been toughened by Paul in light of the Corinthian abuses, whereas the PE represent an older, more liberal usage; or the PE softened a command to silence which stood in both the source and in First Corinthians into a less strict *hēsychia*, which in any case does *not allow a wife to teach in the public worship, didaskein.* If Brooten is right about women around this period occasionally exercising leadership and teaching functions in the synagogue, then the Pauline (and Pastoral) directives may be evidence of a Jewish Christian reaction to these practices, a reaction intended to set the Jewish Christians apart from their Jewish neighbors (see Brooten, *Leaders,* p. 228 n. 83, for examples from Italy).

Centuries later the *Statuta ecclesiae antiqua* §99 (IV Council of Carthage, 398; Bruns, *Canones,* 1, p. 150) indicates a stricter practice than that enjoined by the PE when the North African bishops direct, "Let not a woman *(mulier)* presume to teach men in the assembly, even though she be learned and holy."

Direct literary dependence upon First Corinthians of First Timothy or even of the church order hypothesized here seems improbable, for the author of the PE and his source would then be, for all practical purposes, contravening the text of Paul. Ready as one might be to entertain this possibility as being due to the limitations of this author's grasp of Paul, the point is not one of Paul's subtler notions, and it is difficult to conceive this author's flatly changing an explicit Pauline command. If the composition of the church order posited here postdated First Corinthians (and it very probably did), it is conceivable that the compilers of that order knew the Jewish Christian source that Paul had cited. If its language were as strict as Paul's citation would lead one to think, the church order may have tempered it somewhat, to make it more viable in mixed congregations with their growing Gentile constituency while retaining a distinctively Jewish Christian and Pauline practice.

*and to boss (authentein) her husband.* The ancient etymologists read two elements in the **authent-* terminology, scil. *autos* and either *hiēmi,* "to push, thrust" (thus Phrynichus) or *(h)anyō (*hentēs),* "one who realizes, achieves" (see Hesychius, *synetēs' synergos,* cited by Chantraine, *DELG,* p. 138; see p. 93, *anymi*). The latter is probably historically and scientifically correct. Yet one cannot discount the popular perception that the terms came from "push" (cf. the English "pushy").

As early as Euripides, *Suppliants* 442, the noun *authentēs* is heard as meaning "master" or "the responsible author" (thus also Hermas, *Sim.* 9.5.6). The sense of "real author" or "perpetrator" of a murder or massacre continued in the use of the noun *authentēs* in secular Greek (thus Polybius 22.14.2) as well as Hellenistic Jewish compositions (see Wis 12:6, which the OL translates with *auctores;* Philo, *Det.* 78; Josephus, *War* 1.582; 2.240). Eusebius, *Church History* 8.16.2, uses the noun for the real author of a persecution of the Christians. The use of *authentēs* in the sense of *despotēs,* "ruler," was in the opinion of Phrynichus substandard Greek. However, the pressure from the verbal use was irresistible and spawned a number of later forms that designated or suggested authority and mastery (*authentria* means *kyria;* also see Sophocles, *Greek Lexicon* 1.276).

In 1 Tim 2:12 the apostolic veto on a wife's teaching in the liturgical assembly is explained with the parallel veto on her bossing her husband (who is presumed to be present, according to the directives of vv. 8-9). The colloquial expression may well belong to the old church order which would be giving a popular paraphrase of LXX Gen 3:16: *kai autos* [i.e. *ton andra sou,* "your husband," Adam] *sou kyrieusei,* "and he will be your master." One is reminded of the commonplace from Menander: "The wife *(tēn gynaika)* ought always to take second place in speaking *(legein),* and the husband *(ton andra)* ought in all things to take the lead *(tēn d' hēgemonian).* For there is not a home in which a wife takes first place *(prōteuei gynē)* which has not been utterly ruined" (Koerte 418; 484K). The concrete directives for daily life which the practical nature of the *didaskalia* envisions here are precisely what a wife does not give her husband in the ancient home, Jewish or Greek, and this passage of the PE takes up its archaic Jewish Christian source to ensure, in Paul's name, that the Christian liturgy will not become a platform for a wife to teach her husband a thing or two. The equality of male and female before God and in Christ does not contradict a further ordering within the marriage relationship, also created by God. The equality of the sexes belongs to nature; the subordination of one to the other comes by the choice of the marriage relationship.

As *authentein* is taken up by the Christian Fathers (see Lampe, *PGL s.v.*), it is notable that Chrysostom can also warn a husband not *to boss* his wife just because she is subordinate to him (*In Col Hom.* 10.1; *PG* 62.366c [correct Lampe]), and can say of people in general that they are not to want to have their own way (*me toinyn boulesthe authentein; In Col. Hom.* 11.2; *PG* 62.37a). They also use the verb in the sense, "to hold/act with sovereign authority," "assume authority," "to act on one's own authority," and then "to tyrannize," "to act arbitrarily."

The final, contrasting *(all')* clause of the Greek becomes *That is learning "quietly"* in this version. The *epitrepō* could be construed with the infinitive *einai* (as in *1 Clem.* 1.3 cited above) and the dative *gynaiki* understood from the previous clause. The sense would then be, "I enjoin a wife to be peaceable." The *en hēsychiai* of the preceding verse is simply repeated, perhaps in an attempt formally to round out a somewhat inelegant Greek sentence which is thus informally garbled. The colloquial vigor and awkwardness of the expressions here may reflect the style of the materials assembled in the Jewish Christian church order posited as a source.

13-14. *The reasons for my directive are that God fashioned Adam first, then Eve; and furthermore that Adam was not fooled [by the serpent] but his wife was made a fool of and she turned to sin.* The opening phrase, *the reasons . . . are,* represents the Greek *gar* and refers to the ground and base for the preceding directives. As in 2:5 the taproot for the universality of Christian prayer was found in the Deuteronomic *Shemaʿ* of Israel, so here the directives for a Christian wife are based upon the Torah, specifically the Genesis creation narrative (recall the Pauline appeal to *ho nomos* in 1 Cor 14:34). The author of the PE evinces no hesitation about the value of the created order, about its goodness, about its belonging to the positive will of God for humankind (see 4:4-5). As in Titus 2:3-10 (also with strong Jewish Christian ties), the preservation of nature includes guarding and using responsibly its material gifts and the human relationships that flow from and exist within the created order. At this point in the PE (and in their source) an essay is made to measure the husband and wife relationship over against the great creation account which opened the roll of the Scriptures in Israel and in the Christian churches. The language of verses 13-14 is not that of the formal priestly narrative of the LXX Gen 1 but that of Gen 2–3, from the vivid, earthy, psychologically penetrating, and parabolic narrative of the Yahwist. This venerable etiological account is exploited in two stages, the first fixing on the creation itself of the archetypal man, Adam, and the second drawing upon the history of the primeval violation of God's command to his creatures.

*The reasons for* the directives about the conduct of a Christian wife begin by alluding to LXX Gen 2:7 and its story about God making a human being out of the dust of the earth. Whereas the LXX narrative explicitly mentions God as the fashioner of man, this passage of the PE throws the verb into the passive (thus still implying *that God fashioned* this creature) and makes *Adam* (the name of the man from LXX Gen 2:16) into the subject. The difference is not subtle; *Adam* is unmistakably and exclusively male, and the woman who will be fashioned from his flesh and bone is going to be, by God's will, his wife. The nerve of the argument here is that not only did God freely create both but he chose to create them in the order noted. Consequently, the priority of husband over wife as God's original choice is not to be contravened by his creatures. The same ground of argument is used at Rom 9:20 (quoted in Notes), and almost in the some breath it can be used also to vindicate God when he makes the firstborn subject to one born after, as with Esau to Jacob (Rom 9:10-13). All turns ultimately not on temporal order as such but on the choice that God has in fact made (see 1 Cor 11:8-9 for another application of this Genesis narrative of the creation of man and woman to a Christian husband and wife). In the ancient world, Hellenistic or Semitic, to be a male and to be older was to have a *prima facie* claim to rule (see Aristotle, *Pol.* 1.5.2; 1259b 2-18; 7.13.3; 1332b 36-41); the argument here in the PE goes beyond nature to its personal creator, to whom Adam and his wife (unlike the rest of creation) must personally give an accounting (see F. Maas, *TDOT* 1.85).

The terminology of this verse, and particularly the particle *then, eita,* is by no means characteristic of Pauline (or Lukan) style. Occasional uses of *eita,* e.g., are almost all traceable to a source that is being quoted or alluded to. Again one probably encounters here the language of the Jewish Christian church order, and it is notable that its argument is not expanded upon but, for all its brevity, is taken for granted as familiar and immediately intelligible. No compulsion is felt to draw explicit conclusions from the data; it was apparently enough to cite the sentence to make a point which the reader must grant. There is already a hint here that the Scriptures alone are not carrying the argument. They are being cited from a context in which this congregation uses them, a context that makes the interpretation here inevitable. But more of that later.

At this juncture, one notes that the derived and secondary legal status of the wife in relation to her husband had something to do with the formation of the Yahwistic narrative of Gen 2–3. That account then served to reinforce the model of family relationship among Jewish people and consequently among the first Jewish Christians. The married woman was *hypandros* (see Num 5:20, 29; Prov 6:24, 29; Sir 9:9; 41:21), totally subject to her husband's authority, and this church order as well as the PE took for granted what Roman Christians in the mid-fifties were expected to understand without questioning, that a wife was subject to her living husband's authority (Rom 7:2).

To the preceding principle for the apostolic practice, drawn from the divine will of the creator of the first human couple, a second principle is now advanced in verse 14 from the parabolic salvation history of Gen 3. The argument from silence is first adduced (with all the naivete with which it has been used in theology to this day): ". . . *and furthermore that Adam was not fooled [by the serpent],*" for the LXX Gen 3:13 has only his wife confess obliquely, "The serpent deceived me. . . ." Since the Genesis narrative did not say this of Adam, the omission here takes on positive significance. Adam was not gullible, he *was not fooled.* This left-handed exoneration, even praise, of Adam does not take the shape of Paul's argument in Rom 5–7. It is closer to the tradition of the Lukan genealogy and Acts 17:26, a far cry theologically from Rom 5:12, 15-19. In Ap. Frs. *Adam* is regarded with, at worst, neutrality and, at best, a kind of benevolent respect. Again one would infer here in the PE a non-Pauline tradition (not uncongenial to Luke's point of view) which shows minimal tokens of redaction.

The meaning of the verb *apatan,* here "fooled," and the following *exapatan,* suggest dealing falsely with others (see LXX Exod 8:25 [MT 29 with *pth*]). When a relation between men and women is thus described, the reference may be to sexual seduction (see LXX Exod 22:15; Jth 9:2-3, 12-16; 13:16), though it need not be (see LXX Judg 14:15; 16:5). The sense in the phrase *Adam was not fooled* is in contrast to Eve, who *was made a fool of,* and the serpent is the unnamed agent of the deception. The explicit point is *that Adam was not fooled by the serpent;* the implicit (and uncomplimentary) point is that he was fooled by his wife, or as LXX Gen 3:17 has the Lord God say to *Adam,* "Because you listened to the voice of your wife and you ate from the tree. . . ." The argument takes its point from the fact that it is meant to exclude wives giving religious teaching and directions to their husbands in the Christian liturgical assemblies. That had occurred paradigmatically in Eden. The directive which now receives the Pauline cachet ensures that the Christian husband will not be deluded about God's command by listening to the voice of his wife.

The preceding interpretation is strengthened when one notes the contrast *(de)* that verse 14 has set up between *Adam* and *his wife,* not between Adam and Eve. His wife had been thoroughly deluded by the serpent. How thoroughly deluded? In the light of the other uses in the Pauline corpus as well as in Ignatius and the LXX, it is improbable that *exapatan* bore an obvious connotation of sexual seduction. There was no dearth of speculation in the ancient Jewish and Christian communities on the exact material form which the sin of Eve took. Still, the first explicit allusion to the seduction of Eve by the serpent appears in the Hellenistic Jewish Greek of the first Christian century in 4 Macc 18:6-8, where the mother of the martyrs is portrayed as saying: "I was a chaste maiden and did not leave my father's house; but I kept guard over the rib built into woman's body. No seducer of the desert nor deceiver in the field corrupted me, nor did the seducing and beguiling *(apates)* serpent defile my maidenly purity" (E.T. from Charlesworth, *OT Pseud.* 2.563). The first explicit Christian allusion is in the late second-century apocryphon, *Prot. Jas.* 13.1 (Hennecke and Schneemelcher, *NT Apoc.* 1.381). A. T. Hanson, *Studies,* pp. 65-77, cites other passages from Philo, *The Life of Adam and Eve, The Apocalypse of Moses,* and *2 Enoch.* They are more or less compatible with sexual seduction, but even that observation tends to beg the question, for Greek, like English, used sexual images in speech without intending to designate sexual acts as such. Some sixth-century-C.E. and later rabbinic references interpret Eve's seduction as a sexual act (see D-C, p. 48 n. 25; A. T. Hanson, *Studies,* pp. 74-76).

If Paul and the author of the Pastorals had contact with a Jewish legend of Eve's sexual seduction by the serpent, it looks as if both Second Corinthians and First Timothy encountered it in a form which already was demythologized. Thus 2 Cor 11:3 is explicit and emphatic about the serpent's *panourgia,* "cunning" (cf. 2 Cor 4:2 with *panourgos* in 12:16; Eph 4:14). In all of these passages, plus the one remaining NT occurrence in Luke 20:23 as well as the seven Septuagintal uses, the noun has no sexual overtones. Its connotations cluster rather about teaching or doctrine, shrewd and cunning questions that quite unnerve the simple. In the argument of 1 Tim 2:14 the serpent has disappeared into the anonymity of the Greek passive participle. The reader looking for a hook on which to hang a legendary seducer finds none.

When 1 Tim 2:14 says of Adam's wife, *she turned to sin,* the *parabasis* means, as it does in Hebrews, the contravention of an explicit divine command. This sense of the term to which Paul first witnesses may well have been pre-Pauline, and the source cited here in First Timothy may illustrate how Paul redacted such materials. His original contribution to the interpretation of the narrative of the fall of the first human couple appears to have been his shift of the emphasis from Eve to Adam in his vision of how humankind was plunged into sin. Thus Sir 25:24, in the reflections on a bad wife, asserts, "From a woman sin had its beginning *(archē hamartias)* and because of her we all die *(apothnēiskomen pantes)*" (see W. Goosens, *DBS* 4.314, on the extant Hebrew of this passage). That line of inference, apparently a commonplace of wisdom in late Judaism, is not the line taken by Romans. The choice was quite deliberate, and it looks as if the source cited in 2 Cor 11:3 was edited with an eye to Paul's conviction about Adam's primacy in *parabasis.*

Philo may witness to an interpretation of the woman's part in the fall of humankind that resembles Sirach and the source cited here in First Timothy. He poses the question, "Why does the serpent speak to the woman and not to the man?" (*Questiones in Gen* 1.33; extant only in Armenian, E.T. by R. Marcus in LCL). He answers: "And woman is more accustomed to be deceived than man. For his judgment, like his body, is masculine and is capable of dissolving or destroying the designs of deception; but the judgment of woman is more feminine, and because of softness she easily gives way and is taken in by plausible falsehoods which resemble the truth." In his *Leg. alleg.* 3.61, interpreting the same narrative figuratively, he remarks, "Now observe that, whereas the man says that the woman gave, the woman says not the serpent gave but that he beguiled; for to give is characteristic of sense-perception but to cheat and beguile [is characteristic] of pleasure with its serpent-like subtilty" (E.T. by F. Colson and G. Whitaker in LCL). With Spicq, one also ought to note the way in which Philo explained LXX Gen 4:7, in which God says to Cain, "You sinned. Be quiet *(hēmartes, hēsychason)*": "The oracle utters something very useful. For not to sin at all is the greatest good. But he who sins and is abashed and ashamed is kin to this one and, as one might say, is the younger brother beside the elder" (*Quaestiones in Gen* 1.65). In *Sobr.* 50, commenting on the same passage, he writes, "This implies that while sin, inasmuch as it is movement and activity with vice as its motive, is liable to punishment, stillness *(hēsychazein),* because it is stationary and quiescent, is exempt from arraignment and a means of safety" (see also *Mut.* 195). The Jewish Christian source posited here in the PE appears to make a similar case for the link between Eve being the first to sin as well as the one who spoke about it and the emphatic directive about wives being quiet in the Christian liturgy.

In the centuries around the beginning of the Christian era, with some probability for the latter first century B.C., there appeared originally in Hebrew, probably in Palestine, a work whose extant Greek and Latin versions are called *The Apocalypse of Moses (Apoc. Mos.)* and *The Life of Adam and Eve* (E.T. in Charlesworth, *OT Pseud.* 2.249-295). In *The Apocalypse of Moses* repeatedly one hears Eve asserting that God is angry with Adam "on my account" (29.9), he is ill and "this has happened to you through me; because of me you suffer troubles and pains" (9.2); "I have sinned before you [God] and all sin in creation has come about through me" (32.2). A wild animal, attacking her son, says to her, "The rule of the beasts has happened because of you" (11.1). When the devil conspires with the serpent, he urges, "Rise and come and let us make him to be cast out of Paradise through his wife" (16.3). Even Adam, mortally ill, cries out to Eve, "Why have you wrought destruction among us and brought upon us great wrath, which is death gaining rule over all our race?" (14.2; see *2 Enoch* 30.17). This work became popular among Christians and witnesses to the possibility that forms of this imaginative speculation about Eve and what a later age called original sin were already at home in the first-century Jewish Christian congregations. Paul himself was aware of something like it; the old church order being cited here served as a bastion for it.

The literary links between 2 Cor 11:3 and 1 Tim 2:14 are ultimately the two words *exapatan* and *Heua* as well as the exegetical method used. The latter applies an OT text to a contemporary Christian situation which calls for theological reflection and action. The method was not specific to Paul but is characteristic of certain traditions in contemporary Judaism (thus 1QpHab) and Christianity. One can affirm the possibility (but no more) that First Timothy knew the text of Second Corinthians. Rather more probable is that both Paul and the author of First Timothy were using an old Jewish Christian instruction about the role of Christian wives in the liturgy. Second Corinthians, though the earlier documentary reference, could well be the more typically Pauline in its language, while 1 Tim 2:13-15 may reproduce the instruction more exactly, with its passive verbal forms, Septuagintal terminology, and inelegant Greek. The source, moreover, would have referred to individual wives, as does this passage in First Timothy. The metaphorical application to the church symbolized as bride, wife, and mother is characteristically Pauline (see Gal 4:26-27; 2 Cor 11:2; Eph 5:23-27), though not exclusively so (see Rev 21:2). The PE, on the other hand, presume this imagery at a deeper level when they take up the *oikos/oikia* language for the church.

15–3:1a. "*A person will be saved rearing children, provided they persevere in faithfulness and charity and a sensible holiness." That is the Christian message, meant to be believed.* The awkward, even bizarre Greek of this verse is another signal of a Jewish Christian source which is still glossing the Septuagintal narrative about Eve. Her transgression, for all its enduring effects, is not irreversible. The conclusion here stands in contrast *(de)* to the preceding materials, as the reader moves from the present liturgical assembly in the Jewish Christian house church to the individual home and family. The verb in the phrase *a person will be saved* begins the Greek sentence in Semitic fashion, and its passive voice implies that God is ultimately the agent of the salvation that comes to a Christian husband or wife through parenthood (contrast the preceding *was not fooled/was made a fool of,* i.e. by the serpent). The future tense abruptly shifts the focus from the past and the story about Adam and Eve and her sin to a Christian home in the final age and how God will save wife as well as husband. Genesis 3 similarly moves from the past incident (3:13) to the future lot of Adam as well as of the woman and wife, with some emphasis upon her bearing children (LXX 3:15, "her seed"; 3:16, "I will greatly multiply your pains and your groaning, in pains you will bear your children . . ."). Thus C. Westermann observes, the one fact of "woman's existence is described from two points of view, that of a wife and a mother" (*Genesis* 1.261).

The promise of future salvation here in the PE resembles the gloss that Targum Neofiti I attaches to Gen 3:16. After listing the painful burdens of the mother and wife, it concludes that they will be *byn lmzkh wbyn lmḥt'*, "for justification as [or] for sin" (Macho, *Neophyti* 1.17). A little later God makes practically the same observation to Cain, who is struggling with his vicious inclination: ". . . you have power over it for justification or for sin *(byn lmyzky wbyn lmḥty)*" (p. 21). What the PE mean by salvation here coincides by and large with what the archaic targum meant by "justification" (see Titus 3:5, 7).

The *rearing children, teknogonia,* of 2:15 is a recognizable paraphrase of LXX Gen 3:16, *texēi tekna,* and it reminds one of the meaning that the Yahwist heard in the name *Eve,* i.e. "the mother of all living" (Gen 3:20). Adam while alone "was unable to continue life" (see A. Kapelrud, *TDOT* 4.259). Yet for this document *teknogonia* appears to designate something more than the physical bearing of children (see Clement of Alexandria as cited below and the clause that follows this one). In this connection it may be significant that the LXX employs *teknopoiein* (Gen 11:30; 16:2; 30:3; Isa 65:23; Jer 12:2[?]; 36[MT 29]:6; 38[MT 31]:8) with the meaning "to procreate," a sense that *teknopoiein/teknopoia* had in Greek authors (see MM, p. 628; Spicq, *EP,* pp. 383-384). The Jewish Christian source accordingly avoided the biblical terminology and adopted a rare word from the secular scene, adding a new, Christian aspect to its meaning (see the neologism *antilytron* in 2:6 and the use of *themelion* in 6.19). The novelty was apparently difficult to assimilate, for in the late second century and thereafter the Latin versions were suggesting *creatio, procreatio, generatio,* and even *regeneratio filiorum* as translations (Frede, *VL* 25.477). As early as Clement of Alexandria the apodosis of this sentence was cited of men who *will be saved rearing children* (*Strom.* 3.12.21-22; see Pagels, "Adam," p. 154). *Diognetus* 5.6 says of Christian men and women, in one of the rare uses of the verb in the patristic writers, "They marry as all do, rear children *(teknogonousin),* but they do not expose those who have been born." Apparently in the Hellenistic world at the beginning of the Christian era the husband made the decision to keep the infant or to expose it (see the papyrus from 1 B.C.E. in Deissmann, *LAE,* pp. 154-157). Perhaps a nuance still survives here of the usage of the PE. For a Christian husband and wife, bearing children means *rearing children,* not abandoning them in the city dump. Chrysostom confidently equates *teknogonia* with *paidotrophia,* child rearing (*PG* 62.545; see Menander, *Epitr.* 254 [F. Sandbach]).

Hellenistic societies generally, like many societies, considered the main (or a main) purpose of marriage to be the rearing of children. The Romans, with the Julian and Papian-Poppaean laws, reinforced this conviction with legal penalties for the single state. Tacitus remarks, "But marriages and the rearing of children did not become any more frequent, so overwhelming was the vogue of childlessness" (*Annales* 3.25). For the emphasis here in the PE the Jewish tradition suffices. Thus in LXX Mal 2:15, in the prophetic teaching on marriage, one reads, "What else does God seek but offspring?" (MT has "godly offspring"). Later in the patristic tradition Cyril of Jerusalem has only praise for believers "who have entered into marriage for the sake of rearing children (*dia to teknogonein* [the term would apply to both men and women]), not for love of pleasure" (*Catechesis* 4.25 [*PG* 33.488B]).

The Greek uses a puzzling definite article with *teknogonia* in 2:15, as if awkwardly to underline *the* rearing of a child. In the eleventh century, Theophylact (*PG* 125.40) recalled somewhat impatiently a few exegetes who had taken this as a reference to Mary the Virgin bearing Jesus, the Son of God. As early as Justin (*Dialogue* 100) and Irenaeus (*Adversus haereses* 3.22.4; 5.19 [SC 211.438-444; 153.248, 250]; *Apostolic Preaching* 33) the parallels of Adam with Christ and Eve with Mary were being exploited. A single event, the birth of God's Son "from a woman" (Gal 4:4), undid the sin of Eve and brought salvation to women as well as men. Perhaps because of the redaction of the archaic source employed here as well as our fragmentary knowledge of other ecclesial traditions in the first century, the reasons adduced for this interpretation leave it improbable. In the present state of the evidence, the use of the article may simply be a reproduction of the inelegant Greek of the source, whose authors may have been thinking in a Semitic mode (as is noted above, the sentence begins with the verb) while ostensibly writing Greek.

As awkward, even crabbed, as the preceding clause is, the conditional protasis which concludes *the Christian message, meant to be believed* surpasses it. The gist of the matter is clear. God will save through *rearing children* under certain conditions. The exact meaning hinges on the subject of *provided they persevere, meinōsin.* Who are *they?* The last plural noun in the text was *women* in verse 10, where the reference was to *women* in general and not to a *wife* (the singular *gynē* actually appears in v. 14). Still the shift from singular subject and verb to a plural between apodosis and protasis here is as harsh in Greek as in English. It is scarcely less jarring to take the plural *they persevere* of the offspring implicit in the Greek compound *teknogonia.* In that case, the virtues listed are those which *children* have learned from their mother and in which they persevere, thus witnessing to the power and authenticity of the formation that they have received. Since the PE and their sources use the faithfulness and other Christian virtues of children as a criterion for certain virtues of their father (Titus 1:6; 1 Tim 3:4), it would not be surprising to see a similar criterion proposed for a Christian wife and mother. Still, in 2:15 salvation is at stake rather than election for office in the church. Reprobate children may indeed compromise the credibility of a man's capacity to lead others in Christian virtues, but the sins of the children are not visited upon a parent in any ultimate sense. Fathers and mothers answer for their own sins before the divine judgment (including giving scandal to their children) and thus they gain or lose salvation. That is a far cry from gaining or losing the episcopate.

It is conceivable that *meinōsin* represents a Semitizing usage of the third person plural with a passive or an indefinite sense. Thus this verb which begins the protasis would correspond with the passive which begins the apodosis (see Wilcox, *Semitisms,* pp. 127-128; Black, *Aramaic Approach,* pp. 126-128; N. Turner, *Grammar* 3.292-293). On this interpretation of Semitic interference in the syntax, the list of virtues is for the unspecified *person* who *will be saved rearing children.*

Another possible interpretation of the plural (or even of the impersonal form) would take *they persevere* of both husband-father and wife-mother. Cajetan proposed this (see his *Epistolae Pauli,* p. 142 *ad loc.*), as did Lock, *Commentary,* p. 33. Certainly Clement of Alexandria (as cited above) understood *teknogonia* of the father *rearing children* (not just bearing them). On this interpretation, the third person plural (or the impersonal construction) has its antecedents in Adam and his wife in the preceding verse, and the final clause now explicitly urges the following virtues upon husband as well as wife. Moreover, the initial *will be saved* is understood in the same inclusive, impersonal fashion. This translation has favored this interpretation.

The polysyndetic list of a quartet of virtues *(pistis, agapē, hagiasmos, sōphrosynē)* is bundled together by prepositions *(en, meta)* as well as conjunctions *(kai)*. Such polysyndetic short lists are typical of the PE or their sources (see Titus 3:9 for a quartet of bad acts; 1 Tim 1:5 and 2 Tim 1:7 for triads of good acts and qualities). The closing phrase *meta sōphrosynēs* repeats the opening *sōthēsetai* of verse 15 in another key (see Excursus V, "The PE on Salvation," in AB *Titus*), and it explicitly echoes the opening of this whole section on women at worship, repeating the phrase from verse 9 above (without *aidous kai*). The phrase sounds as if it were in the source and there intended to round off the directives for Christian parents with a reminiscence of the directives proffered to women in general. *En . . . hagiasmōi,* "in holiness," here probably dictated the omission of *aidous* in the phrase from verse 9, since *hagiasmos* already designated substantially the same reality at stake behind the different terms.

This list of virtues in the closing conditional clause amounts to a definition of the way in which the source (and the PE) understood *teknogonia.* It is not simply the physical bearing of children. Christian parenthood is a matter of persevering *faithfulness and charity and a sensible holiness* that suggests sexual self-control and responsibility. *Menein* in this era can mean "without divorce" (see 1 Cor 7:11 and the further material cited by Spicq, *EP,* p. 401 n. 3). Such Christian ways of living transform, by God's saving act, even the commonplace tasks of married life into good works (see v. 10).

The textual problem with *That is the Christian message, meant to be believed* (see Notes) leads into the formal literary problem of the extent and character of the material to which reference is being made. This version has opted to understand *the Christian message* of what has preceded (as in Titus 3:8a) and not of 3:1b alone or of the whole section on the bishop which extends through 3:7. But granted *the Christian message* ends in 2:15, where does it begin? Does it include all the materials on worship cited from the beginning of this chapter? Or simply all the directives for women beginning in verse 9? Or only those for wives which start in verse 10? Or possibly only verse 15?

If one takes *the Christian message* as a quotation formula (thus D-C), there appear to be many indications of a Semitic source and conceptualizations, particularly in 2:13-15. Some have observed that the formula about *the Christian message* has been attached to materials that are concerned more or less explicitly with salvation. *A person will be saved* in 2:15 is thus critical for understanding where one finds *the Christian message* signaled in 3:1a, and 2:15 alone could constitute such a *message* (see Knight, *Sayings,* pp. 52-53, who cautions against constructing an *a priori* argument from what must be established by analysis of each proposed *message*).

Formally it is impossible to justify extending *the Christian message* to the beginning of 2:1 or even to 2:9. The *pistos logos* which results would be long, unwieldy, and diffuse, whereas the other four are very much pithier. Moreover, the church order which is being posited as source for both chapters 2 and 3 offers no convincing reason that here, *in medias res,* half of it should be called *the Christian message.* There is somewhat more reason to see *the message* beginning in 2:11, for from that point on the text deals with the Christian wife. Yet it must be admitted that the other *pistoi logoi* do not use the first person singular as in verse 12 here, for all their uses of the first person plural. The vulgar and awkward Greek of verse 12 also argues against its belonging to *the message* that is being cited. When verses 13-14, with their parenetic application of the Genesis story of the creation and sin of Adam and Eve, are compared to the immediately preceding verses on the conduct of a wife in a Christian liturgical assembly, the line of the argument proposed is clear enough. When they are compared to verse 15, it is equally evident that what is being said in this following verse about salvation takes a new (though not unrelated) tack which only partially coincides with the observations in verses 13-14. This new material, which stands in some contrast with the previous (note the redactor's *de*), introduces a specifically Christian optic for viewing one's home and children. Thus verse 15 is *the Christian message, meant to be believed,* but it is, already in the source, part of the parenesis for a Christian wife.

The linguistic analysis of this parenesis has adverted to the question of literary sources which the PE marshaled here in epistolary form. With another heuristic device one can essay sorting out and bringing into focus some of the social settings and functions of this parenesis (as in Perdue, "Parenesis," pp. 246-256). Functionally parenesis is a potent instrument of socialization, i.e. a verbal means in bringing about "the comprehensive and consistent induction of an individual into the objective world of a society or sector of it" (Berger and Luckmann, *Social Construction,* p. 130). Parenesis regularly implies a setting in which an older and experienced person helps a younger, inexperienced recipient of his or her knowledge to enter a new group or to shoulder new duties. "The liminal period" (V. Turner, *Forest,* pp. 93-111; using Gennep, *Rites,* passim) unfolds in a ritual process of leaving the old order, then a state of suspension or "liminality," and finally entering a new order or social group (V. Turner, *Ritual,* pp. 94-130). Ritual generally is "a public cognitive system" (Price, *Rituals,* p. 9) in which "sacred symbols function to synthesize a people's ethos — the tone, character, and quality of their life, its moral and aesthetic style and mood — and their worldview — the picture they have of the way things in sheer actuality are, their most comprehensive ideas of order" (Geertz, *Religion,* p. 3). Christian ritual or liturgy is no exception. The comments above have suggested that the PE for their parenesis exploited already traditional (though not necessarily stereotyped) liturgical materials.

In terms of a Christian community, parenesis is particularly appropriate for the public recommendations and charges that accompany entrance into the community as such (the primary socialization) or entry into special social roles within the community (secondary socialization). The baptismal sacrament (in its widest sense, including the catechumenate and the readings, hymns, prayers, homilies, and the like which surround the public profession of Christian belief and immersion in water) would be described by the sociologist as belonging to the primary socialization of the person becoming a Christian. The Christian celebrations of marriage and of the dedication of persons to ecclesial ministries (ordinations) are examples of secondary socialization within the Christian social order.

The process of socialization aims at palpable change in the individual as he or she crosses the threshold into a new mode of existence (V. Turner, *Forest*, pp. 101-102). This change becomes evident in the conduct and then the character of the person whose life is being "re-created" by his or her entering this group or assuming a new role within it. Parenesis, positive and negative (see Pseudo-Libanius as cited in Quinn, "Parenesis," p. 497), is one of the means used to urge this transformation, particularly of conduct. It regularly is given, not to be argued with, but to be acted upon. Thus Titus 2:11-14 cites a baptismal confession urging parenetically an ethical transformation of life as the neophyte crosses the threshold into the new order of Christian believers. Titus 3:4-7 ("the Christian message meant to be believed") is from a didactic baptismal oration, whose parenetic force has been increased by its enclosure in a "before (v. 3)/after" schema. The charge given in the course of the ritual of making a new chief among the Ndembu of Africa, which Victor Turner (*Ritual*, p. 101) calls a "harangue," is nothing less than ethical parenesis that is conceived of as irrefutable.

The society or world which the one undergoing socialization is in some sense leaving has become inadequate and unsatisfactory; but leaving it is traumatic, for the former order, too, had its meaning, its directives, its values, its unquestioned presuppositions (see Berger, *Sacred Canopy*, pp. 19-24). The baptismal initiation and the parenetic discourse within it offer another *nomos*, another worldview and concept of order by which a person can structure out life, meaning, and goals (recall Philo's name for Deuteronomy was precisely *paraineseis* [*Agric.* 84, etc.]). In this problematic, one would *a priori* anticipate that the parenesis that occurred within Christian socialization, and specifically within the liturgical expressions of that socialization, would accent strongly the visible, ethical changes expected of the candidate for baptism (not to mention marriage or ordination). *De facto*, that is precisely what we encounter in Titus 2:12 as the parenesis describes the grace that "disciplines us to disown godlessness and worldly lusts, and to live in a sensible, honest, godly way in this present age."

The justification or legitimation of the new world or order into which the neophyte is being inducted is particularly important when the old order still advertises attractive alternatives and the limitations of the new order are coming to light (Berger, *Sacred Canopy,* pp. 29-30). Parenesis makes its case by appeal to nontheoretical processes that are of an intellectual character as well as volitional (Berger, *Sacred Canopy,* p. 21). In general the intellectual grounds which legitimate the new social order involve traditional data, interpretative schemata, and received wisdom (Berger and Luckmann, *Social Construction,* p. 94, cite sapiential and ethical maxims and proverbs). Specifically the parenetic legitimation of the Christian world or roles within it appeals to the OT Scriptures, to the sayings of Jesus, to the texts of public worship — synagogal as well as Christian — and, probably from the first Christian generation onward, to the heroic figures of that generation (Jervell, "Traditions," pp. 19-39).

The volitional grounds for parenesis embrace the norms for conduct in the new order as proposed by an authoritative teacher, as well as the sanctions for breaking the rules and the rewards for keeping them. In this connection it is helpful to recall the function of the "significant other," i.e. the person who introduces the aspirant into the new group and with whom a strong effective bond is established (Berger and Luckmann, *Social Construction,* pp. 130-131). Such a person's life, example, teaching, and directives facilitate the initiate's entrance into the new order or role which he seeks. The "Paul" of the PE is such a figure for Titus and Timothy, and the Pauline ministers of these letters appear at times to function thus for others (so Titus 1:5-9; 2:7; 1 Tim 4:6-16; etc.). With the frequent use of the first person plural, the PE identify Paul and his coworkers with the community into which the one baptized is being initiated. In this perspective, the faith, the worship, and the practice enjoined by the parenesis of the PE are not simply abstract doctrine, empty rituals, and jejune rules; they are the faith as Paul and his generation preached it, the worship they participated in, the conduct that they demanded.

Finally, parenesis aims at reinforcing a sense of identity with a group and a sense of separation from those who do not believe or do not conduct themselves as the group does. Parenetic exhortation sketches in black and white, with clear lines between those inside and those outside. Thus the hearer is forewarned and forearmed for conflict. In a Christian setting parenesis looks to the parousia with its definitive revelation of who is "in" and who is "out" of the new world. Again, as Titus 2:13 puts it, "as we wait for the blessed hope revealed in the glory of Jesus Christ, our great God and savior."

There is no lack in the PE of materials that have some link with Christian liturgy, and some of those materials have their precedents in the practices of Jewish prayer (see Fiensy, *Prayers,* pp. 671-697; Charlesworth, *OT Pseud.* 2, on Hellenistic synagogal prayers, citing parallels to the prayer in 1 Tim 1:17, etc.). Several passages have been or will be encountered whose liturgical origin is argued on stylistic as well as more material criteria (further data will be found at the passages cited) and which exemplify situations for secondary socialization. The charge cited from an ordination liturgy in 1 Tim 6:11-16 and traces of similar charges in Titus 1:6-9; 2:7-8; 1 Tim 3:1b-7; etc., will be discussed first. Then it will be suggested that some of the teaching on marriage in the PE cites the formulas as well as the liturgical charge given in a first-century Christian marriage ceremony.

Over thirty years ago in the R. Bultmann Festschrift, Käsemann argued that 1 Tim 6:11-16 is probably a citation from a liturgical charge at ordination. The text develops in three stages: first an imperatival address to the "man of God" to pursue a sestet of ethical qualities (*tauta pheuge . . . de* belongs to the redaction and not to the source), which shades off into an appeal to the baptismal initiation by which the man of God publicly entered the society of believers (v. 12b). Then the speaker, in the first person singular (*in persona Pauli* in the redaction), with an appeal to God as bestower of all life and to the Christ who was crucified as king (the reference is to the trial as narrated in Luke 23:2-3), urges this "man of God" to keep the Pauline charge unblemished until the parousia (vv. 13-14). Finally, the mention of the parousia becomes an occasion for a solemn doxology that occupies the closing two verses (15-16). The final "Amen" as well as several phrases within this final doxology (the most frequently cited passage of the PE in the second century) may ultimately have come from Hellenistic synagogal liturgy (Charlesworth, *OT Pseud.* 2.682-695). The allusions to synagogal liturgical usage as well as the Septuagintal expressions of the doxology serve to legitimate the worship it urges in the new order of Christian believers. Just as the PE authenticate their epistolary parenesis by citing this traditional text from Christian liturgy, so the liturgical parenesis authenticates itself by an appeal to the previous usage of the OT and the liturgy of the temple and synagogue.

The central parenetic block in this charge includes verses 13-14. At this point, as the PE conceive it, the one who presides over the ordination and who delivers the liturgical charge is the apostle himself. His heroic figure from the previous generation is heard recalling the example of Jesus in his passion and commanding an integral Pauline teaching for which the ordinand must undergo judgment at the parousia. Paul, at least for the PE, has become the "significant other" for the one receiving a new role in the church by ordination, and the apostle effectively eclipses the original deliverer of the charge, placing it beyond a believer's refutation.

The opening imperatival address of this charge urges good conduct upon the "man of God" with a catalogue of six virtues. This parenesis, at the threshold of a new way of life, aims at an evident change in conduct (or a conversion) that ought to characterize the new mode of existence in the Christian community. Warrant for and legitimation of such a charge are grounded in the public baptismal confession of the "man of God" (v. 12b). Nor should one underestimate the theological density of such lists which precisely as sapiential directives of an "intensely concentrated nature" may strike the casual reader as "trite" (Rad, *Hexateuch,* p. 247).

The appearance of the virtue list at the opening of this archaic Christian ordination parenesis suggests a further inference. Certain other lists or catalogues of virtues in the PE may well be from similar sources. Thus, Titus 1:6-9 could be citing its list or lists from the ordination liturgies for presbyter-bishops in other congregations. The charge for the ordination of a bishop may be surfacing in 1 Tim 3:1b-7. First Timothy 3:8-10, 12-13, then, would be from a charge for the ordination of deacons and 1 Tim 3:11, that for single women who had a diaconal role.

There is no particular reason for confining the question to the ordained ministries. If the Christian liturgies for ordinations had parenetic charges to pursue good acts and avoid bad ones, then it is antecedently possible that another area of secondary socialization, i.e. Christian marriage, had similar liturgical parenesis. An example may be found in Titus 2:4-5, where the septet of family virtues (which the older Christian women in the household teach the young women preparing for marriage) may come from the traditional liturgical charge that the older women had learned in the Christian celebration of marriage.

In 1 Tim 2:11-15; 3:1a appears a final example of extended, liturgical parenesis in the PE, and this commentary submits that it is in substance a citation from a Christian, perhaps Roman, liturgy of marriage in the latter part of the first century. *The Christian message, meant to be believed* (3:1a) is in the preceding verse (2:15). *The message* in this instance (as in certain others) is a quotation from a liturgical celebration in a particular church (probably that in which the PE themselves took their origin).

The pre-Christian history of marriage liturgy in Judaism is scanty. There are scattered glimpses of the sacred actions and prayers in Tobit; in 4Q 502; and in the texts assembled in Friedman, *Marriage.* The early Christian sources are just as sparse (Stevenson, *Nuptial,* pp. 3-32; and the studies in Farnedi, *Matrimonio*). Thus Tertullian appears to take for granted that the marriage of Christians is in the presence of the *ecclesia* (see *De monogamia* 11.1-2; *De pudicitia* 4.4 [CC 2.1244, 1287]), and to his own wife he writes: "Where is the store of words that one can draw on to tell the happiness of this marriage which church unites and the offering *(oblatio)* strengthens, [of which] the angels bring back the good news [and] the Father ratifies? For not even on earth do sons validly and legally marry without the consent of their fathers" (*Ad uxorem* 2.8.6 [CC 1.393]).

The scene in a Roman church can be visualized if one recalls the lunette of the *Velatio* in the cemetery of Priscilla (250 C.E.). There a young man, holding an unfolded red-edged veil, stands somewhat behind a young woman who holds a partially unrolled scroll. Both turn slightly to their right toward an elevated, high-backed chair, with low armrests, upon which is seated a bearded, bareheaded elderly man, wearing a long tunic and hooded cloak. He is extending his right hand toward the young woman. The chair, his posture, and the gesture all suggest a teaching situation (Dagens, "Velatio," pp. 124, 126) in a Christian marriage liturgy in which this venerable figure (a bishop or a presbyter? see 4:3 below citing Ign. *Pol.* 5.2) addresses a bride holding the official Roman document listing her duties (as well as her husband's). The young man holds the *flammeum*, the Roman bridal veil, which he will place on his bride's head (a rite symbolizing separation of the man and woman from their former state as well as their incorporation or union in a new one; see Gennep, *Rites*, pp. 130, 132).

*The Christian message, meant to be believed* at the end of 1 Tim 2 is in fact a citation from an already traditional parenetic charge given to the Christian bride as she married before a bishop or presbyter (perhaps in a Roman congregation). Formally, 2:11-15 appear almost as abruptly in their context as does the ordination charge of 1 Tim 6; whereas 2:8-10 have liturgical directions for Christian men and then women generally, verses 11-15 use *gynē* only in the singular and always with the meaning "married woman, wife" (which the singular has everywhere in the PE). The "wife" here has the position of the "man of God" in the ordination charge, though he is addressed with singular imperatives. The ritual for marriage as well as that for ordination is a "public, cognitive system," and within it the bride learns about the new role which Christian marriage gives her. The presiding celebrant (who speaks in the person of Paul in the PE) urges the bride in polite, third person forms to learn quietly and compliantly; in *his* church and its liturgy (perhaps the preexistent document alluded to in 1 Cor 14:34-35; 2 Cor 11:2-3; see Comment above) a wife is not permitted to teach her husband and exercise authority over him. The parenesis is legitimated by an explicit appeal to the data of the Genesis narrative of the creation and the fall of Adam and of his wife, Eve. Commentators have suffered acute, chronic theological dyspepsia about the demonstrative force of this citation. Relief is spelled parenesis. The citation does not and was never intended to prove anything, but the facts narrated illustrate a point that the first-century presider-homilist considered irrefutable because of the interpretation of the Scripture and the practice of his Jewish Christian church.

The reason for dwelling upon Adam and his wife in this archaic marriage charge may be as close at hand as the formula which this marriage liturgy used in expressing the marriage union of a Christian man and woman. AB *Titus*, at 1:6, contended that the spouses promised publicly to be "the husband of one wife/the wife of one husband," basing their married life on their perception of the relation of Christ and the Church to Adam and Eve (see 2 Cor 11:2-3; Eph 5:31-32). Here in 1 Tim 2:13-14 the Genesis narrative is exploited at length for the parenesis which, in the Roman marriage rite, is directed primarily to the bride.

The marriage charge reaches its apogee in its promise that a husband and wife will find salvation in parenthood, *provided they persevere in faithfulness and charity and a sensible holiness.* The PE have no time for Christians who "forbid marrying" (1 Tim 4:3) and thus the task of parenthood which the ancient world, pagan as well as Jewish, believed was the reason for marriage. The purpose had verbal expression in the ancient Greek marriage formulae in which the father of the bride was expected to say to the groom, "I give you my daughter for the lawful begetting of children," . . . *paidōn ep' arotōi gnēsiōn* (Menander, Koerte 682; 720K; see *Perikeiromene* 1014 [F. Sandbach] and the earthy oracle from Delphi cited in Pausanius 9.37.4 as well as Aristotle, *Oeconomica* 3.2 [extant only in the Latin version], and Plutarch, *Moralia* 144B; Advice to Bride and Groom §42; composed in epistolary form, this little treatise illustrates many of the same points that are made at this juncture in First Timothy).

The ancient pagan Latin formula takes a quite different tack which underlines the liminal character of the marriage ceremony. In fact, as Varro, *De lingua latina* 5.61, notes, central elements of the ceremony occur on a threshold *(in limine),* almost certainly that of the groom. The bride is questioned, "What will you be called?" Her answer is, "Where you are Gaius, I am Gaia" (see Cicero, *Pro Murena* 12.27; Quintilian 1.7.28; Corbett, *Marriage,* pp. 68-85). She is freely giving up her former name and the status that it implies. This humiliation makes a new name and status possible. For a study of how such "anti-structural" phenomena, in liminal settings, serve to reinforce social structure, see V. Turner, *Ritual,* pp. 166-201; for betrothal and marriage, see Gennep, *Rites,* pp. 116-145. A ritualized scrutiny of "the central values and axioms" (V. Turner, *Ritual,* p. 167) which Greeks and Romans perceived as underlying their marriages marks the liminal experience. The rites of passage into Christian marriage highlight the values and presuppositions that they shared with their contemporaries, pagan and Jewish, as well as those that were specific to their own worldview.

The basic conviction about the purpose of marriage already noted appears in the Genesis blessing for the human male and female, so that they may fill the land and subdue it (1:28), not to mention in Eve's title as "the mother of all living" (3:20). Tobiah's prayer with Sarah in their wedding chamber takes up the old teaching, as he says: "'Blessed are you, O God of our fathers; praised be your name forever and ever. You made Adam and you gave him his wife Eve to be his help and support; and from these two the human race descended. You said, "It is not good for the man to be alone; let us make him a partner like himself." Now, Lord, you know that I take this wife of mine not because of lust but for a noble purpose. Call down your mercy on me and on her, and allow us to live together to a happy old age.' They said together, 'Amen, Amen,' and went to bed for the night" (NAB). The marriage ritual preserved in the fragments of 4Q 502 seems similarly to refer to "the man" *(h'dm)* and his wife being united "to make descendants" (Groupe 1; fragments 1-3, lines 3-4; see also Groupe 2, fragment 20.3; DJD 7.82, 87; Schürer, *HJP* 3.1461-1462).

The Christian liturgy of marriage cited in the PE refutes in advance those who despise marriage and children. This young couple has chosen to marry, and neither is less a Christian for that; *a person will be saved rearing children* (see 1 Tim 5:14). In the oldest Latin prayer for the Christian marriage liturgy, composed when the Roman sacramentary in Greek was being rewritten between 350 and 400 C.E., the oration for the *velatio* at marriage read, *Adesto, domine, supplicationibus nostris et institutis tuis quibus propagationem humani generis ordinasti, benignus adsiste, ut quod te auctore iungitur, te auxiliante seruetur: per . . . ;* "Lord, look favorably on our prayers and kindly help your own institutions by which you have provided for the propagation of the human race, so that what is joined together with you as its author may be preserved with your help: through Christ . . ." (Nautin, "Rituel," pp. 426-427, 437-442, 454). The prayer laconically joins allusions to the Genesis narrative about God's establishing the marriage bond and the word of Jesus that forbids man to break it (see Mark 10:6-9; *SFG* §252).

The closing list of virtues here in *the Christian message, meant to be believed* reminds one of the opening of the ordination charge below in 1 Tim 6:11. The scrutiny implied here lays bare the ultimate and Christian basis for the final judgment upon the role that this bride is assuming with her husband, the goodness of their married life in Christ. There appear to be antecedents in the marriage ritual at Qumran for the list here. In 4Q 502, after the opening prayers and blessings, Groupe 2, fragment 16, consists of a citation of a passage from the Qumran Rule in which the newly married couple are urged to follow the "spirit of light" which implants in the human heart ". . . a spirit of knowledge informing every *plan of action,* of a zeal for righteous government, of a hallowed mind in a controlled nature, of *abundant love for* all who follow the truth, . . . of a *modesty of behavior* coupled with a *general prudence* and an ability to hide within oneself the secrets of what one knows . . ." (E.T. of Gaster modified; italicized terms occur in 4Q 502; DJD 7.87).

To return to the *Velatio* lunette in the cemetery of Priscilla, it is evocative, in the light of the preceding observations, to notice that opposite the scene of the Christian marriage there is at the right corner of the lunette a painting of the same young woman, seated and holding a baby. In the center of the lunette she is standing as an *orante* figure (Snyder, *Pacem*, pp. 19-20), simply dressed, with head veiled and hands stretched out, flat, with fingers extended, the oldest illustration of the directives about women in 1 Tim 2. This was the way a well-to-do Christian matron at Rome in the latter part of the third century had her tomb decorated, to show that she had married, prayed, and lived according to the Scriptures and the Pauline practice of her church.

## II.B.2. ON THE MINISTERS (3:1B-13)

### *II.B.2.a. The Bishop (3:1b-7)*

*3 1b If anybody aspires to the episcopate, he sets his heart on fine work. 2 Thus a bishop has to be*

*irreproachable,*
*a husband to one wife,*
*temperate,*
*sensible,*
*urbane,*
*one who likes guests,*
*a skilled teacher,*
*3 not a drinker,*
*not a bully,*
*but gentle,*
*not argumentative,*
*not one who likes money.*

*4 He is to be outstanding in his direction of his own home, with children who are obedient and quite reverent. 5 (For if anybody does not know how to direct his own home, how will he take care of God's church?) 6 He must not be a neophyte lest, inflated with vanity, he fall under the devil's condemnation. 7 But he must enjoy also a fine recommendation from outsiders, lest he fall into disgrace and a snare of the devil.*

## ♦ NOTES

3:1b. *If anybody (ei tis)*. On *ei tis*, see Titus 1:6.

*aspires, oregetai,* appears in 6:10 of the craving for money (see also *Ep. Arist.* 211 and Tatian, *Oratio* 11.2; Whittaker, *Tatian*, p. 22). In the one other NT use of *oregesthai,* in Heb 11:16, it describes the desire for heaven (see Philo, *Virt.* 218, and Justin, *Apology* 12 [*PG* 6.344], of those who *aspire* to godliness and philosophy). The term does not appear in Ap. Frs. or in the LXX. Even in secular Greek this verb does not necessarily suggest an inordinate craving. Thus Polybius 5.104.7 has, *ei de pragmatōn oregetai* . . . , "If one *aspires* to a field for activities. . . ." See Spicq, *Lexic.*, pp. 626-627.

*he sets his heart, epithymei,* appears fifteen times elsewhere in the NT but not otherwise in the PE. In its four uses in the other Paulines it is taken in a bad sense of the heart set on evil actions. Thus in Gal 5:17 it describes the flesh desiring what is opposed to the Spirit (though even this dialectical summary does not use the verb of Spirit desiring what is opposed to the flesh). The desire for evil things is designated in 1 Cor 10:6, and the LXX Decalogue (as in Exod 20:17; Deut 5:21) is cited with this verb in Rom 7:7; 13:9. In the Lukan corpus *epithymein* describes a hungry man's desire for food (Luke 15:16; 16:21), including Jesus' own intense desire to eat the Passover with his disciples (Luke 22:15). In the saying transmitted in Luke 17:22 (see Matt 13:17; *SFG* §235), Jesus speaks of his disciples' desiring "to see one of the days of the Son of Man and you will not see it." In these instances the verb is to be taken in a good sense. The case is otherwise in Acts 20:33 (cited above at 2:9). The oscillation in the Lukan connotation resembles that in the rest of the NT, where a good sense (1 Pet 1:12; Heb 6:11), a neutral one (Rev 9:6), and a pejorative one (James 4:2; Matt 5:28) can be discerned.

On *fine work* see Titus 2:7, 14.

*Epithymein* regularly has a bad sense in Ap. Frs., but a good one does appear in Polycarp, *Phil.* 1.3; *Barn.* 16.10; and Hermas, *Sim.* 9.10. The sense of the verb in the Decalogue casts a long shadow over the whole LXX with its dozens of uses (4 Macc 2:5-6), but the good sense remains even in this tradition, particularly of wisdom (see Wis 6:11, 13; Sir 1:26; 24:19), food (Wis 16:3), children (Sir 16:1), and beauty (Sir 40:22). Of the five uses of the verb in the *Testaments of the Twelve Patriarchs, T. Levi* 13.4 and *T. Benjamin* 10.1 use it in a good sense.

*The episcopate, episkopē,* is used only here in the PE, and in the rest of the NT in 1 Pet 2:12 and the Lukan corpus. Luke 19:44 places the term on Jesus' lips in his prophecy over Jerusalem, doomed "because you did not know the time appointed *(ton kairon)* for your visitation *(tēs episkopēs)*." The *episkopē* here is God's own supervisory presence, guidance, and correction when he appears in Jerusalem in Jesus' mission to his people. The meaning is much like that of "the day of divine inquest" in First Peter, on which pardon or punishment awaits God's people (see Selwyn, *1 Pet,* p. 171). Acts 1:20, when it says of Judas, "Let another take his *episkopē*" (citing the language of LXX Ps 108:8), uses a meaning close to the one here in the PE.

Similarly *1 Clem.* 44.1 asserts that "our apostles [i.e. Peter and Paul, who belong in a unique way to the Roman church] knew through our Lord Jesus Christ that there would be wrangling about the title of the episcopate *(tēs episkopēs).*" A little later (44.4) the letter observes that "it is no small fault if we throw out of the episcopate *(tēs episkopēs)* those who have offered its sacrifices holily and without blame." However, in 50.3 *episkopē* refers (in Lukan fashion) to Christ's "visitation." The one remaining use in Ap. Frs. appears in the final blessing of Ign. *Pol.* 8.3, where Ignatius prays for Polycarp to "stay in God's unity and care *(episkopēi)*" (see Schoedel, *Ignatius,* pp. 280-281).

Although *episkopē* does not appear in secular texts before the second Christian century (Lucian, *Dialogue on the Judgment of the Goddesses* 20.6, of Hermes watching over Ganymede), it frequently designates God's powerful manifestations in the LXX. Thus LXX Exod 3:16 uses the word in a gracious sense (cited in Justin, *Trypho* 59.2 [*PG* 6.612]; see 131.3, the only other use in the Apologists [*PG* 6.780]). It designates an appearance for judgment and condemnation upon idols in Wis 14:11. In LXX Num 4:16 *episkopē* refers to a priestly role in an office linked to Israel's worship (see LXX 4 Kgdms 12:12). In *T. Benjamin* 9.2 the author foresees a time when "the Most High shall send forth his salvation through the visitation *(episkopē)* of the unique prophet" (E.T. from Charlesworth, *OT Pseud.* 1.827, modified). See the excursus in Spicq, *EP,* pp. 439-455, for more data on this noun and *episkopos.*

2. *Thus a bishop has to be irreproachable.* For *a bishop has to be* see Titus 1:7 and the excursus in D-C, pp. 54-57, now noting that *episkopos* appears five times in the NT: twice in the singular in the PE, once in the plural in Paul and once in Acts, and once of Christ in First Peter (all cited in the Comment below). In Ap. Frs. (outside of Ignatius) the term appears almost always in the plural. *First Clement* 42.4-5 writes of "bishops and deacons," and the latter passage also cites *episkopous* from a Greek version of Isa 60:17; however, in *1 Clem.* 59.3 God is "creator and *episkopon* of every spirit" (see LXX Job 20:29). *Didache* 15.1 also speaks of "bishops and deacons," and Hermas uses the term only in the plural (*Vis.* 3.5.1; *Sim.* 9.27.2 *bis*). Ignatius contrasts strikingly with this pattern. He writes of the *episkopos* scores of times and in every letter. Even on the two occasions when he uses the plural (*Eph.* 3.2; *Phld.* 10.2), the implication is plain that each *episkopos* leads a separate church.

Besides the passages cited above, the LXX uses *episkopos* a dozen times, in which it regularly suggests the Levites and their care for the place and apparatus of worship (LXX Num 4:16; 2 Chron 34:12, 17; 2 Esd 21:22; pagan sacrifice in 1 Macc 1:51) or the military leadership (LXX Num 31:14; Judg 9:28; 4 Kgdms 11:15, 18; 2 Esd 21:9, 14). In an unusual turn of phrase, in Wis 1:6 the blasphemer is warned that "God is a witness of his thoughts, the real *episkopos* of his mind, who hears his every word" (E.T. modified from Winston, AB *Wisd.,* p. 99).

*Thus* represents *oun,* as in 2:1. *Irreproachable, anepilēmptos,* reappears in the church order for widows in 5:7 and in the ordination charge in 6:14 but not elsewhere in the NT, Ap. Frs., or the LXX. The form *anepilēptos* appears in *Mart. Pol.* 17.1 and Athenagoras, *Legatio* 31.2, as also in the first-century-C.E. Jewish inscription from the Bosphorus by a widow who enfranchised her slave and directed her heirs to leave the man *anepilēpton* (*CII* §683; see p. 65 of the "Prolegomenon"). Philo uses this form regularly (see esp. *Spec. leg.* 3.135; 4.134). For other texts, see MM *s.v.* and D-C, p. 160.

*a husband to one wife, temperate, sensible, urbane, one who likes guests, a skilled teacher.* See Titus 1:6 for *a husband to one wife;* Titus 2:2 for *temperate;* Titus 1:8 for *sensible* and *one who likes guests;* 1 Tim 2:9 for *kosmios,* here *urbane.*

*A skilled teacher* represents *didaktikos,* an adjective which also characterizes Timothy as "the Lord's slave" in 2 Tim 2:24. The term is not otherwise documented in the NT, Ap. Frs., or the LXX. Philodemus seems to speak of a *didaktikos lexis* in his *Volumina rhetorica* 2.22.10, and not long afterward Philo, *Mut.* 83, 88, calls that virtue *didaktikē* which is learned by a receptive disposition and memory as distinguished from that acquired by hard practice *(askētikē).* He makes use of the same distinction in *Congr.* 35, saying that ". . . the virtue that comes through teaching . . . needs the fruits of several studies . . ." (see also *Praem.* 27 as well as Clement of Alexandria, *Strom.* 1.5; O. Stählin, 2.20.8, describing a wisdom which is *didaktikē*). Particularly notable, however, is the sense in *P. Lond.* 1821 (see LSJ *Supplement s.v.*), which describes a man's forefinger as his *daktylos didaktikos,* i.e. his "teaching finger." See the *Velatio* lunette in the cemetery of Priscilla. For the use of forms of *didaktikos* in the ordination charges to and prayers by bishops, see *Const. Apost.* 2.24.7; 2.57.1; 2.58.3 *(logous didaktikous);* 8.1.12 *(logon didaktikon);* 8.16.5 *(logou didaktikou).*

3. *not a drinker, not a bully, but gentle, not argumentative, not one who likes money. Drinker* and *bully* appear in Titus 1:7; *gentle* and *not argumentative* in Titus 3:2. *Aphilargyron,* "not one who likes money," appears otherwise in the NT only in Heb 13:5, though cognates are in 1 Tim 6:10; 2 Tim 3:2 (and once otherwise in the NT, in the *philargyroi* of Luke 16:14). *Didache* 15.1 uses *aphilargyros* in its short list of virtues requisite for bishops and deacons. Polycarp, *Phil.* 5.2, uses the adjective in his longer catalogue of qualities to be sought in a deacon. Cognates in the cluster are relatively frequent in Polycarp; *Second Clement* has a few of them. The LXX does not use *aphilargyros,* though there are a few uses of cognates in the Maccabean corpus. For the papyri and inscriptions see Deissmann, *LAE,* pp. 81-82, and the further references in Spicq, *Lexic.,* p. 169.

4. *He is to be outstanding in his direction of his own home, with children*

*who are obedient and quite reverent.* Lit. "over his own house *(oikou)* finely *(kalōs)* presiding *(proïstamenon).*" See Titus 1:11 on *oikos;* Titus 3:8 for *proïstamenos.* The adverbial *kalōs* appears again in 3:12 (with *proïstamenoi*), 13 and 5:17 (with *proestōtes*). There are thirty-three other uses of the adverb in the NT, which also appears in Ap. Frs. and the LXX, though never with forms of *proïstanai.*

For *children* see Titus 1:4, 6. The phrase here as well as in Titus 1:6 and 1 Tim 5:4 is lit. "having children," which appears otherwise only in the NT in Matt 21:28; 22:24. Out of hundreds of Septuagintal uses of *teknon,* there appear to be only three uses of the phrase *(ouk) echōn tekna* (1 Chron 2:30, 32) or *echein tekna* (Sir 16:3). The expression does not appear in Ap. Frs.

For *who are obedient* see 1 Tim 2:11. For *and quite reverent,* lit. "with all reverence," see 1 Tim 2:2 and Titus 2:7.

5. *(For if anybody [ei tis] does not know how [ouk oiden] to direct [prostēnai] his own home [tou idiou oikou]).* For *ei tis* see Titus 1:6; for *tou idiou oikou prostēnai,* verse 4 above and its references. Unlike 1:8 above, *oiden* is used here with an infinitival phrase as its object, an uncommon construction in the NT, documented otherwise in the Paulines in Phil 4:12, 15 and 1 Thess 4:4, and in the Lukan corpus in Luke 11:13; 12:56 (both Q). Out of the 318 NT uses of *oida,* apparently the only other examples of this construction are in 1 Pet 5:9; 2 Pet 2:9; James 4:17.

*how (pōs) will he take care (epimelēsetai) of God's church (ekklesias)? Pōs* will be used once more in the PE, in verse 15 below. Yet the particle is common enough in the rest of the NT (101 times), with 26 uses in the remaining Paulines and 25 in Luke-Acts. It is regularly used by Ap. Frs. and the LXX.

*Epimeleisthai* appears again in the NT only in Luke 10:34-35 to designate the tender care which the Samaritan showed the half-dead traveler when "he led him to a public inn, and made provision for him there. The next day he took out two pieces of silver, gave them to the innkeeper, and said, 'Provide for him . . .'" (E.T. from Fitzmyer, AB *Lk,* p. 882, perhaps with a medical connotation, as suggested in Spicq, *Lexic.,* pp. 69-70, 273; contrast Menander, *Georgos* 59-62, with *Heros* 26-27). The verb is not documented in Ap. Frs. but the LXX employs it five times, implying care for safety in Gen 44:21; governing locally in 1 Esd 6:26 (27 RSV); care for health in LXX Prov 27:25; Sir 30:25; and even procuring publication of a decree in 1 Macc 11:37. Josephus, *C. Apion* 1.209, quoting Agatharchides of Cnidus (second century B.C.E.), writes that Jews "do not engage in public service in any other way *(allēs epimeleisthai leitourgias mēdemias)*" on the Sabbath, "but pray with outstretched hands in the temples up to nightfall."

A pair of cognates in the cluster of words formed from *melein* appear in 1 Tim 4:14 *(amelein),* 15 *(meletan).* For these and others see the articles of Spicq just cited.

*God's church (ekklēsia). Ekklēsia* (114 times altogether in the NT) appears below in 3:15 in the phrase "the church of the living God," and at the end of the church order for widows as *hē ekklēsia* in 5:16. The noun is most frequently used in Acts and the rest of the Paulines, and it appears regularly in Ap. Frs. There are about 100 uses of *ekklēsia* in the LXX.

The anarthrous phrase *God's church* reappears in this correspondence at 3:15, "the church of the living God." Otherwise in the NT the phrase is always used with the article. It appears nine times in the rest of the Paulines (three of these in the plural) and once in Acts 20:28 in Paul's farewell address to the Ephesian presbyter-bishops, where "God" means the Lord Jesus. Eleven times Ap. Frs. use the phrase "(the) church of God." The inscription of *First Clement* thus designates the church at Rome and at Corinth; for other uses with the article see Ign. *Trall.* 12.1; Polycarp, *Phil. inscr.;* Hermas, *Sim.* 9.18.2, 3, 4. The anarthrous uses are in Ignatius (*Trall.* 2.3 [see BDF §252, 273]; *Smyrn. inscr.; Phld. inscr.* [see BDF §252] and 10.1 [BDF §268]). There is a single, textually disputed, Septuagintal use of the phrase, in the form *en ekklēsiai theou,* in LXX 2 Esd 23:1: ". . . and it was found written . . . that Ammonites and Moabites were not to enter *in the assembly of God* forever. . . ."

6. *He must not be a neophyte (neophyton) lest, inflated (typhōtheis) with vanity, he fall under (empesēi) the devil's (tou diabolou) condemnation (krima).* Lit. "Not a neophyte lest puffed up he fall into condemnation of the devil." See Titus 2:3 for *diabolos. Neophytos* appears only here in the NT and Ap. Frs. as well as the Apologists, who do not use it at all. The term refers literally to a newly planted seedling or the slip of a vine. Thus LXX Job 14:9 uses the term (see also Philo, *Virt.* 28, 156). A transferred sense has begun to appear in the remaining Septuagintal occurrences in LXX Pss 127:3 and 143:12 (of the children in a household) and Isa 5:7 (of the whole people of Judah). The term became technical in Christian Latin and hence remained, like *episkopos* and *diakonoi,* in its Greek form (see Frede, *VL* 25.495; Tertullian, *De praescriptione* 41.6 [CC 1.221.16]).

*Typhousthai* appears again in 1 Tim 6:4, leading off a list of vices of those who oppose the Pauline teaching, and in 2 Tim 3:4 it appears toward the end of a catalogue of vicious characteristics of people in the last days. The verb is not found in Ap. Frs. or the LXX, though it is not uncommon in secular and Jewish Greek, where the root meaning of "to smoke, pour or puff out smoke" is regularly close at hand (see Chantraine, *DELG,* pp. 1147-1148). As early as Alcaeus, LP §336, one reads *pampan d' etyphōs' ek d' eleto phrenas,* "He quite obscured his wits and swept them off." Philo addresses a gourmand with *o tetyphōmene,* "madman" (*Det.* 101), and characterizes as "false and senseless, *tetyphōmenos*" (*Som.* 2.64), an elaborate way of living *(bios)* as well as "the mind of the multitude" (*Conf.* 106). His application of forms of *typhousthai* to teachers who take the credit for already gifted pupils (*Congr.* 127-128) is a particularly appropriate parallel to 1 Tim 3:6.

*He fall* is one of the seven NT uses of *empiptein.* In the Paulines it occurs only in this verse and the following of the PE, as well as in 1 Tim 6:9. In Luke 6:39 the verb poses the question about the blind leading the blind and both falling into a ditch, and in 10:36 is "the man who fell into the hands of robbers." Matthew 12:11 uses this verb of a sheep falling into a ditch. Hebrews 10:31, "It is a fearful thing to fall into the hands *(eis cheiras)* of the living God," offers a parallel to the phrase in 1 Tim 3:6. In Ap. Frs. *1 Clem.* 43.2 uses *empiptein* in an absolute sense of jealousy "arising" about the priestly office; Ign. *Magn.* 11.1 warns about "falling into the fishhooks of false doctrine"; Hermas, *Vis.* 3.2.9, writes of stones "falling into *(epi)* the fire," *Man.* 10.1.5 of "falling into *(eis)* many practices" of secular life, and 12.1.2 of falling into *(eis)* wicked desire. The LXX uses forms of *empiptein* about fifty times and the verb appears four times in the *Testaments of the Twelve Patriarchs,* but the closest one comes in any of these documents to *eis krima empesēi,* the phrase here in the PE, is in Sir 29:19 of the sinner, pursuing gain, who "will fall into lawsuits *(eis kriseis)*." See Spicq, *Lexic.,* pp. 243-244, for more data.

*Condemnation, krima,* occurs once more in the PE, in 1 Tim 5:12, in the church order for widows. There are twenty-six other occurrences in the NT, ten in the remaining Paulines (of which six are in Romans), four in Luke-Acts. For *eis krima* see 1 Cor 11:34 and Luke 24:20 as well as John 9:39 and Jude 4 (with *touto*). In Ap. Frs. seven out of eight occurrences of *krima* are in *First Clement.* In 11.2 and 21.1 it is construed with *eis,* as it is in Ign. *Eph.* 11.1. Although *krima* occurs frequently in the LXX, the phrase *eis krima* seems to be found only in LXX Jer 26:28: "And I shall chastise you for judgment." A basic sense of decision and separation appears already in its earliest use in Greek when Aeschylus has King Pelasgus reply to the request of the maidens by ringing the changes on terms from this cluster: *Ouk eukriton to krima; mē m' hairou kritēn,* "The judgment is not easy to judge; don't pick me as judge" (*Suppliant Maidens* 397).

7. *But he must enjoy (dei de kai echein) also a fine recommendation (martyrian kalēn) from outsiders (apo tōn exōthen).* For *he must, dei,* see Titus 1:7; for *fine, kalos,* see Titus 2:7, 14. An initial note on *martyria* appeared at Titus 1:13. There are thirty-five other NT uses, with the lion's share in the Johannine corpus and none in the rest of the Paulines. Depositions about Jesus are designated by this noun in Luke 22:71 (see Mark 14:55-56, 59), and in Acts 22:18 the term is heard on Jesus' lips in a temple vision in which he assures Paul that the Jews "will not accept your testimony *(martyrian)* about me." In Ap. Frs. *martyria* occurs in *1 Clem.* 30.7, "Let testimony to our good deeds be given by others" (see 38.2); *Barn.* 1.6, "Love of joy and gladness is the testimony of the

works of righteousness"; and Hermas, *Sim.* 5.2.6. The handful of occurrences of the term in the LXX are outweighed by its appearance in the texts of the commandment against false testimony (LXX Exod 20:16; Deut 5:20). Of the man generous with food the LXX Sir 31:23 (RSV 34:23) asserts that "the testimony to his excellence *(kallonēs)* is to be believed."

*outsiders,* lit. "from those outside," *exōthen,* appears only here in the PE and a dozen times elsewhere in the NT, including once in the remaining Paulines (2 Cor 7:5) and twice in the Lukan corpus (Luke 11:39-40), but not used of persons (see *v.l.* in Mark 4:11). Ignatius, *Rom.* 3.2, asks prayer for "strength outside and inside"; the one other use in Ap. Frs. is in Hermas, *Vis.* 3.4.3, of nothing being outside the truth. There are several dozen appearances of *exōthen* in the LXX, but parallels with 1 Tim 3:7 are hard to come by; perhaps LXX Jer 6:11; 9:21 with their references to *nepia exōthen,* "the children outside," are the closest. Josephus, *Ant.* 15.316, uses *exōthen* to mean "foreign nations," i.e. kingdoms other than Herod's; in *War* 179 it means the Romans.

*lest he fall (empesēi) into disgrace (oneidismon) and a snare (pagida) of the devil (tou diabolou).* For *fall, empiptein,* see the preceding verse; for *the devil,* see Titus 2:3.

*Disgrace, oneidismos,* appears only here in the PE and four times otherwise in the NT, once in Rom 15:3 citing LXX Ps 68:10 (pl. with *epipiptein*). The other appearances are in Heb 10:33 (pl.); 11:26; 13:13. The term is not documented in Ap. Frs., but the LXX employs it several dozen times, particularly in prophetic and sapiential documents. *Oneidismos* is used four times in the *Testaments of the Twelve Patriarchs,* and in the singular in *T. Levi* 10.4; 15.2 of the exiled sons of Levi becoming objects of scorn not only to Gentiles but to their friends.

*Snare, pagis,* appears below in 6:9 of those who desire riches and "topple into a temptation and a trap and multiple lusts. . . ." In 2 Tim 2:26 the expression "the snare of the devil" reappears. Otherwise in the NT *pagis* occurs only in Rom 11:9, quoting LXX Ps 68:23, and in Luke 21:35 (see LXX Isa 24:17) of the last day closing on the sinner like *a snare.* In Ap. Frs. it occurs in *Did.* 2.4, "to be double-tongued is the snare of death," and in *Barn.* 19.7, "The mouth is the snare of death." *Pagis* is more common in the LXX and can be documented perhaps threescore times, particularly in the sapiential materials. Tobit 14:10 (Göttingen) has the expression *Aman de enempesen eis tēn pagida,* "Aman fell into the snare," paralleling "the snare of death." The "snare(s) of death" also appears in LXX Ps 17:6; Prov 14:27; 21:6. The linking of *pagis* with the organs of human speech, particularly mouth, tongue, and lips, is notable (see LXX Prov 6:2; 11:9; 18:7; and especially Sir 51:2, of God's rescue "from the snare of a slandering [*diabolēs*] tongue [*glōssēs*]"). For *empiptein eis pagidas,* see also LXX Prov 12:13; Sir 9:3.

## ♦ COMMENT

3:1b. *If anybody aspires to the episcopate, he sets his heart on fine work.* After having construed 3:1a with the final verse of chapter 2, one must ask at this point, "How abrupt a transition does the author of the PE find tolerable as he redacts his materials?" Unquestionably he has used the transitional particles (*de, gar, oun, kai, alla,* etc.) frequently and effectively to assemble his composition, not to mention other terms such as the demonstratives. Still there is no gainsaying the occasionally abrupt, even harsh and ungrammatical, breaks in his writing (see Titus 1:2-3; 2:15–3:1; 1 Tim 1:3-7; 3:16–4:1; 5:22-24; etc.).

Thus these literary criteria do not settle the question. Granted that 3:1a makes a convincing summary conclusion to chapter 2 for the reasons adduced there, one can readily admit that the sententious (though not proverbial) character of the observation in 3:1b would somewhat ease the compositional transition while signaling a major change of subject. The abrupt opening of 3:1b clearly distinguishes the following section of the church order on ministers for a Christian congregation from the preceding section on the Christian men and women, and specifically Christian wives, at worship. The question implicit at this juncture in the church order (which has just described the roles that wives do not have in Christian liturgy) is, "Who does preside and teach in Christian public worship?" The answer is the bishop and the deacons, including women ministers. Whereas the preceding chapter devoted itself to the reasons for Christian prayer and the conduct of the people who participated in public worship, the directives of chapter 3 turn to those whose proper function is ministering by their lives and words to the church at prayer. The leadership which bishop and ministers offer actually places them last in the community envisioned here (see Luke 22:26-27, where this teaching of Jesus is put into a eucharistic context; the situation is otherwise in the parallels, *SFG* §263).

The content as well as the form of *if anybody aspires . . .* makes it very improbable that this saying is a prophetic "pronouncement of sacred law," as Käsemann, *Questions,* pp. 66-81, describes it, for eschatological enthusiasm, legal language, and chiastic structure with an appeal to a *lex talionis* are lacking (see Knight *Sayings,* p. 55 n. 17; Boring, *Sayings,* pp. 130-132, with additional data). If the sententious observation in 3:1b has prophetic roots, it could be classified as a legitimation oracle of recognition (see 1 Tim 1:18 and Aune, *Prophecy,* pp. 68-70, 270-274) in which otherworldly authentication is pronounced upon one who is going to be uniquely important for a people or a society, particularly a ruler. Yet the content of the sentence is far from naive. It serves to introduce a formidable list of qualities requisite for this episcopal leadership, but this leadership (in a problematic presumed by the very arrangement of this church order) presumes that the bishop and his ministers have taken the least desired position as they serve the Christian assembly, for all the demands that this is going to make on their personal and public life. The church order (and the prophetic oracle which it may be citing) reflects a situation in which it was difficult to persuade men to accept *the episcopate.* There is not much esteem for their work, at least in comparison with that of prophets and teachers, as *Did.* 15.2 witnesses with its admonition, "So do not disdain them [bishops and deacons], for they are honorable men among you along with the prophets and teachers." The small original congregations had grown with a corresponding escalation of the demands made upon the generosity of all (see 1 Tim 5:16). The public image of Christians and their leaders was coming under increasingly intense scrutiny. Theological conflicts were heating up with orthodox Judaism as well as with Jewish Christians and other parties within the congregations. Moreover, the administrative charisms were not always held in high regard (Heb 13:17), not least in the Pauline tradition (1 Cor 12:28), which witnesses to certain midcourse corrections in this regard (see 1 Thess 5:12; 1 Cor 16:15-16). The fact that Paul was more than once on the defensive about his own apostolic ministry vis-à-vis the congregations to whom he had first preached the gospel would explain the lack of interest on the part of the local leadership, which may have been disloyal to boot. If that is in fact the case, the ignoring of the local leaders in the great Pauline letters may be due more to apostolic strategy than to theology. The traditional materials cited here in First Timothy could then be as old as the Pauline apostolate. When assessed thus, they can be understood as redressing the balance between apostolate and local leadership which the controversies of the first Christian generation disturbed. In any case, the Pauline apostolate is envisioned in this passage as very much concerned with a ministry in the local church that deserved and needed appreciation, *the episcopate,* with the emphasis on activity or what must be done rather than on authoritative position or status of the body of bishops as such (note the anarthrous *episkopē* as well as the parallelism with *ergon;* Spicq, *EP,* pp. 429, 440 n. 6).

The dangers posed by the growth of an appreciation initially wanting began to crop up in ecclesial life by the last decade of the first Christian century in troubles among the Corinthian Christians as well as with Diotrephes in Third John. In Tertullian's phrase, *episcopatus aemulatio scismatum* [*sic*] *mater est,* "Rivalry for the episcopate is the mother of schisms" (*De baptismo* 17.2: CC 1.291.13-14).

*Episkopē,* found only here in the Pauline epistolary, had probably been adopted by Christians already in the first generation from the LXX tradition for designating leaders, whom they had begun previously to call *episkopoi* (Phil 1:1 addresses "the bishops and deacons" of that congregation). When the narrative of Acts treats of filling "the lot of this ministry," *ton klēron tēs diakonias tautēs,* which Judas had abandoned, "the place *(topon)* of this ministry and apostolate *(apostolēs)*" (Acts 1:17, 25), there is an appeal in Acts 1:20 to words from LXX Ps 108:8, an appeal determined not by the literal sense of the psalm but by the Septuagintal use of *episkopē,* which by the time Luke wrote in the eighties had become, with *apostolē,* part of an established technical terminology for describing the ministry of an *episkopos.* In the Lukan problematic "this ministry" of the Twelve was able to be described not only as *apostolē* but also as *episkopē.* Under certain carefully specified conditions, "this ministry and apostolate" could be shared and transmitted. The narrative implies that something similar could be said of their *episkopē.* The argument of the PE appears to be structured with some of the same elements, though here Paul is the one who receives the ministry of an apostle (see 1:12; 2:7). Just as the primary task of the Twelve is "the prayer" of the Jerusalem church (Acts 6:4), so the *episkopē* appears in First Timothy in the church order devoted, in the name of Paul, to the public prayer of Christians. Just as, in the historical order, there were first persons, then persons who were called *apostoloi,* then the whole task or job of an *apostolē,* so here there were persons, then persons called *episkopoi,* then an *episkopē.* First Timothy and the church order cited here move more systematically, from the task as a whole to the persons who seek it. The procedure presumes a somewhat later stage of development where a job is looking for people who match it rather than vice versa.

In Titus 1:7 the qualifications for a presbyter-bisbop often resemble, formally, terminologically, and conceptually, those of the *bishop* here in 1 Tim 3:2-4. Thus the term *episkopos* itself appears in the PE only in these two passages; *ei tis* is part of the context; the impersonal *dei* introduces a series of qualifications which coincide verbally five times and agree several times more about the reality being designated. Yet there are notable differences in the two treatments, for there is no mention of the presbyter in this chapter of First Timothy and no hint that the presbyter-bishop of Titus *aspires* to the job. Here the *bishop* is listed with the *deacons* (whom Titus does not mention at all). For all the coincidences, the terminology of two lists of qualifications is for the most part different. This passage of First Timothy is conspicuously longer than that in Titus. Accordingly, one is alerted to the fact that, for all that the *episkopoi* of the PE may have in common, there may have been significant, even dramatic, differences in the way in which individual bishops conceived of their *episcopate,* just as in the first generation there is little doubt that the apostolate was understood and lived out by apostles in surprisingly different ways (see Gal 2:8; 1 Cor 9:1-6, 15:10-11; Schnackenburg, "Apostles Before," pp. 287-303). The fact that *episkopē* in First Timothy was transliterated rather than translated in the Old Latin versions indicates that in the West the term was not heard in an abstract or generic way but as a word that designated a concrete, tangible reality that was able to be pointed out in Christian life (similarly, Vg Acts 1:20 uses *episcopatus* whereas it translates Luke 19:44 and 1 Pet 2:12 with *visitatio;* see the studies of Mohrmann, *Études,* passim, identifying this phenomenon in Christian Latin, particularly her *"Episkopos-Speculator"* in 4.231-252).

The historian would relish further hints of how a man was chosen for and inducted into the *episcopate* as the PE conceived it. There is no warrant for the transfer of the delegated apostolic appointment set out by Titus 1:5 into this passage of First Timothy or its source, written ostensibly for different locales. This passage in First Timothy takes for granted that *episcopate* is an existing reality the formalities of entry into which need not be described. If Titus does indeed envision a more embryonic stage in the development of Christian ministry for relatively new, Jewish Christian congregations, then this section of First Timothy, directed to older Christian churches, of mixed origin and in a metropolitan setting, presumes some sort of apostolic, even Pauline, intervention that had long since established and authenticated an *episcopate* in their midst.

Acts has Paul speak to the presbyters of Ephesus as bishops (20:17-35) and describes at length the apostle's relations with that metropolis and its church (see Acts 18:19 through 20:1). The readers of First Timothy may be meant to understand the *episcopate* at Ephesus (the city in which this letter is ostensibly directed to Timothy; see 1:3) against the background of the Pauline instruction to those whom the apostle called bishops and who are understood as shepherds of a flock "in which the Holy Spirit has made you bishops *(etheto episkopous)* to shepherd *(poimainein)* the church of God (*tēn ekklēsian tou theou* [see 1 Tim 3:5, 15]) which he obtained with the blood of his own" Son (Acts 20:28; see 1 Pet 2:25, where the Christ who suffered on the cross is "the shepherd and bishop [*ton poimena kai episkopon*] of your souls," as well as Lohse, "Episkopos," pp. 225-231). The appeal in 2 Tim 3:10-11 to what Paul taught and suffered in Pisidian Antioch, Iconium, and Lystra is not without its parallels to this passage. If the church order hypothesized here in First Timothy originated in the Roman church, one may be encountering the congregation that coined the term *episkopē,* and its quotation in a correspondence directed to the most influential church of Asia Minor would have given wider currency to the new term as it made its way east and found a ready understanding in churches that already used *episkopos.* The advantage of the new word was its inclusive character, for not every person who exercised an *episkopē* had necessarily to have the title *episkopos* (see the letter about the martyrs of Lyons on the subject of Pothinus, Irenaeus's predecessor, cited in Eusebius, *Church History* 5.1.29, and R. Brown, "*Episkope,*" p. 322; *Meaning,* p. 125). The implications of this for understanding the presbyter-bishop of Titus 1:6-7 (not to mention Acts 20:17, 28) are immediately evident; others will appear below.

The *episcopate* is described as the object of a man's fervent aspiration, with a verb that could be read in a bad sense. Yet the good sense of the apodosis of this sentence, identifying the *episcopate* as *fine work,* demands that one take both *aspires* and *sets his heart on* in a good sense, unless one takes the sentence ironically (see Knight, *Sayings,* p. 57 n. 24, critiquing H. B. Swete, *JTS* 18 [1916]: 3). The *episcopate* is a *work (ergon),* and a *fine (kalon)* activity at that. The relation of the *ergon* terminology to the apostolic ministries began in Titus 2:7. The adjective here emphasizes the attractive visibility that ought to characterize the fruit of an *episcopate.* In 2 Tim 4:5 Timothy himself is told, "Do the work *(ergon)* of one who announces the gospel."

2. *Thus a bishop has to be irreproachable, a husband to one wife, temperate, sensible, urbane, one who likes guests, a skilled teacher.* The oracular sentence of the previous verse introduces a list of qualifications for *a bishop* that extends through verse 7. The opening words, *dei . . . ton episkopon . . . einai,* initiate a similar catalogue at Titus 1:7 and sound almost formulaic. Still the term *dei* is not in the Isocrates or Onosander passages cited by D-C, pp. 158-160, though Lucian uses it in *De Saltatione [Pantomimus]* 81.

The transitional *oun,* "thus," has an inceptive rather than an inferential sense (see J. K. Elliott, *Greek Text,* pp. 46-47). The preceding verse has submitted a principle; "so" or "now" one can turn to the requirements for *a bishop.* The term *episkopos* is the title for a person (and thus was, like *episkopē,* transliterated instead of translated already in the Old Latin versions; see Frede, *VL* 25.481-483). It was long heard as a rather vague *nomen agentis* whose exact significance is hard to pin down (Mohrmann, *Études* 4.235).

Did the archaic church order and/or the author of the PE intend the singular form to be taken collectively (note the article and Titus 1:7; Hort, *Ecclesia,* pp. 190-191, 193) or to sketch a model for ministry in which one *episkopos* with several *diakonoi* and women assistants served a given congregation of believers? The meaning in Titus does not determine the meaning here, and in fact a second treatment of the *episkopos* in the small compass of this correspondence probably is meant to show that in some Pauline churches the leaders were called presbyter-bishops and in others they had the title *bishop* (and were assisted by deacons and unmarried women). On the one occasion when the local ministry is addressed by its titles in the rest of the Pauline correspondence, in Phil 1:1, the titles found here in 1 Tim 3 are used. When Polycarp wrote to the Philippian Christians more than a generation after Paul, he called the local leaders "the presbyters and deacons, *tois presbyterois kai diakonois*" (*Phil.* 5.3).

A few years previously, in the last decade of the first Christian century, *First Clement* took it for granted that the Corinthian congregation (and his own?) had by the will of the Lord and his apostles a ministry that was exercised by "bishops and deacons." The terminology was clearly in his possession, for he cited a Greek version of Isa 60:17 for both terms in a way that resembles the

Lukan citation of LXX Ps 108:8 in Acts 1:20. Apparently, according to *1 Clem.* 43.4-5, presbyters also shared "the title of the episcopate" (43.1) and "offered its sacrifices." The faithful in the *Didache* have also as leaders "bishops and deacons" who perform a service *(leitourgousi)* that corresponds with the service *(tēn leitourgian)* of both the prophets (who seem to have been celebrants of the eucharist, 10.7) and the teachers in the communities envisioned by this document (15.1). The term *presbyter,* however, does not appear in the *Didache.* One is thus forewarned about attaching too much weight to a given title in these earliest Christian generations. The titles for those ministering to a church not only varied from one congregation (house church) to another but also varied in the same church from time to time. Again, one congregation may have had a corps of leaders called presbyters, assisted by a group of widows; another, several leaders simultaneously who were called presbyter-bishops; another, only one; another, a presider who had the title *bishop* and who worked with deacons and other assistants, etc. What the author of the PE and his source meant by *episkopos* at this point must be gleaned from text and context. It will be suggested below that the source being cited at this point is a charge from an ordination liturgy, but first the individual components of the list of virtues required for the bishop will be analyzed.

The list leads off with *irreproachable,* which reminds one of the repeated "unimpeachable" of Titus 1:6-7. The use of the term below in the church order for widows (5:7) and the ordination charge (6:14) already signals its currency in the sources utilized by the PE. The unusual word has been formed by the prefixing of an alpha-privative (used twice more as this list concludes, perhaps as a marker for the conclusion) to a derivative of *epilambanesthai,* which not only designates an actual grasping of a reality (as in 6:12, 19) but in its relatively frequent occurrences in Luke-Acts has the sense of (not) catching a person in a mistake in his speech (Luke 20:20, 26). Perhaps the compound was coined in the archaic church order cited here because more than simply verbal errors are to be absent from the conduct of an *episkopos.* His acts and performance as *a bishop* must give no handle to accusation or reproach (note that later this is the sense in Lucian, *De Saltatione [Pantomimus]* 81; for the papyri from the second century B.C.E., see MM *s.v.*).

The term that opened this list, with its emphasis on a way of life that is beyond accusation, serves as a generic introduction for the specific areas in the life of a Christian minister that a leadership charge subjects to enduring, critical attention. The first specific area is suggested by a citing of his promise from the Christian marriage liturgy to be *a husband to one wife.* The older, Jewish Christian part of the list in Titus 1:6 proceeded similarly. As is explained there, only one marriage is envisioned for the lifetime of the man who *aspires to the episcopate* (similarly below for the deacon and the official widow). Their service to the church includes this special witness of faithfulness to one wife, even if she should predecease her one husband. It is helpful to note that here in First Timothy the relations of the husband and father to his home and to his children are no longer joined to the phrase *a husband of one wife* as they were in the perhaps more primitive list in Titus. Here instead, at 3:4-5 below, they have been made into a kind of appendix to this list. The positioning of the marriage relationship in both lists indicates the esteem in which the PE as well as their sources hold the marriage bond as well as the public attention which Christian marriages elicited. Perhaps it is implied also that public irregularities in Christian marriages were frequent enough to warrant a certain primacy for this qualification.

Second only to the demand for married fidelity in *a bishop* is that he be *temperate.* In Titus 2:2 this was the first of the virtues for the older Christian men, and it designates positively what *not a drinker* in verse 3 specifies negatively, though being *temperate* includes self-control in the use of food as well as of drink (see v. 11 also).

*Sensible* is one of the two verbal coincidences between this twelve-entry catalogue and the list of the qualities for a general in Onosander (see v. 3, *not one who likes money,* for the other; *egkratēs,* "self-controlled," in Titus 1:8 offers the only other verbal coincidence between Onosander's list and the PE). The healthy-minded prudence which this adjective suggests is often paired with the following *urbane.* Thus Menander, *Sam.* 343-345 (F. Sandbach), has Demeas complain, "This does not seem credible at all to me, that he who is so urbane and sensible *(kosmion kai sōphrona)* toward all strangers should turn out to be like this toward me. . . ." The Greek *kosmios,* "urbane," designates a certain attractive composure that involves restraint and a sense of order and so a person who is agreeable. What *sōphron,* "sensible," is to the heart, a man's internal presence, *kosmios,* is to the presence he projects to others.

*One who likes guests,* a person who likes and has the means to welcome strangers as guests, coincides again with Titus 1:8. At this point it is appropriate to recall the regular appearance of the *philoxen-* cluster of terms in NT documents that appear to have special ties to the Roman church, thus Rom 12:13; Heb 13:2; 1 Pet 4:9. Among Ap. Frs. it is only in those linked to the Roman church where one encounters *philoxen-* forms (see *1 Clem.* 1.2; 10.7; 11.1; 12.1, 3 [the adjective of Rahab]; 35.5 *s.v.l.;* Hermas, *Man.* 8.10; *Sim.* 9.27.2, "Bishops and people who liked guests at all times gladly and without hypocrisy received the servants of God into their houses"). Though Ignatius received hospitality from the bishops of Asia Minor at every turn and was grateful for it, this terminology was apparently not his, nor that of the Athenian philosopher-apologist Aristides (*Apology* 15). The usage suggests a term that the Roman congregation liked for a quality valued throughout the Christian church, not to mention the ancient world generally (see the texts and the literature cited in Spicq, *Lexic.,* pp. 932-935). Perhaps a hint remains in this term of the Roman provenance of the PE and their source.

The seventh quality of the one who *aspires to the episcopate* is that he be *didaktikon,* "a skilled teacher." Lexically the adjective might mean "teachable" as well as "able to teach," suggesting the one who has been taught as well as who is ready to bring what he has learned to a new situation. Popularly, as a papyrus witness attests, the term suggested one who pointed out what he knew and admonished his hearer in accord with that knowledge. The PE envision others than the one who is called *episkopos* as teaching. In 1 Tim 5:17 the implication is that some who are called *presbyteroi* teach; in Titus 1:9 those called "presbyter-bishops" have a teaching role. As 1 Tim 2:7 made clear, Paul is *didaskalos,* "teacher," for the readers of the PE; and the "gracious gift" which Timothy has received as well as the Scriptures themselves are certainly ordered (among other activities) to teaching the faithful generally as well as his own co-workers and successors (see 1 Tim 4:13-14; 2 Tim 2:1-2; 3:16) according to the Pauline model that he has witnessed (2 Tim 3:10).

Formally speaking, the position in seventh place in this catalogue of *a skilled teacher* may be read with some emphasis, particularly in the source that is being employed, for a different, predominantly negative formal principle appears to govern the next five entries. They may have constituted (at some other point in the source?) a cluster which the author of the PE inserted here without thereby attenuating the importance which the original list attached to teaching (an importance which the manner of listing in 2 Tim 2:24 did diminish).

3. *not a drinker, not a bully, but gentle, not argumentative, not one who likes money.* Some conceptual overlap now appears in the list, with *not a drinker* coinciding largely with *temperate.* Formally, this five-member cluster is structured with negative particles; two negative phrases with *mē* are balanced against two alpha-privative compounds, and an adversative *alla,* "but," introduces *gentle,* the only positive virtue in the cluster. The qualities designated appear to have been arranged chiastically (abcb′a′). A similar construction appears in the five-member negative cluster of Titus 1:7 which concludes the first part of the list there and is followed by an adversative *alla* introducing the seven-member concluding catalogue. The opening pair of vices listed here occur in the same order in Titus 1:7. On the *bishop* as *bully* see the provision in F. X. Funk, *Constitutiones* (8.47.27; 1.571), for the deposition of a bishop (or presbyter or deacon) who attempts to intimidate Christians and nonbelievers from wrongdoing by striking them, ignoring the teaching and actions of Jesus. The closing *not one who likes money* corresponds conceptually with "not money-minded" in the same place in Titus. With the contrasting *but gentle,* the center of this cluster in Timothy is reached and the only positive virtue appears, like a jewel in a dark setting. In Titus 3:2 *gentle* contrasts with a preceding *argumentative,* here with one that follows.

The second alpha-privative here, *aphilargyros,* "not one who likes money," concludes the five-member, negative cluster by singling out another area for self-control beyond that suggested by the opening, *not a drinker.* Moreover, the repeated alpha-privatives echo *irreproachable* at the beginning of this catalogue. For the second and last time this list corresponds verbally with Onosander (see his *Peri Haireseos Stragegou* 1.1, 8), who writes: "For this being free from greed will have the utmost value, because due to it one manages his affairs incorruptibly and high-mindedly. For many, though they faced courageously shields and spears galore, end up blinded by gold, for it is a terrible weapon against enemies and an engine for conquering." Diodorus Siculus (31.26.1-2), after describing the unblemished *aphilargyria* of Lucius Aemilius (d. 160-B.C.E.), feels compelled to note that the freedom from greed characteristic of those old Romans might seem "incredible to some" who "should take into account the fact that we cannot properly judge the freedom of ancients from avarice *(aphilargyrian)* by the dishonest greed of present-day [end of first-century-B.C.E.] Romans. For in our lifetime this people has, it appears, acquired a strong tendency to want more and more" (E.T. from F. R. Walton, LCL). Virgil wrote, *Quid non mortalia pectora cogis/auri sacra fames?* "To what have you not driven human hearts, O cursed hunger for gold?" The theme appears regularly in Horace, Persius, and Juvenal, not to mention the Hebrew Bible (thus 1 Sam 12:3).

The caution about avarice suggests that the Christian *bishop* has access to funds that are not his own. The demand here for a candidate who does not like money is a demand for the virtue of a trustworthy administrator. It has sometimes appeared as a quite ordinary and unheroic holiness. Still the requirement for the virtue may already constitute an unexpressed judgment on a refined, religious arrogance which has ill-concealed contempt for ordinary goodness. Even after generations of reflection upon Judas, the Gospel tradition can find no more damning description of the man than to say he stole from the funds entrusted to him (John 12:6), i.e. he was the very type of the bad steward. On the other hand the great apologia for the Pauline ministry in Acts 20:33 reaches its climax with the declaration, "I coveted no one's silver or gold or clothing," and then the appeal to the apostle's labor for his own support which thus became his gift to the Ephesian church, especially to the weak and the poor.

The question rises, however, about how *a bishop* is to maintain himself and his family. This church order does not broach that subject. The same question will arise with *deacons* below. To anticipate some observations at this point, it appears as if *a bishop* is a man of some means, owning a home in which the congregation can gather and guests can be cared for. He is free to devote his time to serving the church by teaching and studying, by administration and giving leadership.

4-5. *He is to be outstanding in his direction of his own home, with children who are obedient and quite reverent. (For if anybody does not know how to direct his own home, how will he take care of God's church?)* Up to here this list has consisted of very short, regularly single-word entries within one long sentence whose clauses become more complex in Greek as they continue to roll on through verses 4-6. Whereas the editorial intervention of the author of the PE was difficult to ascertain in verses 3:1b-3 (except perhaps at the seam between verses 2 and 3), it is somewhat easier to recognize his observation in the parenthetical verse 5 in this section. The final sentence of this whole section on the bishop, verse 7, appears to echo verbally (with forms of *dei* and *kalos*) the opening of 3:1b-2.

In the more expansive clauses that start with verse 4, the Christian home of the *bishop* becomes a paradigm for the kind of leadership expected of him. The mention of his children reminds the reader of the archaic Jewish Christian requisites for the presbyters in Titus 1:6, though (as is noted above) *a husband to one wife* has gone into the first part of the list here with its sense nuanced somewhat differently in its new context. Here at verse 4 the relation of the husband as household head as well as father comes to the fore. He must manage his home, on a regular, ongoing basis, in a visibly attractive fashion (*kalos;* of deacons and presbyters below, thus making the phrase almost a technical one for describing ecclesial ministries in the PE). *His own home* refers, as regularly in the PE, to the people who constituted the *home,* i.e. the family. The familial model in mind was that in which one man, the *paterfamilias,* headed the household (see H. A. Hoffner, *TDOT* 2.111, 113-115, for details). The explicit parallelism with *God's church* in verse 5 makes it difficult to believe that the comparison was not chosen with an eye to a form of church leadership in which one *bishop* headed a local congregation (setting aside the question whether there were several house churches in a given city or locality). One notes that the plural appears in verse 12: "Deacons are to be husbands of one wife, outstanding in the direction of their own children and homes *(tōn idiōn oikōn).*" The term *monarchical,* etymologically "one-headed," carries so much emotional freight in modern European languages that, for all its technical accuracy for designating the phenomenon here, it is practically useless. Even the most generic and transparent terminology for leadership is indelibly marked and defined by the men who exercise it, as the terms *der Führer* and *il Duce* illustrate to this day.

The terminology of the reference to *children* appears to be typical of a Jewish Christian source used by the PE. The description of the *children* as *obedient, en hypotagēi,* uses the terminology of 2:11 above about the Christian wife. The phrase puts into positive form what the Jewish Christian list at Titus 1:6 meant by excluding presbyteral candidates who had "refractory," *anypotakta,* children. *Obedient* telescopes the three criteria of Titus ("children who are believers, who cannot be charged with debauchery, who are not refractory") into one positive characteristic that includes subordination to God and Christ *(pista),* to the divine commandments *(mē en katēgoriai asōtias),* to legitimate human authority (*anypotakta;* see the Comment there). The parabolic force of this comparison will become plain in the verse following.

The *children* of the *bishop* are in the final phrase to be *quite reverent.* The quality is "humanized" and "Christianized" by being refracted through Christian family relationships. A good father evokes an affection that is mingled with respect and some awe from his children. Again, the attitude is chosen with an eye to what is going to be said in verse 5 about the episcopal ministry to the church, for the rhetorical question of verse 5 is a pendant to the qualification preceding and sounds like a parenthetical observation on already traditional Jewish Christian materials, whose obvious sense pertains to Christian family life and not to an ecclesial leader. The domestic life of the bishop-to-be, so the author of the PE avers, is parabolic of the life in congregations of believers.

The question of verse 5, like the question following a parable, is meant to elicit the reader's agreement to these criteria drawn from domestic life. The protasis of the question takes up the actual terminology of the preceding materials. *For if anybody, ei de tis,* reminds one of the opening of this section in 3:1b. The apodosis, introduced by *pōs,* "how," with the future, expects a negative answer (thus Rom 10:14-15; Luke 1:34; 11:18). The parallels between protasis and apodosis are notable, with the verb *direct* corresponding to *take care,* the noun *home* corresponding to *church,* and the possessives accenting that the comparison is between the household of the one God and that of one human being, i.e. between two social (and thus public) entities which belong each in its own way to the persons named. The contrast is not between private and public but between smaller and greater social responsibilities, with the parenthetical question suggesting an argument *a minore ad maius.* Similarly, a letter of Apollonius of Tyana to a certain Valerius, proconsul of Asia, argues, "You govern 500 cities and are the noblest of the Romans, but with your disposition a person will not even stably manage his own household *(oikias),* let alone cities and peoples" (58.7; E.T. Penella, *Apollonius,* modified, pp. 68-71; see Tacitus, *Agricola* 19). In First Timothy the singular verbs suggest that the author of the PE understood *bishop* above as a true (not a generic) singular, though the opening *for if any, ei de tis,* makes this meaning less than certain.

The key verb for the function of the *bishop* in these verses, *proïstanai,* "direct" or "to preside," is taken to coincide substantially with the meaning of *epimeleisthai,* to "take care of" (see the use of a cognate noun in Acts 27:3 for the care given to the prisoner Paul by his fellow Christians). Though Ap. Frs. do not use the verb, Ignatius admonishes Polycarp, "Do justice to your position *(ton topon)* with all care *(en pasēi epimeleiai)* both of the flesh and of the spirit"

(*Pol.* 1.2; see 2.2). By the time this is written, the episcopal "care" is not simply for material and physical things any more than it is for the purely spiritual. Complete or perfect *(pasēi)* care includes both, and in particular supporting the weak and the sick (see the uses of *bastaze,* "bear," in section 2-3). The adjective *epimeleis,* "careful/attentive," following on "merciful," characterizes the deacons in Polycarp, *Phil.* 5.2 (in 11.2 [Latin] he says of the fallen presbyter Valens, "For how may he enjoin virtues on another person who cannot control himself in these matters?").

The *epimel-* cluster has no lack of documentation in religious contexts, pagan as well as Jewish, as the regular *epimeletai ton mystērion,* "those responsible for the mysteries," bears witness (Spicq, *EP,* pp. 446-447). In Menander's *Dysc.* 36-39 (F. Sandbach) the god Pan says of the heroine, *tas de syntrophous emoi / Nymphas kolakeuous' epimelōs timōsa te / pepeiken autēs epimeleian schein tina / hēmas,* "Cultivating attentively the favor of the Nymphs who dwell with me, she has inclined us to have some care for her" (see also Koerte 321; 379K). First-century Jewish authors witness to a religious nuance. Thus Philo, in the context of a discussion of appointment to the priesthood of Israel, calls Moses "the one responsible for the care and the ruler *(epimelētēs kai prostatēs)* of the nation" (*Praem.* 77). In *Virt.* 57–58, Moses' choice of a successor is being discussed: ". . . he besought and entreated God, who surveys the invisible soul and to whom alone it is given to discern the secrets of the mind, to choose on his merits the man most fitted to command *(eis hēgemonian),* who would care for his subjects as a father *(hoia patēr epimelēsetai).* And stretching up to heaven his pure *(tas katharas),* and, as it might be said, his virgin hands he said, 'Let the God of spirits and all flesh look to find *(episkepsasthō)* a man to set over the multitude to guard and protect it *(eis epimeleian kai prostasian),* a shepherd who shall lead it blamelessly that the nation may not waste away like a flock scattered about without one to guide it'" (E.T., F. Colson, LCL). Equally striking passages from the Essene documents and Josephus correlating care for the community and others with the direction of the congregation will be cited below on the *mebaqqer.*

Here the anarthrous *ekklēsia theou,* "God's church," is the object of the direction and care spoken of. The Christian *home* or household of the *bishop* is a paradigm for *God's church;* in 3:15 "the church of the living God" is explicitly spoken of as *oikos theou,* "God's household." Even the articular *hē ekklēsia* in the church order for widows in 5:16 probably was heard as meaning "God's church," just as "the kingdom" which Paul preaches in Acts 20:25 is understood as "the kingdom of God *or* Jesus" (see variant readings there). In 5:16, too, the church, so the argument goes, ought not to shoulder a task that belongs in the first place to the Christian home (see 5:4). A *church,* in both 3:5 and 5:16, has a local aspect as a home has an address. As a certain kind of home (e.g., the monogamous), it is distinguished from other kinds (e.g., the polygamous) wherever it is found. In any event, local is not antithetically opposed to universal in the analysis of *ekklēsia,* which means an open assembly of people. The explicit addition of *theou,* "God's," in 3:5 serves to distinguish the assembly of Christian believers from the common secular convocations. In 1 Tim 3:15 it is, moreover, "the church of the living God," to preclude any confusion of the Christian religious assembly, worshipping the living God of Israel, with pagan religious assemblies around lifeless material images. Thus there is a bilingual Ephesian theater inscription of 103-104 C.E. describing the statues, including a silver one of Artemis, to be set up *kat' ekklēsian* (see Acts 14:23), "at every assembly" (Deissmann, *LAE,* pp. 113-114). The parallel Latin text simply transliterates in its use of *ecclesia* (*CIL* 3.14195$^{4}$.6). Acts 19:32, 39, 41 remember also that the Ephesian theater was the place for a secular *ekklēsia,* "assembly." Pliny the Younger once uses the transliteration when he writes to Trajan about a financial subvention by a Bithynian *bule et ecclesia* to a private citizen (*Epistles* 10.110.1).

The Greek *ekklēsia* was heard in an inclusive rather than an exclusive sense (MM *s.v.*) and thus was ideally suited for designating the Christian congregation, which was open to the whole people of God and sought to call all people into its assembly. Latin had no term with this particular nuance of meaning, and thus *ecclesia,* with a host of other, particularly sacramental, terms (e.g., *baptisma, eucharistia, episkopos, diakonos, presbyter,* even *charisma*), was simply transliterated into Christian Latin (as the studies of C. Mohrmann have proved at every turn). As *abba, amen,* and a few Semitic words passed from the first Palestinian churches into those of the Greek-speaking world, so these words from the oldest strata of Christian Greek were grafted onto Latin and thus onto many languages in the West, permanent reminders of the Greek origins and culture of many of the early Christian faithful and the tangible, visible character of their key institutions. The anarthrous usage in this chapter in Timothy may be a way of indicating that *ekklēsia theou* is to be heard for all practical purposes as a name (see BDF §257.2), perhaps one current already in Ephesus. The use of the phrase here would constitute a delicate compliment to that local usage, encouraging the house churches there to welcome the Pauline directives of this correspondence as they prided themselves on a specifically Pauline name for their Christian assembly.

6-7. *He must not be a neophyte lest, inflated with vanity, he fall under the devil's condemnation. But he must enjoy also a fine recommendation from outsiders, lest he fall into disgrace and a snare of the devil.* The prerequisites for the *bishop* resume with the closing of the parentheses, though the generally telegraphic and unexplained entries that predominated in the previous Greek sentence now become single-sentence directives with reasons, practical and theological, in a tone that is apologetic and a style that is expansive. The content becomes also more specifically episcopal, i.e. specifically appropriate for one who presides over *God's church.* By and large (except for *a husband of one wife* and *a skilled teacher*), the qualities would be those encouraged in any believer. Now the list focuses upon qualities that ought to characterize a man who leads a *church* and who represents the congregation before nonbelievers.

*He must not be a neophyte.* With this last term one has left the sphere of virtues as such and good conduct to add a qualification based simply on the time elapsed since the baptism of the candidate for *the episcopate.* This unique NT usage applies the word metaphorically to the seedlings newly planted in the Christian house church, and Christian Latin simply transliterated the Greek (on the principle of Mohrmann, noted above). The Qumran community liked to think of itself as God's planting (see Isa 60:21), and this figure is exploited in 1QS 8.5; 11.8, as well as in 1QH 6.15-16; 8.5-26 (see CD 1.7).

The directive in First Timothy has a legal resonance and was incorporated into later ecclesial legislation (see Canon 2 of Nicea in 325 C.E.: Bruns, *Canones* 1. 14; see also F. X. Funk, *Constitutiones* 2.1.2; 1.33 line 23). The implication of this directive is that congregations of Christians had existed long enough so that a suitable pool of believers of long standing could be drawn on; it implies also that the number of adult converts still being received called for a provision such as this one. The Letter to Titus has no room for such a rule since it presumes an area in which the churches are themselves newly founded. This correspondence with Timothy envisions a large metropolitan area, typified by Ephesus, evangelized years before by Paul, but the provision would be appropriate to Roman congregations, to the other Greek cities evangelized by Paul, or even to Syrian Antioch. General applicability is precisely what this correspondence wants to attain.

As a reason was submitted in verse 5 for the demand of an exemplary family life, now one is offered for this rule about neophytes. The former was expressed parabolically, this one in terms of the consequences that are wont to follow on too hasty a promotion to a position of major responsibility. Aristotle had noted the reluctance of any government to permit a citizen a "disproportionate increase" of honor, "but to give moderate honors for long time rather than great honors for a short time. For men are easily spoilt; not every one can bear prosperity" (*Pol.* 5.8.10; 1308 b; E.T., R. McKeon modified; see Tacitus, *Annales* 4.17). Swift promotion exposes to vanity which is qualified in a way peculiar to the PE as *inflated, typhōtheis* (one is reminded of the opposing teachers in 6:4 below). The cognate noun, *typhos,* suggests empty pride (see 3 Macc 3:18; *1 Clem.* 13.1), from a root meaning "feverish and delirious delusions" and so nonsense and vain affectation. "I know what a slave is, prosperous in the eyes of people and inflated, *tetyphōmenos*" (Epictetus 4.1.150). A couple of variants in the transmission of this verb indicate that a few scribes heard it as a form of *typhloun,* to "be blind" (J. K. Elliott, *Greek Text,* p. 50; see Spicq, *Lexic.,* p. 898), but the connotation of delirious delusion, with its suggestion that the vain person thinks he sees something that is not really there, fits the figurative development that follows.

*inflated with vanity,* the *neophyte-bishop* may *fall under the devil's condemnation.* The general sense is clear. He will come to a bad end. The exact character of that end and the relation of this clause verbally to the parallel *lest he fall into disgrace and a snare of the devil* in the next verse are much vexed. Both phrases conjure up judicial settings, the *condemnation, krima,* of 3:6 and 5:12 denoting a sentence of punishment or a *condemnation* that concludes a lawsuit or trial. That judicial sentence is then specified as *tou diabolou,* "the devil's" or "of the devil." However, *diabolos* is not unambiguous in the PE. The anarthrous plural uses surely refer to human slanderers. The articular singular in 2 Tim 2:26 takes up the phrase of verse 7 here when it speaks of escape "out of the snare of the devil," with a reference to the evil spirit elsewhere called Satan in these letters (1 Tim 1:20; 5:15). But if verse 7 refers to the evil spirit with the *ho diabolos,* then it is most likely that the parallel phrase in verse 6 does not refer to the slanderer. To take *ho diabolos* in verse 6 of a human adversary who is in his turn the agent of the demonic adversary of verse 7 strains the text beyond endurance.

In the mind of the author of the PE the *devil* has his human servants (see the church order for widows in 1 Tim 5:14-15). Perhaps here is the key to the meaning of the anarthrous *condemnation* spoken of in verse 6. The reference is not to the sentence passed on the devil (i.e. an objective genitive, which would have been governed by *to krima*) for the pride by which he fell. The *eis krima* here is like that of 1 Cor 11:34 (see 29) with its reference to the Corinthian assemblies taking place "for (their) condemnation" (see Notes). Paul understood the physical chastisements that befell numbers of the Corinthian faithful as signs of God's sentence passed on their sins. The condemnation is not necessarily the final and irrevocable eschatological judgment. In fact, the apostle can say of himself, ". . . that I not be overly exalted *(hyperairōmai),* there was given me a thorn in the flesh, an angel of Satan to abuse me, that I not be overly exalted" (2 Cor 12:7; E.T., Furnish, AB *2 Cor,* p. 513). Conceptually, this passage in the PE accords with the Pauline attitude as it envisions the *neophyte-bishop* stumbling in his feverish delirium into a sentence of chastisement that the devil would carry out. Thus *the devil's condemnation* contains a subjective genitive, insofar as Satan has at his disposal and administers all the evils which afflict humankind, even death (see Job 1–2 and Wis 2:24). The substance of what 1 Tim 1:20 (and 1 Cor 5:5) describe as handing over to Satan becomes in this text the calamities that follow upon that action.

In contrast to *the episcopate* of the vain *neophyte,* evoking censure on every side and bringing down on him even physical disaster, the final sentence about the requisites for *a bishop* returns, in verse 7, to the divine will and plan (see v. 2, *has to be*) that a bishop *enjoy also a fine recommendation from outsiders.* The *recommendation* implies, in the legal practice of the Old Testament, the report of more than one person, and the adjective *fine* suggests the usual pleasing visibility as well as an agreement to the report which practically amounts to public acclamation (Spicq, *EP,* p. 438). But who are the *outsiders* who offer this approbation? Are they Christians from other house churches in the metropolis? Or are they the non-Christian neighbors from the ambient community of nonbelievers? Or even both? The final answer is probably hidden in the intent and the usage of the church order which is being cited at this juncture (other lexical curiosities from it have been noted in 2:6, 15). If so, the usage may well derive, as Spicq has suggested, from Jewish Greek (as early as the prologue, 5, to Sirach, *hoi ektos* means non-Jews). Paul does use *exō/esō* for people "outside/inside" the church (1 Cor 5:12-13; 1 Thess 4:12; Col 4:5). Since the PE attach no small importance to the perceptions of unbelievers (see Titus 2:5, 8, 10), the *outsiders* here more probably are not Christians. Yet if an old Jewish Christian house church in Rome produced this church order, its authors may have considered it desirable to cement good relations with house churches that were predominantly of pagan origin.

The last half of verse 7 coincides largely with the negative clause of result that concludes verse 6, but now the good report from *outsiders* offers a warrant *lest he fall into disgrace and a snare of the devil.* The *disgrace* here refers not to persecution "for righteousness' sake" (as elsewhere in the NT) but to a deserved derision from *outsiders* for not practicing what one publicly proclaims and teaches. In the LXX this reproach comes specifically from the Gentiles (see LXX Ezek 22:4; 34:29; 36:6, 15; 1 Macc 4:58), and here the shame of defeat in battle has been transferred to another holy war in which the *bishop* (who ought to be a good general) can blunder disgracefully and fall *into . . . a snare of the devil.* Thus Satan compromises the mission of the congregation as a whole in the disgrace of its leader and representative.

In explaining *a snare,* Pardee, *RevQ,* p. 177, has noted that the LXX *pagis* translates the Hebrew *ph* and that the Qumran pesher on Ps 37 refers to the "snares of Belial," *pḥy bly'l* (4Q 171; pPs 37.9-10; DJD 5.43), a notable parallel to *a snare of the devil* in the PE. The Qumran psalmist describes the terrors of the end time for himself, saying, "Overwhelming calamities accompanied my steps while all the snares (*pḥy;* see CD 4.14; 1QH 2.8) of the pit were opened and all the nets *(mṣwdwt)* of wickedness spread out and the fishing-net (*mkmrt;* see 1QH 5.8) of the wretched upon the face of the waters . . . while it was the time of wrath for Belial. And the bonds of death tightened leaving no escape . . . ." (1QH 3.25-26, 28; E.T., Dupont-Sommer, *EWQ* modified). The psalmist (1QH 2.29) describes his persecution by "an assembly of vanity and a congregation of Belial" (2.22), saying, ". . . the net (*ršt* [see Ezek 12:13; 17:20]) which they stretched out for me catches their foot; they have themselves fallen into the snares *(pḥym)* which they hid for my soul" (2.29; E.T. D-S modified). Perhaps in this connection one ought to recall also "Belial's three nets *(mṣwdwt)*" in CD 4.15, 17-18, i.e. lust, riches, and defilement of the sanctuary, which appear to have something to do with observance of the OT laws for the marriages of priests. Muted echoes of Qumran such as these, heard in the reference to *a snare of the devil,* perhaps traceable to a Roman Jewish Christian church order, introduce a more general question.

The very term *episkopos* with its etymological overtones of overseeing and inspecting, the qualities sought in his family relationships, and the suggestions of Jewish background encountered thus far make this an appropriate point to review possible links between the Christian *episkopos* and the *mebaqqer,* the inspector or overseer in the Essene communities in the Judean wilderness and elsewhere in the Palestinian area in the last couple of centuries B.C.E. The term *mebaqqer,* for all the familiarity of its root *bqr,* has even less linguistic history than *episkopos,* for it "is not found elsewhere in OT or later Hebrew" (A. R. C. Leaney, *RQM,* p. 189, whose study is being used here). Perhaps the community coined the word to designate a type of leadership that they considered unique to themselves. The *mebaqqer* appears in the Rule in its discussion of the general assembly: "If the superintendent *(mebaqqer)* of the general membership or anyone who is not of the same rank as the person who happens to be raising a question for the consideration of the community has something to say to the company, he is to stand up and declare: I have something to say to the company; and only if they so bid him, is he to speak. If any man in Israel wishes to be affiliated to the formal congregation of the community, the officer at the head *(hpqyd brw's)* of the general membership is to examine him as to his intelligence and his actions and, if he then embark on a course of training, he is to have him enter into a covenant to return to the truth and turn away from all perversity. Then he is to apprise him of all the rules of the community" (1QS 6.12-15; E.T. for this and those following, Gaster, *DSS,* pp. 55-56, modified). During the last half of the aspirant's residency with the community, he is to bring all his possessions and professional tools to the community treasury. "These are to be committed to the community's superintendent of revenues; they are to be entered by him into an account, but he is not to disburse them for the general benefit" (1QS 6.20). A very fragmentary text, 5Q 13.4.1 (DJD 3.183) mentions the *mebaqqer* and then uses a line or two from 1QS 3.4-5 in what may be a meditative composition woven out of strands from the history of salvation and the Rule of the community. The texts thus far appear to describe the chief administrative officer of the community (presumably at Qumran itself). He is emphatically one of the community with limited powers in its assembly. Granted he is the head officer written of, he has extensive discretion based upon his native gifts and acquired training in the recruitment of new members. The text presumes that he is able to read (at least Hebrew and Aramaic) and write (at least financial records). He will have had some title to be a teacher, for his word had to make credible and attractive this congregation's way of understanding and living out the Jewish Scriptures and tradition, a way that must have seemed in many respects far-fetched and abhorrent to their countrymen.

The Damascus Document also envisions a *mebaqqer* in each of the Essene communities scattered about the Palestinian world as well as in the Qumran congregation. In the Comment on Titus 3:10 the legal procedures for taking depositions by the *mebaqqer* (CD 9.18-22) have been cited. In CD 14.11-12 "every dispute and judgment" comes under the jurisdiction of the *mebaqqer* "of all the camps" (i.e. the superintendent at Qumran, who is required to be between thirty and fifty years of age [CD 14.8]). The *mebaqqer* in each camp is expected to instruct even the priest if the latter is unaware of the sect's interpretation of the Torah (CD 13.6). Particularly notable is CD 13.7-19, where the pastoral shape (*pace* A. Leaney) of the *mebaqqer's* task is sketched: "This is the rule for the superintendent of the camp. It is his duty to enlighten the Many about the works of God and to make them understand his marvelous acts. He is to tell them in detail the story of things that happened in the past. He is to show them the same compassion as a father shows for his children. He is to bring back all of them that stray, as does a shepherd his flock. He is to loose all the bonds that constrain them, so that there be no one in his congregation who is oppressed or crushed. He is also to examine every new adherent to his congregation regarding his conduct, intelligence, valor, and possessions, and to register him in his due status, according to his stake in the portion of truth. No member of the camp is to have authority to introduce anyone into the congregation in defiance of the camp's superintendent. . . . No one is to enter into any sort of commercial partnership without informing the camp's superintendent." The emphasis upon the all-important relationship of new members with the *mebaqqer* reappears in CD 15.7-15, where he alone may teach them the rules of the congregation, examine the aspirants, and prepare them for swearing the oaths of entry into the community. Surely an aspect of the work of the congregations and their *mebaqqer* was the care that they lavished on their superintendent and, through him, on the poor. "They [the members of the congregation] shall place the earnings of at least two days out of every month into the hands of the superintendent and the judges *('l yd hmbqr whswptym),* and from it they shall give to the fatherless, and from it they shall succour the poor and the needy, the aged sick, and the homeless, the captive taken by a foreign people, the virgin with no near kin, and the ma[id for] whom no man cares . . ." (CD 14.12-16; E.T., Vermes, *DSS*, p. 116, modified). Josephus notes of the Essenes that "they do nothing without orders from those who are in charge *(epimeleton);* two things only are left to individual discretion, the giving of assistance and mercy. Members may at their own initiative help those who deserve it when they ask an alms and supply food to the destitute" (*War* 2.134).

The phrase above about charities being administered by both the *mebaqqer* and a group called "the judges" ought to be noted. Just as the Christian *bishop* appears with people called *deacons,* so in this ancient Jewish sectarian document the superintendent appears with persons called *judges.* The latter constitute an important body who have a number of duties in administering justice (see CD 9.10; 10.1; 12.3; 15.4). A more complete picture emerges in CD 10.4-10: "This is the rule concerning the judges of the community. Periodically, a complement of ten men shall be selected from the community. Four of them shall belong to the tribe of Levi and Aaron, and six shall be Israelite laymen. They shall be men versed in the Book of Meditation and in the fundamentals of the Covenant. Their minimum age shall be twenty-five, and their maximum sixty. No man over sixty shall occupy judicial office in the community; for through the perfidy of man the potential span of human life has been reduced, and in the heat of his anger against the inhabitants of the earth, God decreed of old that their mental powers should recede before they complete their days" (*Jub.* 23.11; E.T., Gaster, *DSS,* modified). The parallels between these judges and those seven chosen by the Twelve to secure the fair distribution of charity in the Acts narrative about the archaic Jerusalem church hardly need emphasis. The same can be said for the preaching of a Stephen or the teaching and baptizing by Philip. The parallels with those explicitly called *deacons* in 3:8 will be pointed out below.

One does have thus far a striking structural parallel between the Qumran *mebaqqer* and the *bishop* of the PE. Both have a representative function in their communities (which are themselves strongly Jewish), whose hospitality embraces fellow believers and whose charity extends to all in need, whether believers or not. Both answer for funds committed to them (and a limited number of representative colleagues) for charitable distribution. Both are regarded as presiding and caring for the congregation as a father for his family or a shepherd, his flock. Such care involves discipline for the unruly. *Mebaqqer* and *bishop* are expected to explain the Scriptures and the practices of the community to its members. The Qumran documents do not have the *mebaqqer* preside at the worship of the community; interestingly, the description of the *bishop* in the PE does not explicitly direct him to preside at worship. In this connection, the one allusion to baptism in this description (the *neophyte* of v. 6) has nothing to do with an episcopal administration of the sacrament.

Furthermore, while the Qumran *mebaqqer* had charge of the whole process of admission to that community, including teaching, safeguarding of possessions, reception of oaths, etc., this list in the PE does not explicitly link the bishop with the reception of Christian converts. Perhaps it is implicit in the comparison with the father of the family, his requisite skill as teacher, and his representative function with *outsiders.* Still, when the Qumran documents return to the subject of the *mebaqqer* and his role in the admission of candidates regularly, explicitly, and emphatically, one wonders why the subject is not broached in the treatment of the *bishop* in the PE. It must be admitted that the second-century Christian documents hardly emphasize the presence of the *bishop* in the process of receiving converts (see Ign. *Smyrn.* 8.2, where he must "appear"; Justin, *1 Apology* 61 and 65, is even more vague). At the beginning of the third Christian century his involvement is noted and the one anointed with oil of exorcism is handed over "to the bishop or the priest who stands by the water to baptize" (see Cuming, *Hippolytus,* §20, 21). Perhaps the *bishop* of the PE simply was not at that early date expected to administer the sacrament of baptism, in order to preclude any confusion with the Qumran *mebaqqer,* whom he resembled.

As one looks back over this catalogue of requirements of the *bishop,* it appears to subdivide into three sections, with seams detectable at the end of verses 2 and 5. Each part is characterized by unusual, some parts by unique, terminology, none of it "sacral," however (in contrast to *First Clement, Didache,* and Ignatius; see Johnson, *Writings,* p. 385). All three parts have ties, verbal and conceptual, with a similar catalogue for presbyter-bishops in Titus 1:5-9, though the material in Titus appears to be for recently established Jewish Christian congregations outside large metropolitan centers. The Jewish antecedents of many items in this catalogue in Timothy have been indicated. One surmises that texts from an influential Jewish Christian church order (or church orders) have been culled for their notices about episcopal ministry (and the diaconal ministry that follows). Such archaic Christian documents may have resembled the Rule of Qumran or the Damascus Document. The first list (v. 2) sounds as if it were part of a liturgical charge at an ordination (see 6:11). The rougher language of the second section (vv. 3-5) would be less appropriate in an oral setting. The final sentences look like quotations from a rule book.

Granted that the *bishop* appears to have some ties with Christian worship (principally because of the place in which he is introduced in this church order), it is striking to see the emphasis placed on his moral life in these verses. Moreover, the virtues are not feats of simply individual, ascetical prowess (much less of charismatic enthusiasm). They are, as Donelson, *Pseudepig.,* p. 181, has noted, "public virtues," observable conduct that is useful to the community at large, in this case Hellenistic society, which at its best set a high value on such ethics. The specifically Christian virtues of faith, love, and hope go unmentioned, not because the Christian *bishop* conceals them but because society at large is simply puzzled by them.

If the Rule at Qumran and the Damascus Document can be adduced as precedents for the presbyter-bishops in Titus, the *bishop* here in Timothy would probably be sought among those over thirty and less than sixty years of age (see CD 14.8). The regulation excluding the *neophyte* points in this direction, as does the provision forbidding remarriage should the bishop's *one wife* die. His children appear to be young adults also. Aristotle thought the older governed by nature (*Pol.* 7.13.3; 1332b), though he describes the vices of the elderly mercilessly (*Rhetoric* 2.13; 1398b-1390a). The view of old men popularized by Greek New Comedy gives the modern reader some insight into the preceived implications of such a choice for leadership. Thus the old men in Menander are friends, confidants, and helpers (even financial ones), engaged in the business of reconciliation. They are consistent and open (though they may be ignorant and perverse too), dignified and stable, attentive to specific circumstances that qualify general principles (in contrast to the "simplistic enthusiasm and the moral absolutism of youth," who tend to be trivial, predictable, and superficial [MacCary, "Old Men," p. 325; see the whole article for the observations here]).

The provisions for choosing a bishop do not require explicitly that one *first be put to the test,* as verse 10 directs for deacons. Perhaps the bishop came regularly from the ranks of the deacons, and no need was felt to repeat a thorough scrutiny that had preceded his admission into that cadre.

### *II.B.2.b. The Deacons and Women Ministers (3:8-13)*

3 [8]*Similarly, deacons have to be:*

*serious persons,*
*not retailing gossip,*
*not addicted to heavy drinking,*
*not money-minded,*

[9]*but persons who hold the mystery of the faith with a clean conscience.* [10]*Let them first be put to the test; then let those who are unimpeachable serve as deacons.* [11]*(Similarly, the women who are ministers have to be:*

*serious persons,*
*not devils at gossip,*
*temperate,*
*believers in every sense.)*

*[12]Deacons are to be husbands of one wife, outstanding in the direction of their own children and homes. [13]For men who give outstanding diaconal service gain a fine standing for themselves and a right to speak out for the faith that is theirs in Christ Jesus.*

## ♦ NOTES

3:8. *Similarly, deacons have to be: serious persons, not retailing gossip, not addicted to heavy drinking, not money-minded. Have to be . . . persons* has been supplied in the version (see 3:2). For *similarly* see Titus 2:3; 1 Tim 2:9; for *serious,* Titus 2:2; for *prosechein,* Titus 1:14; 1 Tim 1:4; *heavy drinking* appears in Titus 2:3; *money-minded* in Titus 1:7.

*deacons. Diakonos* appears twenty-nine times in the NT (never in Luke-Acts) and describes Christ in Rom 15:8; Paul and workers in the Christian mission in 1 Cor 3:5; 2 Cor 3:6; 6:4; 11:15, 23 (note the plurals); governmental authority in Rom 13:4; and the deacons at Philippi in Phil 1:1, as well as Phoebe, *diakonos* of the church at Cenchreae and Paul's *prostatis* in Rom 16:1-2 (see Pliny the Younger, *Epistles* 10.96.8, "female slaves whom they are accustomed to speak of as *ministrae*"; Brooten, *Leaders,* p. 151). In the PE *diakonoi* are mentioned only in this passage of First Timothy (vv. 8, 12), and the singular *diakonos* describes Timothy in 4:6. All the Old Latin versions took the uses in verses 8 and 12 of the order of deacon (see *diaconos,* etc., of Frede, *VL* 25.500, 504), whereas the title in 4:6 was translated as *minister* (Frede, *VL* 25.531). For the cognate *diakonia,* see 1:12 above.

*Diakonos* in Ap. Frs. occurs often and, whether singular or plural, refers to an order. In *1 Clem.* 42.4-5, as in *Did.* 15.1, they are coupled with bishops. In Hermas they appear in lists along with apostles, bishops, and teachers or prophets (see *Vis.* 3.5.1; *Sim.* 9.15.4). In the numerous references in Ignatius they form the bottom tier of a hierarchy, with a bishop and presbyters occupying places above them (for their functions in Ignatius and Polycarp, see Comment). In the Apologists, Tatian once speaks of Christ as *diakonos* and once of divination (13.3; 19.2). However, Justin, *Apology* 1.65.5 and 67.5, uses the word in the plural for those who screen the communicants at a Roman eucharist and carry the sacrament to the absent.

In the LXX *diakonos* has hardly any precedents. LXX Prov 10:4a uses the term of a foolish servant; 4 Macc 9:17 of the torturers. In LXX Esther 1:10 a council of the king, consisting of seven eunuchs, is called *diakonoi* (see also 2:2; 6:3, 5). In *T. Judah* 14.2 wine is the *diakonos* of the spirit of fornication. Philo does not use the word often, but twice the ears are *diakonoi* (*Post.* 165; *Mos.* 2.199). The attendants at the meal of the Therapeutae are also called *diakonoi*

(*Vita cont.* 75; as is Joseph in *Jos.* 241). The most notable occurrences in Josephus are those that speak of a *diakonos* attached to the prophet Elijah (*Ant.* 8.354) and then to Elisha (*Ant.* 9.54-55).

*Not retailing gossip, mē dilogous,* uses a term which appears only here in the NT and is otherwise undocumented in previous secular Greek or the LXX. Its one appearance in Ap. Frs. and the Apologists is in the list that concerns deacons in Polycarp, *Phil.* 5.2. *Dilogos* may have been coined from the Latin *bilinguis* (Spicq, *EP,* p. 457), used as in Virgil, *Aeneid* 1.661: *quippe domum timet ambiguam tyriosque bilinguis,* "She has reason to fear the cunning house and the double-talk of the Tyrians." *Bilingues* is found in all the Old Latin versions (Frede, *VL* 25.500; see also Sir 5:17; 6:1; 28:15) and was used by Jerome for his Vulgate, Prov 8:13; 18:8. In Pollux 2.118, in the second century C.E., *dilogos* appears for the first time in a secular Greek text. There it means "repeater" (see the cognate verb in Diodorus Siculus 20.37.1, with the sense "to repeat here").

9. *but persons who hold the mystery of the faith.* This marks one of fifteen uses of *pistis* in the PE with the article (versus eighteen anarthrous uses). Just as the appearance of the article does not designate the faith in terms of content in the PE, so the absence thereof does not signal simply the personal act of believing. The use (or nonuse) of the article has less to do with systematic theological distinctions than with the grammatical and rhetorical patterns of Hellenistic Greek.

*with a clean conscience.* For the separate terms, *clean* and *conscience,* see Titus 1:15. The phrase will recur in 2 Tim 1:3 but not elsewhere in the NT or the LXX. *First Clement* 45.7 uses it, and Ignatius, *Trall.* 7.2, writes of the believer who does things apart from the local leaders as "one who is not clean in conscience," *ou katharos estin tei syneidēsei.*

*the mystery. To mysterion* appears once more in the PE, in verse 16, "the mystery of godliness." Nineteen out of twenty-six other NT uses are in the remaining Paulines. In Luke-Acts the author uses "to know *(gnōnai)* the mysteries of the kingdom" (with Matt 13:11; Mark 4:11 has simply, "the mystery of the kingdom"; see *SFG* § 123). The other NT occurrences are in Rev 1:20; 10:7; 17:5, 7 (see R. Brown, *Semitic,* pp. 32-38).

In Ap. Frs. *mystērion* appears once in the vexed passage of *Did.* 11.11, which speaks of a prophet "enacting a worldly mystery of the church," *poiōn eis mystērion kosmikon ekklēsias.* Perhaps a secular mystery is to be contrasted with a mystery of faith, even with a divinely revealed sacramental activity. The text would then be granting a certain freedom to the prophet in the means he could choose to communicate what he perceived as God's revelation, provided he did not confuse the medium with the message, imposing the former along with the latter. This freedom is ultimately warranted by his noting "For it was just in this way that the ancient prophets also used to act." The appeal would include the actions of an Isaiah (Isa 20:2-4), a Jeremiah (Jer 13:1-11; 19:1-2, 10-11, etc.), a Hosea (Hos 1:2-8; 3:1-5). With Audet, *Didache,* p. 452, one opts for something complementary to the ordinary teaching as noted in *Did.* 11.10, perhaps in the tradition of the "revelations" that Paul knew of (1 Cor 14:26; 2 Cor 12:1, 7). This "apocalyptic" tradition, with its bizarre verbal symbolism, could well issue in some sort of mime: Acts 21:10-11 retains the memory of the Judean prophet Agabus (see 11:28) taking Paul's belt and using it to predict his fate.

Ignatius employs forms of *mystērion* regularly. In his *Eph.* 19.1 he writes of "three mysteries of a cry, *kraugēs,*" i.e. the virginity of Mary, her childbearing *(toketos),* and the death of the Lord. When he refers to the Lord's death in *Magn.* 9.1, he asserts, "by this mystery we received faith *(to pisteuein).*" The person of Jesus, his coming into and leaving this world, are the content of the mysteries (or mystery) for Ignatius. Yet he can also say, in *Trall.* 2.3: "and they also who are the deacons *(tous diakonous)* of the mysteries of Jesus Christ must be in every way pleasing to all people; for they are not deacons *(diakonoi)* of food and drink but ministers *(hypēretai)* of God's church *(ekklēsias theou).* So it is incumbent on them to be on guard against accusations as against fire."

In *Diogn.* 4.6, *theosebeias mystērion,* "the mystery of [the Christian] religion," is not to be learned from mere human beings, nor do Christians have merely human mysteries entrusted to them (7.1). Love of neighbor opens up and enables one to speak about "the mysteries of God," *mystēria theou lalein* (10.7).

*Mystērion* appears in the LXX twenty-one times in documents of postexilic origin (see R. Brown, *Semitic,* pp. 2-12, for this and what follows). In Daniel the Greek regularly represents *raz,* the Persian loanword that is presumed for a term in Aramaic or Hebrew which here refers to the symbolic revelation of the divine plan to God's messenger. Behind this lies the Hebrew *swd,* whose root meaning appears to refer to a ruler's council, advisory assembly, or circle of confidants. Then it came to refer to the plan for action that emerged from such a confidential consultation. Even as the kings of this earth, the king of heaven had his *swd* (cf. the use of *mystērion* in Tob 12:7, 11, with the seven angels in 12:15, one of whom is describing his reports to Tobit and Tobias). For the meaning of *mystērion* in *1 Enoch* (especially "evil mysteries"), see Black, *Enoch,* index *s.v.* "secrets"; for the Greek *Apocalypse of Baruch* and 4 Ezra, see R. Brown, *Semitic,* pp. 12-22. In the *Testaments of the Twelve Patriarchs* personal and family secrets are regularly called mysteries (see *T. Judah* 12.6; *T. Zebulun* 1.6; *T. Gad* 6.5), but in *T. Judah* 16.4 the application to God's secret plans is beginning to appear, and in *T. Levi* 2.10 that patriarch hears the angelic promise to enter a sphere in which "you will stand near the Lord. You shall be his priest and you shall tell forth his mysteries to men. You shall announce the one who is about to redeem Israel" (E.T., Charlesworth, *OT Pseud.* 1.788).

10. *Let them first be put to the test.* For *first* see 2:1; the Greek has simply *kai houtoi de,* "but also these persons."

*Dokimazein,* here *let them be put to the test,* does not recur in the PE. Out of the twenty-one other NT uses of the verb, sixteen are in the remaining Paulines but only three in Luke (see Luke 14:19 of trying out a newly purchased yoke of oxen). Fire tests the genuineness of faith in 1 Pet 1:7, and 1 John 4:1 speaks of testing spirits (on cognate adjectives see 2 Tim 2:15 and Titus 1:16).

In Ap. Frs., *1 Clem.* 1.2 uses *dokimazein* of the faith of the Corinthian church, but the other uses in that letter are of the ministry shared by the apostles with their co-workers or with those who succeeded to their task: 42.4 writes of the apostles appointing "their first converts, testing *(dokimasantes)* them with regard to the Spirit *(tōi pneumati)* to be bishops and deacons of those who were going to be believers"; in 44.2 the apostles themselves provided that "other tested men *(dedokimasmenoi andres)* should succeed to *(diadexōntai)* their ministry of worship"; in 47.4, after naming Paul, Cephas, and Apollos, the author says the Corinthians had been "partisans of apostles of high reputation and of a man approved *(andri dedokimasmenōi)* by them," i.e. of Apollos. The coincidences with the language and conceptualization of the PE witness to *dokimazein* becoming a technical term when one discussed sharing in apostolic ministry.

In the *Didache* the prophetic order is involved in a process of being approved and approving (see 11.7-10), which concludes with a passage that was introduced above: "But no prophet who has been tried *(dedokimasmenos)* and is genuine, though he enact a worldly mystery of the church — if he does not teach others to do what he himself does — shall be judged by you, for he has his judgment with God, for so also the ancient prophets used to do." Then in *Did.* 12.1 there is the provision: "Let everyone who 'comes in the name of the Lord' be received, but when you have tested *(dokimasantes)* him, you shall know him, for you have understanding of true and false." *Didache* 15.1, also cited above, directs, "Appoint therefore for yourselves bishops and deacons worthy of the Lord, meek men and not lovers of money, and truthful and approved *(dedokimasmenous),* for they also minister to you the ministry *(leitourgousi tēn leitourgian)* of prophets and teachers." In this context the *leitourgia* surely is eucharistic (see 14.1-3 and Audet, *Didache,* p. 466).

The testing process appears to have become more elaborate in Ignatius, who in *Smyrn.* 8.2, with its directives for sacramental worship, states, "But whatever [the bishop] approves *(dokimasēi),* this is also pleasing to God, that everything which you do may be secure and valid." What the bishop has tested and found wanting is unsafe and insecure. What he has proved safe, he approves, and what he approves, God approves through the sacramental acts in which the church especially asserts its identity.

Hermas uses *dokimazein* ten times, insisting on the part that a person's life and deeds play in the testing of his prophetic inspiration (see *Man.* 11.16).

In the LXX *dokimazein* appears about three dozen times (see Therrien, *Discernement,* pp. 17-31, for an analysis of this word and the cluster to which it belongs). It is from this biblical tradition (and not that of secular Greek) that a connotation of purifying metal with fire attaches itself to this terminology (see Qumran in Comment). A link appears between the *dokim-* cluster and the words for patient endurance *(hypomonē)* in *T. Asher* 5.4 and *T. Joseph* 2.6-7 (see also *Pss. Sol.* 16.13-15). In the Hellenistic Jewish literature, including Philo and Josephus, the *dokim-* cluster does not designate a moral testing or discernment as such (though see 3 Macc 3:5, *eudokimos,* and Sir 41:16, *eudokimein*).

*those who are unimpeachable.* See Titus 1:6-7 for *unimpeachable;* Titus 1:16; 1 Tim 1:13; 2:2 for forms of *ontes.*

*Let those serve as deacons,* from *diakonein,* which will recur in this sense in verse 13, and in a more generic usage in 2 Tim 1:18, of Onesiphorus, "And you know well enough how many services *(diēkonēsen)* he provided in Ephesus." There are thirty-four other NT uses, four in the rest of the Paulines but ten in Luke-Acts. Only Hermas, among Ap. Frs., uses *diakonein.* Of the half dozen occurrences, *Vis.* 3.5.1 and *Sim.* 9.26.2 are notable for their descriptions of the use and abuse of the diaconal office. Justin, *Trypho* 79.2, uses the verb of the angels serving God; Aristides, *Apology* 15.2, of Christians serving the righteousness which they proclaim to others. The verb does not appear in the LXX or the *Testaments of the Twelve Patriarchs.*

11. *Similarly, the women.* For *similarly* see Titus 2:3, and adding *women,* 1 Tim 2:9.

*who are ministers have to be . . . persons* has been added to the Greek.

*serious persons, not devils at gossip, temperate, believers in every sense.* For *serious,* see Titus 2:2; for *devils at gossip,* Titus 2:3; for *temperate,* Titus 2:2. Regarding *believers in every sense, pistos* in the PE is used of both individual believers in Christ and of the body of believers as a whole, or groups within that body. When used in the latter sense the adjective becomes a technical term, but its use of women here (as also of Christ in 2 Tim 2:13, of Paul in 1 Tim 1:12, of men in 2 Tim 2:2, and of children in Titus 1:6) shows that it really belonged to the individuals so designated and was not strictly technical (cf. 2 Tim 2:2 with 1 Tim 1:12).

12. *Deacons are to be husbands of one wife, outstanding in the direction of their own children and homes.* For *deacons,* see 3:8; for *husbands of one wife,* see Titus 1:6; for *outstanding in the direction of their own children and homes,* see 3:4.

13. *For men who give outstanding diaconal service.* See verse 10; for *outstanding, kalos,* see verse 4.

*gain. Peripoieisthai* appears three times in the NT: here in the PE and twice in the Lukan corpus (see Titus 2:14 for the cognate noun). In Luke 17:33 Jesus' saying is transmitted in the form, "Whoever seeks to gain *(peripoiēsasthai)* his life will lose it" (*SFG* §235; see §160), and in Acts 20:28 Paul says in his exhortation to the presbyter-bishops of Ephesus that the Holy Spirit has appointed them "to shepherd the church of God which he gained *(periepoiēsato)* with his own blood." In Ap. Frs. *First Clement* asserts that a person who leaves a congregation for the sake of its peace and unity "will gain for himself *(heautoi . . . peripoiēsetai)* great glory in Christ . . ." (54.3). Only Hermas uses this verb otherwise, notably in *Sim.* 9.26.2, cited above. Forms of *peripoiein* appear more than thirty times in the LXX. The saying of 1 Macc 6:44 about Eleazar reminds one of this verse of the PE: "So he gave his life to save his people and to gain for himself *(peripoiēsai heautōi)* an everlasting name *(onoma aiōnion)*."

*standing. Bathmos* appears only here in the NT and not at all in Ap. Frs. or the Apologists. In the LXX 1 Kgdms 5:5 *bathmos* means the threshold of Dagon's temple, and in LXX 4 Kgdms 20:9-11 it describes the "steps" or degrees "by which the sun had declined on the dial of Ahaz." Sirach 6:36 counsels, "If you see an intelligent man, visit him early; let your foot wear out his doorsteps *(bathmous thyrōn)*." The examples all illustrate the term in its material sense of a raised step. Josephus, *War* 4.171, has a figurative use of the "stages" in a history inevitably reaching a given climax. In the later patristic writers *bathmoi* was the term for the "orders" of bishop, presbyter, and deacon; it looks as if later terminology spun off this very text (see Lampe, *PGL s.v.*, and Swete, *Theodore* 2.132). In Gregory of Nyssa's *Vita Sanctae Macrinae* (*PG* 46.988 D) one reads of "a certain Lampadia, by name, who had been put in charge of the choir of virgins and was in the order of the diaconate *(en tōi tēs diakonias bathmōi)*." *Bathmos* suggests in secular Greek a higher standing or vantage ground in general, including a military promotion, a step in an argument, one's place in a genealogy (see MM; LSJ *s.v.;* BAGD *s.v.* for a text from the mysteries). Eusebius thus writes of Clement's occupying of the "third *bathmon*" in the succession of Roman bishops which becomes the "third *topos*" (*Church History* 3.21 and 5.5).

*a right to speak out. Parrēsia* appears only here in the PE but thirty times otherwise in the NT. The term is particularly characteristic of the Johannine corpus (thirteen times). Mark uses the noun only in 8:32, but it appears five times in Acts. There are seven uses in the remaining Paulines, in 2 Cor 3:12; 7:4 (both with *pollē*); Eph 3:12; 6:19; Col 2:15; Phil 1:20; and a most striking parallel in Philem 8, where Paul describes himself as *pollēn en Christōi parrēsian echōn epitassein soi,* "having much bold freedom in Christ to give you [Philemon] orders." When *1 Clem.* 34.1 employs *parrēsia,* it is of "the good workman [who] receives the bread of his labor with open confidence; the lazy and careless cannot look his employer in the face"; then in 34.5 the term is paired with *kauchēma* when he writes, "Let our boasting and confidence be in him" (see Heb 3:6); and both uses cannot be understood apart from the intervening "Behold the Lord comes . . . to pay each according to his work" (34.3). In *1 Clem.* 35.2, enumerating the gifts that God has prepared for those who wait for him, the writer speaks of "Life in immortality, splendor in righteousness, truth in confidence *(en parrēsiai),* faith in trust, continence in holiness." For the cognate verb see *1 Clem.* 15.7, citing LXX Pss 11:5; 53:5. In *2 Clem.* 15.3 the author exhorts, "Let us then remain righteous and holy in our faith, that we may pray with confidence *(meta parrēsias)* to God. . . ." In the usage of the second Christian century, links between *parrēsia* and persecution even to death begin to appear. Thus *Mart. Pol.* 10.1 has the aged bishop reply to the demand of his Roman judge to renounce Christ: "Listen freely *(meta parrēsias):* I am a Christian." In the letter which Eusebius preserves about the martyrs of Vienne and Lyons, their *parrēsia* is an "apostolic charism" (*Church History* 5.1.49; see the verb in 5.1.18 and *pollēn parrēsian* in 5.2.4).

The dozen LXX uses of *parrēsia* are analyzed in Marrow, "*Parrhesia*," pp. 436-438 (this article will be used for what follows here, as will Unnik, "Background," pp. 290-306). In contrast to Greek secular usage, in Jewish Hellenistic language God himself speaks and acts openly and good people address him thus, particularly in prayer (Philo and Josephus reflect this latter attitude). In Wis 5:1, using the adjectival phrase that appears in 1 Tim 3:13, the author affirms of the just one who dies young, "Then the just man will take his stand with poised confidence *(en parrēsiai pollēi)* to outface his oppressors and those who made light of his sufferings" (E.T. by Winston, AB *Wisd.*, p. 144).

*Parrēsia* and its cognates belong to typically Greek political language (etymologically, "saying everything"), that frank and free speech of a citizen in public assemblies, a freedom which Hellenistic society, especially Athenian democracy, valued highly and which its philosophers and poets celebrated (see Aristotle, *NE* 4.3.28; 1124 b 29; *Athenian Constitution* 16.6; Euripides, *Hippolytus* 422; *Ion* 672, 675; *Bacchae* 668; *Phoenissae* 391). In Menander a slave will profit by having some *parrēsia* (see Koerte 312; 370K), and refutation *(elegchos)* is *parrēsia*'s friend (see Koerte 717; 545K), but the term can suggest insolence and impertinence too (*Epitr.* 1101 [F. Sandbach]). Long after the word became a political fossil, *parrēsia* lived on and was highly valued in the private sector, particularly among friends, where it suggested frankness without flattery (see *Ep. Arist.* 125), plain and (if need be) courageous speech.

*for the faith that is theirs in Christ Jesus.* This (along with 2 Tim 1:13) marks one of two instances in the PE where a further question about the phrase *en pistei,* i.e. in what does this belief consist? is explicitly answered. In both instances the object of the belief is specified in the final adjectival phrase.

## ♦ COMMENT

3:8-10. *Similarly, deacons have to be: serious persons, not retailing gossip, not addicted to heavy drinking, not money-minded, but persons who hold the mystery of the faith with a clean conscience. Let them first be put to the test; then let those who are unimpeachable serve as deacons.* The citation of the church order closes with half a dozen verses devoted to deacons and women ministers, who are spoken of only in the plural and so as a group. The former have the title *deacons;* the latter are simply *the women,* who abruptly (but quite in the style of this correspondence) appear in verse 11, after which the text explicitly returns to *deacons.* The *bishop* of 3:1b-7 appears to be the leading figure in this polity; the *deacons* and *women* ministers are emphatically in second place *(similarly)* and thus his subordinates as well as his assistants (see Leipoldt, *Frau,* pp. 133-134).

The word *diakonos* as it is used here resembles *episkopos* and *apostolos* in its lexical history; it has secular Greek precedents of a sort and hardly any Septuagintal warrant. Philo and Josephus offer a few suggestive parallels, but one must wait for Paul and Phil 1:1 for a use with "bishops" that appears to correspond to this passage in First Timothy. With *First Clement, Didache,* Ignatius, Polycarp, and Hermas references begin to abound and a complex history is well under way.

The prime qualification for *deacons* (and for the *women* ministers in v. 11) is that they be *serious persons,* which was heard, at least in the West, as *graves* (very congenial to the Roman ethos) or *modesti, pudici, casti, honesti,* and *verecundae* with their suggestion of sexual self-control (Frede, *VL* 25.500, 503). As with the judges at Qumran who assisted the *mebaqqer,* it is reasonable to assume that such persons were between twenty-five and sixty years of age. If the *bishop,* and presbyter too, for that matter, belonged to the senior ranks in the leadership, one suspects that *deacons* were as a rule younger men, whose relative youth as well as visibility in charitable works made them rather more popular in the congregation than old teachers were (and prime candidates for the *episcopate*).

The positive virtue of seriousness is followed by a trio of negative phrases, which reminds one of the list in Polycarp.

| *1 Tim 3:8-10* | *Polycarp, Phil.* 5.2 |
|---|---|
| *Diakonous* | *Hōmoiōs* |
| *hōsautōs* | *diakonoi* |
| *semnous* | *amemptoi katenōpion autou tēs dikaiosynēs hōs theou kai Christou diakonoi kai ouk anthrōpōn:* |

| | |
|---|---|
| *mē dilogous* | *mē diaboloi* |
| | *mē dilogoi* |
| *mē oinōi pollōi prosechontas* | |
| *mē aischrokerdeis* | *aphilargyroi* |
| | *egkrateis peri panta* |
| | *eusplagchnoi* |
| | *epimeleis* |
| *echontas to mystērion tēs pisteōs en katharai syneidēsei.* | *poreuomenoi kata tēn alētheian tou kyriou* |

An E.T. of Polycarp's list would read: "Similarly, deacons are to be spotless in the presence of his [God's] righteousness, as deacons of God and of Christ and not of human beings. They are not to be gossips, not slanderers, not persons who are fond of money, self-controlled in regard to all things, compassionate, caring, walking according to the Lord's truth." It is possible on other grounds that Polycarp had read the PE (see 1 Tim 6:7) and used their catalogue in redacting his own. Perhaps both the PE and Polycarp depend upon older church orders which contained charges to be delivered upon the ordination of deacons. First Timothy would then represent an older and shorter form of such a charge; Polycarp, a longer composition marked by another generation of development in a different locale.

Since the Greek *dilogos* would suggest a person who repeats what he has heard or seen to others, the version here has opted for *retailing gossip,* particularly since the *dilogoi* are in tandem with the *diaboloi* in the list in Polycarp. The coinage would be heard as designating a special occupational hazard of the *deacons,* who were the social workers of the ancient congregations. There would be no lack of an audience ready to be entertained by a lively narrative about the latest "case" in which the deacon had intervened. If in fact the Greek term was coined from the Latin for double-talk, a different though related vice is being scored in which the *deacon* does not give a frank report of what he knows to those who have a right to that knowledge. Such deceptive, even hypocritical and lying, speech is no small matter for these first-century believers (as we know from the episode of Ananias and Sapphira).

The second negative qualification, *not addicted to heavy drinking* (is this related to Polycarp's "self-controlled in regard to all things," *egkrateis peri panta?*), with its concern about the abuse of wine, returns to a subject regularly taken up in the PE. The phraseology at this point may suggest that diaconal tasks exposed these men to overindulgence as they visited homes raising funds or distributing food and drink (recall the abuses already at the Corinthian celebration of the Lord's Supper, 1 Cor 11:20-22, 33-34). One also encounters in this prohibition several characteristic ways in which human cultures come to terms with alcohol. "When the fate of many hinges on the action of a single person, that person is usually not permitted to drink before performing the critical activity. The high priests of the Old Testament . . . were particularly forbidden to drink . . . when discharging their priestly duties in the Sanctuary. . . . American pilots today are forbidden to drink for a number of hours before flying as well as during the flight. . . . Yet another ban that appears in various cultures is imposed when it is considered dangerous to heighten the emotions of large numbers of people who gather at the same occasion. . . . [T]here is an inscription at Delphi which forbids the carrying of wine into the stadium on pain of a five-drachma fine. . . . [S]imilar signs are to be seen now at the football stadia of Harvard and Southern Methodist Universities" (Mandelbaum, "Alcohol," p. 18).

The third and final negative phrase, *not money-minded,* puts the accent on profiteering, coming to do good and doing well, in R. L. Stevenson's biting phrase. If the *bishop* is to be above money, *aphilargyros,* his *deacons* have no choice but to be concerned about it, for they must acquire it for and distribute it to the poor, the sick, the distressed (see CD 14.12-16, cited above). In such work, there is danger that some gifts will cling to the hands of those who are to transmit them or that unscrupulous means will be used to acquire goods for the poor. As with the *bishop,* so here with *deacons* and *the women who are ministers,* there is no clue in the text that suggests how they and their families were supported (unlike the regulations that deal with the presbyters and the widows in 1 Tim 5). Perhaps the congregation supported them and the church order simply did not provide for the matter. In the light of 1 Tim 5 this fact appears unlikely. Perhaps *bishop* and *deacons* were expected already to have an income from inherited property and the like and thus the time as well as the financial independence needed for serving their fellow believers. In that case the relationships between benefactor and client, powerful and humane, ought to be conceived according to that model of reciprocal benevolence in the Hellenistic world which Mott, "Benevolence," pp. 60-72, has proposed.

*Deacons* are next described as *persons who hold,* i.e. maintain, *the mystery of the faith with a clean conscience,* a phrase that notably resembles the conclusion of the charge to Timothy in 1:18-19 above, where Paul's co-worker is reminded of the prophetic interventions at his ordination which "were given to help you campaign the fine campaign, with faithfulness and a clear conscience." *Faith* is qualified in 3:9 by prefixing *the mystery,* thus accenting the reality in which one believes more than the act of believing. A similar phenomenon can be seen at the one other occurrence of *mystery* in the PE, in verse 16 below, where *godliness, eusebeia,* the favorite term in this correspondence for authentic religion, is specified as the content of *the mystery,* articulated in the hymnic confession of Christ that follows (Strange, *1 Tim 3:16,* pp. 39-40, has observed an equivalence between these passages and the "fine profession" of the ordination charge of 6:12-13). As the Gospel tradition begins to emphasize knowledge of "the mysteries of the kingdom" and thus the disciples' relation to these mysteries in terms of the hard core of their intelligibility, so the PE concentrate on the contents of the revelation while simply affirming the mysterious and hidden character of their origin and transmission. When 1 Tim 3:9 emphatically adds *with a clean conscience* to this possession of *the mystery of the faith,* the line of thought is not unlike that of 1 Cor 13:2, where Paul describes one who hypothetically can "understand all mysteries and all knowledge"; without charity he amounts to nothing (see 1 Tim 1:5). The unclear Ethiopic text (see Black, *Enoch,* pp. 55, 224) of *Enoch* 58.5 may signal an older Semitic background for *the mystery of the faith* when it speaks of the holy seeking "the secrets of righteousness (and) the portion of faithfulness" (R. Brown, *Semitic,* p. 68). A tantalizing fragment, 1Q 36.16, from a hymnic collection speaks of "the men who guard your mysteries," *'[nšy mšmrt lrzykh]* (see 1 Cor 4:1 and R. Brown, *Semitic,* pp. 27, 45). The "judges" in the Essene councils described above may yet offer the most substantial parallels for what is being required in 1 Tim 3:9 of the Christian *deacons.* The "Book of Meditation," in which the Essene judges must be versed (CD 10.6; see 13.2 and 1QSa 1.7), may have been the community's interpretation of their way of life in terms of revelation (see the fragments of 5Q 13 [DJD 3.182-183]). The fragments of the Rule for the War in 4Q 491.8-10.I.12; 10.II.11; 11.I mention *rzy,* and in line 10 of the last reference, in the canticle of Michael and of the just, the *rzy* are followed by *hgy',* "the meditation [?]," in line 21 (DJD 7.20-29).

Certainly, as R. Brown has shown (*Semitic,* pp. 24-27), the people at Qumran called their special interpretation of the Torah one of the "marvelous mysteries" that the God of Israel had communicated to them. Their language and conceptualization offer some precedent for the way in which the Christian *deacons* here in the PE are expected to have made their own *the mystery of the faith,* the unique Christian interpretation of the OT. An academic, even speculative theological setting for this interpretation is not the setting that this text or the early notices of the diaconal ministry envision. The liturgical celebration, particularly of the eucharist, is a more likely setting, one in which scriptural words and (prophetic?) acts constituted sacramental mysteries in which deacons helped all believers to participate by the public reading and explanation of the Scriptures (originally of the OT) and the distribution of the Lord's body and blood (note the uses of *sacramentum* and *mysterium* in the Old Latin versions; Frede, *VL* 25.501, 513; see Mohrmann, *Études* 1.240-242). Maintaining *the mystery of the faith* is not listed among the requirements for a bishop, but it seems for much the same reason that a testing of the candidate for the episcopate does not appear. As is suggested above, a bishop appears to have been chosen from the deacons of the congregation and is presumed to retain permanently this most important qualification that the diaconal scrutiny originally verified.

If the bishop tended to be an older man, less on the move as physical vigor declined, deacons seem early to have shouldered the burdens of travel to more or less distant believers. Thus Ignatius has an Ephesian deacon to accompany him (*Eph.* 2.1), and one from Cilicia (*Phld.* 11.1). Moreover, he urges deacons, among others, to be sent as ambassadors to the church in Antioch (*Phld.* 10.1-2). Such a network, in which deacons become the ears and eyes of the local congregation in the church at large, is a potent agent for unity in faith among believers. This representative function of deacons is taken for granted in Hippolytus's notice about their ordination in the Roman church: "And when a deacon is ordained, let him be chosen according to what was said above, the bishop alone laying on hands, in the same way as we also directed above. In the ordination of a deacon, the bishop alone shall lay on hands, because he is not being ordained to the priesthood, but to the service of the bishop, to do what is ordered by him. For he does not share in the counsel of the presbyterate but administers and informs the bishop of what is fitting; he does not receive the common spirit of seniority in which the presbyters share, but that which is entrusted to him under the bishop's authority. For this reason the bishop alone shall ordain a deacon; but on a presbyter the presbyters alone shall lay hands, because of the common and like spirit of their order. For a presbyter has authority only to receive; he has not authority to give. For this reason he does not ordain the clergy, but at the ordination of a presbyter he seals, while the bishop ordains" (*Apostolic Tradition* §8; for the presbyter and his relation to presbytery and to the bishop, see 4:14 and 5:17-23 below). In §34 "Each deacon . . . shall attend on the bishop. They shall inform him of those who are ill, so that, if he pleases, he may visit them. For a sick man is greatly comforted when the high priest remembers him" (see Bradshaw, *Canons Hipp.*, pp. 14, 27). In §39 both deacons and priests "assemble daily at the place which the bishop appoints for them" to "teach those who are in church, and in this way, when they have prayed, let each one go to the work which falls to him" (Cuming, *Hippolytus*, pp. 13, 27-28). Evidently this conservative church order of Hippolytus preserved a very archaic view of the deacons and diaconal practices, not least in its ranking of the deacons immediately after the bishop. The defense of the prevailing practice sounds as if it could no longer be taken for granted as it seems to be in First Timothy and *First Clement* and perhaps even the *Didache* (though prophets and teachers appear to be their competitors in this church order). By the time of the Ambrosiaster, what was perceived as the arrogance of Roman deacons had given their order a bad name among some presbyters at any rate (*De iactantia Romanorum levitarum, Liber quaestionum, 101;* CSEL 50.193-198).

The laconic Greek text which is represented by *Let them first be put to the test* serves to attach the directive now appended in verse 10 to the loosely ordered and redacted catalogue of verses 8-9. A similar construction appears in 2 Tim 3:12 and it has classical precedents, with the initial *kai* accenting the link with all that has preceded (including the qualifications for the *bishop* which are suggested by *similarly* in v. 8) and the following *de* emphasizing the point that is about to be added. The meaning is that the qualifications do not offer in themselves sufficient warrant for accepting a person into the diaconal ministry. A testing must occur. As early as 1 Thess 2:4 *dokimazein* has two aspects, that of testing and that of approval; both appear in the use of the adjective of Timothy (2 Tim 2:15; Therrien, *Discernement,* pp. 64-72). Deacons likewise are to be proved and approved. The qualities enumerated in the preceding verses are criteria for the testing aspect of *dokimazein.* One can only make more or less probable inferences on how these criteria were applied to specific candidates for diaconal ministry. The generic character of the virtues inculcated as well as the catalogue genre leads away from an interpretation that would take these qualities as a "checklist" or a "job description." What form then might the testing take? An internship or trial period? An inquiry into the past life of the candidate? A consultation of the community issuing in a favorable judgment on the person who aspired to serve them? To whom did the results of the scrutiny go? To the bishop? To those who were deacons already?

The narrative of the choice of the Seven in Acts 6:3, 5 gives more than a hint of what some representative voices of the second Christian generation thought was prerequisite for a ministry distinct from that of the Twelve. They were to be men (*andras;* see Acts 1:21), of a specified number (i.e. an identifiable body or cadre), who would deal with the material relief of the poor in the congregation, specifically the poor widows. They were to be of good reputation, as witnessed to in public report (i.e. *martyroumenous,* see 1 Tim 3:7). In Acts they interpret the OT in reference to the events that have occurred in the Christ event (thus Stephen's speech; Philip's explanation of the Isaian servant). They also are perforce traveling missionaries, and they prepare men and women for baptism. In the original requirements for their task, they are to be "full of (the) Spirit and wisdom." Thus Stephen in Acts 6:5 is "full of faith and the Holy Spirit"; in 6:8, "full of grace and power." In Acts, as in the PE, there is to be a coincidence of human and divine attestation, with both God and his people witnessing to the candidates for this ministry. The fragmentary ordination prayer over a deacon in Hippolytus has the bishop say: "God, you who created all things and ordered them by your Word, Father of our Lord Jesus Christ, whom you sent to serve your will and make known to us your desire, give the holy Spirit of grace and caring and diligence to this your servant whom you have chosen to serve your Church and to present . . ." (*Apostolic Tradition* §8;

Cuming, *Hippolytus,* p. 13). The divine approval is, at best, implicit in 1 Tim 3:8-10, 12-13, for the passive *let them be put to the test* may include God as well as fellow believers, though Therrien, *Discernement,* pp. 220-221, 225-226, may well be correct in drawing attention to the usage of 2 Tim 2:15 and noting that Timothy's approval has come from God through the imposition of hands of the apostle and of the presbytery (cf. 1 Tim 1:18-19a with 4:14 and 2 Tim 1:8). Similarly in Acts 6:6 an external rite is associated with the qualifications for the Seven which are presumed to be already present (thus the gift of the Spirit precedes baptism in Acts 10:44-46; 11:15-17). Analogously, although the list of virtues here in the PE offers the ground for testing or proof of the diaconal candidates, the concrete means by which the approval is bestowed are not explicitly noted any more than the method for designating the *bishop* was specified above or in Titus 1:5. The case will be otherwise in 1 Tim 5:22. The regular mention of the Spirit and of prophetic phenomena in the texts adduced leads the reader to suspect that those who had received prophetic gifts and insight were involved in verifying the operation of the Spirit in the virtues of aspirants to ecclesial ministries.

*those who are unimpeachable,* with *ontes* accenting the continuing state, has an emphatic position at the conclusion of verse 10 in Greek (see D. Davies, "Position," pp. 106-121). In *then (eita) let [them] serve as deacons,* the particle indicates temporal succession. The jussive form of the verb is notable, indicating that willingness to serve is not enough; an order or commission must initiate the diaconal ministry as this passage envisions it.

11. *(Similarly, the women who are ministers have to be: serious persons, not devils at gossip, temperate, believers in every sense.)*

With this parenthetical sentence one encounters a problem of interpretation that again (see 2:9-15) is rooted in the fact that the Greek *gynē* means *woman/wife* and only the context makes it possible to determine the meaning intended. The first question on this verse is whether *the women* are simply the wives of the deacons just mentioned. In that case, one has another qualification for entry into diaconal ministry, framed in terms of the human person who will be most directly affected by that work. As her husband's *alter ego,* the wife is to have the virtues that he also must bring to diaconal service. Yet it is odd that this qualification is not mentioned for the wife of the bishop here or the wife of the presbyter-bishop in Titus. Moreover, the force of *similarly* in Greek is to place the persons or groups mentioned on a par in some respect. One has to understand the verb *dei,* also, as in 3:8. Finally, the verse following repeats the word *diakonoi,* identifying them explicitly as *andres* and making a provision for their married life in the phrase *husbands of one wife,* characteristic of the ministerial virtue lists of the PE.

Thus the further possibility emerges that the *gynaikes* of the text here are *the women who are ministers,* who correspond to the men who are *diakonoi.* Greek at this time would employ the masculine form for both men and women; thus the repetition with *andres* below (see *peri diakonōn gynaikōn* in Clement of Alexandria, *Strom.* 3.6.53 [O. Stählin 2.220.24]; Greek *diakonissa* appears in Canon 19 of the Council of Nicea [Bruns, *Canones,* p. 19] and thereafter). Since this verse does not explicitly call the women *diakonoi,* one still is left asking whether they are wives of the male deacons, forming teams with them in diaconal ministry. The text inclines one to a negative answer. Indeed, the lack of explicit reference to the family life of these women, to their children, or to their being wives of one husband (see 1 Tim 5:9 on widows), all conspicuous concerns in the lists of virtues for other ministers, makes one suspect that *the women who are ministers* envisioned here are not married or widowed but are single women who had devoted themselves to a form of public ecclesial ministry (see 1 Cor 7:34, observing that "the unmarried woman or virgin is anxious about the affairs of the Lord"). The unmarried state of these women ministers precludes any contradiction of the provisions in 2:11-15 which are explicitly directed to wives. See Lewis, "Women," pp. 167-175, for a somewhat different way of arguing to the same conclusion as the preceding paragraphs. For a brief statement of the question and key bibliographical items, see Gryson, *Women,* pp. 7-8, and Martimort, *Deaconesses,* pp. 20-25.

The qualifications that are noted, four in number, begin with *serious persons,* just as those for the men who are to be deacons began above. *Not devils at gossip* is among the virtues prescribed by the household code for the older women in Titus 2:3, as it is a virtue for deacons in the list cited above from Polycarp, *Phil.* 5.2. *Temperate* is in the household code of virtues for older men in Titus 2:2, as it is in the list of virtues for the *bishop* in 1 Tim 3:2. The final qualification, with its alliteration in *p, believers in every sense,* recalls the description of Paul in 1 Tim 1:12 as well as of the children of the presbyters in Titus 1:6. Luke uses the feminine form of the adjective of Timothy's mother (Acts 16:1) and of Lydia of Thyatira, who opened her house at Philippi to Paul, Silas, Timothy, and Luke with the words "If you [pl.] have judged me to be faithful *(pistēn)* to the Lord, come to my house and stay" (Acts 16:15). Along with 1 Tim 5:16, these are the only NT passages where *pistē* explicitly describes women. The basic sense in all of them is that of a woman who is a believing Christian. No doubt that is why this description in 1 Tim 3:11 adds *en pasin,* thus qualifying *believers* in the widest possible sense. *The women who are ministers* are to be Christian women in every possible sense of that term. A Roman Christian epitaph of 525 C.E. memorializes "a handmaid of Christ, Maxima, . . . friendly, loyal in all things *(fidelis in omnibus),* good, prudent" (A. Gordon, *Epigraphy,* p. 185).

12-13. *Deacons are to be husbands of one wife, outstanding in the direction of their own children and homes. For men who give outstanding diaconal service gain a fine standing for themselves and a right to speak out for the faith that is theirs in Christ Jesus.*

The church order returns now, with its wonted abruptness, to the male *deacons,* whose marital qualifications are now broached in terminology that has occurred, for the most part, in the descriptions of the presbyter-bishop in Titus and the *bishop* here. The qualifications which the archaic order of Titus 1:6 put in the first place and which in 1 Tim 3:2, 4-5 were divided between the beginning and end of the catalogue, are now in the case of the deacons moved to the end. Polycarp, *Phil.* 5.2, and *Did.* 15.1-2 do not mention qualifications from Christian family life for the diaconate. Something similar appears to be occurring in the arrangement of the virtues for bishop and presbyters. Was the domestic image for ministry being more and more discounted? Was the Christian home life considered of less importance for gauging aptness for ministries as the generations passed? Were the ministries that were considered critical being carried on more and more by the unmarried? If, as suggested above, *the women who are ministers* are in fact unmarried, one may be encountering the institutional pressure of that liberation for the Lord's affairs which unmarried Christian women brought to bear on a simply domestic, patriarchal model for ecclesial ministries.

The imperatival *deacons are to be* takes one back to the similar command in verse 10, *let them be put to the test,* commands which alternate with *similarly . . . have to be* in verses 8 and 11. Just as *unimpeachable* stood at the head of the list that turned to domestic virtues in Titus 1:6, so it appears as though the text here in 1 Tim 3:12, after inserting the material on *the women who are ministers* in a deliberate parallel with the *deacons . . . who are unimpeachable* of verses 8-10, has taken up the language of that archaic source at just this point on family life. *Husbands of one wife* is, as in Titus 1:6, a citation from the marriage vows of the man who would be a deacon, promising faithfulness to one wife even should she predecease him. The presbyter's "children who are believers" in Titus 1:6 and the bishop, "outstanding in the direction of his own home, with children who are obedient and quite reverent," in 1 Tim 3:4 have here been conflated, so that both children and households are the object and sign of that manifestly attractive leadership which deacons are to exercise in a forum other than the domestic.

With an explicative *for, gar,* the transition into the final sentence of the church order on deacons occurs. The phrase translated "who give outstanding diaconal service" takes up the verb of verse 10 and the adverb, *kalōs,* of the immediately preceding sentence, thus drawing together the directives in verses 8-10 and 12. One has the impression that the old church order underlying this text did not address itself to *the women who are ministers* and that the author of the PE (who inserted v. 11) respected that fact. The absolute use of the participle *diakonēsantes* here, as well as that of the verb *diakoneitōsan* in verse 10, leaves open the question, "Whom did the deacons (and women ministers) serve?" God? The people of God? The bishop? Unbelievers? These are evidently not mutually exclusive objects. The vagueness may be deliberate, providing for considerable flexibility and adaptability in this cadre of ecclesial ministry.

The aorist tense of the participle *diakonēsantes* suggests that the diaconal service is here being considered as a whole, a complete prologue to the activity denoted by the main verb in the present tense (see Luke 11:8-10), *peripoiountai,* translated here as "gain." This term appears often enough in financial contexts to connote the world of commerce, of buying and selling (see MM *s.v.*). Perhaps here it suggests the diaconal concerns about material goods which have their repercussions beyond this world (see 6:19 below) as they, in a terminology unique in the PE, *gain a fine standing for themselves and a right to speak out for the faith.*

What does this unusual text mean when it speaks of deacons who "acquire rank" or *gain a standing* or "position"? The answer is keyed into the adjective *fine, kalon,* which takes one back not only to the repeated *kalos* of verses 12-13 but also to the beginning of this section (see *kalos* in 3:4) where *the episcopate* is *a fine (kalon) work* (3:1b). In this closing summary about *deacons,* their *fine standing* corresponds to the *fine work* of *a bishop* as the verb *gain* corresponds to *aspires/sets his heart on.* So the *standing* meant here is not primarily the reward of the life to come but the position or vantage that *deacons gain* and hold in the Christian congregation here on earth. As 3:1b accented the value of the apparently thankless task of *the episcopate,* so *a fine standing* emphasizes the appreciation that believers bestow on those who dedicate themselves to serving the needy in the community. Again one surmises that this is a reason that from the diaconal ranks the *episkopos* is normally chosen.

If *a fine standing* is centripetal (note the middle verb, *peripoiounto,* and the pleonastic *heautois*), then *a right to speak out, pollēn parrēsian,* paired with it, is centrifugal. With the verb, a tattoo of *p* sounds begins in Greek which continues through *en pistei* and concludes this church order.

The deacons' service actually gives them extensive freedom "in the faith whose sphere is Christ Jesus," as Moule summarizes the meaning here (*Idiom,* p. 81). Paul himself, not only a prisoner (Philem 1) but also a slave (see Phil 1:1; Titus 1:1), and writing on behalf of a slave (Philem 16) whom he wants to keep with him to take care of him (*diakonēi;* Philem 13), has nothing to lose and thus great boldness (which practically means authority, H. Schlier, *TDNT* 5.883) in making his plea as a follower of Christ of another believer. So the *deacons,* by the humility of their service, acquire that free confidence which ought to characterize the performance of their functions in the congregation of believers.

The link of the diaconal *parrēsia* with prayer ought to be adverted to, since 1 Tim 3:13 deals with *a right to speak out for the faith* and thus refers to both God and human beings. Confidence before the divine judgment and the related confidence in praying (*audemus dicere;* "we dare to say, Our Father . . ." in the old Roman rite) are suggested by the subject of this unit on ecclesial prayer which has occupied 1 Tim 2–3 to this point. Faith in Christ is the ground and matrix of this free confidence and openness of God's children before their Father. Righteousness was the presupposition for *parrēsia* before God, as the Jewish believer understood it (H. Schlier, *TDNT* 5.876); it is a righteousness that comes from *the faith that is theirs in Christ Jesus* (see 2 Tim 3:15).

*The faith* that has issued in *a right to speak out* before God also has issued in a manifestly good and attractive ministry, *kalōs diakonēsantes,* which involves a frank and confident candor before other people, whether believers or not. In Acts as well as in the rest of the Paulines, *parrēsia* is a conspicuous mark of the apostles and of those who share in the apostolic task (H. Schlier, *TDNT* 5.882-883). The term here would suggest that the deacons, for all the fact that their station was last and least in this instruction (note how the women ministers are kept out of last place), still had a participation in the apostolate of Paul himself. In this relationship with their colleagues, their *parrēsia* among fellow Christians becomes in many ways synonymous with *exousia,* i.e. authority. The same bold confidence in confessing their faith among unbelievers lights the fuse that runs inexorably into persecution and martyrdom.

## III. A PIECE IN PAUSE (3:14–4:5)

### III.A. Pauline Introduction (3:14-15)

*3 [14]I am putting these matters in writing for you, Timothy, though I still hope to come to you before long. [15]Still, if I do delay, this letter will let you know how a person has to behave in God's house, which is the church of the living God. [There you, Timothy, are] a pillar and pedestal for the truth.*

### III.B. Hymn (3:16)

*3 [16]And great is the mystery of godliness. There is no denying it!*

*. . . He who was revealed in human flesh,*
*Was made victorious in the Spirit:*

*He who was seen by God's messengers,*
*Was heralded to the pagans:*
*He who was received in faith, in the world,*
*Was taken up in glory.*

## III.C. Prophecy (4:1-5)

### III.C.1. ORACLE (4:1)

### III.C.2. INTERPRETATION OF ORACLE (4:2-5)

#### *III.C.2.a. Doctrines of Opponents (4:2-3)*

#### *III.C.2.b. Refutation from Scripture (4:4-5)*

*4 [1]Here is the Spirit expressly declaring, "In these latter times some people, who dote on seductive spirits and demonic doctrines, will apostatize from the faith." [2]These lying frauds, with their cauterized consciences, [3]interdict marriage and demand abstinence from foods, things that God created for believers and persons who have recognized the truth, to share in thankfully. [4]For everything in God's creation is fine and none is despicable when received with thanksgiving. [5]Every one of them is hallowed by God's word in Scripture and intercessory prayer.*

## ♦ NOTES

3:14. *Timothy.* The name has been added to the Greek to make the second singular address clear.

*Putting . . . in writing. Graphein* appears only here in the PE but 190 times otherwise in the NT. Though Colossians and Ephesians do not use the verb, the rest of the Paulines employ it with some regularity to call attention to the author's writing as such (see Rom 15:15; 1 Cor 4:14; 5:9, 11; etc.). Even more frequently the term designates citations of the OT, a usage unknown to the PE. The meanings in the Paulines also appear in the frequent use of *graphein* in the Ap. Frs. The LXX also uses the verb often, and it is used of correspondence, particularly in First, Second, and Third Maccabees.

*I hope. Elpizon* appears three times more in this letter, hereafter always with *epi* and the dative or accusative (see 4:10; 5:5; 6:17), but not otherwise in the PE. Only Rom 15:12, citing LXX Isa 11:10, uses this construction with the dative in the rest of the NT (only 1 Pet 1:13 has *epi* with the accusative). Of the twenty-seven NT uses of *elpizein* outside of the PE, the verb is uncommon in the Gospel tradition (Luke-Acts share five out of seven occurrences). There is no precise NT parallel to the usage with *elthein* here in 1 Tim 3:14, but close parallels are in 3 John 14, *elpizō de eutheōs se idein,* and in the other Paulines in Rom 15:24; 1 Cor 16:7; Philem 22 (see Phil 2:19, 23). Among Ap. Frs. the verb is used often enough, but parallels to the use at this point in the PE are not frequent. Ignatius, *Rom.* 1.1, writes to the Roman Christians, saying, "For chained in Christ Jesus, I hope to greet you *(elpizō hymas aspasasthai)*. . . ." Perhaps *2 Clem.* 11.5 could be adduced also: "Let us be patient hoping that *(elpisantes hypomeinōmen hina)* we may also receive the reward." The LXX uses *elpizein* often enough but not in the sense here in 3:14, except perhaps in LXX Ezek 36:8, *elpizousi tou elthein, s.v.l.*

*To come to. Pros* has been treated at Titus 3:12.

*Before long* represents *en tachei,* the reading of A, C, D*, P, Psi, 33, 81, 442, 1912. Coptic (Sahidic), and more or less regular Greek usage. *Tachion,* with the meaning here of "as quickly as possible" (see BDF §244.1), is the reading of S, $D^2$, F, G, and the majority of MSS. Other NT documents attest to a comparative sense for the term (thus John 20:4; Heb 13:19). Yet the word also was heard without elative force, though the Atticists preferred *thatton,* "quite quickly" (see BAGD, *s.v. tacheōs*). This more vulgar and so more difficult usage could represent the original text at this point. Still, in the PE generally Sinaiticus is a bruised reed (see J. K. Elliott, *Greek Text,* p. 53, on 1 Tim 3:9), and that may well be the case here (see the variant in 2 Tim 4:9). In this context one also notes the textual problem of a loosely anchored *pros se* which appears now before, now after *elthein* or *en tachei (tachion),* and sometimes drifts completely out of sight (F G 263. 255. etc.; see J. K. Elliott, *Greek Text,* p. 56). In the judgment of Westcott and Hort, this disturbance in the tradition called for brackets in their edition of the Text. Though qualms still run through the apparatus, the solution probably is to be sought in the form of the narrative (see Comment below).

*Tachos* appears only here in the PE and, always in the phrase *en tachei,* seven times in the rest of the NT, once in Rom 16:20, four times in Luke-Acts. In Ap. Frs. *First Clement* uses the term three out of four times in the phrase *en tachei* (48.1; 63.4; 65.1). The one other use is of Moses being told to go down from Sinai quickly (53.2), a quotation taken up also in the two uses in *Barn.* 4.8; 14.3. The LXX uses *tachōs* more than three dozen times, and of these, as many as fifteen are in the phrase *en tachei.*

15. *if I do delay. Bradynein,* to "delay," appears otherwise in the NT only in 2 Pet 3:9 about the Lord's apparent delay of the day of judgment. Hermas alone among Ap. Frs. uses the verb, in *Sim.* 9.19.2, about the peril of delaying repentance. The LXX uses *bradynein* four times: Gen 43:10; Deut 7:10; Isa 46:13; Sir

35:19 (of God's not delaying his judgment, *ho kyrios ou mē bradynēi,* "the Lord by no means will delay"). Of twenty occurrences in Josephus, among the intransitive uses, *Ant.* 6.101 is notable: "But when he [Saul] saw that the prophet delayed *(bradynounta),* he took the victims and himself performed the sacrifices." The few late examples from papyri in MM *s.v.* are not really parallel to the usage here in 1 Tim 3:15.

*this letter will let you know.* "This letter will" has been added to the Greek. The phrase *hina eidēis,* translated here as "this letter will let you know," does not occur otherwise in the PE. The one Lukan usage is in Luke 5:24 (par. Mark 2:10; Matt 9:6), and it does not appear much more often in the remaining Paulines (see 1 Cor 2:12; Eph 6:21; Col 4:16, the latter two offering some close parallels). The combination of *eidenai* with *pōs dei,* "how a person has to," reappears in the other Paulines in 2 Thess 3:7 (see 1 Thess 4:1) and Col 4:6; it does not occur elsewhere in the NT. The shortest, most difficult, and most satisfactory text in 1 Tim 3:15 omits the second singular pronoun, *se,* and reads *dei* impersonally (or as the version here puts it, *a person has to*). Witnesses such as D*, L, Old Latin (some MSS, see Frede, *VL* 25.509) Armenian, Ambrosiaster, Hilary, Origen, et al. inserted the pronoun and thus narrowed the application of the words to Timothy alone. The insertion is already an exegesis whose merits will be discussed below in the Comment.

*to behave, anastrephesthai.* A present, middle infinitive, appearing only here in the PE and eight times otherwise in the NT. The two remaining uses in the other Paulines are comparable (see 2 Cor 1:12; Eph 2:3); the two in the Lukan corpus are not (Acts 5:22; 15:16). The usage in Heb 13:18 is precisely parallel to that here in First Timothy (see the remaining NT uses in Heb 10:33; 1 Pet 1:17; 2 Pet 2:18). The usage in Ap. Frs. is also notable: see *Did.* 3.9; *Barn.* 19.6; *1 Clem.* 21.8 (of the emissary witnesses sent from the Roman to the Corinthian church; see 65.1, where the three of them are named in a passage that has some elements of the apostolic parousia in it); *2 Clem.* 5.6; Ign. *Magn.* 9.1 (speaks of *en palaiois pragmasin anastraphentes* in reference to such Jewish practices as keeping the Sabbath); and finally Hermas, who uses the verb of human conduct, whether evil (*Man.* 11.12) or good (*Sim.* 5.6.6; 9.27.2), and of bishops who *hagnōs anestraphēsan pantote,* "always behaved in a holy way."

In the LXX forms of *anastrephein* appear regularly, and eight times it translates a qal or hitpa'el of *halak.* In LXX Josh 5:6 it designates Israel's desert wanderings in a simply physical sense (see Wis 13:7 of human beings' *anastrephomenoi,* "spending their lives," among God's works). In LXX Zech 3:7 the verb appears in the oracle to Joshua: "Thus says the Lord, ruler of all: 'If you (sg.) proceed in my ways, and if you keep my directives, and if you recognize my house *(ton oikon mou),* and if you also keep watch carefully in my courts, I too will give you (sg.) those spending their lives *(anastrephomenous)* in the midst of those who have been established here.'" A moral sense clearly appears twice in translating *halak.* In 3 Kgdms 6:11-12 *s.v.l.,* in the midst of the description of the building of Yahweh's temple, ". . . the word of the Lord came to Solomon, saying, 'As to this house which you are building, if you walk *(hoduein/halak)* in my statutes and perform my ordinances and keep all my commandments, living *(anastrephesthai/halak)* in them, then I will establish my word with you. . . .'" In LXX Prov 20:7 that translation reads: "He who conducts himself (*anastrephetai/halak* in hitpa'el) in spotless fashion in righteousness, will leave his children blessed." This passage as well as the link of good behavior with the house of God in the preceding makes both relevant to 1 Tim 3:15. The *T. Asher* 6.3 has the dying patriarch urging: "You therefore, my children, keep the Law of the Lord; do not pay attention to evil as to good, but have regard for what is really good and keep it thoroughly in all the Lord's commandments, taking it as your way of life *(anastrephomenoi)* and finding rest in it."

The Greek usage of *anastrephein* for human behavior does not necessarily imply Hebrew influence on a given passage, as the many passages from the Greek papyri and inscriptions show (see Deissmann, *B ST,* pp. 88, 194; MM *s.v.;* Spicq, *Lexic.,* pp. 85-88).

*God's house, (en) oikōi theou,* echoes 3:4-5 with its reference to a bishop's *own home, tou idiou oikou.* Here *oikos* has been qualified with *theou,* a phrase that occurs only here in the Pauline epistolary, though Heb 10:21 uses it when speaking of Christians who "have a great priest [i.e. Jesus] over the house of God *(ton oikon tou theou).*" An articular form of the phrase also appears in 1 Pet 4:17: "For the time has come for judgment to begin with the house of God *(ton oikon tou theou).*" In the Gospel tradition the single use refers not to the congregation of believers (see Luke 6:4 and par.) but to a justification of the conduct of Jesus' disciples vis-à-vis David and his company when they entered Yahweh's tent at Nob (see 1 Sam 21:1-6, where "house of God" does not occur in the MT or the LXX). Otherwise in the Gospels, the narratives of Jesus' cleansing of the Temple use variant forms of the phrase, all with the definite article, to designate the Jerusalem temple. In Ap. Frs. the phrase appears only twice: an anarthrous form in *Barn.* 16.1 asserts that God the creator is himself the true temple of God; Hermas, *Sim.* 9.14.1, questions whether those who repent will "enter into the house of God," *eis ton oikon tou theou.* The phrase *God's house* is Septuagintal in origin (see O. Michel, *TDNT* 5.120). The distinction between the anarthrous phrase at LXX Judg 17:5 and the articular form at 18:31 as well as in LXX 2 Kgdms 12:20 is the difference between *a* sanctuary and *the* sanctuary (wherever the latter is). Still, as Jaubert has noted in "Image," p. 102, the distinction is not consistently carried out. There is a Roman Jewish picture of the Jerusalem temple with the legend *oikos eir[ēn]ēs,* "house of peace," dating from about 250-350 C.E., in *CII* §515; and in §694 and pp. 76-77 of the KTAV edition, there is a Macedonian house synagogue inscription on a white marble column which records the generosity of the man who built the buildings, *tous oikous,* for the holy place, *toi hagioi topoi,* including a dining room (165 or 264/281 C.E.).

*the living God.* The noun *theos,* occurring more than 1,300 times in the NT, appears qualified with *zōn* only a dozen times, half of these being in the Paulines, including here and in 4:10. Similarly, in the LXX, of more than 2,600 occurrences of *theos, (ho) theos zōn* appears less than two dozen times. At this point, the phrase in Ap. Frs. ought to be noted. Thus *1 Clem.* 8.2 cites the divine oath "For as I live *(zo gar egō),* says the Lord . . . ," and a variation on the formula appears in 58.2. The prayer in 59.3 speaks to God as "the one who slays and gives life," *zēn poiounta,* again a Septuagintal formula (see 1 Sam 2:6). *Second Clement* 14.1-2 writes of the church life and the "living church" as the body of Christ; then in 20.2 of the Christian contending "in the contest of the living God," *theou zontos* (recall that the ancient games were held as worship in honor of the gods). Ignatius, in *Phld.* 1.2, praises the quiet, kindly bishop of the congregation for his wrathless disposition "in the complete gentleness of the living God," *theou zontos* (E.T. contra K. Lake; W. Schoedel). The distinctive scriptural connotations of the phrase do not appear in these two latter instances. Hermas, *Vis.* 2.3.2; 3.7.2, seems to cite the phrase from Heb 3:12; but in *Sim.* 6.2.2 one encounters the men who "forget the commandments of the living God *(tou theou zontos)* and walk in deceits and vain luxuries. . . ." Here again the biblical nuances have disappeared.

*[There you, Timothy, are].* This phrase has been added to the Greek.

*a pillar and pedestal, stylos kai hedraiōma,* regardless of its reference, is a unique phrase. Of the individual terms, *stylos* is the more common, appearing 3 times otherwise in the NT, once in Gal 2:9 of James, Cephas, and John, and then in Rev 3:12, where the prophet writes to the church in Philadelphia, of the person "who conquers, I will make him a pillar in the sanctuary *(naoi)* of my God," and in 10:1 with its description of the visionary angel with legs "like pillars of fire." The imagery in this last example reminds one of the divine appearance in (or upon) the pillar of fire during the exodus. Among Ap. Frs. only *1 Clem.* 5.2 uses *styloi* to describe Peter and Paul as "the greatest and most righteous pillars" in the (Roman) church (see *en hymin,* 6.1). The lion's share of the 125 uses in the LXX designate "the pillar of fire" which led the people of God during the exodus (note also Justin, *Trypho* 37.4; 38.1; 64.4; 131.3).

*Hedraiōma,* the second term in the phrase, is a neologism, undocumented in the LXX or Hellenistic Jewish or secular Greek previous to this occurrence (and not found in Ap. Frs. or the Apologists). The Indo-European root **sed-* (thus the Latin *sedes*) has, through the Greek *hedra,* "seat," spawned the adjectival *hedraios,* "sedentary, fixed, firm," which in turn issued in the verb *hedraioō,* whence the late *hedraiōma,* formed with the *-ma* suffix that specifies the result of an action (BDF §109.2 and *Papyr. Lugd-Bat.* 13.63-64, §21.12, *hedreumatōn prosodos,* first Christian century) of fixing in place or seating (see Chantraine, *DELG,* p. 314). A Greek fragment of Irenaeus (*Adversus haereses* 3.11.8; see 3.1.1) paraphrases this passage using *stylos kai stērigma,* understanding the rare *hedraiōma* in the sense of "foundation, support." In the famous letter in 177 C.E. or later about the Lyons martyrs, "solid *pillars,*" as they are called in Eusebius, *Church History* 5.1.6, there is reference to one "Attalus, a Pergamene by race, who had always been *a pillar and pedestal* of the Christians there" (5.1.17; see plate III, vol. 35). In 5.1.43 it said of Attalus that "he had ever been a witness for truth *(martys . . . alētheias)* among us."

16. *And great is the mystery of godliness.* For *megas, great,* see Titus 2:13; for *mystery,* see *mystērion,* 3:9 above; *godliness, eusebeia,* appears ten times in the PE, which constitutes two-thirds of the NT uses, and here denotes the whole Christian life, the faith in practice.

*There is no denying it!* In the Greek, *homologoumenōs* follows the *kai* with which the sentence begins. Since ancient Greek manuscripts did not regularly separate words, it is possible to read this adverb as *homologoumen hos,* "we confess that." A few scribes and ancient versions apparently did read it thus (see D* 1175 Palestinian Syriac). Since the adverb appears only here in the NT whereas the verb is in Titus 1:16, it looks as if a few scribes became confused and understood *hos* as introducing indirect discourse, which is good Greek but not characteristic of NT syntax.

*Homologoumenōs* does not appear in Ap. Frs. or the Apologists (but see *Diogn.* 5.4), and in the LXX it is found only in 4 Macc 6:31; 7:16; 16:1. On the other hand, there is no dearth of examples in Jewish or secular Greek (see Spicq, *Lexic.,* pp. 621-622).

*. . . He was revealed in human flesh.* The beginning of the quotation with *hos* (thus S*, A, $^{\text{vid.}}$ C*, $G^{gr}$, 33, 365, 442, and others in $GNT^{3corr}$) was so abrupt that ancient scribes and translators sought to ease the transition by changing the pronoun so that it would have an antecedent in the preceding introduction. Thus *ho* in D* and presumed in the Old Latin refers to *to mystērion.* Some correctors changed *hos* to *theos,* using the ancient abbreviation for the *nomen sacrum,* OC presuming, ingeniously enough, that *O* had lost a crossbar in transmission (thus $S^c$, $A^2$, $C^2$, $D^c$, K, L, P, Psi, and many others). Macedonius, an early sixth-century archbishop of Constantinople, took this reading, among other things, in a monophysite sense and lost his see for it (J. K. Elliot, *Greek Text,* p. 58; but see Ign. *Eph.* 19.3 and Bousset, *Kyrios,* p. 318 n. 292 [E.T.]). In any case, F. J. A. Hort's defense of *hos* as the more difficult reading and the one which explains the rest of the variants has won the day in textual criticism.

For *ephanerōthē,* "was revealed," see Titus 1:3, adding at this point Ap. Frs.

*First Clement* 50.3 uses this verb of those saved at the final judgment, and *2 Clem.* 14.2-3 employs it when he writes that the church which belongs to the Spirit *(pneumatikē)* "was revealed in the flesh *(en tēi sarki)* of Christ," and then in 20.5 the verb appears in a doxology to the Father who sent the Savior "through whom he revealed . . . truth and life. . . ." Ign. *Eph.* 19.2-3 uses forms of *phaneroun* when describing the incarnation; *Magn.* 8.2 speaks of "the one God who revealed himself through Jesus Christ his Son." In Ign. *Rom.* 8.2 Jesus reveals the truth that Ignatius speaks, and he writes to Polycarp (2.2), "Pray that the invisible things may be revealed to you." In Hermas the verb is used of visionary experiences (*Vis.* 3.1.2; *Sim.* 2.1), including those of the judgment (*Sim.* 3.4.2-3). The parallels in *Barnabas* are particularly apposite at this point to 1 Tim 3:16b (see Comment). The verb also describes visionary experiences in *Mart. Pol.* 12.3; 22.3. In the Apologists, Justin uses the term of the appearances of God to the patriarchs and Moses (*Trypho* 60.3; 75.4; 114.4), and of Christ (*Apology* 56.1). Tatian, *Oratio* 8.2, writes of the pagan gods who have revealed their vile character to humankind by their vile actions.

*in human flesh, en sarki,* with a noun that appears only here in the PE, though *sarx* is used 146 times in the rest of the NT (only First and Second Thessalonians and Third John do not use the noun). There are twenty uses of *en (tēi) sarki* in the rest of the Paulines (a dozen are anarthrous). Paradigmatic are 2 Cor 4:11, "For we [Paul, Silvanus, Timothy] who are alive are constantly being given up to death on account of Jesus, so that the life *(hē zōē)* of Jesus may be revealed *(phanerōthē)* in our mortal flesh *(en tēi thnētēi sarki hēmōn)*" (E.T., Furnish, AB *2 Cor,* p. 252 modified), and Philem 16, where the runaway slave, Onesimus, returns to his master "as a beloved brother . . . both in the flesh and in the Lord *(kai en sarki kai en kyriōi),*" i.e. in his human condition, with the relationships, even those of a slave, which that implies (see E. Schweizer, *TDNT* 7.127), and in the condition before God that faith in Christ has initiated.

*Sarx* occurs in Ap. Frs. regularly, and the phrase *en (tēi) sarki* is not infrequent. *First Clement* 38.2 uses the articular phrase of chastity of life. *Second Clement* has a notable cluster of uses in 9.2-5 and 14.3 (partially quoted above), and *Barnabas* uses the phrase seven times. Ignatius, *Trall. inscr.* 3, applies the phrase to himself; however, in *Eph.* 7.2 Jesus is "in flesh, God" (for the text, see Schoedel, *Ignatius,* p. 61); in *Smyrn.* 1.2 it is Jesus who "was truly nailed in flesh for us under Pontius Pilate and Herod the Tetrarch"; in 3.1 Ignatius confesses, "I know and I believe that he is in flesh after resurrection"; finally in 12.2 he addresses his correspondents "in the name of Jesus Christ and in his flesh and blood." All these uses are anarthrous, as is Polycarp, *Phil.* 7.1: "For every one who does not confess that Jesus Christ has come in flesh is an antichrist." Hermas uses the articular phrase in describing the Spirit whom God has caused to dwell "in this the flesh" (*Man.* 3.1). There appears to be only one use of the phrase in the Apologists when Justin, *Trypho* 16.3 (*PG* 6.509), writes of "the circumcision in your flesh *(en sarki hymōn)*."

Forms of *sarx* appear several hundred times in the LXX, but the unmodified phrase *en sarki* is not found and the modified form is rare (LXX Gen 9:15-16 of the covenant between God and all flesh; LXX Ps 37:4, 8 of no healing "in my flesh"; Sir 44:20 of the covenant in Abraham's flesh). In *T. Benjamin* 10.8 there is an early reading of the text about the judgment of Israel for not believing in the liberator God when he arrived in the flesh *(theon en sarki)*. See Spicq, *Supp. Lexic.*, pp. 591-600.

*Was made victorious in the Spirit.* For *dikaioun,* see Titus 3:7; for *pneuma,* Titus 3:5.

*He who was seen (ōphthē) by God's messengers.* The Greek has no *en* here and no word for God. Forms of *horaō* appear 449 times in the NT, 3 times in the PE (see 1 Tim 6:16; 2 Tim 1:4 below, using *idein*). Of the uses of *ōphthē* in the other Paulines, see 1 Cor 15:5-8; in the Lukan corpus, Luke 24:34; Acts 13:31. Forms of *horaō* are not infrequent in Ap. Frs., but only in Hermas does *ōphthē* appear, in *Vis.* 3.10.3; 3.11.2 of the vision of the seated, elderly lady. The LXX uses *horaō* often, and the appearances of *ōphthē* in the patriarchal narratives are especially notable (cf. LXX Gen 12:7 with Acts 7:2 and see Comment).

*Aggelois,* "messengers," could also be transliterated as "angels," to mean the spirits, good or bad superhuman creatures, who belong to that part of the creation that is superior to human beings to whom they carry messages (hence their name). The church order for presbyters, when it urges, "As God [the Father] and Christ Jesus and the elect angels look on, I adjure you, Timothy, to keep these directives," uses *aggeloi* of the good spirits (1 Tim 5:21). Elsewhere in the NT there are 174 uses of *aggelos,* a dozen in the other Paulines, 46 in Luke-Acts (Revelation with 67 is the only NT document with more). In Luke 7:24; 9:52 the NT uses *aggeloi* of men sent as messengers by men, and also in James 2:25 (see LXX Josh 7:22); *aggelos* in Luke 7:27 (Mark 1:2; Matt 11:10) refers to LXX Exod 23:20; Mal 3:1, and a human, prophetic messenger, the Baptist, sent by God. The other references are to superhuman spirits. References to *aggeloi* in Ap. Frs. are infrequent, except in Hermas, and none seems to designate a simply human messenger. On the other hand the latter meaning is regular in the LXX (thus Gen 32:4, 7; Judg 6:35; 7:24; 1 Chron 14:1; etc.), not to mention Hellenistic Jewish (Josephus, *Ant.* 14.451; and the striking instance in *War* 3.400 where the captive Josephus calls himself an *aggelos* to Vespasian about his imperial destiny) and secular Greek (Sappho L.P. 44.3, of the Trojan Idaeus, "a speedy messenger," *tachys aggelos;* and even of the nightingale, "the messenger of spring," *erōs aggelos,* L.P. 136).

*was heralded. Ekērychthē,* "was heralded," will reappear in the PE only in 2 Tim 4:1-2, "I adjure you, Timothy, . . . herald the message; stand on the alert, when convenient, when inconvenient. . . ." There are fifty-nine other uses in the NT, of which seventeen are in the rest of the Paulines, seventeen in Luke-Acts. Coincidentally, forms of *kēryssein* appear eighteen times in Ap. Frs. *Kēryssein* is used about thirty times in the LXX; Jonah has the most of any single book (1:2; 3:2, 4, 5, 7).

*pagans.* For *ethnē,* see 1 Tim 2:7.

*Was taken up,* from *analambanein* (thirteen times in the NT), recurs in the PE only in 2 Tim 4:11, "Pick up *(analabōn)* Mark and bring him along with you" to Rome (a usage that appears elsewhere in the NT only in Acts 20:13, 14; 23:31; and 7:43 taking up LXX Amos 5:26). Of the seven other uses in the NT, the only ones in the Paulines are in Eph 6:13, 16 of picking up the armor of Christian virtue. The notable parallels with the usage in 1 Tim 3:16 are in the long ending of Mark (16:19) and in Acts 1:2, 11, 22 (and see 10:16). Forms of *analambanein* are used eight times in Ap. Frs. (in Ignatius only in *Trall.* 8.1 but five times in *First Clement*). The closest parallel to 1 Tim 3:16 appears among the three uses in Hermas, in *Vis.* 1.1.5, where the Christian Rhoda, speaking of herself in heaven before God, says, "I was taken up *(anelēmphthēn).*"

In the LXX, out of several dozen occurrences of *analambanein,* the aorist passive *anelēmphth-* appears to be verging on a technical meaning. Thus Elijah's extraordinary mode of departure is designated by *anelēmphth-* in various forms (see LXX 4 Kgdms 2:9, 10, 11; Sir 48:9; 1 Macc 2:58), and even that of Enoch (Sir 49:14). However, LXX Ezek 12:6-7 and Tob 1:20 in S indicate that the ordinary sense circulated also in Jewish circles. They are somewhat rare in Josephus, but *Vita* 15 describes Josephus and his companions as being *taken up* out of the sea and on board a boat.

*in glory, en doxēi,* with the noun governed by *en* as it is in 15 out of 165 NT uses of *doxa* (but here alone in the PE). The phrase appears otherwise in the Paulines seven times (1 Cor 15:41, 43; 2 Cor 3:7-8, 11; Phil 4:19; Col 3:4). The synoptic Gospels have all the remaining uses: Matt 6:29 with Luke 12:27 (Q); Matt 16:27 with Mark 8:38 and Luke 9:26; Matt 25:31; Luke 9:31, with frequent reference to royal splendor, whether of the Father, the Son of Man, Jesus, or Solomon. One must wait until Hermas to encounter the phrase *en doxēi* in Ap. Frs., and in *Vis.* 1.3.2 *en pollēi doxēi* refers to the Lord's glory in which the believer is to share. Out of the 445 uses of *doxa* in the LXX, there is only one textually certain, unqualified use of *en doxēi,* in LXX Ps 111:9; only 14 more uses speak of "in my *or* your *or* his glory," "in all glory," etc.

4:1. *Here is the Spirit expressly declaring.* For *(to) pneuma,* see Titus 3:5; for *declare, legein,* see Titus 2:8. If *to de* is read as *tode,* the demonstrative pronoun serves to usher the Spirit on stage to speak (see *1 Clem.* 63.2; BDF §289 on the literary character of the term).

*Expressly, rhētōs,* is an adverb unattested elsewhere in the NT, the LXX, or

Ap. Frs., although it is used of the explicit citation of God's word in Justin, *Apology* 35.10; 54.7; 63.11 (*PG* 6.384, 409, 424). Philo, *Leg. alleg.* 1.60, notes that Genesis "explicitly *(rhētōs)* says that [the tree of life] is in the middle of Paradise." Josephus, *Ant.* 1.24, describes God as making certain things "expressly clear" in the Scripture; a gloss on his *Contra Apionem* 1.83 also uses *rhētōs,* which appears too in the Epicurean philosopher and poet Philodemus of Gadara (see his *Volumina rhetorica* 1.105 [S. Sudhaus]). Polybius 3.23.5, describing a treaty between Carthage and Rome, notes that in the phrasing about Sicily "they expressly *(rhētōs)* put the case otherwise." O'Callaghan has proposed that 1 Tim 3:16–4:3 (or perhaps its source) has been transmitted in the fragmentary 7Q 4.1, 2, which would have read *[rhē]tōn* at this point (see his "Cueva 7," pp. 34-44). This striking variant may have been a scribal slip for a final *s,* since (as O'Callaghan has observed) it was not unusual for the sounds of *n* and *s* in final position to be confused with each other. The spelling of *daimoniōn* in 7Q 4.5 indicates that the scribe was writing out what he heard rather than what he saw.

Then again, *rhēton* could be the original reading and be understood as a synonym for *rhēmaton. Rhēton,* meaning "word" or "saying," is rather more common than the adverb in secular Greek, and in the LXX it occurs in Exod 9:4; 22:8, as well as in Sym Isa 39:2 and Aq Prov 31:1. In the last instance it translates the plural *dibrey,* "The words of King Lemuel, the oracle that his mother taught him." The parallel suggests that the term was considered an appropriate synonym (at least by the harshly literalistic Aquila) for a prophetic word transmitted from one generation to the next. In this way a very un-Greek phrase, *pneuma rhētōn,* "a spirit of (oracular) sayings," would be parallel to the variant *pneumasin planēs,* "the spirits of error," to be noted below. When the former phrase was very early ironed out of the text, the latter became a candidate for regularization.

There are some other minor but puzzling differences between 7Q 4 and 1 Tim 4:1; thus a nine-space blank would be required before the beginning of this verse and there is no room for *hoti en* before *hysterois kairois.* Given the uncertainty about the identification of these tiny fragments from 7Q 4, it is hazardous to base further exegesis on the variant here. O'Callaghan's case, on the other hand, is more formidable than some admit (see Thiede, "7Q," pp. 538-559, with the literature).

*"In these latter times some people, who dote on seductive spirits and demonic doctrines, will apostatize from the faith."* On *kairoi,* "times," see Titus 1:3; on *prosechontes,* "dote," see Titus 1:14; on *pneuma,* "spirit," see Titus 3:5; on *didaskalia,* "teaching," see Titus 1:9; *pistis,* "the faith," represents one of fifteen PE occurrences with the article, here as the object of a verb describing persons who have abandoned the faith (see also 5:8; 2 Tim 2:18).

*Hysteros,* "latter," appears only here in the NT but not in Ap. Frs. In the LXX there are three uses of the adjective, in 1 Chron 29:29; Wis 19:11; Bar 6:72 (see 3 Macc 5:49 for *hystatēn*). The phrase here in Timothy does not appear in so many words in these documents, though the adverbial *en chronōi de hysteron* of 3 Macc 2:24 comes close. In *T. Benjamin* 11.2 the precise phrase does appear when the dying patriarch says, "And *in the latter times* there shall rise up the beloved of the Lord, from the lineage of Judah and Levi, one who does his good pleasure by his mouth, enlightening all the nations with new knowledge" (E.T. in Charlesworth, *OT Pseud.* 1.828, modified).

*seductive (planois) spirits.* From *planos,* lit. "wandering" and thus "leading astray" (see *planomenoi,* "deluded," in Titus 3:3). The term appears four times otherwise in the NT, but as a substantive: in 2 Cor 6:8, where the deceiver is contrasted with truthful; and in 2 John 7 (twice); as well as in Matt 27:63, which applies the term to Jesus as prophesying his own rising from the dead. Unknown in Ap. Frs., *planos* appears in the LXX only at Job 19:4 and Jer 23:32. The *T. Levi* 16.3 states, "A man who by the power of the Most High renews the law you name 'Deceiver,' and finally you shall plot to kill him, not discerning his eminence" (E.T. in Charlesworth, *OT Pseud.* 1.794).

A few witnesses (P 0241 440 etc. listed by J. K. Elliott, *Greek Text,* p. 61) read *pneumasin planēs* for *planois.* The former is more Semitic and has a parallel in 1 John 4:6, writing of "the spirit of error" (see Justin, *Trypho* 7.3; R. Brown, *Epistles,* pp. 501, 505-506), and *T. Judah* 23.1, speaking of "the demons of deceit" (see below). The closest parallel that the Pauline tradition offers to this expression is the *energeian planēs* which God sends upon the wicked "to make them believe what is false" (2 Thess 2:11). If the harsh *rhētōn* of 7Q 4 was indeed the original reading of this oracle, when that reading was "normalized" there would be little reason to keep the Semiticizing *pneumasin planēs* of this phrase, and one infers that it was the next wrinkle to be ironed out of the text in the name of Greek usage.

*Demonic doctrines* is lit. "the teachings of demons." Only here do the PE use the term *teaching* in a bad sense, and only here do they use *daimoniōn* at all, though there are sixty-two uses elsewhere in the NT, particularly in the Gospel traditions (fifty-three times, twenty-three of which are in Luke). Elsewhere in the Paulines the references to *daimonia* cluster in 1 Cor 10:20-21, with four references to the cup and table of demons in pagan communion sacrifices. The single occurrence in Acts is where some Athenian philosophers describe Paul as "a preacher of foreign divinities *(daimoniōn)*" (17:18). *Daimonion* appears seldom in Ap. Frs. Ignatius has the risen Jesus say, ". . . see that I am not a bodiless wraith *(daimonion asomaton)*" (*Smyrn.* 3.2). Barnabas speaks of the heart as a temple which "was the house of demons through doing things which were contrary to God" (16.7). Hermas uses the term three times, in the singular and in a bad sense. It is in the

LXX that *daimonion* is being forged into a contemptuous word for all that pretends to be divine among the pagans; see LXX Deut 32:17; Bar 4:7 (cf. 35); LXX Ps 105:37 (cf. 90:6; 95:5); Isa 13:21; 34:14; 65:3, 11; and nine times in Tobit. In *T. Judah* 23.3 the dying patriarch says, "My grief is great, my children, on account of the licentiousness and witchcraft and idolatry that you practice contrary to the kingship, following ventriloquists, omen dispensers, and demons of deceit *(daimosi planēs)*" (E.T. in Charlesworth, *OT Pseud.* 1.801). Menander's line from *Kitharistes* fragment 8, Koerte/288K is memorable: "How unstable and deceitful a thing *(poikilon pragm' . . . kai planon)* is Luck."

*Apostatize,* from *aphistan(-ai),* reappears in 2 Tim 2:19 with the sense of keeping away from sin (but note the allusion to Num 16:26-27). Among the dozen other NT uses of the verb, there is only one more in the Paulines, in 2 Cor 12:8, and this is of physical departure. Hebrews 3:12 uses the verb to describe "an evil, unbelieving heart, leading you to apostatize *(apostēnai)* from the living God." The ten remaining NT uses of the verb are in Luke-Acts. Before Hermas, *to apostatize* does not appear in Ap. Frs., though it is common enough in the *Pastor* (*Vis.* 2.3.2; etc.). Justin uses the term of deserting Jesus (*Apology* 50.12) and his words (*Trypho* 8.2) as well as the one God and the faith (*Trypho* 20.1; 111.2). In the LXX *aphistanai* is used not only of putting distance between oneself and another or of political rebellion but also of apostatizing from the God and the religion of Israel (see LXX Deut 32:15; Josh 22:18-19, 23; Dan 9:9; Sir 10:12; Jer 3:14; 1 Macc 1:15 ["from the holy covenant"]; 2:19 ["from the worship of the fathers"]; more in H. Schlier, *TDNT* 1.512). Among the frequent uses in the *Testaments of the Twelve Patriarchs,* one notes in *T. Judah* 18.1-4: "For in the books of Enoch the Righteous I have read the evil things you will do in the last days. Guard yourselves therefore, my children, against sexual promiscuity and love of money; listen to Judah, your father, for these things distance you *(aphistai)* from the law of God, blind the direction of the soul, and teach arrogance. . . . They take away *(aphistai)* sleep from him and utterly waste his flesh." Note in *T. Zebulun* 9.5, "In the writing of my fathers I came to know that in the last days you shall apostatize *(apostēsesthe)* from the Lord. . . ." In *T. Dan* 5.4-5 the dying patriarch asserts: "For I know that in the last days you will apostatize *(apostēsesthe)* from the Lord, . . . To the extent that you apostatize *(apostēte)* from the Lord, you will live by every evil deed, committing the revolting acts of the gentiles, chasing after wives of lawless men, and you are motivated to all wickedness by the spirits of deceit *(tōn pneumatōn tēs planēs)* among you." In *T. Naphtali* 4.1 the patriarch's message is: "I say these things, my children, because I have read in the writing of holy Enoch that you also will apostatize *(apostēsesthe)* from the lord, living in accord with every wickedness of the gentiles and committing every lawlessness of Sodom" (E.T. from Charlesworth, *OT Pseud.* 1.800, 807, 809, 812, modified).

2. *These lying frauds.* Lit. "by the hypocritical preaching of liars *(en hypokrisei pseudologōn).*"

The compound *pseudologos* is otherwise undocumented in the NT, Ap. Frs., or the LXX (though Dan 11:27 has the verb) and is rather rare in secular Greek, where it belongs to the language of the cultivated. Aristophanes, *Frogs* 1521, in the devastating final judgment on Euripides, calls him "a knave ready for anything and a liar *(pseudologos)* and an altar-parasite." Polybius 31.22.9 asserts that the Romans find lying of any kind unpardonable. Strabo 2.1.9 finds most historians of India to be *pseudologoi* (see Spicq, *Lexic.* 2.977).

*Hypokrisis* appears only here in the PE and only five times otherwise in the NT, including once in Gal 2:13 (where even Barnabas was carried away by the hypocrisy of the Antiochene Jewish Christians whose conduct did not square with what they really believed; see U. Wilckens, *TDNT* 8.568-569 n. 50) and once in Luke 12:1 (which equates it with "the leaven of the Pharisees"). *First Clement* 15.1 stigmatizes those whose wish for peace is based on hypocrisy, not on piety; Ign. *Magn.* 3.2 writes of obedience to the bishop without hypocrisy; and Polycarp, *Phil.* 6.3, takes up the phrase of the PE, where immediately after he mentioned the "false brothers," *pseudadelphōn,* he speaks of "those who bear the name of the Lord in hypocrisy *(en hypokrisei),* who deceive *(apoplanōsi),* empty-minded people." As in the PE, the phrase practically means apostates, persons who have really left the church, appearances notwithstanding. In *Did.* 4.12; 5.1 there is a command to avoid "all hypocrisy," and "hypocrisies" figure in the list that constitutes the "Way of Death" (thus also *Barn.* 19.2; 20.1; 21.4). *En hypokrisei* appears also in Hermas, *Vis.* 3.6.1, speaking of evil men who "in hypocrisy believed," which can be distinguished from its meaning in *Man.* 2.5. In *Sim.* 8.6.2, "those who would repent in hypocrisy *(en hypokrisei)*" appear to include "apostates and traitors . . . and blasphemers" as well as those "hypocrites" who introduced strange doctrines (*Sim.* 8.6.4-5).

The single LXX use of *hypokrisis* is in 2 Macc 6:25, but the precise phrase *en hypokrisis* appears in *Pss. Sol.* 4.6 (see 4.22): "Let God remove those that live in hypocrisy in the company of the devout" (the Greek predates 100 C.E.).

*Cauterized,* from *kausteriazesthai,* a variant and perhaps vulgar spelling of *kauteriazesthai,* is undocumented elsewhere in the NT, Ap. Frs., or the LXX, and it is practically unknown to secular Greek before the PE (see Strabo 5.1.9).

*consciences.* For *conscience, syneidēsis,* see Titus 1:15.

3. *Interdict.* "Interdict" is from *kōlyein* and does not appear otherwise in the PE, but it is found twenty-two times elsewhere in the NT, including a dozen in Luke-Acts, as well as in Rom 1:13; 1 Cor 14:39; 1 Thess 2:16 in the rest of the Paulines. In Ap. Frs. only Ign. *Rom.* 4.1 uses this verb, of those who prevent his martyrdom, but it becomes somewhat more common again in the Apologists. There are as many as thirty-three uses in the LXX, none of them particularly il-

luminating for this passage in the PE unless perhaps it be Eleazar's reply to Antiochus about the unclean foods, where the aged Jew says that God "has permitted us to eat what will be most suitable for our lives but he has forbidden *(ekōlyse)* us to eat meat that would militate against this" (4 Macc 5:26).

*Marriage. Gamein,* translated here as "marriage," recurs in the church order for widows in 1 Tim 5:11, 14, where it is translated "remarry." Of twenty-five other NT occurrences of the verb, nine are in First Corinthians, none in the rest of the Paulines. Luke uses *gamein* six times but it does not appear in Acts. In Ap. Frs., apart from five uses in Hermas, the verb appears only in Ign. *Pol.* 5.2: "But it is proper *(prepei)* for the men who are marrying and the women who are being married *(tois gamousi kai tais gamoumenais)* to make their union with the consent of the bishop, so that the marriage *(gamos)* may be according *(kata)* to the Lord and not according to lust" (alluded to in the Comment on 2:15 above; see also Schoedel, *Ignatius,* p. 273). In the LXX there are only three textually certain uses of *gamein:* in LXX Esther 10:3c, "whom the king married and made queen," and in 2 Macc 14:25, where Nicanor urges Judas "to marry (*gemai* [see BDF §101 *s.v.*]) and have children, and so he married *(egamesen),* settled down, and shared the common life." In *T. Judah* 12.2 the widowed Tamar, "decking herself out in bridal array . . . sat at the entrance of the inn in the city of Enan, for there was a law among the Amorites that a woman who was married *(gamousan)* should sit in public like a whore for seven days" (E.T. from Charlesworth, *OT Pseud.* 1.798 modified).

*abstinence.* Abstinence translates *apechesthai,* the only use of this verb in the PE though there are eighteen uses otherwise in the NT, four of which are in other Paulines (see 1 Thess 4:3; 5:22; Phil 4:18; Philem 15). Two out of the half dozen occurrences of the verb in Luke-Acts take the genitive, as it does here in 1 Tim 4:3. The genitive appears with the verb relatively more often in Ap. Frs.; thus *Did.* 1.4 (see 1 Pet 2:11) and Polycarp, *Phil.* 2.2; 6.1, 3. For Ignatius, see the exhortation in *Trall.* 6.1 to "Abstain from strange vegetable food, which is heresy," *allotrias de botanēs apechesthe hētis estin hairesis;* in *Phld.* 3.1 this becomes, "Abstain from evil growths *(apechesthe tōn kakōn botanōn),* which Jesus Christ does not tend because they are not the planting of the Father" (see his *Eph.* 10.3). When Ign. *Smyrn.* 7.1-2 uses *apechesthai,* again with the genitive, it is of staying away from those who themselves stay away from the eucharist and Christian prayer in common. The genitival object appears five times in Hermas. Forms of *apechein* appear about thirty-eight times in the LXX, but in only four instances do they govern the genitive. The closest parallels to the PE are in LXX Jer 7:10 and Wis 2:16, but they are by no means precise. More apposite are the occurrences in *T. Simeon* 2.13 and particularly *T. Asher* 2.8; 4.5.

*foods.* This translates *brōma,* again found only here in the PE but sixteen times otherwise in the NT, including nine times in Romans and First Corinthians. The two uses in Luke (never in Acts) are simply of human food (Luke 3:11; 9:13). In Ap. Frs. Ign. *Trall.* 2.3, deacons do not simply dole out food, *brōmatōn* (cited above in the Notes for 3:9; see the doubtful reading in his *Rom.* 4.1). *Barnabas* 10.9-10 uses *brōma* in discussing dietary laws. Justin, *Trypho* 20.1, picks up language from this passage when he tells his opponent that God "ordered you to abstain from certain foods *(brōmatōn tinōn apechesthai prosetaxen hymin)* so that you would keep God before your eyes when you ate and drank, for you are wont to abandon *(pros to aphistasthai)* his knowledge *(gnōseōs),* as Moses also testifies." Though the word is common enough in the LXX (perhaps seventy-two times), its rarity in the dietary laws is striking.

*created.* This verb translates *ektizein,* and does not appear otherwise in the PE. Of its remaining fourteen NT uses, nine are in the other Paulines. Several of these refer not only to the creation of all things, including the inanimate (see Rom 1:25; Eph 3:9; Col 1:16 [?]), but also to the creation of the Christian believer (see Eph 2:10, 15; 4:24), "according to the image of the one who created him." The last passage, with its citation of the *kat' eikona (theou)* of the LXX Gen 1:26, 27; 5:1, is emphatically paralleled in the OT text with "Male and female he created them" (Gen 1:27; 5:2) and followed by a blessing and command to propagate human life. In 1 Cor 11:9 it is also to the text of Gen 2:21-23 that Paul turns when he writes, "For man was not made *(ektisthē)* from woman but woman from man," with the passive periphrasis for the divine name.

The following verse uses the cognate noun, *ktisma,* "creation," which is best analyzed at this point. Like the verb, it appears only here in the PE, but there are three uses elsewhere in the NT. These refer to living creatures (of the sea in Rev 8:9) and to human and superhuman persons living in this world and the next, who believe in and worship the one true God and his Christ (Rev 5:13; James 1:18). Only Hermas among Ap. Frs. uses this noun, three times (two of them of "God's creations"), always in the plural. The verb *ktizein* is somewhat more frequent in Ap. Frs., appearing in the eucharistic prayer of *Did.* 10.3 as well as in the prayer of *1 Clem.* 60.1 (twice; 18:10 is a quotation of LXX Ps 50:12). In *2 Clem.* 14.1 the church has been created before sun and moon; in 15.2 "God created us"; in *Barn.* 16.8 Christians have been created again by God's forgiveness. Hermas favors the verb.

In the LXX *ktisma* appears half a dozen times, in Wisdom, Sirach, and 3 Macc 5:11. The verb is used over sixty times and is particularly favored by Sirach. Genesis 14:19, 22 has Melchizedek pray to him "who made *(ektise)* heaven and earth." The use of the terminology in Wis 13:3-5 is notable. The verb appears a few times in the *Testaments of the Twelve Patriarchs.* For 1 Tim 4:3 see *T. Naphtali* 2.5: "For there is no form or conception which the Lord does not know since he created *(ektise)* every human being according to his own image" (E.T. from Charlesworth, *OT Pseud.* 1.811).

*To share.* This represents the Greek *metalēmpsis,* which is not otherwise documented in the NT, Ap. Frs., or the LXX, though it is the reading in Justin, *Apology* 67.5 (10, J. Otto), and of A in Hermas, *Vis.* 4.1.3.

A simply orthographical variant with *metalēmpsis* is found in C, D[c], K, L, P, and some minuscules (J. K. Elliott, *Greek Text,* pp. 47-48). More significantly, in the surviving Latin version of the commentary of Theodore of Mopsuestia on 1 Tim 4:3 *ad fruitionem* appears, as if the text being translated were *eis apolausin.* That is in fact the Greek text of 1 Tim 6:17, which the Latin version of Theodore again renders *ad fruitionem* (see Frede, *VL* 25.641 [2]; Swete, *Theodore* 2.186 n. 6; also the eucharistic prayer of *Did.* 10.3, "We give thanks to you, holy Father . . . who created all things [*ektisas ta panta*] . . . [and] gave nourishment and drink to people for their enjoyment [*eis apolausin*], that they might give thanks to you"). There is no trace, however, of *eis apolausin* in the manuscripts of 1 Tim 4:3, and hence Theodore's presumed reading must remain of a tantalizing curiosity.

The secular uses of *metalēmpsis* designate some form of participation, concurrence (MM *s.v.* cite a marriage contract where it is synonymous with *eudokēseōs,* "willing consent"), or sharing, with no particular suggestion of sharing food. From the mid–second century in Christian circles this last sense appears to be coming to the fore.

4. *For everything in God's creation is fine. Ktisma,* "creation," has been analyzed in the verse preceding; *kalon,* "fine," at Titus 2:7, 14.

*despicable. Apoblētos* is not found elsewhere in the NT, Ap. Frs., or the LXX and is hardly found in Hellenistic Judaism. Philo once describes the Palestinian soil as "not despicable nor indifferent but good *(agathon)* . . . land" (*Spec. leg.* 2.169). The term was by no means unheard of in secular Greek. A proverbial line of Homer prescribed: *ou toi apoblēt' esti theōn erikydea dōra,* "The glorious gifts of the gods you are not to consider despicable." Simonides has a vivid example of its use when he writes that nothing that Bacchus has given is *apoblēton,* "despicable" (i.e. to be cast off), even a grape pit (quoted in Athenaeus, *Deipnosophista* 1.32 b-c as from Simonides).

*received. Lambanein* reappears in 2 Tim 1:5, "I have *(labōn)* a reminder of your unfeigned faith . . . ," but not otherwise in the PE, for all of the 258 other uses in the NT, including 32 in the other Paulines and 51 in Luke-Acts. Similarly Ap. Frs. use it at every turn and it is regular in the LXK.

*thanksgiving.* For *eucharistia* see 1 Tim 2:1.

5. *hallowed. Hagiazein* is used once more in the PE in 2 Tim 2:21, "So if a person will only purge himself of that drivel, he will be a utensil for a noble purpose — hallowed, useful to the master, ready for any excellent deed." Of the twenty-six other NT uses, seven are in the other Paulines and three in the Lukan corpus (see Comment below). In Ap. Frs. *1 Clem. inscr.* uses *hagiazein* of

the Corinthian church (alluding to 1 Cor 1:2); in 1.2 the verb appears in the citation of a document now lost that Clement apparently read as Scripture: "Cleave to the holy, for they who cleave to them shall be made holy" (Jaubert, SC 167.176 n. 1); in 59.3, in the prayer to God as Master, the author says that through Jesus Christ, "his child," God "has taught us, made us holy *(hēgiasas),* honored us."

Ignatius, *Eph.* 2.2, describes the Christians as "hallowed" in their subordination to bishop and presbytery; in 12.2 Paul himself has been "hallowed, approved, worthy of blessing"; see also the variant in *Rom. inscr.* In *Did.* 8.2 the verb appears in the Lord's Prayer, and in 10.5 in the eucharistic prayer of the church "hallowed for your kingdom." In practically all of the instances cited thus far, as well as in Hermas, *Vis.* 3.9.1, it is persons who are being *hallowed.*

*Barnabas* 15, however, uses *hagiazein* eight times in the discussion of the Sabbath commandment (see LXX Exod 20:8; Deut 5:12), and 15.6 (see 15.1) apparently takes up LXX Exod 20:11, "You shall hallow it," adding "with clean hands *(chersin katharais)* and clean heart *(kardiai katharai)*" from other OT loci (see 1 Tim 1:5; 2:8). Justin, *Trypho* 21.2, uses *hagiazein* in citing LXX Ezek 20:20 on hallowing the Sabbaths.

Forms of *hagiazein* appear regularly in the LXX. They are especially frequent in the Torah. The verb is a neologism in secular Greek, produced by addition of the factitive or causative suffix, which corresponds to the English *-fy,* to the **hagi-* root. The new word became a technical term among Jews and then among Christians for the specific holiness effected by the God of Israel (to be distinguished from the rather different holiness designated by the *hagnizein* cluster in secular Greek and in Josephus). Thus Philo, *Leg. alleg.* 1.18, wrote of God, who "blessed and hallowed the seventh day"; see also *Spec. leg.* 1.167 on the minute examination of sacrificial animals as meant to teach the one who is offering prayers and thanks that he must have "hallowed" his soul and must bring an unblemished heart before his God.

*by God's word.* For the articular *logos theou,* see Titus 2:5.

*in Scripture.* This phrase has been added to the Greek.

## ♦ COMMENT

3:14-15. *I am putting these matters in writing for you, Timothy, though I still hope to come to you before long. Still, if I do delay, this letter will let you know how a person has to behave in God's house, which is the church of the living God. [There you, Timothy, are] a pillar and pedestal for the truth.* The introduction of this piece in pause is marked by an abrupt return to dialogue between Timothy (who was last addressed in 1:18) and Paul, who continued to give directions in the first person to various groups in 2:1, 7, 8, 12, but who then vanished completely into the subject matter until this section begins. Verse 14 as a whole resumes the line of thought that began at 1:3 with "It was at my explicit encouragement while I was en route to Macedonia that you, Timothy, stayed on in Ephesus"; and, as in 1:18, an earlier dispatch from Paul to Timothy may be surfacing in these reminders. One surmises that at major transitional points the author-redactor of this letter chose this method of giving a Pauline cachet to the developing composition. Just as "This is the charge . . ." in 1:18 refers to the preceding commission that begins in 1:3, now *these matters* has reference to both preceding sections.

The unusual terminology of verses 14-15 and of this whole section alerts the reader to the possibility of a medley of sources here, arranged by the author-redactor for purposes more or less still apparent. The initial inference that the author of the PE wanted his readers to draw was that Paul wrote letters to his co-workers, a thoughtful correspondence meant seriously to be implemented. Some of the material is almost certainly his own imaginative characterization (and to this extent Donelson, *Pseudepig.*, is convincing); some may in fact go back to the last years of the Pauline apostolate (see the letter of recommendation analyzed in Titus; the fragments being proposed here and in the Comment on Second Timothy; and Introduction, p. 7); most materials come from the beliefs and practices of a church (Rome?) which claimed to have strong ties with Paul and to speak for the apostle (Introduction, pp. 21-22). The "autobiographical" character of the little note here may be a creative touch of the author of the PE; however, notes of a similar kind are typical of the Paul of history (see Rigaux, *Letters,* p. 122).

Since the mention of Paul's epistolary activity is hardly necessary for the argument at this point in the PE, or in First Timothy for that matter, and since the author has chosen the epistolary genre to bring Paul, his apostolate, and his teaching to the second Christian generation, it is reasonable to surmise that the author of the PE felt some pressure and precedent out of the Pauline tradition for adverting to the apostle's correspondence; he remembers that Paul wrote letters.

The descriptive *though I still hope to come to you before long* takes up a characteristic element in the form of the Pauline letter called, in R. Funk's happy phrase, "the *apostolic parousia* (cf 1 Cor 5.3-5)" (*Language,* p. 274, postscript; for the following, pp. 264-265, 267; and his essay "Parousia," pp. 249-268, esp. 253-254). Funk has contended that there are three simultaneously present and interrelated aspects of this parousia: the written communication itself, the one whom the apostle has sent with that communication, and behind both, the person of the apostle. In First Timothy the written communication is conceived of as catching up with the emissary who had been left behind at

Ephesus. There is, in addition, an urgent sense of the need for and the meaning of the apostle's presence in this letter to Timothy. The literary reference to the apostolic parousia had been a vital element in the Pauline correspondence, and whoever penned the PE had enough knowledge of the Pauline interests and convictions which expressed themselves in this fashion to prompt him to insert this element into this collection. Titus 3:12-14 and 2 Tim 4:6-18 place an apostolic parousia before the final greetings and after the body of the letter (as it has been transmitted). That position corresponds to Philem 22, also between the body of the letter and the final greetings. Here in First Timothy this element begins the intermezzo between the two lengthy apostolic commissions that constitute the body of this letter.

Is the apostolic parousia a merely formal convention here? With Funk one notes that the one who inserted such an element had more than a superficial knowledge of Paul. The fact that the language is, as has been seen above, both reminiscent of passages in the rest of the Paulines and yet by no means a quotation from any of them makes the use of a passage from an authentic Pauline dispatch an attractive possibility, particularly when one recalls the abrupt and even inelegant character of the insertion that introduces verses 14-15 and the textual disturbances that the awkward repetition of second person address *(soi . . . se)* and the wooden, colloquial style prompted. This note about the apostolic parousia corresponds on the whole with those Pauline passages that Funk has classified under the rubric, "Implementation of the Apostolic *Parousia*." The mention of writing, *graphein,* and its purpose, *hina,* as well as occasionally the reason for Paul's relation to the addressees, preceded the implementation rubric which, according to Funk, may have had as many as six aspects. The mention of the apostle's hope, or wish, or intention is the complement to his eager desire to come and see the churches (thus 1 Thess 2:17; 3:6; Rom 1:11), for the apostle is convinced that his personal presence is the primary means at his disposal in exercising his apostolic power and authority by an oral word. Letters and those who deliver them are, in this problematic, secondary and limited instruments of Pauline communication and direction (though their divine authority cannot be trimmed back, 1 Cor 14:37-38; *pace* R. Funk, "Parousia," p. 260; see Dodd, *More NT,* p. 143). The apostle takes for granted that his personal, physical presence brings the presence of the Spirit and his power (1 Cor 2:1-4; Rom 15:18-19).

*Before long* reminds the reader of a similar usage in another apostolic parousia passage, Heb 13:23: "Know that our brother Timothy has been released, with whom I shall see you if he comes soon *(tachion).*" The advertence to the immediacy of the visit may also pertain to the form, as the uses of *tachion, tacheōs* (1 Cor 4:19; Phil 2:19, 24), *tachy* (Rev 2:16; 3:11!), and *eutheōs* (3 John 14) indicate. When even *First Clement* concludes with *en tachei* and *eis to tachion* (65.1), the reader encounters muted but still recognizable echoes of the Pauline form. See also White, *Body*, p. 50, for *to tachy* and *speudō* in the papyri, as well as MM, p. 627.

If White, *Body*, pp. 41-46, is correct, one may also encounter here in 1 Tim 3:14-15 one of the standard epistolary formulae that grew up around the body of the Greek letter. The language of these verses is that of the "body-closing" in the set phrases that characterize what White calls a "disclosure formula." The example from the letter in P. Mert. 80 (second century C.E.) deserves citation: *dio graphō soi hin' eidēs sy ei ti deon esti ti praxēs* . . . , "So I am writing to you in order that you may know, if there is anything necessary, what you are to do. . . ." Such more or less set phrases (if they are not full-fledged formulae) correspond to the body opening, though the latter looks forward to the matters that will be written whereas the closing takes the opposite perspective. The phrases or formulae address themselves to the motivation for writing, *dio graphō soi hin' eidēis,* "Wherefore I am writing to you that you may know" (P. Mich. 512.6; early third century C.E.). The information that has been put into writing frequently issues in "expressions urging responsibility." That part of the disclosure formula finds expression in *how a person has to behave in God's house* in verse 15.

This formal analysis of verses 14-15 reveals a combination of two elements, the apostolic parousia of l4b-15a enveloped within the disclosure formula of 14a, 15b, which shades off into a description of the obligation of leading a life befitting God's family, i.e. the church. The awkward *Still, if I do delay, ean de bradynō,* is again just the sort of unpolished afterthought that is appropriate to a hurried, personal correspondence. If it is in fact the redactor's insertion, then it may be motivated by the slippage between the Pauline prophecy remembered in Acts 20:25, 38, that the presbyter-bishops of Ephesus would not see the apostle's face again. The phrase would then mean that the redactor did not understand 1 Tim 1:3 to mean that Paul himself had been at Ephesus when he ordered Timothy to stay there. In any case, the allusion to a possible delay of or hindrance to the apostolic parousia is one of the aspects of the implementation of that presence (see Rom 1:13; 15:22; 1 Thess 2:18; even 1 Cor 16:7-9).

*this letter will let you know how a person has (dei) to behave.* Because in the PE *dei* is reserved for observations on apostolic ministries (see 2 Tim 2:6, 24), the reader infers that here the subject of the infinitive following this impersonal verb is the persons who share the Pauline ministry, including Timothy but not Timothy alone. The scribal additions of *se* narrow the focus to Timothy and, in so doing, settle the reference of *a pillar and pedestal for the truth* at the end of the verse. The interpreter thus still has the option of taking the text in a more inclusive sense. In fact, the balance of probabilities inclines in that direction, for this author has certainly not been reluctant pleonastically to repeat the singular address here *(soi . . . pros se . . . eidēis)*. Accordingly, when it does not appear, one infers that the author understood *how a person has to behave* as including all those ministers mentioned in 1 Tim 3, along with Timothy. It is conceivable that the conduct of all believers is in mind at this point (thus Spicq), though even the cognate *anastrophē* in 1 Tim 4:12 refers to the exemplary behavior that ought to characterize Timothy's ministry.

*In God's house* defines the sphere within which the desirable behavior or conduct of the Pauline minister is to occur, a house that is not to be taken simply materially, even of a material temple, but which is to be understood of a household or family, which is synonymous with *the church of the living God.* The language by and large has distinctly Jewish and Septuagintal overtones. The imagery of household or home that has been used to illustrate and inculcate the virtuous qualities needed for ecclesial ministry has been enriched and deepened by an appeal to what belongs specifically to *God's* household. The line of development is Pauline, as Eph 2:19-22 illustrates with different terminology, describing believers (thus the community) first as "members of God's household," *oikeioi tou theou* (see also Gal 6:10, *tous oikeious tēs pisteōs*), then as built "into a holy sanctuary *(naon hagion)* in the Lord" (see 1 Cor 3:16-17; 6:19; 2 Cor 6:16), and finally as "God's dwelling place *(katoikētērion tou theou)* in the Spirit." This is a family which has God as Father, whose house is "a house of prayer," *oikos proseuchēs* (LXX Isa 56:7). The implication is that the proper and primary business of *God's house* is also that of *the church of the living God,* i.e. the prayer of the believing community. Such was the burden of 1 Tim 2; and now the qualifications for those who are going to minister to the worshipping community (3:1-13) are proposed as conduct or behavior that ought to characterize their lives as Pauline ministers who preside, perhaps as a body, at Christian liturgies.

Can the exegete settle the question about where the primary accent falls when this text speaks of *God's house?* Is the emphasis first upon the meeting place or upon the persons who are meeting? Both Semitic and Hellenistic culture used the terminology of a *house* for a building, for a family, even for a religious association (see the inscriptions cited by O. Michel, *TDNT* 5.128 n. 33; also H. A. Hoffner, *TDOT* 2.111-113). The Essenes who composed the Damascus Document were convinced that God had built them "a sure house *(byt n'mn)* in Israel" (CD 3.19), and they twice called their community "the house of the Torah" (CD 20.10, 13). The Qumran rule describes its followers as "the house of truth *(h'mt)* in Israel" (1QS 5.6), "the house of holiness for Israel/for Aaron" (1QS 8.5; 9.6), and "the house of community *(yhd)* for Israel" (1QS 9.6).

Perhaps the person/place antithesis that divides the commentators ought to be resolved in terms of the sign and the signified, each of which has primacy in its own order. All the previous usage in the PE suggests that the actual, individual believers constitute *God's house* or family. This concrete assembly of Christians with God as their Father is the sign of a divine, spiritual house or temple within which the one God is truly worshipped and loved. This protosacramental conception of *God's house* is parallel with the similar conception of God's kingdom. Both have a visible existence and manifestation in the assembly of actual human believers. Their origin as a family depends totally upon the free and antecedent choice and love of the Father. Their reign and goal are not of this world order either (on God as king in the PE, see 1 Tim 1:17; 6:15; on the kingdom, 2 Tim 4:1, 18). In the PE God is the Father who gives life to his family, the church, the congregation of believers, in which he is truly known by faith and which he has called into existence and sustains.

*God's house,* understood in this fashion, can be described further as *the church of the living God.* Just as the *oikos* as sign was the actual, local assembly of believers, that same local assembly could be called *God's church* (as in 3:5 above). But as the local household of the one Father was the sign and revelation of a reality that exists properly and ultimately in the divine order itself, so the local church bodies forth a church which belongs to *the living God* and reveals something of the way in which he is present at all times and in every place. *The living God* is a descriptive phrase that suggests worship of the God of Israel in contrast to that of the dead images of pagan deities. Of all the so-called gods, Yahweh alone actually lives and thus can give life to and protect it in others. Thus *the church of the living God,* in this passage of First Timothy, suggests an assembly who derive their life from the one true God of Israel, who believe in him and worship him as the Father of the Christian family (in contrast to the many false gods of paganism and their lifeless idols; see LXX Dan 14:5-6, 24-25 [NAB]). A polemic note against the temple of Artemis and her cult image which dominated the religion and life of ancient Ephesus has been detected by Spicq. Believers belong to *the church of the living God* as pagans belong to an *ekklēsia* dominated by the lifeless images of Artemis (see the inscription cited in the Comment on 3:5 above). As *God's house* connoted the Christian family as a worshipping entity, so *the church of the living God* implies a church at prayer.

The final phrase of this verse, *stylos kai hedraiōma tēs alētheias,* "a pillar and pedestal for the truth" in the translation here, poses many problems for the exegete, most of which go back, in one fashion or another, to the question, to what or whom does the phrase refer? A few have proposed a reference to the preceding *theou,* but considerations of Greek grammar alone dissolve the desired apposition. Others, beginning with Irenaeus, *Adversus haereses* 3.11.8; SC 211.20, make the gospel and the Spirit the *stylos de kai stērigma* of the church; in Irenaeus, *Adversus haereses* 4.21.3; SC 100.682, the sons of Jacob are the *duodecastylum firmamentum* of the Church. Most interpreters have understood a reference to the *ekklēsia* in the *stylos* of 1 Tim 3:15 and thus *the church of the living God,* his *house,* is *a pillar and pedestal for the truth.* Yet from the days of the Greek Fathers to the present (see Jaubert, "Image," pp. 101-108, for references and also for the argument below), a respectable party of exegetes have contended that the reference is to the unexpressed subject of the verb *eidēis,* i.e. to Timothy himself. The reference is not to the indefinite subject of the infinitive *anastrēphesthai,* for in that case the appositive phrase ought to be construed as an accusative. The choice between a reference to *Timothy* or to the *church* is not eased by one's observing that the reference to the latter is the more obvious in Greek and that the architectural imagery fits the house imagery of the clause, because the figure of the *pillar* was applied through the first Christian century to individuals but not to groups as such (see Jaubert, "Image," pp. 103-104).

The case for referring *a pillar and pedestal* to Timothy finds additional support in Qumran composition (see Jaubert, "Image," pp. 103-104, and Murphy-O'Connor, *PQ,* pp. 219-230). Not only are the members of the Dead Sea sect "to lay a foundation of truth *(mwsd 'mt)* for Israel to make a community of an eternal covenant" (1QS 5.5; E.T. with comment by A. R. C. Leaney, *RQM,* pp. 161, 167), but the legitimate teacher is described in a hymnic composition as "the foundation of the truth," *swd 'mt* (1QH 2.10; perhaps 5.9, 26), precisely "because his role as mediator of revelation demands that he exercise ceaseless vigilance to prevent its contamination by heterodox teaching" (Murphy-O'Connor, *PQ,* p. 229; see Muszynski, *Fundament aus Qumran,* pp. 124-125, 222-223, 232, and below on *themelios* in 2 Tim 2:19). The Septuagintal use of *stylos* would bear out this individual, personal interpretation. Thus Sir 24:4, 36:24, especially the latter, would suggest that *the truth* finds its support in Timothy in the way God's wisdom was enthroned on the fiery pillar or in the way that a husband finds "a pillar of rest," *anapauseōs,* in his wife who has just been called his "helper," *boēthos.* In 4 Macc 17:3 the mother is set like "a roof on the pillars" of her martyr sons. Timothy, as Paul's aide in these letters, is also someone for the apostle to lean on, though he is not simply a human support. *The truth* rests on him, in the sense in which the PE use that term of the Christian revelation, the faith, the gospel of Christ Jesus himself.

The terms constituting the phrase *stylos kai hedraiōma* can be further analyzed. Greek speaks more often of *kiōn* than *stylos,* but the LXX uses the former only four times. *Stylos* usually translates the Hebrew *'md.* Thus far the Qumran texts have produced few examples of the half dozen Hebrew terms that the LXX translates with *stylos* or *kiōn* (and when 3Q 15.6.1, DJD 3.290, and 1QM 5.10 use *'mwd,* it is for a thing, not a person).

*Stylos* has a broad, architectural significance in the ancient world. A column could be set up not only to carry a roof but also (rather less often) to stand free as part of a votive (as distinguished from a funerary or simply honorary) offering, topped by a bronze bowl, image, tripod, or the like. In the ancient Near East the pillar was conceived often enough as a god's pedestal. Some of the difficulty with sorting out the meaning of the *pillar* for the ancients is that there were, even in the Jerusalem temple precinct, freestanding columns at the entrance of the sanctuary building (see LXX 3 Kgdms 7:15-22; Albright, *ARI*, pp. 144, 147; R. B. Y. Scott, *IDB* 2.780-781, *pace* J. Ouellette, *IDBSup*, p. 469). They were almost thirty feet high and probably functioned (as did others in the Near East) as platforms for cressets or fire-baskets in which incense was burned. They were named Jachin and Boaz, probably after the initial words of the royal dynastic oracles which were inscribed on them.

In Greece in the classical period, as L. Vogel points out (*Column*, p. 24, whose study and notes have been used often in this exposition), such columns began to be topped with the donor's statue. They were always put up "within sacred precincts." The use of columns for burial markers is not germane to this passage in the Pastorals, but their use to honor some persons worthy of being raised above others is noteworthy. The honorary column became a typically Roman way of using the freestanding pillar and was considered appropriate for acknowledging a victory gained in battle. Already in Ennius one reads: *Quantam statuam faciet populus Romanus, quantam columnam quae res tuas gestas loquatur*, "What a statue will the Roman people make, what a column to tell your achievements?" (supposedly said of Scipio; the reconstruction is based on *Scriptores Historiae Augusti: Claudius* 7.6, in Warmington, *Remains of Old Latin*, LCL 1.398). The reverse of a Roman denarius shows a small column that was put up in the Roman Forum, commemorating Octavius's victory over Antony at Actium (Nicopolis; see Brilliant, *Art*, pp. 126-127). For the altar and victory columns dedicated in 12 B.C.E. in honor of Augustus at Lyons, see Fishwick, "Ruler Worship," pp. 1204-1206, with plates. Josephus quotes a decree of Augustus favoring the Asian Jews that was engraved on a column in his own temple (*Ant.* 16.165). The elder Pliny, after discussing the erection of statues in Rome, asserts: "The reason for pillars was that statues of people be raised above their fellow mortals. The new discovery of the arch conveys this meaning too. Still the honor first *(primus tamen honos)* began with the Greeks" (*NH* 34.21-27). As Brilliant puts it, "[T]he Greeks were the first to use the independent column to commemorate a glorious achievement or to elevate the emblem of a city in a crowded place, but the Romans turned this simple device into a symbolic image in the service of proud victors," whose purpose is "to present the heroic conqueror as a person of extraordinary distinction, separated from lesser men by the splendour of his deeds" (*Art*, pp. 126, 128). In 113 C.E. Trajan's 100-foot column in Rome, with his gilt bronze statue on top, gave visible definition to Pliny's words of perhaps thirty-five years before. This awesome pillar has outlasted the man whom it was built to honor; now a statue of the apostle Peter stands where that of Trajan once did (see vol. 35, plate 3, and Rossi, *Column,* pp. 12-14). Both illustrate the point, now being made from the Roman world and its literature, that a column honors a person, represents an individual, whose achievements and victories have benefited the people as a whole.

The pillar was used in the old Roman world as a place upon which to inscribe a record of decrees, laws, treaties, public agreements, even a ruler's acts and achievements (see Suicerus below). In the ancient world the reading of a funerary inscription aloud "was thought of thus giving to the dead man a momentary animation" (Nock, *ERAW* 1.358). Thus Augustus in his will provided that his *Res gestae* be written "on bronze columns," *es chalkas stelas,* to be put up around his shrine (Dio Cassius, *Roman History* 56.33.1; in the Ankara inscription they are described as *rerum gestarum divi Augusti . . . incisarum ahenis pilis quae sunt Romae positae,* Volkmann, *Res Gestae,* p. 10). Timothy is conceived of as such a pillar, and the unique reference to Paul's writing finds an explanation in the figure to be used of his co-worker who stands in the Ephesian assembly bearing this Pauline correspondence, the *res gestae divi Pauli,* as did the well-known imperial monuments of Rome. In the ambient Roman view, Timothy is like a freestanding, honorary, victory column, erected in the sanctuary area but not necessarily as part of the sacred building itself. The *pillar* figure accordingly emphasizes the way in which the apostle's co-worker has brought guidance and protection to believers' assembly for worship.

When James, Cephas, and John are called "pillars" of the Jerusalem church, the imagery has shifted a little in the direction of a heavenly sanctuary whose roof is carried by its pillars (see the cautions in Betz, *Gal.,* pp. 99-100 n. 404). However, the use of *pillar* in the singular in 1 Tim 3:15 shows no deep continuity with the *oikos/ekklēsia* language with its emphasis on a group, as such, of people. In the ancient notices, the group is not a *pillar,* even though individuals within it may be so designated. The primary emphasis remains upon the importance of the individual persons, as it still does in Revelation and *First Clement.* In this problematic, when Timothy is called *a pillar for the truth* he is thought of as somehow bearing aloft and honoring that *truth.* Or, in the biblical tradition, he functions as a fiery pillar honoring Yahweh as he brings God's presence and direction to his people.

The neologism *hedraïōma,* "pedestal" in this version, is linked with the **sedrai-* terminology of the LXX, which tends to cluster around the image of the throne of God, immovably fixed. Thus note, with E. Stauffer, *TDNT* 2.362-364, the variant of LXX 3 Kgdms 8:13, *hedrasma tēs kathedras tou aiōnas,* "a seat for the everlasting throne" (see A. T. Hanson, *Studies,* pp. 6-7, for *hedrasma* = *firmamentum* = foundation). The *stylos* imagery would be consistent with speaking now of the base on which the *pillar* is fixed, the stylobate on which a column has its immovable seat (J. C. Suicerus, *s.v.* "*stylos,*" *Thesaurus ecclesiasticus* [2nd ed., Amsterdam: Wetstenias, 1728], col. 1056 [see 1049-1050]). The coinage would have been dictated not only by the desire to avoid the repetition in *stylos kai stylobatēs* but also to accent the stable permanence which Timothy brought to his role as *a pillar,* bearing aloft *the truth.* The Old Latin *firmamentum, stabilimentum,* even *fundamentum,* may have suggested the base for a pillar (see Frede, *VL* 25.511; J. Caesar, *Bellum civile* 2.15.2). The neologism is enough like the Septuagintal terminology connected with the divine throne to make it sound appropriate; it is different enough to distinguish the function here from that of a fixed foundation for God's throne in his sanctuary. A distinction is also made from the *stereos themelios tou theou,* "God's solid foundation," of 2 Tim 2:19 (see *oikia* in 2:20). At 1 Tim 3:15 the author apparently wanted to avoid linking *hedraiōma* with the preceding *oikos.*

On analysis, the imagery of this phrase is distinct from that of the *oikos/ekklēsia* that preceded, and yet it is also consistent with it. Timothy stands within the sacred precinct, the space for worship, like *a pillar,* displaying the revelation for all who come and go while remaining fixed and stable himself. The worshippers are in their turn the throng, the living house, the *ekklēsia,* within whom the God of Israel makes his house, from whom he receives true worship, to whom he gives life as the living God.

Both Suicerus and Jaubert, "Image," pp. 105-107, have gathered ancient patristic texts that understood *a pillar and pedestal* of an individual rather than of the church. The earliest (see Notes) is from the letter of the martyrs at Lyons. Particularly notable is Gregory of Nyssa, *Vita Moysis* 2.184; SC 1.228-230: "And again the divine Apostle bids others to be pillars, saying, *Be steadfast and unmovable.* And he made Timothy into an excellent pillar *(kalon stylon)* when he made him (as he says in his own words) *a pillar and ground of truth*" (E.T. from Malherbe and Ferguson, *Gregory Moses,* p. 101). In Cyril of Alexandria's *Commentary on Zechariah* 91 (*PG* 72.216c), *stylon de kai hedraiōma* refers to Christ, a reminder of how late it was before this particular terminology began to be used christologically (see Gaston, *Stone,* p. 197).

This vexed phrase has been given an ecclesial interpretation since Origen, an interpretation admirably articulated by Spicq, who stresses the building and communitarian imagery of the verse as a whole. The Qumran sectaries used the foundation imagery for their congregation (see Gärtner, *Temple,* esp. pp. 66-70). Still one must admit with A. T. Hanson, *Studies,* p. 17, that no evidence is at hand for the Hebrew terminology being translated with the **hedrai-* cluster of terms. This would have to be said even of the *twr* in the Copper Scroll, 3Q 15.7.15; DJD 3.291, which means something built secondarily for supporting or sustaining the main structure (thus, here a retaining wall; see DJD 3.277 §95).

16. *And great is the mystery of godliness. There is no denying it! . . . He who*

*was revealed in human flesh, was made victorious in the Spirit: he who was seen by God's messengers, was heralded to the pagans: he who was received in faith, in the world, was taken up in glory.* The first part of this verse introduces one of the most attractive texts in the PE, a gem from the treasury of first-century Christian liturgy which has many facets to its surface and fires within it. The introduction is sonorous and stately.

Only here and at 5:7 below do the PE begin a sentence simply with the adverbial *kai* (Spicq, *Lexic.*, p. 622 n. 2), as distinguished from the *kai . . . de* of 3:10 above and 2 Tim 3:12. That this trick of style was not altogether expected here may already be witnessed by the peculiar Irenaean reading of this opening phrase with the last phrase of the preceding verse. The sense here (as well as again in 5:7) is practically equivalent to opening parentheses for the emphatic observation that follows. Though this version has opted for the effect created by an abrupt, opening *and,* Spicq has contended that the meaning is "certainly/really."

The introduction, properly speaking, to the hymn begins in Greek with *homologoumenos,* "There is no denying it!" part of what Hanson has called "An Academic Phrase" (*Studies,* pp. 21-28) which the author of PE introduced here from the Stoic moral philosophy of Fourth Maccabees, which he had read and admired (*pace* O. Michel, *TDNT* 5.213 n. 41). The Bible of this author was an LXX collection; questions of canon belong to a later age. The emphasis, in any case, of Fourth Maccabees is unmistakable. Since the aged Eleazar "despised torments unto the death on account of his godliness, we must admit that godly reason is leader over the passions" (7:16); before the mother of the Maccabean martyrs "we must concede that godly reason is sovereign over the passions" (16:1); the subject of the whole treatise is, "Confessedly then, godly reason is master of the passions" (6:31; E.T. from Charlesworth, *OT Pseud.* 2.552-553, 561 modified). Since the PE value godliness highly, the influence of Fourth Maccabees upon this correspondence is probably more than terminological. Yet, with R. B. Townshend in Charles, *AP* 2.666, one recalls that Fourth Maccabees is a Jewish work in which reason, *logismos,* has been pulled out of Epicurean or Stoic orbit (and the sense of *homologoumenōs* there is not strong; Strange, *1 Tim 3:16,* pp. 32-33), and pulled along after a devout Jewish definition of godliness, *eusebeia,* which was nothing less than a wholehearted adherence to revelation, the Torah, a combination of orthodoxy and orthopraxy which in the ultimate analysis had little to do with philosophy as the Hellenistic world conceived it. In the PE, as in Fourth Maccabees, godliness is not simply a virtue in the Greek sense, though *aretē* has a complex development of meaning (see Spicq, "*Aretē,*" pp. 161-176, esp. p. 174 n. 74) The Torah reveals and teaches the truly godly life (see 4 Macc 1:16-17; 5:17-26; etc.), and for 2 Tim 3:4 *eusebeia* without its *dynamis* is no godliness at all.

In the third Christian century the *Letter to Diognetus* makes substantially the same point when it asserts that "the distinction between Christians and other people is neither in country nor language nor customs . . . yet while living in Greek and barbarian cities . . . and following the local customs in clothing and food and in the rest of livelihood *(bioi),* they show the wonderful and — there is no denying it, *homologoumenōs* — strange character of the constitution of their own citizenship" (5.4).

Similarly, there is *no denying* that *the mystery of godliness* about to be expressed in the latter half of this verse is *great.* The apocalyptic adjective (see Titus 2:13) suggests that *the mystery* involves an eschatological theophany. Belief in this calls forth the behavior that must characterize those who serve God's family, his church. Some have accented the verbal links of *homologoumenōs* with the *homologein* cluster which was often used to confess the Christian faith (including a definite content); thus Neufeld, *Confessions,* pp. 128-133; Strange, *1 Tim 3:16,* pp. 35-38 (this latter work with bibliography to 1970 has been used so often in the following pages that formal citations have been omitted). The rhetorical and juridical connotations of this adverb have been traced by Spicq, *Lexic.,* pp. 621-622. The latter appear particularly in the business papyri, where the *homologein* cluster is a feature of contracts and especially as an answer to the formal question whether one accepted the agreement in question. *Eperōtētheis hōmologēsa,* "The question having been put, I accept the terms," is a contractual formula (see Barclay, "Papyri," pp. 77-78) found even in a deed of adoption. Thus *homologoumenōs* may have here connotations of formal acceptance of a relationship, a new covenant, which God has offered in the person and work of Jesus Christ (see 2 Tim 2:11-13).

Very evocative is the appearance of *homologoumenōs* in a sentence about "Zeus, the greatest *(megistos)* of the gods, *there is no denying it*" (thus the fourth-century-B.C.E. writer of Greek comedy Diodorus of Sinope, as quoted by Athenaeus, *Deipnosophistai* 6.239b). Recalling the acclamation *megalē hē Artemis Ephesiōn* (Acts 19:28, 34) and the frequent use of *mega* in affirmations of divinity, the use of *homologoumenōs* appears to be particularly apt. It is not chosen simply for its elegant, academic sound (though A. T. Hanson, *Studies,* p. 22, contends otherwise for Fourth Maccabees). In the Maccabean essay as well as here in 1 Tim 3:16a the authors are pointing up not a philosophical truth but a revealed one (note *a pillar and pedestal for the truth* in the preceding verse). *The mystery* of the Judeo-Christian faith is at stake here, a truth that is beyond controversy, and thus the somewhat adversative nuance to the adverb here.

The formulation here verges on the polemic as it confronts the Artemision (Acts 19:27), one of the wonders of the ancient world, with *God's house, the church of the living God,* and as it confesses *great is the mystery of godliness* against the chorus of *megalē hē Artemis Ephesiōn.* Yet there ought not to be a dominant emphasis on this aspect. Ephesians 5:32 describes the way in which the Scripture teaches about the relation of Christ with the church in terms of the relation of a husband to his wife by saying *to mystērion touto mega estin,* "This is a great mystery." The Christians in Ephesus had heard a Pauline phrase about a great mystery previous to First Timothy (and regardless of the original, perhaps "circular," character of the letter now called "To the Ephesians"). The phrase already suggested divinity and apocalyptic images. The church was the spotless bride of the kingdom to come (cf. Eph 5:27 with Rev 21:2), as here in the PE the glory of Jesus is the warrant and ground for the great *mystery* whose consummation is still awaited.

The *mystery* here is one *of godliness,* i.e. authentic religion, as in 3:9 above it was "of the faith." Its intelligible content is verbalized but not in a scientific theological form. Rather, to anticipate what will be seen at length below, the liturgical and hymnic character of the following confession reminds the reader that it is not the creative synthesis of an individual theologian that one encounters here. Rather, one hears a community or an order within it singing out its belief in public worship. The noblest act of the church, its faith in and love of God, is cited here in the form in which it has been verbalized and chanted, originally perhaps by one of the prophetic cadre, later by the congregation, perhaps alternating stichs or stanzas (1 Cor 14:26; Pliny to Trajan, cited below; see Delling, *Worship,* p. 86; Hengel, *BJP,* pp. 78-79; Quasten, *Music,* pp. 66-72). The monophonic musical setting and even the specific liturgical action have irretrievably vanished. The modern reader is left holding one leaf of the libretto of an otherwise utterly lost opera. One only surmises the size of the lion from the claw. A veritable library of special studies has been generated by this text. To the materials in J. F. Strange, add Gundry, "Hymn"; Stenger, *Christushymnus;* W. Metzger, *Christushymnus.*

The following formal and philological analysis of 3:16b contends that a quotation has begun *in medias res* with the relative pronoun *hos,* whose masculine antecedent stood in the line(s) omitted. That the lines beginning with *hos* are indeed a quotation has been suggested since the early nineteenth century on the basis of the introductory formula and the discordant *hos,* as well as such internal characteristics as the simply patterned, carefully paralleled, rhythmically composed sentences which appear in 16b. Moreover, the terminology and the meanings which the words bear do not occur or do not coincide on a regular basis with their meaning in the rest of the PE.

Can the formal character or *Gattung* of 16b be specified further? Answers to the question take three basic lines. Most call the composition a hymn; a smaller number have contended for a creedal form; some have combined these and speak of a "creedal hymn" (Falconer, *PE,* p. 138; see also Bousset, *Kyrios,* E.T. p. 300; Delling, *Worship,* p. 88; rejected by Deichgräber, *Gotteshymnus,* p. 133 n. 3).

The poetic character of the source is already signaled by several internal characteristics. On the hypothesis that the quotation in 16b is hymnic in form, James Strange has compiled a list of six formal criteria (as distinguished from those based on content) which are useful for identifying NT hymnic material (see also Barth, "Traditions," p. 10). Applied to verse 16b, they are as follows. First, the opening *hos* of the citation intersects partially with the "relative and participial style" that has characterized at least some of the ancient texts that have been called hymns. Second, the parallelism of the members here is also characteristic of the hymns of the Hellenistic world. This parallelism is worked out antithetically between the concluding nouns of each pair of lines. In this connection, the fivefold repetition of *en* calls for special consideration, since it is missing from the third stich, though the sixfold pattern of an aorist passive verb followed by a noun in the dative remains constant (see Murphy-O'Connor, "Angels," pp. 178-187 below). Third, there is a rhythm based on two stresses per line here, but it is not measurable in the quantitative classical meters and has no particular pattern in the distribution of the unstressed syllables (the second line has seven; the third, three). Fourth, various rhetorical devices such as assonance, homoioteleuton (the six-times-repeated *-the;* see BDF §488.3; Moule, *Idiom,* p. 199), and chiasm (two singular nouns followed by two plural and finally by two singular with the lost stanza containing the "missing" part) are marks of hymnic compositions. Fifth, the third person singular style (along with the first person plural) is a mark of hymnic compositions. Sixth, the reportorial narrative form, employing verbs for declaring the acts of God (as distinct from a proclamation description by means of nouns and adjectives used as titles), is perhaps also characteristic of hymnic composition (for this distinction, see C. Westermann, *Praise,* pp. 31-32, 55-57, 81-90, etc.).

There is a surplus of data that resist the application of these criteria, as James Strange has observed. Thus the so-called relative style (which has also been proposed as a criterion for the confession or the creed) is not a regular characteristic of Hellenistic Greek hymns (see OxyP 15.21; §1786; the hymn to Christ the Educator, Clement of Alexandria, *Paed.* 3.12; the fragment of a liturgical hymn cited in Testuz, *Bodmer X-XII,* p. 76); the parallelism in form found in verse 16b is hard to document in Greek models; the rhythmic patterns are not characteristic of Hellenistic hymnic composition; and other compositional techniques, characteristic of hymnic poetry, are neither plentiful nor at times even in standard form (chiasm of concepts rather than of terms). Attempts to explain the passage in terms of rhythmic prose (E. Norden) and in terms of the rules of Greek rhetorical composition have not produced conviction (see Strange, *1 Tim 3:16,* pp. 55-62). Are there influences from outside the Greek tradition at work here? Or is it that verse l6b does not belong to the hymnic *Gattung?*

The confession, or more narrowly the creedal form, has been suggested (see below, Schweizer, "Creeds") as more appropriate because of the problems just listed. Yet the formal criteria proposed for isolating a confession coincide in no small part with those for the hymn (as Strange observes). Thus the contextual dislocation, the vocabulary peculiar to the passage, the relative or participial style, and the rhythmic style that can be arranged in strophes are notable. Even the positioning of the verb at the beginning of each stich, often found in creedal materials (see Ign. *Trall.* 9.1-2; Schoedel, *Ignatius,* pp. 152-155), belongs rather to the influence of Jewish prayer forms, public and private (on which see J. M. Robinson below), than to a Greek creedal *Gattung* as such.

If that in fact is a clue to a Jewish and even a Palestinian milieu for the origin of the creedal form, several problems may be closer to solution. Christian creeds, in Aramaic, even in Hebrew, perhaps antedated specifically Christian hymns. The latter could have been an attempt of Hellenistic congregations, of Jewish or Gentile origin, to translate and adapt the Palestinian Jewish Christian creedal compositions from a Semitic language.

Granted that verse 16b does not fit snugly into either the hymnic or creedal form, the suggestion of a mixed form of composition issuing into a confessional hymn has appeared to be feasible. The case for this can draw support from J. M. Robinson, "Hodayot-formel," pp. 194-235, who has isolated a strand of literary development from the OT psalms through the formulaic opening of the Qumran *hodayot* (*'wdk 'dwny ky*[']; 1QH passim) into the most archaic Christian prayer texts where the Greek translation of the Hebrew *ydh* bifurcates into either *exomologoumai* or *eucharistō* (as was already the case in the LXX Psalms). The famous Q prayer, the thunderbolt from the Johannine sky, of Matt 11:25 = Luke 10:21 (*SFG* §109) opens with this formula (see Rev 11:17-18 and, less appositely, 1 Tim 1:12). The archaic Christian prayers of thanksgiving expanded into hymns, according to Robinson, under the pressure generated by the enthusiasm of the archaic worship. The directives of 1 Cor 12–14 and of the church order that has preceded this intermezzo in First Timothy are representative of ongoing attempts of the apostolic ministry to bring law and order into a public worship that had admitted in principle spontaneous sung prayer and prophetic exhortation by individuals (see 1 Cor 14:26) alongside the more traditional Jewish singing of the Psalms, reading of the OT, and teaching (see 4:13-14 below and Acts 16:25). This development reached its climax in hymns of thanksgiving quite independent of the more ancient confessional prayer formulae. Independence exacted its toll. The new crops of hymns were no longer hardy perennials but mere annuals.

The content of the Psalms and the Qumran *hodayot* had been, above all, what Yahweh had done for his people, how he had acted in their history, communal and individual. The first-generation Jewish Christians took up the ancient forms and infused a new content, what God had done for them in the act of Jesus the Lord. They sang a "new song" (Rev 5:9; 14:3; Eusebius, *Church History* 5.28.5, quotes an anonymous Christian of about 200 C.E. who wrote, "For who does not know . . . all the psalms or songs [*psalmoi, ōidai*] written from the beginning by faithful brethren, which celebrate the Word of God, even Christ, and speak of him as God?"; Clement of Alexandria, *Protrepticus* 1.4-5, cites Titus 3:3-5 in his comparison of "the new song" of the Christians with the old tunes and songs of paganism, whose music and instruments Christians abhorred; see Quasten, *Music*, pp. 59-62; Delling, *Worship*, p. 87). Their thanksgiving prayers for this act of God were, by reason of this specific content, confessions of their faith as Christians. The form, because it was psalmic and thus a spin-off from the liturgical worship of Judaism, naturally tended to develop in the direction of hymnody in the Greek world. The content, basically christological and a very archaic Christology at that, acted centripetally, so to speak, and kept pulling the form back into a line around itself rather than letting it spin off tangentially.

It is conceivable that both 1 Cor 15:3-5 and 1 Tim 3:16b are archaic creeds (Schweizer, "Creeds," pp. 166-177). Furthermore, if both go back to archaic Palestinian Christian formulations in a Semitic language, one may be meeting here in the PE as well as in First Corinthians two different specimens of confessions of faith that were formulated within the first decade or two of the emergence of the Jerusalem church. The "creed" cited in First Corinthians is far more prosaic than that in 1 Tim 3:16b, which, as is noted above, has more hymnic characteristics.

One cannot establish on principle that prose must chronologically precede poetry, that recitation must precede singing, or that sober listing must precede enthusiastic thanksgiving. Indeed, the history of the emergence of artistic composition in a given culture inclines one to opt for the opposite order (see Albright, *Analogy*, pp. 61-62). In any case, the question of chronological priority simply cannot be resolved on principle but only on factual data.

Another possibility ought to be entertained also for the origin of the creedal texts of First Corinthians and 1 Tim 3:16b. The latter text may document an enthusiastic worship of Jesus as Lord, composed for believing Jews, chanted by them. Perhaps it even began with a pair of confessional stichs (reconstructed below) extolling Jesus as God's Son. In that case, the prosaic and sober articulation of the resurrection faith in 1 Cor 15:3-5 would have been fashioned for a different audience in Jerusalem, i.e. for still-unbelieving (though not necessarily ill-disposed) Jews. If indeed this distinction in audiences lies behind these texts transmitted in the Pauline epistolary, then apparently firm criteria for their relative priority become unfixed.

The same person who composes a song or poem for his beloved can produce a dry legal instrument, a marriage license, and the one neither demands nor precludes the other. An unbelieving and cynical world tends to put more stock in the latter. Justices of the peace are reluctant to accept sonnets in lieu of a license. The beloved may not share their viewpoint. Both compositions have their uses, even in situations quite far removed from those that originally produced them. The case is not much different with these texts from the Pauline tradition. Both are now part of the *didachē,* the further formation of the baptized, which prompted the Pauline letters in the first place as well as their preservation and continued influence after Paul's death. The original purpose of the creed of 1 Cor 15:3-5 was kerygmatic, i.e. the proclamation, the kerygma, of the gospel to those who had not yet believed. First Timothy 3:16 was never anything but a believer's confessional, hymnic prayer about Christ, his Lord. On this analysis (*pace* Schweizer, "Creeds," p. 172), it is difficult to justify the creedal confession of 1 Cor 15:3-5 having been occasioned by and directed to a specifically Jewish, even Palestinian problem ("How shall I get rid of my sins?"), whereas the hymnic creed of First Timothy answered a Hellenistic query from outside of Palestine ("How may I be freed from the powers of blind fate, from necessity? How may I obtain access to the heavenly divine world?"). From a geographical point of view, both questions are Jewish and Palestinian as well as Hellenistic. The Qumran texts illustrate this point, particularly the apocalyptic compositions (see Dupont-Sommer, *EWQ,* p. 98 n. 6, as well as Hengel, *Hellenism,* at every turn). The kerygma cited in 1 Cor 15 may have originally answered a key question from all Jews who had not yet believed that Jesus was the Christ. The text of 1 Tim 3:16b could well have been a hymnic creedal riposte to the misgivings and impatience of Jewish Christian apocalyptists. The kerygmatic text proclaimed to the unbeliever how he could be changed. The hymnic text assuages the impatience of people who, once they have been converted, bridle because the world has not changed. The creedal hymn assures them that the glorified Jesus really is Lord and Christ, whether the merciless might of the Roman *imperium* seems completely to dominate the people of God, or whether the ruthless persecution of a Saul terrorizes the congregations of Christians as a wild beast terrorizes a primitive village.

Where did the *Gattung* or form of hymnic confession exemplified in 1 Tim 3:16b originate? Probably not in Judaism, but in Jewish Christian circles, where it gradually fell into desuetude after the first Christian century. The trajectory traveled by this creedal hymn, now imbedded in verse 16b, may be recoverable, but, granted that one can reconstruct an ecclesial matrix in which the composition was used, is it possible to determine whether that was the original situation which prompted it, to which it was addressed?

Several original ecclesial settings might have transmitted (or even produced) verse 16b. In the language of 1 Tim 3:16a, which introduces this hymnic fragment, there are several hints at a liturgical provenance; thus it was not by chance that *homologoumenōs* was read by some ancient scribes as *homologoumen hos,* and the reference to the Christian *mystērion* may point in the same direction. Similar indicators appear in the section about the Spirit immediately after this hymn. On the other hand, no single life setting in Christian liturgy has been recovered for the body of Christian creedal confessions or hymns. Some favor a setting in baptismal and eucharistic liturgies; others suggest a polemical background. The *Gattung* of creedal confession may reflect a very early stage in the growth of Christian liturgy that favored more improvisation in this area than later generations would find acceptable.

A baptismal liturgy offers possibilities, as does a eucharistic liturgy; some as yet unidentified assembly for public worship could also offer an equal chance (see *Diogn.* 11.3-5, cited below). The lack of convincing evidence for a given ecclesial setting, though frustrating, reminds the literary critic forcibly that verse 16b as it stands is a fragment, a headless torso, and one can only surmise what a preceding (and/or following) strophe contained. The silence about the history and especially the death of Jesus may have no meaning here, since the reader is in the same position with this hymn as he would have been if Paul had quoted only the exaltation strophe of the hymn cited in Phil 2:9-11, omitting the previous verses on the humiliation and crucifixion of Jesus.

When creedal confessions are recorded by various NT authors, they are considered incontrovertible bases for and illustrations of the exhortation, polemic, or practical guidance in which the author is engaged. The hymnic citation enables the author to appeal to the venerable and venerated practices of the congregation to guide that congregation (see Hengel, *BJP,* pp. 85, 89, 95). Thus cited, they have the weight and force of the OT Scripture. The reason appears to lie in the connection of these hymns (as of the Scripture) with the Holy Spirit, particularly the Psalms; they belong with the practically synonymous "spiritual psalms, hymns, songs" of Col 3:16; Eph 5:18 (see Hengel, *BJP,* pp. 79-80, 91-92). It is notable that the composition of Christian hymns (such as the *Odes of Solomon*) began to decline as Christian prophecy began to atrophy. Both the hymns and the prophets appear to have belonged to the Jewish Christian wing of the church. Though their heritage was transmitted and even treasured, the activity that produced it was hardly cultivated. Perhaps the converts from paganism remembered too well the links between their own hymns and the pagan gods to whom they were attributed. Pausanias, 1.21.2, passes on an old tale that Dionysus appeared in a vision upon Sophocles' death to announce that the dramatist had become a Siren; Pausanias adds that "even today attractiveness in poems and in language is still compared to the song of a Siren" (E.T., Levi, *Pausanias*). Julian, "the Apostate," when he wrote to a pagan priest about resuscitating the old religion, could say: "We ought to learn by heart the hymns in honor of the gods — and many and beautiful they are, composed by men of old and of our own time — though indeed we ought to try to know also those which are being sung in the temples. For the greater number were bestowed on us by the gods themselves, in answer to prayer, though some few also were written by men and were composed in honor of the gods by the aid of divine inspiration *(hypo pneumatos entheou)* and a soul inaccessible to things evil" (E.T. by W. C. Wright, LCL 2.329, modified). As Quasten, *Music,* pp. 59-62, 66-68, has shown, the early Christians were taught to abhor the instrumental music and the elaborate, formal hymnody, with its Greek harmonies, meters, and strophic arrangements, all of which flourished in the pagan cults.

The formal characteristics of an apostolic parousia in 1 Tim 3:14-15 have been noted above; now it can be observed that verse 16 does not promise the powerful, personal presence of the apostle but rather recalls an actual hymnic confession of a Christian congregation as the basis for life in *the church of the living God.* The presence of the apostle's co-worker, Timothy, is *a pillar and pedestal for the truth,* i.e. for this creedal confession that is in its turn part of a *monumentum aere perennius,* "a monument more lasting than bronze," occasioned by the Pauline proclamation of and teaching about the risen Jesus.

Thus Paul's co-worker and this correspondence succeed to the presence of Paul. In this problematic it is hard to overestimate the force of this entire passage, from 3:14 through 4:5, for the understanding of the whole of this letter and in fact of this whole correspondence, for it constitutes the center of both, a kind of theological mainspring that keeps the whole exposition moving.

An influential suggestion for understanding the creedal confession of verse 16b contends that its inner coherence and pattern are based ultimately on a putative ancient Egyptian enthronement ceremony which unfolded through the three moments of the exaltation of the new king, his presentation, and finally his enthronement. One couplet in verse 16b is devoted to each of these stages for enthronement (see Jeremias and Strobel, *NTD,* pp. 27-29; Hay, *Glory,* p. 86). Still, even the putative Egyptian ceremony followed a rather different order and had elements that do not appear here (e.g. a hymn by the heavenly beings; see Schweizer, *Lordship,* p. 66 n. 1; Gundry, "Hymn," pp. 207-208). Rengstorf, "Traces," pp. 229-244, has suggested that a Judean ceremony for royal coronation which has left its adoption formula in Ps 2:7 has left traces also on various NT passages as they articulate the way in which Jesus is related to his Father. There is this to be said for hypotheses about form that appeal to the ancient Near East. They have kept open the question about the relation of this creedal hymn in 3:16b to the Semitic and specifically to the Palestinian world.

The extant text of verse 16b is patient of Semitic, specifically Aramaic, retroversion with hardly a qualm. The psalmic tradition of the OT and Qumran attest to putting the verb first in a series of sentences that exhibit the various types of parallelism, as well as to using a past third person form for the verbs (corresponding roughly to the Greek aorist or perfect) and to a positioning of prepositional phrases similar to that in verse 16b. In Aramaic, as in Greek, there would be two stresses in a stich, but each stich in the retroversion also has two words. Perhaps an Aramaic original, using nouns in the absolute state, sounded like the following (with gratitude to J. A. Fitzmyer, who shared all but the gaffes in the reconstruction below with this author in a private communication; for some of the problems of reconstructing Aramaic poetry, see Fitzmyer, *Aramean,* pp. 16-17).

*di ʾitgalli bab*$^{e}$*sar*
*ʾistaddaq b*$^{e}$*ruh*
*ʾith*$^{a}$*zi l*$^{e}$*malʾ*$^{a}$*kin*
*ʾittakraz b*$^{e}$*ʿam*$^{e}$*min*
*ʾithaʾman batebel*
*ʾitgabbî bah*$^{a}$*dar*

A Palestinian Christian origin is quite feasible for a hymn such as this from the point of view of its Semitisms in language and formal structure. The exegetical comment will show the Palestinian links in the content. The case, even for a Palestinian Greek form of the hymn, would be immeasurably advanced if O'Callaghan's identification of 7Q 4 = 1 Tim 3:16; 4:1, 3 were acceptable ("Cueva 7," pp. 34-44, plate IV). These fragments are certainly Greek, as are the other scraps from Cave 7, and can hardly date from after 100 C.E. Yet there are textual difficulties, and the evidence thus far is too light to produce conviction but too heavy simply to brush aside.

The meaning of the terminology of this creedal hymn must now be analyzed. The initial relative pronoun, *hos,* ". . . He who," in this version, probably did not have *theos* as its antecedent, for such NT hymns as this are usually explicitly christological (see Deichgräber, *Gotteshymnus,* pp. 60-61, 207-208; Hengel, *BJP,* pp. 81, 188 n. 8). As was previously noted, *kyrios (Iēsous)* would make a suitable antecedent, though *Christos* would also be appropriate (see Eph 2:13-18; Col 2:8-15; 1 Pet 3:18-22), and even *huios,* "Son" (see Heb 1:1-4). It is possible that a (short) series of christological titles was marshaled in several stichs within an opening formula that can be hypothetically reconstructed from the way in which this genre of composition opens in the hymns and prayers of contemporary Judaism (see J. M. Robinson, "Hodayot-formel," pp. 194-235, and his "Historicality," pp. 130-150). For example:

| | |
|---|---|
| Confess the Lord, | *(Ex-) homologeisthe kyrion* |
| Christ Jesus, | *Christon Iēsoun* |
| God's Son . . . | *theou huion . . .* |

The fragment that constitutes verse 16b does not by any means indicate that the author of the PE lacked access to the whole hymn (whatever the probability of the reconstruction above). The presumption is that he knew the whole text and of set purpose chose not to cite the preceding stich(s). What reason could he have had? One surmises that the omitted section employed a title for Jesus that the author of the PE was reluctant to introduce at this critical juncture into his correspondence. It has already been noted that the name of Jesus dominates the PE and that the correspondence calls him Christ, Lord, even God. However, no form of the title "Son" occurs in the PE. An analogous phenomenon appears in Luke-Acts in the Lukan reserve about using all the "son . . . of" titles for Jesus (see E. Schweizer, *TDNT* 8.380-382).

In the hypothetical reconstruction submitted above, instead of the absolute form of the title, i.e. "the Son," the also very archaic "God's Son/Son of God" has been proposed, for formal reasons as well as its roots in pre-Pauline kerygmatic formulations, familiar to the first-generation congregations in Jerusalem and Rome (on the title, see Fitzmyer, AB *Lk,* pp. 205-208, and, in general, Hengel, *Son*). Pliny's notice (*Epistles* 10.96.7) that the Christians admit that their worship includes "singing alternately between themselves a song to Christ as god," *carmenque Christo quasi deo dicere secum invicem,* suggests that such hymns regularly employed a title such as "God/Son of God" in addressing Jesus. Perhaps the theological approach that suggested omitting the hypothetical reference to "God's Son" here and the notable lack of any form of titles for Jesus' sonship in the PE are a result of "the apocalyptic model of sonship," analyzed by Loader, "Sonship," pp. 525-554. The apocalyptic paradigm was venerable, popular, and Palestinian. As is noted in the comment on Titus 2:14; 3:1-3, 5 in AB *Titus,* the author of the PE had reason to distance himself (and his congregation) from that model. *Diognetus* 11.3-5 (see also *Barn.* 5.11) seems to be paraphrasing the hymn cited here in 3:16b as he writes in a passage that otherwise uses the terminology of the archaic hymn, "He [Christ] is eternal who is today accounted Son. . . ." The reference to "today" points to a cultic setting, perhaps an observance of the baptism of the Lord (later, Epiphany).

Some have seen the stanza cited in Eph 5:14,

Awake, you sleeper,
  rise from the dead,
the Messiah will shine upon you!

(E.T. from Barth, AB *Eph,* p. 554)

as a probable candidate for the strophe missing in 1 Tim 3:16b (see Stanley, *Resurrection,* pp. 236-237; *Church,* pp. 109-110). In this reconstruction Christ is without doubt the antecedent, though on this reading the first extant stich contained in verse 16b becomes banal, for all Jews who hoped for a Messiah presumed that he would be a human being. A final hypothesis about the origin of this hymn is now submitted for testing against the analysis of the content of 3:16b. Did this hymn originate in enthusiastic, ecclesial acclamations in Palestine itself, a prophetic hymnic confession, occasioned by the report of the conversion and apostolate of Paul? Paul himself adverted to such compositions a few years later when he wrote, "And I was still not known by sight to the churches of Christ in Judea; they only heard it said, 'He who once persecuted us is now preaching the faith *(tēn pistin)* he once tried to destroy.' And they kept glorifying (*edoxazon* [note the imperfect]) God because of me *(en emoi)*" (Gal 1:22-24). The direct quotation from a source other than the OT, as Bammel, "Galater," pp. 108-112, has pointed out, is unusual; the usage of *hē pistis* is not the regular Pauline one; and the content does not fit nicely into the argument of the chapter. He opts for a martyr-hymn by Judean Christians, thanking God for the conversion of Paul the persecutor.

Perhaps a wider screen is in order, for one recalls that just a little earlier in Galatians (1:16) Paul had described his conversion-vocation vision by saying that it had been God's good will "to reveal his Son to me *(ton huion autou en emoi)*, so that I might preach the gospel about him to *(en)* the pagans. . . ." The reconstructed first stanza of 1 Tim 3:16b entitled Jesus as "Son of God," and Gundry, "Hymn," p. 221, has noted not only that the extant text has features that are rooted in a persecuted Jewish Christian congregation of Palestine but also that the hymn has a universalistic view about the Christian mission. Evidently the conversion of Paul was not going to end all persecution, but just as evidently it was taken as an irrefutable sign from their risen Lord that the conversion of the nations was his will and not their own arbitrary whim. It is instructive in this connection to recall that, according to Acts 11:18; 21:20, key members of the Jerusalem church "glorify God" because of the conversion of pagans by Peter and Paul. This substantiates from another point of view the case constructed by Hengel, *BJP*, pp. 48-64, that "[t]he earliest community in Palestine was also a missionary community from the beginning: the foundation of this lies in the sending by the Risen Christ" (p. 63). "Furthermore, the first impetus towards the mission among non-Jews came from the 'Hellenists' in Jerusalem" (p. 63; see Martin, "N.T. Hymns," p. 42).

The hymn of 3:16b could have originated, at least in Greek, after the flight of the persecuted Jewish Christian Hellenists to Syrian Antioch and the launching of a systematic mission to the pagans there, with the help of Paul (see Acts 11:19-26 and Gundry, "Hymn," p. 221). An even earlier origin in the Jerusalem congregation, whether in Greek or Aramaic, takes one back closer to that electrifying moment when, after all seemed lost in the persecution and the death of

Stephen, the leader of their missionary efforts, the risen Lord converted Paul, their persecutor, and commissioned him as an apostle to all nations.

To turn to the text of the hymn, the analysis will proceed two stichs at a time, without prejudice (if that is possible) to the question about how the poet first intended them to be sung (singly, in pairs, in triplets).

> *. . . He who was revealed in human flesh,*
> *Was made victorious in the Spirit:*

The initial *ephanerōthē,* "was revealed," as one might expect in dense poetic diction, does not altogether coincide in meaning with the usage in Titus 1:3. If the schema in the latter passage presupposes a descent from heaven to earth, the schema here in 3:16 presupposes an ascent through the humiliation of rejection to heavenly vindication and glory (modifying Martin, "N.T. Hymns," p. 47, and his *Carmen,* pp. xxxii-xxxiii). If the hypothetical first stanza submitted above is accepted, then the hymn indeed had a descent/ascent pattern framing its development of the rejection/vindication pattern. Both patterns appear to have venerable pre-Christian Jewish precedents (see Barth, AB *Eph,* pp. 432-433, 472-477, on the descent/ascent schema which Eph 4:8-10 teases out of Ps 68:18). A combination of both schemata may have belonged to the first Palestinian composition. Still, the text transmitted by the PE appears to fit better into a rejection/vindication paradigm, with the possibility that the opening verb of the surviving fragment once served as a bridge from a now hypothetical first stanza.

The Pauline usage of *phaneroun* is typified in Second Corinthians, where Paul may be taking the term from Jewish Christian adversaries who favored it. In any case, it describes his apostolic ministry (with Timothy and Silvanus) and the revelation of Christ that it brings (2 Cor 2:14; see 11:6). Their proclamation, their very lives have revealed the dying of Jesus (2 Cor 4:10-11), lives through which the revelation has shown and which will be finally judged by Christ (2 Cor 5:10-11; note the perfect infinitives). The work of the apostle, even the correspondence he dispatches, is meant to evoke in response a complementary revelation of Corinthian repentance and "zealous concern" for the Pauline gospel.

Christ Jesus under various titles is the subject of *phaneroun* several times in the Paulines. Thus he is "the Lord" referred to in the quotation in 1 Cor 4:5 and "the Christ" in Col 3:4, both passages referring to the future manifestation of Jesus in glory for the final judgment. In Col 1:26, describing "the mystery hidden for ages and generations but now made manifest (*nyn de ephanerōthē* [see 2 Tim 1:10]) to his saints," a traditional schematization (hidden/revealed) has been taken up and applied to the appearance of Jesus in the past. These passages are of a piece with not only 1 Tim 3:16b but also Rom 3:21, as Lohse, *Col,* pp. 73-74, 134, has shown against R. Bultmann and D. Lührmann, *TDNT* 9.4-5. The content of the mystery is "Christ in you," *en hymin,* which is "the Christ preached among the nations," i.e. "to you," where *en* = *eis* (cf. Gal 1:16 with 2:8; see 2 Cor 1:19, "Christ Jesus whom we preached among you [*en hymin*]"; and Lohse, *Col,* p. 76). The use of *ephanerōthē* to refer to a past appearance of Jesus is not otherwise found in the Pauline epistolary, the first of many indications of a non-Pauline, if not a pre-Pauline, origin for this hymn. That the usage was congenial to Jewish Christian ears may be indicated in Heb 9:26, which says, speaking of Christ the high priest, that he "has appeared *(pephanerotai)* once and for all, at the end of the ages *(aiōnōn)* to put away sin by the sacrifice of himself." The perfect tense here suggests that as the effect of the act of revelation continues into the present time, so the apostolic preaching and the worship it elicits have their roots in a past revelation (cf. Rom 1:17 with 3:21 and Cranfield, *Rom.* 1.91-92, 201-202).

Recalling that the Aramaic reconstruction of 3:16b above used *'itgalli* and that the only LXX occurrence of *phaneroun* translated the Hebrew *glh,* "to uncover, disclose, reveal," it is important to note that the Hebrew Bible has around 180 uses of the verb *galah* and that there are 9 occurrences in biblical Aramaic (for this and the following, see H. Zobel, *TDOT* 2.477, 480-488). It appears particularly in contexts that describe a primarily visionary experience (see Num 24:4, 16). In the light of the Aramaic reconstruction of the hymn in the PE, the Aramaic portions of Daniel have a special relevance, not least the hymnic thanksgiving in Dan 2:22, where God is confessed, saying, "He reveals *(gale')* deep and mysterious things; he knows what is in the darkness, and the light dwells with him." Otherwise, *raz,* "secret" (note the comments on "mystery" in 1 Tim 3:9, 16a), is the object of forms of *glh* in Dan 2:19, 28-30, 47. This linking of specific secrets known only to God and his disclosure of them to privileged intermediaries, particularly in nocturnal visions, becomes characteristic of apocalyptic compositions, continuing from Daniel to the Qumran documents (where forms of *gly* occur about forty times). A passage in 11QtgJob 27.3 uses *ygl'* in a context of God's revealing people's sins; *Enoch* 91.14 in 4QEn$^{g}$ (Milik, *Enoch,* pp. 266-267, 361), in the apocalyptic description of the three final "Weeks," writes, "and thereafter the ninth week, and righteousness [and right] judgement will be revealed *(ytgal')* [in it] for the children of the whole earth . . ." (E.T. from Milik).

The collection of psalmic compositions in 1QH, because of the formal resemblances between them and the hymn in 1 Tim 3:16b, is especially interesting. There is an almost formulaic phrase describing God as the one who has uncovered the ear of the hymnist to God's "marvelous mysteries." Uncovering the ear to revelation implies that it is to be obeyed (see 1QH 1.21; 6.4; 18.4; also CD

2.2, 14-16). Other passages in the *Hodayot* which use forms of *galeh* are also evocative. Thus the hymnist prays in 1QH 5.11-12, "For you, O God, had hidden me from before the sons of man and had sealed up your law *(twrtkh)* within [me], [un]til the time of the revealing *(hglwt)* of your salvation to me" (E.T from Dupont-Sommer, *EWQ*, p. 215). The obscure servant (see Isa 49:2) within whom God's revelation is still further concealed has the answer to his prayer when God discloses his "salvation," *yšʿ*. 1QH 11.15-16, after its formal opening, "I give you thanks, O Lord . . ." for the divine works, specifies them, saying, "For you made me know the secret of truth *(swd ʾmt)* [. . .] [and] have revealed your [wond]ers to me, and I have contemplated [the depth of your mysteries]" (E.T. from Dupont-Sommer, *EWQ*, p. 237). The schema of concealment and revelation hardly needs emphasis, not to mention the concept of the mystery, both at the service of a Palestinian apocalyptic spirituality (see also the mutilated scraps of 1QH 13.2-3 as well as 1Q 26.4 [an otherwise unknown instruction or testament] and 1Q 27.1.5-7, a "Book of the Mysteries" [in which the OT formula "And this for you is the sign that these things shall take place" begins a section, which is continued through an apocalyptic description of the final triumph of righteousness that is concluded with "All who hold fast to the wondrous mysteries will be no more. The world shall be filled with knowledge and there shall be no more folly in it"; this narrative of the sign then ends with "The word will assuredly come to pass and certain is the prediction," *nkwn hdbr lbwʾ wʾmt hmśʾ* (DJD 1.101-104)]; CD 3.13-14; 5.4-5 offers parallels to this schema also). As Zobel notes, for Qumran the secrets involved the scriptural revelation of what was going to happen at the time of the imminent end of this world, an interpretation which made the sect's understanding of the Scripture on this point into revelation (not the sacred books themselves). Thus the prophet Habakkuk writes, "For the earth will be filled with the knowledge of the glory of Yahweh as waters cover the sea . . ." (2:14). The interpretation applies this to the members of the Qumran community, ". . . afterwards knowledge will be revealed *(tglh)* to them 'as the waters of the sea,' abundantly" (1QpHab 11.1; see also 1Q 27.1.5-7 cited above). Here the concepts of glory, of knowledge, and of revelation are of worldwide scope and thus are reminiscent of 1 Tim 3:16b.

In the Rule of the Qumran community, the Torah with its commands is above all that which is revealed (see 1QS 5.8-9, 11-12). The Rule prescribes, "In the Council of the Community there shall be twelve laymen and three priests, perfectly versed in all that is revealed *(bkwl hnglh)* of the entire Law, to put into practice truth, righteousness, justice, lovingkindness, and humility towards one another . . ." (1QS 8.1-2). Here the revelation is source of and motivation for the virtuous activities that follow in a five-member cluster in a way that is reminiscent of the directives for the conduct of the Christian leaders in 1 Tim 3:1b-13, which are ultimately grounded in *the mystery of godliness,* the revelation that occurred in the person and work of Jesus.

When the oracle of Isa 40:3 on the way of the Lord in the desert is explained in 1QS 8.15-16, one reads, "This way is the study of the law which he has promulgated by the hand of Moses, that they may act according to all that is revealed *(hnglh)* season by season [see 1QS 1.9; 9.13, 19], and according to that which the prophets have revealed by his holy spirit" (E.T. in Dupont-Sommer, *EWQ*, p. 92, modified). Here the Mosaic revelation precedes the reference to the prophetic oracles given by God's Spirit, and the arrangement reminds one that the revelation of 3:16b is immediately followed in 4:1 by an oracle of the Spirit. This is the first of several indications that this section of 1 Tim 3:14-16 is to be read in tandem with 4:1-5, constituting together the doctrinal core of First Timothy, the Law and the Prophets, so to speak, for *the church of the living God.*

The act of revelation confessed here occurred *in human flesh, en sarki.* The Son of God, the Lord, has appeared in a condition that the hymn of Phil 2:7 describes as "taking the form of a slave, and being born in the likeness of human beings." Notable in this connection are the passages in *Barnabas* (and only in that document) that link the verb *revealed* with the phrase *en sarki* in describing the life and especially the death of Jesus. In 5.6, 9-11, the author first appears to cite as a saying, "Because it was necessary that he be revealed in human flesh," Jesus lived, died, and rose from the dead; then he specifies that when Jesus chose his apostles as the ones who would proclaim his gospel, then "he revealed himself as God's son, for if he had not come in human flesh people could not possibly have been saved by beholding him. . . . So then the son of God came in human flesh for this reason, that he might draw up the sum total of the sins of those who persecuted his prophets to death." In 6.7, 9, 14, in the midst of prophecies of the passion, *Barnabas* states, "Since therefore he was destined to be revealed and to suffer in human flesh, his passion was foretold." Then he has Moses saying to the people under Joshua (whose name is equivalent to "Jesus"), "Place your hope in that Jesus who is going to be revealed to you [pl.] in human flesh, for a human being is suffering earth, for from the surface of the earth the fashioning of Adam took place." Finally, in explaining the "hearts of flesh" created in us by the Lord, according to Ezekiel, he says this has occurred "because he himself was going to be revealed in human flesh and make his home in us." In 12.10 he exhorts, "Again see [sg.] Jesus, not as son of man but as son of God, revealed in human flesh *(en sarki phanerōtheis)* for a pattern *(typōi).*" For the other uses of *phaneroun* in *Barnabas,* see 2.4; 7.3, 7; 14.5; 16.5. The strong ties between *Barnabas* and Jewish Christian traditions confirm what appears occasionally in the other Ap. Frs., namely that in Greek-speaking Christian circles, *revealed (in human flesh)* suggested the suffering and death of Jesus.

In the latter part of the second Christian century the phrase *en sarki* appears to be translated by Saying §28 of *The Gospel of Thomas* as well as *The Gospel of Truth* 16.31.5. In the former, Jesus is depicted as saying, "I took my place in the midst of the world *(kosmos)* and I appeared to them in flesh *(sarx)*," but in the context his affliction is interior. The latter teaches in an even more explicit context: "For he came by means of fleshly *(sarx)* appearance [lit. "in the flesh of likeness"] while nothing blocked his course because it was incorruptibility (and) irresistibility" (E.T. from J. M. Robinson, *NHL,* pp. 43, 121). The Gnostic evacuation of the cross is under way here in the name of de-Judaizing the tradition. The same generation produced the new "Marcionite" hymnbook to replace the psalms (Muratorian Fragment, lines 82-84) and the Jewish Christian hymns which kept the now archaic, austere teaching of the first apostolic generation on the lips and in the hearts of believers. The anti-docetic nuance which can be seen in the use of *en sarki* in 1 Tim 3:16b seems to have been exploited already in Ignatius and was favored by Gregory of Nyssa *(Contra Eunomium; Contra Apollinarem)* and Cyril of Alexandria *(Quod unus sit Christus; De recta fide)*. On this interpretation, the *en* of *in human flesh* would lend itself to an instrumental interpretation. This is the first of many signals that one is encountering a densely composed, poetic text in 3:16b (and it goes without saying, in the hypothetical Aramaic retroversion proposed above), for superficially the same word is layered with meanings, and *en* may well, even in the next stich, have a different sense.

The same poetic density and ambivalence explain how *phaneroun* can in Christian circles combine theophany and revelation with the suffering and death of Jesus. There is no denying that NT authors used *phaneroun* to designate the whole process of the revelation of Jesus (see Heb 9:26; 1 Pet 1:20; 1 John 1:2; 3:5; 4:9; and R. Brown, *Epistles,* pp. 166-167, 401, 515-516). Such an all-inclusive reference would refer also to Jesus' resurrection and exaltation in (or by) the human nature in which he, the son of God, underwent his passion. Thus Descamps, *Les Justes,* pp. 86-87, takes *in human flesh* as referring to mortal human existence, though not exactly the incarnation but rather the epiphany or transfiguration (for a variation, see Fuller, *Foundations,* pp. 217, 226-227, 246). What previously had been hidden not only in God but in the mortal life and death of Jesus *was revealed in human flesh* when he rose from the dead. There are points of contact between this interpretation and the Pauline usage noted above as well as with later documents of the NT that use *phaneroun* of Jesus' resurrection appearances (the Markan appendix in Mark 16:12, 14; the Johannine appendix in John 21:1, 14) as well as of his final appearance in glory (1 Pet 5:4; 1 John 2:28; 3:2).

Indeed, before one can focus the sense of this first line of the hymn in 3:16b, its formal parallel, *Was made victorious in the Spirit, edikaiōthē en pneumati,* ought to be analyzed. The verb *dikaioun* appeared in Titus 3:7 in the citation of a creedal confession or oration, as here it appears in a hymnic creed. Where the use in Titus had links with the Pauline tradition, the usage here looks distinctly pre-Pauline. In the tradition cited in Titus, the Christian himself is the subject of the whole quotation; here apparently Christ himself is the subject of the verb, a quite un-Pauline usage (and perhaps still another reason that the antecedent of the pronoun subject of this verb is not cited as such). The verb *dikaioun* in this hymnic fragment has the very Hebraic (and un-Greek) sense of "to vindicate, to redress, to give victory, to deliver, to save" (see LSJ *s.v.;* Dodd, *Bible and Greeks,* pp. 47-53, citing LXX Ps 81:3; Isa 1:17 [see *1 Clem.* 8.4; Ign. *Phld.* 8.2] and 50:8; 2 Kgdms 15:4; Mic 7:9 [translating *ryb*]; also see Hill, *Greek Words,* pp. 104-109; Olley, *Righteousness,* pp. 96-101 [qualifying Dodd on Isaiah]; Ziesler, *Righteousness,* pp. 154-155; Reumann, *Righteousness,* p. 15). In 1QM 11.14, "... to vindicate *(lhṣdyq)* the judgment of your truth," Yadin, *War,* has noted that "truth" is, as often in the Scrolls, part of the terminology by which the sectaries name themselves (pp. 274, 312). 11QtgJob 9.7 cites *yṣdq* from Hebrew Job 25:4 (see Beyer, *Texte,* p. 674), but there appear to be no more clear examples in the Aramaic of Qumran. The *'istaddaq* of the reconstruction above may convey a Hebrew contamination of the Aramaic meaning.

To speak of a vindication or victory *in the Spirit* already indicates that *en pneumati* is being understood of the divine Spirit. The Greek *pneuma* could refer also to the human spirit (of Jesus) as such (R. Gundry). The Lukan tradition uses *pneuma* of Jesus' expiring on the cross (Luke 23:46), but it also emphatically has the risen Lord assert that he is not a spirit, because a spirit does not have flesh and blood (Luke 24:37-39). In the Lukan tradition the Baptist goes before Jesus with Elijah's "spirit and power," *en pneumati kai dynamei Ēleia* (Luke 1:17; see 1:15, "But even from his birth he will be filled with a holy Spirit"; Acts 10:38; Fitzmyer, AB *Lk* 1.318-320, 326-327). Spirit here suggests God's prophetic and revelatory gifts (see also Luke 2:27; 4:1; Acts 19:21); it also may designate a creative gift (Luke 3:16; Acts 1:5; 11:16 of being baptized *en pneumati hagioi*); perhaps both when used of the Seven and Stephen in Acts 6:3, 5; 7:55; and of Barnabas in 11:24.

11QtgJob 13.6 has *lrwḥ'*, meaning, it seems, "for the wind," and 33.8 (on the Hebrew of Job 39:26) uses the plural of the hawk spreading his wings, *lrwḥyn,* "in the winds," equivalent to the Greek *en pneumatibus* (see Beyer, *Texte,* pp. 692-693). The Hebrew of Qumran has several uses of *rwh* which refer to the human spirit; particularly notable are 1QH 13.13; 16.9-12; and 17.25. In the initial pair of references the hymnist speaks paradoxically of "a spirit of flesh," *rwḥ baśar,* i.e. the human spirit unable to comprehend revelation and to act upon it. One is reminded of the invocation in Num 16:22, "O God, the God of the spirits and of all flesh, shall one person sin ... ?" which the LXX has already begun to dichotomize with its *theos tōn pneumatōn kai pasēs sarkos* (see Lys, "Connotations," p. 177). In the final reference, God "has made every spirit . . . and allotted the spirit of the just . . . and I have appeased your face because of the spirit which you have put [in me] . . . by cleansing me by your holy spirit" (E.T. from Dupont-Sommer, *EWQ*, p. 248, modified). Here the spirit spoken of can scarcely be called "a spirit of flesh." It is well on the way to designating a spirit that comes from the creator and redeemer God of Israel to dwell in and guide his people. Conceptually this poetically ambivalent usage of *en pneumati,* to designate a gift with a special divine origin and power, is needlessly straitened by one's interpreting it of Jesus' human spirit as such. The densely composed hymnic stich is related to the more expansive archaic creedal statement alluded to in Rom 1:4; the resonances of the Semitic *bᵉ* evidently exercised those who wrote the Greek poem that 3:16b transmits, a poem where several possible senses for *en* can be discerned, even in a single stich, and where the particle is completely lacking in one stich. The poetic sheath of similar sounds around the thought remains substantially intact for all the semantic oscillation within the particle.

If it is difficult to conceive within a biblical and Christian problematic how Jesus attains victory through or in the realm of his human spirit (as distinguished from his flesh), one must still ask what is meant by his having been *made victorious in the Spirit,* i.e. by the Holy Spirit. If *in human flesh* suggests primarily, as was contended above, the suffering and death for which the Son's birth as a human being destined him, then the Holy Spirit brought about the reversal, the victorious vindication, constituted by his resurrection (again see the creedal phrases of Rom 1:4, as well as 8:9-11; 1 Pet 3:18, "For Christ also died for sins once for all, the righteous [*dikaios*], for the unrighteous [*adikōn*] . . . being put to death in the flesh [*sarki*] but made alive in [the] Spirit [*pneumati*]"). He who had gone to death as a wrongdoer is now recognized as right (see the Q logion of Luke 7:35 = Matt 11:19). A further suggestion of honor after dishonor is present, too, in the biblical use of *dikaio-* terminology, which is also associated with victory after battle, exaltation, glorification, even coronation (see *Odes of Solomon* 17.2; 31.5 in Charlesworth, *OT Pseud.* 2.750, 762). Because of the relative lateness of the text of *Corpus Hermeticum* 13.9, the tract *Peri paliggenesias* may have undergone Christian influence on its conceptualization at this point but not vice versa (see Dodd, *Bible and Greeks,* pp. 58-59). Yet it must be admitted that the Paulines speak of people being made righteous by Christ; thus Rom 5:9, *dikaiōthentes . . . en tōi haimati autou,* "made righteous by his blood"; 1 Cor 6:11, *en tōi onomati kyrious hemōn,* "by the name of our Lord"; Gal 2:17, *en Christōi,* "by Christ" (see Acts 13:39).

Nowhere else in the NT except in 1 Tim 3:16b does one read of this victorious vindication taking place *en pneumati. En pneumati* has been taken with a primary reference to the sphere or realm of the divine (and *en sarki* with a primary reference to the human order; see E. Schweizer, *TDNT* 6.416-417, 445). Thus Heb 9:14 speaks of the Christ who had entered the heavenly sanctuary as one "who through the [or his] eternal Spirit (*dia pneumatos aiōniou* [contrast 9:8]) offered himself without blemish to God (*tōi theōi* [i.e. the Father])."

What if one opted for the resurrection's being referred to by the revelation *in human flesh* in the first stich? The victory referred to in the second stich would then stand in a complementary (but not antithetical relation) to the resurrection. The interpretation would understand *en pneumati* instrumentally, but the tension with a locative *en sarki* would be tolerable in an explanatory complement. Just as justification "in Christ" is something more than "by Christ," so here one suspects that *made victorious in the Spirit* denotes more than vindication by the Spirit. The background for the meaning may be allied to the passage from 1QH 16.11-12 where the author writes, "And I know that none is righteous *(yṣdq)* beside you; and I have appeased your face in the Spirit *(brwḥ)* which you put [in me] *(ntth by)* to accomplish your [fa]vors toward [your] servant for[ever] by cleansing me by your holy spirit *(brwḥ qwdšk)*. . . ." In an earlier hymn the author says, "And I, your servant, I know by the Spirit which you put in me *(brwḥ ʾšr ntth by)* [that you are truth] and that all your works are righteousness (*ṣdq* [see *yṣdq* in 13.17])" (E.T. from Dupont-Sommer, *EWQ*, pp. 243, 248 modified).

Against this background, *made victorious in the Spirit* in 1 Tim 3:16b has the nuances of meaning that emanate through a Semitizing Greek use of *brwh.* The vindication would be in the power and works of the Spirit that was in and with Jesus of Nazareth, even *in human flesh* (see Luke 4:14, 18; Acts 10:38), as well as at his disposal in his risen existence (Luke 24:49; Acts 2:33; 10:14, 19 [where the voice of the Lord is the voice of the Spirit]). In this interpretation, not only the revelation but also the vindication of Jesus began in his historical ministry, above all in his *dynameis,* his powerful acts (see Hay, *Glory,* pp. 84, 92). Just as the climax and summation of all that it means to be *in human flesh* appears on the cross, so the ultimate vindication of his powerful acts *in the Spirit* occurs in the resurrection which the Spirit gives him. Just as the risen Lord continues to live *in the flesh,* his vindication continues in the acts that are proper to the Spirit, acts as well as words which God elicits from believers as a testimony to his risen son. Those acts would certainly include prophecies, but prayers, healings, and the moral conduct of believers also are empowered by the Spirit (see the texts from Luke-Acts adduced above; E. Schweizer, *TDNT* 6.409; see also Hill, *Greek Words,* p. 240). In the Pauline corpus outside of the PE, the phrase *en (tōi) pneumati (hagiōi)* occurs as many as twenty-two times (if one counts Rom 1:9; Gal 6:1). The cluster of occurrences in 1 Cor 12:3, 8, *dia,* 13; 14:16 *s.v.l.* illustrates how the phrase is used to designate the matrix for Christian prophetic witness, revelation, faith, healings, tongues, blessings (see Eph 3:5; 5:18-19; 6:18). The Spirit produces the variegated life and works of the body of Christ.

This interpretation of *in the Spirit* would be of a piece with the "spirituality" of Qumran, where the presence of the (holy) spirit can be ascertained by the virtues produced in the lives of the members of the community, where prophecies also flourish, where God's mighty works are perceived, where his secret plan is discerned by the same spirit. Perhaps even that "spirit of chastisement" which God sends on Pharaoh and his family, i.e. grievous physical illnesses which are in turn cured by the laying on of Abraham's hands (1QapGen 20.16-29), should be understood as taking place through a "spirit of healing." The linking of the spirit at Qumran with human understanding and grasp of God's plan and works (as the citations above illustrate) reminds the person who hears the hymn of 1 Tim 3:16b that the revelatory action of the first extant stich has been "nominalized" with the reference to the Spirit. The powerful acts of the Spirit vindicate the revelation borne in the crucified flesh of the risen Lord. That which had been synonymous with weakness and death has become in the resurrection the locus and source of the divine power and life.

In using the Qumran documents as a guide to the background for the parallel between *en sarki* and *en pneumati* in this hymnic fragment in First Timothy, one ought to note, with R. Meyer, *TDNT* 7.114, that ". . . nowhere is it even probable [in the Qumran library] that the flesh is in conflict with the spirit. Denoting man's total personality, the flesh is rather the field of battle between the Holy Spirit and the spirit of iniquity" (see Hill, *Greek Words,* p. 234 n. 4, p. 239). In the archaic hymnic creed of First Timothy, the battle is revealed as won in the crucified flesh of the risen Lord, a victory bestowed and confirmed by the Spirit.

The Lukan use of *sarx* can be reviewed in this connection. The LXX Isa 40:5 on "all flesh" seeing God's salvation is taken up in Luke 3:6; in Acts 2:17 it is again upon "all flesh" that the Lord wills to pour out his Spirit, citing LXX Joel 3:1. When Acts 2:26 cites the LXX Ps 15:9, "My flesh will dwell in hope," it is to apply its language to the risen Jesus whose "flesh did not see corruption" (Acts 2:31; the saying of the risen Jesus on the difference between flesh and spirit in Luke 24:39 has been cited above). All humankind sees its salvation revealed in the risen Jesus, the fulfillment of the prophecy and prayer of Israel. The Spirit and its life pour out upon "all flesh" through the risen "flesh and bones" of Jesus of Nazareth.

In this interpretation of *was made victorious in the Spirit,* the powerful acts of Jesus' ministry, including ultimately the resurrection, as well as the works of the Spirit in those who believe in him, are being acclaimed as acts that vindicated the son of God in human history. Some, on the basis of parallels in

*Enoch* (see J. Strange), have contended that the vindication spoken of here occurred before the Father and the heavenly court, i.e. in the metahistorical realm of the Spirit. A critical difficulty with this interpretation is that the Son somehow has to be vindicated before his Father for fulfilling the Father's will. In the interpretation favored in the comment here, the Spirit vindicates Jesus before a human world where he is still on trial, still able to be doubted, accused, rejected.

The next two stichs of 3:16b read:

*He who was seen (ōphthē) by God's messengers (aggelois),*
*Was heralded (ekērychthē) to the pagans (en ethnesin):*

Literally, "He appeared to messengers, he was heralded among pagans." The verb *ōphthē* is embedded in an archaic Jerusalem kerygmatic formula and its sequel, transmitted in 1 Cor 15:5-8. Here the context as well as the ancient formula make it certain that the risen Christ is the one who appeared or *who was seen.* But by whom or to whom? The kerygmatic formula using the dative (but not a preposition) says, "to Cephas, then to the Twelve, . . . to James, then to all the apostles. Last of all . . . he appeared also to me." Groups as well as individuals are designated; to these Paul had no qualms about suffixing his own name. At first glance it seems odd that the hymnic creed of First Timothy has omitted the preposition *en* in this stich alone, so odd in fact that J. Murphy-O'Connor has obelized the whole line as an interpolation into the original hymn. Rather, one witnesses at this point the authoritative clout of the terminology of the archaic kerygma itself, which takes precedence over the poetic structure and emphasizes what Paul himself had appealed to as warrant for his apostleship to the Gentiles. In this hymnic confession no names are mentioned of those to whom the risen Jesus appeared, but a group of persons are noted under the generic, genuinely datival designation *aggelois* (note the Aramaic *le* hypothesized here), translated with the noncommittal *messengers* (whose anarthrous state belongs to the language of this hymn and contributes nothing to the meaning at this point). The version here preserves the passive form with the instrumental particle *was seen by God's messengers* to illustrate the ambiguity in meaning that the poetic form generated in this stich, an ambiguity that is not resolved by mention of "the elect angels" in the fixed phrase of 1 Tim 5:21.

The Greek term *aggelos* had not yet become simply a technical term for a superhuman spirit. It was a functional noun denoting generically any person who was sent with an announcement. The NT documents (not to mention the later Christian writers) use the word in the great majority of instances of the spirits superior to human beings. Still, they do use it also of human messengers, whether sent by God or by human beings. In this old text of 1 Tim 3:16b the *aggeloi* who saw the risen Jesus are the more prosaic *apostoloi* (including Paul) of the kerygmatic confession of 1 Cor 15:7, 9. A few commentators have argued for this since J. C. Hoffmann (1862-1886) and R. W. Micou (*JBL* 11 [pt. 2; 1892], 201-204), including A. Seeberg (1903); G. Wohlenberg (1906); Murphy-O'Connor, "Angels," p. 186.

In contrast to the usage being argued for in 1 Tim 3:16b, the Qumran texts almost always use *ml'k,* "messenger," as a technical term for a superhuman spirit; thus, 1QM 17.6 of the *ml'k* that God will send, *yšlḥ,* to assist his people in the final apocalyptic battle. Out of more than two dozen uses, only once, in the blessing for the priests in 1QSb 4.25, is an unspecified priest prayed to be "as an angel of the Presence in the abode of holiness." The comparison evidently distances the man from the superhuman messenger-spirit who worships before God. Some such background seems to be required for "the seven angels of the churches" in Rev 1:20, for it is by no means clear that the leaders of the Christian congregations in Asia Minor were all called *aggeloi* in the first Christian century (any more than they all had the title *episkopoi,* which Acts 20:28 documents only for Ephesus). Still, the *aggeloi* of this septet of letters appear to be human beings, for even a prophet does not write to a superhuman spirit about his cooling fervor to summon him to repentance (Rev 2:1-6). One may be encountering here a "sacramentalizing" of apocalyptic language, linking traditional images and personnel of apocalyptic visions (see Jer 1:15 and Matt 19:28; Luke 22:30b) to present Christian leaders ("messengers") who have a task analogous to that of superhuman messenger-spirits. In this connection, one ought to note that in Rev 2:2 the angel of Ephesus has had to discern real apostles from counterfeits. In Rev 21:12-14 twelve angels are at the twelve gates of the New Jerusalem, gates upon whose foundations the names of "the twelve apostles" are inscribed. The gates face in all directions because the messenger-apostles have been sent to all peoples and through them all enter the city of God. What Qumran had affirmed of an apocalyptic messenger-spirit and (with considerable reserve) of a priest of Israel, the prophet of Revelation exploits (with his own reservations) about the leaders of the churches. The great interest of the book of Revelation in *aggeloi,* already clear in the number of uses of the term, shows also the importance of the divine messenger for apocalyptic thought in the composition of the NT. The fact that *aggelos* is a favorite term of Hermas (only ten times in the rest of Ap. Frs.) illustrates how the *aggelos* terminology tended to gather in apocalyptic (and prophetic) compositions. A cognate form appears in a provocative phrase in *T. Naphtali* 2.1 where the patriarch avers, "Since I was nimble on my feet like a deer, my father, Jacob, appointed me to all missionary and messenger work *(eis pasan apostolēn kai aggelian).*" Though later ecclesiastical writers do not appear to have used *aggeloi* as a synonym for *apostoloi,* they did apply the word to men who took up the monastic life (see Lampe, *PGL,* p. 14). The old Latin collect for the feast of St. Catherine spoke of the body of the saint being carried to Sinai *angelis,* i.e. by monks. A striking usage surfaces in Ambrose, *De mysteriis* 6 (SC 25 *bis,* 158), where the bishop of Milan, speaking of the liturgical rite of baptism, says to those who have received it: "There [in the baptismal rite] you saw a Levite, you saw a priest, you saw a high priest. Do not regard their bodily shape but the grace of their ministries. [When you renounced Satan] you spoke in the presence of angels *(praesentibus angelis),* as it has been written that the lips of the priest guard knowledge and they seek the law from his mouth, because he is the angel *(angelus)* of the Lord almighty. There is no mistaking it, there is no denying it, an angel *(angelus)* is to announce the kingdom of Christ, eternal life. You are not to judge him by his outward appearance but by his function." If those who exercise the apostolic ministry, transmitting the gospel and the sacraments, are *angeli,* then *a fortiori* the apostles could have been thus designated.

Are there indications, outside of this hymnic fragment, that *aggeloi* was in fact used very early in the first Christian generation for Palestinian Jewish Christian missionaries? The Pauline warning in Gal 1:8, "But even if we or an angel from heaven *(aggelos ex ouranou)* should preach to you a gospel contrary to that which we preached to you, let him be accursed," has an even sharper bite on this interpretation. In 4:14 the Galatians welcomed Paul "as God's angel," *hōs aggelon theou.* In any case, *aggeloi,* i.e. *apostoloi* on earth and superterrestrial messengers, have one only gospel (note the distinction between "the elect angels" of 1 Tim 5:21, who are with God, and the unqualified *aggeloi* of this hymn in 3:16b). In 2 Cor 11:13-14 pseudo-apostles are disguised as real ones just as Satan is disguised as "an angel of light," *aggelon phōtos.*

A few other glimpses of this old Jewish Christian terminology appear in the Gospel traditions. In the Matthean interpretation of the parable of the weeds and wheat, the reapers of the harvest, managing the final selection and judgment (the *krisis,* etymologically the sifting of grain), become the angels of the Son of Man, *aggelous autou,* whom he sends, *apostelei* (Matt 13:39, 41; see the logion about the eschatological regents, Matt 19:28). Again, "all the angels" with the returning Son of Man (Matt 25:31) are quite understandable as the apostles, "the least of my brothers" and the servants of all (see Matt 18:1-4), hungry, thirsty, ragged, ill, homeless, imprisoned (see 1 Cor 4:9-11), yet bringing salvation to those who showed any solicitude for even their physical needs (note the emphatic *toutōn* of Matt 25:40, 45) and leaving to condemnation those who ignored them. A somewhat less drastically apocalyptic form of Jesus' teaching is transmitted in the Q logion of Luke 10:2 = Matt 9:37-38: "The harvest is plentiful, but the laborers *(ergatai)* are few; pray therefore the Lord of the harvest to send out laborers into his harvest" (note Luke 10:7 = 1 Tim 5:18; see 2 Tim 2:15). Yet when the reception of these emissaries is compared with the reception of those dispatched to Sodom (Luke 10:12 = Matt 10:15 [adding Gomorrah]; *SFG* §177), the reader recalls that a pair (see Luke 10:1) of angels (see Gen 19:1) brought the message of rescue to the only family permitted to escape the fiery end of the cities.

The Gospel narratives about the resurrection of Jesus still join references to a young man (Mark), two men (Luke), an angel (Matthew), and/or two angels (John) that were seen at the empty tomb (note the *optasian aggelon* in Luke 24:23) and gave a message to the women (*SFG* §352). Similarly in Acts 1:10 "two men" appear after Jesus has left this world to convey an order to the Eleven. Perhaps an archaic and infrequent *aggeloi* title for men to whom the risen Lord had appeared and whom he sent has escalated in the transmission of these narratives as the original sense fell into disuse. In that case, the poetic language of the old Jewish Christian hymn would have been taken prosaically as the technical term for superhuman spirits (the literary phenomenon is at least as old as prose paraphrase of the poetry about the sun standing still in Josh 10:12-14). The way would thus be broached for speculation about the relation between the resurrection of Jesus and that nonspatial, nontemporal order where God lives and rules with his angels. The Gospel narratives of the angels at the tomb would represent a cautious and discreet way of linking the resurrection with the angels. A similar exploitation of a hymnic tradition may occur in 1 Pet 3:18-22, where the resurrection confession seems to be explained against the narratives of *Enoch* with their imagery for the topography of the world of the spirits, fallen as well as elect. In this conceptualization, apocalyptic has turned inside out; the final subjection of the whole superhuman order of spirits to the risen Jesus would occur in his descent among the dead and/or in the process of his return from the world of the dead at what corresponds in this world's calendar to the resurrection and exaltation. Comparison with the materials in *Enoch*, not to mention later apocryphal compositions, indicates the exuberance with which this concept could develop as well as the sobriety of its use in First Peter (if in fact it is used there). However, there are critical christological and soteriological deficiencies with reading 1 Tim 3:16b in the light of the *Enoch* ascent. *Ōphthē aggelois* certainly describes generically the appearances of Christ. Superhuman spirits, both those who are appointed to transmit God's revelation and those who oppose it, are described in the Gospel traditions as encountering and recognizing the mission of Jesus in his public life. The good spirits are associated also with his resurrection and exaltation. His appearance to them on a trip through the heavenly spheres to the throne of God strikes one as otiose christological embellishment of the poetic density of this hymnic confession; if, on the other hand, the text is alluding to Christ's appearance on this trip through the spheres to the spirits who withstood the divine plan, the reader wonders what is the soteriological point of thanking God for an appearance of

Jesus to those who are beyond conversion and redemption. In the final balance, to take *God's messengers* as human beings to whom the risen Jesus appeared by God's appointment keeps this hymnic confession's line of development in the historical order as well as formally shaping it with an eye to the following stich.

Was *heralded to the pagans, ekērychthē en ethnesin,* begins with a verb in the passive, as do all the previous stichs. It concludes, however, with a plural noun, as does only the previous line. The content also draws these lines closely together. The *messengers* who have seen the risen Jesus are the ones who *heralded* this news (i.e. *to euaggelion*) to the nations. Like the hymnic text here, Luke can envision a wider group than the actual witnesses of the risen Jesus heralding him. Thus the Baptist heralds a baptism that prepared people for Jesus' appearance (Luke 3:3; Acts 10:37); the cured demoniac heralded "what Jesus did for him" (Luke 8:39). As a rule (though not in Luke 12:3), the ones who do the heralding are Jesus himself (Luke 4:18, 19; 8:1) or his disciples (whether the Twelve in Luke 9:2 or the Eleven and others, as the passive suggests, in Luke 24:47; Acts 8:5; 10:42, particularly Paul, Acts 9:20; 19:13; 20:25; 28:31). Only in Acts 15:21, on the lips of James of Jerusalem, does one hear of those who herald Moses in the synagogues. As a rule, the implication of these texts is that Jesus' appearances constituted a circle of people who heralded him and that others (such as Philip from the Seven) shared in this work by proclaiming the Christ whom those witnesses proclaimed. The language certainly permits Paul to be numbered among *God's messengers* and justifies the titles "herald and apostle" bestowed upon him, with some solemnity, in 1 Tim 2:7.

*To the pagans* is lit. "to (or among) the nations," *en ethnesin.* The usage of *ethnos,* especially in the plural, in biblical Greek, makes it probable (but no more than probable) that this Greek stich was heard as a reference to *ta ethnē,* as Jews used the term, i.e. as a word meaning all of those who were not Jews. It was a characteristic usage, expressing a kind of left-handed universalism that Paul himself exploited on occasion (see Gal 2:15). The use of the Greek particle *en* as an equivalent to a Hebrew or Aramaic $b^e$ (see the retroversion), with the meaning *to* as well as *among,* reminds one of Paul's description of the revelation of the Son "to me *(en emoi)* so that I might proclaim the good news about him to the pagans *(en tois ethnesin)*" (Gal 1:16). The Jewish Christian usage of this hymn, which did leave its mark on the title for Paul in 2:7 above, "the Gentiles' teacher," contrasts with the way in which the PE and their sources generally express the universal scope of salvation (see Titus 2:11, "all human beings"; 1 Tim 2:4, "all human beings"; 2:6, "for all").

Granted that the hymnic fragment here takes up Palestinian Jewish Christian terminology to confess joyfully that the Son has been heralded among non-Jews (see Gal 1:16), is this a reference to an apostolate to the pagans that predated that of Paul (see M. Hengel above on this), or one that included

Paul's, or one that belonged to Paul alone? Acts 11:19 remembers that it was after the death of Stephen that certain Cypriot and Cyrenian Jewish Christians first proclaimed Jesus as Lord to pagans, literally "the Greeks," in Syrian Antioch. The notice is a Lukan flashback, apparently to a time before the conversion of Paul. The conversion of Cornelius forms an elaborate literary prolegomenon to the notice, which in its turn is an introduction to Paul's missionary work in Antioch. A precise relative chronology for these events cannot be recovered. Luke certainly is saying that there were non-Jewish converts in Antioch before Paul arrived to assist Barnabas, and that could have been as long as a decade after Paul's conversion (though Luke probably did not realize that it was *that* long [E. Haenchen]). Luke has not actually stated that pagans were *first* converted in Antioch (this assertion would counter the massive effect of the doubled Cornelius narrative), nor that this happened only in Antioch. There is a laconic notice from Paul's own hand in Gal 1:21, describing a period after his conversion: "Then I went into the regions of Syria and Cilicia." The context leads one to infer that he preached to the pagans in those areas, as he had been commissioned three years before by the risen Lord (Gal 1:16, 18; see Betz, *Gal.*, pp. 71-72, 79-80). Still there is no confirmatory datum available to fix a date for this missionary work within the decade in question or to determine whether Paul's assertion coincides with what Luke knew from another source (or whether Luke knew a period that did not coincide with the one Paul adduced).

A scenario has been proposed above for the reaction of the Judean congregations to Paul's conversion, thankfully praising the wonderful works of God in the resurrection of his Son and in the apostolate that witnessed to him as the Lord, including now the apostolate of one who had been a deadly foe. They thanked God for the reception of that proclamation by Jews and, now particularly, by Gentiles. The oldest Christian churches, as Jervell, "Traditions," pp. 19-39, has shown, received and retained not only a "tradition" about Jesus but also traditions about the apostles (and the apostolate) which brought that tradition to them. The hymn of 1 Tim 3:16b is a fragment of one such tradition from the Jewish Christian congregations of Palestine, probably of Jerusalem itself. It looks as if it originated there in Aramaic during the springtime of the mission to the Gentiles (see Jervell, *Paul,* pp. 13-25, 30-33) and came down to Antioch with Barnabas when the Jerusalem church sent him to monitor the new developments there (Acts 11:22). If the hymn was not already in Greek, this would have been also an opportune time and place for a version. Barnabas found himself so overwhelmed with converts from the Gentiles that he brought back Paul from Tarsus in Cilicia to assist him and the three others whom an archaic list cited in Acts 13:1 names as leading the Antiochene church. At least one, perhaps two, of these men were Cyrenians and thus were probably the founders of the mission to the Gentiles in Antioch (see Acts 11:20), along with Cypriots, which may be intended to include Barnabas (see Acts 4:36; Haenchen, *Acts*, p. 370).

A hymnic composition such as the one in 1 Tim 3:16b, as well as a doxology such as the one to which Paul refers in Gal 1:24, must have been received as somehow authoritatively accredited or warranted, probably as inspired by the Spirit. Solemnly announced (sung) in public worship, the hymn had been in that setting recognized as coming from the Spirit (see 1 Cor 12:10; 14:26, 29, 32). The point of Paul's observation in Gal 1:24 is that the Spirit does not contradict himself. The mission to the pagans for which Paul was converted and for which the Palestinian churches gave public thanks (without any question of influence from a previous acquaintanceship) is the very same mission which some Jewish Christians a few years later were trying to undercut.

On this reconstruction, the hymnic confession of 1 Tim 3:16b originated in the Jerusalem church, probably from one of its prophets, in response to the blessed beginnings of the mission to the pagans. It was also the prophetic thanksgiving called forth in response to a divine intervention that saved the day for that mission, the utterly astonishing and unexpected conversion of Paul the persecutor. As is noted above, the hymn was probably composed in Aramaic but soon was translated into Greek, perhaps in Antioch, whose "Greeks" needed authoritative support and encouragement for their acceptance among Jewish Christians, especially those with ties to the Jerusalem church.

At any rate, when the long hot summer of problems from the mission to the Gentiles came (see Jervell, *Paul*, pp. 33-51), the popularity of the old Aramaic hymn may have declined sharply in Palestine. This decline would have been more than offset by its long use and prestige in the Antiochene church. Meantime it may have traveled from Jerusalem to Rome during the earliest mission to that city (Jews in Jerusalem and Rome tended to keep closer and more direct contacts than used to be thought; see R. Brown and Meier, *Antioch/Rome*, pp. 95-97). Ephesus might well have known the hymn from the Pauline mission there.

In the PE the way in which Paul is described as quoting these lines in writing leads one to infer that the redactor of the correspondence considered the composition as completely Pauline and still not that apostle's own composition. This would explain the appropriateness of citing a hymn like this in a correspondence that deals with second-generation "Judaizing." The ecumenical scope of the hymn is appropriate to the earliest stages of the Jerusalem church and would been at home in the earliest Roman house churches, which sought converts from the Gentiles as well as their fellow Jews. Ephesus, too, gives a sharp counterpoint to such a Christian hymnic creed, for the city's pride was the cult of Artemis, "she whom all Asia and the world *(oikoumenē)* worship"

(Acts 19:27; see Haenchen, *Acts,* p. 573, "the worldwide reverence for Artemis of Ephesus was a fact," citing archaeological evidence from thirty-two places; and Spicq, *EP,* pp. 475-482).

*He who was received in faith, in the world, was taken up in glory.* In these final lines of the hymnic fragment the verb *episteuthē* signals the response that the heralding of the previous stich was intended to evoke. The use of the aorist passive in three out of six uses in the PE is notable; in Titus 1:3; 1 Tim 1:11 the subject of the verb is the *kerygma* or *euaggelion* that has been "entrusted" to Paul. Closer to the usage here in 3:16b is 2 Thess 1:10, ". . . because our testimony *(martyrion)* to you *(eph' hymas)* was believed *(episteuthē)*"; still the subject is not Christ himself but the proclamation of the gospel. The usage in this hymnic stich is not really of a piece with the rest of the PE or the other Paulines. Perhaps the passive here in verse 16b shows that *pisteuein eis* (the specifically Christian usage of "to believe") and *pisteuein hoti* are interchangeable (R. Bultmann, *TDNT* 6.203). Consequently the meaning here is the Son "is believed in," characteristically by receiving the kerygma that heralds the news about him (R. Bultmann, *TDNT* 6.208 n. 258, 209). The "timeless" passive of Rom 10:10 has an almost impersonal note as it states in principle that "one believes with the heart unto justification *(kardiai gar pisteuetai).*" The subject of the passive verb could be expressed by saying, "Christ is believed in by a man with his heart unto justification" (R. Bultmann, *TDNT* 6.214).

The use here of *episteuthē* with *en kosmōi* has no genuine NT parallel; LXX 1 Kgdms 27:12, with its *episteuthē David en tōi Agchous . . .* , is perhaps a better parallel than J. Strange admits, for the *en* phrase is a sort of dative of reference, meant to indicate the subject of the action of the verb (in Hebrew, Achish is the subject of *ya'amen,* "believed," which has *b$^{e}$dawid,* "in David," as its object). If the verb had been active here, the object would have been in the dative (or with *eis* and the accusative; see BDF §312.1). The *en kosmōi* of this stich in verse 16b precludes any misunderstanding about who believed whom. *Kosmos,* as in the traditional material cited in 1 Tim 1:15, means human society, here represented as repenting and believing. *Kosmos* in these passages does not so much mean "man's home" as it does in 6:7 below (*pace* Johnston, "*Kosmos,*" p. 355; see H. Sasse, *TDNT* 3.888, 893, "the theatre of salvation history"). There is no evidence that here *kosmos* is meant to include more than human beings (in other words, superhuman spirits as well). Though Paul used *kosmos* in 1 Cor 4:9 to include "angels as well as men" (*TDNT* 3.892-893), the usage is not determinative for this pre-Pauline hymn, particularly if the *aggeloi* of the third stich are not superhuman spirits but the apostolic *messengers.* Even if those *aggeloi* were to be understood of the fallen angels, it is difficult to understand how they could be numbered as part of a *kosmos* that put its faith in God's Son. Even in James 2:19, the demons "believe" not in Jesus but in one God of Israel.

For hints about the difficulties, see the materials in Wink, *Powers,* pp. 32-35, 43, 113-114.

It is when the Greek *en kosmōi* is translated into a hypothetic Aramaic original that a serious difficulty surfaces. How is one to translate *kosmos* into a Semitic *Vorlage?* It is well known that Hebrew and Aramaic had no single term that meant "universe" (a possible sense for the Greek *kosmos;* see H. Sasse, *TDNT* 1.204 and 3.880-883). However, the Greek *kosmos* could conceivably translate Hebrew and Aramaic terms meaning the inhabited earth or dry land, *'ereṣ/'araʿ* or *tebel,* in contrast to the sky; however, there is no direct evidence for this translation. The poetic term *tebel,* frequently parallel in Hebrew to *'ereṣ,* designates the land and often precisely as dwelt in by human beings. Thus Ps 9:9, where Yahweh "judges the world *(tēbel),*" is synonymously parallel to "ministers judgment to the peoples *(ʿummim)*"; see also Ps 96:13. This earth is, in H. Traub's phrase, "the theatre of human history" (*TDNT* 5.510) and thus can be designated as that which is "under the sky," *hyp' ouranon,* the LXX version of *tebel* in Job 34:13.

Especially notable among the twenty uses of *tbl* in the Qumran documents is 1QS 4.2: "And these are the ways of these [spirits of truth and of perversity] in the world *(btbl).* It is [of the spirit of truth] to enlighten the heart of man. . . ." In 1QH 1.15 one reads of "the spirit of man which you [God] formed in the world *(btbl)* for everlasting days" (see 1QH 3.33, 36). Again, it is fragmentary prayer text which says, "their [the heavenly bodies?; see 1QS 10.1-8] rule is in all the world *(bkl tbl)*" (1Q 34 *bis* 3.2.3; DJD 1.154; E.T. from Dupont-Sommer, *EWQ,* pp. 79, 202, 210, 336).

In Dan 2:10 an Aramaic form of the Semitic root *ybš* appears in the answer of the Babylonian magicians, "There is not a man on earth *('al yabešta')* who can meet the king's demand." The LXX translates *epi tēs gēs* (Theod., *epi tēs xēras,* "on the dry [land]), but the term retains its connotation of man's proper abode. In 11QtgJob 29.3 *tbl* occurs in a phrase describing all that God has created on the surface of the earth, *tbl;* in 24.8 it seems to have stood in a reference to the Lord who "founded the whole ear[th] *(tb[l])*" (see *'rʿ* in 24.7).

For the Aramaic *'rʿ,* see Beyer, *Texte,* pp. 523-524; 4QEnGiants 8.9; Milik, *Enoch,* p. 315, writes of impurities "on the earth," *b/'/rʿ,* of the superterrestrial beings and their families. In Dan 6:28 the king confesses that Daniel's God "works signs and wonders in the heavens and in the earth *(be'arʿa')*" (see 7:23, "the fourth kingdom on the earth"). 11QtgJob 32.5 describes the ostrich as at home in the desert and "in a salt earth *(b'rʿ)*"; see perhaps 35.9 also.

If indeed a form of the Aramaic *tebel* or *'araʿ* stood in the original hymnic confession of the Jerusalem Christians, then every stich of the composition up to this point has the human world as the horizon within which the divine intervention takes place. In this case it is probable that the original translators from

Aramaic into Greek, when they used *en kosmōi* at this point, did not intend to indicate the superhuman, heavenly world so much as the human one.

*The world* in this hymn is certainly not all bad, but it is the human social setting for Christian faith. The poet is not so optimistic as to write that "the world has believed" or that "he has been the subject of faith in the whole world." That indeed is the commission and goal given in Mark 14:9; 16:15; Matt 26:13, and Paul can say that the faith of the Roman church "is proclaimed in all the world *(en holōi tōi kosmōi)*," but the old hymn was no *captatio benevolentiae.* It was creedal, and for all its hymnic enthusiasm it did no more than marvel at what God had done.

The last stich preserved, *was taken up in glory,* moves from earth, the human world, to heaven and superhuman glory. The aorist passive *analēmphthē* is the form of an uncommon verb in the NT which verges on a technical religious usage. One encounters here not simply a euphemism for death (as in Hermas) but, in the Greek biblical tradition, a term to describe an extraordinary departure from this life.

This theme of "translation" from earth to heaven became a commonplace in Jewish literature, particularly apocalyptic, in the centuries just before and after Jesus' birth. Not only Enoch and Elijah but also Moses, Ezra, Baruch, and unnamed people were described as borne off in an extraordinary manner from this world into heaven. God is the one who "picks up" and carries off these people from this earth into another world. Both Fourth Kingdoms and First Maccabees explicitly say, "(as if) into the sky (heaven)," thus explaining the verb's *ana-* prefix in cosmological terms. The language that had been used for Elijah and Enoch was chosen by the translators of this hymn so that the departure of Jesus would be expressed "according to the Scriptures." The Aramaic may have been *hussaq,* as in Dan 6:24, "Daniel was brought up *(hussaq)* out of the pit" (on Aramaic *s$^e$leq,* see Beyer, *Texte,* pp. 646-647), but a basically transitive *'itgabbi* (see 11QtgJob 33.8; Beyer, *Texte,* p. 540) would be better.

The canonical ending of Mark (16:19) uses *analēmphthē* in saying, "The Lord Jesus . . . was taken up into heaven *(eis ton ouranon)* and sat down at the right hand of God." The emphasis here, as in the concluding stich of 1 Tim 3:16b, is upon the *terminus ad quem,* "heaven" and the enthronement at the Father's right. G. Delling (*TDNT* 4.8) has noted Luke's interest in the *transitus* itself, since he took up *analēmphthē* in Acts for describing what had happened at the definitive departure of the risen Jesus (contrast *anaphereto* in Luke 24:51).

It is suggestive that the themes and some of the key terms of the archaic hymn of First Timothy appear in prosaic form at the beginning of Acts (1:3, revelation in the risen flesh; 1:2, 5, 8 and 2:1-4, the Spirit; 1:2-4, appearances to apostles; 1:8, proclamation to the pagans; 2:8-11, 38-41, belief given by the world; and the ascension itself). Luke can sum up the whole passion/resurrection/ascension history as an *analēpsis* when he says in Luke 9:51, "When the days of his being taken up drew near . . ." (see Fitzmyer, AB *Lk* 1.827-828). In biblical Greek only this passage of Luke employs *analēpsis,* which, read with the plural "days" here, includes the day of death (*Pss Sol* 4.18) as well as the day of exaltation (note the singular "until the day on which he was taken up from us" in Acts 1:22; *T. Levi* 18.3 uses *analēpsis* of the "assumption" in a difficult context [see Jonge, *T. 12 Patr.,* pp. 177-179]).

*In glory, en doxēi,* the final surviving phrase of the hymnic fragment, has links with the language specific to the oldest Jewish Christian liturgy and in particular here with LXX Ps 111:9, where this phrase is found as the psalm blesses Yahweh who helps the lowly. The generosity of the just has as its fruit that "his righteousness endures forever; his horn is exalted in glory." Stephen, in Acts 7:55, is said to see the "glory of God and Jesus [*or* that is Jesus] standing at the right hand of God." Ultimately it is this royal imagery that the phrase in glory in 1 Tim 3:16b appears to have tapped, an imagery that envisions the exalted Son clothed in royal splendor "at the right hand" of God. Hay, *Glory,* has shown how this use of LXX Ps 109 runs through the Christian documentation of the first century and thereafter. The same concept of the royal court (but not the same words) lies behind *en doxēi* here and in LXX Ps 109.

*Doxa* as a rule in the NT is the result of God's becoming visible, and the whole dynamic of the relationship between God and Christ can be designated by it (see Titus 2:13), particularly that of Father and Son. The risen Jesus is regularly associated with *glory* (see G. Kittel, *TDNT* 2.247-248). These observations have their force here in the PE. The link between *glory* and sonship is to be considered in the light of the suggestion that, in the omitted opening of this hymn, Jesus may have been confessed as the Son, . . . *he who was revealed in human flesh.* The *en doxēi* of the last extant stich would stand in a continuity with *en sarki* of the first extant stich, serving as a kind of inclusion for all the intervening wonderful acts of God, which thus are seen within the framework of the exaltation of his Son (see Rom 8:17-21; John 1:14; 8:54; 17:2, 5). The *glory* which *was revealed in human flesh,* the life, death, and rising of Jesus, was attested by the extraordinary events that were part and parcel of the first preaching of Jesus as Lord and Christ. This same glory really belonged to another world and another order into which the Son had returned, to which he properly belonged, in which his faithful would join him, first by belief as they worshipped on earth (in creedal hymns such as this one) and finally (after their deaths) in eternal life itself.

If the Aramaic reconstruction of *en doxēi* with *bah$^{a}$dar* is persuasive here, part of its effectiveness lies in its use in Dan 4:27, 33; 5:18 to describe the royal splendor or honor. God challenges Job in 11QtgJob 34.16, "Clothe yourself then with grandeur and with exaltation of spirit and put on splendor and glory *(hdr)* and honor." The same root was current in biblical Hebrew, especially in poetry. Particularly relevant to the thought here is Ps 21:6 of the king receiving from Yahweh honor and majesty. There is a tantalizing Qumran fragment that mentions in a canticle one who will be "r[aised up in splendor of glory and beauty]," *y[ns' bhdr kbwd wtp'rt]* . . . (1Q 19.13.2; DJD 1.85, "The Book of Noah" [?]). *Bhdr* appears in a hymnic context in 1QH 13.17: "It is by your goodness alone that man is justified and by the immensity of your mer[cy]. You will adorn him with your splendor *(bhdrk)* and fill him with abundance of pleasure, with everlasting bliss and length of days" (E.T. from Dupont-Sommer, *EWQ*, p. 243 modified; see also 1QH 12.15; 1QS 4.7-8; 1QSb 3.25).

4:1. *Here is the Spirit expressly declaring, "In these latter times some people, who dote on seductive spirits and demonic doctrines, will apostatize from the faith."* A prophecy now complements the hymn. After the author of the PE has completed his citation of the hymnic confession, he comments upon it, qualifying its understanding with a slightly adversative *de,* which effectively blocks a drift into an enthusiastic theology of glory. Perhaps better, one ought to read a pronominal *tode,* meaning this very Spirit who inspired the hymn and raised Jesus from the dead has spoken also about these last dark days (see Aune, *Prophecy,* pp. 292, 328-330, on early Christian usage of this "prophetic messenger formula"). The Spirit who had, in the Judean and Syrian liturgies, authenticated the hymn and its subject, Jesus the Lord and Son of God, is the author, too, of the following prophetic oracle, for the same Spirit bestows the charism of prophecy upon believers (see 1 Cor 12:10). Such oracles came from the prophetic order in the Christian worship assemblies (see 1 Tim 1:18; Acts 13:2-3; E. Cothenet, *DBS* 8.1313). The form of the oracle itself reminds one of the one-part predictive response oracle, widespread in the Greek world (for analysis, see Aune, *Prophecy,* pp. 55-56). The opening formula referring to *latter times* as well as the content reminds the reader of the apocalyptic oracles of Judaism whose revelation is that even God's own people stand under the threat of proximate divine judgment (see Aune, *Prophecy,* pp. 112-115, 121). The oracle here in 1 Tim 4:1-5 is expanded by the attaching of parenetic directives on conduct to be avoided or to be cultivated. The implication is that the prescribed or proscribed behavior is already subject to debate "and that no suitable authority structure exists upon which to base a more rational appeal" than a direct appeal to the revealing Spirit of God (Aune, *Prophecy,* p. 326).

In the larger perspective, the author of the PE has deliberately joined together hymn and oracle, appealing to the one Spirit (who brings not only good news but bad news) to take some of the sting out of the judgment oracle that follows. The liturgical origin of both hymn and oracle, the joining of them with the demonstrative *tode,* the taking up of the term *pneuma* from one passage to the other, the way in which the content of the passages both complements and yet contrasts with each other, all indicate the forced artificiality of the chapter division at this point. All the literary signals indicate that 3:14-16 is to be read along with 4:1-5 (see Swete, *Theodore,* p. 139, where the transition hints at this). Each of the quotations forms a hemisphere of the globe at the center of this correspondence.

The emphasis upon *the Spirit* at this point, particularly in the light of the correctives given to those who follow Jewish practices, makes it appropriate to recall that in the Judaism of these centuries "the Spirit is essentially the Spirit of prophecy," and it is exactly this "prophetic spirit" that one encounters here in the PE, not to mention in the Lukan writings (E. Schweizer, *TDNT* 6.381, 409, 445; for the rich context of such a summary, see Fitzmyer, AB *Lk* 1.227-231). Here in the PE this prophetic Spirit is *expressly declaring,* i.e. reliably and explicitly reporting, the formula that follows. The force of *rhētōs* implies that the oracle to be cited can be verified, and thus in all probability that it existed in a written source. One envisions a collection in writing of oracles of the Christian prophets of the previous generation, some of which took the form of hymnic confession (as in 3:16b). All was a spin-off of Christian worship in the Spirit (see E. Cothenet, *DBS* 8.1313), recorded and transmitted as of lasting value for a Christian generation to come.

As *legō* is used in Paul's asseveration in 2:7 above and of the directive of the Scripture in 5:18 below, so here in 4:1 *the Spirit* "speaks," *legei,* through the anonymous, prophetic oracle with its dire prediction, *In these latter times some people . . . will apostatize from the faith.* The opening phrase, in this exact form, is quite unusual, though its variant forms, especially with *eschatos,* are common enough (see Aune, *Prophecy,* p. 121; J. K. Elliott, *Greek Text,* p. 60). In the NT, *eschatos* is used with *kairos* in 1 Pet 1:5 or with *hēmera* in 2 Tim 3:1 or with *hōra* in 1 John 2:18 or with *chronos* in Jude 18; 1 Pet 1:20. The phrase then has apocalyptic connotations of the end of human history and of the final judgment. Yet the "last" age has its days and hours too, the smaller, more particular unit tending to stress the shortness of time available. In the phrase here in 4:1, the generic sense of *kairos* in the plural appears, giving the term its widest possible extension (see Titus 1:3), but the *eschatos* that would have been expected has been replaced by the far less common *hysteros* (usually the adverbial *hysteron* in biblical Greek). *En eschatais hēmerais* appears in 2 Tim 3:1, seemingly as a quotation; since the variant phrase here in 1 Tim 4:1 is emphatically linked to a source, one inclines to believe that the formula belonged to the original form of the prophetic oracle. Certainly there is not a trace of this form of the phrase otherwise in the NT.

A further problem has its roots in the comparative form of *hysteros* in this phrase. Is the sense comparative also, as the version *latter times* might imply? The antithetical *proteros* in 1 Tim 1:13 does have a comparative meaning. The comparative "later" (as opposed to "last") would fit the context of the oracle and the situation which produced it. Still the form *hysteros* could be understood in a superlative sense (see 2 Tim 3:1; 4:3 with *kairos;* BDF §62). Evidently the scribes of the Western texts felt the same way about the sense of *hysteros* here as they substituted *eschatos* or translated with *novissimus* or *ultimus* (see J. K. Elliott, *Greek Text,* p. 60; Frede, *VL* 25.517). Still it must be admitted that the unusual and difficult phrase has been normalized by the scribes and translators while the admittedly confused boundaries between comparative and superlative in Hellenistic Greek have here been unduly exploited to phase out the comparative sense.

Granted the strong LXX precedents for using *eschatos* in phrases referring to the end of history, a pressure that has left evident marks on the language of some parts of the NT, the use here in 4:1 of *en hysterois kairois* appears to be a quite deliberate departure from a received terminology, one that gives a different focus to the tradition (in partial agreement with U. Wilckens, *TDNT* 8.595). The Greek phrase here is in no sense stereotyped. Consequently it ought to be taken at face value until there is evidence that it cannot be thus understood and that the language is used loosely. The comparative sense, opted for here, hears a Christian prophet issuing a warning to an exultant young church, perhaps filling with an unexpected harvest of converts, that the present happy situation would later turn sour. The influx of converts to the faith is compared and contrasted with a later apostasy from the faith. That the time in which the prophecy is uttered or the future time to which it is compared is the eschaton, the last age, is neither affirmed nor denied. Probably (in the light of the observations that appear below) a primitive eschatological outlook is simply presumed (as in fact it was presumed in the preceding hymnic fragment). The prophet and his hearers believe in fact that they are living in the last age, which had begun with Jesus' resurrection and will be consummated by his parousia in glory. The prophecy cited here makes the point that this eschatological age will have bad days as well as good, losses as well as gains. The author of the PE takes up the old oracle because he thinks that the days in which he writes are verifying its prediction. The procedure is not un-Pauline, as 1 Cor 10:11 illustrates, with its description of believers as those upon whom "the end of the ages," *ta telē tōn aiōnōn,* has come.

Parallels to this mode of expression appear in the Qumran documents. Thus CD 1.11, in describing the origins of the sect, says that God "raised up for them a teacher of righteousness . . . to make known to the last generations *(ldwrwt 'ḥrwnym)* what he [would do] to the next generation *(bdwr 'ḥrwn),* the congregation of traitors" (E.T. from Dupont-Sommer, *EWQ,* p. 122 modified). In the Habakkuk pesher, a prophecy is interpreted thus: "[those who will be]tray at the end of days *(l'ḥryt hymym);* they are the violent . . . who will not believe when they hear all the things which will be[fall] the last generation *(hdwr h'ḥrwn)* . . ." (1QpHab 2.5-7; E.T. from Dupont-Sommer, *EWQ*, p. 259). This "last generation" has begun for the sectaries, but it is by no means a short period (see 1QpHab 7.7; 9.6) nor is its terminus known (1QpHab 7.2). Indeed, the end for some of the faithful sectaries was tardy in coming (1QpHab 7.12; see Vermes, "Impact," p. 108).

The expression "the end of days," *'ḥryt hymym*, is an important one for understanding the way in which the people at Qumran regarded themselves. It is the mirror image of the critical principle, cherished by the sectarians, that the circumstances of the birth of time are the principles of the end time (see 1QH 12.8, where this dictates thinking about the all-important calendar). Thus, too, "the end of days" appears regularly in the interpretations of the prophetic books as fulfilled in the history and destiny of Qumran; see 1QpHab 7.7, 12; 4QpIsa[a] A.8; Isa[b] 2.1; Isa[c] 10; 4QpHos[b] 1.11; 4QFlor 1.2, 12, 15, 19; DJD 1.77, 79 = 14.6.2 and 14.18.3. The opening of 1QS[a] (see 28[a] 1.1; DJD 1.107-118) uses *b'ḥryt hymym* as part of the descriptive title for the composition that follows: "and this is the rule for all the congregation of Israel at the end of days when they shall join [the community to wa]lk in obedience to the Law . . ." (E.T. from Dupont-Sommer, *EWQ*, p. 104). The way in which the community conceived this period can be glimpsed at 1QS 4.16-17 where, in a programmatic description of the way in which all people live according to "the two spirits," the rule says, "God has allotted these (two spirits) in equal parts until the final end *('d qṣ 'ḥrwn)*" (E.T. from Dupont-Sommer, *EWQ*, p. 81; see J. Carmignac, cited in 2 Tim 3:1, on 11QMelch 4, 15). The reader of 1 Tim 4:1 is reminded of the contrast between the guidance given by *the Spirit* here, which is opposed to the *seductive spirits and demonic doctrines* mentioned in the prophetic intervention.

The eschaton will not be all sweetness and light, but on later occasions within that age *some people (tines) . . . will apostatize from the faith.* As is noted at 1 Tim 1:3, *tines* may be a discreet way of saying "many." In any event, apostasy will be characteristic of the eschaton, as the use of the noun *apostasia* illustrates in LXX Josh 22:22; 2 Chron 29:19; 33:19 (where it is parallel to *hamartiai*); Jer 2:19; and particularly 1 Macc 2:15, where it is used absolutely of the effect of the persecution of Antiochus and designates desertion of the God of Israel and his Law. The deserter himself is *apostatēs*, as in LXX Num 14:9; Josh 22:16, 19; Isa 30:1; 2 Macc 5:8 (see 5:11, where Judea "revolts" against the Antiochene decrees). Two of the Hebrew roots that refer to apostatizing or rebelling against God are *swr*, which is especially frequent in 1QS as well as CD, and *mrd*, which appears in 1QpHab 8.11, 16 and CD 8.4.

The cluster of terms is by no means frequent in the NT. In 2 Thess 2:3 *apostasia* appears when the author, in sketching a scenario for "the day of the Lord," says, "the apostasy comes first" (see Giblin, *Threat*, pp. 81-88, with its further references). His catechesis may even be based on the teaching of an oracle such as the one cited here in 1 Tim 4:1. The one remaining occurrence of the noun in the NT is in Acts 21:21, where the charge against Paul is that he teaches Diaspora Jews "apostasy from Moses, telling them not to circumcise their children or observe the customs." The parallel to Maccabean usage is notable. When Luke does use the verb, it ordinarily means physical separation or departure (see Luke 2:37), but in the interpretation of the parable of the sower this term is used absolutely of deserting the word of God, "in time of trial," *en kairōi peirasmou* (Luke 8:13). In connection with this passage, S. Brown, *AP*, pp. 14-16, has noted that for Luke *peirasmos* has only a pejorative sense (see 1 Tim 6:7) and "is inseparably associated with the sin of apostasy" (p. 21). Since this desertion stands in contrast with "for a time they believe," *pros kairon pisteuousin*, the implication is that they abandon "the faith" or "the way" or "the church," and thus "the notion of apostasy" undergoes "an ecclesialization" (p. 31 n. 115). The usage resembles that of the oracle cited here in the PE, where the apostasy is explicitly *from the faith* (the alliterative *p* sounds underscore this point in the Greek). Moreover, the Lukan usage also understands "to believe" as "to make a profession of belief *or* faith" (p. 47). This usage, archaic and quite Palestinian, as Gal 1:23 illustrates, shows from still another point of view that this prophetic oracle could have emerged from the earliest liturgical assemblies of the Jerusalem Christians.

The difference between the Jewish concept of religious apostasy and the Christian concept which is glimpsed here appears most clearly in the emphasis in the Jewish tradition upon abandoning practice whereas the Christian emphasis tends to focus upon a denial of the faith and the acceptance of wrong teaching (compare Titus 1:16 with 1 Tim 5:8). The two are alike in seeing the practice or the profession in relation to the person of the God of Israel or his spokesman (i.e. Moses or Christ; see 2 Tim 2:11-13 on the total abandonment of Christ by disowning him).

Those *people who apostatize from the faith* are described and defined as persons *who dote on seductive spirits and demonic doctrines*, lit. people who are addicted (note the present tense of *prosechontes*) to "deceitful spirits and the teachings of demons" as others might be to alcoholic spirits (1 Tim 3:8) or "Jewish tales" (Titus 1:14) or "tales and endless genealogies" (1 Tim 1:4). Since up to this point in the PE the term *pneuma* has occurred in the singular and of the Spirit of God (Titus 3:5; 1 Tim 3:16; 4:1a), the use now in the plural and with the adjectival *planois* emphatically distinguishes these *seductive spirits* from the (Holy) Spirit who has authored this prophetic oracle. The continuing alliterative *p*, repeated now in *prosechontes pneumasin planois*, serves to bind the whole phrase together and to distinguish it from the *didaskaliais daimoniōn*, which has its own alliterative unity.

As in other NT contexts which use *planos,* the adjective here suggests teachings about God and Jesus which have no basis in the divine reality and thus, while pretending to be true, authoritative, and credible, are really false, unauthorized, and incredible (and not without a basis that is ultimately satanic). Evidently for the old oracle here and for the author of the PE, the Spirit validates the teaching transmitted (see 2 Tim 1:14). Dualism, ungodly and misleading powers, and apocalyptic eschatology all are linked in varying degrees with the *plan-* cluster of terms (see H. Braun, *TDNT* 6.245). The following materials illustrate these affiliations.

Already at Qumran one encounters a teaching on "the two spirits of truth and perversity," *h'mt wh'wl* (1QS 3.18-19; E.T. in this section from Dupont-Sommer, *EWQ,* modified). These spirits not only are external to a person but also dwell within him. Each spirit, moreover, seems to have a company of "spirits" that belong to it (see "the spirits of Belial" in CD 12.2-3; perhaps in 1QH 17.23-24). They form corresponding "spirits" within human beings (good ones in 1QS 2.20; good and bad in 3.14; good and then bad in 1QH 17.17, 23). A sort of metastasis from the spirits occurs, unto the death or life of the man in whom they grow. There does not appear to be a precise equivalent at Qumran to the *pneumata plana* of the best manuscript tradition of this oracle in First Timothy. It is curious that the variant reading *pneumata planēs* would have an equivalent in the tiny fragments of 1Q 36.25; DJD 1.138, with its *rwḥwt pšʿ* (see the LXX Ezek 33:10, 12 for versions of *pšʿ* using *planē* and *planēthēi*).

The Hebrew *tʿh* stands behind the LXX *planan* in 42 out of 121 uses of that Greek term (H. Braun, *TDNT* 6.233). In 1QH 1.22 a *rwh htw'h* appears in the hymnist's self-description: "Yet I am but a creature of clay and thing kneaded with water, a foundation of shame and fount of defilement, a crucible of iniquity and fabric of sin, *a spirit of straying,* and perverse, void of understanding." The only other use of the nominal form, in CD 20.11, is also notable, for the document is describing sectaries who have deserted the community to side with the Jerusalem high priest. In 1QS 3.21-22, ". . . because of the angel of darkness all the sons of righteousness go astray *(tʿwt).*" For the Qumran hymnist this "straying" is the teaching of the Jerusalem priests on the liturgical calendar (see 1QH 2.14; 4.12, 16, 20 [?], 25; 1QpHab 10.9; cf. 1QS 5.4 with 11). In the light of the connotations noted above in *prosechontes,* one recalls that the Hebrew *tʿh* frequently describes the wandering of the drunkard (see 1QH 4.11-12).

The *Testaments of the Twelve Patriarchs* offer examples of *to pneuma* (or *ta pneumata) tēs planēs* at every turn (see H. Braun, *TDNT* 6.238; E. Schweizer, *TDNT* 6.391). As Braun has noted, the expression is never applied to a thing, only to a person, in the *Testaments.* Moreover, the objects of the deception are the Israelites and much less often the pagans. The former are lured away from the law and its commands into specific types of immorality, headed by sexual sins, *porneia,* and followed by gluttony, anger, hypocrisy, arrogance, lying, injustice (*T. Reuben* 3.2-7). These are the "seven spirits of deceit" (*T. Reuben* 2.1) which tempt people, especially the young. The number is not to be taken arithmetically, for still other "spirits of deceit" are noted in other passages. Thus *T. Judah* 13.3 has jealousy. A spirit named Beliar appears to preside over this host of *pneumata plana* (see *T. Levi* 3.3; *T. Issachar* 7.7; *T. Dan* 1.7; *T. Benjamin* 3.3; and see the Belial, *bly'l,* of 1QM 13.2, *s.v.l.* [Yadin, *War,* pp. 232-233] and CD 12.2; both texts employ *rwhwt*).

The *plan-* cluster of terms appears in the Lukan corpus only when Luke 21:8 uses the verb in the prophetic warning by Jesus which the evangelist edits with an additional note about the irresponsible apocalyptists who are going to say in Christ's name, "The time is at hand." Such prophecy is to be dismissed with contempt (note that Luke simply omits the Markan "and they will lead many astray"; Mark 13:6; *SFG* §288; see H. Braun, *TDNT* 6.242-244, 246).

*Demonic doctrines* takes up the contemptuous Septuagintal usage of *daimones,* a usage that already existed in popular Hellenistic Greek, where it meant spirits hostile and injurious to human beings. The LXX made the term, for all practical purposes, a technical term in the biblical tradition as well as in later Jewish authors for the pagan deities. If the phrase here in the PE is being used in the biblical and even Pauline tradition, then the demons here are the hostile spirits that stand behind pagan polytheistic religion. The *doctrines, didaskaliai,* here fit the meaning discerned otherwise in the PE, i.e. authoritative explanations of the Scriptures of Israel. Here it is not the Pauline interpretation of the Scriptures but those of others, who are contemptuously identified as spokesmen for the evil spirits that animate paganism (note 2 Cor 11:14 with its comparison of the pseudo-apostle with Satan masked as "an angel of light").

Perhaps the sense of the oracle in its original setting is at least partially recoverable. The language is that of a thoroughly Hellenistic Jewish polemic that traced all moral evils back into idolatry and the worship of deities other than the one God of Israel. Thus Wis 14:27, "For the worship of the unspeakable idols is the beginning, cause, and end of every evil" (E.T. from Winston, AB *Wisd.,* p. 270). The *doctrines* here in 4:1 are those that justify aberrations *(planois)* such as those which the author lists in verse 3, *doctrines* which personal and hostile *demonic spirits* that lurk behind paganism inspire. The original burden of the oracle still appears in the excoriation as pagans of those who will abandon the Christian faith. Originally the prophet foresaw the outcome for those converts from paganism who had never really been rooted in the faith and so are exposed to demonic powers that they had never completely abandoned (see Luke 8:12-13). The author of the PE applies another edge of the polemic to heterodox Jewish Christians. They pride themselves on their orthodox purity and seek to persuade other converts, whether pagan or Jewish in origin, to join their ranks, but they are actually tools of the *demonic spirits* which misguide the pagans (note the similar bitter sarcasm in Titus 1:15-16; this tone and language appear in Justin when he tackles Marcion, *Trypho* 35.1-6; *Apology* 58.1-3). See Horbury, "False Prophecy," pp. 492-508, especially pp. 497-499, 505-506, for additional materials.

2-3. *These lying frauds, with their cauterized consciences, interdict marriage and demand abstinence from foods, things that God created for believers and persons who have recognized the truth, to share in thankfully.* The grammatical sequence at this point illustrates how the *spirits* and "demons" are related to their spokesmen, for the hardened liars of this verse are in apposition to the *daimoniōn* of verse 1, though the reference is surely to human beings from this point onward. Thus *lying* here stigmatizes the persons speaking (rather than what they say). Perhaps the harsh transition, which versions are bound to soften, marks the seam where the author of the PE joined the old oracle with his own materials (see 1 Tim 1:3-7).

Since the transition is harsh on any construction, there is a possibility that the phrase *en hypokrisei pseudologōn* is to be taken instrumentally. The transition from the instrumental datives of verse 1 would be very harsh, though there is no denying a certain progression in thought from the *spirits* to their *doctrines* to the deceptive show of virtue on the part of those who speak for the demons. Still there appears to be no parallel for such an understanding of this very rare phrase in Jewish and early Christian Greek, and so the present version has taken it adjectivally.

*Hypokrisis* and its cognates have an ethically bad sense in Hellenistic Jewish Greek, where they begin to appear in the latest strata of the LXX. In classical and Hellenistic Greek otherwise, the terminology was not heard pejoratively. *Hypokrisis* suggested the "deception" of apostasy in the Jewish tradition (see U. Wilckens, *TDNT* 8.565; see Fitzmyer, AB *Lk* 1.642-643; 2.955, for more details, particularly from Qumran, and references). Again with U. Wilckens (*TDNT* 8.569-570), by the time of Ap. Frs., false teachers are by definition apostates and thus hypocrites. Accordingly their use of *en hypokrisei* coincides largely with the adjectival sense proposed here for 1 Tim 4:2, not to mention earlier Jewish Greek.

A firm Hebrew correlative for the Greek *hypokrisis* terminology is hard to come by. The LXX of Job 34:30; 36:13 used forms of *ḥnp,* "godless," but the Hebrew term is very rare in pre-Christian texts (*ḥnwph* in 4Q Testim 28; DJD 5.58). Perhaps the best one can do, in the current state of the evidence, is to note the way in which, at Qumran, the "spirit of truth" stands in antithesis to the "spirit of perversity, *ʿwl*" (1QS 3.18-19), which engenders a vicious brood that includes "falsehood," *šqr;* "falsity and deceit," *kḥš wrmyh;* "a blaspheming tongue, blindness of eye and hardness of heart" (1QS 4.9-11). The titles of choice for the opponent of the teacher of righteousness are "the man of lies," *'ys hkzb* (1QpHab 2.2; 5.11) or "the preacher of lies," *mṭyp hkzb* (1QpHab 10.9; see CD 1.15; 8.13; 19.26; 20.15). In contrast 1QS 10.22 avers, "on my lips shall be found no criminal deceit *(kḥs 'wn)* or falsity *(myrmwt)* or lies *(kzbym)*" (E.T. in Dupont-Sommer, *EWQ,* p. 100).

In a particularly notable passage the Qumran hymnist denounces "interpreters *(mlyṣy)* of falsehood and seers of deceit who devised plans of Belial against me." He goes on to specify these as calendrical deviations anent the celebration of feasts. Those who teach and do such things "are hypocrites (*n'lmym* [see 3.28]); the schemes are of Belial which they conceive and they seek you [God] with a double heart and are not firm in your truth. . . . And they have sought you out among idols . . . and they have gone in to seek you according to the preaching of prophets of falsehood *(kzb),* they who are led astray by error" (1QH 4.9-10, 13-16; E.T. from Dupont-Sommer, *EWQ,* pp. 211-212 modified). Baseless explanation and misleading application of the Law (as the Qumran faithful saw it) often appear to be the issue in this polemic which fits the immediate context here in the PE as well as the Palestinian situation which prompted the oracle originally (Fitzmyer). Granted that one must adduce evidence other than the form of this polemical *topos* to demonstrate the historical existence of the apostates noted here in the PE (see Karris, "Polemic," pp. 549-564), still the Qumran documents indicate that on occasion in the Jewish tradition actual historical deviants were the objects of fierce literary critique. Thus it becomes more probable that apostate teachers were in the mind of the prophet cited here, and still others were in the mind of the redactor.

*These lying frauds* are further described with two participial phrases, the first describing their inner state, *with their cauterized consciences.* The second phrase specifies their teaching. They *interdict marriage and demand abstinence from foods.*

The conscience, *syneidēsis,* has been discussed regularly in the PE thus far. Here it is emphatically *their, tēn idian, consciences,* i.e. the bad conscience which belongs to *these lying frauds* who seek to corrupt the good or clean conscience of those whom they want to teach. The description of the bad conscience as *cauterized* masks a problem with the participle *kekaustēriasmenōn* (which modifies *pseudologōn*). The Greek *kautēr,* "burner," spawned the term *kautērion,* an instrument for burning, a branding iron (which appears in 4 Macc 15:22 as an instrument of torture; *kaustēr* means instruments for cauterizing in Hippocrates, *Peri haimorroidōn* 6). Forms of the verb here in the PE are rare in secular Greek, and it is not immediately clear whether the participle in 1 Tim 4:2 is to be understood as a middle or a passive, i.e. as describing liars who have been seared in their consciences (passive) or who have themselves seared their *con-*

*sciences* (middle). Granted the harsh transition in this sentence from the demons to their human spokesmen, is it possible that the ambiguity was welcome to the author of this passage, who thus could imply simultaneously that these apostates had been branded as slaves by their demonic masters and also that it was their own human choice and fault? If one emphasizes the passive sense, then *kekaustēriasmenōn* calls up the image of the branding iron used on wandering animals, (fugitive) slaves, or deserters from the army. The middle sense would emphasize the medical connotation that accompanies the English *cauterize* to this day. The conscience of these apostate liars has been like an open or suppurating wound that they have closed by searing with a red-hot iron. The former image stresses the relation of these liars to those who really possess them and know them by the brand that they have put on them. The latter emphasizes the drastic measures that these people have taken to rid themselves of their deep-seated infirmities.

With 4:3 a present participle, *kōlyontōn,* begins a second adjectival phrase modifying *these lying frauds.* This participle governs both *gamein,* "marriage" in this version, and *apechesthai k.t.l.,* "abstinence from foods." The zeugma is at best harsh, though not unparalleled in Greek (see *se de kai auton kōlysei energein ta tou thanatou erga kai tēn Ploutōnos archēn zēmioun mē nekragōgounta pollou tou chronou,* "you yourself [Charon] would be prevented from doing the work of death and compelled to embarrass the revenues of Pluto's government by not bringing in any dead for a long time," Lucian, *Charon* 2; E.T. from LCL 2.399-401 modified). With *interdict* the content of the *demonic doctrines* mentioned above is illustrated with the two areas of human activity where *these lying frauds* enounce their own "Thou shalt not. . . ."

The first area of human activity which the *lying frauds interdict* is *marriage* or marrying, *gamein.* Already, from several different points of view, the PE have illustrated the healthy teaching that Christians would marry, establish a household or home, and rear children (see Titus 2:1-6; 1 Tim 2:8-15; 3:2-12). These letters do not command marriage; they can envision circumstances where it is reprehensible (1 Tim 5:11) and when it is strongly to be recommended (1 Tim 5:14). At this point they curtly and contemptuously dismiss any teaching that would forbid *marriage* as such to Christians.

One is left to speculate on what theological justification the *lying frauds* gave for their prohibition. There is a little evidence for the reasons behind the peremptory dismissal of their *demonic doctrines* by the PE. What could have led Christians (Jewish Christians at that, in the problematic presupposed here) to *interdict marriage?* From the use of the Genesis creation accounts earlier in this letter (1 Tim 2:13-14) as well as in the discussion about foods that occupies the rest of this section, the reader infers that the author of the PE (not to mention the church that he addressed) was able to perceive and apply the teaching on the marriage relationship in these chapters of the OT. The teaching of Jesus about marriage was remembered as an application of that of Genesis (see Mark 10:6-7 and Matt 19:4-5 but not Luke; *SFG* §252). In contrast, Paul's teaching on marriage and virginity is grounded on a saying of Jesus about divorce and remarriage as well as Paul's own guidance by the Spirit (1 Cor 7:10, 40). The tack taken by the PE resembles Paul in the appeal to the Spirit. Unlike him, however, there is no reference to Jesus' teaching, probably indicating a Jewish Christian congregation whose "Bible" more or less coincided with what Jews then read as sacred and authoritative. Was there any setting in contemporary Judaism in which marriage was forbidden on a scriptural basis? Perhaps one encounters here a Christian riposte to the Qumran discipline for the holy war (see Titus 1:6) in which the full-fledged covenanter married for a few years for the sake of offspring and then left wife and home to dedicate himself completely to preparation for the imminent apocalyptic battle between good and evil. In the eyes of the one who wrote 1 Tim 4:3, this is to *interdict marriage* as a Christian understands it.

The second area in which the *demonic doctrines* of the apostates lay down prohibitions is in matters of diet as they *demand abstinence from foods.* The zeugma through which *kōlyontōn* governs the second infinitive is less than smooth, and the asyndetic joining of the two infinitives underlines the awkwardness (still one must recall a similar asyndeton in Titus 3:1). Such a verb as *keleuontōn,* "commanding," would have been expected to govern *apechesthai* (see BDF §479.2), and Bentley conjectured that that verb had dropped out of the text in the earliest stage of transmission. As shrewd a critic as F. Hort thought that *apechesthai* was a corrupted form of *kai geuesthai,* "and to taste," or *ē haptesthai,* "or to touch." Yet it is striking that the ancient scribes, whose ear for Greek commended "improvements" for many a turn of phrase in the text before them, managed, as the apparatus witnesses, to transmit the construction here without a qualm, and it is the basis of the version here.

For the meaning of *apechesthai* with the genitive, the Lukan citation in Acts 15:20, 29 of the Jerusalem decision on how much of the Mosaic Law on foods and marriage the Gentile converts were to observe is helpful. They are instructed "to abstain from the pollutions of (*or* from what has been sacrificed to) idols and unchastity (*porneia* [meaning attempts to marry within degrees of relationship forbidden by the law]), from what is strangled and from blood." It looks as if the apostates of the PE ran amuck with this compromise, turning it into a doctrinaire program that tainted matters sexual and dietary. One infers that they appealed to further OT laws on ritual cleanliness (see above on the holy war) and on diet to justify their own directives, explaining and exploiting them according to their own lights and evidently in a completely non-Pauline (and, according to Luke, a "non-Jerusalem-at-its-best") fashion. Considering the course which the argument here will take, it may be significant that the fall of Adam and Eve took place through eating. The apostates could further appeal to God's manifesting his judgment through deprival of food (see M. Ottoson, *TDOT* 1.236-241, esp. 239-240).

The noun *brōma* and *abstinence from foods* remind the reader here of the Pauline controversies with his refractory Corinthian converts (see 1 Cor 6:13; 8:8, 13) and his suggestions on such matters to the parties among the Roman Christians (Rom 14:15, 20). Mark 7:19 uses the term in a controversial logion about Jesus having declared "all foods clean." The controversial sense, involving OT dietary laws, appears again in Heb 9:10 and particularly 13:9: "Do not be led away by diverse and strange teachings; for it is well that the heart be strengthened by grace, not by foods *(brōmasin),* which have not benefited their adherents." By the time of Ignatius, devilish teachings have themselves become the strange fodder of heresy that stands in contrast to "Christian fare," *christianēi trophēi* (*Trall.* 6.1). The combination of heretics, the demonic origins of their teaching, and the link of that teaching with food, actual or metaphorical, makes one wonder if a rhetorical *topos* is in the process of crystallizing during this period, a *topos* to which the author of the PE and Ignatius witness and which each varies for his purpose.

In *things that (ha) God created,* the neuter plural relative *ha* appears to refer to the *brōmatōn* just mentioned. In fact, a few scribes (e.g., $C^c$; see J. K. Elliott, *Greek Text,* p. 63) followed the Attic practice of putting the relative into the case of its antecedent and writing *hōn* at this point. The scruple may have been more than stylistic, however, since the genitive evidently settles the question of the antecedent in favor of *foods;* but the neuter plural could refer to the pair of infinitives that have preceded. In that case, the reasons that are going to be adduced in the relative clause would apply to both *marriage* and *foods.* Perhaps the asyndetic pairing of the infinitives was originally meant to make both read as the antecedents of *ha.* If that is how the phrase ought to be interpreted, the reasons proposed from this point through verse 5 ought to apply to *marriage* as well as to *foods.* The following analysis will offer an opportunity to test that hypothesis.

The author of the PE refutes the teachings of the apostates by appealing to *ho theos,* "God" (the definite article suggests the Father), as the creator who made these things, i.e. *foods* and *marriage.* God's creative act is understood as issuing not simply in human beings in general or persons as male but in persons as male or female and certain of their basic social relationships (see W. Foerster, *TDNT* 3.1026). Even the order of this creative act was exploited by Paul in his argument against the disorderly Corinthian converts, an order and a methodology which appears in 1 Tim 2:13 also. Matthew, in one of only two passages in which the Gospel tradition uses *ktizein* (Mark 13:19; Matt 19:4), transmits Jesus' teaching on marriage by an appeal to the Genesis description of the creation of human beings: "Have you not read that he who made *(ho ktisas)* them from the beginning made them male and female?"

The purpose of these *things that God created* is now explained in terms of their use by *believers and persons who have recognized the truth.* In a word, the ultimate reason for creation is perceived by Christian faith. The members of the phrase here are synonymous to the extent that they describe persons who have committed themselves to Christ, whether of Jewish or pagan origins. The first term, *believers,* emphasizes the internal faith which has brought their hearts to Christ; the following phrase, *persons who have recognized the truth,* emphasizes the external experience and visible acceptance (through sacramental baptism) of the risen Lord and his guidance. In the PE *pistos* refers to teachings and to persons. Only here and at 4:12 does the plural, *pistoi,* occur, using the article and meaning Christian *believers* as a body. Luke has such a usage in Acts 10:45, but there is no precise parallel in the rest of the Paulines (see *hoi hagioi* with anarthrous *pistoi* in Eph 1:1; Col 1:2).

The phrase *epiginōskein tēn alētheian,* which stands behind *persons who have recognized the truth,* does not occur elsewhere in the NT or in Ap. Frs., though one might note the Pauline uses of the verb in Rom 1:32, "they recognize God's decree," and Col 1:6, "from the day you heard and recognized the grace of God in truth." Of the twenty appearances of the verb in Luke-Acts, Luke 24:16, 31 on "recognizing" the risen Jesus is especially notable, not least because the recognition comes in the breaking of the bread, i.e. sharing the eucharistic bread with Jesus (on the cultic overtones of the language used in the Emmaus incident, see Dupont, "Emmaus," pp. 105-121, updated with lavish references in his *Synoptiques* 2.1153-1181). *First Clement* 32.1 employs this verb of recognizing God's great gifts, and *Barn.* 10.3 uses it in giving reasons for the dietary laws of the OT. Pork is forbidden because the animal is one that forgets his master after he eats; thus a certain class of people "when they are in need, recognize the Lord."

*Believers recognize* that they are intended *to share in thankfully* the *things that God created* for them. *Eis metalēmpsin meta eucharistias* is picked up in the following verse here where the participial *meta eucharistias lambanomenon* employs the same root as *metalēmpsis.* The cognate verb, *metalambanein,* occurs in 2 Tim 2:6, of the farmer's right "to be the first to have his share of the crops." Luke uses the verb of sharing food at Acts 2:46; 27:33-34 (somewhat differently at Acts 24:25; see G. Delling, *TDNT* 4.11). The verb in Heb 6:7; 12:10 designates the sharing in the visible blessings as well as in the invisible holiness of God, by the earth as well as the people on it.

In *First Clement* one can share in the "glorious deeds" of the past (19.2); in the "discipline *(paideias)* which is in Christ" (21.8); and in "the promised gifts" (35.4). In a cluster of occurrences of the verb in *2 Clem.* 14.3-5, it has as its object the Spirit and life (see also 15.5 of the sharing of divine benefits and 16.2 of "the mercy of Jesus"). Hermas, *Vis.* 3.7.6, describing those who have lapsed from baptismal grace, says they find a chance to repent "because they shared in the righteous word." Only at *Vis.* 3.9.2 does the verb again appear, in a context that refers to sharing in material food: ". . . do not take a superabundant share of the creatures of God *(ta ktismata tou theou)* for yourselves, but give also a part to those who lack. For some are contracting illness in the flesh by too much eating. . . ."

This use of *metalē(m)psis* for the sharing of food has a striking illustration in Justin, *Apology* 67.5; Goodspeed, *Index*, p. 75, where *hē metalēpsis* is "the participation by each in that over which the thanksgiving has been offered [i.e. in the eucharistic bread and wine; see 65.5 and its use of *metalabein*] and to those who are absent a portion is sent by the deacons." The possibility arises that the usage of 1 Tim 4:3-5 derives from an archaic church order, probably the one whose lines started to appear in 1 Tim 2. Anthony Hanson, *PE*, pp. 88-89, made a case for a sacramental eucharistic reference in 4:5. This analysis will build on his suggestions below.

The phrase *meta eucharistias*, "thankfully," is adjectival to the sharing just mentioned. The noun appeared in a list of names for prayers in 1 Tim 2:1, and will reappear in the verse following. The formal echo of the beginning of the church order is notable in the light of what has been observed in the preceding paragraph.

There is no less reason *a priori* to thank God for marriage than for food. The blessing prayers of Tob 8:5-6, 15-17 and the Qumran ceremony cited on 1 Tim 2:15 remind one of the religious regard for marriage in the Judaism of this period. This passed into early Christian practice, as Ign. *Pol.* 5.2 illustrates (also cited on 2:15 above). Clement of Alexandria cites 1 Tim 4:3 with the comment: "It necessarily follows, then, that it is wrong to forbid marriage and indeed eating meat or drinking wine. . . . But both he who eats with thanksgiving *(meta eucharistias)* and he who does not eat, who also offers thanksgiving *(meta eucharistias)* and has continent enjoyment, should live in accordance with reason." In his discussion of self-control and marriage, Clement says, alluding to this passage, that believers ought to live "as people who are not passionately attached to the created world *(tēi ktisei)* but use it with all gratitude *(meta eucharistias)* and with a sense of exaltation beyond it" (*Strom.* 3.12, 14; O. Stählin 2.235, 240; E.T. from Oulton, *Alexandrian* 2.80, 85).

4-5. *For (hoti) everything in God's creation is fine and none is despicable when received with thanksgiving. Every one of them is hallowed by God's word in Scripture and intercessory prayer.*

*Hoti,* here translated "for," now introduces the principle grounding the

Christian attitude toward *marriage* and *foods* in contrast to that of the *lying frauds* cited in verse 3. The revelation in Gen 1 and the Christian response to that revelation are the bedrock on which this principle builds its riposte. The meaning of the transitional *hoti* is crabbed and obscure (not unlike the usage of the same particle in 6:7 below). The lack of textual variants, however, seems to indicate that the ancient scribes found the meaning clear enough.

*Everything in God's creation is fine* takes one back to the priestly narrative of creation in Genesis, with its refrain of *kalon* at every stage and finally the summary, *kai eiden ho theos ta panta hosa epoiēsen kai idou kala lian,* "and God saw all things that he made and behold [they were] very fine" (Gen 1:31). The importance of this teaching was still being articulated in Jewish circles in Palestine and Alexandria in the intertestamental era, as Sir 39:16, 21, 33 and Wis 1:14 illustrate. Paul expresses the thought in the phrase "Nothing is unclean in itself," *koinon di' heautou* (Rom 14:14). Lukan texts emphasize that what God has cleansed, none is to call unclean (see Acts 10:14, 28; 11:8 and Titus 1:15), though he does not specify whether the cleansing was in the act of creation itself or through some later act. *Kalon,* "fine," here is used as previously in the PE, with an emphasis on visible attractiveness. In the Genesis creation story, "the woman saw the tree was fine for food *(kalon . . . eis brōsin)* and that it was a delight to the eyes . . ." (LXX Gen 3:6). The adjective also describes women in the sacred history, from the wives of the patriarchs (LXX Gen 12:14; 24:16; 29:17) to the chaste Susanna (Dan LXX Sus 2.23).

The second principle adduced by the author, *and none is despicable,* seems to have been as much at home in the Greek world, classical and Hellenistic, as the former was in the Jewish. Lucian appeals to it several times; see *Timon* 37; *Toxaris* 37; *De mercede conductis* 27; *Philopseudes* 29.

*Lambanomenon* (note the present tense), "when received," as was previously observed, echoes *metalēmpsin* in verse 3, as does *meta eucharistias,* "with thanksgiving." Not only is the latter phrase formally significant for the structure of this section, but its sense also is critical for expressing the principle here. The phrase refers to prayer that is in some sense public and substantially synonymous with *in intercessory prayer, dia . . . enteuxeōs,* in the following verse (see 1 Tim 2:1). On this interpretation, the prayer of the church over married couples and over foods corresponds with and reaffirms in the day-to-day life of believers what God did in creating and what he has revealed *in Scripture,* in this instance from the first page of Genesis on. The author appeals to *Scripture* and to the life of the church, to what Christians do in response to revelation, in a word, to apostolic traditions, for these are presented as practices that Paul sanctioned. The constant practice of liturgical prayer in connection with both food and marriage means that the *lying frauds* cannot be right in their prohibitions of these good things.

Can one specify the *thanksgiving* here any more closely? Is it possible that there is a reference to a sacramental eucharistic action at this point in the PE? The resemblances of 1 Tim 4:5 to *Did.* 9–10 as well as to the description of the eucharist in Justin, *Apology* 66.2 (see also 13.1 and 67.2; see Irenaeus, *Adversus haereses* 5.2.3: *PG* 7.1126-1127; SC 153.34-36), appear to confirm the eucharistic reference (see Comment on v. 5 below). Or must one affirm here in 1 Tim 4:4-5, with D-C, that *eucharistia* here means Christian prayers at meals (and no more, a position that Dibelius held for the prayers of *Did.* 9–10 also)? In the late second century there may be a witness to this meaning. Eusebius adds a postscript to his citation of the letter about the martyrs of Lyons, among whom was one whose extraordinarily austere way of life caused misgivings among his fellow Christian prisoners, apparently about his orthodoxy in "not making use of the creations of God," *tois ktismasi tou theou.* The man "was persuaded and began to partake *(metalambanein)* of everything without restraint and gave thanks to God *(kai eucharistei tōi theōi)*" (*Church History* 5.3.2-3). The meaning of verse 5, however, is crucial for answering the questions raised above about such an interpretation.

*Every one of them is hallowed* is in Greek introduced with *gar* as the final summary reason for the goodness of creatures and for the prayer of thanks with which they are regularly *received* (present tense). The reference includes not only the teaching of Scripture that has been adduced but also the public prayer of believers. *Marriage* and *foods* have been sanctified, *everything in God's creation is hallowed (hagiazetai) by God's word (dia logou theou) in Scripture* [not in the Greek] *and intercessory prayer (enteuxeōs).* The verb *hagiazetai* bears the burden of meaning here. The usage of the PE suggests that both persons and things can be *hallowed,* and the passive here is the Semitic circumlocution for saying, "God (*or* the Spirit) has hallowed. . . ." Titus 3:5 used a cognate for naming the Holy Spirit (see also 1 Tim 5:10; 2 Tim 1:9, 14), and 1 Tim 2:15 used a cognate noun for husband and wife persevering "in holiness." In the Lukan corpus the verb appears in a privileged locus, the Lord's Prayer (Luke 11:2). Then it appears twice on the lips of Paul in forms that allude to LXX Deut 33:3. In Acts 20:32 Paul commends the Ephesian presbyter-bishops to that "word of grace" which can give "the inheritance among all those who are sanctified *(en tois hēgiasmenois pasin).*" Then in Acts 26:18 Paul describes the risen Jesus commissioning him to bear witness before the Gentiles that they may have "a place, *kleron,* among those who are sanctified by faith in me, *en tois hēgiasmenois pistei tēi eis eme*" (see Rom 15:16).

It is notable in the passages from Luke that the hallowing is an act of God that is prayed for; it is something that God works through his word (see the *logos tēs charitos,* "the word of grace," in Acts 20:32 with its OT allusion and *God's word* here in 1 Tim 4:5). In the Lukan passages it is also a result or an effect of faith (note *believers and persons who have recognized the truth* in 4:3).

The meaning of *hallowed* in 1 Tim 4:5 intersects at several points with the Pauline meaning, particularly in emphasizing baptism and describing marriage (see 1 Cor 1:2; 6:11; 7:14; 1 Thess 5:23; Eph 5:26). If 1 Tim 4:5 in fact referred only to food being *hallowed,* it would be the only place in the NT where the term was so used (unless the *dōran* of Matt 23:19 is an offering of food). On the whole it is God, Christ, and believers who are *hallowed* in the NT; and even where things are mentioned (the gold and gift of Matt 23:17, 19; the vessel of 2 Tim 2:21), it is by way of examples and comparisons that are meant to correct a heavily materialistic concept of sanctification or holiness (see Notes for use of the Sabbath in Hermas and Barnabas).

In the phrase *by (dia) God's word and intercessory prayer,* the preposition *dia,* "by means of" (Moule, *Idiom,* p. 57), joins both members of the phrase in a manner that closely parallels the allusion to Genesis and to the thanksgiving prayer in the preceding verse. It appears reasonable to take *intercessory prayer (enteuxeōs)* here in the sense of 1 Tim 2:1. There, as here, the meaning substantially coincides between the *thanksgivings (eucharistias)* of 2:1 and verses 3-4 here (see D-C, p. 64 n. 5). On this interpretation, how does the anarthrous *God's word (logou theou)* refer to the actual words of the Genesis passage adduced? In Titus 2:5 and 2 Tim 2:9 the phrase is articular (as normally in the NT; exceptions, 1 Thess 2:13; 1 Pet 1:23). The Comment on Titus 2:5 in AB *Titus* shows that *ho logos tou theou,* "the message of God," in this version means Paul's gospel, i.e. Paul's *kerygma* and *didachē,* by definition "according to the [OT] Scriptures" (1 Cor 15:3-4). It is the Pauline OT hermeneutic, his "wholesome instruction" as the PE conceive it, which they seek to preserve and transmit. So in 1 Tim 4:4-5 it is the message of Gen 1, as understood and applied by Paul, that is *God's word.* The Pauline teaching "according to the Scriptures" and the public prayer of the church have been the means that God has used to hallow Christian marriage and nourishment.

Justin in his *Apology* 13.1-9 describes Christians as worshippers of the creator, ". . . praising him with a word of prayer and thanksgiving *(logōi euchēs kai eucharistias . . . ainountes)* over all the things that we offer. . ." (E.T. from A. T. Hanson, *Studies,* p. 103; see *Apology* 67.2 for the parallel). The famous description of the Christian sacramental eucharist which began in the previous chapter contains in its opening lines (66.2) a notable parallel to the thought of 1 Tim 4:4 when the *Apology* describes the eucharistic bread as "the food *(trophēn)* over which thanks has been given *(eucharistethēsan)* by that word of prayer *(di' euchēs logou)* which has come from" Christ. Justin here is not quoting First Timothy and in all probability not alluding to the PE. Both seem to be adducing "a common source, a common eucharistic and perhaps baptismal tradition" (A. T. Hanson, *Studies,* p. 104). Though one is reluctant to follow Hanson in taking *God's word* in 1 Tim 4:5 as part of the "instituting word" of Jesus, still the parallels are evocative. Perhaps to them one could add the not uncommon use of *hagiazein* in the later Fathers of "consecrating" the eucharistic elements (see Lampe, *PGL*, pp. 16-17). Most notable is Gregory of Nyssa's "the bread hallowed by the word of God to change it into the body of God the Word," *ton tōi logōi tou theou hagiazomenon arton eis soma tou theou logou metapoieisthai* (*Oratio catechetica* 37; *PG* 45.96D).

Needless to say, the later one dates the PE, the more probable becomes the eucharistic allusion at this point. The earlier dating preferred by this commentary leaves little contemporary evidence for specifying the terminology here sacramentally (though evidently it does not exclude it either). The same must be observed for a simple identification with grace at meals, for the language can include marriage as well as food. The best course is to note the liturgical and cultic character of the terminology as well as the explicit reference to marriage as well as foods and then understand grateful, public prayer in a sense that will include both. That prayer might take any number of forms, including blessings, thanksgivings over the food of (eucharistic) meals, ordinations, reconciliation, and the like. More significant for understanding the PE is that they opt for the OT understanding of sanctification as a quality produced in persons and created things, a quality that proceeds from the will and word of the creator God of Israel, a quality that forms a motive for grateful, public prayer. The pagan understanding of holiness in things and people, quite apart from their divine origin and human use, is simply bypassed.

With this programmatic refutation of the apostate liars, this piece in pause which began at 1 Tim 3:14 draws to a close. The language and concepts take up themes that go back as far as Titus as well as touching on the concerns of the church order which began in 1 Tim 2:1.

## IV. THE APOSTOLIC COMMISSION TO TIMOTHY: PART II (4:6–6:19)

### IV.A. As Apostolic Teacher (4:6-16)

#### IV.A.1. PERSONALLY (4:6-10)

*4 [6]When you suggest matters such as the preceding to your brothers, Timothy, you will be a fine minister of Christ Jesus, yourself nourished on the words of the faith and of that fine instruction with which you are quite familiar. [7]Have nothing to do with profane old wives' tales. Train for action that aims at godliness. [8]"Whereas physical exercise is useful for a little, godliness is useful for everything, since it con-*

*tains the promise of a life that is now and that is going to be."* [9]*This is the Christian message, meant to be believed and worth welcoming wholeheartedly.* [10]*Ultimately this promise is the reason for our job and our contest, that we have fixed our hope on the living God, savior of all, particularly of believers.*

## ♦ NOTES

4:6. *When you suggest.* The middle participle, *hypotithemenos,* is a rare term for teaching in the NT. It occurs once otherwise, in Rom 16:4, and there in the active in the phrase "they bowed their neck" with the sense, "to bare one's neck, to risk (one's life)," a phrase that ought to be compared with the one occurrence of the verb in the Ap. Frs. (*1 Clem.* 63.1). Among the thirteen occurrences of the verb in the LXX, this phrase occurs only at Sir 51:26. Twice the middle form and sense attested here in First Timothy occur, at LXX Jer 43:25 (MT 36:25) and 2 Macc 6:8, both times with the meaning of "counsel, suggest, enjoin, instruct." In secular Greek this sense is attested from Homer (LSJ *s.v.*) through the papyri, where there is evidence that the sense is "advising" but not necessarily "reminding" of something previously known (MM *s.v.*). Lock, *Commentary,* p. 50, calls this "a gentle word," and one notes that its meaning appears to be parallel to the *paraggele tauta kai didaske* of 4:11 below.

*Your brothers,* lit. "the brothers," *tois adelphois,* occurs here for the first of four times in this correspondence. Indeed, it is striking that Titus is the only NT book that does not employ the term and that the single occurrence in Second Timothy (4:21) puts that book on a par with documents such as First Peter (5:12) and Jude (v. 1) (both singular; but the latter in a different sense). Second Peter, like Ephesians, has only 2 uses. The 3 uses in First Timothy put it after Philemon, which has 4 occurrences, all in the singular. The 4 uses in the PE stand in contrast to the 129 other occurrences in the Paulines, the 81 uses in Luke-Acts, and the total of 343 NT uses, where the sense is not always the one attested here.

*Timothy, you will be a fine minister (kalos diakonos) of Christ Jesus.* Timothy (added to the Greek) is regularly engaged (note present tense) in the guidance of his Christian brothers. The sense of *kalos* with its stress on the visibly attractive character of a ministry that suggests and enjoins such matters has been explained on Titus 1:16 and 2:7, 14. Here the noun *diakonos* occurs in the singular as well as with the qualification "of Christ Jesus" in contrast to the unqualified *diakonoi* of 1 Tim 3:8, 12. The Pauline correspondence alone in the NT knows the phrase (see 2 Cor 11:23, in the plural as a self-designation of the pseudo-apostles; Col 1:7 of Paul's "fellow-servant [*syndoulos*]" Epaphras; and note the uses of *diakonos theou* in Rom 13:4 of the civil ruler; 2 Cor 6:4 describing Paul, Timothy, and perhaps Sylvanus; and 1 Thess 3:2 of Timothy, *s.v.l.* S. A. P. etc.; see B. Metzger, *TCGNT*).

*yourself nourished. Entrephomenos* is a term attested only here in the LXX, the NT, and Ap. Frs. However, one ought to note the Pauline use of *ektrephein* (Eph 5:29; 6:4) and the Lukan use of *trephein* (Luke 4:16; 12:24; 23:29; Acts 12:20) and *anatrephein* (Acts 7:20, 21, and esp. 22:3, along with Unnik, *Tarsus,* pp. 17-45). The present participle here in the PE stresses the ongoing character of the nourishment, which in turn sustains the teaching of this *diakonos Christou Iēsou.* Spicq, *EP,* p. 502, and D-C, p. 68, cite the passages of secular Greek literature and philosophy which take up this terminology of learning the truth as taking nourishment.

*with which you are quite familiar, hē parēkolouthēkas.* The verb also occurs at 2 Tim 3:10, again of Timothy in relation to the Pauline *didaskalia.* Otherwise the NT uses it only at Luke 1:3 and the canonical ending of Mark (16:17, where "signs" are the subject). Though the Ap. Frs. do not employ the term, the LXX uses it at 2 Macc 8:11 (of the divine judgment *overtaking* Nicanor) and 9:27 (*s.v.l.* ". . . he will keep to my own policy").

7. *profane old wives' tales, bebēlous kai graōdeis mythous.* For *mythous* see Titus 1:14 and 1 Tim 1:4; for *bebēlous* see 1 Tim 1:9. *Graōdeis,* a term not documented elsewhere in the LXX, NT, or Ap. Frs., is documented in philosophical polemic (citations in D-C, p. 68, and Spicq, *EP,* pp. 503-504) for fables that grown men would lend no credence to but that might entertain youngsters. The term does not seem to be documented in the papyri (*nil* in MM), though there are a few uses in secular texts (LSJ *s.v.;* Harrison, *Paulines,* p. 130).

*Train for action that aims at godliness.* This language for bodily exercise is continued in the reference to *gymnasia* in the following verse. These are the only occurrences of this terminology in the PE (though the concept of the athlete and his contest recurs in v. 10 and 6:11-12, and in 2 Tim 2:5; 4:7-8 of both Timothy and Paul). Though the noun does not occur elsewhere in the NT or the Ap. Frs., the verb here is found also at Heb. 5:14; 12:11; and 2 Pet 2:14, as well as in *2 Clem.* 20.2 (all figurative). The LXX attests to *gymnasion* in connection with Jason's gymnasium in Jerusalem (1 Macc 1:14; 2 Macc 4:9, 12; 4 Macc 4:20), but the verb occurs in a figurative sense at 2 Macc 10:15 and the noun *gymnasia* of a martyr's contest in 4 Macc 11:20, where the sixth son cries out from his tortures, "O contest *(agōnos)* worthy of the saints, wherein so many of us brothers, in the cause of righteousness *(dia tēn eusebeian),* have been entered for a competition *(eis gymnasian)* in torments, and have not been conquered" (Charlesworth, *OT Pseud.* 2.557). On the usage of *pros* to indicate the aim or goal of an action, see above on Titus 1:16; 3:1-2, and 1 Tim 1:16; regarding *eusebeian,* the usage of *eusebeia, godliness,* in the NT is concentrated in the PE (ten of fifteen uses), with faint traces running into Acts but not Luke, and in Ap. Frs. the *euseb-* cluster occurs only in *First* and *Second Clement.*

8. *Whereas physical exercise is useful for a little.* The *physical exercise, hē sōmatikē gymnasia,* of this verse is contrasted with the spiritual training just mentioned. The PE never use the noun *sōma,* which the other Paulines use ninety-one times, though not in Second Thessalonians or Philemon; Luke uses it thirteen times but Acts only at 9:40, of a corpse. *Sōmatikos,* on the other hand, occurs elsewhere in the NT only in Luke 3:22 of the Holy Spirit appearing "in bodily form." The adverb occurs in the NT only in Col 2:9 of Christ, in whom "the whole fullness of deity dwells bodily." As Schweizer, *TDNT* 7.1059, has noted, the emphasis in both Luke and First Timothy is upon the physical or corporal character of the action being described. The adjective is unusual in earlier Jewish writing. Only 4 Macc 1:32 and 3:1 employ the word in the LXX, in the former for human desires (*epithymiai,* both bodily and "psychic") and in the latter of bodily passions (*TDNT* 7.1047 n. 286; see also 1050, 1057). Only *Did.* 1.4 uses the adjective among the Ap. Frs., and there is a command to "abstain from carnal *(sarkikōn)* and bodily lusts *(sōmatikōn epithymiōn)*" (Titus 2:12 uses *kosmikos,* "worldly," in a similar negative sense, unlike Greek usage in general, to summarize the convert's disavowal of mere human desires; see also 4 Macc 1:32; 3:1). The usage in Luke and First Timothy does not have the pronounced pejorative nuance of these passages, though the usage in this letter tends toward that nuance. Perhaps just as the description of Abraham's ascent to heaven, *sōmatikos* (*Test. Abr.* 7 [112.7], cited in *TDNT* 7.1050), uses the adverb in a way that is close to Luke (and Colossians), so Josephus, *War* 6.55, with its contrast of the "bodily appearance" of the brave Sabinus with his "heroic soul," resembles the contrast here in First Timothy between "bodily exercise" and that which produces *eusebeia.* MM (*s.v.,* p. 621) cite the documentary papyrus P. Fay 21.10 (134 C.E.) speaking of payment "whether in kind or in money or in bodily labor *(sōmatikais ergasiais).*"

On *useful, ōphelimos,* see Titus 3:8.

*the promise.* The noun *epaggelia* occurs fifty-two times in the NT, with half of those uses in the Pauline epistolary. It is found in the Gospels only in Luke 24:49, and eight times in Acts. All the rest of the occurrences are in Hebrews (fourteen times), except for 2 Pet 3:4, 9, and 1 John 2:25. *Epaggel-* terminology in the PE lacks the Pauline dialectic of promise versus law which characterized the first appearances of these terms among Christians in Romans, Galatians, and Second Corinthians, where they indicated, among other things, the Spirit (cf. Gal 3:14) and life from the dead (cf. Rom 4:13-21). In the PE the verb refers to both the divine promise and human professions that allow considerable slippage between what is professed and the ensuing reality (see Wis 2:13; 1 Tim 2:10; 6:21).

*going to be.* BAGD, p. 501, compares the use of *mellein* here as well as the substantival use in 1 Tim 6:19 with a significant number of parallels in the NT and the Ap. Frs. There are 110 occurrences of the verb in the NT. Though there are the 4 occurrences noted in the Timothy correspondence (1 Tim 1:16; 4:8; 6:19; 2 Tim 4:1), there are only 10 other occurrences in the Paulines. Luke-Acts, however, likes the term, with a total of 46 uses. The phrase *zōē mellousa* does not appear elsewhere in the LXX, NT, or the Ap. Frs., though Acts 24:25 speaks of *to krima to mellon* (cf. commentary on 2 Tim 4:1, 7-8). Although in the LXX there is no mention of a *zōē mellousa* among the 44 uses of *mellein,* the translation of Isa 9:6 in several manuscripts describing the Davidic heir as *patēr tou mellontos aiōnos* (i.e. the messianic age) ought to be noted.

10. *our job.* Lit. "we toil," *kopiōmen.* The Pauline letters use this verb in fourteen of its twenty-two NT occurrences, and also contain eleven of the eighteen uses of the noun (which does not occur in the PE). Hauck, *TDNT* 3.829, has noted that the Pauline usage has given an indelible stamp to this terminology by applying it to Paul's own apostolic "toil" for the churches as well as to that of his colleagues and the local leadership (cf. 1 Thess 5:12; 1 Cor 16:16). This *kopian,* whether directed toward unbelievers in missionary proclamation or toward believers in the various acts of pastoral care, is on the way to becoming a technical term for the apostolic ministry. The *kop-* terminology is not particularly dignified; it seems to have had many of the connotations of the English "job," with its suggestion of hard work, wearisome routine, and lack of recognition. Paul applied it to his practicing his trade of manual labor as well as to his apostolic ministry (2 Thess 3:8; 1 Cor 4:12).

When Luke takes up the verb in Luke 5:5, it is of fishermen's labor that becomes in the same episode the parable for the future toil of Peter, who "will henceforth be catching men" (5:10). In Luke 12:27 *(s.v.l.)* the lilies do not toil for their clothing. The verb is placed on the lips of Paul in the Miletus speech to the Ephesian (presbyter-) bishops, as the apostle, after describing how he engaged in manual labor, says, "In all things I have shown you that by so toiling *(kopiōntas)* one must help the weak . . ." (Acts 20:35). The manual toil here is part of the whole Pauline *modus operandi* and becomes the readiest comparison for what that ministry involves. Second Timothy 2:6, with its comparison to the heavy work of the farmer, is closest to both the Pauline and Lukan usage of the term. However, the Johannine tradition can also describe the disciples' ministry, as "I sent you to reap that for which you did not labor *(kekopiakete);* others have labored *(kekopiakasin)* and you have entered into their labor *(kopon)*" (John 4:38).

The *kop-* terminology is not frequent in the Ap. Frs. (four uses of the verb; ten of the noun at most). *Barnabas* 19.10 is very Pauline in its exhortation to "seek each day the presence of the saints, either laboring by word *(dia logou kopiōn)* and going out to exhort and striving to save souls by the word *(tōi logōi)* or working with your own hands for the ransom of your sins." Though Ignatius never uses the verb, his one use of the noun is in a summary statement describing the office and function of Polycarp as a bishop and a "mature athlete" (also at Ign. *Pol.* 2.3 and 3.1), saying, "Where the toil *(kopos)* is greatest, the gain is great" (*Pol.* 1.3). The link with the figures of the athlete and the games also appears in 2 Tim 2:5 as well as in the immediately following *agōnizometha* here (see above on 4:7).

*our contest.* Lit. "we struggle/contend, *agōnizometha.*" The verb occurs again at 1 Tim 6:12 and 2 Tim 4:7 and, apart from a literal use in John 18:36, the only other NT use of the verb is in Luke 13:24, where the question concerning the number of the saved receives the answer, "Strive *(agōnizesthe)* to enter by the narrow door."

The noun *agōn,* which occurs as an internal accusative in the just cited passages of the PE, is again characteristically Pauline from 1 Thess 2:2 (where it designates Paul's contest for the gospel) through Phil 1:30 (again of Paul's apostolic sufferings, which his converts share; v. 29) to Col 2:1 (of Paul's *agōna* even in behalf of a congregation he has never visited). In the only other occurrence of the noun in the NT, Heb 12:1, the writer urges the congregation who has received the exhortation, ". . . let us run with perseverance the race *(agōna)* that is set before us."

In the Ap. Frs., *2 Clem.* 7.1-5 contains a number of uses of both the noun and verb. But the noun is also found in *1 Clem.* 2.4 of the "contest" in works and prayers of the Corinthian congregation for the salvation of their community, as well as in *1 Clem.* 7.1, where the writer says to the same congregation, "We are in the same arena and the same contest *(agōn)* is before us." The verb occurs in *1 Clem.* 35.4: "Let us then strive *(agōnizōmetha)* to be found among the number of those that wait, that we may receive a share of the promised gifts." *Barnabas* 4.11 has, "Let us strive *(agōnizōmetha)* to keep his commandments."

Though the fifteen uses of the noun and seven uses of the verb in the LXX include other examples of a figurative sense (e.g., Sir 4:28; Wis 4:2), it is Fourth Maccabees that has a striking series of examples, linking this terminology with other references to the athlete and the arena in which he contends unto a martyr's death: see 4 Macc 11:20 (note the sacred character of the games); 13:15; 15:29; 16:16; 17:11, 14 (verb). See Stauffer, *TDNT* 1.136, and also his citations of Philo, pp. 135-136, which compare the struggle for virtue with the contests of athletes. See MM *s.v.,* p. 8, for an inscription which reads *karous agōnas ēgōnisanto* of military warfare, and contrast it with the second-century Ephesian theater inscription *ēgōnisato agōnas treis* (Deissmann, *LAE,* p. 312).

On the reading of *oneidizometha* (we are reviled) for *agōnizometha,* see

B. Metzger, *TCGNT,* p. 641, as well as J. K. Elliott, *Greek Text,* p. 68. This term is found otherwise in the Paulines only in the quotation of LXX Ps 68:10 in Rom 15:3. Luke employs the word at Luke 6:22 (quoting his source?). Thus, unless this whole verse is taken as the citation of the *pistos logos* (cf. Lock, *Commentary,* p. 51), the reading seems unlikely.

*that we have fixed our hope on the living God.* The causal *hoti,* which did not occur in Titus (the only use of the particle in that letter is at 3:11), has occurred in First Timothy at 1:12, 13 as well as 4:4, and will occur below at 5:12; 6:2, 7. In Second Timothy it is used only at 1:16. Thus 8 out of 20 uses in the PE are causal. The Paulines otherwise use the particle 262 times, and as many as 59 uses are causal. Luke-Acts, on the other hand, employ the particle 293 times, with 93 occurrences in a causal sense. In this respect the usage of the PE is closer to Luke-Acts than to the rest of the Paulines.

As was noted on 1 Tim 3:14, *elpizein* occurs with *epi* (plus dative) here, with *epi* and the accusative at 5:5 (otherwise in the NT only at 1 Pet 1:13), and with *epi* plus dative at 6:17. None of these usages can be illustrated from Luke-Acts, and the other Paulines have the construction only at Rom 15:12, citing Isa 11:10. Is this passage the redaction of a creedal statement like that in 1 Tim 2:3-5, which also serves to undergird the apostolate? The theological sense of the verb is predominant in this construction with *epi,* and the activity is that represented in the nominal form, *elpis,* at Titus 1:2; 2:13; 3:7; and 1 Tim 1:1. Confidence in the promise of eternal life for all human beings is the mainspring of the apostolate (with Pfitzner, *PAM,* p. 176). It is curious that once the verb is used in Titus and First Timothy, the noun ceases to occur (Second Timothy employs neither).

*particularly. Malista* occurred at Titus 1:10 and is found again at 1 Tim 5:8, 17, as well as 2 Tim 4:13. Besides Gal 6:10 Paul otherwise employs the term only in Phil 4:22 and Philem 16. Luke uses the word only at Acts 20:38; 25:26; 26:3. The only other NT use is 2 Pet 2:10. In the Ap. Frs., *1 Clem.* 13.1 is close to the sense here in the PE but not 43.6. The Ignatian usage is like that here: Ign. *Eph.* 20.2; Ign. *Phld. inscr.;* and Ign. *Pol.* 3.1 in the context of figurative athletic contests. Spicq, *EP,* pp. 509-510 (noting the usage of the papyri as well as Menander, *Dysc.* 57, 699, 767), has quite rightly emphasized the "nonexclusive" sense of the particle which singles out those to whom something applies preeminently, superlatively, par excellence.

## ♦ COMMENT

4:6. *When you suggest matters such as the preceding to your brothers, Timothy.* The opening *tauta* (cf. the same term in 3:14) of this verse now begins to apply the teachings of the preceding passage (3:14–4:5) to the activity of Timothy himself, and through him to other members of the local church and special groups (orders) in it. The second person singular here and in the following verses links them with the same person and number in 3:14, but with the significant difference that in 3:14 Timothy is primarily the object of the written message whereas here he is the one who will transmit that message in word and action. He appears, first of all, as a teacher, a role that this correspondence highly values.

The objects of Timothy's advice and instruction are called *your brothers (tois adelphois).* The repeated description of the church as an *oikos,* in which the apostolic ministry, whether of Paul or of the *episkopoi,* is described in a paternal sense, almost certainly dictates the description here of the members of the congregation as "brothers" of one another and of Timothy (who is also Paul's "legitimate child," 1 Tim 1:2). This conception of Timothy's relationship to the members of the church is to have its effect on his personal relationship with them, as 1 Tim 5:1 illustrates with its advice to "encourage young men as if they were (your own) [anarthrous] brothers." The implication is that Timothy is considered to be one of the younger generation (in comparison with Paul and the older generation; cf. a similar way of speaking about Titus at Titus 2:6-7). At 1 Tim 6:2 the anarthrous *adelphoi* is clearly used of masters who are believers *(pistous)* and whom Christian servants must respect and serve. Finally at 2 Tim 4:21 "the brothers" *(hoi adelphoi)* are clearly the members of the Roman church who send their greeting to Timothy. This usage in the PE is in accord with the rest of the NT, which has taken up a Jewish usage for the relationship of all Israelites to one another (see von Soden, *TDNT* 1.145-146, and Ringgren, *TDOT* 1.188-193), though both the Near East and the Greek world provide examples of the extension of the term beyond denoting those in a blood relationship.

*you will be a fine minister of Christ Jesus.* The ministry is emphatically of Christ Jesus, not "of the brothers," lest there be any mistaking what specifies the role that Timothy has for the brothers. He is certainly their servant too, but they are not his master. The use of the full title for Timothy at this point in the PE leads one to think that the term *diakonos* is not to be equated simply with the technical term used above at 3:8. Yet the repetition would lead one to infer that the author-redactor saw something in common between the *diakonoi* described above and this *diakonos Christou Iēsou.* Is the reader meant to infer that as Timothy was a *diakonos* with regard to Paul, so the *diakonoi* of the second-generation churches are to be related to the *episkopoi?* Two of the titles given to Timothy in this correspondence strengthen this point, for he is Paul's "child" (*teknon,* 1:2, 18) and he is told to "do the work of an evangelist (*euaggelistou* [as of Philip, one of the Seven, in Acts 21:8]), fulfill your ministry *(diakonian),*" 2 Tim 4:5 (see commentary below *in loc.*). As the Seven shared the work of the

Twelve, and Timothy that of Paul, so the *diakonoi* share that of the *episkopos.* As *diakonia* in the PE certainly refers to the apostolic (Pauline) ministry (see Comment on 1 Tim 1:12), so *diakonos* appears to be one of the titles for those who shared in and succeeded to that ministry. As Paul's *diakonoi* were his couriers, emissaries, representatives, and messengers, so one would infer that the *diakonoi* of the PE were "the roving eyes and ears" of the *episkopos* who could thus stay in one place. It is instructive to recall that into medieval times the (arch)deacons carried out parochial visitations for the residential bishop, and that because of the consequent "visibility" which this task gave them, they were prime candidates for succession to the episcopal office. Their ministration of charity certainly contributed to this visibility and, perhaps, even more so to their popularity.

*yourself nourished (entrephomenos) on the words of the faith and of that fine instruction with which you are quite familiar.* A second participial construction beginning with *entrephomenos* further describes Timothy as *diakonos* and indicates the sources upon which his injunctions to his Christian brothers were to draw. In the Jewish tradition it is the sacred books that give this nourishment. Thus Philo, *Virt.* 195, can speak disparagingly of a man *ē ouk entraphēs oude enēskēthēs tois hierois grammasin,* "not reared or trained in the sacred writings" (see commentary on 2 Tim 4:15), and Josephus, *War* 6.102, addresses the zealot John with *su d' ho Ioudaios ho tois nomois entrapheis,* "while you, a Jew, nurtured in the laws. . . ." This Jewish application of the metaphor, which has precedents in the Hebrew Bible (see Pss 19:10; 119:103 on the law as honey in the mouth), probably lies behind the usage here in the PE, and thus "the words *(logois)* of the faith and of that fine instruction *(didaskalias)*" ought to be understood of the Pauline gospel *(kerygma* and *didachē)* and of the Pauline interpretation of the (OT) Scriptures, for that gospel was by definition "according to the Scriptures."

Here the plural of *logos* occurs for the first of four times in the PE (1 Tim 6:3: "the wholesome sayings that come from our Lord, Jesus Christ"; 2 Tim 1:13: "the model of the wholesome words" from Paul; and 4:15 of defiance to "our [Paul and Timothy's] words"). It is almost certain here that *the words* are equivalent to "my words," i.e. Paul's way of articulating the realities in which Christians put their faith. The apostle had not hesitated to compare his teaching with foods, adapted to the development of his converts (thus 1 Cor 3:1-2), and here the *diakonos* Timothy is to be nourished constantly from that Pauline teaching.

The *kalēs didaskalias* (the adjective, as usual, stressing the visible attractiveness of the Pauline interpretation of the OT) is further qualified here as *hēi parēkolouthēkas,* "with which you are quite familiar." It is significant that Papias, as quoted by Eusebius (*Church History* 3.39.4, 15), uses this term to describe the relation of a disciple to Jesus in his earthly ministry, of Mark to Peter, and of still others to "the presbyters." The relationship here certainly involves receiving a teaching that, because of its origin as well as the immediacy of the witness to it, has considerable authority. Justin, *Dial.* 1.103.8, also uses the verb for the relation of the authors of Gospel documents to the apostles (see Cadbury, *Acts,* p. 162 n. 23). In an earlier study of this term, Cadbury (Foakes Jackson and Lake, *Beginnings* 2.501) has noted that the verb may designate not only "keeping in touch with things done, with a course of events," but that this may be done through correspondence. He cites P.S.I. IV. 411.3 (iii B.C.E.): *hopōs oun parakolouthōn kai sy pros tauta exagagēis tous logous gegrapha soi,* "I have written these words to you so that *upon attending to them carefully* you also might bring forth [the truth] in regard to them" (trans. WCW), which has some resemblances to this passage in the PE. The verb also refers to following what has been said or read with understanding and attention (citations in Cadbury, *Acts*). As MM *s.v.,* p. 485, have observed, this sense of immediate, personal familiarity with the Pauline *didaskalia* (whether oral or written) — and even with Paul himself — is suggested by this use of *parakolouthein.* Dupont, *Sources,* pp. 104-11, has noted how the verb stresses "being present for" and "taking an active part in" events as well as following what one has been taught with attentive understanding. Kittel, *TDNT* 1.215-16, notes that the stress is on "the exactness or constancy of agreement" and that this is the force of *par-* in the compound. Thus one would suggest that here in the PE the sense is that the Pauline *didaskalia,* with which Timothy has had (note the perfect) immediate familiarity, is also the rule for him "to follow." The disciple of Paul has learned from Paul, and what he has learned he in turn is to teach to his Christian brothers.

7. *Have nothing to do with profane old wives' tales.* In contrast *(de)* to *the words* of the preceding verse are the myths, *tous bebēlous kai graōdeis mythous, profane old wives' tales,* that Timothy is now commanded to avoid. The article *tous* with *mythous* conveys scorn and contempt (Stählin, *TDNT* 4.786). The *mythous* must refer to lucubrations on the OT (see 1 Tim 1:4) which are contemptuously dismissed as *bebēlous,* an adjective that occurred above in 1 Tim 1:9. The bitterness of the description can be appreciated when one recalls that the materials proposed were based on Israel's Holy Scriptures and were meant to lead to authentic holiness. Here they are rejected as no better than pagan and profane.

The adjective paired with *bebēlous* is *graōdeis,* a term which conveys a sophisticated, literate contempt for that which cannot be taken seriously. Its recherché sound gives it a nasty sting, as a learned man dismissing a pretentious quack. Timothy is commanded to avoid such myths. The verb *paraitou* is very strong (Spicq, *EP,* p. 503), its present tense stressing the constant, unceasing rejection of this kind of pious persiflage. Here this term is addressed only to the leader, as in Titus 3:10. There the term described the breaking off of a personal association; here it proscribes any association with the heterodox teaching, any attempt to assimilate it or to come to terms with it.

Timothy is rather *(de)*, in a positive perspective, commanded, *gymnaze seauton*, literally *train yourself*. This language for bodily exercise is continued in the reference to *gymnasia* in the following verse. The gymnasium, like the theater, was a preeminently Greek institution that spread throughout the Hellenistic world. Like the theater but less so, the Greek games were explicitly pagan religious activities and were linked at every turn with the worship of pagan gods. Biblical Greek and other early Christian documents may for that very reason have had some reservations about a figurative use of the Greek terminology for these popular institutions (cf. 1 Tim 4:2 above on *hypokrisis*). Even the Pauline uses of these metaphors may have seemed more daring in his age than they do in ours. Yet they did employ the figure of the contest *(agōn)*, as Wis 4:2; 10:12 illustrate (for all the texts see commentary on v. 10, and see also 1 Tim 6:12 and 2 Tim 4:7; for the use of *athlein* and cognates see v. 10 below and 2 Tim 2:5).

If Spicq, *EP*, pp. 160-161, is correct, the Romans of the Republic and early Empire regarded Greek games with something less than admiration. They considered the nudity of Greek athletes degrading and the whole performance as ultimately pointless, the kind of show with which slaves and hired performers might entertain Romans but only to the detriment of Roman moral sensibilities. Augustus liked the games, Horace mentions young Romans at exercise on the Campus Martius, but not without irony (*Odes* 1.8.1-12; cf. 1.1.3-6), and Virgil envisions games in the afterlife (*Aeneid* 6.642), but such activities were never really congenial to the Roman character. The Romans liked their entertainment to be violent, bloody, brutal, and barbaric. But whether games or gladiatorial combats, the Romans only watched and did not directly participate. The ambiguous qualification of *gymnasia* in the following verse here as *useful for a little* is one of the many small indications that the author-redactor of this correspondence wrote from a typically Roman viewpoint (on the many secular Greek texts, particularly of the philosophers, that compare the athletic contest with the contest for knowledge or virtue, see the citations in D-C, pp. 68-69, and Spicq, *EP*, pp. 504-506, as well as Oepke, *TDNT* 1.775, and MM *s.v.*, p. 133).

The exercise or training that Timothy is urged to undertake is to be *pros eusebeian, action that aims for godliness* (BAGD *s.v. pros* III.3.b). The particle *pros* occurs twice again in the verse immediately following; the repetition reminds one of the fivefold repetition in 2 Tim 3:16-17.

8. "*Whereas physical exercise is useful for a little, godliness is useful for everything, since it contains the promise of a life that is now and that is going to be.*"

The reason *(gar)* for the preceding directives is now given by his exploiting the metaphor of gymnastic training that the verb of the previous verse had introduced. Physical exercise *(hē . . . somatikē gymnasia)* is contrasted with an implicit *pneumatikē gymnasia* that issues in godliness (authentic religious life), which in its turn leads into life eternal. Such exercise is *useful (ōphelimos) for a little.*

*Ōphelimos* here qualifies first *gymnasia* and then *eusebeia.* The ambivalence of the term is well illustrated by the contrast between *pros oligon* and *pros panta.* The former phrase occurs otherwise in the NT only at James 4:14, where it certainly refers to the short time that a mist lasts. Indeed, this is the ordinary meaning of the phrase in the Greek authors (see the citations in BAGD *s.v.;* BAGD and Pfitzner, *PAM,* p. 174 n. 2, will not hear of the temporal meaning because of the way *eusebeia . . . pros panta* is interpreted). However, enough weight has not been given to the fact that the *panta* explicitly includes the promise of eternal life, which thus stands in vivid contrast to the transient good effects of bodily exercise in improving the quality of man's physical life (see 1 Cor 9:25 on perishable versus imperishable wreaths; cf. also Dio Chrysostom 9.13 on the wreath of victory as best suited for goat food). The effects of a workout are momentary in comparison with the effects of godliness, which lead one into eternal life (Knight, *Sayings,* pp. 67-68).

The preceding *pros oligon* is contrasted with *the godliness* that *is useful, pros panta.* The *eusebeia,* already defined at 3:16 above as finding its whole meaning in the Son toward whom it is directed, has consequently an absolute or unlimited value. Just as the Father has given all things to the Son (cf. the Q prayer of Jesus at Luke 10:22: *panta moi paredothē*), so authentic religion *(eusebeia)* in relation to the Son makes all things, without exception, useful and profitable for salvation (versus the doctrinaire discrimination scored in 4:3). As Knight, *Sayings,* p. 73, has noted with Spicq, *EP,* p. 507, the phrase here distills the Pauline teaching of Rom 8:28, 32 and 1 Cor 3:21-23: "For all things *(panta)* are yours, whether Paul or Apollos or Cephas or the world *(kosmos)* or life *(zōē)* or death or the present or the future *(eite enestōta eite mellonta),* all *(panta)* are yours and you are Christ's and Christ is God's" (RSV). It is striking how the Lukan, Pauline, and PE traditions seem to be rooted in the Q tradition of Jesus' prayer.

The link between *eusebeia,* "eternal life," and God's promise already appeared in the proemium to Titus (1:1-2). Here in First Timothy, godliness is described as possessing a promise of life, *since it contains the promise* ([anarthrous] *epaggelian) of a life that is now and that is going to be.* The participle has a causal sense (cf. Acts 9:26 and Knight, *Sayings,* p. 73) and in the NT frequently refers to the believer's possession of life (eternal). *Epaggelian* occurs again in the PE only in 2 Tim 1:1, where Paul's own apostleship is not only "by the will of God" the Father, but also "for the sake of the promise of life that is Christ Jesus." Thus the life now and to come is life in Christ.

In the Pauline epistolary, *epaggelia* and *euaggelion* are by and large complementary terms that designate the same reality. It is notable that "the promise" is linked to life as its content (*zōē;* cf. Rom 4:16-21 of the promise to Abraham), as here in 1 Tim 4:8. Though the Paulines use the term in the plural as well as the singular, Luke-Acts, like the PE, use only the singular (see Notes above and AB *Titus* on Titus 1:2).

If this whole verse is in fact the *pistis ho logos* referred to in 4:9, the material may well have been pre-Lukan and evidently quite congenial to that author's understanding of the promise. On the other hand, the material here sounds post-Pauline in its key terminology *(sōmatikē gymnasia; pros oligon; ōphelimos; eusebeia),* and one might surmise that the author of the original *logos* grafted onto *eusebeia* a definition in terms of the later Pauline tradition that he knew.

Though some (Knight, *Sayings,* p. 74) have proposed that the genitive here be taken as a promise *of* life now and hereafter (cf. the genitive at Rom 15:8, speaking of a ministry to the circumcision, and "the promises to the fathers"), the weight of the NT usage persuades most commentators to take *zōēs* as the content of the promise. This content of the implicitly divine promise is life, *zōē,* not *bios* or *psychē.* As Titus 1:2 described this *zōē* as *aiōnios* (there the description of the goal, *ep' elpidi zōēs aiōniou,* is compared and contrasted with the origin of that life in the divine promise "from all eternity," *pro chronōn aiōniōn* [see also 1 Tim 1:16-17]), so here it is *both* now *(nyn) and* to come — a single life that spans two spheres of existence.

This *eusebeia* which issues in *life now — nyn —* should be compared to Titus 2:12, with its *eusebōs zēsōmen en tōi nyn aiōni,* "to live in a . . . godly way in this present age" (see AB *Titus loc. cit.*). The latter phrase with its adjectival *nyn* resembles the nominal *apo tou nyn* that is well known from the LXX, and which is characteristic of Luke in the NT (in Paul only 2 Cor 5:16; cf. Stählin, *TDNT* 4.1107, 1113). Here in First Timothy the usage is adjectival (cf. the parallel participle *mellousēs*), as at 1 Tim 6:17 and 2 Tim 4:10 (both of *aiōn*); "*nyn*" in the PE is in 2 Tim 1:10, which Stählin describes as a *nyn* of eschatological anticipation, the dawn of the day of the Lord, the opening of the acceptable year of the Lord (cf. Luke 4:19, and cf. v. 21 with its "today this scripture has been fulfilled"). In 1 Tim 4:8 the *nyn* has been described as designating "a proleptic first stage of the last things," a combination of possession *(echousa)* and hope *(paraggelia)* for a "[divine] life in which we already participate in the period of Christ, and to which we look forward in fullness then" (Stählin, *TDNT* 4.1120). Cf. 1 Cor 3:22 cited above with its *ta enestōta* and Rom 8:38. The link with the prophetic use of *nyn* ought not to be overlooked (cf. LXX Mic 4:11; Isa 48:7).

Hill, *Greek Words,* p. 189, notes 1 Cor 15:19, where "for this life" means "lifetime."

The *zōē* is also future, i.e. coming, destined, on the way, and its *eschatological* sense is that explained in the commentary on 1 Tim 1:16. As has been noted above, there are a significant number of parallels in the NT and the Ap. Frs. Moreover, *1 Clem.* 24.1 speaks of *tēn mellousan anastasin* (the future resurrection). *Second Clement* 20.2 (cf. above on *theosebeia* in 1 Tim 2:10), in a passage that has multiple echoes of this one in the PE, writes, "We are contending *(athloumen)* in the contest of the living *(zōntos)* God, and we are being trained *(gymnazomethe)* by the life *(biōi)* which now is *(tōi nyn)* that we may gain the crown in that which is to come (*tōi mellonti* [is *biōi* understood here or *zōē?*])." See also *2 Clem.* 10.3-4 with its contrast of present pleasure ("instant pleasure"), *apolausis,* with "the promise to come," *hē mellousa epaggelia.*

In the synoptic tradition this description of a life promised now and in the future has its closest parallel in Mark 10:30 = Luke 18:30 = Matt 19:29 (much abbreviated): *SFG* §255. Both Mark and Luke transmit Jesus' promise to the disciples, who have left all the persons and things that contribute to, extend, and enrich earthly human life "a hundredfold/manifold more (Luke) (*nyn,* 'now' [Mark]) in this time *(en tōi kairōi toutōi)* and in the age to come *(en tōi aiōni tōi erchomenōi)* eternal life *(zōēn aiōnion).*" If the preceding *epaggelia* in First Timothy was Pauline, this description of "the life now and to come" can scarcely be understood apart from the tradition of Jesus' sayings with their inimitable combination of drastic renunciation of present good for the promise of a still unseen, though not completely unexperienced, future good. Knight, *Sayings,* p. 77, has noted how both the Gospel tradition and this *pistos logos* "double" the blessing by placing it in both this life and that to come. With Scott and Parry, he has also called attention to the fact that an *epaggelia* in the NT usually refers to a promise recorded in the NT. The PE apparently regarded the sayings of Jesus as "Scripture" (as in 1 Tim 5:18 below), and it is possible that they were picking up a practice which a *pistos logos* such as this appeared to sanction.

Granted that the *pistos ho logos* is this verse 8 (and not v. 10 below) and that it consists of Christian material that antedates the redaction of this correspondence, one must face two questions: First, is there a pagan source of tradition behind the Christian *logos?* Second, what is the original *Sitz im Leben* of the Christian *logos* here cited?

D-C, p. 68, have noted that verse 8 begins as if it were an aphorism, and they reconstructed a Greek philosophical (cynic-Stoic) critique of the current culture that contrasted the games unfavorably with the exercise of the intelligence. The motif would then have been reworked in Jewish or Christian circles, substituting *eusebeia* for *philosophia* (Gealy, *IB* 11.429; Easton, *Pastoral Epistles,*

p. 148). The hypothesis is tenuous (cf. Knight, *Sayings*, p. 78), for actually only verse 8a *(hē . . . sōmatikē gymnasia pros oligon estin ōphelimos)* would be of secular origin, and no trace of such an aphorism appears to have been cited in the literature that has survived (for all the criticism of athletes in the diatribes of the Hellenistic age, see Spicq, *EP*, pp. 159-161). Easier to imagine (though no more than that) would be a Jewish Christian teacher, sympathetic to the contemporary criticism because of his Jewish background (cf. the citations above from First through Fourth Maccabees and note Philo's lengthy critique of Greek contests in *Agric.*, pp. 111-123, where he fashions the whole *logos* as a kind of parable for use in his moral catechesis; but note Spicq's qualifications, *EP*, p. 161). See Pfitzner, *PAM*, pp. 166, 171-177, also referred to below in the commentary on 1 Tim 6:12.

That brings one to the second question posed above: Can the genre and *Sitz im Leben* of this *logos* be specified any further? As Gealy has implied, the qualified approval of physical exercise here would lead one to think that the original *logos* was composed at a time when the aberrations denounced in 4:1-3 were not yet on the scene, at least in a community where the *logos* originated. The author and/or his audience would have been Jewish Christian or influenced by that segment of early Christianity; moreover, they would have had some contact with the Pauline tradition and its vocabulary as well as with sayings of Jesus (in Mark? in a collection of sayings?). The community would be one that would find a critique of the Greek games congenial. The Roman church would be a strong candidate for such a place of origin. The *logos* would then be an (anonymous) *logos* of that community, part of the materials for postbaptismal formation of believers in Christian life and action (as distinguished from such a *logos* as that in 1 Tim 1:15a, which pertained to their dogmatic formation in the faith itself).

9. *This is the Christian message, meant to be believed and worth welcoming wholeheartedly.* The whole of this verse has been commented upon above at Titus 3:8 and 1 Tim 1:15. The citation formula itself does not provide any clue as to whether what precedes or what follows is the *pistos ho logos.* Most commentators (listed by Knight, *Sayings*, p. 62 n. 1) refer it to verse 8. However, from Alford, through Moffat, Guthrie, and Simpson, to the NEB translation, a significant number have referred the *logos* to the following verse, 1 Tim 4:10 (Knight, *Sayings*, p. 62 n. 2). The *gar* of verse 8 as a transitional particle introducing a quotation, as well as some of the unusual terminology *(gymnasia; sōmatikē)*, are persuasive signs that the reference is in fact to the verse preceding, not to mention its aphoristic nature and its generic application. Yet one ought not to put too much stress on the "subjective" character of verse 10 with its shift to the first person plural as a counterindication for that verse being the *pistos logos*, since Titus 3:4-7 uses the first person similarly (contra Knight, *Sayings*, p. 63).

10. *Ultimately this promise is the reason for our job and our contest.* The *eis touto gar . . . hoti* introducing verse 10 seems best interpreted as a transitional phrase, applying the generic *pistos logos,* "the message . . . to be believed" of verse 9 to the ministry of Paul and Timothy (thus the first person plural). The construction, if not the actual terminology, is quite similar to that of 1 Tim 1:16, where the preceding *pistos logos* is incorporated into the apostle's ministry with the transitional *alla dia touto . . . hina.* That shared ministry is designated here with two verbs, *kopiōmen kai agōnizometha,* "our job and our contest."

The neuter *eis touto* forestalls taking the preceding *eusebeia* alone as the antecedent of this pronoun, though that godliness is evidently not excluded (Pfitzner, *PAM,* p. 176 n. 1). Rather, the *gar* here takes one back to the very beginning of the preceding citation in verse 8 (Knight, *Sayings,* p. 63 n. 5), and the whole complex of training, godliness, and living is now expressed as the goal (D-C and Spicq: i.e. *to telos* understood) of the laboring and struggling of the apostle and his co-worker.

When the verb *kopian* occurs again in this letter at 1 Tim 5:17, it is used in a description of the Christian ministry, but this time that of the *presbyteroi,* whose jobs are preaching and teaching *(kopiōntes en logōi kai didaskaliai).* Similarly, in 2 Tim 2:6 it figures in a series of comparisons meant to illuminate Timothy's ministry. The primary concern evidently at stake (cf. v. 6) is teaching. A ministry of teaching is the wearisome toil being described (see Notes above for a discussion of *kopian*).

With *agōnizometha* the figure of the gymnasium and its exercises again appears in this section. The *kai* is practically epexegetic (which may have given a handle to the variance noted above). The general principle of the *pistos logos* in verse 8 is now applied to the ministry of Paul and Timothy (first person plural). Colossians 1:29 has Paul himself saying, "For this I toil, striving *(eis ho kai kopiō agōnizomenos . . .)* with all the energy which he [God] mightily inspires within me." D-C, p. 68, suggests the possibility that this language for the apostolic ministry had become traditional enough so that the formulation here was a *pistos logos.* The evidence is suggestive but not convincing in the light of the reasons for verse 8 adduced above. Though the Colossians passage is by no means reproduced here, in either terms or tone (D-C is being qualified here), the resemblances are striking. Did the Luke of Col 4:14 have something to do with the formulation of this verse of the PE (cf. 2 Tim 4:7 with v. 11)? In any event the term is surely one of Paul's for his ministry, as 1 Cor 9:25 illustrates, and even for the ministry of prayer of Paul's colleague (Col 1:7), Epaphras (Col 4:12), and the Roman church along with the apostle (Rom 15:30: *synagōnisasthai moi*). This letter uses the term below (6:12) in exhorting the man of God (Timothy) to "contend in the fine contest *(agōna)* . . . of faith" (see Jude 3: *epagōnizesthai tēi . . . pistei*), as 2 Tim 4:7 has Paul himself use that phrase (see

Stauffer, *TDNT* 1.137-138). The latter two passages have somewhat the same resemblances that Col 1:29 has to 1 Tim 4:10.

*that we have fixed our hope on the living God, savior of all, particularly of believers.* The job and contest of the Pauline ministry have proceeded from the hope of Christians. In a similar way, confidence in eternal life is expressed in terms of hope in the *living God (epi theōi zōnti)*, who shares or invites to participation in the life that is properly and specifically his. That participation is a matter of faith expressing itself in worship (see commentary on *ekklēsia theou zōntos* at 1 Tim 3:15).

God is depicted in an expansive descriptive clause that for the sixth and last time in this correspondence applies the noun *sōter* to *theos* (for commentary on this usage, see AB *Titus* on Titus 1:3; 2:10; 3:4, as well as above on 1 Tim 1:1; 2:3). Regarding God as savior "of all men, especially of the faithful," the Greek *anthrōpos* usually does not indicate gender differentiation; it appears twenty times in the PE, occasionally qualified by an ethical consideration for the person in question; no adjective qualifies it more often than *pantes,* "all," as here, thus stressing the importance placed on the universality of the offer of salvation in the PE. *Malista pistōn,* the latter phrase in 1 Tim 4:10, has caused some dyspepsia in commentators, even though it is conceptually no less Pauline than the parallel thought in Gal 6:10, where the charity of Christians is, like that of their God, to extend *pros pantos malista de pros tous oikeious tēs pisteōs,* "to all people and especially to those of the household of faith" (cf. AB *Titus* on the first person plural of Titus 2:13). The particle, in a nonexclusive sense, singles out those to whom something applies preeminently, superlatively, par excellence — the believers.

## IV.A.2. FOR THE FAITHFUL (4:11-14)

4 [11]*These are the matters, Timothy, to charge and to teach.* [12]*No one is to disdain you for your youth. Rather keep on being a pattern for believers —*

*in word,*
*in behavior,*
*in charity,*
*in faithfulness,*
*in purity.*

[13]*Until I arrive, concentrate on your public reading of the Scriptures, on your preaching, on your instruction.* [14]*Do not neglect that gracious gift within you, the one given to you under prophetic direction, with an imposition of the hands of the presbytery.*

## ♦ NOTES

4:11. *These are the matters, Timothy, to charge and to teach.* For the *tauta,* here translated "these are the matters," see R. F. Collins, "Image of Paul," pp. 157-158, on 1 Tim 4:6, where the pronoun has some reference to "the words of faith" as well as "fine teaching." The name *Timothy* is added to the Greek to emphasize the sense of the direct address implied in the imperative.

For *to charge* and the *paraggel-* terminology, see 1 Tim 1:3, 5, 18. On "to teach," *didaske,* see Titus 1:9 and note 1 Tim 5:7 below and 6:2, *tauta didaske kai parakalei,* as well as Titus 2:15, *tauta lalei kai parakalei kai elegche.*

12. *No one is to disdain you for your youth.* Elsewhere in the NT *youth* is the term that Luke 18:21 takes from Mark 10:20 to describe the man, a ruler, who has kept the commandments from youth *(ek neotētos;* Mark adds *mou)* and wishes to inherit life eternal (cf. Matt 19:20, 22 only). Elsewhere in the NT it is only Luke who takes up the term at Acts 26:4, placing it on Paul's lips as he begins his apologia before Agrippa with, "My manner of life *(biōsin)* from youth *(ek neotētos),* spent from the beginning *(ap' archēs)* among my own nation and at Jerusalem, is known by all the Jews." Youth refers to a period in life that began in the early teens and lasted into the mid-forties (see Comment below).

In this letter, "disdain" translates the verb *kataphroneitō* (contrast the *periphroneitō* of Titus 2:15 and Jerome's comment in *Titum* [*PL* 26.589-590], who says the *kata-* compound denotes contempt in its proper sense, as when a martyr despises and scorns all the torments inflicted on him as of no account). In the eight other NT uses, Matt 6:24 = Luke 16:13 (*SFG* §224) as well as Matt 18:10 (in a context of leadership, a little child, and greatness!) have the verb refer to a person, and in the first examples cited, to "masters" *(kyriois),* as in 1 Tim 6:2 below it refers to "masters" *(despotas).* The uses in Rom 2:4 (of the riches of God's goodness) and 1 Cor 11:22 (the churches of God) are somewhat different, as are Heb 12:2 (Christ "despising the shame" of the cross) and 2 Pet 2:10 (persons despising the lordship or rule of authority of Christ? See Schneider, *TDNT* 3.632-633). Ign. *Smyrn.* 3.2 uses the verb of Peter and those with him who saw the risen Jesus and thereafter "despised even death" *(kai thanatou katephronēsan).* The three uses in Hermas, similarly, do not have a personal object (*Man.* 7.2 [but note the passive]; 9.10; and 10.3.1).

*pattern.* For *typos* see Titus 2:7.

*in behavior.* The verb *anastrephesthai* was used of Timothy and other apostolic ministers in 3:15 above. The noun *anastrophē* never occurs in the Gospels or Acts. In the rest of the Paulines it occurs in Gal 1:13 (of Paul's own way of life before his conversion) and Eph 4:22 (of the "former way of life" of the recipients of the letter). The usage here reminds one of Heb 13:7: "Remember your leaders, those who spoke to you the word of God; consider the outcome of their life *(anastrophēs)* and imitate their faith." In addition to James 3:13, First and Second Peter use the noun eight times, of pre- and postbaptismal conduct (often with an adjective such as *kala, agatha, hagnē*). The Ap. Frs. do not employ the noun, and it is documented in the LXX only in Tob 4:14 ("Watch yourself, my son [note his youth], in everything you do, and be disciplined [*pepaideumenos*] in all your conduct [*anastrophēi]*") and in 2 Macc 5:8; 6:23 (speaking of the old Eleazar's "excellent life [*anastrophēs*] even from childhood [*ek paidos*]"). The sense here in First Timothy is best explained in terms of a (Roman) source, a list of virtues employed in the formation of the newly baptized, and thus perhaps especially appropriate for "catechizing" a younger man like Timothy. MM (p. 38) have noted that for all the frequency of this noun in the inscriptions, it is rarely evidenced in the papyri. This "may only mean that it was not current in Egypt."

*in purity. En hagneiai* occurs here and at 1 Tim 5:2 but never again in the NT. The LXX knows the term in Num 6:2, 21 as a translation of the Hebrew *nāzîr/nēzer,* i.e. the one who had consecrated/separated himself as a "nazirite," taking no fermented drink (see 1 Tim 5:23 below), with hair uncut, avoiding any contact with the dead. In LXX 2 Chron 30:19 the term renders the Hebrew *kĕṭohorat haqqōdeš,* with reference to "the sanctuary's rules of cleanliness" (RSV) for those who participated in the Passover celebration. First Maccabees 14:36 (of the "purity" of the Jerusalem temple) is the final LXX usage. Second Maccabees 4:13, on the other hand, is surely an incorrect reading.

The Ap. Frs. do use the term. Thus *1 Clem.* 21.7, in a modified *Haustafel,* uses the term of the purity of married women (and others old and young alike?); again in 64.1 the term occurs in the second to last place (between *egkrateian* and *sōphrosynēn*) in an eightfold list of virtues that begins with *pistin.* The context is a prayer for God's blessing upon Christian souls. Ignatius, *Eph.* 10.3, speaks of his readers remaining "in all purity and sobriety *(en pasēi hagneiai kai sōphrosynēi)* in Jesus Christ, both in the flesh and in the spirit." In Ign. *Pol.* 5.2 one reads, "If any man remains in continence *(en hagneiai)* to the honor of the flesh of the Lord; let him do so without boasting."

In Polycarp, *Phil.* 4.2, Christian wives are exhorted to remain "in . . . faith and love and purity" *(en tēi . . . pistei kai agapēi kai hagneiai),* and in 5.3 the younger men *(neōteroi)* are to care especially for purity *(hagneias).* The seven uses in Hermas are in agreement with the preceding. The occurrence in the twelvefold list at *Sim.* 9.15.2 is notable. The twenty or more uses in Josephus are principally concerned with ritual and priestly purification which extends into the sphere of sexual relations (see esp. *Ant.* 3.78, 152, 224, 273, 276), but he seems never to employ the phrase *en hagneiai.*

13. *Until I arrive concentrate. Heōs* (145 times in the NT) occurs only here

in the PE. As a conjunction it occurs in the other Paulines only in 2 Thess 2:7 and 1 Cor 4:5 (both an eschatological "until"; see Heb 1:13 with 10:13; James 5:7; 2 Pet 1:19; Rev 6:11). The use as a conjunction and preposition is very common in the Gospels and Acts, with Luke 28 times and Acts 22 times. The Greek conjunction (unlike the English *until*) does not necessarily imply that a different *modus agendi* followed the action spoken of. There is no reason to think that Timothy was expected to cease reading out loud the Scripture, exhorting, or teaching after Paul's arrival. This text of First Timothy has accordingly been cited, at least since Jerome, in connection with the much more debated *heōs* of Matt 1:25.

On *erchomai*, "I arrive," see Titus 3:12 as well as 1 Tim 3:14. The present tense instead of the future stresses the certainty of Paul's coming (BDF §383.1; see Hermas, *Sim.* 9.11.1). For the eschatological use of *heōs* with *erchomai*, see Luke 22:18, *heōs hou hē basileia tou theou elthēi*, "until the kingdom of God comes."

The verb *proseche*, "concentrate," has been commented on at Titus 1:14 as well as above in 1 Tim 1:4; 3:8; 4:1. At this point one would stress its occurrence in a context of (apostolic) ministry that emphasizes teaching the OT in a Pauline frame of reference. In contrast to all of the above occurrences, the term here has a quite positive connotation, as also at Acts 16:14 and 20:28.

*your public reading of the Scriptures.* Lit. "the (public) reading." The noun *anagnōsis* occurs in the LXX 1 Esd 9:48 and Neh 8:8 of the public reading of the Torah. The Sirach prologue 9, 13 (Rahlfs, *Sept.*, pp. 10, 17) uses the noun of a personal reading of the Law and the Prophets and then of the Greek version of Sirach's own book. The Ap. Frs. do not use the noun, and the verb occurs, before Hermas, only in *2 Clem.* 19.1: "I am reading *(anaginōskō)* you an exhortation to pay attention to the things that have been written *(prosechein tois gegramenois)* that you may save yourselves and the one among you who reads *(ton anaginōskonta)* them." Josephus knows the noun only in *Apion* 2.147, of reading his own composition, but he twice uses *anagnōstes*, "reader," as a title for Esdras, whose task it is to read the Torah publicly (*Ant.* 11.123, 127). On the Qumran practice of reading and studying the Scripture in an assembly, see 1QS 6.7-8 (Dupont-Sommer, *EWQ*, p. 85); see 7.1 (Dupont-Sommer, *EWQ*, p. 87) and contrast CD 5.2-3 (Dupont-Sommer, *EWQ*, p. 129); A. R. C. Leaney, *RQM*, p. 185.

Though the verb *anaginōskein*, "to read," occurs thirty-two times in the NT, "the reading," *tēi anagnōsei*, is scarcely a common noun, occurring only once otherwise in the Pauline corpus, at 2 Cor 3:14, noting the public "reading of the old covenant" in the synagogue service (see 3:15 for the verb). Acts 13:15 (see the verb in 13:27) uses the term in describing the Sabbath synagogue service at Antioch in Pisidia, where "after the reading *(anagnōsin)* of the law and the prophets," Paul and Barnabas are asked whether they have "any word of exhortation *(logos paraklēseōs)*" for the worshipping congregation. The following kerygmatic proclamation that Luke places on Paul's lips (13:16-41) was probably exactly what Luke conceived of as "an encouraging word" based on the OT, though the phrase has some irony when placed on the lips of the synagogue leadership. Acts 15:31 describes the reading of the Jerusalem letter with its directives as a *paraklēsis.*

*your preaching.* On the verbal cognate of *paraklēsis,* see Titus 1:9 and Schmitz, *TDNT* 5.793-799, especially p. 794 on eschatological consolation. As is noted there, only Luke-Acts (six times) and the Paulines (and Hebrews) use this noun (twenty-three times), and the passages from Acts already cited appear to be as close in meaning to the usage here in the PE as any Pauline passages (see Rom 15:4). Hebrews 13:22 describes the preceding "epistle" as "the word of exhortation *(tou logou tēs paraklēseōs)* that has been written to you briefly," and it also resembles the Lukan usage. On this interpretation, there is a clear line from the *anagnōsis* (the public reading of the OT) to the *paraklēsis* (an exhortation or summons to Christian faith and then to Christian conduct in a way that is recognizably linked to the faith, worship, and conduct of Israel as evidenced by the OT). The Lukan linking of *paraklēsis* with the Holy Spirit should not be overlooked (Acts 9:31; note that the Jerusalem letter stated, "It has seemed good to the Holy Spirit and to us . . ." [Acts 15:28], and thus the Antiochene Christians "rejoiced at the exhortation" [15:31]). The earliest NT document that refers to Timothy describes him as Paul's co-worker "to establish you in your faith and to exhort you" (1 Thess 3:2). Here that function has become "institutionalized" as part of the service in which the apostolic minister presides.

14. *Do not neglect.* The present imperative of *mē amelei* stresses the ongoing character of the command which is the negatively phrased equivalent of the preceding *proseche* and the *meleta* of the following verse. The verb *amelein* is documented otherwise in the NT only in Heb 2:3; 8:9 (= LXX Jer 38:32; MT 31:32); and Matt 22:5. The positive, impersonal *melei* is only a little more frequent (ten times), and it is found in the Paulines (1 Cor 7:21; 9:9) as well as in Luke 10:40; Acts 18:17. In nine out of ten cases it occurs with a negative qualification. *Amelein,* on the other hand, is in litotes, as here, very often in the papyri (Spicq, *EP,* p. 516). The LXX has *melei* five times and *amelein* four times. The Ap. Frs. have *melei* in *Barn.* 1.5 and Ign. *Smyrn.* 6.2 as well as twice in Hermas. *Amelein* occurs in Ign. *Pol.* 4.1, "Let not the widows be neglected," as well as in Polycarp, *Phil.* 6.1, of the presbyters "neglecting neither widow, nor orphan, nor poor."

*gracious gift.* The noun *charisma* will occur once again, of Timothy too, in 2 Tim 1:6. Outside of 1 Pet 4:10, all the other NT uses of the word are in the Roman and Corinthian letters (fourteen times). The LXX has two doubtful occurrences in Sir 7:33 and 38:30 which probably say more of the meaning fourth-century copyists gave the term than what the original text transmitted.

*Didache* 1.5 uses the term of even the material "gifts" which the Father has bestowed on believers so that they can share them with all in need. *First Clement* 38.1 admonishes, "Let, therefore, our whole body be preserved in Christ Jesus and each be subject to his neighbor, according to the charism granted him *(en tōi charismati autou).*"

Ign. *Eph.* 17.2 speaks of "ignoring the gift *(to charisma)* which the Lord has truly sent," which in the context may be a reference to the Holy Spirit as giving life. In Ign. *Smyrn. inscr.* the church of Smyrna is one "which has obtained mercy in every gift *(en panti charismati)* and is filled with faith and love and comes behind in no gift *(anysteretōi ousēi pantos charismatos),* most worthy of God and bearing holy things." Finally, in Ign. *Pol.* 2.2 the bishop of Smyrna is exhorted, "Pray that the invisible things be revealed to you that you may lack nothing and abound in every gift *(pantos charismatos).*" In none of these instances, even the last, is the reference to a charism specific to apostolic ministry.

*given . . . under prophetic direction (dia prophēteias).* On *didōmi* in these letters, see Titus 2:14 and 1 Tim 2:6 above. The *dia* here takes up the *kata tas proagousas epi se prophēteias* of 1 Tim 1:18 and stresses the prophecies as part of the environment of circumstances attendant upon the granting of the charism (see Moule, *Idiom,* p. 57, who acknowledges that, taken as a genitive singular here, it might also be used instrumentally, "through the medium of prophecy," a reading that may have been understood by Theodore of Mopsuestia [Swete, *Theodore,* II, 149: *per prophetiam,* which is commented on as *per revelationem* and then *propter revelationem,* pp. 149-150]). Taken as an accusative plural, it would be read "as a result of," "because of" (see D-C, p. 71). If the singular is read, then one prophecy of the several previously noted is being singled out.

*with an imposition of the hands.* Though the rest of the Paulines do not know this phrase, it does appear in Heb 6:2 in a context that speaks of elementary teaching "about ablutions *(baptismōn),* the laying on of hands, the resurrection of the dead, and eternal judgment." The only other NT occurrence is in Acts 8:18: "the Spirit was given [to the recent Samaritan converts] through the laying on of the hands of the apostles (*tōn apostolōn,* i.e. of Peter and John)." The verbal form of the phrase occurs in that context (Acts 8:17, 19) as well as on eight other occasions in Luke-Acts, and it is found at 1 Tim 5:22 below (as is noted on 1 Tim 2:8 where, and only there in the PE, the term *cheires* occurs without a reference to the imposing of hands).

The Ugaritic root *smk* in the phrase *bsmkt //* to *bšdm* occurs in Ugaritic text 125.35 (C. Gordon, *Ugaritic Textbook,* p. 192; glossary #1771, p. 450). Unfortunately neither phrase is clear in meaning, as Dahood notes (AB *Psalms*

2.304) on Ps 88:8, "Your rage weighs heavy *(sāmĕkāh)* upon me," aptly compared with Ps 32:4, "Your hand was oppressive *(tikbad)* upon me."

*the presbytery.* The term *presbyterion* is by no means common in the NT, occurring otherwise only in Luke 22:66 (where he uses it as a synonym for the *synedrion* which passed judgment on Jesus) and Acts 22:5 of that body in Jerusalem which authorized and empowered Saul to persecute the Damascene Christians. Only here in the NT does the term designate a (Jewish?) Christian body of leaders (*presbyteroi;* see 1 Tim 5:17 on this term). For a more detailed discussion see Comment below.

## ♦ COMMENT

4:11. *These are the matters (tauta), Timothy, to charge and to teach.* The *tauta* expression is part of a typical transitional phrase from dogmatic and moral teaching to parenesis in these letters (except 2 Tim 1:12); see Titus 2:15; 3:8b; 1 Tim 3:14; 4:6, 11, 15; 5:7, 21; 6:2, 11, as well as 2 Tim 2:2, 14. Paul's dogmatic and ethical teaching is to be transmitted to his co-worker's church. R. F. Collins, "Image of Paul," p. 160, observes that the rabbi-disciple relationship is the model that this correspondence uses to show Paul's relation as teacher to his co-workers.

12. *No one is to disdain you for your youth.* The sentence resembles in both its concepts and its terminology Titus 2:7, 15. Thus *mēdeis sou* also opened the latter verse. The comparative youth of Titus was implied in the former citation, and here the term *tēs neotētos* is used explicitly of Timothy.

The phrase is quite natural on the lips of an older leader addressing a younger co-worker, particularly since the term *child* has been employed twice already (1 Tim 1:2, 18; see 2 Tim 1:2 and 2:1 as well as of Titus in Titus 1:4). Indeed, the imagery of Timothy as his "child" was twice used by Paul (1 Cor 4:17; Phil 2:22), and the commendation of Paul to the Corinthian church gives the impression of a man who was by nature shy, if not nervous (1 Cor 16:10), and one whom that hyperaggressive congregation was apt to brush off. "So let no one despise him *(mē tis oun auton exouthenēsēi)*" (1 Cor 16:11).

Granted that the *youth* spoken of in this passage is a relative matter, one can still ask about the rough limits in which this term might apply and where the author of this correspondence thought Timothy belonged within those limits. One gathers from the NT usage already noted that the *terminus a quo* in the Jewish world was the age at which a man was bound to observe the Torah, and thus early adolescence. Such a sense seems to be implied also by *Did.* 4.9 (= *Barn.* 19.5). In *1 Clem.* 63.3 the Roman legates are described as men "who have lived among us without blame from youth *(apo neotētos)* to old age," and here, too, the word seems to denote the earliest age at which one began to take real responsibility for his actions. The condition of *neotēs* thus began in the early teens, but how long was it thought to continue? It seems that one would, in the ancient world, have *neotēs* as long as he could bear arms (see Spicq, *EP*, p. 512) and thus into his mid-forties. In 1 Macc 16:2 a no-longer-young Simon says, "I and my brothers and the house of my father have fought the wars of Israel from our youth *(apo neotētos)* until this day. . . ." See also 1:6 of Alexander the Great and 2:66 of Judas Maccabeus, "a mighty warrior from his youth *(ek neotētos)*." Later in this correspondence Paul will refer to the Jewish childhood of Timothy (2 Tim 3:15: *apo brephous*).

When the historical Paul's apostolate intersected Timothy's life in Lystra and brought him to Christian faith, he was probably already in his teens (1 Cor 4:17; Haenchen, *Acts*, pp. 478, 481). Acts 16:1-3 describes Paul returning to that city a year or two later and taking Timothy into his own apostolic ministry. As a "disciple," he did not have the requirement of circumcision, but the requirements for sharing the apostolic ministry were more stringent, since Timothy's "half-Jewish" background could have compromised the apostolate. The battle over Titus (Gal 2) made Paul sensitive to any criticism on this score. In any event, Timothy could not have been much less than twenty or more than thirty when he joined the Pauline apostolate. If the PE are set within Paul's final year(s) in that apostolate, they are quite correct in presenting Timothy as still within the parameters of *neotēs*, particularly from Paul's point of view. Jerome, *Epist.* 82.8 (*PL* 22.740-741), defending a presbyteral ordination that took place at the age of thirty, points to the example of Timothy (citing this passage) and says, *Certe ipse quando Episcopus ordinatus est, non multum ab ea, in qua nunc frater meus est, distabat aetate,* "Certainly, when he himself was ordained a bishop, he was not much older than my brother is now" (trans. WCW).

It is notable that Luke does not apply the terminology of *neanias/neaniskos* to Timothy in Luke-Acts, though in the PE Timothy is cautioned to avoid "juvenile desires" *(tas . . . neōterikas epithymias,* 2 Tim 2:22; see commentary *in loc.)*, and he is to advise younger men and women (*neōterous . . . neōteras,* 1 Tim 5:1-2) as his brothers and sisters, and thus as his contemporaries.

Spicq, *EP*, pp. 511-512, has noted that every quarter of the ancient world regarded young people as subject to their elders, as listening and obeying rather than speaking and directing. This custom was doubtless shared by the elders *(presbyteroi)* of the Ephesian congregation with whom Timothy had been left (1 Tim 1:3). Their authority, both as elders and as a body of men *(presbyterion?)*, must have been formidable for one whom they could only regard as a young man and alone at that. He is consequently empowered and accredited publicly by a Pauline letter of commendation, and the phrase here might well go back to a dispatch from the Pauline entourage in the mid-sixties to the apostle's co-worker and representative left in the Ephesian church. The Pauline teaching and authorization are conceived as putting even a young man on a par with his elders. Again the Pauline gospel calls into question and reevaluates the distinctions and divisions that are "natural" to human society (as with male-female; slave-free; Jew-Gentile). See Ignatius on the reception to be given a youthful bishop in Ign. *Magn.* 3.1-2.

*Rather keep on being a pattern for believers — in word, in behavior, in charity, in faithfulness, in purity.* Timothy is to counter *(alla)* any contempt for his age through a positive course of conduct and lifestyle that will embody the virtues which usually take years to develop. He is to become permanently (present imperative, not the aorist of many cursives, J. H. Elliott, *Home,* p. 69) a *typos tōn pistōn,* a mold and model (Titus 2:7 also uses *typos* in a similar setting; Titus was to be a "pattern" of the very conduct he would urge on other young men) for believers (on *hoi pistoi* see 4:3 above), a *typos* formed on the *hypotyposis* of Pauline life and teaching (1 Tim 1:16; 2 Tim 1:13; see also Titus 2:7).

The mold or model is then described in terms of its effects or goal, with a fivefold asyndetic list of nouns, each introduced by *en.* Each of the terms refers to an activity or quality in which Timothy is to excel. The five *en* phrases are found only here in First Timothy and in the hymnic fragment above at 3:16 (but there the sequence is interrupted). The closest parallel in the PE to these passages occurs in the threefold repetition of *en* with the town names in 2 Tim 3:11. The one more expansive Pauline list — also a description of the qualities of the apostolic ministry of Paul, Silvanus, and Timothy — occurs in the eighteen phrases of 2 Cor 6:4-7.

The list opens with *en logōi, en anastrophēi,* apparently pairing speech and conduct as audible and visible activities. The use of *logos* here may indicate that a source list is being employed, for even in Titus 2:8 the term tends toward the religious sense of Christian preaching. That meaning is not excluded here, but the more generic sense of all conversation is the easiest meaning of the term (Spicq, *EP,* p. 513). The example given by Timothy is to extend also to his conduct *(anastrophē).*

The next two phrases, *en agapēi, en pistei,* stress the internal effects of the *typos,* as Timothy's own love and faith leave their mark on the hearts of those his ministry touches. The conjunction of *pistis* with *agapē* (in that order) occurs at Titus 2:2 as well as 1 Tim 1:14; 2:15; 6:11; 2 Tim 1:13; 2:22. Only here in the PE is the order *agapē pistis.* The term *agapē* is used here as in the list at Titus 2:2 of the love of neighbor (Spicq, *Agape,* p. 416) rather than in the sense of 1 Tim 1:5, of love for God. The *en pistei* may well be closer to the sense of loyalty or faithfulness (in the grace-charism which God has bestowed on him [4:4]). The usage would resemble that in the great catalogue of the harvest of the Spirit in Gal 5:22, which leads off with *agapē*. Spicq has rightly noted the overtones of confidence in God and a certain "supernatural optimism" that characterize this particular usage. Like *agapē, pistis* here reflects the usage of the catalogue source and is some distance from the *en pistei* = *en Christōi* discussed at 1 Tim 1:14 (see above).

The final phrase in this little catalogue, *en hagneiai,* "in purity," will occur again (with *pasēi*) in the *Haustafel* of 1 Tim 5:2. One could surmise that the source cited here at 4:12 was taking the OT requirements for community and priestly purity and applying them to the priestly people of the NT. In that case the author-redactor of the PE goes a step further in specifying them particularly (but not only) for the one who shares in and exercises a Pauline ministry, a *typos* of "priestly ministry" (see Rom 15:16) that leaves its priestly seal upon the people of God.

13. *Until I arrive, concentrate on your public reading of the Scriptures, on your preaching, on your instruction.* With this verse the first person singular occurs for the first time since 3:14, and the subject matter here is obviously linked with that passage. Both may be fragmentary reminiscences of the original *epistolē systatikē* of the sixties with which Paul shored up the mission of this co-worker, as he had also that of Titus (see AB *Titus* on Titus 3:12-14). One might surmise that if the language here goes back to a dispatch of the mid-sixties, Luke had drafted that letter of commendation.

The three articular nouns in asyndeton that are the object of *proseche* give the impression that the functions so crisply listed need no further definition, that the terms are virtually technical in this context (Spicq, *EP,* p. 514). The order is not accidental, for each function described seems to presume the previous. The final and climactic *didaskalia* (the explanation and application of the OT according to Pauline hermeneutics) to which the Pauline co-worker is to dedicate himself presupposes that he has first read publicly in an assembly the OT Scriptures (and thus, too, has been the first himself to listen to them).

The first-century-C.E. synagogue service began with the *Shemaʿ*, the prayer with eighteen petitions, and the priestly blessing (cf. 1 Tim 2:1-7), which were followed by the reading and translation of a passage of the Torah and, normally but not always, a passage from the Prophets. The Scriptures were read to a standing congregation (as Luke 4:16 reminds); the *ex tempore* exhortation which followed was given to a seated congregation (as Luke 4:20 recalls; Acts 13:16 has Paul *standing* and gesturing like a Greek orator for his "encouraging word," probably a Lukan accommodation of his narrative to the tastes of Greek readers; see Haenchen, *Acts,* pp. 407-408).

The synagogal *ordo servandus* certainly seems to lie behind the terminology and the functions designated at this point in the PE, and the importance of the Scripture reading in that service can scarcely be overestimated. As the famous Ophel inscription of Theodotus says of the synagogue which he erected in Jerusalem, it was to be *eis an[agn]ō/s[in] nomou kai eis [d]idach[ē]n entolōn* . . . , "for the reading of the Law and for the teaching of the commandments, and the guest house and the rooms and supplies of water as an inn for those who are in need when coming from abroad" (trans. I. Sonne, "Synagogue," *IDB,* p. 480, with illustration 94; text from *CII* II, 1404; and Lifshitz, *Donateurs,* §§79-80, pp. 70-71, who notes the Jewish concern for the traveler from abroad — note the *philoxenon* of Titus 1:8). The crisp, almost rubrical, directives in 1 Tim 4:13 remind one of the inscription on the floor of the Sardis synagogue where the reader was to take his stand: *heurōn* (finding your place in the roll); *klasas* (with your voice modulated); *anagnōthi* (read out the Torah); *phylaxon* (keep the commands you read). Spicq, *EP,* p. 514, has noted the skills needed by the public reader in the ancient world. The rolls of typical Greek manuscripts themselves were heavy and hard to handle; the writing was done without punctuation or separation of words; blots, tears, holes, and blemishes accumulated, and other copies by which one could correct a text were liable to be far away. Thus the one who read publicly had to prepare the text carefully in advance to communicate it effectively in the actual process of speaking.

14. *Do not neglect that gracious gift within you.* If the preceding verse described the activities to which Timothy was to devote himself, the admonition here turns to the root and source of those activities, the charism within him *(tou en soi charismatos).* In the PE, *charisma* is used only of the gift that has come from God (see below on *edothē*) through the laying on of hands, whether of the presbytery or of St. Paul or of both. There is nothing particularly non-Pauline or non-Christian in the charism coming through a palpable, visible rite. Thus in Rom 6:23 the *charisma tou theou* of eternal life itself has come through the baptismal act. On the other hand, in these passages of the PE (here and 2 Tim 1:6) there is no evidence that *charisma* is simply equivalent to eternal life or the Holy Spirit. The focus is on the bestowal of one specific gift out of many that the Spirit gives. The visible rite of imposition of hands accordingly gives no monopoly on the Spirit to the apostolic ministers, who in turn would be understood as the sole purveyors of God's gifts. One might tax the author of the PE with a failure to mention the other *charismata* that God has bestowed upon his church, as well as his failure to advert to apostles other than Paul. Yet this correspondence is directed to Timothy (or should the redactor-author also be criticized for not mentioning Titus's *charisma?*). Moreover, there is no lack of a doctrine on grace *(charis)* in this correspondence (see AB *Titus* on Titus 1:4; 2:11; 3:7, 15; 1 Tim 1:2, 12, 14), and the relation of *charisma* to *charis* is more than one of historical etymology.

*the one given to you under prophetic direction.* For the author of the PE the *charisma* is evidently an invisible, internal reality, inhering within Timothy (note the *en soi* both here and 2 Tim 1:6). Whereas the previous exhortation stressed his audible, visible, and ministerial activities, this one turns from the external to the internal, from the outer function to the inner heart of the minister. That heart is what God has touched and empowered, for the aorist passive *edothē* is surely a Semitic circumlocution for the divine name. God at a given moment *gave* or *bestowed* his gift on the person of Timothy (the repeated *soi* is to be noted as well as the conceptual link between the action designated by the verb and the *charis[ma]* to which the relative pronoun refers). Second Timothy 1:6 articulates the relationship with the possessive genitive, *to charisma tou theou,* attributing explicitly to *ho theos* (the Father?) what is left implicit in 1 Tim 4:14. Second Timothy 1:7 (see commentary *in loc.*) also develops explicitly the relation of the *charisma* to *pneuma.* Here the "pneumatic" aspect of the charism is implicit in the *dia prophēteias,* which refers to prophetic interventions and participation in God's bestowing his gift to Timothy. The prophetic "order" is distinguished — but not necessarily separated from — the presbyteral (teaching) order (cf. Acts 13:1, where the five are *both* prophets and teachers).

*with an imposition of the hands.* The prophetic interventions (most probably oral) are distinguished from a visible act, *meta ephitheseōs tōn cheirōn,* "with an imposition of hands," which evidently is to be compared with *dia tēs epitheseōs tōn cheirōn,* "through the imposition of these hands," at 2 Tim 1:6, where the hands are the two hands of Paul himself. Thus the action should be understood as one person (kneeling?) before another, who places both hands (note the plural) on the head of the person before him.

For the exegesis here it will be helpful to review briefly the uses of *epitithenai tas cheiras* in the Gospels and Acts. In Matt 9:18 (= Mark 5:23) the synagogue ruler asks Jesus to lay his hand (note the sg. in Matthew; pl. in Mark) on his daughter to cure her. Again in Matt 19:13, 15 (= Mark 10:13, 16, which reads *hapsētai,* "touch," then *titheis tas cheiras,* "laying on hands" = Luke 18:15, *haptētai* [*SFG* §253]), the phrase describes the action and accompanying prayer for the little children *(proseuxētai).* In Mark 7:32 those who bring the deaf-mute to Jesus in the Decapolis region want him "to lay his hand [note sg.] on him." In Mark 8:23, 25, there may be a distinction in the gesture as Jesus first lays *(epitheis)* his hands on the blind man and then, in the second stage of the cure, "he laid his hands *(ethēken)* upon *(epi)* his eyes." Perhaps this stage envisions the kneeling (?) man looking upward and Jesus' hands touching his eyes rather than the crown of his head (cf. Mark 10:16 cited above). In the canonical conclusion, Mark 16:18 reads, of the believers, "they will lay their hands on the sick and they will recover."

Luke 4:40 says of Jesus and the sick, "He laid his hands on every one of them and healed them," and in 13:13 the phrase is repeated in the narrative of

Jesus' healing the hunchbacked woman on the Sabbath. The phrase is still used of healings in Acts (9:12, 17 of Saul's blindness; 28:8 of the father of Publius), but the gesture in addition signifies and effects a reception of the Spirit (8:17-19; 19:6). Finally, in Acts 6:6 and 13:3 the action occurs in a context of prayer, where men (the Seven, Barnabas, and Paul) are set apart or dedicated to certain tasks. In the former instance the men are already characterized as "full of the Spirit and of wisdom," and in the latter a prophetic word comes from the Spirit, asking for two persons for the work *(eis to ergon)* to which he has already summoned them. The *ergon* is the apostolic mission, the proclamation of the gospel to those who have not yet believed. It is not only the task of Barnabas and Paul but also, as Luke tells the story, of the Seven.

It is notable that, except for the blessing of the children (Matt 19:13, 15), all the Gospel examples of imposing hand(s) are in connection with powerful acts of healing. It has been remarked that neither the OT nor the rabbinic tradition documents such an association (Lohse, *TDNT* 9.428), but the Genesis Apocryphon from Qumran (1QapGen 20.28-29; Fitzmyer, *Gen. Apoc.*, pp. 66-67, 140-141) does describe how, with Abram's accompanying prayer, and his imposition of hands *(wsmkt ydy)* upon Pharaoh's head, "the plague was removed from him and the evil [spirit] was commanded *(w'tgʿrt)* (to depart) [from him] and he was cured." The same Qumran text, 20.21-22, had also written, "Then Hirqanos came to be (Abraham) and begged me to come and pray *(w'ṣlh)* over the king and lay my hands *(w'smwk ydy)* upon him that he might be cured" (Fitzmyer, *Gen. Apoc.*, pp. 64-65, 134).

David Daube, as early as 1956 (*Rabbinic Judaism*, pp. 224-246), called attention to the quite different Hebrew terms for "placing" or "putting" one's hands on another *(śîm; šît)* and "laying (lit. 'leaning') hands" on another *(sāmak)*. He argued that the Greek of both the LXX and NT telescoped different symbolic actions into one with the phrase *epithesis tōn cheirōn* or *epitithenai tas cheiras*. If his observation is correct, then the healing *epithesis* of the Gospels and Acts ought to have corresponded in the *Sitz im Leben Jesu* to the *sāmak* of 1QapGen (contra Daube, *Rabbinic Judaism*, pp. 234-235), whereas that described in the blessing of the children would be *śîm/šît* of old Jacob's blessing (Gen 48:14, 17-18) and of the later rabbis (Daube, p. 231). In one other Qumran text (and that unhappily very mutilated) there survives the phrase *wsmk 't yd[yw* (1Q22 4.9 in DJD 1.95-96; 1QDM; see Dupont-Sommer, *EWQ*, p. 309). If we have here a ritual for the Day of Atonement (so Milik and Dupont-Sommer), then it is conceivable that the text before us, with its "and he shall impose [his] hands," is referring to Lev 16:21-22 with its description of Aaron: "He shall lay both his hands *(wsmk . . . ydw)* upon the head of the live goat" which is to carry all the people's sins into the desert. This would accord with Daube's observations about the "pressing" or "leaning" with the hands that some twenty times occurs with respect to an animal that is to be sacrificed (*Rabbinic Judaism,* pp. 225-226).

The thirteen other occurrences of *smk* in the Qumran literature (six times with forms of *yēṣēr,* cf. Isa 26:3) do not illustrate the imposition of hands, but they do bear out Daube's point on the "forceful" character of the gesture in question, as distinguished from the gentler and more relaxed placing of a hand upon another in blessing (*Rabbinic Judaism,* pp. 227-228). One ought to note that the Hebrew root *smk* denotes an action or activity which is from one point of view a bearing down, a pressure upon; or from another point of view a support, an upholding, a sustaining. The latter sense certainly predominates in the Qumran texts (1QS 4.5; 8.3; 10.25; 1QM 8.7, 14 [of trumpets *sustaining* their sound]; 1QH 1.35; 2.7, 9, 36; 7.6; 9.32; 18.13; and 4QpIsaD 2 [Dupont-Sommer, *EWQ,* p. 275] of God "upholding" the shoot of David). This leaning or supporting syndrome may have something to say about the meaning of this action as distinct from blessing. The person who leans and the one who supports are *both* part of the action, which would be unintelligible apart from the interdependence of the persons involved. On the other hand, the roles within the single action are quite distinct, even contrary; one is active, the other passive; one stands, the other kneels; one gives, another receives.

The Torah also uses the *smk* root to describe the act of the Israelite people dedicating the Levites to the special sacrificial ministry that demanded that the Levites in their turn "lay their hands" upon the sacrificial animals. Indeed, the action seems to be understood as making the Levites themselves an offering before Yahweh (Num 8:10-13, and see Vaux, *Israel,* p. 347). In Num 27:18-23 Moses himself is commanded to "lean his hands" upon Joshua, "a man in whom is the Spirit," with the purpose stated quite explicitly: "You shall invest him with some of your authority [or honor, *mehodekā*]" (RSV). In Num 27:23 this becomes "and he laid his hands upon him and commissioned him (gave him orders, *wayĕsawwēhû*) just as Yahweh said *by the hand* of Moses." In Deut 34:9, "Joshua . . . was full of the spirit of wisdom, for Moses had laid his hands upon him" (RSV) (see Daube, *Rabbinic Judaism,* pp. 226-227). As Lohse has noted, the narrative of the choice and installation of the Seven (Acts 6:1-6) is unmistakably modeled on the former passage (*TDNT* 9.433 n. 55) and meant to say something of the Christian "ordination" of ministers vis-à-vis the Levitical order. In Lev 24:14 the witnesses must "lean" hands upon the head of the doomed blasphemer (Daube, *Rabbinic Judaism,* p. 227).

Daube has observed that even in the first Christian century the rabbis limit the *smk* as a rite to the appropriate temple sacrifices and to the "ordination" of a rabbi. The Levitical "ordination" and the procedure for convicting the blasphemer no longer advert to this ritual (Daube, *Rabbinic Judaism,* pp. 230-231). The laying on of hands among the rabbis took place only on the soil of

Palestine and could have begun before 50 C.E. (Lohse, *TDNT* 9.429, on this and the following). It was performed with an explicit appeal to the action of Moses upon Joshua (citations in Lohse, *TDNT* 9.429 n. 28). The rabbi-teacher (with two assistants and with witnesses present) "leaned his hands" on a student of his that had acquired that mastery of the Scripture and practices of Judaism which would entitle him to be called rabbi and in turn to gather his own students. The rite disappeared from the Jewish world by the mid–third century (Daube, *Rabbinic Judaism,* p. 232). The vigorous debates about the nature, significance, and usage of the *semikah* among contemporary scholars in rabbinics (see Spicq, *EP,* pp. 724-25, with references), as well as the Qumran material, make it necessary to qualify Daube's suggestion in several ways.

As Spicq has noted (*EP,* p. 724), the LXX, the NT, and the Syriac Peshitta have all alike forgotten or failed to note the distinction between *śîm/šît // sāmak.* To put it geographically, the non-Palestinian world either was not aware of or considered insignificant the difference in the physical gesture which the Palestinian world did remember and transmit. Thus the gesture that appears among Christians in the midst of the Greek world in the latter part of the first century may well have had a Palestinian provenance, whether from the sacrificial cult or from the Palestinian method of appointing/authorizing a rabbi (or both). There is no evidence that the physical distinction between "leaning" the hands or putting them on the head ever was consciously adverted to in the Christian documentation.

The inquiry about the meaning of the imposition of hands is a vexed one at every stage of its development. The original Palestinian gesture of "leaning the hands" is scarcely self-explanatory. The reasons for which the Palestinian Christians adopted the ritual are unclear. There is no first-generation, firsthand evidence of the use of the rite, though of course Acts either remembers or retrojects such a rite into the Jerusalem congregation (Acts 6:1-6) and the Pauline apostolate (13:1-3). The PE finally link the rite with Timothy and the presbyters, not with Titus or the *episkopoi/diakonoi.* They also envision that Paul, as well as a *presbyterion,* was involved in its administration to Timothy and then Timothy in his turn administered it to others (and that is the interpretation to be given to 1 Tim 5:22).

As Spicq has noted (*EP,* p. 722 n. 2), the five LXX references to *epithesis* never add *tōn cheirōn,* and thus a "technical" nominal phrase that would correspond to the frequent references to *(epi)tithenai tas cheiras* is not to be found in biblical Greek before the NT; it is not documented in the Ap. Frs., who do not use the verbal phrase either, though *Barn.* 13.5 cites Gen 48:14 where Jacob places his right hand *(epethēken tēn dexian)* on Ephraim's head. MM note only a "hostile sense" for *epithesis* in the papyri, which are in this respect not unlike LXX usage (cf., e.g., 2 Macc 4:41; 5:5; 14:15). One could infer that the nominal phrase was coined by the author of the PE; indeed, it does not appear to occur again in the Christian Fathers until Irenaeus (*Adversus haereses* 2.32.4), and then it is for healing (Lampe, *PGL, s.v. "cheir"* #8, p. 1521). Eusebius, *Church History* 7.32.21, uses the verbal phrase of a bishop's ordination, as well as Serapion, *Euchologium* 27.1 (F. X. Funk, *Constitutiones* 2.189), with its prayer at the "ordination" *(cheirothesia)* of *presbyteroi* which begins *tēn cheira* (note sg.) *ekteinomen* (note pl.). One wonders if the rite is presumed to have occurred in silence and the prayer, with a hand still outstretched, then followed (as to this day in the Roman rite for the ordination of priests).

To return to the imposition of hands by Jesus in his Palestinian ministry, it is historically quite conceivable that he used the *śîm-šît/sāmak* gestures for blessing and for healing. It is notable that the documents do not recall that he ever used either gesture upon the Twelve as a group or individually (cf. Spicq, *EP,* p. 726: Daube, *Rabbinic Judaism,* p. 246). Their enablement or empowerment *(exousia)* for the tasks Jesus gave to them in his historical ministry is simply ascribed to his commanding word (see *SFG* §49: Mark 3:13-13a [see also §142]; 6:6b-13; Luke 6:12 adds a setting of Jesus' prayer to the choice; John 20:22 mentions breathing on them). This would include the command to do what he had done at the supper before his betrayal (1 Cor 11:24-25; Luke 22:19). The replacement for Judas among the Twelve mentions no imposition of hands. The meaning of the "leaning of hands" upon the sick in Jesus' Palestinian ministry ought to be understood within the generic symbolism of the human hand(s) in the ancient world (see on the following Grayston, "Hand," pp. 479-487; Lohse, *ut cit. TDNT s.v.*). The hand stands for a person's power and strength and the work that issues from that, in particular the work of organizing and controlling. The hand can control that which is weaker than it, and thus it can stand for protection, rescue, even salvation. Part of controlling or organizing is working through other persons as one's instruments. Thus God works through men, and those men through other men as delegates or agents (cf. Acts 11:30; 15:23; Grayston, "Hand," p. 481), and this work is said to be "by the hand" of the one delegated. With the suggestion of power goes that of authority and responsibility, as when "hand" stands for an (apostolic) signature (Gal 6:11; 2 Thess 3:17, and other citations in Grayston, "Hand," p. 481; see also Lohse, *TDNT* 9.425). Grayston ("Hand," p. 481) also notes that "for Paul the hand lacked symbolic or figurative quality." This does not seem to be the case with the PE or with Luke-Acts.

Daube has suggested that the "leaning" gesture signified "the pouring of one's personality into another being, the creation of a representative or substitute" (*Rabbinic Judaism,* p. 229; cf. pp. 231-232, 237, 239, 241 and *ANRW* 2.25.3, pp. 2355-2356). The former part of that description seems to be inaccurate; there is no evidence for the rite as transmitting that complex of psychological and psychosomatic attributes which we normally designate as "personality." The various metaphors of pouring liquids, pressing down grain in jars, and lighting one fire from another (pp. 231-232) are not concerned with the transmission of personality, but as the Hebrew text puts it quite baldly, the *hôd* of Moses (Num 27:20) which is to call forth obedience from Israel. That term occurs only there in the Hexateuch (P) and has the sense of visible dignity, majesty, or authority, with overtones of manly vigor and impressiveness. It is parallel with *kbd* in Ps 25:6, and the LXX translated this passage in Numbers with *doxa.* In 1QH 5.32 the Qumran hymnist speaks of "the light of my face" in parallel with "my brightness" *(hwdy).* The reference in Numbers may accordingly be to Exod 34:29-35 with its repeated references to the shining skin of Moses' face (*qaran ʿor,* sending out hornlike rays of light). Since Joshua was not remembered as receiving the same external appearance as Moses, the *hôd* is that part of the gift to Moses which inspired reverence and obedience. It was this *pondus (kbd)* that passed through the hands of the one who leaned upon another, and by accepting it, indeed bearing up under it, the one upon whom hands had been laid shared in the power and authority of the "imposing" one.

Daube's understanding of the rite as in some way signifying substitution, representation, having another "take one's place," a succession to a function or role, seems to be consistent with the biblical texts on the whole (though not with the procedure for the blasphemer). Perhaps the real background is found at a still deeper level in the meaning of bloody sacrifice in Israel, for, as Spicq has noted, the imposition of hands at such sacrifice does not involve transmitting the worshipper's sins to the animal about to be slain (and so a ritual "substitution" of the animal for the man), but rather the worshipper's intent to give the gift to God, "to abandon to Him what belonged to oneself" (*EP,* p. 723 n. 4; see Vaux, *Israel:* ". . . it is a solemn attestation that this victim comes from this particular individual who is laying his hands on it, that the sacrifice . . . is offered in his name, and that the fruits of the sacrifice shall be his" [p. 416]; there is no transfer of one's life-principle or of one's sins to the victim [pp. 448-449]; the rite of imposition and the immolation are both preparatory to sacrifice and are distinct from it [p. 452]. As Milgrom, AB *Lev. 1–16,* pp. 150-153, has pointed out, the basic reason for the placing of the hands on the animal to be offered for sacrifice is to attest to the ownership of the animal. The offerer must give from his own possessions, as otherwise the sacrifice is meaningless. Sacrifice is essentially a gift, and these actions help to make it that, irrevocably and in the divine order; see also Vaux, *SOTS,* pp. 28, 96).

If the power and authority noted above were the gift of God in the first instance, then they were passed on not only by the divine gift but also *precisely* as a divine gift, and the imposition of hands thus enters clearly into the order of effective signs. What God has given to one, he earnestly prays will be given as a gift to another.

The author of Luke-Acts describes an imposition of hands in connection with the establishment of the Seven in their share of the task that otherwise would have defaulted to the Twelve. The similarities in the language of Acts 6:1-6 and Num 27 (noted above) indicate that the author thought of this action in terms of the OT appointment of Joshua, and perhaps of the Levites (Num 8:10; see Vaux, *Israel,* p. 347). This is the only time that this Christian rite (as distinct from Acts 8:17) is described as occurring on Palestinian soil and thus the only one that might have been originally and recognizably a *semikah.* The exact role that is attributed to the Twelve has been disputed, apparently at least since the time that the compilers of the Western text felt constrained to make it quite clear that the Twelve alone imposed hands. Actually, the text as it stands probably means that the whole assembly, *including the Twelve,* prayed and performed the rite. Note that not only do the Twelve speak of seven men "whom we shall appoint" (see the first person plural of 6:3 with v. 4 — *pace* Daube), but the mention of prayer refers precisely to *hē proseuchē,* "the (public) prayer," whose leadership they had reserved to themselves (6:4; see also 1:14; 2:42).

It is of course beyond verification whether the Jerusalem church was actually employing the *semikah* within a decade of the resurrection, not to mention later generations (see E. Ferguson, "Laying on of Hands," pp. 1-12). Yet the very discretion and restraint with which the author of Acts alludes to it allows one to grant at least the fact and to note, with Spicq (*EP,* p. 727), Lohse (*TDNT* 9.433), and Grayston ("Hand," p. 487), the crucial importance of the prayer which accompanies the ritual gesture, for it is the Word of God and prayer that specify the meaning of the OT *semikah* in its new environment (note the prayer accompanying the gesture in 1QapGen 20.28). The text of the prayer has not been transmitted, but the tasks of the Seven, relief service for the poor widows of Hellenist origin, and then the proclamation of the kerygma to non-Judean Jews, were doubtless thought of as the subjects in some fashion of the prayer. As men already equipped with the Spirit, wisdom, and faith (Acts 6:3, 5), all alike prayed for the effective use of these gifts.

If one would ask what form such a prayer might take, Spicq, *EP,* p. 725 n. 2, has suggested that one compare the Qumran "Blessing for the Prince of the Congregation," DJD 1.118-130; 1QSb col. V; Dupont-Sommer, *EWQ,* pp. 112-113, but perhaps the Blessing for Priests *(hkwhnym)* ought to be noted as well (1QSb col. III, 22–IV, 28; Dupont-Sommer, *EWQ,* pp. 111-112; cf. citations on 1 Tim 3:16), with its emphasis upon the judging and teaching functions of these men as well as their leadership in worship. In col. IV, 28, the prayer, moreover, appears to be that God make the priest "an object vowed to infinite holiness *(nzr lqds qwdsym)* for you [sg.] are [con]secrated to him *(. . . tq] ds lw).*" One wonders if the emphasis upon the Isaian "Spirit of the Lord" in the blessings of the Messianic Prince (col. V, 205) as well as of the (Messianic?) high priest (col. II, 24) is taken up in the emphatic references to the Spirit in 2 Tim 1:7. As Spicq has noted, *EP*, p. 724, the language and symbolism of the imposition of hands are not part of the priestly installation in the OT, which was described as "filling the hand." The Seven have no OT "Levitical" functions as such; they do not teach as rabbis, but they do represent and substitute for those who have chosen them, and to that extent they resemble the Levites and the sacrifices of ancient Israel. Like a new Joshua, Stephen proclaimed in his great speech in Acts 7 the true intent of Moses.

Acts 13:1-3 describes an intervention of the Spirit outside of Palestine which commands the Church (prophets and teachers) in Antioch on the Orontes to *set aside (aphorisate)* Barnabas and Saul for the missionary task. They are conceived of as "Levites" (indeed Barnabas is one, Acts 4:36), the "first fruits" of Israel, completely devoted to and a gift to their Lord (LXX Num 8:11: *kai aphoriei Aarōn tous Levitas apodoma enanti Kyriou,* "and Aaron shall set the Levites aside as a gift for the Lord," trans. WCW). They are sent forth not only by the Spirit but by the church. Thus they can receive the title *apostoloi* on this mission (14:4, 14), and as "apostles of the church" (see 2 Cor 8:23), they can be described in the same language as the Twelve (see Haenchen, *Acts,* p. 420, who cites Acts 5:12).

One wonders if, when Paul in Gal 1:1 is so emphatically declaring he is *apostolos ouk ap' anthrōpōn oude di' anthrōpou,* "an apostle not from humans not through humans," he is appealing not to a known, public event in which he had been "sent" by men, but to an anterior and unwitnessed intervention in his life which made him an *apostolos* not simply of the Spirit and the Antiochene church but of Jesus Christ (and thus on a par with the Jerusalem "apostles before me," Gal 1:17). In any event, if Paul did receive an imposition of the hands from the "prophets and teachers" of the Antiochene church, it was for a missionary work from the Holy Spirit and not for becoming a rabbi or a Christian *didaskalos.* He most probably already was a rabbi (and perhaps even by the imposition of hands), and the text already considers him among the Antiochene *didaskaloi.* Note that Paul had received imposition of hands for *healing* after his "conversion" (Acts 9:12, 17). It is the Spirit's word as well as the cultic actions of fasting and prayer by which the church confers a mission (an apostolate) upon certain men, and without prejudice to the question of whether either or both were *apostoloi* in another sense and by a rather different appointment. Note again the almost technical description of the three remaining local leaders as *proseuxamenoi,* "praying" (13:3), and *leitourgountōn,* "worshipping" (13:2), which specifies the meaning of this rite. Luke sees no more difficulty in the newly converted Saul's receiving baptism and the imposition of hands at the direction of the risen Lord and from a leading member of the local church than in his receiving an imposition of hands from a local church at the direction of the

Spirit. On the other hand, he does not record that the Twelve themselves submitted to either rite — or were ever directed to do so.

With this background, when one arrives at the description of Timothy's reception(s) of the *epithesis tōn cheirōn,* 1 Tim 4:14; 2 Tim 1:6, one cannot help being struck by the explicit and implicit references to the *gift (charisma,* with its transparent stress on *charis)* that is given *(edothē; edoken),* a gift that belongs to God *(theou)* and comes from his action. One infers that, however the imposition was given, it was understood as a sacrificial gesture, i.e. as part of the preparation for and expression of the turning over of a gift (in this case of a human person) totally and irrevocably to God. But this method of presentation also emphatically reaffirms that the gift really belongs to the offerer (the apostle and the Church), that it is being offered in his name, "and that the benefits accruing from it will return to him" (Vaux, *SOTS,* p. 28). The divine gift *(charisma)* corresponds to and is signified by the human gift. The latter has not "bought" the former nor extorted it. The gratuitous love and election that has prompted the one has also prompted the other. There is a reciprocity rather like that between the bread and wine given for use in the Lord's Supper and the gift of the body and blood of the Lord. The latter does not come without the former, yet the former in no sense demands that God grant the latter.

The repeated references to prayer with the imposition of hands in the Lukan texts persuade one to make room for this interpretation or specification of the *dia prophēteias* that are described as the context of the imposition of hands in 1 Tim 4:14. Spicq, *EP,* p. 517, understands the prophetic intervention as framed within the liturgy. Cothenet, *DBS* 8.1314, qualifies this to the extent that he, with Spicq, *EP,* p. 727, takes *dia prophēteias* as an instrumental phrase in the singular, but with a wide sense for "prophecy" which includes "the whole Liturgy of the Word which accompanies the imposition of hands and makes its meaning explicit in the course of the ordination ceremony."

The imposition of hands is qualified in terms of those associated with it, a *presbyterion* in 1 Tim 4:14; Paul himself in 2 Tim 1:6. From the level of the final edition of this correspondence, it is most reasonable to presuppose that the redactor was indeed conscious of the difference between the two passages. In fact, the complete omission of mention of any rite associated with the designation of Titus or the *presbyteroi* (bishops) of Crete would lead one to infer that the author-redactor of the PE knew of a leadership by the appointment of the apostle and his co-worker (*hina . . . katastēseis,* Titus 1:5), and without further specification. Then in First and Second Timothy he apparently specifies at least some of the means of designation by citing two different ways in which hands were imposed, noting first the *presbyterion* and then Paul himself. Did the redactor conceive of these rites over Timothy as two separate occasions or as one occasion within which Paul and a *presbyterion* acted together?

Daube has proposed that *presbyterion* here refers not to certain individuals but to an office of leadership, the whole Greek phrase *epithesis tōn cheirōn tou presbyteriou* being a literal translation of the rabbinic phrase *semikat zĕgēnîm* (*Rabbinic Judaism,* pp. 244-45), which has a final sense, i.e. the laying on of hands for the office of elder, "eldership" (Grayston, "Hand," p. 487). Thus Timothy is being reminded of a gift that came to him "with due ordination." Jeremias, "*Presbyterion,*" pp. 127-132, in a study of variant manuscript readings, has noted that B, 88, and 410 in the Theodotion Daniel 12:50 (or Susanna 50) — the unique occurrence of the term in OT Greek texts — have the young Daniel invite the two *presbyteroi* who have borne witness (by imposing hands, v. 34) against Susanna, "Come, sit among us and inform us, because God has given you the right *(hoti soi dedōken ho theos to presbeion* [*presbyterion* is read by all the rest of the manuscripts])." There is every reason, with all questions of authenticity set aside, to infer that the *presbeion* (gift, privilege, prerogative, right; see LSJ) was understood as *presbyterion* and vice versa.

Thus this variant would mean that at least in the first Christian centuries and perhaps as early as Theodotion's version (but not necessarily in the pre-Christian era when the canonical Daniel was produced), *presbyterion* was understood as the elder's prerogative or right. Accordingly, Daube's suggestion would be corroborated and this passage of First Timothy would refer to the (presbyteral) privilege conferred by the imposition of hands. Yet, as noted by Spicq, *EP,* p. 518, with Bornkamm, *TDNT* 6.666 n. 92, the genitive *presbyteriou* in the final sense here is not the simplest way to read the Greek (for all the ease with which the Hebrew construct could be so interpreted), nor is it parallel to the other use of this phrase where the genitive, *mou,* occurs at 2 Tim 1:6 and *tōn apostolōn* at Acts 8:18. If, on our hypothesis, the redactor of the Pastorals is Luke, it is a surprising inconsistency in his usage. The shift from a Jewish *presbyterion* to a Jewish Christian one is no more surprising than his shift from Jewish *presbyteroi* (Acts 4:5; etc.) to Christian ones (Acts 11:30). It is another matter to shift from an actual council to an abstract office or even to a concrete rite.

Sinaiticus in the original hand and a few other witnesses read "with the imposition of the hands of (a) presbyter *(presbyterou)*" (see J. K. Elliott, *Greek Text,* pp. 71-72). If this is not simply an accidental omission of an iota due to the word's being carried from one line to the next *(presbyte/r[i]ou),* it looks like a "learned" correction by a scribe who recalled the Lukan usage (= Sanhedrin) and decided to forestall confusion. Yet one must admit that there are far more references to Jewish *presbyteroi* than to Christian ones in Luke-Acts, and one wonders if the "corrector" who thus avoided Scylla would not note Charybdis. The conjectures of Katz (*ut cit.* J. K. Elliott, *Greek Text,* p. 71 n. 30) have no manuscript evidence in the PE to support them, and precious little elsewhere.

But that takes one back to "the presbytery" as, more probably, the body or group of *presbyteroi,* the assembled leadership of the local church. That is the usual sense in which the letters of Ignatius employ the term on thirteen occasions (and he is the only one of the Ap. Frs. to use it). Since five to seven letters mention a presbytery (not in *Epistle to the Romans* or *Epistle to Polycarp*), this name for the body of *presbyteroi* must have been common enough in Asia Minor. Perhaps that is why First Timothy uses this noun, taking up Ephesian terminology which may not have been understood elsewhere (Crete?). For Ignatius, not only do the *presbyteroi* in the churches he knows correspond to the position of the *apostoloi* a full generation and more previously, but the *apostoloi* in their turn can even be called the "presbytery of the church" (see Ign. *Phld.* 5.1, "making the apostles my refuge," *hōs presbyteriōi ekklēsias*). One recalls that 1 Pet 5:1 has no qualms about numbering "Peter an apostle of Jesus Christ" (1 Pet 1:1) as a *sympresbyteros* with the *presbyteroi* whom he is exhorting. An "apostle" with "presbyteroi" (in a single body *presbyterion*) was apparently quite conceivable in the latter part of the first Christian century.

In that case the so-called contradiction between 1 Tim 4:14 and 2 Tim 1:6 melts away. The author of these letters has no more difficulty conceiving Paul *and* a presbytery imposing hands on Timothy than the author of First Peter has demurred at placing Peter among the *presbyteroi.* The same occasion is being described, but from a different point of view in each passage. First Timothy inserts the passage within a "church order" (see Lohse, *TDNT* 9.434) which the hypothetical addressee is to implement, even with regard to *presbyteroi* (see 5:17-22); what better ground for confidence that his direction will be well received than the recollection that the prophetic order and the *presbyteroi* as a body chose him and imposed hands? On the other hand, 2 Tim 1:6 envisions Timothy in relation to Paul, unsure of himself, sure only that he falls far short of his master. Here, in the testamentary form, he is exhorted, in the light of Paul's participation in the same *epithesis tōn cheirōn,* to remember that he was also Paul's choice for this ministry. It is a significant detail that whereas the acts of the presbytery as a whole are described as *meta epitheseōs tōn cheirōn,* in 2 Tim 1:6 it is *dia tēs epitheseōs tōn cheirōn* that indicates the preponderant role of Paul (Spicq, *EP,* p. 729).

## IV.A.3. SUMMARY EXHORTATION (4:15-16)

*4 15 Let these matters be your study. Be absorbed in them, so that your progress can be perceived by all. 16 Pay attention to yourself and to your instruction. Persevere in these activities; for, if you do this, you will save both yourself and the persons listening to you.*

## ♦ NOTES

4:15. *Let these matters be your study.* Lit. "Meditate upon these things," *tauta meleta.* This verb occurs otherwise in the NT only in Acts 4:25, citing LXX Ps 2:1. There it means "meditate, think upon," in the bad sense of "to conspire," but as LXX Ps 1:2 illustrates, biblical Greek knows it has a good sense too, of meditation "on the law of the Lord" (see LXX Ps 118:16, 47, 70, 117, 148). Only Luke 21:14 knows the form *promeletan* in the NT. In the Ap. Frs. Ignatius once uses the verb in *Eph.* 19.3 for God's *planning* the abolition of death *(dia to meletasthai thanatou katalysin).* Barnabas uses the term five times (4.11; 10.11; 11.5; 19.10, and in 21.7 concludes the letter by saying of all that has gone before, "meditating on these things [*meletōntes tauta*], remember me").

*progress.* The noun *prokopē* occurs only here in the PE and otherwise in the NT only in Phil 1:12, 25. The LXX, too, documents the term very rarely; Sir 51:17, "I made progress therein," *prokopē egeneto moi en autēi* (i.e. in wisdom), and 2 Macc 8:8, describing Judas's gradual success in his rebellion; and the Ap. Frs. do not have it at all. The noun appeared only in Hellenistic Greek, and the Atticists remained uneasy about it (Stählin, *TDNT* 6.704). It was, however, part of the cant of Stoic philosophy and probably had some of the attractiveness that certain existentialist neologisms have in current English. MM, p. 542, note colloquial uses in the papyri of the second Christian century and thereafter. The noun is used in the biblical documentation in a positive sense and usually has a person as its subject.

The cognate verb, *prokotein,* which occurs in the PE at 2 Tim 2:16; 3:9, 13, is always used in a pejorative sense, of "progress" indeed, but from bad to worse, the malignant growth which is no genuine fruit of the organism in which it is flourishing. This usage is further from the Lukan than the Pauline literature. In Luke 2:52 the verb designates Jesus' progress in wisdom and age; in Gal 1:14, Paul's growth in the practice of his Jewish faith; in Rom 13:12, of the night of this age which has "advanced" until the dawn is near. But even these Pauline occurrences do not give the verb the negative connotation it has in the PE. Stählin, *TDNT* 6.716, has suggested that perhaps the opponents styled themselves "progressives" (cf. 2 John 9, of a *proagōn* [progressive] who does not remain [*menōn*] "in the *didachē* of Christ") and the author has turned their own language against them (a quite Pauline procedure), reserving the noun for "true progress" in virtue (cf. Plutarch, *Moralia* 79b, *tēn alēthē prokopēn prokoptein kai atyphon*).

The LXX never uses the verb (cf. Stählin, p. 709, where Sym Ps 44:5 is the only example available from any of the Greek versions of the OT), and in the Ap. Frs. only *2 Clem.* 17.3 offers an instance, but it is in a good sense: "Let us try to make progress *(prokoptein)* in the commands of the Lord" (cf. Stählin, p. 717, who may overstress the "legal understanding of the Christian life" here; see Donfried, *Setting,* pp. 113, 133, 174-176). In Josephus and other Jewish Greek compositions, the noun as well as the verb can refer to progress in either good or evil. For Philo, *Leg. alleg.* 249, "progress" is refracted through Stoic glasses, and his definition of *prokopē* likens it to standing grain, "incomplete, yet earnestly set on its completeness *(ateles ephiemenon tou telous).*"

*perceived.* Though this is the only use of *phaneros* ("evident," "perceptible by the senses") in the PE (out of eighteen in the NT), its sense intersects the Pauline usage (esp. 1 Cor 11:19, though 3:13 and 14:25 as well as Rom 1:19; 2:28; Gal 5:19; and even Phil 1:13 could be compared). Bultmann and Lührmann, *TDNT* 9.3, have noted that, when it is used with *eimi,* "the perception involves understanding," as in Gal 5:19; Rom 1:19; and 1 Tim 4:15.

The same could be observed of the Lukan corpus (see Luke 8:17 [see Mark 4:22]; Acts 4:16 [note that D supplies *estin*]; and much less so 7:13). First John 3:10 resembles this passage of the PE in its use of the term in connection with visible, verifiable action flowing from internal faith and love. Mark 3:12 and Matt 12:16 use the term in the vocabulary of the "messianic secret"; Mark 6:14 for Jesus' "name" coming to public attention. Bultmann and Lührmann, *TDNT* 9.2, aver that this "is not a theological term," but on what basis is not clear. Certainly not on the Gnostic presupposition that what is sense-perceptible is *ipso facto* untheological and can say nothing about the God of creation, precisely the theological context in which Paul uses the term in Rom 1:19 while qualifying it in the context of Rom 2:28.

The term here in the PE is linked with the usage of the cognate *phaneroun* at Titus 2:11, 13; 3:4 (at 2:11 and 3:4 the formally passive *epephanē* and the periphrastic phrase that refers to God imbue the sentence in which they occur with a Septuagintal [cf. Gen 35:7 with Zeph 2:11; 3 Macc 6:39] and therefore "biblical" tone, which is further developed with the occurrence of the cognate noun *epiphaneian,* "appearance," at 2:13). The divine *charis* which dawned on the world in the flesh of Jesus continues to shine out through the flesh and blood of him who has been reborn into Christ and seeks to grow in response to the *charisma* bestowed on him.

The ten uses of the term in the Ap. Frs. are often of visible acts or works (see, e.g., Ign. *Eph.* 14.2 of the good fruit making the good tree visible, and the Latin of Polycarp, *Phil.* 12.3; *2 Clem.* 16.3 of "the hidden and the open deeds [*phanera erga*] of men"). See also Spicq, *EP,* p. 519, for the Priene honorary inscription placed at the most frequented city gate, *hopōs d'an ēi phanera pasin,* "so that it may be known to all" (trans. WCW).

16. *Pay attention to. Epechein* occurs otherwise in the Paulines at Phil 2:16 of "holding fast the word of life" (the verb takes the accusative, not the dative as here; see MM, p. 232, on the text). The only other NT occurrences are in Luke

14:7 and Acts 3:5 (where it does take the dative in describing the way the cripple fixed his eyes on Peter and John) and 19:22. The LXX has as many as twenty-five uses of this verb, and those with the dative are Job 30:26; Sir 34:2 (RSV: "he who *gives heed to* dreams"); 34:15; 35:11 (RSV translates "Do not *trust* in an unrighteous sacrifice"); and finally 2 Macc 9:25 of leaders of foreign nations "watching for opportunities" against Antiochus. The Ap. Frs. have no instance of *epechein.* Here the contemporary P. Fayum 112.11 (99 C.E.) has a striking parallel to 1 Tim 4:16 as well as Acts 3:5 (cited in MM, p. 232): *epechon tōi daktylistēi Zoilōi kai heina auton mē dysōpēsēis,* "Pay attention to Zoilus, the surveyor [thus MM and LSJ] and don't look askance at him." Here in First Timothy the addressee is told to fix his attention first on himself, to pay heed to and to trust himself, to have "a high self-image."

*Persevere.* The verb *epimenein* occurs only here in the PE, but the other Paulines use it on eight occasions, not only of "remaining" physically in a place (e.g., 1 Cor 16:7-8) but also of continuing in a state that is not primarily physical (Rom 6:1 of sin; 11:22-23 of God's kindness and then of unbelief; Col 1:23 of staying grounded on faith). The verb occurs otherwise in the NT (outside of the late text John 8:7) only in Acts, where the six uses are all of physical "remaining." One wonders whether a Pauline fragment has here been fitted, not altogether smoothly, into the redaction as it has come down to us.

In the unique LXX use of this verb at Exod 12:39, it renders the Hebrew *mhh* "to tarry, linger." Hermas uses the verb with some regularity (nine times); otherwise, in the Ap. Frs. only *2 Clem.* 10.5 witnesses the verb, but in a passage that has so many parallels with this verse that one must raise (even while being unable to settle) the question of the relation, more or less direct, between *Second Clement* and the PE (Donfried, *Setting,* p. 89). The passage reads, "But as it is they are continuing *(epimenousin)* in teaching evil (*kakodidaskalountes* [cf. *didaskalia* here in 1 Tim 4:16]) to innocent persons, not knowing that they will incur a double judgment [cf. the double honor at 1 Tim 6:17], on both themselves [cf. *seauton sōseis* here as well as *2 Clem* 15.1] and those listening to them (*hoi akouontes autōn* [cf. *tous akouontas sou* here])." Considering the rarity of the term in other sources (all MM citations are from the Christian era), the usage here in *Second Clement* certainly bears the Pauline imprint and probably that of First Timothy at this point.

*the persons listening.* With *akouontas* one encounters for the first time in the PE a term that will recur in 2 Tim 1:13; 2:2, 14; and 4:17. The verb is common in the NT (427 times). Elsewhere in the Paulines there are 30 uses; Luke-Acts have 65/89 = 154. The Ap. Frs. likewise have abundant examples. Among those passages that resemble the present text, *2 Clem.* 15.1 and 19.1 are so close that some literary dependence can reasonably be suggested (Donfried, *Setting,* p. 89), though it may be to a common source for both rather than *Second Clem-*

*ent*'s depending on First Timothy. Spicq, *EP*, p. 520, suggests that the concept may be a traditional one.

## ♦ COMMENT

4:15. *Let these matters be your study. Tauta* takes one back again to 3:14 and 4:6, 11 above and seems to be a generic reference to the Pauline teaching (R. F. Collins, "Image of Paul," p. 157, and 1 Tim 4:6 and 4:11 above). The governing verb has been different in each case, and here it is *meleta* (present imperative), derived from the same root as the *amelei* of the preceding verse and formally linking the two sentences.

The imperatives which have abounded since 4:6 become a veritable drumroll in their insistence in these two final verses of chapter 4, where four out of twelve uses in this section (6-16) are clustered. The *tauta meleta* is balanced with *en toutois isthi*, and apparently these two pronouns, like the following *autois*, refer also to the content of the apostolic teaching. The imperative of *eimi*, "be," in these teachings apparently is meant to escalate the meaning of the preceding "meditate upon these things." The reflection is to issue in a more than mental or "ideal" attitude. It is part of the activity of "becoming" that issues in a new "being" for the whole person; or rather the apostle commands his disciple "to devote himself" (BAGD, p. 225) *to being* what he contemplates in the Pauline teaching. Again the internal and external, the invisible and the visible, are joined in these commands, and the missionary purpose of both is stressed in the purpose clause, "so that your progress can be perceived by all (persons)." The ecumenical emphasis upon "all" *(pasin)*, i.e. the universal scope of God's saving will, has been examined above (Titus 2:11; 3:2; 1 Tim 2:4).

Here in the PE the reflection upon and assimilation of the Pauline teaching are for the sake of visible "progress" *(prokopē)*. The concept of progress is more common than one might at first imagine in the biblical documents, as the study of Stählin, *TDNT* 6.703-719, has shown. As Stählin remarks (p. 712), this terminology (though not the concept) is more Western and Hellenistic than Eastern and Palestinian. He has also noted not only the visibility of the progress in all of those activities noted in 4:12-13 and the purpose of that visibility (a *typos* for believers; a proclamation of the gospel to *all*), but also that the good acts are ultimately the fruits of the Spirit; i.e. they are part of the divinely empowered response to the charisma which has also been bestowed by the Spirit (cf. 2 Tim 1:6-7 with the link between the *charisma* and a "spirit of power and of love and of prudence"). Note the way in which Serapion's Prayer for the Catechumens (III.3) joins the petition that "they may be protected in things taught and in a clean heart and that they may *make progress (prokoptetōsan)* to become worthy of the 'washing of rebirth,'" citing Titus 3:5 (F. X. Funk, *Constitutiones* 2.160-161; cf. the Comment at Titus 3:5 in AB *Titus* on the work of the Spirit). In the prayer for the bishop and his church (XI, 4, 6), the petition for subdeacons, lectors, "translators" (?), and all ecclesial ministers is "Grant them all kindness and mercy and progress *(prokopēn)*," and a few lines later the prayer for husbands, wives, and children is that they all receive "the blessing of progress *(prokopēs)* and betterment *(beltiōseōs)*" (F. X. Funk, *Constitutiones* 2.168-171); cf. also Serapion's *euchē prosphorou* XIII, 15, 16, 19 (F. X. Funk 2.172-177), as well as 15:2 (F. X. Funk 2.178-179).

16. *Pay attention to yourself and to your instruction. Persevere in these activities.* The further imperatives of this verse, *epeche/epimene,* occur only here in the PE and, like the imperatives of the preceding verse, are paralleled with each other. In the initial charge Timothy is told to fix his attention first on himself. However, the self is not valued for its own sake but insofar as and even to the extent that it is joined to the *didaskalia,* the Pauline instruction and mode of interpreting and applying the OT Scriptures, as has been noted above (see Comment on 4:13).

The parallel imperative phrase, *epimene autois,* "persevere in these things," seems to refer to the same antecedents as *tauta . . . toutois* in the preceding verse, though grammatically it is difficult to exclude the immediately preceding *seautōi kai tēi didaskaliai,* "yourself and your instruction," for all the fact that *seautōi* as a concept fits awkwardly, if at all, with the persevering "in these matters" that is here commanded.

*for, if you do this you will save both yourself and the persons listening to you.* The *gar* clause now provides the purpose and goal of the preceding directive, "pay attention, persevere." The present participle *poion* emphasizes that the preceding acts are conceived of precisely as acts, not as some *status quo* cast in religious concrete but as a dynamic attachment to a living tradition. Note the use of *poiein* at Titus 3:5, as well as 1 Tim 1:13 (cf. 2:1) — all occurrences within texts that have spun off the prayer and worship tradition of the first century of Christian faith or are ordered to it. In the text here, as well as in 5:21 below and 2 Tim 4:5, the "doing" is that of Timothy himself, totally committed to the Pauline teaching and ministry that he shares, exercising an impartial supervision and direction of the presbyters, and conducting an "evangelist's work."

Thus engaged in responding to the divine word, making the progress noted in verse 15, Timothy is promised "you will save *(sōseis)* both yourself and the persons listening *(akouontas)* to you." The verb *save* only here in the PE has a person other than God or Christ as its actual or implied subject (cf. Titus 3:5; 1 Tim 1:15; 2:4, 15; 2 Tim 1:9; 4:18); on the other hand, in the light of all the previous occurrences one ought not to absolutize this one. Just as the ineffectual *poiein* of Titus 3:5 does not formally contradict the fruitful *poiein* of this passage, so the *esōsen hēmas* of Titus 3:5 must be understood as the horizon and ground for *seauton sōseis* here, and accordingly the latter phrase distinctly suggests, with its future tense, final, eschatological salvation, when one will have appeared "before the judgment seat of Christ, so that each one may receive good or evil, according to what he has done in the body" (2 Cor 5:10). The saving initiative of God serves as the ground and horizon for Timothy saving himself and his listeners.

Here *akouontas* refers to those who listen to Timothy's teaching, as in 2 Tim 1:13 and 2:2. Timothy himself is the listener to Paul, and then the one who shares what he has heard with those who will hear him. In 2 Tim 2:14 a "listening" that destroys the hearers is severely criticized; it is the very opposite of the listening in First Timothy that will save them. The final occurrence, at 2 Tim 4:17, refers to a Pauline proclamation of the gospel *(kērygma) hina . . . akousōsin panta ta ethnē,* "so that all the pagans would listen to it." Thus the Pauline gospel *(euaggelion)*, proclaimed *(kērygma)* to unbelievers, explained *(didaskalia)* to believers, will save those who keep listening to it (note the present participle). "Listen" here is, of course, nothing less than the Hebrew *shemaʿ* (listen, hearken) and is equivalent to and implies "believe," i.e. hearing as contrasted with seeing, accepting the word of another rather than visible, tangible experience. The hearing is internal and spiritual as well as a physical phenomenon.

## IV.B. As Apostolic Supervisor of the Orders in the Church (5:1–6:2)

### IV.B.1. DOMESTIC CODE: PART I (5:1-2)

*5 [1]Never scold an elderly man but keep encouraging him as if he were your own father. Encourage young men as if they were your own brothers; [2]older women as mothers; young women as if your own sisters, in complete purity.*

### ♦ NOTES

5:1. *Never scold. Epiplēssō* does not occur elsewhere in the NT or in the LXX or the Ap. Frs., but the noun *epiplēxis* at 2 Macc 7:33 refers to God's "rebuke and discipline *(paideias)*" of his people, and the cognate adjective occurs in the *mē plēktēn* qualification for the (presbyter-) bishop in both Titus 1:7 and 1 Tim 3:3. The verb describes a veritable verbal chastisement, stronger by far than *epitiman,* as in 2 Tim 4:2 (Spicq, *EP,* p. 522). The papyri corroborate this interpretation (see MM *s.v.*, p. 243; also Josephus, *Ant.* 1.246, of the servant's appeal for water [*parakalei*] and Rebecca's rebuking [*epiplēttei*] those who refuse it).

*Encourage young men. Neōterous,* "young men," also appears in the list at Titus 2:6 (also with *parakalei*), although not as an anarthrous comparative, as here. This comparative is not found in the remainder of the Paulines; in the NT otherwise, it designates a group only at Acts 5:6 and 1 Pet 5:5.

On *parakalei* see Titus 1:9.

2. *young women.* The younger women, designated as *neōteras* (cf. *tas neas* of Titus 2:4), are to be exhorted "as sisters" *(hōs adelphas)*. The latter, feminine form occurs only here in the PE, but *neōterai* will appear again in 1 Tim 5:11, 14 below, in the "church order" for widows. Again the terminology seems to pertain to the sources rather than to the author-redactor.

## ♦ COMMENT

It is difficult to tell whether these two verses should be read with the preceding (as differentiating the *akouontas,* i.e. the believers) or as an independent unit (followed by the citation of a church order on widows) or as an introduction to the sections on widows and *presbyteroi.* The oldest MS traditions already attest to the problem, for Sinaiticus seems to mark only a minor transition at the beginning of this verse, with a major transition after verse 2 (where three-fourths of the line is left blank). Alexandrinus, on the other hand, marks a major transition (with a large capital) at 5:1 (and a short blank after 4:16) and a minor transition (a short space within the line) between 5:2 and 3.

This commentary posits a major formal transition before 5:1-2, whose key verb, *parakalei,* not only governs the domestic code which is introduced at this point but also recurs in 6:1-2, where the section on slaves, an integral part of the NT codes, has been placed. Thus, 5:1-2 and 6:1-2 are, on this analysis, quarried from the same source, and the author-redactor has separated the directives for relations to the various domestic classes by inserting two blocks of material, one on widows (5:3-16) and another (5:17-25) substantially on *presbyteroi.* The encircling *parakalei* command, which encloses a large block of traditional materials, hearkens back to the noun, *paraklēsis,* which, along with the public reading of the OT and the Pauline *didaskalia,* was to be Timothy's central task in the Ephesian church. Thus all of 5:1–6:2 is written as a pendant to and specification of that *paraklēsis* to which Timothy was to give his attention. This *paraklēsis* in its turn corresponds with the *paraklēsis* of 1 Tim 2:1–3:13. As we shall note below, the closing section of this letter, 1 Tim 6:3-21a, on false teachers and Timothy's ministry, corresponds similarly to the first part of this epistle (1:3-20), the apostolic *paraggelia,* on false versus true (Pauline) teaching.

In these first verses of chapter 5, Timothy's activity and conduct with respect to four classes of free persons within the believing community are commanded. The persons are placed in an order based upon sex (first male, then female) and, within each sex, age (first old, then young). The order should be compared and contrasted with Titus 2:1-6, where the apostle prescribes what Titus is to teach about the conduct of older men, older women, young women, then young men. The order in Titus 2:7-8 then turned to the addressee himself and his conduct as Paul's emissary; finally, that code turned to slaves. Here in First Timothy, the section on the ministry turns not to Timothy himself but to the way in which he should manage other ministerial "orders," that of the widows, then that of the presbyters. Then, as in Titus, there is a closing section on slaves (6:1-3). Spicq, *EP*, p. 521, has noted that children are not included in the codes of the Pastorals, unlike in Colossians and Ephesians.

5:1. *Never scold an elderly man but keep encouraging him as if he were your own father.* In this passage the conduct of the elderly themselves is not being detailed (as in Titus 2:1-2); rather, the focus is the conduct of Timothy himself toward both the old and young in the (Ephesian) congregation. That conduct is designated first negatively, *mē epiplēxēis*, then positively, *alla parakalei*. The *presbyterōi/presbyteras* of 1 Tim 5:1-2 designate the same class of persons as the *presbytas/presbytidas* of Titus 2:2-3, i.e. older men and women of the church and not church leaders or officeholders as such, though evidently some older men *(presbyteroi)* were also "elders" (*presbyteroi* in the sense of officeholders, as at Titus 1:5; see AB *Titus in loc.*) and some of them must be included among the *presbyteroi* of 1 Tim 5:17-22 below. On the precedence given the older members of the community, see the Comment on 1 Tim 3:6 and especially 4:12. Though this reverence for the aged was widespread in the ancient world at large (see the citations in Spicq, *EP*, pp. 511-512, of classical *loci*), it was also a commonplace in the biblical tradition, thus Lev 19:32: "You shall rise up before the hoary head, and honor the face of an old man [LXX: *presbyterou*]." Deut 28:50 speaks of an inhuman nation "Who shall not regard the person of the old [LXX: *presbyterou*(A) or *presbytou*(B)] . . ." (see Lam 5:12b). The wisdom tradition praises (Prov 20:29) and defends (Sir 8:6, 9) the elderly. In the Qumran community there are the old and the elders. The former, as enfeebled, have their role limited in the community (see 1QSa 1.19; 2.7; Dupont-Sommer, *EWQ*, pp. 106, 108; see CD 14.14-15 and 1QpHab 6.11); the latter appear to be an influential stratum in the community leadership. Thus 1QS 6.8-9 (Dupont-Sommer, *EWQ*, p. 85), when describing the order for assembling the whole Qumran community, prescribes: "Let each man sit according to his rank! Let the priests sit in the first (place), and the elders *(whzqnym)* in the second, and then the rest of all the people." See also 1QS 5.4 (Dupont-Sommer, *EWQ*, p. 129) and CD 9.4 (Dupont-

Sommer, *EWQ*, p. 148). In 1QM 13.1 the fragmentary text reads "and his brother [pr]iests and the levites and all the elders of the Serekh" (*zqny hsrk;* so Yadin, *War*, p. 320: "Serekh probably = the whole congregation as a military unit" or possibly "the camp prefects" of 1QM 7.1; see Dupont-Sommer, *EWQ*, p. 188, who translates as "the veteran officers").

*Never scold.* The approach of Timothy is to be one of persuasive appeal, as continual and regular (present tense) as the chastisement would have been instantaneous and explosive (aorist). As the *mē epiplēxēis* was reminiscent of the *mē plēktēn* of Titus 1:7, so the *parakalei* here reminds one of the qualification of the (presbyter-) bishop in Titus 1:9, that he be *dynatos ēi kai parakalein* (see AB *Titus in loc.* as well as on *parakalein* in Titus 2:6, 15, and 1 Tim 1:3; 2:1). The form in which Timothy's appeal is detailed in ideal familial style has copious parallels from Greek moral philosophy (see D-C, p. 72, for the citations of Plato and other authors as well as the inscriptions that prove how widespread this pattern was, though only Plato notes conduct toward women as does this passage; Spicq, *EP*, p. 522, adds passages from Polybius, Cicero, et al.). On the other hand, there is no precise verbal parallel to this passage and thus no grounds for supposing direct literary dependence on any extant source. Rather, the classifications of the *Haustafeln* were here combined with the directives of popular moral philosophy to become an "Episcopal Mirror" for Timothy.

The passage may well have predated this correspondence, as the vocabulary suggests, though the redactor's touch may be discernible in the singular *presbyterōi* over against the plural *neōterous, presbyteras,* and *neōteras.* The reason may have been that in this correspondence (and its sources) the plural *presbyteroi* designates men with an office or ministry to the congregation. Thus the singular here makes it clear that an older man as such is being spoken of and his private correction, man to man, is to be differentiated from the public correction given to a presbyter (note the singular) numbered among the church officials (cf. 5:19-20).

The appeal to an older man "as to a father" reflects the concepts, though not the exact terminology, of the popular Greek texts noted above (see also Menander, *Georgos* 58-62). The usage may pertain to the source, since the other three uses of *patēr* in the PE (Titus 1:4; 1 Tim 1:2; 2 Tim 1:2) all refer to God the Father (note the way Titus 1:6; 1 Tim 3:4-5 express the relation of a man to his children).

*Encourage young men as if they were your own brothers.* The family paradigm is extended as Timothy's appeal to the younger members of the community is made "as to brothers" *(hōs adelphous).* Implicitly, of course, Timothy is conceived of as belonging to the *neōteroi* himself (see 4:12 above), and the Christian faith in God as Father gives a new realism to the comparison of the members of the believing community with "brothers," "mothers," and "sisters" (cf. Luke 8:19-21, *SFG* §135, as well as Luke 18:29-30, *SFG* §255, noting particularly the way in which *patēr* is treated in the parallels).

2. *older women as mothers; young women as if your own sisters, in complete purity.* The appeal to older women *(presbyteras)* is *hōs mēteras.* One recalls the Pauline "Greet Rufus, eminent in the Lord; and his mother who is also mine *(kai emou)*" (Rom 16:13). The term occurs again in the PE only at 2 Tim 1:5, of Eunice, Timothy's mother. MM, *s.v.,* note how the papyri witness to the word *mētēr* applied as a title of respect and honor to women who were not physically "mothers" of the writers. Michaelis, *TDNT* 4.642, has noted that the ancient world, for all the gradations of opinion expressed on women in general and wives in particular, had the highest estimation of mothers. Thus Philo alludes to (with appropriate discretion) the Stoic Hierocles as holding, "A father and a mother are in fact gods revealed to sight *(emphaneis . . . theoi)* who copy the Uncreated in His work as the Framer of life" (*Dec.* 120; trans. in Loeb VII, 66-67; cf. p. 612).

The appeal to the younger women is to take place *en pasēi hagneiai,* "in complete purity," a phrase that may well pertain to the Christian redaction of the source, whether that redaction occurred before this material was utilized here or is the addition of the author of this correspondence. *En hagneiai* (without *pasēi*) occurs in the list of virtues at 4:12 above, where it seemed to belong to material that dated the Pastorals; the phrase here may have had a similar preexistence. If anything belongs to the final redaction, it is the adjective *pasēi,* which this correspondence favors. If in the ancient world it was only Caesar's wife that must be above suspicion, in the Christian world that responsibility fell upon men as well as women, and, it seems, in a particular fashion upon the Christian ministers (see 4:12 above). Spicq, *EP,* p. 523, has called attention to Aquinas's illustration of this pastoral discretion in the papal style which addresses men as *dilectis filiis,* "beloved brothers," but women as *dilectis in Christo,* "beloved in Christ."

## IV.B.2. THE ORDER OF WIDOWS (5:3-16)

*5 [3]Honor the claims of widows who deserve that title.*

*[4]Thus, in the case of a widow who has children or grandchildren, they should be the first to learn the meaning of reverence for one's own home and of giving recompense to their forebears. For this is a welcome thing in the eyes of God [the Father].*

*[5](The case is otherwise with the widow proper, one who is a completely destitute woman who has fixed her hope in God and stays on night and day in en-*

*treaties and prayers.* [6]*A widow indulging herself voluptuously has died while still living.* [7]*And charge them on these matters, so that they will be irreproachable.)*

[8]*In the case of a man who does not provide for his own people and particularly his immediate family, he has disowned the faith and is worse than an unbeliever.*

[9]*Follow these rules for enrolling a widow on the official roster: she must have lived no less than sixty years; she must have been a wife to one husband;* [10]*she must have public attestation of fine deeds. Thus,*

> *did she rear children?*
> *did she welcome guests?*
> *did she wash traveling Christians' feet?*
> *did she come to the help of the oppressed?*
> *did she set out to do every excellent deed possible?*

[11]*On the other hand, have nothing to do with the younger widows. The reason is that they want to remarry whenever they feel attractions that are incompatible with their commitment to Christ.* [12]*They stand condemned because they broke their previous pledge to him,* [13]*not to mention that, at the same time, they also learn how to be lazy while circulating from house to house, and not just lazy but nosy gossips as well, saying what they have no right to say.* [14]*Now my wish is that younger widows remarry, rear children, run their homes, offer no pretext for reviling to the adversary,* [15]*for some of them have already slipped off after Satan.*

[16]*In the case of a woman who is a believer and who welcomes widows into her home, let her continue to come to their help and the local church not be burdened but free to help the widows proper.*

## ♦ NOTES

5:3. *widows who deserve that title.* Lit. "Widows that are really *(ontōs)* widows." On *widows* see Comment below. For the position of the widow in the ancient world at large and the OT, see Stählin, *TDNT* 9.440-448, as well as Hoffner, *TDOT* 1.287-291.

The one other occurrence of *ontōs* in the Pastorals is at 6:19, where it qualifies *zōē,* i.e. the life which is not the corruptible *bios* but life eternal. The other Pauline uses of *ontōs* correspond with this (Gal 3:21; 1 Cor 14:25). Luke 23:47; 24:34 use this adverb of Jesus being "really" an innocent man and being "really" raised from the tomb. Mark 11:32 uses the term of John being "really" a prophet; John 8:36, of men being "really" freed by the Son.

*Honor.* This is the only use of the verb *timan* in the Pastorals; it is also found only once in the rest of the Paulines, in Eph 6:2 (citing the command of the Decalogue in Exod 20:12, noted below in Comment). Luke 18:20 (= Mark 7:10; 10:19, and Matt 15:4; 19:19; cf. 15:5) also uses it of that commandment, but in Acts 28:10 he uses it of the gifts that the grateful Maltese showered on Paul and his party, literally "they honored us with many honors." Matt 27:9 also uses the verb of setting a price. The remaining NT uses (Matt 15:8 = Mark 7:6; 1 Pet 2:17; John 5:23; 8:49; 12:26) take up the moral-liturgical nuance of honoring without necessarily material, financial overtones (see Schneider, *TDNT* 8.179), a usage that continues in the Ap. Frs., though the concept of (heavenly) reward surfaces at *1 Clem.* 59.3 as well as Ign. *Phld.* 11.2.

4. *grandchildren.* The noun *ekgonos* is otherwise undocumented in the NT. In the latter part of this verse, as well as in 2 Tim 1:3, the term *progonoi* has the sense of "forefathers" or "ancestors" as in LXX Esther 4:17m and as many as eleven other places in the LXX. The *ekgonoi* are descendants as the *progonoi* are forebears, and the LXX uses the former term as many as thirty-one times. LXX Gen 48:6; Sir 44:11 (cf. Hebr); 45:13; 47:22; and 2 Macc 1:20 illustrate, more or less closely, the sense here in 1 Tim 5:4. In the Ap. Frs. one must wait until Hermas, *Man.* 9.9, for the term to occur as a very doubtful reading from pseudo-Athanasius. LSJ note that when spelled *eggonos,* the proper meaning is grandson; thus D*, etc., here. Forms of *eggonos* with this spelling and sense are numerous in the *CII* (see index *s.v.,* p. 631), and apparently *ekgonos* is not documented in such Jewish inscriptions. If, with J. K. Elliott, *Greek Text,* p. 74, *eggona* is original, this fact might be an indication that the source here is not only Christian but *Jewish* Christian and, considering the provenance of many of these inscriptions, *Roman* Jewish Christian.

*they should be the first to learn the meaning of reverence for one's own home. Manthanetōsan* occurs six times in the Timothy correspondence, nine times in the other Paulines, and twenty-five times in the NT (Acts 23:27, of the Lukan corpus, is the only citation of the verb). The word occurs in *First Clement* (8.4; 21.8; 57.2) and Ign. *Rom.* 4.3. and Ign. *Magn.* 10.1. *Barnabas* uses *manthanein* ten times, and the LXX, fifty. The verb in the *Testaments of the Twelve Patriarchs* signifies a learning emanating from God. On the meaning of *prōton* see the commentary on 1 Tim 2:1; 3:10. *Oikon* refers to the family in the personal sense of men, women, children, and slaves that compose a home, whether human or divine, and not to a physical structure as such. The closest correspondence to this personal sense in the other Paulines is in 1 Cor 1:16; Luke-Acts use *oikos* in this sense in thirteen of fifty-eight occurrences (see also above at 1 Tim 3:4, 5, 12 [all with *idios*], and 15).

*the meaning of reverence.* Lit. "to show piety." The verb *eusebein* (ten of the cognate *eusebeia*'s fifteen NT uses occur in the PE; none in the other Paulines) occurs in the NT only here and at Acts 17:23, where Paul is made to say to the Athenians, "What therefore you worship *(eusebeite)* as unknown, this I proclaim to you." The meaning in the latter passage is quite consistent with that of the cognates; the performance of a religious duty toward God is designated. In this passage of the Pastorals a classical Greek sense referring to something more than piety toward the gods as such, i.e. to (religiously inspired) respect for and devotion to one's family, comes to the fore (see the texts cited by Foerster, *TDNT* 7.176, esp. Sophocles, *Oedipus Rex* 1430-1431). The source being cited here reveals its heterogeneity in thus differing notably but not drastically from the sense that the reader has thus far come to expect. Though the verb is unknown in the Ap. Frs., it does occur in the very latest strata of the LXX. Thus Susanna 63 reads, "For young men will be devout *(eusebēsousi)* and there will be in them a spirit of understanding and of knowledge forever." All other uses are in 4 Macc 9:6 *(s.v.l.)*; 11:5, 8, 23; 18:2, and none is parallel to this use in the Pastorals.

*and of giving recompense to their forebears. Apodidonai* (forty-seven times in the NT) occurs also at 2 Tim 4:8, 14 of the Lord himself repaying in the final judgment what has been done for him (see Büchsel, *TDNT* 2.167). The verb is found otherwise in the Paulines only in Rom 2:6 (of divine judgment); 12:17; 13:7; 1 Cor 7:3; 1 Thess 5:15. The Lukan corpus on the other hand has a dozen uses (compared with eighteen in Matthew alone, and only one occurrence in Mark). Repayment to both men and God is denoted by the verb in the NT documents (see, e.g., Mark 12:17 = Luke 20:25 = Matt 22:21). Both the LXX and the Ap. Frs. employ this verb rather often.

Here *apodidonai* has *amoibas* as its object in a phrase that is attested in secular Greek (Büchsel, *TDNT* 2.168 cites Dionysius of Halicarnassus, *Ant. Rom.* VI.73 and *P.Oxyr.* IV, 705.61; the latter is quoted in MM, p. 27, along with several other notable passages, including the Priene inscription 112.17 about a newly made citizen, Zosimus, who "has made [no fruitless] return [for the honor]" [*ouk akarpon tēn tēs timēs*] *dedeichen amoibēn*). The conjunction with *timē* is notable as well; see D-C, p. 74 n. 7, for other citations and Spicq, *EP*, p. 527. *Amoibē* is unattested in the LXX (though used a few times by Aq, Sym, A1) and occurs only in this phrase in the NT. The Ap. Frs. document the term only in Ign. *Smyrn.* 9.2, where the audacious phrase *amoibē hymin ho theos*, "God is your reward," has left a wavering textual tradition that has attempted to change the noun into a verb. Again, the unique occurrence of this term in biblical Greek at this point in the Pastorals leads one to posit the quotation of a source which used this particular phrase that the author-redactor took over unchanged (perhaps it should be noted that both Luke 14:12 [cf. 14] and Rom 11:9 [= LXX Ps 68:23; cf. Col 3:24] use the intensive noun, cognate with *apodidonai*, *antapodoma* with the sense of repayment/retribution).

*a welcome thing in the eyes of God [the Father]*. For *apodekton enōpion tou theou* see 1 Tim 2:3. For *theos* with the article meaning "the Father," see Titus 1:1.

5. *The case is otherwise with the widow proper, one who is a completely destitute woman.* Lit. "However, the (one who is) really a widow and has been left alone *(memonōmenē).*" For *the widow proper, hē ontōs chēra,* see verse 3 above. *Memonōmenē,* the perfect passive participle of the quite classical *monoun/monousthai,* occurs only here in the NT, and it is unattested in the LXX and the Ap. Frs., though Aq, Heb (Job 3:7 = "barren"), and A1 do employ the term in their versions. Hesychius defined this form as *egkataleleimmenos,* one who has been left in the lurch (see Matt 27:46, citing LXX Ps 21:2), i.e. deserted and utterly abandoned. The texts cited in Spicq, *EP,* p. 78 n. 3, are a poignant witness to this utter helplessness, which the perfect tense in this text describes as a state that has perdured to this moment.

*God.* S* reads *epi kn* at this point, as does D* *(ton kn)* with a few other witnesses. J. K. Elliott, *Greek Text,* p. 75, has proposed that the variation is stylistic (avoids repetition of *theos* in these two verses), but it may be theological as well, for *(ho) Kyrios* is the risen "Christ Jesus, our hope" (1 Tim 1:1). Considering the contrast with the young widows of 5:11 who are alienated from Christ, one might argue that the *kyrios* of 5:5 was the original reading, which was pulled into the orbit of the preceding *tou theou* rather than being read with the later *tou Christou.* The *elpizein epi* with the accusative (whether *theon* or *kyrion*) is a Hebraism (Spicq, *EP,* p. 528), documented otherwise in the NT only at 1 Pet 1:13 (of grace coming with Jesus in glory); see 1 Pet 3:5 of "the holy women" of the OT "who hoped in God" *(eis theon).* In the Ap. Frs. the phrase *elpizein epi* . . . is used with reference to God (*Did.* 4.10; *Barn.* 16.1; 16.8 (?); 19.7 = *Did.* 4.10; *1 Clem.* 11.1; 12.7; 16.16 [*epi kyrion* here paraphrases LXX Ps 21:5]; 22.8 [= *epi kyrion* of LXX Ps 31:10]; 59.3, but it also occurs of Christ Jesus (*Barn.* 6.9; 8.5; 11.8 [the cross]; 16.8; Ign. *Phld.* 5.2; and 11.2). If the original reading of the text in 1 Tim 5:5 was *elpizein epi theon,* one would surmise that the source (or the redactor) represented a usage that was Roman (and Jewish Christian). If the source (or the redactor) had *epi kyrion,* then the Jewish Christian influence of the eastern Mediterranean may be surfacing.

*and stays on (prosmenei) night and day in entreaties and prayers. Prosmenei* (see Comment on 1 Tim 1:3), with its present tense, designates a constant, ongoing presence, a perseverance in *tais deēsesin kai tais proseuchais* (on both of these terms see the church order of 1 Tim 2:1).

6. *A widow indulging herself voluptuously.* With the real widow described in verse 5 is contrasted the *spatalōsa* (note the double rhyme with the following *zōsa*), the widow (not in Greek) who lives regularly (present participle) in luxury. The verb *spatalōsa* occurs otherwise in the NT only in James 5:5 of the rich, *etrephēsatē epi tēs gēs kai espatalēsate,* "You have lived on this earth in luxury and pleasure." Among the Ap. Frs. only Barnabas (10.3 of "glutted" swine) and Hermas (*Sim.* 6.1.6 and 6.2.6 of well-fed sheep that were very "frisky") use the

term. The LXX uses the word only at Ezek 16:49, of Jerusalem the prostitute who has "surfeit of food and prosperous case," and again at Sir 21:15 the participle denotes "the reveler" (RSV; cf. the unique LXX use of the noun at Sir 27:13 = wantonness). LXX Amos 6:4 uses the compound *kataspatalōntes* of the rich of Samaria, sprawled on their ivory-inlaid couches.

8. *In the case of a man who does not provide for his own people and particularly his immediate family.* The use of *idioi* here marks the only time in the PE where this adjective is used as a substantive. This substantival use does not appear in the Ap. Frs. For *malista* see commentary on 1 Tim 4:10 and Gal 6:10 with its reference to household. *Oikeioi* occurs only here in the PE.

The form of the verb here, either *pronoei* or *pronoeitai* (active vs. deponent), is uncertain. Because Atticists preferred the latter (cf. BDF §307), it is quite possible that the more vulgar active transmitted by A. S$^{c.}$ D$^{c.}$ L. P. pl is original (thus J. K. Elliott, *Greek Text,* p. 76). If a source is being cited, the form may well go back into that stratum. This verb occurs only in the Paulines in the NT, the other two instances being Rom 12:17 and 2 Cor 8:21, in both instances with *kala enōpion* (*pantōn anthrōpōn/kyriou kai . . . anthrōpōn* = LXX Prov 3:4). The roots of the usage go into a non-NT source and corroborate further the hypothesis that a source is also being cited here in the PE. *Didache* 12.4 uses this verb of providing material provisions for the visiting Christian traveler. In Polycarp, *Phil.* 5.3, the verb occurs in the exhortation to the younger Christian men to "care for purity *(pronoountos hagneias),*" and in 6.1, where the presbyters are told to "neglect neither widow *(chēras)* nor orphan nor poor but to be 'ever providing for that which is good before God and man'" (cf. LXX Prov 3:4 and Rom 12:17; 2 Cor 8:21). Of the eleven LXX uses of *pronoein,* besides that of Proverbs, the closest parallel to our passage appears to be in Wis 6:7 of God, who "himself made both small and great, and he takes thought (*pronoei* [S, *pronoeitai*]) for all alike."

*has disowned the faith.* The meaning of *ērnētai* here is quite parallel to the usage in Titus 1:16 (*arneisthai,* also at Titus 2:12; 2 Tim 2:12-13; 3:5, but not elsewhere in the Paulines; Luke-Acts contain eight of the eighteen other NT uses), and *hē pistis* is the *fides quae,* the revelation of God's will by which a believer must order his actual conduct (as opposed to the *fides qua,* subjective faith, the person who believes, of which faith must also take account; see Spicq *in loc.*).

*and is worse than an unbeliever.* Negative terminology for unbelief is relatively rare in the Pastorals; this is also true of the remainder of the NT, except for *apistos* in the rest of the Paulines. The use of *apistos* here is consistent with its only other use in the PE, in Titus 1:15, where it includes Jews following the OT ceremonial laws but not believing in Jesus as Christ and Lord (cf. also the use of *apistia* of Paul himself before conversion to Christ, 1 Tim 1:13). The adjective *apistos* is found twenty-three times in the NT, and apart from the two occurrences in the Pastorals, the fourteen other Pauline uses are in the Corinthian correspondence, and it appears that all presume (though not all demand) a reference to pagans as distinguished from Jews (is 2 Cor 4:4 an exception?). On the other hand, Mark 9:19 = Matt 17:17 = Luke 9:41 (*SFC* §163) places the adjective on Jesus' lips to describe his Jewish contemporaries. John 20:27 also has Jesus address the adjective to Thomas, in inviting him to accept him as risen from the dead, and so as "Lord and God." Luke 12:46 has a use in Jesus' parable where the reference is unclear (similarly, Rev 21:8), but it could just as well include pagans as Jews. Acts 26:8 has Paul use the word of Agrippa and his party judging the resurrection as *apiston,* "incredible." Here the reference is to an event or thing as an object of unbelief rather than to a person as unbelieving. In the Ap. Frs. this adjective appears in *2 Clem.* 17.5 of the pagans (perhaps including the Jewish nation), as well as in Ign. *Magn.* 5.2 (probably of pagans); *Trall.* 10.1 (Christian heretics — Docetists); *Smyrn.* 2.1 (again Docetists); 5.3 (of the "unbelieving names" of the same Docetists).

There are two, perhaps three, uses of *apistos* in the LXX, in all of which there is some doubt as to what in the Hebrew text corresponds to the Greek (LXX Prov 17:6; 28:25 [*s.v.l.*]; and LXX Isa 17:10 where the translator makes the prophet say to an idolatrous Israel, "You plant a faithless [*apiston*] seed").

The comparative *cheirōn* ("worse") occurs again in the Pastorals at 2 Tim 3:13, but never elsewhere in the Paulines. In the Lukan corpus it does occur once in Luke 11:26 = Matt 12:45 (Q: *SFG* §120) in a saying that is perhaps alluded to in 2 Pet 2:20. The remaining NT uses are at Matt 9:16 = Mark 2:21; Matt 27:64; Mark 5:26 with *eis to* (cf. 2 Tim 3:13); John 5:14; and Heb 10:29. The rare uses in the Ap. Frs. (Ign. *Rom.* 5.1; Hermas, *Sim.* 9.17.5 and 9.18.1) do not add anything to the semantic profile at this point.

9. *Follow these rules for enrolling a widow on the official roster.* Lit. "Let a widow be enrolled *(chēra katelegesthō).*" This verb, undocumented in the Ap. Frs., appears nowhere else in the NT, and its two LXX occurrences (Deut 19:16; 2 Macc 7:30) convey a sense quite different from this passage. In the source the directive was probably to the congregation as such (Stählin, *TDNT* 9.456) and denotes adoption "into a fellowship by election" *(ibid.),* including into a religious association (cf. MM *s.v.* as well as LSJ and the citations by Spicq, *EP,* p. 532). The term meant "registration in a technical sense" (as of troops being called up, D-C), being entered on an official list, designated for an office (Spicq, *EP, in loc.*). Thus Spicq (with others [Héring, *1 Cor,* p. 51; Allmen, *PTM,* pp. 61-62], including Stählin [see *TDNT* 9.455 n. 144]) sees here something like an *ordo viduarum* (cf. Tertullian's *cum viduam adlegi in ordinem nisi univiram [apostolus] non concedat,* "when [the Apostle] does not permit a widow to be admitted into the order unless she is the wife of one man" [trans. WCW], *Ad*

*uxorem* 1.7.4, and note in 1.7.5 his reference to the *sacerdotium viduitatis* even among the pagans, as well as in 1.6.3, *et virginitatis et viduitatis sacerdotia*). Clement of Alexandria, *Paed.* III, 97.2, speaks of the directions that the Scriptures give, "some to priests, some to bishops and deacons, others to widows," and so presupposes an order for widows as for the others named. See Stählin, *TDNT* 9.462-465, for other references from the patristic age, particularly from the church orders (p. 463 n. 210); cf. also F. X. Funk, *Constitutiones*, pp. 182-217, where the widows of *Const. Apost.* III.1.1ff. occur after bishops, presbyters, and deacons and before the section on orphans and martyrs. In the fourth–fifth–century *Test. Domini* I, 40-44 *(Testamentum)*, the order for widows follows that for presbyters and deacons and precedes that for subdeacons and lectors (or vice versa). The qualifications considerably expand on 1 Tim 5; an "ordination" or installation, with its prayer, is furnished; the conduct of the widow afterward, including texts for her nightly vigil and morning praise, is described.

*she must have lived no less than sixty years.* Lit. "(who) has been (living) no less than sixty years." The phrase is otherwise unknown in the NT, but, for obvious reasons, the individual terms are more or less frequent (thus *elasson* otherwise only in Heb 7:7; Rom 9:12 = LXX Gen 25:23; and John 2:10; *hexēkonta* on eight other occasions; *etos* in forty-eight other passages). The assonance of the initial *e*'s ought to be noted.

The perfect participle, *genonuia,* here is equivalent to a (nonexistent) form of *einai* (BDF §165 *ad fin.;* 185.4, citing Plato, *Laws* 6.755A, and also noting the way in which the comparative *ē* has been omitted with *pleiōn* in Acts 23:13, 21; 24:11; 25:6, as well as Luke 9:13 [S*], but also Matt 26:53). The Western tradition (see J. K. Elliott, *Greek Text,* pp. 76-77) took the term with the following phrase; thus the Latin versions read *quae fuerit unius viri uxor,* "who shall have been the wife of one husband" (trans. WCW). The perfect tense does seem to accord better with that phrase. Yet, as BDF note, the example from Plato (also in a "law") still persuades one to take the participle with the phrase preceding.

*she must have been a wife to one husband.* Lit. "a woman of one man." *Henos andros gynē* here has a mirror image in Titus 1:6, "a husband of one wife." *Anēr,* in the PE, refers always to males. It always designates a married man in the singular, and in the plural may refer to men, whether unmarried or married, or husbands in particular. The use of *gynē* in the PE follows nearly the same pattern; the singular signifies a wife (1 Tim 2:10, 12, 14), and the plural designates women, married or not (1 Tim 2:9-10 and 3:11, where the reference may be to unmarried women or wives).

10. *she must have public attestation of fine deeds.* Lit. "in fine deeds well attested *(martyroumenē).*" The participle follows the phrase, as did *gegonuia* in

the previous verse (it is possible that *henos andros gynē* was the redactor's atypical insertion into this church order). Aside from Titus 1:13 (*martyria;* also at 1 Tim 3:7), all uses of **marty-* terminology in the PE occur in the Timothy correspondence: *martyrion* in 1 Tim 2:6; 2 Tim 1:8; *martyres* in 1 Tim 5:19; 6:12; 2 Tim 2:2; the verb here and in 1 Tim 6:13; and *diamartyrein* in 1 Tim 5:21; 2 Tim 2:14; 4:1 (see 1 Tim 3:7, noting also the use with *kalēn*). The verb *martyrein* occurs seventy-six times in the NT (cf. *martyresthai,* five times, including Acts 20:26; 26:22). The Johannine corpus has forty-three of these uses. In the Pastorals the term occurs here in the passive form and at 6:13 below in the active. There are only six other Pauline uses (as well as three of *martyresthai*). Luke 4:22 as well as Acts 6:3; 10:22, 43; 13:22; 14:3; 15:8; 16:2; 22:5, 12; 23:11; 26:5 employ this verb, twelve times altogether (*martyresthai,* Acts 20:26; 26:22). The passive form here is preceded by *en* as at Heb 11:2 instead of the usual *hypo* or *ex* (cf., e.g., Acts 6:3; 10:22; Rom 3:21). See Trites, *NT Concept of Witness,* pp. 72, 208. Note that in Hebrews the older generation *(presbyteroi)* were approved "*in this*" (i.e. in loyal faith), as here the older widows have been approved "in good works." Strathmann, *TDNT* 4.496-497, notes that "direct observation" and readiness to vouch for what one has seen are part of the meaning. The Ap. Frs. do not use *en* with *martyrein,* though the verb occurs rather often and with the sense of approval noted here (cf., e.g., *1 Clem.* 44.3).

Regarding *erga kala* here and *ergon agathon* later in this verse, *ergon* occurs twenty times in the PE, almost always in the plural or to be construed that way; as such *(erga)* it is qualified usually as *kala* (Titus 2:7, 14; 3:8, 14; 1 Tim 5:25; 6:18), but in 1 Tim 2:10 as *agatha.* The emphasis characteristic to the PE occurs when *erga* is qualified by *agatha* or *kala.*

*Thus, did she rear children (eteknotrophēsen)?* Lit. "if she brought up children." This is the first of five conditional protases which increase successively from seven through nine to fourteen syllables in length and convey an impression of mounting intensity. Each one opens with *ei* and ends with *-sen;* the repetition of sounds joins them very closely (cf. the sixfold activity of a pagan toward a Christian which brings the former into a relationship with Christ himself; Matt 25:35-39).

The verb *eteknotrophēsen* never occurs otherwise in the LXX, NT, or the Ap. Frs. MM, p. 628, cite Epictetus, *Discourses* 1.23.3, though Aristotle, *Hist. Anim.* 625b20, uses the verb of raising young animals, and Plutarch of rearing children (*De Amore Prolis* 1 [493.c], 4 [496.c]).

*did she welcome guests?* The second clause, *ei exenodochēsen,* again employs a verb otherwise unattested in LXX, NT, or the Ap. Frs., though the activity designated appeared as *philoxenon,* first in the list of positive characteristics of the (presbyter-) bishop in Titus 1:8 and again of the bishop in 1 Tim 3:2.

*did she wash traveling Christians' feet?* The next condition expands into a phrase, which is literally "if she washed the feet of the saints *(ei hagiōn podas enipsen).*" If the previous verb was a typically vulgar Greek compound to denote the entertaining of guests (cf. MM *s.v.*, p. 433), the phrase here is the equivalent from the eastern Mediterranean world. (See BDF §259.3 on the Semitizing omission of the article.)

The verb *niptein* in the NT is used of pouring water over parts of the body and so of washing the hands and face (eyes) in Mark 7:3 = Matt 15:2 (note Luke 11:38 has *ebaptisthē, SFG* §150); Matt 6:17; John 9:7, 11, 15. Only here and in John 13:5-14 is it used with *podas* as its object (cf. R. Brown, AB *JN* 2.551). The verb is not documented in the Ap. Frs., nor is there an equivalent phrase with *podas,* though the phrase is not unusual in the LXX (Gen 18:4; 19:2; 24:32; 43:24; Judg 19:21; 1 Kings 25:41; 2 Kings 11:8; Cant 5:3). The equivalent Hebrew phrase, *rḥṣ rglym,* has not yet been found in Qumran.

On the translation of *hagiōn* as "traveling Christians," see the Comment below. This is the only use of the plural substantive, *hagiōn,* in the PE. Common as it is in the rest of the Paulines (thirty-eight times), it is rather rare in the Lukan corpus (Acts 9:13, 32, 41 [with widows]; 26:10). The fourteen occurrences in Revelation remind one that the term was particularly dear to the Jewish and Christian apocalyptic tradition (cf. Dan 7:9-27; Matt 27:52; 1 Thess 3:13; 2 Thess 1:10; etc.); cf. Procksch, *TDNT* 1.109-110.

*did she come to the help of the oppressed?* The next conditional clause, *ei thlibomenois epērkesen,* lit. "if she helped the oppressed," again employs a verb, *eparkeō,* that occurs only in this passage of the PE (5:16 below, *bis*) in the NT. The LXX documents the term only at 1 Macc 8:26 (of supplying grain, arms, and money to enemies) and 11:35 *(s.v.l.).* The Ap. Frs. do not use the word. On the other hand, the simple *arkeō* occurs eight times in the NT, with its sense of supplying a sufficiency, including 2 Cor 12:9 as well as Luke 3:14.

*oppressed.* The verb *thlibomenois* appears nine other times in the NT, including 2 Cor 1:6; 4:8; 7:5 and 1 Thess 3:4; 2 Thess 1:6, 7 (but never in Luke-Acts or the Johannine corpus). The cognate noun, *thlipsis,* which occurs forty-five times in the NT, with twenty-four of those uses in the Paulines, is not documented in the PE. In the Lukan corpus, Acts employs this noun five times.

*did she set out to do every excellent deed possible?* On *erga kala/agatha* see Titus 2:14. On *panti ergōi* see Titus 1:15. The compound *epēkolouthēsen* occurs again in the PE, as a conclusion for the companion piece on *presbyteroi* below (5:24, with *erga kala* in 5:25). The only other NT uses are in Mark 16:20 and 1 Pet 2:21. All the other uses keep the connotation of actually "following" upon something or someone at the fore. Only here (and this is still another indication of a source) does that concrete notion practically disappear into a more figurative usage that means "pursuing a matter or concerning oneself with it" (Kittel, *TDNT* 1.215). The NT uses *akoloutheō* ninety times (including twenty-one times in Luke-Acts); *exakoloutheō* three times (all in Second Peter); *parakoloutheō* four times (see above on 1 Tim 4:6); *synakoloutheō* three times (including Luke 23:49). It is striking to note that the single Pauline use of any of this terminology, outside of the PE, is in 1 Cor 10:4 of "the spiritual rock that followed *(akolouthousēs)*" Israel in the desert. Thus one would infer that the language here, if it did not come from the source (and that is more probable), came from the Lukan tradition.

When *epakoloutheō* occurs in the Ap. Frs., at *1 Clem.* 43.1; Ign. *Smyrn.* 10.1; and Polycarp, *Phil.* 3.3, it has the sense of "following" noted above and not the figurative usage noted in this verse of the PE. The same seems to be true of the sixteen LXX uses (*pace* Kittel).

MM, *s.v.*, cite a third-century-B.C.E. papyrus (P Petr II. 40[b][6]) where this verb has the sense of "seeing to" it that a certain job was done, which would parallel the sense here. Cf. also Plato's *Republic* 370c, where it has the force of "to attend to a task."

11. *have nothing to do with. Paraitou* appears twice more in this form in the Timothy correspondence, concerning myths and speculations in 1 Tim 4:7 and 2 Tim 2:23, which Timothy is told to reject, and in Titus 3:10 in regard to divisive people. The other Paulines do not have the verb; of the eight other NT uses, four are in the Lukan corpus.

*The reason is that they want to remarry whenever they feel attractions that are incompatible with their commitment to Christ.* Lit. "for when they become wanton in opposition to Christ, they want to marry." On *hotan* see Titus 3:12 for the only other use of this conjunction in the PE, here with the subjunctive = at a time still determined. On *gamein* see the commentary on 1 Tim 4:3. On *thelein* see 1 Tim 1:7; 24.

12. *They stand condemned.* The participial phrase *echousai krima* is literally "having condemnation." For *krima* see 1 Tim 3:6 *supra.*

*they broke their previous pledge.* The verb *athetein,* disapproved by Atticists (MM) (with the sense of "reject," "nullify," "declare invalid," or set aside), occurs only here in the PE out of fifteen times in the NT. The other Paulines have four uses and there are five in Luke 7:30; 10:16. Ign. *Eph.* 10.3 speaks of Christians imitating their Lord in being wronged, destitute, and rejected *(athetēthē).* Otherwise, in the Ap. Frs. only in Hermas, *Vis.* 2.2.2, of rejecting God, and in *Man.* 3.2: "They . . . who lie set the Lord at naught *(hoi . . . pseudomenoi athetousi ton Kyrion).*" Spicq, *EP,* p. 536, and Maurer, *TDNT* 8.158-159, have called attention to the many parallels in the LXX, of which 1 Macc 6:62 and 2 Macc 13:25; 14:28 are particularly apposite since they refer to setting aside an oath and treaties.

13. *not to mention that, at the same time, they also learn how to be lazy while circulating from house to house.* Here for the only time in the PE occurs

*hama,* a particle that occurs only ten times in the NT, with five in the other Paulines. Luke has the term at Acts 24:26; 27:40. The other uses are in Matt 13:29; 20:1 (both prepositional). Apart from *Barn.* 8.6, only Ignatius uses the particle in the Ap. Frs. (nine times, always prepositionally governing the dative). The term is used here adverbially, as usually in Paul as well as Acts (cf. Moule, *Idiom,* pp. 81-82). In fact, the whole *hama de kai* phrase occurs in Philem 22 (*hama kai* is in both Acts 24:26 and Col 4:3).

On *manthanousin,* see 5:4 above and Titus 3:14. The ellipsis of "to be" here is somewhat irregular (BDF §416.2). On the difficulty of taking the verb with *perierchomenai,* see D-C, p. 75; moreover, Spicq, *EP,* p. 536, has noted examples of this ellipsis when speaking of learning a profession.

*lazy. Argai* never recurs in the rest of the Paulines or the Lukan corpus, though Matt 12:36 uses it of "an *idle* word" and 20:3, 6, of idle laborers. James 2:20 uses it of faith without works (*chōris tōn ergōn;* note the *"erga"* of the real Christian widow in 5:10). Second Peter 1:8 parallels the term with *akarpos,* "fruitless." *First Clement* 34.4 uses this adjective in a passage that seems to allude to Titus 3:1 as well as to 1 Tim 3:13 (commentary *supra*). *Didache* 12.4 uses the term to stigmatize the traveling Christian who fastens parasitically on a community, a *christemporos* (12.5), a man who makes a business out of Christ. *Barnabas* 10.4, in a vivid passage, uses the term to describe people who are like birds of prey, doing no work but waiting for a windfall of carrion. Hermas, *Sim.* 5.4.3-4, uses the word of those who are "weak and idle in prayer" *(argoi pros tēn enteuxin).* Of the four LXX uses, Sir 37:11 is the most apposite here, where an etymological understanding of *argos (a-ergos)* is being played upon (LSJ; cf. Homer, *Iliad* 9.320) for the *aergos anēr,* "the idle man" or "workless" versus the *polla eorgōs,* "the man who has worked many deeds." Delling, *TDNT* 1.452, treats of the verb *argein* (2 Pet 2:3) and *katargein* (see commentary on 2 Tim 1:10).

*circulating from house to house.* The actual terminology, *perierchomenai tas oikias,* has not been met thus far in this correspondence. *Perierchomai* occurs otherwise in the NT only in Acts 19:13 of "itinerant Jewish exorcists" and magicians at Ephesus; perhaps in Acts 28:13 (*s.v.l.,* of a circuitous sea journey; but see Haenchen, *Acts,* p. 718); and finally in Heb 11:37 (of wandering, afflicted members of the people of God). The verb is not found in the Ap. Frs., but there are as many as fifteen uses in the LXX, of which Wis 6:16 (describing wisdom personified as a woman going about seeking worthy persons) and Job 1:6, 7; 2:9 (first of the Satan patrolling the earth, then of Job's children going around *oikian ex oikias*) seem to be particularly appropriate parallels (see the examples in MM *s.v.,* p. 505; Spicq, *EP,* p. 394 n. 2, and esp. Prov 7:11-12 and OxyP 1581.5, *Sarapiōna mēi aphēis argein kai rhembesthai,* "do not permit Sarapio to be idle and roam about" [trans. WCW]).

Though the cognate *oikos* has occurred half a dozen times up to this point, here for the first time in this correspondence one reads *oikias,* which will recur at 2 Tim 2:20 (sg.) and 3:6, which, like Titus 1:10-11, is also reminiscent of this passage. This noun, though common in the NT (ninety-four times) and found thirty-seven times in Luke-Acts alone, occurs in the rest of the Paulines only in 1 Cor 11:22; 16:15; 2 Cor 5:1; Phil 4:22.

*not just.* Literally "not only." This is the first time in the PE that the *ou monon . . . alla kai* construction has occurred, but it will occur again at 2 Tim 2:20 (with *oikia!*) and 4:8. Though the Third Gospel does not use the construction, it occurs in Acts 19:26-27; 21:13; 26:29; 27:10. It is rather frequent in the rest of the Paulines (esp. Romans, Second Corinthians). See BDF §243 on *monon* here as modifying *argai* as a predicate noun.

*gossip.* The adjective *phlyaroi* occurs only here in the NT, though the verb is present in 3 John 10 = "to talk nonsense, to bring baseless charges." In the LXX only 4 Macc 5:11 uses this term of the *phlyaros philosophia* ("preposterous philosophy," Charles, *AP* 2.672) that keeps old Eleazar from eating pork. No form of the term occurs in the Ap. Frs.

*saying what they have no right to say.* Lit. "speaking things that they should not." For all the uses of *dei* in the Ap. Frs., it appears that *ta deonta* occurs only in Hermas, *Sim.* 2.5 and 2.8, of the "necessities" of life.

14. *remarry, rear children, run their homes, offer no pretext for reviling to the adversary.* The apostle's directive is that young widows *gamein, teknogonein, oikodespotein,* "remarry, rear children, and run their homes." The first three infinitives are each one a longer word than the last, and all rhyme with a final *-ein.* The fourth and final phrase is much more expansive (cf. v. 10 above) and regards the whole subject from a rather different perspective.

These first three infinitives are undocumented in the rest of the NT, the LXX, or the Ap. Frs.; one infers that the language at this point is once more that of the source.

*Gamein* has been treated above (4:3; 5:11). *Teknogonein* is, of course, the verbal form of the equally unusual *teknogonia* that appeared above in 1 Tim 2:15 (see commentary *in loc.*), and the sense of "rearing [not just bearing] children" would suit the context here very well. The noun *oikodespotēs* is found a dozen times in the NT, all in the synoptics (note Luke 12:39; 13:25; 14:21; 22:11, and AB *Titus* on Titus 1:7 and the *oikonomos*).

*offer no pretext. Aphormēn didonai* (only occurrence in PE) appears in the form *aphormēn didontes* in 2 Cor 5:12, and the noun is found only in Paul (Rom 7:8, 11; 2 Cor 11:12; Gal 5:13), where its military connotation of a base of operations or the staging site of a foray (thus LSJ; Spicq, *EP,* p. 537) can be discerned. The papyri document the sense of "occasion, opportunity" (MM *s.v.,* pp. 98-99); and Euripides, *Hecuba* 1238-1239 (cited by Bertram, *TDNT*

5.472, as well as the even more apt *Phoenissae* 199-200), has the sense of "pretext."

The Ap. Frs. use the noun (*2 Clem.* 16.1), and the phrase *aphormēn didonai* occurs in a notably similar context in Ign. *Trall.* 8.2: "Give no occasion *(mē aphormas didote)* to the heathen, in order that the congregation of God may not be blasphemed *(blasphēmētai)* for a few fooling persons" (in 8.1 "the snares of the devil" are mentioned). Hermas, *Man.* 4.1.11, says, "I am not giving an opportunity *(ou didōmi aphormēn)* to laxity . . . ," and in *Man.* 4.3.3 an explanation of the "second repentance" is offered "without giving an excuse *(mē didous aphormēn)* to those who are going to believe or to those who have believed already in the Lord."

The rare uses in the LXX are in Ezek 5:7 (see Bertram, *TDNT* 5.472, for meaning) as well as LXX Prov 9:9 and 3 Macc 3:2, in which latter instances the term is also construed with *didonai.*

15. *already.* The adverb *ēdē* (sixty times in the NT) occurs here for the first of three times in the PE (2 Tim 2:18; 4:6), and there are ten other occurrences in Paul. Luke-Acts also have thirteen uses (10/3).

*slipped off after Satan.* Lit. "followed *(exetrapēsan)* after Satan." First Timothy 1:6 also used the verb *exetrapēsan* (with *eis,* as here it occurs with *opisō;* see above and cf. 6:20 *infra* and 2 Tim 4:4, with *epi*). *Opisō* occurs here for the only time in the PE, and on the one other occasion that it occurs in the Paulines it is used nominally, *ta opisō* (Phil 3:13), of past events. Nine of the thirty-five NT uses are in Luke-Acts (7/2), where it often refers to the personal following for goodwill acquired by a master and leader (cf. Luke 9:23; 14:27; 21:8; Acts 5:37; 20:30). See 1 Tim 1:20 on Satan.

The sharp, even harsh, judgment pronounced by this verse may have caused its omission in two manuscripts (1736.6, J. K. Elliott, *Greek Text,* p. 79), though an accident of transmission cannot be discounted.

16. *In the case of a woman who is a believer.* On the *ei tis,* cf. above on 5:4. The *pistē* ("woman who is a believer") whose situation is now described has puzzled many a scribe (see *GNT* and B. Metzger, *TCGNT,* p. 642; J. K. Elliott, *Greek Text,* p. 80, opts for the longer text, and the Western tradition has changed it to the masculine, *pistos,* or has even transmitted both, *pistos ē pistē*). The problem almost certainly goes back to the way in which the archaic (Roman [?]) order was transmitted here.

*who welcomes widows into her home.* Lit. "has widows." For discussion see Comment below.

*let her continue to come to their help and the local church not be burdened but free.* Such a woman is to continue in her good work (note the present tense) of helping (see 5:10 above on *eparkeō*) widows who are in need, "and the church is not to be burdened." One thinks of the Dorcas of Acts 9:36-41. *Hē ekklēsia* here certainly refers to the local congregation (on the term, see 1 Tim 3:5, 15). The command *mē bareisthō* employs a verb that occurs otherwise in the Paulines only at 2 Cor 1:8; 5:4 (though the compounded forms at 1 Thess 2:9; 2 Thess 3:8; and 2 Cor 12:16 are to be noted). Otherwise, in the NT it is documented only in Luke 9:32 (of men weighed down by sleep); 21:34 (of hearts weighed down by worldly affairs); and Matt 26:43 (of eyes heavy with sleep). In the Ap. Frs. the one use of the verb is strikingly similar to the use here, as Ign. *Phld.* 6.3 says, "I thank my God . . . that no one can boast . . . that I was a burden *(ebarēsa)* to anyone in small or in great matters." The LXX has at most two occurrences, at Exod 7:14 (of Pharaoh's heart) and 2 Macc 13:9 *(s.v.l.).* Of special significance is a Roman Christian epitaph in Greek which reads, "Erected by her daughter to the good Regina, her widowed mother, who lived a widow for sixty years and was never a burden to the Church" (Scott, *Pastoral Epistles,* p. 63). Here one gets a glimpse of a woman who certainly was at one time a young widow and who had means herself or was aided privately by others so that she never joined the ranks of those whom this old order would have called "real widows" who received public, ecclesiastical support.

## ♦ COMMENT

The next fourteen verses appear to be based upon a source that provides for an ecclesial order of widows. The transition is abrupt when one considers the disproportion between the telegraphic notes of 5:1-2 and then the massive block 3-16 devoted to one group of women, the widows *(chēras).* However, the transfer from older women to younger women to widowed women is conceptually smooth enough. It is only as one reads on that the quite different character of this material becomes apparent.

5:3. *Honor the claims of widows who deserve that title.* The very first word in this verse, *chēras,* emphatically repeated as *tas ontōs chēras,* serves practically as a title for the whole "memorandum," in the course of which forms of *chēra* occur six more times. The PE never otherwise use the word, and in fact only once elsewhere does it occur in the Pauline epistolary, at 1 Cor 7:8 where the apostle writes, "To the unmarried and the widows *(tois agamos kai tais chērais)* I say that it is well for them to remain single as I do." That is the only glimpse that the first-generation documentation provides of a group of widowed women who are apparently to be distinguished from the (male only?) *agamoi* and who with them form groups within the Corinthian congregation that elicit some direction from the apostle. The plight of the widow in the ancient world left its mark on the NT, as Rev 18:7 indicates from one vantage and James 1:27 from another. Mark 12:40-42 contains a saying about widows and a brief narrative about a widow, emphasizing their being victimized (the only use of the term at Qumran, CD 6.16: Dupont-Sommer, *EWQ*, p. 132, takes up this theme) as well as their generosity.

It is Luke-Acts, however, that contain more references (twelve) to widows than any other NT document. There are not only the parallels to the Markan materials noted above (= Luke 20:47; 21:2-3: *SFG* §284, 286) but also nine other occurrences that belong to special Lukan material (see Stählin, *TDNT* 9.448, who notes that Q contained no reference to *chērai*). These occurrences, as a whole and individually, indicate an interest of that author which in turn bears a striking resemblance to this passage from the PE. If the author of Luke-Acts did not actually insert this "order for widows" at this point, the redactor of the PE must have shared the concerns that motivated Luke.

The woman whose husband has died was in antiquity a veritable paradigm for the helpless and oppressed. Ancient law recognized and enforced the husband's duty to provide for and to protect his wife and family. Thus a woman had legal protection only through her own father and then through her husband. The death of her husband normally left her with the options of returning to her father's household (if he were still alive), or staying with her husband's family, or remaining unmarried and supporting herself (and her children), or marrying again (if particular customs and her circumstances did not preclude doing so). If there were adult sons, their widowed mother was their responsibility. The Levirate law in Israel was an attempt to provide support and protection for a widow who had no son as well as for the name of the deceased husband (Hoffner, *TDOT* 1.290). The widow who was left to support and protect herself (and her orphaned children) was supposed to be the special care of the community and of its leaders (see *CII* #37, cited below), kings and judges in particular. In the Semitic world, but not in the Roman, the gods themselves were particularly concerned for such helpless persons (Stählin, *TDNT* 9.443-444), and the God of Israel was believed to share that concern and to enjoin it upon his people. Indeed, the very frequency with which the widows receive explicit attention in the OT reminds one not only of the plight of the widows in the legal sphere, but also that the OT authors were not unaware of the deficiencies and limitations of the legal structures which were part of their cultural heritage and instruments through which they sought to transmit the revelation and commands of a God who transcended the very law that he promulgated.

As was remarked above, widows are mentioned more often in Luke-Acts than in any other NT document. Moreover, the poor, the lowly, the oppressed, women, and prayer are all important subjects for Luke-Acts. All of these themes crystallize around the figure of the widow. Because of the importance of the Lukan notices on the widow for the NT as whole, including the PE (however one regards the relation of this correspondence to Luke-Acts), a survey of his usage will be helpful.

Already within the prologue to the Third Gospel, when the infant Jesus is presented in the Jerusalem temple, within that setting of Law, cult, and prophecy (Luke 2:22-35), two aged persons, a man and a woman, suddenly appear and, in the power of the Spirit, declare who the child is. The woman, Anna, is described as *prophētis,* "a prophetess," who had been widowed after seven years of marriage, i.e. probably not long after she was twenty years of age. The children, if any, could only have been very young and of no material help to her. In the text she is no less than eighty-four years old (Luke 2:37), evidently more than fulfilling the age requirement for a "real widow" noted in 1 Tim 5:9. Moreover, she never entered another marriage and thus exemplifies the *henos andros gynē* of 1 Tim 5:9; the unmarried state and prophetic activity seem to be linked also in Acts 21:9. Anna "did not depart from the temple, worshipping with fastings and prayers *(deēsesin)* night and day *(nykta kai hēmeran).*" The terminology is strikingly like that of 1 Tim 5:5, and the mention of Anna's fastings reminds one of the publicly known good works at 5:10 below, and her telling about the child Jesus "to all who were looking for *(prosdechomenois)* the redemption of Israel" reminds one of the real widow who in 5:5 *(ēlpiken epi theon)* "has put her hope in God" and accordingly awaits him herself.

In Luke 4:25-26 a saying on Jesus' lips contrasts the many Israelite widows that were bypassed when Elijah the prophet went to the foreign widow of Zarephath. Poverty and oppression do not magically pressure God's help, but even they are relieved or tolerated in accordance with another plan, which includes the mission to all the nations. A similar concern may lie behind the careful regulations of the PE which are concerned that the good works of Christians always say something about the gospel to all people who have not yet believed.

The narrative of the widow of Nain (Luke 7:11-17) turns on the double poignant blow to a woman who lost first her husband, then her only son (Stählin, *TDNT* 9.450). Into her desperate life and tears comes the resurrection in the person and power of Jesus. He is her only hope. The parable of the widow in Luke 18:2-5 is part of how that evangelist recalls Jesus' teaching on how one "ought always to pray and not lose heart" (18:1). If tears were proverbial with widows, so were their petitions for justice and aid against their oppressors (Stählin, p. 451 n. 100), and the unremitting persistence of the widow, in this parable, for justice on earth becomes a mirror of the way in which one must storm heaven, too, with petitions. The correlation with the unremitting prayer of old Anna as well as with 1 Tim 5:5 is evident. The remaining two passages in the Third Gospel have been noted above; here one would add that the widow throwing her pennies into the temple treasury was visibly identifiable because for her whole life as a widow she wore mourning clothes (widow's weeds), including sackcloth, but (at least at times) no veil (see Gen 38:14, 19, as well as Jth 8:5; 9:1; 10:3; 16:8).

In Acts 6:1 Christian widows are the object of the daily charity of the rest of the believing congregation. There are enough so that a distinction can arise in the care for the widows of "the Hebrews" (Aramaic-speaking = Palestinian Jews, Judean and/or Galilean) as distinguished from those of "the Hellenists" (those Jews and, in some cases, Gentile converts from abroad who had come to spend their old age in Jerusalem, had joined the Christians, placed their possessions in the common fund, and then, on the death of their husbands and with no children in the country, needed the support of the church). As women, as widows, and then as foreigners they were particularly liable to suffer from discrimination, and one might suspect that they had been cut off from the normal Jewish relief services in Jerusalem, perhaps their faith furnishing an excuse to the Jewish officials, who thus began to apply pressure on the inchoate church, which in turn responded by setting up its own relief services (see Haenchen, *Acts*, pp. 261-262). *CII* #37 reproduces a Roman Jewish epitaph for an *archōn*, Claudius, who is apparently called "father of widows and orphans." The narrative of Acts appears to presume no small number of widows, since a body of seven is appointed to minister relief. There is no implication in the narrative that these women, as a whole or in part, formed an "order" within the congregation, with a particular service or function. They are simply a large group of extremely impoverished women who must receive equitable assistance. They are apparently all believers and all in need. They must have just judges to satisfy those needs.

The case seems somewhat different with Acts 9:36-41. There not only does the congregation in Joppa appear to have a body of widows ("all the widows" [9:39]; "the saints and widows" [9:41]; see J. Wellhausen *ap* Haenchen, *Acts*, p. 341, "a social class in their own right"), but one would infer that the just-deceased Tabitha-Dorcas was one of their number (*pace* Haenchen, p. 339; following Stählin's suggestion, *TDNT* 9.451 n. 107). In any event she was full of good works and acts of charity *(eleēmosynōn)*, which apparently included sewing garments (to support the group or/and for the poor). The resemblance to 1 Tim 5:10 goes without saying, and the group appears to be formed of a number in like circumstances who have pooled their talents and resources for mutual support and charitable work, perhaps at the commission of the Joppa congregation. With this Lukan background in mind, it seems especially reasonable to understand 1 Tim 5:3-16 as in fact a "church order" for widows that provides the baselines for defining such a body and making it "professional." One is immediately struck by the opening sentence, which not only enjoins the apostolic co-worker to see to the support of widows, but also specifies *tas ontōs chēras*, "real widows" (emphatically reiterated at 5:5 and 16).

The widow's state, like the married state, does not of itself magically produce holiness or automatically put a claim on the congregation. The "real" widow is ultimately a work of God, existing simply and solely for the sake of God, and to that extent makes real claims on the generosity of the church. Indeed, the previous verse, with its injunction to treat all older women as *mēteras*, assumes a special urgency with those really impoverished and dedicated older women, the widows. The church and its leader are to support them as a person ought to sustain his own parents. The use of the imperative, *tima*, "honor," but with the sense of "support" (see Schneider, *TDNT* 8.179), makes the command to Timothy sound like the command of the Decalogue, *tima ton patēra sou kai tēn mētera* (Exod 20:12).

The verb *timan* occurs in the LXX of honoraria for a physician (Sir 38:1), payment for a diviner (Num 22:17, 37; 24:11-13), and material support for Jewish people (Esther 9:3) — see Schneider, *TDNT* 8.172-173. Both this section on the widows as well as the following on the *presbyteroi* begin with the question of support/compensation, and both sections invoke the Torah more or less explicitly in this regard (see 5:17-18, and the noun *timē* as commented on at 1 Tim 1:17). The parallel probably has something to say about the "real" widows as an established body or order as distinct from widows in general, for the "real" *presbyteroi* of 5:17 are not identical with the *presbyteros* of 5:1.

4. *Thus, in the case of a widow who has children or grandchildren, they should be the first to learn the meaning of reverence for one's own home and of giving recompense to their forebears.* After the title and its commandment, the casuistry (note the number of conditional clauses in this section) for determining the real widow is reviewed by this church order. The initial exclusionary criterion is proposed in the case of any woman whose husband has died (and who is thus a *chēra*) but who has "children or grandchildren" *(tekna ē ekgona)*. The implication is not only that the children are old enough to contribute to her support but also that the widow herself is older. The case of the younger is taken up below, 5:11-15. The term for children, *tekna*, has been seen in this "proper" sense at Titus 1:6 as well as 1 Tim 3:4, 12, though the spiritual relationship in Titus 1:4 and 1 Tim 1:2 makes for a "genuine" *(gnēsion)* child, too (cf. the *ontōs* of widows). The term here translated "grandchildren," *ekgona*, was introduced by *ē* = "or," which implies that these descendants are also old enough to contribute to the support of the aged grandmother.

After emphatically distinguishing *(de)* such a widow from "real widows," the apodosis abruptly shifts the subject from singular to plural and from the widow to her children. Some have held (with the scribes of 3. 323. 1319. L etc., who changed this verb to the singular) that widows are in fact still the subject of *manthanetōsan*, but, as D-C have noted, the following *eusebein* can refer only to children fulfilling their duty to God by honoring/supporting their parents, and *progonois* in the next clause must refer to the parents/grandmother mentioned previously. The rather harsh transition is not unexpected in this correspondence (see on 1 Tim 2:15), and accordingly one ought to have no qualms about translating *manthanetōsan* as "Let those children learn. . . ." Its "practical" sense remains here, a learning "to do" rather than "to know." The *prōton ton idion oikon eusebein* reminds one conceptually of Gal 6:10, ". . . let us do good *(ergazōmetha to agathon)* to all men, and especially to those who are of the household of the faith *(malista de pros tous oikeious tēs pisteōs)*."

*and of giving recompense to their forebears.* Parallel to the divinely commanded respect due to one's family *(oikon)* is *amoibas apodidonai tois progonois,* and the two clauses thus correspond to the ethical and material aspects of *tima* already noted above.

The material repayment is now said to be *tois progonois,* the plural perhaps indicating that the *chēra* of the protasis was understood collectively, though more probably because here a general principle is being formulated which covers the particular case of *ei . . . tis chēra.* As is noted above, *progonoi* are contrasted with *ekgona,* and the life and sustenance that the latter have received from their forefathers are to be "repaid" by sustaining them in their need. It is probably this transmission/sustaining of life that brings the parent-child relationship into close comparison with the relation of the Creator God with his creature. What the child owes to his parents is a figure and parable of what he owes to his God, who has ultimately given and sustained his life (cf. Hierocles of Alexandria, quoted by Spicq, *EP,* p. 527).

*For this is a welcome thing in the eyes of God [the Father].* The last clause of this sentence explicitly grounds *(gar)* the respect and support for parents in the order willed by God. Such an activity *(eusebein/apodidonai)* is *apodekton enōpion tou theou,* a phrase that occurred in the church order of 1 Tim 2:3 in a slightly more expansive form, and, as in that passage, suggests an activity (there, prayer; here, generosity) that is pleasing to God the Father (note the article) as he judges human beings. Though the source apparently did not explicitly cite (scriptural) authority for this command to the church and to families to support widows, one notes that covenant commandment and divinely revealed will are the ground for the directives on widows.

5. *(The case is otherwise with the widow proper, one who is a completely destitute woman who has fixed her hope in God and stays on night and day in entreaties and prayers.* In contrast *(de)* to the widows who have children who can and ought to care for them, "the real widow" *(hē ontōs chēra)* is now defined and described in two coordinate, epexegetic clauses *(kai . . . kai)* that specify her basic past and enduring commitment and then her present, ongoing activity.

She is first a woman who, left quite alone, has put her hope in God. The widow is *memonōmenē,* "completely destitute" and utterly abandoned. The complement to this helpless and hopeless condition is the hope that the real widow has just as definitively placed in God, *ēlpiken epi theon.* This verb, followed by *epi theōi zōnti,* described the ground and motivation for the apostolic ministry of Paul and Timothy (see commentary on 4:10). Here the same hope is the basis for the ministry of the real widow; the emptiness of her life humanly speaking has been filled by the hope of eternal life, the life of the resurrection which will see neither marriage nor giving in marriage, as her own life even now manifests (see Luke 20:27-38).

*and stays on night and day in entreaties and prayers.* The second characteristic of the real widow is her total dedication to prayer *(tais deēsesin kai tais proseuchais).* The use of the article here could be meant to include more than simply the private, personal petitions of the real widow, namely, her participation in the public prayers of the congregation, the liturgical assemblies (cf. Spicq, *EP,* p. 528, who stresses the former, however, as well as the Lukan tradition noted above). The phrase *nyktos kai hēmeras* enlarges the temporal horizon of the verb to its limits and thus reinforces the note of persistent dedication of the real widow to a life of prayer. The order of the nouns presupposes the Jewish reckoning of the day as beginning at sunset (cf. Jeremias, *Sayings,* p. 60 on OxyP 840, 34). There is a built-in hyperbole in the phrase, of course, that makes one suspect that it is a hortatory addition of the redactor to the dry provision of the order he used as a source.

*Night and day* was used by Paul as part of a prayer and to describe not only his manual labor but also his prayer in 1 Thess 2:9; 3:10; and 2 Thess 3:8 (but not otherwise in the Paulines). The phrase occurs again in the PE at 2 Tim 1:3, as the thanksgiving prayer of that letter opens with an expansive description of the way in which Timothy has a memento in the apostle's prayers: *en tais deēsesin mou,* "night and day" (reading the phrase with v. 3 and not with v. 4). In the rest of the NT the phrase tends to occur in contexts of prayer and worship (thus Rev 4:8; 7:15, but not 12:10; 14:11; 20:10; Matt 4:2 of fasting but not in the sense that the phrase has otherwise; similarly 12:40; not Mark 4:27; 5:5), particularly in Luke-Acts (Luke 2:37; 18:7; Acts 26:7; in Acts 20:31 the phrase occurs in Paul's description of himself tearfully admonishing [*nouthetōn*] the Ephesian [presbyter-] bishops; only in Acts 9:24 does the phrase occur in a nonreligious context, of Paul's enemies watching the gates of Damascus). The resemblance to the description of Anna in Luke 2:37 is so striking that it has even been proposed that her figure was spun off from this directive. The process may have been more complex. If the author-redactor of the PE was *not* Luke, it is just as credible that the redactor had read Luke-Acts (see Scott, *Pastoral Epistles,* p. 65) and used the language of the Anna episode to articulate his comment here on the source he was employing. The other alternative, that the author of Luke-Acts had read the final form of this correspondence and used its language to define (or create) the figure of Anna, is also conceivable. If the author-redactor of this correspondence was in fact the same person who wrote Luke-Acts, it may well be that this evident interest in widows led him to insert this whole redactional comment into the church order. Still one cannot exclude the possibility that the source contained the whole phrase, which in its turn influenced the language and thought of the author of Luke-Acts-PE at several points.

In the Ap. Frs. *Did.* 4.1 could be using "night and day" in connection with prayer, though this is less likely in the case of *Barn.* 19.10. *First Clement* 2.4 uses the phrase in a context of prayer, but not 20.2 or 24.3. The only other use of the phrase in the Ap. Frs. is Ign. *Rom.* 5.1, of the continual harassment he bears on his journey to martyrdom. Thus only the Roman document shows a real inclination to use the term of constant prayer. Is this due to Clement's knowledge of Luke-Acts-PE? Or the church order as it still stands in the PE? Or both?

6. *A widow indulging herself voluptuously has died while still living.* Again the next sentence is set in contrast *(de)* to the preceding. The seven-times-repeated *de* in 5:3-13 is a tiny but telltale stylistic feature that sets off this section from the preceding chapters of First Timothy, where *de* had been employed fifteen times but never with such a lengthy consecutive concentration. Note that in this chapter the following presbyterial order does not use similar connective tissue. One must wait until 5:24 for another *de,* and the remaining two chapters of First Timothy use the particle only six times (for a total of thirty times in the six chapters of this letter; cf. Titus with eight times in three chapters; Second Timothy with twenty-four times in four chapters); the gradually rising proportion of *de* (from less than three per chapter through five per chapter to six per chapter) may be notable.

The rich, self-indulgent widow is stigmatized as one who has died while still living. The phrase reads almost like the parody of an epitaph, though the funeral inscriptions regularly read the aorist (cf., e.g., *CII* #537 *zēsasa,* of a woman who saw *ek tōn teknōn autōs eggona,* see also *CII* index *s.v.*). The forms of the verb *thnēskō* (to die) are conspicuously absent from *CII* (even *apothanōn* occurs only in #75), and the form *mortuus/mortua est* occurs in only two Latin inscriptions (#614 and #616). Perhaps the Greek perfect here, *tethnēken,* is a Latinism, and an indication of the Roman origin of this church order.

It may also be significant for locating the place in which this church order for widows originated to note that the *spatalāo/spatalē* terminology is documented in Italy and the West both in literary works and inscriptions, and that the Latin loanword *spatalium = spatalē* (meaning a bracelet; see MM) occurs in Pliny, *NH* 13.142, as well as in inscriptions from Nemi in Italy and from Spain *(cit.* LSJ *s.v.).*

The present participle *zōsa,* sandwiched with a double rhyme between *spatalōsa* and *tethnēken,* between self-indulgence and death, is in vivid contrast to the "living God" of the church (1 Tim 3:15) and of Paul and Timothy (4:10), the God in whom the real widow has put her hope (5:5). From that living God has come quite a different kind of life "now and to come." That life always designated *zōē* in the PE, and which the PE prize, is life in the last age, defined as the period between the present time, the now, the eschatological age initiated with the resurrection of Jesus and the future world wherein believers will join the risen Lord in the age that is to be. During that eschatological age "Godliness is useful for everything" (1 Tim 4:8) because it contains the promise of this life. The *zōsa* here is one of those who are "living" in the sense that they await the judgment of Christ upon "the living *(zōntas)* and the dead" (2 Tim 4:1).

The simple *thnēskein* occurs only here in all the Pauline epistolary. Indeed, it is not common in the rest of the NT, where Luke-Acts (7:12; 8:49/14:19, 25:19) have half of the eight uses (all of which are forms of the perfect). Only Hermas of the Ap. Frs. employs the verb (five times), always in the phrase "neither are they alive nor have they died," except in *Sim.* 9.28.6, where the phrase "you would have died to God *(tethnēkeite an tōi theōi)*" occurs. All these instances parallel the meaning here in First Timothy, where alone in the NT this verb is used of a moral or spiritual "death." Again there may be an indication of a usage of *thnēskein* that was peculiar to the Roman church. In the LXX Bar 3:4 speaks of "the prayer of the dead of Israel" as parallel to that "of the sons of those who have sinned." *To tethnēkos tēs psychēs* is a phrase of the second-century-C.E. Aelius Aristides (cited BAGD *s.v.*), and Philo, *Fug.* 55, with its striking parallel to 1 Tim 5:6, reads: ". . . some people are dead while living *(zōntes enioi tethnēkasi)* and some alive while dead *(tethnēkotes zōsi)*. . . . Bad people, prolonging their days to extreme old age, are dead men, deprived of life *(bion)* in association with virtue, while good people, even if cut off from their partnership with the body, live forever, and are granted immortality." The whole passage that follows illustrates the sense of this verse of First Timothy, ending with "This is the most noble definition of deathless life, to be possessed by a love of God and a friendship for God *(erōto kai philiai)* with which flesh and body have no concern" (58). See also *Sentences of Sextus* #7 and the passages cited by Spicq, *EP,* p. #530, and Bultmann, *TDNT* 3.13 n. 52: "The wicked are *eti zōntes nekroi*" (*Somm.* 2.66, etc.). The letter to the church of Sardis brands that church as one that has the name of living whereas it is dead, "*onoma echeis hoti zēis kai nekros ei*" (Rev 3:1). See 2 Tim 1:10; 2:11 on *thanatos: apothnēskein.*

7. *And charge them on these matters, so that they will be irreproachable.* The *kai tauta paraggele* takes up the *paraggele tauta* of 4:11 (see Comment above and references there) and marks a transition from a moral principle to an exhortation. It is possible that this sentence was not in the source, at least in this

form, for the language seems typical of the redaction as it reminds one that the apostle is addressing Timothy and directing the latter to implement the instruction or ordo that is being cited. The purpose of the insistent exhortation *(hina)* is that the real widows be *anepilēmptoi* (irreproachable), an adjective that led off the list of virtues in the "episcopal mirror" of 1 Tim 3:2. The word itself may well have stood in the source (perhaps heading the list of qualities that are marshaled in vv. 9-10 below), but the redactor has detached it to form part of his parenthetical remark at this point. On the other hand, he may also have simply borrowed it from the source he had cited above in 1 Tim 3. The "real widows" are a church order parallel to that of the *episkopos* with his *diakonoi,* and they are to be similarly "beyond reproach."

8. *In the case of a man who does not provide for his own people and particularly his immediate family, he has disowned the faith and is worse than an unbeliever.* The *de* here is somewhat awkward and probably the redactor's addition to ease the transition from his parenthetical directive back into the directives of the source. He is faithful to the "letter" of the source that began with an identical *ei de tis.* If the previous verse is redactional, then this second "case" followed immediately on that of the *spatalōsa.* The former was to receive no support because she was already quite "dead" and thus needed no support. This second case is the widow whose children have *de facto* not followed out the directives in 5:4. If the *spatalōsa* stood in contrast to the "real widows" of 5:3, 5, then "the man [anyone: *tis*] who does not provide *(ou pronoeitai)* for his own people *(idiōn)* and particularly *(malista)* his immediate family *(oikeiōn)*" is to be read in the light of 5:4. The *idioi* here are evidently to be coordinated with and to some extent coincide with the *oikeioi.* The passage surely presupposes that both the family and the one who provides for it are all believers, and perhaps that is the particular nuance of the nominal *idioi* at this point (contra Stählin, *TDNT* 9.454 n. 128), a usage that occurs at Acts 4:23 and 24:23. Just as the church is described by the familial model (the *oikos*), so one's fellow believers become *idioi,* one's own family, and thus the Christian widow has a double claim on her believing children, who must provide for her as a mother in Christ as well as their mother in the flesh. On the other hand, the Lukan usage is not the only key for understanding this passage, for John 1:11 uses *idioi* for Jesus' own people (cf. D-C *in loc.*) as well as for his disciples (John 13:1).

The word *oikeioi* reminds one that at every turn in these letters and their sources the *oikos* was a central concern of and a paradigm for the church (see commentary on 1 Tim 3:4, 5, 12, 15). Only the Paulines speak of *oikeioi;* Gal 6:10 of "the members of the household of the faith"; and Eph 2:19 of "fellow citizens with the saints and members of the household of God." Both passages evidently use *oikeioi* to designate Christian believers. The usage here in First Timothy is primarily of the flesh-and-blood relationships of the human *oikos* and to that extent is un-Pauline and another indication that a source is being cited (cf. Michel, *TDNT* 5.134-135). The unique use of *oikeioi* in the Ap. Frs., at *Barn.* 3.3, is a quotation of LXX Isa 58:7 which also has a primary reference to the flesh-and-blood "household" but not without presupposing that those relatives are fellow believers in Yahweh and members of his people.

The apodosis of this sentence and the judgment passed on the case proposed in the protasis is in two parts that correspond with the *idiōn* and *oikeiōn*. One who fails to care for his *(idioi)* fellow believers *has disowned the faith,* and one who does not look after his own (believing?) relatives is worse than those who do not have the Christian faith but do thus provide (e.g., the Jew, who keeps the Decalogue; the devout pagan). Believers incarnate "the faith," and to fail to care for their relatives is to fail to care for revelation and the God who revealed.

9. *Follow these rules for enrolling a widow on the official roster.* The church order again turns to defining the real widow *(chēra),* but this time without the *de* contrast with the previous verse (as had been done at 5:5). The definition-description is articulated in an eightfold list of qualifications that extend through the following verse. The first three qualifications actually belong to the main clause and apodosis of a fivefold list of conditions that follow.

The text here in the PE was evidently a base on which later organizations for widows were founded. As Spicq, *EP,* p. 532, has noted, moreover, the PE also presuppose an organized institution in their own day. There is a public enrollment with corresponding responsibilities both on the part of the community, which has elected and accepted the candidates, and of the candidates themselves, who have pledged their lives to Christ in this particular role as well as to the charitable service of others. The careful prescriptions indicate that entrance into the "order" was both public and solemn, and brought, apparently, a certain honor *(timē!)* from the community (cf. *Const. Apost.* 11.57.12 and 8.13.14), in which their works were not only good *(agathon)* but visibly and attractively so *(kalon).* This visibility would be enhanced not only by the place given these women in the assemblies for worship but also, in all probability, by their clothing, for the "widow's weeds" were a feature of ancient life, as was noted above.

The apodosis continues with three phrases that describe more fully the widow who is eligible for the order. The first qualification pertains to her age, the second to her previous marriage, and the third to her reputation.

*she must have lived no less than sixty years.* If *gegonuia* is to be taken with the first qualification (see Notes above), the widow to be enrolled must be sixty or older. In the ancient world, sixty was the beginning of old age, as forty-five was the end of youth (cf. on 1 Tim 4:12). It was an age when marriage and fathering children were notable (cf. Gen 25:26 of Isaac; 1 Chron 2:21, *s.v.l.*) and when one's life was no longer worth much. (See Lev 27:3, 7, where a male from twenty to sixty is valued at fifty silver sanctuary shekels; once over sixty, at fifteen! Women drop from thirty to ten. Cf. also Smallwood, *Jews,* p. 373, on women over sixty being exempt from the tax rolls.) Thus the age chosen here is not simply in terms of fitness for marriage but also in terms of the poverty imposed by the weakening effects of advancing years. It is presumed in the light of the foregoing verses that this sixty-year-old woman is really without support from a family and quite alone.

*she must have been a wife to one husband.* The *henos andros gynē,* obviously a variant on the qualification for the (presbyter-) bishop of Titus and the *episkopos* as well as the *diakonos* of 1 Tim 3, would imply that the widows are an "order" and a ministry. The full force of this passage for determining the sense of the others ought to be exploited, for here unquestionably the marriage partner of the *chēra* is dead and a further qualification is added that there has been only one such husband (cf. the paradigmatic description of Anna in Luke 2:36-37 above at 5:3). The point of the provision would be quite lost if it referred simply to fidelity in successive marriages, for a widow is a widow and the number of her previous marriages would be irrelevant. The provision is obviously meant to exclude certain widows from the order of real widows with a provision that turns on number, as was the case with preceding provision on age. Widows below sixty are not to be enrolled with the "real widows"; widows of a second marriage are similarly disqualified. Second marriages were advisable in some circumstances (e.g., 1 Tim 5:11-14) but were not to be countenanced in candidates for the public ministries. The roles widows, as also presbyters, bishops, and deacons, fulfilled for the believing community publicly and permanently shaped the way they lived; one such role being to witness to the permanent union of Christ and the church by their one Christian marriage.

10. *she must have public attestation of fine deeds.* The final qualification for the real widow, and one step beyond the previous chronological and sociological description to the explicitly legal order, connoted by *martyr,* is that she be highly respected for her fine deeds, *en ergois kalois martyroumenē.* These "deeds," as Spicq, *EP,* p. 534, has noted, are not so much the virtuous activities of widows as they are the carrying out of the obligations of their state and their dedication to charitable activity. The following conditional clauses then specify the activities of widows that produce the attestation of others. Spicq, p. 533, cites a particularly apposite inscription to illustrate the language here (*MAMA VIII,* 414): *tas epi tēi kosmiōi anastrophēi martyrias kai teimas (sic) apodidonai,* "to give testimony and honors for a way of life above reproach" (trans. WCW). See also 1 Tim 5:4 above and 2:9; 4:12. The *CII* contains no entry under *ergon, agathon,* or *kalon,* though *kalōs (sy-) biosas(a)* is frequent enough for an irreproachable life in Judaism (see #9, #23, #28, #82, #117, #118, #119 [where it is parallel to *kalōs akousas,* "enjoying a good reputation"], #123 [*ezēsas,* "lived a

fine life"], #144 [*antizōsas,* but see p. 30], #336 [?], #353, #374 [*ezēsen*], #377 [*ezēsen*], #509, #537).

*did she rear children?* The lead position of "rearing youngsters" in these conditional clauses reminds one that this source (like the one cited in 1 Tim 2:15; note the repeated *de* at that point also) puts a high value on bearing and bringing up children. The presumption here seems to be not only that the widow has outlived her own offspring (cf. 5:4), but also that she did rear those born to her and did not expose them (Lock, *Commentary,* p. 60). The rearing of youngsters probably should be understood as extending to those not her own, the orphans and foundlings whom the "real widow" had adopted as her own. The *-trophein* element in the compound would include giving more than physical sustenance for such children (as in Epictetus, *Discourses* 1.23.3). The real widow would educate them in faith and virtue. Note that in the ancient world most foundlings and abandoned children were infant girls (cf. the statistics in Spicq, *EP,* p. 534), and thus the widow would be the natural teacher for such growing girls (cf. Titus 2:3-4) to prepare them for Christian marriage and family life (see Stählin, *TDNT* 9.457 n. 162). The heroic charity involved in this generosity by one already quite destitute herself to those even more abandoned is striking. The passage in Hermas, *Man.* 8.10, on the charity a man must show to widows, orphans, and the poor ought to be compared with *Vis.* 2.4.3, where the two little books by the prophet are to go one to Clement (the Roman bishop?) for distribution to churches abroad and the other to a woman, *Graptē,* who "will exhort widows and orphans" (is she the head of the widow's "order" as Clement is of the Roman presbytery? Stählin, p. 461, suggests "probably a deaconess").

*did she welcome guests?* As was mentioned in the notes above, the activity designated by *exenodochēsen* appeared as *philoxenon,* first in the list of positive characteristics of the (presbyter-) bishop in Titus 1:8 and again of the bishop in 1 Tim 3:2. In Matt 25:35 the least of Christ's brothers (his ministers?) are themselves traveling strangers whom pagans had received into their homes *(xenos ēmēn kai synēgagete me).* It is not only James 2:25 that puts a high value on the kindness of an otherwise disreputable woman to strangers who were of God's people, but Paul certainly recalls the service of Christian women (possibly widows; cf. Stählin, *TDNT* 9.451 n. 107) to his own apostolate (Rom 16:1-2; Phil 4:2-3). The Lukan tradition has the old Anna welcoming the stranger family in the Temple (Luke 2:38), and Jesus himself accepts the hospitality of women (Luke 10:38), even a disreputable one who compensates for what the actual host had neglected (Luke 7:44-46; washing the feet [cf. below], anointing the head, a welcoming kiss). In Acts 12:12 it is at "the house of Mary" (apparently a widow; cf. Stählin, *ibid.*) that the church has assembled for prayer, and the Thyatiran Lydia who welcomes Paul's entourage is apparently a single woman, if not a widow, of means (Acts 16:14-15). The real widow of the Christian community, like her OT counterpart (cf. the widow of Zarephath in 1 Kings 17:8-16), is willing to share her starvation rations with the "foreign" prophet who has appeared at her door (note Luke 4:25-26). If she has more, it is so that she can give more generously to indigent Christians.

*did she wash traveling Christians' feet?* "Washing the feet" was the first kind service that a host extended (through his servants; cf. 1 Sam 25:41 of Abigail, widow of Nabal). When he welcomed a guest into his home, he took off the guest's sandals and bathed the feet, hot and dusty from trudging the unpaved roads and streets of the ancient world. The action is one of humble service (Hauck, *TDNT* 4.947), and Weiss, *TDNT* 6.631, suggests that this passage in the PE is to be understood in the same way as in the Johannine tradition. In fact, he suggests that both texts may have spun off the same tradition. If the Johannine Gospel did indeed originate in the Ephesian area, it is conceivable that the tradition of Jesus' washing the feet of his disciples was known and that the Hellenistic language of the previous phrase in the source was here expanded upon and given a Gospel precedent when the (Roman) order for widows was adapted for this correspondence. Still, the fact that neither the Lukan (cf. Luke 12:37, which stops short of saying this; cf. R. Brown, AB *JN* 2.564) nor the Pauline tradition knows of this phrase leads one to think that the phrase appeared in the source before the redaction that we have before us.

The term *hagiois* makes quite clear that the ministry of the widows described here is to believers, and the whole phrase implies that it was receiving as guests believers who traveled from one congregation to another (cf. the prophets, teachers, and apostles as in *Did.* 11–13; itinerant preachers as in 3 John 5-8; and the Jewish Christian Palestinians of Titus 3:12-14). Hebrews 6:10 uses the term of those who were the object of a charitable service *(diakonēsantes tois hagiois),* as in this passage of the PE. R. Brown, AB *JN* 2.564, 569, notes how disciples might give this service to their rabbinic teacher, even though it could not be required of a Jewish slave.

The term "holy ones" can designate not only human beings but also the heavenly beings called angels, an apocalyptic usage that Christian believers exploited (Procksch, *TDNT* 1.109 n. 68) and which also appears in the Qumran phrases *ml'ky qwdš,* "the holy angels" (1QSa 2.8-9, Dupont-Sommer, *EWQ,* p. 108), and *wqdwšy 'l,* "and the holy ones of God" (11QMelch 9, Fitzmyer, *ESBNT,* pp. 247, 261). CD 20.8, Dupont-Sommer, *EWQ,* p. 140, says of the unfaithful member of the sect, "for all the saints of the Most High *(kl qwšdy ʿlywn)* have cursed him." Here a clear line cannot be fixed between the members of the sect in whose assembly the angels are present and the members themselves — all are "holy ones" (Fitzmyer, *ESBNT,* p. 261). The term never is far from its base in worship of the one God of Israel who is holy and makes holy the men who confess and obey him. Thus, both angels and humans, in heaven and on earth, are *hagioi* to the extent that they are caught up in worship. The saints here are guests in the church, the house of the living God, and the widows welcome them at the door and, for the sake of the Lord of the house, wash the feet of his guests.

*did she come to the help of the oppressed?* The aiding action was directed toward "oppressed persons" *(thlibomenois)*. In Paul the term denotes the sufferings of Christians (by persecution) and particularly the affliction of the apostle and his co-workers. Again one would infer that the redactor, if not the original church order, would have understood the phrase here of a widow's ministry to traveling and probably harassed Christian apostolic teachers whose bodily sufferings would have called for their being nursed back to health again (cf. the commentary on 2 Tim 3:11 and the contexts of the Pauline passages noted above as well as the great catalogue of 2 Cor 12:23-27). As Schlier, *TDNT* 3.143-146, has pointed out, this oppression of God's people, and particularly of the apostles, is presented not simply as a fact but as a necessary continuing feature of calling into Christ and his eschatological work, above all into his passion and cross (Col 1:24; 2 Cor 1:5; Phil 3:10; cf. Rev 7:14). Thus the widow's aid to the oppressed and persecuted Christians, particularly to apostolic ministers, would be understood as a ministry to the Lord crucified and suffering in his least members (cf. Matt 25:35-40; Mark 9:41). If the *thlibomenoi* here are thought of as those afflicted by poverty (and even poorer than the widows who care for them), as Schlier hesitantly proposes (p. 147, cf. 2 Cor 8:13 and contrast *Did.* 5.2 = *Barn.* 20.2), then even this poverty is an aspect of their apostolic ministry (2 Cor 6:10).

In *Barn.* 7.11 the suffering necessary to lay hold on the crucified Christ and his kingdom is taken up. In Ign. *Phld.* 6.2, the verb refers to those "harassed" by a devilish plot (i.e. the teachings of Judaizers), and in *Smyrn.* 6.2, Christian love is described as care "for the widow . . . for the orphan . . . for the distressed . . . for the afflicted *(thlibomenou)* . . . for the prisoner or for him released from prison, . . . for the hungry or thirsty." The list reminds one conceptually of the PE here, but the only verbal coincidence is in the use of *thlibomenou*. Of the eighteen uses in Hermas, most are concentrated in *Sim.* 7.1-7, which is a veritable prophetic catechism on the function of affliction for believers.

*did she set out to do every excellent deed possible?* The final and longest conditional clause is a generic summary that describes the widow as one who *panti ergōi agathōi epēkolouthēsen*. "Every excellent deed" here complements in meaning the *en ergois kalois* of the apodosis above. If the widow has devoted herself to all kinds of really good work, that work in its turn *will* be visible and verified by others and will thus certify the widow's worthiness to be enrolled among the "real widows."

11. *On the other hand, have nothing to do with the younger widows.* Once more the *de* reverses the field in this church order, and the negative injunction "have nothing to do with *(paraitou)* younger widows" stands in antithesis to the *katalegesthē* of 5:9. *Paraitou* is practically a technical term here for not giving a hearing to someone in the sense of not opting for or electing an individual. The widows to be bypassed are described as *neōteras* (cf. 1 Tim 5:2), which, as the following explanation makes clear, means of marriageable and childbearing age. Spicq, *EP,* p. 535, notes the provisions of the patristic age that envisioned the "consecration" of virgins at no earlier than forty.

*The reason is that they want to remarry whenever they feel attractions that are incompatible with their commitment to Christ.* The reason or basis for the injunction *(gar)* is frankly grounded on the normal sexual drives, which are all too liable to undermine the public and permanent commitment of the widow who has been precipitately admitted to this order only to discover that she really still wanted marriage. The phrase *katastrēniasōsin Christou* employs a verb undocumented otherwise in the LXX (contra Schneider, *TDNT* 3.631), NT, or the Ap. Frs., though Rev 18:7, 9 employs the simple form of the verb to describe Babylon the great, the widow, who "clothed herself in splendor and went awhoring *(estrēniasen),*" and "the kings of the earth who committed fornication with her and went awhoring *(strēniasantes)*" (cf. 18:3 for the noun *strēnos;* the translation here is Ford, AB *Rev in loc.*). The term suggests not only lust but violence and arrogance as well (cf. the etymologically related Latin *strenuus* and the English *stern,* and LXX 4 Kings 19:28 for the only use of the noun in that translation; in his translation of Isa 61:6 Symmachus uses the verb of Zion glorying in the riches of the Gentiles, probably with the obtuse naivete that the translator cultivates). The compound with *kata-* not only emphasizes an already vigorous term but also governs the object in the genitive *(tou Christou),* i.e. they wax wanton "against (the) Christ" or "in opposition to Christ" (Schneider, *TDNT* 3.631; see also BDF §181, and Spicq *in loc.*). MM, *s.v. strēniaō,* p. 593, note that this is a verb of the middle comedy (see LSJ for citations), where its basic sense of "feel strong and hearty" is near the surface as in fact it is in this passage in the PE. Schneider, *ibid.,* notes that the *-iaō* suffix is that of verbs signifying illness, and again that may be just the nuance that the source wished to convey: the weakness of nature eroding the enthusiastic but ill-considered commitments of an immature and inexperienced person.

The articular *tou Christou* in this passage is the more conspicuous for the fact that this is the only time in the PE that the name of Jesus does not accompany that of (the) Christ, which occurs thirty-two times in these letters. Again the usage of the source appears, though of course there are examples of the usage in the rest of the Paulines, in the Lukan corpus, etc. Grundmann, *TDNT* 9.562, speaks of an absolute use of *Christos,* typical of Paul, that does not occur in the PE except in this passage. Yet in view of what he says about Luke-Acts and First Peter, it does not seem that he wants one to infer that 1 Tim 5:11 is actually taking up Pauline usage.

When sensual impulses spring up, *they want to remarry, gamein thelousin.* The conclusion is stated simply as a fact of experience, and the author-redactor apparently senses no incompatibility with 4:3 above nor with 5:14 immediately below and its "my wish is that younger widows remarry. . . ."

12. *They stand condemned because they broke their previous pledge to him.* The participial phrase *echousai krima* then describes these young widows as "standing condemned," i.e. receiving (adverse) judgment, from God and (apparently) from their fellow believers. The reason for this *(hoti)* is that their admission to the ranks of the "real widows" involved a public promise, agreement (see Chrysostom in Spicq, *EP,* p. 536, and Cramer, *Catena* 7.40), and commitment which had in turn been publicly accepted by the local church. Marriage after this meant *tēn prōten pistin ēthetēsan,* "they broke their previous pledge." At first sight the reason might look as if it referred to the second marriage breaking the faith that had been pledged to the first husband. The reason would then reflect the widespread ancient unease with second marriages. Yet it is difficult to sustain that interpretation in the light of a context (v. 14) which evidently accepts and even encourages the marriages of young widows, provided only that they have not been publicly enrolled in the widows' order.

The use of *pistis* here only partially coincides with the other uses in this correspondence that are far more "theological." Here one is concerned with the faith — the troth — that one person pledges to another, the agreement (*synthēkē;* cf. Chrysostom *in loc.* and the other passages cited by Spicq, *EP,* p. 536) to which one is expected to be loyal (cf. the usage in the virtue catalogue of Gal 5:22), in this case the agreement to remain unmarried which has been publicly given to Christ, through the Church. This "previous pledge" ought not to be followed by a second pledge, and to marry after this is "to break faith." Maurer, *TDNT* 8.158, has noted, "In the LXX, *atheteō* has strongly the character of wilful repudiation of an institution and even more so of a person." Those two aspects seem to be telescoped into each other in this passage of the PE where the widow's second marriage is obviously a desertion of the ranks of the widow's order and, not so obviously, a rejection of the person of Christ (cf. 1 Thess 4:8, where what is not so obvious to the bodily eye is plain to the believer's vision).

13. *not to mention that, at the same time, they also learn how to be lazy while circulating from house to house, and not just lazy but nosy gossips as well, saying what they have no right to say.* The adversative *de,* "not to mention that," here contrasts the lesser vices that are about to be listed with the preeminent sin, the breaking faith with Christ that has just been mentioned, "along with

that . . ." or "at the same time they also *(kai)* learn [to be] lazy." Here the young widows are supposed to be learning how to be "real widows" (i.e. the actual duties of their order) but in fact are becoming experts in sloth. The adjective *argai* that is emphatically repeated in this verse occurred above in Titus 1:12 in the hexameter cited from Epimenides (there men of Crete are characterized as brutes that "live to eat," *gasteres argai*, lit. "lazy bellies"). The use of the term in an explicitly cited source in Titus makes it all the more believable that the usage here is still another indication that a preexistent church order for widows is being quoted.

*Perierchomenai tas oikias* is reminiscent of Titus 1:10-11 and the Jewish Christian men who "overturn entire households *(oikous)*." Greek could and did distinguish between *oikos* and *oikia* (all that belonged to a person vs. his actual residence; cf. the English *home* vs. *house*), and the NT witnesses to the meaning "family" or "household" for *oikia* as well as the "house" or "possessions" (Mark 12:40 = Matt 23:13 [*s.v.l.*] = Luke 20:47, of those who devour "the house of *widows*"; cf. Michel, *TDNT* 5.131). Luke-Acts normally use the term of an actual residence, and that sense is certainly at the fore in the PE. The older widows who circulate from house to house are apparently engaged in a ministry that the "real widows" also performed. These younger women, however, turn such charitable visits into a pastime and worse than that *(ou monon de argai)*, for they also become *nosy gossips (phlyaroi kai periergoi)*.

The adjective *phlyaroi* was quite classical, and the uses by the comedy writers et al. (Aristophanes, *Clouds* 365; Menander 541.2; *Dysc.* 831 [verb], 892) may indicate its popularity for the literate expression of contempt. The verb is found occasionally in the papyri (MM); examples of the adjective/noun have been adduced by Spicq, *EP*, p. 395, from the papyri, where it refers to the babbling of babies and nonsense words. Josephus, *Vit.* 150, uses *phlyaron* = "the absurdity" of blaming military setbacks on sorcery.

The next adjective here, coupled with *phlyaroi*, is *periergoi*, and that word, in its one other NT use in Acts 19:19, does refer to magical arts, *ta perierga* (see Note on *perierchomai* above), as also do the papyri (MM *s.v.*, p. 505, and Deissmann, *B ST*, p. 323 n. 5). The cognate verb occurs in the NT only in 2 Thess 3:11, of some Christians "living in idleness, mere busybodies, not doing any work *(mēden ergazomenous alla periergazomenous)*."

The LXX does not use the adjective, though verbal and nominal cognates occur in Wis 8:5 (*s.v.l.* and in a good sense) as well as in Sir 3:23 (RSV, "Do not meddle [*mē periergazou*] in what is beyond your tasks [*ergōn*]") and 41:22 (of "meddling" with another's maidservant). One must wait until Hermas, *Vis.* 4.3.1.66-67, to read *periergos* in the Ap. Frs. (in the sense of "curious"; cf. the verb in *Sim* 9.2.7). There is no doubt that the basic denotation of the adjective is "meddlesome" or "officious," again a sense that Attic comedy documents (cf.

Menander, *Epitr.* frag. 849 K; and line 262 as well as *Dysc.* 836 *s.v.l.;* note Gomme and Sandbach, *Commentary,* pp. 262, 293, for comments on both places). Note Gorgias's eavesdropping in 821-822; cf. also in *Sam.* 300. Whether the connotation of indulging in magical practices was implied in the source and/or thus understood by the redactor can only be conjectured. If indeed Luke was the redactor, it is quite possible in the light of his usage that he thus understood it. While Spicq, *EP,* pp. 395-396, favors the meaning "indiscreet," the English "nosy" combines the ideal of diligent, close examination of a matter which is after all none of one's business; he also suggests how magical practices may have arisen in connection with the visitation of the sick, distributing amulets and charms (cf. 2 Macc 12:40), and pronouncing incantations (cf. the following phrase here).

*Lalousai ta mē deonta,* "saying what they have no right to say," takes up and expands the *phlyaroi* of the preceding phrase, specifying at least some of the baseless talk as about things that should not even be mentioned. *Lalein* is used in this correspondence (Titus 2:1, 15) of the Pauline co-worker's teaching of healthy, Pauline doctrine, and Titus 1:11 wrote of Jewish Christian men *didaskontes ha mē dei aischrou kerdous charin,* "who teach things they ought not . . . for their own financial gain, shame to say." One would infer that the redactor, at least, took this phrase as referring to some sort of teaching that was totally alien from the Christian faith, perhaps the magical formulae and prayers which were so dear to ancient Ephesian religious tastes.

14. *Now my wish is that younger widows remarry, rear children, run their homes, offer no pretext for reviling to the adversary.* The phrase *boulomai oun* occurred in the church order of 1 Tim 2:8, as now it occurs in this order for widows (cf. Titus 3:8), and it probably belongs to the pen of the redactor (cf. Acts 17:20), speaking *in persona Pauli,* rather than to the source. The Pauline cachet is probably needed at just this point, since the directives that follow coincide only partially with those of 1 Cor 7 and one can imagine an appeal being made to the "historical Paul" for setting aside these directives. The author-redactor of these letters is apparently convinced that the old church order for widows which he is reproducing at this point is not in conflict with the Pauline tradition — indeed, that the apostle would have subscribed to it.

The subject of the four infinitival phrases that summarize the apostle's regulations is *neōteras,* "young women" (as in 5:2) or "young widows" (as in 5:11). If one takes the former alternative, then a general rule is being proposed for all young women, and young widows are no exception to it. If *neōteras* does understand *chēras* (and the source would certainly have so understood it, if the term was in the source), then young widows (anarthrous; hence not *all,* but as a general rule) are once more to establish homes.

Since *teknogonein* is the verbal form of the equally unusual *teknogonia* that appeared above in 1 Tim 2:15 and the sense of "rearing [not just bearing] children" would suit the context here very well, one surmises that some early Christians sought and fashioned a "new" vocabulary to express their veneration for *human* life, and that as more than simply physical life. Christian faith was not a fertility cult; it could not tolerate infanticide. Accordingly, rearing of children, i.e. nurturing and educating them, was the complement of marriage *(gamein)*. The order is probably not only chronological but also morally irreversible, i.e. the author does not envision having children and then marrying. The advice here does not advert to any children by the young widow's previous marriage, probably because if there were any, they would be too young to care for their widowed mother (cf. on 5:4 above).

The third infinitive, *oikodespotein,* would complement the educative-nurturing activity with a guidance-directive role for the wife and mother within her home *(oikos)*. One recalls that the church order of 1 Tim 3:4-5 (cf. Titus 1:6) spoke of the father's presiding over the household. Here the mother's unique role is denoted with a unique term, which appeared in late Hellenistic Greek (usually of astrological phenomena; see Harrison, *Paulines,* p. 132), though the use of the noun in Plutarch, *Roman Questions* 271 E, is precisely parallel to that of the verb here, and that text illustrates how the *anēr-kyrios-oikodespotēs* cluster was complemented by the *gynē-kyria-oikodespoina* cluster. Considering the possible Roman provenance of the source cited here in the PE, it may be significant that Plutarch is inquiring about the reasons for a peculiarly Roman custom, "Why do they, as they conduct a bride to her home, bid her say, 'Where you are Gaius, there am I Gaia'?" To which the author first answers, "Is it her entrance into the house upon fixed terms, as it were, at once to share everything and to control jointly the household, and is the meaning then, 'Wherever you are lord and master *(kyrios kai oikodespotēs)*, there am I lady and mistress *(kyria kai oikodespoina)*'?" The emphasis in this whole section upon stable commitment reminds one of Plutarch's remark later in the same treatise (288 E) that "a woman . . . should be stable, domestic, and difficult to remove from her place" *(hedraion kai oikouron* [cf. the *v.l.* at Titus 2:5, and J. K. Elliott, *Greek Text, in loc.*] *kai dysmetakineton)*.

The sonorous and expansive infinitival phrase with which this four-member series closes uses a terminology not otherwise found in the PE. Bertram, *TDNT* 5.473, has rightly noted that what gives a pretext here is the young widow's state itself, as in Gal 5:13 it was Christian freedom and in Rom 7:8, 11 the divine law itself. That understanding in its turn enables one to explain the mysterious *tōi antikeimenōi* that exploits this state, for "the opponent" would then correspond to the *sarx,* the flesh (as in Galatians), or *hē hamartia* (as in Romans). The verb *antikeitai* occurred above in 1 Tim 1:10. In the NT the closest parallel to the usage here in the PE is 2 Thess 2:4, with its description of "the man of lawlessness . . . the son of perdition who opposes *(antikeimenos)* and exalts himself. . . ." The only use of the word in the Ap. Frs. is in *1 Clem.* 51.1, where the author writes, "Let us pray that for our transgressions and for what we have done through any attacks of the adversary *(tou antikeimenou)*, forgiveness may be granted to us." Here "the adversary" is Satan (Jaubert, SC, 167, 183 n. 3, who also notes *Mart. Pol.* 17.1; the letters of the Martyrs of Lyons in Eusebius, *Church History* 5.1.5, 23, 42). If the source employed by First Timothy is indeed of Roman provenance, the sense of the term in *First Clement* may be particularly significant for understanding our text. If McCasland's suggestion that *hē hamartia* in Rom 7 is also a synonym for Satan is sound, then the Roman church may well have understood Rom 7:11, *hē gar hamartia aphormēn labousa,* as "Satan took occasion . . ." ("The Black One," p. 78). Of course, *antikeimenos* is the Greek translation of the Semitic *Satan,* and the use of Satan in the following verse here in the PE may indicate that the source was aware of that.

The case for "the adversary" = Satan would be all but certain if one could explain how the phrase *loidorias charin* fitted into the picture. *Loidoria* occurs otherwise in the NT only in 1 Pet 3:9 (at the end of a household code [?]; note that Polycarp, *Phil.* 2.2, takes up the same phrase in the only use of the noun in the Ap. Frs.). The cognate verb occurs at 1 Cor 4:12, and the noun *loidoros* in 1 Cor 5:11 and 6:10 (vice lists). Acts 23:4 knows the verb, too (as does John 9:28 and 1 Pet 2:23). As H. Hanse, *TDNT* 4.293, has noted, such reviling or insults were "especially forbidden in relation to superiors," and perhaps that observation ought to be kept in mind in the PE, *scil.* the adversary finds a pretext to rail at one who is his superior. If the adversary is in fact Satan, then he makes the young widows' abuses into an occasion for insulting God or mocking him for having received the frail pledges of persons who could not keep them. Indeed, the adversary both leads the susceptible into temptation and then makes their sin into an occasion for reviling God.

On the other hand, commentators have also taken the *loidoria* as a reviling of Christian widows/women/believers in general by unbelievers or even fellow Christians who have fastened on the indiscretions of some younger widows with a certain malicious glee (cf. Hanse, Bertram, Hendriksen, Boudou, and Barrett). One would have expected "adversaries," in the plural and even anarthrous, if that were the interpretation. Of course, the human agents of Satan could be included here, those people who, ultimately under demonic influence, blaspheme God and his Spirit under any pretext. In any event, the concern of this correspondence, as it was the concern of the historical Paul, is that the good name of the church not be compromised by her members (cf. Titus 2:5, 8, 10). Here one would surmise that this was also the concern of the source being cited.

The characteristic of this last phrase that leads one to think that the redactor's hand may be showing is the distinct change in point of view between the first three infinitives and this concluding phrase. Not only are the others positive and this negative, but also the others describe the role of the widow-wife and this last phrase actually describes the result which this role will have upon another. Such changes, nevertheless, in point of view have been even more abrupt in other sources cited (cf. 1 Tim 2:15), and thus one can only submit the possibility here of redaction.

15. *for some of them have already slipped off after Satan.* This verse proceeds to document the opposite of what has just been stated as positively desirable in principle, the *gar* introducing the reason for the apostolic directives that have just been laid down in the name of Paul. The *ēdē* introduces a contemporary sort of tone into the text of the order that is being cited authenticating the Pauline directives of the preceding verse from the actual experience of the community. The use of *opisō* in the sense of the personal following for goodwill acquired by a master and leader fits precisely here except that here the person followed is not a man but Satan (it is striking that "Satan" is the address used for Peter in Mark 8:33 = Matt 16:23, where he is told, *hypoge opisō mou,* i.e. "be my disciple and learn what my mission is; don't try, like the devil, to teach me what it is"). Recall that the link between Satan and magical practices may be an element here as well as women's breaking their commitment to a widow's way of life in following Christ. The five sibilants in this verse give it an ugly, hissing, serpentine sound too.

16. *In the case of a woman who is a believer and who welcomes widows into her home, let her continue to come to their help and the local church not be burdened but free to help the widows proper.* After the edited and redacted materials of the previous two verses, the dry, casuistic terminology of the source reappears and brings the reader up short. A final entry on widows adverts to still another situation in which widows received care and support apart from the communities of "real widows." This case (as distinguished from the situation of 5:4, 8 above) envisions a Christian woman who is well-to-do if not wealthy and who has control of her property, a woman who is probably a widow herself. She in turn and out of her own generosity "has widows"; i.e. she has gathered widowed believers who were in less fortunate circumstances than hers, given them hospitality, and supported them (note this sense of *echein* already in *Odyssey* 17.515 and 20.377). One need not envision them as living under one roof, but that situation is not to be excluded either. An inscription that seems to presuppose the kind of relationship that the archaic order presumes reads *mētri agapētēi, philotheōi kai philochērai kai philan kai philoteknōi,* "to beloved mother, devout, a friend of the widow, and one who loved her husband and children" (trans. WCW; *Suppl. Ep. Gr.* II, 521 *ap.* Spicq, p. 393 n. 1).

A final explanatory purpose clause *(hina)* makes it clear that the previous procedure is meant not to excuse the congregation from the material support of widows but rather to make it possible to concentrate that support (note the verb repeated in the form *eparkesēi*) on the order of "real widows" whose qualifications have already been noted (vv. 5, 9-10).

The final mention of *hai ontōs chērai* serves as an inclusion framing this whole section on widows (cf. 5:3), which in turn, and no doubt because it was incorporated into this correspondence under the aegis of Paul, furnished the basic guidelines for the later church order of the patristic age when they come to this subject (see Stählin's survey, *TDNT* 9.459-465). The task of supervision, which Paul is here conceived of as giving to Timothy, was by the beginning of the second century the special responsibility of the local bishop, as Ign. *Pol.* 4.1 indicates with its directive to Polycarp: "Let not the widows be neglected. Be yourself their protector *(phronistēs)* after the Lord." Ign. *Smyrn.* 13.1 records his greeting to the households of Christian families and then, in parallel, *tas parthenous tas legomenas chēras,* "the virgins called widows," who apparently also constitute a group (or groups). The term *parthenoi* is evidently qualified lest it be misunderstood, but there is no question that here it denotes women presently living a single life. The qualification refers to the fact that they had not always so lived. The episcopal task of overseeing widows, doubtless an onerous one, was shared with *presbyteroi,* as Polycarp, *Phil.* 6.1, indicates. Stählin notes (p. 461) how eventually deacons, too, shared the task (with an appeal to Acts 6:1-4) of the *episkopoi* (cf. Hermas, *Sim.* 9.26.2, of deacons who abuse their office of caring for the poor, including widows, with *Sim.* 9.27.2 of the *episkopoi* who "ever ceaselessly sheltered the destitute and the widows by their ministration [*tēi diakoniai*] and ever behaved with holiness"). The teaching of Polycarp, *Phil.* 4.3, ought to be noted here too, for after outlining what moral guidance ought to be given to Christian families, he then turns immediately to the teaching that "We [himself with his *presbyteroi* and the Philippian church] ought to give to the widows" (again the plural and perhaps a group; cf. the citation above of Ign. *Smyrn.* 13.1). The catalogue of virtues that follows is terminologically quite different from the one cited in 1 Tim 5:3-16 (except possibly for the term *pistis*), though the activities noted more than once coincide with those mentioned in First Timothy. The text of Polycarp reads, "Let us teach the widows to be discreet (*sōphronousas* [here with the sense, "to be virtuous, chaste," BAGD]) with regard to the faith *(peri tēn . . . pistin)* of the Lord [the reference may be, as in 1 Tim 5:12, to the troth pledged to Christ and not to the deposit of faith], praying (*entygchanousas* [cf. the *prosmenei tais deēsesin k.t.l.,* 1 Tim 5:5]) ceaselessly (*adialeiptōs* [cf. *nyktos kai hēmeras* of 1 Tim 5:5]) for all persons, being far from all slander *(diabolēs),* evil speaking *(katalalias),* false witness *(pseudomartyrias),* love of money *(philargyrias),* and all evil [cf. 1 Tim 5:13-

14], knowing that they are an altar of God (*thysiastērion* [Stählin, pp. 460 n. 183, 464]), and that all offerings are tested (*mōmoskopeitai* [cf. 1 Tim 5:9-10]), and that nothing escapes him of reasonings or thoughts, or of 'the secret things of the heart' [1 Cor 14:25]." In Polycarp, *Phil.* 5.2, the next group spoken of are the deacons; then the younger, single men (5.3). The terminological difference between Polycarp and the PE on widows is especially striking when one notes that it was Polycarp, *Phil.* 4.1, who cited the actual terms that appear in 1 Tim 6:7, 10. If the quotation does not depend on a common source, then one would infer that Asia Minor had a *didachē* for widows different from the Roman one cited in 1 Tim 5:3-16, and that did not yield to the later.

## IV.B.3. THE ORDER OF PRESBYTERS (5:17-25)

*5 17The presbyters who have given outstanding direction deserve to get double pay, particularly those whose jobs are preaching and instruction; 18for the Scripture says, "You shall not tie shut the mouth of the ox that is threshing grain," and "The workman is deserving of his wage."*

*19Do not give a hearing, Timothy, to a charge against a presbyter, unless the evidence comes from two or three witnesses. 20Those who are sinning you are to refute while all the presbyters look on, to put fear of wrongdoing into the rest of them.*

*21As God [the Father] and Christ Jesus and the elect angels look on, I adjure you, Timothy, to keep these directives without prejudice, that is, not doing anything out of partisanship.*

*22Be in no hurry, Timothy, to impose hands on anyone.*

*Incur no responsibility for the sins of others.*
*Keep yourself chaste.*

*23Drink only water no longer, but take wine, moderately, for your bad stomach and your frequent bouts with illness.*

*24The sins of some people are obvious enough, escorting them to judgment; others trail their sins behind them.*

*25Similarly also, fine deeds are obvious, and those that are not obvious cannot stay hidden always.*

## ♦ NOTES

5:17. *The presbyters who have given outstanding direction.* Lit. "The elders who have presided well *(kalōs proestōtes).*" On *kalōs* see 1 Tim 3:4. On *proestōtes* see Titus 3:8.

*deserve to get.* The verb *axiousthōsan* (imperative), found seven times in NT, occurs only here in the PE and only at 2 Thess 1:11 otherwise in the Paulines ("make worthy," Foerster, *TDNT* 1.380). Luke 7:7; Acts 15:38; and 28:22 also use this verb. The other NT uses are Heb 3:3; 10:29. The LXX uses the verb about fifty times but never with *timē.* Of the ten uses in the Ap. Frs., the closest parallel to this passage in the PE is Ign. *Eph.* 21.2, where the martyr-to-be says, *ēxiōthēn eis timēn theou heurethēnai,* "I was considered worthy to be found for the honor of God."

*double pay.* Lit "double honor." On *timē* cf. above on 1 Tim 1:17 and the verb in 1 Tim 5:3; the *entimous* of Phil 2:29 ought also to be noted. For the papyri and inscriptions with *timē* = "stipend," see Spicq, *EP,* p. 542, D-C, p. 78; as well as Schneider, *TDNT* 8.169-174, 176-177. The Third Gospel does not use *timē,* but all six occurrences in Acts (4:34; 5:2, 3; 7:16; 19:19; 28:10) refer to price/value, and in the last example to gifts.

*those whose jobs are preaching and instruction.* Lit. "the ones who are laboring in word and teaching." For *jobs, kopiōntes,* as the term for the apostolic ministry of Paul and Timothy, see 1 Tim 4:10. The use of *en logōi* here is quite parallel to its use of Timothy in 1 Tim 4:12, where it specifies the oral activity of one sharing in the Pauline ministry (see also Titus 2:8).

On *didaskaliai* see Comment in AB *Titus* on Titus 1:9.

18. *the Scripture says.* This is the first of two uses of *graphē* in this correspondence (also in 2 Tim 3:16; see commentary there for further statistics). For the use of *legei* see Titus 2:8. This is the only use of this formula in the PE and (even more surprising) the first of only three explicit quotations of the OT Scriptures in these letters (otherwise, without a validating formula, at 5:19 and 2 Tim 2:19).

"The workman is deserving of his wage." The initial *axios* of the saying here takes up the verbal *axiousthōsan* of the preceding verse, as *ergatēs* corresponds to *hoi kopiōntes* and *misthou* to *timēs.* On the adjective itself, see 1 Tim 1:15; 4:9, as well as 6:1 below. The *ergatēs* occurs once again in the PE, of Timothy himself, sharing in Paul's teaching and trials, "a workman *(ergatēn)* who has no reason for shame" (2 Tim 2:15; cf. 2:1-7, esp. v. 6 with its reference to "the hardworking [*ton kopiōnta*] farmer [who] ought to be the first to have his share of the crops"). Elsewhere in the Paulines, *ergatēs* occurs only of the *pseudapostoloi ergatai dolioi* of 2 Cor 11:13 and the *kakous ergatas* of Phil 3:2, in both cases of Jewish Christian missionaries whose teaching is perverted. The use of an adjective with *ergatēs* in each instance indicates that the term itself did not have a pejorative sense for Paul. In Luke-Acts the term can designate manual laborers (Acts 19:25) as well as those who do evil (Luke 13:27), but in Luke 10:2 *(bis),* as well as verse 7, *hoi ergatai* are the farmer laborers toiling in God's harvest, i.e. men engaged in bringing other persons into the kingdom of God. The language seems to go back again to a collection of Jesus' sayings on the subject (= Matt 9:37-38; 10:10), and Matt 20:1, 2, 8 uses the noun of all those who worked for the same pay *(misthos)* in the householder's vineyard. The parable stands just halfway between the "secular" usage of James 5:4 (cf. Deut 24:14-15) and the application of the term to the Christian ministry that is most common in the NT.

*Didache* 13.1-2 takes up this same saying, but in the Matthean form, and applies it to the "genuine prophet" as well as the "genuine teacher," each of whom is worthy of his food, *axios esti tēs trophēs autou.* On the use of the term in *1 Clem.* 34.1, see the commentary on 1 Tim 3:13 (see Donfried, *Setting,* pp. 62-68, for the term in *2 Clem.* 4.5, *ergatai anomias,* comparing Matt 7:23, *ergazomenoi tēn,* with Luke 13:27, *ergatai adikias*). The passage of *Didache* is especially illuminating not only because the saying is again adduced to justify support for those who minister to the Christian congregation but also because that *trophē* is spelled out (13.3-7) in terms of wine, grain, beef, lamb, bread, wine, oil, and then extended to clothing and money *(argyriou).*

Of the twenty-nine uses of *misthos* in the NT, this is the only use in the PE. The five other uses in the Paulines are in Romans (4:4) and First Corinthians (3:8, 14; 9:17, 18). In First Corinthians all four uses are in contexts of the recompense for apostolic ministry. In the Third Gospel, apart from 10:7, the term also appears in two passages of a heavenly recompense, 6:23 (= Matt 5:12, *SFG* §78[Q]) and 6:35 (*SFG* §80), apparently a Lukan expansion of Q based on the logion just cited. In Acts 1:18 the money taken by Judas is *misthos tou adikias,* in a Semitizing phrase that means "ill-gotten gain" (cf. Haenchen, *Acts,* p. 160 n. 6, for LXX references). Every work for which an apostle takes pay is not necessarily a good work for his Lord; indeed, the money may be only a down payment toward damnation. Preisker, because he is arguing with rather than explaining the PE, is less than helpful (*TDNT* 4.723-724) on this term. Of the twenty-one occurrences of *misthos* in the Ap. Frs. (never in Ignatius), only Hermas, *Man.* 11.12, clearly uses the word of a material honorarium for the (prophetic) ministry.

19. *Do not give a hearing, Timothy, to a charge against a presbyter.* The *mē paradechou* with its singular imperative brings the reader sharply back to Timothy (not in the Greek text), who is not to "give a hearing" in the sense of "acknowledge as correct" or "receive" an accusation against a presbyter "unless the evidence comes from two or three witnesses." *Paradechou* occurs only here in all the Paulines. The only other NT uses are in Acts 15:4; 16:21; and 22:18. That last passage also provides the closest NT parallel to this passage in the PE, for Paul hears Jesus, in a vision, say of the Jews, "They will not accept your testimony *(paradexontai . . . martyrian)* about me." The only other NT uses are at Mark 4:20 of welcoming the word and Heb 12:6 (citing LXX Prov 3:12; also

*1 Clem.* 56.4). Of the eight uses in *First* and *Second Clement,* Hermas, and Ignatius, only Ign. *Smyrn.* 4.1 offers a rather remote parallel to this passage in First Timothy with its directive "not to receive" *(mē paradechesthai)* heretical teachers. MM furnish no parallel for the phrase here from papyri, nor does Spicq, *EP,* p. 544, give more than the *dechesthai egklēmata* ("to receive charges or accusations") from C. Ord. Ptol. n. 61.

*charge. Katēgoria,* "charge or accusation," occurs also in Titus 1:6 (*en katēgoriai,* lit. "not under accusation"). Elsewhere in the NT only John 18:29 uses the word, referring to the formal accusation lodged against Jesus by Pilate. The LXX and the Ap. Frs. do not use it, although cognates of the word appear in Acts and the Maccabean corpus.

*unless the evidence comes from two or three witnesses.* The initial particles *ektos ei mē* that introduce the Deuteronomic law cited here (Deut 19:15) are found in this combination only in the Paulines in the NT (1 Cor 14:5; 15:2), though *ektos* alone and as a preposition is found not only in 1 Cor 6:18; 15:27; 2 Cor 12:2, but also in Acts 26:22 and Matt 23:26.

Where the LXX Deut 19:15 reads *kata anthrōpou,* this text in the PE specifies *kata presbyterou;* similarly where Deuteronomy reads *epi stomatos duo martyrōn kai epi stomatos triōn martyrōn stathēsetai pan rhēma,* this text telescopes that into *epi duo ē triōn martyrōn* (J. K. Elliott, *Greek Text,* pp. 83-84). The longer text of the sources makes it quite clear that the *epi* is to be understood as "on the evidence of" (i.e. on the oral testimony, the "mouth" of) the witnesses to the acts and not in the sense of an accusation from only one, received "before/in the presence of" several witnesses (BDF §235; Spicq, *EP,* p. 545; Vliet, *Testimony,* p. 88, who cites *Test. Abr.* 13.23). Delling, *TDNT* 8.221, notes that "two or three" here does not necessarily mean a few but rather is contrasted with "one" *(testis unus, testis nullus!).*

20. *Those who are sinning you are to refute.* The other use of *hamartanein* in this correspondence is in Titus 3:11 (the noun, *hamartia,* occurs in 1 Tim 5:22, 24; 2 Tim 3:6; *hamartōlos* in 1 Tim 1:9, 15). The NT contains forty-one other uses of the verb, fifteen of which occur in the Paulines, and of those, fourteen in Roman and First Corinthians. Hermas, the LXX, and other Jewish Greek documents, including the *Testaments of the Twelve Patriarchs,* use the verb frequently. The verb can even apply to inadvertent wrongdoing, in Menander (Koerte 432/499K; see Herodas 5.27, in *Mimiambi,* ed. I. C. Cunningham [Oxford: Clarendon, 1971]) and *1 Clem.* 2.3.

*refute. Elegchein* occurs also at Titus 1:9, 13, but only a dozen other times in the NT. The verb is characteristic of the sapiential and prophetic traditions of the LXX (see occurrences in *First Clement*), but appears only infrequently in the Ap. Frs.

*while all of the presbyters look on.* Lit. "in the presence of all." The simple phrase *enōpion pantōn* occurs elsewhere in the NT only at Acts 19:19; 27:35, where in the former instance "all" are fellow believers and in the latter, all persons whether believers or not, on the endangered ship (cf. Luke 8:47 for *enōpion pantos tou laou* as well as Rom 12:17 for *enōpion pantōn anthrōpōn*, referring to believers and nonbelievers alike). The use here in the PE is the first of two instances where *enōpion* refers to merely human persons (cf. 6:12 below). In the six other instances it refers to God, to Christ, even to the angels (as in 5:21; see 1 Tim 2:3). For reading "presbyters" see the Comment below.

*to put the fear of wrongdoing into the rest (hoi loipoi) of them.* Lit. "in order that the rest also may have fear." Only at 2 Tim 4:8 does *loipon* occur again in this correspondence, and then in an adverbial usage that is rather colloquial. On the other hand, the term is not uncommon in the rest of the NT (fifty-three times), and *hoi loipoi* occurs in several different strata (e.g., Acts 28:9; Eph 2:3; 1 Thess 4:13; 5:6; Rev 11:13 [with *emphoboi*]).

*fear.* The term *phobos* occurs only here in the PE, although frequently enough in the rest of the NT (forty-six times). Yet this is the only time in the NT that it is used in this phrase, *phobon echein* (though Luke 8:37 does write *phobōi . . . syneichonto,* of LXX Job 3:24). In the Ap. Frs., *Barn.* 11.11 may speak of "having fear and hope," but the rest of the uses are in Hermas (as many as six). Balz, *TDNT* 9.205, has noted an example in *Test.* XII, B.4.5 *(s.v.l.),* and BAGD, *s.v.,* cite P. Lond 1914.12, *phobon theou echontes . . . ,* but there does not appear to be an example in LXX.

21. *As God [the Father] and Christ Jesus and the elect angels look on.* Lit. "in the presence of God and of Christ Jesus and of the elect angels." On "God and Christ Jesus," who begin the triad, see Titus 1:4 and 1 Tim 1:2, noting with Spicq, *EP,* p. 546, that the omission of the definite article with Christ Jesus places his person on the side of the divine Father rather than among "the elect angels." Thus one might well read the triad as a dyad, with Father and Son in one division and all the holy angels in another.

*the elect angels.* The one other occurrence of *aggelos* in the PE referred to the apostolic messengers (1 Tim 3:16). On "elect" see Titus 1:1.

*I adjure you, Timothy.* Lit. "I charge." The name "Timothy" is not in the Greek text. With *diamartyromai* the text returns again to the first person singular, last seen at 5:14 *(boulomai).* In this correspondence this verb always occurs with a form of the phrase *enōpion tou theou* (2 Tim 2:14; 4:1, also in first person sg.). The phrase is not otherwise documented in the NT or in the Ap. Frs. (where the verb is not found). However, note LXX Deut 4:26, where Moses says, *diamartyromai hymin sēmeron ton te ouranon kai tēn gēn,* "I call heaven and earth as witness against you today" (cf. 31:28 and Jth 7:28), where sky and earth are at least personified if they do not actually stand for the forces that put in operation the covenant curses. In the impassioned peroration and climax of the speech that Josephus (*War* 2.401) placed on the lips of Herod Agrippa II, he has that king say, "As for me, I call to witness *(martyromai)* your sanctuary and God's holy angels *(tous hierous aggelous)* and our common fatherland, that I have kept back nothing that could conduce to your preservation." On the other hand, Josephus never uses the phrase *enopampion tōn aggelōn.*

In the Paulines, only 1 Thess 4:6 employs *diamartyromai;* apart from Heb 2:6, the ten other NT occurrences are in Luke (once) and Acts. It is in Luke 16:28 that the closest parallel to the meaning here in the PE is found (but cf. Acts 2:40 also), as the rich man asks Abraham to send Lazarus to his brothers "to warn *(diamartyrētai)* them so that *(hina)* they do not come into this place of torment" (Strathmann, *TDNT* 4.512). The fact that in both cases the "charge" or emphatic warning is described as coming from another world makes the parallel more striking.

*to keep these directives.* On *tauta* see the Comment below. This is the first of 5 occurrences of *phylassein* in the PE (1 Tim 6:20; 2 Tim 1:12, 14; 4:15). There are 3 other Pauline uses (Rom 2:26; Gal 6:13; 2 Thess 3:3). No NT document uses the verb more frequently than Luke-Acts (6/8 = 14 times). The 9 other NT uses are scattered through the other Gospels and the Catholic Epistles. The verb *phylassein* occurs 471 times in the LXX (Bertram, *TDNT* 9.237). The Ap. Frs. witness to *phylassein* governing God's *entolas* (*Barn.* 4.11) as well as those of the Lord (*2 Clem.* 8.4), and, perhaps more significantly, in the light of the "deposit" of the PE (see Comment below), *Did.* 4.13 (= *Barn.* 19.11) writes, "You shall not forsake the commandments of the Lord *(entolas kyriou)* but you shall keep what you received *(phylaxeis de ha paralabes).*" In Hermas *phylassein tēn entolēn/tas antolas* occurs very frequently indeed.

22. *Be in no hurry, Timothy, to impose hands on anyone.* This is the only textually certain use of *tacheōs* in the PE (cf. below on 2 Tim 4:9 and J. K. Elliott, *Greek Text,* p. 161, for use of other forms of the *tach-* root; cf. above on 1 Tim 3:14). The adverb is Pauline enough, occurring in 1 Cor 4:19; Gal 1:6; Phil 2:19, 24; 2 Thess 2:2, but it also occurs in Luke 14:21; 16:6 (as well as John 11:31). Timothy is not found in the Greek. For the nominal form of the "imposition of hands," see 1 Tim 4:14.

*Keep yourself chaste.* This is the first of three occurrences of *tērein,* "keep" (6:14 below and 2 Tim 4:7), in this correspondence (sixty-eight times otherwise in NT). The other Paulines use the verb five times; in the Lukan corpus, only Acts employs the word (eight times). In 1 Tim 6:14 Timothy is to keep "the commandment *(entolēn)* beyond blemish," and in 2 Tim 4:7 Paul avers that he has "kept (the) faith" (cf. commentary *in loc.*). The closest NT parallels to the reflexive use here in 5:22 are 2 Cor 11:9 where Paul, recalling that he supported himself, assures the Corinthians, "So I refrained and will refrain *(emauton . . . etērēsa kai tērēsō)* from burdening you in any way," and in the Catholic Epistles

James 1:27 describes real worship as "to keep oneself *(heauton tērein)* unspotted *(aspilon)* from the world" and Jude 21 admonishes, "Keep yourselves *(heautous . . . tērēsate)* in the love of God." In both the latter passages the stress is on worship and prayer (Jude 20), and the *aspilon* of James is conceptually near the *hagnon* of 1 Tim 5:22. The stress in all of these reflexive uses is on the responsible activity of the individuals being exhorted (Riesenfeld, *TDNT* 8.143), and the imperative here in 1 Tim 5:22 is to be taken not as an inceptive ("begin now to keep . . .") but as a complexive ("henceforth, in all things, keep yourself . . ." [BDF §337.2]).

The reflexive use really stands behind the striking occurrences of *tērein sarka* in the Ap. Frs. (see Riesenfeld, *TDNT* 8.143 n. 23). Thus Ign. *Phld.* 7.2 writes, "Keep your flesh *(tēn sarka hymōn . . . tēreite)* as God's temple," in his only use of this verb. *Second Clement* 8.4, 6 (cf. 9.3 with *hōs naon theou phylassein tēn sarka)* teaches, ". . . if we keep the flesh pure *(tēn sarka hagñen tērēsantes)* . . . we shall obtain eternal life," and concludes, "Keep the flesh pure *(tērēsate tēn sarka hagñen)* and the seal [of baptism; cf. 6.9; 7.6; Donfried, *Setting,* pp. 123-126] unstained *(aspilon)*. . . ." This teaching has its summary climax in *2 Clem.* 14.3: "Guard the flesh *(tērēsate tēn sarka)* that you may receive the Spirit."

Wisdom 10:5 is close to First Timothy when it says of Wisdom that "It preserved him (*ētēresen auton* [i.e. Abraham]) blameless *(amempton)* before God." Perhaps in LXX Proverbs one ought to note 4:23: "guard your heart" *(tēreisēn kardian);* 13:3: "He who will guard *(phylassei)* his mouth will keep *(tērei)* his soul (*tēn heautou psychēn* [cf. 16:17; 19:16])."

23. *Drink only water no longer.* The compound verb *hydropotei,* otherwise undocumented in the NT, does occur in LXX Dan 1:12, but not in the Ap. Frs. It may be employed because it sounds stronger than *hydōr pinein* and suggests a firm, constant practice (Spicq, "1 Tim 5:23," p. 145 n. 2). *Mēketi,* "no longer," is only here in the PE; of the twenty other NT occurrences, nine are in the other Paulines and four in Luke-Acts.

*but take wine.* The *alla* stands in contrast to the preceding admonition and introduces the expansive positive direction with which this fivefold series closes. The second occurrence of *chraomai* in this correspondence (see Notes on 1 Tim 1:8) is completely within the Pauline usage (cf., e.g., 1 Cor 9:12, 15). The closest parallels to this usage in the Ap. Frs. are in Ign. *Eph.* 9.1, "using as a rope the Holy Spirit" (cf. his *Rom.* 9.1, the Syrian church "uses God as shepherd"); *Trall.* 6.1, "Use only Christian food and abstain from strange *(allotrias)* food, which is heresy" (cf. Ign. *Phld.* 4.1, "Be careful therefore to use [*chrēsthai*] one eucharist").

*for your bad stomach.* Lit. "for the sake of the stomach." On *dia* with the accusative in the PE, cf. Titus 1:13. Note that J. K. Elliott, *Greek Text,* p. 86, would keep the *sou* of D^c. F. G. K. L. etc. against S. A. D*. P. 33. 1739 etc. The term *stomachos* is not found elsewhere in the NT or in the LXX or the Ap. Frs. Spicq, "1 Tim 5:23," p. 146 n. 2, has remarked that the Hebrews were the one people in the ancient world, East or West, who for all practical purposes never wrote about or used metaphors concerning the stomach (cf. Harrison, *Paulines,* p. 133, for citations of *T. Naphtali* and Philo).

*your frequent bouts with illness.* Along with Timothy's stomach, the text notes his frequent illnesses. Though this is the only time that the PE use these terms, *asthenia* occurs on twenty-three other occasions in the NT: the cognate verb *asthenein* occurs of Trophimus in 2 Tim 4:20 (a passage that, like this one, probably goes back to the circle of the "historical Paul" of the mid-sixties; see commentary *in loc.* for LXX and Ap. Frs.), and thirty-two times in the rest of the NT. *Asthenēs* occurs twenty-five times in the NT but never in the PE. Only Rom 15:1 uses *asthenēma.* The terms basically refer to weakness (a-privative + *sthenein,* to have strength, power; cf. Latin *in-firmus;* Engl. *in-firmity*) and then specifically to the weakness brought on by illness or disease. The Lukan writings use the noun of physical illness only (Luke 5:15; 8:2; 13:11-12; Acts 28:9, all objects of miraculous healings; thus also the two uses in John 5:5 and 11:4; not in Mark; Matthew only in 8:17, citing Isa 53:4, though that text is applied to Jesus' healings). A similar usage characterizes the verb in Luke 4:40; Acts 9:37; 19:12; but not 20:35 (on the lips of Paul). Mark uses the verb once and Matthew three times of physical healing; John uses it eight times, especially of Lazarus.

Paul, on the other hand, uses the noun of moral and/or physical weakness in general (cf. Rom 6:19; 8:26; 1 Cor 15:43; 2 Cor 13:4) as well as illness (1 Cor 2:3 [?]; 2 Cor 11:30; 12:5, 9-10), and the verb similarly (cf. Rom 4:19; 8:3; 14:1-2 with 2 Cor 12:10; Phil 2:26-27). The PE remind one of Luke in their application of the terminology almost always to physical illness. Luke-Acts do the same in their four uses of the adjective *asthenēs.*

The illnesses of Timothy are here further qualified as *pyknas,* an adjective that only Luke employs otherwise in the NT (Luke 5:33, adverbially of the fasts of the Baptist's followers; Acts 24:26, of Paul's rather frequent audiences with Felix). The LXX uses this adjective at Ezek 31:3; 3 Macc 1:28; 4:10; 4 Macc 12:12 (cf. the adverbial *pyknoteron* at Esther 8:13; 2 Macc 8:8; 3 Macc 4:12; 7:3). In the Ap. Frs., Ign. *Eph.* 13.1 and *Pol.* 4.2 employ the term in the adverbial *pyknoteron,* as *2 Clem.* 17.3 also does (cf. *pyknōs* also at Ign. *Eph.* 13.1; *Did.* 16.2; Hermas, *Man.* 11.4). Only at 1 Tim 5:23 among these citations is this adjective applied to illnesses, though as Spicq, "1 Tim 5:23," pp. 146-147 n. 3, has observed, this is a common enough usage in medical literature.

24. *The sins of some people are obvious enough, escorting them to judgment. Prodēloi* occurs otherwise in the NT only at Heb 7:14 (of an "obvious" genealogical fact). (See also *ekdēlos* in 2 Tim 3:9.) The LXX uses the term only in Jth

8:29 (of her wisdom) and 2 Macc 3:17 (of the physical symptoms of interior distress) and 14:39 (of Nicanor making his hatred obvious by the force he sent to arrest Razis). The verb appears in 3 Macc 4:14 in the sense of "that previously described." Among the Ap. Frs. only *First Clement* uses the adjective, at 11.1; 12.7; 40.1; and (closest to 1 Tim 5:24) 51.3, where the author writes of the men who had opposed Moses, namely Korah, Dathan, Abiram, and On (Num 16), "and their condemnation *(to krima)* was made manifest *(prodēlon)*." That terminology is notably like the phrase in 1 Tim 5:24 that describes the "obvious sins" as "going before [the men just mentioned] to judgment," *proagousai eis krisin.* The participle is from *proagein,* 1 Tim 1:18 (see Notes, *in loc.*). Where in that passage the prophetic interventions (the acts of the Spirit) led the way to Timothy's "ordination," here the sins of a candidate for laying on of hands lead the way to a *krisis,* a judgment against those sins, a judgment that Timothy must make on earth (contra D-C: with Spicq, Dornier).

*Proagein* occurs as many as fourteen times in LXX, with six in the Maccabean corpus. Judith 10:22 offers a vivid parallel to the sense in 1 Tim 5:24 when, describing the meeting of Holofernes with Judith, one reads, "he came forward to the front of the tent, with silver lamps carried before *(proagousai)* him." Thus do good and evil deeds conduct men to judgment. The only occurrences in the Ap. Frs. are Ign. *Rom.* 9.3, where Ignatius speaks of the messengers of the churches who, on his journey to death, "went before me *(proēgon me)* from city to city"; and in Polycarp, *Phil.* 3.3, it is love of God and neighbor that goes before *(proagousēs)* and hope that follows (*epakolouthousēs;* note also in 1 Tim 5:24) the faith. D-C, p. 81, cites several other passages where this thought but not the actual terminology occurs (LXX Isa 58:8; *Barn.* 4.12).

*Krisis* occurs only here in the PE, and only once in all the rest of the Paulines, at 2 Thess 1:5, where persecutions and afflictions are "evidence *(endeigma)* of God's righteous judgment *(tēs dikaias kriseōs)*." Of the forty-five other NT uses of *krisis,* five are in Luke-Acts, where the noun refers not only to the final, divine judgment (Luke 10:14; 11:31-32) but also to the present "judgment and love of God" as well as to the human judgment passed on Jesus (Acts 8:33, citing LXX Isa 53:8).

25. *Similarly also.* On the connective phrase, this is the last of a half dozen occurrences of *hōsautōs* in the PE (see Titus 2:3, 6 and 1 Tim 2:9; 3:8, 11), and the only one with *kai* = also (cf. 1 Cor 11:25).

*and those that are not obvious cannot stay hidden always.* Lit. "and those that are otherwise cannot be hid *(kai ta allōs echonta krybēnai ou dynantai)*." The phrase is somewhat unusual. *Allōs* occurs only here in the NT, though there are nine occurrences in LXX, and, in the Ap. Frs., six in Hermas. The impersonal use of *ta . . . echonta* here, with the sense "it is" or "the situation is," can be paralleled in Acts 7:1; 12:15; 17:11; 24:9, and cf. 25, and apparently in other places in the NT according to Spicq (BAGD *s.v.*, p. 334; II.2 cites *1 Clem.* 14.2 and LXX Tob 7:11, but no other NT uses; note the uses with compounds of *echō* in BDF §308).

Forms of *dynamai* will occur five more times in the PE (1 Tim 6:7, 16; 2 Tim 2:13; 3:7, 15). There are 209 uses of the verb in the NT, with 26/21 = 47 in Luke-Acts. The remaining Paulines use the verb 32 times, though it is not documented in Colossians, Second Thessalonians, or Philemon.

Forms of *kryptein* occur nineteen times in the NT, but the use here in the PE is unique, and indeed the only other occurrence in the Paulines is in Col 3:3. Luke uses the verb three times in his Gospel (13:21; 18:34; 19:42). Matthew 5:14 uses the phrase here in the PE when he says *ou dynatai polis krybēnai* in exhorting the disciples to let their light shine before men "so that they can see your good works *(ta kala erga)* . . ." (Matt 5:16).

The verb *kryptein* occurs only in *First Clement* among the Ap. Frs.; 12.3 of Rahab hiding the spies (cf. LXX Josh 2:4, 6); 28.3 in a non-LXX form of Ps 139:7-8; and 56.10, citing LXX Job 5:21.

On *kryptos,* which does not occur in the PE, see especially Luke 8:17; 11:33; 12:2, all with the "revelation" theme of that which is hidden coming to light and public knowledge, as well as Rom 2:16; 1 Cor 4:5; 14:25 (cf. Ign. *Eph.* 15.3; *Phld.* 7.1; as well as Polycarp, *Phil.* 4.3, cited above on widows).

## ♦ COMMENT

With verse 17 a second church order begins abruptly, a presbyteral one that has some striking formal parallels with the previous one for widows; *ontōs chērai* of 5:3 corresponds with *kalōs proestōtes presbyteroi* here, the *tima* of that verse with the *diplēs timēs* here; the distinction between good and sinful *presbyteroi* corresponds to that between good and bad widows. This presbyteral order extends through verse 25 and the end of this chapter, as Meier, "*Presbyteros,*" pp. 325-337, has argued, against, e.g., D-C, and with Spicq. The steps in the positive (vv. 17-18) — negative (vv. 19-22 [23]) — negative (v. 24) — positive (v. 25) chiasmus, discerned by Meier (cf. p. 336), will be the grid upon which the following notes will be coordinated.

5:17. *The presbyters who have given outstanding direction deserve to get double pay, particularly those whose jobs are preaching and instruction.* The *presbyteroi* of this section are all but certainly not simply the older men of the community (contra Jeremias) any more than the "real widows" were simply women whose husbands had died. As Titus 1:7 (see also 1 Tim 3:1b-7) already indicated, the group or order of *presbyteroi* had terminological distinctions made concerning it, since at least one of those called *presbyteroi* was also entitled *episkopos* in the Jewish Christian congregations envisioned by that letter, and, if Meier is correct (pp. 337-339), everyone of the *presbyteroi* of the Cretan congregations could be called an *episkopos.* The terminological qualifications probably go back to the problems created by an undifferentiated earlier terminology's being picked up to designate the specific role and function of certain persons in and for the congregation. Because these functions were quite specific, the terminology became technical and tended to crowd out the earlier usage as well as to attract qualifying terms to differentiate the new use from the previous one (cf. Mohrmann, *Études* 1.116-119, on the way the terms for Christian office pass from Greek into Latin without change because the terms named persons who defined their meaning; also true of the sacramental acts).

Here in First Timothy the *presbyteroi* are not explicitly called *episkopoi,* though from the point of view of the outline of this letter, they do correspond with the church order on the *episkopos* in 1 Tim 3. Here the *presbyteroi* are specified by the participle *proestōtes,* i.e. those who have presided. If that is the basic distinction, then *presbyteroi*-presidents are being distinguished from the ranks of older men as such (as in 5:1 above). In a word, the technical term for officials is being distinguished from the generic designation for chronologically older men. Then *presbyteroi*-presidents are in turn distinguished in a sort of *cursus honorum:* those who simply preside, those who do a good job of it, and particularly those who preach and teach. Thus there are managers, good managers, and good ones who can explain why they do it (note that this distinction does not follow Bornkamm, *TDNT* 6.667, or Meier, "*Presbyteros,*" p. 326). Basically, however, a *presbyter* is here defined in terms of his *proïstanai,* and this in turn was precisely the term that 1 Tim 3:4-5 used to illustrate the relationship of the *episkopos* to the church (see Comment *ad loc.*).

The adverb *kalōs* here, which, as was noted at 1 Tim 3:4, is construed three of four times in this correspondence (and alone in the NT) with *proïstanai.* On the one other occasion (here of the deacons *kalōs diakonēsantes,* 1 Tim 3:13) it qualifies the "presiding" of certain *presbyteroi* as of visible and verifiable excellence and thus "outstanding." This need not mean that the other *presbyteroi* were necessarily the dubious/controversial ones to whom this church order next turns (v. 19). As we shall see, they were considered a small number in proportion to the whole order. The contrast is much more probable between those who devoted only part of their time to the tasks of leadership and those who devoted themselves full time to that ministry (Bornkamm, *TDNT* 6.666-667, is not quite so clear on this). Michaelis (*ut cit.* D-C, p. 78) has correctly observed that the church order of 1 Tim 3:4, 12 presumes that the church leaders have retained other jobs by which they support themselves. The point here is that some (and they are relatively few, one would surmise, because of the doubling of the honorarium) have obviously devoted all their time to this service and have done it well. All of these men, "particularly those whose jobs are preaching and instruction," "deserve to get *(axiouthōsan)* double pay." As in the other uses of *malista* in this correspondence (cf. Titus 1:10; 1 Tim 4:10; 5:8; 2 Tim 4:13), the term is not used in an exclusive or prejudicial sense.

Of the full-time *presbyteroi,* all of whom receive the same double stipend, some are regularly laboring (*kopiōntes;* note present tense) *en logōi kai didaskaliai.* This correspondence obviously puts a high premium on preaching and instruction, not to mention the study and reflection that those activities imply. It is conceivable that the congregation addressed did not fully share that conviction, or at least the fellow *presbyteroi*-presidents who spent full time in "administration" and questioned whether colleagues who studied and taught full time ought to be supported by the congregation.

Full-time presbyter-presidents, whether managers or manager-teachers, are all to be considered worthy of "double pay." At this point in the PE, the qualification of *timēs* as *diplēs* ("double") alerts the reader to a special sense for the "honor" being earned. This adjective occurs only here in the Paulines and only at Matt 23:15 (adverbial) and Rev 18:6 elsewhere in the NT. The latter passage refers to the eschatological double recompense meted out for the evil deeds *(erga)* of fallen Babylon. 1QpHab 7.15, Dupont-Sommer, *EWQ,* p. 263, has "twofold" judgment for the evil. The adjective is frequent enough in the LXX (as many as twenty-eight times); the passages that offer the most illuminating parallels to this are Gen 43:15 (*to argyrion diploun,* cf. 43:12, to buy food in Egypt) and perhaps Deut 21:17 on the firstborn receiving *dipla,* a double share of his father's estate. In the Ap. Frs. only Hermas employs the term, on four occasions, the closest parallel being in *Sim.* 2.8, which speaks of the vine bearing "double fruit" *(diploun ton karpon)* for itself and the elm tree that supports it (= the rich support the poor, who in turn pray for them).

18. *for the Scripture says, "You shall not tie shut the mouth of the ox that is threshing grain," and "The workman is deserving of his wage."* This verse makes it clear beyond a shadow of a doubt that the preceding "double honor" was indeed an honorarium. The ground for the previous directive *(gar)* is now stated in terms of *legei hē graphē,* "the Scripture says."

This formula "the Scripture says" occurs principally in the Paulines (Rom 4:3; 9:17; 10:11; 11:2; Gal 4:30) but also in James 2:23; 4:5 (where the identification of the "Scripture" is uncertain). In the Gospels the phrase can be documented only in John 19:37 (cf. 7:38, 42) and never in the Lukan corpus. According to Spicq, *EP,* p. 792 n. 3, the earliest use of *graphē* = Scripture is *Ep. Arist.* 155, 168; cf. *T. Zebulun* 9.5. Schrenk, *TDNT* 1.742-773, has noted the way in which single texts from the scriptural collection are designated by *graphē* as well as the collection as a whole (pp. 752-754), and particularly to the point here is his observation that the "personification" of Scripture implied in such verbs as *speaks, knew beforehand* (Gal 3:8), *consigned* (Gal 3:22; cf. Rom 11:32) presupposes that God *says* what the reader can see in the written text. The one God has transmitted his will and plan in Scripture, and the text, in each of its parts and as a whole, reveals that deeply consistent and unified will of God. Here the voice of Scripture joins the voice of the apostle and of the prophetic Spirit (1 Tim 2:7; 4:1) in giving authoritative direction to human judgment and action.

*"You shall not tie shut the mouth of the ox that is threshing grain."* It is not only the formula here that is Pauline but even the application of the text of Deut 25:4 to the problem of support for apostolic ministers. Paul appealed to the same text in his argument on the matter in 1 Cor 9:9, where *kēmōseis* ("muzzle") B*. D*. F. G. (cf. Philo on Deut 25:4 cited in Brooke-McLean, LXX *in loc.*) replaces the LXX *phimōseis* ("tie shut"). MM *s.v.*, p. 672, note that this term was subliterary and perhaps even considered a vulgar term for nagging persons or animals. A. T. Hanson, *SPTT*, p. 162, suggests that the difference between the verbs was that *kimoun* was more technical and specific ("to muzzle" an animal) and *phimoun* was more generic. The citation here in First Timothy reproduces every word of the LXX but changes the order from verb-object to object-verb (i.e. to a less Semitic pattern?). The scribes of A C P I 33 pl brought the word order into conformity with the LXX (J. K. Elliott, *Greek Text*, pp. 81-82).

The term *bous* occurs in Paul only when this passage is cited. The only other NT uses are peculiar to Luke 13:15; 14:5, 19 (all relating to the care for these animals); and John 2:14-15 (sacrificial offerings; cf. *Did.* 13.3, the only use in the Ap. Frs.). The verb *aloaō*, meaning threshing by trampling over the sheaves of grain spread on the threshing floor, occurs in the NT only in these two Pauline passages (note the way it is taken up in the Pauline argument in 1 Cor 9:10) and never in the Ap. Frs. Finally, the verb *phimoō* occurs in the Paulines only in this passage of the PE, and, in its other NT occurrences (six times, including Luke 4:35), refers to silencing men, demons, and once the stormy sea (Mark 4:39). Again, it is not documented in the Ap. Frs.

A. T. Hanson, *SPTT*, pp. 163-165, has assembled rabbinic and Philonic texts that illustrate the way in which inferences were made to other spheres of human conduct from this provision for the humane treatment of animals (cf. esp. Philo, *Virt.* 145-146). The text here would immediately suggest the gifts of food for nourishment in return for the work expended in leading worship, managing charities, and giving instruction. The Pauline interpretation of the OT, even to its application to apostolic ministers, is here taken for granted as needing no further explanation or proof. With Hanson (p. 165) there is no need to assume that the text of First Corinthians was before the eyes of the man who wrote this passage in the PE. Yet the coincidence with the Pauline teaching is so striking that one can assume that the writer knew of the way in which Paul actually argued on this point, even to the OT *locus* that he referred to (though not to the *text*) as well as Jesus' teaching (cf. *infra* on 1 Cor 9:14).

*"The workman is deserving of his wage."* A second citation is joined to that from Deuteronomy by *kai,* and with no differentiation it is apparently to be read as *hē graphē.* However, the actual quotation appears nowhere in the LXX nor does it translate any passage of the Hebrew Bible. Deuteronomy 24:14-15 illustrates how Hebrew expressed the divine will that a hired man receive his wages; the language is not that of 1 Tim 5:18. The quotation in First Timothy could come from some book, now lost, that was received as Scripture and was on a par with the collection that we call the OT (cf. Preisker, *TDNT* 4.698 n. 5). In that case, as in James 4:5, the formula "the Scripture says . . ." designates a document that eventually was not included by the rest of the churches in the collection that was to be read out as the word of God.

However, a further possibility must be reckoned with, for the quotation appears word for word (but without *gar* in First Timothy) on the lips of Jesus in Luke 10:7 (*axios gar ho ergatēs tou misthou* [Matthew, *tēs trophēs*] *autou; SFC* §177, Q). A collection of Jesus' sayings addressed to those who were being sent out in his name is being cited. Paul seems to allude to it in 1 Cor 9:14: "The Lord commanded that those who proclaim the gospel should get their living *(zēn)* by the gospel" (see Conzelmann, *1 Cor.,* p. 157; that Paul might have known this as an isolated saying, cf. Tuckett, "Paul," pp. 376-381). This saying has a proverbial ring (cf. Harvey, "The Workman," p. 209) and may have been taken up from the lost source just mentioned. Yet the wording of the Matthean form, with its mention of food, is more earthy and Semitic than the Lukan "wage" *(misthou).* Indeed, Matthew's predilection for *misthos* (ten times vs. one time in Mark, four times in Luke-Acts, one time in John [4:36, also on apostolic ministry]) would lead one to suspect that he has preserved the original Greek wording of the saying, since it is difficult to imagine his changing *misthos* to *trophē.* In that case, the Lukan form of the saying, with *misthos,* would represent Luke's adapting the language to a Greek-speaking world (note Spicq's [*EP,* p. 543] citations of Euripides, *Rhesus* 161-162; *oukoun ponein men chrē, ponounta d'axion misthon pheresthai,* as well as the lyricist Phocylides, *misthon mochthēsanti didou,* "Give pay to the toil-worn," frag. 17), and see J. K. Elliott, *Greek Text,* pp. 82-83, for the texual tradition (S* had *trophēs* here).

Of course, it is possible that both Luke and the author of the PE took the quotation from the same lost source or that the PE took it from the Third Gospel or vice versa. On the hypothesis offered by this commentary, the author of the Third Gospel took up and adopted the logion from a Greek collection of sayings of Jesus on those who were to carry on *his* work, and then repeated the same saying when he composed and redacted the section of the PE on the presbyteral ministry. One would infer, in that case, that the collection of Jesus' sayings was, in Luke's mind, on a par with the Scripture of Israel, and that Paul's interpretation of those Scriptures was consistent with the teaching of Jesus (whatever the ultimate origin of the saying, whether Jesus quoted it or created it). See *2 Clem.* 2.4 for a similar joining of a saying of Jesus to an OT citation, as *hetera de graphē* (Donfried, *Setting,* pp. 56-60, 79-81). The repetition of the saying here may, on our hypothesis, have been needed because of the way in which Paul's own ministry to the Ephesians is recalled with its explicit invocation of an otherwise unrecorded saying (Acts 20:35) that justifies Paul's having taken no support from believers in Ephesus. Since the speech is conceived as being delivered to the (presbyter-) bishops of Ephesus, this later, forceful argument for the support of full-time presiding *presbyteroi* becomes the more necessary, since Paul's foregoing a stipend would be cited as a precedent of his own will for the ministry in general. Cf. the "farewell" of Acts 20 with the evidence in PE of a further visit.

19. *Do not give a hearing, Timothy, to a charge against a presbyter, unless the evidence comes from two or three witnesses.* With this verse the presbyteral order turns from the good and even excellent *presbyteroi* of the preceding directives to one who, in contrast, is not among the *kalōs proestōtes.* The development of the order by means of contrasts has already been noted in the preceding one on widows, but in this one the particle *de* scarcely figures at all (only in 5:24). Here the principle for receiving charges against an erring presbyter is stated. One notes here not only the unique use of *kata* with the genitive in the PE (common enough in the rest of the Paulines as well as Luke-Acts) but also the use of *presbyteros* in the singular. The presiding presbyters, including the *kalōs proestōtes,* are noted in the plural, the backslider in the singular, already implying that this was the exceptional case (note the similar use of the singular in Titus 2:8; the convention is as old as the Hebrew of the blessing of Abraham in Gen 12:3). Moreover, Timothy is commanded by Paul to take the role of judge in the case of denunciation. The negative form of the directive is instructive: Timothy is as a rule not to entertain an accusation against a presbyter.

In Titus 1:6 the term *katēgoria,* "charge or accusation," occurs in the context of the virtues prerequisite not only in the *presbyteroi* but also in their children. The latter are not to be subject to any charge of public profligacy. The inference in Titus 1:6 is that one who has taught his own children in the faith is thus capable of teaching it to another household, the church, but the intemperance of children in matters of sex and food and drink, when public, contradicts the faith professed by the family. In First Timothy, of course, at this point the presbyteral order is concerned not about prerequisites but about conduct that could even disqualify a presbyter already in office from continuing to preside. Thus the charge or accusation must be against him personally, for his own conduct, not that of his children. The precise character of the misconduct is not specified here, though it is fair to infer from the ethical lists that concern candidates for presbyteral-episcopal ministry in Titus 1:6-9 as well as 1 Tim 3:2-7 that a rather wide spectrum of public acts was subject to review.

As Büchsel, *TDNT* 3.636-637, has noted, the NT usage of *katēgor-* terminology has, by and large, a formally judicial connotation and a legal sense, referring to the persons, the process, the content of delation and accusation. The Roman Empire from the first Christian century was a hotbed for intrigue and delation, with their attendant ills, and the first Christians were to become a prime target. One has only to recall Tacitus on Nero (*Annales* 15.44.6) or Pliny's correspondence with Trajan (*Epis.* 10.96.5-6). Needless to say, Jesus had himself been trapped in the same web of betrayal and delation (cf. Luke 6:16; Acts 1:16; 7:52). There was no lack of disgust and protest (Spicq, *EP,* p. 142 n. 2).

The Christians were by no means immune themselves from the malaise; precisely because the possibilities for delinquency in ministry were many and the office tended to throw even the lesser shortcomings of its incumbents into high relief, only an accusation brought by two or three witnesses is even to be given a hearing. With this provision for evidence one encounters a principle of Jewish law, for even the terminology here (almost legalistic in its redundancy, cf. Moule, *Idiom,* p. 83) is basically that of LXX Deut 19:15 (cf. 17:6 and Num 35:30) on the witnesses requisite for legally establishing a crime or wrongdoing, particularly on a capital charge. That provision and the mentality that it created have left their traces on many strata of the NT (cf. 2 Cor 13:1; Heb 10:28; Matt 18:16; John 8:17), and not least on the way in which the apostolic ministers themselves bore witness in twos and threes. If the Christian presbyteral institution was radically (in the historian's sense) a Jewish institution, then it is appropriate that legal procedures related to it be those of the Jewish tradition. That such procedures had to be explicitly spelled out and "proved from Scripture," so to speak (since an explicit formula is lacking and the text is not a word-for-word citation of Deuteronomy), may be an indication that the congregation from which these provisions originated or to which they were directed (or both) was not accustomed to such a legal procedure. Rome would qualify above all, but Ephesus would not lack credibility by any means. Still it must be remembered that it was only in Palestinian Judaism that the Deuteronomic directive was systematically implemented (cf. the witnesses at Jesus' trial), and then as a reaction, in Maccabean times, against the incursions of Hellenistic legal influence. Paul, in other words, reflects a typically Palestinian rabbi's point of view when he cites this passage at 2 Cor 13:1; and even the Gospel's memory of the way in which Jesus grouped his emissaries indicates that a Palestinian custom was being employed that was by no means taken for granted in the Mediterranean world, even in Alexandria (see Vliet, *Testimony,* pp. 41, 63).

The use of pairs and trios in this correspondence (thus Paul and Titus; Paul and Timothy; Zenas and Apollos, Titus 3:13; Hymenaeus and Alexander, 1 Tim 1:20; Phygelos and Hermogenes, 2 Tim 1:15; Hymenaeus and Philetus, 2 Tim 2:17; Jannes and Jambres, 2 Tim 3:8) reminds one that this pairing of witnesses was a particular concern of Luke-Acts and perhaps linked with that *asphaleia,* "full truth," which the whole composition was to give (Luke 1:4). For a presentation of this theme, see Morgenthaler, *Die lukanische Geschichtsschreibung;* cf. Vliet, *Testimony,* pp. 96-97 n. 19, which notes some of the criticisms of this work. In the light of our hypothesis, it is interesting to see this same pattern of grouped witnesses (true and false) appearing in the PE.

20. *Those who are sinning you are to refute while all the presbyters look on, to put fear of wrongdoing into the rest of them.* With this verse one moves from the singular *(presbyteros)* of the preceding to the plural, and from the one against whom a charge is lodged to those *presbyteroi* who are actually continuing in proved wrongdoing, *tous hamartanontas.* For forty years and more Galtier maintained that at this point the author of these letters turned to sinners in general (see Meier, "*Presbyteros,*" p. 330 n. 22, for literature; see also Fuller, "Elders"). As Galtier noted, Chrysostom and Origen already took this "generic" line of interpretation (see also Cyprian, *Testim.* III, 76-77; Fahey, *Cyprian and the Bible,* p. 509). Yet it must be admitted that the present participle here is not so easily taken as the generic substantival *hamartōlos* (cf. 1 Tim 1:9, 15). Since the whole preceding context is concerned with *presbyteroi* who are qualified by participial constructions *(proestōtes; kopiōntes),* the overall parallelism outweighs the fact that the *presbyteros* closest to this participle is in the singular.

Indeed, such abrupt shifts from singular to plural are rather characteristic of the PE and their sources not only in this chapter (5:13-16) but also in 2:9-15. Meier (pp. 331-332) has also pointed out that a section on sinners in general would be quite out of context at this point, a context that is describing Timothy's relation with various believers who have been classified according to sex, age, and ministry. When sin and virtue have been considered, this has been done precisely with an eye to the function that the person ought to exercise in the church (cf. 5:5-15 on the "real widows").

The one other use of *hamartanei* in this correspondence, at Titus 3:11, also in the present tense, reminds one that there a procedure was laid down for Titus to follow in dealing with the refractory. The verb here may imply that the procedure of repeated admonition of Titus 3:10 is presumed to have taken place after the verification of the charge by two or three witnesses. With the ordinary troublemaker, that procedure concluded with Titus's being instructed to avoid the man. Here, apparently because of the public responsibility of the presbyter, those who persist in wrongdoing are to receive a public refutation from Timothy. The verb *elegchein* was used in Titus 1:9 of the negative aspect of the teaching ministry of the (presbyter-) bishop, and again in Titus 1:13 and 2:15 of the way in which Titus himself was to deal with Judaizers and any who opposed the Pauline teaching.

These previous uses as well as the final occurrence in 2 Tim 4:2 lead one to infer that a refutation of a false teaching was involved in disowning the sin of delinquent presbyters. In other words, they refused to accept the correction offered and went on to justify the activity that had provoked the charge in the first place. Such rationalization must receive public refutation "in the presence of all."

In all the occurrences of *enōpion pantōn* (see Notes above), the phrase suggests a solemn and publicly witnessed statement, authoritative and legally binding, before God and his court as well as before men and theirs. How far does *pantōn* extend? Certainly to *all* the presbyters (not just the delinquent ones), who would thus correspond to the *pollōn martyrōn* of 6:12 below. The following *hina* clause appears to corroborate this fact with its use of *hoi loipoi* (see *infra*). But *pantōn* could be interpreted of the whole congregation and thus of more than just the presbyteral order within it. It could also extend to all people, whether believers or not (cf., e.g., 1 Tim 2:1, 6; 2 Tim 2:24; 3:9). Indeed, usually in the PE various qualifications make it quite clear when *pantes* refers to all believers (cf. Titus 3:15; 2 Tim 2:19, 22) as distinct from all mankind. Perhaps in that light one ought not to extend *pantes* here in 1 Tim 5:20 beyond the *presbyteroi,* innocent as well as delinquent, who are surely being spoken of in this context. In that case the correction/refutation is publicly given to the assembled presbyteral order so that its innocent members will be equipped to neutralize the bad example/teaching of their erring fellow presbyters. Still that is not the reason or purpose explicitly proposed by the text, which states that the correction is given in the presence of all, literally "that the rest *(hoi loipoi)* also *(kai)* may have fear." Here the reference is almost certainly to "the rest of the presbyters," i.e. the innocent as distinct from (note the *kai* = also) those who persist in public sin (D-C, p. 50; Spicq, *EP,* p. 545). One cannot exclude, of course, that the reference is to all the other believers in the community (thus Balz, *TDNT* 9.216, and D-C, p. 78 n. 22), but that seems less likely in the light of the preceding observations. The public refutation is seen as producing fear *(phobon echōsin)* in the innocent as well as the guilty (cf. Rev 11:13; *hoi loipoi* [of those who underwent the earthquake] *emphoboi egenonto*).

The motivation adduced here is Pauline enough, as not only Rom 13:1-7 makes clear (cf. Balz, *TDNT* 9.214-215), but especially 2 Cor 7:11-15 with its description of the (useful) fear that Paul's letter and his emissary, Titus, generated in the Corinthian church. Here again in the PE the Pauline emissary, backed by this epistolary guidance, is to correct in such a way that it elicits reverent obedience.

21. *As God [the Father] and Christ Jesus and the elect angels look on, I adjure you, Timothy, to keep these directives without prejudice, that is, not doing anything out of partisanship.* This verse marks a climax in solemn, emphatic expostulation as the apostle is conceived as laying a most serious charge upon Timothy in his task as judge. In that capacity Timothy would be receiving the oath-authenticated testimony of men telling the truth before God himself. Now abruptly the tables are turned and the judge is told to remember that he is simultaneously being judged. His earthly court is under the judgment of a higher court. The solemnity and authenticity of the charge here are emphasized by the threefold witnessing to the Pauline admonition (cf. 1 Tim 2:3; 5:4; 2 Tim 2:14 with God alone; 1 Tim 6:13; 2 Tim 4:1 with God and Christ). The previous mention of "two or three witnesses" also links up with tripartite division here.

Here one encounters not an archaic hymnic fragment but an edited section of a presbyteral order, and lest there be any confusion, the *aggeloi* are now qualified as *ekletoi.* The latter term used nominally has designated, in Titus 1:1 and 2 Tim 2:10, Christian believers; here it qualifies *aggeloi* as another group that God has chosen. The nominal use is by far the commonest in the NT (cf., e.g., Luke 18:7; 23:35 [of the Messiah]). The use with "angels" is not otherwise documented in the NT, the Ap. Frs., or the LXX (though Tob 8:15 A, B has "all your angels and your chosen ones" in parallel), but *Odes of Solomon* 4.8 does write of "the elect archangels" clad with the divine seal (or "sign"; see Charlesworth, *OT Pseud.* 2.736), and Henoch 39:1 (Charles, *AP* 2.210, not extant in Greek, but cf. 6:2; 61:10; etc., in Schrenk, *TDNT* 4.185 [cf. 190]) speaks of God's "elect and holy children" who unite with "the children of men." 1QM 12.5 speaks of "the elect of heaven" *(bḥyry šmym)* in a broken text, where the context could lead one to infer that celestial beings are thus designated (cf. Yadin, *War,* pp. 314-315; Fitzmyer, *ESBNT,* p. 155) but where it is also quite possible that the reference is to the former members of the earthly community who have joined the heavenly court and are numbered with the spirits (Yadin, *War,* pp. 240-242). The usage in any case is in the Jewish and even the Palestinian tradition and apparently (cf. the Enoch passage) distinguishes the "elect" spirits from the reprobate. It is such "good angels" that are associated with the appearance of the Son of Man as judge, and it is striking in this connection to note that Luke speaks of the glory of the Son of Man, of the Father, and of the holy *(hagiōn)* angels, thus articulating the Markan "when he comes in the glory of his Father with the holy angels" (Mark 8:38; *SFG* §160) into three distinct elements that remind one of the tripartite formulation here in the PE. Luke 12:9 (cf. 8) and 15:10 have *enōpion* governing *aggelōn,* a usage that is otherwise documented in the NT only at Rev 3:5 (where again the triad of the PE is illustrated, for it is Christ who says, "I will confess his name before my Father and before his angels [*enōpion tōn aggelōn*]") and 14:10, "in the presence of the holy angels and in the presence of the Lamb."

From every point of view the phrase has an eschatological tone and even apocalyptic content. The genius of its use here is that it brings the final judgment into the day-to-day life and judgments of the church, subjecting the latter to the former without a qualm, even though an apostolic co-worker exercises that earthly judgment.

The charge has as its purpose *hina tauta phylaxēis,* "to keep these directives" (note the *hina* clause in the previous verse). It is qualified first adverbially by *chōris prokrimatos,* "without prejudice," and then with an adjectival clause referring to the subject of the verb, Timothy himself, *mēden poiōn kata prosklisin,* "not doing anything out of partisanship," where the last phrase again modifies adverbially the particle *poiōn.* The adverbial phrases are parallel for a reason that will be noted below. The antecedent to "these directives," literally "things *(tauta),*" seems to be the directives of the preceding verses, 17-20 (cf. B. Weiss, *ut cit.* Bertram, *TDNT* 9.241 n. 27), for the repeated *enōpion* certainly links this verse with verse 20, as the triad of heavenly witnesses links with verse 19. The emphatic return to the first person singular implies that all the preceding directives on the presbyteral ministry are to be received and acted on as authentic Pauline teaching (cf. R. F. Collins, "Image of Paul," pp. 162-163), not just verses 19-20 on delinquent presbyters. Indeed, it is precisely 5:18 that is indisputably Pauline teaching.

D-C, following Galtier, proposes a complete change of subject in 5:22 and understands verse 21 as a transition into that subject and refers one to his comments on 1 Tim 4:6 (p. 68). The commentary here has taken its lead from Collins, pp. 157-158, however, and understands *tauta* in the summary function that it typically has in the PE.

The sense of *tauta phylakēis* here is best inferred from the usage at 6:20 below, as well as 2 Tim 1:12, 14, for in all of these cases it has as its object *parathēkē,* "the deposit," and that is precisely what is at stake here in *tauta,* the Pauline "deposit" of teaching and guidance that is to be watched and defended. On the meaning in 2 Tim 4:15 see commentary *in loc.,* and note also Acts 21:25. Ignatius knows only this sense; see his *Eph.* 7.1; *Trall.* 2.3 and 7.1.

In the LXX, particularly in the Torah, *phylassein* designates the way in which one is to be on the alert to respond to the covenant laws and the exhortations of God's spokesmen. That meaning was current in the Qumran community (Bertram, *TDNT* 9.238) and passed into the Gospel tradition (Mark 10:20 = Luke 18:21 = Matt 19:20) and the Pauline letters (Rom 2:26; Gal 6:13). The Lukan usage is particularly instructive, for it includes not only keeping the Law (Acts 7:53; 21:24) and its commandments (Luke 18:21; note that *tauta* is the pronominal object with the previously quoted commandments as antecedent), even Gentile converts "keeping" prescriptions of the Torah (Acts 16:4 and cf. 21:25, qualifying Bertram, *TDNT* 9.240), but also extends to "hearing the word of God *(ton logon tou theou)* and keeping it *(phylassontes).*" Thus, one observes or keeps not only the Law (or the Scriptures) but also that good news which is *kata tas graphas* and which has been announced and transmitted by Jesus (Luke 5:1; 8:21), the Twelve (Acts 6:2; cf. 11:1), and those who shared their ministry (Acts 8:4, 14), including Paul and Barnabas (Acts 13:5, 7, etc.). Indeed, the church itself becomes, to the mind of Luke, *ho logos tou theou,* in its visible growth and transmission of revelation (see Haenchen, *Acts,* p. 568). Moreover, the directives of church leadership and/or of the leading church can summon even Gentiles to *observe* some commandments that were meant only for Jews (Acts 16:4, *phylassein ta dogmata*).

The usage here in the PE is quite consistent with this Lukan pattern, for Timothy is being told to "observe" not only the OT prescription but also the Pauline interpretation of it and the further Pauline instruction on the management of the *presbyteroi.*

Timothy's observance of the Pauline directives is then qualified as *chōris prokrimatos* ("without prejudice"). The preposition occurred only once in the PE, at 1 Tim 2:8, in a phrase that belonged to a source. One is inclined to offer a similar observation here in the light of what will be noted about *prokrimatos.* Luke uses the particle only in Luke 6:49, whereas the Paulines employ the term fourteen times (NT total forty-one). *Prokrima* is a noun otherwise undocumented in the NT, the LXX, or the Ap. Frs. P. Flor. 1.68 (from 172 C.E.) is the first witness to its use anywhere outside of the PE (MM *s.v.,* p. 542), to which Spicq adds P. Hermop. 18.15. The phrase is a legal formula, translating the Latin *absque praejudicio* (Aulus Gellius, cited by Simpson, *Pastoral Epistles,* p. 79). It may be suggested that the original Roman presbyteral church order used this phrase in some connection in its directives and that it here bobs to the surface in this Lukan redaction of how he thought Paul would have expressed this injunction for the man who must judge *presbyteroi.* Perhaps the fact that the Roman church used the phrase was for the redactor of this correspondence practically equivalent to saying Paul used the phrase. The redactor himself recognizes its obscurity, for the participial phrase following really explains its meaning. Though BAGD *s.v.,* p. 708, says second century B.C.E. for IG V [I] 21 II, 7, this seems unknown to Spicq and to Büchsel, *TDNT* 3.953. Harrison, *Paulines,* p. 133, has correctly "Sparta II cent. CE." With Büchsel one must agree that the technical legal sense of a prior decision that has to serve as a norm for a later one is not to be pressed here. Rather, the phrase is to be understood ethically of "a preconceived opinion in favor of the accused or accuser" that would hinder the administration of justice. The concern (but not the terminology) is quite at home in the Jewish tradition, as Spicq, *EP,* p. 546, has noted, citing Sir 11:7; 19:13-17.

The participial phrase that follows rewords the preceding in a negative form, describing now Timothy as subject *mēden poiōn* (cf. the *touto gar poiōn,* also of Timothy, at 4:16) *kata prosklisin.* The final phrase, though found only here in the NT, is somewhat better documented, for a single LXX use of the noun occurs of preferring athletics to worship in 2 Macc 4:14 (*s.v.l.;* cf. the unique LXX use of the verb at 14:24 of the close attachment of a friendship). The *Ep. Arist.* 5 (Charles, *AP* 2.94) may use the noun (see BAGD *s.v.*). Among the Ap. Frs. only *First Clement* uses the term, but on four occasions: One is in *1 Clem.* 21.7 of women bestowing their care and concern *mē kata proskliseis,* "not by factious preferences but in holiness." In *1 Clem.* 47.3-4, referring to Paul's First Corinthians, the author writes: "With true inspiration he charged you concerning himself and Cephas and Apollos, because even then you made *(pepoiēsthai)* yourselves partisans *(proskliseis).* But that partisanship *(hē prosklisis)* entailed less guilt for you, for you were partisans (*proseklithēte* [the only use of the verb in the Ap. Frs.]) of apostles . . . and of a man approved by them." The final example is *1 Clem.* 50.2, where the author speaks of *agapē* (as in 21.7) "without human partisanship," *dicha proskliseōs anthrōpinēs.* The sense in all of these passages in LXX, NT, and the Ap. Frs. is unfavorable (with BAGD; contra D-C, who thinks the last example is "neutral"). The one NT use of the verb is in Acts 5:36 of the partisans who rallied around the revolutionary Theudas.

MM cite no inscriptional or papyrus materials for the noun *prosklisis,* but LSJ *s.v.,* p. 1517, note its uses not only of the physical actions of leaning or genuflecting but also of an inclination or predilection (Polybius 5.51.8; 6.10.10). Note also the definition of *hairesis* as *prosklisis dogmatōn* cited in v. Arnim, *Stoicorum Veterum Fragmenta,* vol. 2, p. 37.

22. *Be in no hurry, Timothy, to impose hands on anyone. Incur no responsibility for the sins of others.* From the dispositions with which Timothy should dispense justice to the *presbyteroi,* the text turns to that ounce of prevention which can forestall the embarrassment of public correction: *cheiras tacheōs mēdeni epitithei,* "Be in no hurry to impose hands on anyone." Whatever the imposition of hands may refer to, the action is not one to be readily bestowed. A certain responsible deliberation is presupposed for it.

But what precisely does the imposition of hands refer to here? The verbal form of the phrase, as distinguished from the nominal *epithesis tōn cheirōn* of 1 Tim 4:14, may indicate that the gesture, ambivalent in itself, refers to something other than the designation for and constituting of an apostolic ministry. On the other hand, if there is a difference at all, it may be between Timothy's receiving his share in the apostolic ministry through the intervention of Paul himself whereas the *presbyteroi* under discussion here are to be "ordained" by Timothy (see Quinn, "Ordination," p. 366).

In any event, as Coppens, "L'Imposition," has noted, the gesture here has been associated not only with ordination but also with confirmation (Ehrhardt, *Framework,* p. 147), with healing, and with penance (Coppens *ap.* Meier, "*Presbyteros,*" p. 333), not to mention baptism (Tertullian, *De baptismo*). The second last named seems to be the only serious competition against ordination, and Galtier, "La réconciliation," long argued that the reference is in fact to a rite of penitential and sacramental reconciliation. D-C inclines to follow that interpretation (along with Lock, Falconer, Easton, Boudou). In accessing this interpretation one ought to review the following data. From the point of view of external evidence, the earliest surviving Christian "exegesis" of this text, Tertullian, *De pudicitia* 18.9; CC Ser. lat. II, 1318; *PL* 2.1017, interprets the imposition of hands in the contemporary rite of reconciliation in North Africa in terms of this text (cf. a generation later, Cyprian, *Epistula* 74.12, and the description of the controversy in Eusebius, *Church History* 7.2, who notes that "A custom, which was at any rate old, having prevailed in such cases [of reconciling penitent apostates and heretics] to use only prayer [*tēi . . . euchēi*] with the laying on of hands [*dia cheirōn epitheseōs*]"). It is notable that, for all Cyprian's allusions to avoiding association with sinners (*Epistula* 67.9; 73.19; *Lapsis* 34), he never actually cites 1 Tim 5:22 (see Fahey, *Cyprian and the Bible,* p. 509, as well as the index, p. 694); neither does Eusebius nor *Const. Apost.* 2.18.7; F. X. Funk, *Constitutiones,* p. 67 (according to the index, this verse, however, is never cited in *Constitutiones*). It looks as if there are two questions: one, the association of the rite of reconciliation with an imposition of hands; the other, the association of this mode of effecting reconciliation with the actual text of 1 Tim 5:22. The former is witnessed to from 200 C.E. on. That Tertullian witnessed to the latter is indisputable. Whether he meant it to be exegesis is debatable. Whether it represented the exegesis of the North African church, much less the Catholicum, is even more doubtful since in fact this text was not actually taken up in this sense when later authors spoke of an imposition of hands in reconciliation. Tertullian's "exegesis" is "eisegesis" (not least in his Montanist discontent) and actually little more than describing a current practice with a verbally appropriate sacred text. His understanding here is no more or less convincing than his citations of this same verse in the context of his discussion of baptism (see below).

Do the internal data of the text vindicate the penitential interpretation? Galtier appeals to the use of *mēde koinōnei hamartiais allotriais* that follows immediately upon the previous admonition against hasty laying on of hands and is coordinated with it by *mēde* (Ambroggi, *Le Epistole Pastorali,* p. 163, who observes that it is not to be taken as final, *hina,* or consecutive, *hōste*). He maintains that the verb normally refers to a participation in a reality already present, and the present tense of the verb here stresses that. He then further maintains that "the sins of others" are not the future sins of hastily promoted presbyters but the present sins of penitents who are not hurriedly to be reconciled. Even if, with Lock, one combines penitent and presbyter, the reference of the whole verse is to the reconciliation, not the ordination, of that presbyter (cf. also Meier, "*Presbyteros*," p. 334).

Does the language of 1 Tim 5:22b bear the weight that Galtier puts on it? This is the only use of *koinōnein,* "incur responsibility for/share in," in the PE. The cognates only occur in this correspondence when Titus 1:4 speaks of "the faith all share" *(koinēn)* and 1 Tim 6:18, of rich people being *koinōnikous* ("munificent" in the sense of ready to share their goods: see commentary *in loc.,* and see the only use of *koinōnein* in the Ap. Frs., *Barn.* 19.8). The reality of faith is one shared in at the present moment; in the second instance the rich are to be *(einai)* here and now ready to share their wealth. The Gospels and the Lukan corpus do not use *koinōnein* (but note there are uses of *koinos, koinoō, koinōnia*). There are four other instances in the Pauline corpus (Rom 12:13; 15:27; Gal 6:6; Phil 4:15) and one in Heb 2:14. The two remaining NT occurrences are also the most helpful for understanding the usage in First Timothy. First Peter 4:13 can say, ". . . you share *(koinōneite)* Christ's sufferings," evidently asserting that the past sufferings of the Lord are participated in by those undergoing present persecution. Second John 11 declares, ". . . he who greets him [who teaches false doctrine] shares his wicked work *(koinōnei tois ergois autou tois ponērois)*." Here, too, a present act brings one into communion with the past (evil) deeds and teaching of another. Galtier is quite correct, accordingly, in stressing that the *koinōnein* here in First Timothy refers not to future sins but to past and present evil acts.

This is the first of 3 occurrences of *hamartiai,* "sins" (all pl.), in these letters (compared with 170 in the rest of the NT). The second is at 5:24 below, and it seems to take up again the thought of this verse. The last is at 2 Tim 3:6. When one notes the 45 other occurrences in the Paulines (but not in Second Thessalonians, Colossians, Philemon!) against the 19 in Luke-Acts, one senses again that the terminological preferences of the PE are with the former. This noun in the PE, as otherwise in the NT, particularly when in the plural (as it also is in Luke-Acts, except at Acts 7:60), designates particular sinful actions rather than the state of sin or guilt as such. The text here is accordingly warning Timothy off from participation in the sins of others and a certain solidarity in evil that would follow upon a hasty imposition of hands.

The *others (allotrias)* are not further specified at this point. Again this is the only use of this word in the PE (thirteen in the rest of the NT). Of the four other Pauline uses, 2 Cor 10:15-16, with its *en allotriois kopois,* is quite parallel with the usage here. In the Lukan corpus there are occurrences at Luke 16:12 as well as Acts 7:6 (note LXX Gen 15:13 here has *idiai*). The adjective can have the connotations of the English "alien" or "foreign" ("entangling foreign alliances"), and thus the sense here suggested is that the sins are not simply those of others but are quite uncharacteristic of and alien to Timothy.

The whole phrase, "Incur no responsibility for the sins of others," certainly refers primarily to past and present evil acts rather than to future sins. In conjunction with the preceding phrase on the hasty *(tacheōs)* imposition of hands, the admonition leads one to infer that a careful examination of the previous life of the one receiving the ritual gesture is presupposed (cf. on vv. 24-25 below; Meier, "*Presbyteros*," pp. 333-335; Ambroggi, *Le Epistole Pastorali*, p. 163).

Thus, linguistically, the imposition of hands is not defined by the succeeding phrase as a gesture effecting reconciliation (that is not to be given too readily), but it could just as well refer to a hasty ordination making one into an (involuntary but real) participant in the sinful acts that still cling to the candidates. Evil acts, in this correspondence, could be acts of bad teaching as well as other evil human deeds (cf. 2 John 11). But that takes one back to the context in order to settle the question, To what does the laying on of hands refer? Galtier proposes to make the context speak of the reconciliation process by positing a change of subject in verse 20, from the sinful presbyter of verse 19 to sinners in general in verse 20. Yet, as was noted above, *hamartanontas* in that verse is not a synonym for *hamartōloi*, and one can make quite as good a case if not a better one for this whole section's (17-25) referring to *presbyteroi* (Meier, "*Presbyteros*," pp. 335-336). In that case the contextual argument tells in favor of referring the imposition of hands to presbyteral ordination. Thus, even though Chrysostom and Origen did take verse 20 as referring to sinners in general, neither they nor any other Greek Father took verse 22 as referring to anything other than ordination (Spicq, *EP*, p. 547).

In fact, even the evidence from Tertullian deserves a review in the light of the one other passage in which he cites 1 Tim 5:22, and that is in his Catholic work *De baptismo* 18.1, where he is speaking about the discretion that should be exercised in bestowing that sacrament, a discretion that he authorizes not only in terms of the pearls to pigs in Matt 7:6 but also with a quotation from an archaic Latin translation of 1 Tim 5:22, "*Manus ne facile inposueritis nec amartiis alienis communicaveritis*" (see Kilpatrick, "1 Tim 5:22," pp. 127-128). The manner in which the passage is cited is recognizably parallel to the way of citing Scripture in *De pudicitia* 18.9 (where a different translation is used). Yet here the laying on of hands is associated with the baptismal rite (cf. *De baptismo* 8.1-2; CC, p. 283). But in that case Tertullian saw two quite different meanings in the same text, or he felt quite free to bring to a current baptismal as well as penitential practice the same Scripture text, probably without committing himself to either rite as being actually designated by the text itself. Certainly he would not have excluded applying the text to ordination too, though he does not appear to have applied NT texts on the imposition of hands to ordination. In fact, he never associates this rite with ordination (see Beneden, *Aux Origines,* pp. 60-62, 150, who notes that Tertullian tells nothing of *how* the *sanctificatio* in ordination was conferred beyond that it occurred *per ordinis consessum* [*Exhor. Cast.* 7.3]; cf. Beneden, pp. 24-34, for an explanation of the passage).

LeSaint, *Tertullian,* pp. 162-163 n. 108 and p. 266 n. 539, has called attention to these two passages in which Tertullian cites 1 Tim 5:22, though he has not made the inference above on Galtier's argumentation. R. P. C. Hanson, "Interpolation," p. 218, has called attention to the way in which the baptismal narrative of Acts 19:5-6 has been glossed with "for the forgiveness of sins," perhaps linking that grace with the imposition of hands mentioned in verse 6. On Hanson's suggestion, the interpolation would have originated in the Roman church between 120 and 150 C.E. (p. 223) and would reflect the liturgical usage and belief of that congregation. Thus one ought to distinguish the earlier sporadic and *ad hoc* uses of this text by occasional, principally (or only?) Western witnesses from the later but consistent and formally exegetical comments of Chrysostom, Theodore of Mopsuestia, et al. of the Greek Fathers, not to mention Ambrosiaster.

*Keep yourself chaste.* The third imperatival phrase of the fivefold series that goes through verse 23 is a positive admonition. The pattern has been two negatives, then a positive; in the following verse, first one negative, then one positive.

"Keep yourself chaste," *seauton hagnon tērei,* takes up an adjective that figured in the list of virtues for the young women in Titus 2:5 (*hagnos;* the **hagn-* root is regularly linked with ritual and cultic requirements in the NT, thus a liturgical background is recommended for the usage there), and the ritual sense may well be at the fore in this passage with its previous mention of a ceremonial gesture and the sins of the men upon whom hands might be hastily imposed. The term *tērei* here in 5:22 is not unrelated in meaning to the *hina tauta phylaxēis* of verse 21, for the verbs are partially synonymous when they designate a "watching over" (see Riesenfeld, *TDNT* 8.140-141, for examples in secular and LXX Greek), as the Western variant at Acts 21:25 illustrates.

23. *Drink only water no longer, but take wine, moderately, for your bad stomach and your frequent bouts with illness.* With this verse and its first negative, then positive admonition, the fivefold series of commands that began in 5:22 and that have become progressively more "personal" (from an objective warning not to ordain hastily, to a warning about becoming entangled in others' sins, to keeping oneself undefiled), here become entirely individual. So "personal" at this point is the advice that Falconer conjectured that the whole

verse was interpolated. Yet all the MSS are against this, and among the patristic witnesses only Ephraem of Syria moved this verse to the very end of this chapter (Spicq, "1 Tim 5:23," p. 143 n. 3).

As D-C and Spicq, "1 Tim 5:23," pp. 143-144, have noted, the command to "holiness" *(hagnon)* in the previous verse gives an opening into the subject of abstaining from wine and drinking only water, a practice to which the OT tradition witnesses in the legislation for the Nazirite (cf. esp. LXX Num 6:2, 21) as well as the practice of the Rechabites (Jer 35:2, 5-6, 8, 14) and of Daniel and his companions (Dan 1:12). The popular presuppositions are summed up adequately in 2 Macc 15:39: "It is harmful to drink wine alone, or again, to drink water alone, while wine mixed with water is sweet and delicious and enhances one's enjoyment. . . ." The passages on *vinum temperatum* in the classical world are too well known to need citation. Spicq, "1 Tim 5:23," p. 144 n. 6, cites the passages from Philo and notes that the Qumran sectaries drank lightly fermented must.

In the light of our hypothesis, it is notable that Luke 1:15; 7:33 has the Baptist described in Nazirite terminology as one who drinks "no wine or strong drink" *(oinon kai sikera).* Spicq has suggested that Timothy has (or was known to have) undertaken this practice of religious self-denial. The present imperative of the command and the initial *mēketi* give a firm reversal to Timothy's practice and again emerge easily from the preceding command, "Keep yourself chaste but not to the extent that you drink only water" ("1 Tim 5:23," p. 145 n. 2).

The "little wine" counseled here is in contrast to the warning against "much wine" *(oinōi pollōi)* at 1 Tim 3:8 and Titus 2:3 (cf. also the *mē paroinon* of Titus 1:7; 1 Tim 3:3 [Spicq, "1 Tim 5:23," p. 149 n. 4]). The frequency of these warnings on the abuse of wine in the correspondence (though not a peculiarly Lukan or even Pauline concern in the rest of the NT) seems to have called for the qualification *oinōi oligōi,* the latter term otherwise found in the PE in the adverbial phrase *pros oligon* in 1 Tim 4:8. Spicq, "1 Tim 5:23," p. 145, suggests that the remedy proposed would discomfit Judaizing ascetics, whose real abnegation stood in function of false principles, even gnosticizing ones.

Still, it must be noted that the text proposes no doctrinaire or theological grounds for its directive but simply notes that this course of action will be "for your bad stomach and your frequent bouts with illness." The concern here is very Hellenistic (see Notes above), though of course the ailment the "nervous stomach," the queasy acidity that tense perfectionists are always prone to and that administrative pressures have been known to cause even in the most stolid and placid, is by no means a monopoly of Greeks or Sumerians. Indeed, when one looks back over the management and personnel problems that have been broached and then committed to the addressee's care, the reference to a "bad stomach" does not look as utterly at variance with the context as it did at first sight. As Chrysostom noted, what the "angel of Satan" was to the apostle (2 Cor 12:7-10), so these frequent illnesses are to his colleague and co-worker. Aquinas already noted that the apostle worked no sign and wonder to deliver his "beloved child" (2 Tim 1:2; indeed, he does not even tell him to pray as he had when he learned that sometimes God's answer to prayer is "No"). He simply gives the standard prescription of his day, perhaps along with Luke, his "beloved physician" (Col 4:14) — cf. Spicq, "1 Tim 5:23," p. 148.

24. *The sins of some people are obvious enough, escorting them to judgment.* With this verse the watershed is past and the highly personal conclusion of the preceding verse and the series of admonitions to Timothy is over. The text now returns to the third person with which this whole section on the *presbyteroi* had begun (5:17-18) and makes two closing observations, on bad *presbyteroi* and then the good, thus sending a glance backward first to 5:19-22 (23) and finally to 17-18.

If the variation in the person of the verbs is indeed a key to structure in this section, one ought to note the pattern here:

| | |
|---|---|
| verse 17: | 3rd pl. |
| 18: | 3rd + 2nd sg. indicative in first quotation (which thus prepares for 19) |
| 19: | 2nd sg. imperative |
| 20: | 2nd sg. imperative + *hina* and 3rd pl. subjunctive |
| 21: | 1st sg. + *hina* and 2nd sg. subjunctive |
| 22: | 2nd sg. imperative |
| | 2nd sg. imperative |
| | 2nd sg. imperative |
| 23: | 2nd sg. imperative |
| | 2nd sg. imperative |
| 24: | 3rd pl. |
| | 3rd pl. |
| | 3rd pl. |
| 25: | 3rd pl. |

This pattern appears to confirm that proposed by Meier on other, more conceptual, grounds. This arrangement might offer the advantage of giving a "context" to verse 23 in the imperatival series as well as a formal and conceptual emphasis to verse 21. Whether that verse was an insertion into a preexisting sevenfold series represented by the imperatival directions of verses 19-20, 22-23 is more difficult to ascertain.

"The sins *(hai hamartiai)* of some people *(tinōn anthrōpōn)*" takes the reader back to the *hamartiais allotriais* of verse 22 (Meier, "*Presbyteros,*" pp. 334-335), and more remotely to *tous hamartanontas* of 20, which referred to *presbyteroi* who were sinning persistently. The involvement in "the sins of others" in verse 22 referred to the perils of hasty ordination, and now verse 24 returns to that subject with a comment on the reason for testing candidates for the presbyterate. The author certainly supposes that they will be men, but the Greek *anthrōpōn* is used generically without particular stress on gender (as would be the case, e.g., with *andrōn* or a form of *arsēn*). The *tinōn anthrōpōn* here could mean "many" or "few"; it contrasts with the frequent *pantes anthrōpoi* of the PE (*pantes* is the most frequently used adjective qualifying *anthrōpoi* in the PE, thus underlining the significance imbued to the universality of the offer of salvation in the PE; see above on 1 Tim 2:1, 4; 4:10). The fact that *anthrōpoi* rather than *presbyteroi* are spoken of implies that the persons described are Christian believers but not yet ordained, and supports the contention above that verse 22 refers to the past and present *hamartiai* of the candidates, not their future ones (for which vv. 19-20 provide a judicial procedure). The one in charge of such testing (on which this correspondence puts no little stress; cf. 1 Tim 3:10, as well as the extensive lists of prerequisite virtues for presbyteral-episcopal ministry) will find that the sins of some "are obvious" *(prodēloi)*, others not so. This adjective is repeated in the following verse of *erga kala.*

What Timothy binds on earth will be bound in heaven, and his *krisis* is a proleptic glimpse of the final judgment for such sinners. Here the "judgment" is going on now even though God is performing it. The usage here is, as Spicq suggests, a Latinism — *producere reum in jus,* comparing the *proagagein* of Acts 12:6 and 25:26 (Haenchen, *Acts,* p. 677) of bringing a Peter or a Paul to formal trial. Here the *presbyteral* candidates who have sinned are the *delatores,* the denouncers, appearing before the tribunal and preferring charges in the light of which Timothy must proffer judgment (BAGD cite Eusebius, *Pr. Evang.* 5.24, *PG* 21.369, where *ekeina dei mallon eis tēn krisin proagein* = "to come before the court").

*others trail their sins behind them.* Not all sins are so obvious; on the contrary *(de),* they lit. "also *(kai)* follow after some [other] persons *(tisin . . . epakolouthousin).*" The verb occurred at 5:10 above, but here it has a somewhat different and more common sense, like that of 1 Pet 2:21 or especially *1 Clem.* 43.1 (cf. Ign. *Smyrn.* 10.1). The sense here appears to be that the sins of certain candidates for the presbyterate trail them like a shadow (Spicq) and are not at all obvious (as were those previously noted). Accordingly, the period of trial and examination can only be lengthy and the previous admonition (v. 22), "Be in no hurry . . . to impose hands on anyone," is further justified.

25. *Similarly also, fine deeds are obvious, and those that are not obvious*

*cannot stay hidden always.* The final sentence proceeds to contrast emphatically the good works *(ta erga ta kala;* note the repeated article [Spicq]) of other presbyteral candidates with the sins just mentioned. *Erga kala* are the attractively visible fruits of the Spirit in the lives of believers (contra Simpson; cf. Spicq). They, too, are "obvious" *(prodēla)* in the exact same way *(hōsautōs kai)* as the sins previously noted.

What the anti-Christ is to Christ, bad works are to good ones. The visibility of the former is unto demoralization and destruction; the latter for the sake of encouragement and building up. Thus the good works of a presbyteral candidate ought to be verified (not just the absence of sins) to ensure his presiding well (cf. the *kala* here with the *kalōs* of v. 17). This is not to say that all good *(agatha)* works are immediately obvious. Again, as with the sins of verse 24, some good actions are not immediately and visibly attractive *(kala).* They are *ta allōs echonta,* i.e. not *prodēla,* not *kala.* Perhaps no passage in the PE illustrates more vividly the distinction between *kala* and *agatha.* There are *obviously* fine works *(prodēla* stressing the nuance of visibility in *kala).* Still not all good *(agatha)* works are *prodēla,* but that does not mean that they cannot be ascertained. *Krybēnai ou dynantai,* the writer (or his source) says flatly: "[They] cannot stay hidden."

If God's revelation and the gospel cannot and ought not to be hidden, the works that emanate from and depend upon that revelation and its grace ought to be publicly verifiable. The God of Israel and the God of Christians is a "hidden" God, i.e. utterly transcendent while knowing all that men consider hidden (cf. Oepke, *TDNT* 3.967-968; also 1 Tim 1:17; 6:16). Thus human knowledge of him and his will depends upon his revelation and direction. That revelation is of a God reaching out to and seeking to guide *all* men. Thus the line from hidden to revealed terminates (for the NT) in world mission (Oepke, p. 977), not in the esoteric, even doctrinaire and egotistical, elitism of, e.g., Qumran or Gnosticism (cf. the *Gospel of Thomas,* sayings #5 [= OxyP 654.27-30 and 32, 33]; see the notations in Grant and Freedman, *Secret Sayings,* pp. 44-48, esp. 47, and 118, 142-143).

## IV.B.4. DOMESTIC CODE: PART II (6:1-2)

6 [1] *Those Christians who are bound in slavery are to regard their masters as deserving all esteem. Thus God's name and the instruction will not be defamed.* [2] *Moreover, slaves that have masters who are believers are not to disdain them. After all, they are brothers. Instead they are to be even better slaves because they have masters who practice kindness as men who are believers and beloved.*

*These are things, Timothy, for you to teach and encourage.*

## ♦ NOTES

6:1. *Those Christians who are bound in slavery.* Lit. "Whoever *(hosoi)* are slaves under the yoke." *Hosoi* occurs once again in this correspondence at 2 Tim 1:18 (*hosa . . . diēkonēsen,* as object of a rather different "service"). The term appears 24 times in the other Paulines; there are 27 occurrences in Luke-Acts (10/17). There is a total of 110 NT uses of the word, and a good many in the Ap. Frs. as well. The usage here of number/quantity appears in both the Lukan and Pauline corpus (see BAGD *s.v.* for examples: note that the absolute use of *hosa* as in 2 Tim 1:18 has parallels in Luke-Acts, but BAGD give none for Paul; however, Rom 3:19; 15:4; Phil 4:8 may be examples). The term stresses that every one of those who are *douloi* are objects of the following directives. The *douloi* are further specified as *hypo zygon,* "under [the] yoke."

*bound in slavery (hypo zygon douloi).* This is the only use of *zygon* in the PE. It is notable that the one other Pauline use, at Gal 5:1, is the apostle's admonition, "Do not submit again to the yoke of slavery *(zygōi douleias),*" where the reference is to the metaphorical yoke and slavery of the Mosaic law. It is precisely this usage that appears in the one occurrence in the Lukan corpus, at Acts 15:10, where Peter speaks of "putting a yoke upon the neck of the disciples which neither our fathers nor we have been able to bear" (cf. Rengstorf, *TDNT* 2.899). In contrast to this "yoke" is the one that the Matthean tradition has Jesus speak of (Matt 11:29-30; cf. 2 Cor 6:14, *heterozygountes apistois*). The one other NT use (Rev 6:5) is of the balance-bar or beam of a scale. With both the usage of Galatians and that of Acts, the application of the term to those sociologically "subjugated" (as in PE) has passed over to denote those religiously "subjugated" by divine laws. The link between the yoke and slavery is attested both in classical Greek (Rengstorf, *TDNT,* p. 899 n. 20) and in the Palestinian world from Genesis through Maccabees (citations in Spicq, *EP,* p. 552; Rengstorf, *TDNT,* p. 899 n. 20).

*First Clement* 16.17 with its "under *(hypo)* the yoke *(ton zygon)* of grace" and *Did.* 6.2 speaking of "the whole yoke of the Lord" are in the tradition of the Matthean logion cited above. *Barnabas* 2.6 with its "yoke of necessity" is in the Galatians-Acts sphere of meaning. Neither is really parallel to this verse in the PE.

The phrase *hypo zygon* occurs in the LXX Zeph 3:9 (with *douleuein,* of the freeing of the captive nation) as well as in Sir 51:26 (of Wisdom and instruction), and *hypo ton zygon* at Jer 34(MT 27):8, 11 (of the captivity of a nation to Babylon).

When Josephus uses *zygon,* it is of an actual yoke (*Ant.* 12.194, 100-101); on one out of the three occasions that he employs *zygos* it is in the phrase *hypo (ton) zygon.* Thus *Ant.* 8.213, retelling the accession story of Rehoboam (cf.

LXX 2 Chron 10:4-14 with seven occurrences of *zygos*), speaks of the tribes of Israel as having carried a heavy yoke (note *douleia* twice in the context) under Solomon *(hyp' ekeinōi),* and *War* 5.365 speaks of "shaking off the yoke" of Roman domination (note the use of *douleuein* in 5.364). *War* 7.87 uses the phrase *hypo ton auton palin zygon* of the Germans submitting again to Domitian after a revolt.

*to regard their masters as deserving all esteem.* The slaves are first directed to "regard (*hēgeisthōsan* [third pl. imperative]) their masters *(tous idious despotas)* as deserving *(axious)* of all esteem *(pasēs timēs).*" *Hēgeisthai* occurs at 1 Tim 1:12, and here also stresses the free initiative of the persons who are subjects of the action. In the Ap. Frs. *First Clement* uses the term in the participial form = "leaders" eight times; *2 Clem.* 5.6 and Ign. *Smyrn.* 8.1 use the verb in the sense that it has here. It is Hermas, however, who uses the phrase *axion (-ous) hēgeisthai* six times, with the Lord (*Vis.* 2.1.2; *Man.* 4.2.1) or God (*Sim.* 9.28.5) or the visionary Lady = Church (*Vis.* 3.3.4) as subject.

Büchsel, *TDNT* 2.907-908, concentrates his whole treatment on the participial sense = "leaders," noting little more than the meaning "think, believe, regard as," with advertence to 1 Thess 5:13 and its sense "esteem, regard as important."

On *axious* here cf. above, 1 Tim 1:15 and 4:9, as well as 5:17-18 above on the presbyters, *axiousthōsan . . . axios.*

An *archōn pasēs timēs* occurs in *CII* 85, 324, 337, and almost certainly in the *archon pases tessimen* ([*sic*], in Latin script) of #216. As the introduction by Lifshitz explains, this phrase = the man in charge of receiving all funds, taxes, gifts for the synagogue — the cashier. Unfortunately, there is no apparent link with this Jewish phrase and the one here in this *Haustafel.*

See 1 Tim 1:17 for *timē.* Material service is of course not excluded, but the emphasis extends beyond that to showing esteem and respect.

The use of *idious* with *despotas* illustrates the considerably weakened force of this possessive adjective in *koinē,* as was mentioned already at Titus 2:5, 9 (cf. Deissmann, *B ST,* pp. 123-124; D-C, p. 82).

*Thus God's name and the instruction will not be defamed.* For "defamed," *blasphēmētai,* see Titus 2:5. On the two other occasions when "God's name," *to onoma tou theou,* is used in the NT, it is also used with a form of *blasphēmein* (Rom 2:24, citing LXX Isa 52:5, uses the word to indicate pagan abuse for "the name" of the God of Israel, as well as Rev 16:9). Because the phrase is so unusual in the NT, it is difficult to argue, with J. K. Elliott, *Greek Text,* pp. 88-89, that the *onoma Kyriou* of D*. 33. is original. Rather, it is a Western "normalizing" that makes the usage here conform to the many other places in the NT that speak of *to onoma (tou) Kyriou,* not to mention 2 Tim 2:19.

The phrase *to onoma tou theou* is found only three times in the Ap. Frs.:

Ign. *Phld.* 10.2 speaks of sending a legate to his Antiochene congregation *hyper onomatos theou; Eph.* 1.3, of a bishop-representative of the congregation; Hermas, *Vis.* 3.4.3, citing LXX Pss 85, 9, 12, but adding *theou* in place of *sou,* "that the name of God might be glorified." It is notable, however, that *1 Clem.* 1.1 speaks of the "name" of the Corinthian church being reviled *(blasphēmēthēnai),* and then in 47.7 avers that the story of their factiousness has reached the ears of those who do not share the faith "so that you bring blasphemy *(blasphēmias)* on the name of the Lord *(tōi onomati Kyriou).*" *Second Clement* 13.1-4 (cf. Donfried, *Setting,* pp. 53, 86-88) is an elaborate reflection and exhortation based on this text. Ign. *Trall.* 8.2 seems to base his exhortation to ungrudging charity on the same text too. Bietenhard, *TDNT* 5.279-280, remarks that just as believers are defined by their relation to the name of God in their faith, worship, words, works, even sufferings for that name, "so unbelief is manifested in *blasphēmein.*"

Among the Ap. Frs., *1 Clem.* 47.7 speaks of the Corinthians bringing "blasphemies on the name of the Lord through your folly *(aphrosynēn),*" and *2 Clem.* 13.3 describes the pagans turning "from wonder to blasphemy" as they compare the divine oracles with Christian deeds. Ign. *Eph.* 10.2 exhorts his readers to offer prayers "for the blasphemies *(pro tas blasphemias)*" that other men inflict.

*Didache* 3.6 teaches, "Be not a grumbler, for this leads to blasphemy *(blasphēmian),* nor stubborn, nor a thinker of evil, for from *(ek)* all these are blasphemies engendered *(blasphēmiai gennōntai).*" For Hermas, see *Man.* 8.3 and *Sim.* 6.2.3.

2. *believers. Pistos* = "Christian" here because, for the PE, what identifies and sets apart God's elect from unbelievers, Jews or pagans, was faith in Jesus. Galatians 1:23, taken in parallel with Gal 1:13, suggests that from very early on "the faith" was defined in terms of those who composed the church (or churches) of God (cf. 1 Tim 4:3).

*After all, they are brothers.* Lit. "Because they are brothers."

*Instead they are to be even better slaves.* Lit. "but rather *(alla mallon)* to continue as slaves *(douleutōsan).*" On *mallon* see 1 Tim 1:4; for its somewhat adversative force, cf. Acts 5:14, *mellon de,* weaker than the *alla mallon* here (cf. Mark 5:26, the only other NT use of the phrase); *douleuein* occurred, of slavery to lusts, at Titus 3:3.

## ♦ COMMENT

With these verses the Domestic Code of 5:1-2, which was "interrupted" to receive the long directives on widows and presbyters, is now taken up again and concluded with the directives for slaves (cf. the arrangement, e.g., at Titus 2:2-10, where there is also a much briefer "digression" on the ministry of Titus himself [vv. 7-8] just before the commands for slaves). The continued and repeated use of the third person in 6:1-2 places the passage in formal continuity with the last verse of chapter 5, and thus in contrast with the second person singular with which this code began at 5:1-2, as well as with the second person singular address to Timothy that resumes at 6:2b and that closes the parentheses around this whole section (cf. commentary *in loc.;* note $GNT^{3corr}$ and Nestle$^{26corr}$ put v. 2b with v. 3!). Barrett, *Pastoral Epistles,* p. 82, has proposed that the continuity between 6:1-2 and 5:24-25 is more than formal; he submits that the case of *presbyteroi* who are also slaves is now taken up and that the initial *hosoi* of 6:1 = "Such of the above as. . . ." This commentary will not take up that suggestion for reasons that will become apparent below. That does not mean that the suggestion is linguistically unreasonable or even materially impossible. It is both reasonable and possible. It has not been demonstrated, and another more reasonable explanation is given below.

The repetition in 6:1 of the adjective can remind the reader of the use of this terminology of the *presbyteroi.* Yet the formal resemblance (which would lend support to Barrett's suggestion that 6:1-2 deals with presbyters-slaves) seems to be merely formal. In the passage above the concern was with the *honorarium* of the presbyters, with their being "deserving of [their] wage." Here the concern is emphatically with slaves and the *timē* that they ought to give rather than the stipend they ought to get.

6:1. *Those Christians who are bound in slavery are to regard their masters as deserving all esteem.* The slaves *(douloi)* were taken up in the same relative position in the *Haustafel* of Titus 2:9-10. There the section preceding closed by including both Paul and Titus in the phrase *peri hemōn,* indicating they were the last free persons of the Christian household and the first of the slaves who appeared thereafter. That placement of the apostolic ministers was purposeful, as the positioning of the bishops and deacons at the end of the 1 Tim 2–3 church order, and that of the presbyters in the one here, indicates. At both Titus 1:1 and 2 Tim 2:24 *doulos* is a title for the apostolic minister, Paul or Timothy. Here there is no mistaking the reference to the ancient social institution; the slaves are explicitly *hosoi eisin hypo zygon . . . ,* "whoever is under the yoke. . . ." The expression seems otiose, but, when one notes the use of *doulos* to designate the apostolic ministers, the phrase here sets off and distinguishes the *douloi* about to be mentioned from the *presbyteroi* who have just been treated at length. The distinction is not unlike that between "real widows" and "widows" in 5:3 or between "presbyter" and "presbyter(s)" (5:1, 17, 19). Here the author turns from the Lord's *douloi* to those who are sociologically slaves, literally "subjugated," men.

The usage of the phrase "bound in slavery," in the light of the other documentation, appears to stress the politico-sociological meaning of *douloi* at this point and thus to preclude taking that term in its "ministerial" sense. *Hosoi* would then refer not to the *presbyteroi* of 5:17-25 but to the old and young men (and women?) of 5:1-2. No exceptions are made; every Christian slave is to act in accord with the following directives, which make a distinction only on the basis of whether the master is not (v. 1) or is (v. 2) himself a believer.

The *despotēs* in Greek usage was the counterpart of *doulos,* and the sense here is that of Titus 2:9; i.e. a "master" could be any free person, young or old, male of female, with, as the Greek term suggests, unqualified ownership and the right of undisputable disposal of a particular property. The word order as 6:1 opens, with verb *(eisin)* plus qualifying phrase plus noun, is reversed in this section, beginning with the noun, *tous idious despotas* (note how the alliteration binds it to the preceding *douloi*), then the qualifying phrase, then the verb (abccba).

*Thus God's name and the instruction will not be defamed.* The reason for the reverence and respect is expressed in terms of the Christian's mission to unbelievers, which, at the very least, is not to block the grace of God on its way to all. Thus, negatively put, pagan masters receive all esteem "so that the name of God and the teachings are not insulted." The *didaskalia* here is the OT teachings (on slaves) as interpreted by Paul, and *to onoma tou theou* is the name of the one God of Israel who has revealed himself through the Scriptures of Israel. Where Titus 2:5 had urged virtues on young women, *hina mē ho logos tou theou blasphēmētai* ("the message of God," thus indicating that the missionary character of Christian revelation was to motivate their freely chosen subordination), here *ho logos* has been further differentiated, to emphasize the person of the God who spoke as well as the apostolic preaching and teaching of what he had commanded. Note also how God is distanced from the envisioned insult by the phrasing and the use of the passive form.

2. *Moreover, slaves that have masters who are believers are not to disdain them. After all, they are brothers.* In contrast *(de)* to the previous masters, the case is now proposed of those slaves "that have *(echontes)* masters who are believers *(pistous despotas)*." Slaves with such masters are directed "not to disdain them," *mē kataphroneitōsan,* a verb that appeared above when Timothy was exhorted to let no one look down on his youthfulness (see 1 Tim 4:12). As Spicq has observed, the verb designates an unwillingness to consider and to take a real interest in another, the very opposite of charity (*agapē;* see Matt 6:24 and *Agape* I, 18). Thus, in positive form, the slaves are being told to love their Christian masters because *(hoti)* "they are brothers *(adelphoi)*." Here the reason for the command *(hoti)* turns to the inner nature of the Christian community as a family (a household) of equals — of brothers — with a common father (see

Comment on 1 Tim 4:6) rather than to the mission of Christians to unbelievers. Both are acts of charity, but charity must begin at home, must be "especially for those who are of the household of faith" (Gal 6:10).

*Instead they are to be even better slaves because they have masters who practice kindness as men who are believers and beloved.* In contrast *(alla)* to the indifferent disdain just noted, slaves are "instead to be even better slaves." The following *hoti* clause (parallel to the one in the previous verse) now gives the reason or ground for continuing as slaves. There is, however, an ambiguity built into the Greek, perhaps even a deliberate one. Is the reason (1) that the Christian masters are kind to them or (2) that the slaves are performing a work of charity for their masters? The former line has been taken by commentators from Chrysostom and Theodore of Mopsuestia to D-C and J. K. Elliott; the latter by many through Spicq, Barrett, and Kelly.

The initial adjectives in the clause *pistoi kai agapētoi* are surely predicate (J. K. Elliott, *Greek Text,* p. 89) and thus ought to be explained in terms of *hoi tēs euergesias antilambanomenoi. Antilambanein* occurs in the NT only in the Lukan corpus. Luke 1:54 speaks of God's helping *(antelabeto)* his servant *(paidos)* Israel, and the parallel with the first interpretation of 1 Tim 6:2 ought to be observed. In Acts 20:35 the verb has been placed on Paul's lips as he explains how his practice of self-support shows how "one must help *(antilambanesthai)* the weak *(asthenountōn).*" Here it is the apostolic "servant" (*douleuōn,* Acts 20:19 and cf. 16:17) whose physical labor is considered a gift and service to the community (cf. Haenchen, *Acts,* p. 594). One must wait until Hermas for the one occurrence of this verb in the Ap. Frs. (*Vis.* 3.9.2), where the Church tells her children, "look after (*episkeptesthe* [cf. perhaps *mē kataphroneitōsan* above]) one another and help one another *(antilambanesthe allēlōn)*"; care for material needs is stressed in the latter phrase (one recalls in this connection among the gifts of the Spirit to the Corinthian church, *antilēmpseis, kybernēseis,* 1 Cor 12:28). This verb is frequent enough in LXX, where it renders as many as fourteen Hebrew roots (see Spicq, *EP,* who with D-C also marshals the examples from the papyri and inscriptions, as do MM *s.v.,* pp. 47-48). As BDF §170 discusses the NT verbs that take the genitive, it notes that in this passage of the PE *antilambanomenoi* means "to take part, share in," or, better, "to devote oneself to," and thus is parallel to the Lukan uses.

"[Those] who practice kindness *(euergesias)*" employs a compound that is otherwise in the NT used only by Acts 4:9, where Peter describes the healing of the cripple at the Beautiful Gate as *euergesia anthrōpou asthenous,* "a benefiting of a sick man." It is only Luke in the NT who uses the cognate compounds: *euergetein* in Acts 10:38 of Jesus "benefiting and healing," and *euergetēs* in Luke 22:25 of pagan rulers who take the title "benefactors."

In the Ap. Frs. *First Clement* uses *euergetikos patēr* of God (23.1): *euergetēs s.v.l.* in 59.3, again of God, in relation to spirit; and *euergetein* in 20.11, of God as *despotēs* "benefiting" all things (Ign. *Rom.* 5.1 describes his guards as becoming worse for their having been treated kindly [*euergetoumenoi*]). Only *First Clement* uses *euergasia,* at 19.2, of God's "benefits."

LXX Ps 77:11 (MT 78:11) uses this noun for God's miracles for his people (cf. Acts above). Wis 16:11, 24 similarly employs the term for God's wonders in the exodus. In 2 Macc 6:13 even the calamities that befall God's people are "a sign of great kindness *(megalēs euergesias),*" and in 9:26 a letter of Antiochus Epiphanes has him speak of "the public and private services *(euergesiōn)* rendered" to the Jewish people. Fourth Maccabees 8:17 has a hypothetical conversation of the seven martyr brothers in which they speak of the "kind treatment" or "benefit" that the tyrant proposes. Thus in biblical Greek *euergesia* is, in the great majority of cases, the kindness/benefit(s) that God bestows as master of the world, and in the few remaining cases the "benefit" bestowed by an earthly king. In the Ap. Frs. it refers only to God's benefits. On the basis of these parallels one would infer that *euergesia* here in the PE would be understood as the master's benefits or kindnesses to his slaves. A similar case could be made from the papyri; thus "*plēn mallon philanthrōpiai te kai euergesiais synauzein tautēn tēn archēn,* but rather by liberality and benefits increasing the welfare of this empire" (MM *s.v.,* p. 260, citing P. Fay 20.16 [iii/iv a.d.], and see Spicq, *EP,* p. 554, for a dozen other texts). In that case, however, *antilambanomenoi* could refer to slaves "accepting" or "taking" the benefit of their Christian masters' kindness rather than "devoting themselves" to benefiting their masters. But it could also refer to the masters' devoting themselves to the benefit of their slaves.

Does the meaning of *pistoi . . . kai agapētoi* shed any light on which interpretation to follow? *Pistoi* almost certainly has the same sense as at the beginning of this verse; i.e. it means a believing Christian as distinguished from a Jew or pagan. In the first part of the verse it certainly modified *despotas.* Moreover, *hoti pistoi eisin* here is formally parallel to the *hoti adelphoi eisin* of the first part, just as *douleuetōsan* is antithetically parallel to *mē kataphroneitōsan.* But in that case those who are designated *pistoi* here in the second part of the verse are most probably the same as in the first, i.e. the masters, and in that case, since *pistoi* is a predicate adjective to *hoi . . . antilambanomenoi,* that participle would be understood of masters devoting themselves to the benefit of those Christian slaves who serve them. Thus the clause would mean, "because those who devote themselves to the benefit (of their slaves) are (themselves) Christian believers and beloved *(agapētoi).*"

That last adjective occurs in the PE again at 2 Tim 1:2 (see commentary *in loc.*) of Timothy himself as Paul's "beloved child." Is the sense here that the slaves are "beloved" by their Christian masters? Or if the masters are the subject of one clause, are they being described as beloved by their slaves as also they were fellow believers with them? Or is it understood that the Christian masters are beloved by God, *theou* (cf. Spicq, *Agape* 2.435-436)? D-C opt for the last, noting the parallel usage in Rom 11:28 (see also Rom 1:7) as well as Ign. *Phld.* 9.2 of "the beloved prophets" of the OT. Luke 3:22 (cf. 20:13) also witnesses to this sense, which would be contrasted to his one other use of this adjective, in the letter of the Jerusalem church to Antioch (Acts 15:25) where Paul and Barnabas are *agapētois hēmōn,* a usage quite parallel to 2 Tim 1:2. However, D-C's reason is unacceptable: "the slaves who must be admonished to serve cannot, in the same injunction, be expected to act out of love for their masters." This combination of slavery with love is not only found in the OT tradition (cf. Exod 21:5; Deut 15:16 [*TDOT* I, 105]; Deut 10:12, 11:13, where the Hebrew *'hb/'bd* becomes the LXX *agapan/latreuein*), but Gal 5:13 also finds Paul exhorting his refractory Galatians, "Through love *(dia tēs agapēs)* be servants *(douleuete)* of one another." In Col 4:7 Tychicus is not only "a beloved brother," *ho agapētos adelphos,* but also "fellow servant in the Lord," *syndoulos en kyriōi* (cf. 1:7). The adjective *agapētoi* here takes up the directive of the first half of the verse, for, as was noted, *mē kataphroneitōsan = agapate,* and here the reason for the slaves' love of Christian masters is that those masters are "beloved" by God.

If *antilambanomenoi* does in fact mean slaves who accept the benefits given by their masters or who devote themselves to their benefit, then *pistoi . . . kai agapētoi* would more naturally refer to their being faithful to such masters, as well as beloved by them. By and large the parallelism between the two parts of this verse and the other uses of the terminology found here incline this commentator to side with the Greek Fathers and D-C in taking this whole *hoti* clause as referring to Christian masters.

*These are things, Timothy, for you to teach and encourage.* The final sentence of this verse, *tauta didaske kai parakalei,* is taken by many editors to begin a new paragraph and to belong accordingly with the following verse. The terminology has been studied above at Titus 1:11; 1 Tim 2:12; 4:11 (where *didaske* also occurred with *tauta*), as well as Titus 1:9; 2:6, 15. In the last instance *parakalei* occurred with *tauta lalei,* and at the conclusion of a domestic code to which a creedal confession had been appended. That formal parallelism as well as the other uses of *tauta* in this correspondence (cf. above on 4:11 and R. F. Collins, "Image of Paul") lead one to think that the appearance of the second person imperative phrase here (after the third person from 5:24 up to this point) is meant not only to link up with the second person imperatives of the section on presbyters but to hark back to the very beginning of the previous chapter, 5:1-2, and thus enclose the two "orders" for widows and presbyters. Indeed, the *didaske* would take one back to the formula of 4:11 and thus summarize the whole intervening *paraklēsis,* with its healthy Pauline teaching.

## IV.C. In Relation to Problems (6:3-19)

### IV.C.1. THE HETERODOX (6:3-5)

*6 [3]In the case of a man who propounds strange teachings and has no recourse to the wholesome sayings that come from our Lord, Jesus Christ, nor to the godly instruction, [4]one can only conclude that he has become a conceited ignoramus with a morbid craving for speculations and quibbling about terminology. These in turn produce —*

*jealousy,*
*controversy,*
*vituperations,*
*vicious insinuations,*
*[5]the incessant bickerings of men*
*whose minds are a shambles and*
*who have been robbed of the truth;*
*they think godliness is a means*
*for gain.*

### ♦ NOTES

6:3. *In the case of a man who propounds strange teachings.* Lit. "If anyone *(ei tis)* teaches another doctrine *(heterodidaskalei).*" On the *ei tis* that introduces this long sentence (vv. 3-5) see Titus 1:6. On *heterodidaskalei* see 1 Tim 1:3.

*and has no recourse to the wholesome sayings that come from our Lord, Jesus Christ.* Lit. "and does not agree *(proserchetai)* with the healthful words which [are those] of our Lord, Jesus Christ." Not *(mē)* is quite classical as contrasted with the "literary" *ou* in 3:5 and 5:8; BDF §428.1; Moule, *Idiom,* p. 148. J. K. Elliott, *Greek Text,* p. 90, prefers the *ou* reading of one MS Ψ. The verb appears here for the only time in the Pauline corpus, though there are eighty-six other NT uses, twenty of them in Luke-Acts (fifty-two in Matthew). The use with the dative of things is not paralleled in the Gospels and Acts but does occur in Heb 4:16; 12:18, 22. *First Clement* uses the verb only with the dative, whether of persons or things (23.1; 29.1; 33.8; 63.1). Other constructions are found in *2 Clem.* 17.3; *Did.* 4.14; and Ign. *Rom.* 10.2. Hermas, *Vis.* 3.1.5; 3.12.3, again witnesses to the dative of person, while *Man.* 5.1.3 has an intransitive use without an object. Common as the verb is in the LXX, and often enough with the dative, there is no verbal parallel with this passage in the PE, though such passages as Sir 4:15; 6:19, 26, where "giving heed to" or "approaching" wisdom means giving heed to the Torah, are conceptually and grammatically parallel to 1 Tim 6:3. Parry, *Pastoral Epistles, ad loc.*, cites a few classical *loci* where this verb can be rendered "to engage in, to busy oneself with." LSJ *s.v.* list "apply oneself to philosophy, to law," or "to have recourse to." D-C, p. 83, cites Epictetus, *Discourses* 4.11.24, "adhere to philosophy." Menander uses the verb in *Sik.* 9; *Sam.* 241, 451, 457; *Aspis* 361, 528, 534, but none is parallel to PE.

It is evident that *proserchetai* does not fit with complete ease into the text. As J. K. Elliott, *Greek Text,* p. 90, citing Field, has noted, as well as MM *s.v.*, p. 547, there is no justifying the meaning "consent to" for *proserchetai,* nor does the protasis following in verses 4-5 conceive of the false teacher's making any "approach" to the truth. If the meaning proposed in the preceding paragraph is not justified, then a textual variant as old as S* 181. 1912 (Vg and OL: *acquiescit*) Theod. Mops *(intendit)*, Cyp. Luc. Ambst. ought to be reviewed, for they all read or presume *proserchetai.* In that case the language here in 6:3 would echo that of 1 Tim 1:4 (not to mention Titus 1:14 and 1 Tim 3:8; 4:1, 13) as *heterodidaskalei* echoed 1:3. However, the middle form is unattested in the NT, though documented otherwise (LSJ *s.v.*).

The attested meaning of *proserchetai,* as well as its MS attestation and its being the *lectio difficilior* in sense, leads one to judge that the original reading of Sinaiticus was indeed a copyist's error or "correction." The latter would in turn have been congenial to the Western tradition of the text.

*wholesome sayings (hygiainousin logois).* On the plural *logois,* see above on 1 Tim 4:6. The qualification of the words as "wholesome" is to be understood as the identical qualification of the *didaskalia* in Titus 1:9; 2:1; 1 Tim 1:10; 2 Tim 4:3 (cf. Titus 2:8, the *logon hygiē*). The added clause here, specifying the healthy words as literally "which [are those] of our Lord, Jesus Christ," is necessary because elsewhere in this correspondence the *logoi* are always those of the Pauline gospel (cf. 2 Tim 1:13).

4. *one can only conclude that he has become a conceited ignoramus.* The apodosis now begins with the verb *tetyphōtai,* i.e. the verb used in 1 Tim 3:6 (see commentary *in loc.*) of the neophyte prematurely promoted to an episcopate. The heterodox teacher has become "conceited." He is further described as an "ignoramus," *mēden epistamenos,* lit. "understanding nothing," with a verb that occurs only here in the Paulines but that is attested nine times in Acts, as well as in Mark 14:68; Heb 11:8; James 4:14; Jude 10. The sense is that of personal acquaintance, knowledge by experience and encounter (as, e.g., Acts 19:15, 25; 20:18, and the *mē epistamenos* of Heb 11:8). Of the five occurrences of the verb in the Ap. Frs., those in *1 Clem.* 45.3 and 53.1 are notable, for they refer to the genuine knowledge of OT Scripture, and that sense is close to the surface here in First Timothy also.

*a morbid craving for speculations (nosōn peri zētēseis).* The participle *nosōn* (contrasted with *hygiainousin* above) is attested only here in the NT and the Ap. Frs. Oepke, *TDNT* 4.1095, has emphasized the Hellenistic affinities of *nosein* in its figurative usage, the character of the following list (D-C), and "the strong emphasis on ignorance as the source of aberration. . . ." For "speculations," *peri zētēseis,* see Titus 3:9.

*speculations. Logomachias* occurs only here in the NT, though it is exegetically significant that the scribes of Pap. 61.F. Lat. G read this noun also at Titus 3:9 (J. K. Elliott, *Greek Text,* p. 193) instead of *genealogias,* apparently indicating that they understood the latter term as quibbling about names.

The cognate verb *logomachein* occurs in 2 Tim 2:14, but neither this verb nor the noun is otherwise attested in the NT, the LXX, or the Ap. Frs. Lampe cites several later patristic uses of the verb. The secular attestation for the verb begins in the twelfth century C.E. (Eustathius *opusc.* pp. 47, 96; *ap.* Harrison, *Paulines,* p. 131, this is curious and may be an error), but the noun was used by Varro as the title for a satire on the debate between Stoics and Epicureans (first century B.C.E.), and then by Porphyry (third century C.E.), *ad Horat. Sat.* 2.4 (Kittel, *TDNT* 4.143). Though the word is Greek, it seems to have been "popular" in Rome and the West (cf. Harrison, *ibid.*); note Plautus, *Asin.* 307 (2.2.41), *verbivelitationem fieri* (Spicq).

*These in turn produce jealousy, controversy, vituperations, vicious insinuations.* For "these in turn produce *(ex hōn ginetai)*" see Titus 3:7 as well as 1 Tim 2:14; 4:12; 5:9; cf. Rom 1:3; Gal 4:4 (note the way in which Western texts read this verb, J. K. Elliott, *Greek Text,* p. 91).

*jealousy.* For *phthonos* see Titus 3:3.

On *controversy, eris,* see Titus 3:9, and on the Western "plural" reading *ereis* see J. K. Elliott, *Greek Text,* p. 92, and Titus 3:9.

*vituperations (blasphēmiai).* Though this is the only use of this noun in the Pastorals out of its eighteen NT occurrences, it does occur in Luke 5:21 (also pl.) as well as in the singular in Eph 4:31; Col 3:8. The plural is also witnessed in Jude 9 and Rev 13:6 as well as in Mark 3:28 and Matt 15:19. The cognate verb *blasphēmein* occurs at Titus 2:5; 3:2; 1 Tim 1:20; 6:1; *blasphēmos,* "blasphemer," in the lists of 1 Tim 1:13 and 2 Tim 3:2.

*vicious insinuations (hyponoiai ponērai). Hyponoiai* is not otherwise attested in the NT. The verb is found only in Acts, three times, of which 25:18 is instructive for the PE. LXX Dan 4:19, 33b; 5:6 indicate that the noun, without further qualifications, can mean vision as well as suspicion (Behm, *TDNT* 4.1018). On the one other occasion that the LXX employs the term, it is qualified precisely as here in the PE, for Sir 3:24 writes, "Wrong opinion *(hyponoia ponēra)* has caused their thoughts to slip" (cf. Sir 25:7 and its *ennea hyponoēmata*). The Ap. Frs. do not use the noun, for all the frequency of their use of the adjective *ponēros.* The papyri document the sense "suspicion" with its connotations (MM *s.v.*, p. 659), which is classical enough. Both Plato, *Republic* 378[d] (where the note in LCL I.180-183 calls *hyponoia* "the older word for allegory"), and Plutarch 2.19[e] thus speak of the "deeper meaning" of myths and allegories (LSJ *s.v.l.*, 1890; cited with many others in Behm, *TDNT* 4.1017-1018).

The adjective *ponēros* here also occurs in the PE below at 2 Tim 3:13; 4:18, and on seventy-five other occasions in the NT. Of these, ten are scattered through the other Paulines (*nil* in Second Corinthians, Philippians, or Philemon — or Titus), and twenty-one are in Luke-Acts (thirteen/eight). Harder, *TDNT* 6.546-566, treats of this passage on p. 556, where (n. 69), with Weiss, he rejects Hofmann's view (p. 185) that *ponērai* here must be read apart from *hyponaiai.* He notes that "evil reservations or insinuations" here in the PE are not unlike the *dialogismoi ponēroi (kakoi)* of James 2:4 and Matt 15:19/ Mark 7:21 (cf. LXX Dan 5:6, *phoboi kai hyponoiai,* with Theod. Dan 5:6, *hoi dialogismoi autou synetarasson . . . ;* cf. *TDNT* 4.1018).

5. *the incessant bickerings.* Only known occurrence of *diaparatribai* in the rest of the NT, the LXX, the Ap. Frs., and profane Greek (see Comment).

*of men whose minds are a shambles.* Lit. "of men *(anthrōpōn)* having been ruined *(diephtharmenōn)* as to their mind *(ton noun).*" The Greek verb occurs only five times in the NT: once again in the Paulines at 2 Cor 4:16 of man's visible, flesh-and-blood constitution "wasting away *(diaphtheiretai)*" and also in Luke 12:33 of the moth's destruction of a garment (cf. the noun, found only in the Acts in the NT, six times). Revelation 8:9 and 11:18 are the other NT examples of the verb. Cf. God as *aphthartos* in 1 Tim 1:17. Harder, *TDNT* 9.93-106, treats the Hebrew equivalent *šḥt* in the OT and the Qumran scrolls, pp. 96-97, and the LXX on pp 98-100. On *nous* here as an accusative with the passive, see BDF §159.3. See AB *Titus* at Titus 1:5.

*who have been robbed of the truth.* The perfect passive participle of *aposterein* pertains to a verb attested only here in the PE, and only at 1 Cor 6:7, 8; 7:5 in the rest of the Paulines. Only Mark 10:19 employs the word otherwise in the NT. Of the eight LXX uses, five are in Sirach (4:1; 29:6, 7; 34:21, 22), and all refer to a deprival of the means of livelihood, particularly of wages (Exod 21:10; Deut 24:14; Mal 3:5). For *truth* see note on 1 Tim 2:4 above.

*they think godliness is a means for gain.* The verb *nomizontōn,* whose present participle occurs here, is not attested elsewhere in the PE and occurs only at 1 Cor 7:26, 36 in the rest of the Paulines. Of the twelve other NT uses of this verb, three are in Matt 5:17; 10:34; 20:10, and the remaining nine are in Luke-Acts. Acts 8:20 is a particularly notable parallel as Simon Magus hears the Petrine rebuke, ". . . you thought *(enomisas)* you could obtain the gift of God with money *(dia chrēmatōn).*"

This verb occurs only in the latest strata of the LXX, Wis 13:2; 17:3; Sir 29:4 (of money loaned); 2 Macc 4:32; 7:19; 8:35; 14:4; and 4 Macc 2:14; 4:7, 13;

5:16, 18, 19; 9:4, 7. In the Ap. Frs. only *First Clement* uses the word, at 1.1; 26.1; 44.3, but not in the sense of supposing that which is not true.

The noun *porismon,* "gain," occurs only in this and the following verse in the NT; see Comment for further discussion.

## ♦ COMMENT

6:3. *In the case of a man who propounds strange teachings and has no recourse to the wholesome sayings that come from our Lord, Jesus Christ, nor to the godly instruction.* In contrast to the good teaching, the next and final section of this letter turns to those who teach otherwise, *ei tis heterodidaskalei.* One recalls that First Timothy began with the apostolic *paraggelia* on false versus true teaching (1:3-7 vs. 8-17) and Timothy's relation to both (1:18-22). Now this letter closes by returning to a further *paraggelia* on false teaching (6:3-5, 20-21); cf. the *paraggellō/paraggelle* of 6:13, 17, and its relation to Timothy's ministry (cf. 6:11-16 with 1 Tim 1:3).

The parallel clause in the protasis here describes and defines one who "propounds strange teachings" as having "no recourse to," *proserchetai,* a twofold body of teaching that consists in *logois* and *didaskaliai.* The heterodox do not have recourse to (1) "the wholesome sayings that come from our Lord, Jesus Christ," *hygiainousin logois, tois tou kyriou hēmōn Iēsou Christou,* or to (2) "the godly instruction," *kai tēi kat' eusebeian didaskaliai.*

The distinction, once made, immediately poses the question of to which "words" of the Lord Jesus this text refers. One recalls Acts 20:35 where the Ephesian (presbyter-) bishops are exhorted by Paul "to remember the words of the Lord Jesus *(tōn logōn tou Kyriou Iēsou),* how he said, 'It is more blessed to give than to receive.'" If Haenchen, *Acts,* pp. 594-595, is correct that here the author of Luke-Acts placed a Greek proverb on the lips of Jesus (via Paul), still one must come to terms with the importance that was attached to having certain "words" or sayings come from Jesus himself. In light of the logion cited in 1 Tim 5:18 in this correspondence (which explicitly cites the OT on only two other occasions), one would infer that the author-redactor was referring here in 6:4 to at least a collection of Jesus' sayings. There is no gainsaying the importance that the author of Luke-Acts attached to such a collection when one recalls the amount of material purporting to be Jesus' teaching that he incorporated into his form of the Gospel.

In the hypothesis proposed in this commentary, the reference here in the PE to recorded and collected words of Jesus (the only such reference in the NT according to Kittel, *TDNT* 4.109) takes the reader back (via Paul) to the opening roll of this composition with its "definitive" collection of precisely these materials. It may support the hypothesis that only this passage of the PE and Acts 20:35, in the NT, use the actual terminology *logoi tou Kyriou . . . Iēsou* (cf. Kittel, *ut cit.*, pp. 105-106, on the sayings of Jesus). Notable, too, is *1 Clem.* 13.1, which apparently echoes this passage in Acts when it exhorts the Corinthians to "do that which is written *(to gegrammenon)* . . . especially remembering the words of the Lord Jesus *(memnēmenoi tōn logōn tou Kyriou Iēsou)* which he spoke . . ." and there follow citations of sayings of Jesus that seem to come from a sayings source rather than the Gospel texts now extant (cf. Jaubert, pp. 122-123, as well as p. 52). Equally striking is *1 Clem.* 46.7-8, where again one reads, "Remember the words of the [*or* our] Lord Jesus *(mnēsthēte tōn logōn tou Kyriou Iēsou)*, for he said . . . ," and again sayings of Jesus follow that do not correspond to the transmitted texts of the Gospels.

"The wholesome sayings that come from our Lord, Jesus Christ" here can be compared and contrasted with "God's word" in 1 Tim 4:5, as well as with the saying of Jesus cited as *graphē* in 5:18 above. The contents of such sayings are the antithesis of the heterodoxy just mentioned. To these sayings of the Lord is joined "the teaching according to godliness," the *didaskalia*, the Pauline interpretation of the OT Scriptures that has been commented on previously. The additional qualification of the *didaskalia* here as *kat' eusebeian* takes up a phrase that stood in the description of Paul's apostolate "for the faith of God's elect and for the knowledge of the truth," that is, *kat' eusebeian* in Titus 1:1. As is noted in the commentary there, the sense of the phrase is "that which accords with real religion" or "genuinely religious," and here likewise the concern is with a "genuinely religious teaching" about the OT Scriptures, which is opposed to the one who *heterodidaskalei* and who has a rather peculiar appreciation of *eusebeia* in any case, as the conclusion of verse 5 makes clear.

4. *One can only conclude that he has become a conceited ignoramus with a morbid craving for speculations and quibbling about terminology.* The heterodox teacher just described "has become a conceited ignoramus." In contrast *(alla)* to real knowledge of the word of God, the heterodox has rather "a morbid craving *(nosōn)* for speculations and quibbling about terminology." In the LXX (cf. Oepke, *TDNT* 4.1092, for Sym.) *nosōn* occurs only in Wis 17:8 of magicians "who promised to drive off the fears and disorders of a sick soul *(psychēs nosousēs)*, were sick *(enosoun)* themselves with ridiculous fear." The figurative use here in the Pastorals is notably similar to the imaginative polemic of Wisdom. The controversial stance of the opponents is itself symptomatic of their sick minds. They really are seeking not knowledge but the prickly satisfaction of hostility and rejection. This morbid craving finds its outlet in religious controversies and wranglings about words. Just as in Titus 3:9 all four terms including the *machas nomikas* (see AB *Titus in loc.*) referred to scriptural (OT) matters and their interpretation, so here the *zētēseis kai logomachias* appear to refer to

religious controversies principally about what we would call the OT but perhaps here extend to disputes about the sayings of the Lord (cf. the previous *logoi . . . tou kyriou* with *logomachias*).

*These in turn produce jealousy, controversy, vituperations, vicious insinuations.* Out of these scriptural wranglings is produced a fivefold asyndetic series of evils, described in a series of gradually lengthened words and phrases that extend throughout verse 5. The first of the series is *phthonos,* "jealousy," which figured above in the list of the vices at Titus 3:3. A special sharpness must have been felt in this polemic of the Pastorals if this section was redacted at a time when the memory of the death of Paul, as occasioned by intramural Christian strife that eventuated in his denunciation and betrayal to the Roman authorities, was still fresh in the mind of the Roman church (cf. 2 Tim 1:15; 4:10-11, 14, 16). Joined immediately to *phthonos* is "controversy," *eris,* which was paired with *phthonos* in Rom 1:29 and Phil 1:15 (of some who preached Christ "from envy and rivalry").

With *blasphēmiai,* "vituperations," and after, not only are the terms in the list longer, they also are in the plural (on the minor variants see J. K. Elliott, *Greek Text,* p. 93). The noun here surely refers to abusive, slanderous speech, but its object is not unambiguous. Is it abuse and insult for God himself and his revelation or primarily for those who are his spokesmen? Both possibilities can be argued on the parallels in this correspondence, and of course the author-redactor may not have intended any real distinction to be made between the two.

With *hyponoiai ponērai* and the fifth member in the series, the plural noun is now augmented with an adjective. As here, human conjectures can be and are branded as morally reprehensible at 2 Tim 3:13 where *ponēroi* is a term for the people *(anthrōpoi)* who have rejected Paul and his teaching (cf. Acts 17:5), and at 2 Tim 4:18 the apostle is assured that "the Lord will deliver me from any one of these vicious attacks *(apo pantos ergou ponērou)*" of the persons who are encompassing his death (the intensifying *pantos* = *kwl* is a characteristic Qumran way of qualifying *rʿ* [*TDNT* 6.551]). Thus the uses in the PE refer to man as such as well as to his internal thoughts and his visible works. The Lukan corpus also likes to use *ponēros* to modify *pneuma* (*-ta*) (Luke 7:21; 8:2; 11:26; Acts 19:12-13, 15-16.

5. *the incessant bickerings of men whose minds are a shambles and who have been robbed of the truth.* The fifth and final member of the series expands to fill a whole verse of fourteen words. The initial noun, *diaparatribai,* is unknown to the rest of the NT, the LXX, the Ap. Frs., and even profane Greek. It is an "intensive" compound of *paratribai,* a term that refers to mutual friction and irritation. Lampe, *PGL,* p. 357, cites Clement of Alexandria, *Strom.* 1.8 (*PG* 8.736c, quoting this passage), as well as Chrysostom in his commentary on this passage

(*PG* 11.648c) and Antiochus Monachus (+ 619 or thereafter), *PG* 89.1841c, for this noun. *Paratribē* occurs in Polybius 2.36.5 of the relations between Rome and Carthage, "Characterized by mutual suspicion *(hypopsiais)* and friction *(paratribais)*." Lampe, p. 1027, adduces an example from Socrates Scholasticus *H.E.* 4.29.6 (*PG* 67.541c) where the noun describes a jostling so violent that it caused death to many, as well as another from pseudo-Athanasius, *Apoll.* 2.19 (*PG* 26.1165A), that refers to the aberrations/strayings from the paths by heresies.

The "incessant bickerings" (cf. the *knēthomenoi tēn akoēn,* those with "itchy ears" at 2 Tim 4:3) are the peculiar possession of persons (*anthrōpon;* cf. Titus 1:14 [pl.]; 3:10 [sg.]; 1 Tim 5:24 [pl.]) "whose minds are a shambles *(diephtharmenōn ton noun)*." The perfect passive participle suggests the progressive mental spoilage (Spicq, *EP*) that has occurred in these troublemakers who in the English idiom are "spoiling for a fight." The use of *nous* in this passage and in the *katephtharmenoi ton noun* of 2 Tim 3:8 is comparable to that in 2 Cor 11:3: "But I am afraid that as the serpent deceived Eve by his cunning, your thoughts will be led astray *(phtharēi ta noēmata)* from a sincere and pure devotion to Christ." The link between intellectual and moral corruption can be read in conjunction with 1 Cor 15:33 with its proverb from Menander, where evil teaching in its turn spoils the moral conduct of those who listen to it (cf. Conzelmann, *1 Cor.,* pp. 278-279 nn. 139, 141).

In Ign *Eph.* 19.3 one reads of the star of Bethlehem that "by this, . . . ignorance was removed and the old kingdom was destroyed *(diephtheireto)*." In *Magn.* 10.2 he exhorts, "Be salted . . . [in Christ] that none among you may be corrupted *(diaphtharēi)*," in a context that enjoins his readers from Jewish practices. In his *Rom.* 7.1 he declares, "The prince *(archōn)* of this world *(aiōnos)* wishes . . . to corrupt my mind towards God *(tēn eis theon mou gnōmēn diaphtheirai)*." This last example is particularly close to the PE and resembles the usage also of Hermas, *Sim.* 4.7, "For his understanding *(dianoia)* is not corrupted *(ou diaphtharēsetai)* away from the Lord, but he will serve him with a pure mind." There are seven other uses of this verb in Hermas, but not otherwise in the Ap. Frs.

The "men whose minds are a shambles" are further described in a parallel phrase in which the connective *kai* is rather conspicuous after the long asyndetic series that has preceded. They are "robbed of the truth *(apesterēmenōn tēs alētheias)*." The sense of this verb is to defraud someone of that to which he has a right (see Notes). A Christian may suffer that willingly, of material or ephemeral goods, as in Ign. *Eph.* 10.3, but Hermas, *Vis.* 3.9.9, can admonish, "See to it, therefore, children, that these disagreements do not rob you *(aposterēsousin)* of your life *(tēn zōēn)*," but the sense of material fraud predominates in the papyri (MM *s.v.,* p. 69). These men have been robbed of the truth, i.e. precisely and profoundly robbed of faith in the person of Christ. Ironically that fact does not mean that they have lost their livelihood, for in a delicious and sardonic final characterization, a veritable scorpion's sting, they are persons "who think *(nomizontōn)* godliness is a means for gain." In their confused state of mind they suppose that which is in fact not so.

*they think godliness is a means for gain.* These men suppose that "godliness" pays. The *eusebeia* here is, of course, a counterfeit of true religion, the "appearance of godliness *(morphōsin eusebeias)*" of 2 Tim 3:5, all the externals without the Spirit, the words without the music, the letter without the living voice. Note how the Western addition here tried to make this quite clear (*GNT*$^{3corr}$, and B. Metzger, *TCGNT,* p. 643) with the addition of *aphistaso apo tōn toioutōn,* "withdraw from such people." This role-playing gets them an actor's salary and for them religion is a livelihood, not a life. In this verse *porismon* is the material profit that accrues to a "material" religion; in the following it is "profit" in another order, as the *eusebeia* there is also "real" *eusebeia.*

In the LXX only Wis 13:19; 14:2 use *porismos,* of the human desire for turning a profit and moneymaking. The noun does not occur in the Ap. Frs. MM *s.v.,* p. 529, cites Artemidorus, p. 254.20, *to ergon lusiteles men eis porismon,* "the work is advantageous for profit." Spicq, *EP,* p. 559, has adduced a notable example from Philo, describing the Sabbath observance as one in which men are to refrain from "works that pertain to seeking and gaining *(porismon)* a livelihood *(biou),* and giving their time to the one sole object of philosophy with a view to the improvement of character and submission to the scrutiny of conscience" (*Op. Mund.* 128). The contrast between religious observance that does not pay and other works that do is deliberate. In *Det.* 55 Philo adds, "But it would be impiety to say that religion *(eusebeian),* which is caring for God, is a way of providing *(poristikēn)* what will benefit the deity, for he gains benefit from nothing." This principle does not really figure in the argumentation of the PE. The author is intent upon branding the false teachers with precisely that fondness for money that he found so abhorrent in candidates for sharing the apostolic ministry (Titus 1:7; 1 Tim 3:3, 8).

## IV.C.2. RICHES: PART I (6:6-10)

6 [6]*No question of it. Godliness brings gain, great gain — for someone contented with what he has.* [7]*The reason is that we brought nothing into the world; as a result we cannot take anything out of it.* [8]*So then if we have keep and covering, with them we shall be content.* [9]*Those, however, who want to be wealthy topple into a temptation and a trap and multiple lusts, senseless and injurious, the kind that engulf people in utterly ruinous destruction.* [10]*The root that lies under all evils is the*

*love of money. Certain persons who have craved it have strayed off from the faith and have skewered themselves with multiple tortures.*

## ♦ NOTES

6:6. *No question of it. Godliness brings gain, great gain — for someone contented with what he has.* Lit. "However *(de),* godliness with contentment is a great gain." "Great gain," *meta autarkeias,* occurs once otherwise in the NT, in 2 Cor 9:8, of God who provides so richly "that you may always have enough of everything *(pasan autarkeian)* and may provide in abundance for every good work." For its use in the LXX and Ap. Frs., see Comment below.

7. *we brought nothing into the world; as a result we cannot take anything out of it.* The terminology of 1 Tim 6:7, "we brought nothing," *ouden . . . eisēnegkamen,* uses a verb that occurs only here in the PE, but twelve of its remaining occurrences in the NT are in Luke-Acts (five times/seven times; and note that Luke 11:4 = Matt 6:13 is the Q ending of the Lord's Prayer). Though Heb 13:11 also uses *eispherein eis . . . ,* this also occurs in Luke 11:4 as well as Acts 17:20. The verb is common enough in the LXX, but not so in the Ap. Frs. *Didache* 8.2 uses it in the conclusion of the Lord's Prayer, and Polycarp, *Phil.* 4.1, in quoting this passage of the PE as well as (in 7.2) in quoting the conclusion of the Lord's Prayer. Hermas alone uses the term independently, so to speak, of those who "introduced *(eispherontes)* strange doctrines and corrupted the servants of God" (*Sim.* 8.6.5).

On the phrase *eis ton kosmon,* cf. 1 Tim 1:15 (as well as the *en kosmōi* of 3:16). Wisdom 7:6, in a context that resembles this verse of First Timothy, writes, "there is for all mankind *(pantōn)* one entrance into life (*bion* [Sinaiticus reads *kosmon!*]) and a common departure," and the variant reading reminds one that human life in its visible and material aspects could be understood as *kosmos.*

The latter member of this saying is formally parallel to the former. The verb again is in the first person plural, and thus the speakers identify themselves with all humankind. Where the previous member has *ouden* as object, in this member *oude* is used adverbially and the indefinite *ti* has become the object of *exenegkein . . . dynametha.* On *dynamai* cf. 1 Tim 5:25. *Ekpherō* occurs eight times in the NT, but only here in the Paulines; five of the remaining seven uses are in Luke-Acts (Luke 15:22 of a stored garment; Acts 5:6, 9, 10 of corpses; 5:15). Mark 8:23 and Heb 6:8 are the other two. In the Ap. Frs., outside of Polycarp, *Phil.* 4.1, cited above, this verb is used only by *1 Clem.* 24.5, in the sower parable where the decayed seeds "bring forth fruit *(ekpherei karpon),*" and again at 52.2, citing LXX Ps 68:32, of a sacrificial calf "putting forth *(ekpheronta)* horns and hooves." In more than a column of entries under *eispherō* in H-R, there is no parallel for the phrase here in the PE. *Nil* in *TDNT* 9 for this verb, though Weiss, *TDNT* 9.64-65, treats of *eispherō,* noting that the NT use is ordinarily of things rather than persons (contrast the end of the Lord's Prayer).

*as a result.* On the translation of *hoti,* see Comment below.

8. *keep and covering. Keep, diatrophas* (cf. the *misthou* of 1 Tim 5:18 = Luke 10:7 and the *trophēs* of Matt 10:10), occurs only here in the NT, and in the LXX it is found only in 1 Macc 6:49 (of provisions for a siege) and in the singular (note all the examples in MM *s.v.,* p. 156, are singular). It is not found in the Ap. Frs. Indeed, the Western text (D. F. G. K. P. 061 pl) reads the singular here in First Timothy, and J. K. Elliott, *Greek Text,* p. 96, notes that the cognate *trophē* is in fifteen out of sixteen NT occurrences in the singular. He believes that the Alexandrian text changed the term into the plural in order to tidy up the parallelism with the following *skepasmata.* Yet that argument is really double-edged, for the plural is the more difficult and unusual reading and thus stands every chance of having been "normalized" by the Western scribes in spite of the parallelism. In the papyri (MM), as here, the term designates the provisions or "keep" for a person, his "board."

If *diatrophas* was unusual in biblical and early Christian Greek, *covering, skepasmata,* is quite unheard of in the rest of the NT, the LXX, and the Ap. Frs. The term derives from *skepas,* "shelter," and thus (means of) shelter and clothing (i.e. covering).

*we shall be content.* This verb (cf. Kittel, *TDNT* 1.464-466) takes up both the thought of and the term *autarkeia* in 1 Tim 6:6 (see above). Of the eight NT occurrences, this is the only one in the PE. It occurs once otherwise in the Paulines, on the lips of the risen Jesus telling Paul, "my grace is sufficient for you" (2 Cor 12:9). Luke uses the term only of the Baptist's telling soldiers to be content *(arkeisthe)* with their wages (Luke 3:14). Of the other NT uses, 3 John 10 says of the arrogant Diotrephes, *mē arkoumenos epi toutois,* i.e. "not content with these [harsh words]," he has resorted to the physical exclusion of his opponents (cf. 2 Macc 5:15). Much closer to the thought of the PE is Heb 13:5: "Keep your life free from love of money *(aphilargyros ho tropos)* and be content with what you have *(arkoumenoi tois parousin).*" The latter expression was popular enough in Greek philosophy (Teles, third century B.C.E., *ap.* Kittel, p. 465).

The LXX uses *arkein* a dozen times and in Exod 12:4 and Num 11:22 of a sufficiency of food, but without a close verbal parallel to PE.

In the Ap. Frs. this verb occurs in *1 Clem.* 2.1, describing the Corinthians as once having been "satisfied *(arkoumenoi)* with the provisions *(tois ephodiois)* of Christ"; and Ign. *Pol.* 5.1 wants Christian women to "love the Lord and be content *(arkeisthai)* with their consorts *(symbiois)* in the flesh and in spirit." Of the two uses in Hermas, *Vis.* 3.10.8 and *Sim.* 5.2.9, the latter with its reference to food and its distribution offers some illustration of the PE use.

9. *Those, however, who want to be wealthy.* In contrast *(de)* to those satisfied with a modicum are *hoi . . . boulomenoi ploutein,* "those who want to be wealthy." The participial form, *boulomenoi,* takes up the verb *boulesthai* for the last time in the PE (Titus 3:8; 1 Tim 2:8; 5:14), and one notes that this use of the participle is rather frequent in Acts (six of fourteen uses of the verb), though not found in Luke. Previously the executive will of the apostle had been the subject. Here it is the determined mind and will of those seeking wealth — *ploutein,* "to be wealthy." This verb will occur again in the PE at 6:18 below, in a good sense, of becoming rich "in fine deeds" (cf. vv. 5-6 *supra* on "gain"). In the rest of the Paulines it is used in Rom 10:12 of the one Lord who "bestows his riches *(ploutōn)* upon all who call upon him"; in 1 Cor 4:8 ironically of the Corinthians, "Already you have become rich"; in 2 Cor 8:9 of Jesus himself, who became poor "so that by his poverty you might become rich." Apart from Rev 3:17, 18; 18:3, 15, 19, only Luke 1:53 and 12:21 *(s.v.l.)* use the verb of the rich, whom God sends off empty and who lays up treasure for himself and will not be "rich *(ploutōn)* toward *(eis)* God." On the cognate *plousiōs* see Titus 3:6 and 1 Tim 6:17 (which also has *plousiois* and *ploutou*). In general see F. Hauck and W. Kasch, *TDNT* 6.318-332, especially 328-330.

In the Ap. Frs., *2 Clem.* 20.1 writes of "the unrighteous enjoying wealth *(ploutountas).*" Hermas has the four other uses of this verb (cf. further on 6:17-19 below).

*topple into a temptation and a trap.* On *empiptousin eis . . . pagida* cf. above on 1 Tim 3:6, 7 for the neophyte who might "fall into disgrace and a snare of the devil." See also Comment below.

*temptation. Peirasmon* is a noun that out of twenty-one NT uses occurs only here in the PE and only twice otherwise in the Paulines (1 Cor 10:13 *bis;* cf. Seesemann, *TDNT* 6.28-29; Gal 4:14 of Paul's broken health as a "trial" for his converts-to-be in Galatia; cf. BAGD *s.v.,* p. 277). Of the eighteen remaining NT uses, seven are in Luke-Acts (six/one). Korn, *PEIRASMOS,* pp. 76-88 (cited in Seesemann), has shown the roots of the NT conception of *peirasmos* in the LXX, where the noun occurs nineteen times (five times in Deuteronomy; four times in Ecclesiastes; six times in Sirach).

In the Ap. Frs. *peirasmos* occurs, apart from two citations of the Lord's Prayer (*Did.* 8.2; Polycarp, *Phil.* 7.2), only in *2 Clem.* 18.2, where it is parallel to the devil's devices, and Hermas, *Man.* 9.7, where a slow answer to a prayer is *dia peirasmon tina ē paraptōma ti,* "on account of some trial (testing?) or some sin." The latter usage seems close to that of Luke and PE.

*multiple lusts.* On *epithymiai* see Titus 2:12 and 3:3 (where *anoētoi* also occurs). To the previous comments at Titus 2:12, add here (with S. Brown) that the usage of *epithymia* in Luke is psychological and that the one occurrence in Acts (20:33) where it does refer to an unethical desire for money has no suggestion that this was a *peirasmos* for Paul. Of the 353 NT uses of *polys*, 82 are in the Paulines (none in Second Thessalonians); 51/46 = 97 are in Luke-Acts.

*injurious.* See Comment below.

*the kind, haitines.* "The kind who/which" *(hostis)* is used seven times in the PE: in a denigrating sense and always in the plural as here, Titus 1:11; 1 Tim 1:4; and 2 Tim 2:18; and in a positive sense in 1 Tim 3:15 and 2 Tim 1:5 in the singular, and in 2 Tim 2:2 in the plural. Cf. also 1 Tim 1:4; 3:15.

*engulf.* The verb *bythizousin* occurs otherwise in the NT only in Luke 5:7 (of sinking boats), and in the LXX only in 2 Macc 12:4 (of drowning several hundred Jews). In the Ap. Frs. only *1 Clem.* 51.5 uses this verb, of the Egyptian army being sunk in the Red Sea. For the same sense, Josephus, *Apion* 1.306, 308, 314. The figurative sense here in the PE can be paralleled in a few secular texts (see D-C *in loc.* for Alciphro, and MM *s.v.*).

*utterly ruinous destruction.* Lit. "ruin and destruction." See Comment below for detailed discussion.

10. *root.* The noun *rhiza* (sixteen times in NT) occurs only here in the PE. Otherwise in the Paulines only Rom 11:16, 17, 18 and 15:12 (= LXX Isa 11:10) use the noun. Luke 3:9 (= Matt 3:10) takes it up from Q, and 8:13 from Mark 4:17. Maurer, *TDNT* 6.985-990, has noted that only four of fifty-seven LXX uses actually refer to the roots of plants (p. 985), and the NT similarly uses this noun only in comparisons, except Mark 11:20 (p. 988). The figurative senses that approach this usage in First Timothy are LXX Deut 29:17, of an idolater in the land as "a root coming up *(rhiza anō phyousa)* in gall and bitterness" (cf. Heb 12:15); Sir 40:15, "The children of the ungodly . . . are unclean roots *(rhizai akathartoi)* upon sheer rock"; and 1 Macc 1:10 of Antiochus Epiphanes as "a sinful root (= shoot)" *(rhiza hamartōlos)*. The Qumran sectaries called themselves "a root *(šwrš)* of planting" (CD 1.7, Dupont-Sommer, *EWQ*, p. 121), and their hymns particularly favor this term (1QH 3.31 of the stone "roots" of mountains; 4.14 of hypocrites and idolaters, "a root is in their thoughts bearing fruits that are poisoned and bitter" [Dupont-Sommer, *EWQ*, p. 212]; 6.16 of the community whose "roots go down to the abyss" [Dupont-Sommer, *EWQ*, p. 219]; 8.7, both verb and noun, of the community; 8.10 of the proud whose root does not reach the stream of living water; 8.23 of the members of the community), usually for the community but occasionally for its enemies.

Of the uses in the Ap. Frs., *1 Clem.* 16.3 = LXX Isa 53:2, and 39:8 = LXX Job 5:3, and *Barn.* 12.9 = an addition to LXX Exod 17:14. Polycarp, *Phil.* 1.2, speaks to the Philippians of "the firm root *(bebaia . . . rhiza)* of your faith" that "bears fruit," just as the evil root here in First Timothy bears evil fruit (Maurer, *TDNT* 6.990). More striking, indeed, is the fact that Polycarp, *Phil.* 4.1, uses different terms from 1 Tim 6:10 when he expresses the same concept, saying *archē de pantōn chalepōn philargyria.* On three/four uses in Hermas, see Maurer, p. 990.

*evils.* The adjective *kaka* (Titus 1:12) has here become nominal, as it will also be at 2 Tim 4:14. The NT has 50 uses of this term, and in the rest of the Paulines there are 23. Of the 6 times in Luke-Acts, the neuter plural occurs in Luke 16:25 of the "evils" — i.e. hunger, disease, abandonment — suffered by Lazarus, and in Acts 9:13 of the "evils" that Paul has inflicted on the Jerusalem church. Grundmann, *TDNT* 3.469-487, has noted 371 uses of *kakos* in LXX, in 227 instances = the Hebrew *raʿ/rāʿa*], and also the use there of *kaka* = disasters, personal and national, that are punishments for moral evil, for sin (p. 477). In Job 2:10 one has moved beyond this to a usage very much like that of Luke, where the disasters (evils) are not considered a necessary consequence of moral evil (sins).

*love of money.* The noun *philargyria* does not occur elsewhere in the NT, but the cognate adjective occurs at 2 Tim 3:2, as well as Luke 16:14. Moreover, the antonym *aphilargyros* was used in 1 Tim 3:3 (as well as Heb 13:5; see commentary *in loc.* for all uses by LXX and Ap. Frs. of this cluster of terms). Rare as this noun is in biblical Greek (*nil* in *TDNT* except for Delling, 6.270-271), there is no dearth of examples in the secular and religious literature, as D-C, Spicq, LSJ, MM *s.v.* illustrate.

*have craved.* On *oregesthai* see 1 Tim 3:1.

*have strayed off. Apeplanēthēsan* occurs otherwise in the NT only at Mark 13:22, of false christs and false prophets "leading astray," if possible, the elect. The verb *planan* occurred above in Titus 3:3, and three additional times in the PE (2 Tim 3:13 *bis;* 1 Tim 4:1); the verb in the other Paulines is known only in the warning "Be not deluded" (1 Cor 6:9; 15:33; Gal 6:7; the sole Lukan usage [Luke 21:8] is similar); of the other thirty-three NT uses, almost half are shared by Matthew and Revelation (see also commentary at 2 Tim 3:13). In the seven LXX occurrences, the term denotes straying from the faith of Israel in 2 Chron 21:11; Jer 27(MT 50):6; 2 Macc 2:2, with explicit mention that the Babylonian idols are silver and gold, thus implying a link between greed and idolatry; in Prov 7:21 the adulteress leads astray; in Sir 13:6, 8 the rich man himself strays away from wisdom (the Law).

In the Ap. Frs., Polycarp, *Phil.* 6.1, 3, described as part of the presbyters' responsibility "bringing back those that have wandered" *(ta apopeplanēmena),* and he noted hypocritical Christians "who lead astray *(apoplanōsi)* empty-minded *(kenous)* men." The next paragraph would lead one to infer that these men taught heretical views.

Hermas, in his half dozen uses of this verb, uses it of the way in which bitter ill-temper "leads away" the vain *(apokenous)* and doubled-minded but not "those who are filled with faith" (*Man.* 5.2.1 *tris*), as well as in a contest where Christian men *(hoi pisteusantes)* are deceived *(apoplanōntai)* through wealth and business relationships (*Man.* 10.1.5). In *Sim.* 6.3.3 one reads of "those who wandered away from God and walked in the lusts and deceits of this world." In *Sim.* 9.20.2 the verb occurs again to describe the way in which wealthy businessmen "do not cleave to the servants of God but are choked by their work *(praxeōn)* and go astray *(apoplanōntai)*."

*skewered.* The verb *peripeirein,* here in the aorist active as the previous verb was in the aorist passive, occurs only here in the NT. It is not documented in the LXX or the Ap. Frs. It is attested in its literal sense of "to pierce with swords and spears" or "with a stake" in Diodorus Siculus 16.80, 19.84 (*ap.* LSJ and Harrison, *Paulines,* p. 133), in the first century B.C.E. (cf. Josephus, *War* 3.296). The metaphorical sense is attested in Philo, *Flacc.* 1, where of Flaccus it is said, *athroous anēkestois periepeire kakois,* "He put crowds (of Jews) on the spit of utterly ruinous evils"; *Som.* 2.103 of being "*pinned* in impassable ravines"; and *Praem.* 20 of being "*pinned* in nets."

*multiple tortures.* The avaricious have spitted themselves on *odynais pollais,* "many pangs," a noun found elsewhere in the NT only in Rom 9:2 of Paul's own heartfelt and constant "anguish" (*odynē* in the sg.) at the failure of Israel to believe in Jesus. The LXX uses the noun sixty times, especially Job (seventeen times) and Psalms (Hauck, *TDNT* 5.115), but apparently never with *pollai* (see S* *poikilais* and J. K. Elliott, *Greek Text,* p. 98). The Ap. Frs. do not use the noun.

## ♦ COMMENT

6:6. *No question of it. Godliness brings gain, great gain — for someone contented with what he has.* The unusual word order of this sentence, with its initial *estin,* characteristic of definitions and very solemn affirmations with an oath (cf. 2 Cor 11:10; Spicq, *EP,* p. 560), places the following statement in emphatic contrast (*de,* here translated "no question of it") with what the false teachers suppose. "Godliness *(hē eusebeia)* is gain, great gain *(porismos megas)* — for someone contented with what he has *(meta autarkeias)*." Here the term *porismos* is redefined in the way *ōphelimos* was at 1 Tim 4:8: the specifically Christian "gain" or treasure is being spoken of (cf. the treasure in heaven of Luke 12:33-34 and 18:22, a treasure already in the heart of the good man, Luke 6:45; cf. the Matthean parable of the kingdom, Matt 13:44, "like a treasure hidden in a field"). The "gain" is here further qualified as "great," *mega,* and here, too, the eschatological connotations of the adjective ought not to be overlooked (of its hundreds of NT uses, eighty occur in Revelation — the most of any NT book).

In Titus 2:13 the *megas* fortified the eschatological thrust of the confession in which it appeared while also hinting at its triumphal, public character; cf. also above on 1 Tim 3:16, "great is the mystery of godliness *(eusebeia)*." As God and his plan are great, so is the reward or gain that he offers in the world to come.

Here *eusebeia,* real religion, is further described in a phrase, *meta autarkeias.* The noun does not occur in the LXX, and one waits until Hermas, *Man.* 6.2.3; *Sim.* 1.6 (cf. also the *arketon tēs trophēs* of *Vis.* 3.9.3 in context), to encounter the word in the Ap. Frs. The LXX does use, however, the cognate *autarkein* (Deut 32:10) and *autarkēs;* Prov 30:8, "Give me not wealth or penury but prescribe the necessities and a sufficiency of things *(ta autarkē)*"; Sir 5:1; 11:24, "Do not say 'I have enough (wealth)'"; 31:28 of temperance in drinking; 40:18, "Life is sweet for the self-reliant worker *(autarkous ergatou)*"; and 4 Macc 9:9, "But you shall suffer for our cruel murder . . . sufficient *(autarkē)* torment by fire forever." Paul also uses the adjective when he writes to the Philippians (4:11), "Not that I complain of want; for I have learned, in whatever state I am, to be content *(autarkēs einai)*." MM *s.v.,* p. 93, remark that the sense here and in Sir 40:18 is to be found in the literary (philosophical) sources rather than popular idiom (where it means simply "enough"). The noun occurs in the papyri only with the meaning of a concrete, tangible sufficiency of something (MM *ibid.*), and, of course, that is quite possible at this point in the PE. In that case the reference is to authentic religion along with a sufficiency of material support being indeed a "great profit." In that case the last phrase has an ironic nuance, for the modest support needed by the genuinely faithful is not the high-yield market at which the false teachers aim.

The use of the cognate *toutois arkesthēsometha* at 6:8 below (see commentary *infra*) would indicate that the author here understood at least a sufficiency of material goods such as food and clothing when he used *autarkeia.* But did he understand more than that material sufficiency? Kittel, *TDNT* 1.466-467, has suggested that the usage here extends beyond rolling with the punch of material fortunes, for *autarkeia* is a constituent part of and a complement to *eusebeia.* Real religion accepts *all* things, not just the hard things, from the Lord of creation, and one encounters here, as in Phil 4:11-13, a profound affirmation of all God's good gifts in this world (cf. Phil 4:8), in the sufficiency of which all men are to share (cf. 2 Cor 9:8). Hengel, *PREC,* pp. 54-59, has noted the link between the Pauline attitude toward possessions and that "inner freedom" which he valued so highly (cf. 1 Cor 6:12), an attitude which he shared not only with the wandering Cynic and Stoic philosophers of his own day but also with the rabbis of the first century (*ap.* Hengel, p. 54). "The wise man is self-sufficient" (Antisthenes *ap.* Diogenes Laertius 6.11) epitomized and articulated an "ideal of complete self-sufficiency [that] was essentially derived from Socrates" (Hengel, *PREC,* p. 55). (For Menander, *Dysc.* 714, see 6:8, *arkesthēsometha, infra.*)

What differentiated Pauline self-sufficiency and inner freedom was that it was not an end in itself but a freeing for apostolic service to God, to God's Christ, and to all men. If Socrates had seen his service in poverty as bringing men to realize that they are not wise (cf. Plato, *Apology* 36c), Paul saw his as bringing to the foolish the wisdom of God, Christ crucified (1 Cor 1:22-25). With Hengel one notes that the passage of First Timothy does not represent the doctrinaire, rigoristic asceticism of a Tatian, but perhaps it is closer to the Pauline tradition than Hengel admits, for this whole passage on perils of possessions and yielding to avaricious desires is set in the context of the apostolic teaching ministry and a Paul and Timothy who are content (*arkesthēsometha,* note the first person plural) with their food and clothing as they teach and exhort (cf. 6:2). Moreover, they choose men to share and continue this apostolic task who are not money-grubbers (Titus 1:7, etc., *supra*).

To take up Kittel's point, the *autarkeia* here is actually part of the complement of that *eusebeia* which for this correspondence designates authentic Christian religion. There is a sort of parity established between godliness and contentment by the preposition *meta* here, which, as Spicq, *EP,* p. 560, has noted, is used in the way that the Hebrew *'im* was employed (cf. also the *meta sōphrosynēs* of 1 Tim 2:15 as well as 1 Tim 1:14; 4:3-4), and this usage denotes more than simply accompaniment (as at Titus 3:15; 2 Tim 4:11). Hengel would call this moderate asceticism of the PE "a bourgeois element" (p. 58) without any pejorative connotations, or so he claims. That, unfortunately, is like trying to use the term *myth* without any derogatory sense. Moreover, even the neutral "middle-class" meaning of *bourgeois* implies a certain stable security and an ensured *status quo* that is far from the minimal and precarious "sufficiency" of food and clothing that this correspondence envisions for apostolic ministers and teachers who are going to live in the world with scarcely more than they were born with (see commentary on vv. 7-8 below).

Hengel is certainly right in observing that early Christianity drew its main support from the middle class of the day, but the PE, like Paul, are probing, questioning, critiquing the "conventional morality" that those people brought to faith and baptism. This correspondence will not have Christian morality transmuted into a simply Jewish morality, much less a legalism. Just as emphatically it is not giving a *nihil obstat* to the popular philosophical teaching of the day on ethics. The vocabulary of the latter is exploited, but so is that of Hellenistic (including Palestinian) Judaism.

The one thing that specifies and identifies the morality of the PE is the person of Christ as preached, taught, and interpreted by Paul, by Paul's collaborators, and by Paul's congregations. The materials and vocabulary, whether from the OT or the Christian churches or popular Hellenistic ethics, are placed on the lips of Paul, attributed to his pen. It is his gospel and his apostolate that are the lasting measure and norm of all the rest. These letters do in and for the second generation — in the name and power of Paul — what his original correspondence had done for his churches (and others) of the previous generation. *Paulus redivivus* here calls the second generation to order, through his coworkers and successors, through his correspondence, as he had called the previous generation to order in the same way.

7. *The reason is that we brought nothing into the world; as a result we cannot take anything out of it.* The ground and reason *(gar)* for the great profit of the preceding *autarkeia/eusebeia* are an observation on the universal human condition: "We brought nothing into the world; as a result we can take nothing out." The gap between nothing and something is infinite, and in that respect to have anything at all, even in this life, is already "a great gain."

The thought or concept here, as all the commentators note (cf. D-C, pp. 84-85), is found in the OT (Gen 3:19, "You are dust [LXX *gē*] and to dust you shall return"; Eccles 5:15, cf. 3:19-20; Job 1:21; Wis 7:6; Sir 40:1; 41:9-10), in Jewish literature from the Hellenistic age and later, including Philo, *Spec. leg.* 1.294-295, "Naked you come and naked will you again depart . . ." (note the rather different use of the same image in *b. Yoma* 96$^{b}$ [D-C, *in loc.*, n. 12]), not to mention classical literature, Greek (cf. *Anthologia Palatina* 10.58), and Latin (Horace, *Odes* 2.14.21-24, and Seneca, *Ep. Mor.* 102.24-25). In the light of such wide dispersion of the *thought*, it is notable that the only passage in the ancient sources that actually approaches *the words* of 1 Tim 6:7 is Polycarp, *Phil.* 4.1. That passage begins with an allusive paraphrase of 1 Tim 6:10 (see below) and then continues, "Knowing therefore that we brought nothing into the world (*ouden eisēnegkamen eis ton kosmon* [verbatim in First Timothy]), but we have not a thing to take out (*all' <u>oude exenegkein ti</u> echomen* [the underlining is for words in First Timothy]), let us. . . ."

When one considers the verbal disparity in expressing the basic concept in the other sources (not to mention its rather late appearance in the Greek literary tradition — D-C), it is difficult to resist the inference that there is a literary relationship between this passage in the PE and Polycarp, or between the two of them and a common written source. Since the *all' . . . echomen* of Polycarp makes it easier to read the saying than the *hoti . . . dynametha* of First Timothy, one would further infer that either the source contained this latter expression and that First Timothy quoted it exactly and that Polycarp paraphrased the source and eased the reading; or that Polycarp paraphrased the text of First Timothy itself; or that Polycarp also wrote the PE. Von Campenhausen once proposed but has not sustained the last hypothesis. Since there is no linguistic reason for positing a source for First Timothy at this point, and since the text of First Timothy already associated itself in some fashion with Ephesus and Asia Minor (cf. 1 Tim 1:3; 3:14-15), this commentary prefers not to multiply entities but rather to see in Polycarp an actual citation of the PE. It is more difficult to affirm that the PE quoted Polycarp and made his easier text more crabbed and difficult to understand. The fact that the citation in Polycarp occurs in a context that explicitly recalls the letters ([*sic*] in 3.2) of Paul to the Philippians, and within a veritable cento of allusions to and quotations of the PE and other Paulines, makes it reasonable to suppose that his church at Smyrna already knew and read one (or several) collections of Pauline correspondence.

Still another form of the folk wisdom expressed here was placed on the lips of Jesus in the collection of sayings that was titled the *Gospel of Thomas.* What existed in a tantalizing fragment in an early third-century Greek copy of a sayings collection (OxyP 1) has appeared in a Coptic version (adaptation? or vice versa?) of the same document, where the saying #28 (Guillaumount, *Gospel according to Thomas,* pp. 18-21) reads:

> Jesus said: I took my stand in the midst of the world *(kosmos)* and in flesh *(sarx)* I appeared to them; I found them all drunk, I found none among them athirst. And my soul *(psychē)* was afflicted for the sons of men, because they are blind in their heart *and do not see that empty they have come into the world (kosmos)* (and that) *empty they seek to go out of the world (kosmos) again.* But *(plēn)* now they are drunk. . . . [italics Quinn's]

Fitzmyer, *ESBNT,* pp. 392-396, has critically examined this saying and proposed a reconstruction of the lost Greek that for the italicized lines could read:

. . . *kai [ou] blep*
i [*ousin hoti hēkousin eis*
ii [*ton kosmon kenoi: zē —*
iii [*tousi de palin exel —*
iv [*thein ek tou kosmou ke —*
v [*noi . . .*

On the extant Greek, see Jeremias, *Sayings,* pp. 69-74, as well as Hennecke and Schneemelcher, *NT Apoc.* 1.106-107. Grant and Freedman, *Secret Sayings,* pp. 44-45, have no reference to 1 Tim 6:7, though they and Fitzmyer do to 1 Tim 3:16 (see commentary *in loc.*). Fitzmyer, *ESBNT,* p. 396, translates the Coptic *šoueit* with the Greek *kenoi,* noting 1 Cor 15:58. Grant and Freedman called attention to 1 Cor 15:34 and its context in connection with the drunkenness image of this whole logion. One might also note how the theme of blindness of heart in this logion figured also in 1 Tim 6:4-5. Apart from the *eis ton kosmon* phrase, however, the Coptic passage is not close enough to First Timothy to warrant positing literary relationship between the two. It is possible that there was a saying of Jesus floating in the first-century (oral?) tradition that First Timothy has here redacted in one way (cf. the reference in 6:3 to the healthy words of the Lord) and that *Gospel of Thomas* redacted in another (cf. the way in which *kosmos* = *men* or *human society,* with Jesus "standing" and "revealing" in their uncomprehending midst and contrast the first person plural of First Timothy where "we" = "all of us human beings" who do see the way in which men come into and leave the world).

Gärtner, *Gospel of Thomas,* p. 28, has noted that Sayings 28-29 are to be interpreted together in the mind of the one who arranged them because of the repeated key term *sarx.* But Saying 29 concludes by saying, "But I marvel at how *(pōs)* this great wealth [of the spirit] has made its home in this poverty [of the flesh, *sarx*]." The sons of men, in the flesh, are described in Saying 28 as "drunken" (as well as blind), Gnostic language for those who cannot grasp (or are ignorant of) the saving truth (Gärtner, *Gospel of Thomas,* pp. 130-131). This christologically critical saying seems deliberately to distance itself somewhat from the canonical affirmations that the preexisting Word became flesh (John 1:14; cf. 1 John 4:2; 2 John 7) or that the Son of God "was revealed *(ephanerōthē)* in human flesh" (1 Tim 3:16).

The extant Greek of this part of Saying 28 makes it quite clear that one is encountering in Jesus someone from the supernatural order who stands behind what appears as flesh to other sons of men (Gärtner, pp. 141-143). There men are ignorant of their *termini ex quo* and *ad quem,* and this ignorance is not only to be drunk and to be blind but also to be empty (cf. *Gos. Truth* 19.9-25; cf. 20.34-35), a typically Gnostic description for a person, which has a parallel in James 2:20: "O vain man," *O anthrōpe kene* (Gärtner, p. 192). The Lukan usage in Luke 1:53; 20:10-11 of men empty of food or produce would be closer to what the PE are describing than what the *Gospel of Thomas* means by "empty men" or, for that matter, by "poverty" in the following saying (cf. Gärtner, pp. 194-196). On the PE use of *kenophōnia* see 1 Tim 6:20 and 2 Tim 2:16. Perhaps Saying 29 does contain a remote parallel to 1 Tim 6:6 when it describes "How this great wealth" of the heavenly world or kingdom "came to dwell in this poverty," for "great wealth" here designates at least partially what *porismos megas* designates in 1 Tim 6:6 (Gärtner, p. 196, may be too drastic in saying that "wealth as a symbol of the heavenly" has "no direct analogy in the NT" [cf. not only this passage of the PE but also the parables on treasure, pearl, talents, not to mention the dominical command to lay up treasures in heaven, Matt 6:19-20]).

The language of both members of this saying has Lukan rather than Pauline affinities (see Notes). It is the particle(s) by which the two halves are coordinated that pose(s) the greatest problem for the intended meaning of the verse. The textual history indicates from the very earliest witnesses (see on Polycarp above) that the *hoti* of S*, A, F, G, pl (see apparatus of *GNT*$^{3corr}$; Metzger, *TCGNT, in loc.;* and J. K. Elliott, *Greek Text,* p. 95) was interpreted as *all'* ("but") or *dēlon hoti* ("it is obvious that") — thus S$^c$, D$^c$, K, P.Psi, pl, or *alēthes hoti* ("it is there that") — thus D* and many Western witnesses; not to mention those who apparently cut the Gordian knot by simply omitting the particle altogether (Ephraem, Jerome, et al.). Hort proposed a primitive dittographic error that produced an otiose *hoti* from *kosmon* (*KOCMONOTI:* note the way in which that noun is divided from line to line in S, A). However, those who argue for an omitted *dēlon* also argue from a homoioteleuton with the *kosmon* [*dēlon*] *hoti.* Actually a primitive *hoti* alone best explains all the other variants, and the best course seems to be explaining precisely that text. The *dēlon (alēthes)* variants may have been originally not so much variant readings as marginal notes on how a very difficult particle was to be understood (perhaps recalling 1 Cor 15:27; Gal 3:11; and even Heb 7:14). The hardly less difficult *all'* of Polycarp represents a similar attempt.

If the *hoti* has its common causal sense, the relation of the two members verges on nonsense. If it has the weakened meaning "just as, in the same way," then the meaning of the whole is more intelligible. BAGD *s.v.,* p. 589, note that at times the subordination introduced by this particle is "so loose that the translation *for* recommends itself (BDF §456.1)." Examples are given not only from Paul (1 Cor 1:25; 4:9; 10:17; etc.) but also from Luke (Luke 9:12; 13:31; 16:24). Yet one must admit that a weakened but still real causal tone can be heard in these passages and it is difficult to justify any such nuance in 1 Tim 6:7. It would be particularly harsh in view of the *gar* in the former member. Spicq has also noted the possibility of a *hoti-recitativum* at this point and thus simply a "quotation mark" (cf. BDF §470) for the last member of the sentence here, which would then be cited in the same fashion as the latter verse in Gal 6:7-8. Yet such a "quotation" is here so brief and apparently so dependent upon the previous member of the sentence that is difficult to see why the *hoti* would be used at this point except for a very well-known phrase (and there seems to be no case for this phraseology being in wide circulation). If Bernard, 95, is correct about a "resumptive" *hoti,* equivalent to an understood but still emphatic "I say," one would have a more viable way of explaining a *hoti-recitativum* at this point. Even though *alla* is used rather than *hoti* (as in Polycarp), see Philo, *Spec. leg.* I, 294-295 (the latter part was cited above: ". . . you who brought nothing into the world, not even yourself," *ton mēden eis ton kosmon alla mēde sauton eisenēnochota*). None of the examples cited by Bernard (or J. K. Elliott) uses *hoti.*

Parry has suggested that *hoti oude* here is written for *oud' hoti,* i.e. *nedum* = "not to speak of" or "nor even is it the case that," which occurs elsewhere in the Paulines in the form *ouch hoti* (2 Cor 1:24; 3:5; Phil 3:12; 4:11, 17; 2 Thess 3:9). Yet there does not appear to be another example of such an inversion in word order with this phrase.

One is left with a "final" or "consecutive" sense for the particle: Spicq seems to prefer the former, with the poverty of human birth really being ordered to the poverty of death, showing that one cannot take any more out of the world than he brought into it. No examples with *hoti* seem to substantiate this. One is left with the "consecutive" use of a result (= "so that"), which BAGD consider probable here and which Spicq notes is common enough in the papyri and can be documented in Heb 2:6 (citing LXX Ps 8:5) and probably in Luke 7:47 (cf. *Agape* I, 131 n. 4, French edition). The *hoti* might resemble the Hebrew *ky* when used with the meaning, "as a proof *or* sign for. . . ." See the example in MM *s.v.* #4, p. 463.

The shift from the aorist tense of the first clause to the present of the second, as well as the conceptual movement from the fact of having entered with nothing to excluding even the possibility of taking something out, seems to make the *hoti* meaning "result" the most probable here. Note that Polycarp 4.1 changed the *dynametha* (possibility) to *echomen* (the fact).

8. *So then if we have keep and covering, with them we shall be content.* In the light of the previous principle and its emphasis upon "nothing," the text in contrast *(de)* turns to "something": "So then if we have *(echontes)* keep (the means of subsistence, *diatrophas*) and covering *(skepasmata)*, with them we shall be content *(arkesthēsometha)*." As the previous saying touched on the past and present, so now this conclusion turns to the future. As was noted previously, the first person plural no longer refers to all humankind but to the apostolic ministers and even all believers whose concrete way of life will be dictated by the preceding principle. Here they are persons who *have (echontes)* food and covering, a favorite participial construction of these letters (cf. Titus 1:6; 2:8; 1 Tim 1:19; 3:4, 9; 4:8; etc.). The whole phrase has a certain sonorous, sesquipedalian gravity about it that reminds one of those who in English cannot say "sweat" but speak rather of "perspiration."

Something of the same phenomenon seems to appear in the Q Greek of Matt 8:20 = Luke 9:58, SFG §176: *ta peteina tou ouranou kataskēnōseis,* lit. "the winged ones of the sky (have) tents over them." The term here could refer to "covering" in the sense of a roof over the head as well as clothing on the body (see Philo *infra;* D-C), and the concept of the bare sufficiency that was required for a man was common enough as in the visionary lines of Menander, *Dyscolos,* that begin with *autarkēs* (714) and conclude with *echōn d'an metri' hakastos ēgapa,* "each man would have enough to live on, and he'd be satisfied" (745; trans. LCL), and in the philosophers, Stoic or Cynic (see texts in D-C), who use the actual terminology of *autarkei* (see on *arkēsthesometha* below) but not the phrase for food and covering encountered here. Indeed, the closest one comes to the phraseology here is in Philo, *Praem.* 99, where he says, "Now the simple wealth of nature is food and shelter *(trophē kai skepē)*. . . . Shelter is of two kinds, raiment and housing. . . ." The latter is the sense of *skepasmata* in Philo, *Mig. Abr.* 215, "They make *places of shelter* and security fit for virtue-loving souls." The former is the sense at *Leg. alleg.* 3.239, "As clothes are the *coverings* of the body, so are food and drink *(sitia kai pota)* of the living being." His *Det.* 19 notes the man "who is careless about the coverings of his body," and in *Sacr.* 84 the "coverings" of the soul (false conjectures) that must be taken off. Josephus, *War* 2.129, speaks of the Essenes vesting "with linen cloths *(skepasmasin)* around their waists" for their purificatory bath.

*With them* (*toutois* [for the things mentioned previously, cf. 4:15 above]) *we shall be content (arkesthēsometha)*. If the progression from aorist to present to future in the verbs of these two verses is deliberate (and it seems to be), then this is a final determined statement (as the previous two were) rather than a hortatory or imperative one (though Spicq inclines to the latter and D-C perceive no data for a decision). The contrast with that which awaits the rich in verse 9 would further substantiate this interpretation.

The parallels to the thought here in the PE from the popular philosophical ethics of the Hellenistic world have long been cited (cf. Kittel, *TDNT* 1.465, as well as Hengel, *PREC*, pp. 8-9, who notes the way in which Luke's rhetorical education in Greek modes of thought and expression "stylized" such early Christian practices as holding goods in common; in fact, even the similar practice at Qumran appears to have been influenced "by the ideals of the Hellenistic spirit of the age" as well as by Hebrew biblical traditions). Perhaps if the Greek New Comedy had survived in the same quantity as the philosophers, one would encounter there the really potent force in shaping the popular mind and ethic of the Hellenistic age. In any case, the text of Menander's *Dyscolos* contains a most persuasive argument for detachment from wealth and self-sufficiency (cf. Hengel, *PREC*, p. 10, citing *Dysc.* 797-812, fragment 128K [in Handley, ed., pp. 110-111] as well as 713-747 noted above).

In contrast to the food and clothing phrase of this verse, consider 4QpHos$^{b}$ 2.12 (Dupont-Sommer, *EWQ*, p. 278) with its mention of "famine and nakedness." Also cf. Josephus, *War* 2.133, on "the [Essene] limitation of their allotted portions of food and drink *(trophēn kai poton)* to satisfaction *(mechri korou)*." In his *Ant.* 2.90 he speaks of Joseph's distributing grain to the Egyptians, "such as would suffice for sowing and sustenance *(ton arkounta pros te sporan kai diatrōphēn)*." In *Ant.* 15.378 he speaks of Herod *toutois arkestheis*, "satisfied with these [words]."

9. *Those, however, who want to be wealthy topple into a temptation and a trap and multiple lusts, senseless and injurious.* The warnings here about those

who want to be rich are to be distinguished from the admonitions below in 6:17-19 to those who are *de facto* rich (Kasch, *TDNT* 6.329-330). Those who seek wealth "fall into a temptation and a trap and multiple lusts, senseless and injurious," *empiptousin eis peirasmon kai pagida kai epithymias pollas.* With Michaelis, *TDNT* 6.164-166, note that, like *piptein,* this cognate compound does not refer to "falling" into specific sins and cannot mean "to sin." In fact, in the NT only at 1 Tim 6:9 does *empiptein* refer to sins even generically. With the term thus qualified, one can take up Kuhn, *Scrolls,* pp. 95-96, when he notes the link among *peirasmos, piptein,* and *paraptōma,* comparing, e.g., Gal 6:1; 1 Cor 10:6-13. The present tense here in First Timothy stresses the constantly repeated falls (Spicq, *EP,* p. 563).

Spicq has noted the recurring *p* sound in this verse (nine times), and not least in this list of what awaits the avaricious, which leads off with *eis peirasmon.* In the Lukan usage of *peirasmon* the plural refers to the perils endured by the apostolic witnesses (Luke 22:28; Acts 20:19 of Paul; S. Brown, *AP,* p. 9); according to S. Brown, pp. 15-16, all the uses in the singular (except Luke 4:13) have negative overtones associated with falling into sin because of a certain carelessness. James 1:2, 12 would not have this sense, but cf. 1:13-15. *Peirasmos* in Luke-Acts represents a term taken by Luke from his sources, with a meaning that those sources gave it (Mark, Q for Luke; probably Lukan compositional activity in Acts 20:19). As S. Brown notes (p. 13): "so far from regarding *peirasmos* as the inescapable fate of Jesus' followers, Luke *never* represents faithful Christians as suffering *peirasmos* [contra Kuhn, p. 96]. In the account of the apostolic church in Acts the singular use of the word is entirely absent." On the hypothesis proposed in this commentary, 1 Tim 6:9 may represent still another source where the term was thus employed, or, more probably, a Lukan usage based upon that in the previous volumes of his composition. It seems to support S. Brown's thesis when one notes that in this passage of the PE "the snare" is *not* described as the devil's (as it was in 1 Tim 3:7; cf. Seesemann, *TDNT* 6.32; Schneider, *TDNT* 5.595, inclines to think that the snare here is thought of as the devil's, even though not said as such).

After *eis peirasmon kai pagida* the polysyndetic list continues with *kai epithymias pollas anoētous kai blaberas,* "into . . . multiple lusts, senseless and injurious." The "lusts" are not only "foolish" (*anoētous;* see Titus 3:3; Spicq cites the *aphrōn* of Luke 12:20 for the linking of desire for wealth with lack of intelligence) but "many" *(pollas),* an adjective that occurred in Titus 1:10; 2:3 and in 1 Tim 3:8, 13. But here and in the following verse it is used both of things and in the plural, a usage that will recur at 2 Tim 4:14, *polla . . . kaka.* In all these three instances the adjective occurs in a phrase that must be understood *in malam partem,* which is not always the case when it refers to things in the singular (1 Tim 3:13) or persons in the plural (1 Tim 6:12; 2 Tim 2:2).

The lusts are finally characterized as *blaberas,* "injurious," an adjective that occurs only here in the NT and only at LXX Prov 10:26. In the Ap. Frs. *1 Clem.* 28.1 and Hermas use the adjective, the latter five times. In *Vis.* 3.9.4, ". . . lack of sharing is harmful *(blabera)* to you who have (possessions, riches) and do not share with the poor." In *Man.* 6.1.3 a steep, thorny, crooked path is "harmful to those who walk on it." In *Sim.* 6.5.5-7 the "harmful luxuries *(tryphai blaberai)*" are noted, including adultery, drunkenness, slander, lying, and *covetousness* (*pleonektēs;* cf. 1 Cor 5:10-11; 6:10; Eph 5:5, but not in PE).

In the papyri (MM *s.v.*, p. 112) there is a medical note on fresh fruits being *blaberōṭeron,* "very harmful" (cf. LXX Prov 10:26 on vinegar being harmful, i.e. irritating, to the teeth as is smoke to the eyes). Josephus uses the term at least four times (*War* 3.218 and 533; *Ant.* 7.322 [adverb] and 13.240). In secular Greek the noun *blabē* (damage) can be used not only in a general sense but also in a juridical way (cf. *DELG, s.v.*, p. 177; Spicq, *EP,* p. 563), and the latter nuance may appear here in First Timothy.

The greed for wealth noted here with its attendant evils is a charge that the Qumran sectaries brought against their opponents. Thus, 1QpHab 8.3-13 denounces the Wicked Priest as insatiably greedy and so ending "in every kind of unclean defilement." CD 4.15-19 avers that the "three nets of Belial" are "lust," "riches," and "defilement of the sanctuary" *(znwt; hwn; ṭmʾ hmqdš).* For a study of the whole passage see Kosmala, "Three Nets," pp. 91-113. On *hwn,* particularly, meaning private property of all kinds, including money or wealth, the attitude of the sectaries "is utterly negative" (Kosmala, p. 101), and in this respect they initiate a quite new development of a rather less prominent theme in the Hebrew Scripture (cf. Prov 11:4; Kosmala, p. 106), which on the whole considers *hwn* a blessing from God. For the Qumran elect, *hwn* = *bṣʿ* (booty; unjust profit; gain from violence) and coincides in meaning with the rather neutral *mmwn* (1QS 6.2; CD 14.20; and the mutilated 1Q27; 1.2.5; cf. with the *hwn* of the 1QS 6.17, 19). The *mamōnas adikias* of Luke 16:9 (cf. 16:11, 13) takes up the same term and represents the basic outlook of Qumran by the way in which it is qualified. "The Sect did not understand the expression *beṣaʿ raʿ* . . . [1QpHab 9.12 and cf. with 9.8-12 cited above] simply as unlawfully acquired gain; for them it was fundamentally evil" (Kosmala, pp. 101-102, *q.v.* for the texts, as well as p. 106). The fragmentary 1QH 10.22-25, Dupont-Sommer, *EWQ,* p. 235, has the psalmist say, after affirming that he puts his hope in God's mercy and forgiveness:

> For it is you who formed the inc[lination of your
> servant] [and] established me according to your will.
> And you have not put my support in gain *(bṣʿ)*
> And in the ri[ches] (*h*[*wn*]) [of wickedness]

my h[eart has found no pleasure].
And you have not set a creature of flesh
to be my strength
(but) the hosts of the valiant.
[The ungodly lean] on abundance of plea[sure],
[on ab]undance of grain and new wine
and oil,
And because of (their) possessions
*(mqnh)* and fortune *(qnyh)*
they are proud.

As Kosmala has noted, both Luke 12:15 and 1 Tim 6:9-10 exploit the same theme.

*The kind that engulf people in utterly ruinous destruction.* A final expansive phrase further describes the preceding *epithymiai* as the kind that literally plunge people "into ruin and destruction," *eis olethron kai apōleian.* The former noun occurs in the NT only in the Paulines (1 Thess 5:3; 2 Thess 1:9; 1 Cor 5:5). Schneider, *TDNT* 5.168-169, notes that the sense of "eschatological destruction" appears in the twenty-three LXX occurrences in both prophetic and sapiential texts, and on the only occasion when the term appears with an adjective, in 4 Macc 10:15, it is to swear an oath "by the eternal doom *(ton aiōnion . . . olethron)* of the tyrant," as well as "by the blessed death" of his previously executed brothers and "by the glorious life of the righteous" (Charles, *AP* 2.677). Second Thessalonians 1:9 uses the same adjective with *olethros.* In eight of twenty-three LXX uses, this noun is construed, as here and 1 Cor 5:5, with *eis.*

In the one use of the noun in *1 Clem.* 57.4, it is in part of a lengthy citation that includes LXX Prov 1:26, where wisdom foresees the ruin *(apōleiai)* and destruction *(olethros)* that will overtake those who ignore her. In Ign. *Eph.* 13.1 the Christian assemblies enable Satan's powers to be destroyed and his destructiveness (*ho olethros autou;* note here the active sense of the noun) to be nullified *(leutai).* In addition to Schneider's examples from profane literature, one ought to note Menander, *Dysc.* 366, where in comic exaggeration a man can be called *olethron argon,* "an idle pest" (or, perhaps separately, "a pest [and] idler" [Handley, *Dyskolos,* p. 193]), and *Sam.* 348, Sandbach (136), where a woman is "a pest," *olethros;* cf. his *Aspis* 21. A very strong term could thus become attenuated in popular usage.

To *olethron,* 1 Tim 6:9 adds *kai apōleian* (eighteen times in NT), which is parallel to and coincides substantially in meaning with the preceding terms. If, in fact, *olethros* had weakened in meaning, the added noun drives home the original force of the term and the *kai* becomes practically epexegetic. Though this is the only use in the PE, *apōleian* occurs in the Paulines; at Rom 9:22 (with *eis*); Phil 1:28; 3:19; 2 Thess 2:3. The one Lukan use is in Acts 8:20, but there, significantly, it is Peter's saying to Simon Magus, "May silver perish *(eis apōleian)* with you, because you thought you could obtain the gift of God with money." This usage as well as that in the rest of the NT (see Oepke, *TDNT* 1.396-397) and in the LXX implies more than simply the loss of what one has gained or even the ending of mortal life. It includes "an everlasting state of torment and death" (Oepke, p. 397). This noun occurs in *1 Clem.* 57.4 (just cited *supra*) as well as *2 Clem.* 1.7 of God's having mercy on "the great error and destruction *(apōleian)* in us." The term reminds one of what the astronomers call a "black hole" in a microcosm that is man. In Hermas, *Sim.* 6.2.4, "Death has eternal destruction *(apōleian . . . aiōnion),*" the eschatological sense is clearly at the fore.

10. *The root that lies under all evils is the love of money.* The preceding teaching is grounded *(gar)* in an observation that has all the characteristics of folk wisdom and a proverbial expression: *rhiza . . . pantōn tōn kakōn estin hē philagyria,* lit. "root of all evils is money-love." The anarthrous *rhiza* implies that there may be other sources. For all the occurrences of the thought of this maxim in Greek literature and in Latin (see the citations in D-C and Spicq), one must really begin by noting that the terminology with which it is articulated here is unique in the Hellenistic world (*pace* Delling, *TDNT* 6.270 and 271 n. 17, who is citing pseudo-Phocylides 42, "Love of money is the mother of all evil," *hē philochrēmosynē mētēr kakotētos hapasēs,* whose every word differs from First Timothy). Cf. the unmistakable citation of 1 Tim 6:10 in Clement of Alexandria, *Paed.* 3.11-12; *PG* 8.437-440, with the accompanying elegant variation on Bion the Sophist, whose *mētropolin . . . pasēs kakias* becomes *akropolis tēs kakias* in Clement.

The adjective *kaka* (Titus 1:12) has here become nominal, and the sense at this point in First Timothy is in the practice of using the neuter plural for moral evils or sins (Rom 1:30; 3:8; 1 Cor 10:6), and it was thus that James 1:13 used this form. That the author of this correspondence was aware that *kaka* could also be understood as disasters, personal and national, that are punishments for moral evil is illustrated by 2 Tim 4:14, where the reference is quite parallel to Acts 9:13 (cf. 9:16) and where Paul is now depicted as enduring what he had once inflicted.

Thus the root of all sins (and perhaps of all the punishments that they bring) is (*estin,* for a permanent situation or condition) *hē philargyria.* The article identifies the subject that has been kept for this emphatic final position (cf. John 1:1: *theos ēn ho logos*) and the predicative, generic character of the anarthrous *rhiza* with which this clause began.

*Certain persons who have craved it have strayed off from the faith and have skewered themselves with multiple tortures.* A final relative clause rounds off this expository section that began at 6:3. One notes that the third person verbs give a more formal, didactic tone to this whole paragraph (contrast the second person phrase in 6:2b as well as the frequent second–first person of 6:11, 21). The proverbial wisdom of 6:10a is now verified from the actual experience of the community. The *tines,* as was noted previously in this correspondence (cf. 1 Tim 1:3, 6, 19, as well as the singular at 6:3), may refer to "many."

The *hēs . . . oregomenoi* takes up formally the preceding *philargyria,* with *oregomenoi* emphatically verbalizing the initial *phil-* in terms of desire (cf. the *boulomenoi ploutein* of 6:9) while the pronoun actually and materially refers to the riches *(-argyria).* From the evidence at 1 Tim 3:1 one would infer that the verb is not to be, as such, taken *in malam partem* of inordinate desire. The context here does color the way in which the desire is understood, and the meaning becomes practically equivalent to the English "craving."

This passage of First Timothy is quite in the LXX tradition when it uses this verb of being led away "from the faith *(apo tēs pisteōs),*" i.e. from the God of Christian revelation and from the believer's commitment to him (see Notes above). The Pauline letters do not otherwise use this prepositional phrase, though Acts 13:8 does. It is not found in the rest of the NT. Haenchen, *Acts,* p. 399, favors taking Acts 13:8 of "objective 'faith,' i.e. the Christian religion," comparing Acts 6:7 (though, as he notes, that view is not certain). One could make the same observation about this phrase in 1 Tim 6:10 with the same reservations.

The final member of this compound relative clause describes the same greedy persons as having "skewered themselves *(heautous periepeiran)* with multiple tortures *(odynais pollais).*" Here the avaricious have spitted themselves on *odynais pollais,* "many pangs" (see Rom 9:2 of Paul's own heartfelt and constant "anguish" [*odynē* in the sg.] at the failure of Israel to believe in Jesus). It is notable that Luke alone in the NT uses the verb *odynaomai* of parents' anguish at the loss of their child (Luke 2:48); of the rich man's anguish in hell (Luke 16:24-25); and in Acts 20:38 of the anguish of the Ephesian presbyter-bishops over Paul's saying that they would never see him again. *First Clement* 16.4 uses the verb only in quoting LXX Isa 53:4 on the Servant (= Christ) in anguish for us *(peri hēmōn odynatai).* The term, as Hauck, *TDNT* 5.115, notes, is used for the intense pain, accentuated here by the plural, associated with a stab or cut and can apply to either bodily or mental anguish, though perhaps he moralizes too much when he speaks of the "self-accusations and pangs of conscience" that will overtake avaricious apostates.

Here one would suggest that the riches themselves, so eagerly sought, leave those who have acquired them in desperate frustration and anguish, neither satisfying their greed nor healing their hearts. Thus they torture themselves with the things that they hope will cure them; cf. the interpretation of the sower parable (*SFG* §124; Mark 4:19 = Matt 13:22). See especially Luke 8:14, "and as for what fell among thorns [note the emphasis on that which is piercing and sharp], they are those who hear [i.e. believe], but as they go their way they are choked by the cares and riches *(ploutou)* and pleasures of life *(biou)*, and their fruit does not mature." Spicq, *EP*, p. 565, cites aptly the career of the prodigal son, Luke 15:12-17. Indeed, it is striking, as one notes this final appeal to the experience of the community, to recall the persons in Luke-Acts who cannot hear God because of money, the desire for it, and the power it brings (Judas, the Pharisees, the parabolic figures of the prodigal don, and various rich men, Ananias and Sapphira, Simon Magus, the owners of the girl with a divining spirit [Acts 16:19], Demetrius the silversmith and his colleagues [Acts 19:25-27], not to mention Felix the Roman governor, whose anticipation of a bribe kept Paul imprisoned [Acts 24:26]). The PE, of course, speak of a nameless crowd of the avaricious, apparently Jewish Christians, and perhaps thus brand Demas in 2 Tim 4:10 (see commentary *in loc.*).

## IV.C.3. AN ORDINATION CHARGE (6:11-16)

6 11 *You, O man of God, must shun these things. Instead pursue —*

> *upright conduct,*
> *godliness,*
> *faithfulness,*
> *charity,*
> *steadfastness,*
> *gentleness.*

12 *Contend in the fine contest, the contest in the arena of faith. Lay hold on eternal life. You were called into that life and for it you made that fine profession before the eyes of many witnesses.*
13 *Before the eyes of the God who keeps all things alive and of Christ Jesus who publicly attested to the fine profession before Pontius Pilate, I charge you*
14 *to keep the apostolic command beyond blemish, beyond reproach, until the revelation of our Lord, Jesus Christ.*
15 *That revelation God will make in due time, he who is —*

> *the blessed and only suzerain;*
> *the king of those who act as kings*
> *and lord of those who act as lords;*
> 16 *the only one who possesses immortality,*
> *who inhabits inaccessible light;*
> *the one whom no human being ever saw*

*or can see*
*to whom belong honor*
*and might eternal.*
*Amen.*

## ♦ NOTES

6:11. *You.* On *sy de* see Titus 2:1. The phrase also occurs in Second Timothy at 3:10, 14 and 4:5, along with *sy* (1:18; 4:15) and *sy oun* (2:1). In the rest of the Paulines, only Rom 11:17, 20 and 14:10 employ the phrase. In Luke-Acts it occurs only in Luke 9:60; 16:7, 25 (never in Mark, John, Acts; twice in Matthew; in Heb 1:11-12 = LXX Ps 101:27-28 and James 4:12).

*O man of God.* Luke uses the exclamatory *ō* most frequently in the NT (six of seventeen times), not only of persons in general (Luke 9:41; Acts 18:14; 27:21) but also of individuals with names (Luke 24:25; Acts 1:1; 13:10). BDF §146 speaks of a typically Attic "polite, unemotional *ō*" found only in Acts, but 1 Tim 6:11 could also qualify. The scribe of P omitted the word, possibly because it was felt to be superfluous with the following vocative (cf. J. K. Elliott, *Greek Text,* pp. 98-99, who puts the opposite interpretation on the omission). The use with "Timothy" at 6:20 below resembles the usage of Acts too, but with an emotionally charged command (BDF §146.2).

For the Pauline usage of *ō* see the Comment below; otherwise in the NT *ō* is used of the "unfaithful generation" addressed by Jesus (Mark 9:19 = Matt 17:17 = Luke 9:41 and for a woman of great faith in Matt 15:28).

*shun.* See Comment below for the NT use of *pheuge.* In the Ap. Frs. *pheuge* is used much the same as in the Paulines; cf. *Did.* 3.1; *Barn.* 4.1, 10; *1 Clem.* 30.1 (with its reference to *neōterismous . . . epithymias* reminding one of 2 Tim 2:22), but not 4.10; 28.2; or 58.1; *2 Clem.* 10.1; 18.2; Ign. *Trall.* 11.1; *Phld.* 2.1 ("division and wrong doctrine"); 6.2; 7.2; *Pol.* 5.1. Hermas does not seem to use the verb in this sense, but rather of the devil and lust fleeing from a faithful man.

Only the latest strata of the LXX, and even then rather rarely, use *pheugein* of a flight from evil: thus S of Tob 4:21 *(s.v.l.);* Wis 1:5; Sir 21:2, "Flee from sin *(hamartias)* as from a snake."

*upright conduct.* On *dikaiosynē* see Titus 3:5. Here, as at 2 Tim 2:22 and 4:8, the term occurs without a preposition. In the last instance noted, "the crown of righteousness" employs the noun in a quasi-adjectival sense (see Pfitzner, *PAM,* p. 184, and Ziesler, *Righteousness,* p. 155). As D-C, p. 88, has noted, the usage here (presupposing the doctrine of Titus 3:5) is similar to that of Luke (contrast Luke 1:75 with Acts 17:31; cf. also Acts 10:35; 13:10; 24:25) when he uses the noun of "good conduct" or an upright life. Of course, that is also a Matthean usage (cf. Matt 5:10; 6:1; 21:32) and is also common enough in the Ap. Frs. (cf., e.g., *1 Clem.* 5.7 of Paul teaching "righteousness to the whole world"; 33.8, ". . . let us work the work of righteousness . . ." [cf. Acts 10:35]; 48.4; 60.2 [*s.v.l.*] on those who "make straight their way in holiness and righteousness" [*en hosiotēti kai dikaiosynēi,* cf. Luke 1:75]). *Second Clement* 4.2 has a variation on Matt 7:21 that concludes by saying that one who will be saved will be "*ho poiōn tēn dikaiosynēn*" (cf. 19.2-3, especially *praxōmen oun tēn dikaiosynēn hina eis telos sōthōmen;* 18.2 was cited above).

*godliness. eusebian.* This is one of ten instances of *eusebeia* in the PE (out of fifteen in the NT); the **seb/m-* language often occurs in traditional materials, e.g., in the virtue list of Titus 2:2-7 and the baptismal confession of 2:11-14; in the vice list of 1 Tim 1:9-10 and the church order of 2:1–3:13; and in the list here. Moreover, the sixfold list of virtues that are to be sought is, in its number, unlike any seen thus far. Previous lists have had three, four, five, seven, even twelve members. The six negatives of Titus 1:7 offer the closest parallel, though they are part of a longer catalogue. In this connection one must weigh the omission of *eusebeian,* the second member of the sextet, in S* as well as 1908. Cop (sah). L (vg/Z*). J. K. Elliott, *Greek Text,* p. 99, notes the difficulty that such lists pose in manuscript transmission and suggests either a mechanical error or a deliberate assimilation of this list to the one in 2 Tim 2:22 (which has only four members). If a source (liturgical) is being cited at this point, the anomalous number is explained, and in that case the original hand of S (unaware of the source as such) is bringing the shape of the list more into conformity with the rest of this correspondence. He then would have chosen to drop a virtue that had occurred in the exposition of 6:3, 5 above. But on the other hand, the combination of a shorter reading with both Alexandrian and Western witnesses for the "noninterpolation" makes it just as plausible that the quintet of virtues was original (even in the source) and that the *eusebeia* here is a spillover from the previous exposition.

One more possibility must be noted: that the source had five virtues and that the final redactor inserted *eusebeian* in the light of the previous material (cf. Pfitzner, *PAM,* p. 178, on this list as "a concise commentary" on the *eusebeia* of 1 Tim 4:7-8 and 6:6). After all, the numerical patterns are those of the sources here, not of the redactor, and the latter may have felt quite unconstrained by their pattern. In that case the scribal tradition represented by S* etc. was still aware of the liturgical source (perhaps it was still in use in some form in their churches), and the copyists brought their MSS into conformity with the text that they used in worship. In the final analysis, the original reading of the text is quite uncertain.

*charity. Agapē* occurs ten times in the PE (nine in the Timothy correspondence). The word always appears coupled with one or more virtues in the PE; when it appears with only one, that one is faith (cf. also commentary on 1 Tim 1:5 above).

*steadfastness.* Elsewhere in the PE *hypomonē* appears only in Titus 2:2 and the list of 2 Tim 3:10. Romans has six of the thirteen uses in the remainder of the Paulines; Luke 8:15 and 21:19 constitute the noun's occurrences in the Gospels and Acts.

*gentleness.* On the variant spelling of *praüpathia (-thia* or *-theia)* cf. J. K. Elliott, *Greek Text,* p. 99, and BAGD *s.v.*

12. *Contend in the fine contest, the contest in the arena of faith.* Lit. "Fight the fine fight of the faith."

*Lay hold on.* The same verb occurs in 6:19 of the rich being taught to grasp that which is "really life" *(tēs ontōs* [*s.v.l.*] *zōēs).* The rest of the Paulines never use this verb. Luke-Acts share twelve out of seventeen remaining NT uses of this term, which often has the sense of taking (grasping) by the hand (Matt 14:31; Mark 8:23; Acts 23:19; Heb 8:9, quoting LXX Jer 38:32). There does not appear to be a precise NT or LXX parallel for the usage here in the PE, though Wisdom in Prov 4:13 can say to her "son," *Epilabou emēs paideias . . . phylaxon autēn seautōi eis zōēn sou,* "Lay hold on my instruction . . . keep it for yourself, for your life" (trans. WCW), where "life" is somehow at stake in a man's attitude toward wisdom. In Bar 4:2, after wisdom is said to be "the book of the commandments of God and the law that endures forever; all who hold her fast *(kratountes autēs)* will live *(eis zōēn)* . . ." (4:1), there follows, "Turn, O Jacob, and take her *(epilabou autēs)*. . . ." Only Hermas (*Vis.* 3.2.4; *Sim.* 9.10.5) uses the verb in the Ap. Frs., and neither occurrence offers a parallel to 1 Tim 6:12, 19. G. Delling, *TDNT* 4.9, notes the use of the privative form of this root in the *anepilēmptos* of 6:14 below (also 1 Tim 3:2; 5:7). LSJ and MM offer no precise parallels in secular Greek.

*You were called into that life.* Lit. "(. . . the eternal life) into which *(eis hēn)* you were called *(eklēthēs).*" *Eklēthēs* occurs 148 times in the NT, but only here and in 2 Tim 1:9 in the PE (in a prayer that seems also to be taking up liturgical language; see commentary *in loc.*). The other Paulines use the verb 31 times, with not a few parallels to these passages in the PE (cf. 1 Cor 7:20; Eph 4:1 for "the calling with which you were called" language; Rom 8:30). Luke-Acts (43/18) use the verb 61 times. Luke 14:7-24 with its invitation parables offers the best parallels to the usage here in the PE. Revelation 19:9 has a beatitude for "those called to the wedding banquet *(eis to deipnon tou gamou)* of the lamb" in which the verb is construed with *eis* (cf. also 1 Pet 5:10: "He who called [*kalesas*] us into [*eis*] his eternal glory"; 1 Pet 2:9: "who called us out of darkness into his own wonderful light [*eis to . . . phōs*]"; as well as the *eis touto eklēthēte* of 1 Pet 2:21; 3:9). In Paul the verb is construed with *eis* in 1 Cor 1:9 *(koinōnian);* Col

3:15 *(eirēnē . . . eis hēn eklēthēte);* 2 Thess 2:14 (*en hagiasmōi pneumatos . . . eis ho ekalesen hymas* — if the Spirit *is* the antecedent); but apparently never thus in Luke-Acts.

In the Ap. Frs. the verb is frequent enough, but only in *1 Clem.* 59.2 is it construed with *eis,* speaking of Jesus "through whom the creator called us *(ekalesen)* from darkness to light" (*eis phōs;* cf. Acts 26:18 as well as 1 Pet 2:9 *supra cit.*). The usage of *Second Clement* resembles that of 2 Tim 1:9; see commentary *in loc.* K. L. Schmidt, *TDNT* 3.488-489, in commenting on the technical theological force of this verb when God (as here in the PE) or Christ is the one calling, has noted that it denotes "the process of salvation" (cf. 2 Tim 1:9 "of God who *saved* and *called* us with a holy *calling*"). He has also noted how when used with *eis* it refers to an invitation to a banquet or celebration (LXX Esther 5:12: . . . *eis tēn dochēn;* OxyP 12.1487.1: . . . *eis tou gamous,* fourth-century C.E.; also MM *s.v.,* p. 318).

*you made that fine profession.* The phrase *hōmologēsas tēn kalēn homologian,* lit. "you professed the fine profession," with its cognate accusative is formally quite parallel to the preceding *agonizou ton kalon agōna,* with the same adjective stressing the resemblance further. The verb has occurred of professing God in Titus 1:16 (cf. the adverb *homologoumenōs* at 1 Tim 3:16). Here in 1 Tim 6:12 it appears to be construed with *eis hēn (zōēn aiōnion),* as in Rom 10:10, "one confesses with the mouth unto salvation *(eis sōtērian).*" For this use of *eis* = result or condition "so as to receive," see BAGD *s.v.* There does appear to be one parallel in Luke-Acts at Acts 10:4; outside of the Paulines, cf. 1 Pet 1:7; 2:2. Cf. LXX Jth 6:21 for *epekalesanto ton theon . . . eis boētheian. . . .* Perhaps the usage is the "vocation, use, or end indicated for" classification of BAGD *s.v.*

One may surmise accordingly that here in the PE, as also in Rom 10:9-10, the terminology of a (liturgical) source is being cited. The terminology (as the constituents of the compound imply) designates *agreement* with something/someone, agreement that was public (hence in words/actions that witnesses could hear and/or see as well as between the two persons involved) and permanently binding (cf. Michel, *TDNT* 5.200-202, 211; cf. also Beasley-Murray, *Bapt. NT,* p. 205). Here in the PE the verb surely means "to make a solemn public statement of agreement to the Christian faith," and the addition of the adjective *kalēn* to "the confession" *(tēn . . . homologian)* stresses that what was in some way previously hidden and unknown became manifestly visible and publicly known (though not necessarily accepted) in the *homologia* (cf. Michel, *TDNT* 5.211 with n. 35).

*profession.* The noun *homologia* does not occur in the Ap. Frs. (but cf. *homologēsis* in Hermas, *Sim.* 9.28.7, and Michel, *TDNT* 5.217, 219). The verb is not used in *Didache, Barnabas,* or *First Clement* but is common enough in *2 Clem.* 3 and 4 where the problem of confession by deeds as well as words is discussed (in Titus 1:16 the person whose lips confess the faith is solemnly repudiated by his contemptible works; cf. also Michel, *TDNT* 5.217-218). In Ign. *Magn.* 8.1; *Smyrn.* 5.2; 7.1; and Polycarp, *Phil.* 7.1 *(bis),* the content of the confession when mentioned is that Christ has come in the flesh, a flesh with which one is confronted in the eucharist, a flesh that was crucified and rose again. These concerns are not those of this passage in the PE; however, considering the way in which this correspondence welds together faith and works, the insistence of the source here on the virtues of a man of God must have made it congenial to the redactor.

*many witnesses.* The term *martyres* will occur again in this correspondence only at 2 Tim 2:2, of the Pauline teaching that Timothy heard *dia pollōn martyrōn* and that he in turn is to transmit. In the rest of the Paulines, except when 2 Cor 13:1 cites Deut 19:15 and in 1 Thess 2:10 (where *both* men and God are witnesses), the term *martys* occurs in the singular and of God bearing witness to the truth of what Paul writes (Rom 1:9; 2 Cor 1:23; Phil 1:8; 1 Thess 2:5). In the PE the noun is always plural and refers to men who are apparently presumed to be believers (cf. the *enōpion pantōn* of 1 Tim 5:20). Whereas nine of thirty-five NT uses of *martys* are in the Pauline epistolary, fifteen are in Luke-Acts (two/thirteen). In the Lukan usage, as in the PE, men are witnesses, almost always in the plural and almost always believers (especially apostolic witnesses). Mark 14:63 = Matt 26:65 uses the noun of there being no need of witnesses at Jesus' trial. The one other use in the Gospels is again a citation of Deut 19:15, in Matt 18:16 (see Strathmann, *TDNT* 4.489-490). For the remaining NT passages, see Strathmann, *TDNT* 4.489, 494-496.

The word *martys* occurs in the Ap. Frs. only in *1 Clem.* 63.3 (of the messengers from Rome to Corinth "who will be witnesses between you and us") and Ign. *Phld.* 7.2, where Christ is invoked as "martys de moi" (cf. *Barn.* 15.4) that Ignatius received no coaching on what he was to say to that church. Of the no more than seventeen uses of the verb *martyrein* in the Ap. Frs., none appears to be completely parallel to 1 Tim 6:13, though *1 Clem.* 5.7 (cf. 5.4), speaking of Paul, "who gave his testimony before the rulers *(martyrēsas epi tōn hēgoumenōn),*" is formally identical while the meaning is somewhat different.

13. *God who keeps all things alive.* God is here designated *ho theos* = "the Father" and then described as *tou zōiogonountos ta panta.* The Greek verb *zōiogonein,* in the NT otherwise only at Luke 17:33 and Acts 7:19, always included both giving life and sustaining it. In the LXX (eleven uses) it signifies a return from serious illness and the door of death, even in the one usage where God is the subject (1 Kgdms 2:6).

*Pontius Pilate.* There are three other occurrences of the double name Pontius Pilate in the NT (Matt 27:2; Luke 3:1; Acts 4:27). According to Metzger, *TCGNT,* p. 65, the reading at Matt 27:2 is very probably a harmonization. He also notes that the double name became more common beginning with Ignatius, who employs only this form, *Magn.* 11.1; *Trall.* 9.1; *Smyrn.* 1.2. Like Josephus, *Ant.* 18.2, who employs the double form upon the first mention of this prefect of Judea (cf. inscription of Caesarea), so Luke writes in his Gospel, where the name occurs in the form "Pilate" thereafter eleven times. In Acts 3:13 (with *arnein,* the opposite of *homologein*) and 13:28, "Pilate" also occurs.

*I charge you.* For the *paraggellō soi* that opens this verse, see 1 Tim 1:3 as well as 1 Tim 4:11 and 5:7.

14. *the revelation.* On *epiphaneia* see Titus 2:13.

15. *That revelation.* Here the antecedent of the relative pronoun *hēn* is *epiphaneias* (not repeated in the Greek).

*will make.* The verb *deixei,* "to make or show," occurs only once otherwise in the Paulines (1 Cor 12:31, of Paul himself "showing" the "more excellent way" of charity). Of its thirty (thirty-one) other NT uses, six (seven, *s.v.l.*) are in Luke-Acts, and the Q narrative about Satan's temptation of Jesus, when "he showed *(edeixen)* him all the kingdoms of the world in a moment of time" (Luke 4:5; cf. Matt 4:8), offers a kind of antithetic "epiphany" to the one here in the PE. The eight uses of the verb in Revelation (and perhaps John 14:8-9) indicate that the apocalyptic connotation here in the PE is by no means unique. Its cognate *endeixētai,* of the risen Lord showing mercy to Paul, ought to be noted (1 Tim 1:16). H. Schlier, *TDNT* 2.26, suggests that the use here in the PE has come to mean "to bring to pass," with the original sense of God making Christ visible in the final epiphany. He cites several lines of Euripides as illustrating *deiknymi* = "to create, fashion; to cause (bring) to experience," as well as LXX Num 16:30, *yibra'* = *deixei,* but BAGD have not taken up the suggestion. Indeed, this sense seems to reduce itself to making something (someone) visible to someone else whether that process be unusual or not. It belongs to the vocabulary of revelation.

This verb is conspicuous in the vocabulary of Hermas and fits in with the other visionary, apocalyptic interests of that work. Otherwise the verb occurs infrequently. *First Clement* 5.5 speaks of the martyred Paul, who "showed ([*hyp-*]*edeixen, s.v.l.*) the way to the prize of endurance"; in 10.3 he cites LXX Gen 12:1 (as above, Acts 7:3); and at 10.7 LXX Gen 22:2 is being alluded to; at 16.12 LXX Isa 53:11 is quoted. At 26.1 God "shows" with the example of the Phoenix "the greatness of his promise [of final resurrection]." At 35.12 the author is again citing the LXX Ps 49:23, "the sacrifice of praise will glorify me, and therein is a way *(hodos)* in which I shall show the salvation *(sōtērion)* of God to him." Thus in the two instances where *First Clement* is not using the LXX, the verb takes on an eschatological nuance.

Barnabas uses the verb four of five times in the phrase *hina deixēi* (5.6, 9; 7.5; 12.6) of God's showing one reality with or through another (including the OT; cf. also the lines of Menander, *Sikyonios,* pp. 148-149, *tōn emōn logōn gar oiseis eutheos ta symbola/kai parōn deixeis ean tis auta boulētai skopein,* "For straightaway you will bring the evidence of my words, and you will personally show it if someone wishes to inspect them" (trans. WCW). Barnabas's final usage in 13.3 involves a similar "showing" from the OT narrative a further reality.

*in due time.* On *kairos idios* see Titus 1:3.

*blessed and only suzerain. Makarios* occurred above of God in 1 Tim 1:11 (see above) and of hope in Titus 2:13 (the only use of the word in the PE to qualify an entity other than God). On *monos* see the doxology of 1 Tim 1:17.

*the king of those who act as kings.* On God as *basileus,* see the comments on the doxology of 1 Tim 1:17; cf. Philo, *Dec.* 41. The verb *basileuein* occurs on twenty other occasions in the NT but only here in the PE. The term occurs on nine other occasions in the Paulines, six in Romans and three in First Corinthians (with human beings, or sin or death or grace or Christ as subject, but never God). The Lukan usage is similar: the Christ in Luke 1:33 "will rule over the house of Jacob"; the only other occurrences in the Lukan corpus are in Luke 19:14, 27, of a human being, who is to be understood parabolically (of God as judge?). The one other use in the Gospels is in Matt 2:22 of Archelaus ruling Judea. The usage here in First Timothy is evidently of men exercising kingship (note the present tense) here and now in the world within which this doxology is offered; it is in Revelation (and the apocalyptic usage that it represents) that on occasion God himself is the subject of this verb (cf. Rev 11:15 with 17; 19:6, and note the prayer contexts; cf. K. L. Schmidt, *TDNT* 1.590).

In the Ap. Frs. this verb is used only twice: in Ign. *Rom.* 6.1, where the martyr-to-be writes, "It is better for me to die in Christ Jesus than to be king *(basileuein)* over the ends of the earth," and again in *Barn.* 4.4, also of human rule. In the numerous LXX uses of this verb it is in the Psalms that this term is particularly employed of God/the Lord (LXX Pss 9:37; 46:8; 92:1; etc.).

*those who act as lords.* The verb *kyrieuein* occurs only here in the PE and otherwise in Paul only five times (in Romans with death, sin, the law, and Christ as subject and in 2 Cor 1:24 of Paul and Timothy and Silvanus not "lording it over the faith" of the Corinthians). The one other NT use, in Luke 22:25, is precisely parallel to the meaning here in the PE where "the kings *(basileis)* of the gentiles exercise lordship *(kyrieuousin)* over them." The verb is even less frequent in the Ap. Frs., found only in Barnabas (three times) and Hermas (twice). In the former's closing prayer (*Barn.* 21.5), God *(theos)* is "exercising lordship *(kyrieuōn)* over all the world"; and Hermas, *Sim.* 9.23.4, speaks of "the God and our Lord who rules over all *(ho pantōn kyrieuōn).*" Even in the other instances where men are the subject, the verb does not have the bad sense that it usually has in the NT. W. Foerster, *TDNT* 3.1097, has noted that this verb is frequent in the LXX, whether of God ruling or of foreign tyrants, as well as simply to designate political leadership.

16. *immortality.* The noun *athanasian* is documented otherwise in the NT only in 1 Cor 15:53-54, where it = *aphtharsia* (cf. 2 Tim 1:10 as well as *aphtharsia* in 1 Tim 1:17). In the LXX it occurs only in the latest Hellenistic (Alexandrian) Jewish strata. In Wis 3.4; 4:1; 8:13, 17; 15:3 it describes the object of the hope of the righteous dead; the divine memory of a man's virtue is identified with it; it denotes the fruit of association with wisdom; it springs from the root of the knowledge of God's power. In 4 Macc 14:5 "the road to immortality" lies through the martyrs' death, and in 16:13 the term is used of the martyrs' mother bringing forth her sons "a second time into immortality." Bultmann, *TDNT* 3.22-25, has noted (p. 24) that the OT has no term that corresponds to this, for all of its secular Greek literary usage. It seems to be rather unusual in the papyri and inscriptions; cf. MM *s.v.* and the examples in Bultmann, p. 23. The example cited by MM from W. Ramsay, *Studies in the E. Roman Provinces,* p. 129, is parallel to the thought but not the precise terminology here in the PE, *oudis* [*sic*] [*atha*]*natos ei mē monon is* [sic] *theos autos* . . . , "No one is immortal except only the one God himself. . . ." The noun is common in Philo; of the seven uses in Josephus, *War* 7.340, 348 is notable for speaking of the immortality of the soul *(psychēs)* (Bultmann, p. 24).

In *1 Clem.* 35.2 the first of the "blessed and wonderful gifts of God" is "life in immortality *(zōē en athanasiai).*" For Ign. *Eph.* 20.2 the eucharistic bread is "the medicine of immortality *(pharmakon athanasias),* the antidote *(antidotos)* that we should not die but live *(zēn)* forever in Jesus Christ." The opposite is the *thanasimon pharmakon* of Ign. *Trall.* 6.2 of the "strange food which is heresy" (cited *supra* on 1 Tim 4:3). A curious ague seizes some exegetes when they encounter this phrase, as though the image were somehow more shocking than washing away sins with water or anointing with oil for health and strength.

In *Did.* 10.2 the thanksgiving prayer for the eucharistic rite begins with an expression of gratitude for "the knowledge and faith and immortality which you made known to us through Jesus, your child." This linking of *athanasia* and the eucharistic act appears thus to be quite early. There is no evidence, however, that this eucharistic nuance appears in 1 Tim 6:16. Rather, with Bultmann, pp. 24-25, one notes in this passage not simply God's perduring endlessly but his "mode of existence . . . equivalent to what is elsewhere called *doxa,*" in contrast to the mortal existence of flesh and blood.

*inhabits.* The verb *oikein* occurs only here in the PE, and elsewhere in the NT only in Rom 7:18, 20 (of evil and sin dwelling in man); 8:9, 11 (of the Holy Spirit dwelling in believers); 1 Cor 3:16 (also of God's Spirit dwelling in the believer as in a temple); 7:12-13 (of living as husband and wife). The single occurrence of the term in the Ap. Frs., Hermas, *Vis.* 5.1.2, describes the vision of the Shepherd coming to dwell *(oikēsō)* with Hermas for the rest of his life.

*inaccessible light.* On the fifteen occurrences of *phōs* in the Ap. Frs., see Conzelmann, *TDNT* 9.356-357, noting the "local" or spatial sense in Ign. *Rom.* 6.2 and comparing the liturgical language of *1 Clem.* 59.2. *Acts of Thomas* 27 writes, "Beyond our comprehension, Lord, is your light, and we are not able to bear it; for it is greater than our sight" (Hennecke and Schneemelcher, *NT Apoc.* 2.457). The light is qualified as *aprositon,* a term not otherwise attested in the NT, the Ap. Frs., or the LXX.

*saw. Eidon* occurs 336 times in the NT (67/49 in Luke-Acts) but is comparatively rare in the rest of the Paulines (16 times). W. Michaelis, *TDNT* 5.324, has noted some 930 LXX uses of *eidon.*

*honor and might eternal.* On the use of *timē* in the phrase *timē kai kratos aiōnion,* see above on 1 Tim 1:17. The noun *kratos,* "might" (twelve times in NT), occurs only here in the PE and, as was already noted, figures especially in doxologies. There are three other Pauline uses — Eph 1:19; 6:10; and Col 1:11 (see Lohse *in loc.,* p. 30) — where, as always in the NT, this term is used of a power beyond man's (Heb 2:14 of the devil). In the Lukan corpus the word occurs twice: in Luke 1:51 in the hymn placed on Mary's lips, and in Acts 19:20 of "the Word of the Lord" that "grew *(kata kratos)* mightily." In the Ap. Frs. only *First* and *Second Clement* employ *kratos.* In addition to the *loci* cited above, see *1 Clem.* 27.5 (cf. Wis 11:21 with 12:12); 33.3; 61.1. In the last citation the term is used in a prayer that describes how the divine *despotēs* has endowed earthly leaders with "the power of kingship *(tēn exousian tēs basileias).*" The final use in the Ap. Frs. is in *2 Clem.* 17.5 where the author describes the judgment day when even unbelievers will see "the glory and might" of Jesus and "will be astounded when they see the sovereignty *(basileion)* of the world given to Jesus." Here one encounters evidence that the liturgical formula was understood in a fundamentally eschatological sense. The "letter" contained in the *Mart. Pol.* 20.2 concludes with a prayer for *doxa timē kratos megalosynē* to God the Father. Michaelis, *TDNT* 3.906, has noted that for all the frequency of *kratos* in NT and later doxologies (p. 908), this is not the sense in which it is used in LXX Greek, though it is used often enough there in prayers and commonly applied to God. Even in secular Greek it is seldom used in acclamations that would in their turn be a sort of matrix for the doxological genre among Christians. There does not seem to be a doxological use of *ʿwz* in the Qumran documents either.

## ♦ COMMENT

6:11. *You, O man of God, must shun these things. Instead pursue — upright conduct, godliness, faithfulness, charity, steadfastness, gentleness.* With this verse begins a paragraph (11-16) that Käsemann, *Essais,* pp. 111-118, has suggested is a set piece of exhortation that had its *Sitz im Leben* in an ordination ceremony of the second Christian generation. There is no denying the unmitigated abruptness of the transition from the warnings on avarice that preceded to the second person singular parenesis for Timothy that follows, not to mention the equally abrupt return to the subject of the rich in 6:17-19. As Käsemann has noted, some have considered verses 11-16 an interpolation (e.g., Falconer, *PE,* p. 158), whereas others (e.g., Jeremias and Strobel, *NTD,* p. 82) have considered verses 17-19 as a sort of appended afterthought on how Timothy ought to guide those who actually are rich. If logic were the grounds for arranging this whole section, one would find it easier to read 6:3-10 with 17-19, leaving 11-16 to stand with minimal adjustments just before concluding verses 20-21 of this letter. There was evidently something more pressing and persuasive than internal logical sequence that guided the author-redactor of this section of the PE. Before Käsemann's suggestion is tested, the language and concepts of the whole paragraph ought to be analyzed.

The introductory *sy de* of this verse was addressed to Titus in Titus 2:1, following a lengthy section on true and false teaching that had been couched in the third person, as was the preceding instruction here in First Timothy. In almost all of the instances of *sy (de)* outside of the PE (see Notes above), the phrase occurs of an unnamed individual, who usually stands as a typical instance (cf. Rom 11:17, 20; 14:10; Luke 9:60; 16:25; James 4:12) or an interlocutor summoned up for a rhetorical purpose. The use of the vocative *anthrōpe* also functions as a rhetorical device (see Fiore, *Function,* p. 13). Thus here the abrupt shift to the second person singular does not necessarily mean that a more personal or intimate section is to follow. Rather, the "man of God" to whom it is addressed is typified by Timothy, and the portrait sketched is less what the historical Timothy ought to be than what any "man of God" ought to be.

The exclamatory *ō,* which here introduces the "man of God" phrase, will introduce the name of Timothy himself at 6:20. The rest of the Paulines use the term to introduce things (Rom 11:33) as well as persons (Gal 3:11), but even the persons, in the singular, are unnamed rhetorical constructs (Rom 2:1, 3; 9:20). Here at 6:11 the *anthrōpe theou* leads one also to think of the other Pauline usages as parallel where three of five times *ō anthrōpe* occurs of a "rhetorical man" summoned forth for the occasion (cf. also the "*ō anthrōpe kene*" of James 2:20).

The phrase "man of God" occurs otherwise in the NT only at 2 Tim 3:17 (cf. the *apo theou anthrōpoi* of 2 Pet 1:21), where it is certainly employed in a generic sense and not just of Timothy personally. In this correspondence, the singular *anthrōpos* occurred at Titus 3:10 in a generic sense. The use of *anthrōpos* with the name of Jesus Christ at 1 Tim 2:5 is specific, but the very fact that the name was added indicates that the word tended to be understood in a general fashion. N. Bratsiotis, *TDOT* 1.233-235, has distinguished as many as seventy-five occurrences of the phrase *'ish (ha) 'elohim* in the MT, predominantly in Deuteronomic strata of the OT (especially the Former Prophets). The only explicitly named "men of God" are Moses, Samuel, David, Elijah, Elisha, Shemaiah, and Igdaliah (Jer 35:4), and the phrase never occurs in the form "men of Yahweh," nor are there "women of God." For all the frequency of the phrase in the OT, it has not yet appeared in Qumran. As Bratsiotis has remarked, the Hebrew phrase has a reverential tone and is applied to persons divinely commissioned to bring God's message to men; thus the phrase most frequently designates prophets and is associated with the spirit (*ruaḥ;* cf. LXX Hos 9:7 on the prophet/"man of the spirit," *pneumatophoros;* see Käsemann, *Essais,* p. 118, on the Hellenistic *pneumatikos*) and holiness (cf. 2 Kings 2:9, 15; 4:9).

Perhaps most striking in connection with 1 Tim 6:11 and its admonition to the man of God, *tauta pheuge,* i.e. flee the greedy desires and avarice just noted (*tauta,* as usual in the PE, referring to matters previously mentioned), is the refusal of the OT "man of God" to seek any recompense for his ministry (cf. 1 Sam 9:7-8 with 12:3-4; 1 Kings 13:7-9; 2 Kings 5:15-16 with 4:8-10). Of course the actual practice may have made this all the more praiseworthy (cf. Hallevy, "Man of God," p. 239). On usage in Philo, Aristeas, and Sextus, see D-C, pp. 87-88.

*Pheuge* occurs once again in the PE at 2 Tim 2:22, also addressed to Timothy, with *neōterikas epithymias* as its object (note that *tauta* here would include the *epithymias* of 6:9 above). Paul uses *pheugein* only in 1 Cor 6:18 and 10:14, in a plural imperative to flee fornication and idolatry. In the five occurrences in Luke-Acts it is not used of fleeing vice or sin except insofar as that is implied in fleeing the approaching wrath of the divine Judge in Luke 3:7 = Matt 3:7 (Q). There are no real parallels to the use in the Paulines of the twenty other NT references. On the other hand, the Ap. Frs. almost always use the term in the Paulines' way, of fleeing from various vices and evils (see Notes above).

Antithetically *(de)* coupled with the vices that are to be fled are the virtues that are to be pursued. The alliteration of *diōke de dikaiosynen* is striking. The whole phrase recurs in 2 Tim 2:22, and the verb also occurs in 2 Tim 3:12 to designate persecution rather than a striving after something in a good sense (note also the use of the noun in 1 Tim 1:13). In the NT there are forty-one other occurrences of *diōkein,* eighteen in the other Paulines, twelve in Luke-Acts (three/nine). Luke uses the verb of persecution except in Luke 17:23, where it refers to "following" false prophets. The Paulines, on the other hand, employ the term of pursuing virtue (1 Cor 14:1; Rom 12:13; 14:19; Phil 3:12, 14 [of a goal wider than virtue]; 1 Thess 5:15) as well as of persecution (1 Cor 15:9; Rom 12:14), and the most notable parallel to the phrase here in 1 Tim 6:11 is

Rom 9:30-31: "Gentiles, who did not pursue righteousness *(ethnē ta mē diōkonta dikaiosynēn),* have attained it, i.e. righteousness through faith, but Israel, who pursued the righteousness that is based on the law *(Israēl de diōkōn nomon dikaiosynēs),* did not succeed in fulfilling that law."

The base of the use of *diōkein* as the pursuit of virtue seems to go back to the LXX Ps 33:15, *zētēson eirēnēn kai diōxon autēn,* alluded to in Rom 14:19 and Heb 12:14 as well as quoted in 1 Pet 3:11. Perhaps LXX Isa 51:1, where *dikaion* is parallel to *kyrion,* is even more basic. Oepke, *TDNT* 2.230, has a few other LXX examples of "pursuing" good, especially Deut 16:20, *dikaiōs* to *dikaion diōxēi,* which is linguistically closer to 1 Tim 6:11. See also the athletic imagery of the race in the LXX passages adduced by Bauernfeind, *TDNT* 8.229-230 (e.g., LXX Ps 118:32). The same citation crops up again in *1 Clem.* 22.5, who otherwise uses *diōkein* = to persecute (as do *Didache* and *Barnabas* except when they speak of *diōkontes anatapodoma,* "pursing rewards," in a bad sense, as LXX Isa 1:23 [*Did.* 5.2; *Barn.* 20.2; cf. *2 Clem.* 20.4]). *Second Clement* 10.1-2 writes of "following after virtue" *(aretēn)* and thus of peace *(eirēnē)* "following after us." In *2 Clem.* 18.2 he can write, after the sentence cited above on *peirasmos,* "Yet I am striving to follow after righteousness *(tēn dikaiosynēn diōkein)* that I may have the strength at least to draw near to it, in fear of the judgment to come."

*Dikaiosynē,* "upright conduct," leads off the list of virtues. Ziesler, *Righteousness,* p. 155, notes that every instance of the noun in the PE, including Titus 3:5, has a mention of human conduct or ethics and all are taken in reference to God. Titus refers to conduct before faith and baptism, whereas 1 Tim 6:11; 2 Tim 2:22; and 3:16 refer to the postbaptismal conduct of believers. The "crown of righteousness" in 2 Tim 4:8 may refer to the reward for the apostle's works or to the life of heaven and its righteousness as complementing that of the good works done in this life (see commentary *in loc.* for further discussion).

In 1 Tim 6:11 the reference certainly is a believer's uprightness of life (without prejudice to the question of the origin and sustaining cause of that holiness), and one can adopt Chrysostom's comment on the same phrase in 2 Tim 2:22 (*PG* 62.631): "Virtue in general *(tēn katholou aretēn)* he calls 'uprightness.'" It is difficult to determine whether the following *eusebeian* is to be paired with *dikaiosynēn* (Spicq notes how Titus 2:12 speaks of living *sōphronōs kai dikaiōs kai eusebōs*), or whether it serves as a title for the following trio, "faithfulness, charity, steadfastness," and perhaps for the concluding "gentleness" as well. In that case, *eusebeia* telescopes out of *dikaiosynē,* and this godliness is in turn described in a variation on the triad of faith-hope-love that may have had a liturgical provenance before it appeared in Paul (1 Thess 1:3; 5:8), specifically perhaps a (thanksgiving) prayer offered to the Father as object of belief, the Son as source of hope, the Spirit as bringing the love of Father and Son into and out of the praying church (cf. Delling, *Worship,* pp. 60-61). In that case, *pistis* is used here of the subjective adherence of the believer to God, and *agapē* could well be understood primarily of the love for God with one's whole being (with prayer being the privileged expression of that *agapē*). In that case the final *praüpathian* would have been called for to preclude misunderstanding on the importance of *agapē* toward one's neighbor as well.

As in 1 Thess 1:3 and Titus 2:2, so here in 1 Tim 6:11, *pistis* and *agapē* are followed by *hypomonē*, a term that was commented on when it occurred in Titus 2:2. Hauck, *TDNT* 4.583-584, in discussing the LXX (and corresponding Hebrew) terminology, has noted that Israel is the one who waits *(hypomenei)* and that it is God, the hope of Israel, for whom his people wait (cf. Jer 14:8 with 22; and cf. 1 Tim 1:1 on Christ as "our hope"). In this tense, persevering wait, there are trials to endure (note the fourteen occurrences of the **hypomen-* root in Job; cf. James 5:11). One of the rare cases where the NT takes up the LXX terminology of *hypomenein ton kyrion (tōi theōi)* is 2 Thess 3:5 on the *hypomonē tou Christou* that is parallel to *agapē tou theou* (Hauck, *TDNT* 4.585-586). The "waiting for Christ" here is in contrast to the *theos tēs hypomonēs* of Rom 15:5, where God is the source of Christian patience in afflictions that are not "self-selected burdens" but part of the human society's rejection of the Word of God and those in whom that Word lives and speaks (Hauck, *TDNT* 4.587). In the NT and here in the PE, *hypomonē* emphasizes the present sufferings and trials that the one who believes in and loves God endures, whereas *elpis*, "hope," stresses the future goal and reward toward which the believer strains (cf. the *hypomonē tēs elpidos* of 1 Thess 1:3 as well as 2 Tim 2:12).

The sixth and final term in this catalogue is *praüpathia*, a term that is otherwise undocumented in the NT or the LXX but that does occur in the Ap. Frs. in Ign. *Trall.* 8.1, where in a warning against the devil's snares *(enedras)* the recipients are charged to "adopt gentleness *(praüpatheian)* and be renewed in faith . . . and in love. . . ." Philo, *Abr.* 213, speaks of the "gentleness" *(praüpatheian)* of Abraham influencing that of his servants as they suffer from the quarrelsome aggressiveness of the servants of Lot. On the cognate *praütēs* see Titus 3:2 as well as 2 Tim 2:25.

With this final term one notes the recurring alliteration with the *p* sound that has occurred in each term of this list since *pistis*, binding these last four words together through this repeated consonant.

12. *Contend in the fine contest, the contest in the arena of faith.* In 1 Tim 4:10 it is said of Paul and Timothy, *agōnizometha*, "we contend," and in 2 Tim 4:7 the first person singular perfect ("constative": Moule, *Idiom*, p. 16) takes up the same phrase found here in 6:12 in the form *ton kalon agōna ēgōnismai.* The second person singular present imperative *agōnizou* is given further emphasis with the internal accusative of the phrase *ton kalon agōna.* The emphasis upon an agreeable visibility in *kalos* here, too, suggests too that the game or contest is

one visible to and assessed by a judge. Pfitzner, *PAM*, pp. 166-167, has observed that *ho kalos agōn* is quite parallel in usage to *hē kalē strateia* of 1 Tim 1:18 (cf. *kalos stratiōtēs* of 2 Tim 2:3), and perhaps the latter phrases were consciously modeled on the former. Originally there was a note of polemic against athletics in the *kalos agōn,* but it has really faded out of sight in these passages of the PE (cf. 1 Tim 4:8 above). That is not to say, however, that the athletic imagery in this terminology had become so commonplace that the metaphor was no longer alive (Pfitzner, *PAM,* p. 179 n. 1, contra MM *s.v. agōnizomai,* p. 8) and the "game" of warfare was for all practical purposes identical with the games of the athletes.

The qualification of the *agōn* here in First Timothy as *tēs pisteōs* is not transparent. It is difficult to take the genitive here as denoting the object or goal for which the man of God strives, since precisely as *fides quae* ("revelation") it is a reality that he already possesses. If "the faith" were to be understood as the revelation "on behalf of which" the contest (with the heretics of vv. 3-10) is occurring, one would have expected the dative rather than the genitive (cf. Phil 1:27; Jude 3). There is less reason, with B. Weiss, *Handbuch,* p. 236, to take *pistis* as a personification here (*apud* Pfitzner, *PAM,* p. 179). Pfitzner is correct in taking the genitive as an appositive to *agōn.* Thus "the faith" is the arena in which the contest occurs (cf. *1 Clem.* 6.2), the whole life of the believer as he strives to remain true to the revelation that God has given him. Whereas the *pistis* of the preceding verse stressed deepening the subjective commitment, *hē pistis* here brings both the subjective and objective aspects of the faith into play.

*Lay hold on eternal life. You were called into that life and for it you made that fine profession before the eyes of many witnesses.* Parallel to "contend in the fine contest" is "lay hold on eternal life," and *epilabou* corresponds to *agōnizou* in the way that "the fine contest" does to *hē aiōnios zōē.* The aorist *epilabou* designates the decisive act of laying hold on eternal life in this life (not just at the end of this life and thus only in another order or world; Pfitzner, *PAM,* p. 180 n. 2, calls attention to 1 Tim 4:8). Pfitzner, *PAM,* pp. 179-180 n. 1, is correct in noting that the athletic imagery does not continue with the use of *epilabou.* The connotation of personal contact and fellowship, however, ought not to be overlooked.

What the short, appositive *tēs pisteōs* was to the preceding *agōn,* a lengthy descriptive clause now is to *zōē,* "the eternal life into which *(eis hēn)* you were called *(eklēthēs)* and (to receive it) you professed the fine profession before many witnesses." The suggestion here is of an invitation to the banquet of eternal life — a messianic banquet (the calling vocabulary uses the language of invitation, particularly to share with a wealthy, generous host a banquet and life-giving food [see parables of Luke 14:7-24 and the beatitude of Rev 19:9]; cf. also Notes above) that the man of God has received and in which he has already begun to share.

However, there is no evidence that the author-redactor had the eucharist in mind, though the original liturgical setting of this composition (whether baptismal or an ordination) may in fact have had a eucharistic setting.

Since "the fine profession" of the man of God is here taken up in and evidently parallel to "the fine profession" of Christ Jesus bearing witness before Pontius Pilate in the next verse, it is reasonable to expect that the content of the *homologia* here has something to do with what Jesus publicly admitted in the trial(s) that precipitated his crucifixion under the charge, "This is the king of the Jews" (Luke 23:38). Since the Lukan tradition alone speaks of *Pontius Pilate* (see Note on v. 13), one turns there first to explain "the profession." Once Jesus has admitted to the Sanhedrin that he is "the son of God," that body declares that it needs no further "*martyria*" (Luke 22:70-71; cf. the *Martyrōn . . . martyrēsantos* of 1 Tim 6:12-13) and takes Jesus forthwith to Pilate, where he is then charged with fomenting sedition, refusing to pay taxes, and saying that he was *Christon basilea.*

That last charge caught Pilate's ear, and Luke has him inquire, "Are you the king of the Jews?" (*ho basileus tōn Ioudaiōn* = title on cross cited above), and Jesus' reply is *Sy legeis,* i.e. an admission with the reservation that he had not actually used the terms. Thus Jesus' "fine profession" was his public admission that he was "Christ," the anointed king, and that in turn must be the nucleus of the "fine profession" of a man of God, that "Jesus is the Christ." This concept leads naturally into the final overwhelming doxology of God as "King" in verse 15. Perhaps the reading of the name "Christ Jesus" in 6:13 is prompted by this consciousness of the central importance of that title for belief in Jesus. Since the "profession" of Jesus is explicitly the one before Pilate and not that before the Sanhedrin, the reference is to the Christ/King title, not to the title Son (of God) (*pace* Michel, *TDNT* 5.211). That fact would correspond with the way in which these letters have preferred to speak of Jesus as Christ, Savior, or/and Lord, but never as Son *(huios).*

The phrase "before many witnesses," *enōpion pollōn martyrōn,* has a solemn juridical tone, and as *enōpion* here introduces human witnesses (cf. 1 Tim 5:20) in the following verse, it governs "God" *(tou theou),* as is usual in this correspondence (1 Tim 2:3; 5:4, 21; 2 Tim 2:14; 4:1). Whether God or man is the object, the phrase connotes an authoritative, legally binding statement, publicly and solemnly witnessed in heaven and on earth. Here the witnesses are called *martyres,* reminding one of the previous use of this term in 1 Tim 5:19 citing the Deuteronomic law demanding two or three witnesses on a capital or serious charge. The importance of this term for the understanding of this passage is stressed by the appearance of the cognate verb in the following verse when the author invoked "Christ Jesus who witnessed *(martyrēsantos)* before Pontius Pilate. . . ." That verb was studied when it occurred at 1 Tim 5:10 (see above).

Here, with Strathmann, *TDNT* 4.492-494, one distinguishes between the witness to a fact and a witness to the truth, a distinction that was exploited particularly by Luke, for whom the Twelve and others are "witnesses" to the public events of Jesus' life, including his resurrection (cf. Luke 24:33 with 48 [where *toutōn* = "that the Christ should suffer and on the third day rise from the dead" in 24:46]; Acts 1:8, 22). Here in 1 Tim 6:12 as well as 2 Tim 2:2 (not to mention 1 Tim 5:19), the *martyres* are witnesses to the fact of the man of God's (or Timothy's) public act of confessing the faith. The verb in the following verse has a somewhat different nuance, for there Jesus' "fine profession" witnesses to a hidden reality, the truth of his being a king, the anointed son of David (cf. Strathmann, p. 499, who would add, a "*suffering* messiah"). That of course is the *content* of the man of God's confession, but the *martyres* in verse 12 are to the *fact* that he made such a confession, not to the content as such. Moreover, Jesus' *martyrein* is to a historical individual who did not believe, whereas Timothy's confession is apparently before witnesses who are presumed to be believers (cf. Strathmann, p. 497 n. 63, who also observes that all *martyrein* is ordered to evangelizing the unbeliever and involves *homologein;* but not all *homologein* is immediately so ordered but may take place before believers who thus become witnesses [*martyres*] to a *homologia* that is not a *martyria*).

13. *Before the eyes of the God who keeps all things alive and of Christ Jesus who publicly attested to the fine profession before Pontius Pilate, I charge you.* The *paraggellō soi* with which this verse opens reminds one of the opening of this letter, 1 Tim 1:3 *(paraggeilēis),* and the apostolic *paraggelia* (1 Tim 1:5, 18) given to Timothy. From a formal point of view, both here and at 6:17 below, the repeated use of the verb serves to signal the reader that the "*paraklēsis*" (cf. 1 Tim 4:13) which began in 4:6 is now drawing to a close.

The omission of *soi* in S* as well as F, G, 33, 1739, Ambrose, Augustine, Theodoret, Theodore of Mopsuestia, and Basil is, as J. K. Elliott, *Greek Text,* p. 100, suggests, an attempt to take the teaching of this correspondence out of the "person to person" framework and make it generally applicable. The question still remains, however, whether the original source (the liturgical homily or exhortation) had the more general form without *soi.* If that was in fact the case, then the *soi* may have been the insertion of the redactor of this correspondence, who "personalized" and "individualized" a more generic parenesis. In that case, Sinaiticus again (cf. on *eusebeia* above) may have been "remembering" the still available liturgical source when its scribe dropped the pronoun at this point (cf. the way in which *se* was omitted in D*, 326, Lect, 185, Didymus at 6:14: note also 5:23 above).

D-C, p. 88, propose that the whole phrase from *enōpion tou theou* through *kai Christou Iēsou tou martyrēsantos epi Pontiou Pilatou* here is a fragment of an archaic creedal formula (see Käsemann's summary, *Essais,* pp. 112-

113). If that is the case, we have before us a redactor's citation of a liturgical homily that in its turn was taking up a creed that had been or was to be employed in the liturgical service at which the exhortation was to be delivered. The mention of Pontius Pilate recalls not only the Lukan way of speaking but also the most ancient Roman creed (cf. Kelly, *Creeds,* pp. 143-144). The creed here has essentially two members, the former a profession of faith in God the creator and the latter in Jesus as the Christ (cf. D-C and citations there).

Spicq, *EP,* p. 570, noting the emphatic phraseology of this text, including *ta panta,* which certainly stresses the all-inclusiveness of the divine King of kings' (cf. v. 15) power to give life, has suggested a deliberate opposition to the imperial cult (*pace* D-C) in which the emperor's subject was to regard his leader "as the origin of his life and his existence" (*Inscr. de* Priène 105.10.32). D-C, p. 88, cite *Joseph and Aseneth* 8.2, 10, describing God as *zōopoiēsas ta panta kai kalesas apo tou skotous eis to phōs.* Cf. *Acts of Thomas* 10, *ho theos ton kosmon zōopoiōn* (Hennecke and Schneemelcher, *NT Apoc.* 2.447).

God as the one who gives life is conceived of as creator; as the one who preserves or keeps alive, he is protector, rescuer, savior. The second sense is particularly appropriate in the light of the following clause, for the Father is the protector who preserves the life of his Son, Christ Jesus, when the latter reveals his kingship to Pilate. Men may inflict death on "the king of the Jews," but God gives life (keeps alive) in the resurrection. D-C raise the question whether the "witnessing" of Jesus is understood as in words or as in deeds (or, one might add, as in both). The final *tēn kalēn homologian* certainly indicates that the redactor understood the *martyrēsantos* in terms of words. If that final phrase is not his own (and D-C argue that it is, on the analogy of *1 Clem.* 5.4, 7, cited above), then the liturgical homiletic source thus understood the creedal statement. Of course, the creed itself preexisted the homily and indeed may well have ended with *martyrēsantos epi Pontiou Pilatou,* which was not further specified but which could certainly be taken of the whole course of action that Jesus persevered in to the cross.

It is notable that again S as well as K. L. T. R. 69. et al. read *zōopoiountos* (J. K. Elliott, *Greek Text,* p. 101). Again one wonders whether S knew the liturgical source being cited and "corrected" what actually was the editorial adjustment of the (Lukan) redactor of this correspondence. Recall that the II Constantinople Creed of 381 calls *to pneuma . . . zōopoion* (DS 150).

In secular Greek also, the gods are invoked as having power to bestow life through nature *(physis).* Hobart, *Medical Language,* p. 155, has noted the use of the term in medical texts (MM *s.v.,* p. 275) to mean "to bestow life." Spicq suggests that in this passage of First Timothy both senses of the verb may have been intended, and, on the hypothesis of a source redacted by Luke, this becomes easier to understand, for the original homily would have used the term in its normal secular Greek sense whereas the redactor read it in the sense that he had learned in LXX Greek. If S is correct in "restoring" the liturgical source to *zōopoiountos* (which would in turn be a more "Pauline" term; cf. Rom 4:17, *theou tou zōopoiountos tous nekrous;* 8:11; 1 Cor 15:22; etc.), then the redactor's hand appears in the use here and the meaning is, more probably, "the God who keeps alive." For the thought here, cf. Acts 17:25.

14. *to keep the apostolic command beyond blemish, beyond reproach, until the revelation of our Lord, Jesus Christ.* The *paraggelia* or charge is *terēsai se tēn entolēn . . .*, "that you (sg. = 'man of God' = Timothy) keep the command. . . ." The Western omission of *se* has been noted above in 6:13. The verb *tērein* has been analyzed above in 1 Tim 5:22, and just as there "*keep* yourself holy" partially coincided in meaning with the very solemn *(enōpion tou theou k.t.l.) diamartyromai . . . hina tauta phylaxēis,* so here the similarly solemn admonition to keep "the command" may refer (at least in the source) to the actual command (negative and positive) with which this parenesis began: "Flee these things but pursue righteousness etc." (Thus B. Weiss, *Handbuch, pace* D-C, who take *entolēn* in 6:14 = *parathēkēn* of 6:20.) From his point of view, the final redactor of the PE may well have understood that the concluding *parathēkēn* of all that "Paul" had transmitted in this correspondence, including, of course, this homiletic material and the *entolēn,* equaled the command of 6:11 contained within it. One cannot proceed in the reverse order, from *entolē* to *parathēkē* with the same confidence.

The meaning of *entolē* here would be better understood, even from the point of view of the final redactor, by reference to its one previous use in the PE, at Titus 1:14, where the "commandments of (Judaizing) people" are implicitly contrasted with the commandment that is placed on the lips of Paul and is to be received as God's own directive through the apostle (cf. the Lukan use of the verb *entellomai* in Acts 1:2; 13:47 of the command of the risen Lord "through the Holy Spirit" to his apostles; otherwise in his writing, Luke 4:10, citing LXX Ps 90:11). Though the Pauline correspondence normally uses *entolē (-ai)* of the OT commandments, the apostolic directives on women's silence in liturgical assemblies are to be recognized as a command of the Lord *ha graphō hymin hoti kyriou estin entolē,* 1 Cor 14:37 (*s.v.l.* with $p^{46}$. $S^{c}$ [* has *entolē estin*] A. B; see B. Metzger, *TCGNT,* p. 566, *pace* Schrenk, *TDNT* 2.553). This passage is parallel to 1 Tim 6:14 in its calling the apostle's written directive the Lord's *entolē* (as distinct from the written OT directives that are *entolai theou,* as in 1 Cor 7:19. Cf. also Mark 7:8-9; Matt 15:3; Rev 12:17; 14:12, *hoi tērountes tas entolas tou theou kai tēn pistin Iēsou,* "those who keep the commandments of God and the faith of Jesus" [RSV]. Luke 1:6 uses *poreuomenoi en pasais entolais kai dikaiomasin tou kyriou,* "walking in all the commandments and ordinances of the Lord" [RSV], to describe the good lives of Zachariah and Elizabeth according to the

OT). Though 1 Tim 6:14 does not read *hē entolē tou kyriou,* its irreproachable observance is "until the manifestation of our Lord Jesus Christ" in the very next phrase of this sentence.

G. Schrenk, *TDNT* 2.545-546, has noted that both secular Greek and the LXX employ this noun for the orders of human kings, a usage that Josephus, too, favors, though he (like secular texts) employs the noun for the commands of God (the divine king) too. The term also can designate in secular Greek the "education" that a teacher gives his pupil, an ordinary command or commission (cf. Acts 17:15 of an *entolēn* for Timothy and Silas to rejoin Paul promptly; Col 4:10, "instructions" [RSV]), and an authorization for representation or a mandate for an official's installation (cf. MM *s.v.,* pp. 217-218, and Schrenk, *ut cit.*). Käsemann, *Essais,* p. 117, rightly sensed that the singular *entolē* in 1 Tim 6:14 was unusual in its indeterminate usage and that it referred to "the charge committed to him" (Schrenk, *TDNT* 2.555), and that accordingly it was to be taken in the same way as in the papyri that use the term to speak "of installation as the supervisor of a village" (Schrenk, p. 546). Here the *entolē* is "the charge" being given to the man of God when he is installed in his office, and this meaning goes back into the liturgical text that is being cited here. Since there is no evidence for the noun's being used to designate the form rather than the content, one ought to understand the term here of the directive as such, which in its turn is to be kept "unspotted, irreproachable" *(aspilon anepilēmpton).*

*Aspilos,* "beyond blemish," occurs only here in the PE. Its three other NT appearances are in the Catholic Epistles, at 1 Pet 1:19 of Christ the Lamb; 2 Pet 3:14 of Christians; and James 1:27 where the Christian is exhorted, *aspilon heauton tērein apo tou kosmos,* "keep oneself without blemish from the world" (Dibelius, *James,* pp. 121-122, is to be noted). The use of the term for persons in these texts has led some commentators to take these adjectives here of *se* (the man of God) rather than of the commandment. D-C and MM illustrate convincingly that the adjective was able to apply to things as well as persons in secular Greek from 300 B.C.E. Moreover, even though the LXX contains no use of the term, Sym. Job 15:15 applies this adjective to the heavens. *Second Clement* 8.6 (cited on *tērein* at 1 Tim 5:22 above) writes of keeping *(tērēsate)* "the seal *(sphragida)*" of baptism "undefiled *(aspilon).*" The two uses in Hermas are both of men/the human nature of Christ (*Vis.* 4.3.5 and *Sim.* 5.6.7). The "ritual" overtones of the term make it particularly appropriate here for describing the *entolē* laid upon a man of God, and the Jewish Christian connotations of the terminology ought to be noted (cf. Dibelius, *James,* p. 122, who dismisses this Jewish Christian mode of speaking because of his hypothesis on the late, Hellenistic origin of James). The *Second Clement* passage cited above witnesses surely to a baptismal context, in which this term was quite at home. That may be the liturgical context for the homily cited here as well as an ordination (see further *infra*).

The second adjective, paired formally with *aspilon* by an alpha privative, *anepilēmpton,* "beyond reproach," occurred above in the catalogue of qualifications for the *episkopos* (1 Tim 3:2; see commentary above) as well as in the *ordo* for widows at 5:7. The use of this very rare term in two other source strata for this correspondence makes a *prima facie* case for its belonging to source material here also, but note there of persons; cf., however, *Mart. Pol.* 17.1 of the *anepilēpton politeian* (career) of that old bishop. The asyndetic joining of the terms reminds one of the way in which Titus 3:1 joined a pair of nouns, and 1 Tim 4:3, two infinitives.

The keeping of the charge inviolate and irreproachable is placed immediately in an eschatological horizon with the phrase "until *(mechri)* the revelation of our Lord Jesus Christ." The preposition *mechri* occurs only eighteen times in the NT and again in the PE at 2 Tim 2:9, where it means "up to *and including* chains." The same inclusive sense seems to be required here, as is also the case in Luke 16:16 (contra Conzelmann) and Acts 20:7; Acts 10:30 really *says* this but the text may be corrupt (Haenchen, *Acts,* p. 350). In the six other Pauline uses, the exclusive sense ("up to but not including") seems to predominate (cf., e.g., Phil 2:8 with 30). In the Ap. Frs. both senses are found, once even in the same sentence (*1 Clem.* 4.9). The usage here in First Timothy is surely that of the source, but it is also closer to Luke than to Paul.

The *epiphaneia* here is the appearance of Jesus in glory at the end of time (thus Bultmann and Lührmann, *TDNT* 9.10) as Lord of the church *(tou Kyriou hēmōn).* Bultmann and Lührmann, pp. 8-9, have noted the sense of "helpful divine intervention" in this term in its Hellenistic usage, pagan as well as Jewish (almost always in Josephus; cf. Vermeulen, "*EPIPHANEIA,*" p. 15; often in LXX; but never in this sense in Philo, who uses the noun regularly but does not use *epiphainesthai* in a sense that is religious, of God or the Logos becoming "visible" to men's souls or minds [see Vermeulen, pp. 13-15; cf. also p. 23]). The context is frequently that of a military encounter, a battle in which the *epiphaneia* ensures victory. It is thus an appropriate term for the decisive and final appearance of the Messiah-Lord who rules all other kings (cf. v. 15 below).

In 1QM 12.(6)7 the high priest's prayer exhortation for the final battle says, "And you, O God, are terrible *(n[wr'])* in the glory of your majesty, and the congregation of your holy ones are among us for eternal help *(l'zr)*" (cf. Ps 121:2 and Isa 45:17; Yadin, *War,* p. 316, translates "alliance"; Dupont-Sommer, *EWQ,* p. 187, "succour"). If the *n[wr']* restoration is correct (cf. Yadin, *War,* p. 316), it would be notable that the LXX uses the *epiphan-* cluster to translate the Hebrew *yarē'* (cf. LXX 2 Kings 7:23; Deut 33:2; etc.; and see Dupont, *Syn Christōi,* p. 76).

Vermeulen has stressed that there are only two secular uses of *epiphania* that refer to the arrival of a king or sovereign (p. 16), both from areas that already regarded these men (Caligula, Hadrian) as gods. Thus he is reluctant to receive the term as commonly designating the happy advent *(parousia)* of a Hellenistic king (*pace* Deissmann, Mohrmann), noting that the LXX as well as the other Jewish literature of the period does not favor the secular, political connotation for the terminology that rather is linked with light, truth, revelation, training, and display of power (p. 17) and is thus used by Paul (see p. 17 n. 3). He goes on to observe, however (p. 18), that other Hellenistic terminology for the happy advent of the sovereign *(kyrios, sōtēr, philanthrōpia, basileus)* does occur along with the *epiphan-* cluster.

With Dupont, *Syn Christōi,* pp. 75-77, one notes that the *epiphania* here and elsewhere in the PE is never (as in 2 Thess 2:8) linked with the destruction of God's enemies. Here there is no controverting, no resistance to "the king of kings and lord of lords" of verse 15. Here the Hellenistic sense predominates; the *epiphania* in Second Thessalonians may betray the Hebrew Bible's stress on the fearful *(yr')* divine vengeance on the nations, a root that the LXX confused regularly with both *r'h/'wr* (to [make] see [n]/light). Note also the mention of God, "who inhabits inaccessible light," in 6:16.

Dupont particularly notes the inscription on the "epiphanies" of Asclepius where that deity's appearances in his sanctuary were to bring healing (cf. *sōtēr*) to his clients (p. 74). He also adverts to "the extraordinary power" (p. 75) that is being described as at work when 2 Thess 2:8 uses the noun in the phrase "by the epiphany of his parousia" (where neither the terms are synonymous nor the phrase pleonastic).

15. *That revelation God will make in due time.* With the relative pronoun *hēn (= epiphaneias),* a great concluding doxology begins (cf. the fragment of 1 Tim 3:16 that begins also with a relative, *hos*) in seven members (Spicq, *EP,* p. 572) that reach their climax in "to whom belong honor and might eternal. Amen," in 6:16. "The epiphany of Jesus Christ" is that which God (under no less than seven titles) "will make/show" *(deixei).*

God will "show" the epiphany in his own good time *(kairois idiois).* In the exordium of Titus 1:3, as in 1 Tim 2:6, this unusual phrase referred to the occasions set by God for the apostolic proclamation. Here in 6:15 the phrase has a more archaic apocalyptic sense of "the time" set by and known to God the Father alone for the glorious final appearance of his Son (the hendiadys *chronoi kai[e] kairoi* recurs in 1 Thess 5:1 as well as Acts 1:7, but in Titus 1:2-3 a wedge is driven into the hendiadys [*chronoi* appears in v. 2; *kairoi* in v. 3] and the two terms are reinterpreted, perhaps to disabuse Christians from reading into it a forbidden apocalyptic calendar). Also note LXX Dan 2:21-22, where in Daniel's thanksgiving prayer for the revelation of the mystery (of the king's dream) to him, he blessed God who ". . . changes seasons and times (*kairous kai chronous* [order *sic* in Theod. also]), he removes kings and sets up kings . . . he knows what is in darkness and the light dwells with him" (thus MT and Theod; cf. 1 Tim 6:16). Already in this traditional ordination homily the apocalyptic language is being detoxified, but not as elaborately as in Titus 1:2-3.

D-C, p. 89, have noted at this point the resemblance between the PE and the Lukan writings on the distinction of two "advents" for the Christ, one in the incarnation and historical ministry of Jesus (cf. the *epiphaneia* of 2 Tim 1:10) and the other at the end of time in the judgment of all humankind (as here in 1 Tim 6:14-15). In Luke-Acts, as here, the "right time" for these manifestations is totally at God's disposal (cf. Delling, *TDNT* 3.459-461, for passages), and the distinct separation of the two comings of Christ corresponds to the lengthening period since the actual Palestinian ministry of Jesus of Nazareth. The coming of Christ is no longer felt as *imminent,* and perseverance over the long haul of earthly life takes precedence over enthusiastic but short-term commitments. The difference is that between the idealistic generosity of the engaged girl and the advice she gives her own engaged daughter a generation later — the difference between Q and Matthew/Luke and especially Luke.

The generation after the PE saw the receding past and the "delayed" future being drawn together in the sacramental celebrations of the church and particularly that of the eucharist as both memorial of the cross and pledge of future glory. The sense of eschatological (and even psychological) imminence and immediacy is thus caught up and preserved in the sacramental order as it fades in the historical order because of the lapse of time. Perhaps a hint of this or at least an opening for this understanding can already be seen in the plural *kairoi* here, for the one *epiphaneia* has not only its final historical consummation but also its proleptic pledge in the sacramental interventions of the Lord Jesus in the ongoing life of his church. His ministers in particular come before his judgment every time they teach and act in his name, not just on the last day.

*he who is the blessed and only suzerain; the king of those who act as kings and lord of those who act as lords.* The great sevenfold naming of God is one of the most elaborate in the NT. A. R. C. Leaney, *RQM,* p. 258, classifies it as "an adaptation of an elaborate and self-conscious *berakah*" in the OT and Qumran tradition, not to mention, e.g., Luke 1:68. It falls into the following arrangement in sense lines (with syllable counts in parentheses):

1. *ho makarios kai monos dynastēs* (11)
2. *ho basileus tōn basileuontōn* (10)
3. *kai kyrios tōn kyrieuontōn* (9)
4. *ho monos echōn athanasian* (10)
5. *phōs oikōn aprositon* (7)
6. *hon eiden oudeis anthrōpōn* (8)
7. *oude idein dynatai* (7)

8. *hōi timē kai kratos aiōnion* (10)
9. *amēn*

The initial *ho(n/oi)* of lines 1, 2, 4, 6, 8 is scarcely accidental. The alliteration of *m*(1), *b*(2), and *k*(3), as well as the rhyme *(tōn . . . ontōn),* is also striking. The first line and the closing doxology (line 8) serve as a horizon around the expansive but gradually shortening central stanzas. There are nineteen syllables in lines 2-3, with the conjunction emphasizing the compound phrases; then seventeen syllables in the asyndetic lines 4-5; finally, fifteen syllables in the final stich, which is joined together by a chiasmus *(eiden oudeis — oude idein).* The closing *dynatai* of 7 reminds one of the *dynastēs* of line 1, not only formally but also because of the contrast between the one whom man is *powerless* to see and what that *Powerful* one makes visible, the epiphany of Jesus Christ.

The term here for God, *dynastēs,* occurs otherwise in the NT only of men, in Luke 1:52 ("He has put down *the mighty* from their thrones," also a poetic prayer passage) and Acts 8:27 (the title of the Ethiopian treasurer in that nation's court). W. Grundmann, *TDNT* 2.286, has noted that this old Greek *nomen agentis* for a human ruler was already applied to a god in Sophocles, *Antigone* 608, where the chorus thus hymns Zeus. Josephus seems to use *dynastēs* only of earthly rulers (eighteen times), never of the God of Israel; an interesting contrast occurs in his use of *despotēs,* for in *War* 7.410 he describes the *sicarii* as persuading their Jewish protectors "to look upon the Romans as no better than themselves and to esteem God alone as their Lord *(theon de monon hēgeisthai despotēn).*"

The link with the *dyna-* stem (= power, compatibility) is transparent. The LXX usage is notable, for although the great majority of occurrences are of human *dynastai,* in the latest strata of that collection the noun begins to be used of the God of Israel. Thus Sir 46:5-6, 16 describes an invocation *(epikalesato)* of God in prayer as *ton hypsiston/kyrion dynastēn.* In Second and Third Maccabees, eight of thirteen uses of the noun apply to God. Thus in 2 Macc 3:24 the terrifying manifestation *(epiphaneian)* to Heliodorus is made by "the sovereign *(dynastēs)* of spirits and of all authority." In 2 Macc 12:15 the noun describes the Jewish people invoking *(epikalesamenoi)* "the great sovereign of the world *(ton megan tou kosmou dynastēn).*" In 2 Macc 15:3-5 Nicanor's blasphemous remarks on the Sabbath turn on whether there is indeed a God who is *dynastēs* in competition with this earthly ruler. In 2 Macc 15:23 this noun is used in a prayer for victory against Nicanor, and finally in 15:29, when that tyrant has fallen, the victors "blessed the sovereign *(dynastēn)* in the language of their fathers." Again in 3 Macc 2:3, in the great prayer of Simon the high priest that begins, "Lord, Lord, king of the heavens . . . ," God is also addressed as "a righteous ruler *(dynastēs dikaios)*" (Charles, *AP* 1.164). Then in 3 Macc 5:51 the doomed

Jews are described as "beseeching the ruler of all power *(ton tēs hapasēs dynameōs dynastēn)* by a manifestation *(meta epiphaneias)* to show pity upon them, now that they were come to the gates of death." The use of this noun in connection with prayer (particularly doxological prayer; cf. Grundmann, *TDNT* 2.294) is quite in harmony with this passage in the PE, not to mention the link with *epiphaneia.*

The Ap. Frs. did not take up *dynastēs,* and Lampe does not carry a single entry in patristic Greek. One might infer that the usage in the PE does in fact represent that of the source which reproduced the prayer language of an old, strongly Jewish Christian congregation that drew upon the same prayer tradition as the LXX Sirach and Second and Third Maccabees, if it did not actually employ those books.

The God who is called *dynastēs* is further qualified as "the blessed and only *(makarios kai monos)* suzerain." The alliteration tends, with the conjunction *kai,* to bind this whole phrase tightly together. *Makarios* occurred above of God in 1 Tim 1:11 and of hope in Titus 2:13, and, as is noted there, the application to God is unusual. The language of the source is probably evident here, and the immediate, alliterative addition of *monos* precludes the *makarios* being taken in its pagan sense of "the blessed gods" but demands that the term be understood of the one, only God of Israel. Like *dynastēs* above, *monos,* too, was especially associated with the vocabulary for doxological prayer in Israel, and its use here not only fumigates the preceding *makarios* but also makes certain that the following *dynastēs* will not be taken of any earthly ruler (cf. the use of *monos* in v. 16 below as well).

The title *basileus* is alliteratively expanded with *basileuontōn,* which in its turn is a unique (Spicq) variation upon the more customary formula, *basileus basileōn,* just as the following *kyrios kyrieuontōn* offers a deliberate variation on *kyrios kyriōn.* The standard phrases occur together in the NT at Rev 17:14 and 19:16 (order inverted from one to the other), and in both cases they are titles for the Lamb/Word who is Christ Jesus (see K. L. Schmidt, *TDNT* 1.577; see Ford, AB *Rev,* pp. 282, 291, 314, for the OT references to these titles, as well as D-C, p. 89, and Spicq, *EP,* p. 573; especially note Deut 10:17 and cf. Dan 2:37 with 2:47). Spicq has noted 1QM 14.16 (cf. 4QM), where the psalmic prayer (cf. Ps 21:14 [RSV 13]) begins, "Rise up, rise up, O God of angels, and raise yourself in power, O King of kings" (*Mlk hmlkym* from 4QM$^a$ 13; Yadin, *War,* pp. 328-329). 1Q 19 *bis* "Book of Noah" (DJD 1.152) contains an angelic petition apparently addressed to the "[Lord] of lords *(ʾdwnym)* and the pow[erful of powerful ones] *(wgb[wr gbwrym]),*" and the editor notes the parallel to 1 Enoch 9.1-4; *sy ei kyrios tōn kyriōn kai ho theos tōn theōn kai basileus tōn aiōnōn* (Black, *Apoc. Henochi,* p. 23). To this one might add, from the prayer of Abraham in 1QapGen 20.15-16 (Fitzmyer, *Gen. Apoc.,* pp. 64-65, 130, with the OT parallels cited, plus Enoch 63.4, "the Lord of kings and Him who is king over all kings"), "you are Lord of all the kings of the earth *(mrh lkwl mlky 'r')*."

Thus the terminology and its arrangement are quite at home within the Jewish and even Palestinian style of address to God in prayer. The unique variations here in First Timothy to *basileuontōn/kyrieuontōn* in all probability permit one to infer something of the interests and intent of the author of the source and the community to which this composition was addressed.

The way in which this passage varied the traditional liturgical phrase may be a conscious attempt to "realize" the epiphany of the Lord in the historical process, stressing that the rule of God and his kingdom are actually superimposed over those exercising kingship and lordship on earth at any given moment. The God who is really ruling now over the rulers of this human society will in his good time reveal and manifest that rule in the "epiphany" of the Lord Christ.

16. *the only one who possesses immortality.* Taking up the *monos* of line 1, the fourth title for God in this doxology describes him as "the only one who possesses *(echōn)* immortality *(athanasian)*." The adjective again unmistakably roots the doxology in the monotheistic faith of Israel. This is the only time in the PE that *echō* has God as subject (out of twenty-two uses) and again may indicate that the usage of the source appears here.

The rarity of the use of *athanasia* (see Notes above) and the nonuse of *athanatos* in the NT are at first surprising until one recalls that the resurrection/everlasting life of the Christian faith was not to be confused terminologically with the *athanatos/athanasia* concepts of Hellenistic paganism and its philosophers. Here again the *monos* of this title is an almost polemical riposte to that usage, taking it up only to redefine it totally, not to assimilate it. The *Kerygma Petri* (see D-C, p. 90 n. 25) is a conceptual but not a verbal parallel to this passage in the PE (it is closer to 1 Tim 1:17; see *PG* 9.257).

*who inhabits inaccessible light.* The next title, *phōs oikōn aprositon,* parallels the previous one, *echōn = oikōn, athanasia [doxa] = phōs . . . aprositon.* What the one God *has,* in the former title, he now *dwells within.* This passage in the PE is quite Pauline in having God as subject. It is unique in the NT in denoting the place of God's dwelling in another order and outside of man (cf. Tob 5:16). O. Michel, *TDNT* 5.135-136, notes that the phrase here in First Timothy "has an antique ring" and cites the exuberant, apocalyptic description of God's dwelling in Enoch 14.10-20 (Charles, *AP* 2.197). Here the text is comparatively sober in its calling the divine place of dwelling *phōs . . . aprositon.* As D-C, p. 90, have noted, this use of *phōs* for a place rather than for the divine nature (as in Clement of Alexandria, *PG* 9.664, cited by D-C) or the Christian inheritance is unusual. H. Conzelmann, *TDNT* 9.347, has called attention to *phōs* = a "transcendent sphere of light," the kingdom of the Christ, "a realm of power" in Col 1:12 (Lohse, *Col,* p. 36, "a domain . . . a spatial orientation").

One recalls the self-designation at Qumran of "the Sons of light" (1QS 1.9; 2.16; 3.13 and 24-25, and 1QM 1.1, 3, 9, 11, 13; 4QFlor 1.9, *s.v.l.*) that is evidently meant to denote their belonging to God's side and company (cf. Luke 16:8), though the use of *'wr* (light) serves also to distance the relationship in the way that "Sons of God" does not. In 1QS 4.7-8 "the sons of the truth" (= the sectaries) are bound for endless blessing and happiness in life everlasting and "the glorious crown and garment of honor in everlasting light *(b'wr 'wlmym).*" 1QM 13.5-6, in a prayer of blessing and cursing, contrasts the spirits of the lot *(gwrl)* of Belial and of darkness with "the lot of God *(gwrl 'l)* for light [eter]nal *(l'wr ['wlmym).*" See Yadin, *War,* pp. 320-321, who has a note on *gwrl* on p. 207 and references on "sons of light" on p. 242. In 1QM 17.6-7, God "has magnified the authority of Michael through eternal light *(b'wr 'lmym)* to light up in joy [the house of I]srael, peace and blessing for the lot of God *(lgwrl 'l)*" (Yadin, pp. 340-341). God's lot or portion consists of the spirits and men whom he has chosen and who belong to him (cf. A. R. C. Leaney, *RQM,* p. 129, on 1QS 2.2, who adduces Lev 16:8, 10 as a possible source for this figure; the Greek term for this is *klēros* [cf. Acts 1:17, 26], cognate with Hebrew *gwrl* and from which come the English "cleric, clergy"!). They live or will live in God's light.

In the Qumran prayer book God is identified with light (1QH 7.25; 9.26-27; 4.5) in a way that reminds one not only of LXX Pss 26:1, *Kyrios phōtismos mou kai sōtēr mou,* "The Lord is my light and my salvation," and 35:10, *en tōi phōti sou opsometha phōs,* "in your light we shall see light," but also of the Hebrew conviction that one could not see God and continue to live (Exod 33:20; cf. *aprositon* here in First Timothy as well as the following title). As A. R. C. Leaney, *RQM,* p. 41, has noted, the image says far more about the way in which God was conceived of as bringing truth to man (revelation) than it says about God's nature (cf. the very fragmentary 1QH 12.14-15; Dupont-Sommer, *EWQ,* p. 240, which concludes with ". . . the shining of your glory (shall be) an ev[erlasting] light *(l'wr '[wlm]) . . .*").

The *phōs* is qualified here with *aprositon.* As Spicq, *EP,* p. 574, has noted, the positive and privative form are associated with (in-)accessible mountains. Thus, Philo, *Mos.* 2.70, and Josephus, *Ant.* 3.76, use the adjective of Mount Sinai and the revelation there of Israel's God. Josephus, *War* 7.280, thus describes the Masada citadel; *War* 7.435 uses the term of the closing of the Jewish temple at Leontopolis (Heliopolis). A variant reading in *C. Apion.* 2.167 (which does not adopt the reading) applies the term to the God of Israel; cf. also the *(a)prositon* reading to describe the wall around Jerusalem in *War* 3.162. Clement of Alexandria *ut cit.* uses the phrase, and the late second-century *Acts of Peter* 20 speaks of Jesus as one "through whom we have light unapproachable *(lumen inaccessibile).*" The adjective gives the whole phrase a recondite quality literarily that corresponds to the remote and majestic splendor of the divine reality, bathed in light like a massif in the sunset.

*the one whom no human being ever saw or can see.* The next stich begins as did each of the preceding with *ho,* but on this occasion not as the article but as the accusative pronoun, *hon,* which has as its antecedent the Sovereign, King, and Lord previously mentioned. The immediately preceding stich had emphasized the inaccessibility of the (region of) light in which God dwells. That inaccessibility is now defined in terms of the human faculty that gives man his farthest and swiftest extension, sight. The mention of "light" could be taken to mean that a human being had or could *see* what he could not otherwise reach. The light, however, in which God dwells has not revealed but has concealed him. No merely human being, moreover, is even capable of seeing him. One meets here the reverse side of the divine will to rescue all men that was encountered in Titus 2:11 or 1 Tim 2:4-5. Man alone cannot see, much less effectively desire to see, the true God.

The *oudeis anthrōpōn* is a rather pleonastic phrase that stresses the universality of the assertion here and perhaps contrasts with the opening of this parenesis addressed to one "man of God." The chiastic *eiden oudeis . . . oude idein,* noted previously, binds the two phrases very closely together. This form of the verb *eidon* occurs again in the PE at 2 Tim 1:4 (see commentary *in loc.*) of Paul's desire to see Timothy again, and that parallel makes it quite clear what is being said here of God. The use here in First Timothy would again be more likely that of the source, and a source that could be reflecting Jewish Greek biblical usage at this point. Thus 1 Enoch 14.15-22, cited above, as well as the biblical tradition from Exod 19:21; 33:20, "But you cannot see my face for no one shall see me and live"; Lev 16:2 and Isa 6:5 (cf. Michaelis, *TDNT* 5.332-333) stress not only the *de facto* invisibility of God (see 1 Tim 1:17 on God as *aoratos*) but the radical incapability of man to see him. As Michaelis notes, the principle remains valid even though God can and has dispensed from it. That "dispensation" is nothing less, of course, than the gift of revelation itself, and it shares in the characteristics of God's grace that radically escape man's grasp.

In connection with this stich of the divine titles one cannot ignore the famous Acts of the Scillitan Martyrs of North Africa (Musurillo, *Acts,* pp. 86-89), where a Roman court record of July 17, 180 C.E., records the dialogue between a dozen Christians captured along with their "books and letters of a just man named Paul *(libri et epistulae Pauli viri iusti)*" (p. 88, 1.15) and the Roman proconsul, P. Vigellius Saturninus, in Carthage. At one point the Christian Speratus, taking up the proconsul's description of Latin religion as "*simplex est religio nostra,*" says, "If you give me a calm hearing, I shall tell you the mystery of simplicity *(mysterium simplicitatis).*" The proconsul replies, "If you begin to malign our sacred rites, I shall not listen to you. But swear rather by the Genius of our Lord the Emperor *(per genium domni [sic] nostri imperatoris).*" That reply and its closing words apparently reminded Speratus of a passage from those letters of a just man, Paul, that he was carrying in a *capsa,* and he answered, "I do not recognize the empire of this world *(ego imperium huius seculi non cognosco)*" (cf. 1 Tim 6:13 on the final confession of Jesus witnessing before Pontius Pilate and Luke 23:2-3). He continued, "Rather, I serve that God whom no man has seen, nor can see, with these eyes *(illi Deo servio quem nemo hominum vidit nec videre his oculis potest).*" The use of *servio* meaning "to worship, to invoke God in prayer" has been suggested by the previous demand to call upon "our lord, the emperor" in the proconsul's demand. The prayer that comes to Speratus's mind is this one of the PE (or of their source?), which places all visible human sovereignty under that of the unseen God. With a certain pathos he has glossed the text and applied it to himself with *his oculis.*

He then continues his defense by saying, "I have not stolen; and on any purchase I pay the tax, for I acknowledge my lord who is emperor of kings and of all nations *(quia cognosco domnum [sic] meum, imperatorem regum et omnium gentium).*" The denial of theft is prompted not so much by its civil repercussions as by its figuring in the Decalogue that Speratus observes (perhaps the OT was among the *libri*). His statement poses implicitly the question: "Is there a law against honesty? Am I being prosecuted because I do good?" (cf. Gal 5:23 with 1 Tim 1:8-11). He then cites his payment of taxes *(teloneum reddo)* as a positive, visible sign of his loyalty to the head of state. He gives Caesar what is Caesar's (see Mark 12:17, *SFG* §280, and Rom 13:6-7; he appeals to both *libri* and *epistulae*) and acknowledges in words just what he means by that tribute — the emperor is *dominum meum* (not *domini nostri,* as in the proconsul's command), his ruler and master on this earth, but not his *dominus* in the sense of his God. He is quite willing to acknowledge the emperor as ruler of kings and of all peoples provided that doing so does not compromise his faith in the God who is King of those exercising kingship and Lord of those exercising lordship (Speratus's use of the noun *Regum* would be in contrast to *basileuontōn*/OL [?] *regnantium* [note Vg here has *rex regum*]).

Barnes, *Tertullian,* pp. 277-278, has noted this passage from the Scillitan Acts as "a direct biblical quotation" and has suggested that it comes from a Latin translation of at least part of the Pauline epistolary that was in circulation in North Africa before 180 C.E. (cf. Wordsworth and White, *NTL* 2.611). Even the description of the Scillitan epistolary as that "of Paul, a just man" appears to be influenced by 2 Tim 4:8 with its play on the *dikaios-dikaiosynē* terminology in relation to Paul, facing legal condemnation and death while really innocent (cf. *1 Clem.* 5.2 of Peter and Paul as *dikaiotatoi*). When a tiny congregation in North Africa has a Latin translation of the PE available in 180 C.E., it is difficult to believe that the translation itself was quite new, and that its existence in turn certainly demands an even older, generally accepted Greek text (surely no later than 150 C.E.; also note the apologetic concern over Paul, executed even though a Roman citizen). But if that is the case, it is scarcely conceivable that Marcion did not know of the PE. It is far more probable that Tertullian was quite correct in asserting that Marcion rejected *(respuit)* them. O'Malley, *Tertullian,* p. 63, agrees that the Marcionite *Evangelium-Apostolicum* was in circulation in Latin in North Africa by the time Tertullian wrote.

*to whom belong honor and might eternal. Amen.* The final stich of this invocation, beginning with *hōi,* which thus puts it into the series of pronouns above, all referring to the one God, now becomes explicitly doxological with the anarthrous and averbal "to whom belong honor and might eternal, Amen." The formulaic character of the ending is manifest in the use of *aiōnion* as well as the concluding *Amēn,* though the use of the adjectival *aiōnion* indicates that the terminology was not simply and thoughtlessly formulaic, as indeed the phrase *timē kai kratos* itself is a variation that combines the *timē kai doxa* formula with the *doxa kai kratos* formula that also is documented in 1 Pet 4:11; Rev 1:6; 5:13 (cf. 1 Pet 5:11 and Jude 25) as doxological prayers conclude.

Käsemann, *Essais,* p. 112, has reviewed the elements in 6:11-16 that point to a liturgical source that has been redacted and inserted at this point (as other sources have been used to mark a "caesura" at other points in this correspondence) by the author of the PE, noting particularly the formal alternation of nouns, relative pronouns, and participles that typify liturgical composition as well as the grandiloquent doxological acclamation and final *Amen.* Delling, *Worship,* p. 63 n. 2, has noted how both rhyme and rhythm were characteristic of popular poetry in this period and thus are indicative of a popular liturgical text as a source. Even the choice of titles for God betrays the eclecticism typical of the liturgy, as archaic (Jewish, even Palestinian) devotional language is joined to expressions that the Hellenistic world used for deities (though there is no convincing evidence that this language was the precipitate of Gnostic dualism, contra Bultmann, Käsemann). There is little question that such a melding of materials (both in form and content) had Christian converts within the Diaspora synagogue as its originators. The creedal confession of 6:13 is, however, one of the elements from which the source document was fashioned and stands in some tension, as has been noted above, with the preceding parenesis.

What then precisely was the situation that produced 1 Tim 6:11-16? The question has its sharpest focus in the *homologia* of 6:12-13. Are we to envision the fearless confession of one's Christian faith before the pagan judges of the empire? That was already an "exegesis" that the Scillitan martyrs found helpful, and it has often been proposed since (cf. Neufeld, *Confessions,* pp. 130-133, and Beasley-Murray, *Bapt. NT,* pp. 204-206). Or is it rather the profession of faith in the moment of baptism that is spoken of here and on which this exhortation comments? An overwhelming number of exegetes appear to have accepted this solution (Käsemann, *Essais,* p. 113). Or, finally, are we encountering here the charge from an ordination ritual that the redactor linked with his composition by inserting *tauta pheuge* into the opening sentence (Käsemann, p. 119)? The final hypothesis appears to explain more data than the preceding two.

There are, unquestionably, baptismal elements in this parenesis, as the command of verse 11 illustrates and the teaching on the contest for eternal life in verse 12 reinforces. Käsemann, *Essais,* p. 114, has noted, too, how the two-member formula of verse 13 fits into a baptismal exhortation that stresses how the original creation and the new eschatological one have been telescoped into each other in the sacramental act. Yet it is notable that Jesus is not spoken of as Son in this text nor is God explicitly entitled Father — matters that are of critical importance at least for later baptismal confessions (cf. G. Bornkamm as cited by Käsemann, p. 114 n. 1). It is, indeed, the avoidance of the "Son" title that makes it easier to speak of the *homologia* of Jesus and of the "man of God" in the same breath, an association which, as Käsemann has noted, is completely atypical of baptismal language, which usually stresses the abyss between the one baptized and his Lord. Other tensions have also appeared in the commentary above, where (for all the formal, compositional parallels) the terms (e.g., *martyrōn-martyrēsantos*) designate different realities.

These tensions and conceptual stresses appear far more reasonable when one posits an appointment to (designation for) a role of Christian ministerial leadership as the *Sitz im Leben* for 6:11-16. The "man of God" in verse 11 is surely being addressed as a mature individual who is being told to keep on doing (present imperatives) what is presumed to have begun at a previous time when "he made [aorist] the fine [i.e. orthodox, thus Käsemann] confession" (v. 12). But in that case, the past baptismal *homologia* is indeed being referred to, but as the ground and motivation for a distinct role and ministry over and above that of the Christian vocation in general. The redactor in any case certainly understood Timothy in the role of the "man of God" addressed here, and Timothy is a "man of God" not as a baptized believer but as one who has received "the charism of God" through the imposition of hands (cf. 1 Tim 4:14; 2 Tim 1:6) and the intervention of the prophetic Spirit (1 Tim 1:18) for a ministry of the word of God such as that described in 2 Tim 3:16-17. He is head of a community of believers, one who has learned Paul's gospel (cf. 2 Tim 1:8-14) and who transmits it to others and who provides for its continuing transmission (2 Tim 1:1-2). In that ministry he must be prepared to suffer (2 Tim 2:3-13), to meet opposition from within the community and without.

Here "Timothy" is being reminded of the commitment in his ordination, a commitment that on that occasion was grounded on the baptismal commitment with which his Christian life began. One is reminded that Paul's conversion and apostolic commission coincided (cf. 1 Tim 1:12). They were theologically inseparable as they had historically coincided. Here, for the "man of God," the baptismal conversion has eventually and irrevocably issued in the ordination commitment to an apostolic ministry. Ordination puts an optic on baptism that is irreversible. Jesus' suffering as the Christ was his "fine profession," into which believers have been plunged by faith and baptism. For some believers that baptismal participation in the cross of the Lord has issued in a further call to share the apostolic ministry, and doing this involves a renewal of the fine profession with which his life as a believer began. The tension between the two *homologiai* here is the tension between the historical and the sacramental orders, between the order of signs and the realities signified.

Käsemann, *Essais,* p. 116, has stressed the compactly integrated character of this whole parenetic charge, with its archaic, apocalyptic terminology (calling attention to "the times of refreshment" in Acts 3:20; see not only Haenchen, *Acts,* p. 208, but also MacRae, "Heaven," pp. 151-165). There is no trace of embarrassment at the "delay" of the Lord's epiphany, but simply solid assurance of belonging to a plan that God alone knows. Delling, *Worship,* p. 81, has called attention to the fact that these "formulaic" expressions are actually never repeated but are formed *ad hoc.* The source was accordingly an "original" composition.

Perhaps the "exegesis" of the Scillitan martyrs (not to mention Delling, *Worship,* pp. 80-81) was not as far from the mark as might first appear, for we have not yet really answered the question as to why the redactor included this ordination charge (with its baptismal taproot) in a letter to "Timothy" long after his "ordination." The answer lies in the persecutions to which the apostolic minister and leader is above all exposed. The PE know a harassed, persecuted, and martyred Paul. They assure and encourage one who shares Paul's ministry as he faces similar persecution. He must find strength and heart in his sacramental baptismal and ordination charism (cf. 2 Tim 1:6) as Paul found it in his historical conversion-commission by the risen Jesus (cf. 2 Tim 4:17-18 with 1 Tim 1:12). If Speratus was indeed the ordained leader of the Scillitan martyrs (and his having some sort of leadership seems evident, for his name heads the list, he speaks first, and several times he speaks for all), then the passage from First Timothy had a special resonance for him as he renewed his baptismal and ordination commitment before his Roman prosecutor. What had begun in history in the confession of Jesus and had entered his life in sacramental acts now had come full circle and was becoming part of his own personal history before a Roman judge. One cannot rule out the possibility that this very charge (apart from First Timothy) had been used at his own ordination and that he is not quoting First Timothy but the source itself, still in liturgical use (cf. above on readings of S).

## IV.C.4. RICHES: PART II (6:17-19)

6 [17]*Timothy, charge the wealthy of the present age —*

*not to be snobbish,*
*not to have set their hope on precarious wealth,*
*but on the God who lavishly provides*
*everything for our satisfaction;*
[18]*charge them to do good;*
*to become wealthy in fine deeds;*
*to be munificent,*
*sharing all around,*
[19]*making their deposits in an*
*excellent fund for the future,*
*so that they can lay hold*
*on the life which deserves*
*that name.*

## ♦ NOTES

6:17. *Timothy, charge the wealthy.* Timothy (not in the Greek) is directed to give orders to the "wealthy" *(plousiois).* The noun *plousios* occurs only here in the PE. Of its twenty-seven other NT uses, only two are in the Paulines (2 Cor 8:9 and Eph 2:4, of God/Christ being "rich"), whereas there are eleven uses in Luke (but none in Acts; in fact, Acts, like John, does not appear to use any of the *plout-* family of words).

*of the present age.* Regarding the almost formulaic phrase *en tōi nyn aiōni, aiōn* occurs also in 1 Tim 1:17 *(tris);* 2 Tim 4:10, 18 *(bis);* and Titus 2:12 (in this same phrase). Elsewhere in the NT the word appears 114 times, 30 of which occur in the other Paulines; in Revelation it appears 26 times, thus signaling its apocalyptic connotations. *Nyn,* "present," occurs four times in the Timothy letters (once in Titus). The present age is, for wealthy believers, the scene, present and spatial, for living "in a sensible, honest, godly way" (Titus 2:12). It contains nothing that is not ephemeral, contingent, and mortal; it offers neither hope nor security.

*precarious wealth.* Lit. "the uncertainty of wealth." The noun *adōlotēs* does not occur otherwise in the NT (though Luke 11:44 uses the adjective of "*unseen* graves" and 1 Cor 14:8 of an "*uncertain* note" on a trumpet; 1 Cor 9:26 uses the adverb *adēlōs* of Paul not running "aimlessly" in the race for an imperishable crown). The noun does not occur in the LXX, though 2 Macc 7:34 describes

Antiochus as "puffed up by uncertain hopes *(adēlois elpisin)*." The Ap. Frs. likewise do not use this term (though *1 Clem.* 18.6 does quote the adjective in citing LXX Ps 50:6). *Nil* in Josephus, but Philo, *Quod Deus imm.* 29, speaks of God having no "uncertainty about future events *(hē tōn mellontōn adēlotēs)*." In secular Greek the term occurs as early as the philosopher Protagoras (fifth century B.C.E.; cf. LSJ *s.v.* and Freeman, *Ancilla*, p. 126, for a translation of this famous dictum on the existence or not of the gods, knowledge of which is precluded by "the obscurity of the subject and the shortness of human life"). Polybius 5.2.3 employs the noun for "the swiftness and unexpectedness *(tēn adēlotēta)*" of an enemy's arrival *(parousias!)* by sea. Plutarch, *De Crasso* 2.4, is most appositely cited by Spicq, *EP*, p. 576, with its description of the owners of buildings, threatened by fire, letting them go for a song "because of fear and uncertainty *(dia phobon kai adēlotēta)*." The closest parallel to the thought of 1 Tim 6:17 on a man's depending on *ploutos* is Menander's *Dysc.* 812 (Handley, *Dyskolos*, pp. 111, 274; Sandbach, *Menandri*, p. 83) with its gnomic *pollōi de kreitton estin emphanēs philos/ē ploutos aphanēs hon sy katoryxas echeis*, "It's much better to have a friend you can see before your eyes than any treasure you've got buried out of sight." Casson, *Ancient Comedy*, p. 100, and Danker, "Menander and the NT," p. 368, also cite *Dysc.* 797-802; 808-810, and cf. 1 Tim 6:19 below.

There is a Semitic turn of phrase in the genitive of quality here (BDF §165) where "uncertainty of wealth *(ploutou)*" = "uncertain wealth." Of the twenty-two uses of *ploutos* in the NT, this is the only one in the PE (cf. its single use in Luke 8:14 and parallels; it is not found in Acts at all, or John). Of the fourteen Pauline uses outside the PE, it is striking to see that they redefine wealth in terms of "the being of Christ, the work of God in Christ, and the eschatological situation of Christ's community" (Hauck and Kasch, *TDNT* 6.328-329) and thus are in striking contrast to the usage of the synoptics/PE. This Pauline usage is also that of Heb 11:26 and Rev 5:12; however, Rev 18:17 and especially James 5:2 are in line with the PE (cf. Hauck and Kasch, *TDNT* 6.330). In the Ap. Frs. before Hermas (who uses *ploutos* rather frequently), only *1 Clem.* 13.1 writes *mē kauchasthō . . . ho plousios en tōi ploutōi autou*, "do not let the rich man boast in his riches" (trans. WCW), citing LXX 1 Kings 2:10. By far, most of the LXX uses of *ploutos* occur in the wisdom literature, such occurrences indicating that the proper use of wealth was a concern of the sapiential tradition (see Hauck and Kasch, pp. 323-325, for statistics and comment on this; recall the way in which the statistics for the use of *plout-* cognates start to rise significantly in the biblical prophets).

*lavishly provides.* On the adverb *plousiōs* see Titus 3:6 (note first person plural there too). *Parechein* recurs at Titus 2:7 and 1 Tim 4:1 in the PE, and in the remainder of the Paulines only twice, notably in Col 4:1, of the household code there. Of the eleven other NT uses, nine occur in Luke/Acts. The LXX uses the verb fifteen times; Ap. Frs., nine.

*satisfaction.* The one other NT use of the noun *apolausis* in Heb 11:25 has the bad sense of "enjoyment of the fleeting pleasure of sin *(hamartias apolausin).*" The single LXX use of the word, in 3 Macc 7:16, is of "the (Jews') full enjoyment of safe delivery" from their persecutors. *First Clement* 20.10 writes of "the everlasting springs, created for enjoyment *(pros apolausin)* and health, which supply *(parechontai)* unfailing sustenance for the life of man." *Didache* 10.3 (cited p. 883) in its eucharistic prayer says, "You, Lord almighty, did create all things *(ektisas ta panta)* for your name's sake and did give food and drink *(trophēn te kai poton)* to men for their enjoyment *(eis apolausin)*, that they might give thanks to you. . . ." In *2 Clem.* 10.3-4, however, present (sinful) *apolausis* entails future torment.

The phrase is Hellenistic (D-C, p. 91), but MM *s.v.*, p. 65, cites *OGIS* 669.8 (first century C.E.) *koinēn apolausin heortēs parechetō* when both the noun and the verb used in the PE occur in an eastern Mediterranean ambience. A use in Philo is *Mos.* 2.70 (cited above on *aprositon*) on Moses' "taking nothing that is needed to satisfy *(eis . . . apolausin)* the requirements of bare sustenance" up onto the "inaccessible mountain." Josephus uses the term nineteen times, once with *eis* in *Ant.* 4.298 of the "enjoyment" of the fruits of one's land and of marriage; in *Ant.* 1.46, with *pros*, of paradise furnishing spontaneously everything "for man's enjoyment and pleasure *(pros apolausin kai hēdonēn),*" as well as in 12.98 of turning "to feasting and enjoying *(pros euōchian kai tēn apolausin)* the good things that had been prepared" for Ptolemy's banquet. In Josephus, *War* 7.388, one reads of the Roman's "hoped-for enjoyment *(elpizomenēs . . . apolauseōs)*" at capturing those who had held out in Masada.

18. *charge them to do good.* While not repeated in the Greek, the *paraggelle* is repeated in the translation for emphasis. *Agathoergein,* "to do good," is the uncontracted form of *agathourgein* (cf. Acts 14:17, cited above, of God), and occurs only here in the NT, LXX, and Ap. Frs. The contracted form is also not documented elsewhere in that literature. In secular Greek the verb is very rare (BAGD cite Pythagoras, *Ep.* 10, p. 607, sixth century B.C.E.).

*to be munificent, sharing all around.* The rich are "to be generous *(eumetadotous),*" an adjective not attested elsewhere in the NT, LXX, or Ap. Frs., and sharing "what is one's own *(koinōnikous)*" that is apparently to be taken almost epexegetically, though it, too, is found only here in the NT, the LXX, and the Ap. Frs. See Comment below for a further discussion of both terms.

19. *making their deposits in an excellent fund for the future.* Those who surrender material goods "are treasuring up for themselves *(apothēsaurizontas heautois)* a fine foundation *(themelion kalon)* for the future *(eis to mellon)*. . . ." *Apothēsaurizein* occurs only here in the NT; in the LXX it is found only in Sir

3:4, where the one honoring parents is "like one who lays up treasure *(apothēsaurizōn)*." The Ap. Frs. do not use the term.

The cognates, *thēsauros/thēsaurizein,* occur seventeen and eight times, respectively, in the NT. Of the five Pauline uses, Rom 2:5 uses the verb of storing up the eschatological judgment, wrath of God, whereas 1 Cor 16:2 and 2 Cor 12:14 use it of saving up money. The noun is used in 2 Cor 4:7 as well as Col 2:3 of God's/Christ's immaterial treasures. On the Lukan use of the cognates see Comment below. On the *themelion kalon* see Comment below. On *mellein* in the PE see above on 1 Tim 1:16; 4:8.

*on the life which deserves that name.* Lit. "(that which is) really life *(ontōs zōē)*." The weightiest MSS here read *ontōs,* a term that is typical of the vocabulary of the PE and here would distinguish the *zōē,* as "the real widow" of 5:3, 5, 16, and she is not just any woman whose husband has predeceased her. A number of Byzantine witnesses here read *aiōniou,* probably because of the rather more difficult *ontōs* as well as the pressure of that fixed phrase *zōē aiōnios,* which had just occurred above with the same verb (J. K. Elliott, *Greek Text,* pp. 108-109; B. Metzger, *TCGNT,* p. 644).

## ♦ COMMENT

6:17. *Timothy, charge the wealthy of the present age not to be snobbish.* With an abruptness that has been called brutal (Käsemann, *Essais,* p. 112), the text returns to the subject of riches that had been left at 6:10. The thirteen repetitions of *p(h/s)* in this verse and the following recall the same assonance in 1 Tim 6:9. The author turns from the danger of desiring wealth to counsel for those who actually are wealthy.

The links with the intervening parenesis are of the most formal character: the repetition of catchwords *(paraggellō/paraggelle; aiōnion/aiōni; epilabou tēs aiōniou zōēs/epilabōntai tēs ontōs zōēs),* the introductory imperatives. The insertion of a liturgical piece in pause within another list or exhortation had occurred in 3:14–4:5 and in the *Haustafel* of 5:1-2 (3-24: *ordines* for widows and presbyters) and 6:1-2; here the phenomenon has appeared once more with the ordination charge serving as an interlude within the catechesis on riches.

The formal variations with *plousiois, ploutou, plousiōs* (v. 17), and *ploutein* (v. 18) as well as the assonance with *p* leave no doubt about the inner coherence of this paragraph, for all its curious separation from 6:3-10. Indeed, the emphatic repetition and the assonance leave little doubt that the author-redactor wanted these verses to be read with the *ploutein* of 6:9.

Here for the fifth and last time in First Timothy the verb *paraggelle* recurs (cf. commentary on 1 Tim 1:3), this time introducing a sevenfold (or even eightfold if one counts the participial clause of 6:19) catalogue of virtues for those believers who are *de facto* wealthy. If 6:7-10 verged on the doctrinaire in its teaching on riches (D-C, p. 91, note the "ideological" character of the Lukan teaching on riches, e.g., Luke 12:21), this passage is more humane, though in its realistic way it is no less demanding. The apostolic minister who has heard the command *(paraggellō)* of the apostle Paul (6:13) is now in his own turn to command *(paraggelle)* the wealthy *(plousiois)* Ephesian believers "in this present world/age *(en tōi nyn aiōni)*" to be on guard for the dangers that riches bring.

It is notable that although the *plout-* family of words does not occur in Acts, the author of this letter shares with the author of Acts the opinion that there were quite a few wealthy believers in Ephesus (cf. 1 Tim 2:9 on the women's jewelry too). Thus Acts 19:25 with its frank admission of the economic motive for the agitation against believers could be read as an illustration of 1 Tim 6:9-10, whereas 1 Tim 6:17-19 reads like advice for persons like those Ephesian magicians who became believers and destroyed books of magic worth 50,000 silver pieces (Acts 19:19), i.e. 50,000 days' wages. The point at issue here is neither whether the incident happened in 54 C.E. nor the price of magic books on the Big Board that day in Ephesus (Haenchen, *Acts,* p. 567). Rather one sees that the author of Acts thought it quite reasonable to usher rich Ephesians onto the stage of his narrative to make his point, and that the author of the Pastorals thought that Christian Ephesus was a suitable *Sitz im Leben* for admonitions about the use and abuse of wealth (one recalls the warnings on rich clothing in 1 Tim 2:9). Revelation 2:9; 3:17 show how the rich/poor language had a sort of mirror image in apocalyptic exhortation, where the rich in this world's goods may be ultimately poor (Rev 3:17) whereas the poor are actually wealthy (2:9). The Magnificat (Luke 1:53; cf. 12:21 and Comment on 1 Tim 6:9 *supra*) uses the same poetic paradox, and it is just below the surface of the play on *plousiōs/ploutein* later in 1 Tim 6:17-18 as well as the *en tōi nyn aiōni* that here qualifies the wealthy and implies that there is another age/place in which they might not be so rich (cf. James 2:5).

Hauck and Kasch, *TDNT* 6.328, remark that for Luke *ploutos* (i.e. "wealth," occurring in the Gospels only at Mark 4:19 = Matt 13:22 = Luke 8:14 and there "psychologized" in terms of men's desire/care/anxiety for riches) is of far less concern than the *plousios* (the wealthy). Even then it is a concern about not simply the owner of this world's goods as such but the wealthy precisely as opposed to Jesus' person and teaching (cf. also Matt 27:57). The resemblance to the approach of the PE is notable.

The teaching on the rich and their riches here in the PE has some resemblances to the parenesis of James 1:9-11; 2:5-12; 5:1-6, though as Dibelius, *James,* pp. 39-45, has noted, the latter tends to be rather more systematic and doctrinaire than the PE (and, in my judgment, Luke-Acts). One might infer that James envisioned a community of Jewish believers who were all poor, oppressed, and mocked (even because of their faith, James 2:7) by their fellow Jews. Luke-Acts as well as the PE know of well-to-do (Gentile [?]; cf. Acts 16:14) believers. Already in Paul the Palestinian churches, and especially that of Jerusalem, are by definition poor (cf. Rom 15:26-27), whereas the pagan (and Jewish) converts from outside Palestine are (relatively speaking, cf. 1 Cor 1:26) better off.

Timothy is to command those who have an abundance of this world's goods to cultivate seven (eight) virtues, the first two of which are couched in negative form *(mē . . . mēde),* the remainder, in strong contrast *(alla),* expressed positively.

The rich are, first of all, "not to be snobbish," *hypsēlophronein,* a verb that is otherwise undocumented in the NT, the LXX, or the Ap. Frs. and that remains so until well into the Christian era (cf. Harrison, *Problem,* p. 133; Lampe, *PGL s.v.,* citing Hippolytus, *Dan* 3.10.4). Romans 11:20 (cf. 12:16) uses *(ta) hypsēla phronein* in warning the converted Gentiles not "to become proud but to stand in awe *(phobou)*" and to counsel the Roman Christians "not to be haughty but associate with the lowly *(tapeinois).*" Spicq, *EP,* p. 576, hits off the meaning of the verb precisely when he cites the English *snob* for a person who disdains ordinary little people. It is no small hazard for the rich, especially the *nouveaux riches.*

*not to have set their hope on precarious wealth, but on the God who lavishly provides everything for our satisfaction.* The second quality and the third, antithetically balanced *(alla),* turn on the verb *ēlpikenai* (perfect infinitive), which here governs the uncertainty of "wealth" in the negative phrase, and then, positively, "God" *(epi theōi,* as in 1 Tim 4:10, *epi theōi zōnti,* and 5:5, *epi theon).* A perversely "realized" eschatology is thrown into high relief by this contrast that sets the whole secure and certain content of Christian hope into the scales against the "uncertainty of wealth." The latter as the object of "hope" becomes practically an idol, a material substitute and replacement for the living God, and thus quite abominable.

Hoping in wealth stands in contrast, as is noted above, to hoping in God. As the wealth was "uncertain," now God is characterized as "granting *(parechonto)* us all things richly for enjoyment." The present participle here stresses the continuous character of God's provision for those who hope in him, in contrast to the sporadic, uncertain help provided by riches. God is the subject here as at Acts 17:31 (but unlike all the other NT uses of the term, including Titus 2:7 and 1 Tim 1:4). In the Ap. Frs. *1 Clem.* 20.10 (cited at Titus 2:7); 23.1; 63.2 use the term only with creatures as subject; this is true also of Ign. *Eph.* 19.2 and *Rom.* 2.2 *(s.v.l.),* but *Smyrn.* 11.3 can say, "For if you desire to do well, God is ready to help you *(theos hetoimos eis to parechein)*" *(v.l., paraschein).* God is not the subject in the three occurrences in Hermas, *Vis.* 3.3.2; *Man.* 11.20; *Sim.* 2.7. The LXX has God as subject on several occasions in its fifteen uses of the verb. The most apposite to 1 Tim 6:17 are Wis 16:20, saying of God, "You supplied *(paresches, s.v.l.)* them with bread from heaven, ready to eat . . . ," and 18:3, "You provided *(parasches)* a flaming pillar of fire as a guide for your people's unknown journey."

The *hēmin* includes here not only the apostle and Timothy but also this whole apostolic church, including the rich believers, who are to be instructed that it is God "who gives *(parechonti)* us all things *(panta)* richly *(plousiōs)* for enjoying *(apolausin)*." The repeated *p* sounds *(p, ps, ph)* of these verses are concentrated at this point, giving a staccato stress to the thought. Whereas in 1 Tim 4:3-4 God created *pan ktsima, eis metalēmpsin meta eucharistias,* here *eis apolausin* adds a further note to that divine purpose.

The phrase suggests by and large the human satisfaction that comes from adequate food and drink, a happiness that this author does not hesitate to place in God's gift (cf. 4:3-5). The concept is basically a variant on the "Give us each day our daily bread" of the Lord's Prayer (Luke 11:3; cf. Matt 6:11). Acts 14:17 speaks of the living, creator God as one "who did good (*agathourgōn* [cf. the *agathoergein* that occurs next in this list, in 1 Tim 6:18]) and gave you from heaven rains and fruitful seasons, satisfying your hearts with food and gladness *(trophēs kai euphrosynēs)*." Thus the rich man is to hope for happiness and satisfaction even in this life from God and not from wealth.

18. *charge them to do good; to become wealthy in fine deeds; to be munificent, sharing all around.* The wealthy man is to be urged "to do good," *agathoergein.* It is tempting to see in this unusual compound (see Notes above) a quite Lukan articulation of themes that were most congenial to him (cf. Luke 6:35-36 on doing good, *agathopoiountes,* to all without discrimination; *SFG* §80), and particularly that human beings must treat one another as God has first treated them.

With the next quality to be urged on the wealthy, "to become wealthy in fine deeds," the verb *ploutein* has now taken on a good sense, the sense that it has in the other Paulines of God's own "wealth" and the "riches" that he bestows on believers. If God "lavishly provides everything for our satisfaction," he also makes us rich in the visible attractiveness of our actions. *Erga kala,* in the PE, are not "our works" (they are never qualified as *hēmōn* or *hymōn,* "ours" or "yours") but are God's work. Although we do not do them in the deepest sense, they are yet verifiably, palpably, and attractively good; they comprise "works of charity" and other acts of honest, everyday living. The materially wealthy in the church are not by the fact of that wealth rich in good works. Being that demands their cooperation with God's initiative.

The next two (three) qualities are governed by the infinitive *einai.* The rich are "to be generous *(eumetadotous),*" an adjective not attested elsewhere in the NT, LXX, or Ap. Frs., though one ought to note, among the five NT uses of *metadidonai,* Rom 12:8 ("he who contributes in liberality"), Eph 4:28, and Luke 3:11 on the person with two garments "sharing *(metadotō)*" with the man who has none. Since both Luke and Paul have a predilection for *eu-* compounds, one cannot say here in which direction this particular one points. Josephus has no instance of this adjective, though Spicq can cite Marcus Aurelius 1.14.4; 6.48.1, and LSJ note Vettius Valens, the second-century-C.E. philosopher. Do these Roman references say something about the provenance of this Pastoral parenesis? In any event the unusual term highlights the unusual generosity that is being urged here upon the wealthy.

Perhaps because the term was so unusual, it is joined immediately with *koinōnikous,* which is apparently to be taken almost epexegetically, though it, too, is found only here in the NT, the LXX, and the Ap. Frs. The adjective is common enough in secular Greek (LSJ *s.v.* notes Aristotle, *Rhetoric* 1401/a/20, citing a Greek proverb about the god Hermas who "shares all around"), and Philo, *Det.* 72, has a stinging observation on the sophists who demonstrate "the social character *(koinōnikon)* of righteousness" but do nothing about it. In the one use of the term in Josephus (*War* 2.122), he speaks of "an astonishing community of goods *(thaumasion . . . koinōnikon)*" among the Essenes that results in their complete equality in possessions, with neither "abject poverty or inordinate wealth" among their number. It is such a generous surrender of goods to the community of believers that is being envisioned here, not without a touch of the same idealism that painted the picture of Acts 4:32-37 with its *ēn autois panta koina,* "they had everything in common."

19. *making their deposits in an excellent fund for the future.* The voluntary turning over of one's surplus goods to one's poorer brothers leads to the final expansive participial phrase that is both a seventh or eighth quality and a motivation for all the preceding. Those who surrender material goods are "making their deposits *(apothēsaurizontas heautois)* in an excellent fund *(themelion kalon)* for the future *(eis to mellon). . . .*" *Apothēsaurizein* occurs only here in the NT. The Third Gospel (but never Acts) has five uses of the cognates, *thēsaurus/thēsaurizein* terminology, in contexts that are strikingly reminiscent of this passage in First Timothy (for the other NT uses see Notes above). The verb occurs in Luke 12:21 in the conclusion drawn from the story of the rich fool (12:13-20), and the noun is in 12:33-34 in the Q sayings (= Matt 6:19-21: *SFG* §202) on the "treasure in the heavens" that awaits those disciples who have sold everything and given the proceeds to the poor (also Luke 18:22 = Mark 10:21: *SFG* §254). Luke 6:45 = Matt 12:35 (*SFG* §118) has "the good man out of the good treasure of his heart produces good." Using the goods one has received to qual-

ify for receiving other goods is by no means foreign to Luke (cf. the crafty steward of Luke 16:1-9; the three who receive deposits in Luke 19:12-26). Indeed, it is Luke 13:9 that uses the phrase *eis to mellon* that also occurs here in 1 Tim 6:19 and nowhere else in the NT. Luke uses it of the future time at which the owner hopes the barren fig will produce fruit.

Behind this figurative mode of speech lies the concept of the temple in the ancient world, Palestinian as well as Hellenistic. The building represented the house or dwelling of the divinity, and it was a place in which men deposited treasures, under the god's protection, for a time of need. The earthly building was of course only an image of the real temple, i.e. God's dwelling beyond this world (= the heavens), and there, too, men could deposit their treasures, their good lives and works for the day when they enter into "real life," i.e. eternal life with God (cf. F. Hauck, *TDNT* 3.136-137).

That which the rich Christians are to treasure up for the age to come is designated as *themelion kalon,* "a fine fund," using a Greek noun that resembles another cognate term, as the English *foundation* (Spicq, *EP,* pp. 578-579, compares the French *fonds, fondation*) has a double meaning of the base for a building and a deposit of money that produces interest. A *fund* and a *fundament* are etymologically derived from the same root, just as from the Greek *themo* have come *themethla* = lower part, base, foundation (*DELG,* p. 428) and *themeilia/themelios* as well as *thema* = money deposited (cf. LSJ *s.v.* for examples). But does *themelion* have the sense of *thema* (not in the NT)? Of the sixteen NT uses of the former (again in the PE at 2 Tim 2:19, also sg., as well as five other Pauline uses: Rom 15:20; 1 Cor 3:10-12; Eph 2:20), none has this meaning, including the four Lukan uses (Luke 6:48-49; 14:29; and Acts 16:26, pl.). LSJ *s.v.* and MM, p. 286, do not document such a meaning. Yet, as BAGD note, there is little question that the sense here is practically equivalent to a (hidden) reserve of money, a treasure (note the conjecture *keimelion* by Junius, *ap.* Nestle, *app. crit.* [K. L. Schmidt, *TDNT* 3.63, as well as J. R. Harris, "Tobit and the NT," p. 31], *thema lian kalon* for *themelion kalon,* comparing Tob 4:9, *thema . . . agathon thēsaurizeis seatōi*); Ign. *Pol.* 2.3 speaks of "the prize money on deposit" (i.e. the *thema*) that awaits "God's athlete," namely "immortality and eternal life." On the other hand, *themelios (-on)* appears in the Ap. Frs. always to refer to a foundation in the sense of a base for a structure. The same seems true of Josephus, as well as of the papyri (MM *s.v.*) and the LXX. However, Schmidt, *TDNT* 3.63 n. 7, observes that in the legal papyri the word does mean "purchase," a sense that would fit here in the PE. Perhaps here one encounters not a *hapax legomenon* but a *hapax* in this particular meaning, etymologically quite intelligible but otherwise undocumented. This trick of style is not alien to this correspondence (cf. *henos andros gynē; hedraiōma* [3:15 *supra*]; etc.). See Hauck, *TDNT* 3.137, for the rabbinic references to laying up treasure with God: *Pss. Sol.* 9.5 (9);

Charles, *AP* 2.642; J. R. Harris, *Psalms,* p. 149, "for he who does righteousness lays up (a treasure of) life for himself with the Lord." On "the gatherers of the treasures of faith" in 4 Esd 6:5, see the note in Charles, *AP* 2.574, for the way in which the Latin tradition understood this in terms of *eorum merita.*

*so that they can lay hold on the life which deserves that name.* The *hina* clause takes up the very terminology of 6:12 above (see commentary *in loc.*) as it describes the result/purpose of "treasuring up a fund for the future," namely, "so that they can take hold of *(epilabōntai)* that which is really life *(tēs ontōs zōēs).*"

Philo, *Quis Her.* 53, writes, "Those who are really living *(hoi de zōntes ontōs)* have Wisdom for their Mother" and thus have not died with respect to "the life of the soul *(ton psychēs . . . bion).*" Hill, *Greek Words,* p. 176, citing *Det.* 84, says that for Philo "Life in accordance with reason . . . is the real life of man *(ontōs zēn).*" Spicq, *EP,* p. 579, compares his *Congr.* 87: "So then true life *(hē pros alētheian zōē)* is the life of him who walks in the judgments and ordinances of God."

## V. CLOSING SUMMARY (6:20-21A)

6 [20]*O Timothy, keep what has been deposited with you. Keep your distance from the profane drivel and dialectic of so-called knowledge.* [21a]*Some, who profess to have this at their disposal, have in fact deviated in their faith.*

### ♦ NOTES

6:20. *keep what has been deposited with you.* Lit. "keep the deposit." The noun *parathēkē,* unknown in the Ap. Frs., occurs in LXX Lev 6:2, 4 (MT 5:21, 23) (*pqdwn,* of a deposit of money), as well as Tob 10:13 (of a wife "entrusted as a trust" to her husband) and 2 Macc 3:10, 15 (of deposits for widows and orphans in the Jerusalem temple). When used of persons, this term means "hostage" (cf. LSJ *s.v.*).

The Ap. Frs. do not use the Hellenistic *parathēkē,* but once Hermas, *Man.* 3.2, employs the Attic *parakatathēkē* of the spirit that believers have received from the Lord, a "deposit" of which God is defrauded by lies.

In Philo, *Spec. leg.* 4.30-33, the characteristic note of the *parakatathēkē* that is singled out for extensive comment is the complete confidentiality of the transaction between depositor and depositee. The object is transferred without witnesses or receipt. God alone knows it, and only he can vindicate one who finds his trust violated. Philo favored the *parakatathēkē* comparison in the religious sphere, as Spicq, *EP,* p. 583, has noted (cf. *Spec. leg.* 4.71; *Ebr.* 213 [a curious allegorization of Deut 23:1 where "the deposit of truths" has been cut off]; *Quis Her.* 104-105 of all the created gifts that God has placed at man's disposal as a trust; *Sacr.* 60 of "the knowledge of divine rites").

*Keep your distance from the profane drivel.* The verb *ektrepein* occurred in a similar context in 1 Tim 1:6 as well as 5:15. The adjective *bebēlous* was used nominally in 1 Tim 1:9 (see above) and as an adjective at 4:7. The "drivel," *kenophōnia,* of this verse occurs again at 2 Tim 2:16 but not elsewhere in the NT, the LXX, or the Ap. Frs., though Dioscurides, *De Materia Medica* praef. 2 (first century C.E.), uses the term (other later citations, LSJ *s.v.;* Harrison, *Paulines,* p. 131; Lampe *inter alia* notes Eusebius, *Church History* 5.18.5, citing Apollonius). The term is unattested thus far in the papyri (MM; *nil* in *TDNT s.v. kenos* or *phōnē*).

*dialectic.* The term *antithesis,* like its companion *kenophōnia,* is undocumented otherwise in the NT, the LXX, or the Ap. Frs., though common enough in secular Greek (cf. Harrison, *Paulines,* p. 129, citing Plato, Aristotle) and attested in Philo, *Ebr.* 187, as he illustrates the dialectic by which understanding is sought through comparing and contrasting of opposites (Josephus does not use the noun at all). One is reminded of the *logomachia* of 1 Tim 6:4, and perhaps even the dialectical prattle of the opponents of the Pauline *parathēkē* has been the regular contretemps in this letter to the authentic Pauline *didachē.*

*so-called knowledge.* The *gnōsis* the Christians propose and that which had issued in their *epignōsis alētheias,* "knowledge of the truth," is contrasted with a knowledge of God that is *pseudōnymos* (Bietenhard, *TDNT* 5.282-283). First Timothy 1:10 had noted the *pseustais* among those for whom the OT *nomos* was intended (cf. Titus 1:12 also). In 1 Tim 2:7 the verb occurred of the apostles not lying, and in 1 Tim 4:2 the teachings of demons are *en hypokrisei pseudologōn.* This particular term occurs only here in the NT, LXX, or Ap. Frs., though in secular Greek Aeschylus likes it (*Prom.* 85-86, 717; *Seven against Thebes* 670-671, *ap.* Bietenhard, p. 283), and Philo uses it (*Dec.* 53, of calling things by "false titles [*pseudōnymous prosrēseis*]" that would make them gods; *Abr.* 25, of "bastard governments falsely so-called [*tas nothous kai pseudōnymous archas*]).

21a. *deviated.* On *ēstochēsan* see 1 Tim 1:6.

*in their faith.* Lit. "with respect to *(peri)* the faith (*tēn pistin;* see 1:19 for the phrase, as well as 2 Tim 3:8; for other uses of this preposition with the accusative see Titus 2:7; 1 Tim 6:4; 2 Tim 2:18)."

## ♦ COMMENT

6:20. *O Timothy, keep what has been deposited with you.* The poignant "O" of 6:11 is now taken up and explicitly addressed to Timothy, with whose name this letter had begun (1:2) and with which it now draws to a close. The final two verses here balance the first two of the epistle, enclosing all the intervening materials of such varied form and provenance within the personal written discourse of the apostle to his co-worker, a discourse that is intended to be "overheard" by the church, as the final greeting (v. 21, *hymōn*) makes clear. Some (Lock, Parry, Schlatter) have suggested that these final verses were added by Paul's own hand, as certainly was the case in other letters of his (cf. Gal 6:11-18). Still it was conventional to add such a subscription in the correspondence of the ancient world, and the redactor could just as well have composed this conclusion with some formal resemblance to the practice in actual correspondence. The abruptness of the conclusion, its dry summary character, and its vocabulary (?) all tend to make the latter alternative more credible.

The final imperative of this epistle, *tēn parathēkēn phylaxon,* takes up the verb of 5:21 with the sense seen there of alert response to the OT and Pauline (scriptural and apostolic) teaching and directives that have been proposed. Here as well as in 2 Tim 1:12, 14, this verb has *parathēkēn* as its object. Since these are the only NT uses of *parathēkē,* the whole phrase tends to be drawn into the characteristic usage of the PE, and already in the LXX (e.g., cf. Exod 22:7, 9-10) one notes the *phylassein/paratithēmi* terminology occurring in the same context (cf. C. Maurer, *TDNT* 8.162-168). The verb *paratithenai,* from which *parathēkēn* derived, takes one back to 1 Tim 1:18 and the opening section of this letter. It may be no accident that this letter opened with the verb denoting all that Paul is entrusting (note present tense) quite explicitly *(soi)* to his co-worker, and now as the letter concludes the nominal form "substantizes" the whole process of transmission to "Timothy" recorded in the document. Then the Pauline *parathēkē* that Timothy has received (2 Tim 1:12, 14), he is in turn to transmit *(parathou)* to others who will also teach it (2 Tim 2:2). Spicq has shown (*EP,* pp. 327-355) how the Roman laws on trusts are presumed here rather than the Attic, another indication of the provenance of this correspondence. One notes with Maurer, p. 163 n. 8, that a Jewish biblical mentality underlies it too, but that was because there was such a strong Jewish Christian cadre in the Roman church.

The inclusive *paratithemai* (1:18) / *parathēkēn* (6:20) would lead one to define the content of the term here as the content of this whole letter, with its Pauline prayers, parenesis, and teaching about the OT; its church orders; liturgical materials from the celebration of sacraments (hymnic, confessional, creedal, homiletic); catechetical materials. All these materials in their turn could be designated as "the gospel," the faith, the mystery of godliness, etc. More important than the generic name by which the theologian now might wish to designate this content is the conviction of these letters that the *parathēkē* is Paul's, that it has come from that apostle and his mission, and suffering, and actions, and teachings (2 Tim 1:8-14; see commentary below). There is no question that the Spirit has a role to play in keeping this "deposit" (2 Tim 1:7, 13-14).

*Keep your distance from the profane drivel and dialectic of so-called knowledge.* The participial clause *ektrepomenos tas bebēlous kenophōnias . . .* expresses antithetically the previous command to "keep the deposit." One meets here a linguistic and rhetorical variation on the *mataiologia* of 1 Tim 1:6 (as well as Titus 1:10; see above on 1 Tim 1:6), both of which belonged to the polemical arsenal of the popular philosophers (Spicq, *EP,* p. 582), as did the *v.l. kainophōnia* of F. G. H. pl. Western witnesses (J. K. Elliott, *Greek Text,* pp. 109-110). With Campenhausen, *Tradition,* pp. 35-36, one notes here the concern to defend the Christian faith as consonant with culture, popular philosophy, with all that is sane and reasonable (and to put on opponents the burden of the senseless, irrational, and uncouth, though of course *they* thought of themselves — and must have appeared — no less sophisticated than those loyal to the Paul of the PE).

Timothy is to avoid, along with the "profane drivel," *antitheseis tēs pseudōnymou gnōseōs,* "dialectic of so-called knowledge." The article that governs *kenophōnias* also governs *antitheseis,* and that fact alone makes it impossible to see here a citation of the title of Marcion's *Antitheseis* (see Spicq, *EP,* p. 583). Indeed, one would scarcely be surprised if that audacious theologian did not plan this trilogy of documentation for the Christian faith on the Luke-Acts–PE plan, substituting the "historical Paul" for Acts and his own *Antitheseis* for the appended PE, taking his title from the very correspondence he had rejected. He was surely, on other grounds, the master of the bold offensive as the best defense.

This "profane drivel and dialectic" are further stigmatized as "of so-called knowledge." It has been noted that the PE prefer to speak of *epignōsis alētheias,* and this passage contains the sole use of *gnōsis* in this correspondence. That the term did not yet have a bad sense, as such, is certainly indicated by the qualifying *pseudōnymou* here. D-C, p. 92, propose that the term is being taken from the "technical" vocabulary of the opponents, in which it designated their peculiar teaching. If so, it had not been indelibly stained (as *Gnostic* or *Gnosticism* in English) by those who used it. Bultmann, *TDNT* 1.689-714, has noted how in secular Greek this terminology denotes the act of knowing as well as the knowledge of things as they really are *(alētheia* vs. *doxa)* (pp. 690-691). The biblical and Septuagintal usage (Bultmann, pp. 696-701) stresses the personal involvement in "detecting or feeling or learning by experience" over "the element of objective verification." For biblical language *gnōsis* is simply not "science." "Knowledge has an element of acknowledgment" and involves a "movement of the will," which from God's point of view issues in his election or choice of those he knows and from man's point of view issues in worship, confession of

God, "the fear of the Lord" (Bultmann, p. 698). The noun *gnōsis* is rather less frequent than the verb *ginōskein* in LXX, but it is well on the way to meaning "knowledge *of* God," revelation (Bultmann, p. 700), and thus to being used for *religious* knowledge rather than human experiential knowledge in general. For the biblical tradition as it enters the NT, accordingly, *gnōsis* designates not a purely speculative knowledge of God but "a knowledge which accepts the consequences of knowledge," as in 2 Tim 3:1 (Bultmann, p. 704); and "the knowledge of God attained in Christianity is a service of God" (Bultmann, p. 705). "Intrinsically the usage is that of popular Greek and we may always translate 'knowledge.' If the theoretical element determines the concept, the practical consequences are always implied" (Bultmann, p. 708).

It is by no means clear that a real distinction can be drawn between *gnōsis* and *epignōsis,* even though the latter "has become almost a technical term for the decisive knowledge of God which is implied in conversion to the Christian faith" (cf. Titus 1:1; 1 Tim 2:4; 4:3, as well as 2 Tim 2:25; 3:7; Bultmann, p. 707).

Bultmann (p. 708) has shown that the theoretical aspect of *gnōsis* can involve theological reflection upon the OT Scriptures, particularly in terms of the allegories, mysteries, and parables encountered in the texts. It also can issue from a theological probing of the sacramental actions (e.g., Rom 6:6 on baptism). Such reflection, speculative and practical, did run amok, even in the first generation, among converts from Judaism as well as from paganism, in Pauline as well as Palestinian churches (cf. James 2:20). Yet there is no hard line of evidence that enables one to link the various forms of theological dyspepsia of the first Christian generation (or even the second) with the more developed malignancies that metastasized throughout the Catholic church of the second century.

The *gnōsis* here in First Timothy is certainly to be taken in its religious sense of knowledge *of God,* and specifically of God as he had revealed himself to Christians through Jesus and those whom Jesus sent. The *gnōsis* the Christians propose and that which had issued in their *epignōsis alētheias* is contrasted with a knowledge of God that is *pseudōnymos* (Bietenhard, *TDNT* 5.282-283).

21a. *Some, who profess to have this at their disposal, have in fact deviated in their faith.* Some (*tines,* the indefinite as in 1:3, 6) who are professing/promising (*epaggellomenoi:* see Titus 1:2 and 1 Tim 2:10, esp. the parallels from Ignatius, and also LXX Wis 2:13) this knowledge (*hēn* has *gnōseōs* as its antecedent) have actually "missed the mark" with respect to their faith. The use of *tines peri tēn pistin ēstochēsan* here is parallel to *hoitines peri tēn alētheian ēstochēsan* in 2 Tim 2:18, where a false concept of the resurrection is condemned. Though one cannot infer that as precisely the content of "the faith" here, yet it is suggestive. There is no question that what this correspondence considers the content of *hē pistis* is not the content of the *gnōsis* which the opponents of Paul claim.

## VI. FINAL PRAYER (6:21B)

*6 [21b]Grace be with you all.*

### ♦ NOTES

6:21b. *all.* While the word *all* does not occur in the Greek, this final blessing is invoked on all the faithful, who are addressed with the plural *hymōn,* "you." See Comment below.

### ♦ COMMENT

6:21b. After the summary of 20-21a, the final *hē charis meth' hymōn* comes with striking abruptness. As the opening greeting of this letter had prayed for *charis* for Timothy (1:2), now that *charis* is invoked on all the faithful who are conceived of as listening to the letter (through Timothy?). The same closing formula occurred in Titus 3:15, with the addition of *pantōn,* and it will conclude 2 Tim 4:22 also. In both of the Timothy letters the Byzantine and Western traditions of the text have changed the plural *hymōn* to the singular *sou,* very probably because on every other score the letter is addressed to an individual (B. Metzger, *TCGNT,* p. 644). J. K. Elliott, *Greek Text,* p. 110, opts for the singular here, noting how scribes tended to "generalize" letters addressed to individuals. The omission of the greeting altogether in several ancient versions and patristic witnesses (including Chrysostom) could be due not only to inadvertence (B. Metzger, *TCGNT,* p. 644) but also to the letters being written one immediately after the other (note the complete omission of the final blessing in $P^{72}$ 1 Pet 5:14). Indeed, one wonders if the original redactor simply transferred the ending that was in the original dispatch which ended at 2 Tim 4:22 to this point as well, or are we dealing with a blessing added in the liturgical assembly? In any event the identical endings of the letters to Timothy as they stand in the prime witnesses serve to underline their common unity and to distinguish them from that of Titus.

In the rest of the Paulines, the closing blessing normally mentions (the Lord) Jesus (Christ), as it always mentions *hē charis.* Colossians 4:18 is the only one of the Paulines that closes exactly as do First and Second Timothy (cf. Lohse, *Col,* p. 177). It is also the letter that witnesses (4:14) to the presence of Luke in the entourage at the time of dispatch.

# Notes and Comments on the Second Letter to Timothy

# Outline of Second Timothy

I. An Apostle's Greeting (1:1-2)
II. Thanksgiving Prayer (1:3-14)
  A. The Past (1:3-5)
  B. The Present (1:6-12)
  C. The Future (1:13-14)
III. Personal Note One (1:15-18)
IV. Testament of Paul (2:1–4:8)
  A. The Legator (2:1-13)
  B. The Challengers Challenged (2:14–3:9)
    1. The Errors (2:14-26)
    2. The Erring (3:1-9)
  C. The Legatee (3:10–4:8)
    1. Paul's Life (3:10-13)
    2. Timothy's Imitation of Paul (3:14–4:4)
    3. Paul's Death (4:5-8)
V. Personal Note Two (4:9-21)
  A. News for Timothy (4:9-15)
  B. Paul at Law (4:16-18)
  C. Pauline Greetings to Ephesus (4:19-21a)
  D. Roman Greetings (4:21b)
VI. Final Prayers (4:22)

# Introduction to Second Timothy

The epistolary diptych direct to Timothy closes with a second parenetic letter that assumes the form of an epistolary testament in the name of Paul on the eve of his death to Timothy as his child and heir. The apostle is no longer conceived of as in passage (as in Titus and First Timothy) but as under arrest in Rome (1:16-17; 2:9). Thence he writes to summon Timothy from Asia Minor, probably from Ephesus, where the previous letter had left him (1:16, 18; 4:9, 11-12, 19).

Second Timothy opens with a brief apostolic greeting and blessing for Timothy that corresponds closely (but not exactly) with the opening of First Timothy. A lengthy prayer of thanksgiving follows immediately, reminding one of the regular practice in the rest of the Pauline corpus but not in the PE. The prayer rehearses Timothy's faith-history as a basis for his present courageous stand with Paul, who is suffering for being herald, apostle, and teacher of the gospel that the Lord of history and his indwelling Spirit will guard through the apostle and his co-worker until the day of judgement.

The body of the epistolary testament has been inserted between two personal notes (see Outline III and V) that can be read together. A similar preexisting envelope appears to have been used in composing the Letter to Titus as we now have it. The notes here transmit news about what has happened to Paul since his arrest, transfer to Rome, and imprisonment there, as well as his instructions for Timothy to join him and greetings for house churches in Ephesus.

The testament within this framework falls into three major sections: the first, devoted mainly to the testator, Paul himself; the next, to those whose teachings and lives are a threat to the validity of the will proposed; the third and final section turns to the legitimate heir, Timothy.

It is Paul himself who is depicted as mandating the transmission of his apostolic teaching and his gospel. Timothy and those he picks to carry on this apostolic work must be ready to suffer as Paul did in union with the Lord of the church.

The second section of the testament prepares Timothy to withstand those who would overthrow the Pauline heritage, particularly by evacuating the reality from the final resurrection and the accompanying judgment. The Lord's servant must not give up hope for such persons, but their vices in fact verify the grim oracles about the kinds of people who will multiply in the last days, which they imagine will never come. Their opposition to Paul is like that of the Egyptian magicians to Moses as he began to bring the plagues on Pharaoh's land. An initial, superficial resemblance to Paul's work and his success is destined for early frustration and failure.

The third and final section of the testament turns to the legatee, Timothy, in his relation to the legator, Paul. Three subdivisions are marked in Greek by a recurring *sy de,* "You, however, . . ." The first recalls Paul's apostolic life and sufferings from the first days when Timothy witnessed them in Pisidian Antioch, Iconium, and Lystra. Then Timothy is urged to continue living out the faith he received through Paul and through his mother and grandmother, a faith fully grounded in the Septuagintal form of the Scriptures of Israel. With this heritage he has to prepare for the Lord's judgment by indefatigable proclamation of the Pauline word to erring Christians. The closing section turns from Paul's heir to the apostle, who is about to die to this life but who is alive with hope in and love for "the upright judge, the Lord" (4:8) who will recompense him.

After the personal notes mentioned previously, Second Timothy ends in 4:22 with a double prayer, first for Timothy and then for all believers who have heard the extended conversation between Paul and his child that has occupied the whole epistolary diptych that has preceded.

# To Timothy (2 Tim)

## I. AN APOSTLE'S GREETING (1:1-2)

*1 [1]Paul, apostle of Christ Jesus, by the will of God and for the sake of the promise of life that is in Christ Jesus, [2]writes this to his dear child, Timothy. Grace, mercy, peace from God the Father and Christ Jesus, our Lord.*

### ♦ NOTES

1:1. *by the will of God.* On the use of *dia* with the genitive here, cf. Titus 3:5, 6, as well as 1 Tim 2:10, 15; 4:5, 14 (of prophecy linked to ministerial appointment). Second Timothy favors this usage, as 1:6, 10 *(bis),* 14 (of the Holy Spirit); 2:2; 3:15; 4:17 illustrate.

The noun *thelēma,* "will," occurs sixty-two times in the NT, with twenty-four in the Pauline epistolary and four/three in Luke-Acts. In the PE, note the use of the verb *thelein* in 1 Tim 1:7; 5:11 (of what human persons "want," *in malam partem* in context); 2 Tim 3:12 (of human persons, in a good sense); and especially 1 Tim 2:4 of God's universal will for men's salvation.

The Ap. Frs. use *thelēma* of God's guiding men and calling them to his service often enough (Schrenk, *TDNT* 3.61), but particularly notable is *1 Clem.* 32.3-4, as the author writes of the way in which all authorities and leaders of God's people gained their position "Not through themselves or their own works or the righteous actions that they wrought, but through his will *(dia thelēmatos autou),* and therefore we who by his will *(dia thelēmatos autou)* have been called in Christ Jesus are not made righteous by ourselves . . . but through faith *(dia pisteōs)*. . . ." One is an apostle as one is a Christian, by the divine will and choice that precedes all human deserving (cf. 2 Tim 1:8-12 as well as 1 Tim 1:12-14) and belongs to no man by right.

On the LXX usage, see Schrenk, pp. 53-54, noting particularly LXX 1 Esd 8:16 with its quotation of Artaxerxes' written commission to Ezra that he is to employ the royal gifts of gold and silver "in accordance with the will of your God" in restoring the temple and its sacrificial worship. The LXX Psalms use *thelēma(-ta)* more frequently than do the other books of that translation (for Hebrew *ḥpṣ, rṣwn,* and once *'lylh*).

The Qumran documents appear to use *ḥpṣ* of predominantly human needs or desires (but in CD 3.15: Dupont-Sommer, *EWQ,* p. 126, "the desires of his will" [*rṣwnw:* the other uses at 2.21; 3.3, 11, 12; 11.4, 21 do not refer to God] refers to God). *Rṣwn* is the preferred term in 1QS for God's (good) will (1QS 5.1, 9, 10; 8.6, 10 [?]; 9.4 [contrast 5], 13 [explicitly *rṣwn 'l*], 15, 23, 24 [again *rṣwn 'l*]). Note 11.17-18, where the piety of the sectaries reaches a high pitch, "For without you no way is perfect, and without your will, nothing is done. It is you who have taught all knowledge, and all that is brought into being exists by your will" (Dupont-Sommer, *EWQ*, p. 103). In 1QM 2.5 incense obtains "the good will of God *(rṣwn 'l),*" and apparently at 18.14 the reference is to God's will. Of the sixteen uses in 1QH, all refer to God's (good) will, creating, revealing, purifying, directing, giving peace (see Vogt, "Peace among Men," pp. 114-117; R. Brown, *Semitic,* pp. 22-30; Lohse, *Col,* pp. 25-26, on Col 1:9).

On the Essene devotion to the will of God, see Philo, *Quod omn. pro.* 84 (*to pantōn men agathōn aition, kakou de mēdenos nomizein einai to theion,* "their belief that the Godhead is the cause of all good things and of nothing evil" [trans. LCL]), and Josephus *Ant.* 13.172, who writes that the Essenes hold that "Fate *(heimarmenēn)* is mistress of all things and nothing befalls men unless it is in accordance with her mandate" (trans. WCW), as well as Josephus, *Ant.* 18.18. Cf. 1QS 3.15-17, and G. F. Moore, "Fate and Free Will," pp. 371-389, where fate appears as equivalent for all practical purposes to what the Christian tradition means by "providence." Josephus, curiously enough, never uses the noun *thelēma.*

*for the sake of the promise.* On the meaning of *epaggelian zōēs* here, see the phrase in the form in which it is used in 1 Tim 4:8; see also Excursus IV, "The Terminology for Life in the PE," in AB *Titus.* The prepositional phrase *kat' epaggelian* occurs elsewhere in the NT only in Acts 13:23, "God has brought to Israel a Savior, Jesus, as promised," and Gal 3:29, "heirs according to the promise." In the LXX the phrase occurs only in 1 Esd 1:7, with the sense, "in accord with his promise." There are no instances with *kata* among the nine uses of the term *epaggelia* in Josephus.

The phrase *kat' epaggelian* is not documented in the Ap. Frs., though the term *Epaggelia* is used by *1 Clem.* 10.2 of "God's promises" (pl.) to Abraham; 26.1 of the promise of resurrection; 27.1 of the divine promises (pl.); 34.7 of God's "great and glorious promises." *Second Clement* 5.5 speaks of "the promise of Christ" that issues in "everlasting life"; in 10.3-4 and 11.1, 7, God's promise is an object of faith, and, in the plural, they are "what ear has not heard nor eye seen, etc."; in 15.4 God's saying that he is present to one praying is "the sign of a great promise." The one use in Ign. *Eph.* 14.2 is of a *present* human profession *(nyn epaggelias)* that stands in some contrast to a perseverance in faith to the end. The uses in *Barn.* 5.7; 6.17; 15.7; 16.9; and in Hermas, *Vis.* 1.3.4; 2.2.6; 3.2.1, and *Sim.* 1.7 do not add anything to the understanding of the usage of the PE.

For more on the *epaggel*, "promise," terminology, see note on 1 Tim 4:8.

*in Christ Jesus.* Thirty-two times forms of "Christ Jesus" occur in the PE, twenty-six in the order used here. "Christ" occurs alone only once in the PE (1 Tim 5:11), and never is the name "Jesus" employed alone. The use of "Jesus Christ" may signal a Jewish Christian emphasis (Hebrews uses the words thrice, but never in reversed position; the Catholic Epistles always use it). On the phrase "in Christ Jesus," see 1 Tim 1:14; 3:13.

2. *dear. Agapētōi* is a term that this correspondence used otherwise only at 1 Tim 6:2 (see Spicq, *Agape* 2.429-431, for NT inventory). *Agapētos* occurs in the Ap. Frs. in *First Clement* (always pl.); Ignatius, four of six times plural, but singular in *Pol.* 7.2; 8.2; and once in Hermas, *Sim.* 5.2.6, of a parabolic "beloved son" (who is never explained in the text as it stands; cf. LCL 2.165 n. 1).

## ♦ COMMENT

The opening verses of Second Timothy take up those of 1 Tim 1:1-2 with a striking identity in terminology that, literally speaking, forges a bridge between the two epistles and invites the reader to see them as a unit distinct from Titus. Twenty of the twenty-nine words in 2 Tim 1:1-2 occur also in 1 Tim 1:1-2, in the same order and in relatively the same positions. Both greetings repeat the name "Christ Jesus" three times. First Timothy 1:1-2 has a few words and phrases that are not used here *(kat' epitagēn; sōtēros hēmōn kai Christou Iēsou, elpidos hēmōn; gnēsiōi;* and *en pistei).* This greeting substitutes or adds the few terms and phrases that are to be noted here.

The resemblances with Titus 1:1-4 are not as striking as with First Timothy, but the *kat' epaggelian zōēs* of 2 Tim 1:1 does take up the language of Titus 1:2, *ep' elpidi zōēs aiōniou hēn epēggeilato ho . . . theos* (which First Timothy does not).

1:1. *Paul, apostle of Christ Jesus, by the will of God and for the sake of the promise of life that is in Christ Jesus. Paul* is used 158 times in the NT, 128 of those in Acts, which also uses the name for someone other than the apostle once (13:7). The name is used at least once in every document of the Pauline epistolary, including the PE. Outside of the Paulines and Acts, the name is used only once, linked with Simon Peter in 2 Pet 3:15.

*Apostolos,* "apostle," occurs seventy-nine times in the NT, with thirty-four of those appearing in the Paulines. Six times it occurs in Luke, twenty-eight in Acts, and one each in the other Gospels. It is used more than thirty times in the Ap. Frs., and in *1 Clem.* 5.3; 44.1; 47.1 (with the definite article), 4; Ign. *Rom.* 4.3; and Polycarp, *Phil.* 9.1, it includes or applies to Paul.

The phrase *dia thelēmatos theou* stands for the *kat' epitagēn theou* of

1 Tim 1:1. The term *thelēma* has not previously occurred in this correspondence; it will be used again at 2:26 below (probably of God's will also, but others hold for the will of the devil; cf. Luke 23:25 of men and the diabolic *thelō* of Luke 4:6). On the latter interpretation, that stark contrast in usage places the whole apostolate and the life of the church between two superhuman "wills" and sets up a dialectical tension that will enable one to probe and assess what one sees happening even in the church.

The whole phrase *dia thelēmatos theou* is found only in the Pauline epistolary and almost always as part of the opening apostolic greeting (1 Cor 1:1; 2 Cor 1:1 [cf. 8:5 of the response to the apostle]; Eph 1:1; Col 1:1) describing and qualifying the *apostolos* title. As Lohse, *Col*, p. 6 n. 10, remarks of its use in Colossians, the will of God is seen as a choosing/electing will as distinguished from a will commanding a certain course of conduct and action. Of course the apostolate is itself a way of life undertaken at the divine imperative, and thus the distinction proposed is not radically a separate meaning for the term.

Paul favors the phrase "will of God" (cf. in addition to the above, Rom 1:10; 12:2; 15:32 [with *dia*]; Gal 1:4; Eph 6:6; Col 4:12 [cf. 1:9]; 1 Thess 4:3; 5:18, not to mention the cases where *autou* = *theou*). Luke-Acts never employ it, though *thelēma kyriou* does occur (Luke 12:47 [parabolic, of stewards and Christ]; Acts 21:14 [= Lord Jesus of v. 13]), and there are indirect references to God's will (Luke 22:42, "Not my will but yours be done"; Acts 13:22 of David, "who will do all I will [*thelēmata mou*]"; and 22:14-15 where Ananias is described as saying to Saul, "The God of our fathers appointed you to know his will [*gnōnai to thelēma autou*], to see the Just One and to hear a voice from his mouth, for you will be a witness to all men of what you have seen and heard"). Though Luke can use *thelēma* of simply human whim (Luke 23:25), here knowing God's will is the experience of the risen Lord, and this in turn is ordered to the apostolate.

The "will of God" throws the shadow of suffering onto a man's life (cf. Schrenk, *TDNT* 3.55-56, 58-59), and that connotation is particularly appropriate to Second Timothy, where Paul's sufferings in his apostolate are adverted to at every turn.

Paul has his apostolic leadership at God's antecedent good pleasure, which has elected him, purified him, directed him "for (according to) the promise of life which is in Christ Jesus." The *kat' epaggelian* (note Sinaiticus has accusative plural) for which the apostle has been called stands in contrast to those *epaggelomenoi* (announcing/promising) a false knowledge with which the last lines of the preceding letter closed.

The use of *kata* with the accusative here is reminiscent of *kata pistin* in Titus 1:1, 4, and it is quite possible that the redactor of this correspondence meant Paul's apostleship from the risen Jesus "through the will of God" as "*for* the life which is in Christ Jesus," i.e. both the apostleship and the divine plan have as their *raison d'être* the risen life (thus, e.g., Theodoret as cited in D-C, p. 97). Still one cannot altogether discount the nuance "in accord with" or "corresponding to" (Kelly, *Commentary,* p. 153, renders it "in reference to"), and Spicq is probably to be followed in keeping the ambivalence in suspension.

2. *writes this to his dear child, Timothy. Grace, mercy, peace from God the Father and Christ Jesus, our Lord.* The first part (of the two parts or members) of the prescript continues as did 1 Tim 1:2, by naming Timothy, described again as Paul's *teknon,* as the recipient of this letter. This part of the prescript varies from 1 Tim 1:2 in a single term; whereas that letter had described Timothy as *gnēsion teknon,* "true child," this one characterizes him as "beloved" *(agapētōi),* which is a designation of Timothy in 1 Cor 4:17. Paul called his converts his "beloved children" (1 Cor 4:14; Spicq, *Agape* 2.432-433), and that may be one of the connotations of the phrase here, though it could equally well suggest "beloved by God" (cf. Eph 5:1 and Rom 1:7). The other Paulines use *agapētos* of his friends (Rom 16:5, 8, 9, 12; Col 4:9, 14; Philem 16) as well as of those who shared his apostolate (Eph 6:21; Col 1:7; 4:7; Philem 1 [?]).

It may be suggestive in this regard that on the one occasion when *agapētos* in Luke-Acts does not modify *huios* ("son," and refer directly or parabolically to Jesus, as in Matthew-Mark also), it occurs in a *letter* from the Jerusalem church where it characterizes Barnabas and Paul (Acts 15:25). Thus Luke, at any rate, knew of the term as an epistolary convention. Spicq, *Agape* 2.434, and *EP, in loc.,* would add that *apagētos* often, in both secular and biblical texts, has the connotation of "authentic, genuine" (cf. *gnēsios*) as well as "unique" (cf. the use of *huios agapētos* in the synoptics). Thus here in the PE Timothy is a child of predilection.

The second member of this epistolary greeting is word for word that of 1 Tim 1:2.

## II. THANKSGIVING PRAYER (1:3-14)

### II.A. The Past (1:3-5)

*1 [3]I give thanks to the God whom I, like my forebears, worship with a clean conscience, as I make unceasing mention of you in my entreaties, night and day. [4]When I remember your tears, I yearn to see you and so to have my fill of joy. [5]I have a reminder of your unfeigned faith, the very same as that which first dwelt in your grandmother, Lois, and in your mother, Eunice, and in you too, I am convinced.*

## ♦ NOTES

1:3. *I give thanks.* For the phrase *charin echō* see above on 1 Tim 1:12.

*worship.* Of the twenty-one NT occurrences of *latreuein* (five of *latreia*), this is the only use of this terminology in the PE (which also do not speak of *idōlolatria (-rēs),* though that figured in Pauline vice lists). The other Paulines used *latreuein* three times (Rom 1:9, 25; Phil 3:3; *latreia* at Rom 9:4; 12:1), and the verb (alone) appears in Luke-Acts eight times (three/five) — in the rest of the Gospels only in Matt 4:10, citing LXX Deut 6:13 (= Luke 4:8 also).

In the Ap. Frs. *latreuein* occurs three times (the noun only once, in *Did.* 6.3); *1 Clem.* 45.7, cited but not quoted in the commentary on 1 Tim 3:8, in a context that explains persecution and suffering, writes, "the Most High is the defender and protector of those who worship *(latreuontōn)* his excellent name *with a pure conscience (en katharai syneidēsei).*" Ign. *Smyrn.* 9.1 stigmatizes the man who does not let his bishop know what he is doing as a man who "worships the devil *(tōi diabolōi latreuei).*" In Polycarp, *Phil.* 2.1, God is "the one whom all breath worships *(hōi pasa pnoē latreuei).*"

*like my forebears.* The phrase *apo progonōn* is lit. "from ancestors." *Progonōn* occurred above at 1 Tim 5:4 (of parents and grandparents; see commentary *ad loc.*) but is not documented elsewhere in the NT or the Ap. Frs. The LXX has a dozen uses, of which eight are in Second, Third, and Fourth Maccabees, and most of those refer to the forefathers of the Jews and in fact to rather more remote ancestors than grandparents. The context is frequently the Jewish way of life, i.e. their conduct (including formal worship) before their God. The construction with *apo* occurs in 3 Macc 6:28. The term *progonoi* is frequent in the inscriptions (citations in Spicq, *EP,* p. 701; cf. references in D-C, p. 98), but interestingly there is no example in *CII.*

*as I make unceasing mention of you.* Lit. "as I have unceasing remembrance of you." The initial term in *hōs adialeipton echō . . .* here appears for the only time as a conjunction in this correspondence, though there are ten other uses of the particle in the PE (cf. Titus 1:5, 7; 1 Tim 5:1 *[bis],* 2 *[bis];* 2 Tim 2:3, 9, 17; 3:9). It has the sense of time/circumstance. Luke-Acts favor the conjunction (twenty-six times/thirty-four times) whereas there are only eleven other Pauline uses (but one is precisely Rom 1:9).

The phrase *echō tēn peri sou mneian* is, as Spicq, p. 703, notes, a Latinism *(memoriam habeo),* as was the preceding *charin echō.* The noun *mneia* occurs in the NT only in the Paulines (seven times total). Usually it is construed with *poiein* and associated with prayers (Rom 1:9; Eph 1:16; 1 Thess 1:2; Philem 4), but in 1 Thess 3:6 Paul wrote *echete mneian hēmōn agathēn.* The LXX uses the noun fifteen times (four times with *poiein*) but never with *echein* (contra Spicq, who cites Zech 13:2; Bar 4:27, both of which have *estai*). The Ap. Frs. use the term three times. *First Clement* 56.1 says of intercession for sinners, that "they will have *(estai autois)* fruitful and perfect remembrance *(mneia)* before God and the saints. . . ." In *Barn.* 21.7 the exhortation closes with "If there is any memory *(mneia)* of good, remember *(mnēmoneuete)* me. . . ." Hermas, *Vis.* 3.7.3, also uses the term but with no particular point for 2 Tim 1:3. See MM *s.v.* for examples of *mneia* in prayers (but not with *echein*).

*in my entreaties.* On *en tais deēsesin mou* see the study of *deēseis* at 1 Tim 2:1, which recurs along with the *nyktos kai hēmeras* phrase at 1 Tim 5:5. Here in 2 Tim 1:3 the *adialeipton,* "unceasing," stresses still further the constancy of the memento in the prayer of the apostle. In Rom 9:2 (the only other NT use of this adjective) Paul uses this term to describe the "unceasing anguish in my heart" at the refusal of his countrymen to believe in Jesus. The four Pauline uses of the adverb, *adialeiptōs,* ought to be noted, for as in Rom 1:9, so in 1 Thess 1:2; 2:13; 5:17, the term always refers to the apostolic recollection of and thankful prayer for believers that is to call forth a similarly constant prayer from them. It is the formal grammatical structure rather than the actual meaning that distinguishes these adverbial uses from the adjective of 2 Tim 1:3.

In the LXX the adverb alone occurs six times in the Maccabean literature. In 1 Macc 12:11 the high priest Jonathan's letter to the Spartans declares, "we therefore remember you *constantly (adialeiptōs)* on every occasion both in our feasts and on other appropriate days, at the sacrifices that we offer and in our prayers, as it is right and proper to remember brothers" (cf. 1 Tim 2:1). In 2 Macc 3:26 the adverb is used of blows; in 9:4 of a nonstop chariot journey; in 13:12 (cf. 10) of three days and nights of public intercessions and fasting before joining battle; in 15:7 of Maccabeus's unceasing hope for God's aid. In 3 Macc 6:33 it is said of King Ptolemaeus Philopator himself that he "unceasingly gave thanks in exalted terms to heaven for their [i.e. the Jews'] unexpected deliverance" (Charles, *AP* 1.172).

In the Ap. Frs., Ign. *Pol.* 1.3 uses the adjective in exhorting his colleague, "Be diligent with unceasing prayers." He uses the adverb in *Eph.* 10.1, "Pray unceasingly for other men. . . ." In Polycarp, *Phil.* 8.1, the adverb refers to constant perseverance in Christ Jesus. Hermas uses the adjective in *Sim.* 2.6, cf. 8, where it appears to refer to the constant prayer and intercession of the poor man. He employs the adverb in *Sim.* 5.4.4 of the Lord's giving unceasingly in answer to prayer, in *Sim.* 9.27.2 of bishops "ceaselessly" sheltering the poor and the widows in their homes.

4. *I remember.* This verb, *mimnēiskomai,* which takes up the nominal *mneian* of the preceding verse and prepares for the *hypomnēsin* of the following, occurs only here in the PE and only once otherwise in the Paulines (1 Cor 11:2: ". . . you remember me in everything . . ."). Of its twenty-one other NT uses, eight are in Luke-Acts (six/two), where its use in connection with prayers

is notable (Luke 1:54, 72; 23:42; Acts 10:31), as well as its connotation of merciful compassion and concern (Spicq).

This verb is found in the Ap. Frs. *Didache* 4.1 instructs the catechumen, "You shall remember, day and night, him who speaks the word of God to you . . . ," which recalls 2 Tim 2:8 also. *Didache* 10.5 prays, "Remember, Lord, your church. . . ." *First Clement* 13.1 and 46.7 use the verb of the words of the Lord Jesus (cf. Luke 24:6, 8; Acts 11:16), and in 50.4 it occurs in a nonscriptural sentence joining two OT prophetic oracles: "And I [God] will remember a feast day (*hēmeras agathēs* = Pasch). . . ." See also *Barn.* 13.7; 19.10, "You shall remember day and night the day of judgment"; Hermas, *Vis.* 3.1.5; 4.1.8.

*tears.* The noun *dakryon* has ten other NT uses. In Paul it is otherwise found only in 2 Cor 2:4 of Paul's tearful letter to his converts. In Luke-Acts the term is used of the sinful woman (Luke 7:38, 44), and, most notably, in Acts 20:19, 31 of Paul's own fervent exhortation to the Ephesian Christians, who in turn are described as weeping *(klauthmos),* embracing, and kissing Paul as he parts from them who will not see his face again (Acts 20:25, 37-38). One wonders if the details of the final arrest scene have been conflated with this Miletus scene.

*Dakryon* in the LXX, though frequent enough, offers no precise parallel to this passage (but cf. LXX Pss 41:4 and 55:9). The Ap. Frs. do not employ this noun.

*joy. Chara* occurs fifty-nine times in the NT and twenty times in the Paulines outside of this single occurrence in the PE. There are a dozen occurrences in Luke-Acts (eight/four). *Plēroō* occurs only here in the PE but eighty-five times elsewhere in the NT, including twenty-two times in the other Paulines and twenty-five times in Luke-Acts (nine/sixteen). For the phrase *charas plērōthō,* see Comment below.

The LXX uses the phrase only in 2 Macc 3:30 and 3 Macc 4:16, though the individual terms are not infrequent. In the former instance, the phrase describes the effect in the temple of a divine epiphany, and in the latter, the king merrily preparing to destroy the Jews of Alexandria, ordering feasts in the pagan shrines.

The Ap. Frs. use both terms, but the phrase *charas plēroun* does not appear in their text (but cf. *Mart. Pol.* 12.1). H. Conzelmann, *TDNT* 9.360, has noted that the phrase does occur in Josephus, *War* 3.28, and that the effect of the verb is to stress the merry rejoicing that the *nomen actionis* designates. The term *chara* appears often in contexts of the joy of recognition, reunion, and meeting (including meeting with God on festal occasions in worship: Conzelmann, p. 363). The NT usage turns regularly on the paradox of joy in suffering (Conzelmann, pp. 367-371), and in Paul *chara* is linked with the apostolic work itself (Conzelmann, p. 369).

5. *first.* On *prōton* cf. 1 Tim 2:1; 3:10; 5:4.

*grandmother, mother.* Eunice is described as Timothy's *mētēr,* a term that occurred in 1 Tim 5:2 in a metaphorical sense but that certainly here refers to physical generation. The term *mammē* for "grandmother," not otherwise attested in the NT or Ap. Frs., occurs in LXX 4 Macc 16:9 where the mother of the seven martyred sons laments that now she will "not be called by the name *mammē*" by her son's children. The word belongs to the vocabulary of children, an affectionate term, not unlike the American "gramma." For the usage of the papyri and inscriptions, see Spicq, *EP,* p. 705, and MM *s.v.*, p. 387, where it is noted that in modern Greek the term means "midwife." Harrison, *Paulines,* p. 131, cites examples from earlier Greek authors (e.g., Menander, *Samos* 28, Sandbach 243 [p. 241], *hē mammē de pou;* "where's its mammy gone?") where the term is used for a mother.

## ♦ COMMENT

Formally speaking, the thanksgiving prayer that begins at 1:3 is a readily identifiable part of the Pauline epistolary schema (see Lohse, *Col,* pp. 12-13), yet there is no agreement on where the prayer ends. Of course, this problem is no surprise in the Pauline correspondence, which confronts the exegete with this problem even in First Thessalonians, where the prayer may go from 1:2 to 3:13. The positioning of the prayer here in Second Timothy is the customary place for prayer in the Paulines, but its placement is different from that in First Timothy (where it is placed later) and in Titus, which has no thanksgiving (cf. Galatians).

The opening of the prayer here in Second Timothy, *charin echō,* is identical with that in 1 Tim 1:12 (see commentary *ad loc.*), but the thanks are here addressed not to the risen Jesus but to God the Father (note the articular *tōi theōi*), who is mentioned four times through verse 8. The prayer turns to "our Lord" in 1:8, using the name Christ Jesus three times thereafter (vv. 9, 10, 13), and concludes (?) with the mention of the Holy Spirit in 1:14. The "trinitarian" framework appears to be unique for the PE. This letter and thus the apostolic communication are conceived of as emerging from the unceasing apostolic worship and prayer of Paul, a prayer that includes those who share not only his faith but also his apostolate.

1:3. *I give thanks to the God whom I, like my forebears, worship with a clean conscience, as I make unceasing mention of you in my entreaties, night and day.* The thanksgiving prayer is directed *tōi theōi hōi latreuō.* The phrase takes up the anarthrous *theos* of 1:1-2, who is there (1:2) designated *patēr.* Here the articular form (repeated in 1:6-7 below, anarthrous in 1:8) reinforces that identification.

The phraseology here is reminiscent of the LXX (cf. Exod 3:12, and rather often there, as well as Deuteronomy, Joshua, Judges, though never in the first person singular, the closest being LXX 2 Sam 15:8 of Absalom's vow, *latreusō tōi kyriōi*), where the verb *latreuō* occurs ninety times (Strathmann, *TDNT* 4.59). As Strathmann has pointed out (pp. 60-61), the verb (and the noun *latreia*) practically always refers in the LXX to public worship, to the liturgical cult, whether directed to the God of Israel or the pagan deities. Yet the *latr-* cluster never appears in Psalms. It also normally refers to the cult of a community or a people (including Levitical priests), whereas *leitourgein* is practically reserved to the sacerdotal functions of the Levitic tribe. S. Daniel, *Le vocabulaire*, pp. 55-92, furnishes a detailed study of the ways in which the *ʿbdh* of the MT has entered the LXX, and she also notes the way in which *latreuein* is used of the cult by the people as a whole whereas *leitourgein, leitourgia* is practically reserved for designating the specific (sacerdotal) tasks of the Levites and priests (cf. pp. 76, 91-92).

Like the LXX, the NT uses this terminology only in a religious sense, of worship, and the connotation of sacrifice is never far away (cf. Strathmann, p. 65). Considering the prominence that is given to suffering in Second Timothy (1:8, 12, 16; 2:3-13; 3:10-12; 4:5-8, 16-18), that connotation is important here. The other Paulines employ *latreuein (-reia)* of false worship of material idols (Rom 1:25), of Israel's worship of the one God (Rom 9:4), of the Christian believers' worship of God in the Spirit and a way of life sustained by the Spirit (Rom 9:4; 12:1, perhaps as contrasted with Israel's temple *latreia* according to "the letter" and with material creatures; see Phil 3:3).

It is, however, the thanksgiving prayer that opens Romans that shows the most resemblances to the language of 2 Tim 1:3-14, without the latter being an actual quotation:

| **Romans 1:8-11** | **2 Timothy 1:3-6** |
| --- | --- |
| 1:8 *eucharistō tōi theōi* "I thank my God" | 1:3 *charin echō tōi theōi* "I give thanks to God" |
| 1:9 *ho theos hōi latreuō* "God whom I serve (worship)" | 1:3 *tōi theōi hōi latreuō* "to the God whom I worship" |
| 1:9-10 *hōs adialeiptōs mneian hymōn poioumai pantote epi tōn proseuchōn mou* "that without ceasing I mention you always in my prayers" | 1:3 *hōs adialeipton echō tēn peri sou mneian in tais deēsesin mou nyktos kai hēmeras* "as I make unceasing mention of you in my entreaties, night and day" |
| 1:11 *epipothō gar idein hymas* "I yearn to see you (pl.)" | 1:4 *epipothōn se idein* "I yearn to see you (sg.)" |

| | |
|---|---|
| 1:11 *hina ti metadō charisma hymin pneumatikon* "that I may impart a spiritual gift to you (pl.)" | 1:6 *to charisma tou theou ho estin en soi dia tēs epitheseōs tōn cheirōn mou* "the gracious gift of God the Father, which is within you through the imposition of these hands of mine." |

It is as if the thanksgiving prayer for the Roman church was here set in a new key as a thanksgiving prayer from Rome (2 Tim 1:17).

One cannot pass by the Lukan usage of *latreuein*, for with him, too, this verb designates the public (though not necessarily strictly liturgical) worship that the faithful Israelite gives to the only true God (Luke 1:74, Zechariah the priest's prophetic blessing psalm; Luke 2:37 of Anna — note also *deēsesi* as well as *nykta kai hēmeran;* Luke 4:8 = Matt 4:10 [Q], based on LXX Deut 6:13 in answer to Satan's request for worship). Stephen takes up the term in an allusion to LXX (?) Exod 3:12 in Acts 7:7, and in 7:42 he uses this verb for the worship of the stars.

In its last three occurrences in Acts, the verb is placed on Paul's lips in contexts that, on other grounds as well, call this prayer of Second Timothy to mind. Thus in Acts 24:14-16, in Paul's apologia before the Roman governor in Caesarea, he says, "According to the way, which they call a sect, I worship the God of our fathers *(latreuō tōi patrōiōi theōi)*" according to the Scriptures and in the hope of the resurrection; "so I always take pains to have a clear conscience (*aproskopon syneidēsin echein* [cf. Acts 23:1]) toward God and toward men." Then in Acts 26:6-7, speaking of the resurrection, before Agrippa, he describes it as being on trial for "hope in the promise (*epaggelias* [cf. 2 Tim 1:1]) made by God to our fathers *(eis tous pateras hēmōn)* to which our twelve tribes hope to attain, as they earnestly worship night and day *(en ekteneiai nykta kai hēmeran latreuon)*," and cf. 26:22. The complex of concepts and terminology coincides notably with 2 Tim 1:3. The final occurrence in Acts, at 27:23, is Paul's assurance to the 275 mortally endangered passengers with him that "an angel of the God to whom I belong and whom I worship *(tou theou hou eimi, hōi kai latreuō)*" had promised their deliverance. The passage is significant, for it presumes that the apostle's prayer and worship are the setting for the answering word of God.

The prayer of Paul is here explicitly linked with his ancestors, *apo progonōn,* and this connection in turn prepares the way for the mention of Timothy's mother and grandmother. The term appeared in the ordo for widows at 1 Tim 5:4, with the same sense as here of parents and grandparents. D-C, p. 98, appear to separate the concept of "salvation history" from the references here and in verse 5 to the religious rearing of children. Since in Israel religious upbringing consisted essentially and specifically in making Israel's history of salvation one's own (cf. Deut 6:20-25; the Passover meal; etc.), and since this letter links Timothy's religious upbringing with the Scriptures *apo brephous,* "from childhood" (2 Tim 3:15), D-C's contrast between this passage and the concept of salvation history in Luke-Acts appears arbitrary. Granted there is no systematic development of "the relationship between Israel and the church" at this point, it is still notable how the elements that are here are coherent with the Lukan view on the history of God's one people (see Jervell, *Paul,* p. 42). The praying and suffering apostle, along with his co-workers, are the living shoots of a tree long planted.

While the apostolic worship is *kata tas graphas,* "according to the Scriptures," *apo progonōn* stresses the once living human vessels by which revelation has been transmitted, as *graphai* stresses the record of once living words. The *en katharai syneidēsei* is a ministerial qualification for the deacons in 1 Tim 3:9 (persons whose consciences, and very way of thinking, have been polluted are incapable, in turn, of determining what pollutes and edifies ecclesial life) and links worship with the moral life. A clean conscience is again a characteristic note of the religion of Israel (cf. Ps 51:2-4, etc.)

4. *When I remember your tears, I yearn to see you and so to have my fill of joy.* The *epipothōn se idein* now describes the grateful, worshipping, remembering apostle as "longing to see you, (Timothy)." This is the only use of the verb *epipothein* in the PE, but, as was already noted, forms of this phrase occurred in the thanksgiving prayer of Rom 1:11 with *epipothō gar idein hymas* (of a Christian church that Paul had not seen; cf. also the noun in 15:23) and in the conclusion of the thanksgiving prayer of 1 Thess 3:6, *epipothountes hēmas idein,* of the Thessalonian converts longing to see their apostles (cf. 2:7). In 2 Cor 9:14 the collection for the poor Christians of Jerusalem finds that the latter "long for you and pray for you *(autōn deēsei hyper hymōn epipothountōn hymas).*" In Phil 1:8 the apostle writes in the opening thanksgiving, "For God is my witness, how I long for you all with the affection of Christ Jesus *(hōs epipothō pantas hymas en splagchnois Christou Iēsou),*" and then in 2:26 of Epaphroditus, who "was longing to see you all *(epipothōn ēn pantas hymas idein).*" The one other Pauline usage, 2 Cor 5:2, is of the Christian's longing to put on the risen body and life with God.

The verb occurs in the strange citation of James 4:5, of "the spirit dwelling in us," and in 1 Pet 2:2 of the longing for the pure milk of teaching. It is otherwise undocumented in the NT and does not occur in the Ap. Frs. (for the adjective see *1 Clem.* 65.1; and *Barn.* 1.3, *hē emoi epipothētē opsis hymōn*).

Of the twelve LXX uses of *epipothein,* seven are in the Psalms, the most famous of which describe the thirsty longing for God and his temple worship (LXX Pss 41:2; 83:3). Spicq has noted (*Agape* 3.237) that in the ten cases where there is a corresponding Hebrew text, eight different Hebrew terms are being translated! The Timothy who was *agapētos* above is now the object of *epipothōn,* reminding one that *agapaō/epipotheō* can be synonymous (cf. Suidas: *epipothia = hē agapē, ap.* Spicq, *Agape* 3.101 n. 3, French ed.), with the *epi-* prefix adding an intensive note (even of anxiety) in the *epipoth-* terminology (which is not yet documented in the papyri and may appear in one broken [fifth-century-C.E.] epitaph, cited by Spicq, *Agape* 3.99 n. 4, French ed.).

After the present participle *epipothōn,* the perfect participle *memnēmenos* introduces the next phrase, "having recalled your tears." This verb takes up the nominal *mneian* of the preceding verse and prepares for the *hypomnēsin* of the following. O. Michel, *TDNT* 4.675-683, has noted that in the LXX the verb "to remember," when God is the subject, designates "an efficacious and creative event" (p. 675), particularly when he remembers his covenant and the patriarchs. Man, on the other hand, when he is the subject, remembers God's acts, his commands *(ibid.).* The verb is particularly characteristic of OT prayer (the Psalms use this verb more than any other OT book), and one notes again LXX Ps 41:4, 6, where the psalmist "remembers" his God and the temple worship. Luke-Acts appear (along with Hebrews) to be especially affected by the OT usage (cf. citations in Notes above), and Michel, p. 676, has noted that in Acts 10:31 "to remember" practically means "to mention." That meaning might apply to this prayer in Second Timothy, though Paul is described as recalling not Timothy himself but his tears.

The memory that Paul retains of Timothy is that of a tearful parting, almost certainly, Spicq has noted, an allusion to Paul's arrest by imperial officers and his enforced separation from his entourage (though 2 Tim 4:10-11, 20 would indicate that no small number managed to stay near him; cf. also 2 Tim 1:17). Perhaps another part of that fragmentary tradition has been preserved in 2 Tim 1:15-16 (see commentary *in loc.*).

The purpose clause *(hina)* comes with some abruptness as the remembered sorrow of Timothy at parting is contrasted with the apostle's longing to see him again "so to have my fill of joy *(charas plērōthō).*" The phrase found here occurs otherwise in various forms in the Paulines; thus Rom 15:13 where Paul prays, "May the God of hope fill you with all joy *(plērōsai hymas pasēs charas . . .)* and peace in believing, so that by the power of the Holy Spirit you may abound in hope." The phrase also occurs in Phil 2:2 in the form *plērōsate mou tēn charan* (cf. also 2 Cor 7:4). The phrase is most characteristic of the Johannine corpus (cf. John 3:29; 15:11; 16:24; 17:13; and 1 John 1:4; 2 John 12). It also occurs once in the Lukan corpus, in Acts 13:52, where, after describing the persecution of Paul and Barnabas in Pisidian Antioch, with an abruptness that reminds one of 2 Tim 1:4, the author writes, "And the disciples were filled with joy *(eplērounto charas)* and the Holy Spirit." The passive here as well as in

Second Timothy reminds one that God ought to be understood as the unexpressed subject of *plēroun* (as in Rom 15:13).

5. *I have a reminder of your unfeigned faith.* Again a participial phrase describes the apostle, subject of the preceding *plērōthō,* as "receiving a reminder of the unfeigned faith" in Timothy. The phrase *hypomnēsin labōn* (note second aorist and the variants; J. K. Elliott, *Greek Text,* p. 114, calls attention to the *analabōn* for a single act in 2 Tim 4:11 but does not recognize such a situation here) does not occur elsewhere in the NT, the LXX, or the Ap. Frs. Indeed, the noun is not common (on its cognate verb see Titus 3:1 and 2 Tim 2:14), occurring otherwise in the NT only in 2 Pet 1:13; 3:1 (of the letter being written); in LXX Ps 70:6; Wis 16:11; and 2 Macc 6:17 (of the author's preceding comments); and in the Ap. Frs. in Hermas, *Vis.* 3.8.9 (of a revelation/vision). The term is used of concrete reminders from an external source (MM *s.v.,* p. 659) in writing often enough, to justify Spicq's suggestion that some communication, perhaps in writing, from Timothy is being referred to at this point. (See MM and LSJ for *hypomnēma* used in the sense of the English "memo.") The second-century-C.E. Giessen Papyri, 67.3 *(ap.* LSJ *s.v.),* write of *epistolē hypomnēseōs tōn ergōn.* Here in Second Timothy the communication that Paul received has served to remind him of "the unfeigned faith within you *(tēs en soi anypokritou pisteōs).*" First Timothy 1:5 wrote of *pisteōs anypokritou* (see commentary *in loc.*) in the same sense as here.

*the very same as that which first dwelt in your grandmother, Lois, and in your mother, Eunice, and in you too, I am convinced.* That "unfeigned faith" of which Paul has just received a reminder is the very same (*hētis* = simple relative; BAGD say it's typical of Luke; cf. 1 Tim 3:15) as "that which first dwelt *(enōikēsen prōton)* in your grandmother, Lois, and your mother, Eunice." *Enoikein* occurs below in 1:14 with the Holy Spirit as subject. This verb occurs in the NT only in the Paulines, at Rom 7:17 (sin dwelling in man); 8:11 (of the Spirit); 2 Cor 6:16 (of God, referring to a non-LXX form of Lev 26:11-12); and Col 3:16 (of "the word [*logos*] of Christ"). See the form *oidein* that occurred above, in 1 Tim 6:16, of God. The passage here in the PE seems to be particularly close to the sense of Col 3:16 where "the *logos* of Christ" is the revelation (gospel) as preached (Lohse, *Col,* p. 150). Only a variant reading in *Barn.* 16.10 documents this term in the Ap. Frs. It occurs about forty-four times in the LXX with by far the greatest number in Isaiah and Jeremiah, but with no close parallel to the usage here, except for the fact that it is *persons* who are the usual subject of this verb. This may say something of the way in which the PE conceived of both the Spirit and the faith, not to mention the way in which the church is "the house" of the living God (cf. 1 Tim 3:15).

That faith had its dwelling first (i.e. before it came to Timothy) in his grandmother *(en tēi mammēi sou),* Lois *(Lōïdi),* and in his mother, Eunice *(kai tēi mētri sou, Eunikēi).* It cannot be settled whether an order of conversion (first, second, third) or a comparison (= *proteron*) between Lois/Eunice and then Timothy is intended. The PE here enlarge with further details the memory of Paul's visits to Lystra (cf. below on 3:11) that are otherwise documented only from Acts 14:6-22 and 16:1-3. The narrative of Acts 16:1 explicitly contrasts Timothy's Greek (= pagan) father with his Jewish mother. That narrative, however, does not transmit her name, though she can be described as *pistēs,* i.e. a (Jewish) *Christian,* on Paul's return visit (Acts 16:1). Timothy, on the same occasion, is *mathētēs,* which in Acts means a Christian believer (cf., e.g., 14:20, 22, 28; and 15:10). Thus either upon the first visit of Paul and Barnabas to Lystra or in the interim, Acts understands that Timothy and his Jewish mother (but apparently not his father; was he already dead?) had become Christians. To these facts this passage of the PE now adds the name not only of that Jewish mother but also of the grandmother, indicating that both had become Christians before Timothy himself. Perhaps one is to think of these women as accepting the Pauline preaching when they heard it in a Jewish gathering for worship (an actual synagogue is not mentioned in connection with Lystra) and then gradually convincing the young son who was growing up as a pagan. If in fact we are dealing with two widows (cf. minusc. 1838 of Acts 16:1 as well as gig and p; Haenchen, *Acts,* p. 479 n. 1) supporting and rearing a child, the scene becomes quite intelligible.

The proper names of the two women may have something to contribute. The mother's name, Eunice, is indisputably Greek but does not occur often (cf. citations in Spicq, *EP,* p. 705). It would be roughly equivalent to the English Victoria. The name is not documented in LXX or *CII* and does not appear to have been taken by Jewish women. Thus its occurrence here may say something to the question of the quality of Judaism from which Timothy's mother came, for her marriage to a pagan was contrary to Jewish law as well (Yebamoth 45b; Haenchen, *Acts,* p. 478 n. 3). If the *mammē* Lois here is actually the mother of Eunice (and not of Timothy's father), one might infer from her name (possibly a Hellenized form of a native Cilician *Lais* [?] — cf. Spicq, *in loc.,* but cf. J. K. Elliott, *Greek Text,* p. 115 — which is also not documented in Jewish sources [i.e. LXX, *CII*]) that the family had not been conspicuous for its observance of the Jewish law. This fact would not really be as inconsistent with their teaching their child about the Jewish Scriptures as W. L. Knox and Haenchen (p. 478) would aver. The women draw upon the one religion that they know for stories to regale their youngster (2 Tim 3:15). Their doing so does not make him a *bar mitzvah!* If their Judaism was lax by some standards (women, after all, were not bound by the Law), it need not have been so by all ("from their fruits you shall know them"), and in this case the home that produced a Timothy was observant enough. In any event, it is their *Christian* faith that is being recalled with joy at this point, a conversion that was the setting for Timothy's own coming to belief. Whether Paul on that first journey through Lystra actually converted Timothy is beyond proof (even though in 1 Cor 4:17 he calls him his "child in the Lord"). It is of course equally conceivable that Lois was the pagan mother of Timothy's pagan father and that after his death she was attracted to the Jewish faith of her daughter-in-law, which appears to have been attractively accommodating (D-C seem to imply this is why she is not mentioned in Acts 16:1). Spicq notes other possibilities *in loc.;* also Gealy, *IB,* pp. 462-463.

The slightly adversative *de,* as the prayer turns to Timothy, makes certain that the preceding comparison will not be taken as critical of Timothy, of whom Paul can say, "I am persuaded *(pepeismai)* that (it is) also *(kai)* in you (*en soi* [which had occurred as this whole clause began])." The perfect passive of *peithein* occurs only here and in 1:12 below in the PE, but on fifty other occasions in the NT, where the Pauline epistolary (with twenty) and the Lukan literature (with twenty-one) have the lion's share. Bultmann, *TDNT* 6.1-11, has noted (with G. Bertram) how the LXX occurrences of *peithein* bring a typically Hellenistic concept of convincing persuasion into the Hebrew biblical tradition where this one Greek verb renders at various times about a dozen different Hebrew roots (according to H-R; Bultmann, pp. 1, 3). In the NT the passive, as here in the PE, has the meaning "to be convinced," which appears not only in the Paulines (e.g., Rom 8:38; 14:14; 15:14) but also in the Lukan corpus (Luke 16:31; 20:6; Acts 5:40; etc.). The Ap. Frs. employ *peithein,* and the closest parallel to the use here in the PE is in Ign. *Trall.* 3.2, *peri hōn pepeismai hymas houtōs echein,* "I am confident that you accept these things" (*Pol.* 2.3; and in Polycarp, *Phil.* 9.2).

The faith that Timothy has received within his Jewish and then Christian home has been paralleled with Paul's own faithfulness to the God of his fathers. The typically Jewish (and OT) stress upon family and forebears as the privileged bearers of divine revelation and direction of their children is behind this parallel.

## II.B. The Present (1:6-12)

*1 6So I, with good reason, remind you, Timothy, to rekindle that gracious gift of God the Father, which is within you through the imposition of these hands of mine; 7for God gave us not a dastard spirit but one of dynamic strength and of charity and of discretion. 8May you not be ashamed about the testimony to our Lord or about me, his prisoner. Instead, along with me take your share of suffering for the gospel, as God gives the strength, 9the God who saved us and called us for a holy life. That saving call did not correspond to our deeds. It corresponded with his own design, his own grace, given us in Christ Jesus from all eternity.* [10]*That gracious design, however, has now been made clear through the revelation of our savior, Christ Jesus. He broke the power of death. He made life and immortality shine forth through the gospel,* [11]*for which I in turn was appointed herald and apostle and teacher.* [12]*Thus I, with good reason too, am undergoing these afflictions, but I am not ashamed of them, for I know the one in whom I have put my faith and I am convinced that he has the power to keep for that Day what has been deposited with me.*

## ♦ NOTES

1:6. *Timothy.* Not in the Greek.

*remind.* The verb *anamimnēiskō* occurs only here in the PE and on five other occasions in the NT, two of which are in the Paulines. In 1 Cor 4:17 it is Timothy who will remind the Corinthians of Paul's "ways"; in 2 Cor 7:15 it is Titus who remembers the conduct of the Corinthians. Hebrews 10:32 with its exhortation, "Recall *(anamimnēskesthe)* the former days when after you were enlightened, you endured a hard struggle with sufferings . . . ," is actually closer to this passage in the PE. Mark 11:21; 14:72 use the word of Peter "being reminded." One must wait until Hermas, *Vis.* 2.1.1, for the single use of this verb in the Ap. Frs. The twenty-five (or fewer) LXX uses do not add anything to understanding this passage in Second Timothy.

*to rekindle. Anazōpyrein* occurs only here in the NT, but twice in the LXX. See also Excursus IV, "The Terminology for Life in the PE," in AB *Titus.*

7. *gave, edōken.* Titus 2:14 uses this verb in the aorist in the phrase "he laid down his life for us," which recurs in 1 Tim 2:6 with the aorist participle *dous* (cf. on 1 Tim 2:6 and 4:14).

*dastard spirit.* Lit. "spirit of cowardice." The noun *deilia* does not otherwise occur in the NT. The cognates of *deilia* are not frequent in the NT (cf. the verb in John 14:27 and the adjective in Mark 4:40 = Matt 8:26 [not in Luke: *SFG* §136]; Rev 21:8), but in all instances they designate the opposite of trusting faith (Spicq). The LXX uses the *deil-* family of terms more frequently, with perhaps ten occurrences of *deilia.* In Sir 4:17 it is parallel to *phobos* (cf. the verbs in LXX Deut 1:21; 31:6, 8; Josh 1:9; 8:1; 10:25). In 1 Macc 4:32 Judas's prayer when he is faced by the enemy is that God "fill them with cowardice *(deilian).*" In 2 Macc 3:24 the effect of the divine epiphany is to throw Heliodorus's bodyguard "into faintness and cowardice *(eis eklysin kai deilian* [cf. Lev 26:36])." In 3 Macc 6:19 another epiphany "filled the army of the adversaries with confusion and terror *(tarachēs kai deilias).*" Finally in 4 Macc 6:20 the aged Eleazar speaks of "being mocked of all men for cowardice *(epi deiliai)*" in the short time of life that would remain for him in any event should he capitulate to his persecutors. The meaning of "personal cowardice" is illustrated by Sostretus's *deilian legeis,* "what do you think I am, a coward?" *Dyscolos,* 123 (Sandbach, *Menandri,* p. 52; cf. the isolated line of *Sikyonios* [441 K, Sandbach, *Menandri,* p. 285]; perhaps only first words are Menander's; cf. Gomme and Sandbach, *Commentary,* p. 671), *kakē men opsis, en de deilaiai phrenes,* "as fierce as his appearance was, the heart was cowardly within."

The Ap. Frs. use the noun *deilia* only in Hermas, *Sim.* 9.21.3, where "the double-minded, when they hear of affliction, become idolators *(eidōlolatrousi)* through their cowardice *(dia tēn deilian),* and they are ashamed of the name of the Lord." The cognates *deilos* and *deilainō* occur only in *Sim.* 9.28.4; 9.1.3; and Ign. *Rom.* 5.2. On the fourteen (fifteen) uses in Josephus, see Concordance, as well as Spicq, who has gathered the secular Greek materials *in loc.* (including Philo).

*dynamic strength.* The PE have not previously employed the noun *dynamis,* though it will occur again in the very next verse as well as in the definition of real versus apparent *eusebeia* at 3:5 below. Of the 118 uses of *dynamis* in the NT, 45 are in the other Paulines (outside of those here in Second Timothy or in Philemon) and 25 in Luke-Acts (none in John or First, Second, and Third John). The PE tend toward the Lukan rather than the Pauline proportion in their usage. It takes over eight columns in H-R to list the LXX uses of *dynamis* that translate as many as two dozen Hebrew roots. In 164 of these instances the root *ḥyl* is being rendered (Grundmann, *TDNT* 2.285). The Ap. Frs. use *dynamis* often enough of God the Father and of Jesus, of faith, even of devils, but one must wait until Hermas, *Man.* 11.2, 5, 6, 10, 11, 17, for its explicit linking with the Spirit. On the verb *endynamoō* see 1 Tim 1:12 as well as 2 Tim 2:1 and 4:17; on *dynatos,* 2 Tim 1:12; Titus 1:9.

*charity. Agapē,* in its nine uses in the Timothy correspondence (also Titus 2:2), is always linked with one or more other virtues (if only one, that one is faith) in the PE (see also above on 1 Tim 1:5).

*discretion. Sōphronismos* is found only here in the NT. For discussion of the *sōphro-* cluster of words see Excursus V, "The PE on Salvation," in AB *Titus.*

8. *May you not be ashamed.* The verb *epaischynomai* occurs only in this context in the PE (cf. vv. 12 and 16 below, second person singular). See 2 Tim 2:15 for *anepaischynton.* It is found otherwise in the Paulines only in Rom 1:16; 6:21, the former notably close to this passage of Second Timothy. In the Gospel tradition it occurs only in Mark 8:38 = Luke 9:26, *SFG* §160, but in a collection of Jesus' sayings on the scandal of his disciples sharing their master's suffering and cross. The only other NT uses, Heb 2:11 and 11:16, speak of God or his Son as "not ashamed." The PE do not employ *aischynō, kataischynō, aischynē* (but see 2 Tim 2:15 for *anepaischynton*); however, Titus 1:11 does write of *aischrou kerdous;* Titus 1:7 and 1 Tim 3:8 employ *aischrokerdēs.*

*prisoner.* The term *desmion* occurs only here in the PE (cf. commentary on 2 Tim 1:16 where *tēn halousin* is the object of *ouk epaischynthē*) but fifteen times elsewhere in the NT. In the Paulines it is used only of Paul himself (Eph 3:1; 4:1; Philem 1, 9, always as "prisoner *of Christ Jesus/in the Lord*"). In the Lukan corpus there are six uses of the term, all in Acts (16:25, 27 pl.; 23:18; 25:14, 27; 28:17) and, whenever in the singular, referring to Paul himself (even one of the plural uses includes Paul). The only uses in the Gospels (Mark 15:6 = Matt 27:15-16) refer to the practice of releasing a prisoner on Passover. Hebrews 10:34 refers to the recipients of that letter as having been kind to prisoners, and 13:3 highly commends the practice. The only use of the noun in the Ap. Frs. is in *1 Clem.* 59.4, where the author prays to God, "ransom our prisoners."

The *desm-* cluster of terms is found with some regularity though not frequently in the LXX. None appears to add anything substantive to the usage here in the PE.

*Instead, along with me take your share of suffering for the gospel, as God gives the strength.* Lit. "Join in suffering *(sygkakopathēson)* for the gospel *(euaggeliōi)* according to God's power *(kata dynamin theou)*." The verb *sygkakopathein,* which will recur at 2 Tim 2:3, is not otherwise documented in the NT, the LXX, or the Ap. Frs. and resembles nothing more than the *syn-* neologisms in the other Paulines. There seems to be no secular Greek use of the term outside of the scholion on Euripides, *Hecuba* 203 (*apud* Harrison, *Paulines,* p. 133), and only a few fourth-century and later Christian works (Lampe, *PGL s.v.,* p. 1267).

9. *called us for a holy life.* Lit. "called (us) with a holy calling *(katesantos klēsei hagiai)*." The noun *klēsis* (eleven times in NT) is otherwise not found in the PE. Though there are eight other Pauline uses (K. Schmidt, *TDNT* 3.491-493, calls it a technical Pauline term, p. 492), the noun is not found in the Gospels or Acts.

The LXX uses *klēsis* only three times: in Jth 12:10 (A) of Holofernes' ill-fated banquet, ". . . he did not call for the invitation (*ouk ekalesen eis tēn klēsin* [cf. LSJ *s.v.*]) of any of his officers" (B here reads *chrēsin,* in the sense of "acquaintance, intimacy"; cf. LSJ, *s.v.*). LXX Jer 38:6 (contrast MT 31:6) reads: "There will be a day of calling (= invitation) for those defending *(apologoumenōn)* in the hill country of Ephraim. Rise up and go up to Sion, to the Lord our God." Finally in 3 Macc 5:14 the term is in the plural for the man in charge of *invitations* to the royal banquet (Charles, *AP* 1.169). The usage of the LXX corresponds rather closely to that of secular Hellenistic Greek and obviously differs from that in Paul (Schmidt, pp. 492-493). This passage of the PE, on the other hand, is quite Pauline in the way in which it understands the "holy calling," extended by the saving God and lived out in response to his election.

In the Ap. Frs., *1 Clem.* 46.6 contrasts the fragmented church of Corinth with their *mia klēsis en Christōi* (the whole section is filled with allusions to Eph 4:4-6). *Barnabas* 16.9 lists "the calling of his [God's] promise" immediately after "the word of faith" as the means by which God dwells in each Christian as in his temple. Hermas, *Man.* 4.3.6, uses the term to describe the baptismal repentance, and *Sim.* 8.11.1 reads, "But the Lord, being long-suffering, wishes *(thelei)* those who were called *(tēn klēsin tēn genomenēn)* through his Son to be saved *(sōzesthai)*." They never speak of "being called with a calling."

On God's call into eternal life *(eis hēn eklēthēs)*, see 1 Tim 6:12.

*It corresponded with his own design, his own grace.* Lit. "but according to his own purpose and grace." *Prothesis*, "design," is used in four of twelve NT occurrences of "the bread offered to God" (Heb 9:2; Mark 2:26 = Matt 12:4 = Luke 6:4). Paul uses the word in Rom 8:28; 9:11; Eph 1:11; 3:11; only he, in the NT, employs the verb, *protithemai*, in Rom 1:13 of Paul's intention to come to Rome; 3:25 of Christ Jesus, whom God had put forward as an expiation; and Eph 1:9. The only other uses of the noun are in Acts 11:23; 27:13. C. Maurer, *TDNT* 8.165, has noted that the nineteen LXX uses of the noun are not usually of purpose or design and even when they are, the design is that of men (cf. 2 Macc 3:8 of "the king's purpose" and 3 Macc 1:22; 2:26; 5:12, 29), not of God. This sense appears in Rom 1:13 (verb) as well as the two uses of the noun in Acts *ut cit. supra* and in 2 Tim 3:10 below. The one use of the noun in the Ap. Frs., in *1 Clem.* 45.7, is similar, as it describes the men in the fiery furnace "who served God with a holy and faultless purpose."

10. *made clear.* On *phaneroō* see Titus 1:3 where "the infallible God" is the subject of *ephanerōsen de . . . ton logon autou* in a schema that resembles the one here in Second Timothy.

*the revelation of our savior, Christ Jesus.* In nine of the PE's ten uses of *sōter*, it is preceded by "our," for apart from the community of persons that he has saved, the savior is inconceivable.

*Epiphan-* terminology, apart from that in the PE, occurs in the NT only in Luke 1:78-79, of Zechariah's hymn about "the Dawn from on High" giving light to those sitting in darkness, and in Acts 27:20, referring to the despair that overtook Paul's shipmates on the storm-tossed sea, who were lost in darkness "when for days on end neither sun nor stars appeared." The most frequent use of the term in the LXX refers to the Lord's face *(prosōpon)* being revealed to worshippers of him; only *First Clement* of the Ap. Frs. takes up this Septuagintal use of the term (59.4; 60:3). *Epiphaneia* itself appears only once outside the PE, in 2 Thess 2:8, "the appearance of his presence *(parousia)*"; in the PE it also occurs attached to one or more (pro-)nouns which signify Jesus: 1 Tim 6:14, "of our Lord, Jesus Christ"; 2 Tim 4:1, 8, "his revelation"; and here, "of our savior, Christ Jesus." In the Ap. Frs. it refers only to the future "day of revelation" of the God of Israel in judgment. Of the dozen LXX uses, Amos 5:22 and Esther 5:1c alone designate the arrival or appearance of a human being (see also commentary at 1 Tim 6:14).

*broke the power of death.* Christ Jesus is first described as the person who "broke the power *(katargēsantos)* of death *(ton thanaton).*" Neither term appears otherwise in the PE. Of the twenty-seven NT uses of *katargein,* twenty-five are in the Pauline epistolary. In the only LXX uses of the verb, in 2 Esd 4:21, 23; 5:5; 6:8, the meaning is not "to destroy" but "to stop" or "make [persons] cease" to act in the way they had been acting (in this case rebuilding the walls of Jerusalem).

In the Ap. Frs., Ign. *Eph.* 13.2 writes, "There is nothing better than peace, by which every war in heaven and on earth is abolished *(katargeitai).*" Otherwise the verb occurs only in *Barnabas,* but five times there, including 5.6, which appears to take up the terminology of 2 Tim 1:10 in describing Christ's suffering "in order that he might abolish death *(hina katargēsēi ton thanaton).*"

The noun *thanatos* (on the verb, *thnēskein,* see 1 Tim 5:6) occurs 120 times in the NT and on 46 other occasions in the Paulines outside of this single articular use in 2 Tim 1:10 (note the anarthrous "life and immortality" that follow). Still the term does not occur in Galatians, Ephesians, First and Second Thessalonians, or Philemon. Luke-Acts share 15 (7/8) occurrences of the word.

*life and immortality.* On *zōēn* see Excursus IV, "The Terminology for Life in the PE," in AB *Titus.* The cognates of *aphtharsia* are found principally in the Pauline and Petrine correspondence, and the usage in 2 Tim 1:10 presumes the Pauline usage of the term, specifically that of Rom 2:6-7, wherein God renders "to every person according to his works: to those who, by patience in well-doing, seek for glory and honor and immortality *(aphtharsian),* he will give eternal life *(zōēn aiōnion).*" What is called *aphtharsia* from the human viewpoint is *zōēn aiōnios* in the eyes of God.

*shine forth.* The verb *phōtizein* (both transitive and intransitive) occurs only eleven times in the NT, and this is the one use in the PE (another hint that a source is being cited). In the Ap. Frs. the one use of this verb is in the inscription to Ign. *Rom.* where that church is described as "beloved and enlightened *(pephōtismenēi)* by the will (*en thelēmati* [cf. 2 Tim 1:1]) of him who has willed all things that are," i.e. God the Father. Of the LXX uses of *phōtizein,* Neh 9:12, 19 are notable for comparison to this passage in 2 Tim 1:10, for they describe the pillar of fire at the exodus lighting the way *(tēn hodon)* for the refugees from Egypt. See Spicq, *EP,* p. 717, for others.

12. *Thus I, with good reason too, am undergoing these afflictions.* The opening phrase of this verse is, literally, "on account of which reason I also suffer these things." The verb *paschō* occurs only here in the PE, though there are thirty-nine other NT uses, of which six are in the other Paulines and eleven in Luke-Acts.

*he has the power to keep for that Day what has been deposited with me.* Lit. "he is able to keep my deposit unto that day." The only uses of *dynatos (einai)* in the PE occur here and at Titus 1:9. For the Pauline and Lukan use of this phrase see Comment below. The adjective occurs otherwise in the NT thirty times, with ten other uses in the Paulines and ten in Luke-Acts (four/six).

In the Ap. Frs. *dynatos* becomes more frequent in Hermas, but in *1 Clem.* 61.3 God "alone is able to do these things *(ho monos dynatos poiēsai tauta),*" i.e. make rulers govern well, reminding one that God shares his power with men (cf. *1 Clem.* 48.5, "Let a man have power to utter knowledge").

The verb *phylassein* was analyzed above on 1 Tim 5:21, and *parathēkēn/ phylassein* (which will recur at 2 Tim 1:14) at 1 Tim 6:20.

The phrase "that day/those days" occurs forty-nine times in the whole NT, and in the singular form (including here in the PE) twenty-six times. It is notable that in the rest of the Paulines the phrase occurs only when 2 Thess 1:10 says of Jesus, ". . . when he comes on that day *(en tē hēmerai ekeinēi)*. . . ." Moreover, the singular is never found in Hebrews, the Catholic Epistles, or Revelation.

## ♦ COMMENT

1:6. *So I, with good reason, remind you, Timothy, to rekindle that gracious gift of God the Father, which is within you through the imposition of these hands of mine.* With this verse Spicq opens a new section of parenesis, extending to verse 14, as distinct from the preceding thanksgiving prayer. As he notes, however, the terminology here goes back into the preceding verses (thus *anamimnēiskō* to the preceding *mnē* terms; *tou theou* to *tōi theōi;* etc.) and the conjunctive phrase *di' hēn aitian* tightly joins what follows with the preceding verses, just as it does at 1:12 below (this phrase recurs in Titus 1:13, as well as five times in Luke-Acts [Luke 8:47; Acts 10:21; 22:24; 28:18, 20] and once in Hebrews [2:11]). As was noted previously, the phrase is quite Lukan (and non-Pauline). The repetition of it in this context leads one to suggest that it is being used as a formal marker for an inclusion among three closely joined sections of one compositional unit rather than simply as a bridge between two quite separate forms of composition (cf. the way in which it is related to the quotation in Titus 1:12 and the prescriptions for dealing with true and false teaching in the context). If that is really the case, then verses 6-11 or 12 as well as 13-14 are constituent parts of the thanksgiving prayer, whose central dogmatic core (as Spicq aptly notes) is the lengthy sentence that takes up verses 8-11 (cf. the similar theologoumenon in 1 Tim 1:15).

The faith that has just been spoken of becomes the ground and basis now for Paul's personal reminder *(anamimnēiskō)* to his young co-worker to renew the divine gift that has come to him through an act of the apostle. Paul's reminder is "to rekindle *(anazōpyrein)* the gift of God *(to charisma tou theou).*" The latter phrase was analyzed when it occurred in 1 Tim 4:14. *Anazōpyrein* occurs only here in the NT, but twice in the LXX. First Maccabees 13:7 has a form of this verb when it says after Simon's speech, "He rekindled *(anezōpyrēsen)* the spirit of the people as they listened to these words." LXX Gen 45:27 says of the aged Jacob, when he received the news from his sons that Joseph was indeed alive, "The spirit of their father Jacob revived *(anezōpyrēsen to pneuma).*" In the Ap. Frs., *1 Clem.* 27.3 writes, "Let therefore faith in him be rekindled *(anazōpyrēsatō)* in us." Ign. *Eph.* 1.1 writes of the Ephesians, "You are imitators of God and having rekindled *(anazōpyrēsantes)* your natural work in the blood of God, you completed it perfectly." Spicq reviews the use of the verb in the Hellenistic texts, including the five in Josephus (cf. the noun in *Ant.* 12.327) as well as several texts in Philo that are related conceptually though not verbally to 2 Tim 1:6 (*Joseph* 4, 124, the latter being particularly apt). The OT association of this verb with the human "spirit" *(pneuma)* made it also an appropriate one for describing a rekindling of the gift of the divine Spirit *(tou theou)* that will be explicitly described in the verse following. This *charisma,* a fire from heaven, burns as long as there is fuel, but it requires man's attentive concentration to make it flare up with light and warmth.

The *charisma* is described as that "which is within you *(en soi)* through *(dia)* the imposition of these hands of mine." The repetition of the second person singular yet again (the eighth time) in this prayer stresses the highly personal and individual character of the relationship between the apostle and his co-worker/successor (D-C). The *charisma tou theou* is *en soi* as faith was *en soi* in verse 5 *(bis).* This was also the phrase in 1 Tim 4:14, which went on to speak of the *charisma* as that "given to you under prophetic direction *(dia prophēteias),* with *(meta)* an imposition of the hands of the presbytery." Here in Second Timothy the preposition *dia* has replaced *meta* and we read that the charism has come *dia tēs epitheseōs tōn cheirōn mou.* What occurred through the instrumentality of prophetic interventions can also occur "through" the (ritual) action of Paul. D-C, p. 98, probably protest too much when they aver that *dia* "must not be accorded too much importance."

7. *for God gave us not a dastard spirit but one of dynamic strength and of charity and of discretion.* God the Father *(ho theos),* to whom this whole thanksgiving prayer is addressed (v. 3) and whose gift *(charisma)* is in Timothy, is next described as the one who "gave (*edōken* [aorist]) us *(hēmin)* a spirit *(pneuma). . . .*" Here for the first time in this prayer, which has thus far shuttled between "I-you" (sg.), the first person plural occurs, joining both Paul and Timothy as the personal objects of the divine operation, and from this point on

*hēmōn* (8, 9, 10), *hēmas* (9), and *hēmin* (9, 14) occur regularly (along with "I-you").

Timothy as well as Paul received *pneuma* that in this anarthrous form refers to the gifts or effects of the Holy Spirit rather than the Spirit personally (cf. Titus 3:5; 2 Tim 1:14; Spicq, *EP*, p. 709). Just as the divine *charis* produced *charisma,* the divine "breathing" *(pnein)* into a man produces *pneuma* (cf. God's breathing into Sacred Scripture, making it all *theopneustos,* 2 Tim 3:16). This gift is first described negatively, "for God did not give us a dastard spirit *(pneuma deilias).*" The whole phrase sounds like Rom 8:15, *ou gar elabete pneuma douleias,* and conceptually it is not far off either. D-C, p. 98, hold for "a genuine Pauline thought" being deliberately pressed into service at this point. Again one is tempted to infer that the author-redactor had some knowledge of Romans, perhaps via the community that received that letter rather than from the text itself. It may be no accident that Second Timothy professes to have a Roman origin (cf. 1:17; 4:19, 21).

The "spirit" bestowed by God is next defined, in opposition *(alla)* to a cowardly spirit, as one "of dynamic strength and of charity and discretion *(dynameōs kai agapēs kai sōphronismou).*" It is almost pleonastic to join *pneuma* with *dynamis* (and in fact that may be why *pneuma* is not repeated at this point; contrast Rom 8:15). W. Grundmann, *TDNT* 2.284-317, has pointed out that in the Lukan literature as well as for the Pauline epistolary the apostles are filled with *pneuma/dynamis* that manifests itself in wonderful acts ("signs and wonders") as well as in words (cf. pp. 310-313). In the Paulines the link between Spirit-power *(dynamis)* and miracles is verified not only in the apostle's ministry (cf. Rom 15:18-19 with 2 Cor 12:12 and 1 Cor 2:4) but also in the lives of his converts (Gal 3:5; 1 Cor 12:7-12, 28-30). It is notable that in Luke it is not only Jesus (Acts 2:22; 10:38; Luke 4:14, 36) and the Spirit-filled apostles who receive and exercise *dynamis,* working miracles (cf. Acts 1:8; 4:7-10; of Paul in 19:11), but also those who share the apostolic ministry. Thus Stephen is introduced as "a man full of faith *(pisteōs)* and Holy Spirit [anarthrous]," but after the imposition of hands is said to be "full of grace and power *(charitos kai dynameōs),*" so that "he kept doing great signs and wonders among the people" (Acts 6:5, 8). The parallel with 2 Tim 1:6-7 hardly needs mentioning. If this explanation of a *pneuma dynameōs* here in the PE is correct, then one is encountering here the only reference in this correspondence to Paul as a worker of miracles. In the reluctance to emphasize this aspect of the apostolic ministry the PE are in harmony with the rest of the Pauline epistolary and are, so to speak, "in character." As 2 Tim 3:8 will give occasion to note, this correspondence, not to mention Luke-Acts (cf. Acts 8:10, 13), is quite aware of the ambiguities of the miraculous.

Here in 2 Tim 1:7 the contrast with a spirit of cowardice is further heightened by description of the spirit that God has bestowed on the apostle and his co-worker as one "of charity *(agapēs)*." The polysyndetic *kai* that joins this trio of virtues ensures that charity will be taken with the preceding *dynamis*. Spicq has observed that this is the only time in the PE that *agapē* is not listed with *pistis* (*Agape* 2.411), but the whole preceding section was precisely on Timothy's faith. Here *agapē*, which *per se* could refer to God's love for man, to man's love for God, or to man's love for neighbor, surely refers to man's *agapē* and probably to man's love for neighbor, as in "the harvest of the Spirit" in Gal 5:22 (cf. Rom 12:11) — thus Spicq, *Agape* 2.412. If indeed the preceding *dynameōs* was a reference to apostolic miracles, then the immediate mention of charity toward neighbor is in the best Pauline tradition, as 1 Cor 13:1-2 illustrates.

The final term in this trio, *sōphronismou*, is otherwise undocumented in the NT, the LXX, or the Ap. Frs., and because the other terms were familiar "biblical" terms, this final noun has a startling sound in its context. The *sōphrō-* terminology, of course, is familiar in the PE, and the term here ought to be read in the light of Titus 1:8; 2:2, 4, 5, 6, 12; 1 Tim 2:9, 15; 3:2 (see commentary *in loc.*). Spicq (*Agape* 3.50 n. 1, French ed.) has noted that the word is somewhat stronger than *sōphrosynē* and is related to it as *logismos* (reasoning) is to *logos* (reason). In secular Greek this noun begins to appear in the first centuries B.C.E. and C.E. with Strabo 1.2.3 and then in Philo, *Leg. alleg.* 3.193, "And if you consent to become a slave of the wise one, you shall cast from yourself ignorance and boorishness . . . and be partaker of admonition and correction *(nouthesias kai sōphronismou koinōnēseis)*." Josephus uses the noun in *War* 2.9 = *Ant.* 17.210 of an officer trying to persuade people to act reasonably and sensibly *(epi sōphronismōi)*. The uses in Plutarch (Spicq, *EP*, p. 710; Harrison, *Paulines*, p. 133; cf. LSJ *s.v.* for references) vary between an intransitive and a transitive sense (self-control/teaching of moderation).

The stress here is upon a *charisma* that is ordered to fearless service of others (miracles; fraternal charity), in which case the question is not Timothy's (or Paul's) personal moderation but their grace for persuading others to adopt it (on *charis* teaching one to live *sōphronōs*, cf. Titus 2:12, and note the older women giving formation in sensible living to the younger in Titus 2:4). There is no more reason to divorce this charism for teaching from the apostolic office (or ministry) than to disassociate miracles or charity from it. Obviously to have said that these functions belong to that office is not to say that *only* those who have that office can work miracles, engage in charity, or teach.

8. *May you not be ashamed about the testimony to our Lord or about me, his prisoner.* With this verse begins the long (seventy-nine-word), densely written sentence that extends through verse 11, to form the generative dogmatic core of this prayer. The conjunctive *oun* here grounds the *mē . . . epaischynthēis* upon the preceding pneumatic charism conferred by laying on of hands (cf. and contrast the uses of *oun* in 1 Tim 2:1, 8; 3:2; 5:14; as well as below at 2:1, 21).

Bultmann, *TDNT* 1.189-191, has described and documented the way in which the NT usage takes that of the LXX ("to shame," "to be shamed, confounded, exposed" by the judgment of God); however, he has observed (p. 190) that here in 2 Tim 1:8, 12, 16 the old basic secular sense of "being ashamed . . . of a dubious person or cause" is at the fore. In these verses it is the witnessing to Christ and the prisoner-apostle, herald, and teacher in handcuffs that is viewed as a cause for shame and that occasions the negative injunction for Timothy, *mē . . . epaischynthēis.* Note the uses of the verb in the Ap. Frs. where Ign. *Smyrn.* 10.2 refers first to the fact that the Smyrnean believers did not regard his fetters *(ta desma . . . oude epēischynthēte)* as shameful and then promises that Jesus Christ "shall not be ashamed of you *(epaischythēsetai),*" apparently on the day of judgment (cf. the citations of Mark 8:38 = Luke 9:26 in notes and below on Barrett). Hermas writes only of (not) being ashamed of "the name of the Lord" (*Sim.* 8.6.4; 9.14.6; 9.21.3).

But what precisely then does the negative injunction here in 2 Tim 1:8 mean? What sort of action (or nonaction) is being counseled? Something more than a rhetorical litotes seems to be involved (Spicq) which would amount to an exhortation to be proud of (to make your boast about — cf. 2 Cor 10:8, 17; 11:30) the apostolic witness *(martyrion).* The second and parallel half of this verse makes joint suffering for the gospel the equivalent of not being ashamed of the apostolic witness, and it has been repeatedly noted that the allusion to "I am not ashamed of the gospel, for it is the power of God . . ." *(ou gar epaischynomai to euaggelion, dynamis gar theou estin . . .)* in Rom 1:16 is "probably intentional" (D-C, p. 99). But that passage, too, is not crystal clear. Again a mere litotes does not seem satisfying. From Chrysostom to Barrett exegetes have suggested a "psychological" horizon for understanding this passage, contrasting the provincial Jew, Paul, with the metropolitan pagan colossus astride him. There is really no evidence that this romantic, Promethean mentality was actually shared by Paul. He after all was actually writing to his brother believers in the capital, not to Rome itself (cf. Rom 1:13, 15). There is no hard evidence that they suspected his credentials. This lack of a ready answer drives the interpreter back to Paul's theology for an understanding of the phrase, and two studies must be noted: Grayston, "Not Ashamed" 2.569-573, and Barrett, who has returned to the subject in his *NT Essays,* pp. 116-143. With Grayston one could say that Paul is here declaring that he is quite unaware of having done any wrong by announcing a gospel of God's grace for *all* men, all alike sinners. He has not thus encouraged sin. He has not canceled the promises to Israel. He has nothing to be ashamed of in his teaching. Yet one could criticize this suggestion as still over-psychologizing.

Barrett's far more complex and comprehensive argument appears to offer a more solid theological ground for the Pauline affirmation. At the same time, and as a happy side effect, it seems to explain what this passage of the PE wants to say (regardless of who wrote the PE). Barrett submits that the reason for Paul's confidence in not being put to shame is grounded "in the nature of the gospel," antecedent to his social and psychological condition (p. 117), and with this in mind he analyzes closely not only Mark 8:38 = Luke 9:26: *SFG* §160 (cited above), but also the great Q logion on the confession/denial *(homologein/arneisthai)* in Matt 10:32-33 = Luke 12:8-9 (cf. above on Titus 1:16; 1 Tim 5:8; and 6:12-13; as well as 2 Tim 2:12, *infra*). He concludes that the Pauline "I am not ashamed of the gospel" is closely related to the teaching of those sayings of Jesus that linked a man's shame over or denial of Jesus on earth with the shame/denial that will meet that man on judgment day. That shame or denial can extend not only to the person and life of Jesus but also to his teaching (p. 131). The "precise opposite" (p. 141) of this denial is the confession of faith. A person's future fate before God is determined by that person's attitude at this moment toward Jesus of Nazareth. Thus Paul's "I am not ashamed of the gospel" means "I confess my faith in the crucified and risen Christ, in what he did and taught."

That meaning in Romans coincides with the meaning here in 2 Tim 1:8, as well as at 12 and 16 below. Here Timothy is exhorted "not [to] be ashamed about the testimony *(to martyrion)* to our Lord or about me, his prisoner." *To martyrion* refers, as above in 1 Tim 2:6, to the *apostolic* witness to what God has done for humankind in Christ Jesus. That witnessing appears to include not only words but actions (D-C). Here that is all packed into the objective genitive of the phrase *tou kyriou hēmōn* (cf. the same phrase used possessively in 1 Tim 1:14, also in a thanksgiving prayer, of the abounding grace "of our Lord," as well as its use along with the title Jesus Christ in 1 Tim 1:2 and 2 Tim 1:2; the omission of *hēmōn* in S*. 104. 1908 is probably not original according to J. K. Elliott, *Greek Text,* p. 118).

That apostolic witnessing, which Timothy is to believe and not be ashamed of, is then exemplified/specified in terms of Paul himself *(mēde eme)*, suffering as the Lord's own prisoner *(ton desmion autou)*. The final touch is startling. Even as a prisoner Paul is to be regarded with faith, for he is Christ's prisoner (not Nero's). His visible fate constitutes an embarrassment and a compromise that could tempt a man to apostasy. But he asks Timothy to face that squarely and to believe in the prisoner witness to a crucified Christ.

The usage of *desmios,* "prisoner," here is to be compared with 2 Tim 2:9, where the persecuted apostle speaks of "my gospel for which I am suffering *(kakopathō)* even to fetters *(mechri desmōn)* as if a criminal *(hōs kakourgos)*." There are seventeen other uses of *desmos* in the NT, of which seven are in the other Paulines, always in the plural and usually with the first person singular possessive (Phil 1:7, 13, 14, 17; Col 4:18). The chains *(desma)* are Paul's and the prisoner Paul *(desmios)* is Christ's. In Philem 10, Paul, the *desmios Christou,* has begotten the slave Onesimus *en tois desmois,* and in verse 13 these become "the chains of the gospel *(en tois desmois tou euaggeliou),*" i.e. what Paul suffers because of the gospel.

The Lukan literature uses *desmos* seven times. In Luke 8:29 (note the verb *edesmeueto* there; also in Acts 22:4, as well as Matt 23:4) it refers to the actual fetters on a demoniac, and in 13:16 to the "bond" by which Satan had hunched a woman's spine (the only other use in the Gospels refers to the "bond" on a deaf-mute's tongue, Mark 7:35). In Acts (16:26; 20:23; 23:29; 26:29, 31) Paul is always the one in bonds (though in the first citation so also are Barnabas and the other prisoners). In Heb 11:36 the OT men of faith "suffered . . . even chains and imprisonment *(desmōn kai phylakēs)*" that could be contrasted with "the chains of the netherworld *(desmois aïdiois)*" that bind the disobedient angels in Jude 6. Note the predominantly Lukan usage of the rest of the *desm-* cluster: *desmophylax* — Acts 16:23, 27, 36; *desmōtērion* — Acts 5:21, 23; 16:26 (also Matt 11:2); *desmōtēs* — Acts 27:1, 42. On *deō* see 2 Tim 2:9.

In the Ap. Frs. forms of *desmos* are rather more frequent than of *desmios.* Thus *1 Clem.* 5.6 writes of Paul *heptakis desma phoresas,* "seven times he was in bonds." One wonders what sources, if any, were used for this count, since 2 Cor 11:23 (cf. 6:5) speaks generically *en phylakais perissoterōs,* and in Acts only two imprisonments are recorded, the short one in Philippi, Acts 16:23-26, and the long one, from Jerusalem through Caesarea to Rome, that began in Acts 21:33. Or is this just a way of saying that there are seven documents available to Clement that describe Paul as a prisoner, regardless of whether some documents come from the same imprisonment or describe more than one? In this case *First Clement* knows of Acts, Second Corinthians, Ephesians, Colossians, Philippians, Philemon, and Second Timothy. *First Clement* 49.2 writes of "the bond of the love of God," and 55.2 speaks of Christians who, to ransom others, have surrendered themselves *eis desma.* In *2 Clem.* 20.4 God loads the unjust spirit "with bonds *(desmois).*" It is, of course, in the letters of the prisoner-bishop Ignatius that references to his bonds abound (Ign. *Eph.* 11.2, cited above on 1 Tim 2:9; *Magn.* 1.2; *Trall.* 12.2; *Smyrn.* 10.2, cited above on *epaischynein;* 11.1; and *Pol.* 2.3), though he also uses the term in *Eph.* 19.3 of "the bond of wickedness"; and *Phld.* 8.1, similarly. Polycarp, *Phil.* 1.1, notes how that church "has helped on their way (*propempsasin;* cf. Titus 3:13) . . . those who were bound in chains. . . ." "The leading out from their fetters those who were bound" in *Barn.* 14.7 is substantially a citation of LXX Isa 42:7. It is notable how references to the actual, historical imprisonments of the apostle and of his fellow believers in the next generation predominate in these patristic uses of *desmos.* One recalls, with Jervell, that the history of the apostles and of their churches was conceived of as part of the history of salvation, and above all the actual sufferings of the apostles and believers were seen as an integral part of the suffering of Jesus.

*Instead, along with me take your share of suffering for the gospel, as God gives the strength.* In strong contrast *(alla)* to the preceding negative injunction (with its sensitively hesitant aorist subjunctive; cf. Luke 7:23 = Matt 11:6; Q in *SFG* §106), there now follows a forthright aorist imperative directed to Timothy. As was noted above in connection with not being ashamed of witnessing to our Lord, that apostolic witnessing appears to extend beyond witness in speech to witness in action, including Paul's imprisonment. Here Paul's co-worker is summoned to endure sufferings himself along with Paul, for to share the apostolic ministry is to share not only the work of the apostle but the world's reaction to that work (cf. W. Michaelis, *TDNT* 5.937).

This co-suffering with Paul is specified as *tōi euaggeliōi,* a noun that occurred in the opening of First Timothy (1:11) and that will recur here in verse 10 and finally at 2:8. D. Hall, "Fellow Workers," pp. 119-120, has suggested that the dative here is not that of advantage/disadvantage (thus meaning suffering for the good of the gospel). Rather, he suggests, it is the object of the *syn-* in this compound, and thus the phrase means "share suffering with the gospel" that is thus practically personified as a living word that cannot be bound (2 Tim 2:9). He has compared the usage of Phil 1:27 and 3 John 8. One might add that the most influential parallels for this construction are the context here and that *sygkakopathein* is to *euaggeliōi* what *epaischynesthai* is to *martyrion/eme.* Thus the witnessing to the Lord, the imprisoned apostle, and the gospel are parts of a single reality that is to be confessed, believed in (i.e. not be ashamed of), and suffered with. Yet one must admit that the personification of the gospel is not close to the surface in any of its uses in the PE and the concept of a "suffering gospel" is even more unexampled. Indeed, the point of 2 Tim 2:9 is precisely that the word of God *has not been* (and presumably cannot be) put in prison. Moreover, since the verb is used absolutely in its one other occurrence at 2:3 below (with at most a reference back to the speaker being understood), this translation still opts for the dative of advantage.

Suffering for the gospel is here described in an adverbial phrase like *kata dynamin theou.* The anarthrous usage here may be due to the preposition (J. K. Elliott, *Greek Text,* p. 118), but in any event the reference must be to the spirit of power *(dynameōs)* that God *(ho theos)* had bestowed on Timothy through Paul's ordaining him (1:6). Here the gospel is likewise filled with "the power of God" who has originated and who sustains it. The phrase again takes one back to Rom 1:16, "I am not ashamed of the gospel," where *to euaggelion* is immediately defined as *dynamis gar theou estin eis sōtēriān panti tōi pisteuonti.* Here in 2 Tim 1:8, *euaggeliōi kata dynamin theou* is immediately followed by *tou sōsantos hēmas.* Thus gospel-power-salvation have an inner linkage that the term *dynamis* expresses (cf. Barrett, *NT Essays*, pp. 139-140) and that calls forth a responding *dynamis* in the believer (cf. 1:7 and 2:1 below).

9. *the God who saved us and called us for a holy life.* It is "God who saved us *(tou sōsantos hēmas)*," i.e. the Father (cf. the savior God *esōsen hēmas* in Titus 3:5); and, as will be said in verse 10, this has occurred *dia tēs epiphaneias tou sōtēros hēmōn Christou Iēsou*, "through the revelation of our savior, Jesus Christ." As the Titus passage had many characteristics of a liturgical confessional composition, so verses 9-10 in 2 Tim 1 have traits that seem to lead back to a liturgical source that is being recalled and alluded to if not actually cited. Spicq notes (with D-C, Norden, et al.) the participial constructions, the careful balancing of clauses, the antitheses, as all pointing in this direction. *Per se* one cannot determine from literary analysis whether one is dealing with a Pauline (and Lukan) reworking of a liturgical confession or a liturgical confession that, of set purpose and with no little success, summarized the Pauline teaching, especially as found in Paul's letter to the Roman church. This commentary opts for the latter, submitting that one reads here a Lukan redaction of a (Roman?) liturgical confession (used at an ordination ceremony [?] even for "Timothy" [?], thus Gealy, *IB*, *in loc.*) that was in its turn based on the Pauline teaching (not necessarily written teaching) to a Christian congregation between 55 and 65 C.E.

The first person plural, *hēmas*, here surely refers to the church of which Paul and Timothy are part, and that God has saved and called with a holy calling *(kalesantos klēsei hagiai)*. It is difficult to say whether the cognate *ekklēsia* is being suggested by the *kalein-klēsis* terminology here. The phrase "to call with a calling" occurs only in the Paulines in the NT, and then only in 1 Cor 7:20 ("Everyone should remain in the calling in which he was called," referring to single/married state; Jew/Gentile; free/slave) and Eph 4:1 ("I, therefore, a prisoner for the Lord, beg you to lead a life worthy of the calling to which you have been called," that is certainly Christian conduct in general after baptism, cf. 4:4). Barth, AB *Eph*, p. 151 (on *klēsis* in Eph 1:18), notes (with K. L. Schmidt and H. Schlier) that "calling is an act of creation and election. . . . In the Pauline letters the instrument of the call is the gospel. The call is more than an offer: it goes out in the power of God and is effective."

Here in Second Timothy the calling is "holy *(hagiai)*" (cf. the *Holy* Spirit of Titus 3:5 as well as 2 Tim 1:14; the only other use of *hagioi* in the PE is nominal, at 1 Tim 5:10) and thus refers to the baptismal vocation (and that empowered by the Spirit). The Semitism involved in repeating the root of the verb in the object noun has made the sense of the dative *klēsei hagiai* hard to recover. Spicq proposes an instrumental or a modal meaning; i.e. God "called us by means of a holy (baptismal) invitation" or God "called us for a holy calling [i.e. way of life]." The aorist *kalesantos* would lead one to think of a divine call that came at a given past moment in Timothy's life (baptism, ordination?), and thus one might favor the noun's reference to the mode of living out that call in the moral life. Cf. the datives at 2 Tim 3:10; D-C, p. 99, cite 1 Thess 4:7, where . . . *ekalesen hēmas . . . en hagiasmōi* means, "He called us . . . to be holy." (On the distinction from secular or profane callings or states in life, and the debate over the meaning of 1 Cor 7:20 in comparison with 1 Cor 1:26, see K. L. Schmidt, *TDNT* 3.491-492; Condon, "Calling," pp. 71-84.)

*That saving call did not correspond to our deeds. It corresponded with his own design, his own grace, given us in Christ Jesus from all eternity.* The mention of the divine rescue and call to a holy way of life evokes immediately a Pauline description of the ground or basis of that divine act. Negatively put, it "did not correspond to our deeds *(ou kata ta erga hēmōn).*" The phrase (see 4:14 below) recalls the similar one of Titus 3:5, *ouk ex ergōn tōn en dikaiosynēi ha epoiēsamen hēmeis,* "no thanks to any upright deeds that we performed ourselves." Salvation does come in accord with (God's) own design *(kata idian prothesin)* and grace *(charin):* that again is reminiscent of Titus 3:5, *alla kata to autou eleos esōsen hēmas,* "but because of his own mercy, save us."

God's rescue is here in Second Timothy "in conformity with his purpose and grace," as in Titus it fitted "his mercy." The term *charis* has been seen often enough in this correspondence thus far (see esp. Titus 2:11 and 1 Tim 1:14), but here it is in hendiadys with *prothesis,* a term that occurs only once otherwise in this correspondence, at 3:10 below. The *idian* reinforces the contrast of the conjunction *alla,* stressing that it is the *divine* purpose, not man's, that brings about salvation.

The use of *prothesis* here in 2 Tim 1:9 is in the specifically Pauline meaning of the altogether and in every sense antecedent plan of God that originated and stood behind all that happened in the life and death and rising of Jesus. The thought as well as the terminology of this verse recalls Rom 8:28, "we know that in everything God works for good with those who love him, who are called according to his purpose *(tois kata prothesin klētois* [cf. 2 Tim 1:9 *kalesantos klēsei*] *ousin).*" The same phrase, *kata prothesin,* recurs in Rom 9:11 (see Käsemann, *Rom.,* p. 264, on its relation to justification) to describe the antecedent character and origin of God's love and call. In Eph 1:11 the phrase again recurs, this time as synonymous with the *kata tēn eudokian autou hēn proetheto* of 1:9. The "purpose" of God is "his good will" that is quite antecedent to his creation (cf. the last occurrence of the phrase, in Eph 3:11, *kata prothesin tōn aiōnōn,* referring to the apostolic mission to bring the Gentiles into God's people).

In this text of Second Timothy the hendiadys of *prothesis* with *charis* practically means "gracious purpose" (cf. the *eudokia* of Eph 1:9) and thus corresponds conceptually with *to auto eleos* in Titus 3:5. This meaning quite precludes any understanding of the divine purpose as an absolute predestination to damnation. Here in Second Timothy, as in the great Pauline texts, it is the personal God of Israel, not an impersonal, mechanistic fate, that is intervening with love in the history of his alienated creatures.

The aorist participial phrase *tēn dotheisan hemin,* "which was/were given to us," could refer to the immediately preceding *charin,* or more likely to the hendiadys *prothesin kai charin,* though the latter term now dominates the thought (as though in English one spoke of "purposeful grace"). The passive here, of course, conceals the divine agent who "gave us" grace, and one notes the use of the active above in verse 7 (cf. the passive 1 Tim 4:14), as well as the *charisma* of verse 6. Behind all this stands Jesus' "giving himself" (Titus 2:14; 1 Tim 2:6). What God gives is mercy *(eleos)* to the living and the dead (2 Tim 1:16, 18), understanding *(synesin)* to his ministers (2 Tim 2:7), and repentance *(metanoian)* to sinners (2 Tim 2:25). Here God's "design . . . [and] grace [were] given us in Christ Jesus *(en Christōi Iēsou),*" a phrase that appeared as this letter opened (2 Tim 1:1) as well as above in 1 Tim 1:14; 3:13. The general prayer context here, as well as the creedal-confessional source, would favor the phrase's being taken in a more personal, unitive sense than some (e.g., Allan) would countenance.

The final phrase of this verse, *pro chronōn aiōniōn* ("before the eternal times," exactly as in Titus 1:2; cf. Käsemann, *Rom.,* p. 425), takes up the *pro-* of *prothesis* (as *dotheisan* took up the free gift aspect of *charis*) and in the fashion of Eph 1:9-11 places the divine plan for the incarnation-redemption before all the long ages of the divine promise (see Reicke on temporal "*pro*" in *TDNT* 6.685; also 2 Tim 4:21 below).

10. *That gracious design, however, has now been made clear through the revelation of our savior, Christ Jesus.* That gracious purpose that was a free gift in another order and world (and thus hidden from and inaccessible to humans) has, however (*de* gives a slight contrast here), "now been made clear *(phanerōtheisan . . . nyn)* through the revelation *(dia tēs epiphaneias)* of our savior, Christ Jesus. . . ." This second participial phrase qualifying *prothesis kai charis* adopts a "then/now" schema for the revelation process with some contrast between the divine and human orders, between eternity and time, between the unseen and the seen (cf. on *nyn* in Excursus IV, "The Terminology for Life in the PE," in AB *Titus*). The use of the passive here is paralleled by 1 Tim 3:16, of the Son *hos ephanerōthē en sarki,* which again implies the eternity/time schema. What was there articulated in a dense, hymnic acclamation has here been put into a creedal form which in turn has been laminated into a thanksgiving prayer.

With another form of the Semitizing internal object that was encountered in verse 9, *dia tēs epiphaneias* nominalizes the process designated by *phanerōtheisan.* What 1 Tim 3:16 expressed by *en sarki* is here *dia tēs epi-*

*phaneias tou sōtēros hēmon Christou Iēsou.* The *sōtēr* is the term of God *sōsantos hēmas* (v. 9) as *epiphaneia* was the term of *phaneroun.* Here in 2 Tim 1:10, as was noted previously, *epiphaneia* designates the incarnation, the "manifestation" of God's gracious purpose in the life and death and rising of Jesus, whereas on all other occasions (including 2 Tim 4:1, 8 below) it refers to the glorious manifestation of Jesus for the final judgment. The usage is by no means contradictory to the other passages in this correspondence (which already use the verb *epiphainein* of the incarnation, Titus 2:11; 3:4), but it is different enough to make one suspect that the usage of the creedal source has survived here. Lampe, *PGL s.v.,* p. 538, notes this sense in the Greek Fathers as early as Clement of Alexandria (*Protrep.* I, *PG* 8.61 c), who after quoting Titus 2:11-13 writes, of the Word and Savior, *touto estin to aisma to kainon, hē epiphaneia hē nyn eklampsasa en hēmin . . . ,* "This is the new song, the epiphany that now has shown forth among us. . . ." In his *Stromata* 6.17; *PG* 9.393b, he speaks of teaching by giving commands and says, *toioutos kai ho kata tēn epiphaneian tou kyriou tropos,* "such also was the Lord's way *when he came,*" literally, "And such is the manner in accord with the Lord's epiphany."

*He broke the power of death. He made life and immortality shine forth through the gospel.* Two further participial phrases next telescope out of the name of Christ Jesus and are set within the classic *men . . . de* correlative particles, which, curiously, occur in this correspondence only in Second Timothy (also below at 2:20; 4:4), though some other Pauline letters do not use the construction either (Colossians [see Lohse, *Col,* on 1:23], First and Second Thessalonians, Philemon). When the PE do use *men* it is always correlated with *de.*

Christ Jesus is first described as the person who "broke the power *(katargēsantos)* of death *(ton thanaton).*" Neither term appears otherwise in the PE, another clue perhaps to the use of a source at this point. Luke 13:7 uses the term of the barren fig tree "idling" or "making useless" the ground on which it grows. Hebrews 2:14, however, uses the term along with *thanatos* to speak of the mortal nature taken by the Son "that through death *(dia tou thanatou)* he might make powerless *(katargēsēi)* him who has the power of death *(to kratos . . . tou thanatou),* that is, the devil." For all the Pauline uses of *katargein* (in relation to faith, the law, the promise, the sinful body, prophecy, knowledge, etc.; cf. G. Delling, *TDNT* 1.452-454), only once, in 1 Cor 15:26 (cf. 24), does he write of "nullifying" death: "the last enemy to be made impotent is death *(eschatos echthros katargeitai ho thanatos).*" The passage in Second Timothy is parallel with this in its terminology, in its quasi personification of death, in its attributing the action to Jesus (cf. Conzelmann, *1 Cor.,* p. 273). The passages differ in that Second Timothy has an active aorist versus First Corinthians's passive, present (= future). Thus what in First Corinthians is going to happen finally, here in Second Timothy is confessed to have occurred *in Christ Jesus,* crucified and risen. The translation of *katargein* with the English "to destroy" may convey the wrong impression, for the basic sense of the verb is "to make completely inoperative, to put out of use" (Delling, *TDNT* 1.453; see also Wink, *Powers*, p. 52 n. 37).

R. Bultmann, *TDNT* 3.7-25, has noted (p. 18) how in this passage of the PE as well as elsewhere in the NT the inevitable destructive power of death is the horizon for human existence, a horizon that Jesus crossed and recrossed. All we know of what is beyond that horizon of mortality comes through him. Indeed, the horizon itself, death, loses its absolute character, becomes relativized and ultimately inoperative, because of Jesus' passage through the worst death men could fashion into indestructible life. This passage stresses what occurred when *he* shared in our human death; at 2 Tim 2:11 the emphasis will shift to *our* share in his dying (*synapethanomen:* see commentary *in loc.*).

What turned off the power of death also turned on the light *(phōtisantos)* of life *(zōēn)* and immortality *(aphtharsian).* Here in 2 Tim 1:10 Christ has made to "shine forth through the gospel" life and immortality (cf. Conzelmann, *TDNT* 9.349, on parallels to *Corpus Hermeticum*). The aorist participle *phōtisantos* points to a given, once-for-all action that brought light, just as the preceding *katargēsantos* indicated a single action that nullified death. The cross did that; the resurrection brought to light life (as opposed to the preceding *ho thanatos*) and immortality (i.e. as opposed to the corruption that death entails).

In the three Pauline uses outside of the PE, 1 Cor 4:5 speaks of the Lord on the day of judgment bringing to light (also transitive) things hidden in darkness *(hos kai phōtisei ta krypta tou skotous).* Ephesians 1:18 speaks of "the eyes of the heart having been enlightened *(pephōtismenous)*" by the Spirit to see the hope in store for believers (see Barth, AB *Eph,* pp. 148-150), and 3.9 speaks of Paul the apostle as one who "makes visible (makes *all men see* [*phōtisai*]) what is the plan of the mystery hidden for ages in God" (see Barth, pp. 342-343, for a discussion of the shorter reading; see also B. Metzger, *TCGNT,* p. 603). In these contexts the light is that of the eschaton, of Easter morning bringing the glorified Christ and his life into the night and "death" of merely human existence. It is the light of the Lord, of the Spirit, and of the apostle, each in his own role, and the parallels to the confession here in 2 Tim 1:10-11 are evident. The eschatological connotations of this verb are especially evident in Rev 18:1; 21:23; 22:5, where the (Lord) God himself or his messenger illumines heaven and earth. That eschatological sense may be telescoped back into the sacramental "enlightenment" (baptism? Conzelmann, *TDNT* 9.355, thinks so, not Barth) in Heb 6:4, 10:32. John 1:9 seems to take the enlightening by the Word back to the beginning of each person's existence. The one use of this verb in Luke (11:36) is in his redaction of the puzzling logia on lamps, eyes, and light (*SFG* §192-193). Conzelmann, *TDNT* 9.348-349, proposes that the verb here in the

PE, as elsewhere in the Paulines, designates "disclosure" of knowledge of "the economy of salvation" and that Christ has "effectively manifested" life.

The final phrase of this verse, *dia tou euaggeliou,* seems to include Christ as both conqueror of death and giver of life "through the gospel." On the use of *dia,* cf. above on 2 Tim 1:6 where the charism came "through the imposition of . . . hands." The *euaggelion* has an instrumentality that must be understood "sacramentally"; i.e. it, too, is a sign willed by Christ for bringing forgiveness and life to humankind. On this noun, see the commentary on 1 Tim 1:11. At this point the usage of the Ap. Frs. ought to be introduced. It is notable that there is only one use in *First Clement* (47.2, of the beginning or opening of Paul's preaching mission to the people of Corinth) and one in *Second Clement* (8.5, of a citation of a logion transmitted also in Luke 16:10-12; cf. Donfried, *Setting,* pp. 72-73). It is Ignatius who employs the term most often (eight times), but only in two of his seven letters; see Ign. *Phld.* 5.1-2 *(tris);* 8.2; 9.2 *(bis);* and *Smyrn.* 5.1; 7.2, in the latter of which he writes, ". . . the gospel in which the passion *(to pathos)* has been revealed *(dedēlōtai)* to us and the resurrection has been accomplished *(teteleiōtai).*" For the other uses, see *Did.* 8.2; 11.3; 15.3-4; and *Barn.* 5.9; 8.3.

11. *for which I in turn was appointed herald and apostle and teacher.* The mention of "the gospel" furnishes the transitional element into the final phrase of this long sentence that brings the reader out of the confessional material *(euaggelion)* and back to the first person singular of the confessing, praying apostle. The language is that of 1 Tim 1:12 (also a thanksgiving prayer) and especially 2:7 where, but for a single *kai,* this whole verse appeared previously and with a similar function with regard to the traditional material that had just been cited (see commentary above). The shorter form here is less emotional, more formulaic, than the one in First Timothy. It is also much more cunningly fitted into the total structure of this sentence where each part has telescoped out of the other in the order: God-Grace-Christ-Gospel-Apostle. The Pauline job description, his *ergon* for the gospel, is summed up in the three nouns "herald, apostle, teacher," and one must not fail to note that this task is described literarily within an apostolic prayer.

12. *Thus I, with good reason too, am undergoing these afflictions, but I am not ashamed of them, for I know the one in whom I have put my faith and I am convinced that he has the power to keep for that Day what has been deposited with me. Di' hēn aitian* here corresponds with the opening of verse 6 above, as does *ouk epaischynomai* with *mē . . . epaischynthēis* in verse 8, and *pepeismai* later in this sentence with that word in verse 5. One could infer that the text is deliberately throwing its references across the intervening source materials in order to take up the themes that had been introduced in the first part of this prayer. The opening phrase would thus signal an "inclusion" of all the intervening materials, including this verse 12.

The apostolic work for the gospel is the reason also (*kai:* almost = "naturally"; cf. Michaelis, *TDNT* 5.920) for the apostle's suffering these things *(tauta),* and the neuter plural takes one back to the bound, suffering prisoner of verse 8, as the first person singular in *di' hēn aitian . . . paschō* ("I am undergoing": note the present tense) alludes to the aorist imperative, *sygkakopathēson tōi euaggeliōi,* of verse 8. It is notable that a cluster of cognates formed on the *path-* stem is found here in Second Timothy: *sygkakopathēson* will occur again at 2:3 (as was already noted), *kakopathein* at 2:9 and 4:5, and *pathēma* at 2 Tim 3:11. Otherwise in the PE one meets only *praüpathia* in 1 Tim 6:11.

In this correspondence, the whole cluster always refers to the sufferings of the apostle and the one who shares the apostolic ministry. Michaelis, pp. 912, 920, has noted that Paul does not normally use *paschein* of himself to describe his own sufferings as an apostle but usually employs that term for the sufferings that Christians as a group have to endure (he does use *pathēmata* of his own afflictions; cf. Michaelis, pp. 931-934). Here, however, it is certainly the apostolic task that has just been described that is the reason for his personal suffering and that just as emphatically is no cause at all for personal shame *(all' ouk epaischynomai),* reluctance to confess Christ, and, ultimately, apostasy (cf. exegesis of *epaischynomai* above on 1:8). Indeed, the gospel is really advanced through these afflictions (cf. also 1:8; 2:3).

Already in Luke-Acts as well as in the Ap. Frs. (see Michaelis, pp. 913, 923, for references) *paschein* has the meaning "to die" (also in Hebrews, First Peter) when used of Christ's suffering. More relevant for this passage in Second Timothy, however, is Acts 9:16 (cf. Michaelis, p. 919) where, in the vision to Ananias, the risen Jesus says of Paul that he is the chosen instrument for the apostolate to the Gentiles, "and I will show him how much he must suffer (*dei . . . pathein* [cf. Luke 9:22; 17:25; 24:26; Acts 17:3 where Jesus is spoken of with forms of this phrase, but never anyone else, except Paul here]) for the sake of my name *(hyper tou onomatos mou).*" This passage of the PE appears deliberately to complement this passage in Acts, and both affirm that "only he who suffers for the name (of Jesus) is its bearer" (Michaelis, p. 919), and that apostolic ministry is validated by the apostolic affliction through which the gospel shines. On the ambivalence of *paschein* for Luke, cf. Luke 13:2 and Acts 28:5.

The repeated *p* sounds of this verse tie its terms together, even when they are strongly contrasted as here, *paschō all' ouk epaischynomai.* Then the reason *(gar)* for this inflexible resistance in suffering is grounded in the personal knowledge and experience (*oida;* cf. the use of this verb in Titus 1:16 of "knowing God," and 1 Tim 1:8 of "knowing that the law is fine") of "the one in whom I have put my faith and I am convinced *(hōi pepisteuka kai pepeismai hoti . . .)* that he has the power to keep for that Day what has been deposited with me."

Again the reduplicated *pep-* sounds link this clause together as the prayerful thought of the apostle is depicted as turning in faith and trust (contra Lock, *Commentary,* p. 88, which seems forced; cf. *pisteuein* with the dative at Titus 3:8) to Christ (cf. below on reference of the pronoun). That faith issues in his personal conviction ("and I am persuaded," *pepeismai;* see above on 1:5, which also dealt with *pistis,* but that of Timothy's family rather than Paul's) "that he has the power *(hoti dynatos estin)* to keep *(phylaxai)* for that day *(eis ekeinēn tēn hēmeran)* what has been deposited with me *(parathēkēn mou).*" In Titus 1:9 the phrase *hina dynatos ēi* referred to the presbyter-bishop whose firm grasp on the Christian preaching and teaching would *make it possible* to help his hearers and refute opposing teachers (see Comment at AB *Titus* 1:9). The phrase *dynatos einai* in various forms occurs in both Pauline and Lukan passages, usually of human beings being able (or not) to do something, being capable, having power or strength (as in Titus 1:9; cf., e.g., 2 Cor 12:10; 13:9; Luke 14:31; Acts 11:17). Luke 1:49 uses *ho dynatos* as a divine title (contrast Acts 18:24), and the term is used in relation to God in Luke 18:27 = Mark 10:27 = Matt 19:26 *([panta] dynata para tōi theōi).* Jesus is also *dynatos* in the Lukan tradition (Luke 24:19; cf. Acts 7:22 of Stephen).

It is in the Paulines, however, that it is explicitly said of the Jews, "God has the power *(dynatos gar estin ho theos)* to graft them in again" (Rom 11:23), or of Abraham that he was unwaveringly and "fully convinced *(plērophorētheis)* that God was able to do what he had promised *(ho epēggeltai dynatos estin kai poiēsai)*" (4:21). It is Heb 11:19 that writes of Abraham's faith when told to sacrifice Isaac, that he thought "that God was able to raise someone even from the dead *(kai ek nekrōn egeirein dynatos ho theos).*" This passage of 2 Tim 1:12 is in the Pauline tradition if God is the one who is being spoken of as having the power to preserve his apostle unto judgment day. Yet the text itself, as well as such passages as 2 Tim 2:11-12; 4:1, 8, 17-18, would lead one to submit that the *dynatos* here is the Lord Jesus who has "empowered" and will "empower" his apostle (cf. 1 Tim 1:12; 2 Tim 4:17) with a *pneuma dynameōs* (note the *dyna-* stem) that comes ultimately from the Father, *ho theos* (2 Tim 1:7), for whom all things are possible (cf. *"Abba, ho patēr, panta dynata soi,"* Mark 14:35-36). On God's making Paul's equipment for battle, *dynata,* see 2 Cor 10:4.

Christ is able *tēn parathēkēn mou phylaxai,* which may mean either "to keep my deposit" or "to keep the deposit for me." That is, the *mou* may be either a possessive or an objective genitive. Whereas in 1 Tim 6:20 *parathēkē* had no other qualification than the article, here in Second Timothy it is *kalē* at 1:14 and *mou* at 1:12. The parallel would naturally lead one to prefer the subjective, possessive sense for *mou* (= my) and to interpret the *parathēkē* in the same way whenever this phrase occurs. The objective sense of *mou* would refer to Paul's life, his soul, his salvation as the deposit in Christ's keeping, and this meaning would agree with the immediately preceding context (cf. the authors cited by Spicq, *EP,* p. 719, from Ambrosiaster to J. Dupont). Yet *mou* occurs nine times in this letter (and not elsewhere in the PE!), at 2 Tim 1:3, 6 above as well as at 16; 2:1, 8; 3:10; 4:6, 16 below. When *mou* occurs before nouns in 3:10 and 4:16, it could conceivably be taken objectively, though the position is quite in accord with the possessive sense (BDF §284). In the remaining instances when it follows its noun, it must be interpreted subjectively. Thus *parathēkē mou* is conceptually parallel to *euaggelion mou* of 2 Tim 2:8: it is the Pauline apostolate, the Pauline gospel, the Pauline method and content of preaching and teaching that the Lord keeps watch over "even to that day *(eis ekeinēn tēn hēmeran).*" Paul belongs to the gospel more than the gospel belongs to Paul, and thus the complete confidence that the Lord of the gospel will keep intact the apostolic transmission of that gospel and this correspondence that is a Pauline transmission.

The phrase *eis ekeinēn tēn hēmeran* occurs in the form *en ekeinēi tēi hēmerai* at 2 Tim 1:18 and 4:8 (both dealing with the *kyrios* Jesus and the day of his judging believers, thus leading one again to hold that the Lord Jesus is the one who "keeps the deposit"). In the many occurrences of the singular in the Gospels and Acts it may refer to a given moment in past history (cf., e.g., Acts 2:41; 8:1; Matt 13:1), but more frequently the reference is to "that day" of the final judgment (cf., e.g., Luke 10:12; 17:31; 21:34, and contrast Luke 6:23 of "that day" when one suffers persecution). The phrase in itself could be either Pauline or Lukan; the frequency of its use here in Second Timothy inclines one to see it as Lukan. But note that with *eis* = until (BAGD *s.v.*, p. 228) it is parallel to Phil 1:10 = *eis hēmeran Christou.* In the Ap. Frs., for all the many uses of *hēmera(i),* one reads only twice of "that day," in *2 Clem.* 17.6 ("of judgment") and Hermas, *Sim.* 5.3.7 (of "that day" when one keeps a fast).

In the PE the term *hēmera* itself, which has thus far occurred in the bound phrase "night and day" in 1 Tim 5:5 and 2 Tim 1:3, occurs in the twice-repeated phrase already noted in Second Timothy as well as in 2 Tim 3:1 (see commentary *infra*), where it is used for the only time in the plural in another phrase, *en eschatais hēmerais,* which is conceptually related to 1 Tim 4:1 and its oracle about the apostates *en hysterois kairois.* The phrase in the singular refers to that final day of history, the judgment day of the Lord; in the plural it designates the period of time (the "days") that immediately precede "that day." G. von Rad, *TDNT* 2.943-947, notes that the eschatological phrase "that day" usually refers to a future time in which Yahweh's intervention, judgment, and victory in human history will be manifest in a definitive and ultimate fashion. G. Delling, as he continues that study (*TDNT* 2.947-953), notes the eschatological sense of both *eschatai hēmerai* (as LXX, p. 950) and *ekeinē hē hēmera* "which denotes the all-embracing day of judgment" (p. 952). LXX Isaiah and Zechariah speak most often of "that day" as a time when God definitively intervenes in human history. Delling also notes that the day is defined not in terms of its length or chronological situation but in terms of its content, in this case the judgment. Thus *whenever* Christ judges, that (future) day will have arrived — not vice versa. Time is subject to God and Christ, not vice versa.

The adjective *ekeinos* had been used in Titus 3:7 to designate Christ, but it was not used at all in First Timothy. Here in Second Timothy, outside of this phrase, it will occur again in 2:13 of Christ, in 2:26 of God, and in 3:9 of the magicians Jannes and Jambres.

## II.C. The Future (1:13-14)

*1 [13]With that faith and charity which are yours in Christ Jesus, stick to the model of the wholesome words that you heard from me. [14]Keep that fine deposit, Timothy, through the Holy Spirit who dwells in us.*

### ♦ NOTES

1:13. *With that faith and charity which are yours in Christ Jesus.* Lit. "in faith and charity that (are) in Christ Jesus." On the form of the phrase at this point and its terminology see 1 Tim 1:14, where it occurs with the unusual *meta* instead of *en.*

*model.* On *hypotypōsin* see Notes at 1 Tim 1:16.

14. *through the Holy Spirit who dwells in us.* Regarding *dia pneumatos hagiou,* the Holy Spirit is mentioned explicitly for the first time in the PE at Titus 3:15, in this same phrase (although not governed by *dia* as here). One reads regularly of the Holy Spirit elsewhere in the NT (apart from Second and Third John), and particularly in Luke-Acts and the other Paulines. *To pneuma to hagion* occurs only twice in the LXX (Ps 50:13; Isa 63:10-11), but is used regularly in the Ap. Frs. *Hagios* also qualifies the Christian vocation in 2 Tim 1:9, and is used nominally in 1 Tim 5:10 for Christian travelers who are welcomed by a devout widow. Elsewhere in biblical Greek and early Jewish and Christian literature, the term appears hundreds of times. Noteworthy is the more than seventy citations in both Luke-Acts and the rest of the Paulines, respectively. On *who dwells, enoikountos,* cf. on 2 Tim 1:5 above, of faith.

*Timothy.* Not in the Greek.

### ♦ COMMENT

1:13. *With that faith and charity which are yours in Christ Jesus, stick to the model of the wholesome words that you heard from me.* With the second person singular imperative of this new sentence one is reminded of the similar imperative that in verse 8 began the long dogmatic construct that reached its conclusion in verse 12. Here, however, in the present tense Timothy is commanded, *hypotypōsin eche hygiaionontōn logōn hōn par' emou ēkousas,* "stick to the model of the wholesome words that you heard from me." *Hypotypōsis* occurred above in the Pauline thanksgiving prayer in 1 Tim 1:16 of the life of the apostle himself as example of what the immeasurable mercy of God can do for all. Here the anarthrous *hypotypōsin* is a model or paradigm of "healthy words" (for the phrase see 1 Tim 6:3, where it is the [written?] words of Jesus, and the further references there) that are explicitly described and defined (cf. BDF §270.3) as "those which you heard from me."

The stress upon Timothy's having heard (aorist) at a given past point ensures that the *written* words of this correspondence are not the *logoi* spoken of here (though they are conceived of as a base for a *hypotypōsis* such as that provided here). The *logoi* heard from Paul are in a different order from the written collection of the Lord's *logoi.* One recalls that Luke-Acts do not know of a Pauline correspondence and that the one reference to writing in the PE (1 Tim 3:14) makes the written word of the apostle a stopgap until his personal arrival. E. K. Lee, "Words," pp. 166-173, has described (p. 169) the interrelation of the *deigma/hypodeigma* (sample/suggestion) terminology with the *typos/hypotypōsis* (pattern/outline) terms, singling out the way in which *typos,* referring to written materials, designates the literary form or tenor of a composition (cf. 3 Macc 3:30; Acts 23:25 of letters). The suggestion of a "mold" for casting an image or statue is never far away when *typos* is employed, and that nuance makes the term particularly attractive for denoting ethical training (cf. Titus 2:7; 1 Tim 4:12; cf. also Donelson, *Pseudepig.,* p. 93, for the use of *hypotypōsin* in ethical formation). Moreover, the *typos* is the visible reality that more or less adequately represents at least one aspect of an invisible reality that belongs essentially to another (divine) order.

Can the concrete occasion of Timothy's "hearing" Paul be further specified? One would already infer, from the one previous use of *akouein* in this correspondence at 1 Tim 4:16 (see commentary *in loc.*), that it was the identifiably public teaching of Paul in the (liturgical?) assembly of believers that is being adverted to here in 2 Tim 1:13. This notion seems to be supported by the recurrence of the phrase *ha ēkousas par' emou* in 2 Tim 2:2 below, where *dia pollōn martyrōn* may hint at the complexity of this transmission setting (a Pauline entourage that became a Pauline "school"?). In 2 Tim 2:14 *akouontōn* is used of those who put their faith in the caviling and quibbling of non-Pauline teachers and suffer catastrophe. Finally, in 2 Tim 4:17 it is used of all the pagans "hearing" Paul's public confession of his faith in the setting of his trial (see commentary *in loc.*).

But what then precisely is the sense of *eche* if the *hypotypōsis* here is indeed a visible, written sketch of what Paul once taught orally, an outline of that

Pauline *parathēkē* that the Lord Jesus will protect until judgment day? *Echein* could be understood quite concretely of actually preserving and keeping a written document that has been entrusted to another (cf. Luke 19:20 of the man who kept [*eichon*] the master's *mina* wrapped up in a napkin). *Eche* is here understood as in 1 Tim 3:9 of the deacons, *echontas to mystērion tēs pisteōs en katharai syneidēsei,* where also the final phrase precludes a simply material understanding of *echein.* The usage of 2 Tim 3:5, describing those *echontes morphōsin eusebeias, tēn de dynamin autēs ērnēmenoi,* appears to presuppose an analogous situation among those who "have" (i.e. observe, keep) the visible palpable conventions of religion (the *morphōsis* there would correspond to the *hypotypōsis* here) whereas they deny its real power (i.e., of course, the Spirit of God; cf. 2 Tim 1:7-8).

Here in 2 Tim 1:13 Timothy must keep in "faith and charity which are [his] in Christ Jesus" the *hypotypōsis* of the Pauline teaching. Some commentators have linked this phrase to the immediately preceding *ēkousas* and thus to Timothy's hearing in faith and love (Theodoret), or to *par' emou* and so to Paul's teaching in faith and love (Jeremias?). Some have even understood the whole phrase with the next verse (Weiss). However, in the light of the preceding comments here, it seems best to take it of "keeping" in the fullest sense the Pauline teaching (as here recalled in writing).

14. *Keep that fine deposit, Timothy, through the Holy Spirit who dwells in us.* With this final sentence of the prayer-exhortation, *parathēkēn mou phylaxai* of verse 12 becomes *tēn kalēn parathēkēn phylaxon,* the concluding exhortation of 1 Tim 6:20, with the addition of *kalēn,* which has that suggestion of pleasing visibility which has been noted previously of works, testimony (1 Tim 3:7), and persons (pl.?) (1 Tim 4:6). As Christ sustained and watched over Paul's deposit in verse 12, now Timothy is to do the same, i.e. to act *in persona Christi* with respect to the Pauline apostolate that he shares. Neither Paul nor Timothy performs such a task by virtue of his human powers, and so the final phrase specifies explicitly that this keeping the deposit is "through the Holy Spirit who dwells in us *(en hēmin).*" The same spirit dwells in both the apostle and his coworker, empowering each for his role in visibly transmitting (hence *kalēn*) what Christ invisibly is sustaining and protecting.

## III. PERSONAL NOTE ONE (1:15-18)

*1 [15]You know this, of course, that all those in the province of Asia — to name only Phygelus and Hermogenes — abandoned me. [16]May the Lord, however, grant mercy to the family of Onesiphorus, for time and again he revived my spirits and was unashamed about this manacle on me. [17]Instead, when he came to Rome he hunted for me right away and he found [me]. [18]So may the Lord grant him to find — indeed, he will find mercy from the Lord on that Day. And you know well enough how many services he provided in Ephesus.*

## ♦ NOTES

1:15. *to name only Phygelus and Hermogenes.* Lit. "among whom is Phygelus and Hermogenes." The name Hermogenes does not occur elsewhere in the PE, the NT, the LXX, or the Ap. Frs. The same is true of Phygelus. The names are probably not the result of the author's learned conjecture or fantasy based on Jewish materials (see Comment below; cf. D-C, p. 128, who correctly note at this point the way in which the *Acts of Paul* fantasizes on 2 Tim 4:10 [Hennecke and Schneemelcher, *NT Apoc.* 2.383]). The *Acts of Paul* does not use the name Phygelus (nor Hymenaeus nor Philetus), though it does employ Hermogenes as well as Onesiphorus (Hennecke and Schneemelcher, *NT Apoc.* 2.353-355, 357, 359-360, 364) and Alexander (see Comment).

The name Hermogenes does occur once in a crudely inscribed Roman Jewish epitaph (*CII* 324), but its blatantly pagan meaning ("born of Hermes") may have precluded its widespread use in devout Jewish circles. It is very frequent in the papyri (Spicq). Phygelus is not documented in *CII,* though it does occur in the inscriptions and usually with the spelling here rather than the *Phygellos* of A, the Byzantine tradition generally (J. K. Elliott, *Greek Text,* p. 124). MM *s.v.*, p. 677, note only the *Phygelios* of *CIG* 2.3027. BDF §42.3 note the name in the inscriptions of Ephesus and of Miletus. It appears to be a non-Greek name for a place/person that was confined to the province of Asia. If it is an invention at this point, it is certainly one of the most accurately erudite touches in ancient pseudonymous composition. The balance of probabilities is evidently on the side of this actually being the quite "Asian" name of a man, probably a convert from paganism (BAGD: "Christian") on whom Paul had counted in vain.

*abandoned me.* See Titus 1:14 for this very strong verb, there with "the truth" as its object.

16. *grant mercy to the family of Onesiphorus.* On *didōmi,* "grant," see above in 1:7, 9. For "mercy" *(eleos)* see Titus 3:5; 1 Tim 1:2; and 2 Tim 1:2. On *oikos,* "family," see Titus 1:11; 1 Tim 3:4-5, 12. Nowhere else in the NT does the name Onesiphorus occur, nor in the LXX nor in the Ap. Frs. The name was borne by a Christian martyr at Parium in Mysia (about 175 miles north of Ephesus) in the early second century (see MM *s.v.*, p. 450; and see Spicq, *EP,* pp. 732-733), and the still later legends of the *Acts of Paul* have been noted above. There is no con-

trol whatsoever for even the sober data proffered by that source (e.g., that he came from Iconium: Hennecke and Schneemelcher, *NT Apoc.* 2.353). Even D-C, p. 127, think it "quite possible" that 2 Tim 1:16-18 is transmitting the actual name and actions of this person.

*for time and again he revived my spirits.* The adverb *pollakis,* rendered "time and again," occurs only here in the PE, but of its sixteen other NT occurrences, seven are in Paul (and only one in Luke-Acts, at Acts 26:11). Of the dozen LXX uses of the term, five are in the Maccabean books, and in no instances can a corresponding Hebrew term be identified. In the Ap. Frs. only Hermas, *Vis.* 3.1.2, employs this adverb.

The verb *anapsychein* (classically, to cool by breathing or blowing on; cf. *anazōpyrein* above, 1:6) does not otherwise appear in the NT, but there are seven LXX uses: Exod 23:12 (of the Sabbath rest for slaves); Judg 15:19 (of the refreshment of the thirsty Samson); 1 Sam 16:23 (of David's music refreshing Saul); 2 Sam 16:14 (of David's fleeing entourage refreshing themselves at the Jordan); LXX Ps 38:14 (praying to God, *anes (aniēmi) moi hina anapsyxō pro tou me apelthein kai ouketi mē hyparxō*); 2 Macc 4:46 (the king takes refreshment in a colonnade); and 13:11 (the people beginning to revive from their suffering).

In the Ap. Frs. the verb appears in Ign. *Eph.* 2:1, where the old bishop on his way to martyrdom has been visited by a certain Crocus, who relieved *(anepausen)* him, and he in turn prays, "May the Father of Jesus Christ refresh *(anapsychai)* him in like manner. . . ." In *Trall.* 12.2 that congregation with its presbyters is "to refresh *(anapsychein)* the bishop" with their harmony and prayer.

*unashamed about this manacle on me.* On *epaischynthē* see above on 1:8, 12. Here the *desm-* terminology seen above in 1:8 is specified more closely with *halysis,* the noun for the chain(s) around a prisoner's wrists and/or ankles. There are ten other NT uses, one of Paul in Eph 6:20 as an ambassador "in chains *(en halysei)*" for the mystery of Christ. It is in the Lukan corpus that this term occurs most frequently (five times): Luke 8:29 (cf. Mark 5:3-4: *SFG* §137) writes of the Gerasene demoniac as "kept under guard *(phylassomenos)* and bound with chains *(edesmeueto halysesin)* and fetters *(pedais),* but he broke the bonds *(ta desma).*" In Acts 12:6-7 Peter, arrested and imprisoned by Herod, has been "bound *(dedemenos)* by two chains *(halysesi dysi)*" which fall off "his hands *(ek tōn cheirōn).*" Normally a prisoner was handcuffed to a single guard (hence normally the singular *halysis,* cf. *infra*); here the security is doubled and "fail-safe" (Haenchen, *Acts,* p. 383 n. 5, cites Josephus, *Ant.* 18.196 [which does not employ *halysis*], and Seneca, *Ep. Mor.* 5.7; cf. the scene of Vespasian chopping off Josephus's chain [*diekopse tēn halysin*] with an axe [*War* 4.629, cf. 626]). In Acts 21:33 Paul is treated by the Roman tribune exactly as Peter had been and is "bound with two chains" (Haenchen, *Acts,* p. 617) and thus to two soldiers. In Acts 28:20, where Paul is under a relatively milder confinement, the text has him describe himself as "bound with this chain *(tēn halysin tautēn)* on account of the hope of Israel." One is intended to visualize the single soldier guard at his side.

The one other NT use of this noun is in the vision of Rev 20:1 on the binding of Satan. Unlike all the uses above, it is evidently there part of the figurative language of apocalyptic.

17. *Instead, when he came to Rome he hunted for me right away and he found [me].* Far from being "ashamed" and apprehensive, Onesiphorus "rather *(alla)* when he came to Rome *(genomenos en Rhōmēi)* right away (*spoudaiōs* [see Titus 3:13, cf. 12 = speedily]) hunted for *(ezētēsen)* me and found *(heuren).*" The aorist participle, *genomenos,* = when he came or when he arrived and took up his residence (cf. the *paragenomenos* of MS 642 and J. K. Elliott, *Greek Text,* p. 125), as in Acts 7:38 and especially 13:5, *genomenoi en Salamini,* "When (Barnabas and Paul) arrived in Salamis . . ." (though also see Mark 9:33; Matt 26:6). The use of *en* = *eis* is a Hellenistic (papyri in Spicq) and Septuagintal colloquialism (BDF §218; cf. Tob 5:5). Though the Paulines, including the PE, use *ginesthai en* often enough, there does not seem to be an exact parallel to the meaning here (contrast, e.g., 2 Cor 1:8 as well as 2 Tim 3:11 with this passage).

On the comparative *spoudaioterōs (-on)* here in A. 88 (Ψ, $D^c$, K, L, etc.), see J. K. Elliott, *Greek Text,* p. 125, who favors the reading.

The verb "sought" or "hunted," *zētein,* occurs only here in the PE, but 116 times elsewhere in the NT, including 19 times in the other Paulines (except Galatians and Second Thessalonians) and 35 times in Luke-Acts (25 and 10).

*he found.* The verb *heuren* occurs in these two verses (17-18) of the PE, and 174 times elsewhere in the NT. There are 15 other uses in the Paulines (Romans, First and Second Corinthians, Galatians, Philippians), but 80 in Luke-Acts (45 and 35). Though *heuriskein* is frequent in the Ap. Frs., the "seek/(not) find" schema is relatively rare; cf. *1 Clem.* 57.5 (rather remote) and 21.6 (somewhat closer, esp. with its *hina heurethēte en hēmerai kriseōs*).

18. *on that Day.* On the phrase *en ekeinēi tēi hēmera* see on 1:12 above.

## ♦ COMMENT

These next four verses (15-18) have a notably different character and tone from the preceding, due not least to the names of persons (Phygelus, Hermogenes, Onesiphorus) and places (Asia, Rome, Ephesus) that crop up at every turn, as well as a crabbed and broken style that is rather unlike the smooth, even, sonorous paragraphs that have preceded.

The opening "You [sg.] know this, . . . that . . . *(Oidas touto hoti)*" is evidently transitional and similar to the *oidamen de hoti* . . . and *eidōs touto hoti* . . . of 1 Tim 1:8-9 and cf. even 2 Tim 1:12, *oida gar.* As in the latter passages, *touto* refers to what follows, not to what has preceded (as *tauta* in the PE does). Since this passage closes with a similar *hosa . . . sy ginōskeis* in verse 18, the intervening notices take their special function within this composition from the conceptual framework within which they are presented. As the preceding prayer had emphasized memory, this next section turns to Timothy himself, beginning and closing with what he is well aware of, intending to align the factual notices for a parenetic purpose. The mention of the province of Asia as the notice opens and then the principal city of that province, Ephesus, as this section closes, seems to have a similar "framing" effect, enclosing the lone figure of Onesiphorus (in contrast to the *pantes* of v. 15) in Rome. Of what had happened in Asia and Ephesus, good and bad, Timothy was aware. Of what had occurred in Rome he is here made aware (16-18a).

1:15. *You know this, of course, that all those in the province of Asia — to name only Phygelus and Hermogenes — abandoned me.* What Timothy is aware of must be that day on which Paul was trapped and arrested (not necessarily the tearful day that Paul recalled in the preceding prayer [1:4] that may have preceded the arrest at Troas). Further details are now added. "All who [are] in Asia repudiated me, among whom is Phygelus — and Hermogenes." *Pantes hoi en tēi Asiai* is hyperbolic, even if *all* refers to the Christian believers of the province of Asia (obviously Timothy and Onesiphorus's whole family are exceptions). The point is that the great majority of those Christians who could have helped would have nothing to do with the apostle upon his arrest, and the few who had the courage to remain loyal as a result could do little enough for him. The exaggeration is a natural one for a lonely prisoner and has an undeniable rhetorical effectiveness as well, throwing into high relief the loving loyalty that is about to be narrated.

The elusive character of the incident adverted to here as well known to the recipient of this correspondence can be seen in the various explanations of just who and where are *pantes hoi en tēi Asiai.* The reference to *Asia* here is surely to that great Roman senatorial province, now at the western end of modern Turkey, which extended from the Aegean Sea to the mountains of Pisidia and from Bithynia south to Lycia, an area studded with five hundred cities. The Attalids had willed this kingdom to Rome, and their royal seat, Pergamum, was the "metropolis" of the province, though, as Mommsen has noted (*Provinces,* p. 329), "Ephesus was the *de facto* capital of the province where the governor was obliged to enter on his office, and that boasts of this 'right of reception at landing.'" One can recall how Luke has the Ephesian elders go down to receive Paul when he landed at Miletus in Acts 20:16-17.

To say that "all those Christians from Asia repudiated me," with the aorist *apestraphēsan* referring to a specific occasion known to Timothy, would most naturally refer to the time of Paul's arrest somewhere in that province (Troas?), when to his disappointed surprise he discovered that his Christian brothers did not stand by to help him. The phrase could also mean that the Asian Christians who did stand by and accompany the prisoner apostle to Rome eventually gave up and left for home again, or, finally, that the Asian Christians who already lived in Rome and who could have been expected to help Paul actually left him in the lurch. The latter two interpretations require taking *en tēi Asiai* as equivalent to *apo (ek) tēs Asias,* either a Semitism or a koine colloquialism (cf. Spicq, *EP,* p. 732). Since there is no evidence that the PE or Luke or Paul (cf. their uses of *en tēi Asiai* in Acts 16:6; 20:16; and 2 Cor 1:8, as well as Luke's use of *apo [tēs] Asias* in Acts 6:9) actually used such a construction, the first interpretation is the one preferred here. The one weakness in this explanation is the inexplicable abandonment of the apostle by those with whom he had worked for years. Yet it is no more surprising or unexampled than the analogous abandonment by the Roman Christians and even by his own entourage that is described in 2 Tim 4:9-11, 16.

In this verse, two of Paul's bitter enemies are singled out by name, Phygelus and Hermogenes. In 2:17 another pair, Hymenaeus and Philetus, presumably in Ephesus or its neighborhood, are named. In 4:14 "Alexander, the coppersmith" may also be an Asian and even an Ephesian (or from Troas). Is he the same Alexander whom, along with Hymenaeus (2 Tim 2:17), Paul delivered "to Satan" in 1 Tim 1:20? The names in 1 Tim 1:20 as well as 2 Tim 1:15; 2:17 are all introduced by *hōn estin,* a phrase that is peculiar to the PE (Spicq) and that could indicate that, where the names do recur, the author-redactor of this correspondence, at any rate, takes them as designating the same persons. If that is in fact the case, then "Alexander, the coppersmith" in 2 Tim 4:14 is so styled precisely in order to distinguish him from the Alexander mentioned previously. Both Alexanders are most probably Christians, though whether of Jewish or pagan origin the names do not betray. *CII* 85, 92, 140, 370, 501, 84 (?) illustrate that Jews took this name, as does Acts 4:6, that was very common in the Hellenistic world at large. The famous *crux interpretum* at Acts 19:33 (see Haenchen, *Acts,* p. 574) is quite explicitly about a Jew (19:34), and perhaps that Ephesian is so designated precisely to distinguish him from the Alexanders that are going to be noted in the PE. It is notable in the light of our hypothesis on authorship that the divers Alexanders are nicely distinguished in Acts and the PE.

The one other use of the name in the NT (Mark 15:21), also of a Jew, shows no concern about any confusion. The situation is different in Acts and the PE and probably goes back to a historical situation in which different persons with the same name had to be differentiated. If the PE were inventing the name(s), it is difficult to imagine why this meticulous differentiation would be called for. The author would just pick another name. Such may well be the case in the apocryphal *Acts of Paul and Thecla* 1, where *ho chalkeus* is Hermogenes (Hennecke and Schneemelcher, *NT Apoc.* 2.353, 356-357; a pagan Syrian Alexander occurs also: Hennecke and Schneemelcher 2.360). D-C's extrapolation from this late second-century document and its fantastic lucubrations of Paul's apostolate to substantiate the plausibility of the invention of the names in 2 Tim 1:15; 4:10 (p. 128) is far-fetched. The PE obviously knew of and used legendary materials without a qualm, as 2 Tim 3:8 illustrates. That they were in writing probably gave such materials sufficient "authority" for the use that was being made of them. One cannot exclude the possibility that the names of Paul's enemies belonged to the tradition and even written traditions about the apostle after his death. The author-redactor of these letters may have taken up that tradition or even documents containing it without verifying the facts. It is most unlikely, considering the way in which he handled the names, that he himself invented them. It is unlikely that traditions about Paul's last days that already were in circulation in 80-85 C.E. contained much fiction (as *First Clement* and Ignatius illustrate in the few, sober details that they offer: the closer the "Acts" of the martyrs are to their execution, the less legendary accretion they suffer).

16. *May the Lord, however, grant mercy to the family of Onesiphorus, for time and again he revived my spirits and was unashamed about this manacle on me.* With the *dōiē eleos ho kyrios* . . . and its second aorist optative (repeated in v. 18), another prayer begins, in two parts, for "the household of Onesiphorus *(tōi Onēsiphorou oikōi)*" and then (in v. 18) for the man himself.

The prayer is that the Lord, i.e. the risen Jesus, would give mercy to, i.e. have pity on and help, the members of a household perhaps in Ephesus, but in any case a family that needs no introduction to Timothy (cf. 1:18b) beyond the name of Onesiphorus. At the end of this letter the same household is to be greeted by Timothy for Paul (2 Tim 4:19; cf. commentary *in loc.* for Ign. *Smyrn.* 13.1-2). But why the prayer here for the Lord's mercy on this family that is to be greeted in any case as this letter closes? The most plausible reason, in the light of all the details that follow, is that Onesiphorus had died unexpectedly and that these sentences transmit that news in as delicate a manner as possible and not without some linguistic awkwardness as well (though even that serves to underline the authenticity of the feelings of the one who sends on the sad news).

The name itself of Onesiphorus means "the one bringing advantage" or "beneficial" (LSJ), and thus in Greek his name already stands in vivid contrast to the names just cited in verse 15 of the men who brought no aid to Paul. For this man's household Paul prays because (*hoti:* causal, as in 1 Tim 1:12, 13; 4:4,

10; 5:12; 6:2, 7 [?], though this letter and Titus do not otherwise use the particle in a causal sense) "often he refreshed me *(pollakis me anepsyxen)*." The verb here is in the aorist, as are the three that follow *(epaischynthē ezētēsen: heuren)*, and thus, emphatically, the actions described belong to a point in the past and have not continued up to this writing. Particularly with this initial verb one would have anticipated a perfect (or even a present tense) if Onesiphorus were still with Paul. The implication is that the man is no longer with him, and the prayer for his family gently informs Timothy and reminds them that Onesiphorus did not leave Paul to return to help them.

But true to his name, he often revived Paul's spirits, *pollakis me anepsyxen*. The verb implies an exhausted and even harried person as object as well as a ministry to the physical needs for drink and food, though evidently not excluding support for the spirit *(psychē!)* as well (cf. E. Schweizer, *TDNT* 9.663-664). In this latter connection it is notable that the unique NT use of *anapsyxis* is in Acts 3:20, where it is part of an apocalyptic expression for the final age of salvation and redemption (Schweizer, pp. 664-665). The unique LXX use is of the relief from the plague of frogs in Exod 8:11. The nominal form is not documented in the Ap. Frs. In Luke 16:24 *katapsychein* refers to the drop of cool water that Lazarus could give the rich man.

The refreshment that Onesiphorus brought has been offered in the setting of Paul's arrest and imprisonment: "and he was not ashamed of my handcuffs *(tēn halysin mou)*." The use of the singular here in the PE would mean that when Onesiphorus ministered to Paul a Roman guard always observed and witnessed this service and the person who gave it. This gives a special point to Onesiphorus's not being "ashamed," for his kindness to the prisoner could have tainted him with the crime for which Paul had been arrested. If Paul was indeed being persecuted for the gospel, then anyone who showed concern for the apostle was liable to suffer for the gospel as he did. Indeed, only a non-Christian would have no reason for apprehension (another reason for taking the reference in v. 15 to the Christians of Asia).

17. *Instead, when he came to Rome he hunted for me right away and he found [me].* In a few swift, vivid strokes the events that led up to Onesiphorus's relief are sketched in. Onesiphorus no sooner had arrived in Rome, a city name that only Paul (Rom 1:7, 15) and Luke use in the NT (Acts 18:2; 19:21; 23:11; 28:14, 16), than he quickly (cf. Titus 3:13 and Phil 2:28) and/or diligently (as in Luke 7:4) began the search for the imprisoned apostle. Whether other business had brought him to the city or whether visiting Paul was the express purpose of the trip from Asia Minor is not settled.

The aorist *ezētēsen* again stresses the past over-and-done character of the action, as does the second aorist of the following *heuren*. H. Greeven, *TDNT* 2.892-896, studies only the religious sense of this verb, but his observation on the search's being done in "patient and hopeful expectation" rather than with "pitiless rigor" applies here to Onesiphorus's inquiry for Paul (cf. Acts 9:11 with its command to Ananias, *zētēson en oikiai Iouda Saulon . . .*). Lock, *Commentary, in loc.,* has noted that the emphasis here on earnest inquiry seems to presuppose a relatively less accessible Paul than that depicted in Acts 28:30; cf. 11:25-26 on Barnabas's hard search for *(anazētēsai)* and finding *(heurōn)* Saul in Tarsus; this assessment is not highly persuasive in itself. Note how the variant readings with *ana-* and *epi-* seek to increase the force of this verb (J. K. Elliott, *Greek Text,* p. 126). D-C, p. 106, see here a reference to Paul's "first and only imprisonment," an eisegesis that the text does not support.

The final *kai heuren* is abrupt (cf. the positioning of *me* in some MSS [J. K. Elliott, *Greek Text,* p. 126], and note the similar omission of the pronoun in v. 9) and closes the sentence on an almost exclamatory note (Spicq). The *zētein/(ou) heuriskein* schema, rare in Paul (cf. Rom 10:20, citing Isa 65:1; and the somewhat superficial parallels at 1 Cor 4:2 and Gal 2:17), is rather frequent in the Gospels and Acts (cf. esp. Luke 11:9, 10, 24; 13:6, 7; Acts 17:5-6, 27). H. Preisker, *TDNT* 2.769-770, has noted how frequently the term is used to denote the surprising discovery of the unseen and unexpected within and through that which a person thought he "knew." That is what has happened to Onesiphorus. He "found" Paul, in prison, visited him, cared for the needs of this "least of the apostles" (cf. Matt 25:36, 39-40).

18. *So may the Lord grant him to find — indeed, he will find mercy from the Lord on that Day.* No sooner had he done this than the Lord "found" him, surprised him like Milton's Persephone to carry him off to another world, and now the apostle's prayer turns from the household that this man left behind to Onesiphorus himself with the prayer that the risen Lord *(ho kyrios)* of life (who has conquered death; cf. 1:10 above) would grant Onesiphorus "to find mercy from the Lord on that Day." The *heurein eleos* is evidently taking up the *heuren* of the brief history of Onesiphorus's merciful visit to Paul that is now to issue in his finding the ultimate mercy "with the (risen) Lord" as he had given mercy to that Lord's apostle. What Onesiphorus has done on earth is not unrelated to what he is to discover at the judgment seat of Christ (2 Cor 5:10). The one "who brought help" to Paul has the latter's prayer that he will in turn find help with Paul's Lord.

The phrase *para kyriou* comes with a certain harsh awkwardness after the *dōiē . . . ho kyrios* with which this part of the prayer began, a roughness that the textual tradition sought to iron out by changing the second "Lord" to "God" (D* etc.) or omitting the phrase altogether (C. 241. Tert.; see J. K. Elliott, *Greek Text,* p. 127). It is more likely, however, that at least one formulaic expression is found here, the opening *dōiē . . . ho kyrios* (cf. the previous verse; the optative, so rare otherwise in the NT [see BDF §65.2, noting that it is most frequent in the Lukan corpus] but here expressing an attainable wish or prayer [cf. BDF

§384] and thus attested in the Paulines [BDF §95.2; cf. Rom 15:5], and found also in the LXX Wis 7:15; Ps 19:5; etc.). Luke-Acts never employ the form *dōiē*. In the Paulines, however, *ho kyrios . . . dōiē* is documented at 2 Thess 3:16, but only there. For all the uses of *didonai* in the Ap. Frs., one does not encounter this exact phrase (cf. the *theos dōiē* of *Barn.* 21.5). Nor is any form of it found in *CII*. Thus there does not seem to be enough evidence in Christian or Jewish materials to say certainly that the phrase "May the Lord grant . . ." was so common in prayer that the one using it would be practically unaware that he had said *kyrios* and thus be untroubled by the following *para kyriou*.

But perhaps *para kyriou* is the formulaic expression that was used automatically, without adverting to the awkward repetition? *Par' emou* has already occurred in 1:13 and will recur at 2:2. *Para tinōn* will be read at 3:14. Only here do the PE use this particle with the genitive of the Lord (anarthrous). The Paulines use *para kyriou* only in Eph 6:8, and the Lukan corpus only at Luke 1:45 and Acts 20:24 (in the form *para tou kyriou Iēsou*). Otherwise in the NT the phrase occurs in Matt 21:42 = Mark 12:11, citing LXX Ps 117:23, and James 1:7 *(para tou kyriou)*. The phrase seems not to appear in the Ap. Frs. before *Barn.* 14.2 *(s.v.l.)*. Again the phrase is not documented in *CII*. Thus again the evidence for a stereotyped formula seems tenuous. Nor does Easton's appeal (*Pastoral Epistles*, p. 46) to an Aramaic background, "May *Mara* grant him to find mercy from *Elohim*," comparing Mark 12:36 and its citation of LXX Ps 109:1, seem much more convincing. Jeremias's suggestion (*NTD*, pp. 116-117, Italian) that we meet here a rough conflation of two formulas founders on the fact that one cannot make a very convincing case for even one formula so stereotyped that the repetition would sound unforced.

Perhaps there is an anacoluthon here, due to a deliberate abandoning of the optative and suddenly affirming, with typically Pauline certitude after the mention of "mercy," "(which is) from the Lord on that Day." Paul has no doubt that his prayer will be answered and that the Lord will indeed have mercy on his merciful servant.

*And you know well enough how many services he provided in Ephesus.* The final clause tumbles back into the history of Onesiphorus again, the Asian milieu from which he came (*en Ephesōi;* see 1 Tim 1:3) and to which this letter is directed, a milieu in which Timothy can remember very well *(beltion)* whatever services Onesiphorus gave *(hosa . . . diēkonēsen)*. On *hosa* cf. the *hosoi* of 1 Tim 6:1. *Diakonein* was used in 1 Tim 3:10, 13 of the function of the diaconal ministry or order. There seems to be no reason in this text, however, to infer that Onesiphorus belonged to that order, though what he did in visiting and caring for a prisoner was certainly a task that we find *diakonoi* performing at the beginning of the second century (Ign. *Eph.* 2.1; *Magn.* 2.1; *Phld.* 11.1). But obviously such tasks were not reserved to the diaconal order.

The comparative *beltion* that occurs only here in the NT probably has the positive sense of "(very) well" (cf. BAGD; BDF §244.2; cf. the D reading in Acts 10:28 and Haenchen, *Acts,* p. 350 n. 3), though the comparative sense would also be intelligible (contra BDF). Cf. the uses in the Ap. Frs.: *1 Clem.* 19.1 (a true comparative); *2 Clem.* 6.6 (*could* be positive, but probably not); Hermas, *Vis.* 3.4.3; 3.7.1; and *Sim.* 1.9. The effect of this clause is to draw the thought back to the addressee (note the emphatic *sy*) and to tie off neatly the inserted note that began with *oidas touto* in verse 15.

## IV. TESTAMENT OF PAUL (2:1–4:8)

### IV.A. The Legator (2:1-13)

*2 1Now, my child, find strength in that grace which is in Christ Jesus; 2and those*
*things that you heard from me, through many witnesses, set out for trustworthy*
*men, the kind who will also be competent to teach others. 3As a fine soldier of*
*Christ Jesus take your share of suffering along with me. 4No one on active duty in*
*the military gets involved in the business of civilian life. He avoids this to please the*
*man who called him to arms. 5Moreover, take the case of a man who competes in*
*the public games: he does not get the winner's crown if he does not compete accord-*
*ing to the rules. 6Or again: the farmer on the job ought to be the first to have his*
*share of the crops. 7Consider what I am saying here, Timothy; for in every way the*
*Lord will grant you insight.*

*8Keep in mind Jesus Christ,*

*risen from the dead,*
*from the line of David.*

*That corresponds to my gospel 9for which I am being wronged, put into chains as*
*though a wrongdoer — but the word of God has not been chained. 10For this very*
*reason, that is, for the sake of the elect, I am submitting to everything. My purpose*
*is that they too reach the salvation which is in Christ Jesus with eternal glory.*

*11The Christian message, meant to be believed, is this:*

*". . . for if we shared in his death,*
*we shall share in his life.*
*12If we submit now,*
*we shall share in his reign.*
*If we ever disown him,*
*he is the one that will disown us.*

*[13]If we are faithless,*
*he is the one who stays faithful,*
*for he cannot possibly disown himself."*

## ♦ NOTES

2:1. *find strength in that grace.* For *endynamou* see Note at 1 Tim 1:12. For *charis* see Titus 1:4. The demonstrative "that" translates the Greek article *tēi.*

2. *set out.* On *parathou* see 1 Tim 1:18; when immediately following the Pauline eucharist for the apostolate, Paul "sets out" the apostolic *paraggelia* to his child, Timothy; and cf. the noun *parathēkē* of 1 Tim 1:18 and 6:20 and 2 Tim 1:12, 14.

*trustworthy men. Anthrōpos* in the Greek generally connotes no differentiation according to gender, similar to the English word *anthropology.* It occurs twenty times in the PE, occasionally attended by ethical qualifications (only Christ Jesus is referred to in the singular unqualified). *Anthrōpoi,* the plural, generally compares mere humans to God and, when qualifications occur, they usually underline moral deficiencies in the former; only this passage in the PE refers to "trustworthy men." *Pistos* appears in the NT sixty-seven times, of which seventeen are in the PE (sixteen in the other Paulines; ten in Luke-Acts). It can designate either the body of believers, a group within that body, or an individual in the PE. This phrase does not otherwise occur in the rest of the NT. The closest parallel seems to be the "*. . . pistois adelphois*" of Col 1:2 (cf. 4:7, 9).

*the kind who will also be competent to teach others.* Lit. "such as will be competent *(hikanoi esontai)* also *(kai)* to teach others *(heterous* [see the singular at 1 Tim 1:10, Zerwick, *Analysis,* p. 640] = *allous).*" On *hoitines* see Titus 1:11 and 2 Tim 2:18. On the meaning of *didaskein,* here for the last time in the PE, see on Titus 1:11 (AB *Titus*); 1 Tim 2:12; 4:11; 6:2. The adjective *hikanoi,* "competent/worthy/fit," occurs only here in the PE out of its forty NT uses. It is not common in the rest of the Paulines (only Romans once, First Corinthians twice, Second Corinthians thrice), but there are twenty-seven uses in Luke-Acts (nine and eighteen). On the other hand, in 1 Cor 15:9 and 2 Cor 3:5 the term is used with a dependent infinitive (as here in the PE) whereas that occurs in the Lukan corpus only at Luke 3:16 (= Mark 1:7/Matt 3:11).

Before Hermas, the only use of *hikanos* in the Ap. Frs. is in *1 Clem.* 50.2 of being "*able* to be found" in charity *(hikanos heurethēnai).*

3. *fine soldier.* The noun *stratiōtēs* appears only here in the PE and never otherwise in the Paulines (which do have *systratiōtēs* in Phil 2:25; Philem 2). Fifteen of twenty-five other NT uses are in Luke-Acts (two and thirteen). Only this passage of the NT uses the expression "fine soldier" figuratively. The cog-

nates in 1 Tim 1:18, *strateuēi . . . tēn kalēn strateian,* are also addressed to Timothy (see commentary *in loc.*), and, there as here, *kalos* refers to the visible excellence of the role being adduced for comparison. In the Ap. Frs. *stratiōtēs* may occur in Ign. *Rom.* 5.1 but not elsewhere. The term occurs rather rarely in the LXX, six times in Second, Third, and Fourth Maccabees and in 2 Kings 23:8; on this comparatively rare usage see O. Bauernfeind, *TDNT* 7.706.

4. *No one on active duty in the military gets involved in the business of civilian life.* Lit. "No one doing military service *(oudeis strateuomenos)* is entangled *(empleketai)* in the activities of life *(tais tou biou pragmateiais)*." See Notes at 1 Tim 1:18 on *strateuomenos:* present tense here = "on active duty." The present tense of *empleketai* lays down a general rule. The verb occurs otherwise in the NT only in 2 Pet 2:20 of "the defilements of the world." In the LXX the verb occurs at Prov 28:18 and 2 Macc 15:17. LXX Prov 28:18 reads, "He who travels on crooked roads will become entangled in hand-to-hand combat." In the Ap. Frs. only Hermas uses this verb, of sheep getting their wool tangled in thorns (*Sim.* 6.2.6-7). MM *s.v.* cite Epictetus 3.22.69 and Polyb. 25.9.3 *(tois hellēnikois pragmasin emplekomenos)* as relevant texts from secular Greek. Cf. *en plegnasin* of hair in 1 Tim 2:9.

*business.* This is the only NT use of *pragmateia.* Of the eight LXX uses of the noun, half are in First Kings (7:33; 9:1; 10:22 *bis* [B]). First Chronicles 28:21 uses it of the work of building the Solomonic temple. Cf. also LXX Ps 70:15 (B, *s.v.l.*); Dan 6:3; and 2 Macc 2:31. In the Ap. Frs. the noun is documented only in Hermas, but there as many as eleven times. The phrase *tais tou biou pragmateiais* contains one of two occurrences of *bios* in the PE (the other is in 1 Tim 2:2). The usage here resembles that in the Gospels, wherein the material necessities of life are referred to (see esp. Luke 21:4 = Mark 12:44). If a soldier is to provide the needed protection of a society, that society must provide his livelihood, his material means, albeit small compensation for the hardships of military life.

*to please.* This is the only use of *areskein* in the PE (though cf. the cognate *euarestous* in Titus 2:9, of slaves toward masters). Out of seventeen other NT uses, thirteen are in the other Paulines, where the distinction between pleasing human beings (including oneself) and pleasing God is notable (cf., e.g., 1 Thess 2:4, 15; 4:1, etc.). The one use in the Lukan corpus is in Acts 6:5 of the advice *(logos)* of the Twelve that pleases the assembly of believers. As W. Foerster, *TDNT* 1.455, has noted, the verb came originally out of a legal problematic with the basic sense of reconciling or making peace between persons. In the LXX (one column in H-R) the term always means "to please," whether of men or God (cf., e.g., Num 23:27 with Josh 9:25) and usually stands for some form of the Hebrew *ṭwb/yṭb; bʿyny; lpny,* "(to be) good in the eyes of; before the face of." *First Clement* 52.2 takes up this verb in quoting LXX Ps 68:31. *Second Clem-*

*ent* 13.1 exhorts, "Let us not be men-pleasers *(anthrōpareskoi)* and let us wish to please *(areskein)* by our righteousness not ourselves alone but also those who are without. . . ." Ign. *Trall.* 2.3 says that deacons "must be in every way pleasing *(areskein)* to all men." Then in Ign. *Rom.* 2.1 he writes, "For I would not have you 'men-pleasers' *(anthrōpareskēsai)* but pleasing God *(theōi aresai)* even as you do indeed please him *(areskete)*." The most striking parallel to 2 Tim 2:4 is Ign. *Pol.* 6.2, *areskete hōi strateuesthe,* "please the one in whose ranks you serve" (trans. WCW).

*the man who called him to arms.* Lit. "the one who enlisted him," *stratologēsanti,* the aorist participle of a verb not otherwise documented in the NT, the LXX, or the Ap. Frs.

5. *competes. Athaleō* occurs only here in the NT and the LXX, but in *1 Clem.* 5.2 the greatest apostles, Peter and Paul, "competed until death *(heōs thanatou ēthlēsan)*." In *2 Clem.* 20.2 the parallel to 2 Tim 2:5 is notable: "we are contending *(athloumen)* in the contest of the living God . . . that we may gain the crown *(stephanōthōmen)*. . . ." It is noteworthy that in the LXX the whole cluster of the *athl-* terms is found in Third and Fourth Maccabees, except for Wis 4:2, which writes of virtue *(aretē),* "throughout all time it marches crowned in triumph *(stephanēphorousa),* victor in the contest for prizes *(athlōn)* undefiled."

*does not get the winner's crown.* Lit. "he is not crowned." The only other NT use of the verb *stephanoun* occurs in Heb 2:7, 9. In the Ap. Frs. the verb *stephanoun* is used in *2 Clem.* 7.1-3 (four times), as well as in 20.2 cited in connection with 1 Tim 4:8 and 2 Tim 2:5. *Barnabas* 7.9 interprets the "crowned" and accused scapegoat of the crucified Jesus. Hermas uses the verb in *Man.* 12.2.5; *Sim.* 8.2.1; 8.3.6 *(bis);* 8.4.6.

Of the seven LXX uses, that in 4 Macc 17:15 is particularly noteworthy with its summary statement, "righteousness won the victory and gave the crown to her athletes *(tous heautēs athlētas stephanousa)*." The crown is that for a victory dance in Jth 15:13 and of the royal bridegroom in Cant 3:11. In LXX Ps 5:12, "You crowned (Hebrew *ʿṭr*) us with goodwill as with a shield." See Grundmann, *TDNT* 7.624, who notes here the root sense of *ʿṭr* = to surround (cf. 2 Tim 4:8 on the Greek root too). See LXX Ps 102:4, of the Lord "who crowns *(stephanounta: ʿṭr)* you in mercy." See also Ps 8:5. Third Maccabees 3:28 describes slave-informers who were to be "crowned (*stephanōthēsetai* [i.e. rewarded]) with freedom" (Charles, *AP* 1.167, and note *ad loc.* as well as Deissmann, *B ST,* p. 345). For the LXX use of the noun, see Notes on 2 Tim 4:8.

*according to the rules.* For *nomimōs* see 1 Tim 1:8.

6. *Or again: the farmer on the job ought to be the first to have his share of the crops.* The third comparison stresses the result of the co-suffering even more than the previous one as it declares (lit.), "the hardworking *(kopiōnta)* farmer

*(ton . . . geōrgon)* ought *(dei)* to be first *(prōton)* to receive his share *(metalambanein)* of the fruits *(tōn karpōn)*." For *kopiōnta* see 1 Tim 4:10 (note the connection with the athletic imagery there as well).

On *geōrgos*, "farmer," in the NT see Comment below. The Ap. Frs. do not use the noun (though Ign. *Phld.* 3.1 uses the cognate verb with Jesus Christ as subject). The LXX uses this noun only ten times at most; thus Noah is *geōrgos gēs* (note that etymologically *geōrgos* is "working the earth," as the Latin *agricola* is one who "cares for a field") in LXX Gen 9:20 (cf. 49:15). Uzziah, who loved the soil, had "many farmers and vinedressers" (2 Chron 26:10). For the uses in the Prophets see LXX *Amos 5:16;* Jer 14:4; 28:23 (with shepherds); 38:24 (with shepherds); *52:16;* Joel 1:11; the italicized texts couple farmers with those who care for the vineyards. In Wis 17:17 (16, Rahlfs) farmer, shepherd, and desert workman (miner?) are joined in a trio.

The Hebrew *'ikkar* most frequently is the root translated by *geōrgos*, and it is yet to be documented in Qumran.

The "hardworking farmer" of this comparison in the PE is one who ought *(dei)* to receive his share *(metalambanein)* of the crops *(tōn karpōn)*. *Dei* occurs eight other times in the PE (Titus 1:7, 11 [*bis*]; 1 Tim 3:2, 7, 15; 5:13 [*deonta*]; 2 Tim 2:24), and nearly half its remaining NT uses occur in Luke-Acts; see also 2:24 below and on 1 Tim 3:2, 7, 15; note how the verb in the PE always occurs in passages about what *ought* to be first (*prōton:* J. K. Elliott, *Greek Text*, p. 130, on classical sense of first in a series, and cf. Luke 2:2: note S* had *proteron* but see Elliott). Both this infinitive and its object occur only here in the PE. However, the noun *metalēmpsis* occurs in 1 Tim 4:3, as does *akarpoi* at Titus 3:14.

With *metalambanein* one encounters a verb that in the other Paulines might have been compounded with *syn-* (cf. Phil 4:3), as Moule, *Idiom*, pp. 61-62, has remarked (recalling Falconer, *PE*, p. 7) that the *meta* of the PE = *syn* of the Paulines. In any case the rest of the Pauline corpus has no use of *metalambanein*. In the NT otherwise it occurs only in Heb 6:7; 12:10; and in Acts where, except for 24:25, it designates the partaking of food (2:46; 27:33-34). Though Heb 6:7 uses this verb in speaking of a cultivated field receiving a divine blessing, the language of Acts is closer to that of the PE, for the *trophēs* (nourishment) there is synonymous with *tōn karpōn* (the crops) here. Of the fourteen LXX uses of *metalambanein*, twelve are in Second, Third, and Fourth Maccabees. In Second Maccabees it has the meaning "gathered" in the sense of "learned" or "heard," but in none of its occurrences in the LXX does it mean partaking of or sharing in food. In the Ap. Frs. the verb is used in *First* and *Second Clement* and in Hermas, but only one of eleven occurrences refers to partaking of food, Hermas, *Vis.* 3.9.2-3: ". . . do not take a superabundant share of the creatures *(ta ktismata . . . metalambanete)* of God yourselves but give also a part to those who lack. For some are contracting illness in the flesh by too much eating. . . ." G. Delling, *TDNT* 4.10-11, prefers to take this use in Second Timothy as "to receive the portion accruing to one," though he also notes the link with taking food.

The noun *karpos* occurs on sixty-five other occasions in the NT outside of the PE. Thirteen are in Luke-Acts (twelve/one); ten are in the other Paulines, where the term is always in the singular and always in a figure or comparison. In the Lukan corpus the plural occurs only in Luke 3:8 and 12:17. This latter instance is notable, for it is the speech of a rich landlord who does not have granaries enough to store "my crops *(tous karpous mou).*" The only other plural use in the NT epistolary is a figurative one in James 3:17. The only other plural uses in the Gospels are Matt 7:16-20 (on good trees producing good fruits, etc.; cf. Rev 22:2) and again in the parable of the vineyard, where all the uses of *geōrgos* were concentrated (Matt 21:34, 41, 43; also Mark 12:2).

Among the numerous occurrences of *karpos* in the LXX, there is curiously not a single instance where it is used with *geōrgos.* See Hauck, *TDNT* 3.614, for a survey of its meanings. It is usually the translation of the Hebrew root *pry/prh.* The *prwt* ("fruitfulness of seed") in 1QS 4.7 may, in the context (which mentions "a crown of glory"), be moving beyond this visible world (cf. A. R. C. Leaney, *RQM,* p. 152). 1QH 8.20 apparently speaks of "the fruitful planting" that prospers and becomes an "everlasting [fount]ain for the glorious Eden and it shall bear fr[uit forever] (*wpr*[ . . .)" (Dupont-Sommer, *EWQ,* p. 228, who cites *Odes of Solomon* 38.17-21). In the same hymn (1QH 8.11, 13) there were previous references to the fruit *(pryw)* produced by the teacher of righteousness, who, for all his ignominy and suffering, irrigates the desert and brings forth a great, sheltering tree (Dupont-Sommer, *EWQ,* pp. 225-230). The suffering-to-fruit pattern is suggestive for the understanding of 2 Tim 2:6. Unfortunately, the tiny fragment from what appears to be sapiential/Deuteronomic "testament" with appropriate instructions to a (beloved or only?) son is too mutilated to determine just what are "the fruits in your possession" (1Q26.2.4; DJD 1.102).

In the Ap. Frs., *karpos* occurs forty-six times, with thirty of these in Hermas. *Second Clement* 19.3 (cf. also 20.3) is quite apposite to this passage of Second Timothy when it says, "Blessed are those who obey these instructions: though they suffer *(kakopathēsōsin)* for a short time in this world, they shall gather the immortal fruit of the resurrection *(ton athanaton tēs anastaseōs karpon).*" In Ign. *Trall.* 11.2 those who are the planting of the Father are to appear as "branches of the cross [cf. Ign. *Smyrn.* 1.21] and their fruit *(karpos)* will be incorruptible *(aphthartos).*" Here, too, the *karpos* is beyond this worldly order and sounds more like the harvest signified by the metaphor in Second Timothy than by the other uses in the epistolary.

7. *Consider what I am saying here, Timothy.* The threefold comparison

completed, the author now reviews it with an admonition. The words *here, Timothy* are not in the Greek, which is literally "Understand *(noei)* what I am saying *(ho legō)*." This phrase occurred in a negative form in 1 Tim 1:7 of those *mē noountes mēte ha legousin* . . . , "not understanding either what they are saying. . . ." On *noeō* see 1 Tim 1:7.

*for in every way the Lord will grant you insight.* Lit. "for *(gar)* the Lord (*ho kyrios* [i.e. Christ Jesus, in the usage of the PE]) will give you (*dōsei soi* [note the sg.; on *didōmi* with the Lord as subject, 2 Tim 1:16, 18 and cf. 1:7, 9]) insight *(synesin)* into all things *(en pasin)*." Though J. K. Elliott, *Greek Text,* p. 167, would hold for an original *dōēi* (subjunctive) here, the attestation for the future seems overwhelming (S, A, C*, D, F, G, pl). The Semitic word order in the sentence seems also to make the future more credible as the original reading (cf. LXX 3 Kgdms 3:9, 11). One can easily discern the theological scruples that would have prompted the less risky subjunctive. *En pasin* appeared above in Titus 2:9-10; 1 Tim 3:11, and will recur below at 2 Tim 4:5; in all cases it modifies what precedes it (see also 1 Tim 3:11).

There are half a dozen other NT occurrences of *synesin,* which the PE use only here. Of these, four are in the other Paulines (Eph 3:4, cited above; 1 Cor 1:19, citing Isa 29:14 in a non-LXX form and with a pejorative sense; Col 1:9; 2:2). For a fuller discussion see Comment below.

8. *Keep in mind.* Though other terms in the *mne-* cluster were comparatively frequent in the thanksgiving prayer at the opening of this letter (cf. 2 Tim 1:3, 4, 5, 6), this is the only use of *mnēmoneuein* in the PE. There are twenty other NT occurrences, with six in the other Paulines and three in Luke-Acts (one/two). Nine of twenty-one uses are in the imperative, with only this passage of Second Timothy and Rev 2:5; 3:3 in the singular.

There are as many as twenty-one uses of this verb in the LXX. When a positive command, it means to remember the exodus events (LXX Exod 13:3; contrast Isa 43:18) or God's wonderful acts (1 Chron 16:12) or God himself (Tob 4:5; cf. 14:7). It is also used of a son's duty to remember his father's commands (Tob 4:19) and of prayer (LXX 2 Kgdms 14:11). As Michel, *TDNT* 4.683, has noted, one remembers God's acts, which in turn summon forth faith and grateful prayer (confession). To assist this remembering and worship, a written "memorial" can be made (cf. Exod 17:14 and Esther 9:32; 10:2).

In the Ap. Frs., *2 Clem.* 17.3 uses this verb of "the commands of the Lord." Ign. *Eph.* 12.2 employs the term of Paul's "remembering" these believers in his correspondence; in 21.1 he asks *(mnēmoneuete)* to be "remembered" by them as they are "remembered" by Jesus. In Ign. *Magn.* 14.1 he directs, "Remember me in your prayers . . . and remember the church in Syria," and the latter admonition appears later in *Trall.* 13.1 and *Rom.* 9.1; *Smyrn.* 5.3 is an interesting passage because it links writing with memory and thus with an unwillingness to put down the actual names of heretics (cf. the various passages in the PE). Polycarp, *Phil.* 2.3, introduces a saying of Jesus with "remembering what the Lord taught."

On *Barn.* 21.7, cf. above on 2 Tim 1:3. For the usage of Hermas, see *Vis.* 1.3.3; 2.1.3; 4.3.6; *Man.* 4.1.1; *Sim.* 1.7 and 6.5.4.

*risen from the dead.* The verb *egeirō* (cf. Oepke, *TDNT* 2.333-337) occurs 142 times otherwise in the NT, with 40 in the other Paulines and 30 in Luke-Acts (18/12). The term *nekros* occurs 126 times (though never in Second Thessalonians; Philemon; Second Peter; First, Second, and Third John; and Jude!), and the phrase *ek nekrōn* or its equivalent is met at every turn in describing Jesus' deliverance and exaltation (and that of others: cf. Luke 16:30-31; 20:35). Cf. Sir 48:5, *ho egeiras nekron ek thanatou* (of Elijah).

In the Ap. Frs., though *egeirein* does occur of God's raising up the fallen in *1 Clem.* 59.4 (who always uses *anistanai/anastasis* for the resurrection), in all other instances except the four uses in Hermas it refers to the resurrection of Jesus and his followers and then often with *ek/apo nekrōn;* cf. Ign. *Magn.* 9.2 (of the effect of Jesus' entry into the world of the dead); *Trall.* 9.1-2, after speaking of Jesus' death (including his being *ek genous Daueid,* also in *Smyrn.* 1.1; *Eph.* 20.2), says of him, "who was also truly raised from the dead *(ēgerthē apo nekrōn),* when his Father raised him up *(egeirantos auton),* as in the same manner his Father shall raise up *(egeirei)* in Christ Jesus us who believe in him. . . ." In *Smyrn.* 7.1 he describes those who "abstain from the eucharist and prayer, because they do not confess that the eucharist is the flesh *(sarka)* of our savior, Jesus Christ, that flesh that suffered for our sins and that *(hēn)* the Father by his goodness raised up *(ēgeiren).*" Polycarp, *Phil.* 1.2, refers to the faith of the Philippians in Jesus Christ, who suffered and died "for our sins" and "whom God raised up *(ēgeiren),* having loosed the pangs of Hades [cf. Acts 2:24]," and in 2.1-2 he exhorts his readers who "believe in him who raised up *(egeiranta)* our Lord Jesus Christ from the dead *(ek nekrōn),*" saying, "Now he who raised him from the dead *(hode egeiras auton ek nekrōn)* will also raise us up *(egeirei),*" and in 5.2 he appeals to the Lord's promise "to raise us from the dead *(egeirai hēmas ek nekrōn).*" There are many LXX uses of *egeirein,* including Sir 48:5 of raising the dead, but they never seem to take posterity/seed/children as object.

*from the line of David.* Lit. "from the seed *(spermatos)* of David." This is the only occurrence of either noun in the PE. The noun *sperma* occurs 44 times altogether in the NT. For its use outside of the passages noted in the Comment below, see Schulz, *TDNT* 7.545. The term is most frequently used in transferred meanings, whether in comparisons, figures, or parables.

For the uses of *sperma* in the Ap. Frs. other than those noted in the Comment below, see *Barn.* 3.3 and Hermas, *Vis.* 2.2.2; *Sim.* 9.24.4, none of which refers to the patriarchs or David. For other passages on David in these documents, see *Did.* 9.2 (of Jesus in the context) and 10.6, as well as *Barn.* 10.10; 12.10-11 (of Jesus as Christ).

G. Quell and S. Schulz, *TDNT* 7.536-547, have noted that this noun occurs 217 times in the LXX, and often figuratively for the family (descendants) and the nation (p. 538) as historical, human entities and thus as nonmythical constructs (p. 542). There are relatively few references in the LXX to the *sperma David/autou/sou,* but note LXX 2 Kgdms 7:12; 22:51; 3 Kgdms 2:33; 1 Chron 17:11; Ps 88:4, 29, 36; Sir 47:22.

Among the relatively rare uses of *zrʿ* in Qumran, there is one notable passage in connection with 2 Tim 2:8 which occurs in 4QPBless 4: Dupont-Sommer, *EWQ,* p. 315. There occurs a pesher of the Blessing for Judah in Gen 49:10, which begins, ". . . a monarch will [not] be wanting to the tribe of Judah when Israel rules [and] a (descendant) seated on the throne will not be wanting to David . . . *Until* the Messiah of righteousness comes, the branch of David; for to him and to his seed *(wlzrʿw)* has been given the covenant of the kingship of his people for everlasting generations"; cf. 4Q*Flor* 10: Dupont-Sommer, *EWQ,* p. 313.

9. *I am being wronged, put into chains as though a wrongdoer.* Lit. "I am bearing hardship *(kakopathō)* to the extent of bonds *(mechri desmōn)* as though an evildoer *(hōs kakourgos).*" *Kakopathō* takes one back to the *sugkakopathēson* of 2:3 above, though this form of the term occurs elsewhere in the Paulines only at 2 Tim 4:5 below (as a command to Timothy). Its one other NT use is in James 5:13 (where the only NT use of the noun is in 5:10).

In the Ap. Frs. only *2 Clem.* 19.3 uses this verb in its beatitude, "Blessed are they who obey these instructions: though they suffer *(kakopathēsōsin)* for a short time in this world, they shall gather the immortal fruit (*karpon,* of 2 Tim 2:6) of the resurrection."

The unique LXX use is in Jon 4:10 of the plant for which the prophet "underwent no trouble" or "took no pains" (Michaelis, *TDNT* 5.936). On the meanings in Philo ("to take pains, exert oneself") and Josephus ("to run into military misfortune/difficulty"), see Michaelis, pp. 936-937. The Hebrew *ʿml* (cf. Jon 4:10) has in Qumran on occasion referred to the sufferings and persecutions of the righteous. Perhaps the most striking is 1QpHab 8.2-3: Dupont-Sommer, *EWQ,* p. 263, "God will deliver them from the House of judgment because of their affliction *(ʿmlm)* and their faith in the teacher of righteousness" (cf. also 1 QH 11.1 (?), 19 (?), and 4QDibHam 6.12).

This verb is common in secular Hellenistic Greek, and the usage of Menander is particularly interesting (*Dysc.* 348, 371). MM *s.v.* cite only four examples, but Spicq, *EP,* p. 746, has more.

On *mechri* see 1 Tim 6:14. Here for the only time in the PE the *desmoi* are encountered, on which cf. above on *desmios,* 2 Tim 1:8. On *hōs,* which occurs ten times in the PE as a particle (vs. once as a conjunction, 2 Tim 1:3), see above at 2 Tim 1:3.

The noun *kakourgos* occurs only here and in Luke 23:32-33, 39. It occurs four times in the LXX: in Prov 21:15, "the holy man is unclean among criminals *(para kakourgois)*"; in Sir 11:33, "Beware of a scoundrel *(apo kakourgou)*, for he devises evil"; and 33:26 (RSV, 27 Rahlfs), "Yoke and thong will bow the neck and for a wicked *(kakourgōi)* servant there are racks and tortures" (cf. the fetters, *tas pedas*, of v. 29); in Esther 8:13, *heuriskomen ou kakourgas ontas.* The Ap. Frs. do not use this noun. It is common in secular Greek in the Hellenistic period. Thus of Menander, *Dysc.* 258 (*kakourgos euthys apo tou blemmatos,* "One look and you can see he's up to no good," Casson, *Ancient Comedy,* p. 79), and its technical, legal sense of one guilty of a seriously criminal action is documented from the papyri in Spicq, *EP,* pp. 746-747, and MM *s.v.*, and one notes that the *kakourgos* is consigned *eis to desmotērion* (cf. Philo, *Quis Her.* 109). In Josephus, *Ant.* 2.59, the slandered Joseph is cast "into the malefactors' prison *(eis tēn tōn kakourgōn heirktēn)*"; cf. 2.69 where "in bonds *(en desmois)*" he is suffering *ta tōn kakourgōn,* "the things that happen to criminals," and note also 2.74, "for two full years he suffered in bonds *(tois desmois kakopathounta)*."

*but.* On the WH suggestion for reading *alla* as if it began a new sentence, see J. K. Elliott, *Greek Text,* p. 132, who considers this "unlikely."

*has not been chained.* There are forty other NT uses of the verb *deō,* of which four are in the Paulines and fourteen in Luke-Acts (two/twelve). In Luke 13:16 Satan has "bound" a woman in her physical affliction; in 19:30 (= Mark 11:2, 4 = Matt 21:2) a donkey has been tied up to prevent its wandering off. In Acts 9:2, 14, 21; 22:5 the verb describes the way in which Saul is determined to bring believers bound as prisoners to Jerusalem. In Acts 12:6 Peter is the one "bound with two chains" in prison, as in 21:33 it is Paul. In Acts 20:22 Paul describes himself as "bound by the Spirit" *(dedemenos egō tōi pneumati)* to go to Jerusalem, and in 21:11 an oracle from the Spirit prompts the prophet Agabus to bind his own feet and hands as a prophetic gesture of Paul's fate, which the apostle willingly accepts (21:13). In 22:29 the tribune who has ordered Paul bound is dismayed to learn that he had done this to a Roman citizen (see Haenchen, *Acts,* p. 634 n. 4, for data and references). In the last use of the verb, in Acts 24:27, it is still of Paul, "bound" for two years in Ceasarea. It is striking that in Acts, eleven of twelve uses of this verb refer to Paul, whether as binding or as bound, whether directly or indirectly. Moreover, in eleven of twelve instances the one who binds is human; in the single instance in Acts where there is a nonhuman agent, it is the Spirit (cf. and contrast Satan in Luke 13:16).

In the other Pauline uses of *deō,* three of four refer to the bond between husband and wife (Rom 7:2; 1 Cor 7:27, 39), but in Col 4:3 it is "the mystery of

Christ on account of which I am bound *(di' ho kai dedemai),*" and the reference there is evidently to Paul's status as prisoner (cf. Col 4:10, 18).

In the Ap. Frs., *1 Clem.* 40.5, "the layman is *bound* by the ordinances for the laity," and in 43.2 the term is used of binding rods into a bundle (cf. Num 17). Apart from a single use in *Barn.* 6.7 (= LXX Isa 3:10), "Let us bind the just one, for he is unprofitable to us," all the other fifteen uses of *dein* are in the Ignatian epistolary (*Eph.* 1.2; 3.1; 21.2; *Magn.* 12.1; *Trall.* 1.1; 5.2; 10.1; *Rom.* 1.1; 4.3; 5.1 [*s.v.l.*]; *Phld.* 5.1; 7.2; *Smyrn.* 4.2; 6.2 [not specifically of Ignatius]; 11.1) and with one exception refer to the actual bonds of the old prisoner bishop, who wears them much as the apostle did in the previous generation.

10. *For this very reason, that is, for the sake of the elect, I am submitting to everything.* Lit. "Because of this *(dia touto)* I endure all things *(panta hypomenō),* because of the chosen ones *(dia eklektous).*" *Eklektos,* used twenty-two times in the NT, occurs in the PE here and at Titus 1:1 in the nominal and at 1 Tim 5:21, and thrice otherwise in the Paulines (Rom 8:33; 16:13; Col 3:12; in the first and last of these a phrase otherwise undocumented in the NT occurs: *eklektoi (tou) theou*). Notable is the language of Luke 18:7: "And will not God *(ho . . . theos)* vindicate his elect *(eklekton autou)*?" See also Luke 23:35, where "the Christ of God" is "the elect *(ho eklektos).*" Acts does not use *eklektos.* The LXX uses it over one hundred times, but it does not use the phrase "God's elect," although "the Lord's elect" does appear in LXX 2 Kgdms 21:6, of Saul (see also Note on 1 Tim 5:21 of angels). On *dia touto,* "for this very reason," see 1 Tim 1:16.

The verb *hypomenein* occurs again in the PE only at 2:12 below (there in first person plural as here the first person singular). There are fifteen other NT uses of the verb. The noun *hypomonē* occurs only in the lists of Titus 2:2; 1 Tim 6:11; and 2 Tim 3:10 in the PE, and of the thirteen other Pauline uses, six are in Romans; in Acts and the Gospels it occurs only at Luke 8:15 and 21:19, and most of its twenty-four Septuagintal occurrences fall in Psalms, Sirach, and especially Fourth Maccabees. As Hauck, *TDNT* 4.584, has noted, in the LXX Job *hypomenein* occurs thirteen times (the noun once), and perhaps as many as fifteen times in Fourth Maccabees, a book that, again in Hauck's phrase (p. 585), is "a great hymn of praise to steadfastness" under persecution for the faith of Israel.

In the Ap. Frs., *1 Clem.* 45.8 uses the verb of the persecuted righteous of the OT. His other three uses are of waiting for the Lord and his gifts. *Second Clement,* in two of three uses of the verb, designates the sufferings of Christ (1.2) and of the faithful (17.7).

Ignatius's seven uses of the verb always refer to suffering or bearing with some affliction, even in the unique case of *Pol.* 3.1 (cf. 2) where, after writing at some length on what athletes endure, he says, "But especially must we endure all things (*panta hypomenein* [the same phrase occurs in *Smyrn.* 4.2; 9.2, cited below]) for the sake of God, that he also may endure *(hypomeinēi)* us." (This unusual attribution of *hypomenein* to God is not found in the NT; cf. Hauck, *TDNT* 4.587).

Polycarp, *Phil.* 1.2, uses the verb of the sufferings of Jesus, of whom in 8.1 it is said, "He endured all things *(panta hypemeinen)* for our sakes, that we might live in him *(zēsōmen en autōi).*" In 9.1, to the Philippians themselves, he then says, "Now I beseech you all to obey the word of righteousness and to endure with all the endurance *(hypomenein/askein pasan hypomonēn)* that you also saw before your eyes . . . in Paul himself and in the other apostles."

The one use in *Did.* 16.5 seems to take up Matt 10:22; 24:13; and Mark 13:13. The one use in Hermas, *Vis.* 2.2.7, is of "the tribulation to come *(tēn thlipsin tēn erchomenēn).*" For *Barnabas* see 5.1, 5 *(bis),* 6, 12 and 14.4 (all of the suffering of Jesus).

*reach the salvation, sōtērias tychōsin.* The unusual phrase *sōtērias tygchanein* does not occur elsewhere in the LXX, NT, or Ap. Frs., but the verb's use here reflects its usage in Luke-Acts rather than in the other Paulines. The phrase is the conceptual equivalent of the *eis sōtērian* of 3:15 below, which is rather more Hebraic and Septuagintal (see LXX Exod 15:2; Num 6:14; 2 Kgdms 10:11; 1 Chron 19:12; 2 Chron 12:7; etc.). On *tygchanein,* of the eleven other NT uses, six are in Luke-Acts (see Luke 20:35 of "that age" whose content is the resurrection; Acts 19:11; 24:2 of "much peace"; 26:22 of help from God; 27:3 of care from friends; 28:2). The usage of Heb 8:6; 11:35 resembles this, but not the three other Pauline uses (1 Cor 14:10; 15:37; 16:6). Of the ten uses in the Ap. Frs., perhaps the most notable are in Ignatius, and particularly *Smyrn.* 9.2, which also uses *hypomenein* (partially cited on 1 Tim 5:4): "God is your reward *(amoibē)* and if for his sake you endure all things *(panta hypomenontes),* you shall attain to him *(autou teuxesthe).*" For the rest, see Bauernfeind, *TDNT* 8.242.

*with eternal glory.* On *doxa* see Titus 2:13. *Doxa* is qualified with *aiōnias,* otherwise in the NT only in 1 Pet 5:10. In the LXX see Wis 10:14; Bar 4:24 (with *meta*); 5:2. In the seventy-one uses of the adjective *aiōnios* in the NT, forty-three times it modifies *zōē;* it applies in the remaining twenty-eight occurrences to fire, torment, sin, and judgment, as well as to unseen things (salvation, redemption, the covenant, the inheritance, kingdom, gospel, the Spirit, and God himself). The usage here in the PE reflects that of other strata in the NT. On the phrase, see Comment below.

11. *The Christian message, meant to be believed.* The phrase *pistos ho logos* occurs a half dozen times in the PE (Titus 1:9; 3:8a; 1 Tim 1:15; 3:1; 4:9; and here), qualifying the message Paul was entrusted with. The phrase is unique to the PE, absent from the NT, the LXX, or the Ap. Frs., and quite rare in Greek otherwise. See also Titus 1:9 and 3:8a.

*shared in his death.* Other than its use in Rom 6:8, *synapothanein* occurs in the Paulines only in 2 Cor 7:3, where it is followed by "and live together *(kai suzēn),*" but it refers to the Corinthian believers who are united in "our" heart, i.e. the heart of the apostle and his co-workers, and so with Christ. The other NT use of this compound is Mark 14:31 of Peter's declaration of loyalty even to physical death with Jesus, where "If I must die with *(synapothanein)* you" is followed immediately by "I will not deny you" (*SFG* §315, *aparnēsomai,* of the *arnēsometha . . . arnēsetai* in verse 12b below here; cf. John 11:16 as well as 2 Cor 4:10; 5:14-15). The PE never employ any form of *apothnēiskein* (though the verb is frequent enough in Luke-Acts — ten/four times — and the other Paulines — forty-two times), but they do once employ *tethnēken* of one dead in sin (see commentary on 1 Tim 5:6). The apostolic fathers never use the verb, and in the LXX it is documented only in Sir 19:10: "Have you heard a word? Let it die with *(synapothanetō)* you. Be brave! It will not make you burst!" cf. Bultmann, *TDNT* 3.19, proposing that this terminology has been borrowed from the mystery religions.

*share in his life. Syzēsomen* is a verb found only in the Paulines in the NT, in Rom 6:8 and 2 Cor 7:3, as was noted above. It is not found in the LXX, and in the Ap. Frs. it is not documented before Hermas (*Man.* 4.1.4-5, 9 of a husband and wife cohabiting; *Sim.* 8.9.1, 3 of those who lived with the heathen); cf. *sybiōsasa, CII* 28 of wife with husband. LSJ noted *symbiōsis* = "club/society"; see *CIG* quoted on Alexander the coppersmith below (from Cook, *Troad*). In profane Greek, besides the passage in Athenaeus noted above, the term is found in a fragment of the fourth-third–century-B.C.E. comedian Philemo *(apud* LSJ *s.v.)* as well as one of Aristophanes (LSJ). Aristotle's usage includes the absolute form found here; thus *NE* 1126a 31; 1157b 7; 1172a 23, as well as his *Pol.* 1278b 21; and 1280b 38 (where he observes, "The will to live together is friendship," McKeon 1189). The linking of life together, of friendship, and of death (with/for another) is of course frequent enough in the NT (cf. John 13:37; 15:13; Rom 5:7; Mark 14:31 — *SFG* §315 cited above).

12. *we shall share in his reign.* In the NT only Paul otherwise uses the verb *symbasileuō,* "co-reign," and then only once, in 1 Cor 4:8. This verb is found once in LXX 1 Esd 8:26 of those who "co-rule" along with Artaxerxes. In the Ap. Frs. only Polycarp, *Phil.* 5.2, uses the term when he writes in a passage that otherwise has conceptual links with this pastoral letter: "For if we please him in this present world, we shall receive from him that which is to come; even as he promised us to raise us from the dead, and, that if we are worthy citizens of his community *(politeusōmetha),* we shall also reign with him *(symbasileusomen autōi),* if we have but faith *(eige pisteuomen).*" D-C, p. 109, suggest a common source, a hymnic composition or even Rom 6:8. D-C, in the same context, are quite wrong on the way in which Polycarp uses *logos* (cf. 3.2; 6.2; 7.2; 9.1, where

not even one instance certainly refers to a saying of Jesus). MM *s.v.* cite Polybius 30.2.4, who speaks of Attalus who "for the present shared the throne *(symbasileuei)* with his brother, differing from him only in this, that he did not wear a crown and had not the title of king, but otherwise having equal and in fact identical power."

*disown.* The *arnēsometha . . . arnēsetai* terminology has occurred previously in the PE in Titus 1:16 and 1 Tim 5:8. *Arneisthai* recurs in Titus 1:16; 2:12; 1 Tim 5:8; 3:5, but not elsewhere in the Paulines. Of the eighteen other NT uses, eight are in Luke-Acts (see also Riesenfeld, "*Arneisthai*"). The LXX employs *arneisthai* only six times: in Gen 18:15 (= Hebrew *kḥš*, of Sarah denying that she laughed at the prediction of her pregnancy), and then one must wait until the very last strata of that work for further examples of its use. Thus, Wis 12:27 says of frustrated idol worshippers that "they saw and recognized as the true God him whom they had before refused *(ērnountai)* to know." Again in 16:16 that author speaks of *arnoumenoi gar se eidenai asebeis*, "the ungodly, refusing to know you [i.e. God]" (cf. Riesenfeld, pp. 212-213, which stresses the subjective "not *wanting* to know" the proffered reality). The midrash on the utter panic of the Egyptians in 17.10 has them "refusing *(arnoumenoi)* to look even at the air, though it nowhere could be avoided." The only other uses are in 4 Macc 8:7 and 10:15 of denying the Law of Moses and "the brotherhood" of the famous family of martyrs. Riesenfeld, p. 210, has suggested that this denial is tantamount to "not wanting to have anything to do with" or "to deny one's interest in something/person."

Evidently a religious sense for the verb began to emerge in Alexandrian Jewish circles as the Christian era approached. (Note the secular authors cited by Riesenfeld, p. 210 n. 12 and p. 215 n. 26.) The new sense was signaled by the unclassical but Hellenistic use of an accusative of person after the verb (Riesenfeld, p. 210 n. 12; MM *s.v.*), once it had begun to signify a denial of interest in relation to another (Riesenfeld, pp. 209-210). The compound *aparneisthai* occurs only in LXX Isa 31:7 (= Hebrew *m's*) of men rejecting their handmade idols (cf. Riesenfeld, p. 211, which stresses "denying their interest in/or approval of them" and cites Lucian *De morte, per.* 13, of Christians "denying" Greek gods; Schlier, *TDNT* 1.471 n. 2). Apparently none of the thirty-three uses in Josephus takes the accusative of person.

In the Ap. Frs., Ign. *Magn.* 9.1 writes that "there are some who deny him (Christ)" *(hon tines arnountai;* note the *v.l., ho)*. In *Smyrn.* 5.1 he observes, "there are some who ignorantly deny him *(hon tines agnountes arnountai)*, but rather were denied *(ērnēthēsan)* by him," which sounds like an allusion to this passage of Second Timothy or its source(s), or the saying of Jesus on confessing/denying him. In *Smyrn.* 5.2 Ignatius continues, speaking of the man who fails in "confessing (the Lord) clothed in the flesh *(homologōn auton sarko-*

*phoron)*. But he who says this has denied *(apērnētai)* him absolutely" (his only use of the compound).

*Second Clement* 3.1, in the context of a rejection of idolatry, speaks of "knowing" *(egnōmen)* the Father through Christ and goes on to ask, "What is the true knowledge concerning him except that we should not deny *(arneisthai)* him through whom we knew him?" This statement in turn evokes the paraphrase of Jesus' saying, "Whosoever confesses me before men, I will confess before my Father" (cf. Matt 10:32 = Luke 12:8: *SFG* §101). *Second Clement* 17.7 writes of those who have "denied Jesus by word and deed" (cf. Riesenfeld, p. 217 n. 29).

Hermas employs *arneisthai* eighteen times (*aparneisthai*, five times). *Vision* 2.2.7-8; 2.3.4; and 3.6.5 are instructive, as are *Sim.* 1.5 and 8.8.2, 4. *Similitude* 9.28.4-8 is the final summary of Hermas's doctrine on this subject.

See also *Mart. Pol.* 9.2.

13. *are faithless.* The verb *apistein* (the noun *apistia*, "unbelief," occurs only once in First Timothy in the PE, and four times elsewhere in the Paulines [eleven NT uses total; none in Luke-Acts]; *apistos*, "unbeliever," appears twice in the PE, and fourteen of its twenty-three NT occurrences fall in the Paulines [three in Luke-Acts]) is not common in the NT, occurring eight times, including Mark 16:11, 16 (of response to the report of the risen Jesus and to the gospel; it should also be noted that these verses are in the postscript and not part of the original Gospel of Mark). In the Paulines the only other use is Rom 3:3, where basically the same question is posed as in this final stich of the *pistos logos:* "What if some (Jews) were unfaithful *(ēpistēsan)?* Does their faithlessness nullify the faithfulness *(tēn pistin)* of God? By no means. Let God be true *(alēthēs)* . . ." (cf. Rom 11:29-32). The other NT uses stress unbelief over unfaithfulness (cf. Knight, *Sayings*, p. 126). Luke (cf. Mark 16:11, 16) uses this verb of the apostles' unbelieving response to the women's report of the resurrection (Luke 24:11) and initially to the appearance of the risen Jesus (Luke 24:41), and then of the response of some of the Roman Jews to Paul's proclamation (Acts 28:24). The one other NT use, 1 Pet 2:7, is also of disbelief in Jesus as the Christ.

*Apistein* occurs in the very latest strata of the LXX, in Sir 1:27 (*s.v.l.*, RSV 28); Wis 1:2 (= "distrust"); 10:7 (of the failure of Lot's wife); 12:17 (= "men doubt" the divine power); 18:13 (of Egyptian refusal to believe in God's word to them through Moses). Finally, in 2 Macc 8:13 this verb describes those cowards who distrusted "God's justice *(tēn dikēn)*" and fled before Nicanor.

The one use of this verb in the Ap. Frs. is Ign. *Eph.* 18.1, of "the cross that is an offense to unbelievers *(skandalon apistousin)* but to us salvation."

In Hellenistic Greek the term can signify incredulity, even about divine interventions (healings, e.g., see MM and LSJ, *s.v.*).

*possibly.* For the use of *dynatai* cf. the commentary above on 1 Tim 5:25 and 6:7, 16.

## ♦ COMMENT

2:1. *Now, my child, find strength in that grace which is in Christ Jesus.* The initial *sy oun* of this new section takes up the second person singular pronoun with which the previous parenthetical note had concluded. The conjunction *oun,* which occurred in 1:8 above, could be simply transitional at this point (cf. 1 Tim 2:1, also after a personal note), particularly if this whole section transmits preexisting material. However, from the point of view of the redactor-author of this correspondence, it could be understood as basing the following parenesis upon the preceding references to Timothy's parents (*teknon mou* here), to the *dynamis* (*endynamou* here) that he has received as a *charisma* (*chariti* here), to the Pauline teachings that he had heard (*ha ēkousas par' emou* here).

The *teknon mou* here applied to Timothy takes one back to 1:2 *(agapētōi teknōi)* as well as 1 Tim 1:2, 18 (cf. Titus 1:4), but only here in the PE is the first person singular possessive pronoun attached, with the resultant nuance of paternal predilection, concern, and tenderness. On the two occasions when *teknon (mou/emou)* occurs otherwise in the Paulines, it refers to Timothy (1 Cor 4:17) or to Onesimus (Philem 10; there certainly as one whom Paul had brought to the Christian faith; cf. the use of the plural in 1 Cor 4:14). Only 3 John 4 otherwise in the NT speaks of *ta ema tekna* (cf. and contrast Matt 27:25, *ta tekna hēmōn*).

In the present, passive imperative (Zerwick, *Analysis,* p. 640), Timothy is told to find strength, literally "be strengthened *(endynamou).*" The verb appeared in the Pauline thanksgiving prayer in 1 Tim 1:12, where Christ Jesus was the subject. The continuing empowerment of Timothy is to come from (the grace of) God. The *en tēi chariti* takes the reader back not only to *to charisma tou theou* of 1:6 and the "grace, given us in Christ Jesus" of verse 9 above, but also to the thanksgiving prayer of 1 Tim 1:14 where Paul extols the abounding *"hē charis tou kyriou hēmōn . . ."* that reached him. The grace gave Paul not only his life in Christ but also his apostolate. Now Timothy is to continue drawing strength and power for his part of the Pauline apostolate from the same abounding grace, "in (= by means of) that grace which is in Christ Jesus *(tēi en Christōi Iēsou).*" The latter phrase appeared in 1:13 above and, in a slightly different form, in the previously cited thanksgiving of 1 Tim 1:14. In Timothy as in Paul, in son and in father, the baptismal grace and the grace for apostolic ministry are complementary; and as the risen Christ empowered Paul both as a believer and as an apostle, so God is to continue "empowering" Timothy as both baptized and ordained. This correspondence considers that divine support and power as a "given," a *datum,* a *charis,* and thus Timothy is told to draw upon it, to be strengthened. God has reached out to him and continues to grasp him; Timothy must now react and correspond humanly to that divine act (cf. the *anazōpyrein* of 1:6).

2. *and those things that you heard from me, through many witnesses, set out for trustworthy men, the kind who will also be competent to teach others.* Part of that "reaction" to the divine empowerment is the second imperative of this parenesis, lit. "and give over *(parathou)* those things that you heard from me *(ha ēkousas par' emou)* through many witnesses *(dia pollōn martyrōn)*." The divine *dynamis* not only has touched Paul and Timothy, but it demands and compels Timothy to transmit what he has received. What he has received are the explicitly and specifically Pauline teachings that are again described in terms of an oral formation rather than the study of a written record (or collection of Paul's letters: cf. Comment on 1:13 above).

The oral formation is no special wisdom or elite gnosis but one that had been given *dia pollōn martyrōn,* which reminds one of the OT provision for "two or three witnesses" (1 Tim 5:19, with *epi*) as well as the ordination homily in 6:12 that speaks of a confession *enōpion pollōn martyrōn.* Moule, *Idiom,* p. 57, has suggested that perhaps *dia* here has the sense "supported by," and others that it means "in the presence of" (N. Turner, *Grammar* 3.267; BAGD *s.v.,* citing Philo, *Leg. ad Gai.* 187, and who notes this as coming from the personal "mediation" nuance in this particle; see also D-C, p. 108). The difficulty is created by the preceding *par' emou.* What is the point of adding *dia pollōn martyrōn* when it has just been stated that Timothy heard Paul himself? What is the difference between the *para* and *dia* here? The MS tradition apparently felt no discomfort with the sense here (see J. K. Elliott, *Greek Text,* pp. 127-128, for Hippolytus's *paraklēsōn*), and the other uses of *dia* in the PE do not mean "in the presence of," though some could conceivably be interpreted as meaning "supported by" (cf. 1 Tim 4:14; 2 Tim 3:15). See Spicq, *EP,* p. 738, for still further alternatives.

If one opts for the normal instrumental sense of the construction, however, Timothy has heard from Paul (as source or origin, cf. *para kyriou* in 1:18 above) through (or by means of) intermediaries who have both heard Paul and tell Timothy what Paul did and said. Thus, at this point the text would be deliberately expanding the Timothean experience of Paul, previously described as "immediate," now described as "mediated" too. The purpose of this further qualification or nuancing of the way in which Timothy received the Pauline teaching would serve as precedent and authentication for Timothy's own transmission of that teaching to others. It is quite conceivable that the observation is only literary-theological and that it does not intend to describe an actual historical setting, e.g., an ordination (thus D-C), in which Timothy received the Pauline instruction "through many witnesses." It may, however, be based upon the memory of the way in which the Pauline entourage during Paul's actual apostolate learned from one another as they learned from the apostle. The recollection of a "Pauline school" deriving from his apostolate and surviving it may also be at work here. Thus Timothy would be understood here as transmitting Pauline teaching in agreement with other disciples of Paul and not simply as a unique student of the apostle. "Through many witnesses" accordingly gives a collegial verification to those teachings *(tauta)* that Timothy in his turn is to pass on to "trustworthy men *(pistois anthrōpois).*"

Though the individual terms are frequent in the PE, this phrase does not otherwise occur in the NT. The addition of *anthrōpois* to *pistois* here adds, at least materially, an element that was not present when *pistoi* alone was used to designate the whole community of believers, regardless of sex (cf. 1 Tim 4:3, 12 with 4:10, *sōtēr pantōn anthrōpon malista pistōn*). Evidently *anthrōpoi* does not mean "men only," an "improvement" that the scribe of "2" sought to make in 2 Tim 2:2 with his *andrasin* (J. K. Elliott, *Greek Text,* p. 128; cf. also Spicq's examples referring to the soldiers of the guard, *andras pistous*). The *anthrōpois* here could be simply a literary or rhetorical flourish; it may have been chosen to mean "persons," regardless of sex; it could indicate this author's preference for taking the *pistois* as "men" but a reluctance to settle the question at this point. The masculine in the following phrase is not determinative of the question. In light of the exegesis of 1 Tim 2:12 and 3:11, the last alternative is followed here.

The persons to whom Timothy is to transmit the Pauline teaching not only are to be "believers" themselves but also will be able to teach others, *hoitines hikanoi esontai kai heterous didaxai.* The aorist infinitive here is dependent upon the phrase "(those) who will . . . be competent" and thus has a comprehensive scope. The term *hikanoi,* which denotes fitness or capability, presupposes that some evaluation has been made of the *pistoi (anthrōpoi)* and that not all believers are *ipso facto* "suitable" for the teaching task that this correspondence envisages. The *kai* = "also" implies that Timothy has given an advanced teaching to these men and they transmit this. K. Rengstorf, *TDNT* 3.293-296, notes the Pauline (e.g., 1 Cor 15:9) and Lukan (e.g., Luke 3:16; 7:6) passages where a man professes his unworthiness and incapability (pp. 294-295) over against the divine power and authority. This passage of the PE is in another order, that of determining human capability in relation to human incapacity, and reminds one of the testing of the deacons in 1 Tim 3:10.

In this verse, as D-C and others have noted, the authoritative sharing/transmission of the Pauline apostolic ministry is being described. What had been described with a different terminology and at much greater length in Titus 1:5-9 is now in summary fashion enjoined upon Timothy. *First Clement* 42.1-4 sketches the sharing/transmission process in a way that is conceptually identical with the PE (*pace* D-C), though the actual verb "to succeed" (i.e. the *diadexōntai* of 44.2) does not appear in the PE (the noun, of course, appears even later of apostolic "succession," *diadochē*). One wonders whether a concept that was first gathered from the Pauline apostolic practice and described here in the PE was within a decade of their publication applied to "our" apostles (i.e.

*Peter* as well as Paul) and then to *hoi apostoloi* generally. In a word, were the concept and even the terminology of succession a spin-off from the determination of those who shared the Pauline apostolate to institutionalize and perpetuate it?

Second, at this point one ought to note the way in which this closing letter of the PE has from this point on to 4:8 its own distinct character (within the epistolary form) as a farewell address or last testament. The parenesis that in Titus and First Timothy had a rather more objective and legal tone, here, precisely because of the testamentary character of the format, sounds far more personal, poignant, and persuasive. It is the form of the testament that of course is the clue to the paradigm chosen to explain the transmission of the Pauline apostolate. There is no chain, no pipeline, no aqueduct. There is an inheritance, a Pauline inheritance that the apostle transmits to his *teknon,* who in turn is to give it over to others. (On *paratithēmi/parathēkē* see above on 1 Tim 1:18 and 6:20, recalling that there are no examples cited in LSJ or MM of a legal, testamentary usage of this terminology.)

3. *As a fine soldier of Christ Jesus take your share of suffering along with me.* The third imperative in this triad (the next occur in 2:8, 14, 15, 16, 22, 23), *sygkakopathēson,* "join with me in suffering," takes up into this testamentary parenesis a concept and even the exact term that appeared in the opening prayer (see above on 1:8). That co-suffering is then explained with a triple comparison to the suffering of the soldier, the athlete, and the farmer. If Timothy is to share in apostolic leadership, he must take up his share of apostolic suffering.

Timothy is to join Paul in bearing suffering *hōs kalos stratiōtēs,* "as a *fine* soldier of Christ Jesus." Bauernfeind, *TDNT* 7.706, has noted that the Greek term in its technical sense designated professional mercenaries since Herodotus (see p. 703) and thus did not really translate the Hebrew texts. The term, however, did not have the pejorative connotation that the English *mercenary* carries and thus was used more easily when there was no Hebrew text (and practice) to make one look for a more accurate term. That a soldier was paid was taken as a matter of course (that there were abuses in such an arrangement was also common knowledge; cf. Matt 28:12; Luke 3:14 [*strateuomenoi*]). The soldier's obedience seems to have been the characteristic that singled him out in the ancient world, and the special oath taken by Greek and Roman soldiers gave this obedience a peculiar religious significance and set them apart as a special order within the Hellenistic world.

Granted the frequency of this rhetorical *topos* in the diatribe, comparing human life to that of the soldiers, the athlete, and the farmer (see D-C, pp. 32-33, 108 n. 5), one is struck here by the fact that Luke-Acts do not document a figurative use of *stratiōtēs/strateuomenos* for a believer, whereas the Paulines know only a figurative *(sy)stratiōtēs* (Phil 2:25; Philem 2; 2 Tim 2:3), always of persons linked in some special way with Paul's entourage and its apostolic work. Notable also here, from the literary point of view, is the fact that both this passage in the PE and 1 Cor 9:7 use a triple figure leading off with the soldier to drive home rather different points about the apostolic ministry. When First Corinthians speaks of soldier-vinedresser-shepherd, Second Timothy speaks of soldier-athlete-farmer. There is some coincidence in concept between vinedresser and farmer, but none in terminology or order in the list. Thus one can scarcely make a case on these data for the direct dependence of this passage in Second Timothy on that one in First Corinthians (which does use the athletic comparison in 9:24-27). Rather, one might posit a common Christian rhetorical *topos,* loosely organized around common occupations in the ancient world, that sought, by marshaling several paradigms, to drive home the practical reality of the apostolate while at the same time showing its "otherness" and complexity. The *topos* could be partially rooted in the practice and language of Jesus himself, who could call men who shared his work "fishers for men," laborers in the harvest, plowmen and shepherds as well as personal domestic servants (Luke 17:7 and see Minear, "Note on Luke," pp. 82-87), stewards, messengers, scribes. The triple pattern is certainly present in Luke 17:7 as the plowman-shepherd-personal servant, but the soldier is nowhere to be found. On the other hand, the absence of the figurative *stratiōtēs* in the Lukan corpus ought not to be overestimated, since the actual devout centurions and soldiers of Luke 7:8; Acts 10:1, 7 act on their orders and wait on their superiors in a way that would make the comparison in Second Timothy come out plainly if the PE came from the same author as Luke-Acts.

The immediate association of the soldier with suffering, misunderstanding, even mockery (Pfitzner, *PAM,* p. 169) was proverbial in the Hellenistic world as Menander, *Sikyonian* fragment 439 K, illustrates: "Open to reproach *(euloidoreton),* as is natural, seems the figure of the soldier *(to tou stratiōtou schēma)* and of the stranger *(xenou)*"; reproach of the former seems better known.

4. *No one on active duty in the military gets involved in the business of civilian life. He avoids this to please the man who called him to arms.* The comparison of Timothy with "the fine soldier" is expanded by observing, "No one doing military service gets entangled in the affairs of life, so that he might please the one who enlisted him." The entanglements are specified as *tais tou biou pragmateiais.* Hermas, *Man.* 10.1.4, offers the best parallel to this passage of the PE when he speaks of persons who are believers only and "mixed up *(empephyrmenoi)* with business *(pragmateiais)* and riches and heathen friendships and many other occupations of this world *(pragmateiais tou aiōnos toutou).*" Thus *pragmateia* is the business of earning a *living* (see Philo, *Mos.* 2.211) and the objective genitive *tou biou* has the sense of "livelihood" here, as it

also has in Luke 21:4 (= Mark 12:44), but not in 1 Tim 2:2, though external occupation is being designated there too. The mobilized soldier has an all-encompassing responsibility bestowed on him that precludes the everyday business of providing for his own food and shelter. The community or society that needs his protection provides for that.

The purpose or motive proposed here for the warrior's avoiding the ordinary business of earning a livelihood is *hina tōi stratologēsanti aresēi,* "to please the man who called him into arms." The clause comes abruptly and presumes a verb such as "he avoids [these entanglements]. . . ." According to Second Timothy, the good soldier wants to please the man who called him to arms. We might have expected "his general" or "his commanding officer." The turn of the thought here is a little unexpected though one must recall that the one enlisting or levying the troops could also be the general himself (cf. Plutarch, *Caesar* 35, of soldiers levied by Pompey [*stratologoumenous*] and then taken over by Caesar himself; cf. also Josephus, *Ant.* 5.114, of Joshua). For figurative use of the verb, cf. Josephus, *War* 5.380. There is no question that the comparison is meant to suggest that as the soldier seeks to please the person (general) who enlisted him, so Timothy is to please Christ, his king. His motivation thus radically differs from that of the Stoic (Pfitzner, *PAM,* p. 164). The figure of Paul, however, is not to be completely discounted here: it was Paul who had enlisted Timothy for this mission (cf. Acts 16:1-3; 2 Tim 1:6-7) in the name of God and Christ. Timothy is a soldier in the holy war, bound by his public confession (= oath) and moving in obedience to his commanding officer (cf. 1 Tim 1:3-7 with 2 Tim 4:21).

5. *Moreover, take the case of a man who competes in the public games: he does not get the winner's crown if he does not compete according to the rules.* A second example is adduced with an introductory *ean de kai . . . tis,* proposing an additional *(kai)* case *(ean . . . tis)* in some slight contrast *(de)* to the preceding. Cf. the *ean tis* protasis in 1 Tim 1:8, which also uses *nomimōs,* as does the second protasis here. The case is that of any man engaged in athletic contests. The present subjunctive indicates the general situation of all athletic competitions. The verb *athlēi* is repeated in the aorist, *athlēsēi,* in the second protasis here in order to specify one situation within the general one (see Zerwick, *Analysis,* p. 640; D-C, p. 108).

The comparison of the apostolic ministry to the Greek athletic contests occurred, with a different terminology, in 1 Tim 4:7b-10 as well as 6:12. The *athlein* terminology here might lead one to suspect that the concept of endurance unto death, martyrdom, is not far from the surface. In any event, the comparison makes clear that the contest alone (i.e. suffering alone) is not enough. If he has not competed according to the rules, he is not crowned *(stephanoutai).* Pfitzner, *PAM,* p. 170, observes rightly that *nomimōs athlein* is the crucial point of this second comparison and that somehow it ought to illuminate that co-suffering with Paul that Timothy is to endure. The previous metaphor of the soldier certainly stressed the suffering associated with obedience, and that nuance is suggested by *nomimōs* also (Pfitzner, p. 171; see examples cited by Spicq, *EP*, p. 743). The precise point is the same one at stake in the various beatitudes pronounced on suffering in other strata of the NT. Suffering alone is not enough; it must be "on account of the Son of Man"/"falsely on my account" (Luke 6:22/Matt 5:11); "on account of righteousness" (Matt 5:10; cf. 1 Pet 3:14); "for the name of Christ . . . not . . . as a murderer or a thief or a wrongdoer . . . yet if one suffers as a Christian, let him not be ashamed (*aischynesthō* [1 Peter 4:14-16]). . . ." Thus the athlete's painful struggling according to the regimen is compared to Timothy's willingness to submit to the hardships that flow from an evangelical ministry.

The athlete who has not accepted the discipline necessary for successful competition, *ou stephanoutai,* "is not crowned." This unique use of *stephanoun* in the PE reminds one of the similarly unique use of the noun *stephanos,* of "the crown of righteousness" (see 1 Tim 6:11) in store for Paul himself, who has fought the good fight and run the race in 2 Tim 4:7-8. In 1 Cor 9:7 these figures were certainly used to justify the wages taken by an apostolic minister in this life. Here in Second Timothy there is no question that the primary emphasis of the comparisons is on the co-suffering with Paul, but that apostolic passion is also to lead to living and reigning with Christ (2:11-12 below), always provided that one has suffered for the gospel and not for his own bad manners or bad theology. The "concept of reward" is not "simply presupposed" in 2 Tim 2 (*pace* D-C) but is integral to the examples proposed and to their terminology *(stephanoutai; tōn karpōn metalambanein)* as well as to the *pistos logos* of 2:11-13 below. Just as the wages taken by the apostle on earth are completely out of proportion to the grace that he has shared with believers, so too are the "wages" given at last by the Lord to his soldiers, athletes, and farmers all out of proportion to their human contribution to his work.

The verb *stephanoun,* passive in this metaphor, reminds the reader that in the primary reference the crown is given by God. The only other NT use of this verb, in Heb 2:7, 9, offers a suggestive parallel to this passage in Second Timothy, for there the LXX Ps 8:6, "You [God] crowned him with glory and honor *(doxēi kai timēi* [cf. *supra* on 1 Tim 1:17] *estephanōsas),*" is interpreted of Jesus "crowned with glory and honor because of the suffering *(pathēma)* of death." Thus one must realize in reading these comparisons that they are *ex convenientia* and *post hoc.* A suffering Paul and Timothy do not get their crown *because* athletes are awarded. They receive it because they are suffering in Christ and Christ was crowned because of his mortal suffering. The athlete's crown is an illustration and a parable for quite another order and causality.

6. *Or again: the farmer on the job ought to be the first to have his share of the crops.* It was Paul and Timothy themselves that were the subjects of *kopiōmen* (followed by *kai agōnizōmetha*) in 1 Tim 4:10 (see commentary *in loc.*). In 1 Tim 5:17 it was the *presbyteroi.* As there, so here the emphasis is upon the grueling, wearisome, permanent (present participle) routine of the job being described. Moule, *Idiom,* pp. 95, 104, suggests that one translates the participle here as "industrious." As was noted in connection with 1 Tim 4:10, the comparison of the apostolic task with that of harvest workers occurs in several strata of the NT tradition. Not only the plowman or the thresher but even the ox treading out the grain helps bring in the harvest and gets his living from that task in the Pauline tradition (see 1 Cor 9:1-11 and above on 1 Tim 5:18). First Corinthians 9:7 takes its illustration from the grape crop. Here in 2 Tim 2:7 the actual term *geōrgos* appears for the only time in the Pauline epistolary (though *geōrgion* occurs as an NT *hapax* in 1 Cor 3:9). Its one other epistolary use is in James 5:7. The remaining seventeen NT occurrences of the word are in the Gospels (none in Acts), sixteen of them concentrated within a single pericope of the triple tradition (Mark 12:1-9; Luke 20:9-16; Matt 21:33-41, *SFG* §278), the parable of the tenant farmers who kill the son of the owner of the vineyard that they work. In the single use in John 15:1 the Father himself has become the *geōrgos* for his vine. In fact, in every NT use of this noun, it is part of a parable or comparison. Here in the PE we encounter a characteristically Pauline concept being joined to a term that belongs in quite another tradition (including the Lukan).

The *Georgics* of Virgil give an idealized Roman portrait of life on the farm for a society that did not particularly relish it. The *Dyscolos* of Menander presents what was probably a far more popular and unforgettable picture of the farmer in Knemon, the antihero of that play (cf. Handley, *Dyskolos,* pp. 11-12, 22-24) who "spends his days hauling wood, digging, slaving — and hating everyone in town" (Casson, *Ancient Comedy,* p. 71; Handley 1.31-32: *xylophorōn, skaptōn, t' ae[i /ponōn . . .*). The rather Utopian view of farmer and soldier here may be another slight indication of the Roman provenance of this correspondence.

F. Hauck, *TDNT* 3.614-616, has observed how the term *karpos,* "fruit," is used on occasion of the outcome of the apostolic task, as in Rom 1:13; Phil 1:22, even of the collection for the Jerusalem poor (Rom 15:28), and as a figure for the material nourishment that the apostolic minister receives for his work (1 Cor 9:7). The figure here in Second Timothy has moved beyond that, for "the crops" are surely here that final harvest that the farmer-minister has labored to bring in and in which he is the first to share, but always the first of a great company (cf. below 4:8 on "the crown of the upright life" that the Lord will give to Paul "on that Day," "and not only (to) me but also to all who have their hearts set on his revelation"). Perhaps the eschatological harvest of the sower parable ought to be noted in this connection (Mark 4:7-8 = Luke 8:8 = Matt 13:8) as well as Mark 4:29 (which emphasizes the divine action in contrast to the "inaction" of the sower). In Matt 13:26 a distinction is made between the appearance of the *karpos,* filled with weeds, and the harvest still to come. This passage in Second Timothy visualizes the farmer's share in one completed harvest.

7. *Consider what I am saying here, Timothy; for in every way the Lord will grant you insight.* The threefold comparison completed, the author now reviews it with the admonition "Consider what I am saying here." The perception of the realities signified by the words and figures just employed is urged upon Timothy. The implication is that they have not been casually chosen and that they will repay continuing analysis (present imperative) in terms at least of the *sygkakopathēsan* on which they depend and perhaps of more.

The use of *ho legō* here is significant. First, the singular *ho* includes certainly the materials in verses 3-6 and could extend to all that has been adduced under the three imperatives that opened this parenesis (thus 2:1-2 as well as 3:3-6; see J. K. Elliott, *Greek Text,* p. 131, on *ha* in many MSS and note the use of *ho prepei* in 1 Tim 2:10 also). It is even possible that *ho legō* refers to the following sentence. Second, the verb, on the face of it, means "what I am saying," though it evidently refers to "what I am writing" (cf. the *graphō* of 1 Tim 3:14 as well as the forms of *legein* in 1 Tim 2:7; 4:1; 5:18). In this connection Eph 3:3-4 ought to be noted where the author avers: ". . . the mystery was made known to me by revelation, just as I have briefly written above *(proegrapsa).* When you read this *(pros ho anaginoskontes)* you can perceive my insight (*tēn synesin* [cf. *infra* in 2 Tim 2:7]) into the mystery of Christ." As Barth, AB *Eph,* p. 330, has noted, the reading here is the public reading out of the written text to a group that was, by and large, unlettered. Thus, both "to speak/to read" had soft edges that made them suitable to designate "to write/to listen."

The power to understand as just commanded is no linguistic-literary critical insight but an understanding and penetration in faith. Christ's gift of *synesin en pasin* is what makes the commanded understanding of *noei* possible (note that the minuscule MSS 1836 actually reads *dynamin* here). It should also be noted that "insight" is a gift (grace) along with "mercy" and "charisma."

If the *ho* above did not refer to verses 1-2, or if it actually referred to this very promise, then *en pasin* surely embraces all the matters in the preceding exhortation. But what is meant by *synesin,* a term that the PE use only here? In Col 1:9 Paul prays that the members of that church may "be filled with the knowledge of his [God's] will *(tēn epignōsin tou thelēmatos)* in all wisdom and insight *(sophiai kai synesei)* worked by the Spirit (*pneumatikēi* [Lohse's trans., *Col,* p. 24])." Conzelmann, *TDNT* 7.895, says that for Paul "Understanding and conduct are an indissoluble unity." Lohse, *Col,* p. 26, has noted how understanding of (or insight into) the will of God "is always connected with the command to follow God's will and to do it," not only in the first generation of Christianity but also in Judaism. Moreover, this insight is God's gift, as is the power to implement it. Thus when Mark 12:33 (cf. 30) makes his unique addition to "the greatest commandment," it is to say that one must love God not only with heart and soul and strength but also *ex holēs tēs syneseōs,* thus ordering the intellectual perception signified by *synesis* to the activity designated by *agapan.*

The one occurrence of *synesis* in Luke (2:47) is of the astonishing insight or perception of the boy Jesus as he questioned the religious teachers of Judaism. Of the eight Lukan uses of the verb *syniemi* (which does not occur in the PE), the usage of Luke 24:45, where the risen Jesus opens the mind *(noun)* of the disciples "to understand the Scriptures *(tou synienai tas graphas),*" is particularly pertinent to this passage of Second Timothy, where "the Lord (*Kyrios* = the risen Jesus)" is to give insight into what has just been written. Again one must envision a perception of the link between what was being taught and what ought to be done.

H. Conzelmann, *TDNT* 7.888-896, has noted how in secular Greek generally this terminology was associated with hearing or listening (cf. the preceding *legō* in 2 Tim 2:7) that issued in understanding judgments (p. 889). The LXX witnesses to the belief of Israel that (at least in matters pertaining to God) such a power to hear/understand was a divine gift that did not figure in man's natural faculties but one that he must strive to obtain. *Synesis* was paired with *sophia* (as in Col 1:9) as an endowment that a man prayed the Lord would give (1 Chron 22:12), and it was frequently linked with the Spirit of God (cf. LXX Exod 31:3; 35:31; Deut 34:9). The great description of the messianic endowments in LXX Isa 11:2 leads off with, "And the Spirit of the Lord shall rest upon him, the spirit of wisdom and understanding *(pneuma sophias kai syneseōs)*. . . ." The wisdom and insight here as elsewhere in the OT are not speculative, theoretical, or abstract. They refer to practical insight into what is actually happening with the ability to take appropriate action (cf. the great Solomonic prayer of LXX 2 Chron 1:10-11, *sophian kai synesin dos moi,* and what follows, with the parallel 3 Kgdms 3:9, 11-12, *kai dōseis . . . kardian akouein kai diakrinein,* which become *synesin* [*s.v.l.* or *syniein*] in v. 11 and *kaidian phronimēn kai sophēn* in v. 12).

It is particularly the Hebrew roots *byn,* "to understand," and *śkl,* "to be prudent; consider; ponder," as well as *ydʿ* and others that have been translated by *syniēmi/synesis,* and in the Qumran texts these roots are practically synonymous. Conzelmann has assembled the texts (cf. also Lohse, *Col,* pp. 25-27) that illustrate the conviction of the sectaries that "all insight comes from 'the God of perceptions'" (p. 891) whose deeds (mysteries) are the source of knowledge and of life. In Qumran, too, there is a role for the Spirit and for the legitimate teacher, authorized interpreter of the law and of how to put it into practice (p. 892). In the light of 2 Tim 2:2, it is important to note how the Qumran rule (1QS 1.1 and 3.13: Dupont-Sommer, *EWQ*, p. 77; cf. also 9.12, 21) provides for those insightful persons *(mśkylym)* who are to transmit that authentic teaching to the community (cf. A. R. C. Leaney, *RQM*, pp. 72-75, 118).

In the Ap. Frs., *1 Clem.* 16.12 uses the noun in quoting LXX Isa 53:11, and then in 32.4 and 33.3. The former is a declaration in the Pauline tradition that "we . . . are not made righteous by ourselves or by our wisdom or understanding or piety *(sophias ē syneseōs ē eusebeias)*. . . ." The latter is a description (with some Stoic echoes) of God the creator: ". . . by his infinitely great might did he establish the heavens, and by his incomprehensible understanding *(akatalēptōi . . . synesei)* did he order (*diekosmēsen* [Conzelmann, p. 896]) them." Ign. *Pol.* 1.3 exhorts his colleague: "Be diligent with unceasing prayer. Entreat *(aitou)* for wisdom *(synesin)* greater than you have," and thus takes up that typically biblical theme of seeking insight through prayer. Of the three uses in *Barn.* 2.3; 10.1; and 21.5, the last is the most apposite to Second Timothy, for it is a prayer, "Now may God *(theos)*, who is Lord over all the world, give you wisdom, understanding *(dōiē hymin sophian, synesin)*, prudence, knowledge of his ordinances and patience." *Didache* 12.1, 4 uses the noun to designate that power of discernment necessary in testing, caring for, and providing work for the itinerant Christians who ask for the hospitality of the local church. The passage may be relevant for 2 Tim 2:7 since there Timothy is to discern and choose the men suitable for transmitting the Pauline teaching.

8. *Keep in mind Jesus Christ.* With the solemn present imperative "Keep in mind *(mnēmoneue . . .)*," the exhortation moves to a new level. The singular imperative of Rev 3:3, which matches the singular of this verse, is particularly notable where the church of Sardis is told, "Remember then what you received and heard *(eilēphas kai ēkousas)*; keep *(tērei)* that and repent." In the Pauline tradition the readers are commanded to remember the work *(kopon)* by which Paul and his confreres supported themselves while preaching (1 Thess 2:9), to remember his chains that are badges of his authority (Col 4:18; see Lohse, *Col*, p. 177 n. 63) and his whole ministry, to remember their own condition as pagans outside of God's grace and covenant (Eph 2:11). In 1 Thess 1:3 the members of the apostolic entourage are "unceasingly remembering" the Thessalonian believers in prayer, and 2 Thess 2:5 asks whether those believers remember the actual teaching *(tauta elegon)* of Paul in their midst. The usage in Gal 2:10 of "remembering the poor" is important, for it illustrates the immediately practical effect that any "remembering" was to have.

"Remember Lot's wife" of Luke 17:32 is an appeal to an "act of God" cited from "the Scriptures" that ought to guide the present conduct of those who hear the teacher. In Acts 20:31, 35 it is Paul himself who is depicted as exhorting the Ephesian churchmen to remember the way in which the apostle had unceasingly exhorted *(nouthetōn)* them as well as the way in which Paul's conduct of his work had been in accord with "the words of the Lord Jesus" that they remembered.

It is not only the Pauline and Lukan traditions that join a remembering of the apostle with a remembering of the works of God and his Christ; the concept appears also in the command of Heb 13:7, "remember your leaders, those who spoke to you the word of God; consider the outcome of their life and imitate their faith" (cf. Michel, *TDNT* 4.682). *Didache* 4.1 uses a cognate verb when it directs, "My child, you shall remember *(mnēsthēsēi),* day and night, him who speaks the word of God to you, and you shall honor him as the Lord. . . ."

Here the object of the act of memory is the person of "Jesus Christ" (on the order of the names see Titus 1:1). The order here probably belongs to a source that is being cited, possibly a creedal confession based upon the apostolic (in this case, Pauline) kerygma. To the name of the man, Jesus, the title "Christ," i.e. the anointed king of the Jews, has been added. Two further phrases modify the name with its title. The Christ "raised from the dead *(egēgermenon ek nekrōn)*" who was Jesus "from the seed of David *(ek spermatos Dauid)*." Spicq, *EP,* p. 746, suggests a quotation here of an archaic Palestinian credo or a kerygmatic formula (cf. D-C).

*risen from the dead.* The fact that the PE only here use the term *egeirō* may again indicate a quotation of a source. It is especially used for describing the resurrection of Jesus, in both passive and active forms, the former always implying and the latter often saying explicitly that God (i.e. the Father, *ho theos*) raised the Lord Jesus (cf., e.g., Acts 3:15; 4:10; 5:30; 10:40; and for the last time in Acts, 13:30, 37; Rom 10:9; 1 Cor 6:14; etc.), and it may well go back to the most archaic articulation in Greek of the Jerusalem kerygma (cf. 1 Cor 15:4; *anistanai* would be more Hellenistic). Curiously, there is only one other occasion in the PE when the resurrection is explicitly spoken of, and that is in 2 Tim 2:18, and then the noun *anastasis* is used (see commentary *in loc.* and note that the PE never use the verb *anistēmi,* which occurs 107 times in the NT but never *anestēken* of Jesus' rising — for the term had too much of a present meaning; BDF §342; cf. on *estēken* of 2 Tim 2:19). The formulation here keeps the passive of the primitive formula but condenses "died and was buried" into the adverbial phrase "from the dead *(ek nekrōn)*" that presumes the brute facts of physical death and burial and speaks explicitly of the world of the dead, i.e. the shadowy but real human existence beyond the grave (cf. R. Bultmann, *TDNT* 4.892-893). Not only from physical death and burial but from this world of the dead, God raised Jesus Christ. The one other use of *nekroi* in the PE is at 4:1 below, also a (bipartite) formula that speaks of "Christ Jesus who is going to judge the living and dead *(zōntas kai nekrous).*" There one clearly sees that two human societies are being spoken of, those who live in this order and those who are in another order beyond this life, the *nekrōn.* Jesus of Nazareth entered both orders, the former by his incarnation, the latter by his death on the cross. Because he brought salvation to both, he will also bring judgment to both. The PE are in contrast to much of the rest of the NT in their rare mention of the *nekroi.*

*from the line of David.* The second phrase of this creedal confession describes Jesus as "from the seed of David *(ek spermatos Dauid).*" Neither noun occurs otherwise in the PE, a possible indication of the formulaic source being adduced here. Indeed, though the phrase *sperma Abraam/autou* is not unusual in Luke-Acts and the other Paulines (Luke 1:55; Acts 3:25; 7:5-6; Rom 4:13, 16, 18; 9:7-8; 11:1; 2 Cor 11:22; Gal 3:16, 19, 29; and otherwise in NT only Heb 2:16), the description of Jesus as *ek spermatos Dauid* is again explicit only in Rom 1:3 (where the phrase of 2 Tim 2:8 also occurs) and implicit only in the *apo tou spermatos* of Acts 13:23 (also placed on Paul's lips). This phrase appears otherwise in the NT only in John 7:42. Ign. *Rom.* 7.3 speaks of "the flesh *(sarka)* of Jesus Christ, who was of the seed of David *(ek spermatos Dauid),*" and in his *Eph.* 18.2, of "our God, Jesus, the Christ *(ho Christos),* who was conceived by Mary according to God's plan *(oikonomian),* on the one hand of the seed of David *(ek spermatos men Dauid),* on the other of the Holy Spirit. . . ." See Notes above for Ignatius's uses of *ek genous Daueid* and note in all this usage the repeated emphasis on the *sarx* (*kata sarka,* also in Rom 1:3 = "man, human nature"), i.e. Jesus as a mortal human being. *First Clement* 10.4-6; 32.2 use the term *sperma* in citing the Genesis promises to Abraham; in the promise to the suffering servant (LXX Isa 52:10); in alluding to Mark 4:3 in 24.3; and in 56.14, citing LXX Job 5:25; but never of David, who is mentioned in *1 Clem.* 4.13; 18.1; 52.2 but never as Jesus' ancestor.

*That corresponds to my gospel.* The creedal quotation is then authenticated not with the *kata tas graphas* of the archaic Jerusalem schema but with *kata to euaggelion mou,* i.e. as "in accord with" or "corresponding to" the Pauline gospel (on *eugggelion* see 2 Tim 1:10 and further references there to 1 Tim 1:11). This is the only time in the PE that *mou* qualifies *euaggelion,* but it is a Pauline phrase, as Rom 2:16; 16:25 illustrate and as the first person plural possessive *euaggelion hēmōn* confirms (2 Cor 4:3; 1 Thess 1:5; 2 Thess 2:14), not to mention the conceptualization in 1 Cor 15:1-3, 11. The kerygma is to the OT Scriptures as the creed is to the apostolic (and specifically Pauline) *euaggelion.* There is correspondence but not identity while each corroborates the other.

9. *for which I am being wronged, put into chains as though a wrongdoer — but the word of God has not been chained.* As above in the thanksgiving prayer the thought moved immediately from the summary of the gospel (1:10) to the apostle and his sufferings (1:11-12), so here the preceding mention of "my gos-

pel" leads immediately to literally "in which *(en hōi)* I am patiently bearing hardship *(kakopathō)* even to bonds *(mechri desmōn)* as though (I were) an evildoer *(hōs kakourgos)*." The gospel and its content, Jesus Christ, could be so closely identified that here *en hōi* would mean *en Christōi* (cf. the *en hōi* of Eph 1:7, 11, 13; Spicq, *EP*, p. 746). However, it seems preferable to retain the distinction between the proclamation and the one proclaimed, and in that case *en hōi* here would mean "because of which/for the sake of which proclamation" (cf. Spicq; BAGD *s.v.*, citing Rom 8:3; Heb 2:18; 6:17; cf. 1 Cor 7:14).

Paul's suffering is *mechri desmōn,* i.e. up to and including bonds. The fetters make the apostle's suffering like that of an evildoer, a criminal, *hōs kakourgos. Kakourgos* (one who does the very opposite of the *kala erga* that the PE promote; the *male*factor as opposed to the *bene*factor) is known otherwise in the NT only in Luke 23:32-33, 39 to designate the two criminals crucified with Jesus (whom Mark 15:27 with Matt 27:38 calls *lēistai,* "robbers," *SFG* §§344-346). Note how Luke as a rule palliates what would be taken offensively or scandalously, hence also the weak language here in the PE.

W. Grundmann, *TDNT* 3.484, has called attention to the way in which the apostle is thus "inserted" into the scene of the Christ's death (see the following verse here for the significance of this).

*but the word of God has not been chained.* From the midst of this utterly demoralizing fate and in dramatic contrast with it *(alla)* comes the triumphant and bold confession "but the word of God has not been chained." On *ho logos tou theou* see Titus 2:5; note especially the phrase with "God/Lord" in 1 Thess 1:8; 2:13 *(bis);* 2 Thess 3:1. The sense here, which practically means "the whole Christian enterprise" or "the Church," is more characteristic of Luke than of any other Christian writer (cf. Haenchen, *Acts,* p. 264). As the preceding *kakourgos* took up *kakopathō,* so now *dedetai* takes up *desmōn* and the Pauline gospel is conceived of as going freely on while its proclaimer languishes in chains.

10. *For this very reason, that is, for the sake of the elect, I am submitting to everything. My purpose is that they too reach the salvation which is in Christ Jesus with eternal glory.* 1QS 8.6 speaks of the community as "the elect of (= by) loving mercy appointed to offer expiation for the earth and to bring down punishment on the wicked." Note how the latter motivation seems to be avoided in 2 Tim 2:25, which occurs in a context of Christian community as foundation and temple. As was noted above on 1:15, *touto* refers to what follows, and in this case the repeated *dia* with *eklektous* stresses the writer's conviction that the apostle's afflictions are to be understood as being for the sake of those whom God has called to faith and life (cf. also on the following *hina* clause here).

The *panta* takes up a favorite theme of the PE, universality and all-inclusiveness, and sees it exemplified even in all the sufferings of the apostle.

*Hypomenō,* "endure/undergo/submit to," occurs twice in the parenetic sections of the other Paulines: Rom 12:12 of "every trial *(thlipsei)*"; and especially 1 Cor 13:7, where in the actual phraseology of this text of the PE one reads of "love *(agapē)*" that "hopes all things *(panta elpizei),*" "endures all things *(panta hypomenei).*" There are only two uses of this verb in the Lukan corpus (Luke 2:43; Acts 17:14), both in the basic intransitive sense of "stay behind" (Knight, *Sayings,* p. 120). Thus the extended usage here in 2 Tim 2:10, 12 is distinctly Pauline and non-Lukan, and in fact the *hypomenō* of this verse seems to be the formal verbal link with the "faithful saying" that is cited below as the "text" that vindicates and justifies what has happened to Paul as an individual historical figure (cf. Knight, pp. 116, 121). The present tense in both passages puts the stress on what is happening now (in the life of the one who sends this correspondence; in the life of the community that composed the "Christian message, meant to be believed [*pistos logos*]"), and the shift from first person singular here to plural below puts Paul's individual sufferings in the context of the sufferings of the believing community, the church (cf. Knight, p. 121).

Hauck, *TDNT* 4.587-588, notes that the exemplary character of Paul's sufferings is being taught here in 2:10 and that the ecclesial suffering-coreigning of 2:12 is not unrelated to the Pauline suffering for the salvation of believers. Both phenomena are rooted and based in the suffering of the Lord of the apostolic church and thus can really lead to victory and life with him (cf. the *hina* clause of 2 Tim 2:10b).

Here the apostle's suffering is ordered to salvation of "the elect"; it is "that *(hina)* they too *(kai autoi)* reach the salvation *(sōtērias tychōsin)* which is in Christ Jesus (*tēs en Christōi Iēsou* [see on 2 Tim 1:1])." One notes that the order here is election-salvation in contrast to 1:9 above, where it was God saving and calling (G. Foerster, *TDNT* 7.995 n. 130). The critical terms in this clause are *sōtērias tychōsin,* neither of which occurred before in the PE, though, of course, the cognates of *sōtēria* have been frequent enough (*sōtēr,* "savior," with ten occurrences, and *sōizein,* "to save," with seven; *sōtērios,* "rescuing," also occurs once). As Foerster, pp. 994-995, has noted, comparing the use of the verb in 2 Tim 4:18, the *sōtēria* of Second Timothy definitely belongs to the eschatological consummation of history and is distinguished (though scarcely separated) from the glory of it *meta (= syn) doxēs aiōniou,* "with eternal glory." Though Foerster, p. 995, is nervous about it, the placing of *sōtēria* in the coming consummation and really associating it with the missionary activity of men appears to make the usage here in the PE quite in harmony with the earlier Paulines. See Beasley-Murray's *Bapt. NT,* p. 208 n. 2, on salvation in the PE belonging to both past (Titus 3:5; 2 Tim 1:9) and future (1 Tim 4:16), noting that these are *verbs.*

O. Bauernfeind, *TDNT* 8.238-242, has noted how prominent in the most ancient Greek texts is the sense of hitting a target and remarked that in all the various archaic uses there "is regard for what man cannot ordain or control" (p. 238). Thus, between all the human marksman's skill and the actual bull's-eye another element enters in: for later Greeks this element was *tychē*, "chance," and the verb, *tygchanein,* came to designate simply what happened. Perhaps this nuance made the verb rather a rare one for translating the Hebrew Bible. There is nothing by chance, nothing that just happens when one deals with the God of Israel. (One should note that in the Hebrew Bible there is a realm of chance; see 1 Sam 6:9 for the misfortunes of the Philistines happening by "chance *(mkrh)*" if God was not smiting them.)

In LXX books that were written in Greek originally, the verb becomes more common (though not the noun, *tychē*). The NT texts cited from the PE, Luke-Acts, and Hebrews (see Notes above) are deeply consistent with the most archaic Greek usage in which salvation and resurrection (even the "liturgy" of Heb 8:6) are a target that a man does not hit by his own skill. However, there is no room for "chance" in this schema either: God provides the element that brings the arrow to its target (cf. Phil 2:12-13 and Bauernfeind, *TDNT* 8.241-242).

The *sōtēria* toward which the elect aim is "in Christ Jesus," i.e. in the faith-relation to the person of Jesus the Messiah-King, and it is further associated "with eternal glory *(meta . . . doxēs)*." This is a phrase that is otherwise documented in the NT only in Jesus' saying about the end of history in Luke 21:27 and its parallels, "And then they will see the Son of Man coming in a cloud *with* power and great *glory (meta dynameōs kai doxōs pollēs)*." The parallels in Matt 24:30 and Mark 13:26 read *pollēs* with *dynameōs.* The association of salvation, the person of Jesus, and the heavenly light breaking over the world has been seen at Titus 2:11-14 (not to mention Luke 2:8-12). Further, the phrase conceptually and in the term *aiōnios* practically equals eternal life.

11. *The Christian message, meant to be believed, is this: ". . . for if we shared in his death, we shall share in his life. . . ."* With the *pistos ho logos* of this verse, one encounters the last of the five "faithful sayings" of the PE and the only one in Second Timothy. As the phrase stands, it could refer to what has preceded or to what will follow. Knight, *Sayings,* pp. 112-114, has surveyed the suggestions of those who understand "the faithful saying" phrase to refer to material that has preceded. Thus, N. J. D. White proposed verses 4-11; B. Weiss, verses 8-9; Ridderbos and Fausset, verse 10. The particle *gar* with which the following sentence begins indicates some kind of break with what has preceded (cf. the *gar* of v. 13b). If that is the case (the argument goes), then what has preceded is "the faithful saying" and verses 11b-13 furnish the basis for that teaching. However, *gar* could also mean "namely" or, even more probably, it could refer to material that has not been cited (cf. *infra*). Whether it was carried over from the original

material or the author-redactor inserted it, the *gar* still makes sense as a particle that explains the relation between what has preceded (esp. v. 10 on salvation) and the belief of the community. The repeated first person *singulars* of verses 8-10 make them less suitable for the more impersonal "teaching" that has characterized the faithful sayings thus far and that also characterizes verses 11b-13.

Thus, in this commentary *pistos ho logos* is taken as an introduction to a quotation that begins with the words *ei gar synapethanomen.* Commentators have long noted hymnic characteristics in the four conditional sentences that constitute verses 11b-13. All begin with the particle *ei;* all have a protasis in the first person plural; the first three have an apodosis that begins with *kai,* the last two use *ekeinos* in the apodosis to contrast strongly with the first person plural of the apodosis of the first two sentences. The first three sentences have thirteen/thirteen/fifteen syllables apiece, and the fourth conditional sentence has twelve syllables plus another twelve for the final *gar* clause (cf. Knight, *Sayings,* p. 134 n. 63).

If all are read together, the sonorous and expansive conclusion would be typical of the PE redactor's style (though not necessarily particular to it). The repeated *ei, kai, syn-,* and *-omen* bind the first two sentences very tightly together (cf. Knight, p. 114). Perhaps the fragmenting and loosening of this structure in the remaining stichs is deliberate, heightening as it does the concept of separation from and denial of Christ Jesus. The protases move from aorist to present and then from future to present; the apodoses are all future until the last one, which is present.

The abrupt shift to this final conditional sentence completely in the present tense may again indicate the redactional expansion of this final member of the whole *pistos logos* by the final editor of the Pastorals. It is possible, too, that the *pistos logos* was based on an even more archaic (even Palestinian Aramaic) hymn, perhaps an oracle composed by a member of the prophetic order (cf. Spicq, *EP,* p. 748). This in turn could lie behind not only the Pauline teaching in Rom 6:8, but also a catechetical summary that originated in the Roman church as it reflected on its own Pauline letter and explained the old Jewish Christian hymn (now translated into Greek; see Knight, p. 136). Further qualification of this proposal depends upon the data that emerge from a detailed analysis of the text of verses 11-13.

The hymn-catechesis of verse 11b seems to begin *in medias res,* though the context and particularly verse 10 make unmistakable the reference to Christ Jesus as the one with whom believers died and will live (Knight, p. 116). Yet the text itself simply declares, "If we co-died, we shall also co-live . . . ," and there is not even a pronoun to make the transition less abrupt (cf. the abrupt beginning of 1 Tim 3:16). When Rom 6:8 offers conceptually the same affirmation, the text actually reads *ei de* (cf. *gar* here) *apethanomen syn* (cf. *synapethanomen* here) *Christōi, pisteuomen hoti* (cf. *pistos ho logos* here) *kai syzēsomen* (as here) *autōi* (not found here).

The repeated *sy(n)-* in this whole passage certainly underscores the solidarity of believers as a community (first person plural) with Jesus Christ, but in *synapethanomen* the question is to what "dying" the text refers. Is this a hymn that glorified martyrdom (in the later technical sense of that term)? Though Bernard, Bouma, Holtzmann, and von Soden thought so (*apud* Knight, p. 116), and Jeremias too (*apud* Beasley-Murray, *Bapt. NT,* p. 207), yet the aorist here surely contrasts a "dying" in the past with a future life. Besides, the past "dying" is followed by a present enduring and a future denial, which again rules out a reference to martyrdom (Knight, p. 117; emphatically in Beasley-Murray, pp. 207-208). When the same language occurs in Rom 6:8, it is in reference to the sacramental dying and burial with Christ that occurred in the believer's baptism.

As Spicq documents, this verb is common enough, particularly in Hellenistic Greek, and even the phrase here is echoed in *toutous d' hoi basileis echousi syzōntas kai synapothnēiskontas,* "such as these, kings keep to live and die with" (trans. WCW; see MM *s.v.*), cited by Athenaeus 6.249 B, about a certain Adiataunus whose 600 bodyguards were bound by vow like liege men to live and die with him. When Cicero wrote to Atticus on February 5, 49 B.C.E. (7.20.2), he quoted the Greek tag as he described himself awaiting the advancing Caesar: *Ego autem in Italia kai synapothanein,* "Now if it [the impending war] is to be in Italy, I am ready to die with her [Italy]. . . ."

It was not only the philosophical tradition that spoke of parents dying with their children (*tois teknois synapothnēiskein;* Stobaeus 2.7.13, *ap.* Spicq) but the dramatic tradition as well (Euripides, *Suppliant Women* 1007), asserting that "death is sweetest when one dies along with *(synapothnēiskein)* those dear ones who have died already" (cf. *ibid.* 1040). Unfortunately, only the title of the comedy of Diphilus (fourth-third century B.C.E.), *synapothnēiskontes,* has survived, but significantly, in the prologue of the *Adelphoe* (6-10) of Terence: *Synapothnescontes Diphili comoedia est:/eam Commorientis Plautus fecit fabulam,* "There is a comedy by Diphilus called Synapothnescontes: from it Plautus has fashioned his play *Commorientes*" (trans. WCW; the Latin *commorior* means "to die with" or "die at the same time as," OLD, *s.v.*, hence the Latin *Commorientes* could be rendered into English "Companions in Death"). The term seems to have been bandied about in Roman comedy and in Latin correspondence in a way that leads one to infer that it was the locally popular language that the Roman church took up to articulate the believers' co-dying with Christ.

The initial *ei* with the indicative in the first conditional clauses of this *pistos logos* stresses the reality of the dying/endurance without implying that the following apodoses have been caused or restricted by the preceding conditions (BDF §372.2a; cf. Moule, *Idiom,* p. 149). The *kai* that introduces these apodoses further stresses the disjunction between the past/present condition and its future fulfillment; cf. *infra* on the omission of *kai* in verse 13.

In the first stich of this saying, the paradoxical complement of the past, sacramental dying with Christ is that "we shall also co-live (with him)." The "co-living" here, like that of Rom 6:8, is a sharing of Jesus' living for his Father (cf. Rom 6:10-11). See also "And he died for all, that those who live might live no longer for themselves but for him who for their sake died and was raised" (2 Cor 5:15). Just as Jesus' life for the Father began in a fully human history without sin that passed through human death into a risen life with and for the Father, so the believer's co-life with Christ begins in his human, mortal existence joined to Christ's death, followed by a life of love of God and neighbor (thus without selfishness, which is sin), and this existence passes into the life of the resurrection without any real interruption because of that believer's death as an individual human being. The only *"real"* death was the death of Christ; the only *"real"* life is the one he led and leads and shares with those who have died with him (cf. Gal 2:20). The believer's present life in Christ can thus be inseparably united with the life to come (thus Bultmann, *TDNT* 2.869). For a heterodox misinterpretation of this, see 2 Tim 2:18 below.

12. *If we submit now, we shall share in his reign.* The second stich, which begins with the condition *ei hypomenō,* links this citation verbally with the *hypomenō* of 2:10 above. The community of believers, "left behind" by its Lord and thus holding out while enduring affliction in the present order (cf. Rom 12:12), will "also *(kai)* co-reign *(symbasileusomen).*" Knight, *Sayings,* p. 122, calls attention to the *diamemenēkotes* of Luke 22:28-30, applied to the apostles. In the NT only Paul otherwise uses this verb "co-reign," and then only once, in 1 Cor 4:8, as he ironically scores the Corinthians' misunderstanding of what it means really to share God's rule (and thus inevitably the cross; cf. Knight, *Sayings,* pp. 121-122; Conzelmann, *1 Cor.,* pp. 87-88). One current of Christian speculation carried this resurrection/reign concept into the backwaters of Gnosticism (see below on 2:18 and Conzelmann's citations, p. 87 nn. 28, 30). The line of thought articulated here has developed the historical/sacramental framework for Christian existence. Like the "co-living" of the previous stich, the "co-reigning" of this line is certainly inchoate in this life (above all in the "reign" of virtue), but its consummation belongs ultimately in another order, where God rules in the fullest sense (cf. commentary on 1 Tim 1:17 and 6:15).

*If we ever disown him, he is the one that will disown us.* With the third stich, while the form remains parallel to that of the preceding pair, the content stands in sharp contrast, as the hymnic composition turns to the future and darkly declares, literally, "If we (shall) deny (him), that one also *(kâkeinos)* will deny us."

The initial *arnēsometha* of 2 Tim 2:12 surely refers to Christian apostasy (Riesenfeld, "*Arneisthai*," pp. 214-215), the personal repudiation of Jesus on the part of one who had previously been baptized and believed, and thus is the equivalent in parallel to *apisteuomen* (cf. below and Riesenfeld, p. 216, on the spectrum between "practical neglect and formal apostasy"; cf. also Schlier, *TDNT* 1.470, though there is no evidence that this was a failure to meet the needs of one's neighbors). Still it does not explicitly have the person of Christ as an object (as God was not explicitly named in Titus 1:16; cf. Riesenfeld, p. 215; see also Knight, *Sayings*, p. 125). The second use of the verb, where Christ is emphatically *(ekeinos)* the subject *(arnēsetai)*, does employ the personal pronoun *hēmas* in a usage that has already been noted as Hellenistic and classical. Here again Jesus' repudiation of a personal relationship with or knowledge (cf. Matt 7:23) of a onetime believer who had repudiated him makes it quite clear that it is a reciprocal religious (faith) relationship that is being described and that that relationship is breakable. Moreover, the break has been (and will be) public, i.e. before witnesses who can verify its having occurred (cf. Riesenfeld, pp. 213-214). Just how one goes about this repudiation is not at this point specified — whether in words or by deeds or by both. The PE as well as later authors elsewhere explicated this (cf. Titus 1:16; 1 Tim 5:8; 2 Tim 3:5; *2 Clem.* 3–4 [see Notes above], and see Knight, *Sayings*, pp. 124-125). The point here is that the believer's denial in whatever form is met by the Lord's denial on a day to come, and here this brief poetic line condenses the whole logion of Matt 10:33; Luke 12:9 (Knight, p. 125).

13. *If we are faithless, he is the one who stays faithful, for he cannot possibly disown himself.* The believer's denial in turn lays bare the whole problem of the relation between faith and works. To repudiate the Lord is to lapse from the faith *(ei arnēsometha* is parallel to and partially synonymous with *ei apistoumen* [*pace* Knight, *Sayings*, p. 126], as the preceding *synapethanomen* is parallel to and partially synonymous with *ei hypomenomen)*. For this evil act in the flesh one cannot escape answering before the judgment seat of Christ (cf. 2 Cor 5:10). But does not that action evacuate the sense of justification by faith? The hymnic *logos* simply denies this. Human apostasy is a fact (note the present tense of *apistoumen*); so is the faithfulness of Christ Jesus (*ekeinos* is again emphatic).

In 2 Tim 2:13 human infidelity and abandonment of Christ are contrasted paradoxically with his (note that *kai* is here omitted [Knight, *Sayings*, p. 127], but again the emphatic pronoun occurs and the singular contrasts with the plural of the protasis) "remaining faithful" *(pistos menei)*. There is an avoidance of making Christ the subject of a contrasting *pisteuein.* He does not "have faith" in anyone. He does "remain faithful" to himself and to his own promises, to his covenant (cf. D-C, *in loc.*). As Knight observes (p. 217, with D-C, *in loc.*), this is Christ's faithfulness *to us* in a favorable sense. It is not assuring those who have failed in faith that Christ will in turn honor his promises to punish. Rather, God's enduring, saving will is put into dramatic contrast with men's falling away (the omission of *kai* = "also" underscores this, as its previous repeated use in each apodosis affirmed some correspondence and relationship between the actions described in the protasis and apodosis).

Here *pistos* characterizes the person of Jesus (for the only time in the PE), as above (2:11) it characterized this *logos* (and the other "faithful sayings") as well as believers (2 Tim 2:2; 1 Tim 3:11; 4:3, 10, 12; 5:16; 6:2; Titus 1:6), including the apostle himself (1 Tim 1:12). Though the other Paulines (1 Cor 1:9; 10:13; 2 Cor 1:18; 1 Thess 5:24; 2 Thess 3:3) and other NT works (e.g., Rev 1:5; 3:14) apply this term to God/Christ (see Knight, pp. 128-130, on all of them), there is no example in Luke-Acts, a slight indication that this part of the *pistos logos* is not particularly Lukan in language or thought. Similarly, *menei* here has Christ as its subject in 1 Tim 2:15 (see Comment above), as in 2 Tim 3:14; 4:20 human persons are the subject. The one who summons his faithful to endure *(hypomenein),* himself endures *(menei)* (Knight, p. 127).

The paradoxical statement of this final conditional sentence cries out for further explanation, and the closing clause (which exactly doubles the length of the stich) submits as a reason (*gar:* J. K. Elliott, *Greek Text,* p. 135, omits) "For he is not able to disown himself." This is the only time in the PE where God/Christ is subject (2 Tim 3:15 approaches this with the Sacred Scriptures as subject), and even here it is an assertion of what Christ is incapable of doing. The final use of *arnēsasthai* again takes up the personal religious sense noted above but now applies it to Christ's being unable to deny or repudiate his own person. The reflexive use of the verb in Matt 16:24; Mark 8:34; Luke 9:23 of the necessity of a man's "disowning himself" means disregarding, even abandoning as irrelevant, all that belongs to a human person by nature (Riesenfeld, "*Arneisthai,*" p. 218). This person who cannot deny himself is *ipso facto* not like all other human persons; he is like God. In this person, God's unchangeable covenant relationship with men has been revealed (cf. Num 23:19). Men's refusal of and withdrawal from that personal relationship cannot bring God/Christ to change. God/Christ has freely chosen to be what he is to men and he cannot deny his own person (cf. Titus 1:2 with Heb 6:17-18), particularly in regard to the offspring of David (Ps 89:33-35). Men can and do freely destroy their own personal relationship with the faithful Christ. God always remains a savior: men refuse to be saved.

With the *tauta* of verse 14 there is no question that the citation of the *pistos logos* has, in the mind of the redactor-author of the PE, been completed (cf. on the uses of *tauta* above, on 1 Tim 4:6, 11, 15, etc.). There is for all practical purposes no question that it began in verse 11b above. The question is: Can any redactional additions or adjustments be isolated within this citation? There is a consensus that the first two stichs (vv. 11b-12a) belong to the hymnic source. Easton, *Pastoral Epistles, in loc.*, proposes that a redactional addition begins already in verse 12b (see Knight, *Sayings*, pp. 132-133). A good many commentators have submitted that verse 13b with its previously unparalleled expansion of the preceding stich is the addition of the author of the PE (Knight, p. 134, citing von Soden, Lock, Spicq, Gealy, and Hanson; also Moffat). Thus, Spicq proposes that not only the *gar* of verse 13b but also the whole stich could well come from the apostle's own hand (on his hypothesis for composition of the PE).

Yet Easton's division has not carried the day. He has noted correctly the rhythm, the assonance, the triumphant tone of verses 11b-12a, though even here the form is not quite identical from stich to stich (note the change of tense in the protases). With Knight, p. 132, one must observe that certain of these formal characteristics do continue throughout the remaining lines (*ei* + first plural verb), that the rhythm does not alter so drastically that one is obliged to posit a different author, and that the changes from a triumphant to a threatening tone in the last stichs is by no means inconsistent with a poetic development of the first two lines. Indeed, if the redactor added verses 12b-13, one ought to be able to see how the addition fits into the context here in 2 Tim 2. Particularly with verse 13 this link cannot be demonstrated (cf. D-C, *in loc.*). One accordingly infers that verses 12b-13 do not come from the redactor-author of the PE. One cannot thus exclude the possibility of additions and accretions to the most archaic (Aramaic?) form of the hymn as it was translated and transmitted through the first and into the second Christian generation. Still it is another matter convincingly to isolate these redactional elements. Even verse 13b ("for he cannot . . . disown himself") corresponds in length to the preceding stichs, and its striking variation in structuring the thought flows out of the reality that is being affirmed, i.e. Christ's faithfulness derives not from our faithfulness but from his own person (Knight, pp. 134-136).

With Knight, p. 136, and Beasley-Murray, *Bapt. NT*, p. 208, a baptismal setting for this hymn is proposed, and the baptismal ceremonial of the Roman church seems the most plausible place. The eschatological urgency given to the composition by its use of Jesus' logion on denial as well as the fact that Paul can allude without further explanation to the composition when he writes to the Roman church (Rom 6:8) indicates that this hymn probably was already there before 50 C.E.

## IV.B. The Challengers Challenged (2:14–3:9)

### IV.B.1. THE ERRORS (2:14-26)

*2 [14]Bring these matters to mind, Timothy, I adjure you, as God looks on. Shun quibbling over words — good for nothing except the utter ruin of the listeners. [15]Do your best to make yourself a fit offering to God, a workman who has no reason for shame, one who clears the way for the message of the truth. [16]Steer clear, however, of "profane drivel," for it progresses ever more deeply into godlessness [17]and its message spreads like gangrene. Take Hymenaeus and Philetus as examples. [18]It is men like those who have deviated from the truth when they say that the resurrection has already occurred, and so they overturn some people's faith.*

*[19]God's solid foundation stands, nevertheless, bearing this seal:*

*"The Lord knows those who are his,"*
*and*
*"Let everyone who names the Lord's name abandon wickedness."*

*[20]Still in any great house there are not only the utensils of gold and silver but also wooden ones and earthenware, for noble and ignoble purposes. [21]So if a person will only purge himself of that drivel, he will be a utensil for a noble purpose —*

*hallowed,*
*useful to the master,*
*ready for any excellent deed.*
*[22]Shun juvenile desires. Rather pursue*
*upright conduct,*
*faithfulness,*
*charity,*
*peace,*

*in company with those who invoke the Lord from a clean heart. [23]Steer clear, however, of foolish and undisciplined researches; as you are well aware, they breed only wranglings. [24]The Lord's slave ought not to wrangle. Instead, he has to be —*

*gentle with all,*
*a skilled teacher,*
*forbearing,*

*[25]considerate in correcting the unmanageable, just in case God may grant them a change of heart that will lead back into full knowledge of the truth. [26]Then their heads would clear and they would find their way "out of the snare of the devil in which he has been keeping them alive" and into the will of God himself.*

## ♦ NOTES

2:14. *Bring these matters to mind, Timothy, I adjure you, as God looks on. Shun quibbling over words — good for nothing except the utter ruin of the listeners.* This difficult sentence is literally, "Call to mind these things *(tauta hypomimnēiske)* charging *(diamartyromenos)* before God *(enōpion tou theou)* not to dispute about words *(mē logomachein)* [which is] useful for nothing *(ep' ouden chrēsimon)* [but] for [the] ruin *(epi katastrophēi)* of those hearing."

*bring these matters to mind.* This verb occurs four times in the Ap. Frs., in *1 Clem.* 7.1 and 62.2-3, in the last instance with the phrase *kai tauta . . . hypemnēsamen* but, as in *Barn.* 12.2, the sense is "to remind" (on the noun see above on 2 Tim 1:5).

In LXX 3 Kgdms 4:3 (cf. 2 Kgdms 8:16) a form of this verb denotes the recorder, i.e. the one who wrote memoranda in Solomon's court. In Wis 12:1 it refers to the *reminding* and warning Spirit of God, and in 18:22 to Moses' *reminding* God of the promise to the fathers. In 4 Macc 18:14 the father of the Maccabean Seven is described as one who "called to your minds the saying *(graphēn)* of Isaiah." The link with written materials in two of four uses ought not to be overlooked. MM *s.v.* give examples that all mean "to remind."

On *diamartyromenos* ("charging") here, see above on 1 Tim 5:21, where the sense is also that of a solemn, judicial warning. This warning is "not to word-wrangle *(mē logomachein)*," a *hapax legomenon* in the LXX, NT, and Ap. Frs.; it has not yet been documented in any pre-Christian Greek texts (but Menander, *Dysc.* 250, has been noted as a remote possibility with its *gomachōn*, though almost certainly this is the *zygomachōn* of line 17, cf. Sandbach, *Menandri*, p. 58; Handley, *Dyskolos*, p. 132; see also Danker, "Menander and the NT," pp. 365-366). On this term and the cognate noun, see 1 Tim 6:4. The neologism ought to be understood in this context in terms of 2:16 *(kenophōnias) infra.*

The adjective *chrēsimos* is not found elsewhere in the NT, though there are as many as fifteen LXX uses. MM *s.v.* list examples from the papyri and inscriptions, but there seems to be none that corresponds verbally with the phrase "good for nothing" here in the PE. In classical usage the term is employed with the dative as well as with *eis, pros,* and *epi* (cf. the variants listed by Spicq, *EP,* pp. 308-309; J. K. Elliott, *Greek Text,* pp. 137-138; and LSJ *s.v.*), and in Plato, *Gorgias* 480b, one reads, "Rhetoric is of no use to us at all . . ." *(ou chrēsimos ouden hē rhētorikē hēmin),* which approaches the phrase in the PE rather closely.

Recalling that LXX Ezek 15:4 translates the Hebrew *ṣlḥ* with *mē chrēsimon eis ergasian,* it is worth noting that 1Q27 1.2.5 (DJD 1.105) can write *lw' yṣlḥ lkwl* (apparently of the ephemeral success of the wicked; cf. Dupont-Sommer,

*EWQ*, pp. 327-328). In CD 13.21, again with the negative *l'*, this verb describes those "unfit" (cf. Dupont-Sommer, *EWQ*, p. 158, "to dwell in the land [when the Messiah . . . comes . . . (?)]; but cf. Gaster, *DSS*, p. 87, "shall not succeed in reoccupying their native soil").

15. *Do your best.* On *spoudason* see Titus 3:12, where it has the sense of "hasten." Here it has more the meaning of moral effort (see Comment below).

*to make yourself a fit offering to God.* In this exhortation Timothy is to do his best morally, lit. "to present yourself *(seauton . . . parastēsai)* as 'tried and true' *(dokimon)* to God (*tōi theōi* [i.e. to the Father])." See J. K. Elliott, *Greek Text*, p. 138, on the *heauton* of a few cursives.

*Paristanein* is used below in 4:17 intransitively. There are thirty-nine other NT uses: fourteen in the rest of the Paulines, sixteen (three/thirteen) in Luke-Acts (once in Matthew; six times in Mark). See Bertram, *TDNT* 5.838-839, for LXX use of *paristanein*, including Deut 10:8, *enanti Kyriou;* 18:5, 7, *enanti tou theou/kyriou tou theou;* 21:5, *parestēkenai autōi;* cf. also Jth 4:14; Job 1:6; 2:1. The use with the dative is frequent, including references to the God of Israel, e.g., Ps 5:3, "In the morning I present myself *(parastēomai)* to you *(soi)*" (MT differs, Bertram, p. 839); Zech 4:14; 6:5, with *kyriōi;* 4 Macc 17:18 of the martyrs who "now stand before the throne of God *(tōi theōi nyn parestēkasi thronōi)*," but the precise phrase of the PE, *parastēnai tōi theōi*, is not documented in the LXX.

In the Ap. Frs., where this verb occurs seven times, *1 Clem.* 34.5-6 employs it of serving God (though not using *theōi*). The other uses are *1 Clem.* 23.4 = *2 Clem.* 11.3 and *1 Clem.* 35.10. Polycarp, *Phil.* 6.2, apparently alluding to Rom 14:10 cited above, writes, "We must all appear before *(parastēnai)* the judgment seat of Christ." Hermas, *Sim.* 8.4.1, uses the verb of his taking his stand beside the shepherd to serve him. *Martyrdom of Polycarp* 2.2 is closer in sense to 2 Tim 4:17.

This is the only use of *dokimos* in the PE, a term that is documented otherwise in the NT five times in Paul and again in James 1:12 (cf. 1:3). The cognate *dokimazein* was discussed when it occurred at 1 Tim 3:10. For *adokimos* see Titus 1:16 and *infra* at 2 Tim 3:8.

Therrien, *Discernement*, pp. 17-26, has analyzed the whole cluster of *dokim-* terms in the LXX (thus *dokimazein*, thirty-seven times; *adokimos*, two times), including the half dozen uses of *dokimos* to which one might want to add the *eudokimos* of 3 Macc 3:5. This last passage, however, uses the term in an ethical sense whereas the other half dozen refer to refined precious metal or genuine money (cf. LXX Gen 23:16; Therrien, p. 19, and cf. pp. 17 n. 3, 25-26). He has noted how the LXX adds the connotation of trial (purification) by fire and in a crucible to the secular Greek meaning of the *dokim-* cluster (pp. 19, 21, 26).

In the Qumran texts the usage of *bḥn* in 1QM 5.11; 16.11; 15.17, 19, as well as 1QS 8.7; 9.2; 1QS[b] 3.23; 4.20 (isolated fragment); CD 13.3; and 1QH 2.13; 6.26; 7.9 (cf. commentary below on "foundation" in 2:19) is notable (cf. Therrien, pp. 27-29, 31, who compares 1QS 4.19-21; 6.16–17.21, and notes that the usage at Qumran, like that of the LXX, stresses the proof/purification that comes in the Qumran novitiate). Qumran is in the biblical tradition in its linking of the test with the crucible or furnace in which metal is refined.

Therrien (pp. 29-30) has noted the link of the *dokim-* cluster with the terminology for endurance/patience *(hypomonē)* in *Pss. Sol.* 16.12-15 and the *Testaments of the Twelve Patriarchs, T. Joseph* 2.6-7; *T. Asher* 5.4, a link that appears in this context of Second Timothy as well as James 1:3-4, 12. For Philo and Josephus, as well as other Hellenistic Jewish literature, see Therrien, pp. 30-31, who observes that in neither the secular nor the Jewish texts does this terminology denote a moral discernment/testing as such (though cf. 3 Macc 3:5, *eudokimos,* and Sir 41:16, *eudokimein:* Therrien, pp. 25-26).

*a workman.* On *ergatēs* see 1 Tim 5:18.

*clears the way for the message of the truth. Orthotomein* is not otherwise documented in the NT or the Ap. Frs. The *phrase* "the word of truth *(logos tēs alētheias)*" is not otherwise used in the PE, though the individual terms have the sense that they bore in Titus 1:1, 3, 9, etc. *Logos* appears twenty times in the PE; four of these are plural, five appear in the phrase *pistos ho logos.* The PE contains nearly half as many uses of *alētheia* as the rest of the Paulines (fourteen to thirty-three), wherein the meaning entails "the opening up of the divine world and its claim" (Käsemann, *Rom.,* p. 38, paraphrasing R. Bultmann in *TDNT* 1.243) and not simply knowledge in a generic sense (cf. 2 Tim 2:9, "The Word of God").

16. *profane drivel.* On *tas bebēlous kenophōnias* see 1 Tim 6:20.

*for it progresses ever more deeply into godlessness.* Lit. "for in an ever greater measure *(epi pleion gar)* they will make progress in ungodliness *(prokopsousin asebeias).*" *Asebeia* occurs only here and at Titus 2:12 in the PE, and six times total in the NT; the cognate *asebēs* is found once in First Timothy.

The verb *prokoptein* describes men who forge/cut their way ahead (cf. LSJ *s.v.,* noting the use of roads and comparing the connotation of *orthotemein* in the previous verse). The one use of the noun in the PE, at 1 Tim 4:15, is in *bonam partem* and of an individual (G. Stählin, *TDNT* 6.713, as in Luke 2:52). The verb will occur again in the PE below, at 2 Tim 3:9, 13, there also in a pejorative sense (as is noted on 1 Tim 4:15) and of a collectivity (*TDNT* 6.713, 715-716, and cf. 704), which perhaps has designated itself as "progressive."

The idiomatic *epi pleion,* "at an ever greater measure" or "more and more," will recur below at 3:9 (also with *prokopsousin*), and the negative *prokopsousin epi to cheiron* at 3:13. The phrase recurs otherwise in the NT only in Acts 4:17 (with *dianemethei*, "spread"); 20:9; 24:4 (with *egkoptō*) (though forms of *pleion* occur fifty-two times otherwise, including seven times in First and Second Corinthians and Philippians). BAGD *s.v.* distinguish the use here in 2 Tim 2:16 (as though the partitive genitive *asebeias* depended upon *epi pleion*) from the more clearly adverbial uses in Acts as well as those of 3:9, 13 *infra*. Basically, however, all are grammatically of a piece, and the partitive genitive of things *(rei)* can be explained simply from the dependence on *prokoptein* (cf. LSJ *s.v.*).

*First Clement* 18.3, citing LXX Ps 50:2, used *epi pleion*, and in 55.1 the phrase recurs to denote ever increasing controversies. The phrase is not otherwise documented in the Ap. Frs., though the term *pleion* occurs in *Barn.* 11.2 and Hermas, *Vis.* 3.6.4 and *Sim.* 8.1.16 (adjective). MM *s.v.* cite only *epi to pleion* . . . in a papyrus from after 175 C.E. (*BGU* 1.282[29]).

17. *and its message spreads like gangrene.* Lit. "and their word will have *(hexei)* a spreading (*nomēn* [lit. "a pasture"; cf. the Texan "spread"]) as gangrene *(hōs gaggraina)*." The noun *nomēn* occurs only once otherwise in the NT, in John 10:9, with its normal Greek sense of a pasture, a place for grazing sheep and other animals; thus all the uses cited in MM *s.v.*, cf. the English *nomad*, i.e. one who roams for pasture, a meaning that the LXX employs in over thirty occurrences (the reading in Job 20:27 is doubtful) and that is taken up in the two uses in Ap. Frs., *1 Clem.* 59.4 (where Christians are "your people and the sheep of your pasture" = LXX Ps 78:13 or 99:3), and *Barn.* 16.5, citing Henoch 89.55, 66, 67 as "Scripture," of the Lord's people as "the sheep of his pasture" destined for destruction.

The noun *gaggraina* is not otherwise documented in the papyri, the LXX, the NT, or the Ap. Frs., though its meaning is clear, both etymologically (*graein*, "to eat," plus the pejorative *aina* suffix: Spicq citing Chantraine) and descriptively from its use in ancient medical works (citations in Spicq, D-C) as well as in Plutarch (quoted in D-C), where it is used figuratively as here in PE.

*Hymenaeus and Philetus.* On the name "Hymenaeus" see 1 Tim 1:20. The name "Philetus" is otherwise undocumented in the NT, the LXX, the Ap. Frs., or *CII*. Preisigke, *Namenbuch*, *s.v.*, notes a *dia Tiberiou Jouliou Philētou* in Oxy 1.72.17 (first century C.E.) and the dative *Philetōi* in *Stud* 20.106.15 (fourth century C.E.). On the meaning of these two names see the Comment below.

18. *It is men like those.* On *hostis* see Titus 1:11; cf. also the use of *hētis* of the faith, adducing as examples the proper names of Lois and Eunice in 2 Tim 1:5 (*hētis* of the "house of God" in 1 Tim 3:15) as well as the *hoitines* of 2 Tim 2:2 and Titus 1:11 and the *haitines* of 1 Tim 1:4; 6:9.

*have deviated from the truth.* Lit. "have missed the mark *(ēstochēsan)* with regard to the truth *(peri tēn alētheian)*." In 1 Tim 1:6 those who "have wandered away into vain discussion *(eis mataiologian)*" (RSV, cf. the *kenophōnias* of 2 Tim

2:16) are *hōn tines astochēsantes* (on this verb see Notes at 1 Tim 1:6), and that letter closed (6:21) describing *tines . . . peri tēn pistin ēstochēsan,* where *tēn pistin* is surely synonymous with *tēn alētheian* here in 2 Tim 2:18 (see above). On "truth" see Excursus II, "Truth and *epignōsis alētheias* in the PE," in AB *Titus.*

*resurrection. Anastasis* occurs only here in the PE (cf. the use of *egēgermenon* in 2:8 *supra*). Of the forty-one other NT uses of the noun *anastasis* (see Oepke, *TDNT* 1.368-371, on the verb), seven are in the Paulines: Rom 1:4 *(nekrōn),* 6:5: 1 Cor 15:12 *(nekrōn),* 13 *(nekrōn),* 21 *(nekrōn),* 42 *(nekrōn);* Phil 3:10 (with *tēn exanastasin* of the final resurrection in 3:11; cf. Oepke, *TDNT* 1.371-372).

19. *God's solid foundation stands, nevertheless.* Lit. "Still God's firm foundation stands . . . ," *ho mentoi stereos themelios tou theou hestēken. . . .* The vocabulary is not typical of the PE. The postpositive *mentoi* occurs only here in the Pauline epistolary. Unknown in the synoptic tradition or Acts, the particle does occur five times in John and again in James 2:8 and Jude 8. As Dibelius, *James,* p. 141, has observed, *mentoi,* concessive in sense, "points to a specific connection with what precedes."

The adjective *stereos* occurs otherwise in the NT only in 1 Pet 5:9 (of being "firm *tēi pistei*") and in Heb 5:12, 14 (of "solid" food), though Acts 3:7, 16; 16:5 (of faith) use the cognate *stereoun* and Col 2:5, *stereōma* (of faith). In the Ap. Frs. only *Barn.* 5.14, 6.3 use *stereos* in quoting LXX Isa 50:7 (of Rock; cf. *Odes of Solomon* 22.12 in Charlesworth, *OT Pseud.* 2.755: "and the foundation of everything is Thy Rock. And upon it Thou has built Thy kingdom, and it became the dwelling place of the holy ones"; Bertram, *TDNT* 7.611); *1 Clem.* 27.7 uses *stereōma* in quoting LXX Ps 18:2 (= "firmament" of the sky, on which see G. Bertram, *TDNT* 7.609-610). The LXX use of the adjective (sixteen times) tends to have a negative connotation when the term is used of people (Bertram, p. 610, citing the *paideian sterean* of LXX Jer 37:14), though for illustrating this passage of the PE one ought to note the relatively frequent occurrences of the fixed phrase *sterea petra* (LXX Deut 32:13; Isa 2:21; 5:28; 50:7 [cited above]; 51:1) and once *lithous . . . stereous* (Lev 14:42, though R has *heterous*), though the term in the LXX never qualifies *themelios* or any other foundation (even if the stones of a house wall are being spoken of in Lev 14:42).

Of the 152 NT uses of the verb *hestēken,* this is, as was noted, the single use in the PE. It is also the only time in the NT that it has *themelios* as subject. There are 15 other uses in Paul (though none in Galatians, Philippians, First and Second Thessalonians, Philemon) and 61 in Luke-Acts (26/35). Yet the Paulines prefer the perfect form (= present tense; BDF §341 and §342 with its reference to 2 Tim 2:8) relatively speaking far more often (six times) than does the Lukan corpus (about five times), and explicitly in connection with grace (Rom 5:2), faith (Rom 11:20; 2 Cor 1:24), the gospel (1 Cor 15:1); but twice of a human determination or "stand" (1 Cor 7:37; 10:12) as such. The Pauline sense is a strong one (Grundmann, citing Schlier, *TDNT* 7.651 n. 35). The Lukan uses (Luke 8:20; 9.27; Acts 1:11; 26:6, 22) all refer to persons standing physically in place.

In the Ap. Frs. only Hermas uses *he(i)stēk-* in various forms, except for a single use of the participle in *2 Clem.* 2.6 (*ta hestōta stērizein,* "to give strength to the things that are standing" is no great wonder). W. Grundmann, *TDNT* 7.641, notes that the abundant LXX use of this verb is in line generally with its sense in secular Greek and that, when used of Yahweh, "it makes plain that God's word and work establish a fact that has validity, on which one may rely, and that possesses the character of a divine statute." In the light of this passage of the PE, LXX Isa 51:16, *estēsa ton ouranon kai ethemeliōsa tēn gēn,* is noteworthy. Grundmann, pp. 645-646, in surveying the Qumran materials, notes that for the Qumran psalmist it is God who makes a man stand and that "this rising up is also a being raised up" before God and among his angels (cf. what was noted above on the spiritual character of the resurrection among the sectaries). Of the Teacher of Righteousness in 1QH 7.7-9, moreover, one reads, "But you have set me up as a stout tower *(wtśymny kmgdl ʿwz)* and as a steep rampart, and you have established my fabric (i.e. the body of his community: Dupont-Sommer, *EWQ, in loc.*) upon rock; and everlasting foundations serve me for my ground (*wʾwšy ʿwlm lswdy* [contrast 7.4]) and all my walls are a tried rampart that nothing can shake" (Dupont-Sommer, *EWQ,* p. 222, and cf. the analysis of "foundation" below). Grundmann, p. 651, observes that the *hestēken* of Second Timothy means that the faith and life of the church are "impregnable and indestructible." The English *establishment* and *institution* are both etymologically and in usage what the Greek means by this use of *histēmi.* This has occasioned and does occasion some theological skittishness (cf. Bertram, *TDNT* 7.614).

*bearing this seal.* Lit. "has this seal *(echōn tēn spragida tautēn).*" The term *sphragis* is used sixteen times in the NT, only here in the PE but elsewhere in Paul in Rom 4:11 (of Abraham's circumcision as a "sign of righteousness") and in 1 Cor 9:2 (of the Corinthian church as a seal set on Paul's apostolic gospel [note the resurrection in 9:1]). In both of these instances the "seal" is nonverbal. Here it is emphatically *(tautēn)* the text that follows, and one is reminded that the usage in Revelation (which has the thirteen other NT uses of the noun) is of a book (Rev 5–6, passim, and 8:1) and of "the seal of the living God" on the foreheads of the redeemed (Rev 7:2; 9:4; see G. Fitzer, *TDNT* 7.951, and Ford, AB *Rev,* pp. 116-117, 121-124), doubtless to be conceived of as an alphabetical or other symbolic mark (cf. the symbolic mark or number [*charagma/arithmos*] of the beast in Rev 13:16-18 on hand or forehead). See also Ezek 9, where the scribe is ordered to place a mark on the foreheads of those who are to be spared in the threatened slaughter.

The twenty-five LXX uses of *sphragis,* almost always for the Hebrew *ḥtm,* have been surveyed by Fitzer, *TDNT* 7.943-946. Of particular note for this passage in the PE are the passages where the seal consists of words inscribed on stones (apparently always relatively small, precious ones = cf., e.g., LXX Exod 28:21 [proper names]; 36:21 and cf. 36:13 [again of the names of the twelve sons of Israel], as well as Sir 45:11). Sirach uses the term more than any other LXX book (nine times), but the use most apposite to 2 Tim 2:19 is Sir 42:6: "where there is an evil wife [i.e. a poor housekeeper who loses things] a seal is a good thing [i.e. to lock up one's valuables]." Again it is in the Bel and the Dragon appendix to Daniel that one hears of the house (Theod. v. 10, *oikos*)/ temple (*naos* LXX, vv. 13-14) of the pagan god, Bel, on the bars of whose doors the king's seal is impressed (here a signet ring [*daktyliōi,* Theod. vv. 11, 14; LXX v. 14] stamped on the clay or wax *bullae* that enclose the ends of cords wrapped around the bolt and latches; cf. the *sphragides* [pl.] of v. 17 [Theod. and LXX], meaning "several objects bearing the impression of the seal," with the *sphragis [bis]* in LXX meaning the unique royal sign itself). Fitzer, *TDNT* 7.943, after speaking of the sealing of houses and graves, cites an example of ritual closing of a pagan temple with clay seals, but there seem to be no examples precisely parallel to the carving on a foundation stone being spoken of as a seal.

In Qumran the hymnist says, "And he, who causes the shoot of ho[li]ness to grow into a planting of truth, has remained hidden with none to consider him, and his mystery *(rzw)* has been scaled *(ḥwtm)* with none to know it" (1QH 8.10-11; cf. Isa 53). Thus here God's secret plan has been concealed with the legitimate teacher and his "institute," and the *ḥtm* root stresses the divinely willed hiddenness and inaccessibility of that mysterious secret locked within the sect. Apart from very mutilated fragments (1QH 11.3 and 4QpIs$^{c}$ 15 + 1.3, Charlesworth, *Concordance*), the one other occurrence of *ḥtm* is of the Sacred Scripture itself as "the sealed book of the Law *(bspr htwrh hḥtwm)* in the ark (of the covenant)," CD 5.2, where apparently the chestlike ark is thought of as locked and sealed, with the consequence that the Sacred Scripture (the Law) was not read out or acted on for many generations (including "nature's principle" on marriage cited above). Again the hiddenness/inaccessibility of God's revelation is stressed in Qumran. The mottoes on the banners carried for the eschatological war by the people of God are suggestive of the function of the inscription being spoken of here in the PE (cf. 1QM 3.13–4.14; also there are inscriptions on the battle trumpets in 1QM 2.16–3.11). However, the *ḥtm* terminology is not used, but forms of *ktb* are.

In the Ap. Frs., *1 Clem.* 43.2, 3, 5 uses the *sphragi-* terminology for a midrashic narrative based on Num 17; *2 Clem.* 7.6 (cf. 6.9); 8.6 twice uses forms of the phrase *tērein tēn sphragida,* "to keep the seal (undefiled)," almost certainly of baptism but perhaps at the same time of the Holy Spirit (Fitzer, p. 951, tends to consider them mutually exclusive). In *Barn.* 9.6 the concept of circumcision as a (uniquely identifying) seal is critiqued, and for that interpretation its secret ordering to Christ is substituted (cf. Fitzer, *TDNT* 7.951-952, cf. 947-948). Hermas never uses the verb, but he does employ the noun a dozen times and explicitly of baptism (cf. *Sim.* 9.16.3-7, and Fitzer, p. 952).

*names the Lord's name.* Common as is *onoma* in the whole NT (228 times), *onomazein* is rather rare (nine times), and the *onoma- onomazein* phrase occurs only here in the PE. *Onomazein* does not occur in the Ap. Frs.; MM *s.v.* have no examples of the phrase here. On the terminology see H. Bietenhard, *TDNT* 5.242-283.

*abandon wickedness.* The verb *aphistēmi* was analyzed above in 1 Tim 4:1 (its use in Luke 13:27 will be discussed below). This is the only use of *adikia* or any of its cognates in the PE, though of the twenty-four other NT uses of this noun, eleven are in the other Paulines and six are in Luke-Acts (four/two). Matthew-Mark do not employ the noun; John does so only once. It is not found in Galatians, Ephesians, Philippians, Colossians, First Thessalonians, or Philemon, not to mention First Peter, Jude, or Revelation. On this word group, see G. Schrenk, *TDNT* 1.149-163, who has noted that what *asebēs* is against God, *adikos* is against men in profane Greek texts (p. 150), a distinction that LXX usage tended to qualify in the light of the Hebrew faith in a God who commanded social justice. In profane as well as biblical Greek, *adikia* and *anomia* are often synonymous, whereas the opposite of *adikia* is *dikaiosynē* and, significantly for this passage of Second Timothy, *alētheia* (usually opposite of *adikon* [-*a*]). The plural appears to emphasize the multiple separate acts of lawlessness, whereas the singular includes what we designate as "guilt" as well as a certain "presence" (destructive or alluring, enticing?) that blocks out the good men (cf. LXX Isa 57:1).

In the Ap. Frs. *adikia* is not common, occurring in *1 Clem.* 35.5, where it leads off a list of vices and contrasts with *alētheia,* and 60.1, where it is plural and parallel to *anomias.* In *2 Clem.* 19.2 it occurs in a description of a person who "admonishes us and turns us from unrighteousness *(epistrephēi apo tēs adikias eis tēn dikaiosynēn).*" *Barnabas* 3.3 uses it in quoting the LXX Isa 58:6 cited above. Polycarp, *Phil.* 2.2, writes (in a resurrection context) of *apechomenoi pasēs adikias pleonexias k.t.l.,* where again the term heads up a vice list.

20. *great house. Megas,* although used hundreds of times in the NT, occurs only thrice in the PE and five times in the remainder of the Paulines (Luke-Acts uses forms of the term fifty times plus). No biblical book employs the term more than Revelation (eighty times), thus imbuing the term with apocalyptic connotations (see the commentary on 1 Tim 3:16). The *oikia* has occurred in the plural in 1 Tim 5:13 (along with the *ou monon . . . alla kai* correlatives that also occur here).

*utensils of gold and silver but also wooden ones and earthenware.* In the PE *skeuos,* "utensils," occurs only here and in the verse following with a quite deliberate juxtaposition of the literal and figurative meanings of the term. Of the twenty-one other NT uses, five are in the Paulines. The various vessels in the great house are of varying value, "not only gold and silver but also wood and clay," and the four adjectives, none of which occurs otherwise in the PE, are arranged in a decreasing order of value. See Plutarch, *De Caesare* 48.7 (I 730-731), for all four adjectives (Maurer, *TDNT* 7.358).

The adjective "golden" (*chrysa;* on *chrysion* see 1 Tim 2:9) is a favorite in Revelation (fifteen times, once in the phrase "golden and silver idols," 9:20), but otherwise in the NT there are only the occurrences of the incense altar and urn of Heb 9:4. In the Ap. Frs. the adjective *chrysous* occurs only in connection with the vision of the great future persecution in Hermas, *Vis.* 4.1.10; 4.3.4 (which also twice uses the noun). *Second Clement* 1.6 among the Ap. Frs. uses *chrysos* where it is followed by *argyros* (see *Mart. Pol.* 15.2 for the pair in a quite different context). In *Second Clement* the terms describe the pagan idols, "stone and wood *(xyla)* and gold and silver and copper, the works of men."

In the NT the adjective *argyreos* is found only here in the PE, in Rev 9:20 (cited above), and in Acts 19:24 of the souvenir "silver shrines of Artemis." It is not documented in the Ap. Frs. The cognate *argyrion/argyrokopos* (also Acts 19:24)/*argyros* (four times in the phrase "gold and silver") occurs twenty-six times in the NT (almost half in Luke-Acts but in the other Paulines only in 1 Cor 3:12, describing the *themelion* of the apostolic building, preceded by "gold" *chrysion,* followed by "precious stones, wood, hay, straw," *lithous timous, xyla, chorton, kalamēn*). In the Ap. Frs. *argyrion* does occur, but only in *Did.* 11.6, 12 and 13.7, and only with the meaning "money." 4QOrd 2.6, 11 may use the word *ksp* (silver) in its practical directives on implementing the Torah.

*for noble and ignoble purposes.* Lit. "those that are on the one hand *(men)* for honor *(eis timēn)* and those that on the other hand *(de)* are for dishonor *(eis atimian).*" On *men . . . de* see above on 2 Tim 1:10. Only here in the PE is *timē* (which occurred in 1 Tim 1:17; 5:17; 6:1, 16) construed with *eis;* indeed, only once elsewhere in the NT does this phrase occur in the form *eis timēn skeuos,* in Rom 9:21. The one other occasion in the NT when *eis* is construed with *timēn* is in a doxological list at 1 Pet 1:7. In the LXX, similarly this precise phrase *eis timēn* is relatively rare (Gen 20:16; Exod 28:2, 36; Isa 10:16 ["dishonor into your honor," *eis tēn sēn timēn atimian*]; Dan 4:27, 33 [Theod.]) and on occasion corresponds to Hebrew *lkbwd.* For this reason it is striking that Ignatius alone among the Ap. Frs. uses the phrase "for the honor," *eis timēn* (of God, *theou;* of the father, *patros;* of the flesh, *tēs sarkos;* of the Lord, *tou kyriou;* of us, *hymōn*) on eight occasions (*Eph.* 2.1; 21.1, 2; *Magn.* 3.2; *Trall.* 12.2; *Smyrn.* 11.2; *Pol.* 5.2 [*bis*]).

The correlative phrase *eis atimian* occurs also in Rom 9:21, and the noun on five other occasions in the Paulines (Rom 1:26; 1 Cor 11:14; 15:43 [opp. *doxa*]; 2 Cor 6:8 [opp. *doxa*]; 11:21) but not elsewhere in the NT or the Ap. Frs. The LXX, however, uses *atimia* forty-eight or forty-nine times but *eis atimian* only three times: Jth 8:23; Hos 4:7 *(bqlwn);* Isa 22:18 *(qlwn).*

In Qumran, *lkbwd(-ka* or *'l)* occurs in 1QS 10.9; 1QH 1.10; 6.10; 7.24; 8.5; 9.17; 10.12; 11.27; 18.22; f 2.5, 16; 1QS$^b$ 4.25; *4QDibHam* 3.4; and 1Q19 13.1. On the other hand, *qlwn* occurs in 1QH 12.25; 13.15 in passages that describe the legitimate teacher/man in general as one "drawn from the dust and [out of clay] I was sh[aped] as a fount of defilement and ignominious shame *(qlwn),* a container *(mqwy* [reservoir as in Isa 22:11?]) of dust, a thing kneaded with water," and "He is a fabric of dust and a thing kneaded with water [who]se counsel *(swd)* is nothing but [uncleann]ess, ignominious shame *(qln-sic).*" When "the vessels for honor/for dishonor" are contrasted with "the receptacle of glory" in 1QH 12.29, Dupont-Sommer, *EWQ,* p. 241 *(mqwy kbwd,* cf. 1QS 11.6, *mqwh gbwrh),* the parallels become intriguing, for the process of making clay pots is surely being alluded to with the terminology here that describes God's creation of men. In 4QpHos$^b$ 2.12, Dupont-Sommer, *EWQ,* p. 278, the commentator explains that God "has smitten them with *famine and nakedness* that they may become an object of sham[e] *(lqlw[n])* and ignominy in the eyes of the nations on which they have leaned." Then in 1QpHab 11.12, 15 a commentator explains Hab 2:16, "You will be sated with contempt instead of glory *(qlwn mkbwd)*" of "the priest whose ignominy *(qlwnw)* became greater than his glory *(mkbwdw)* . . . and the cup of fury of [G]od will swallow him up by heap[ing] up his [humilia]t[ion] *(q]l[w]nw)* [upo]n him. . . ." Here the antithesis of shame/glory in the career of the wicked priest is suggestive in the light of 1QH passages on men as clay vessels full of shame.

21. *purge.* The verb *ekkatharēi* (from *ekkathairein,* cf. *ekkatharizein* and F. Hauck, *TDNT* 3.430) occurs otherwise in the NT only in 1 Cor 5:7, of the old leaven that must be purged out, "the leaven of malice and evil" (5:8), which in the context refers to those believers disassociating themselves from the incestuous man (5:1-5) and immoral believers generally as defined in 5:9-11. The Ap. Frs. do not use the term, but it does occur in LXX Deut 26:13 with *ek tēs oikias;* Josh 17:15 (cf. *v.l.* A, with *katharizein*); and Judg 7:4 (for *katharizein* see LXX Deut 32:43); Josh 17:15, 18; Judg 20:13 *(ponērian apo Israēl);* and Isa 4:4 *(to haima ek mesou autōn),* but only in Josh 17:15 with the dative of the reflexive (cf. accusative here in the PE). This reflexive in the PE precludes understanding this purge as having "evil" *(adikian)* as its implicit object and *apo toutōn* referring thus to removing the evil "*from* these (opponents)." The person being described is certainly the one being cleansed (LSJ, BAGD).

Note that *kathar-* terminology is well represented in the PE; thus the adjective in Titus 1:15 (2:14, verb); 1 Tim 1:5; 3:9; 2 Tim 1:3; and 2:22 *infra.*

*useful to the master. Euchrēston* is found elsewhere in the NT only in 2 Tim 4:11 of Mark as "useful" to Paul, *eis diakonian* (i.e. sharing in the apostolic ministry or service; cf. Paul's description of his own conversion/vocation at 1 Tim 1:12, *eis diakonian*), and Philem 11 of the actual "slave" Onesimus, once a "useless" *(achrēston)* runaway, now "useful" *(euchrēston)* both to his onetime *despotēs* (the actual term is, of course, not used) and to the apostle himself *(gar moi . . . diakonēi).* The cognate *chrēstotēs* occurs of Christ in Titus 3:4.

The term occurs only twice in the LXX, at Prov 31:13 of the good wife who "made (a) useful thing(s) with her hands," and again in Wis 13:13 in the polemic against image worship: the wood finally used for an idol is "a cast-off piece . . . useful *(euchrēston)* for nothing." See Wis 13:11 of a *chrēsimon skeuos.* Spicq has called attention to Ep Jer 58, where in a similar polemic the author writes, "So it is better to be a household vessel that serves its owner's needs *(skeuos en oikiai chrēsimon)* than to be these false gods."

*First Clement* 37.5 writes, "The smallest members of our body are necessary and valuable *(euchrēsta)* to the whole body, but all work together and are united in a common subjection *(hypotagēi)* to preserve the whole body." Here, too, the suggestion of service and subordination accompanies the use of this adjective, which appears again only in Hermas (e.g., *Vis.* 3.5.5; 3.6.1, 7, to God, to the Lord). On the adjective *chrēstos* only in *1 Clem.* 14.4; 60.1, *s.v.l.,* in the Ap. Frs., see Weiss, *TDNT* 9.488-489.

On the *despotēs,* "master," see Titus 2:9.

*ready for any excellent deed.* Lit. "prepared for every good work *(eis pan ergon agathon hētoimasmenon).*" *Hetoimazein,* which occurs only here in the PE, is found forty times otherwise in the NT, but in the Paulines only twice: 1 Cor 2:9 and Philem 22 (of preparing a guest room for the apostle; cf. *proetoimazein,* Rom 9:23; Eph 2:10; the *hetoimasia* of Eph 6:15; *Mart. Pol.* 18.3; and the *hetoimos* of Titus 3:1, the only use of that term in the PE, although the other Paulines employ it in 2 Cor 9:5; 10:6, 16). The Lukan usage is almost confined to his Gospel (fourteen of fifteen times). W. Grundmann, *TDNT* 2.704-706, has noted that even in Homer's Greek the verb can refer to preparation for cultic worship and liturgical sacrifice, as it can in the LXX (2 Chron 35:4, 6, 12, 14-16), and he has also noted certain "taboo-like features" (p. 706) that are linked with this preparedness. The LXX has most frequently used the *hetoim-* terminology to render the Hebrew root *kwn* with its basic sense of to establish, to found, to set up (thus another of the foundation/institution terms that have dominated this passage of the PE). Cf. the Qumran usage of *kwn* in 1QS 3.9, 15; 8.5, 10 cited above; 10.12, 20 (= "begins" there: Dupont-Sommer, *EWQ,* p. 100); 11.10-11, 13, 16; 1QH almost passim; 1QS[b] 3.20 cited above.

For the uses of *(pro-) hetoimazein* in the Ap. Frs. (in addition to those cited above where used with *eis*), see *1 Clem.* 34.8; 35.3; 39.9 (*pro-* 33.3 *s.v.l.* 38.3); *2 Clem.* 14.5; Ign. *Rom.* 5.2; *Did.* 4.10; 10.5; *Barn.* 3.6; 5.7; 14.6; 19.7 (*pro* in Hermas, *Vis.* 4.2.5); and *Mart. Pol.* 13.2: 14.1.

The *pan ergon agathon* phrase has occurred at Titus 1:16: 3:1 (with *pros*); 1 Tim 5:10 (with dative); and again at 2 Tim 3:17 (with *pros;* Moule, *Idiom*, p. 68, submits that *eis* here is a merely stylistic variation). It may be idiomatic with *hetoimazein* that takes *eis* in Rev 9:7, 15 (as does *proetoimazein* in Rom 9:23) and as many as eighteen times in the LXX; it is not construed with *pros* in biblical Greek (cf. the instructive variant of Tob 5:17).

In the Ap. Frs. *hetoimazein* is construed with *eis* in Ign. *Eph.* 9.1 of the Ephesian Christians "as stones of the temple of the Father, made ready for the building *(hētoimasmenoi eis oikodomēn)* of God the Father." Cf. the adjective in Ign. *Smyrn.* 11.3 of God as "ready to help *(hetoimos eis to parechein)*" and Ign. *Pol.* 7.3 *(hetemoi este eis eupoiïan)*, "you are ready to do good deeds . . . ," and *1 Clem.* 2.7 (both cited on Titus 3:1); *2 Clem.* 15.4 of the Lord as "more ready to give *(hetoimoteron . . . eis to didonai)* than we to ask"; *Didache* and Hermas, *Vis.*, though they use the adjective, do not construe it with *eis* or *pros.* The only other uses of *hetoimazein eis* are in *Barn.* 14.5 and Hermas, *Sim.* 1.2, though the verb is found seventeen times altogether and is represented in each of the Ap. Frs. (plus twice in *Martyrdom of Polycarp*), and the adjective is never construed with *pros.* Thus the *eis pan ergon hētoimasmenon* here in Second Timothy looks as if the use of the verb has dictated the use of the particle *eis;* with the cognate adjective, apparently the pressure was not so strong and thus the *pros pan ergon agathon hetoimous* was acceptable. See on 2 Tim 3:11 for *pros* with *artizein.* In any event, Moule is correct. The variant belongs primarily in the order of contemporary Greek idiomatic style and is of no consequence conceptually.

22. *Shun juvenile desires.* Here the *epithymias* (translated "lusts" in Titus 2:12; 3:3; 1 Tim 6:9; it appears only in the plural in the PE [also in 2 Tim 3:6; 4:3], and always in the NT, the Ap. Frs., and the *Testaments of the Twelve Patriarchs* carries a pejorative sense) are qualified as *neōterikas,* a term otherwise undocumented in the NT but found in the LXX 3 Macc 4:8 of the newly married deprived of *euōchias kai neōterikēs rhaithymias* ("mirth and youthful ease," Charles, *AP* 1.168). In the Ap. Frs. only Ign. *Magn.* 3.1 uses the term of "the outwardly youthful appearance *(tēn phainomenēn neōterikēn taxin)*" of the Magnesian bishop. MM *s.v.* note the usual contrast with *presbyteros,* "the older man," as well as an example of things "in the latest style" (cf. also Spicq, *EP, in loc.*). See Behm, *TDNT* 4.896-901, for the secular Greek usage; see also 1 Tim 3:6 for *neophytos;* 4:12 for *neotēs*).

*in company with those who invoke the Lord from a clean heart.* On *ton kyrion* see Notes on 1 Tim 1:2; on the phrase *ek katharas kardias* see above on 1 Tim 1:5.

The NT texts that use various forms of the phrase *epikalein to onoma kyriou* have been noted above at verse 19. Here one must observe that the actual phrase *epikalein ton kyrion* does not occur elsewhere in the NT. However, a few times various forms of the phrase *kalein kyrion* do occur: thus Matt 22:43, 45 = Luke 20:44; Luke 6:46 (cf. 1 Pet 3:6 of the relation of Sarah to Abraham). The compounded form, *epikalein,* appears to be emphatic and perhaps to mean genuinely worship the Lord Jesus, as distinguished from saying, "Lord, Lord," without really knowing/believing/living out what that title signifies, and perhaps from following David, who called the Messiah "Lord." Note the relation between *gnōsis* and *epignōsis.*

The LXX uses forms of the phrase *epikalein (ton) kyrion* in 1 Kgdms 12:17, 18; 2 Kgdms 22:4, 7; 3 Kgdms 17:21; Esther 4:8; Job 5:8 (not MT); Pss 13:4 (negatived); 17:3, 6; 98:6; 117:5; Sir 46:16; 47:5; 48:20; 51:10; 2 Macc 8:2; 12:36; 13:10; 15:21, and in every instance the LXX understands the phrase to refer to prayer to and worship of the one God of Israel.

The Ap. Frs. do not use the phrase *epikalein* (or *kalein*) *(ton) kyrion.*

The relative rarity of the phrase *epikaloumenoi ton kyrion* has exerted some pressure on scribes who remembered Rom 10:12; 1 Cor 1:2; or Eph 6:24 (e.g., A). However, with Metzger, *TCGNT,* p. 648, and J. K. Elliott, *Greek Text,* p. 144, the reading of S, D, K, P. pl is almost surely correct (and deserves a higher rating than the "C" of *GNT*$^{3corr}$).

23. *Steer clear, however, of foolish and undisciplined researches.* On the verb *paraitou,* lit. "go around," and the phrase "foolish speculations/researches," see Titus 3:1. The adjective "undisciplined *(apaideutous)*" is unique not only here in the PE but in the NT at large. In the Ap. Frs. only *1 Clem.* 39.1 employs the term in a flash of assonant and polysyndetic polemic against men who are *aphrones kai asynetoi kai mōroi kai apaideutoi,* "mindless and witless and foolish and uninstructed," where one observes also that *mōros* precedes *apaideutos* as here in the PE. The LXX, as is noted on Titus 3:9, uses *mōros* thirty-six times, but never coupled with *apaideutos,* which occurs sixteen times.

*as you are well aware, they breed only wranglings.* Lit. "knowing that they produce wranglings." The *eidōs hoti gennōsin machas* uses an introductory phrase that also occurred in Titus 3:11 as well as the *machai* of Titus 3:9. Other forms of *eidōs hoti* also were used in 1 Tim 1:8-9; 2 Tim 1:15. The verb *gennaō* occurs only here in the PE out of its 97 NT uses (45 in Matthew; 18 in John; 1 in Mark). Luke-Acts use the verb 11 (4/7) times, and there are 6 other Pauline uses. There are 10 uses in 1 John; 4 in Hebrews; and 1 in 2 Pet 2:12.

24. *to wrangle.* The verb *machesthai* is as infrequent as the preceding *machas.* It is found only here and in Acts 7:26 (and only there of physical bat-

tle: Bauernfeind, *TDNT* 4.527); James 4:2 (where it similarly takes up the noun preceding); and John 6:52. All passages that offer data (including Ap. Frs.; see below) refer to battles between believers (whether between Jewish ones or Christian ones), and that is the most reasonable inference in the rest; cf. also on the *amachous* of Titus 3:2 and note that the same term is a qualification for the *episkopos* in 1 Tim 3:3, as here *ou . . . machesthai* is for "the Lord's servant."

The whole word cluster has a pejorative connotation in the NT (also the one use of the verb in the Ap. Frs., *Did.* 4.3 = *Barn.* 19.12), something that is not true in the vast majority of LXX uses (twenty-one of the verb; thirty-two of the noun, including *v.l.*), which are generally of physical combat in any case (see Bauernfeind, *TDNT* 4.527-528). The Hebrew *ryb* is usually rendered by the LXX *machē/-esthai,* and one observes how in the Qumran documents the good and evil spirits "battle" *(yrybw)* in human beings who are engaged in religious controversy *(ryb)* with one another (1QS 4.18, 23: Dupont-Sommer, *EWQ,* p. 82), while the instructor of the community is directed, "And let him not rebuke the men of the pit nor dispute *(wlhtrwbb)* with them," 1QS 9.16: Dupont-Sommer, *EWQ,* p. 95; 1QS 5.6 seems to refer to a more formal *ryb,* i.e. a "trial" conducted by the community that leads to a decision *(lmšpṭ),* as also 1QS[a] 1.13, 20, and CD 14.12. In 1QS 10.19 the perfect sectary declares, "I will not engage in strife *(ryb)* with reprobate men" (Gaster, *DSS,* p. 139; Dupont-Sommer, *EWQ,* p. 100, apparently read *rb* instead of *ryb* at this point). The term *ryb* designates the eschatological war in 1QM 4.12; 12.5. In the hymns, the psalmist himself, i.e. the legitimate teacher, is "a man of dispute *(ryb),*" i.e. one who provokes controversy all round (1QH 2.14; 5.22, 30; 7.23), though he also uses this *ryb* terminology of the divine judgment (1QH 9.15, 23; 10.35; cf. CD 1.2). In CD 1.21: Dupont-Sommer, *EWQ,* p. 123, the enemies of the sect will incur God's anger "because they persecuted them [the sectaries] with the sword and because they stirred up civil strife *(wysysw lryb ʿm).*"

*gentle. Ēpion* is a term that occurs only once otherwise in the NT, but there very significantly, for in 1 Thess 2:7 Paul says of himself, Silvanus, and Timothy that "as apostles of Christ we might have made demands on you, but we were gentle (*ēpioi;* note *v.l. nēpioi* and B. Metzger, *TCGNT,* pp. 629-630; Bertram, *TDNT* 4.919) among you, like a nurse, taking care of her children." This adjective is not documented in the LXX, though LXX Esther 3:13b does use *meta ēpiotētos* where the king's letter describes him as "not elated with presumption of authority but always acting reasonably and with kindness." Similarly, the Ap. Frs. do not employ the adjective, but *1 Clem.* 23.1 uses the adverb of God the Father, who "kindly *(ēpiōs)* and lovingly bestows his favors on those that draw near to him with a simple mind." The noun may occur, *s.v.l.* in Hermas, *Sim.* 9.24.3. MM *s.v.* note the use in an epitaph of a man *ēpion anthrōpoisi* and also in an invocation of Isis; see Spicq, *Agape* 3.107-109 (French ed.), as well as the Bulgarian inscription that he cites *ad locum.*

*forbearing.* The adjective *anexikakon,* patient or "forbearing," is again a NT and LXX *hapax,* though Wis 2:19 employs the noun when it writes of the just man, "Let us test him with insult and torture that we may find out how gentle *(epieikeian)* he is and make a trial of his forbearance *(anexikakian).*" No form of the term is documented in Ap. Frs. or *CII.* MM *s.v.* and Spicq note the use of the word in a medical papyrus of a patient's tolerance of symptoms; see LSJ for secular usage, especially Lucian. Only the noun occurs in *War* 1.501, 624, and 4.166 of Josephus.

25. *considerate in correcting the unmanageable.* Lit. "with considerateness *(en praütēti)* correcting *(paideuonta)* those who oppose *(antidiatithemenous)*" (nine of sixteen *praü-* terms occur in the Paulines). However, the precise phrase *en praütēti,* used adverbially with forms of *dechesthai* and *deiknynai,* occurs in the NT only in James 1:21; 3:13, where, as Dibelius, *James,* pp. 112, 209, noted, it designates the "accompanying circumstance" of "a meek and good-tempered life in general." Of the perhaps thirty-two LXX uses of the *praü-* cluster, most are in the sapiential strata, with one use of the adjective for Moses in the Pentateuch (Num 12:3), and perhaps five uses of the adjective in the Prophets, of which the most significant for 2 Tim 2:25 is LXX Joel 3:11: *ho praüs estō machētēs,* "Let the good-tempered be a fighter" (where evidently the same antithesis as here in the PE is supposed). Of the (ten) LXX uses of the noun *praütēs* (cf. the *lect. dub.* in Esther 3:13b), six are in Sirach, which four times uses forms of *en praütēti,* in 3:17; 4:8; 10:28; and 45:4 (*en pistei kai praütēti;* also of Moses).

Those who are opposed to the Lord's servant are "unmanageable" *(antidiatithemenous),* an unusually long word, otherwise undocumented in the NT, LXX, and Ap. Frs. The term seems to have appeared first in the higher *koine* (BAGD *s.v.*), for it is in Longinus, *On the Sublime* 17.1, of one who "steels himself utterly against persuasive words" (MM *s.v.,* who cite no other uses). LSJ *s.v.* notes first-century-B.C.E. Diodorus Siculus 34.12 with the active sense "retaliate" and the twelfth-century-C.E. Eustathius 546.28; cf. also J. K. Elliott, *Greek Text,* p. 145, noting how F, G pick up the diabolic *antikeimenous* (cf. 1 Tim 5:14).

*just in case God may grant them a change of heart that will lead back into full knowledge of the truth.* Lit. "whether God may perhaps grant them repentance *(metanoian)* unto knowledge of the truth." The conjunction *mēpote* occurs here for the only time in the Pauline epistolary, though there are twenty-four other NT uses, distributed among the four Gospels, Acts, and Hebrews (Luke-Acts having seven and two, respectively). See Comment below for further discussion.

*Metanoia* occurs only here in the PE. Of the 21 other NT occurrences, 3 are in the Paulines (Rom 2:4; 2 Cor 7:9-10), but 11 (5/6) are in Luke-Acts, which also have 14 uses of the verb (9/5) against a single Pauline use (2 Cor 12:21). The verb has a total of 34 NT uses. The LXX uses (apart from the 3 in Wisdom noted above) are Prov 14:15, *panourgos de erchetai eis metanoian,* "The Knave (ready for anything) comes to regret it" (no corresponding Hebrew, cf. *TDNT* 4.991), and Sir 44:16 where Enoch is proposed as a *hypodeigma metanoias,* "an example of repentance to all generations" (the Hebrew, happily extant here, means "a portent of knowledge to all generations" [also Armenian, some Greek and OL MSS — thus *NCCHS,* p. 559], an Alexandrian, anti-apocalyptic put-down for the fantastic lucubrations that Gen 5:24 had spawned [cf. Philo, *Abr.* 47; cf. 17 and *Praem.* 17-18 on Enoch's *metanoia*]). The term *metanoia* does not occur in Greek Enoch.

On "full knowledge of the truth" see Excursus II, "Truth and *epignōsis alētheias* in the PE," in AB *Titus.*

26. *Then their heads would clear and they would find their way "out of the snare of the devil in which he has been keeping them alive" and into the will of God himself.* This very difficult passage is literally, "and they may become sober again *(ananēpsōsin)* [escaping] out of the snare of the devil *(ek tēs tou diabolou pagidos),* having been kept alive *(ezōgrēmenoi)* by him *(hup' autou)* unto the will of that one *(eis to ekeinou thelēma).*" The verb *ananēpsōsin* does not occur otherwise in the NT or LXX. It is used once in the Ap. Frs., in a passage that has several verbal and conceptual links with 2 Tim 2:26. After writing on how the congregation ought to be with their bishop, Ign. *Smyrn.* 9.1 says, "moreover it is reasonable for us to sober up *(ananēpsai)* while we still have time to repent towards God *(eis theon metanoein).* It is good to know God and the bishop . . . he who does anything without the knowledge of the bishop is serving the devil *(tōi diabolōi latreuei).*"

The appearance of this verb (unknown in the papyri, according to Spicq, and *nil* in MM) in the PE is not surprising, since the *neph-* terminology is common enough in this correspondence compared with the rest of the NT (see Titus 2:2; cf. O. Bauernfeind, *TDNT* 4.936-941, who does not treat *ananēphesthai*). The English "sober up" catches the nuance of *ananēphein* rather nicely, though apparently the Greek compound was a more cultivated word than the English phrase (cf. the uses in Aristotle et al., LSJ *s.v.*). In Josephus, *War* 1.619, it is used absolutely; in *Ant.* 6.241 it is used with *ek.* Philo, *Leg. alleg.* 2.60, expounding on Noah's drunkenness, says, "So he becomes sober again *(ananēphei),* that is to say, he repents *(metanoei)* and recovers as from an illness." There is not a shred of evidence that it ever meant "to escape" (*pace* D-C, RSV, etc., who use the translation "escape").

The use of the cognate *eknēpsate dikaiōs . . . agnōsian gar theou tines echousin* in 1 Cor 15:34 is of more than passing note since it addresses members of that church who do not believe that the dead are raised (see Conzelmann, *1 Cor.*, p. 279, who notes that this usage of *nēphein* "is a standard term of eschatological parenesis"); cf. *Gospel of Thomas* §28(86), pp. 20-21 (cited at 1 Tim 3:16 above).

The perfect passive participle *ezōgrēmenoi* is from a verb, *zōgreō,* that occurs otherwise in the NT only in Luke 5:10, where it is used figuratively of the way in which Simon Peter will henceforth catch men as he has just taken a shoal of still-living fish in his nets. With *Iliad* 6.46; 10.378, the verb conveys the plea to be taken prisoner and returned for rich ransom. The LXX uses the verb chiefly of prisoners of war (LXX Deut 20:16; 2 Kgdms 8:2; 2 Chron 25:12; cf. Num 31:15, 18). The Ap. Frs. contain no use of this verb.

The phrase *eis . . . pagida tou diabolou* occurred in 1 Tim 3:7 (see commentary; of riches as a snare, 1 Tim 6:9). Here it occurs as *ek tēs tou diabolou pagidos* with the addition of the article *tēs* required by the change in word order. *Ho diabolos* here is certainly not to be translated as slanderer or calumniator (cf. W. Foerster, *TDNT* 2.80-81; 7.161) since the opponents are being punished for their public sins.

## ♦ COMMENT

2:14. *Bring these matters to mind, Timothy, I adjure you, as God looks on. Shun quibbling over words — good for nothing except the utter ruin of the listeners.* With *hypomimnēiske* the genitive would have been expected (as in Luke 22:61; Moule, *Idiom,* p. 37) though by no means required (cf. John 14:26); moreover, the sense of the verb here is somewhat different from that at its other use in the PE, in Titus 3:1, where it meant "remind," not "recall" as here. The present tense stresses constant, regular practice (Spicq).

The sense of *diamartyromenos,* here translated as "I adjure you," is that of a solemn, judicial warning. This warning is "not to word-wrangle," *mē logomachein,* a *hapax legomenon* in biblical Greek. The following phrases, introduced by *ep(i)* with their drastic asyndeton, have been difficult to construe. Some of the manuscripts, A C lat*, have tried to ease the sense by reading *mē logomachei,* i.e. an imperatival "Do not word-wrangle," but this, too, can be read meaningfully only with the second *epi* phrase (BDF §389 suggest hesitantly an original imperatival infinitive, which would be subject to the same criticism). The unspecified character of the persons who are to be reminded does not make the situation here any clearer, but an object infinitive dependent on *diamartyromenos* still seems to be the least difficult choice (J. K. Elliott, *Greek Text,* p. 137).

The phrase *ep' ouden chrēsimon,* not so much a gloss (a possibility suggested by D-C) as an ejaculatory exclamation, is quite clear in itself for all the obscurity of its grammatical relation with the rest of this sentence. Of the LXX uses, Tob 6:4 (S), "The gall is useful *(chrēsimon)* for medicine," and Wis 8:7, "Nothing in life is more profitable *(chrēsimoteron ouden)* for men than these (virtues)," are quite apposite to the use here. Cf. the use of a vessel (Ep. Jer. 59 and Wis 13:11) with 2 Tim 2:21 *(skeuos . . . euchrēston)* below.

In the Ap. Frs., Ign. *Eph.* 4.2 writes, "It is therefore profitable *(chrēsimon)* for you to be in blameless unity, in order that you may always commune with God." The only other use is in Hermas, *Vis.* 4.3.4, of those who "will be made pure and become useful *(chrēsimoi)* for the building of the tower."

The second *epi* phrase governs the dative (for purpose or result: BDF §235.4; Lock speaks of result treated [ironically] as purpose whereas D-C speak of an "accompanying condition," citing the *eph' helpidi* of Rom 8:20), *katastrophēi,* "for the ruin of those listening" (*akouontōn;* see commentary on 1 Tim 4.16 for this verb). *Katastrophē* occurs elsewhere in the NT only at 2 Pet 2:6 of the exemplary ruin of the cities of the plain, Sodom and Gomorrah, a usage that takes up LXX Gen 19:29 (= Hebr. *hpkh*), though there are sixteen other LXX uses, mainly in the Wisdom books (Job, Proverbs, Sirach) and the Maccabean literature. The term is often linked with the fate of the godless and sinners (e.g., Job 8:19; 27:7; Prov 1:18, 27; Sir 9:11; 1 Macc 2:49). Seven of the eight uses of *hpk* at Qumran are in 1QH (3.7 of a beleaguered fortress).

In the Ap. Frs. this noun is found only in *1 Clem.* 7.7 (Jonah to the city of Nineveh) and 57.4, citing LXX Prov 1:27 noted above.

In Menander, *Perikeir.* 12 (already noted by MM *s.v.*, p. 333), the goddess Agnoia (Misapprehension) speaks of an old woman: *ēdē d' apeirēkuia kai/ proōromenē tou zēn katastrophēn tina/hautēi parousan,* "At length, her powers failing, and foreseeing now at hand some *sudden end* of life," where the term = "death." That is certainly not far from the meaning here in Second Timothy where the opponents fasten like a gangrene *(2:17)* on those they teach (cf. 1 Tim 1:3-6, 6-7; *6:4-5;* Titus *1:13-16;* 3:9, noting especially the terminology of illness/ health in the italicized passages).

15. *Do your best to make yourself a fit offering to God, a workman who has no reason for shame, one who clears the way for the message of the truth.* This verse stands in positive contrast to the preceding and following, a shaft of sunlight between banks of storm clouds. The singular aorist imperative *spoudason* is directed to Timothy as in Titus 3:12 it was to Titus, but here in a moral sense, which, as Harder, *TDNT* 7.559-560, has noted, telescopes out of "the external sense of quick movement in the interests of a person" to the meaning of "high estimation" and then "for ethical motivation" as well as "for taking things . . . seriously." A papyrus of 318 C.E. uses the term of getting "intensively involved"

in a liturgical action. MM *s.v.* cite a papyrus of 22 B.C.E. where the verb means "that you do your best." Harder, pp. 562-563, has noted how the LXX apparently did not take up this ethical sense of "moral exertion" from contemporary Hellenistic usage, even in the latest strata where there is generally no Hebrew original. Josephus does use the verb of Isaac "practicing every virtue" and being filled with zeal *(espoudakōs)* for God's worship (*Ant.* 1.222), and in Philo the adjective at any rate is used at every turn, of moral exertion. A Roman Jewish epitaph describes a Jewish wife as *spoud(ai)a philentolos,* "diligent and loving the law," *CII* §132, and so the thought of moral exertion is certainly not totally alien to Jewish thinking here at this time — *pace* Harder, p. 563.

In this exhortation Timothy is told to do his best "to make yourself a fit offering to God *(seauton dokimon parastēsai).*" Already in nonbiblical Greek this verb can be used forensically, of bringing a person before a judge or court, as well as cultically of bringing worship (sacrifices); cf. texts cited by B. Reicke, *TDNT* 5.837, as well as MM *s.v.,* and Therrien, *Discernement,* p. 219.

In the hundred LXX uses of *paristanein,* perhaps the most apposite to this passage of the PE are those that refer to the royal servants/ministers/priests who present themselves/their worship "before him," i.e. God or the Lord. In the light of this LXX usage it is notable that it is Luke who writes (1:19) of Gabriel as *ho parestēkōs enōpion tou theou* and the infant Jesus being brought *parastēsai tōi kyriōi* (2:22). Otherwise in the NT it is only in the Paulines that one reads, "Food will not commend us to God" (*parastēsei tōi theōi,* which MM renders "affect our standing with") (1 Cor 8:8) as well as "Yield yourselves to God *(parastēsate heautous tōi theōi)* as men who have been brought from death to life" (Rom 6:13; the baptismal context ought to be observed in light of the comments above on 2 Tim 2:11-13). Here the actual terminology of *paristanein* + *tōi theōi* appears, and a variation on it appears in an explicitly forensic setting in Rom 14:10: "For we shall all stand *(parastēsometha)* before the judgment seat of God *(tōi bēmati tou theou).*" Reicke, p. 840, has noted how the secular (royal) court and the divine court illustrate each other in the NT use of this verb (cf., e.g., Acts 23:33; 27:24).

The sacrificial offering of oneself may be suggested by the usage here in Second Timothy, for that, too, belongs to the Pauline way of speaking (Rom 12:1; cf. 6:13, 16, 19 of the baptismal immolation of one's self with the crucified Jesus). This very Hebraic way of speaking of virtue in sacrificial language can be contrasted with the Greek discussion in terms of what is pleasing to the eye and attractive in a visible way (Bultmann, *Primitive Christianity,* p. 47).

That Timothy is exhorted "to make yourself a fit offering *(dokimon)*" may lend further support to this nuance or connotation. Dibelius, *James,* p. 88, on James 1:12 notes only that the metaphor of refining metal or an athlete's testing need not be adduced to explain the term that describes the *hypomenōn* (i.e. the one enduring a trial). Therrien, *Discernement,* p. 220 and n. 3, suggests that here in Second Timothy the work well done is precisely the work of the apostolic ministry in which Timothy shares and that he brings as a sacrificial offering to the Father (cf. 2 Tim 4:6 of Paul's being "sacrificed" [*spendomai*] as in Phil 2:17), who will recognize its refined and tested purity. The sacrifice represents the offerer himself, who thus comes before his judge and master to receive final approval of the apostolic work that he has done by virtue of the divine gift (charism) that God has himself first bestowed (cf. 1 Thess 2:1-7, where Silvanus and Timothy are with Paul "approved" as "apostles of Christ," as well as the description of Timothy's link with Paul in 2 Tim 2:6-14). Thus the bivalence of prove/approve or test/attest is present in this passage as in other Pauline uses (Therrien, pp. 64-72).

The title given to Timothy at this point, *ergatēs,* was also applied to every apostolic minister in 1 Tim 5:18 (see Notes *in loc.*). Though certainly used of missionaries (2 Cor 11:13; Phil 3:2), it by no means follows that the congregation to which this correspondence is addressed is (conceived of as) a mission congregation (*pace* D-C). As an apostolic "workman" he is *anepaischynton,* i.e. has no need to be ashamed (thus BAGD) or is to have nothing of which to be ashamed (cf. Spicq, *EP,* p. 754, on active/passive of this verbal adjective). This *hapax legomenon* in biblical and pre-Christian Greek is cognate with the verb of 2 Tim 1:8, 12, 16 (see Notes *in loc.*), and this passage strikingly confirms the explanation proposed there that the "unashamed" here means that Timothy is to come to God's judgment as an apostolic minister who has confessed his faith in the crucified and risen Jesus, in what he did and taught.

Though this adjective is not documented in the Ap. Frs., it does occur in Josephus, *Ant.* 18.243 (MM *s.v.*); in Agapetus, *De Officio Boni Principis* 57, p. 174, Groebel *ap.* BAGD, who employs it adverbially. When Agapetus, the deacon of S. Sophia, wrote his *Ekthesis Kephalaiōn Parainetikōn* for Justinian, he exhorted the latter to learn from others *anepaischyntōs* as well as to follow up the advice without delay (§57 in *PG* 86[1], 1181). The advice seems to be meant for the emperor, not for a bishop (contra BAGD), though obviously it could, *ceteris paribio,* apply.

The third and final descriptive phrase for Timothy, *orthotomounta ton logon tēs alētheias,* again uses a terminology that is unusual; LXX Prov 3:6; 11:5 employ *orthotomein* to translate the Hebrew *yšr,* for making a straight road (path) (see Plato, *Laws* 810$^{e}$, cited by D-C for a metaphorical "way cleared [*tetmēmenēn hodon*]"). BDF §119.1 propose "to cut straight ahead" or "to lead." H. Koester, *TDNT* 8.111, has noted the passages from Thucydides and Herodotus to Josephus and Plutarch, where *temnein hodon* = "to build a road," and has observed how the LXX use of *orthotomein* takes up the secular Greek figurative use of *temnein hodon,* but with mounting stress on the *orthō* of the compound. There are no other uses of *orthotomein* in Hellenistic Jewish Greek (Koester, p. 112, who comments on other terms for the same concept); yet one ought to note how the metaphorical figure of "the way" (of moral conduct) continued to flourish in the Qumran literature (Koester, *TDNT* 8.112, cites 1QS 4.2; 1QH 12.34) as well as the NT (cf. Fitzmyer, *ESBNT*, pp. 281-283, on absolute use behind this) and the Ap. Frs. This use of the phrase "the way" makes it difficult to explain why here in Second Timothy *tēn hodon* (which would have been expected) is actually *ton logon.* Indeed, one would with Koester take *orthotomounta* as if it were the *orthopodousi* of Gal 2:14.

One surmises that the former would have placed too great a stress on Timothy's personal moral conduct at this point whereas the author in this whole passage wishes to accent the undeviating accuracy of his public teaching and confession of the apostolic deposit (*pace* Koester). Thus one can agree with MM *s.v.*, who cite *kainotomein*, "to make a new or strange assertion," that the stress in *orthotomein* has settled on the *ortho-*, with the meaning here accordingly to "teach the word (of truth) aright." See the passages of Tatian and Lucian cited by D-C, which support this contention that the metaphorical force of *temnein* (to cut) in this compound has so faded out of consciousness that the term can appropriately be used with *ton logon tēs alētheias* as its object.

But then, what is *ho logos tēs alētheias?* The phrase has not occurred otherwise in the PE. It is not found in the Gospels or Acts. It does occur in James 1:18, where it has the same anarthrous form as in 2 Cor 6:7 (and perhaps the same meaning if one follows Dibelius, *James*, p. 105 n. 187, who considers the lack of article insignificant, but cf. below). The phrase occurs with the article in Eph 1:13 and Col 1:5. In both passages "the gospel" *(euaggelion)* is in apposition with "the word of truth." Truth and salvation are complementary aspects of the same basic reality for Paul (cf. Barth, AB *Eph*, pp. 95, 134-135, esp. 134 n. 332), and it is quite possible that "the word of truth" is here a pre-Pauline phrase, taken up also in two of the Captivity Letters (Barth, p. 95).

Lohse, *Col*, pp. 18-19, as well as Dibelius, *James*, p. 105, have noted the appearances of the phrase, in anarthrous form, in LXX Ps 118:43; *T. Gad* 3.1 (pl.); comparing *Odes of Solomon* 8.8 (cf. Charlesworth, *OT Pseud.*, p. 741, "Hear the word of truth and receive the knowledge of the Most High," who notes the plural imperatives and suggests that the "Ode" may have been a collect for the liturgy). Dibelius, *James*, p. 105 n. 186, is doubtless correct in tracing the phrase back into a Jewish milieu, but that origin does not explain the meaning(s) in the Jewish Christian literature of the apostolic age, for it is difficult to equate the almost incidental usage in a list by Paul in 2 Cor 6:7 with the dense meaning of James 1:18 *(pace* Dibelius *ut cit. supra)* and the equally weighty usages of the now arthrous phrase in the Captivity Letters and the PE. Dibelius, p. 105, is correct in opting for the meaning "gospel" in James 1:18; that, moreover, is the meaning in the Captivity Letters; it is most probably the basic meaning here in 2 Tim 2:15, where a phrase already part of the Pauline school's terminology is taken up.

Its very familiarity papers over the awkwardness of its use with *orthotomein,* for it was heard and understood as meaning "to teach the gospel rightly." This link of the phrase with the Pauline tradition is verified in the single instance in which a form of the phrase occurs in Polycarp, *Phil.* 3.2, where the old bishop of Smyrna disclaims his ability "to follow the wisdom of the blessed and glorious Paul who . . . taught *(edidaxen)* accurately and steadfastly the word about the truth *(ton peri alētheias logon)* and also when he was around wrote letters to you. . . ."

As Lohse, *Col,* p. 18, observed on Col 1:5, so here in Second Timothy the *logos* refers to the already "fixed, traditional formulas (cf. 1 Cor 15:3-5; Rom 1:3)" of the exposition in which the gospel *(euaggelion = alētheia)* was proclaimed to unbelievers and taught to believers. With Lohse, p. 19, and Barth, AB *Eph,* pp. 134-135, one can stress that this "word of truth" is the apostolic (i.e. here the Pauline) exposition and expression of the saving truth. Eusebius, *Church History* 4.3.1, referring to the early second-century Quadratus's *apostolikē orthotomia,* thus isolates the sense of 2 Tim 2:15 quite precisely (*pace* Koester, *TDNT* 8.112 n. 11).

16. *Steer clear, however, of "profane drivel," for it progresses ever more deeply into godlessness.* With an abrupt contrast *(de),* the correct exposition of the apostolic gospel by Timothy is coupled with the once-for-all (aorist) admonition *periïstaso,* "Steer clear," that was directed to Titus in Titus 3:9 in an admonition that likewise stood in contrast to a *pistos ho logos* the apostolic minister was to inculcate. Here, however, the things to be avoided are not the four activities noted in Titus 3:9 but "the profane drivel," "*tas bēbelous kenophōnias.*"

The twofold reason *(gar)* for giving theological jargon (Easton, *Pastoral Epistles*) wide berth is now stated (through v. 17a). The first reason, where variations on the *p* sound link the words together half a dozen times, is the ironic "for it progresses ever more deeply into godlessness." The "ungodliness" here in Second Timothy is within the Christian congregation, not that which characterizes the condition before conversion.

These purveyors of theological gossip are ironically stigmatized as men who "are going to go somewhere," who are "progressives," for the verb *prokoptein* describes men who forge/cut their way ahead (cf. LSJ *s.v.,* noting the use of roads and comparing the connotation of *orthotomein* in the previous verse).

17. *and its message spreads like gangrene.* The second *(kai)* reason for avoiding the sloganeers describes *their* exposition (*ho logos autōn* — could be of the "drivel" [pl.] in v. 16) in stark contrast with *ton logon tēs alētheias* of verse 15. That *logos* had been healthy and healing; cf. on the *hygiainein/hygiēs* of Titus

1:9, 13; 2:1-2; 1 Tim 1:10; 6:3 *(logois);* 2 Tim 1:13 *(logōn);* 4:3; Titus 2:8 *(logon hygiē);* the *logos* of these "advanced" believers "spreads like gangrene."

This seems to be the only case in biblical and Jewish Greek (see Notes above) where the term *nomēn* assumes the metaphorical sense of a spreading (as of fire, baldness, sores, ulcers) that can be documented rather more frequently in profane Greek (LSJ *s.v.*). Polybius, *Histories* 1.81.6, has *poieitai tēn nomēn* of ulcers spreading, which he then compares with moral disorders in the human soul. There is no use with *echein* in the LXX, not to mention this medical idiom. It is perhaps more than a coincidence that Acts 4:17 has the Sanhedrin describe the report of the miraculous healing as "spreading" *(dianemēthēi),* a verb (*nemō;* cf. LSJ *s.v.* for use of both pasturing and ulcers/gangrene) cognate with *nomē,* which Luke alone uses in the NT (Haenchen, *Acts,* p. 219 n. 3, is possibly misleading when he notes the meaning in its only LXX use, Deut 29:25, "to distribute," as the strict one, for both "to deal out" and "to pasture" already occur in Homer for *nemein* and it is quite possible that the author of Acts is using *nemomai* compounded with *dia* in the medical sense of the root word; the *dia* would then emphasize the spreading of the report *through* as well as *to* [*eis*] the people at large); cf. Hobart, *Medical Language,* pp. 196-197. Cf. also Acts 14:2 of "poisoning the minds of the pagans" *(ekakōsan),* where the meaning is also not that of the LXX (Haenchen, p. 420; Hobart, pp. 205-206).

In any case, the teaching of the sloganeers will spread out like a flock of grazing animals and *hōs gaggraina,* i.e. as gangrene spreads out in a previously healthy limb, "pasturing" on the still-living flesh. The root sense of that which "eats" or "consumes" is significant in light of the figurative *nomē* ("pasture") that follows this phrase in the Greek text. In the light of 3:9, 13 *infra,* D-C prefer to understand this of the deterioration of the individuals who propose/accept the teaching. Yet at this point it seems to envision the gangrenous doctrine as eating its way into the congregation as a body, whose numbers, like limbs, decay as the deadly teaching spreads. The application to individuals below then follows quite simply from the "corporate" sense here. Note also the comment on *tinōn* in 2:18, "the faith of *some.*"

*Take Hymenaeus and Philetus as examples.* After a full stop (whether colon or period), 17b abruptly announces the names of Hymenaeus and Philetus. Unlike the rest of the Pauline correspondence, which contemptuously ignores the names of the apostle's opponents, the PE here, as previously (cf. 1 Tim 1:20 for two names in a similar construction — also enemies), supply exemplary names out of a larger number *(hōn estin)* of those whose teaching is being stigmatized. Perhaps this is still another indication of the conventional character of this correspondence, actually transmitting historical data from another generation in the epistolary genre. In a genuine correspondence the names would needlessly dignify the opponents (cf. Ign. *Smyrn.* 5.3 refusing to put the names of the heretics in writing). In the genre to which the PE belong, the names have been transmitted to document and certify the kind of teaching that is being scored.

Hymenaeus was, along with an Alexander, handed over to Satan in 1 Tim 1:20 (see commentary above). Hymenaeus was not that easy to dislodge, for it is almost surely the same person whom we meet here. Since the name itself is Greek, not Semitic, and makes the bearer a client of the pagan marriage god Hymen (cf. LSJ *s.v.*), one would infer that he was a Gentile convert. W. Michaelis (*apud* Spicq and D-C, p. 112 n. 11) surmised that he belonged to the leadership (episcopate or perhaps presbyterate) of the Ephesian church, and thus the apostle's sentence was deserved in its severity and hard to make stick — hence the double mention of his name as well as the following summary of his poisonous *logos.* In both passages his name occurs first in the pair.

The name of Philetus *(Philētos)* is coupled with that of Hymenaeus in this passage, as is that of an Alexander in 1 Tim 1:20. It is a thoroughly Greek term (= beloved, worthy of love; cf. *Agapētos*), and again one might surmise that its bearer was a Gentile convert. Note that the Alexander of 1 Tim 1:20 could be a Jewish name (cf. *CII;* LXX). If that is actually the case, then Hymenaeus is in one case coupled with a Jewish Christian opponent of Paul and then with a Gentile convert opponent. Again his link with two different groups would indicate his influential position.

18. *It is men like those who have deviated from the truth when they say that the resurrection has already occurred, and so they overturn some people's faith.* The *hoitines* not only is a resumptive *hoi* but indicates that both the preceding names and the following teaching are concrete examples of the "gangrene" just scored. Such men as those just named "have deviated from the truth." These men have their own *logos,* but it is not *ho logos tēs alētheias* of 2:15. That truth/faith their exposition has definitively (aorist) missed, like an arrow off target, "and they overturn (*anatrepousin;* see Titus 1:11, where households are the object) the faith of some *(tēn tinōn pistin).*" The once-for-all error in a matter of revealed, saving "truth" *(alētheia,* i.e. *fides quae)* has ongoing effects in the present (note present tense of *anatrepousin*) on the faith, i.e. the personal adherence *(fides qua)* of a number of believers to Christ. The author of the PE sees this as touching many, discreetly called "some" (*tines;* cf. *supra* 1 Tim 1:6). Once someone like Hymenaeus has made shipwreck of the faith (see 1 Tim 1:19-20), many passengers go down with their captain. The *tines* also implies (as does the contrasted *themelios* of 2:19) that a congregation or body of believers is presupposed here of which some fall away.

Between the mention of the past error and the present damage, the author of the PE has cited an example of the gangrenous *logos,* introduced with the cognate *legontes* that refers certainly to Hymenaeus and Philetus and probably to the whole circle that they exemplify. The statement is to be understood as a probative quotation (cf. the use of *legei* in 1 Tim 4:1 of the prophetic Spirit, and 5:18 of the OT and the saying of Jesus). It involves a textual problem on whose solution depends the precise meaning of the teaching that is being quoted. Did the author of the PE actually write, "Resurrection already has occurred" (*anastasin ēdē gegonenai;* as in S, G, 048.33 Cyril), or did he say, "The *(tēn)* resurrection already has occurred" (with the rest of the witnesses, cited in *GNT*$^{3corr}$, *ad loc.*)? The evidence for the anarthrous noun is scarcely overwhelming, especially in the light of the other omissions by the scribe of S in the PE. Following the lead of J. K. Elliott, *Greek Text,* pp. 139-140, the article probably ought to be retained, while acknowledging that it is conceivable that S, G, etc. have preserved the original anarthrous form of the citation (cf. B. Metzger, *TCGNT,* pp. 647-648).

That one does encounter a quotation here may be signaled not only by the second perfect infinitive, *gegonenai,* a very rare form in the NT (J. K. Elliott, *Greek Text,* p. 139), but also by the use of *anastasis,* which occurs only here in the PE (cf. the use of *egēgermenon* in 2:8 *supra*).

In the Paulines two of the three arthrous uses of *anastasis* refer to Jesus' resurrection (cf. Rom 6:5 and Phil 3:10). The references to the final resurrection are, with the exception of 1 Cor 15:42, anarthrous. The Pauline letters that do not use the term indicate that it was by no means the one technical term that the author felt compelled to use for Jesus' rising or the general resurrection, though it does always refer to one or the other of these. In the rest of the NT epistolary, this noun occurs only in Heb 6:2; 11:35 *(bis)* (both anarthrous and referring to the general resurrection); and in 1 Pet 1:3; 3:21 (both anarthrous and referring to Jesus' rising). The only occurrences in Rev 20:5-6 are the arthrous references to "the first resurrection" (= the general resurrection).

In the synoptics the uses of this term cluster in the narrative of Jesus' dispute with the Sadducees on the nature of the general resurrection. Thus Mark 12:18 *(hoitines logousin anastasin mē einai)* and 12:23 *(en tēi anastasei)* use the noun only of the general resurrection but first without, then with, the article. Matthew 22:23, 28, 30, 31 follows the Markan pattern, using the anarthrous term first and thereafter with the article (thus almost certainly taking the article as meaning "the resurrection mentioned previously"; cf. BDF §252 and BAGD *s.v.*). For the Johannine usage (John 5:29, anarthrous; 11:24-25, arthrous, of general resurrection, then of Jesus himself), see R. Brown, AB *JN, in loc.*

In Luke-Acts the first of seventeen uses of *anastasis* refers to a rising in its most generic sense as opposed to a fall (Luke 2:34, anarthrous; also the verb has not so dramatically narrowed its meaning in the NT: Oepke, *TDNT* 1.368-371). Thereafter this noun in the Third Gospel always refers to the general resurrection; thus Luke 14:14, "of the just" with the article, and finally in Luke 20:27, 33,

35, 36, where in the narrative of the controversy with the Sadducees, Luke follows the same pattern in the use of the article that was seen above in Mark-Matthew. In Acts a new and instructive variant appears. "*The* resurrection" *(hē anastasis)* is that of Jesus or the promise of the final resurrection as intimately linked with that of Jesus: Acts 1:22; 2:31; 4:2 (see Haenchen, *Acts,* p. 214); 17:18. Thereafter in Acts 17:32; 23:6, 8; 24:15, 21; 26:23 (where Jesus is *prōtos ex anastaseōs nekrōn*) the noun is always anarthrous and refers simply to the general resurrection.

The noun *anastasis* occurs as many as twenty-five times in the Ap. Frs. (including *Mart. Pol.* 14.1, but never in Hermas). About half (eleven or twelve) of these passages refer to the general resurrection, and again about half of those employ the definite article; the rest (seven) do not (thus *Did.* 16.6; *Barn.* 21.1; *1 Clem.* 24.3; 26.1; Ign. *Smyrn.* 5.3; Polycarp, *Phil.* 7.1; and *Mart. Pol. ut cit.*). When this term refers to Jesus' resurrection, it almost always takes the article (thus twelve times in Ignatius, nine refer to Jesus' resurrection, and only two of nine are anarthrous: Ign. *Eph.* 20.1; Ign. *Smyrn.* 12.2). The one clear reference to Jesus' *anastasis* in *First Clement,* at 42.3, has the article (cf. *Barn.* 5.6-7).

From these data one might infer that there was a distinct tendency for Christian authors to use the arthrous *anastasis* to designate Jesus' resurrection, but that the general resurrection could be spoken of with or without the article, with variations in meaning occurring for other reasons.

In that framework, the heretics here in Second Timothy most probably said, "*The* resurrection has already occurred," which could mean "The resurrection (of Jesus) has occurred" or "The resurrection (of all) has already occurred." The former statement was of course unimpeachable; the latter was proving to be quite unacceptable. The heretics took shelter in the crevices of ambiguity. They really meant what the Sadducees had meant in discussion with Jesus (Luke 20:27 and others *ut cit. supra*), and stripping away the article unmasked their teaching for what it was. The scribes of S. G. etc. were quite correct in discerning precisely what the heretics in Second Timothy *meant;* the body of textual witnesses is correct in transmitting what the author of the PE said that they *said.* The articular reading is actually the *lectio difficilior* (*pace* Spicq), and its omission a scribal attempt to refract precisely the meaning of the heretics through the actual term of the text.

The proposition cited is far from a random choice. The witness to the resurrection of Jesus has been introduced already as the center of the Pauline gospel, incontrovertible and indispensable (2 Tim 2:8; cf. 1:10-11). If the fact could not be denied, the meaning of the fact for all the dead could be denied. That denial had in the first generation been the ploy at Corinth, and Paul's reply was completely to reverse the field on his opponents, saying time and again, "But if there is no resurrection [anarthrous] of the dead, then Christ has not been raised" (1 Cor

15:13, 16). Here in the PE (and in the second generation) the opponents are, on the one hand, emphatically declaring that Christ has been raised, that the witness of Paul and the other apostles to the fact is acceptable, but they are saying that that resurrection has been and always will be the only one, that the whole meaning and power of *hē anastasis* is confined to what happened years before "on the third day" after Jesus' death. There is no other rising of the dead to look for, to hope for. They have effectively reduced Jesus' resurrection to "an isolated miracle," as in the Greek authors cited by A. Oepke, *TDNT* 1.369, and thus have struck a reasonable compromise with the drastic, materialistic pessimism of Greek culture; cf. Aeschylus, *Eumenides,* pp. 648-650, who has Apollo say, "Death is once for all and there is no rising *(outis est' anastasis),* for this my Father has provided no remedial spells" (*epōidas;* cf. *infra* on magic). Another way of leaving the dead quite dead and yet having them live on in the flesh was to maintain that a man's "resurrection" occurred in his offspring, who carried on his name (person) into later generations (Sir 11:28 — LXX against Hebrew — and 30:4-6). That this was the line taken by the Sadducees is vividly illustrated in Jesus' controversy with them cited above, even to the *anastasin mē einai . . . exanastēsēi sperma* of Mark 12:18-19 = Matt 22:23-24 = Luke 20:27-28.

The Qumran sectaries (of priestly conservative background, though not Sadducees) do not appear thus far to have entertained any teaching on the resurrection of the flesh. The closest that a text comes to that is 1QH 11.10-14: Dupont-Sommer, *EWQ,* p. 237 (1QM 12.5: Dupont-Sommer, *EWQ,* p. 187, who sees reference to Dan 12:2, but not so Yadin, *War,* pp. 314-315), where the critical lines speak of God's having cleansed "this vermin that is man" so that "he may be raised from the dust *(lhrym mʿpr)* to [thy] mystery [of truth]" and somehow join the company of angels (cf. 3.22 and 1QS 11.7-9, all of which call for a figurative "resurrection" [Spicq] that corresponds to the metaphorical "rebirth" that these texts also speak of [cf. Gaster, *DSS,* p. 562]). These lines of thought were sharply rejected by the Pharisaic tradition (cf. Acts 23:7-8; the rabbinic texts are cited by Oepke, *TDNT* 1.370; cf. also the name Anastasius (-a) in *CII* index, though noun and verb are not found, but it is notable that neither Philo nor Josephus uses *anastasis* of the resurrection of the flesh, though in his *War* 2.163 the latter takes the Pharisaic approach to the reality signified by the term [Oepke, *ibid.,* p. 370]). The Sadducaic "compromise" surely survived among heterodox Christians of the second century; see *Acts of Paul* 14 (quoted in D-C, p. 112 n. 13, as well as the commentary of Theodore of Mopsuestia and Theodoret).

The letter to Rheginus 45.23 and 49.15-16, as well as the Gnostic Menander quoted in Justin and Irenaeus (all cited in D-C *ad loc.* and Oepke, *TDNT* 1.371), witness to a persistent teaching that no more general resurrection can be hoped for than what has already occurred.

It is difficult to believe that an author with the devotion to Paul that is evinced at every turn in the PE, and one faced with the blatant contradiction of Paul's teaching in 1 Cor 15, could have resisted quoting or at least paraphrasing the devastating Pauline refutation cited above. In a situation such as this, the argument *ex silentio* has its force. One can reasonably infer that the author of the PE did not have access to/had not studied the text of First Corinthians. Of course, on our hypothesis, since a collection of Paul's letters to the churches had not yet been formed, this is not surprising. Nor is the persistence of the heretical teaching surprising. There is no reason to believe that the Pauline argumentation swept the field in Corinth in his own day. There is some reason to believe that Paul's star declined in the decades immediately following his death. That the "rehabilitation" of Paul that we now can witness in Luke-Acts-PE involved a confrontation with the spreading of the same heterodoxies that the apostle had attacked is historically no more surprising than that Clement of Rome, a few years later, confronted the same schismatic turmoil to which Paul had addressed himself in First Corinthians.

What inner logic urges this denial of the general resurrection? It seems too simple to put all the blame on the external pressure of contemporary pagans or even on certain parties within unbelieving Judaism (Sadducees; Samaritans: Oepke, *TDNT* 1.370). That pressure was there, and it was certainly eased by the course taken. Yet the apologetic motive itself aims at making the preaching offered attractive, at bringing the unbeliever to adherence to Jesus. The resurrection of the dead was no doubt an intellectual scandal, a "scientific" absurdity for the ancient world. But that was not the real scandal, the practical down-to-earth scandal, about the general resurrection. The scandal inherent in the resurrection of all is that it involves the judgment of all (cf. Acts 17:31). No resurrection accordingly meant no judgment (thus Polycarp, *Phil.* 7.1: *mēte anastēsin mēte krisin,* "neither resurrection nor judgment"; cf. Oepke, *TDNT* 1.371, on the "two resurrections, of the just [cf. Luke 14:14; Rev 20:5-6] and of sinners; and cf. Origen, *In Rom* 5.9, *PG* 14.1047-1048, on the *duplex resurrectio,* the rising in faith complemented sacramentally by baptism and the rising on the last day). There was no judgment (= condemnation) because there was no sin — only ignorance and the anguish of the gathering coils of material mortality, and one cannot do other than what he does.

19. *God's solid foundation stands, nevertheless.* The refutation of the gangrenous doctrine takes on a quasi-parabolic form with quotations of/or allusions to the Law (Torah). Here in Second Timothy the truth in what has been quoted is conceded while it is added that the apostolic gospel actually proclaimed more than the opponents admit and their assertion has not undermined or shaken that fact, though they indeed "overturn the faith of some" (cf. also 2:14, *katastrophēi*). What the heretics have not overturned is precisely what

God has established. "Still God's firm foundation stands, . . . *ho mentoi stereos themelios tou theou hestēken.* . . . The vocabulary is not typical of the PE (as *mentoi* already presaged); the one previous use of *themelios* (1 Tim 6:19) had its own problems; see commentary *in loc.; stereos* occurs only here in the PE, as does *hestēken;* in the clause that follows, "seal" *(spragida)* occurs for the only time in the PE, and the quotation of an OT text took place only once before in this correspondence, and even there in the citation of a source (1 Tim 5:18). Thus one can ask whether at this point the author of the PE begins to cite or quote a source that answers the preceding quotation. The logical speculation of the opponents is countered by theological speculation, and here the strong Jewish and OT character of that riposte may be in deliberate contrast with the Hellenistic philosophical character of the preceding teaching, which makes no pretense of being "according to the Scriptures."

The heart-word of this parabolic reply is certainly *themelios,* "foundation." It is God's, i.e. the Father's *(tou theou).* It is "firm" *(stereos)* and it "stands" *(hestēken).* Here in the PE the adjective is in the LXX tradition to the extent that the "solidity" being spoken of is nothing less in origin than that of God himself, "the hard rock" (thus LXX Isa 51:1) from which his people have been quarried (Bertram, *TDNT* 7.612-613; see Notes above). From God comes the firmness of the foundation; because of him *hestēken,* "it stands" (cf. Philo as cited by Bertram, p. 612 n. 37, and quoted by Grundmann, *TDNT* 7.644-645).

All the analyses thus far (see Notes) have led back to the observation with which this explanation of 2 Tim 2:19 began, the critical importance of the meaning of *themelios,* the Greek use of which, secular and biblical, was surveyed in the commentary on 1 Tim 6:19. At this point, where the term is certainly used in its ordinary sense, one can further observe that the noun is unknown to the Gospel tradition outside of Luke-Acts (cf. the verb in Matt 7:25 = Luke 6:48: Q), where it occurs ordinarily in the singular and in parabolic materials (Luke 6:48-49 [of a house]; 14:29 [of a tower]). As was noted above, the five Pauline uses outside of the PE cluster in 1 Cor 3:10-12, plus Rom 15:20 and Eph 2:20, all related to the work of apostles, including Paul. Conzelmann, *1 Cor.,* p. 75, notes that by this figure Paul means "the community itself" as well as "the rudiments of doctrine" (see the Greek materials cited in *ibid.* n. 58 and the Qumran texts in n. 67), and both he and Barth, AB *Eph,* p. 271, note how in First Corinthians Paul is at some pains to remove any impression that "he himself can be regarded as the foundation" (Conzelmann, p. 75; cf. Rom 15:20 of Paul not wanting to build on another man's foundation) whereas in Eph 2:20 "the apostles and prophets" are the foundation (cf. Barth, pp. 314-317). In Paul the cognate verb, *themelioun,* occurs in Eph 3:17 (of believers being "grounded in love") and Col 1:23 (of believers being "stable and grounded in faith"; cf. Lohse, *Col,* p. 66, esp. nn. 33-34 on OT and Qumran background).

Otherwise in the NT *themelios* occurs in Heb 6:1, of the teaching/preaching that issued in repentance/faith; 11:10, of the city of God (verb in 1:10 citing LXX Ps 101:26 of God's "laying the foundations of the earth"); and in Rev 21:14, 19 *(bis)* (note the link of the foundations of the eschatological city of God with the twelve apostles). Finally, 1 Pet 5:10 *(s.v.l.)* uses the cognate verb.

Among the Ap. Frs., before Barnabas and Hermas only *1 Clem.* 33.3 uses *tou idiou boulēmatos themelion,* of the earth resting on the foundation of God's creative will. Hermas, on the other hand, uses the terms *themelios (-on), themelioun* rather often (thirteen times). *Barnabas* 6.2 uses only *themelion,* and that only in citing LXX Isa 28:16 of "the foundations of Zion" laid by God.

With Schmidt, *TDNT* 3.64, and Lohse, *Col,* p. 66 n. 33, one observes that LXX Greek used the *themeli-* cluster of God to describe his founding (creation) of the physical universe and of his own people, conceived of as a city (i.e. a human society), or their temple (where they were most obviously his people) on Mount Zion (cf. LXX Isa 28:16, cited above), the solid rock mountain itself created by God on which the city of God finds its foundations. The LXX seems not to use this noun with any form of *histēmi.* In the great majority of instances it renders a form of Hebrew *ysd.*

The Qumran material as well as other documentation on the community of believers as house/temple was discussed at length on 1 Tim 3:15 (see commentary *in loc.,* though because of the direction the explanation of *stylos/hedraiōma* took, discussion of the *themelios/oikia* terminology has been transferred to this point).

In the Qumran documents the root *ysd* and its cognates furnish the terminology for found(-ation), establish(-ment), constitute (constitution), institute (institution), fundament(-als), base (basis/principle), as well as discipline, instruction, regulatory teaching, and mystery. In some instances this terminology refers to the individual (and in particular the legitimate teacher), in others to an assembly/council/community/company (particularly that of Qumran).

The community (foundation) and its teacher (founder) are mutually illustrative and explain each other. That which has been created reveals the intent and will of the creator (thus the male/female of Gen 1:27 is "nature's principle" [Dupont-Sommer, *EWQ,* p. 129] for later human conduct, "the true basis of their being created," *yswd hbry'h,* CD 4.21). That which has been done by God in creating thus becomes in its turn the criterion for judging what should be done now as the end time approaches. Cf. 1QH 1.8, in my translation, "the circumstances of the birth of time (a season) are the principles (bases) of the end-time"; cf. also 1QS 10.1-8. Thus creation and creatures are the repository of the will and intent of their creator. They are *(y)swd,* foundation/mystery simultaneously, both institution and institute (in the English sense of place where learning takes place), and hence their constant link with "truth" (cf., e.g., 1QH

1.27; 2.10; 5.9, 26; 10.4 *s.v.l.;* 11.4, 9, 12, *s.v.l.,* 16, etc., as well as vanity, violence, hypocrites: 1QH 2.22; 6.5; 7.34; the dark side of "institution/establishment" was also recognized among the sectaries, and in, for them, the highest earthly places, the Jerusalem priesthood). See 1QS 5.5-7 and 8.5-9 (Dupont-Sommer, *EWQ,* pp. 83, 91) as well as 9.3-4 (Gaster, *DSS,* p. 63; cf. 1QS 3.25), where it is evident that the community or congregation is not only God's house/temple but also God's "foundation" = "establishment/institution" (1QS 7.17-18, where *yswd* = "the institution of the community" [Dupont-Sommer, *EWQ,* p. 89] or its "whole basis" [Gaster, *DSS,* p. 59], i.e. its principles). The tracing of this thought into Isa 28:16; 54:11 has been commented on in Gärtner, *Temple,* pp. 134-136 and 42-43, 78-79 (cf. Gaster, *DSS,* p. 309), and to his observation on the way the MT "tested stone" has become "the tested stones" of 1QH 6.26, one might add the LXX Isa 28:16 with its repeated *eis ta themelia* (i.e. neuter pl.) in rendering the MT *ylssād . . . mûsad mûsad,* though it keeps the singular *lithon.* Thus it illustrates the same oscillation from singular to plural that the Qumran sectaries apparently found quite natural.

In Qumran the "legitimate teacher" is the creature (foundation) of God and also the repository of God's will, i.e. the plan/mystery that God has for his creatures. Those who follow that teacher's regulations/discipline, those who make them the basis/principle for their actions (cf. 1QS 8.10 where Gaster, *DSS,* p. 61, has "*fundamentals* of the community"), become in their turn a divine creation/foundation that is again the repository/revelation of the divine plan for the end time (cf. 1QS$^a$ 1.12-13: Dupont-Sommer, *EWQ,* p. 105, for the candidate at twenty-five years of age "taking his place among the foundations of the congregation . . ." [*lht[yṣ]b byswdwt ʿdt*]). A community that came into being as an expression of God's intent and will also leads its members into the divine order and joins them with the angelic denizens of that order (cf. 1QS 11.8). One has practically no more room to doubt the teacher/community founded by God than the Creator/creation themselves. To reject any one of them is to reject or reduce to nonsense the others.

*bearing this seal.* It is against that background that the devastating force of 2 Tim 2:19 comes into focus. The Pauline gospel, the gospel as received by Paul's churches, has been and continues to be "God's solid foundation." The community of believers in the risen Jesus, preached by the apostles (cf. 1 Cor 9:1), stands like a house/temple (cf. the *oikia* of v. 20) on a foundation of solid rock, unshaken in the spate (cf. Luke 6:48-49) of heresy. Paul is "the legitimate teacher," and believers in the risen Jesus form the congregation of the new covenant. To have controverted the Pauline gospel is to have rejected the principle and basis, the constitution and institution, the revelation and mystery of the church. To that a Hymenaeus and Philetus might say, "But *you* cannot judge that; only God can judge that we have abandoned the Gospel." The author of the PE anticipates the objection by asserting that God's "institution" or foundation "has this seal *(echōn tēn spragida tautēn)*" — and not the heretics — namely, "The Lord knows those who are his."

The seal in the ancient world at large had its whole meaning from its relation to the owner. His seal openly claimed some thing as his own, within his power, accessible to him and those duly authorized by him but secret from others, something (for a reason perhaps known only to the person who sealed it) costly and precious. This provocative combination of making secret and public is never far from the surface. Fitzer, *TDNT* 7.946, also notes the nuances of validity, reliability, and inviolability that accompany this terminology of sealing. The fact that Israel, at least in her religious literature (as contrasted with seals actually found), preferred the carving on a seal to be a personal name and thus a written sign rather than an image of some creature probably is rooted in the covenant commandment that no image be fashioned of Yahweh (cf. Fitzer, p. 942). Thus the words by which he calls men, above all, their personal names, are on the stone seals by which he can claim his people as his own, marking them like soft clay or wax as containing something secret but valuable to him. When Philo calls the Word of God "the archetypal seal" (*Op. Mund.* 25, where the whole of creation is a copy of God's image), he is articulating a very Jewish way of regarding the seal (Fitzer, p. 946).

*"The Lord knows those who are his."* Thus "the foundation" is "God's" in 2 Tim 2:19 and that divine possession is publicly recognized in God's seal, which in Jewish fashion is conceived of in verbal (rather than image) form. But instead of the expected personal name of God, the divine king, being carved upon his foundation/house/temple (as the *lmlk* seal is stamped on the clay jars containing the produce that belonged to the king of Israel or Judah), and rather than the actual names of the twelve sons of Jacob (as on the high priest's breastplate), here "the seal" contains a provocative citation of the word of God from the words of Moses to the rebellious Korah and his crowd of leading men. On that occasion the LXX Num 16:5 understands Moses to have said, *Epeskeptai kai egnō ho theos tous ontas autou kai tous hagious kai prosēgageto pros heauton kai hous* (sg., MT) *exelexato heautōi prosēgageto pros heauton*, "God has visited and knows those who are his and who are holy, and he brought them to himself, and those whom he chose he brought to himself" (trans. WCW). (The MT reads "in the morning," *boqer*, for the LXX *epeskeptai* [= **biqqēr*], also YHWH for the LXX *theos* [= *'elohîm*], and the singular for the plural.)

It is notable that the part of this text cited in Second Timothy does not take up the otherwise appropriate *epeskeptai* of the LXX and that it names YHWH of the MT with the *Kyrios* that was the normal Greek rendering of the *qere* here. It is evident that the author of this passage either knew the MT himself or had a Greek text other than the one the LXX has transmitted to us. Of course, the LXX had before it a Hebrew text that read *'elohîm,* a text that the author of this passage did not know of or did not choose to use. It is possible that the author simply changed a LXX *theos* to *kyrios* in his quotation for his own doctrinal purpose. The plural *ontas* here belongs to LXX, not MT, and the latter quotation *(kai apostētō)* is virtually a paraphrase of Num 16:26. Yet the practice of choosing a variant Hebrew text to make a midrashic point has been amply documented in 1QpHab, and it is not to be dismissed that in this instance the text chosen varies from the much more commonly known LXX and has its *Vorlage* in the text that eventually became the MT. In this instance the MT translated by *Kyrios* added another sense to the text that the PE adduce, for God's (i.e. the Father's) seal explicitly witnesses to the *Kyrios,* i.e. to the Lord Christ as knowing who really belongs to him. The sense of anarthrous *Kyrios* here is then taken as in harmony with its other arthrous uses in First and Second Timothy (see commentary on 1 Tim 1:2), whereas the form of the term respects its original designation of Yahweh, the God of Israel.

In this quotation, "the Lord knows those who are his *(egnō kyrios tous ontas autou),*" the present participle stresses the here-and-now condition of men in relation to Christ, their *Kyrios,* their actually belonging to him at this moment (cf. the adverbial *ontōs* of 1 Tim 5:3, 5, 16; 6:19). The verb in the form *ginōskeis* occurred above in 2 Tim 1:18. Here the second aorist, *egnō,* emphasizes the antecedent elective character of the divine creative choice of those who actually have been incorporated into his building (cf. Gal 4:9; another cluster of images but with the same basic sense of *ginōskein,* John 10:14, 27). Here the LXX form of the text casts into the past what the MT makes a matter of the Lord's future revelation, "In the morning the Lord will show *(weyodaʿ)* who is his . . . ," and that LXX interpretation was more congenial with the argument of PE here, so the LXX is now adopted without a qualm. The Greek not only has its native sense of full, experiential knowledge (cf. *Odyssey* 1.2 of Odysseus, who "knew the mentality [*noon egnō*] of many men") but carries with it the connotations of the Hebrew *ydʿ,* "to choose" and "to love."

Where Moses appealed to a future sign against Korah and his rebels, the PE appeal to a once-and-for-all divine intervention in which Christ has known (i.e. loved and chosen) his own, the resurrection and his appearances to his apostles. If Hymenaeus and Philetus do not teach what the apostles taught about the resurrection, then they do not belong to their company — and that company was constituted by the appearances of the risen Christ. It is that company which has been sealed to the Lord; he knows them all by name and has publicly marked them off as his own possession. Thus to be apart from them is to be part of Korah's rebellion against the leadership that God has given his people. Their specious theology of holiness (cf. Num 16:3) and pious disclaimer of the judgment of the apostolic teacher is met as Jesus met the Pharisees: "God knows your hearts" ([Luke 16:15] *ho de theos ginōskei tas kardias hymōn*). What had once happened in Israel is happening again in God's people (cf. 1 Cor 10:1-11; Schlatter *ap.* D-C). On other texts, especially *Odes Sol.* 8.14-15, see D-C's quotations, p. 112.

*and "Let everyone who names the Lord's name abandon wickedness."* The author of the PE and/or his source now warms to his subject, and the lapidary text from Num 16:5 is now complemented *(kai)* with a second allusion to the climax of that rebellion narrative in which Moses addresses "the congregation" *(hāʿēdāh;* LXX *tēn synagōgēn):* "Depart ([LXX] *aposchisthē-e*), I pray you, from the tents of these wicked men. . . . so they got away *(apestēsan)* from about the dwelling of Korah" (Num 16:26-27). Here in the PE the text reads, *Apostētō apo adikias, pas ho onomazōn to onoma kyriou,* and it is a veritable potpourri of allusions to LXX texts that D-C think might be "early Christian poetry."

As was just noted, it is actually used to describe the withdrawal of the people from the rebels in Num 16:27. Frequent as forms of *aphistanai* are in the LXX, even with *hamartia(i),* only Sir 7:2 ("Stay away from wrong," *apostēthi apo adikou*) and 32 (RSV 35):3 ("To keep from wickedness is pleasing to the Lord and to forsake unrighteousness [*apostēnai apo adikias*] is atonement") employ forms of *adik-* as object, the latter passage alone using verbally the same phrase as here in the PE, though with the infinitive rather than the imperative found here. *T. Dan* 6.10 reads, "forsake all unrighteousness *(apostēte oun apo pasēs adikias),*" which is contrasted with "the righteousness of the law of the Lord *(tēi dikaiosynēi tou nomou kyriou).*"

In the Pauline usage *adikia* emphatically leads off the vice list of Rom 1:29 and usually stands in opposition to *dikaiosynē* (Schrenk, *TDNT* 1.155-156), and that perhaps is the more remote contrast set up between the *apostētō apo adikias* of this passage in Second Timothy and the *diōke de dikaiosynēn, pistin, k.t.l.* in verse 22 below. Paul too, however, knows of the contrast with *alētheia* which is nearer the surface here in Second Timothy (cf. Rom 1:18; 2:8; 2 Thess 2:10, 12; 1 Cor 13:6, though "the truth" is not the proposition or statement as such but the quite concrete reality of the resurrection (of Jesus and of all people) signified by the words.

The parallels with Lukan usage are notable too. The author of the PE employs the term always in a genitive singular that often reflects the Semitic construct (thus Luke 16:8-9, *ton oikonomon tēs adikias,* lit. "steward of unrighteousness" = "dishonest steward" [RSV]; *ek tou mamōna tēs adikias,* lit. "in the mammon of unrighteousness" = "in the unrighteous mammon" [RSV]; 18:6, *ho kritēs tēs adikias,* lit. "the judge of unrighteousness" = "the unrighteous judge"; Acts 1:18, *ek misthou tēs adikias,* "reward of his wickedness"; 8:23, *syndesmon adikias,* "bond of wickedness" = LXX Isa 58:6). The *ergatai adikias,* "workers of wickedness," in Luke 13:27 are in a parabolic parenesis, peculiar to Luke, that has manifold links with this passage and others in the PE (cf. the commentary on *ergatēs* in 1 Tim 5:18 and 2 Tim 2:15 above; the exiled Jewish Christian teachers of Titus 1:10-11, the displaced persons of their time, seeking hospitality among believers in Crete, came from towns that had been witness forty years earlier to the ministry of Jesus [cf. Luke 13:26]; recall Lock's suggestion of an early sayings collection being employed at this point in Luke; see G. Fitzer, *TDNT* 7.948 n. 80). Here the house has been shut up, and those locked out cry to get in. However, the *oikodespotēs-kyrios* replies, *ouk oida hymas pothen este,* "I do not know where you come from" (RSV; Luke 13:25). Then to their appeal to their onetime physical proximity to him comes the riposte *ouk oida pothen este,* "I do not know where you come from" (RSV), this time followed by the citation of Ps 6:9, *apostēte ap' emou pantes ergatai adikias,* "depart from me, all you workers of iniquity!" (RSV), in its LXX form except that the latter reads *pantes hoi ergazomenoi tēn anomian,* "all (you) who work wickedness" (trans. WCW). The use of the house imagery with its drastic distinction of those outside and inside, the scriptural word of the *Kyrios,* and the verbal and conceptual coincidences lead one to the conclusion that the source quoted in the PE may have inspired the parenesis placed on Jesus' lips by Luke 13.

The final phrase of the seal designates the subject of the third singular imperative *apostētō* as *pas ho onomazōn to onoma kyriou.* The *onoma (tou theou)* has been commented on at 1 Tim 6:1. Here occurs the far more frequent "name of the Lord," used as the internal object of *onomazōn,* a Hebraizing usage that occurs in various forms as many as twelve times in the LXX in over two dozen uses of this verb. Close to the phrase here in the PE is Lev 24:16, where the death penalty is prescribed for *onomazōn de to onoma kyriou,* "the one who names the name of the Lord" (trans. WCW), which has become blasphemy (cf. 1 Tim 6:1; 1QS 6.27; Bietenhard, *TDNT* 5.263, and perhaps it is significant that the Qumran texts thus far only once employ [of Yahweh] *nqr' šmkh 'lynw* in *4QdibHam* 2.12, "The Words of the Luminaries," from a lovely liturgical morning prayer, which Gaster, *DSS,* p. 273, renders ". . . remind Thyself also of the peculiar favors [wonders] which thou hast [always] wrought for us in the sight of the nations, *because thou hast claimed us as thine own* [lit. because thy name hath been called over us])." LXX Amos 6:11 has *siga heneka tou mē onomasai to onoma kyriou,* "keep silent so that you don't mention the Lord's name" (trans. WCW), most of which recurs in LXX Jer 20:9 of the prophet refusing to mention the name of Yahweh. LXX Jer 32:15 speaks of "the name [of God] being named upon this" city of Jerusalem, and in 1 Macc 14:10, "the name of his glory was named up to the end of the earth."

It is LXX Isa 26:13 (which has few contacts with MT) that furnishes most of the terminology of this phrase in the PE in its most persuasive setting, for there one reads, *Kyrie, ho theos hēmōn, ktēsai hēmas; Kyrie, ektos sou allon ouk oidamen, to onoma sou onomazomen,* "O Lord our God, take possession of us; O Lord, we know no other except you, (and) we call upon [lit. 'name'] your name" (trans. WCW; note the *zkr* of MT as in 1QS 6.27). Here prayer to and public worship of the one *Kyrios* of Israel are designated (cf. Bietenhard, p. 255; "naming the names" of false gods in, e.g., LXX Josh 23:7), and thus the meaning comes very close to "those calling on the Lord *(epikaloumenōn ton kyrion)*" in 2 Tim 2:22 below (cf. BAGD *s.v.*). "We know no other except you" is the response to "The Lord knew those who were his," and the PE understood the *Kyrios* in both these OT passages as Christ (see Bietenhard, *TDNT* 5.271-272). Moreover, the appeal to God as creator (*ktisai;* cf. 1 Tim 4:1) reminds one of the building imagery here in the PE. *Every (pas)* true Israelite, i.e. worshipper of the one real God, is to break away and keep away from that *adikia* which surrounds and breaks against God's solid foundation upon which he has been built, from which his prayer and worship rise.

The *onoma- onomazein* phrase occurs only here in the PE in a form that is not quite paralleled in Eph 1:21 (cf. Barth, AB *Eph,* p. 155), and in a much closer parallel in Acts 19:13 of certain Jewish exorcists who "named the name of the Lord Jesus *(onomazein to onoma tou kyriou Iēsou)* over those who had evil spirits" and to whom came the ironic query, *"Hymeis de tines este?"* "But who are you?" (v. 15). If the "faith" of Hymenaeus and Philetus is to be compared with that of those uncommitted magicians, perhaps they will face the same discomfiture. The one who really belongs to the Lord not only "names the name of the Lord" but abandons evil (cf. Luke 6:46 and 13:25 and Matt 7:21-22: *SFG* §74). The PE typically refuse to allow any real separation between genuine faith and Christian living.

20. *Still in any great house there are not only the utensils of gold and silver but also wooden ones and earthenware, for noble and ignoble purposes.* With the adversative *de* the haggadic parable turns from the "foundation" and its provocative inscriptions to comment on the problems raised by those texts. Those problems are not precisely those of verses 16-18, and this fact, in its turn, is another indication that these verses (i.e. 19-20 [21]) were not composed *ad hoc* but were derived from an authoritative source, not to be changed or redacted simply to bring it into alignment with the argument at hand. It more than demolished the position of the adversaries, and it is perhaps that very overkill which gave it the position it has in the PE. The quotations, especially the first one in verse 19, had left the opponents of verses 16-18 completely on the outside. The quotation, however, had raised a question for those left on the inside, a question made more acute by the second "seal." How does one come to terms with the obvious differences, patent moral differences, among believers? How does one explain that somehow the abandonment of *adikia* still finds some clinging to the fingers that have cast it off? It is to those problems that the ex-

pansion, almost allegorical, of the parable now addresses itself: "However *(de)*, in a great house *(en megalēi . . . oikiai)* there are not only vessels of gold and silver . . . *(ouk estin monon skeuē chrysa kai argyra . . .)*."

Here the physical "house" has become a figure for another "house" that God has founded, "a great house," not only physically spacious (a *megaron*) but the eschatological dwelling of God and his people, the house to end all houses. In this great house, as in any great complex built for the assembly of many persons, there are utensils of every kind (cf. the rooms full of smashed pottery in the ruins of Qumran), and these vessels *(skeuē)* inside the building now suggest a reply to the questions posed by the inscriptions carved on the outside.

In the PE *skeuos* occurs only here and in the verse following with a quite deliberate juxtaposition of the literal and figurative meanings of the term. Romans 9:21-23 juxtaposes literal/figurative senses as here and speaks of an *eis timēn skeuos,* "vessel for noble use," as 2 Tim 2:21 of a *skeuos eis timēn* (again an indication that if the PE knew of the text or even the gist of any Pauline letter, it was Romans). In 2 Cor 4:7 the apostolic ministers are clay vessels for the gospel treasure *(en ostrakinois skeuesin)*. The Lukan writings use *skeuos* seven times (two in Luke; five in Acts); the one figurative use is that in Acts 9:15 of Paul as the risen Jesus' *skeuos eklogēs,* "chosen vessel," a striking coincidence in its way too, with the significance of the parable here in the PE. Among its warnings for the last day, Luke 17:31 includes one addressed to the man on a rooftop not to go down after "his vessels in the house *(ta skeuē autou en tēi oikiai)*" where "his vessels" (RSV: goods) are evidently the valuable ones, thus "the plate," silver and gold, his "best clothes," and perhaps even the tools of his trade (cf. the secular and LXX uses cited by Maurer, *TDNT* 7.358-359). Of course, the vessels par excellence were those used in worship, in the temple, and the precious metals of which they were made dramatized the importance of the actions and the places in which they were used (cf. Maurer, p. 359, for texts). Two nuances of meaning appear often when *skeuos* is used figuratively: one is associated with the form of vessels, their being ordered to contain and "control" something else that would otherwise escape or be destroyed (wine, grain, oil, water, etc.); the other is their fragility, of easily shattered clay, of easily bent or punctured metal. Both nuances are often prominent where the term is used to designate human beings, particularly as bodies (the concept comes full circle when clay jars are fashioned in the form of human bodies for their burial).

Wisdom 15:7-8 (cf. 13) combines the connotations already noted in what may represent the commonplace, exploited in the Pauline letters and their sources. There, in the polemic against false worship, the author writes: "For when a potter kneads the soft earth and laboriously molds each one [i.e. vessel] for our service, he fashions out of the same clay both the vessels *(skeuē)* that serve clean uses *(ta te tōn katharōn ergōn doula)* and those for contrary uses, making them all in like manner, but what shall be the use of each of these the worker in clay decides. With misspent toil he forms a futile god from the same clay — this man who was made of earth a short time before and after awhile goes to the earth from which he was taken, when he is required to return the soul that was lent him." In the Ap. Frs., *2 Clem.* 8.2 has a development of this image in another line; for the three uses in Barnabas and two in Hermas, see Maurer, *TDNT* 7.367.

The adjective "golden" (*chrysa;* on *chrysion* see 1 Tim 2:9) is a favorite in Revelation (see Notes above). Perhaps, like *megas,* it has apocalyptic connotations; it is often, but by no means always, linked with worship contexts. In Qumran the mention of gold is usually paired with that of silver and in that order, with two exceptions; moreover, all the texts except 1QH 5.16 *(s.v.l.)* and 4*QdibHam* 4.10 (Gaster, *DSS,* p. 275) are in 1QM 5.5, 8, 10, 12, 14; and *12.12.* The adjective *argyreos* is found in the NT only here in the PE, in Rev 9:20 (cited above), and in Acts 19:24 of the souvenir "silver shrines of Artemis."

The polysyndetic list introduces the second pair of adjectives with a coordinate *alla kai,* and the lowliest vessels of the great house are now described as *xylina kai ostrakina.* The former term occurs in the NT once again in Rev 9:20 (noted above) as the last adjective in a list of five for idols (following *chalka . . . lithina,* so again the least valuable material in that list). The LXX has thirty uses of the term, ten in Ep. Jer. (mostly for idols), and it modifies a form of *skeuos* in Lev 11:32; 15:12; Num 31:20; 35:18 (here of a wooden weapon, but previously of wooden utensils that contract impurity). The Ap. Frs. do not use the term.

Finally, the commonest, the frailest, and the cheapest vessels in the house are *ostrakina,* those made of baked clay. It was Paul's term for the apostolic ministers, including himself, but there is no other NT use apart from the one in 2 Cor 4:7. The Ap. Frs. do not use this adjective (though Diognetus 2.7 does use it ironically of cheap idols). The LXX employs it as many as fifteen times, modifying *skeuos* in Lev 6:28; *11:33;* 14:50; *15:12* (in italicized texts note *lithinos* in context), usually of vessels contracting impurity. The link with ritual impurity may influence the choice of *ekkatharēi/katharas* in verses 21-22.

With still another *kai,* this time epexegetic or explicative (Maurer, *TDNT* 7.364 n. 42), the arrangement according to the value of the material is followed by the observation that certain vessels are "for honor *(eis timēn)*" while others are "for dishonor *(eis atimian).*" With the particle *eis* the vessels are classified now according to their purpose, and the phrase *eis timēn* is taken up again in verse 21, along with the *eis pan ergon agathon* (cf. *pros* in 3:17 below, a difference which Moule, *Idiom,* p. 68, submits is purely stylistic).

Here in the PE the division according to purpose, "for honor/for dishonor," would most readily be taken as applying to "gold and silver vessels for honor," "wooden and clay vessels for dishonor"; i.e. the intrinsically more valuable materials are used for more dignified and worthwhile purposes. Yet one must note that in the argument of Rom 9:21-29 "the vessel for menial use," even "the vessels of wrath," the pagans, were the ones whom God first exalted in preference to "the vessel for honor," and of course in 2 Cor 4:7 the apostle and his ministerial colleagues are "clay vessels." Thus the epexegetic phrase here in verse 20b is intended to remind the reader that the purposes of God, his priorities, are quite distinct from human evaluations and that God may use gold and silver vessels for menial tasks in his house and cheap materials for noble ends. Both classifications exist and rightly in God's great house, but God's is the critical one for salvation (lest the gold feel ill used or the clay become arrogant).

21. *So if a person will only purge himself of that drivel, he will be a utensil for a noble purpose — hallowed, useful to the master, ready for any excellent deed.* The conditional clause that opens this sentence *(ean oun tis . . .)* suggests that we are no longer in the source material of verses 19-20 (note that *GNT*$^{3corr}$ uses a colon at the end of v. 20, as does *NTG*$^{26corr}$) but that material is now being applied by the redactor to the situation envisaged by this correspondence. This last of seven uses of *oun* in First and Second Timothy (not in Titus) would accord with previous usage if a distinct break from the preceding sentence was envisaged (cf. 1 Tim 2:1, 8; 2 Tim 2:1) for a more personal intervention of the author-redactor in regard to background material (cf. 1 Tim 3:2; 5:14; 2 Tim 1:8). This is the only time in the PE (and the NT) that *ean . . . tis* or *ei tis* frames *oun* (though Phil 2:1 opens a paragraph with *ei tis oun*). However, when *ean tis* was used in 1 Tim 1:8 *(nil* in commentary *in loc.)* and at 2 Tim 2:5 (see above), a distinct or separate case was being adduced (note the use of *kai* to draw them more closely together in the latter instance). The use of *de* for *oun* in some MSS (J. K. Elliott, *Greek Text,* pp. 141-142) may be an attempt to paper over the separation.

Even more indicative of the separation between this sentence and the source just cited is the demonstrative pronoun with which this protasis concludes: "So if a person will only purge himself of that drivel [lit. *from these (apo toutōn)*], he will be a utensil for a noble purpose . . . [etc.]." There is no plural noun in verses 19-20 that could conceivably be the antecedent of *toutōn;* the one noun that could be is the feminine singular *apo adikias.* Granted that a not dissimilar oscillation from singular to plural occurred in the *ean* clause of 1 Tim 2:15 (referring to the *gynē* of 2:14) and that there too a (just-)cited source is in question, still it is notable that the real break in the thought development occurred immediately after this in 1 Tim 3:1b with the *ei tis* sentence, followed by *dei oun* (see commentary above). If it is the case that the antecedent of *toutōn* occurred previous to the source citation, then Hymenaeus, Philetus, and their ilk (vv. 17-18) are the most conspicuous candidates, and the gangrenous character of their doctrine would evoke the purification vocabulary (if in fact it is that; cf. *infra* on *ekkatharēi; hēgiasmenon;* and the *katharas* of v. 22). If, however, the cleansing process must involve cleansing from things rather than persons, then the words *profane drivel* of verse 16 are the antecedent.

The generic *ha (skeuē) eis timēn* of verse 20 are now specified in terms of the believer who uproots (cleanses?) himself from these (men or/and their opinions); this person "will be a utensil for a noble purpose" (*estai skeuos eis timēn;* note now the singular). The parabolic phrase is taken up and defined or explained asyndetically in three gradually lengthening phrases in which a final *-on* occurs five times.

> *hēgiasmenon* (five syllables)
> *euchrēston tōi despotēi* (seven syllables)
> *eis pan ergon agathon hētoimasmenon* (twelve syllables)

The *hēgiasmenon* takes up a term analyzed above in 1 Tim 4:5, and here it reinforces the worship and temple connotations of verses 19-20 and makes the point unmistakably that the holiness being spoken of inheres in persons rather than things. Man is the vessel sacred to God, "sanctified" by God for himself alone. Such a vessel is then *euchrēston tōi despotēi,* "useful to the master," here quite transparently God for whom all men are "living instruments" as slaves were to their masters in ancient society (to use the Aristotelian phrase, *NE* 8.11). The usage, as is noted on Titus 2:9, is quite Lukan. Of particular note is the relational connotation of the useful or serviceable good (cf. *chrēsthai*) as distinguished from the intrinsically or naturally good *(agathos)* and the externally attractive good *(kalos).* Since even bad things can be *chrēstos* (= serious; examples, Weiss, *TDNT* 9.483), the *eu-* prefix is not otiose, especially since the term sounded practically the same as *Christos* when spoken (the pronunciation of *i* and *ē* was nearly identical in *koine* Greek). In profane Greek, offerings can be *chrēsta,* and the term also takes on a moral sense. The examples from the dramatists, especially Menander (*ut cit.* Weiss, pp. 483-484), show how the adjective applied to human conduct that was "kind, gentle, friendly, as in the master-slave relation" (Weiss, p. 484). Here in the PE the *despotēs* has already manifested and performed his excellingly useful work for man (Titus 3:4); this passage now describes a servant like his master who responds to *chrēstotēs* by becoming *euchrēston* in his turn.

Finally, the vessel that has been consecrated and has become usefully serviceable has that consecration and usefulness defined and described as "ready for any excellent deed." The eschatological perspective or horizon for this *hetoim-* cluster ought to be observed. The "readiness" of the vessel "for every good work" cannot be understood apart from the Pauline *skeuē eleous ha proētoimasen eis doxan,* "vessels of mercy, which he has prepared beforehand for glory" (RSV; Rom 9:23; cf. 1 Cor 2:9); or preparing the way for the Lord as

Luke understands that (cf. Luke 1:17, 76; 3:4; 9:52; 12.40 [adj.], 47 [parabolic]; 14:17 [adj. in parable]; 17:8 [parabolic]; 22:8-9, 12-13 of preparing a place for Passover with Jesus). The future tense of *estai* begins from the moment of God's merciful election, which orders his vessel to good services, and carries forward to final glory *(eis doxan)*. That which is honorable now *(eis timēn)* ends in the divine glory.

22. *Shun juvenile desires. Rather pursue upright conduct, faithfulness, charity, peace, in company with those who invoke the Lord from a clean heart.* If the preceding verse belongs to the source used in verses 19-20, then the opening *tas de neōterikas epithymias pheuge* of this verse begins a new paragraph which the *de* sets off from the preceding quotation. If, however, the interpretation proposed above is followed, then the *de* at this point marks the transitional contrast between the quasi-allegorical interpretation/application of verses 19-20 and the more pointed and direct address that resumes at this point with the three second-person singular imperatives of verses 22-23 (note the three that occurred in 2:14-16 above).

The chiastically positioned imperatives *pheuge diōke de* are addressed here to Timothy as in their previous occurrence in 1 Tim 6:11, where Timothy was conceived of as "the man of God" to whom the ordination charge was given. As there, so here the generically mentioned vices are first, and a list of specific virtues beginning with *diakaiosynēn* follows *diōke.* In 1 Tim 6:9 *epithymias pollas* had been noted; here the words *tas . . . neōterikas epithymias* are the explicit object of *pheuge* (see commentary above). In 1 Tim 6:11, as here, the asyndetic virtue catalogue not only begins with *dikaiosynēn* but later includes *pistin agapēn* together and in that order (though 1 Tim 6:11 adds *eusebeian* before the pair and *hypomonēn praüpathian* [see commentary on *en praütēti* in v. 25 *infra*]). The coincidences of language here make it difficult to resist the inference that Second Timothy is here quoting First Timothy or the source that First Timothy also employed.

J. Behm's remark, *TDNT* 4.897, that *neos* refers to age "up to 30 at most" is incorrect. Forty would be closer to the mark (see above on 1 Tim 4:12). His remarks on the association of youth with temptation to sin, particularly in the Jewish-Greek tradition (pp. 897-898 n. 16), are particularly apposite to this passage of Second Timothy as well as the others in the PE just noted. The lusts are not just the sexual excesses to which youths may be particularly inclined but also to that impatience, self-assertion, and self-indulgence (Lock), not to mention the hunger for novelty; the contempt for routine; the obdurate, implacable intransigence; the agitation verging on violence; the lack of prudent measure (Spicq, Boudou, Barclay, Gealy), which mark the immature (of any chronological age!). It is possible that too much has been made of this passage in reconstructing the view of the PE on the age of the man to whom Paul writes. The vices just noted are no monopoly of the young; indeed, they are particularly abominable in "a dirty old man." Timothy's relative youth with respect to Paul makes the admonition credible, but it by no means demands that one who is admonished to flee youthful lusts be himself below forty.

*Dikaiosynēn,* "righteousness," one of the virtues Timothy is to pursue, recurs in Titus 3:5 and 1 Tim 6:11 as "upright deeds," and in 2 Tim 4:8 in the phrase "the crown of the upright life" (see also on 1 Tim 6:11). On *pistin/ agapēn* see Excursus I, "*Pistis* Terminology in the PE," in AB *Titus,* and 1 Tim 1:5. On *eirēnēn* see Titus 1:4; 1 Tim 1:2; 2 Tim 1:2.

The final phrase, *meta tōn epikaloumenōn ton kyrion ek katharas kardias,* with its fivefold assonance on *k,* is that expansive conclusion to lists that has been characteristic of PE. Timothy is to seek the virtues that the whole company of Christian worshippers seeks; the pursuit of virtue is a community task, and ecclesial work, to be done with peace (*meta* = "in company with," "together with" [BDF §227.3], not "peace with," which W. Foerster, *TDNT* 2.413-414, 416-417, noted would call for *pros* as *pros pantas* in 2:24 *infra*). To be joined with those who call the Lord is to be joined with Moses, Aaron, Samuel, David, Elijah, Esther, the Maccabean heroes; it is to be joined with Christian believers now (note the present tense) engaged in real prayer and worship. The phrase serves to identify them as both Jews and Christians.

23. *Steer clear, however, of foolish and undisciplined researches.* As the terminology of the preceding sentence had links with that in 1 Tim 6:11, this sentence reminds the reader of Titus 3:9-10, which also used the verb *paraitou* and spoke of *mōras . . . zētēseis* and *machas.* Where the previous admonition began with *epithymias pheuge,* this one begins with the more properly intellectual vices (cf. G. Bertram, *TDNT* 4.832) and counsels, *zētēseis paraitou.* The "researches" being scored are foolish *(mōras)* and undisciplined *(apaideutous).* Both adjectives are typical of the sapiential strata within the LXX collection; thus *mōros* has all but six of its uses in Sirach, Job 16:7, and Ps 93:8; *apaideutos* has only two uses (Isa 26:11; Zech 2:1) outside of Proverbs, Sirach, and Wisdom.

*Mōros* and its cognate in the LXX correspond to the Hebrew roots meaning "the fool," where the lack of knowledge designated is primarily the lack of a genuine knowledge of the God of Israel and his will for his people (cf. Bertram, *TDNT* 4.833-836, esp. on Sirach, which in LXX may "intellectualize" this terminology more than the other biblical documents). This religious concept appears also in Philo (Bertram, p. 837). The *mōra-* cluster of terms is predominantly Pauline, often used paradoxically, ironically to describe the cross and the apostolate. In Rom 1:22 idolaters "became fools *(emōranthēsan)*"; in Eph 5:4 "silly talk *(mōrologia)* and levity" are not even to be mentioned among believers. The former affirmation can apparently be made without fear of qualification from that dictum of the Matthean Sermon on the Mount, about calling no man "Fool" (*mōre;* Matt 5:22), but that use should occasion no more surprise than Matt 7:26; 23:17, 19 *(s.v.l.);* 25:3, where Jesus himself thus designates several classes of persons. The note of contempt with which Greek and Jew used (and exchanged) this designation ought to be observed (Bertram 4.840). The contemptuous dismissal here in the PE of specious theological (OT?) research reminds one of the way in which Matt 23:17 (19 — *lect. dub.*) scores the theologians and teachers of the law themselves as *mōroi kai typhloi* (cf. 1QH 1.37 "[but those that are foo]lish of heart *(ks]yly lb)* cannot understand these things").

Though, as noted above, the phrase *mōros kai apaideutos* does not occur in biblical Greek other than in the PE, Sir 42:8 writes, "Do not be ashamed to instruct the stupid or foolish," *peri paideias anoētou kai mōrou,* and the continuation shows that merely intellectual enlightenment is not meant: "or the aged man who quarrels with the young." Similarly, LXX Prov 17:21, "A father has no joy over an undisciplined son *(epi huiōi apaideutōi)*" (where the Hebrew is *nbl* = fool), has more to do with the rebukes and rods that have been spared (cf. Prov 15:12 and 13:24) than the scion's IQ (*pace* Bertram, p. 834) and intellectual acuteness. In fact, the *apaideutos* here in 2 Tim 2:23 ought to be understood in terms of the grace of God "disciplining *(paideuousa)* us" in Titus 2:12 (i.e. in a school of chastisement and suffering, of scourges and blows, wherein Paul and his colleagues exercise a leadership comprised of sharing their own experience in the school of the cross to which the remainder of the Christian family belong). Note also how the *paideuonta* of 2 Tim 2:25 is "gentled" by *en praütēti* (see below), and, with Bertram, *TDNT* 5.625, observe that the researches are being dismissed as unfit for nurturing growth in Christ and the Spirit. They are salt that is not salty, directives that lead nowhere — except into controversies.

*as you are well aware, they breed only wranglings.* The verb *gennōsin* normally designates (human) begetting and birth, but Paul already employs it of a man's birth into Christ and according to the Spirit of which he is an agent (1 Cor 4:15; Philem 10; Gal 4:23-24, 29). The figurative use here of "giving birth" to *machas* seems to be unique in the NT (cf. F. Büchsel, *TDNT* 1.665-675). Still the concept figures vividly in James 1:15 (cf. 4:1-2 and Dibelius, *James,* pp. 93-94; 215-219, esp. for the secular Greek texts). Polybius 1.67.2 can speak of *stasis egennato;* Philo, *Jos.* 254, "joy . . . begat fear," and Josephus, *Ant.* 6.144, "begetters of crime," also use *gennan* figuratively (BAGD *s.v.*).

In as many as twenty uses of this verb in the Ap. Frs., Ign. *Trall.* 11.1 uses it figuratively when he warns against the heretical teachers, "Fly *(pheugete)* from these wicked offshoots which bear *(gennōsas)* deadly fruit, which if a man eat he presently dies." The most striking parallels to the usage here in the PE are in *Did.* 3.2-6 with its detailed description of the biogenesis of vices. The antithesis of this usage is in Hermas, *Vis.* 3.8.7, of the generation of virtues. Other uses are of physical birth, even extraordinary ones like that of Jesus, whether in the flesh (thus Ign. *Eph.* 18.2; *Trall.* 9.1; *Smyrn.* 1.1) or from the Father (cf. *1 Clem.* 36.4, citing Ps 2:7). The use for the origin of the fabled phoenix is actually not figurative in the mind of *1 Clem.* 25.3 (cf. Josephus, *Ant.* 9.7; *War* 4.469; Büchsel, *TDNT* 1.665, does not respect the intent of the ancient authors in this respect — they knew well enough the difference between literal/figurative language; they often took without question for natural history what has since proved a fable).

24. *The Lord's slave ought not to wrangle. Instead, he has to be gentle with all, a skilled teacher, forbearing.* In some contrast *(de)* to the preceding controversial researches, "a servant of [the] Lord ought not to battle," *doulon de kyriou ou dei machesthai,* where the *machesthai* has evidently spun off the preceding *machas.* Here, as in James 4:1, 2, the distance between controversy and bloody violence has been short indeed.

Thus here Timothy, in his role as *doulous kyriou,* must by the divine will (*dei,* cf. *supra* on Titus 1:7, 11 [*mē*]; 1 Tim 3:2, 7, 15; 5:13 [*mē*]) not become involved in factious controversy with his fellow believers. The Lord's servant, in the strongest contrast to *(alla) machesthai,* is to be characterized by four qualities (or five if the preceding negative quality is included). The list, couched in rare terms, has some formal characteristics of previous lists in the PE, e.g., the assonance on *p* and on *k.* On the other hand, the terms or phrases do not become gradually longer.

The servant-minister of Christ is first of all "to be gentle with all (persons)," *ēpion einai pros pantas.* If Jewish Christians were to be "gentle" *(amachous einai),* "to show *every* consideration *(pasan . . . praütēta)* toward *every* person *(pros pantas anthrōpous),*" as in Titus 3:2, *a fortiori* an apostolic servant of Lord must be "gentle," *ēpion.*

The next quality of the Lord's servant, *didaktikos,* is an even rarer term than the former and was used to characterize the *episkopos* in 1 Tim 3:2 (see commentary above). Still this is the only verbal link (apart from *machas . . . machesthai* with *amachon*) between this list and the "episcopal mirror." J. Jeremias, *TDNT* 3.752 n. 82, has observed that the PE, for all their emphasis on community disciplines, intensely stress the need for a tolerant, patient, loving leadership, notably in this passage.

25. *considerate in correcting the unmanageable, just in case God may grant them a change of heart that will lead back into full knowledge of the truth.* The final descriptive phrase, which runs off expansively through the following verse, qualifies "the Lord's servant" as *en praütēti paideuonta,* "considerate in correcting the unmanageable *(antidiatithemenous).* . . ." Again, as is noted on Titus

2:12, *paideuein* implies rigorous action as much as, if not more than, words (Bertram notes that *elegchein* would highlight verbal correction: *TDNT* 5.625), and here *en praütēti* must be read very closely with the participle as the alliteration already suggests, so that the harsh connotations of *paideuein* (closely associated in the Hellentistic world with cudgeling and whipping the recalcitrant student; therefore, corporal punishment) are gentled with the adverbial *en praütēti,* a noun that occurred on Titus 3:2.

*Praütēs* here reminds one again of the final qualifications of the "man of God" in 1 Tim 6:11, *praüpathian,* and one recalls that the cluster of terms was characteristic of the Pauline epistolary (see Titus 3:2). The LXX usage (see Notes for references) illumines the meaning of 2 Tim 2:25; the first three words are in the sapiential father-to-son form of discourse and the last is part of the portrait of the greatest leader of Israel, meant to inspire and form the reader many centuries later. The one who is great must humbly do his tasks, must listen meekly to those who (think they) are poor and oppressed, and must not arrogantly overestimate his wisdom. In the LXX this terminology never certainly applies to God (as it does in profane Greek texts; cf. Hauck and Schulz, *TDNT* 6.647), probably because it usually translated the Hebrew *ʿnw,* which designated a person without property who had to earn his bread by serving others.

More significant is the way in which LXX Ps 89:10 speaks: *hoti epēlthen praütēs eph' hēmas kai paideuthēsometha,* "lowliness has come upon us and we shall be disciplined" (trans. WCW), where the lowliness (*nil* in MT) of painful labor that has come upon men who are at best rather short-lived has been a divinely given discipline/learning experience. Learning (becoming educated) is a humbling experience, and thus one who transmits what he has learned should do so with the humility and lowliness that the acquisition imposed. In this view, the Semitic connotations of *ʿnw* predominate in *praütēs* rather than the Indo-European ones of gentle friendliness. The Qumran use of "the spirit of lowliness" in its list of virtues in 1QS 4.3 *(rwḥ ʿnwh)* has not gone unobserved (cf. Lohse, *Col,* p. 147 n. 105; Hauck and Schulz, *TDNT* 6.649), as well as the other uses of *ʿnwh:* 1QS 2.24 (a list of virtues also); 3.8 *bis* (once with Spirit); 5.3, 25 (also lists); 9.22 (of absolute poverty); 11.1 (of Spirit); and 1QH 5.21 (the humble); 17.22 (where there is some link with the divine discipline [*byswryk*]); thus Dupont-Sommer, *EWQ,* p. 250, renders "teachings," but cf. Gaster, *DSS,* p. 204).

The text of Ign. *Trall.* 4.2 (cited also by Hauck and Schulz, *TDNT* 6.650 n. 31) is particularly apposite in the light of the purpose adduced for the "kindly discipline" of 2 Tim 2:25, for the old bishop says, "I have need therefore of meekness *(praotētos)* by which the prince of this world is brought to nothing." Indeed, it has been noted (Hauck and Schulz 6.650) how Ignatius stresses *praotēs* [*sic*] as the virtue for a bishop (*Trall.* 3.2; as well as of Polycarp in *Pol.*

2.1; 6.2, where both times the phrase *en praötēti* is employed, otherwise in Ap. Frs. only in the prayer for all earthly leaders to fulfill their task *en eirēnei kai praütēti* in *1 Clem.* 61.2). In Ign. *Eph.* 10.2 all believers are admonished, in a context that has many conceptual and a few verbal links with 2 Tim 2:23-26, "Be yourselves gentle *(praeis)* in answer to their wrath *(orgas).*"

Those believers constantly and unswervingly (present tense) opposed to the Lord's servant are now designated as *antidiatithemenous.* Spicq has noted how the PE favor *anti-* compounds though they never use the particle as such; the Lukan writings similarly found such compounds congenial, though so do the other Paulines. Considering the unusual character of so much of the terminology in this passage, one could reasonably infer also that this word was cited from a source (the ordination parenesis?) being redacted in verses 24-26.

If the terminology has often been exotic thus far, with "*mēpote dōiē* [following *GNT*$^{26corr}$] *autois ho theos metanoian eis epignōsin alētheias kai ananēpsōsin . . . ,*" the syntax too becomes, with the use of the optative *dōiē,* "strangely archaic" (D-C, p. 113 n. 23), and with the following subjunctive *ananēpsōsin* (in v. 26) somewhat harsh if not "clumsy" (D-C). The Byzantine texts and 33 (followed by *GNT*$^{3corr}$) early smoothed out this inconsistency (as they saw it) by reading *dōēi(dōi).* Yet the optative-subjunctive sequence can be documented from papyri as well as biblical Greek (see 2 Macc 9:24 in A; and D-C, p. 113 n. 23, for P. Reinach); the optative is the reading of excellent witnesses (cf. list in BDF §95.2 as S* A. C. D* P for *dōēi,* not *dōiē,* and J. K. Elliott, *Greek Text,* p. 167); it is the most difficult reading that explains the later variations of other witnesses; it is a reading consistent with the usage of this author, as the prayer(s) at 2 Tim 1:16, 18 witness. In any event, if this passage of the PE is indeed the redaction of a liturgical source, e.g., an ordination charge, the "strangely archaic" optative becomes rather more familiar as an echo from the prayer setting (again note the prayers in which *dōiē* is used in 2 Tim 1:16, 18).

*Mēpote* is a particle that comes out of a sense of doubtful apprehension that practically wishes something were true (cf. Luke 3:15), as though construed with *phobeisthai* (cf. the explicit use at Heb 4:1 and also the Latin *timeo ne* [positive, vs. *ut,* negative] and BDF §370.1), and practically equivalent to the English "if possibly" or "so that perhaps" (cf. Moule, *Idiom,* p. 157), to which the following admittedly rare optative gives a poignant prayerful tone.

This tenth and final use of *didōmi* in the PE is in a phrase with *metanoian* as object, a phrase that only Luke employs otherwise in the NT (Acts 5:31; 11:18). The LXX (which uses *metanoia* only five times in any case) has this phrase at Wis 12:19 (in a context that has conceptual links with this passage of the PE): "through such works you [God] have taught your people that the righteous man must be kind *(philanthrōpon)* and you have filled your sons with hope because you give repentance *(didois . . . metanoian)* for sins (v. 20) . . .

granting them [God's enemies] time and opportunity *(topon)* to give up their wickedness" (cf. 12:10, "But judging them little by little you gave them a chance to repent [*edidous topon metanoias*]," and 11:23, which uses *metanoia* too). Significantly the terminology of Wisdom recurs in *1 Clem.* 7.5 (note *1 Clem.* 7–8 are about *metanoia* and the noun occurs six other times, the verb twice here; the only other uses are *1 Clem.* 57.1; 62.2) in the form, "Let us learn that the Master *(ho despotēs)* has given an opportunity for repentance *(metanoias topon edōken)* to those who are willing to turn to him." Otherwise the phrase occurs in *Barn.* 16.9 in his exhortation to believers (under the figure of a temple) to whom God gives repentance *(metanoian didous hēmin)* and in Hermas, *Vis.* 4.1.3; *Sim.* 8.6.2 (twice, *s.v.l.*); and 8.11.1.

This phrase, which also occurs in *Syb. Orac.* 4.168 (cited by D-C; Spicq), though it has a Semitic sound and may in fact be a Semitizing construction, can be documented only (it seems) from Jewish and (Jewish) Christian Hellenistic Greek sources. Also note the Latin of Polycarp, *Phil.* 11.4, who says of Valens, the presbyter, and his wife, *quibus det dominus paenitentiam veram,* "may the Lord grant them true repentance" (trans. LCL).

J. Behm, *TDNT* 4.1004, observes that the repentance here in the PE is God's gift (*didonai; pace* D-C, p. 114) while noting (p. 1005) how the Paulines usually rearticulate *metanoia* in terms of resurrection/new creation/rebirth (cf. Titus 3:5). But what is a *metanoia* that is (note that A adds *elthein* here: J. K. Elliott, *Greek Text,* p. 145) *eis epignōsin alētheias,* "into knowledge of the truth"? That latter phrase (note Moule, *Idiom,* p. 112, comparing Heb 10:26) had become and in the PE surely can be a designation for the faith-conversion that terminates in the baptismal confession (cf. Excursus II, "Truth and *epignōsis alētheias* in the PE," in AB *Titus*). But if that is the case, do we meet here an affirmation (apprehensive and doubtful, to be sure, but still an affirmation) of the possibility of another *metanoia* after a believer has abandoned his baptismal commitment and life? Hebrews 6:(1-)4-6 took a less optimistic view (cf. Heb 10:26, which also uses *epignōsis alētheias*): it was beyond human possibility to be "converted" again, and apparently not part of the divine plan either (thus Heb 12:7; Behm, *TDNT* 4.1005-1006).

In this passage of the PE, rather than 1 Tim 5:22 (*apud* Galtier), the first links are forged between the apostolic servant of the Lord and the divine gift of *metanoia* even to those who had fallen away from genuine faith in Christ Jesus (vv. 17-18 above). The statement is prayer, hoping against hope perhaps, finding its authority in a liturgical charge given to the Lord's servant on his ordination, a charge that originally referred to leading men to baptismal repentance and that has now been readapted to suggest tentatively and apprehensively the inextinguishable hope for the salvation of even the greatest sinners (cf. the prayer of Paul in 1 Tim 1:12-17).

26. *Then their heads would clear and they would find their way "out of the snare of the devil in which he has been keeping them alive" and into the will of God himself.* There are few verse divisions in the NT that have wreaked so much havoc with exegesis as this one, for (along with the shift from optative to subjunctive) the division has obscured the parallel in the compound *mēpote* clause and reduced an already overextended syntax into a semantic shambles. Even the particle *kai* with which the verse begins is not a simple conjunctive but is practically epexegetic, specifying in the clause that follows exactly what the preceding technical terms, "a change of heart that will lead back into the full knowledge of the truth," meant. It could also be understood (particularly in the light of the following subjunctive) as proposing the positive purpose/result of the preceding gift of *metanoia* or the condition/circumstances for it (cf. BDF §442.9 and esp. 471.3 on the epexegetic *kai;* with *mēpōs,* 2 Cor 9:4; as well as with *mēpote,* Mark 4:12 and Acts 28:26-27; cf. Luke 8:10 where Luke edits out some of these Semitizing *kai*s).

Granted (but not conceded) that *ananēphein ek* is the expected Greek idiom with this verb and that the *diabolos* here is in fact the devil, then the real crux lies in the noun *pagidos.* Its basic sense as that by which something/-one is fastened, and so a *trap* or *snare,* is incontrovertible. Moreover, its image seems to be exploited still further (D-C) in the description of the opponents as *ezōgrēmenoi,* an unusual verb that only Luke uses in the NT (on whose meaning see *infra*).

The LXX usage (though always active; the LXX, in Deut 20:16; 2 Kgdms 8:2; 2 Chron 25:12 [cf. Num 31:15, 18], refers to sinners as prisoners of war) may be the key to the actual understanding of the passive *zōgrēmenoi* in 2 Tim 2:26, literally for "those who have been left alive *by him*" *(hyph' autou);* this would then most naturally refer to those imprisoned but not put to death by the devil, and the *eis to ekeinou thelēma* would explain the reason for that survival, i.e. it was *eis to ekeinou thelēma,* "for the will of that one" (God: *ho theos*) mentioned in the former clause (see J. K. Elliott, *Greek Text,* p. 146, for a survey of the problem for one who accepts this position). The construction with the *autou . . . ekeinou* would then be quite parallel to the *autōn . . . ekeinōn* of 3:9 below. Moreover, *thelēma* would be used precisely as it was used in 2 Tim 1:1, the only other use in the PE (cf. commentary above), of the merciful, saving will of God.

Does the solution to the intolerable harshness of this verse lie in the source that was being redacted at this point? But that possibility, of course, still does not really explain the very difficult transition between *ananēpsōsin* and *ek tēs tou. . . .* Was the source cited without an essential term before *ek?* That solution would be a last recourse and counsel of despair. It seems preferable to make a distinct pause after *ananēpsōsin,* then to take the whole phrase *ek tēs tou diabolous pagidos ezōgrēmenoi* as a quotation from the source that has cropped up at every turn in this passage.

Finally, the redactor has added two telegraphic explanatory notes to the quotation; the *hyp' autou* emphasizes that the devil who has trapped men still does not have his prisoners completely at his disposition, still cannot execute them forthwith and pack them off to hell (cf. on Satan as God's "functionary," 1 Tim 1:20 and *TDNT* 5.624 n. 179). But that little note provoked the afterthought, "Why does he keep them alive?" and that question is answered not in terms of their usefulness for the devil's work (which would be completely against the thrust of this passage). However, because *God,* who alone has authority over life and death, has a use for them, they are to show forth his saving good will, *eis to ekeinou thelēma* (a phrase parallel to and explanatory of *metanoia eis epignōsin alētheias* in 2:25b). *Eis to thelēma* does not otherwise occur in the NT, but note Heb 13:21, *eis to poiēsai to thelēma autou,* as well as Luke 12:47, *mē . . . poiēsas pros to thelēma autou.*

On this reconstruction the parallel clauses of 2:25b-26 read:

just in case God may grant them a change of heart
  that will lead back into full knowledge of the truth.
Then *(kai)* their heads would clear
  and they would find their way "out of the snare of the devil
    in which he (the devil) has been keeping them alive"
    and into the will of God himself.

Quite different interpretations, particularly of the pronouns *autou* and *ekeinou,* have been common (J. K. Elliott, *Greek Text,* p. 146). Thus BAGD *s.v.* holds that *autou* = devil and that *ekeinou* also = devil *(s.v.);* for the abrupt shift in pronouns referring to the same antecedent, Wis 1:16 would offer precedent (though its more expansive form makes the transition rather less harsh and puzzling). BDF §291.6 notes instances in John and the Markan ending where *ekeinos* refers to an antecedent just mentioned (Mark 16:19-20: *autois, ekeinoi*). D-C; G. Schrenk, *TDNT* 3.61; J. Schneider, *TDNT* 5.594; and many others (listed in Spicq) prefer to take both pronouns of the devil. The real weakness of this solution is that it does not accept the meaning of *ananēpsōsin* and still insists on taking *ek* with that verb. In the solution proposed above the three phrases

*ek tēs diabolou pagidos,* "Out of the snare of the devil"
  *ezōgrēmenoi hyp' autou,* "those kept alive by him (the devil)"
    *eis to ekeinou thelēma,* "into the will of that one (God)"

are in one sense parallel as they telescope out of one another, all explaining the participial subject *ezōgrēmenoi,* "those kept alive." The crabbed and telegraphic development of the thought stems not only from the quotation of the words of the source (apparently considered so authoritative that any change, in such a delicate question, would be challenged) but also from the painful character of the subjects touched, i.e. the problem of evil (and that among believers) and the problem of postbaptismal repentance.

## IV.B.2. THE ERRING (3:1-9)

*3 [1]Realize this, however, that in the last days rough times will be at hand; [2]for then people will be —*

*intent on themselves,*
*intent on money,*
*pretentious,*
*arrogant,*
*blaspheming;*
*to those who bore them,*
*undutiful,*
*ungrateful,*
*irreligious,*
*[3]unaffectionate,*
*irreconcilable;*
*devils at gossip,*
*uncontrolled,*
*uncouth,*
*uncaring about goodness;*
*[4]renegade,*
*reckless,*
*conceited,*
*intent on pleasure*
*rather than intent on God.*

*[5]These people hold onto the appearance of godliness but they have repudiated its dynamic. Keep people like that at a distance too. [6]For from their ranks come those who are worming their way into homes to captivate the idle women,*

*loaded with sins*
*and driven by diverse cravings,*
*[7]ever learning*
*and never turning to full knowledge*
*of the truth.*

*[8]Just as once Jannes and Jambres defied Moses, so too these numbskulled counterfeiters of the faith are defying the truth, [9]but they will not progress far. Their own stupidity is going to become just as obvious to everyone as the stupidity of those two.*

## ♦ NOTES

3:1. *Realize.* On the verb *ginōske* see 2 Tim 1:18 and Comment on 2:19; as well as R. Bultmann, *TDNT* 1.689-714. The plural of A. 33. pl is rejected by J. K. Elliott, *Greek Text,* pp. 146-147, as a typical scribal "generalizing" of the text; cf. James 1:3; 5:20 (cf. Dibelius, *James,* pp. 72, 258, and note that he opts for the singular imperative, against B. 69 et al.), where such a general admonition is given. Cf. the use of *ginōske(-te) hoti* in the Ap. Frs., *2 Clem.* 5.5; 16.3 (both in eschatological, even apocalyptic teaching), and Hermas, *Man.* 6.2.3, 5 *(bis),* where its meaning is psychologized.

*rough times will be at hand.* "In the last days rough times *(kairoi chalepoi)* will be present *(enstēsontai).*" *Kairoi,* in the PE, are always modified (see commentary on 1 Tim 2:6; 4:1; 6:15 [as well as the only uses of the singular in the PE at 2 Tim 4:3, 6]). Here these *kairoi* are genuinely plural and are described with *chalepoi* (cf. English "rugged," "rough"), a term that the NT uses only once otherwise, in Matt 8:28, of a pair of demoniacs. In the Ap. Frs., Polycarp, *Phil.* 4.1, cited above on 1 Tim 6:10, uses this term to say, "But the beginning of all evils *(chalepōn)* is love of money." *Barnabas* 4.5, citing Theod. Dan 7.7, glosses the description of the fourth beast by adding that it is "fiercer *(chalepōteron)* than all the beasts of the sea." Hermas, *Vis.* 1.4.2, describes a prophetic reading as "hard and difficult" *(chalepa kai sklēra),* and in *Man.* 6.2.10 "the works of the angel of wickedness are bad" *(chalepa). Martyrdom of Polycarp* 11.1 (cited above on 2:25 for its use of *metanoia/-noein)* has Polycarp reply to the proconsul, ". . . but it is good to change from bad things *(chalepōn)* to good ones *(dikaia).*"

The eleven LXX uses of *chalepos* are, with the exception of Isa 18:2 (= Hebrew *yr',* niphal), in the Greek (Alexandrian) strata; thus Sir 3:21; Wis 3:19, "For the end *(ta telē)* of an unrighteous generation is grievous *(chalepa)*"; 17.11; 19:13 (of the harsh oppression of strangers); 2 Macc 4:4 (of a sharp rivalry), 16 (of a hard disaster); 6:3 (of "the harsh . . . onslaught of evil"); 4 Macc 7:24 (of tortures); 9:4 (of a choice worse than death); 16:8 (of the problems of rearing children). The closest the term comes to qualifying a time or season is *ta telē* of Wis 3:19. A survey of LSJ *s.v.* showed no use of time, but often of various forms of angry, aggressive, harsh, and severe behavior. See Menander, *Dysc.* 325 (Handley, *Dyskolos,* p. 189; Sandbach, *Menandri,* p. 61); *Epitr.* 720-721,

Sandbach, *Menandri,* p. 127; see also adverbial in LCL, p. 88 (566 K); also Menander, *Sikyonos* 343, Sandbach, *Menandri,* p. 280, where Theron says to the old man, Kichēsias, *chalepos ēsth'-*, "you were a difficult customer" (see Gomme and Sandbach, *Commentary,* pp. 663-664, where the adj. is "singularly flat" and may = "a difficult customer"). MM *s.v.* cite OxyP X.1242.36 (third century-C.E.) where the references are to the *chalepa* ("outrages") inflicted on the Alexandrian Jews; also of "harsh" or "fierce" persons in a sixth-century-B.C.E. text in Dittenberger, *Syll.*[3] 780.31. Perhaps the English "rough times" would catch the unusual character of the Greek phrase here with two common words in an uncommon combination.

The "rough times," *enstēsontai,* "will be present" or "will enter," a verb that occurs only here in the PE. Its six other NT occurrences are in the Paulines and Heb 9:9. Oepke, *TDNT* 2.543-544, reviews most of the fourteen LXX uses of this verb. Particularly notable in connection with 2 Tim 3:1 would be 2 Macc 3:17; 4:43; 3 Macc 1:16 (*tēi enestōsēi anagkēi* [*s.v.l.* cf. 1 Cor 7:26]; see Charles, *AP* 1.164). The third-century-B.C.E. P. Petr. II, 19.2.5 (*ap.* Oepke), speaks of *dia tēn enestōsan kakian.* LXX 1 Esd 9:6 with its "impending winter" is notable too.

2. *intent on themselves.* Lit. "self-lovers." *Philautos* is a NT *hapax,* not used in the LXX or the Ap. Frs. MM *s.v.* cites Philo, *Leg. alleg.* 1.49, *philautos de kai atheos ho nous oiomenos isos einai theōi,* "but the mind considering itself equal to God loves itself and is without God" (trans. WCW), and also cites one use of noun in papyrus; cf. Plato, *Laws* 5.731E, and Aristotle, *NE* 9.8 (1168B). See the Philo references in Spicq, who submits that all the other vices in this list unfold what is implicit in *philautia* (cf. Cramer, *Catena*), which is more than just narcissistic egotism. It is an atheistic and drastic humanism that knows no measure or value beyond the individual man, and according to Philo, *Fug.* 81, the *philautoi* are the very opposite of the *philotheoi* (note 2 Tim 3:5, *philotheoi, infra*). Spicq notes that this is conceptually close to the *authadē* of Titus 1:7.

*intent on money.* Lit. "money-lovers" *(philargyroi).* The adjectival form here in 2 Tim 3:2 occurs elsewhere in the NT only in Luke 16:14, of the Pharisees (cf. commentary on 1 Tim 6:10 for the rest of usage profile). Spicq notes *T. Levi* 17.11 (Charles, *AP* 2.314), where the Jerusalem priesthood is scored with this term in a sevenfold list of vices that will bring on its failure. See Menander, *Aspis* 123, 149, 351 (Sandbach, *Menandri,* pp. 7, 8, 16).

*pretentious.* The only NT uses of *alazones* are here and in Rom 1:30, but *alazoneia* occurs in 1 John 2:16 and James 4:16 (of the plans to make money in 4:13) as well as *T. Joseph* 17.8 (cited in Dibelius, *James,* p. 234). In the LXX the noun *alazoneia* occurs perhaps as many as seven times, only in the latest strata of works composed in Greek (Wis 5:8 with "riches"; 17:7 of the vaunted insight given by Egyptian magic; 2 Macc 9:8 of Antiochus's arrogance; 15:6; 4 Macc 1:26; 2:15; 8:19). For the verb see Prov 25:6 and Wis 2:16, and for *alazōn* cf. Job

28:8 Prov 21:24; Hab 2:5 (cf. 1QpHab 8.3-12, where this link between the avarice and arrogance of the wicked priest is exploited at length).

In the Ap. Frs. it is *First Clement* particularly that employs *alazōn* (57.2 with *hyperēphanon*) and its cognates: *alazoneuomai,* 2.1; 38.2; *alazoneia,* 13.1; 14.1; 16.2; 21.5; 35.5; and as a variant in 57.2 (both with *hyperēphania*). Otherwise the noun is found in the list in *Did.* 5.1 as well as Hermas, *Man.* 6.2.5 (with *hyperēphania*) and 8.5.

*arrogant.* The word *hyperēphanoi* occurs in the Paulines only in Rom 1:30 *(ut cit. supra),* but elsewhere in the NT it appears in Luke 1:51 in Mary's song, of the discomfiture of the arrogant, as well as in the citation of LXX Prov 3:34 by James 4:6 and 1 Pet 5:5 (cited also by *1 Clem.* 30.2; Ign. *Eph.* 5.3. Dibelius *James,* p. 225). The noun occurs elsewhere in the NT only in the vice catalogue of Mark 7:22.

*to those who bore them, undutiful.* Lit. "disobedient to parents *(goneusin apeitheis).*" The adjective *apeithēs* occurred at Titus 1:16 and 3:3 (in the NT otherwise only at Luke 1:17 and Acts 26:19; of the eight LXX uses, nearly all refer to the rebelliousness of God's people), both times in series with other vicious qualities. LXX Deut 21:18 is quite parallel to this passage of Second Timothy as it envisions the case of a son *apeithēs kai erethistēs* (provocative) toward father and mother.

*Goneis* occurs only here in the PE out of twenty NT uses. There are four other uses in the Paulines besides the already cited Rom 1:30, all of parents/children *(tekna);* 2 Cor 12:14 *(bis)* is parabolic. Of the seventeen LXX uses, as many as eight are in the Maccabean corpus, with 4 Macc 2:10 offering an interesting counterpoint to this passage of Second Timothy when it remarks that "the Law ranks above affection for parents *(tēs pros goneis eunoias).*" In the Ap. Frs. only Hermas uses the word, *Vis.* 1.3.1; 2.2.2, in the latter passage describing Hermas's own children as having betrayed their parents *(proedōkan tous goneis . . . prodotai goneōn).*

*ungrateful. Acharistoi,* a term found otherwise in the NT only in Luke 6:35 of the Father who is "kind *(chrēstos)* to the ungrateful and the selfish *(acharistous kai ponērous).*" The four LXX uses of this term are in the latest Greek strata. Thus Sir 29:17, 25 qualifies a person ungrateful for benefits received, and Wis 16:29 writes, "the hope of an ungrateful man will melt like wintry frost. . . ." Finally, in 4 Macc 9:10 the attitude of the seven martyrs seems to the enraged Antiochos to be that of "disobedient *(apeithountōn)*" as well as "ungrateful *(acharistōn)*" men.

This adjective is not documented in the Ap. Frs. Of the secular uses, LSJ notes *Od.* 8.236 for "ungracious"; Conzelmann, *TDNT* 9.375, notes, with LSJ, Xenophon, *Anabasis* 2.1.13, for "without charm" and Herodotus 1.90.4 for "ungrateful" or "thankless gods" (cf. also MM *s.v.*).

*irreligious.* On *anosioi* see 1 Tim 1:9 above.

3. *unaffectionate, irreconcilable. Astorgoi,* "unaffectionate/loveless," occurs at Rom 1:31 but nowhere else in the NT, LXX, the Ap. Frs., or Josephus. Romans 12:10, however, does write of *tēi philadelphiai eis allēlous philostorgoi,* "be devoted to one another in brotherly love" (trans. BAGD, p. 861). *Aspondoi,* "unreconcilable," is a NT *hapax,* undocumented in the LXX, the Ap. Frs., and the papyri (thus Spicq). See the Comment below for more on both terms.

*devils at gossip, uncontrolled, uncouth, uncaring about goodness.* "Devils at gossip" is simply *diaboloi* in Greek. The ethical lists at Titus 2:3; 1 Tim 3:11; and 2 Tim 3:3 also contain this anarthrous plural. The noun *diabolē* (slander) occurs ten times in the LXX, but the plural as here does not. "Uncontrolled *(akrateis),* uncouth *(anēmeroi),* and uncaring about goodness (*aphilagathoi,* lit. 'unloving of good')" occur nowhere else in the NT, LXX, or Ap. Frs., with the exception of *akratēs,* which occurs in LXX Prov 27:20: *hoi apaideutoi akrateis glossēi,* "the undisciplined do not control their tongue" (trans. WCW; cf. Aeschylus, *Prom.* 884: *glōssēs akratēs,* "tongue uncontrolled," as Io describes her anguished hysteria; of speech also in Josephus, *Ant.* 15.229 and 16.399). Note Spicq's Philo citations: twelve times in Josephus (cf. above; add *Ant.* 5.277 for sexual jealousy); cf. the third-century-B.C.E. inscription (medical) of "powerless fingers *(daktylous akrateis),*" MM *s.v.*

4. *renegade, reckless.* Both *prodotai* and *propeteis* occur otherwise in the NT only in the Lukan corpus. In the LXX *prodotēs* occurs only in 2 Macc 5:15 of Menelaus leading Antiochus into the Temple to pillage it; 10:13 of Ptolemy called Macron, charged falsely as a traitor; and 10:22 of soldiers who took bribes to let some besieged escape; 3 Macc 3:24 has the letter of Ptolemy Philopator charge the Jews with this term.

In the Ap. Frs. only Hermas employs *prodotai* (always pl.): *Vis.* 2.2.2 (cited above); *Sim.* 8.6.4; 9.19.1, 3 *(bis).* MM *s.v.* cite *Ep. Arist.* 270: "The man bent on advancing his own interests is a born traitor."

*Propetēs* occurs in LXX Prov 10:14; 13:3; and Sir 9:18, always of rashness in speech. In the Ap. Frs. only *1 Clem.* 1.1 uses this term, coupled with *authadē* (cf. Titus 1:7), to describe the "rash and self-willed persons" who provoked the Corinthian schism. MM *s.v.* cite a second-century-C.E. epitaph that speaks of *hē propetēs moira* ("untimely," LSJ). See Menander, *Perikeir.* 441; *Epitr.* 306, for adverb of loose speech and Menander 574 K of acting precipitately.

*rather than.* On the typically Lukan *mallon ē* in this phrase see the Comment on 1 Tim 1:4.

5. *appearance.* The term *morphōsis* is not found in the LXX (cf. Behm, *TDNT* 4.754 n. 2) or the Ap. Frs. Indeed, the *morph-* cluster is very sparsely represented in the NT (Gal 4:19, *morphoō;* Phil 2:6-7, *morphē* [a hymn]; Mark 16:12, *morphē,* of the risen Jesus). LSJ *s.v.* give several uses of cognates. There is

a striking parallel to this verse of the PE in Philo, *Plant.* 70: *kai nyn eisi tines tōn epimorphazontōn eusebeian,* "for even now there are those who simulate piety" (trans. WCW); though Philo does not use *morphōsis,* it is all the more intriguing in view of the "citation" in the previous verse here. See also *T. Benjamin* 10.1 (Behm, p. 754; Charles, *AP* 2.359): "I longed to see . . . the form of his countenance *(tēn morphōsin tēs opseōs).*"

*repudiated, arneomai.* Except for Titus 1:16; 2:12; 1 Tim 5:8; and 2 Tim 2:12-13, *areneisthai* does not otherwise appear in the Paulines; of eighteen other NT uses, eight occur in Luke-Acts. Uses in the LXX are late and rare, but cf. Wis 12:27; 16:16; 4 Macc 8:7; 10:15. *Arneisthai,* in Hellenistic and biblical usage, can also take a personal object, as it does in 2 Tim 2:12b-13 (see the Notes and Comment on 2 Tim 2:12-13 above).

*Keep people like that at a distance too.* Lit. "and avoid these [men] *(kai toutous apotrepou).*" The verb used here, *apotrepou,* occurs nowhere else in the NT (cf. the *ektrepein* of 1 Tim 1:6; 5:15; 6:20) or the Ap. Frs. Some LXX MSS read it at Sir 20:29; 48:18, as well as 3 Macc 1:23; 4 Macc 1:33 (of "pleasures," *hēdonas*); 16:12 (of death). MM *s.v.* cite the verb from a woman's private (and quite fragmented) letter that indicates that this term, common enough in literary texts, actually had wider use in the second century C.E. LSJ cite several later authors for the middle meaning "to dissuade, deter," Polybius, *Histories* 7.13.1; and "beat off, repulse," Plutarch, *Brutus* 42. The present tense may have a durative aspect here, "Keep on repulsing such persons."

6. *to captivate.* "To make captives" (*aichmalōteuontes;* $D^2$. et al.; *aichmalōtizontes* in D. F. G et al.; J. K. Elliott, *Greek Text,* pp. 148-149). In the Ap. Frs. the form in *-teuein* does not occur, but Ign. *Eph.* 17.1; *Phil.* 2.2 employ that in *-izein,* of the "prince of this world" leading the Ephesians away captive and of wolves "who lead captive with evil pleasures *(hēdonēi kakēi)* the runners in God's race."

The figurative use of these verbs in the Christian documents has some precedent in LXX Jth 16:9: "Her beauty captivated his mind" *(ēichmalōtisen);* contrast 5:18, "They were led away captive *(ēichmalōteuthēsan)* to a foreign country" (RSV).

*sins.* On the noun *hamartia* see Comment on 1 Tim 5:22.

7. *ever. Pantote* is used only here in the PE but forty times otherwise in the NT and twenty-six times in the other Paulines, especially of prayer. Luke has the word only twice: Luke 15:31 (of the elder son); 18:1 (also of prayer). In the LXX the only uses are in Wis 11:21; 19:18. In the Ap. Frs., Ign. *Eph.* 4.2; 11.2 use the term; otherwise and rather often Hermas does.

8. *just as once.* Instead of *hōs,* the phrase *hon tropon* is used and understood as if it were one word (cf. Latin *quemadmodum*), and thus *de* follows *tropon* (BDF §475.2). *Tropos* occurs only here in the PE, and twelve times other-

wise in the NT. Of these uses, five are in Luke-Acts and all are a form of the phrase here in Second Timothy (Luke 13:34 = Matt 23:37 [Q]; Acts 1:11; 7:28 = LXX Exod 2:14; 15:11; and 27:25 [both with *kath'*]). When *tropos* occurs in the other Paulines, this phrase is not used (Rom 3:2; Phil 1:18; 2 Thess 2:3; 3:16), nor does it occur in Heb 13:5 or Jude 7. The phrase occurs at every turn in the LXX, but it is relatively rare in the Ap. Frs. (who use the noun only seventeen times anyway): *1 Clem.* 4.10 (citing LXX Exod 2:14 *ut supra*) and *2 Clem.* 8.2; 9.4; 12.4.

*defied.* Here this verb occurs for the first time in the PE; it will be used again at 4:15 of the opposition of the coppersmith Alexander to the words of Paul and his colleagues. Of the eleven other NT uses of this verb, five are in the Paulines: Rom 9:19; 13:2 *(bis);* Gal 2:11 (Paul against Cephas); Eph 6:13. The Lukan usage is also quite parallel to that in the PE: Luke 21:15 (with *anteipen,* "contradict"); Acts 6:10 (against Stephen) and 13:8 of Elymas, the *Magus,* opposing Barnabas and Paul. Indeed, in Luke it is always a matter of the opposition to the preaching (as here in the PE); in the other Paulines the passage that comes closest to the situation here is in Gal 2:11. In the other NT uses of the verb it refers to resisting evil (the devil): Matt 5:39; James 4:7; 1 Pet 5:9.

Of the as many as seventy-one LXX occurrences of this verb, it once has *tois logois* as its object (Jth 8:28 of her words on how God tries his people) as in 2 Tim 4:15, but it never is used of opposition to Moses in the Pentateuch. In the Ap. Frs., *1 Clem.* 27.5 uses the term in citing Wis 12:12 (cf. 11:21). The other uses are in *Barn.* 4.9; 6.1; and Hermas, but none offers notable parallels to the usage here in the PE.

*these numbskulled counterfeiters of the faith are defying the truth.* These opponents of the last days are lit. "people (*anthrōpoi* [cf. 3:2 above]) corrupted as to the mind (*katephtharmenoi ton noun* [a permanent state; see 1 Tim 6:5]) unqualified (*adokimoi,* lit. "untested" and so "qualified," recurs in the vice catalogue of Rom 1:2; the remainder of the NT uses, except for Heb 6:8, fall in the Corninthian letters [1 Cor 9:27; 2 Cor 13:5, 6, 7]) with regard to the faith (*peri tēn pistin* [*peri* with the accusative occurs frequently in the PE; in the Paulines otherwise, only at Phil 2:23])."

*Kataphtheirein* does not otherwise occur in the NT (though *phtheirein* occurs nine times: in 1 Cor 3:17 [*bis*]; 15:33 [the Euripides-Menander quotation]; 2 Cor 7:2; 11:3 [with *ta noēmata* as object]; Eph 4:22; as well as in 2 Pet 2:12; Jude 10; and Rev 19:2). The eight uses in the Ap. Frs. are in Hermas; in none is it used with *nous,* but *Sim.* 6.2.4 speaks of *katephtharmenoi eisin apo tēs alētheias,* "these then have been corrupted from the truth." The thirty-one LXX uses again offer no illustration with *nous,* though Spicq, *EP,* p. 779, has noted how in 1 Macc 8:11 *katephtheiran* occurs in a context with *antestēsan* of the Romans destroying those who opposed them. For further observations on this terminology as well as on *nous,* see the commentary above on 1 Tim 6:5 and the data noted there from Harder, *TDNT* 9.93-106, especially p. 103; also Therrien, *Discernement,* pp. 276-278, on *nous* as "the anthropological principle of moral discernment," as well as pp. 228-229 comparing Rom 1:28.

9. *Progress.* On *prokoptein* see Note at 1 Tim 4:15.

*Their own stupidity.* The noun *anoia* here (taking up the *katephtharmenoi ton noun* of v. 8; cf. the *anoētoi* of 1 Tim 6:9 and Titus 3:3) is a term that occurs otherwise in the NT only in Luke 6:11, of the furious reaction of scribes and Pharisees to Jesus' healing on the Sabbath in the synagogue. The at most thirteen LXX uses twice have a Hebrew *Vorlage,* Prov 14:8 and 22:15 *('iwwelet),* with the sense of "folly" (cf. H. Cazelles, *TDOT* 1.137-140, though he has *nil* from Qumran). No Hebrew corresponds to LXX Job 33:23; Ps 21:2; Eccles 11:10. In Wis 15:18 *anoia* refers to "the lack of intelligence" in animals and in 19:3 to a "foolish decision." In 2 Macc 4:6 Simon's treachery and slander are "folly," and in 4:40 one reads of a man "advanced in years and no less advanced in folly." In 2 Macc 14:5; 15:33; and 3 Macc 3:16, 20 the noun also occurs. The Greek term often reflects the Hebrew connotation of *'wl,* i.e. foolish speech or words (Cazelles *ut cit.*). See also J. Behm, *TDNT* 4.962-963, for classical usage, as well as Philo and Josephus.

CD 15:15 (Dupont-Sommer, *EWQ,* p. 161 n. 6; cf. Gaster, *DSS,* p. 90) envisions the case of a sectary so stupid that he cannot grasp the plain meaning of the law, and so it legislates, "The stupid, the mad, the foolish *('wyl),* the demented, the blind, the crippled, the lame, minors: none of them shall enter in the midst of the Community . . ." (cf. 1QS[3] 2.3-8: Dupont-Sommer, *EWQ,* pp. 107-108). 1QS 4.10: Dupont-Sommer, *EWQ,* p. 80, in its long list of the qualities produced by "the spirit of perversity," includes "abundant wickedness, impatience, and much folly *(wrwb 'wlt)* and burning insolence." 1QS 4.23-24: Dupont-Sommer, *EWQ,* p. 82, describes the "spirits of truth and perversity" warring within man and thus leading to conduct "in wisdom and folly *(bḥkmh w'wlt).*" Only a fragmented reference remains in 1QH 13.4. But 1Q27 1.1, 7 (The Book of Mysteries, DJD 1.183) writes, "The world will be filled with knowledge and ignorance exist no more" (Gaster, *DSS,* p. 429; cf. Dupont-Sommer, *EWQ,* p. 327). Here the "eschatological folly" is swallowed up in the final sunrise of righteousness over the world.

In the Ap. Frs. *anoia* occurs only in *2 Clem.* 13.1, where in a summons to repentance the author writes, "for we are full of much folly *(anoias)* and wickedness."

In A as well as 330. 2400 (J. K. Elliott, *Greek Text,* p. 151) one reads *dianoia autōn.* Since neither *anoia* or *dianoia* occurs otherwise in the PE, it is not possible to argue strictly from the usage of the author. *Dianoia* is the more "reasonable," neutral term, much less harsh and polemical in its designating the "understanding" or "thought" or "intelligence" or "disposition" of the opponents (cf., e.g., Luke 1:51; Col 1:21; and Lohse, *Col,* pp. 63-64), though it can be taken in a bad sense too (cf. the pl. in Eph 2:3 and in *1 Clem.* 39.1). *Anoia* has, however, the better external attestation, and it is also the more difficult reading in this instance with its unmitigated fierceness, as well as consistent with the reliance on *alpha* privative compounds in the PE (cf. esp. *anoētos* cited above, 1 Tim 6:9; Titus 3:3).

*obvious. Ekdēlos* occurs only here in the NT, and in the LXX only in 3 Macc 3:19; 6:5, and not at all in the Ap. Frs. The intensive form of the adjective here (thus LSJ *s.v.;* Spicq; cf. BDF §318.5 on "perfectivizing" prepositions prefixed to verbs) is found in several inscriptions from the late second century B.C.E. and first century C.E. (MM *s.v.*), as well as in a text of Vettius Valens, p. 92.10. However, *Iliad* 5.2-3 describes Diomedes as receiving strength and courage *hin' ekdēlos meta pasin/Argeioisi genoito,* "that he might be conspicuous among all the Argives." Of the four uses in Josephus, *Ant.* 20.41, "if the matter becomes obvious to all *(tou pragmatos ekdēlou pasin genomenou)*" is notable.

See above on 1 Tim 4:15 concerning his progress being "evident *(phanera)* to all *(pasin)*" for the meaning of *pasin* here in Second Timothy. It looks as if the author reserved the *dēlos* compounds for describing sins and stupidity while *phaneros* was reserved for "progress" in virtue.

## ♦ COMMENT

3:1. *Realize this, however, that in the last days rough times will be at hand.* With a slight contrast to what has preceded *(de),* the *touto . . . ginōske* now directs Timothy's attention to the following teaching. Bultmann, *TDNT* 1.704, has noted that the admonition "to know" here has the Hebraic overtone of being ready to act on what one has learned (cf. Luke 10:11). The present imperative of this verb is typical of the epistolary genre (Spicq), and the verb itself implies that what follows is in some sense already familiar to the reader, that he is already aware of it (Dibelius, *James,* pp. 72, 258, on James 1:3; 5:20). The link of this verb with recalling what one has already learned about events that are still to come is notable (see Giblin, *Threat,* pp. 159-166, and the *oidate* of 2 Thess 2:6).

The teaching of which Timothy is already aware is not here described as Paul's own gospel or deposit. It is introduced with *hoti,* which suggests (or is meant to suggest) a citation, and one is reminded of the prophetic oracle that introduced a very similar section of the previous letter, 1 Tim 4:1-3. Here in Second Timothy, as D-C have noted, the motif of the testament and farewell discourse of the famous man is at the fore, and Spicq has noted that where 2 Tim 1 put particular stress on the past and 2 Tim 2 on facing the present problems, this chapter now turns to a future that is (if possible) even more somber, a characteristic motif of the testament form (Munck, "Discourse d'adieu," pp. 155-170).

The phrase *en eschatais hēmerais*, "in the last days," occurs only here in the Pauline epistolary, though conceptually its counterpart is certainly *en hysterois kairois*, "in these latter times," in 1 Tim 4:1. The phrase does occur twice otherwise in the NT, when Acts 2:17 adds these words to its citation of LXX Joel 3:1 (with the article *tais*), and in James 5:3, in a context of the terrifying judgment in store for the greedy rich. Cf. the *ep' eschatōn hēmerōn* of 2 Pet 3:3 as well as the seven uses of the singular in John (e.g., 6:39-40, 44, 54, and see R. Brown, AB *JN, in loc.*). In the LXX *ep' eschatōn/eschatou (tōn) hēmerōn* is the standard form of this phrase (Gen 49:1; Num 24:14; Deut 4:30; 8:16 [cf. 31:29]; 32:20; Josh 24:27 [cf. Neh 8:18, *heōs tēs hēmeras tēs eschatēs*]; Hos 3:5; Mic 4:1; Jer 23:20; 25:18; 37:24; Ezek 38:16; Dan 2:28, 45; 10:14). In some of these instances the LXX has heightened the eschatological sense of the passage. The form *en hēmerais eschatais* occurs only in Prov 31:25; Isa 2:2; and Dan 11:20 (cf. Kittel, *TDNT* 2.697-698; G. Delling, *TDNT* 2.943-953, esp. pp. 947 and 950-951). The Hebrew root *'ḥr* in some form is being translated by these Greek phrases, and that root appears in the favorite Qumran phrases about "the last generations/days" analyzed above at 1 Tim 4:1. As Delling noted (p. 951), later Jewish apocalyptic tended not only to use the phrase of the actual content of the eschaton rather than its simply temporal framework (pp. 947, 952), but also to specify that contrast "unequivocally" of "the divine action in the last days," whether that be tribulation, judgment, etc. (cf. above on 2 Tim 1:12, 18).

Carmignac, "La notion d'eschatologie," pp. 17-31, has noted that in the NT when *eschatos* qualifies a noun indicating time *(day, hour, season)*, it may mean not only "last day, etc." but also the present or immediate past (from the writer's point of view). Acts 2:17; Heb 1:2; and 1 Pet 1:20 are certainly examples. Other instances grammatically speak of the future (e.g., 1 Tim 4:1; 2 Tim 3:1) but really are speaking within and about the situation being predicted. Thus NT use of *eschatos* with temporal nouns is conceptually very close to *hysteros* and the *'aḥarôn/'aḥarît* terminology of the OT and can designate a more or less lengthy period, considered as yet to come by the OT but now in the process of realization (cf. also U. Wilckens, *TDNT* 8.595, who compares 2 Tim 3:1 with 4:3, *estai gar kairos hote*). Stählin, *TDNT* 4.781 n. 117, summarizes the argument for all the opponents of the PE, present and to come, as belonging to the same genre, propagating the similar "myths," living similar lives (cf. 4:4 *infra*).

In the Ap. Frs. the phrase occurs in the form *en tais eschatais hēmerais* in *Did.* 16.3 (cf. 16.2) and *Barn.* 4.9, the former of which, in a strongly eschatological context, says, "In the last days the false prophets and corrupters shall be multiplied and the sheep shall be turned into wolves . . . (4) and they shall . . .

persecute and betray (*paradōsousi* [cf. 2 Tim 3:4, *prodotai* below]). . . ." The phrase also occurs with *ep'* in *2 Clem.* 14.2 (of the time of the incarnation); *Barn.* 12.9; 16.5 (in the latter Enoch is apparently "the Scripture" being cited); 89.55-56, 66-67; Charles, *AP* 2.255-256; and Hermas, *Sim.* 9.12.3 (a parable apparently of the time of the incarnation).

A. Oepke, *TDNT* 5.868, submits that both 2 Tim 3:1 and 1 Tim 4:1 "are weaker statements (of the hopeful expectation of the end) than one finds in Paul," though just what "weak" means is problematic. The "realism" of Paul and that of first-generation Christian apocalyptic are not *ipso facto* beyond criticism, and that indeed is what the second generation (including Luke-Acts-PE) proceeded to administer as it isolated what (in its judgment) still was applicable to the second generation. The Church publicly admits that it must live in the present age. Doing this, too, takes strength.

In the last days bad times will be present. The stress of the term *enstēsontai,* "will be present" or "will enter," is on that which is here and now present, with perhaps (according to BAGD, LSJ) a nuance of threatening or menacing harm still to come (cf. Gal 1:4, *ek tou aiōnos tou enestōtos ponērou,* "of the present evil age," with 2 Thess 2:2 on the mistaken notion *hoti enestēken* [but note *v.l.* here too] *hē hēmera tou kyriou,* "that the day of the Lord has already come"; see Conzelmann, *1 Cor.,* p. 132, on 1 Cor 7:26, esp. the examples in n. 14: he prefers the meaning *imminent* that straddles the present/future aspect that the verb conveys). A. Oepke, *TDNT* 2.543-544, is quite emphatic about the absence of the *menacing* connotation from this verb, "at least with the perfect," but he does say that 2 Tim 3:1 is "the only possible instance" in the NT of this nuance, and even then by no means necessary.

In the Ap. Frs., *1 Clem.* 55.1 writes of kings who consulted oracles "when a time of pestilence has set in *(loimikou tinos enstantos kairou).*" Ign. *Eph.* 11.1 writes, "Let us either fear the wrath to come or love the grace that is present *(tēn enestōsan charin)* — one of the two." Otherwise the verb is found only in *Barn.* 1.7, of prophets revealing things past, present *(enestōta),* and to come; 4.1, also of present matters; 5.3, present as distinct from past and future; 17.1 *(lect. dub.),* 2, present as distinct from future. These passages bear out Oepke's observation that the nuance of menace does not accompany the verb as such.

2. *for then people will be intent on themselves, intent on money, pretentious, arrogant, blaspheming.* The "rough times" to come (at hand) are explained *(gar)* in terms of disastrous persons *(anthrōpoi),* not the standard disaster images of apocalyptic (earthquake, flood, eclipse, etc.). The repeated *anthrōpoi* (vv. 8, 13) appears to coincide with the subsections here, marking off verses 1-9 from verses 10-13 and both from verses 14-17 and its *theou anthrōpos.* The vice catalogue that follows is the most stunning in this correspondence (and second only to that of Rom 1:29-31 in the rest of the NT), stretching through the next

three verses in nineteen sonorous, assonant asyndetic entries (Delling, *TDNT* 1.227, says eighteen). The *-oi* ending gives a rhyme to almost every member of the list, which opens and closes with alliteration/assonance on *ph(il)* sounds *(philautoi, philargyroi . . . hyperēphanoi, blasphēmoi,* and at the conclusion, *tetyphōmenoi, philēdonoi . . . philotheoi . . . morphōsin).* In the middle of the catalogue occurs a seven- (or perhaps eight-) member list of terms beginning with the alpha-privative, a list itself divided by the occurrence of *diaboloi* after the fourth (or fifth) entry *(aspondoi).*

There is no discernible ethical or theological principle on which the list is being ordered. This is not to say, by any means, that the individual terms are meaningless or vague or that a given term is not quite deliberately paired off with another by alliteration and/or final assonance in complementary or antithetical fashion. We can affirm that the list (or the lists used as sources) had practical rhetorical and/or catechetical goals that did not include a speculative ethical/theological synthesis. Here the terminology designates actions and attitudes that are quite alien to life in Christ. They are not being adduced for their own sake for purely academic reasons. They have in the context an apologetic polemic function, identifying and stigmatizing specific lifestyles and attitudes as really quite alien from that to which believers are called (and for whose instruction this list is intended, since it is hardly a brief to be presented in a court that will judge and sentence those who live in the way described).

D-C's directive to take the list "as a whole since it is traditional" is both simplistic and overly rational (idealistic), as is the observation that the opponents are not being accused "of having committed any or all of the particular sins mentioned" (p. 115). There is, of course, no question that the opponents have not committed all these sins, whether as a group or individually (as BDF §460.2 note, the asyndeton already indicates this). It is quite another matter to affirm that the author-redactor thought that none of the items applied to any of the opponents. Indeed, it is almost inconceivable when one recalls that his purpose was practical rather than speculative. It is even more difficult to believe when one notes that the list(s) proffered have been taken from sources that have been edited with that practical end in mind. Thus the list was not "a whole," even though its materials were "traditional."

The apologetic polemic goal demands that the author of the PE thought that one or another of the opponents had really been hit by one or another of the vices that he had chosen from the traditional lists at his disposal. One cannot reasonably infer from the form or genre that he thought any or all of them were guilty of all the vices listed; one can reasonably infer that he thought some of the entries applied (as even D-C admits for v. 5). One cannot from the form alone determine which ones applied or to whom the author thought they applied.

The first two entries are paired by their opening and closing syllables, *philautoi, philargyroi,* a pattern that will reappear as the list closes in verse 4. Perhaps the source of these entries was one brief catalogue constructed in this way as distinct from the alpha-privative catalogue at the heart of the list as it now stands. Grundmann, *TDNT* 1.18, has noted that *philautoi,* which leads off this whole list, would correspond with the *aphilagathoi* that concludes the alpha-privative list (cf. commentary on this term below).

Coupled with "self-lovers" by identical prefix and ending is "money-lovers" *(philargyroi).* Again in Titus 1:7 a different term, *aischrokerdē,* designated the same quality as one that ought not to be found in the (presbyter-) bishop. In 1 Tim 6:10 *hē philargyria* was "the root of all evils."

The next quality, *alazones,* separates the preceding pair from the following *hyperēphanoi, blasphēmoi,* whose internal and final assonance *(ph. oi)* link them together. With this term the list here intersects verbally with that in Rom 1:30-31, where one also reads of *hyperēphanous, alazonas . . . goneusin apeitheis . . . astorgous* (the latter also in a group of alpha-privatives). There is every reason in Romans to infer that a pre-Pauline tradition (Jewish and then Jewish Christian) was being redacted by the apostle, and similarly, here in Second Timothy the verbal coincidences lead one to think that either Romans or (more probably) the traditional material behind Romans was being exploited.

G. Delling, *TDNT* 1.227, notes how magicians and officers are described as braggarts, especially the latter (as in Plautus, *Miles Gloriosus*), as promising what in fact they cannot deliver. The term is peculiarly apt for describing men who think they really have ultimate control of the future (cf. James 4:16 *ut cit. supra*) that really belongs only to the God whom they refuse to acknowledge. Spicq is reluctant to see here the braggarts of Greco-Latin comedy, but it is difficult to imagine the (Roman) readers of this correspondence not thinking of such "clowns" when the term was used. Cf. Menander, *Perikeiromenē* 78, for *alazōn* (Sandbach, *Menandri,* p. 202); note that the term does not occur in the papyri (Spicq).

G. Bertram, *TDNT* 8.526-527, traces the LXX usage of *hyperēphanoi,* "arrogant," and notes how the plural of the Magnificat (Luke 1:51) envisions the arrogant as "a group or party" (p. 528), a suggestion that might apply to all the plurals of this list in Second Timothy. In the Markan list (7:22) *hyperēphania* follows *blasphēmia,* as here in Second Timothy it precedes *blasphemoi,* again probably because each term was thought to complement the meaning of the other and the links in sound were thought to underscore those in the sense (on *blasphēmoi* see 1 Tim 1:13), *blasphēmoi* here adding the note of verbal insult to an attitude of contemptuous arrogance. The verbal insults would contrast with boasting about oneself *(alazones).*

This term may have come into the vice lists of Jewish and/or Jewish

Christian communities under Stoic pressure (Bertram, *TDNT* 8.525), but not without the conceptual substance that the LXX precipitated from the Jewish faith. *Hyperēphania* and its cognates occur many times, with the great majority of uses in the sapiential (including Psalms) and Maccabean collections where the terminology designates human contempt for and deliberate resistance to the divine plan for his people. It is notable that the LXX does not pair *hyperēphanos* with *blasphēmos,* an indication perhaps of the contribution of those who fashioned the catalogue itself as distinguished from the individual terms that constitute it.

In the Ap. Frs., *First Clement* uses the *hyperēphan-* terminology most frequently (cf. *supra* and 16.2; 30.1; 35.5; 57.2 [*s.v.l.*] for noun, and 30.2; 49.5; 57.2; 59.3 for adjective, but never paired with *blasphēm-* terms). Ignatius once uses the adjective *(cit. supra),* and he alone the verb (*Eph.* 5.3; *Smyrn.* 10.2; *Pol.* 4.3), but again neither is paired with *blasphēm-* terminology. This is true also of *Did.* 2.6 (adj.) and 5.1 (noun) as well as *Barn.* 20.1. In Hermas, in addition to *Man.* 6.2.5 cited above, *Man.* 8.3 contains *blasphēmia* in the context; *Sim.* 8.9.1 uses the noun of the rich apostates. Thus again the pairing with *blasphemia/-oi* is specific to the NT catalogues found here in the PE and in Mark.

P. L. Schoonheim's *"hyperēphanos"* study of Luke 1:52 has an important table (pp. 237-239). He isolates "self-exaltation" as the center of meaning of *hyperēphanos,* as opposed to humility that means "readiness to do God's will." The link with the *philautoi* here in the PE is obvious.

2-3. *to those who bore them, undutiful, ungrateful, irreligious, unaffectionate, irreconcilable.* The sixth entry in this list, and the one that marks a kind of caesura as the series of alpha-privatives begins, is a phrase, *goneusin apeitheis,* "disobedient to parents," that also occurred in Rom 1:30 *cit. supra.* Both Eph 6:1 and Col 3:20 are in *Haustafeln* that direct obedience to parents *(hypakouete tois goneusi),* and the former (Eph 6:2) explicitly adduces LXX Exod 20:12, the command of the Decalogue to "honor your father and mother." Luke has the term six times (*nil* in Acts!), compared with once in Matt 10:21 which = Mark 13:12. John 9 uses the term six times. All instances are of human parents, including those of Jesus (Luke 2:27, 41, 43). In the light of the biblical and other usage, those "disobedient to parents" here in Second Timothy are surely being described against the background of the Decalogue, though neither here nor in Romans does this reference furnish any schematic key for the list as a whole (cf. and contrast 1 Tim 1:9-10 and commentary *in loc.*). To modern Western ears, the charge sounds curiously banal and flat in comparison with the other pungent, polemical characterizations of the opponents. Since they are scarcely dependent minors, one wonders in what sense the phrase could have applied to any of the opponents. The problem is the opposite of that posed by the patricides of 1 Tim 1:9, where the enormity of the crime made it anomalous. Here in Second Timothy one wonders where there were grounds for any crime at all. Perhaps Spicq is to be followed when he calls attention to the place and privilege of parents in the ancient world and takes *apeitheis* as really equivalent to ignoring and condemning one's mother and father. Another possibility is suggested below.

The first clearly independent quality in the alpha-privative list is *acharistoi,* a term found in Luke 6:35 of the Father, who is "kind *(chrēstos)* to the ungrateful and the selfish *(acharistous kai ponērous).*" H. Conzelmann, *TDNT* 9.393, thinks the term there may belong to Luke's redactional activity. In any event, it contrasts verbally with the *charis of* 6:32-34 (cf. Conzelmann, p. 392). Perhaps more illuminating is the third- or second-century-B.C.E. grave inscription cited by Conzelmann, p. 374 n. 9, of a boy prematurely dead who thus has cheated his parents out of the gratitude that would have been theirs *(tas goneōn pseusamenos charitas).* This epitaph derives its pathos from its presupposing the grateful thanks given to parents by their grown children. When one recalls the linking of disobedience with ingratitude in Fourth Maccabees (see Notes above), it is possible that the use of *acharistoi* here in the PE is a redactional explanation of the preceding phrase on those "disobedient to parents." If that is the case, a phrase that appeared as less than apt as it stood in the original catalogue was here appropriately glossed so that it would home in on some of the opponents.

The next alpha-privative, *anosioi,* occurred also in the list at 1 Tim 1:9, where it was paired with *bebēloi.* F. Hauck, *TDNT* 5.492, suggests that here the term, because of the phrase and terms that precede, might mean "devoid of piety" (toward parents). Oedipus is stigmatized with this adjective in *Oedipus Rex* 353. Josephus, *Ant.* 2.22, uses the adjective with the dative ("toward God and men") to qualify murder, especially of one of the family, a brother (*scil.* Joseph). MM *s.v.* (and Spicq) note that in second-century-C.E. Alexandrian papyri the adjective was aimed at the Jews in their great revolt there in 115-117 C.E.

The *astorgoi* ("loveless") also occurs in the list in Rom 1:31. LSJ *s.v.* notes Menander 522 for the noun, "the austere life involves a certain lack of natural affection" *(astorgian),* observing that the adjective normally means lacking in natural affection (particularly familial, as parents for their offspring, Clytus 1 [fourth-third–century-B.C.E. historian]) but that it can mean pitiless, "cruel" of "death" (cf. MM *s.v.* for third-fourth–century-C.E. epitaph). See Spicq, "*Philostorgos,*" pp. 497-510, and his *Prolégomènes,* p. 4 n. 3, citing Aeschines 2.146; 47.29; Antiphon §73: and esp. Theocritus 2.112 and 17.43.

On *aspondoi* MM, *s.v.,* note the Priene inscriptions where it means "without formal treaty" as a condition between friends. Of course, "implacable" foes are by definition unable to come to terms, as friends do not have to (thus MM). The term means literally "without a drink-offering," "without a libation," an indispensable characteristic for Greeks of a treaty or agreement between persons, divine or human (cf. the *spendomai* of 4:6 below and commentary *in loc.* as well as Michel, *TDNT* 7.528-536, though there is *nil* on this privative adjective). See the LSJ entries, p. 260, that refer to Ares, to war and battle, to enemies, especially in the dramatists. Note Spicq's references to Philo. See also Josephus, *Ant.* 4.264; 15.146, 220, especially 15.146, where it is the second in a fourfold list along with *anosious* (= "sacrilegious toward envoys"), as Herod encourages his troops against the Arabs. It is possible that all four of these alpha-privatives refer to parents.

*devils at gossip, uncontrolled, uncouth, uncaring about goodness. Diaboloi* now apparently interrupts the chain of alpha-privatives. The term has already occurred, in the plural and in ethical lists, in Titus 2:3 and 1 Tim 3:11, with the sense of slanderer/calumniator. Here in this list the basic Greek sense of "opponent, attacker, adversary" may be at the fore. When one considers the rather exotic term that has preceded, it is possible that this term that appears so abruptly in the list of alpha-privatives is actually a gloss on the preceding *aspondoi,* which as a result could be read as a phrase, "implacable adversaries" or even "implacable devils," with the more common and still ambivalent *diaboloi* both explaining and intensifying the recondite *aspondoi.* This gloss would then balance off against the *goneusin apeitheis acharistoi* with which this section of the list began. However, this commentary understands the previous adjectives as applied to parents, hence *diaboloi* mark a new grouping.

The opponents are then scored as *akratēs,* "uncontrolled, incontinent," another NT *hapax.* The cognate noun, *akrasia,* occurs of lack of sexual self-control in 1 Cor 7:5 (note that *Satan* tempts through this and cf. *diaboloi* here in the PE). In Matt 23:25 the Pharisees are denounced as full of "extortion and rapacity *(harpagēs kai akrasias).*" W. Grundmann, *TDNT* 2.342 n. 5, suggests for the meaning here in Second Timothy "undisciplined" or in Matthew "a lack of moderation or control" that includes more than sexual misconduct. Still the concern of these letters with sexual self-control (cf. *egkratē* in Titus 1:8 for the [presbyter-] bishop; the directives for the widows in 1 Tim 5:6, 11-15; for Timothy himself in 1 Tim 5:2) inclines one to believe that the author-redactor, if not the original vice list, interpreted the "incontinent" as "sexually uncontrolled." Spicq proposes that the term describes those who are unable to control themselves.

On *anēmeroi,* D-C, p. 116 (and MM), quote Epictetus on men who have forgotten their divine origin and so have become "wild, savage, untamed *(anēmeroi)* lions." The romantic penchant for the undomesticated and undomesticable was not popular in the ancient world. It certainly did not appeal to the author of the PE, who could find no worse condemnation of the Cretans than the infamous verse of Epimenides (Titus 1:12) calling them wild beasts.

*Aphilagathoi* is a neologism, occurring only here in the NT, undocumented previously in LXX and secular Greek, not occurring in the Ap. Frs. However, *philagathon* was one of the virtues for a (presbyter-) bishop in Titus 1:8, and W. Grundmann has noted with Aristotle (*TDNT* 1.18) that *philagathos* is the opposite of *philautos.* In that case, the last of the privatives here takes the reader back to the very beginning of this whole catalogue.

4. *renegade, reckless, conceited, intent on pleasure rather than intent on God.* With *prodotai propeteis* the list again links two terms by their initial syllable *(pro-)* and internal assonance (on *t*). Otherwise in the NT, these words occur only in the Lukan corpus: *prodotai* in Luke 6:16 (of Judas) and Acts 7:52 (of the "betrayers and murderers" of "the righteous one"); *propetes* in Acts 19:36 where the Ephesian town clerk advises the tumultuous crowd, "You ought to be quiet and do nothing rash (*propetes prassein* [note the alliteration here too])."

With the appearance of the perfect passive participle *tetyphōmenoi,* there begins a verbal change in the catalogue itself, whose entries after this become less telegraphic, more expansive, as they signal the conclusion of the list. This verb occurred in 1 Tim 3:6 (see commentary *in loc.*) of the bishop and in 1 Tim 6:4, again part of a list of vices of the opponents of Pauline teaching.

The next descriptive phrase, *philēdonoi mallon ē philotheoi,* literally "pleasure-lovers rather than God-lovers," with its repeated opening *phil-* and final *-oi,* reminds one of the opening of this whole list as it now comes full circle to a close. The *phil-* compounds are of course frequent enough in the PE (as they are in Luke-Acts), but they seem especially characteristic of the ethical lists. G. Stählin, *TDNT* 9.134 n. 191 and p. 169, has observed that the verb *philein* in the NT never denotes man's love for God, but that in the adjectival *philotheos* here in 2 Tim 3:4 that active sense is practically unavoidable in the light of the parallel *philēdonoi,* "pleasure-lovers." Neither term occurs in the LXX nor Ap. Frs. Stählin, *TDNT* 2.918, observes that the *philēdonos* compound is a Hellenistic construction that in the secular sphere means "intent on pleasure" as contrasted with *ponos,* "pain" (cf. Sirach prol. 15, 23). It is Philo who repeatedly works from the contrast *philēdonos . . . philotheos* (*Agric.* 88; *philēdonon kai philopathē mallon ē philareton kai philotheon,* "a lover of pleasure and passion rather than a lover of virtue and God," trans. WCW). On this verse Stählin notes the combination of Stoic and biblical antithesis; cf. *Fug.* 81; also *Leg. alleg.* 2.50 of one preferring *philopathes* to *philotheou;* the verbal coincidence is so exact that Spicq, *EP,* p. 776, considers that the phrase in the PE is *certainement empruntée à Philon.* See Stählin, *TDNT* 2.920 nn. 69-70, on Clement of Alexandria's uses of *philēdonos/-ia,* especially his defining it as totally alien to the divine nature.

The love of pleasure rather than of God is the love of one's own will rather than God's revealed will. To have chosen thus is to have a life of greedy unrest, of internal strife, of frustration and bitterness. This entry provides a drastic climax of a stunning list of vices.

5. *These people hold onto the appearance of godliness but they have repudiated its dynamic.* The opponents are "people who hold on to (*echontes* [cf. 1 Tim 3:9; 6:2, 8]) the appearance *(morphōsin)* of godliness *(eusebeias)* but *(de)* they have repudiated *(ērnēmenoi)* its dynamic *(tēn . . . dynamin autēs).*" The whole charge turns on the meaning of *eusebeia,* as the PE understand and define that term (see Excursus III, "*Eusebeia* and Its Cognates in the PE," in AB *Titus*). In this author's mind *eusebeia* has a *morphōsis* and a *dynamis* proper to it. The opponents have and continue to have (present tense) the former; they have denied up to the present (Spicq notes perfect passive) the latter.

*Eusebeia,* as was already noted, involves giving God his due. What is the *morphōsis* of that activity? The term occurs otherwise in the NT only in Rom 2:20. There the apostle is addressing his fellow Jew as one who "has in the law the form of knowledge and of the truth *(echonta tēn morphōsin tēs gnōseōs kai tēs alētheias en tōi nomōi),*" but who does not really do what he knows the Law teaches. "The knowledge and the truth" (about the one God) is a more Hebraic way of putting what *eusebeia* says to a born Greek, and J. Behm, *TDNT* 4.754, suggests that this expression along with others in Rom 2:17-20 are from a Pharisaic catechesis for Hellenistic proselytes that Paul knew from before his conversion to Christ Jesus.

In that case 2 Tim 3:5 might be alluding to this source and not to Romans, a source that perhaps was taken up and adapted already in the vice list cited here. The catalogue would in that instance have been modeled on the Jewish catechetical tradition that used such lists to score the pagan world and its ways (cf. Rom 1), but it would also have been edited with an eye to controversy with Jewish opponents as well as pagans. The redactor of the PE, who seems on other grounds to have knowledge of the tradition of Romans and who surely carries on the battle with Judaizing Christians into the second generation, may himself have added this tip to the long lash that he had taken up, perhaps from the Jewish Christian (but not necessarily Judaizing) congregation from which he wrote.

The use of *morphōsis* (see Notes) and the contrasting distinction between the outward appearance and the heart of man is thoroughly Hebraic and biblical (cf. 1 Sam 16:7: "For the Lord sees not as man sees; man looks on the outward appearance [MT: *lʿynym,* but LXX: *eis prosōpon*] but the Lord looks on the heart" [RSV]). Matthew 7:15 has a saying of Jesus on false prophets who are parabolically described as wolves in sheep's clothing (Matt 7:15 only), and Paul himself, 2 Cor 11:13, stigmatizes his opposition among the "apostles" as *pseudapostoloi,* with the further drastic observation, "Even Satan disguises himself *(metaschēmatizetai)* as an angel of light" (v. 14). The PE also presume this distinction in the rules for those who are "really widows" (1 Tim 5:3, 5-6, 16).

The charge here is that the opponents have the *morphōsis* of genuine religion, i.e. they have (as teachers) the right words and expressions (cf. 2:18 *supra*), they have the external forms (words, gestures) of Christian worship, but they have all this as "outside" with no "inside," a face with no heart. Their teaching and their prayer are just words, empty sounds and gestures, for they have denied *(ērnēmenoi)* the power *(tēn . . . dynamin)* of godliness *(autēs)*. Here real, ongoing, solemn repudiation of the personal relationship with Christ is envisaged by this verb, and that relationship or that which constitutes it is called "the power" of godliness.

There is one other passage that uses *dynamis* in the PE, and that is 2 Tim 1:7-8, where Timothy is urged to stir into flame "the gift of God" that is specified in terms of *pneuma,* and that spirit is one "of power *(dynameōs)* and love and self-control"; he is then told to "co-suffer for the gospel according to God's power *(kata dynamin theou)*. . . ." As above, *dynamis* is ultimately the empowering Spirit, giving life and strength (even miraculous strength) to those upon whom God bestows him. From another point of view, the risen Christ "empowers" *(endynamoō)* those in whose lives he has intervened (1 Tim 1:12; 2 Tim 4:17 of Paul; 2 Tim 2:1 of Timothy) and who have put their faith in him.

Gealy, *IB* 11.499-500, has suggested that here in 2 Tim 3:5 it is precisely *tēn* (*the;* note definite article) *dynamin* of the resurrection that the false teachers have disowned (cf. 2:18 *supra*) and, in so doing, they have rejected the God who will raise all the dead as he raised Jesus, by the power of the Spirit (see Phil 3:10 and W. Grundmann, *TDNT* 2.316 n. 108). So for the author of the PE, the risen Jesus and his Spirit are the unseen heart (dynamic) of genuine religion, of godliness, and those who have denied that reality have only the external forms, "the dead letter," of religion and worship left. There is no breaking the circuit between the divine power that raised Jesus and that which will raise all; to deny part is to deny all; to have accepted one is to accept all. The link between this heretical denial of the resurrection and of the Spirit's power and the vices just listed is not articulated, though it may be presupposed.

*Keep people like that at a distance too.* With a glance backward over the whole list, the author now admonishes, literally, "and avoid these (men)," *kai toutous apotrepou,* which is the complement to the introductory *touto de ginōske* of 3:1. Here it is explicitly the men or persons just described above (*toutous* = such as these; BAGD) who are to be avoided, not the controversial researches (as in 2:23 above). This directive to avoid or shun certain persons has occurred previously in the PE at Titus 3:10 (contrast Titus 3:9 [teachings]; 1 Tim 4:7 [doctrines]; 6:11 [vices], 20 [doctrines]; 2 Tim 2:22 [lusts]), but the verb used here, *apotrepou,* occurs nowhere else in the NT (see Notes above).

6. *For from their ranks come those who are worming their way into homes.* The reason *(gar)* for the preceding directive is given: *ek toutōn gar* (i.e. from

such men as those just mentioned as *toutous*) *eisin hoi edynontes eis tas oikias*, "for from their ranks come those who are worming their way into homes. . . ." Titus 1:11 witnessed to Judaizing Christians who "overturn whole households *(holous oikous)*," but the terminology now is somewhat different. In 1 Tim 5:13 idle young widows circulate from house to house *(perierchomenai tas oikias)* as here heterodox and vicious men insinuate themselves into houses and households. It has been noted above how frequently the vices listed here are those qualities that elsewhere in the PE disqualify a candidate for (presbyter-) bishop or the diaconate. The reason may be that the opponents were members of the leadership, charged with the public prayer and worship of believers *(morphōsis eusebeias)*, and that their position in turn opened the doors of (believers'?) homes to them. For the author of the PE their entry is made *endynontes*, "creeping" or "slipping into" (as one "slips into" clothing, for which action the same verb is used).

This poetic form of the verb does not otherwise occur in the NT (cf. *endyō*, twenty-eight times in the NT), but cf. Luke 4:40 (BDF §101) using *dynontos de tou hēliou* of sunset as well as Jude 4 describing those who are upsetting the congregations to whom that letter is directed as *pareisedysan gar tines anthrōpoi k.t.l.* (though here a form of *-dyein* rather than *-dynein* may be [is?] employed; cf. BAGD *s.v.*). In Ap. Frs. only *Barn.* 4.10 uses the term, of men who go to live alone, "retiring within yourselves *(kath' heautous endynontes)*." MM *s.v.* note one (restored) use of this verb in a third-century-C.E. magical papyrus (P. Lond 121.271 [= 1.931]), but without context. One wonders whether this unusual, "literary" form of the verb was meant to suggest the pretentious obsequiousness of the heterodox leaders as they enlisted support for their party in the local church. The occurrence of the term in a late magical text just might suggest an older tradition of its use and so link up with the Egyptian magicians of verse 8 here.

*to captivate the idle women.* After slipping into Christian houses the opposition leaders "make captives of idle women *(gynaikaria)*. . . ." The verb *aichmalōtizontes*, whose form in *-euein* suggests that the opponents do this with professional skill (cf. BDF §108.5), occurs in the *-euein* form in Eph 4:8, taking up LXX Ps 67:18. In the *-izein* form it is used on three occasions in the NT: in Rom 7:23 (of Paul's becoming a prisoner of war to the law in his members) and 2 Cor 10:5 (of the apostolic ministry as engaged in a holy war, taking minds captive for Christ) as well as Luke 21:24 (of the inhabitants of Judea who "will be led captive among all nations").

The usage here in the PE is closest to that of Romans, and that may be the reason for the less well-attested reading. J. K. Elliott, *Greek Text*, p. 149, thinks that the more Hellenistic *-izontes* is original here (as do *GNT*, Nestle, Spicq, et al.). Both forms of the verb are well attested in the LXX, with *-teuein* being somewhat more common. In 1 Macc 1:32; 5:13; 8:10 it has *tas gynaikas* as its object, but in each case one or another major MS reads the *-izein* form (which Rahlfs always adopts). However, in LXX Gen 34:29 there are no variants in favor of *-izein*. In LXX 1 Kgdms 30:2 "women" *(gynaikas)* are understood as object (A adds them), and in 30:5 (cf. 3) they are subject of the passive form. In 4 Kgdms 5:2 *neanida* is object. Perhaps it ought to be noted that outside of the reading in First Maccabees there is no evidence that LXX *-izein* took "women" as an object. Perhaps one encounters here in the PE a Septuagintal idiom that the Western tradition made conform to popular, Hellenistic usage.

The diminutive *gynaikaria,* with its derogatory overtones (BDF §111.3), occurs only here in the NT and is not documented in the LXX or the Ap. Frs. D-C notes its use in Epictetus; MM *s.v.* cite 4.1.86 (= LCL 2.272-273; "wenches" is the translation there) and also the Greek comedian Diocles (fifth century B.C.E.); LSJ also cite Marcus Aurelius 5.11. MM also suggest that "the *gynaikaria* of 2 Tim 3:6 would then be society ladies, borne by caprices in various directions and full of idle curiosity." A. Oepke, *TDNT* 1.785, suggests that one may glimpse here the Jewish and Gnostic propagandizing of women that the early Christian congregation abhorred for all its openness to women in its life and worship (cf. 1 Tim 2 above).

*loaded with sins and driven by diverse cravings.* These women are characterized with four participles, of which the first is *sesōreumena hamartiais,* "loaded with sins." The perfect passive participle here is from *sōreuein,* a verb otherwise documented in the NT only in Rom 12:20, which is in turn a citation of LXX Prov 25:22 (Hebrew *ḥth*) on heaping fiery coals on an enemy's head. The cognate *episōreuein* (*epi-* for stress) occurs in the NT only in 2 Tim 4:3; it is not found in the LXX (but in Sym Job 14:17 [of sin: Lang, *TDNT* 7.1096] and Cant 2:4) but occurs once in the Ap. Frs., *Barn.* 4.6, "Be not made like unto some, heaping up your sins *(episōreuontas tais hamartiais)* and saying that the covenant is both theirs and ours." There is only one other LXX use of *sōreuein,* Jth 15:11, of piling loot on carts. The verb does not occur in the Ap. Frs.

Lang, *TDNT* 7.1094-1096, notes that the verb first appears in Greek only with Aristotle, the compound verb only in the early Christian era. The verb denotes the action of making a heap (*sōros;* esp. of grain) and with *epi-* means to "overload," e.g., "the excessive heaping up of business." Lang, pp. 1095-1096, notes that there is no secular Greek example of a personal object (in a figurative sense) for this verb, as in 2 Tim 4:3, and even the use here in 3:6 does not seem to be paralleled.

In contrast to the previous perfect participle, the second of the four participles describes the "idle women" in the present passive as "being driven *(agomena)* by diverse cravings *(epithymiais poikilais).*" *Epithymiai* occurs only in the plural in the PE, and always with a pejorative sense. Apart from here and in Titus 3:3, *poikilos* does not occur otherwise in the Paulines, but its use in most of its occurrences in the rest of the NT (in which it designates diseases, lusts, pleasures, odd doctrines, trials) is in unattractive contexts but with an inconsistent semantic pattern. In Titus 3:3 *poikilos* also modifies *hēdonai,* "pleasures."

On *agomena,* which occurs only here and at 4:11 in the PE, note that there are sixty-four other NT uses: five in the Paulines and thirteen/twenty-six in Luke-Acts (fourteen times in the Ap. Frs.), but no exact parallel to the phrase here in the PE (cf. Rom 8:14 of being led by God's Spirit; Gal 5:18 and 1 Cor 12:2 of being led into idolatry). Note also the NT *hapax, agōgē,* at 2 Tim 3:10 below. Spicq cites a very apt parallel from Clement of Alexandria, *2 Strom.* 20.113.4; in *PG* 8.1057A it is in the singular, *tēs tōn kakōn epithymias autos hēgēsamenos.*

7. *ever learning and never turning to full knowledge of the truth.* The women are next characterized in parallel phrases whose rhyming assonance, "ever . . . never," *pantote manthanonta . . . mēdepote . . . dynamena,* binds them closely and mockingly together to make the contrast in thought still more acute.

Here "the idle women" are "ever learning," *manthanonta,* as in Titus 3:14; 1 Tim 2:11; 5:4, 13; and 2 Tim 3:14. *Manthanetōsan,* "learn what it means," is used twenty-four times otherwise in the NT, nine times in the other Paulines (once in the Lukan corpus [Acts 23:27]). In First Timothy all the uses of the verb are connected with women (wives in the worship assembly; children learning to care for widowed mothers; young widows learning to be idle), and Rengstorf, *TDNT* 4.410, has noted the officious and pseudo-intellectual character of the religious life being fostered here, probably legalistic as well (he had previously noted the link between *nomos* and *manthanō;* cf. pp. 401, 408, 409). The regular use of the verb here in reference to the practical knowledge of God and his will for moral life is striking. If the PE are in harmony with this later usage, then it is moral learning that the idle women are ever acquiring, never practicing.

"And never *(kai mēdepote)* turning to full knowledge of truth *(eis epignōsin alētheias elthein dynamena).*" *Mēdepote* occurs only here in the NT (cf. on *mēpote supra* 2 Tim 2:25); it is very rare in the LXX (Sir 19:7 and 3 Macc 3:16; 7:4, 11) and in the Ap. Frs. (*Barn.* 16.10; Hermas, *Man.* 2.3; 10.1.4; *Sim.* 8.7.2).

On *dynamena,* which also occurs at 2 Tim 2:13, see the commentary above on 1 Tim 5:25 (see also 6:7, 16). On the whole phrase *eis epignōsin alētheias elthein* see above on 1 Tim 2:4 and Excursus II, "Truth and *epignōsis alētheias* in the PE," in AB *Titus.* In Titus 1:1 and 1 Tim 2:4 the *epignōsis alētheias* is the baptismal profession in which the process of conversion reaches its term. In 2 Tim 2:25 it could refer to a postbaptismal return to Christ. Spicq is emphatic that that is the case in this passage, and thus he starts up the real problem in this long description. Are the "idle women" pagans? It does not sound as if they were Jewish, either in manner of life or interests. If so, this description of the opponents' mission to nonbelievers is unique in the PE. Here we see persons under the burden of a sinful past (note *sesōreumena*) still being swept on (present *agomena*) by a variety of lusts, going through an unending catechesis *(pantotē manthanonta)*, but never undergoing a genuine conversion (never receiving baptism?).

8. *Just as once Jannes and Jambres defied Moses.* With this phrase the previously described situation (3:1-7 certainly; probably 2:14-16 as well, on which cf. below) is set for comparison *(houtōs kai)* into the great redemption story of the OT. The (present and) future bad days are to be evaluated in terms of the exodus history and its bad moments. What happened "in the beginning" happens again "in the end."

The central point of the comparison is the activity of opposition, as the repeated *antestēsan . . . anthistantai* makes unmistakable. This verb, *anthistēmi*, occurs here for the first time in the PE; it will be used again at 4:15 of the opposition of the coppersmith Alexander to the words of Paul and his colleagues. In the PE the opposition of (at this point) unnamed opponents to the truth *(tēi alētheiai)* is exactly parallel *(houtōs kai)* to the opposition that *Iannēs* and *Iambrēs* once offered to Moses.

The incident referred to as if well known and needing no explanation would be quite unknown if one had to confine oneself to the canon of Scripture, for the names of Jannes and Jambres do not occur elsewhere in the NT or the LXX. Indeed, as one reads the testimonies in chronological order, one wonders whether more details appeared as the basic story became less popular. These names are not documented in the Ap. Frs. or in Philo and Josephus (though there is a generic hint at *Ant.* 2.9.2; cf. McNamara, *NTPT*, pp. 94-95, who cites the Pseudo-Jonathan Targum on Exod 1:15, where the names of Jannes and Jambres are noted explicitly).

Still the first hint of the incident referred to occurs in a Hebrew text of Palestinian provenance, CD 5.18-19 (Dupont-Sommer, *EWQ*, p. 130), where the author cites a precedent for what is occurring in his own troubled times, i.e. the "last" times, by appealing to the exodus period: "For formerly Moses and Aaron arose by the hand of the Prince of Lights (cf. 1QS 3.20); but Belial raised up Jannes *(yaḥaneh)* and his brother, in his cunning, when Israel was saved for *the first time*" (note the phrase). Even in that venerable text the other brother's name can apparently be taken for granted as well known.

Chronologically the next references emanate from the first-century-C.E. Roman scene, where in 77 C.E. Pliny, *NH* 30.2.11, writes in his section on medical zoology of a magic *(magices)* derived "from Moses and Jannes *(a Mose et Janne)* and Lotapes and the Jews." The next reference, apart from this one in the PE, takes one into the age of Hadrian and is in Apuleius, *Apology* 90 (c. 150 C.E.), where, again in a context of magic, that cosmopolitan Latin author-raconteur writes, "I am ready to be any magician *(inter magos)* you please . . . Moses or Jannes *(Moses vel Johannes)* or Apollobex. . . ." One notes here that the spelling transcribes the Hebrew consonants of CD more closely than Pliny but at the price of a different vocalization.

In the second century C.E. Pythagorean Numenius Apamensis, cited by Eusebius, *Pr. Evang.* 9.8 (also Origen alludes to this in *Contra Celsum* 51 [Chadwick, *Chr. Thgt.*, p. 226], saying, "He also quotes the story [*tēn . . . historian*] about Moses and Jannes and Jambres [*Iannou kai Iambrou*]"), offers further details, including the name of the brother. "Next were Jannes and Jambres *(Iannēs kai Iambrēs)*, sacred scribes of the Egyptians, considered to be inferior to no one in magical art (*mageusai;* cf. *Did.* 2.2 for this verb in a perhaps Jewish list; Nock, *EGC*, p. 325]) at the time when the Jews were being driven out of Egypt" (D-C modified; cf. Chadwick, *Chr. Thgt.*, p. 226 n. 3). Here for the first time, if one were reading the extant testimonia in chronological order, one could pinpoint the first datable reference to some narrative that embroidered the Exodus story of Moses' confrontation with the Egyptian magicians before the pharaoh and the OT narrative of the first three plagues (cf. Exod 7:11, 22; 8:7, 18-19).

The earliest Christian texts outside the PE that advert to narratives about these persons are in Origen's *Contra Celsum* 51 (noted above). In his commentary on Matt 27:9: §117 (244-249 C.E.) he remarks, . . . *Sicut "Jamnes et Mambres restiterunt Moysi" non invenitur in publicis Scripturis sed in libro secreto qui suprascribitur "Jamnes et Mambres liber,"* ". . . as 'Jamnes and Mambres resisted Moses' is not found in the public Scriptures but in a secret book that is inscribed 'the book of Jamnes and Mambres'" (text in *PG* 13.1769; slight variants in *TDNT* 3.193 n. 17; trans. WCW). Origen goes on to note that some have rejected Second Timothy for this reason. In his comment on Matt 23:37 he notes, *Nec enim scimus in libris canonizatis historiam de Janne et Mambre resistentibus Moysi,* "Nor indeed do we find the story about Jannes and Mambres resisting Moses in the canonical books" (*PG* 13.1637; trans. WCW).

Thus at least one written source comes into view. There may have been several, if the variants in transmitting the names, especially of Iambres/Mambres, are an indication of different written sources behind the surviving notices (*TDNT* 3.990). It is distinctly possible that when the Gelasian *Decretum de Libris recipiendis et non recipiendis* 1.303 notes, *liber qui appellatur Paenitentia Jamne et Mambre apocryphus,* "the apocryphal book that is called the Penitence of Jamnes and Mambres" (text *ap. TDNT* 3.193; trans. WCW), the book described is quite distinct from the one that Origen called *Jannes et Mambres liber* (*pace* McNamara, *NTPT*, p. 89). Again, the whole cycle *(liber* or *historia)* may have contained several "books" *(libri)* with their own titles.

Cyprian cites these names in his quotation of 2 Tim 3:1-9 (in an Old Latin version) in *De Unitate* 16 (CC 3:1, p. 261); cf. Fahey, *Cyprian and the Bible,* p. 515. They also occur in the *Acta Pilati* 5 (Hennecke and Schneemelcher, *NT Apoc.* 1.456) in Nicodemus's plea for Jesus in which, adverting to his miracles, he calls upon Acts 5:38-39 as well the Jannes and Jambres story. It is said of the latter that the Egyptians considered them gods but that "they perished themselves and those who believed them." D-C, p. 117, also cite *Martyrdom of Peter and Paul* 34; *Const. Apost.* 8.1.6 (F. X. Funk, *Constitutiones,* p. 462) cites the incident in its directives on charisms and ordinations, noting that Moses' wonders were resisted by Jannes and Jambres as Christ's by Annas and Caiaphas.

The rabbinic notices about Jannes and Jambres (with many variants in the Hebrew spelling of their names; cf. *TDNT* 3.192 nn. 1-8 and McNamara, *NTPT,* pp. 90-91) could indicate an extensive romance or cycle of tales that stretched from Moses' birth through Pharaoh's court and beyond Sinai to the Balaam episode, where in the Pseudo-Jonathan Targum to Num 22:22 they are "pages" (cf. *TDNT* 3.193 and McNamara, *NTPT,* pp. 90-96). The difficulties in dating targumic materials are notorious. Martin McNamara advocates that some of this material on Jannes and Jambres goes back into the first Christian century and the Palestinian targum called Pseudo-Jonathan (see McNamara, *NTPT,* pp. 82-96, and his *Targum,* pp. 89, 179). The Pseudo-Jonathan on Exod 7:11-12, Walton, *Polyglotta* 4.113 (quoted by McNamara, *NTPT,* p. 85), reads:

> And Pharaoh also called
> the wise men and sorcerers *(ḥršyy')*
> and they also — Jannes and
> Jambres *(Yan's we Yambr's),*
> the sorcerers *(ḥršyn)* who were in Egypt —
> did likewise with their magic
> charms. (12) And every man threw
> down his staff and they became
> basilisks, and immediately they
> were changed to become as they
> were at first and the staff
> of Aaron swallowed up their staffs.

The names are spelled in this text in the Hellenistic fashion already noted in Pliny as well as in 2 Tim 3:8; the more Hebraic transliteration of CD and

Apuleius can be contrasted (cf. McNamara, *NTPT*, pp. 85-88) with this. No form of these names is found in *CII*, but Preisigke, *Namenbuch*, notes in Col. 145, *s.v.*, "*dia Ianne*" where he supplies *(Iōannēs)* in Lond. IV, 1432.43, and cf. the *Iannos* of Lef 657; there is no sign of *Iambrēs/Mambrēs* in his lists, however.

In the Jewish as well as the pagan sources they were associated with magic and sorcery *(magi, ḥršyn)* and astrology (*'sṭgnyn* etc.; Jastrow, *Dictionary*, p. 89; and cf. *Ps. Jon. Targ.* on Exod 7:22; 8:3, 14, 15 in Walton, *Polyglotta* 4.114-115). On "Paul and the Magus" see Nock, *ERAW*, pp. 308-330, especially pp. 324-325, where he gathers the texts of Tacitus, Tibullus, and Virgil that link the *magus* and magic with evoking the dead, which in its turn reminds one that this conjuring up the dead was linked with Mambres in a fragment of the lost *Poenitentia Ianne et Mambre* (Hengel, *Hellenism* 1.212; 2.140 n. 659). The Roman contempt for magic (cf. Servius *ad Aen.* 4.493 cited in Nock, p. 324 n. 87) certainly breathes out of the Latin tradition, and it is perhaps that Roman distaste that molds this polemic against those who deny the resurrection on one hand and then offer as a "substitute" for the Christian revelation and apostolic preaching of the resurrection the tricks of necromancers and the pseudoscience of astrologers.

One cannot avoid comparing the confrontation here with that between Paul and the Jewish "pseudo-prophet magus" Elymas in the presence of the still unconverted Sergius Paulus (Acts 13:6-12). Nock, *ERAW*, pp. 325-326, happily describes Elymas as a sort of domestic philosopher or private chaplain in the entourage of the great man and thus reminds one that in the ancient world at large the magician was not just a cheapjack but could be considered a "sacred scribe" *(hierogrammateus;* cf. Josephus, *Ant.* 2.205; see also below on 2 Tim 3:16, *hiera grammata)*, i.e. a learned theologian. It is in this guise, i.e. as learned men of God, that the opponents here in the PE insinuate themselves into households, promising to bring back the dead by their recondite arts as the apostolic preaching had not done.

On the later Greek and Latin authors on Jannes and Jambres, cf. McNamara, *NTPT*, p. 90; Lampe, *PGL*, p. 661; and on Theodore of Mopsuestia, Swete, *Theodore* 2.218.

If Jannes and Jambres have almost vanished below the horizon of history, the name of the one whom they opposed, Moses, rides high to this day. This is the only appearance of his name in the PE, but there are 78 other NT occurrences, with the 9 other Pauline uses concentrated in Romans (5:14; 9:15; 10:5, 19) and the Corinthian correspondence (1 Cor 9:9; 10:2; and 2 Cor 3:7, 13, 15). In Luke-Acts his name occurs 29 times (10/19), compared with 7 in Matthew, 8 in Mark, 12 in John (or 27 altogether). There is 1 use in Jude 9 (also a reference to an apocryphal legend), and 1 in Rev 15:3; the remaining 11 are in Hebrews.

In the Ap. Frs., apart from the reference to "the Law of Moses" in Ign.

*Smyrn.* 5.1, the references are clustered in *First Clement* and Barnabas, with most in the latter. *First Clement* 4.10, 12 describes Moses, "servant *(theraponta)* of God," as object of hatred and rebellion; in 17.5 he is faithful *(pistos);* in 43.1, "a faithful servant" *(pistos therapōn);* and in 43.6 he knows beforehand about a budding rod that figures in an episode from an otherwise lost legend connected with Num 17. In 51.3, 5 there are references to the rebellion of Num 16 as well as the reception accorded to the wonders he worked in Egypt. Finally, in 53.2, 4 he is mentioned for his intercession for Israel when they sinned at Sinai.

J. Jeremias, *TDNT* 4.848-873, has sketched the richly fantastic *bios* of Moses in Hellenistic Judaism, whether in Palestine or abroad (pp. 850-855). However, where diaspora Judaism extolled him as "the hero and ideal man," the Palestinian traditions saw him as "primarily the mediator of revelation" (p. 852; cf. pp. 855-856). Significant for this passage of the PE is the Moses typology of pre-Christian and rabbinic Judaism, where the principle "as the first redeemer (Moses), so the final redeemer (the Messiah)" controls the expectation and portrait of the Christ (pp. 860-861). Particularly notable in this regard is CD, which portrays the leader of this community of "the new covenant" as one who has led a new exodus for a community in which he is the lawgiver and teacher (cf. p. 861 with nn. 157-168, recalling that this was in print half a dozen years before the first Qumran materials were unearthed, not to mention 6 QD).

As was already noted, his name figures along with that of Aaron when the opposition of "*Jḥnh* and his brother" is mentioned in CD 5.18-19 as well as 5.21–6.1 with its "they preached rebellion against the commandments of God (revealed) by the hand of Moses and also (by the hands of the) anointed (*bmšyhw* [read *bmšyḥy*]) of holiness" (i.e. the prophets: Dupont-Sommer, *EWQ,* p. 131, modified), and this opposition reminds one of the theme of the suffering of the patient Moses in the later rabbinic traditions (cf. Jeremias, *TDNT* 4.863-864). In 1QS 1.2, Dupont-Sommer, *EWQ,* p. 73, Moses, along with the prophets, mediates the divine commands in their writings (note "*by the hand of* Moses" — *byd*); in 1QS 5.8 the reference is to "the law *(twrh)* of Moses" (as frequently in CD, and cf. 1QS 8.15, 22, as well as 1QM 10.6 and 1QH 17.12). 4QFlor 2.3 seems to speak of "the book of [Moses . . ." and 4QTestim 1 has Moses as the object of God's speaking. 1Q 22.1.1, 11; 2.5, 11; 4.3 is a collection of "The Sayings of Moses" (see Dupont-Sommer, *EWQ,* pp. 307-309), in which he is the speaker or the one to whom God speaks in a kind of "Farewell Exhortation" (Gaster, *DSS,* pp. 373-376) or even last testament, at the end of the wilderness wandering. His name may occur again in 4QOrd 2.17; cf. Gaster, *DSS,* p. 92; and it certainly figures in 4QDibHam 2.9; 3.12; 5.14; Gaster, *DSS,* pp. 273-274, 276, as the "Prayer for intercession" notes Moses' prayers and predictions for God's people. In all of these texts he is conspicuously the "Mediator of revelation," above all in his teaching, oral and written, but also in what he has done.

As in the Qumran documents, so in the NT, "Moses" often stands for the documents attributed to him by pre-Christian Judaism (cf. Rom 10:5, 19; 1 Cor 9:9; 2 Cor 3:15, as well as Luke 2:22; 5:14; 16:29, 31; 20:28, 37; 24:27, 44; Acts 3:22; etc. There is no lack of examples in the other Gospels). He is, in the tradition of Luke-Acts, also the ruler and deliverer (Acts 7:35; *archonta kai lytrōtēn*), a performer of miracles, and a prophet (Acts 7:36-37 and cf. Jeremias, *TDNT* 4.865), one to whom the God of Israel had spoken and through whom came that God's "living oracles" (cf. Acts 7:31-32, 38). He is also remembered as one who met misunderstanding and resistance from every side (Jeremias, p. 865) for all the fact that he was "beautiful *(asteios)* before God" and "was instructed in all the wisdom *(sophiai)* of the Egyptians and he was mighty *(dynatos)* in his words and deeds *(en logois kai ergois)*" (Acts 7:20 [= LXX Exod 2:2], 22); cf. the latter phrase of Jesus, in singular, Luke 24:19; cf. Haenchen, *Acts,* p. 281 n. 1, and Jeremias, p. 865, who note that the legendary Moses becomes a great orator, in spite of Exod 4:10; note how Philo made him an Egyptian savant (*Mos.* 1.23-24).

Particularly revealing in this connection is the citation of the Alexandrian-Jewish tragedian Ezekiel of the second century B.C.E. (Hengel, *Hellenism* 1.69, 109, and 2.52 n. 139; 71 n. 352; 109 n. 396, and the excerpts in Eusebius, *Pr. Evang.* 9.28; *PG* 21.756-757), who must have sought to give the *Heilsgeschichte* a new impact on the Hellenistic world by giving it dramatic form. The success of the effort is immaterial. Its importance lies in its following up on an insight into the popular impact of the Greek theater and an attempt to grasp the nettle that had thus far been the vehicle for popularizing paganism. The missionary zeal that prompted such an experiment cannot be overlooked.

Though the controversy on the general resurrection belongs to the triple tradition in the synoptics (*SFG* §281), it is notable that whereas Matt 22:31 omits the Mark 12:26 mention of "the book of Moses," Luke 20:37 personalizes it by saying, "But that the dead are raised even Moses showed" (see *infra,* p. 2140). In Luke 16:29, 31 as well as, more generically, in 24:27, 44 and Acts 26:22-23, Moses is linked with the resurrection. All this is significant in the light of the error on the resurrection scored here in the PE. Moreover, with Jeremias, *TDNT* 4.865, one notes that it is also in Luke-Acts (passages just cited above) that Moses is said to have predicted the sufferings and death of the Messiah (cf. Luke 9:31, of Moses and Elijah speaking "of his *exodus*"), though the Pentateuch contains no such notice. In Jeremias's opinion, p. 867, the "Moses/Christ typology" is "plainly formulated" in Acts as well as in Hebrews and John.

Acts contains other data that appear to derive from the Moses legends of Hellenistic Judaism (forty years old when he escaped to Midian, and his forty-year stay there in Acts 7:23, 30; an angel addressed him on Sinai in Acts 7:38; cf. 53 as well as 30, 35; see Jeremias, pp. 865-866) but none that is decisively from outside of the Palestinian milieu. Some of the data in Acts that bring the figures of Moses and Christ into a complementary or typological relationship are due to primitive Christian and/or to Lukan shaping of the Jewish tradition (cf. esp. Acts 3:22-23 and 7:22, 25, 35, 37, and Jeremias, p. 868 n. 226).

*these numbskulled counterfeiters of the faith are defying the truth.* Here in the PE, according to Jeremias, p. 869, "Moses is a type of the Messianic community of salvation," and in this respect the comparison is thoroughly Pauline, for only the apostle (in the NT) makes Moses "a type of the community rather than Christ." Granted the oscillation between individual and community, between founder and foundation, already noted in comments on 2:19 above, it may be better to say that Moses here is a type of the church/apostle/Christ, for each telescopes into the other in this section.

Thus the heretics in verse 8b here "defy *the truth (tēi alētheiai)*" as Jannes and Jambres once "defied Moses," and the reader recalls the "pillar and pedestal for the truth" in 1 Tim 3:15 with its deliberately ambiguous reference, both the community *(ekklēsia)* and the apostolic minister (Timothy) as the *locus* for "the truth," i.e. the place where Christ and his gospel are truly revealed. The rebels of the final age, among whom belong those who deny the resurrection (2:18), have put themselves into competition with "the truth," i.e. they are really offering another revelation, a non-Pauline and nonapostolic one. In this competition they are bound eventually to lose to the church, to Paul, to Christ, as Jannes and Jambres lost to Israel, to Moses, to God. Therrien, *Discernement,* p. 228, notes that the emphasis at this point is not so much on their teaching as such but on their "opposition to the official representatives of God and perhaps also on the manner of this opposition."

The crisp, asyndetic joining of *adokimoi peri tēn pistin* to the preceding phrase, "numbskulled counterfeiters," is meant to leave no question about the inner relationship between the decerebrate condition of the opponents and their consequent incompetence to communicate the revelation (*hē pistis = fides quae* [Therrien, *Discernement,* p. 229], the *alētheia* so frequently referred to in this context, and cf. 1 Tim 6:5). As Therrien has observed (pp. 229-230), *adokimoi* here designates the opponents as "unqualified," i.e. lacking apostolic approval and thus well on the way to "reprobation" (cf. Rom 1:28 and Vg *reprobi circa fidem* here). Accordingly, these false teachers are "without guarantee in matters of faith," for they have no mandate, apostolic or divine, for their teaching.

9. *but they will not progress far. Their own stupidity is going to become just as obvious to everyone as the stupidity of those two.* The statement ". . . but *(alla)* they will not progress far *(ou prokopsousin epi pleion)*" takes up again the phraseology that had appeared in 2:16 above (note that *dokimon* was in 2:15) and that will appear again in a variant form at 3:13 below.

These self-styled "progressives" can go only so far, "because *(gar)* their own stupidity (*anoia autōn* [note the reference to the subject of *prokopsousin,* i.e. the numbskulled, unqualified men of v. 8b]) will be quite evident *(ekdēlos estai)* to everyone, as also the (*hōs kai hē* [= article as pronoun, 'that,' referring to folly; J. K. Elliott, *Greek Text,* p. 151, and cf. the *ha* of 2:20, *supra*]) of those men (*ekeinōn* [i.e. Jannes and Jambres; cf. 2:26 *supra*])."

"Their own stupidity is going to become obvious *(ekdēlos)* to all." One recalls the *hamartiai prodēloi* of the errant presbyteral candidates of 1 Tim 6:24, preceding them to the divine judgment. The *stupidity* of opponents now is on its way to being unmasked, "just as that of those" men noted above, Jannes and Jambres, "became *(egeneto)*" obvious. Spicq notes that the aorist here is ingressive; it corresponds conceptually with the *prokopsousin* of the first part of this verse. Contrast the same form in 2 Tim 3:11.

## IV.C. The Legatee (3:10–4:8)

### IV.C.1. PAUL'S LIFE (3:10-13)

3 [10]*You, however, Timothy, were quite familiar*

*with the instruction,*
*with the approach to living,*
*with the design,*
*with the faithfulness,*
*with the patience,*
*with the charity,*
*with the steadfastness*

*that were mine,* [11]*along with the persecutions, with the sufferings, such as happened to me in Pisidian Antioch, in Iconium, in Lystra. What persecutions I bore! Still, from all of them the Lord delivered me.* [12]*Moreover, all who want to live in a godly way in Christ Jesus will be persecuted.* [13]*However, vicious people and charlatans will progress — from bad to worse, deluding and deluded.*

### ♦ NOTES

3:10. *You, however, Timothy, were quite familiar with the instruction.* Lit. "You, however, faithfully followed *(parēkolouthēsas)* my teaching . . . *(mou tēi didaskaliai . . .).*" On the verb see 1 Tim 4:6 (on the variant in tense to perfect, J. K. Elliott, *Greek Text,* pp. 151-152 and 65), where it also occurs with *didaskalia* (note how 1 Cor 4:17 describes the relation of Timothy to Paul's "ways").

11. *the persecutions.* For the NT use of *diōgmos* see Comment below. *Diōgmos* is found only three times in the LXX: in Prov 11:19 (MT *rdp,* of one who "pursues" evil); Lam 3:19 (MT *mrwd,* which means "restlessness," BDB, *s.v. rwd*); and 2 Macc 12:23, again of a military "pursuit" of a routed enemy (on the verb — *only* — see Oepke, *TDNT* 2.229 [with Bertram]-230; *nil* MM). This noun is not found in Josephus, *CII,* and it is not especially common in classical Greek, where in any case it usually means a pursuit or chase (LSJ *s.v.*), though already in Aeschylus, *Suppliants* 148, 1046 (in the maiden's choruses), and in Euripides, *Orestes* 412 (of the Furies), the uses in the plural suggest harassment and persecution that are ultimately unjustified. In Plutarch, "On Brotherly Love," if the reading *diōgmois* is correct, there is a reference to brother harassing brother in dividing their inheritance. From its use in the NT and then from *Mart. Pol.* 1.1 on (see below and Lampe, *PGL s.v.*), one would infer that this noun was becoming part of the inner-Christian vocabulary for the persecution the Christians underwent at the hands of unbelievers (cf. *martys,* etc.)

In the Ap. Frs., *1 Clem.* 3.2, listing the woes that have fallen upon the factious Corinthians, notes "persecution and disorder *(diōgmos kai akatastasia).*" One must wait until *Mart. Pol.* 1.1 to encounter the term again in a Christian document: "We write . . . the story of the martyrs and blessed Polycarp who put an end to persecution *(ton diōgmon)* by his martyrdom. . . ."

The ordinary Qumran usage of *rdp* is for the pursuit of a routed army (cf. 1QM 9.5-6; 18.2, 12). Once, God "pursues" with goodness (1QS 10.18), but most significant is the use of this term for the pursuit-persecution of the teacher of righteousness and his followers (1QpHab 11.5), a persecution that became violent ("with the sword," CD 1.21). All of these usages are documented in the OT (see BDB, *s.v. rdp*) too, but it is instructive to see the sense of "persecution" appearing in Palestinian Hebrew on the verge of the Christian era and then appearing in a regular sense in Christian Greek (as distinguished from Jewish and pagan Greek).

*the sufferings. Pathēma* occurs in the plural fifteen of sixteen times altogether in the NT, but it is not used at all in the Gospels or Acts. Though it is found only here in the PE, there are eight other Pauline uses in Romans, Second Corinthians, Galatians, Philippians, and Colossians; three occurrences in Hebrews (2:9 [the only singular use], 10; 10:32); and four in First Peter (1:11; 4:13; 5:1, 9). The term is not documented in the LXX. See *1 Clem.* 2.1 (of Christ's sufferings) and Ign. *Smyrn.* 5.1 (of Ignatius's own sufferings, which have failed to convince some, just as the Scriptures and the gospel have not led them to belief).

*such as happened to me in Pisidian Antioch, in Iconium, in Lystra. What persecutions I bore.* Lit. "such as *(hoia)* happened to me in Antioch, in Iconium, in Lystra, what sort of persecutions I (have) endured *(hypēnegka)*. . . ." The uses of *hoia-hoious* in this verse are the only occurrences of the adjective in the PE; it occurs twelve times otherwise in the NT, eight times in the other Paulines, and never in Luke-Acts. See also 1 Thess 1:5 and especially Phil 1:30 with its reference to the Philippians' sufferings for Christ that are "of a piece with that conflict in which you saw and now hear me to be engaged *(auton agōna echontes hoion eidete en emoi . . .)*."

There are eighteen uses of *hoios* in the LXX, and as many as eight are in contexts of trial and hardship, even of the eschatological trials (cf. Dan 9:12; 12:1 with Rev 16:18 as well as Mark 13:9 = Matt 24:21). The Ap. Frs. employ the term only in *Barn.* 10.8; *2 Clem.* 10.4 ("they do not know . . . what *(hoian)* is the joy of the promised future"), and eight times in Hermas.

For the identification of Antioch as Pisidian Antioch see Comment below.

With the repeated exclamatory *hoious* followed by *diōgmous,* a chiastic parenthesis (*tois diōgmois . . . hoia* above) is set around the names of the cities that have evoked the cry, "What persecutions I bore *(hypēnegka)!*" The second perfect here is equivalent to the aorist (cf. BDF §80-81), and the verb occurs otherwise in the NT once in the Paulines, 1 Cor 10:13 (of "bearing" temptation/trial; see Conzelmann, *1 Cor.,* pp. 168-169), and once in the Catholic Epistles, 1 Pet 2:19, of one who "endures pain *(hypopherei . . . lypas)* while suffering unjustly." F. Hauck, *TDNT* 4.582, has noted that the verb describes one who stands erect under and bears a burden.

In the Ap. Frs. the verb occurs in *1 Clem.* 5.4 of "the many trials *(ponous)*" that Peter "suffered *(hypēnegken)*"; then in 7.4 with the sense of "brought" and in 14.2 of incurring "great danger *(kindynon hypoisomen megan)*" by precipitate schism. The eight uses in Hermas add nothing.

There are as many as twenty-one LXX uses of the verb. Where there is a corresponding Hebrew, it is four of ten times a form of *nś'*, "to bear up," "to carry." The use of Eleazar's torments in 2 Macc 6:30 (cf. 7:36 *s.v.l.*) is an especially apt parallel (see also 4 Macc 14:12; 17:3).

*Still, from all of them the Lord delivered me.* Lit. "But (*kai* adversative, as in the Hebrew *we:* Spicq) out of them all (*ek pantōn* [the phrase does not occur otherwise in the PE]) the Lord (*ho kyrios* [the risen Jesus, in the final emphatic position in the sentence]) delivered me *(me errysato)*." The verb here, which recurs at 4:17-18 below, signals the liturgical provenance of this whole phrase. *Rhyesthai* occurs 141 times in the LXX, and it is significant that almost half of these uses are in the Psalter, where it usually translates a form of *nṣl.* Mordecai in LXX Esther 10:3f says *kai errysato kyrios hēmas ek pantōn tou kakōn toutōn* (of persecutions), "the Lord has delivered us from all these evils" (RSV), and

LXX Ps 33:5, 18, 20, *ek pasōn autōn rhysetai autous,* "[the Lord] delivers them from all of them [i.e. their afflictions]" (trans. WCW), comes very close to the terminology here (cf. LXX Ps 141:7, *rhysai me ek tōn katadiōkontōn me,* "deliver me from those who persecute me"; trans. WCW). First Maccabees 2:60, speaking of Daniel, says *errysthē ek stomatos leontōn,* "was delivered from the mouth of the lions" (RSV), and resembles 2 Tim 4:17 below. G. Harder, *TDNT* 6.561, has noted that in the NT documents the verb commonly refers to deliverance from men and their acts, not from the devil (though Col 1:13 somewhat qualifies this). W. Kasch, *TDNT* 6.998-1003, has noted that in secular Greek *sōizein* can always be substituted for *rhyesthai* but that the reverse holds only when the former means "to deliver, protect." He has also observed, pp. 1001-1002, how already in LXX usage the reference is to the personal historical deliverance of actual persons by the God of Israel, not to any magical or material protection.

In comparison with *sōizein* (106 times) in the NT, *rhyesthai* is rather rare, occurring outside of these 3 instances in the PE only 13 times, of which 8 are in the other Paulines: Rom 7:24; 11:26 = LXX Isa 59:20; 15:31 (of Palestinian Jewish persecutions); 2 Cor 1:10 (*bis* with a change in tenses that is reminiscent of 2 Tim 4:17-18); Col 1:13 (the domain of Belial; cf. Lohse, *Col,* pp. 36-37, and qualify Harder above); 1 Thess 1:10; 2 Thess 3:2. The occurrence in the Matthean conclusion to the Lord's Prayer (Matt 6:13) is again a reminder of the liturgical connotation of the verb, as is the single use in Luke 1:74 in the hymn of Zechariah. Matthew 27:43 uses the verb in the mockery of the crucified. The final NT uses are in 2 Pet 2:7, 9 (of the persecuted Lot as precedent for the Lord's deliverance of the godly). Men are always the direct object of this deliverance as God is its source (Kasch, *TDNT* 6.1002), and Kasch, p. 1002, has noted the influence of LXX language and conceptualization on 7 of 15 NT uses of this verb and has pointed out that the NT extends the meaning of the "deliverance" being spoken of to the eschatological order just as do the Qumran documents (p. 1003 n. 8 cites 1QpHab 8.2; 12.14, as does Lohse, *Col,* pp. 36-37, who adds CD 14.2; all use forms of *nṣl* that occur in similar contexts in 1QH 2.31; perhaps 3.5; 5.13 with the reference to Daniel [?] among the lions). Note commentary on 4:17 below for 5.18-19; 7.17, also cited by Kasch; 4QpPs 37.1.9 (2.10), Dupont-Sommer, *EWQ,* p. 271 (cf. Gaster, *DSS,* pp. 326-327); 4QDibHam 2.16; 6.12; 7.2 (cf. Gaster, *DSS,* pp. 274, 278, who apparently does not read this verb at 6.12).

12. *Moreover, all who want to live in a godly way in Christ Jesus will be persecuted.* Lit. "And *(kai)* all persons *(pantes),* moreover *(de),* wishing *(hoi thelontes)* to live in a godly way in Christ Jesus will be persecuted *(diōchthēsontai).*" "To live," *zēn,* occurs 140 times in the NT, 53 of which fall in the Paulines (6 in the PE; 21 in Luke-Acts [9/12]). The verb connotes living not simply in a biological sense but also in an ethical sense, bound up in one's personal conduct.

*Eusebōs* occurs only here and in Titus 2:12 in the NT. The **seb/m-* cluster in the Greek denotes awe always and suggests religious devotion and respect frequently. For "in Christ Jesus" see Notes and Comment on 2 Tim 1:1, 9, 13; 2:1, 10; and 1 Tim 1:14. On *hoi thelontes* compare and contrast the usage in 1 Tim 1:7; 2:4; 5:11.

13. *vicious people and charlatans.* Lit. "evil men and charlatans *(ponēroi . . . anthrōpoi kai goētes).*" See 1 Tim 6:4 on the adjective. The noun *goēs,* a NT *hapax,* is not documented in the Ap. Frs., though Diognetus 8.4 writes of "the miracle-mongering and deceit of the magicians *(terateia kai planē tōn goētōon)*" where the *planē* also reminds one of 2 Tim 3:13. There is no occurrence of this noun in the LXX, but the cognate *goēteia* (lit. "witchcraft") occurs in 2 Macc 12:24 with the sense of cunning guile in speech (cf. Aquila's *goētikos,* "skilled in witchcraft," for Prov 26:22 = "whisperer," *nirgān,* "talebearer" in Hebrew or "murmurer"). There are no examples in Menander, but note other classical examples in LSJ *s.v.* MM *s.v.* have no example of this noun but a peculiar use of a cognate. See Nock, *ERAW,* pp. 309-310, 314-315, 318 ("No one would call himself a *goēs;* it meant quack and had no background" in contrast to *magus*).

For the usage in Philo, see Delling, *TDNT* 1.737. Josephus uses the term ten times: in *War* 2.261 *(goēs kai prophētou pistin epitheis),* 264 (*lēistrikoi,* brigands); 4.85; 5.317; and in *Ant.* 20.97 (cf. Theudas), 160, 167, 188; and *C. Apion* 2.145, 161 of those who call Moses "a magician and deceiver *(apateōn).*"

*deluding and deluded.* The verb *planaō* recurs in Titus 3:3, and is known in the other Paulines only in the warning "Be not deluded" (1 Cor 6:9; 15:33; Gal 6:7); it is used similarly in the one citation in the Lukan corpus (Luke 21:8). Of the other thirty-three NT uses, Matthew and Revelation share almost half between them. In the LXX and Jewish Greek, the **plan-* cluster of terms regularly characterized what was viewed by the authors as spurious prophecy.

## ♦ COMMENT

3:10. *You, however, Timothy, were quite familiar with the instruction, with the approach to living, with the design, with the faithfulness, with the patience, with the charity, with the steadfastness that were mine.* With the *sy de* of this verse a phrase recurs that was seen in Titus 2:1 as well as in 1 Tim 6:11. It will appear at 3:14 and again at 4:5 below, and it seems to introduce three sections or paragraphs of this epistle, i.e. 3:10-13; 3:14–4:4; and 4:5-8 (contra Spicq's division). The sufferings of Paul form a kind of frame around the parenesis on false versus true teachers (cf. D-C, p. 118).

The author appeals to Timothy as one who participated in the life and work of the apostle Paul, as one who "followed" his words and deeds. "The instruction" occupies pride of place in the nine-member list that follows and that Spicq calls "a little biography of Paul." Cf., on the whole list, Spicq, *Agape* 2.419-420. The list is held together by the seven-times-repeated *tēi,* followed by *tois . . . tois.* The displacement of the possessive *mou* to precede the whole catalogue, rather than to modify a single entry, serves to stress the unity of all the individual things noted in the person of the apostle.

With the apostle's teaching is immediately linked *tēi agōgēi,* his approach to living, lit. "practice" . . . (or "orientation"), a term that occurs only here in the NT. Its two occurrences in the Ap. Frs., in *1 Clem.* 47.6 and 48.1, have the sense of "practice" or "training." The schismatic behavior of the Corinthian believers is *anaxia tēs en Christōi agōgēs,* "unworthy of your training in Christ" (thus at *1 Clem.* 47.6; note the *v.l. agapēs*). In *1 Clem.* 48.1 one reads of "the holy and seemly practice *(tēn semnēn . . . hagnēn agōgēn)* of brotherly love." The links between this term, with its basic sense of "guidance, direction," and the process/result of education have been explained by K. L. Schmidt, *TDNT* 1.128-129, who also cites the six uses in LXX Esther 2:20; 10:3; 2 Macc 4:16; 6:8; 11:24; and 3 Macc 4:10. In most of these references there is a contrast between the Jewish and pagan (Greek) *agōgē* (the latter including their games).

Of the six or seven uses in Josephus, *Ant.* 14.247 cites the Decree of Pergamum that opens with "As the Romans in pursuance of the practices of their ancestors . . . *(katakolouthentes tēi tōn progonōn agōgēi . . .)*." In *Ant.* 14.195 a Roman decree of Julius Caesar speaks of "the Jews' manner of life" *(peri tēs Ioudaiōn agōgēs);* cf. *Ant.* 12.10, "determined to keep alive their fathers' way of life and customs" *(tēn patriōn agōgēn tōn ethōn).* The other textually certain occurrences are in *Ant.* 18.169 and *War* 1.462 and 3.109 (of the Roman army).

The next term in the list, *prothesis,* "design," occurred in 2 Tim 1:9 (see above) of the utterly antecedent divine grace and purpose. Here that grace and purpose have touched Timothy's experience through Paul's apostolic grace and purpose. What in 1:9 was emphatically *God's* purpose is here emphatically *mine,* i.e. Paul's. I doubt that the term means "opinion" here; *pace* G. Kittel, *TDNT* 2.237. C. Maurer, *TDNT* 8.166, proposes "aspiration, mind," which is too weak. The alliterative *p* sounds bind *tēi prothesei* to *tēi pistei,* "faithfulness," as do the identical endings in *-ei.* Paul's purpose, i.e. his apostolic mission and goal, cannot be separated from his own faith (*fides qua* here, despite the article), i.e. his loyal attachment to and trust in the Lord who had sent him (cf. 1 Tim 1:12-14).

His own patience *(tēi makrothymiai),* like his *prothesis* in connection with that of the Father, stands in function of the *makrothymia* of Christ Jesus (cf. 1 Tim 1:16 and commentary *ad loc.*), and the reason for that forbearance is now documented in the way in which the apostle's patience in its turn touches the man who "follows" him, as will be seen when the term recurs in 4:2, coupled there with *didachē.* The reference is to the apostle's (and his co-worker's) forbearance with the people whom he teaches, as the gospel is opposed and the apostolic teaching contested, a patience that waits without surrendering, as indeed God himself does (cf. J. Horst, *TDNT* 4.385).

The love *(tēi agapēi)* and the steadfastness *(tēi hypomenēi)* that are next noted may be suggested by the preceding *makrothymia* (cf. Titus 2:2, where they follow *pistis,* and 1 Tim 6:11). The apostle's forbearance is the product not of weakness and cowardice but of *agapē,* that total love of God which enables a man to love even his enemies. This enables him to put up with not only persons *(makrothymia)* who oppose his gospel but also external trials, persecutions, and burdens, and the latter are in particular the objects of *hypomonē* (as the next verse illustrates).

11. *along with the persecutions, with the sufferings, such as happened to me in Pisidian Antioch, in Iconium, in Lystra. What persecutions I bore!* The last two items in the catalogue are both introduced by the plural *tois,* which sets them off from the preceding nouns in the singular and binds the pair closely together. If *hypomonē* suggested external trials, this pair of terms, *diōgmois* and *pathēmasin,* specifies what was endured even more precisely — Paul's own "persecutions," his own "sufferings."

The term *diōgmoi* (ten times in the NT), used at this verse's opening and closing, is employed only here in the PE. It occurs three times otherwise in the Paulines, twice in the plural, in 2 Cor 12:10 and 2 Thess 1:4, of the persecutions that overtook Paul and also his converts. In Rom 8:35 the singular occurs in a list of sufferings that will not separate one from the love of Christ. In the rest of the NT there are occurrences in Mark 4:17 = Matt 13:21 and Mark 10:30. Acts 8:1 and 13:50 employ the term (in the singular) of the persecution of the Jerusalem church and of that against Paul and Barnabas (cf. *infra* on Antioch, Iconium, and Lystra).

The irony of this mention of Paul's *diōgmoi* will not be lost on one who recalls his unique designation as *diōktēs* in 1 Tim 1:13. The one who had inflicted trials now suffers them, and from his own *diōgmoi* he can see that all believers will be persecuted (v. 12, cf. commentary below; for further discussion on *diōgmos* see Notes above).

The ninth and final term in this list, *tois pathēmasin,* is to be read very closely with the preceding *tois diōgmois.* W. Michaelis, *TDNT* 5.930-935, has noted that the sense predominant from the first use of the word in the Greek tragedians, i.e. sufferings/misfortunes, is also the predominant sense in the NT. The Pauline texts that are closest to this passage of Second Timothy are 2 Cor 1:5-7, which is to be read with Col 1:24 (Lohse, *Col,* pp. 68-72, noting esp. p. 70 n. 19, contra Michaelis, p. 933) as well as with Phil 3:10. As Lohse, *Col,* p. 70, has noted, "the sufferings of Christ" in Col 1:24 are the sufferings that usher in the messianic age and the (final) appearance of the Messiah. They are signs not only of a future coming but of a *parousia* that began with the death and resurrection of Jesus of Nazareth.

Among all these sufferings of believers, those of the apostle are "far more significant" (Lohse, *Col,* p. 70), precisely because the apostle and his ministry are a distinctive sign of the gospel of the crucified and risen Jesus. The apostle suffers *hyper hymōn* (Col 1:24; cf. 2 Cor 1:5-7), a phrase that goes to the heart of the Jerusalem kerygma of the Christ's death "for our sins" (1 Cor 15:3) and to the most primitive celebrations of the Lord's Supper (1 Cor 11:24: *sōma to hyper hymōn,* "my body which is for you"; cf. Mark 14:24 of the blood poured out *hyper pollōn,* "for many," and Quinn, "Propitiation"). Here in 2 Tim 3:11, as in Col 1:24, the stress on the first person, on "*my* sufferings," emphasizes the apostle's unique role in comparison with that of all other believers (cf. Lohse, *Col,* p. 72). It is finally and above all in his sufferings that the apostle's ministry is consummated. In his correspondence, as in this list in Second Timothy, Paul appears on the scene as a teacher, but in the end, as here, he appeals to his persecutions and sufferings to authenticate and validate that apostolic task (cf. 1 Cor 4:9-13; 2 Cor 11:23-33; 12:10). Sufferings are "the signs of an apostle" par excellence (cf. 2 Cor 12:12 and Barrett, *Signs* 8.42). Second-generation believers learned this lesson well, perforce, and found support for it in the way later Judaism elaborated the persecutions of the prophets (Lohse, *Col,* p. 72). It is sketched on a vast canvas through Luke-Acts and (not by chance on our hypothesis) through the PE (cf., e.g., Luke 11:49; 21:12-19; 22:28; Acts 5:40-41; 8:1; 9:16; 12:1-3; etc., as well as 2 Tim 1:8; 2:3, 9-10, etc.). The sufferings that belonged to the essence of apostolate were to become a principle of composition for edifying literature in the second century, as the numerous "Acts" in Hennecke and Schneemelcher, *NT Apoc.,* illustrate at every turn. Imagination supplied to later writers about the apostles what Paul's memory of his own and others' history contained.

The *pathēmata* of Paul are now particularized with concrete places. "Such (*hoia:* sufferings) as happened to me in Pisidian Antioch, in Iconium, in Lystra." Here the "persecutions and sufferings" are "of the kind that happened (*egeneto;* aorist for particular occasions) in Antioch, in Iconium, in Lystra. . . ." There is no mistaking which Antioch of the ancient world (there were no fewer than seventeen) is being referred to here, for the same trio of cities, in that order, with Derbe added, occurs in the description in Acts 13–14 of the initial mission of Barnabas and Paul into what is modern Turkey. They had set out from Antioch on the Orontes; they reached "Antioch of Pisidia," about one hundred miles north of Perga (Acts 13:14), and on successive Sabbaths preached in the local synagogue (Acts 13:14-44). The Jews reacted against the proclamation and, while Paul and Barnabas turned all their efforts to the pagans, the Jews (again, as Acts remembers it) incited important pagan women and men against the Christian preaching "and stirred up a persecution (*diōgmon* [cf. 8:1 and Comment *supra*]) against Paul and Barnabas and drove them out of the city" (Acts 13:50). Iconium (modern Konya) lay almost eighty miles, as the crow flies, to the southeast on the Via Sebaste (Haenchen, *Acts,* p. 415 n. 2). The name of Pisidian Antioch will recur again in the narrative of the Iconium persecution (Acts 14:19, cf. below) and then in the reverse order as Paul and Barnabas, returning from Derbe, revisit the new congregations of Lystra, Iconium, and Antioch (Acts 14:21). No other NT document even mentions any of these cities, not to speak of listing all three in the same order as do Acts and 2 Tim 3:11.

The ancient city of Pisidian Antioch rambled over seven hills on a plateau overlooking Yalvaç plain, and in a deep gorge along its east side ran the river Anthius. A Seleucid foundation of the early Hellenistic period (before 261 B.C.E.), the city came into Roman hands by 25 B.C.E. It was colonized by Roman veterans and became a center of Romanization, as the great *Monumentum Antiochenum* with its *res gestae* of Augustus and the magnificent aqueduct that carried water out of the hills to the north into the acropolis bear witness. There were large city squares in honor of Augustus and Tiberius and a Corinthian tetrastyle temple of Mên and Augustus; even the wards of the city were named after those in Rome. Curiously, the man Augustus sent to bring peace to this area in 10-7 B.C.E. was Publius Sulpicius Quirinius, who was a few years later to be "governor of Syria" (Luke 2:2); on this imperial legate and his census see Schürer, *HJP,* pp. 381, 399-427; S. Sandmel writes of his career in *IDB s.v.*

New Roman roads ran along the shores of nearby Lakes Egridir (Limnai) and Beyşehir. By the latter was the Via Sebaste (mentioned above), completed in 6 B.C.E. by the propraetor, Cornutus Aquila, perhaps using the older royal road of the Persians (see Foakes Jackson and Lake, *Beginnings* 1.225-226). Around 40 C.E. the Pauline mission reached the town (and there is no real reason to doubt the historicity of the event of Paul's bringing the gospel there, for all the verbal "special effects" in the Lukan narrative and the PE; contra Haenchen, *Acts,* p. 417, whose skepticism becomes almost pathological in its single-minded and drastic dismissal of any historical events behind the Lukan narrative). It must have been a multilingual community, with the native Phrygian dialect being used alongside Greek and Latin. In this melting pot a Jewish community also existed, which could conceivably have dated from the foundation of the city under Seleucus Nicator, who, according to Josephus, *Ant.* 12.119, gave Jews citizenship "in the cities that he founded in Asia *(en tēi Asiai).*"

With the great ridges of the Sultan Dağ to the northeast and Lake Beyşehir to the southwest, Paul took the Via Sebaste to Iconium (modern

Konya, which is a Turkish provincial capital and had 65,000 inhabitants in 1958) at the edge of a great plain whose fertility was proverbial in the ancient world. The late second-century *Acts of Paul* 2.3 (Hennecke and Schneemelcher, *NT Apoc.* 2.353-354) describes Onesiphorus waiting for Paul (whom he has never before seen) to enter Iconium: "And he went along the royal road (the old name for the Via Sebaste? see Foakes Jackson and Lake, *Beginnings* 1.226) which leads to Lystra, and stood there waiting for him, and looked at [all] who came according to Titus' description (cf. 2.2). And he saw Paul coming, a man of small stature, with a bald head and crooked legs, in a good state of body, with eyebrows meeting and nose somewhat hooked, full of friendliness; for now he appeared like a man, and now he had the face of an angel." The personal description for all its persuasive detail is "the typical portrait of a Jew, admittedly adapted to the eminence of the Apostle" (W. Michaelis, quoted by Hennecke and Schneemelcher, *NT Apoc.* 2.333; cf. Haenchen, *Acts,* p. 426 n. 6).

Iconium, inhabited already in the Chalcolithic period, had a checkered history as a Phrygian village and city that stretched back over a thousand years when Paul entered it. Hellenized under the Seleucids, it became part of the Province of Galatia in the Roman Empire in 25 B.C.E. (Kepler, *IDB s.v.*). The imperial munificence touched the town so that, around the time of Paul's visit, Claudius (41-45 C.E.) had it called Claudiconium. Into the synagogue of the Romanized town came Paul and Barnabas (Acts 14:1), and Luke patterns the sequence of events on those of Antioch, except that the apostolic mission in Iconium perdures rather longer and miracles accompany it (Acts 14:3). Again unbelieving local Jews are pictured as conniving with the pagans "to molest and stone them *(hybrisai kai lithobolēsai autous)*" (Acts 14:5). It is no accident that in this description of the signs and wonders, along with regular harassments of Paul and Barnabas, Luke now gives them the title "apostles" (14:4; cf. 14 *infra* also). In any event, this time they eluded the stoning and once more headed down the Via Sebaste and then over to the west to the Lycaonian town of Lystra and then east to Derbe (Acts 14:6).

The name of *Lystra* (*en Lystrois* in 2 Tim 3:11) is plural in the dative, singular in the accusative (thus a Hellenized and heteroclite noun that belonged to a non-Greek language, probably Anatolian; BDF §57), and occurs five times in Acts (14:6, 8, 21; 16:1-2). The town was identified through a Latin inscription found in 1885 (text in Foakes Jackson and Lake, *Beginnings* 1.226; *CIL* 3.6786) calling it *Julia felix gemina Lystra* (i.e. "twin Lystra," as we say Twin Cities? perhaps the reason for the shift from plural to singular forms for the name in its transmission). It was about eighteen to twenty miles from Iconium, and the tell on which it was built rose on the north bank of the River Kopri. The site is now called Zoldera (Zordula), and across the river on its southern bank is the modern village Hatunsaray of Khatyn Serai. Is a second tell nearby the twin city? A few scattered blocks and sections of foundations are all that survive now of this village in a fertile plain that came under Augustus's rule in 25 B.C.E. and by 6 B.C.E. was well Romanized with a settlement of veterans that made it a colony (*colonia;* cf. the inscription cited above) and a sister to the one in Pisidian Antioch (Mellink, *IDB* 3.194, notes a statue of Concord sent to the latter as a gift).

There is no indication of a synagogue in the town in the narrative of Acts 14:6-20, though one must presume some not noticeably strict Jewish inhabitants in the light of the fact that Timothy and his family lived here (Acts 16:1-3). Perhaps the reader is meant to infer that Paul and Barnabas had found the two previous synagogue "beachheads" less than profitable in the long haul and so decided to change their strategy by going into this rather rustic and devoutly pagan area. The rather more direct and sensational approach narrated by Luke had equally sensational drawbacks as the excited locals, led by "the priest of Zeus whose temple was in front *(pro)* of the city," called them gods in an elaborate patois and tried to sacrifice to them. Then, according to Luke, the organized opposition of the synagogues of Antioch and Iconium invaded Lystra and precipitated the stoning of Paul within the city itself (but apparently not of Barnabas).

The peculiar horror of the event lived on in his own mind, as the *hapax elithasthēn* of 2 Cor 11:25 bears witness. Even Haenchen, *Acts,* p. 429 n. 4, is ready to admit that this refers to what actually had happened at Lystra (and thus presumably that there were historical materials in the traditions utilized by 2 Tim 3 and Acts 14). Timothy, if he did not personally witness it, would have heard of it from his family and neighbors. It must have touched his experience immediately, for when Paul came back to Lystra on his "second" mission he found him already a convert (Acts 16:1-3). Luke recalls that on the occasion the unconscious if not dead body of the apostle was simply dumped outside the city and left unburied to be eaten by scavengers; then disciples came, gathered around, and inexplicably Paul "rose up and entered the city; and on the next day he went on with Barnabas to Derbe" (Acts 14:20), another Lycaonian town that stood about fifty-three miles to the east-southeast at Kerti Hüyük, on the once marshy plain southeast of the massif Kara Dağ.

12. *Moreover, all who want to live in a godly way in Christ Jesus will be persecuted.* In this verse, as a reflective appendix to and justification for the long list that has preceded, with its final stress on apostolic sufferings, the author now adds *(kai),* "Moreover, all who want *(hoi thelontes)* to live in a godly way in Christ Jesus will be persecuted."

Here particularly "the (human) will to live" in Christ is the complement of the divine "will to save (rescue)" through Christ. Of the many uses of *thelein* in the Ap. Frs., the most notable parallels to this passage are *1 Clem.* 22.21, citing LXX Ps 33:13; and 62.1, *tois thelousin eusebōs kai dikaiōs dieuthynein,* "for those who wish to guide their steps in piety and righteousness" (see Titus 2:12). Ign. *Rom.* 8.1 writes, "I no longer desire to live after the manner of men *(ouketi thelō kata anthrōpous zēn),*" and note that most of his uses of *thelein* are concentrated in this letter. *Barnabas* 7.11, speaking of suffering, has Jesus say, "Those who want to see me *(hoi thelontes me idēin)* and attain to my kingdom must lay hold of me through pain and suffering." In *Barn.* 9.2, "Again the Spirit of the Lord prophesies, 'Who is he who wants to live *(ho thelōn zēsai)* forever? Let him hear the voice of my servant *(paidos),*'" with allusions perhaps to LXX Ps 33:13 and Exod 15:26; cf. also *Barn.* 19.1. Hermas, *Sim.* 8.2.9, writes, "He who created *(ho . . . ktisas)* this tree (God's law) wishes all to live (*thelein pantas zēn* [cf. 1 Tim 2:4])," which could be compared with the use of *thelein* in connection with repentance and baptism in *Vis.* 3.5.5 and 3.7.3.

With *diōkthēsontai,* which takes up in verbal form the root of the repeated *diōgmous* of this passage, one meets this term for the third time in the PE (1 Tim 6:11; 2 Tim 2:22), but for the first time with the sense of "persecuting," a sense that is common in Luke-Acts but unusual in the Paulines. As was noted also above, the Ap. Frs. incline to use the verb with the meaning "to persecute." Oepke and Bertram, *TDNT* 2.229, have noted the LXX usage particularly in the Psalms, of both simple and composite *(ek- kata-)* forms of *diōkein,* with the sense "to persecute" (cf. the *v.l.* of Luke 11:49). Perhaps the English term *hunt(ed)* comes closest to containing the double meaning of the Greek. LXX Eccles 3:15 also uses the term of the "persecuted" man (cf. Jer 15:15; 20:11).

The most notable conceptual parallel to 2 Tim 3:12 is in the passage already noted on the persecutions that befell Paul and Barnabas in Antioch, Iconium, and Lystra. No sooner is that painful mission completed than Luke has the apostles return to Lystra, Iconium, and Antioch, "strengthening the souls of the disciples, exhorting them to continue in the faith, and saying that through many tribulations *(thlipseōn)* we must *(dei hēmas)* enter the kingdom of God" (Acts 14:33). The suffering of the apostle and that of the rest of the believers are intimately conjoined. Haenchen, *Acts,* p. 436, remarks on the Lukan style of this verse in Acts, and one could observe the same for 2 Tim 3:11-12.

13. *However, vicious people and charlatans will progress — from bad to worse, deluding and deluded.* In contrast now *(de)* to those who strive for holiness and thus suffer persecution are "vicious people and charlatans *(goētes).*" The final term, a NT *hapax,* refers to sorcerers and swindlers, cheapjack magicians, and here almost certainly refers to those compared with Jannes and Jambres in 3:6-8. G. Delling, *TDNT* 1.737-738, has noted the derogatory nuance in the term that *magos/mageia* did not necessarily have in the ancient world. The *goēs* was a charlatan and a quack, spouting verbal formulae for vicious ends (cf. Euripides, *Bacchae* 234, where Pentheus thus stigmatizes Dionysus).

With the phrase "they will make progress for the worse *(prokopsousin epi to cheiron)*" one meets a verb that was analyzed above (2 Tim 2:16; 3:9) with the same pejorative sense (cf. G. Stählin, *TDNT* 6.704, 714-716), reinforced here by the *epi to cheiron* phrase, unique in the NT but found in Mark 5:26 with *eis* (the adjective *cheirōn* occurred in 1 Tim 5:8). Josephus uses *prokopē/prokoptein* with *epi to cheiron* in *Ant.* 4.59, of rebellion against Moses; *Ant.* 20.214 and *War* 6.1 of the sufferings of besieged Jerusalem (cf. Stählin, p. 712).

The "progress" of these quacks and charlatans who are sorcerers, not prophets, is ironic indeed, for in the very act of "misleading" they are "misled," *planōntes kai planōmenoi,* "deluding and deluded." Here the expression *planōntes kai planōmenoi* forms an alliterative and memorable climax to a sentence that has been bound together with *p* sounds. Here the sounds fix the phrase in the memory in the same way that the vivid image of the blind leading the blind into the pit sticks in the imagination (cf. Matt 15:14 and *TDNT* 7.351 n. 67).

H. Braun, *TDNT* 6.249, is incorrect in observing that these "evil men and quacks" do not attempt to propagate their teaching among unbelievers (cf. the obvious reference of *goētes* here to Jannes and Jambres, who in their turn are a paradigm of those who "evangelize" pagan women with their false doctrine of the resurrection). The other contexts in which the *plan-* cluster is used in the PE would suggest that the opposing teachers here are propounding a proto-Gnostic spirituality (cf. 1 Tim 4:1-4) and that they are being charged with avarice (1 Tim 6:10); cf. Braun, *TDNT* 6.249. From Titus 3:3 one might infer that they were of Jewish Christian background or at least had certain interests in common with the Jewish Christian churches. It remains striking that there is no mitigating the culpability of the error — the wandering — of the opponents. They are not tragic figures (cf. Braun, *TDNT* 6.251) but vicious charlatans.

## IV.C.2. TIMOTHY'S IMITATION OF PAUL (3:14–4:4)

*3 [14]You, however, Timothy, persevere in the things you learned and became sure of. You are well aware of the people you learned from [15]and that from your tenderest years you have known the sacred letters which have the power to make you astute in attaining salvation through faith which comes from union with Christ Jesus. [16]All the Scripture is inspired by God and useful —*

*for instruction,*
*for censuring,*
*for straightening people out,*
*for giving training in upright conduct,*

*[17]so that the man of God may be complete, that is, completely equipped for every excellent deed.*

*4 [1]As God the Father looks on, and Christ Jesus who is going to judge the living and dead, I adjure you, Timothy, while bearing witness to his revelation and his kingdom:*

> *[2]herald the message;*
> *stand on the alert, when convenient*
> *when inconvenient;*
> *refute;*
> *reprove;*
> *encourage —*

*with the utmost patience in the task of teaching. [3]For there will come a time when they will not put up with this wholesome instruction. Instead, they will load themselves with teachers who answer their craving to get relief for their itchy ears. [4]Furthermore, as they turn a deaf ear to the truth, they will slip off after tales.*

## ♦ NOTES

3:14. *You, however, Timothy, persevere in the things you learned and became sure of. You are well aware of the people you learned from.* Lit. "But you keep staying *(mene)* in the things that you learned *(emathes)* and became convinced of *(epistōthēs)*, knowing *(eidōs)* from *(para)* whom [pl.] you learned *(emathes)*." On *mene* see Note at 1 Tim 2:15. Regarding *manthanein, manthanetōsan* occurs six times in the Timothy correspondence (also at 1 Tim 2:11; 5:4, 13; 2 Tim 3:14), along with once in Titus (3:14), and nine times in the other Paulines (twenty-five total in the NT). The learning urged in Titus 3:14 is in the style of that of Phil 4:9 and 11, where first the apostle writes, "What you have *learned* and received and heard and seen in me, do *(prassete)*," and then adds, "Not that I complain of want; for I have *learned* in whatever state I am, to be content." This is learning charity by acting charitably, not an abstract, theological systematization.

The NT *hapax epistōthēs* occurs seventeen times in the LXX in both active and passive forms to designate a fixed and lasting assurance (cf. LXX Pss 77:8, 37; 92:5). *First Clement* 15.4 = LXX Ps 77:32; and in *1 Clem* 42.3 the author writes of the apostles that, "being fully assured by the resurrection of our Lord Jesus Christ and with faith confirmed *(pistōthentes)* by the word of God *(en tōi logōi tou theou)*, they went forth." These are the only uses in the Ap. Frs. LXX 3 Macc 4:20 offers a good "secular" parallel to the meaning of the passive here in the PE, "to be assured of" (MM *s.v.*, who also note the *v.l.* of 2 Thess 1:10 and *Ep. Arist.* 91). See also Excursus I, "*Pistis* Terminology in the PE," in AB *Titus*.

As H. Riesenfeld, *TDNT* 5.729, has noted, both this passage and 1:13 above use *para* in the way that is customary after Greek verbs of hearing and answering (cf. also Acts 24:8).

On *eidōs* see above at 1 Tim 3:15, which also has the indirect question, as well as with *hoti* (the italicized verses contain *hoti*), Titus 1:16; *3:11; 1 Tim 1:8, 9; 3:5;* and *2 Tim 1:12, 15; 2:23.* The verb occurs for the last time in the PE in 2 Tim 3:15 of Timothy's "knowing" the OT Scriptures — see below.

15. *from your tenderest years.* Lit. "from infancy." The noun *brephos* occurs only here in the Paulines, but six of seven remaining NT uses are in Luke-Acts. Thus Luke 1:41, 44, of a child still in the womb; 2:12, 16, of the newborn Jesus; 18:15, of the babies brought to Jesus for his blessing; and Acts 7:19, of newborn babies in Pharaoh's Egypt. First Peter 2:2 uses the term in a comparison that involves the hunger of unweaned children for their milk.

The five LXX uses are in Sir 19:11 (of giving birth to an infant) and the Maccabean literature (1 Macc 1:61; 2 Macc 6:10; 3 Macc 5:49; 4 Macc 4:25, all of children just circumcised or still at the breast). In the Ap. Frs. only Hermas employs the word (*Sim.* 9.29.1, 3 [*bis*] of innocent babies [i.e. those who have never deliberately chosen evil]).

*the sacred letters.* On the phrase as a whole as well as the word *hiera,* see Comment below. The noun *gramma* occurs only here in the PE but on thirteen other occasions in the NT, of which seven are in the Paulines and four in Luke-Acts (two/two). The other two uses are in John 5:47 (of Moses' writing); 7:15 (here anarthrous and with *oiden* = "to know how to read"; was this what influenced the anarthrous reading in Second Timothy [see Comment below]?). In Luke 16:6-7 *ta grammata* are the receipts for goods kept by the steward; in Acts 26:24 *ta polla . . . grammata* is Paul's "great learning," and in 28:21 it is "letters" (anarthrous) about Paul from Palestine. If Luke wrote or redacted the PE, one would see why *ta hiera grammata* would be needed to designate the Scriptures, for he never uses *grammata* of the Bible. The case is otherwise with the rest of the Paulines, where in Rom 2:27, 29; 7:6; 2 Cor 3:6 *(bis),* 7 (all except once in the singular) it refers to the Mosaic law. Only in Gal 6:11 does it refer to Paul's own subscription to that letter. In all of these instances except 2 Cor 3:7, the noun is anarthrous (another reason for the anarthrous reading in Second Timothy noted below).

As was noted above, *gramma* in the LXX never refers to the Jewish Scripture. In other Jewish Greek texts it can scarcely be used without further qualification to mean Scripture (Schrenk, *TDNT* 1.763, cites Josephus, *Ant.* 5.61, but even there the qualification is present in context; Spicq, *EP,* p. 791, does not note any), but with some qualification (*hiera, Ioudaïka, hēmetera,* etc.; Schrenk, pp. 763-764) it is so used commonly.

In the Ap. Frs. *gramma* occurs in Ign. *Magn.* 9.1 (a very doubtful reading but, if correct, a reference to OT commandments); *Rom.* 8.2 of his own "short letter"; *Pol.* 7.3 also of his own letter; Polycarp, *Phil.* 13.1, of correspondence; *Barn.* 9.7-8, interpreting the "3 letters" of "318" (cf. Yale Papyrus 1). Hermas uses the term in *Vis.* 2.1.4 of the "little book" of prophecy that he is to deliver. Thus there is no certain use of *gramma* = Scripture in these authors. According to Lampe, *PGL*, p. 322, the earliest uses of *gramma(-ta)* in this sense appear to be in Clement, *Protrep.* 9 (*PG* 8.197[c]), who is commenting on this passage of Second Timothy, and Origen, *Contra Celsum* 4.27 (*PG* 11.1068[a]), both with *hiera* (in fact the term appears regularly to be qualified with some attributive).

*the power to make you astute in attaining salvation through faith.* Lit. "the power (*ta dynamena*) to make you wise *(se sophisai)* unto salvation *(eis sōtērian)* through faith." On *dynamis* see 2 Tim 1:7 above. Here Second Timothy does not actually employ the *didask-* terminology (as does the following verse) but states that the Scriptures have the power *se sophisai,* "to make you wise." The one other use of this verb in the NT, in 2 Pet 1:16, is in a pejorative sense of "cleverly devised myths *(mythois).*" That ambivalence in meaning goes back to the Greek philosophers and to the LXX (see Wilckens, *TDNT* 7.527). There are twenty-two LXX uses of this term, of which ten are in Sirach and all but three in the Wisdom literature (the wisdom theme of 3 Kgdms 4:31 is obvious; 1 Kgdms 3:8 is the only instance where the Hebrew text is not a form of *ḥkm*). The bad sense is found in Sir 7:5; 10:26; 35 (RSV 32):4; and 37:20, especially in the phrase *mē sophizou* (cf. Eccles 7:17). A notable example of the good sense is in Sir 47:14 where, of Solomon, the author exclaims, "How wise you became *(esophisthēs)* in your youth *(neotēti).*" The Psalms, too, are close to the thought here in 2 Tim 3:15, especially LXX Ps 18:7: *hē martyria kyriou pistē sophizousa nēpia* (cf. LXX Ps 104:22, of old men; 118:98, surpassing enemies).

Ign. *Smyrn.* 1.1 praises "Jesus Christ, the God who has thus given you wisdom *(hymas sophisanta),*" i.e. faith in his cross and rising. The only other uses of *sophizein* in the Ap. Frs. are in *Barn.* 5.3; 9.4, first in a good sense, then in a bad.

*Salvation through faith* marks one of only two uses in the PE of *sōtēria,* contrasted with sixteen uses in the other Paulines and ten in Luke-Acts (four/six). As the trials of the apostle were for salvation in the only other PE usage of *sōtēria* (2 Tim 2:10), so here the letter of the OT is for salvation. The *sōtērias tychōsin* of 2:10 is the equivalent conceptually of the somewhat more Hebraic and Septuagintal *eis sōtērian* here (see LXX Exod 15:2; Num 6:14; 2 Kgdms 10:11; 1 Chron 19:12; 2 Chron 12:7; etc.)

16. *inspired.* E. Schweizer, *TDNT* 6.454-455, reviews the history of this term, which occurs only here in the NT, LXX, and Ap. Frs. Indeed, all usage of the compound in Greek appears (outside of this text in the PE) after 100 C.E. (Spicq, *EP,* p. 793 n. 2). Schrenk, *TDNT* 1.758, Spicq, D-C, and Schweizer cite passages, secular (Plutarch; Vettius Valens; Pseudo-Phocylides), Jewish (? *Sibyl-*

*line Oracles*), and Christian (Origen, *On John* 6.48; *PG* 14.284A, Lampe; Theodore of Mopsuestia; Maximus Confessor; Gregory of Nyssa, *Eun.* 7; *PG* 45.744-745 [744 D for *pasa graphē theopneustos*]). Lampe also notes Clement of Alexandria, *Strom.* 1.21; *PG* 8.853A; 7.16; *PG* 9.540C, who writes of how God leads men to the heights *kata tas theopneustous graphas* and in 9.544A of men whose lust for notoriety (he cites Marcion and Prodicos) makes them play the sophist about the things that are in accord "with the divinely inspired words *(tois theopneustois logois)* handed down by the blessed apostles and teachers." It is notable that the second-century-C.E. Epitaph of Abercius of Hieropolis can be called *theopneuston epigramma;* and Gregory of Nyssa can designate his colleague Basil's *Hexaemeron* (*PG* 44.61A) as *tēn theopneuston ekeinēn . . . theōrian.* It is also used of the Conciliar decision condemning Nestorius.

E. Stauffer, *TDNT* 3.121, notes how this term in 1 Thess 4:9 qualifies the Christian believer, as *theopneustos* here in Second Timothy qualifies the Scripture. G. Bertram, *TDNT* 3.123, has listed the seven uses of the *theo-* compounds in the NT, all in the other Paulines (Rom 1:30, *theostygēs;* 1 Thess 4:9) or in Acts (5:39, *theomachos;* 23:9, *theomachein;* 1 Tim 2:10, *theosebeia*), with *theosebēs* in John 9:31 (though perhaps one should note the proper name *Theophilus* as well, Luke 1:3 and Acts 1:1, especially since the first element is object of the second).

*and useful for instruction, censuring, for straightening people out, for giving training in upright conduct.* Lit. "and useful *(ōphelimos)* for teaching *(pros didaskalian),* for reproof *(pros elegmon),* for correcting *(pros epanorthōsin),* for training in righteousness *(pros paideian tēn en dikaiosynēi). . . .*" *Ōphelimos* occurs also in Titus 3:8 and 1 Tim 4:8, in the latter of bodily exercise and godliness, but not otherwise in biblical Greek (but see the Roman connection in the Ap. Frs. [*1 Clem.* 56.2; 62.1; Hermas, *Vis.* 3.6.7]). *Anōpheleis,* the antonym, occurs in Titus 3:9. On *didaskalia* see Notes and Comment on Titus 1:9 in AB *Titus.*

The next two phrases, *pros elegmon* and *pros epanorthōsin,* use terms not documented elsewhere in the NT or in the Ap. Frs. *Elegmos,* "rebuking," does occur as many as twenty-one times in the LXX; cf. especially, in the singular, Lev 19:17 (18 is the second "great command"); Ps 38:11, "You chastised *(epaideusas)* man with rebukes *(en elegmois)* for sin"; and of the dozen uses in Sirach, note 21:6, "Whoever hates reproof *(elegmon)* walks in the steps of the sinner, but he that fears the Lord will repent in his heart" (cf. 35 [RSV 32]:17), and 48:7 of Elijah hearing Yahweh's "rebuke" on Sinai.

*Epanorthōsis* ("correcting") occurs only in LXX 1 Esd 8:52 and 1 Macc 14:34. In the latter case it is used of the restoration of cities, a sense that has frequently surfaced in the inscriptions (see L. Robert *ap.* Spicq *in loc.*), where it is also used of raising statues and restoring sanctuaries (LSJ Suppl.; MM *s.v.;* and Spicq also). H. Preisker, *TDNT* 5.450-451, cites (as do D-C *in loc.*) a passage of Epictetus (*Diss.* 3.21.15) describing the mysteries as established *epi paideiai* (cf.

the next phrase here in Second Timothy *kai epanorthōsei tou biou*). Polybius 1.35.1, commenting on the rout of Regulus, remarked that those events have "much to contribute to the better conduct of human life *(pros epanorthōsin tou tōn anthrōpōn biou)*." When Philo, *Mos.* 2.36, explains why God answered the prayer of the translators of the LXX on the island of Pharos in the harbor of Alexandria, he notes that it was so "that the greater part, or even the whole of the human race might be profited *(ōphelēthēi)* and led to a better life *(eis epanorthōsin biou)* by continuing to observe such wise *(philosophois)* and truly admirable ordinances." Here the link with *pasa graphē* is notable.

Josephus uses this noun in *Ant.* 11.157 and 16.263 (of Ezra's "rectifying [*tēs epanorthōseōs*] the offenses against the laws of the state," i.e. putting the newly restored exiles on the road to effective reform, and of "setting to rights [*tēn epanorthōsin*] the unfortunate state of affairs" with Herod).

The noun *paideian* occurs here for the only time in the PE; its one other Pauline use is in the domestic code of Eph 6:4. All the other NT uses are in Hebrews (12:5, 7, 8, 11), which at 12:5 is taking up LXX Prov 3:11. This noun is frequent in the LXX, occurring as many as 102 times, with the vast majority of instances in Proverbs and Sirach. The verb *paideuein* occurs at Titus 2:12; 1 Tim 1:20; and 2 Tim 2:25 in the PE, and in its two other Pauline uses connotes the effects of severe illness and life-threatening trials (1 Cor 11:32; 2 Cor 6:9). Luke 23:16, 22, however, contains the most vivid example of the term's connotation to Hellenistic readers when it refers to the scourging of Jesus (although cf. Acts 7:22 and 22:3, where this verb emphasizes intellectual activity, not the physical hardship that accompanies it). For the cognate *apaideutos,* "undisciplined," see above on 2 Tim 2:23.

17. *complete. Artios* occurs nowhere else in the NT or in the LXX (though the adverbial *artiōs* = "until now" occurs in LXX 2 Kgdms 15:34; cf. Symmachus Ezek 11:3) or in the Ap. Frs. It is to date undocumented in the papyri (Spicq; though see MM *s.v.* for the adverb). Josephus knows only the adverb (*War* 4.245; *Ant.* 13.282), but Philo uses the adjective several times (with *plēres*) to mean "balanced and complete" (*Plant.* 125 of four as an "even" number; *Det.* 7). The term is often employed in secular Greek for well-proportioned and balanced bodily faculties, of that which is well adjusted and healthy, full grown and sound (citations in Spicq and LSJ). Note that D* and L originally read *teleios* for this rare term (J. K. Elliott, *Greek Text,* p. 156, proposes assimilation to James 3:2; cf. the vulgate *perfectus*).

*completely equipped.* "The complete man of God" is one who has been "completely equipped for every excellent deed." The LXX Exod 28:7 (A.) uses *exertizein* of the two shoulder-pieces of the Aaronic ephod, "joined to" its two edges, but the verb is not documented in the Ap. Frs. MM *s.v.* cite papyri that speak of an olive press "in working order *(energon)* and completely furnished *(exērtismenon hapasi)*" as well as of a boat "supplied *(exērtismenon)* with two oars" (again the balanced, even number). Josephus, *Ant.* 3.139, uses the term of the way in which the legs of the table of shewbread were "finished" in the Doric style (cf. the *lect. incer.* of 3.43). Thus the term here in Second Timothy has a certain elative sense, adding the note of "*perfectly* equipped" to *artios.*

*for every excellent deed.* On *pros pan ergon agathon,* see Titus 1:16; 3:1, and (with *eis*) 2 Tim 2:21.

4:1. *As God the Father looks on, and Christ Jesus who is going to judge the living and dead, I adjure you, Timothy, while bearing witness to his revelation and his kingdom.* Lit. "I charge, in the presence of God *(tou theou)* and of Christ Jesus who is going to judge living and dead, both his manifestation and his kingdom." See the Comment below for an explanation of the translation adopted by this commentary.

*who is going to judge the living and dead.* To the name "Christ Jesus" this formula appends "who is going *(tou mellontos)* to judge *(krinein)* living and dead *(zōntas kai nekrous)*. . . ." This entire phrase is an inchoate formula of the second Christian generation (see Acts 10:42; 1 Pet 4:5; note also Rom 14:9, an earlier variation of it). LXX Isa 8:19 and Tob 5:10 (S) can be cited as precedents for its Jewish and Christian usage, as can the dominical logion in Mark 12:27 par. (*SFG* §281), which refers to "the God not of the dead but of the living." A Jewish source, *Ep. Arist.* 146, documents almost this precise phrase. This is the only time in the PE that *mellōn* modifies Christ, though it was used of future believers in 1 Tim 1:16 and of the future (life) in 1 Tim 4:8; 6:19 (see above). Here it governs the verb *krinein* (note the *v.l. krinai*), as in Acts 17:31 (cf. James 2:12, *mellontes krinesthai*), but not elsewhere in NT, in any of the 110 uses of *mellein* and the 114 of *krinein.* Note that it is only Acts 24:25 that uses the phrase *peri . . . tou krimatos tou mellontos* in the NT (on *krima* see 1 Tim 3:6; 5:12). *Krinein,* which occurred previously in the PE only in Titus 3:12, of Paul's personal decision on where to spend the winter, occurs 113 times elsewhere in the NT; between them, Romans and First Corinthians share 35 of the other 39 Pauline uses. Luke-Acts employs the verb in 28 instances.

*his revelation.* On *epiphaneian autou* see Titus 2:13; 1 Tim 6:14; 2 Tim 1:10 (as well as 4:8 *infra*).

2. *herald the message.* Lit. "Proclaim the Word *(kēryxon ton logon).*" The verb used here as an aorist imperative occurs in the hymn fragment cited in 1 Tim 3:16; it is a verb that often has "the kingdom (of God)" as its object (e.g., Luke 8:1; 9:2; Acts 20:25; 28:31), or "the gospel," but only here in the NT, *ton logon* (which has been analyzed in the commentary on Titus 1:3, 9; 2:5, 8; 3:8 and which figured through 2 Tim 2:9, 11, 15, 17). Paul is for these PE the *kēryx* as he is *apostolos,* par excellence (1 Tim 2:7; 2 Tim 1:11). (See G. Friedrich, *TDNT* 3.704, for the various objects of the verb "proclaim.")

*stand on the alert, when convenient, when inconvenient.* The next imperatival phrase, lit. "Stand by *(epistēthi),* when convenient, when inconvenient *(eukairōs akairōs),*" uses a verb that recurs at 4:6 below and only once otherwise in the Paulines, at 1 Thess 5:3. All the other NT uses are in Luke-Acts (seven and eleven = eighteen times). Evidently in the NT this verb often has a threatening nuance, though not necessarily so, as it depicts one person peering down on another or standing over another.

Of the as many as seventy-six LXX uses (which correspond to twenty Hebrew verbs in MT), the senses noted above for the NT also occur. With Spicq, note the *epistēthi kai hetoimason* of LXX Jer 26:14: "Stand ready and be prepared, for the sword shall devour round about you" (cf. LXX Jer 51:11: "Behold I will set my face [*ephistēmi to prosōpon mou* (cf. Lev 17:10; 20:3, 5, 6, etc.)] against you for evil . . ."). LXX Hag 2:6 reads, "My spirit *(pneuma)* abides ([RSV for MT "stands"] *ephestēken*) among you: fear not."

In the Ap. Frs., *1 Clem.* 12.4 uses the verb in the royal inquiry about the Israelite spies coming to Rahab (cf. Sir 41:22), but one waits until Hermas, *Vis.* 3.1.9 *(s.v.l.)* and *Sim.* 9.6.2, for the term to occur again but without notable relevance to the PE. The asyndetically paired *eukairōs akairōs* (cf. BDF §460.1, though Spicq proposes this as a typically Latin rather than Greek oxymoron, *nolens volens*) draw out both the threatening and the more neutral sense of *epistēthi,* which has no object here. What is good news, sudden surprising good news from a divine messenger (cf. the "heralding" above), for some, is also bad news for others. Whatever the effect, the herald must be at his task "in season, out of season." The *kairos* root will reappear in verses 3 and 6 *infra* (where there are references to the other uses in the PE). Here it is prefixed with *eu-* and *a-;* cf. the English *timely/untimely.*

*Eukairōs* occurs otherwise in the NT only in Mark 14:11 of Judas seeking a good time to betray Jesus (Luke 22:6 uses the noun *eukairian* of this, as does Matt 26:16; for *eukairein* see Acts 17:21 as well as 1 Cor 16:12 and Mark 6:31, with the sense "to have an opportunity"). The adjective *eukairos* modifies *hēmera* in Mark 6:21, and in Heb 4:16, *boētheia.* In the LXX the adverb *eukairōs* is documented only in Sir 18:22 of fulfilling a vow "promptly," though the adjective is found in LXX Ps 103:27 (of food at the right time) as well as in the Maccabean corpus (2 Macc 14:29; 15:20, 21; 3 Macc 4:11; 5:44). The noun *eukairia* occurs not only in Sir 38:24 (of leisure giving opportunity for wisdom) and 1 Macc 11:42 but also in LXX Pss 9:9, 22; 144:15 (also of food). The Ap. Frs. do not employ any form of *eukair-.*

The antithetic *akairōs* occurs nowhere else in the NT (though note the verb in Phil 4:10), and in the LXX only in Sir 32 (RSV):4, of the unseasonable display of cleverness (cf. *akairos* in Sir 20:19; 22:6, as well as the *akairios* read by A in 2 Macc 6:25). The one occurrence in the Ap. Frs. is when Ign. *Rom.* 4.1 alludes to a proverb of Zenobius on "an unseasonable kindness *(eunoia akairos)*" and uses the adjective, not the adverb. G. Delling, *TDNT* 3.462 n. 1, has noted the extreme rarity of *akairios* as well as of the verb *akairein*. Even the papyri have only one, late example of *akairos*, but see MM *s.v.* for the adverb in the letter of the prodigal (second-century-C.E. B G U 111, 846.14-15, in the form *akairiōs, s.v.l.*). The adjective also occurs in a second-century-B.C.E. inscription about *hai lian akairoi dapanai*, "the exceedingly inopportune expenses" (*Syll.* 730.12). On *eukairōs* see MM *s.v.*, who cite several examples from third–second-century-B.C.E. papyri.

*refute.* On *elegchein* see Titus 1:9.

*reprove.* The fourth imperative, *epitimēson*, occurs twenty-nine times in the NT, but only here absolutely. In Jude 9 it appears to be in a citation from the lost *Assumption of Moses* where Michael prays that the Lord will rebuke the devil; the actual terminology also occurs in LXX Zech 3:2 *(epitiman, bis)*. All the other NT uses are in the synoptics, with twelve in Luke versus six in Matthew and nine in Mark.

There are ten LXX occurrences of this verb, five in the Psalms. Where the LXX corresponds to MT, it is translating *gʿr*, a term that also occurs a few times in Qumran. Thus 1QM 14.10 (cf. 4QM[a] 7) reads, "His spirits of destruction thou hast chided *(gʿrth)* [away from us, and when there acted evilly the me]n of his dominion, thou hast preserved the soul of those to be redeemed by thee" (Yadin, *War*, p. 328, for translation, restoration). In 1QH 9.11: Dupont-Sommer, *EWQ*, p. 231, the psalmist says of God, ". . . thou hast put/ a supplication in the mouth of thy servant and hast not threatened *(gʿrth)* my life nor driven away my gladness" (see 1QH4 1.6: "[yo]u give rebuke to every opponent [*(tgʿr bkwl śṭn)*; cf. f 45.3 and 1QS[b] 1.8; cf. Zech 3:2, which also has *gʿrb* with respect to *śṭn* of destruction *(mšḥyt)*, i.e. every corrupt opponent])." Apparently here in Qumran as in the OT it is God who rebukes, above all.

No form of *epitimaō* occurs in the Ap. Frs.

3. *wholesome instruction.* The word used here is *hygiainousā*, as also in Titus 1:9; 2:1; 1 Tim 1:10. Otherwise in the PE the term refers to words (*logoi:* 1 Tim 6:3; 2 Tim 1:13), and to faith (Titus 1:13; 2:2), as the cognate *hygiēs* refers to *logos* in Titus 2:8. Luke employs *hygiainein* of physical health (5:31; 7:10; 15:27), but in the NT otherwise only the epistolary greeting of 3 John uses the word.

*itchy ears.* Lit. "itching as to the ears." *Knēthesthai* is a rare Hellenistic verb not otherwise documented in the NT, the LXX, or the Ap. Frs. MM *s.v.*, noting that Attic used *knaō*, cite Clement of Alexandria, *Strom.* I.3.22.5; *PG* 8.712. Clement scores the jargon of the Sophists "scratching *(knēthontes)* and tickling, in what I consider an unmanly way, the ears *(akoas)* of those who long to be scratched *(knēsasthai)*." See also Herodas 4.51, "The day will come when you will scratch *(knēsēi)* your dirty poll (*bregma* [= front part of head])" (cf. also the Attic *knō* in

8.8, "grumble and scratch your head"; *apud* MM). Spicq has noted that Hellenistic literature frequently refers to the *knēsis ōtōn* as a metaphor for any bittersweet desire that combines both pleasure and pain (especially Plutarch; also Lucian; see LSJ *s.v.*). The figure fixes memorably on the exasperated desires that impel these pitiful believers to pile up teachers. LSJ do not note any specifically medical usages, *s.v. knēthiaō k.t.l.*, but Galen is cited *s.v. Knaō* (p. 964). The noun *tēn akoēn* is found only here and in the next verse in the PE. Here it is the object of itch/scratch; there it is the object of "turning away *(apostrepsousin).*" G. Kittel, *TDNT* 1.221-222, refers to neither of these passages.

The noun is found twenty-two times otherwise in the NT. Eight of these occurrences are in the other Paulines. In the Lukan corpus the term appears in Luke 7:1; Acts 17:20 (pl. = ears); 28:26 (= LXX Isa 6:9). As Kittel has noted (p. 221), *akoē* can be a technical term for the gospel proclamation (cf. the *logos akoēs* of 1 Thess 2:13; Heb 4:2; and cf. Rom 10:16-17 [citing LXX Isa 53:1]; Gal 3:2, 5). That is certainly not the meaning in 2 Tim 4:3, and it is very difficult to justify it for the following verse, where it is the direct object of *apostrepsousin.* The LXX, which employs *akoē* as often as forty-six times, never uses it as the object of *apostrephein.*

In the Ap. Frs., *1 Clem.* 16.3 uses the term in quoting LXX Isa 53:1 and again in 47.7 of the report *(akoē)* about the Corinthian dissensions reaching the Roman church. Barnabas uses the term four times in 9.1-3, in a cento of LXX texts and allusions, and again in 10.12 (in the latter two it surely means "ears").

4. *as they turn a deaf ear to the truth.* Lit. "and, on the one hand, they will turn away the ear from the truth." The verb here, *apostrephō,* occurred above in Titus 1:14 of "abandoning the truth" and in 2 Tim 1:15 of abandoning the apostle himself. In the NT otherwise, it is used only six times, including in Luke 23:14; Acts 3:26; and Rom 11:26, quoting LXX Isa 59:20. This concept of resisting the truth occurs in the PE in Titus 1:14; 1 Tim 6:5; 2 Tim 2:18; 3:8; 4:4).

*they will slip off after tales.* Lit. "on the other they will turn to myths." *Mythoi* occurs only in the plural in the NT, the PE (Titus 1:14; 1 Tim 1:4; 4:7; 2 Tim 4:4), and 2 Pet 1:16. The single LXX appearance is in the singular, in Sir 20:19, of a *mythos akairos,* "thought expressed at the wrong time" (see also 1 Tim 1:4; 4:7).

## ♦ COMMENT

3:14. *You, however, Timothy, persevere in the things you learned and became sure of. You are well aware of the people you learned from.* With the second *sy de* (cf. 3:10 *supra*) the parenesis returns emphatically to Timothy, who stands in contrast *(de)* to the quacks of 3:13, as they in their turn were contrasted to the suffering believers (3:12) and the apostle himself. As the previous section (3:10-13) had sent Timothy back to his relationship with the apostle, this section refers him to his Jewish and Christian family background (cf. the prayer in 2 Tim 1:3-5 where the same order is followed), with particular stress on the Jewish Scriptures as the matrix for good teaching.

As in 2 Tim 2:13 Christ "stays *(menei)* faithful," here Timothy is exhorted, "persevere *(mene)* in the things you learned *(en hois emathes)* and became sure of *(epistōthēs)* . . ." in a "psychological abiding . . . in the things which belong to salvation" (J. Hauck, *TDNT* 4.576). This is the final occurrence of *manthanein* in the PE (Titus 3:14; 1 Tim 2:11; 5:4, 13; 2 Tim 3:7), and K. Rengstorf, *TDNT* 4.410, proposes that the sense here is much the same as in Rom 16:17, with its reference to the apostolic *didachē,* though here the *didachē* in question has been received under (*para: TDNT* 4.409 n. 140, the usual preposition for expressing this relation) familial auspices (note how the variant *para tini* below would obscure the point). The content is evidently conceived of as involving a number of matters *(en hois),* but they are not further specified.

The final clause of this verse is *eidōs para tinōn emathes,* lit. "knowing from whom [pl.] you learned" the realities of the faith noted previously. If the previous *en hois* stressed the discreteness within the revelation, "the articles of the creed" (cf. Plummer *ap.* Spicq, *EP,* p. 785) which must all be accepted, this participial clause emphasizes that Timothy recognizes fully "from whom" *(para tinōn)* he has received his knowledge of revelation. The Western reading of the singular here (*para tinos:* in C$^c$. D. K. L. T. R. most minuscules etc. cited by J. K. Elliott, *Greek Text,* p. 20) deliberately exalts Paul (3:10-11 would justify the change) and simplifies the complex process of tradition here sketched. Thus Timothy speaks for Paul, the whole Paul, and nothing but Paul. No room is left for the thin edge of criticism and distinction to be inserted into the teaching of the PE. However, the repeated *sy de* introduction would lead one to infer that the author is now turning from the one who was of primary importance in Timothy's formation, the apostle himself (the previous *sy de* section, 3:10-13), to those who were of secondary importance, though chronologically prior, *scil.,* Timothy's family (cf. 2 Tim 1:5 with Acts 16:1-2). Reference to other religious teachers is also conceivable (Lock notes the witnesses of 2:2 *supra*).

15. *and that from your tenderest years you have known the sacred letters which have the power to make you astute in attaining salvation through faith which comes from union with Christ Jesus.* A second reason for Timothy's persevering stability is now adduced, dependent on the causal *eidōs* participle of the previous verse and introduced (as often in the PE; cf. references adduced at *eidōs* above) with *hoti.* It is coordinated with the previous reason (i.e. the persons who taught him the faith) and explains how Timothy's acceptance of their teaching was not just a personal or even familial eccentricity but was according

to the Scriptures, i.e. it was measured by the publicly documented revelation to the whole people of God.

*from your tenderest years you have known* (*oidas* [past action still occurring, Moule, *Idiom,* p. 8]) the (*ta* [*s.v.l.*]) *sacred letters (hiera grammata)*. . . . The repeated *eidōs* . . . *oidas* serves to bind the coordinate clauses more closely together (as the present verse division blurs that coordination). Timothy's knowledge of and experience in the Scriptures are said to date from infancy. The use here in Second Timothy is obviously hyperbolic and meant to heighten the basic affirmation to the utmost. There was never a moment in his conscious life that the teaching of Scripture had not touched.

The phrase *ta (s.v.l.) hiera grammata* is anarthrous in S. $C^b$. D*. F. G. 33 etc. (J. K. Elliott, *Greek Text,* p. 155), and Nestle[22] followed this text. Yet A. C*. and the Byzantine text at large have opted for *ta* (which *GNT*[3corr] prints in brackets). Since the NT offers no other occurrence of the phrase, one may with Schrenk, *TDNT* 1.761-769, especially 751 and 765 n. 13, hold that the phrase in Second Timothy is already a technical formula, practically a book title, and thus the article has been omitted in accord with standard Greek usage (BDF §257.2; cf. 252). Yet that form should be documented from Jewish Greek usage, and none of the 26 LXX uses of *gramma* is modified by *hiera;* the one anarthrous usage in Esther 6:1 refers (*pace* Schrenk, pp. 763-764) to secular "chronicles," and not one LXX use of *gramma* refers as such to the Scripture of Israel. Of the at most 181 uses of *gramma* in Josephus, the phrase *(ta) hiera grammata* occurs as many as 11 times. Of the two anarthrous uses, that in *Ant.* 3.178 refers to the tetragrammaton, not to the Scriptures as such (cf. *War* 5.235). The 8 remaining occurrences in Josephus all refer to the Scriptures of Israel (except perhaps *C. Apion.* 1.228 = Egyptian sacred chronicles) and use the article *ta.* Spicq remarks in his Excursus 10 (*EP,* p. 791) that he has never found an example of the phrase without the article designating the Scriptures. It is found only in the nominative and accusative.

In this linguistic horizon, *ta hiera grammata* was not heard in the first century C.E. as a technical phrase or title as such (the *phrase* is not documented in Ap. Frs.), and thus there was no pressure to drop the article. But if that is the case, the longer reading here in Second Timothy is more probably the original, and the omission of the article in S. $C^b$. D*. etc. is a stylistic "correction" that occurred in the third century and later when the anarthrous *hiera grammata* was indeed heard as the title for the Bible. Thus, agreeing with J. K. Elliott, *Greek Text,* p. 155, *ta* belongs to the original text of Second Timothy here.

The individual terms of this phrase have not occurred previously in the PE. Indeed, other forms of *hiera* occur in the NT only in 1 Cor 9:13 (= the sacred tasks of the Levitical priesthood) and Col 4:13 (= the city Hierapolis; Lohse, *Col,* p. 174 n. 38, and BDF §115.2 on reading); though there are numerous uses of the term in compounds (particularly, of course, in forms of the city name Jerusalem), it is notable that the PE employ only *hieroprepēs* (Titus 2:3). In the Ap. Frs. this adjective, *hieros,* occurs only in *1 Clem.* 33.4, of the Creator's "sacred and faultless hands"; 43.1 of that which Moses wrote "in the sacred books *(en tois hierais biblois)*"; 45.2 of studying "the sacred writings *(eis tas hieras graphas)*"; and 53.1 of a good understanding of the same.

The profile of LXX usage may furnish the clue for the relative unpopularity of this adjective, for out of at most 122 uses of this term (including those = temple), all but 16 are in First Esdras and the Maccabean corpus. Thus the oldest and most influential strata of the LXX chose not to use this term to render the Hebrew *qdš* etc. (but preferred forms of *hagios;* cf. G. Schrenk, *TDNT* 3.226). The reason was probably that the use of the term in pagan Greek for all the apparatus of idolatry led to a conscious decision to choose a terminology for Jewish religious practice that would clearly set it off from paganism. The precedent was obviously highly influential, but just as evidently, individual authors felt free to depart from it for their own purposes, particularly when they were convinced that the earthly reality being described was in fact one that bordered on the divine order or world, a "place" or time in which the true God was really present and revealing his will (thus, for the Jerusalem sanctuary and its furniture; for feast days; for Scriptures). See Schrenk, *TDNT* 3.226-229, on Philo, Josephus, and First through Fourth Maccabees.

The NT documents and the Ap. Frs. followed the mainline Jewish practice, using *hieros* seldom and, when they did, employing it usually for their Scriptures (the Jewish collection). The only "image" of God is the word of God.

Here in 2 Tim 3:15 that written word is designated as *grammata,* literally "letters," which, in Greek as in English, can stand for "literature" (see the texts cited in Schrenk 1.762, 764) as well as education (i.e. knowing how to read and write [Acts 4:13: *agrammatos*]), which in Jewish circles was to learn to read the Law; thus *T. Levi* 13.2: *didaxate de kai hymeis ta tekna hymōn grammata hina echōsi synesin en pasēi tēi zōēi autōn, anaginōskontes adialeiptōs ton nomon tou theou,* "And do ye also teach your children letters, that they may have understanding all their life, reading unceasingly the law of God" (Charles, *AP* 2.311 [note the directive is to priests] and cf. *T. Reuben* 4.1 where the patriarch exhorts his children to "expend labor . . . on study" [Charles, *AP* 2.298]). See also Spicq, *EP,* p. 791 n. 1, for Philo and Josephus.

It may well have been this context of the education of a youngster that dictated the choice of *grammata* here as the designation for the Scriptures (rather than the far more usual *graphē* that occurs in 3:16 below). Then *hiera* was prefixed to this noun so that it would not be taken of literature in general but the sacred books of Judaism. As was seen above, this usage was Jewish though not Septuagintal. It is instructive to note that imperial decrees (especially in the East) could be called *hiera grammata* (Schrenk, *TDNT* 1.763 and 3.225). Spicq, *EP*, p. 792, notes the epistolary and juridical connotations of the term with abundant citations. In the context here in the PE, the use of books of magic may be significant (Spicq, p. 791 n. 4; *ta Ephesia grammata* would be in striking contrast to *ta hiera grammata* here in the PE).

These are "sacred letters," "which have the power *(ta dynamena)* to make you wise *(se sophisai)* unto salvation *(eis sōtērian)*. . . ." Here the letters are signs that contain and conduct a power that is quite beyond them *qua* visible marks with ink or audible human words. There is a *dynamis* with which they are charged (cf. the *dynamis* of 2 Tim 1:7-8 and 3:5), the divine *dynamis*, the *Spirit* (cf. *theopneustos* in v. 16 *infra*) which "empowers" the Scriptures to make a man wise "for salvation" (contrast the *dynamena* of 2 Tim 3:7; on the other uses of *dynamai* see 1 Tim 5:25; 6:7, 16; and 2 Tim 2:13, which are particularly instructive for grasping what a man can/cannot do, in the mind of this author). A provocative parallel to this passage is the remark of Josephus in *Ant.* 20.264 that the Palestinian Jews "aver that in their opinion only those men have wisdom *(sophian)* who know the Law well *(sophōs)* and who are able *(dynamenois)* to interpret *(hermēneusai)* the power of the sacred letters *(tēn tōn hierōn grammatōn dynamin)*." Here *dynamis* refers to the meaning, i.e. the life and power, within the dead letter, and that meaning is understood as becoming *human action* or life in response to the word (command) properly understood.

Here Second Timothy does not employ the *didask-* terminology (as does the following verse) but states that the Scriptures have the power *se sophisai*, "to make you wise." "To become wise" here is to be taken in the practical sense; the OT shows one what to do and what to avoid in the real order, in one's personal life. It is not quite accurate to say that the OT is here transferred "without a break" (Wilckens, *TDNT* 7.527; cf. Rengstorf, *TDNT* 2.147) into Christian instruction, for it comes with *Paul's* teaching and interpretation and as taken up in Christian faith (cf. the rest of the phrase here). The practical goal *(eis)* of this scriptural wisdom is "salvation" *(sōtērian)*, final, eschatological rescue and redemption. The one other occurrence of *sōtēria* in the PE was at 2 Tim 2:10, where it was observed that the *eis sōtērian* phrase is the more Septuagintal and Hebraic way of stating purpose (see LXX Exod 15:2; Num 6:14; 2 Kgdms 10:11; 1 Chron 19:12; 2 Chron 12:7; etc.).

16. *All the Scripture is inspired by God.* There has probably been no more influential theologoumenon in the PE than this verse in which the author explains still further why the Scriptures have the power that he asserted in the previous sentence. The first reason is grounded in their origin (opting for the passive and attributive interpretation of *theopneustos*); the second, in their manifold practical usefulness for the apostolic ministry. In these practical letters, though the divine origin has in fact pride of place, pastoral usefulness gets the space.

The sentence begins with one of the universal affirmations that are congenial to this author: *pasa graphē,* "all Scripture" or "every Scripture." The term *graphē* occurred in 1 Tim 5:18 with an unmistakable reference to a passage of the Torah and a more problematic one to a saying of Jesus. If that sense of specific passage inheres in *graphē* here, then *pasa graphē* means "any passage of Scripture" (D-C compared Acts 8:35, *apo tēs graphēs tautēs,* cf. 8:32; Acts 1:16 could also be cited, along with Luke 4:21). Yet the anarthrous usage here as well as the evident reference to the previous *ta hiera grammata* inclines one to take *pasa graphē* as meaning "the whole collection of sacred writings." This use of *graphē* referring to the collection does not occur in Luke-Acts, which use the plural *graphai* for this purpose (Luke 4:27, 32, 45; Acts 17:2, 11; 18:24, 28).

Of the fifty NT uses of *graphē,* there are only a dozen Pauline uses outside the PE, and these are concentrated in Romans, First Corinthians, and Galatians. Once in Rom 1:2 Paul qualified *graphai* with *hagiai* (as the PE qualified *grammata* with *hiera*). He normally employs the singular for a specific *locus,* the plural for the collection (whatever its limits). Yet in Gal 3:8, 22, he uses *hē graphē* of the whole Jewish collection of sacred books (G. Schrenk, *TDNT* 1.753-754, and cf. Ellis, *Paul's Use of OT,* p. 21, though n. 13 is misleading). Although there is no possibility outside of 2 Tim 3:16, it is conceivable that here *graphē* means "book," i.e. "every book" of the sacred literature. Schrenk, p. 754, notes the examples of this usage in LXX 2 Esd 6:18; 2 Chron 24:27, as well as *T. Zebulun* 3.4. Spicq, *EP,* p. 787, has observed that article + *pas* + substantive = collective; anarthrous *pas* + substantive = distributive, i.e. "each and every . . . ," and this is particularly verifiable in the PE (cf. with *ergon,* Titus 1:16; 1 Tim 5:10; 2 Tim 2:21; 3:17; 4:18). Though here in 2 Tim 3:16 no particular verse has just been cited, it may be that (see Acts 2:36 and N. Turner, *Grammar,* p. 199) one can take *pasa graphē* as meaning "the whole of Scripture," not "every inspired scripture" (see Moule, *Idiom,* p. 95). Still, as Spicq has observed, most exegetes understand the phrase as "each and every (book of, passage of) Scripture. . . ."

The ultimate meaning converges (cf. Heb 9:19), and the stress of the author on the collectivity or on each of its parts depends on the particular form of aberration that he had in mind; *scil.* persons who rejected on principle the whole OT (Marcionites: gnostics) or persons who rejected one or another book (again presumably on some theological criterion); note the way Tertullian uses the passage to justify Enoch (*De Cultu Feminarum* 1.3.3)! The earlier the date of the PE in the first century, the more chance that the author had in mind the rejection of one or another book of what we call the OT.

If Luke is the author of the PE, it is conceivable that *graphē* refers to one or another part of the OT collection which he knew as threefold (cf. Luke 24:27 with 44 and perhaps also the way in which the controversy with the Sadducees is handled in Luke 20:37, where the Markan mention of "Moses' book" [Mark 12:26: *SFG* §281] which highlights the Sadducean rejection of all beyond the Torah has been transformed into a simple reference to a given passage). B. Reicke, *TDNT* 5.888, also holds for the distributive sense of *pasa graphē* here in Second Timothy (note esp. his Lukan citations).

As early as Theodore of Mopsuestia and Ambrosiaster, exegetes were proposing that *theopneustos* could be understood as an epithet modifying *graphē* and this phrase would then be understood with an unexpressed *esti,* whereas *kai* would mean "also." Thus the sentence would mean "Every book of Scripture, inspired by God, [is] also useful. . . ." On the other hand, not a few commentators have opted for *theopneustos* as an attribute (Schweizer, *TNDT* 6.454) with *esti* understood as preceding while *kai* would have its conjunctive sense; thus "Every book of Scripture [is] inspired by God and useful etc." Spicq, *EP,* pp. 794-795, has opted for the former, marshaling the arguments pro and con with erudition and clarity while noting that the question is one of stress rather than of different concepts. Perhaps the omission of *esti* was not an oversight but was deliberate. In that case the author was of set purpose leaving open what his commentators have sought to close. The question keeps recurring because the text has been written without *esti.* Making the insertion is like unrolling a watch spring; once the spring has been released, it snaps back because it was made that way. But in that case the twofold emphasis of the written text must be preserved in its translation, and both explanations belong to the commentary. Some have proposed that *graphē* here is so solemn and religious a term that it would be pointless or pleonastic to say *graphē esti theopneustos* (cf. D-C; Barrett). Yet that is to read the term anachronistically. *Graphē* was not, by the first century C.E., such a firmly fixed designation for the sacred books as a whole (cf. the examples noted above and see also 1 Tim 5:18). There is no denying the parallels between the preceding *ta hiera grammata* and the *graphē theopneustos* here, yet *hiera* preceded *grammata* and was obviously adjectival. Here that *hiera* is being further explained by a neologism that in turn would make a preceding *esti* quite in order.

But precisely what does *theopneustos* mean? Some have proposed that it be interpreted "actively," i.e. of the Scripture as "breathing God" or "blowing God's Spirit" into men. Grammatically that interpretation is possible with this term, as it surely is the case with some other compounds (cf. Theophilus: *theosystatos, theosyedetos, ap.* Spicq, *EP,* p. 793 n. 2). Yet there is no evidence that this term was actually thus understood, even though the other *theo-* compounds in the NT usually understand *theo-* as the direct object of the latter, verbal element in the compound, except for *theodidaktos* in 1 Thess 4:9 (cf. John 6:45). Yet that latter compound is by far the closest conceptual parallel in the NT to this verse of the PE. With a neologism such as *theopneustos* one may again note that the author's intention may have been to leave the question open, or, better, to affirm both meanings, since the Scripture has its value and usefulness because it comes from God ("*cujus Deus auctor,*" as Ambrosiaster notes), and it brings God (his Spirit; his will) into the believer's mind and personal life. Spicq, *EP,* p. 793 n. 2, aptly speaks of the Scripture, thus understood, as a sacrament, a visible sign, divinely instituted to bring the grace of God into the believer's life. It is its relation to the will of Christ that differentiates it from "the seven sacraments" of the Church.

The formation of *theopneustos* from the verb *pneō* (to breathe on, to blow on) is perhaps patterned on the formation of *pneuma* from the same verb. The basic image of breath (vitality)/wind (unseen power; cf. the uses of *pnoē,* [*ek-*], and [*em-*] *pneō,* esp. in Luke-Acts: *TDNT* 6.452-453) has led to the formation of this verbal adjective which aims at describing the relation between the invisible God and the visible Scripture, precisely as a material body of literature. With this term the PE made their most original and creative contribution to Christian theology. The Scripture has its power (cf. *dynamena* in v. 15) because of the Spirit/breath that produced it and presumably continues to vivify it (cf. the way in which the *charisma* of God and "Spirit of power" are related to Timothy in 2 Tim 1:6-7). The teaching of the PE on the relation of *pneuma* to the Scripture is seen within the same problematic that governed the relation of the Spirit and baptism and ordination.

Thus the author of the PE unites "the Spirit and the letter" in a way that transcends the Pauline antithesis of the pair. The author's sacramental doctrine is the key for understanding his doctrine on Scripture. Oepke, *TDNT* 5.868, mistakes the sacramental doctrine for "the beginning of establishment in the world."

Of course literature does not drop out of the heavens. Letters are in the most profound sense human creations: visible, palpable signs that people are (for one reason or another) out of reach of the senses (whether for the moment or forever). Thus to have said that the Scripture is "enspirited by God" is to have implicitly said that men have been thus "enspirited," and in fact it is to that aspect of the process that 2 Pet 1:21 addresses itself. Schweizer, *TDNT* 6.345 n. 49, noted that the pagan world spoke of inspired men but not inspired writings.

*and useful for instruction, for censuring, for straightening people out, for giving training in upright conduct.* The Scripture, precisely because it is sacred (cf. *hiera* above) and because that holiness derives from its divine origin *(theopneustos),* is also (cf. *kai* and Spicq, *EP,* p. 795) "useful *(ōphelimos)* for instruction *(pros didaskalian),* for censuring *(pros elegmon),* for straightening people out *(pros epanorthōsin),* for giving training in upright conduct *(pros paideian tēn en dikaiosynēi)*. . . ." An asyndetic four-member list, with its alliteratively repeated *pros,* describes the usefulness of Scripture under four headings in which the causal/final nuances of *pros* (Spicq, p. 796 n. 1) color the sense of every mounting step in the catalogue, whose last member predictably expands throughout the following verse.

The term *useful* might also be rendered as "efficacious" (Spicq, *EP*, p. 796 n. 1) or "effective" since here, as in its previous uses, it describes that which is valuable not for its own sake but for the service it gives to men and to God. Note that the dative was used to describe usefulness to persons in Titus 3:8; here and in 1 Tim 4:8 *pros* is used for impersonal realities or processes.

Scripture is "useful" in the first place "for teaching." Note how the use here corroborates the proposal that in the PE this term always refers to the Pauline way of instructing about and through the OT. The Pauline *didaskalia* is the first and immediate complement of "every book of Scripture," which is here seen as efficacious in that apostolic doctrinal formation. The *ōphelimos* here for Pauline teaching about the OT can be contrasted with the *anōpheleis* of the controversies and battles about the OT law in Titus 3:9.

The next two phrases, *pros elegmon* and *pros epanorthōsin,* use terms not documented elsewhere in the NT or in the Ap. Frs. The term *elegmos,* "censuring," is cognate with the *elegchein* of Titus 1:9, 13; 2:15; 1 Tim 5:20; and 2 Tim 4:2 *infra* (where the terminology and concepts of this passage are applied personally to Timothy's ministry), and one could infer that the setting right and pointing to repentance implied by this rebuke/correction/proof are to proceed from the OT Scripture itself, as here stated in principle.

The sequence of phrases here in Second Timothy is not random, and thus the restoration/correction that follows upon proof/reproof is in its turn ordered "to training in upright conduct." All three phrases use terms that combine suggestions of that which is displeasing and harsh with that which is good and useful. Here the correction and restoration imply that which has fallen into ruins and which must with effort be put together again.

Thus when the author continues to describe the pastoral usefulness of the whole of Scripture, in his final expansive phrase, he begins *pros paideian tēn en dikaiosynēi. . . .* There is only one occurrence of the noun in the Pentateuch — Deut 11:2 (cf. 8:5 for the verb, as well as 4:36; 21:18; 22:18; 32:10) — but an exceedingly significant one, for the concrete incidents in which Yahweh dealt with opposition from the Egyptians and from Israel are proposed as a *paideia* that the children of the desert generation had not witnessed (cf. LXX Hos 5:2 where Yahweh has become the *paideutēs,* "trainer," of Israel).

Bertram, *TDNT* 5.612 n. 89, has stressed the basic familial model behind the concepts of education in the ancient world. In the Hebrew tradition the fathers of the family and the Law itself are the means ultimately that the God of Israel uses to teach and discipline *his* family. In this Israelite model the state had no educational function; even that of the priesthood was stringently limited; it was the head of the household who had the obligation to educate his children in the Law. This model lies behind the use of *paideia kai nouthesia Kyriou,* "discipline and training of the Lord," that the father must administer to his children in Eph 6:4.

The *Kyrios* is the educator of believers as Yahweh was of Israel, and he uses the head/father of the Christian family as his instrument or agent for this task (cf. Heb 12:9). As Bertram has observed (5.624), what the Jewish Christian tradition, taken up by Ephesians, considered good for the family, the PE consider as a suitable *paideia* for the community of believers that is conceived of as a household in this correspondence. In this family the OT Scripture is still the privileged instrument, now of the *Kyrios* and his apostolic ministry (and thus not contradictory to Gal 3:24).

The usefulness of the OT for discipline is now specified with *tēn en dikaiosynēi,* a term met above and analyzed in Titus 3:5 (with *en* in the *pistos logos)* and 1 Tim 6:11 (the list that opens the ordination parenesis). Here "in righteousness" means "in upright conduct" (cf. *Barn.* 4.11, 13, and Schrenk, *TDNT* 2.210), the "actualization" of God's free gift of righteousness in the personal history of each believer (cf. Bertram, *TDNT* 5.624). The Scripture is useful for training in good conduct because its commands and its examples are both an encouragement and a warning about the life one chooses to lead after baptism.

17. *so that the man of God may be complete, that is, completely equipped for every excellent deed.* The preceding sentence continues, expanding the final notice of the preceding list, and probably referring to the whole fourfold usefulness, when it concludes with a final clause of purpose (cf. E. Stauffer, *TDNT* 3.323-333, and note p. 328 n. 52), *hina artios ēi ho tou theou anthrōpos . . . ,* "so that the man of God may be complete (or fit). . . ." "The man of God" is the ordained apostolic minister in general (cf. D-C, "the leader of the congregation," and Spicq) and Timothy in particular (as in 1 Tim 6:11, where that phrase is analyzed; J. Jeremias, *TDNT* 1.364, glosses it as referring to the Christian in the generic sense, as does G. Delling, *TDNT* 1.475-476).

It is notable that already in Homer (*Iliad* 14.92; *Odyssey* 8.240) the term *artios* is employed of "speaking to the purpose *(artia bazein),*" and that could be exactly the sense here, *scil.* the Scripture is useful because it enables that man of God to match his words to the needs of people, it enables him to speak to the purpose for which he was ordained, it fits him exactly for his ministry of teaching, reproof, correction, and discipline. Thus the clause here could be translated, "so that the man of God may be adapted ('complete!') equipped for every good work *(pros pan ergon agathon exērtismenos).*"

The final phrase, of course, explains and defines the unusual *artios* by the cognate perfect passive participle from *exartizō,* which does occur on one other occasion in the NT, in Acts 21:5, of finishing out the days of a stay in Tyre. There Haenchen, *Acts,* p. 600 n. 9, notes that the verb belongs to the studied elegance that Luke on occasion brought into his narrative, and that may be the case here in 2 Tim 3:17 as well, where the dense theologoumenon of the preceding two verses ends with this elegant verbal play on *artios-exērtimenos.* Cf. the *katartisei* of 1 Pet 5:10.

That equipment in its turn is ordered "to *(pros)* every excellent deed," where *pros* is to be taken as in the preceding list. There the stress lay not on the minister's receiving teaching, reproof, etc. (though this is obviously presupposed), but on his using the Scripture to give these things to others. Here the Scripture has completely equipped him for guiding men similarly to every good work.

4:1. *As God the Father looks on, and Christ Jesus who is going to judge the living and dead, I adjure you, Timothy, while bearing witness to his revelation and his kingdom.* With this long sentence (extending through v. 4) and its return to the first person singular in *diamartyromai,* one notes first of all that the whole opening phrase, literally "I charge, in the presence of God and of Christ Jesus . . . ," occurred word for word in 1 Tim 5:21 (see commentary above and other references there; cf. 2 Tim 2:14 as well). For the author of the PE it has formulaic character (D-C). If its position in the development of 1 Tim 5:17-25 is a clue as to how the phrase is to be taken here, it is transitional within a paragraph but does not mark the opening of a new subject. The same could be said for the return to the first person singular, which also alternated with the second singular in 2 Tim 3:10-11 above. The sentence here does not mark a new paragraph so much as a different tack with the same thought that has been developing since the second *sy de* of 3:14 *supra.* The next new paragraph actually begins with the third *sy de* of 4:5 *infra.*

Spicq has correlated this solemn opening, in its admonition/protestation, with the legal procedure for choosing successors in the Greek world. The description of Christ as the coming judge of this world and the next has probably been taken from a liturgical setting, perhaps a baptismal confession already fixed in the first Christian generation. If so, the phrase may have originated in the proclamation to unbelievers, even in the earliest Palestinian kerygma (cf. Acts 10:42, which also uses *diamartyrasthai;* also Wilcox, *Semitisms,* p. 169; Dalton, *CPS,* pp. 263-266), taken up in the baptismal rite where it would highlight the eventual judgment upon the life and acts of the one whom Christ had touched in the apostolic word and sacraments (cf. 2 Cor 5:10).

The opening formula, repeated from 1 Tim 5:21, and the further, appended citation from a liturgical source are perhaps the reason for the apparently abrupt change to the correlative *kai . . . kai* phrases in the accusative. So harsh was the transition that the original reading of S. A. C. D. G. 33. et al. was changed to *kata tēn epiphaneian autou kai tēn basileian auton* (S$^c$. D$^c$. K. L. P. etc.; B. Metzger, *TCGNT*, p. 649; J. K. Elliott, *Greek Text*, pp. 157-158). The apparent dependence of these nouns on *krinein* may have tempted the scribes to cut the Gordian knot and write *kata* for the former *kai* and thus "clarify" the relation of the following nouns to *krinein* or to *diamartyromai* (cf. J. K. Elliott, *Greek Text*, p. 158). BDF §442.16 propose interpreting the second *kai*, joining "his revelation" with "his kingdom," as a hendiadys with *kai* = "through" or "in." The usage would be quite in the Lukan tradition; cf. Luke 2:47; 21:15; Acts 1:25; 14:17; 23:6, as well as Titus 2:13 (also with *epiphaneia*).

However, to have said that the second *kai* means "in" or "through" does not make it any more likely that the first one has that meaning. Indeed, that would involve an intolerably harsh hendiadys followed by another hendiadys. Actually the formulaic character of the words from *diamartyromai* through *nekrous* makes the shift into the simple accusative somewhat less harsh, and of course *diamartyromai* can take a noun in the accusative as its object, as it does in the LXX not only in forms of the stock phrase "I call heaven and earth to witness today . . ." (Deut 4:26; 8:19; 30:19; 31:28; and Jth 7:28) but in Deut 32:46, where it refers to the words *(logous)* spoken by Moses; in Ezek 16:2; 20:4 to *anomias;* etc. Even more striking, however, is the usage of Luke, for this verb not only takes an accusative in Acts 8:25 (the word [*ton logon*] could be the object of *lalēsantes* alone); 20:21 *(tēn . . . metanoian)*, 24 *(to euaggelion);* 23:11 (*ta peri emou* = Jesus), but in 28:23 one reads of Paul *diamartyromenos tēn basileian tou theou*, "testifying to the kingdom of God." The last example is quite parallel to 2 Tim 4:1, as again the Lukan Paul speaks out in distinction from the formulaic expressions that have preceded. Thus, as we understand it, *diamartyromai enōpion* . . . has first of all its sense in the formula cited, but it takes on its typically Lukan sense as his language and phraseology surface in the hendiadys *kai tēn epiphaneian autou kai tēn basileian autou.* Thus one ought to translate *diamartyromai* initially as "I admonish . . ." and then repeat "I bear witness to both his revelation and his kingdom."

Here the *epiphaneian autou* "coincides with" *basileian autou* (K. L. Schmidt, *TDNT* 1.583). Both "the epiphany" and "the kingdom" are emphatically those of the Christ coming in judgment. This is the first of two uses of *basileia* in the PE. The qualification of the kingdom as *epouranion* occurs only in 2 Tim 4:18 in the NT; the adjective occurs only here in the PE but ten times otherwise in the Paulines (in 1 Cor 15:40 [*bis*], 48-49; Eph 1:3, 20; 2:6; 3:10; 6:12; Phil 2:10). There are six uses in Hebrews and one in John 3:12. H. Traub, *TDNT* 5.538-542, has noted that the prefixed *ep-* in this adjective means "at," and so "in heaven," and was thus used not only of the gods who dwell "in heaven" from Homeric Greek onward but also of those things that belong to the divine order (as early Pindar, Fragmente 132.3). The spatial or local paradigm is never far from the text when the term is employed. The adjective occurs at most six times in the LXX and once in Theod. Dan 4:23 (A but not B).

The term *basileia* will be modified by *epouranios* at 4:18 below, where it is also the kingdom of the risen *Kyrios.* The qualification of the kingdom as *epouranion* occurs only in 2 Tim 4:18 in the NT. Apart from LXX Ps 67:14 (scarcely the most pellucid verse in the Psalter), all the occurrences are in the Maccabean literature (2 Macc 3:39 [of God's dwelling]; 3 Macc 6:28 [of "the almighty, living, heavenly God"]; 7:6 [of "the heavenly God"]; and 4 Macc 4:11 [*s.v.l.* of the heavenly host]; 11:3 [*s.v.l.* of heavenly justice]; cf. Traub, p. 539).

In the Ap. Frs. *1 Clem.* 61.2, the prayer addresses God as "heavenly master, king of the ages *(despota epouranie, basileu tōn aiōnōn)*" where the conjunction with *basileus* reminds one of the PE. The final doxology of *2 Clem.* 20.5 describes Jesus "the Savior" as the one who "manifested *(ephanerōsen)* to us the truth and the life of heaven *(tēn epouranion zōēn).*" Ignatius employs the term five times, always in the plural: *Eph.* 13.2 (of wars in heaven and on earth); *Trall.* 5.1-2 (of the content of his own letters that he can comprehend); 9.1 (of the inhabitants of heaven); and *Smyrn.* 6.1 (of judgment for even heavenly beings). Polycarp, *Phil.* 2.1, also uses the word in the plural for "heavenly beings," as contrasted with "earthly *(epigeia).*" *Martyrdom of Polycarp* 14.3, in its great prayer, addresses Jesus as "the everlasting and heavenly *(aiōniou kai epouraniou)* high priest." In 20.2 *(s.v.l.)* and in Epilogue 6 there is reference to believers being brought/gathered "into his heavenly kingdom," and a doxology follows immediately (cf. 22.3 and *Diognetus* 10.2 for the *ouranios basileia/en ouranōi basileia*).

It seems quite evident that the usage of 2 Tim 4:18 is a more Hellenistic way of expressing "the kingdom of heaven *(hē basileia tōn ouranōn)*" that occurs so often in that highly Semitic form in Matthew in contrast to the usage of Mark and Luke-Acts (and the rest of the NT), which always speak of "the kingdom of God *(hē basileia tou theou).*" See K. L. Schmidt *TDNT* 1.582 (as above), on the use of attributes with *basileia.* Yet Traub's comment, *TDNT* 5.541, ought to be noted too, that this adjective adds the note of consummation and perfection, implying that the kingdom is more than Jesus' bringing God's rule into this world but is a reality that exists "with him in heaven," a reality into which God introduces men.

To this eschatological kingdom Paul here in 2 Tim 4:1 bears witness, in the presence of the Father and the Son. The term *kingdom* itself, as was noted above, has only 2 uses in the PE; indeed, there are only a dozen other uses in the Paulines, with none at all in Second Corinthians, Philippians, or Philemon, in striking contrast with the 148 other NT uses of *basileia.*

Moreover, the Ap. Frs. use *basileia* with some frequency: thus *1 Clem.* 42.3 (of God); 50.3 (of Christ); 61.1 (of earthly rulers); *2 Clem.* 5.5 (of the future);

9.6 (of the future and of God); 11.7 (of the future and of God); 12.1 (of the future and of God); 12.2 (of Christ and future); 12.6 (of the Father). Ignatius speaks in *Eph.* 16.1 of the future "kingdom of God" (cf. *Phld.* 3.3) and in 19.3 of "the old kingdom" (of superstition and magic).

In Polycarp, *Phil.* 2.3, the beatitudes on "the kingdom of God" are cited, and in 5.3 Polycarp also speaks in Pauline terms of those who will not inherit the kingdom of God. Hermas uses *basileia* 13 times, always with *tou theou.* In addition to the references of *Martyrdom of Polycarp* cited above, see 22.1, "in the kingdom of Jesus Christ." The *Didache* always speaks of "your [i.e. God's] kingdom" (8.2; 9.4; 10.5). For Barnabas, see 4.4 (pl.); 4.13 (of the Lord); 7.11; 8.5 (on the cross); 8.6; 21.1 (future, of God).

The PE used the cognates *basileus* and *basileuein* in 1 Tim 1:17; 6:15 of God and in 1 Tim 2:2 of secular rulers. See Kleinknecht, von Rad, Kuhn, and Schmidt for the *"basileus k.t.l."* study in *TDNT* 1.564-593. Schmidt has noted the rather rare LXX uses of the *basileia theou,* as in Wis 6:4 *(autou)* and particularly 4 Macc 2:23, where the divine law makes possible a kingdom of prudence, justice, goodness, and fortitude. This ethicizing of the concept of God's kingdom was carried out systematically in Philo, whose stylistic habit of employing *basileia* in hendiadyses is comparable with the usage here in 2 Tim 4:1 (Schmidt, pp. 574-575, for citations), though only once does he ever write of a kingdom to come (*Mos.* 1.290, interpreting LXX Num 24:7, the Balaam oracle). Josephus, probably deliberately (Schmidt, p. 576), never uses the expression "the kingdom of God" and only once alludes to God's *basileia* (*Ant.* 6.60, and then to its being rejected by Israel, as he retells the Samuel story).

For the NT teaching on the highly complex concept of the kingdom, see Schmidt's article (which aptly notes on pp. 580-581 that one has to contend not only with the kingdoms of men [cf. Luke 4:5 = Matt 4:8] but also with the kingdom of Satan [Luke 11:18 = Matt 12:26; cf. the devil's *exousia* in Luke 4:6]). See also the work of Schnackenburg, *God's Rule.* He treats the Qumran texts on the kingdom of God on pp. 50-54, and on p. 51 he notes particularly the way in which "heaven," inhabited by God's saints and angels, "appears to be God's particular dominion" (1QM 12.1-2: Dupont-Sommer, *EWQ*, p. 187). Of 2 Tim 4:1, Schnackenburg notes, pp. 297-298, that kingdom of God and kingdom of Christ are quite interchangeable, that the present rule of Christ in power can be called God's rule (cf. 1 Cor 4:20), and that the kingdom to come (as here in Second Timothy) "can also be called the kingdom of Christ." In commenting on 1 Tim 4:18, Schnackenburg notes, pp. 318-319, that there *epouranios* is used appropriately (for all its Hellenistic resonances) of the kingdom's "true and appropriate place" (cf. the usage in Ephesians noted above), which stands in dramatic contrast to the apostle's threatened existence. The royal rule of God that has begun in human history ends in "a special sphere, where it is manifest in glory," and for that heavenly order "spatial images" are in order. That is God's kingdom, as what went before it is his rule. In fact, as Wis 10:10 uses the phrase "kingdom of God," it is precisely to refer to the world at the top of Jacob's ladder, God's special sphere and order.

The hendiadys here, "both his manifestation and his kingdom," which has already been noted as not only Philonic but Lukan, suggests taking the whole phrase as "manifest kingdom" or "royal epiphany," the former stressing the spatial image, the latter, the personal character of the "kingdom" to which the apostle bears witness.

2. *herald the message; stand on the alert, when convenient, when inconvenient; refute; reprove; encourage — with the utmost patience in the task of teaching.* With the solemn introduction of the preceding verse, the drumroll of five imperatives in this verse comes as no surprise. The form of the list is not cut fully on the patterns to which the reader of the PE has been accustomed; thus the members do not gradually increase in length, and alliteration and assonance are minimal. Yet there is a recurring use of *-on* endings, with the paired *-kairos;* the last phrase does expansively dilate the final concept; the asyndetic construction gives urgency and energy to the imperatives (cf. *infra* on parenetic style). The first of the "five commandments" for "the man of God" is "proclaim the word." Here Paul's "child" and heir is to take up his apostolic task, to proclaim the gospel word to those who have not yet believed (G. Friedrich, *TDNT* 2.719-720, 737, and 3.711, would also include congregations of believers).

In commenting on the second imperatival phrase, both D-C and Spicq note that the assembling of verbs in a parenetic line that has no inner, conceptual coherence is typical of the hortatory genre, and they cite 1 Pet 5:10 (note the variant readings there) as well as Plutarch, *Lib. educ.* 16, with its advice to fathers "to be vigilant and alert and to bring young men to reason by instruction, by threats, by entreaties, by pointing out examples. . . ."

The verb *ephistēmi* is used otherwise in the NT of an "eschatological vigilance" in view of the sudden, unanticipated return of the Lord (cf. 1 Thess 5:3 and Luke 21:34, both with *aiphnidios*), as well as the sudden advent of an angel (Luke 2:9; cf. 24:4; Acts 12:7) or of the Lord in a dream (Acts 23:11) or of a human messenger from God (thus Ananias in Acts 22:13) or from other men (Acts 10:17; 11:11). In Luke 2:38; 10:40 the verb describes the way an Anna or a Martha comes to Jesus, and in Luke 4:39 the way in which Jesus himself is present to Simon's sick mother-in-law. In Luke 20:1; Acts 4:1; 17:5 the manner in which the enemies of Jesus and his apostles come upon them is described with this term; and in Acts 6:12; 22:20 the same verb describes the manner in which Stephen's enemies (including Paul) closed in. In Acts 23:27 the letter of Claudius Lysias says that he and his troops "came upon" Paul in the midst of a murderous mob. In some ways the usage of Acts 28:2 of a wintry Malta rainstorm settling in on the shipwrecked Paul and his companions illustrates the sense of the term most vividly (cf. Haenchen, *Acts*, p. 713).

Spicq has noted the link of *eukairia* with rhetorical terminology. Delling has noted that as the classical sense of *kairos* for "a favorable time" faded, *eu-* was prefixed to the term in order to restore that nuance or connotation. Delling has also called attention to the fact that "timely/untimely" may refer not only to those who hear the preaching but also to the convenience/inconvenience of the preacher himself. Plato, in *Phaedrus* 272a, in a context of adapting speech to the varied psyches of men, speaks of the necessity of distinguishing the times that are favorable for speech from those that are not *(tēn eukairian te kai akairian diagnonti)*. In fact, the whole paragraph is relevant to this counsel of the PE and illustrates Spicq's observation that the *eukairōs/akairōs* terminology has special links with the rhetorical arts.

With the third imperative, *elegxon*, the *pros elegmon* of 3:16 above is taken up and applied to the "complete" minister there and is addressed specifically to Timothy (cf. the way in which the generic ordination address of 1 Tim 6:11-16, which also begins with *sy de*, is directed individually to Timothy). Note with F. Büchsel, *TDNT* 2.474, that it is precisely as leader of the congregation of believers that Timothy is "to reveal to someone his sin and to summon him to repentance." That the proof/reproof here pertains to the moral order is practically certain in view of the profound moral concern of the PE; this interpretation, however, would not exclude extirpating non-Christian opinions and intellectual positions that encouraged or grounded un-Christian conduct. The *pasa graphē* of 3:16 above is of course the armory from which Timothy is to draw his proofs and reproofs, *à la mode paulienne.*

About the fourth imperative E. Stauffer, *TDNT* 2.623-627, has observed that in the LXX it is "a technical term for the powerful divine word of rebuke and threat" (p. 624; cf. Zechariah *supra* and 3 Macc 2:24). Here in the PE, however, Sir 11:7 is a notable parallel with "Do not find fault before you investigate; first consider and then reprove *(noēson prōton kai tote epitima)*" (cf. also the rebukes in Gen 37:10 and Ruth 2:16). It is not accidental that the rebuke is called forth by conduct and activity (even the sea in LXX Ps 105:9, insofar as it offers an obstacle to the march of Israel to freedom), and the link with the devil, where *diabolos,* precisely as opponent, ought to be noted (Stauffer, pp. 624-625).

In the synoptics, as Stauffer, *TDNT* 2.625-626, has noted, it is God and Jesus, precisely as Lord, who rebuke demons (cf. Luke 4:35, 41; 9:42) and men. When men, even disciples, administer rebuke on their own initiative and according to their own lights as to what is fitting, they are almost always rebuked by Jesus in turn (cf. Luke 9:55; 18:15; 19:39). Even illness and storm are subject to the rebuke of Jesus (Luke 4:39; 8:24). The only rebuke that the disciples are to give is that to a sinning brother: "if your brother sins, rebuke him; and, if he repents, forgive him . . ." (Luke 17:3), and that must be the ground for the injunction here in the PE where the leader in the congregation, "the man of God," Timothy, must rebuke in the name of the Lord and as God rebukes. Here again the importance of *pasa graphē* comes into sharp focus. The rebuke is to come through a man indeed, but out of the word of God and with the authority of the God who authored that Word.

The fifth and final imperative of this list, *parakaleson,* was seen above of the parenetic activity of Paul (1 Tim 1:3; 2:1), of Timothy (1 Tim 5:1; 6:2), of Titus (Titus 2:6, 15), and of the (*presbyter*-bishop [Titus 1:9]). Cf. commentary *in loc.* Here one ought to note that in S*. F. G. 69.462 and various versions and patristic citations, *parakaleson* precedes *epitimēson.* Almost certainly the variant is due to understanding the phrase *en pasēi makrothymiai kai didachēi* with the immediately preceding verb rather than the whole series. In that case, the phrase would best modify *epitimēson,* here used absolutely for the only time in the NT, and needing some such qualification as this phrase gives, to forestall its being taken of an arrogant correction given on simply human initiative. But if this is the case, then the reading of A etc. is the more difficult and explains the variations.

The closing, expansive phrase, *en pasēi makrothymiai kai didachēi,* could be taken simply with the preceding *parakaleson* (*epitimēson, s.v.l.* S* etc.) or with the whole series of imperatives that preceded. The latter option seems more satisfactory — the whole activity of the apostolic ministry is to be characterized "by all patience and instruction." Again the phrase is a hendiadys that could be rendered as "patient instruction" or "a teacher's patience." The terminology recalls not only the *didaskalia-makrothymia* of Paul in the opening *sy de* paragraph of this whole section (3:10), but also the use of the individual terms in 1 Tim 1:16 (see Comment *in loc.* of Christ's patience with Paul and Titus 1:9 [*didachē:* note how the terminology of Titus 1:9 and of these verses coincides]). One recalls the description of a medieval archbishop of Canterbury hearing out with endless patience stubborn rustics, cosseting their irrational heterodoxies.

3. *For there will come a time when they will not put up with this wholesome instruction.* For the third time in the PE (above, 1 Tim 4:1; 2 Tim 3:1) the author turns to a realized future (cf. *TDNT* 4.782 n. 117) to ground *(gar)* his directives. Here the *estai gar kairos hote* . . . plays on the sound and the root meaning of the preceding *eukairōs akairōs,* and the noun *kairos* here designates a predicted season or a decisive point whose content is characterized by the following negative and positive temporal clauses (G. Delling, *TDNT* 3.461-462, and cf. the *kairoi chalepoi* of 2 Tim 3:1 *supra*). The five previous uses of *kairos* in the PE have all been plural; now here and in 2 Tim 4:6 the noun is in the singular and in each instance designates a time that (by human standards) is a bad

time, a time of apostasy, a time of death. All *kairoi,* however, are under the providential direction of God and his Spirit, all are foreseen and fixed points in his plan (cf. Delling, p. 459). Thus the thorn of pessimism has been drawn and the author retains a basic equanimity in the midst of straitened circumstances.

The predicted season that has arrived is one "when (*hote* [cf. Titus 3:4, and with the future, Luke 17:22]) they will not put up with *(ouk anexontai)* this wholesome instruction *(tēs hygiainousēs didaskalias).*" The contrast with "itching as to the ear" brings out the nuance of "healthful" quite clearly. Then that wholesome instruction will get no welcome: "they will not put up with it." See H. Schlier, *TDNT* 1.359. This verb, which occurs fourteen times otherwise in the NT, twice in Luke-Acts (Luke 9:41; cf. 10:12, 14; and Acts 18:14) and nine times in the Paulines outside of the PE, is placed on Jesus' lips in Luke 9:41 (= Mark 9:19; Matt 17:17): "How long am I to . . . bear with you," and on the lips of Gallio in Acts 18:14 as he says, ". . . I should have reason to bear with you, O Jews."

Of the Pauline usages, that of 2 Cor 11:4, describing how that congregation "submits readily enough *(kalōs anechesthe)*" to "another gospel *(euaggelion heteron),*" is strikingly close to this passage in the PE. Hebrews 13:22 is the only other close parallel in the NT with its "I appeal to you, brethren, bear with my word of exhortation *(anechesthe tou logou tēs paraklēseōs),*" where the object is also in the genitive as that which caused the emotion (BDF §176.1); usually, as in the LXX, it is the person that is in the genitive and a thing that is in the accusative. Menander, *Dysc.* 60: Handley, p. 81, also illustrates this structure in a sentence where a string of verbs occurs (cf. also lines 547-550) in Chaereas's opening description of himself as matchmaker: "I go right out and grab the girl to haul her off to him; I get drunk, I burn down her door, I don't listen to reason [Casson, *Ancient Comedy,* p. 72] *(euthys harpasas pherō/methyō katakaō logon holōs ouk anechomai).*" Yet in the sixteen LXX uses of *anechein,* the genitive of things occurs also (2 Macc 9:12). LXX Job 6:26, *oude gar hymōn phthegma rhēmatos anexomai,* "For I shall not endure the utterance of your word," is the closest LXX parallel to this passage of the PE. As many as eight different Hebrew roots are translated by LXX *anechein.*

In the Ap. Frs., *1 Clem.* 49.5 uses this verb to say, "Love bears all things," and Ign. *Pol.* 1.2 writes, "Bear with all *(pantōn anechou)* in love as I know you do." It is the reproach of God in LXX Isa 1:13, "I cannot bear your sabbaths . . . ," that *Barn.* 2.5; 15.8 cites, with some variants, though one notes the accusative for the direct objects, which is also the case in Hermas, *Man.* 4.2.1, *oliga mou rhēmata eti anaschou,* "Yet bear with a few words of mine" (contrast *Man.* 4.4.1 with its genitive of person).

*Instead, they will load themselves with teachers who answer their craving to get relief for their itchy ears.* The allergy to sound teaching is then contrasted strongly *(alla)* with a simultaneous movement: "according to their own lusts they will amass for themselves *(heautois episōreusousin)* — itching as to the ear *(knēthomenoi tēn akoēn)* — teachers." The opening *kata tas idias epithymias* (cf. above on Titus 2:12; 3:3 [AB *Titus*]; and 1 Tim 6:9; 2 Tim 2:22; 3:6) refers to the whole battery of disordered desires that must be rationalized and that accordingly lead to frenetic gathering of "teachers *(didaskalous),*" which here means practically "false teachers" and has an ironic glint; cf. *gurus* (K. Rengstorf, *TDNT* 2.152; p. 158 n. 66). One notes that in 1 Tim 4:1 it was the *teachings* that were false; here it is the *teachers.* For *kata* with *tas (idias) (heautōn) epithymias (autōn),* see Eph 4:22; Jude 16, 18; and 2 Pet 3:3.

The subject of the verbs in both of these clauses is left unexpressed and indefinite. They are stigmatized, however, as having an itch in the ear, *knēthomenoi tēn akoēn.* These persons with itching ears "will load *(episōreusousin)* themselves with teachers." This compound form of *sōreuō* occurs only here in the NT. The LXX does not use it but Sym. Job 14:17; Cant 2:4 do. In the Ap. Frs. it is found only in *Barn.* 4.6 describing those who pile up their sins by admitting that Jews and Christians have the same covenant bond. Here in the PE, as F. Lang, *TDNT* 7.1096 n. 12, has noted, the prefix *epi-* adds emphasis to the ironic use of the verb *sōreuō,* which was commented on at 2 Tim 3:6 (pp. 2027-2028). Spicq cites Epictetus 1.10.5, of a vacillating Roman official who "has piled up *(episesōreuken)* one property after another."

4. *Furthermore, as they turn a deaf ear to the truth, they will slip off after tales.* The "positive" activity of the preceding verse is now complemented *(kai)* with compound *men . . . de* clauses that sharply (note the asyndeton) correlate and contrast the way in which these persons "will on the one hand turn their ear *(tēn akoēn apostrepsousin)* from the truth *(apo men tēs alētheias)* but on the other hand they will turn to myths *(epi de tous mythous ektrapēsontai).*" G. Stählin, *TDNT* 4.765, 786-788, has noted that the myths being scored here must have made some sensual appeal, in the mind of the author of the PE at any rate; they are in complete contrast to the *alētheia* in this verse and wholesome instruction in the previous; note the similar double contrast with *logois tēs pisteōs* and *kalē didaskalia* in 1 Tim 4:6-7.

## IV.C.3. PAUL'S DEATH (4:5-8)

*4 [5]You, however, Timothy,*

> *keep calm, in every sense;*
> *accept being wronged;*
> *do the work of one who announces the gospel;*
> *carry out fully the ministry that is yours.*

[6]*For now my own blood is to spill as a wine-offering. The time set for my embarkation has come.* [7]*I have contended in the fine contest. I have run the whole track. I have kept faith.* [8]*Whatever happens, there lies in store for me the crown of the upright life with which the upright judge, the Lord, will recompense me on that Day — and not only me but all who have their hearts set on his revelation.*

## ♦ NOTES

4:5 *You, however, Timothy, keep calm, in every sense.* Lit. "You, however, be self-possessed *(nēphe)* in all things/under all circumstances *(en pasin).*" Though the cognate adjective *nēphalios,* "temperate," occurred in Titus 2:2; 1 Tim 3:2, 11 (of older men, the bishop, the deaconesses; otherwise the term is undocumented in biblical Greek or the Ap. Frs.), and the cognate *ananēphein* in 2 Tim 2:26, this is the only use of this verb in the PE, though in the Paulines it is found in 1 Thess 5:6, 8. The only other NT uses are in 1 Pet 1:13; 4:7; 5:8. O. Bauernfeind, *TDNT* 4.939 nn. 15 and 20, notes that in 2 Tim 4:5 this verb designates "acknowledgment of the reality given with God's revelation," an acknowledgment that involves hardship (the following *kakopathēson*). The verb *nēphein* does not occur in the LXX. It does occur in *2 Clem.* 13.1, "Let us be sober for (our) good *(nēpsōmen epi to agathon),*" and also in Ign. *Pol.* 2.3, "Be sober *(nēphe)* as God's athlete," as well as in Polycarp, *Phil.* 7.2, "Watching unto prayer (*nēphontes pros tas euchas* [cf. 11.4 and 1 Pet 4:7])."

On the *en pasin,* see Titus 2:9, 10; 1 Tim 3:11; 2 Tim 2:7; and G. Delling, *TDNT* 8.75, who compares the *nēphontes teleiōs* of 1 Pet 1:13 with the *en pasin* here.

*accept being wronged.* The second verb in this quartet, *kakopathēson,* does not occur in S*. L. (vg S). Pel$^{B}$. This is probably a parablepsis due to homoioteleuton with all the *(-ēs-) ou* terminology from this point on in the verse. S* was probably fatigued at this point, as the uncorrected *MASĒ* for *PASĒ makrothymiai* in verse 2 indicates, as well as perhaps the preceding metathesis (but less probably; cf. *supra in loc.*). On *kakopathein* see 2 Tim 2:9 where it is placed on Paul's own lips, and cf. 2:3 where it becomes as here an apostolic charge to one who shared Paul's apostolic ministry, a succession in suffering, not just in teaching. BDF §337.2 note the complexive use of the aorist at this point and hereafter, a contrast with the simple present imperative *nēphe.*

*one who announces the gospel.* Lit. "evangelist *(euaggelistou).*" This noun, which is not documented in the LXX or the Ap. Frs., is practically unknown to pre-Christian Greek. G. Friedrich, *TDNT* 2.736, cites the fragmentary Rhodian inscription (IG 12.1.675.6, cited by MM *s.v.,* p. 259) where the term seems to describe the pagan high priest of Daphne as one who pronounces oracles. The two Christian texts cited by MM are of the fifth-sixth century C.E. and use the term of the apostle John. For the later patristic texts (beginning with Clement of Alexandria) that use this term of God, Christ, and angels as well as of men, see Lampe, *PGL,* p. 559, and the Comment below.

*carry out fully.* Of its four other NT uses, three are in the Paulines (Rom 4:21; 14:5; Col 4:12) and the other in Luke 1:1. The noun occurs only of spiritual goods in 1 Thess 1:5; Col 2:2; and Heb 6:11; 10:22 (Delling, *TDNT* 6.311, and cf. *1 Clem.* 42.3). On the secular Greek data for *plērophorein,* see Delling, *TDNT* 6.309. He also notes that the one LXX use is Eccles 8:11, where the sense seems to be that men are "convinced" that they can sin when punishment for evil is tardy (cf. *T. Gad* 2.4).

In the Ap. Frs., *1 Clem.* 42.3 uses the verb for the apostles' being "fully assured" by the resurrection, and 54.1 of a man "filled with love *(agapēs).*" Ign. *Magn.* 8.2 writes of the OT prophets inspired "to convince *(eis to plērophorēthēnai)* the disobedient," and in 11.1 of being "convinced of the birth and passion and resurrection" of Jesus. The *inscr. Phld.* also writes of that church as "fully assured *(peplērophorēmenēi)* in all mercy in his resurrection." Ign. *Smyrn.* 1.1 writes of those Christians as "being fully persuaded *(peplērophorēmenous)* in respect to *(eis)* our Lord." Hermas employs this verb in *Man.* 9.2 and *Sim.* 2.8 *(bis)* (the Lord "will fulfill the petition of your soul") of the rich and the poor "complementing" each other with their material and spiritual gifts. It is here that the sense of Luke and the PE and (perhaps Colossians) appears again.

*the ministry.* On the use of *eis diakonian* in 4:11, see commentary *infra.*

6. *For now my own blood is to spill as a wine-offering.* Lit. "For I am already being poured out as a libation *(Ego gar ēdē spendomai).*" On this last of three occurrences of *ēdē* in the PE, see above on 1 Tim 5:15; 2 Tim 2:18, and note with Spicq that here it means "now," i.e. the event is imminent (cf. Rom 1:10; 1 Cor 4:8).

The verb *spendomai,* here in the present passive (contrast the rest of the verbs in this verse), occurs otherwise in the NT only in Phil 2:17, *ei kai spendomai epi tēi thysiai kai leitourgiai tēs pisteōs hymōn,* "even if I am to be poured as a libation upon the sacrificial offering of your faith," where the cultic and liturgical nuances of this verb are explicitly articulated. What Paul and Timothy wrote together in Philippians (1:1) is here reorchestrated, and only the verb itself corresponds from one passage to the other.

O. Michel, *TDNT* 7.528-536, has noted the use of *epispendō* in connection with inheritance in the Gortyn inscriptions (p. 528 n. 2) as well as the notable language of Euripides, *Bacchae* 284-285, where Teiresias says of Dionysus, "He is the gods' libation (*houtos theoisi spendetai* [probably passive]), though a god *(theos gegōs)*/so that through him do men obtain good things" (cf. 280-282).

Michel, p. 529, notes also that the libation offering is particularly linked with prayer in the secular Greek texts.

The twenty-one LXX uses of *spendein* translate the Hebrew *nsk* (where there is a Hebrew text), and frequently the term takes a form of *spondē* (a term not found in the NT) as an internal accusative, but this pattern is one that is not confined to Hebrew, as Michel's citation of Thucydides 5.14.4 (p. 531 n. 23) illustrates. The half dozen uses in the Pentateuch all refer to actual cultic libations, as do all the other LXX occurrences, though not necessarily in temple worship by priests. The mention of libations of false gods (cf. LXX Jer 7:18; 19:13; 39:29; 51:17, 19, 25) reminds one that this rite, along with the other apparatus of worship in Israel, came from the ambient pagan culture and its cult (Michel, p. 532). David's use of water apparently caught Israel's imagination (LXX 2 Kgdms 23:16; 1 Chron 11:18; 4 Macc 3:16), but the normal use of wine by the high priest can be read in Sir 50:15, which stresses the sacrificial connotations of the verb by describing the libation as "from the blood of the grape *(ex haimatos staphylēs)*." Though *nsk* has not been found in Qumran, see Michel, p. 534, for their concept of sacrifice; p. 535 for Josephus and Philo. *TDNT* 2.467 n. 1 contains further references on libations in Hebrew worship, including that of water on the Feast of Tabernacles.

*Spendesthai* is not documented in the Ap. Frs., though note the cognate in Ign. *Rom.* 2.2, "Grant me nothing more than that I be poured out *(spondisthēnai)* to God, while an altar is still ready."

*The time set for my embarkation has come.* Lit. "And the time *(ho kairos)* of my departure *(tēs analyseōs mou)* has approached *(ephestēken)*." On the verb *ephestēken* cf. commentary on 4:2 above, noting that here the threatening nuance of the term has surfaced. On *kairos* see 4:3 above.

That time is here specified as *tēs analyseōs mou,* a noun that occurs only here in the NT, though the cognate verb occurred in Phil 1:23 of Paul's "desire to depart *(eis to analysai)* and to be with Christ" in death (cf. Phil 1:21, "to die is gain"). The only other NT use of the verb is in Luke 12:36 in the parable of the master "coming home *(analysēi)* from the marriage feast" (F. Büchsel, *TDNT* 4.337, posits a "special sense" here of "return," though that seems unnecessary; the believer's "citizenship is in heaven" [Phil 3:20], and Paul conceives of his death as going home to the city to which he had really belonged — as the Philippians were "citizens" of Rome even though they had been born and lived all their lives in Macedonia; cf. the *apolyeis* of Simeon's canticle in Luke 2:29). The LXX does not employ *analysis,* but the verb *analyein* is used eighteen times (never with a Hebrew original). In the light of the preceding paragraph, Wis 2:1, "no one has been known to return [i.e. come home again] from Hades," is notable (cf. also Tob 2:9; 3 Macc 5:21, 44).

In the Ap. Frs. only *1 Clem.* 44.5 uses this noun, of the "fruitful and perfect release *(analysin)*" that the now-deceased presbyters of the Corinthian church enjoyed (in contrast to those whom the Corinthians were now dismissing while still alive).

7. *I have contended in the fine contest.* Lit. "I have fought the good fight *(ton kalon agōna ēgōnismai)*." The terminology was analyzed at 1 Tim 6:12 above. See J. K. Elliott, *Greek Text,* p. 160, on the Semitic word order in an unnamed MS. The internal accusative is a Hebraic way of escalating the action to a superlative degree (Spicq).

*I have run the whole track.* Lit. "I have finished the race *(ton dromon teteleka)*." On the noun see Comment below. The verb *telein* occurs only here in the PE, but twenty-seven times in the rest of the NT. There are four other uses in the Paulines (Rom 2:27; 13:6; 2 Cor 12:9; Gal 5:16) and five in Luke-Acts (four/one: Luke 2:39; 12:50; 18:31; 22:37; and Acts 13:29). The apocalyptic connotation of the term may be seen in the eight occurrences in Revelation. Delling, *TDNT* 8.58, has pointed out that in secular Greek this verb can refer to carrying out "religious acts; e.g., . . . games, *Inscr. Magn.* 56.11-15," and thus one is reminded again of the explicitly religious character of the ancient Greek athletic competitions. The Greek poets, notably Sophocles, used this verb of the ending of human life: *Antigone* 1114, *ariston ēi sōizanta ton bion telein* ("it may be best to save the life that is ending") and cf. 1064-1065; *mē pollous eti/trochous* [*sic* with Jebb *in loc.*] *hamillētēras hēliou telein* ("you are not to finish many rapid courses of the sun"); *Trachiniae* 79, *hōs ē teleutēn tou biou mellei telein /ē touton aras athlon* . . . ("that either he should find his death, or when he had achieved this final task . . ."). See also Simonides 36 et al. in LSJ *s.v.*

On the as many as twenty-eight LXX uses of this verb, see Delling, pp. 58-59; the closest parallel to the usage for a human life or career, as here in the PE, is Wis 4:16, of "the youth that is quickly perfected (ended: *neotēs telestheisa tacheōs* [cf. 4:13-14])," where the reference also is to premature death.

In the Ap. Frs., apart from *Barn.* 7.3 (and a variant at *1 Clem.* 37.2), all the uses of this verb are in Hermas (as many as twenty-three times, and several times with *diakonia* as object; cf. *Man.* 2.6 [*tris*] and see Delling, *TDNT* 8.60-61).

*I have kept faith.* On the verb *tērein* see 1 Tim 5:22 and 6:14, where it has *entolēn* as object in an ordination exhortation. Here for the only time in the NT and the Ap. Frs. this verb has *tēn pistin* as its object. However, in both secular and Jewish Greek texts *tērein (tēn) pistin* refers to remaining faithful to one's word, loyal and completely committed (D-C and Spicq cite Polybius 6.56.13; 7.12; 10.37.9, as well as Josephus, *Ant.* 15.134; and *War* 2.121; and 6.345: the former is particularly notable since it says that the Essene judgment of women was that *mēdemian tērein . . . tēn pros hena pistin,* "not one keeps faith with one husband" [the comparison with 1 Tim 5:12 and the repeated *mias gynaikos anēr/henos andros gynē* of the PE ought to be recalled]). A second-century-C.E. inscription from the theater in Ephesus has a certain M. Aurelius Agathopos, a grateful client of Artemis, declare *hoti tēn pistin etērēsa,* "that I kept the faith" (MM *s.v.*, p. 633; Deissmann, *LAE,* p. 312; D-C; Spicq). Cf. also *tous tēn pistin eusebōs te kai dikaiōs tērēsontes,* "those who will keep the faith in a godly and upright manner" (trans. WCW; Dittenberger, *Syll.* 339.47, *ap.* Spicq, *EP,* p. 806).

8. *Whatever happens, there lies in store for me the crown of the upright life.* Lit. "As for the rest *(loipon),* there is laid away *(apokeitai)* for me the crown of righteousness *(ho tēs stephanos)*" (cf. the adjective at 1 Tim 5:20). There are nine of thirteen uses of the adverbial *(to) loipon* in the Paulines. Of the others, one is in Acts 27:20, the others in Matt 26:45 (= Mark 14:41, *to loipon*) and Heb 10:13.

The forty-nine LXX uses of *stephanos,* surveyed by Grundmann, *TDNT* 7.624-626, show that the imagery of the crown was conspicuously less prevalent in Israel than in Greece but that it became more common in the later strata of the LXX as Hellenistic language and concepts became acceptable and even the high priest wore a golden crown (cf. Zech 6:11; Sir 45:12; 1 Macc 10:20; cf. Josephus, *Ant.* 3.172). In the wisdom literature, particularly Proverbs and Sirach, the crown is the recompense for and public acknowledgment of virtue; and in Wisdom of Solomon this imagery (but not the term *stephanos*) is used in 4:2 of virtue: "throughout all time it marches crowned in triumph *(stephanēphorousa),* victor in the contest for prizes *(athlōn agōna nikēsasa)* that are undefiled," and in 5:16 of the righteous: "they will receive a glorious crown *(to basileion tēs euprepeias)* and a beautiful diadem *(diadēma tou kallous)* from the hand of the Lord." From this wisdom tradition of the crown, the line goes into the martyrological compositions (4 Macc 17:15, and Grundmann, *TDNT* 7.627). It is the *Ep. Arist.* 280 (Charles, *AP* 2.119) that uses the actual phrase found in the PE when the author says to Ptolemy, "This is what you do, O mighty King [i.e. you hate wickedness and act righteously], and it is God who has bestowed upon you the crown of righteousness" (Charles, *AP* 2.119). *Testament of Levi* (de Jonge, 8.2; *ton stephanon tēs dikaiosynēs*), cf. 9 (Charles, *AP* 2.308), also uses this phrase in a list of the high-priestly regalia. *Testament of Benjamin* 4.1 has "crowns of glory." For the rabbinic texts on the next world as a "crown with great glory" (S. Bar. 15.7f) and others, see Grundmann, p. 628, who also there surveys the Philonic usage.

In the NT, *stephanos* occurs eighteen times: only here in the PE; never in Luke-Acts, though the proper name occurs seven times in Acts (the other Gospels use it only of the crown of thorns: Matt 27:29; Mark 15:17; John 19:2, 5). The other Paulines use it three times: in 1 Cor 9:25 of the victorious athlete's crown; in Phil 4:1 and 1 Thess 2:19 of those churches as Paul's "joy and crown."

As was noted above on 1 Tim 6:11, "the crown of life/glory" is mentioned in James 1:12; Rev 2:10; 1 Pet 5:4 (cf. Heb 2:9), and the conceptualization is the same as here with the "crown of righteousness" after suffering. There are seven further references to crowns in Revelation (see Grundmann, pp. 630-631).

The verb *apokeitai* occurs only here in the PE (but note *keitai,* 1 Tim 1:9) and only three times otherwise in the NT, in Col 1:5 of "the hope laid up *(apokeimenēn)* for you in heaven," and in Luke 19:20 of the *mina* of which the servant to whom it was entrusted says, "I kept [it] laid away *(apokeimenēn)* in a napkin"; Heb 9:27 uses this verb in the phrase *apokeitai tois anthrōpois hapax apothanein,* "it is appointed to men once to die." The Ap. Frs. do not employ this verb.

The four LXX uses are in Gen 49:10, "until that which is laid up for him comes" (*heōs an elthēi ta apokeimena autōi* [trans. WCW]); Job 38:23, "and it is stored for you against the hour of your enemies" (*apokeitai de soi eis hōran echthrōn* [trans. WCW]); 2 Macc 12:45, ". . . he was looking to the splendid reward that is laid up *(kalliston apokeimenon charistērion)* for those who fall asleep in godliness"; 4 Macc 8:11, "If you disobey me there is nothing before you but death in torments (*ouden . . . plēn tou meta streblōn apothanein apokeitai* [Charles, *AP* 2.675])."

See Lohse's texts on Col 1:5 (*Col,* pp. 17-18). Spicq notes how (as in Luke 19:20 *supra)* the accent is on security or sureness of safety in this laying away of a precious thing, and he cites "crowns deposited in the temple of Athena-Thoeris," *P. Ludg. Bat.* 16.3.4. MM *s.v.* have other references to things "stored" in a sanctuary, a granary, a library. LSJ cite Sophocles, *Oedipus Colonus* 1751-1753 (cf. 1727), where Theseus says, *En hois gar/charis hē chthonia xyn' apokeitai/penthein ou chrē,* "There is no point in mourning those for whom the common gift of the earth is reserved," and this should be contrasted with the crown that the judge gives not only to Paul but "to all who have loved his epiphany." Houlden, *Pastoral Epistles,* p. 133, suggests that the registers of the victors' names are kept in heaven (cf. 2 Tim 2:19 as well as the "Book of Life," Phil 4:3; Rev 21:27).

Of the eighteen uses of this verb in Josephus, *Ant.* 15.403 speaks of the high priest's vestment for sacrifice kept *(apokeisthai)* in the fortress north of the Temple area (cf. *Ant.* 18.91, 93). *Antiquities* 6.368 speaks of Saul and his sons fighting "as though their entire glory *(tēs holēs autois doxēs)* rested (*apokeimenēs, or* depended) solely on their dying nobly *(en monōi tōi kalōs apothanein)*. . . ."

*with which the upright Judge, the Lord, will recompense me on that Day.* Lit. "which the Lord will give as a reward *(hon apodōsei)* to me on that day, the just judge *(ho dikaios kritēs)*." On *apodidonai* see 1 Tim 5:4 as well as 2 Tim 4:14 below. The noun *kritēs* occurs only here in the PE, out of nineteen times in the

NT. There is no other Pauline use, but there are ten uses in Luke-Acts (six/four; otherwise in the Gospels only three times in Matthew). Of the seventy-five uses of *kritēs* in the LXX, only nine apply the title to the God of Israel: with *Kyrios,* Isa 30:18; 33:22; 63:7 *(agathos);* with *theos,* LXX Pss 7:11 *(ho theos kritēs dikaios);* 49:6; 67:5; 74:7. Sirach 32 (RSV 35):12 writes *kyrios kritēs esti,* and 2 Macc 12:6 writes of Judas Maccabeus "calling upon God the righteous judge *(ton dikaion kritēn theon).*" Thus only twice is *dikaios kritēs* said of *theos* (both in a prayer context) and never of *kyrios.*

In the Ap. Frs., *1 Clem.* 4.10 takes up this term, citing Exod 2:14 (not in the LXX). *Second Clement* 1.1 and Polycarp, *Phil.* 2.1, describe Jesus Christ as "judge of living and dead." Hermas, *Sim.* 6.3.6, cites *dikaios kritēs* of God from LXX Ps 7:12. *Didache* 5.2 = *Barn.* 20.2 refers to corrupt human judges *(anomoi kritai).* On *dikaios* see Titus 1:8 and 1 Tim 1:9.

*and not only me but all who have their hearts set on his revelation.* Lit. "not only to me, however — but also to all *(pasi)* who have loved his appearing *(tois ēgapēkosi tēn epiphaneian autou).*"

The great majority of witnesses (S. A. C. D$^{c.}$ G. et al.) have *pasi* after *alla kai.* Western witnesses particularly, beginning with D*, old Latin, and Vg. Syriac, etc., omit *pasi.* B. Metzger, *TCGNT,* p. 649, notes that the majority of editors for *GNT*$^{3corr}$ found the attestation too varied and strong to support a scribal addition at this point, though scribes did indeed like to add forms of *pas.* J. K. Elliott, *Greek Text,* p. 161, notes that *pasi* balances the preceding *emoi* and that the order *pas* + article + noun not only is Semitic but is quite in the style of the PE (cf. 1 Tim 6:10; 2 Tim 3:12; 4:17), which in any case emphasize universality at every turn. The fact that S* omitted *tois ēgapēkosi* while keeping *pasi* indicates that the exemplar of S* certainly had *pasi,* which cannot stand without the participle, though the participle certainly makes sense without *pasi.* The scribe of S* was tired when he copied the PE, but here his fatigue itself witnesses to the longer reading as the more ancient one. D. N. Freedman has suggested (in a private communication) that the omission could also be explained as a case of homoioteleuton.

On the verb *agapan,* which occurs 143 times altogether in the NT, see Notes at 1 Tim 1:5.

In the secular Greek usage of this term see Spicq, *Prolégomènes,* pp. 32-70, and in particular p. 70 n. 2, where he stresses the *external action* that *agapan* regularly implies. To the citations of Menander, p. 59 n. 1 (cf. LCL, pp. 438-439, for his unique *agapēsmon* = affection), add *Misoumenos* 307-308, *ēgapēsa se/ agapō, philō, krateia philtatē* (Sandbach, p. 191), and *Sam.* 247, 278, 385, and 617. Cf. the sense of "to be content" in *Dysc.* 745 cited at 2 Tim 4:10, *infra;* also Plato, *Republic* 330c, cited there.

For a survey of the LXX usage see Spicq, *Prolégomènes,* pp. 71-119, noting in particular that in the Israelite creed of Deut 6:5-6, "Listen . . . and love," the *agapēseis* "comprises faith, worship, and moral life" (p. 95) and that a basic LXX meaning of *agapan* is "to treat with honor/respect/reverence" (cf. p. 119). It presupposes a free, conscious choice that must remain radically unchangeable.

For a survey of the Qumran use of *'hb,* see *Prolégomènes,* pp. 140-143, and for the other Jewish writings of the period, pp. 131-139. To the materials from the *Testaments of the Twelve Patriarchs,* add (with Spicq, *EP,* p. 808) *T. Levi* 8.15, *hē de parousia autou agapētē estin,* "and his presence is beloved," speaking of the establishment and "presence" of a new priesthood in Judah, apparently a reference to the Maccabees and specifically to John Hyrcanus (see Charles, *AP* 2.309).

## ♦ COMMENT

4:5. *You, however, Timothy, keep calm, in every sense; accept being wronged.* With *sy de* and the four singular imperatives, the third and final block of parenesis, which extends through 4:8, is introduced. This section is sixty-five words, the same length as the first section, 3:10-13, and almost exactly double that number is in the central section just completed. D-C, p. 121, have noted only verses 6-8 as "the solemn conclusion of the parenesis"; the schema adopted here includes verse 5.

Spicq, *EP,* p. 802, has noted how the term *nēphe,* here translated "keep calm," takes up *epistēthi* in 4:2 and has further observed that *nephein* is a technical term in the rhetorician's lexicon for the speaker who is in complete control of himself, his subject, and his vocabulary in contrast to the frenetic vaporings of the emotional opposition. He cites Longinus 16.4; 34.4: "The orator proceeds to measure his language, choosing his very words so as to give no handle to his opponents, thus showing that even in the midst of Bacchic Revels we ought to remain sober *(nēphein),*" and of Hyperides: "He never exhibits strong feeling *(kardiēi nēphontos),* has little energy, rouses no emotion."

*do the work of one who announces the gospel.* The phrase *ergon poiēson euaggelistou,* lit. "Do (the) work of (an) evangelist," with its use of *ergon* in the singular, reminds one that in the singular in the PE (Titus 1:16; 3:1; 1 Tim 3:1; 5:10; 2 Tim 2:21; 3:17) *ergon* almost always seems to refer to a special ministerial work, whether by men or women (2 Tim 4:18 is certainly an exception and Titus 3:1 could be another, though even in the latter one is dealing with exiled Jewish Christian leaders). A similar observation could be made of some uses of *poiein* in the PE, except in Titus 3:5, which is the citation of a source in any event, and 1 Tim 1:13 in the Pauline prayer. Thus in 1 Tim 2:1 the term refers to the public service of prayer by all Christians; 1 Tim 4:16, to Timothy's performance of his tasks as Paul's co-worker; 1 Tim 5:21, of Timothy's observing the prescribed *modus agendi* with the presbyters. In any event, the "work" that Timothy is here told to "do" is explicitly described as *euaggelistou,* that of an "evangelist."

The later patristic texts (beginning with Clement of Alexandria) use this term of God, Christ, and angels as well as of men. Of those that refer to people (apart from the NT), Eusebius, *Church History* 5.10.2, speaking of Pantaenus, the first recorded head of the catechetical school in Alexandria, notes that "he was appointed as a herald *(kēryka)* for the gospel of Christ to the pagans in the East" (India), "for indeed there were until then [late second century C.E.] many evangelists of the word *(euaggelistai tou logou),* men who had earlier thought to use inspired zeal on the apostolic model *(apostolikou mimēmatos)* for the increase and building up of the divine word *(tou theiou logou).*" In *Church History* 3.37.2-4 he remarks, among other things, "It is impossible for us to give the number and the names of all who first succeeded *(diadochēn)* the apostles and were shepherds or evangelists *(poimenes ē kai euaggelistai)* in the churches throughout the world." He had just distinguished between the itinerant and "founding" preaching of "the evangelists" and the local, stable ministry of "the pastors" whom they left behind. He then notes the names of men like Ignatius, Clement, Polycarp, Papias, et al. who left documents from that period. Lemaire, *MOE,* pp. 106-107, thinks with G. Bardy (cited in n. 111) that Eusebius may here be relying on an anti-Montanist source from Asia Minor. It is notable that Chrysostom, Basil Seleucensis, and an anonymous sixth-century hymn use *euaggelistria* of women (citations in Lampe, *PGL,* p. 559).

*Euaggelistēs* occurs twice otherwise in the NT, once in the Paulines (Eph 4:11), once in Acts 21:8. In the latter instance it designates Philip, one of the seven appointed to a ministry at tables (cf. Acts 6:1-2) by the laying on of hands of the apostles and of the assembly in Acts 6:3-6. Acts remembers a ministry of preaching and baptizing for this man, in Samaria, then on the road to Gaza, then in Caesarea (Acts 8:4-40), whose Jewish Christian congregation he may have founded (cf. Haenchen, *Acts,* pp. 313, 601). In Eph 4:11-12, "And he (Christ) gave the apostles, the prophets, the evangelists, the pastors *(tous de euaggelistas tous de poimenas),* and the teachers for equipping (*katartismon* [cf. 2 Tim 3:17]) the saints for a work of ministry *(eis ergon diakonias). . . .*" Here the later terms "the evangelists, the pastors," have been inserted into the more archaic listing of apostles, prophets, teachers found in 1 Cor 12:28-29 (so Dibelius, *apud* Barth, AB *Eph,* p. 437 n. 72 *ad finem;* cf. the foundation of apostles and prophets in Eph 2:20 [*epi tōi themeliōi . . .*]). Barth, AB *Eph,* pp. 436-437, 483, stresses that all of these "orders" have something to do with speaking. Lemaire, *MOE,* pp. 106-107, 187, proposes that "the evangelists" of Eph 4:11

(along with "the pastors") are a second-generation Christian gloss on the archaic first-generation list, denoting those who carried on the tasks of apostles, prophets, and teachers in that second Christian generation.

On Philip "the evangelist," Lemaire, *MOE,* p. 69, submits that he ended with a permanent ministry in Caesarea, based in his own house, surrounded by his own family (among whom his four virgin prophetess daughters were particularly recalled). He apparently offered regular hospitality to traveling fellow believers, and this was a duty of a Christian community leader (cf. Titus 1:8; 1 Tim 3:2; as well as the Cypriot Mnason receiving Paul and his party in his house in Jerusalem, Acts 21:16; cf. Haenchen, *Acts,* p. 607). Lemaire suggests that the title *euaggelistēs* was given to Philip by the Caesarean church after he had settled in his ministry there (p. 69 n. 126). When Lemaire comes to the same term in the PE, he suggests very tentatively (p. 187) that Timothy is given the title because he, too, is conceived of by the author of the PE as having a more or less permanent ministry (cf. 1 Tim 1:3; 3:14-15) in an influential Christian church in a large urban center, a ministry that was conceived of as a collaboration with Paul, as the ministry of Philip was in collaboration with that of the Twelve (and perhaps in a particular way with the ministry of Peter if that apostle indeed brought the first pagans directly into the Christian assembly at Caesarea, whether before or after Philip's arrival; there is no question of his collaboration with Peter and John in Acts 8:14-25). An evangelist would have responsibility for promoting and coordinating the evangelization of the surrounding area. Lemaire calls "the collaborators of Paul — the 'evangelists'" and gives the title to Titus as well as Timothy.

The way in which Timothy is urged to "an evangelist's work" in the PE would lead one to think that this was in fact the title of a ministerial office in the Ephesian church in the second Christian generation and that perhaps popularly it was thought to go back to a ministerial title for one of the seven in Caesarea (note the Philip traditions associated with Hierapolis in Asia Minor). In any case the author of the PE (and in our hypothesis, of Luke-Acts) used the title of the office or task to nail down the collaboration of Timothy with the apostle Paul, a participation in the apostolic work that within a decade of these letters was to be spoken of as "succeeding" the apostles *(1 Clem.* 44.2: *diadexōntai . . . dedokimasmenoi andres).*

*carry out fully the ministry that is yours.* The fourth and final imperative to Timothy is *tēn diakonian sou plērophorēson,* "fulfill your [sg.] ministry." In 1 Tim 1:12 *diakonia* referred to Paul's apostolic ministry granted by the powerful intervention of the risen Jesus, though, as was noted there, the term was anarthrous and without the possessive; here the articular use with the possessive indicates the particular form of *diakonia* that fell to Timothy. Here Timothy's ministry is again the object of an aorist imperative, in this case the verb *plērophorein* (which occurs again at 4:17 *infra* but not otherwise in the PE). Of its four other NT uses, three are in the Paulines (Rom 4:21; 14:5; Col 4:12) and the other is in Luke 1:1. Here in the PE the verb is active; in 4:17, as in the other NT occurrences, it is passive. Here it takes the object *diakonian* (cf. G. Delling, *TDNT* 6.297, who notes Col 4:17, *diakonian . . . plērois*). In the Pauline usage outside of the PE it is used in the sense of being fully convinced or assured, unless perhaps Col 4:12 may be read in the sense of "brought to full measure" (thus G. Delling, *TDNT* 6.310; also Lohse, *Col*, p. 173, "to be filled with").

In Luke 1:1 the reference is to the acts of God that "have been fulfilled among us," i.e. *pragmata* that were "according to the Scripture" (and so "fulfilled" the word of God) and that found their consummation in the salvation of the believing community *(en hēmin)* (Delling, p. 310). The sense here in 2 Tim 4:5 is evidently closer to this Lukan usage than to the Pauline in Romans and First Corinthians. Timothy is to consummate, to bring to complete achievement a ministry that has been given him by God, a ministry that is to use "all the Scripture" (2 Tim 3:16-17) and that is to issue in the salvation of his hearers and of himself (cf. 1 Tim 4:11-16). The same is true of the usage in 4:17 below where Paul avers that "the proclamation (*to kerygma* [see Titus 1:3]) was fulfilled *(plērophorēthēi)* through me," i.e. his office of *kēryx* (1 Tim 2:7; 2 Tim 1:11) reached its divinely willed (note passive) consummation by means of his public defense before the Roman authorities (cf. G. Friedrich, *TDNT* 3.717, who suggests that the concept of "office" here may indicate a later usage, but he probably suffers from the German allergy to *Amt*). The framing effect of this terminology that brings Luke 1:1 into the last chapter of the epistolary roll that we call the PE gives an uncanny unity to what we have suggested is actually one massive literary project.

6. *For now my own blood is to spill as a wine-offering.* With this verse and *egō gar ēdē spendomai*, the parenesis returns to the first person singular, which complements the second person singular exactly as in the preceding two sections (3:10-13 and 3:14–4:4). Here the ground and reason *(gar)* for Timothy's *diakonia* is that Paul's own ministry is coming to an end. The concept of succession to the apostle and his work has determined the form of the parenesis; the first of these three *sy de* sections dwelt on the present "collegiality in suffering" *with* Paul; this last section now turns to a continuance of that same witness *after* Paul.

The emphatic pronoun *egō* (cf. Titus 1:3, 5; 1 Tim 1:11, 15; 2:7; and 2 Tim 1:11; 4:6) is "the apostolic *egō*," the person of Paul precisely as apostle, as sent by the risen Lord to become the teacher of the pagans. (The comparative frequency [forty-three times] of first person singular pronouns in the PE is notable. Thus Titus has four [above + 3:12, 15, *me, emou*]; First Timothy has six [above + 1:12 *(bis)*, 16, *emoi, me*]; whereas Second Timothy has no fewer than thirty-three [above + *emou,* 2 Tim 1:13; 2:2; 4:11, 17; *mou,* 1:3, 6, 12, 16; 2:1, 8; 3:10; 4:6, 16; *emoi,* 4:8; *moi,* 3:11; 4:8 *(bis),* 11, 14, 16, 17; *eme,* 1:8; *me,* 1:15, 16, 17; 3:11; 4:9, 10, 16, 17, 18].)

As Michel, *TDNT* 7.536, suggests, the apostle here is conceived as voluntarily pouring out his lifeblood as a priest (Sir 50:15 above) poured out wine at the foot of the altar of holocausts, as a complement and appendix to the principal sacrifice (cf. Michel, p. 532). In that case the historical death of the apostle is here joined to the actual death of Jesus, complementing and putting the finishing touch on the unique sacrifice of the cross as it affected his own existence as an apostle. The apostle's history has thus become part of Jesus' own history, even to death. The priestly ministry of the apostle to the pagans (Rom 15:16; cf. 1:9) has reached its consummation in the sacrifice of his own life (cf. *TDNT* 3.185) in the service of the good news that "Christ died for our sins . . ." (1 Cor 15:3). Spicq has noted the possibility of an expiatory nuance to this language and the way in which the Qumran sectaries regarded their lives of priestly piety (cf. 1QS 9.3-5: Dupont-Sommer, *EWQ,* p. 93); the way the author of 4 Macc 6:28-29; 17:22 (*hōs antipsychon;* cf. 1:11; Charles, *AP* 2.683; cf. pp. 663, 667) regarded the deaths of the martyrs; and the way rabbinic Judaism regarded the death of the high priest (*Makkot* 2.6). Plutarch, *Moralia* 494 D, writes of the lion prepared *spendesthai peri tōn teknōn,* "to pour out (its life) for its offspring."

*The time set for my embarkation has come.* As at 4:3 above, the "appointed time" is from a human point of view a frightening moment, a threatening occasion, that of death. Because it has been appointed by God as a rubric in the lifeblood of his witnesses, it is a time that has been planned, a marked festival in the calendar of their lives.

The basic sense of the verb *analyein,* here translated "embarkation," is "to loosen up," i.e. to undo ropes or thongs, such as those that hold a ship to its wharf and so "to leave" (cf. Polyb. 3.69.14; Babrius 42.8 in LSJ, *analyō;* Philo, *Congr.* 30, of "the cables of life are fastened on," but no form of *analyein* occurs there). Philo, *Flacc.* 187, speaks of death on the land as better than death at sea, for the land "received them when they first came into existence; it should also receive them when they finally depart from life *(tēn ek tou biou teleutain analysin).*" Josephus uses the noun only once, *Ant.* 19.4.1 or §239, of "retirement" or "departure" (LSJ). Secundus, *Sententiae* 19 (LSJ *s.v.*), speaks of death as the *analysis sōmatos.*

The nautical imagery seems most appropriate at this point in Second Timothy, as Paul indicates that the ineluctable time for his last voyage has come, a voyage that makes that requested from Timothy in 4:9 appear much less formidable. Note that in ancient navigation all depended on when the right wind *(pneuma)* blew; men went as soon as the wind came or shifted.

7. *I have contended in the fine contest.* With this sentence the glance of the apostle shifts to the past, and three powerful telegraphic phrases serve to condense his apostolate. In the first phrase, lit. "I have fought the good fight," the perfect *ēgōnismai* traces a line to a terminal point (cf. Moule, *Idiom,* p. 16). It occurred above with the present imperative addressed to Timothy and every apostolic minister in 1 Tim 6:12 (cf. 1 Tim 4:10 of Paul and Timothy together).

*I have run the whole track.* In the second phrase, lit. "I have finished the race *(ton dromon teteleka),*" the previous image is further defined and the contest *(agōn)* is exemplified by the *dromos,* its "most impressive part" (cf. Bauernfeind, *TDNT* 8.233-234). There are only two other NT uses of this noun, both in Acts. The former is in Acts 13:25 of the Baptist's "finishing his course *(eplērou . . . ton dromon),*" and the latter is in Paul's farewell at Miletus, where he says in 20:24, "I do not account my life of any value or precious to myself; if only I may accomplish my course *(hōs teleiōsai ton dromon mou)* . . . ," where the verb is a cognate of the *teteleka* of 2 Tim 4:7 (see below).

There are as many as ten LXX uses of *dromos,* normally of actual running (e.g., LXX 2 Kgdms 18:27) or of the "course" of the sun and the passing days (cf. LXX 2 Esd 4:34; Job 17:11). In LXX Jer 8:6; 23:10 the metaphorical application to human life begins to surface (cf. Eccles 9:11, "The race is not to the swift . . .").

In the Ap. Frs., *1 Clem.* 6.2 writes that the martyred Christians of the first century "steadfastly finished the course of faith *(epi ton tēs pisteōs bebaion dromon katēntēsan),*" and in 20.2 writes of "the course *(dromon)* of day and night" (cf. LXX above and Diognetus 7.2 [*bis*]). Ign. *Pol.* 1.2 writes, "I exhort you *(parakalō se)* to press forward on your course *(tōi dromōi sou)* . . . ," in reference to Polycarp's exercise of his ministry (cf. Bauernfeind, *TDNT* 8.234).

From LSJ and MM one would infer that there are no secular Greek references to *dromos* = the course of human life, except those that take up the sense of Latin *cursus* (cf. *Aeneid* 4.653) for life, public or private (citations LSJ *s.v.,* p. 450). Bauernfeind cites on p. 233, Herodotus 8.74.1 (cf. 8.140 and 9.37.2 and cf. LXX Prov 7:23) as an example of a figurative use. It has an almost proverbial ring as Herodotus uses it, a kind of snail shell metaphor that has no inner life. In any event it does not yet mean the span of life or a lifetime (in the sense of "career," a term that comes from *currere,* "to run"). Haenchen, *Acts,* p. 409, speaks of "a peculiarly Christian (Hellenistic) language of devotion . . . in the making" as he examines this terminology in Acts 13:25. For later Christian usage in this sense, see Lampe, *PGL,* pp. 387-388.

In the light of the cultic language of the previous phrase, one ought to note that *dromos,* too, came to mean the *order (dromos)* of Christian feasts as opposed to the Jewish (in Eusebius, *Vita Constant.* 3.18; *PG* 20.1076A, where he speaks of the coincidence of Easter with the Passover). Bauernfeind, *TDNT*

8.234, has noted Philo, *Leg. alleg.* 3.48, about the good man "who wins a noble race *(kalon dromon)* and proves victor in this grandest of all contests *(agōnisma),*" that of seeking the one God. In the light of the texts cited above, one could suggest that the concept and language were of Roman provenance, originally ministerial and due to the influence of the Pauline imagery (e.g., 1 Cor 9:24-26, where *trechein* is a key metaphorical term).

Bauernfeind, p. 234, has noted that all three NT uses of *dromos* (cf. *supra*) have as their specific content a life that has been devoted to a God-given task, i.e. proclaiming the good news: the Baptist heralding the coming of Jesus; the apostle Paul that he had come and will come again. The verb *teteleka* affirms that the task has been brought to perfection, consummated, and one notes that in the Lukan lexicon *dromos* is the object of *plēroō* (Acts 13:25) and *teleioō* (Acts 20:24). The latter verb means "to fulfil . . . a received commission" (G. Delling, *TDNT* 8.81), and the former one also refers to a divinely willed time of activity (G. Delling, *TDNT* 6.297; cf. 8.59 n. 11 with 81 n. 13; he seems hesitant about this).

In the Lukan usage of the NT (cf. citations above), as well as in Revelation, the verb refers to an execution or accomplishment of the divine ordering will, which has prescribed (by a prophetic word, often transmitted in writing) certain acts and a certain course (cf. *dromos*) of events (Delling, 8.59-60). Here Paul conceives his career as a divinely established race (cf. the divine origin of the Greek games) whose course he has finished — victoriously. BDF §342.1 note how the perfect here indicates an action up to the present from which one expects a permanent effect.

*I have kept faith.* The third phrase, *tēn pistin tetērēka,* if it had occurred in a context like this in a pagan inscription, would surely have been taken to refer to the contestant's having kept the oath/pledge linked to competition in the Greek games (cf. Easton, *Pastoral Epistles,* and 2 Tim 2:5 above). Here for the only time in the NT and the Ap. Frs. this verb has *tēn pistin* as its object. However, in both secular and Jewish Greek texts *tērein (tēn) pistin* refers to remaining faithful to one's word, loyal and completely committed. Thus almost certainly in this passage of the PE *hē pistis* does not stress the creed, the *fides quae,* but rather (with *tērein*) the subjective and enduring loyalty of the apostle (R. Bultmann, *TDNT* 6.208).

The course that began with Paul's baptismal confession has now come to its close. The goal is at hand. Spicq stresses the peculiarly Roman concern for *fides* as the basis for all human relationships and contracts, whether between individuals or nations. Plutarch, *Numa* 16.1, treats the temple to *Fides (Pistis)* that the legendary Numa first erected in Rome, and the all-important oath of the Romans by their *fides.*

8. *Whatever happens, there lies in store for me the crown of the upright life*

*with which the upright Judge, the Lord, will recompense me on that Day.* As verse 6 assessed the present and verse 7 surveyed the past, this verse with an adverbial accusative *loipon* turns to the future. This rather colloquial usage means "finally" or "it remains that" (Moule, *Idiom,* p. 161), though because of the inner link between what has gone before and what awaits the apostle, it could be rendered "therefore" (Moule, p. 207). Where the previous two verses stressed, with the first person singular pronoun and verbs, the activity of Paul, this verse now regards the apostle as object *(moi . . . emoi)* of the divine action of Christ. In verses 9-11 Paul is the object or the one affected by the varied activity of various colleagues *(pros me . . . me . . . met' emou . . . moi).* The imagery of the games is carried a step further at this point with the figure of *ho tēs dikaiosynēs stephanos,* "the crown of righteousness" (i.e. of victory; cf. 1 Cor 9:25) that "is reserved for" *(apokeitai)* the apostle. In 2 Tim 2:5 the same image was exploited in the verb *stephanoutai.*

W. Grundmann, *TDNT* 7.615-636, has called attention (p. 615) to the etymological sense of that which encloses or encircles (*stephein,* of walls around a city; of persons around one person) and has noted the many species of leaves and flowers used in plaiting the crowns of the Hellenistic world. The crown of gold transformed into the medium of precious and imperishable metal what had been inexpensive and ephemeral (Grundmann, pp. 616-617). In the ancient world the use of the crown was ultimately cultic, marking and setting aside a person or thing for worship (Grundmann, pp. 617-618), and crowns were particularly linked with the cultic honoring of the dead, who received a reverence and homage like that for the divine images (cf. the wreaths carved on sarcophagi, and Grundmann, pp. 618, 623-624). The crown or wreath was a memorial for the dead, as it is still in the American Memorial Day. One of the most archaic Greek customs for honoring the dead was the celebration of athletic contests (*Iliad,* book 23). The games, of course, came to be celebrated also in honor of the gods, but in any case "The god or the deceased is honored when the victor is crowned" (Grundmann, p. 620), and no greater honor came to a man in this life than the crown for winning in these games. The crown thus is a messenger's sign of joy and so of good news in the ancient Greek world (cf. Sophocles, *Oedipus Rex* 80-83, and *Trachiniae* 178-179), worn so that the one waiting for the messenger would already *see* at a distance that the news was good.

Grundmann, *TDNT* 7.633-634, traces the application of the crown imagery to martyrs through the first Christian centuries. Particularly interesting, in the light of the inner conceptual coherence of "crown of life/of righteousness," is the second-century Gnostic Christian hymnbook (Hennecke and Schneemelcher, *NT Apoc.* 2.809) called the *Odes of Solomon,* 17.1-2: "Then I was crowned by my God, and my crown is living. And I was justified by my Lord, and my salvation is incorruptible." Dibelius, *James*, pp. 88-89, does not adduce this text in his collection of materials on "the crown of life." He proposes that the metaphor was hackneyed and that the use of dependent genitives (of life/of righteousness) was quite unreflective. Yet the terminology is not that frequent in Jewish and Christian Greek literature and the phrases are rare (cf. the Notes above).

Accordingly, the objective or subjective interpretations are live options, and the phrase here in Second Timothy means either "the crown that bestows holiness" (cf. Grundmann, *TDNT* 7.629) or "the crown that belongs to righteousness." The former interpretation would be in the line taken by *Odes Sol.* 17.2. If, however, "righteousness" here is synonymous with "victory," then the subjective usage is more likely. In favor of the latter is the athletic imagery that has dominated verses 6-7 as well as the *stephanos* figure itself (cf. also 2 Tim 2:5 with its *nomimōs*). Spicq understands the phrase as a Hebraism and thus = "the justified crown, i.e., due in justice to the victorious athlete and because it has been promised by God" (cf. the *dikaios kritēs* below). A causal genitive is also possible; i.e. the crown is given because of a holy life (cf. "the training in righteousness" in 2 Tim 3:16; cf. G. Schrenk, *TDNT* 2.210, "the crowning of the state of righteousness"). Finally, some opt for an appositional genitive, which would mean the crown that consists of final justification, i.e. eternal life. In this case the phrase is exactly equivalent conceptually to that in James 1:12 or 1 Pet 5:4. The first option is the most obvious in the context, but one can by no means exclude the possibility that the way was deliberately left open for one or both of the other meanings. Spicq cites the phrase "the crown of righteousness" from the Egyptian *Book of the Dead* 19, "a crown of victory and glory, 'symbol of the new quality of the man who has victoriously undergone the test of the judgment.'"

F. Büchsel, *TDNT* 3.655, has noted how the term *apokeitai* is used to stress the divinely willed and certain character of the future (including death) that awaits man. The root is frequent enough in the NT (cf. 1 Tim 1:9), especially as compounded with *ana-*, *synana-*, *anti-* (1 Tim 5:14), *epi-*, *kata-*, *para-*, and *pro-*, as well as *apo-* here. D-C note that forms of *apokeisthai* had become practically technical terms in royal "edicts of commendation" and, with Spicq, cite the texts.

The *apokeitai* of the main clause is then taken up in the *hon apodōsei* adjectival clause that modifies "the crown of righteousness," just as the *dikaios kritēs* takes up the cognate *dikaiosynē*. The initial position of the verb gives a Semitic turn to both clauses. See the references to the papyri in Spicq, where *apodidonai* means paying a debt or recompensing a service.

In both occurrences of *apodidonai* in 2 Tim 4 *ho kyrios* is the subject, and an eschatological distribution of reward/punishment is envisioned for the apostle who has served his master and for the opponent of the apostle's mission (*en ekeinēi tēi hēmerai,* as in 2 Tim 1:18; with *eis,* 1:12). As Alexander the coppersmith is to receive *kata ta erga (polla . . . kaka),* so Paul is to receive the victor's crown (which is apparently *kata ta erga polla kala k'agatha* that the apostle has done). The future tense in both verses 8 and 14 reminds one that for the NT "retribution belongs essentially to the future world rather than the present" (Büchsel, *TDNT* 2.168) and that it extends to external acts as well as internal dispositions, even the least. Thus both good and evil fortune in this life lapse into relative insignificance. The criteria for success and failure are reserved to "the upright judge," *ho dikaios kritēs,* a phrase that here in verse 8 stands in apposition to *ho kyrios* (cf. Christ's *krisis dikaia,* John 5:30, and G. Schrenk, *TDNT* 2.189). As above (2 Tim 1:8) Paul was the Lord's prisoner, not Nero's, so here he has a just judge in that Lord but not in the Roman court (cf. 16-17 *infra*).

Ziesler, *Righteousness,* pp. 156, 163, has observed that when the adjective *dikaios* is applied to God's "just judgment" and "just repayment" in 2 Thess 1:5-6, it refers to God's retribution in the final judgment for those who have suffered for their faith as well as for their persecutors (cf. the application to God in Heb 12:23, "to God the judge of all"). Cf. also *Pss. Sol.* 2:19, "God is a judge and righteous, and accepts no man's person" (J. R. Harris, *Psalms,* p. 142); 9:4, "For you [O God] are a just judge over all the peoples of the earth" (p. 149); in 4:28, "the Lord our God is a strong judge in righteousness" (p. 145); and in 8:29, "God is to be praised who judges all the earth in his righteousness" (p. 148).

But does 2 Tim 4:8 refer to God *(ho theos)?* Evidently *ho kyrios* is the actual term used here and in 4:14 below. In the light of the usage of *kyrios* in the PE generally, and particularly in the light of 2 Tim 1:16, 18 *(en ekeinēi tēi hēmerai)* above, the Lord who is here described as "the Upright Judge" is none other than the risen Jesus, appearing as "judge of the living and the dead" (*kritēs zōntōn kai nekrōn:* Acts 10:42), not to mention 2 Tim 4:1, "Christ Jesus who will come to judge the living and the dead *(krinein zōntas kai nekrous).*"

Acts 10:42 has Peter speak of Jesus as the one established by God *(tou theou)* as "judge of living and dead," and in Luke 18:6 the parable of the unjust judge (*ho kritēs tēs adikias;* genitive of quality and a Semitism; see BDF §165 and *TDNT* 3.943 n. 2) stands in striking contrast to *ho dikaios kritēs* here in the PE. Luke 12:14 has Jesus in his historical ministry fending off the task of the *kritēs* (= umpire; cf. Büchsel, *TDNT* 3.942 n. 1). The usage of the PE corresponds exactly with the kerygma of Acts in making the Lord Jesus *kritēs.*

The intensely individual mold of this whole confessional declaration about the crown is in the last phrase completely shattered. Paul does not see his apostolate as working out simply and only his individual final salvation. He will not win the race alone — *ou monon de emoi;* the crown of victory will be given, literally "not only to me but also (*alla kai* [cf. 1 Tim 5:13; 2 Tim 2:20]) to all (*pasi* [see *infra* on *v.l.*]) who have loved *(ēgapēkosi)* his epiphany *(tēn epiphaneian autou)*." Spicq has noted how in Paul's correspondence his congregations of converts are his "crown" (gathered around him in a circle, listening to his teaching and direction) and his joy (cf. 1 Thess 2:19; Phil 4:1). Here that Pauline usage has reminded the author of this passage that when Paul receives the victor's wreath, it will not be alone but with the whole circle of those who have earnestly desired the glorious arrival of the Lord Jesus.

With *tois ēgapēkosi,* those "who have their hearts set," one encounters this verb for the first of two occurrences in the PE (see 4:10 *infra* of Demas, "who loved [*agapēsas*] the present age [*ton nyn aiōna*]"). The contrast here between verses 8 and 10 is instructive: a believer can "love" "this age, here and now," or he can love the next, *tēn epiphaneian,* which comes with the glorified Jesus. He cannot love both and stay with Paul. As Spicq, *EP,* p. 808, has noted, the verb *agapan* here in the PE has its classical and Hellenistic sense of seeking, desiring, or aspiring after, a sense that also appears in LXX Pss 4:3 (loving vanity) and 33:13 (loving to see good days; cf. Spicq, *Prolégomènes,* p. 78; cited in 1 Pet 3:10 in a different form).

In the NT usage of *agapan,* it is notable that Luke 11:43 has this verb take the accusative of a thing as object, a usage not found outside of the PE in Paul (except Eph 5:25 of the Church) or in the other synoptics, though often enough in the Johannine literature and the rest of the NT. The Lukan use noted has the sense of "prefer" or "aspire after," which is found here in the PE, with the pejorative connotation that appears in 4:10 (cf. 1 John 2:15 on not loving the world [*kosmon*]). Spicq, *Agape* 1.150 (E.T. 120), seems to opt for this sense of "to prefer" in his final summary on Luke 11:43. It may be significant that in Luke 11:42-43 there is first the mention of "love *(agapē)* of God *(tou theou)*" (the only use of *agapē* in Luke), and then this verb is used (rather than *philein* as in Matt 23:6-7; see Stählin, *TDNT* 9.128-129) in order to stress the radical incompatibility of the two "loves," just as here in 2 Tim 4:8, 10.

*and not only me but all who have their hearts set on his revelation.* Thus Paul and all who follow his teaching "have their hearts set" (faithfully persevering for a lifetime, as the perfect implies: Spicq); "his revelation *(epiphaneian autou)*" is certainly a reference to the *prosdechomenoi tēn makarian elpida kai epiphaneian tēs doxēs tou megalou theou kai sōtēros hēmōn Iēsou Christou,* "as we wait for the blessed hope revealed in the glory of Jesus Christ, our great God and savior," of Titus 2:13 (cf. also 1 Tim 6:14 and 2 Tim 1:10). As was noted above on 2 Tim 4:1, the noun *epiphaneia* can refer to the incarnation and historical ministry of Jesus, but the future orientation of this whole verse makes that sense improbable. For excellent material on the secular usage of *epiphaneia* and cognates, see Spicq, *Agape,* E.T., 2.396-406.

G. Bornkamm, *Early Christian Experience,* pp. 169-176, especially 170-171, in his study of the anathema in primitive Christian worship, has noted the pre-Pauline, formulaic character of the "sacral law." "If anyone has no love *(ei tis ou philei)* for the Lord, let him be accursed." He sees here a citation of a fixed liturgical dialogue in which *philei* appeared instead of the normal Pauline usage of *agapan* (cf. Eph 6:24, *ton kyrion,* and 2 Tim 4:8). Stählin, *TDNT* 9.136, agrees (note also the literature cited in his nn. 204-210), noting that the only other Pauline usage of *philein* is in the set epistolary formula of Titus 3:15. See Spicq, *Agape* 3.81-86, for an excellent gathering of citations for *philein* and for the literature on this passage (E.T. 3.224-228, without the full citations). Here in the PE the *philei* of the old formula has become *tois ēgapēkosi* and the *Maranatha* (Our Lord, come!) has become *tēn epiphaneian autou* (still another indication that the *kyrios* here in the PE is the Christ). Thus here "to have loved" the Lord who is coming as judge is basically to have hoped for and aspired after that coming and to have done so in a public, confessional fashion, particularly in the liturgical (eucharistic) assembly. To have prayed for the Lord to come there in worship (and prayer = *agapē* for Luke 6:27-28) is to have prayed for his final coming in judgment.

## V. PERSONAL NOTE TWO (4:9-21)

### V.A. News for Timothy (4:9-15)

*4 [9]Do your best to come here soon; [10]for Demas, his heart set on this present world, left me helpless and set out for Thessalonika. Crescens has gone to Gaul; Titus, to Dalmatia. [11]Only Luke is with me now. Pick up Mark and bring him along with you, for he can be helpful to me in my ministry. [12]I have appointed Tychicus to go to Ephesus.*

*[13]When you come, bring along that cape which I left behind in Troas at Carpus's home — and bring the books, too, particularly the notebooks. [14]There in Troas, Alexander, the coppersmith, brought many false charges against me. (The Lord will give him the recompense that corresponds to his deeds.) [15]Watch out for him yourself now, because his defiance of our words was frenzied.*

### ♦ NOTES

4:9. *Do your best to come here soon.* Literally, *"hasten," spoudason;* this word also occurs at Titus 3:12; 2 Tim 2:15; 4:21. The whole phrase *spoudason elthein pros me* occurred in Titus 3:12. Second Timothy 4:21 will again say, *spoudason . . . elthein. Spoudason* otherwise appears in the NT seven times — three times in the Paulines (Gal 2:10; Eph 4:3; 1 Thess 2:17) and Second Peter (1:10, 15; 3:14), and once in Hebrews (4:11, with *eiselthein*). The variant reading in Ign. *Eph.* 1.2 is alone of the verb's thirteen uses in the Ap. Frs. to parallel the PE usage. No parallels exist in the dozen Septuagintal uses. (See 2 Tim 2:15 for *spoudazein* in the moral sense.) *Elthein,* "to come," occurs 636 times in the NT, and is frequent in Paul. Eight times forms of the verb occur in the Timothy correspondence, usually referring to the comings and goings of Paul and the members of his entourage (1 Tim 3:14; 4:13; 2 Tim 4:9, 13, 21). The final adverb, *tacheōs,* "quickly," occurred in 1 Tim 5:22 (see above); *tachion* occurred in 1 Tim 3:14.

10. *for Demas, his heart set on this present world, left me helpless and set out for Thessalonika.* The reasons for the prompt trip of Timothy are now adduced: "For Demas left me *(Demas gar me egkatelipen),* having loved the present age *(agapēsas ton nyn aiōna).*" See 4:8 above on *agapan,* and Titus 2:12 (AB *Titus in loc.*); see commentary at 1 Tim 6:17 on *en tōi nyn aiōni.*

*Egkatelipen* will recur with *pantes me* in 4:16 below, and the term, not otherwise found in the PE, occurs eight times otherwise in the NT: twice in the Paulines, Rom 9:29 (citing Isa 1:9) and 2 Cor 4:9 (of the apostles "persecuted but not abandoned"); and twice in the Lukan corpus (Acts 2:27 [= LXX Ps 15:10] and 31). Matthew 27:46 = Mark 15:34 is also a citation of LXX Ps 21:1. Hebrews 10:25; 13:5 (= LXX Josh 1:5) are the other NT uses.

In the Ap. Frs., *1 Clem.* 11.1; 33.2 use the verb of God not abandoning his own and of men not abandoning love *(agapēn).* The other uses are *Did.* 4.13 (= *Barn.* 19.2); *Barn.* 4.14; 11.2; 19.2; and Hermas, *Man.* 9.2; *Sim.* 2.9.

*Dēmas* appears to be a shortened form of the common masculine Greek name *Dēmētrios* (cf. BDF §125.1 and *s.v.* Preisigke, *Wörterbuch,* pp. 85-86; Lohse, *Col,* p. 174 n. 42), which was borne by Jews in the Hellenistic age (cf. *CII* §682) as well as by pagans (Acts 19:24, 38) and Christians (3 John 12). Spicq, *EP,* p. 811, quotes an epitaph of 117 C.E. of an Egyptian Jewish physician named Demas. Demas, however, appears nowhere in the LXX or *CII* or in the Ap. Frs.

*and set out.* See 1 Tim 1:3 for *eporeuthē.*

*Crescens has gone to Gaul.* "Crescens *(Krēskēs)* left for Gaul *(eis Galatian).*" The name is a Latin one, not found in Preisigke or in Livy but borne by one of Nero's freedmen (Tacitus, *Hist.* 1.76) and a centurion (*Annales* 15.11) and others cited by Spicq *in loc.,* including *CII* 68 (a Jewish proselyte), 218, and perhaps 421 (both Roman). There are no other LXX or NT uses of the name, nor is it used in the Ap. Frs., except in the Latin ending of Polycarp, *Phil.* 14.1, where he is secretary-messenger. On the frequency of Latin names here in Second Timothy, see on 4:19, 21 *infra.*

On *eis Galatian* see Comment below.

11. *Only Luke is with me now.* Lit. "Luke alone is with me *(Loukas estin monos met' emou).*" On *monos* of God see 1 Tim 1:17; 6:15.

*Pick up Mark and bring him along with you.* The terminology has occurred above in this correspondence: *analambanein* in the hymn of 1 Tim 3:16; again in 2 Tim 3:6; *euchrēstos* in 2 Tim 2:21; *diakonia* in 1 Tim 1:12; 2 Tim 4:5. For the philological profile of these terms, see the commentary *in loc.*

*Analabōn* has here its quite ordinary, secular sense of "pick up" (cf. citations in Acts and Spicq, *EP,* p. 813, for papyri; also Delling, *TDNT* 4.8).

*Age,* in the sense of "bring" (someone) when it has a nominative participle also governing the object, appears to be peculiar to Luke in the NT; cf. Luke 19:30; 22:54; Acts 11:25 and 23:18 (both esp. apropos here). BAGD *s.v.* (1.b) cite P Petr II, 32 [2a], 13, *agōn meth' autou* (also in MM *s.v.*).

On the name "Mark" in secular sources, Philo, and Josephus, see BAGD, *s.v.* BDF §41.3 note that the long penult "is established in Latin" and so the circumflex must be used.

12. *I have appointed Tychicus to go to Ephesus.* "Tychicus, however, I dispatched to Ephesus" *(Tychikon de apesteila eis Epheson).* Ephesus is the city mentioned in 1 Tim 1:3 and 2 Tim 1:18.

The verb *apostellein* occurs only here in the PE (though the cognate *apostolos* has been applied to Paul five times). There are 130 other uses in the NT, 3 other uses of the verb in the Paulines (see Comment below). In Luke-Acts this verb is used 49 times (25/24), compared with 20 times in Mark, 22 times in Matthew, and 28 times in John. For the LXX, Qumran, and Ap. Frs. see Comment below.

13. *When you come.* On the uses of *erchomai* in the PE, cf. Titus 3:12 (cf. 1 Tim 3:14; 4:13, as well as 4:21 *infra;* other senses than physical journeying, 1 Tim 1:15; 2:4; 2 Tim 3:7).

*bring along.* This is the only use of *pherō* in the PE, though there are 68 NT occurrences. There is only 1 other Pauline use, Rom 9:22, in a figurative sense of God's "bearing" the vessels of wrath. The Lukan corpus employs the term 14 times (4/10), whereas John uses the verb 17 times; Matthew, 6 times; Mark, 15 times. The sense of physical carrying or bearing is frequent enough in the Lukan literature (cf. Luke 5:18 = Mark 2:3; Luke 23:26; 24:1; Acts 5:2, 16, etc.). For the LXX usage, see K. Weiss, *TDNT* 9.56-57. For *eispherein,* cf. 1 Tim 6:7 (and Weiss, p. 64). The verb occurs often enough in the Ap. Frs., particularly in Hermas, who uses it of carrying actual objects (cf. *Vis.* 3.2.7 of stones; *Sim.* 8.2.1 of crowns; etc.); otherwise see Weiss, pp. 59-60.

*that cape which I left behind in Troas at Carpus's home.* Lit. "the cloak *(ton phailonēn)* which I left behind *(hōn apelipon;* see Titus 1:5) in Troas *(en Trōiadi)* with Carpus *(para Karpōi). . . .*"

On *phailonēn* see the texts assembled in D-C, p. 123, and Spicq, *EP,* p. 814.

Greek borrowed the term from Latin *paenula* (cf. Spicq, "Pèlerine," p. 390 n. 5), and often with metathesis of the liquid consonants (cf. BDF §32.2; cf. also 25) but not always (LSJ: *phainolēs* is the usual spelling, p. 1912), and J. K. Elliott, *Greek Text,* p. 165, noting the *phelonēn* of S. A. C. etc. with the *phailonēn/phailōnēn/phelōnēn* of others, submits that the spelling of the original author is unidentifiable. Most papyri favor *phain-*, but there are enough exceptions to preclude a final choice. Etymologically the Latin term seems to have come from the Greek *phainolis* (light-giving) or *phainein* (to show forth), which may have designated the garment as bright in color or perhaps "showy," i.e. conspicuous (cf. Buck, *Indoesyn,* p. 417; Spicq, "Pèlerine," p. 390 n. 5). Ernout and Meillet, *DELL,* p. 474, say that it was borrowed by the Greeks at a very early stage, since in Latin the aspirate has been lost (cf. *ampulla*), and that the word appears as early as Plautus for a hooded cloak. Harpers cites *paenulam in caput induce, ne te noscat:* Pomponius, d. 138 C.E., *apud* Nonius the Grammarian 537.8 (third century C.E.), and see G. Lucilius (180[?]-102[?] B.C.E.) there too; L. *Remains OL* III, 162-163, *Paenula, si quaeris, cantherius, servus, segestre / utilior mihi quam sapiens,* "If you ask me, a cloak, a gelding, a servant, or a straw coat is more useful to me than a wise man" (trans. WCW). The Vulgate simply transliterated the term into the current Latin spelling, *pēnulam* (the only use of the term in Vg). *Phailonēs* is not found in the LXX or Ap. Frs.

*which I left behind.* There are only four other uses of the verb *apoleipō* in the NT, in Heb 4:6, 9; 10:26; and in Jude 6. Only the last, describing the angels "leaving" their proper habitation, resembles the usage here in the PE. The closest LXX parallels are in the Maccabean literature (1 Macc 9:65; 10:79; 2 Macc 4:29; 10:19, esp. apt; 13:23; 3 Macc 1:17). In the Ap. Frs., *1 Clem.* 3.4 uses the term of abandoning the fear of God; 7.2, of abandoning "empty and vain cares"; 9.1, abandoning "vain toil, strife, jealousy"; 28.1, abandoning "foul desires"; Polycarp, *Phil.* 2.1; 7.2, speaks of abandoning vain speech and foolishness. *Barnabas* 5.12 has this verb as a variant for the sheep of the flock being abandoned (apparatus in *Clavis,* 55 *s.v.*). MM *s.v.* cite the legal sense in wills, and a Phrygian gravestone of 114 C.E. that describes "a woman who left *(apolipous[a])* four sons on earth and a daughter."

*in Troas at Carpus's home.* Lit. "in Troas with Carpus." In this port town, Paul had left his cloak (and his books, as will be seen) *para Karpōi.* This is the only occurrence of this preposition with the dative in the PE; the accusative is not found at all; the use with the genitive has been seen in Second Timothy only four times (1:13, 18; 2:2; 3:14). In the Paulines otherwise, only 1 Cor 16:2 has the sense "at his home," but it is found in Luke 19:7; Acts 9:43; 10:6; 18:3; 21:7, 8, 16; 28:14. The other synoptics do not so use *para* with the dative of persons, but John does (John 4:40; 14:17). Though *para* with the dative occurs often enough, it is never used to mean "at the home of . . ." in *First* and *Second Clement,* Ignatius, Polycarp, or *Barnabas.*

The proper name *Karpos* (accented on the first syllable to distinguish it from the common noun *karpos,* sixty-six times in the NT) occurs only here in the NT, the Ap. Frs., and the LXX. The Greek term meant "produce, harvest, fruit," though that sense was normally as remote as it is in English proper names such as *Ham* or *Applebaum.* MM *s.v.* note the use of the name on a Magnesian coin of 230 C.E. *(M. Aur. Karpos),* and Spicq notes its use in a Corinthian inscription (*Inscr. d. Cor* 8.3.68). Preisigke, *Namenbuch s.v.,* p. 166, notes Pet III, Teb I.230, Teb II, OxyP X (along with *Karpoun* and *Karpophoros;* cf. Acts 14:17 for the common adjective). It is possible that the accent on the penult points to a Latin origin for this name (as well as distinguishing it from *karpos* in Greek), which, as *Carpus,* means "carver" (*carpere;* see Petronius 36, *ad fin.* and 40, *obsonium carpit,* "he plucks fruit," cited in Harpers). Here again the etymological sense was as far from the surface as in the English cognate proper name *Carver.*

*the books. To biblion* occurs thirty-four times in the NT (with twenty-three in Revelation). The plural, *ta biblia,* occurs only here and at John 21:25 and Rev 20:12. This is the only use in the PE; there is only one other use in the Paulines, at Gal 3:10 = Deut 27:26 in the form *en tōi bibliōi tou nomou,* "in the book of the law" (not in MT or LXX), where the reference is to Deuteronomy and thus to the whole Pentateuch (or Torah). Neither the MT nor LXX has book or its equivalent; both read *words* (MT *dibre;* LXX *logios*). Also the word *bibliōi* in Galatians is not plural.

The only Lukan usage of the word is in the singular, of the Isaiah roll that Jesus read from in the Nazareth synagogue (Luke 4:17 [*bis*], 20). In both Mark 10:4 = Matt 19:7 the term refers to the divorce document prescribed by Deut 24:1 (cf. G. Schrenk, *TDNT* 1.617). In John 20:30, "in this book *(bibliōi)*" refers to the Gospel document, as the plural in John 21:25 refers to all the possible volumes that could be penned about Jesus' words and deeds. Hebrews 9:19; 10:7 use *biblion* of or in connection with the rolls that we now call parts of the OT (Schrenk, p. 617: the Covenant Law, the Psalms).

On the Egyptian origin of this Greek term *(byblos; biblos)* for papyrus (rolls) see Schrenk, *TDNT* 1.615-616, 618, noting especially the use of *biblos* in Luke 3:4; 20:42; Acts 1:20; 7:42; 19:19 (only this use of Ephesian books of magic, all the others of OT books, whether of individual ones or a book containing several authors [prophets]). Luke 3:4 uses *biblos* of Isaiah, but in 4:17 and 20 uses *biblion* to refer to Isaiah; thus one infers that the terms for Luke could be used interchangeably. That does not exclude either term's having a hieratic nuance for the author, since even "books" of magic were holy for those who believed in them! Schrenk, p. 617 n. 8, has noted how, for the LXX, *biblion* designates the written *torah,* though Sirach's Prologue speaks of the reading of the Law and of the Prophets and of the other ancestral books *(tōn allōn patriōn bibliōn)* and here *ta biblia* embraces the whole Jewish collection (whatever its exact boundaries might be). The usage that appears in *Ep. Arist.* 28 and 30 (Charles, *AP* 2.97-98) seems to refer to the Torah (alone) as the Jewish *biblia.*

In Josephus, however, there is no question that the plural can refer to the Torah (*Ant.* 3.74, etc.) and perhaps to the whole collection. Cf. *Ant.* 1.15, cited by Schrenk, which *could* refer to the Torah alone; this might also be the case with *Ant.* 8.159; certainly the reference in *Ant.* 8.55 to "our books *(bibliois s.v.l.)*" refers to a collection that included what we call Second Kingdoms. In *Ant.* 10.210 Daniel is *to biblion . . . en tois hierois grammasin* (cf. 2 Tim 3:14), and in 10.218 *en tois archaiois . . . bibliois* (such as Daniel) is synonymous with *tas Hebraiōn biblous* that Josephus has been paraphrasing throughout this work. Josephus also uses the term for extracanonical Jewish compositions as well as secular documents, of which the most interesting example is in the description of the Essenes (*War* 2.142, 159), where "the books *(ta biblia)* of the sect" could be distinguished from *bibliois hierais* or could coincide with them, at least partially.

On *biblion* in the Ap. Frs., see *2 Clem.* 14.2; the plural certainly refers to the OT Scriptures (coupled with *hoi apostoli*). Donfried, *Setting,* pp. 93-94, holds for a collection of the Law and the Prophets, noting the quotations from Genesis and Jeremiah in the context. The only other uses are in *Barn.* 12.9 (of a sheet of papyrus for recording an oracle — cf. LXX Exod 17:14 and note *chartion bibliou* cited by Kraft, *Clavis,* p. 76, as a *v.l.*) and in Hermas, *Vis.* 1.3.2, of "the books of life" in the next world containing the names of the just (also in *Sim.* 2.9).

14. *There in Troas, Alexander, the coppersmith, brought many false charges against me.* Lit. "Alexander the coppersmith *(ho chalkeus)* showed *(enedeixato)* many evils *(polla . . . kaka)* in regard to me *(moi)*." On the name Alexander, so frequent in the Hellenistic world (cf. Alexandria Troas itself) and found six times in the NT, see its use in 1 Tim 1:20, the only other Pauline occurrence (see commentary above). Luke writes of an Alexander of the high-priestly family in Jerusalem in Acts 4:6 and another (Ephesian? Asian?) Jewish Alexander in Acts 19:33-34. Both apparently are to be differentiated from the one mentioned in 1 Tim 1:20, and at this point in 2 Tim 4:14. With addition of the phrase *ho chalkeus,* it looks as if the author of the PE (at least) does not want the Asian (Christian?) opponent of Paul in First Timothy to be confused with this Alexander the coppersmith of Troas (?). The only other NT use of the name is in Mark 15:21 for a son of the Cyrenian who helped bear the cross.

The only LXX use of the name is in 1 Macc 10:58. It is not found in the Ap. Frs. For its use by Jews see *CII* $85^2$, 92, 140, 370, and perhaps 84, 501 (all in the neighborhood of Rome); for the use in Latin, 210, 219, 677. Since Paul's enemies were usually from his own people and since this name was in common Jewish usage, the presumption is that this Alexander was of Jewish origin. Whether he was a Jewish Christian is a further question. The identification supplied by the text is *ho chalkeus,* with the article indicating that the trade (as is usual in the NT, J. K. Elliott, *Greek Text,* p. 165; not the cognomen) is being referred to.

The noun *chalkeus* occurs only here in the NT, and the cognates are not particularly frequent there either (cf. 1 Cor 13:1; Rev 18:12; etc.). The term is found seven times in the LXX (Gen 4:22 of Tubal-Cain; 2 Chron 24:12; Neh 3:32 [RSV, "goldsmiths"] for MT *ṣrp;* Job 32:19 [*nil* in MT]; Sir 38:28; Isa 41:7 [RSV, goldsmith]; 54:16). In the Ap. Frs. it is documented only in Hermas, *Vis.* 1.3.2, in a comparison illustrating the effect of persistence in labor.

*Enedeixato,* "bore witness to," is also used in the PE at Titus 2:10 *(endeiknymenous);* 3:2; and 1 Tim 1:6. It is used seven other times in the NT (in the Paulines and at Heb 6:10, 11). The verb is used only in *1 Clem.* 21.7 and 38.2, of the Ap. Frs., for manifesting wisdom or purity in a public, verifiable way. Cf. also Titus 3:2; 1 Tim 1:16.

Regarding *polla,* this is the last of its nine uses in the PE (often in a bad sense as in Titus 1:10; 2:3; 1 Tim 3:8; 6:9-10).

*(The Lord will give him the recompense that corresponds to his deeds.)* Lit. "The Lord *(ho kyrios)* will repay him *(apodōsei autōi)* according to his works." The Semitic tone and word order in this parenthesis have led to a number of the variants noted by J. K. Elliott, *Greek Text,* pp. 165-166. The most important is the variant *apodōē* for *apodōsei* in a series of Western and other texts beginning with D$^c$ (list in Elliott, p. 166). It is conceivable that this subjunctive/optative (see Elliott) was original but that the consequent wish or curse sounded altogether too harsh. Thus the scribes consciously assimilated the remark in the Paulines to the language of LXX Ps 61:13 (MT and Rahlfs, v. 12): *sy (kyrie) apodōseis hekastōi kata ta erga autou,* "For you (O Lord) will repay each one according to his works" (trans. WCW; cf. Prov 24:12). Yet it must be admitted that ancient scribes, too, had vengeful impulses and would have found it easy and altogether justifiable to escalate the Pauline phrase (abrupt and in its Semitizing a little difficult to fit into the development of the thought here) into a prayer whose conceptualization is quite in the apocalyptic, martyrological tradition (cf. Rev 6:9-11). This would be particularly likely if the citation of LXX Ps 61 did not occur to the scribe. Stählin, *TDNT* 8.268 n. 63, cites this passage in commenting on Paul's prophetic judgment on the high priest in Acts 23:3.

15. *Watch out for him yourself now.* Lit. "Whom you also *(hon kai sy)* be on guard against *(phylassou).*" On this verb, see its uses at 1 Tim 5:21; 6:20; and 2

Tim 1:12; 14, which yield a somewhat different sense. The meaning in this verse is, however, quite Lukan (cf. Luke 12:15 and Acts 21:25); 2 Thess 3:3 has *phylaxei apo tou ponērou.*

*because his defiance of our words was frenzied.* The reason *(gar)* for the preceding command is that Alexander "exceedingly *(lian)* opposed *(antestē)* our words *(tois hēmeterois logois).*" This is the only use of *lian* = "vehemently" in the PE, and it is not otherwise documented in the Paulines. Of the eleven other NT uses, one is Lukan, Luke 23:8, of Herod's exquisite joy at seeing Jesus (cf. 2 John 4; 3 John 3, also of joy; as well as Matt 2:16 of Herod the Great's rage). Matthew 27:14 and Mark 6:51 also use this adverb of heightened emotional reactions. There are twenty LXX occurrences of *lian,* though none especially notable for defining further the meaning here in 2 Tim 4:15. The uses in the Ap. Frs. (all but five in Hermas) do not add anything.

On *anthistanai* (cf. J. K. Elliott, *Greek Text,* p. 168, for perfect read in S^c.^ D^c.^ etc.), see the uses in 2 Tim 3:8 and the commentary *in loc.*

## ♦ COMMENT

4:9. *Do your best to come here soon.* A few witnesses use the unclassical and unliterary (BDF §102) *tachion* here (I.33), and J. K. Elliott, *Greek Text,* p. 161, considers it the likely original here. However, the weight and variety of traditions against this form make *tacheōs* almost certainly the form originally written. With BDF §244.1 note that the sense may be "very quickly" or "as quickly as possible," and note the papyri cited in Spicq, *EP,* p. 810. He has observed the urgency of the language here, though its quasi-formulaic character as "an epistolary cliché" ought also to be weighed.

However, the pleonastic *tacheōs* serves precisely to revitalize the formula and to alert the reader that its language is not simply conventional. A further reason for the formula's repetition at this point may be adduced: as it rounded out the letter to Titus above, so now the same phrase serves to conclude the correspondence with Timothy. It introduced the final *personalia* in Titus; it now introduces the concluding *personalia* of the letters to Timothy (First Timothy had no such *personalia* precisely because it was to be read with Second Timothy in redaction).

10. *for Demas, his heart set on this present world, left me helpless and set out for Thessalonika.* As it did in 1 Tim 6:1, "the present age" has here a pejorative sense. *Egkatelipan* will recur with *pantes me* in 4:16 below, and the term, not otherwise found in the PE, gives its tone to this whole closing section of this correspondence. The precise sense of the verb is "to leave one helpless."

The first person pronoun *me* as object is not to be overlooked. It is Paul who has been abandoned or left helpless, and the obvious presupposition is that Demas belonged to the Pauline entourage, the traveling *curia* who served him, implemented his directives, were dispatched by him. What is certainly true of Crescens, Titus, Luke (in the next verse), and Tychicus (v. 12) must be true of Demas here. He was numbered among those who shared Paul's ministry in a special way (again the *met' emou* of v. 11). His departure from Paul differed from that of the rest, for only of him is it said *egkatelipen,* "he deserted." Of Demas, Crescens, and Titus *eporeuthē,* "he went," can be predicated; Paul "sent Tychicus *(apesteila).*"

The letter here aims precisely at restaffing the Pauline entourage (v. 11, with Mark as well as Timothy). A glimpse of its normal complement can be surmised from the two additional names in 4:20 *infra.* The Pauline staff is obviously to be distinguished from those local Roman Christians named in 4:21. *Pace* D-C, it requires no "literary critical manipulations" to perceive the quite different intentions of 4:9-12 compared with 4:19-21. The *pantes* of verse 16 versus the *Loukas . . . monos* of verse 11 is rather more worthy of analysis (cf. *infra in loc.*).

Colossians 4:14 and Philem 24 both contain the name Demas; in both instances his name is joined to that of Luke and both are called *synergoi,* though Demas is not otherwise described in these places (unlike the others, who appear in both Colossians and Philemon: Lohse, *Col,* p. 176). If, however, the only Jewish Christians who stayed on Paul's staff when Colossians was written are Aristarchus, Mark, and Jesus Justus (Col 4:10-11), then the *synergoi* are all (including Luke and Demas) converts from paganism. Needless to say, that does not settle the question whether they were *Semites* rather than Indo-Europeans, nor whether they had been "God-fearers" on the periphery of the synagogue in their pagan days (cf. Luke in 4:11 *infra*). Demas could have been a Samaritan (see *infra* on Thessalonika)!

Here in Second Timothy, Demas has left Paul in the lurch because, in the apostle's judgment, he "preferred" this world and its security to the next. In Menander, *Dysc.* 745, Cnemon's meditation on the advantages of his frugal life climaxes in saying all strife would disappear when *echōn d'an metri' hekastos ēgapa,* "all would *be content* with modest lives." Perhaps that is how Demas's "preference" is to be understood, as a satisfaction or contentment with material goods (Danker, "Menander and the NT," p. 368, translates, "But each would be satisfied [*ēgapa*] to have his own modest share"). Considering the subject matter of 1 Tim 6:17 (cf. 6:7-10) when it spoke of *en tōi nyn aiōni* (not to mention how 1 John 2:15-16 defines *agapan ton kosmon*), one surmises that it was the precarious poverty of the apostolate that eroded Demas's zeal (cf. also Plato, *Republic* 330c: *moi edoxas ou sphodra agapan ta chrēmata,* "You appear to me not to be overfond of money"). Note how the only uses of *agapē-agapan* in

Luke (11:42-43, cited above) are in a context of scrupulous tithing and relentless craving for honor on the part of men who really loved money (cf. Luke 16:14, *hoi pharisaioi philargyroi*). If Demas had somehow provided for the imprisoned apostle and then left with the purse, using an "apostolic" trip as an excuse for his departure, the reason for this open and devastating declaration of Paul's judgment on him becomes clearer. The apostle will have no misunderstanding. Some, indeed, he has sent off deliberately, but his present straits have been brought on not by his own imprudence but by the deliberate selfish choice of one co-worker. He does not say that Demas has abandoned the Lord, but that implication is not far from the surface. If Luke indeed penned this passage, there is little doubt as to what he considered the "French leave" of his colleague (cf. Ananias and Sapphira).

In the earliest Christian generations Thessalonika was the most populous city in Macedonia (and northern Greece; cf. Strabo, *Geography* 7.323). Founded about 316-315 B.C.E., it was named after the sister of Alexander the Great and became the best port in Macedonia. The beautiful Gulf of Salonika (on Thermaic Gulf) lies to the southeast of the peninsula on which the walled city was erected. Rivers and hot springs (cf. the name *Therma,* seven miles southeast, Finegan, *IDB* 4.629) increased the attractiveness of the site. When Macedonia became a Roman province (148 B.C.E.), the city became the Roman administrative center and free city (cf. Pliny, *Naturalis Historia*).

Recent excavations (see Thompson, *IDBSup,* pp. 901-902, for bibliography) have unearthed a Roman Forum, with a double stoa. The great Via Egnatia touched, if it did not run through, the city (cf. Makaronas, "Via Egnatia," pp. 380-388, esp. 388). The earliest extant Pauline correspondence, First and Second Thessalonians, witnesses to an established Jewish colony in the city in 50 C.E. Acts 17:1-9 also knows of this. More surprising is the witness unearthed to a Samaritan synagogue in the city, documented by the fourth-century-C.E. bilingual inscription (see Purvis, "Paleography," pp. 121-123; cf. also *CII* 108). In this text, lines 8-9, the priestly blessing is not only that "the Lord (K[yrio]s) will make his face shine *(epiphanei)* upon you *(se)*" but also "and will love you *(agapēsei se)*."

Acts 17:5-7 remembers that Paul and Silas stayed at the house of one Jason (= Joshua, and so a Jew? Haenchen, *Acts,* p. 507 n. 9) in the city. Though there is no explicit statement that he was a convert to Christ, yet it has been inferred from 17:6, "Jason and some of the brethren." Acts 20:4 remembers Aristarchus (19:29 with Gaius; 27:2) and Secundus as Thessalonikan Christians (if Aristarchus is also mentioned in Col 4:10; Philem 24 — cf. Haenchen, *Acts,* p. 628 — then he was a convert from Judaism; Secundus with his Latin name would then have represented the converts from paganism on the occasion of bringing the collection to Jerusalem).

Demas "returned to Thessalonika" because it was (or was conceived of as) his native city and home (Spicq). Whether he was a convert from Samaritanism or paganism is beyond solution, but it may be necessary to leave the option open when sketching other matters on the background of the Pauline entourage. Bauer, *Orthodoxy,* pp. 74-75, conjectured that the Thessalonikan congregation had in the second Christian generation wandered into "heterodoxy" and that the author of Second Timothy is here stigmatizing that community by making it the refuge of the worldly Demas. The Thessalonian correspondence certainly witnesses to the activity of refractory local opponents to Paul's mission within months of his departure. Yet there is no actual evidence that the community had anything like the continuing factions that plagued the Corinthian church into the nineties, and Acts in the second generation certainly makes a point of remembering the contribution that Thessalonika made to the personnel of the Pauline mission.

*Crescens has gone to Gaul.* The bad news was first in the list. With a certain abruptness due to taking up the *eporeuthē* of the statement about Demas, the next items are about less drastic departures from Paul's entourage. Crescens went *"eis Galatian,"* the reading of the vast majority of MSS from neutral, Western, and Byzantine witnesses. At first sight the meaning seems evident. The reference is to the area of Asia Minor that in Gal 1:2 (3:1, *Galatai*); 1 Cor 16:1, as well as in 1 Pet 1:1, is called *Galatia.* There the case would probably have rested were it not that S. C. 81. 104. 326. 436, as well as Vulgate, Coptic, and Ethiopic witnesses, in addition to Eusebius (*Church History* 3.4.8: *Krēskēs men epi tas Gallias steilamenos hyp' autou,* "Crescens was dispatched by him into Gaul") and Epiphanius (*PG* 41.109: *ou gar en tēi Galatiai hōs tines planēthentes nomizousin alla en tēi Galliāi,* "not to Galatia, as some who are mistaken think, but to Gaul"), read "to Gaul." Two questions must immediately be distinguished: (1) Did the original text of the PE read *Galatia* or *Gallia?* (2) To what did that term refer? On the basis of the MS witnesses, *Galatia* is almost certainly correct (note "B" in *GNT*$^{3corr}$). But to what region did *Galatia* refer? One who reads the PE as part of the Pauline collection naturally defines the region as the one to which Galatians and First Corinthians refer *(cit. supra).* But if the PE and their terminology are not necessarily Pauline, then *Galatia* here in Second Timothy could designate another region.

The MSS cited above as well as Eusebius and Epiphanius had no doubt that the region was Gaul, not Galatia, and they even felt compelled to put that meaning into the text by reading *eis Gallian(-s).* That their "exegesis" was correct is indicated by two related phenomena. First, Luke-Acts never speak of *Galatia (-ēs);* on the two occasions when Acts speaks of the Pauline mission in central Asia Minor, he uses the phrase *Galatikēn chōran* (coupled both times with *Phrygian:* Acts 16:6; 18:23). What at first sight seems to be a curious periphrasis results from a second linguistic phenomenon. Into the second century C.E., as Spicq has noted with extensive documentation, both the diplomatic and literary tradition used the term *Galatia* for ancient Gaul, (roughly) modern France and Switzerland. Even the LXX 1 Macc 8:2 — Goldstein, AB *1 Macc,* p. 347 (and see Goldstein, AB *2 Macc,* on the more problematic 2 Macc 8:20) — uses *Galatai* = the European Gauls; the scribe of the Q Ez 38:5 has added *Galatai* in the lower margin according to H-R, *suppl.* II, p. 44, but Göttinger LXX has *nil ad loc.* (vol. 16.272). Neither *Gallia* nor *Galatia* occurs in the Ap. Frs.

The "Galatian country" in Asia Minor was so named because it was colonized by European Gauls in the third century B.C.E. That Paul could in popular and occasional language call it *Galatia* was intelligible. Yet this was quite rare in formal, official terminology (cf. Schlier, *Galater,* p. 5). Magie, *Roman Rule* 1.453-454 and 2.1305-1306 n. 5, notes that the official title seems in the first-century C.E. to have been *provincia Galatica,* which later became *provincia Galatia.* On the oscillation between *Galatia/Gallia* for designating the European province, cf. *Ant.* 17.344 (where MM have *Galilaias!*), where Augustus dispatches the Jewish ethnarch Archelaus into exile in Vienna, *polin Galatias;* later in 18.252 he writes that Caligula sent Herod into exile in Lyon, *polin tēs Gallias.*

That the author of Luke-Acts was aware of the situation, the two citations above show. But in that case, Galatia in the PE may be used in its normal sense in the Roman world (cf. Haenchen, *Acts,* pp. 483-484) and thus really designate Gaul. If the PE and Luke-Acts actually had the same author, the distinction fits perfectly into the two works and distinguishes both from the normal Pauline usage. In any case, the early scribes and historians left a warning that *Galatia* in the PE did not mean what it had in Paul (Spicq).

That *Galatia* = Gaul here may further be inferred from the content of this section, for in verse 12 Tychicus has been sent to Ephesus (with this letter?). There would be little reason to send two men by the same route when one could have carried the message to Ephesus and then gone on to Galatia. *Acts of Paul,* Hennecke and Schneemelcher, *NT Apoc.* 2.383, has "Luke from Gaul and Titus from Dalmatia" awaiting Paul in Rome as he comes for martyrdom.

*Titus, to Dalmatia.* Lit. "Titus (set out) for Dalmatia *(Titos eis Dalmatian).*" There is little doubt that the Titus here is the one to whom the initial letter in this correspondence was addressed (see Titus 1:4), and the mention of him here serves to round off the whole collection. In Titus 3:12 he had been the one told to hasten to join the apostle in Nicopolis for the winter season, just as here Timothy is to hasten to Paul's side "before winter" (v. 21). Here Titus is said to have gone "to Dalmatia," a name not otherwise attested in the NT, LXX, or Ap. Frs., though frequently enough documented in other Greek and Latin texts. The most striking, in this context, is that of Augustus's *Res Gestae,* Ancyra

29.1, which mentions "Spain, *Galatia,* Dalmatia," where *Galatia* is evidently the formal name of Gaul and then "Dalmatia" refers to the Roman senatorial and later imperial province that corresponded with much of what was until recently Yugoslavia. It, too, had not only Greek colonists but also many Gallic settlers. (See Spicq, *EP,* p. 55 n. 9, for bibliography including Hammond, *Epirus,* pp. 614, 700.) Romanization had begun as early as 168-167 B.C.E., a process that reached its peak under Augustus, Tiberius, and Claudius (Spicq, p. 55: see J. Finegan, *IDB* 1.757, who notes some of the bloody cost of this colonization).

The term *Dalmatia* specifies those inhabitants of the southern part of the larger area designated as *Illyria* or *Illyricum* (Finegan, *IDB* 2.681). In Rom 15:19 Paul writes that he has carried the apostolic preaching from Jerusalem *kai kyklōi mechri tou Illyrikou,* "and as far round as Illyricum" (RSV), which certainly means up to that area as "the W limit of the Eastern world" (Finegan) and could mean in that area. By the time Titus was written, at least in the oldest stratum of the redaction, Paul is (recalled as) about to winter in Nicopolis (which is two hundred miles south of Illyria and in the province of Epirus). This Nicopolis, one of many a "Victory City" in the Hellenistic world, was the largest city on the western coast of Greece at that time; it boasted a double harbor, minted its own coinage, and hosted quadrennial athletic games that equaled those of Olympia. The notice here in Second Timothy would lead one to infer that Titus had indeed joined Paul there, that there had been a successful mission that had reached two hundred miles to the north (i.e. into Dalmatia), and that now Titus had been sent back there from Rome to reinforce and consolidate what had been begun as long as a year (?) previous.

11. *Only Luke is with me now.* The *met' emou,* "with me," refers to the members of Paul's own circle or staff, the entourage that traveled with the apostle (cf. the greeting to Titus from *hoi met' emou pantes* in Titus 3:15). Those local Christians who send along greetings in verse 21 are not "with" the apostle in this sense. The only one of his entourage left at this point is *Loukas,* a name documented otherwise in the NT only in Col 4:14; Philem 24, where he is listed among the non-Jewish co-workers *(synergoi)* of Paul and described further as "the beloved physician *(ho iatros ho agapētos)*." The name does not occur in the LXX or the Ap. Frs.

BAGD *s.v.* give the references to inscriptions, one of which is from Pisidian Antioch, where it was found in conjunction with another that calls the same boy *Loukios.* The name could be an abbreviated (and affectionate) nickname for the Latin name *Lucius* (BDF §125.2 also suggests *Lucanus*), and attempts have been made to identify the *Loukas* of the Paulines with the *Loukios* of Cyrene in Acts 13:1 (thus Ephraem of Syria cited by Haenchen, *Acts,* p. 374 n. 7; BDF §268.1 note that the "incorrect" use of the article with *ho kyrēnaios* here in Acts 13:1 may be due to the author's [or a redactor's] wanting to distinguish the *Loukas* = *Loukios* who wrote this work from the Cyrenian Lucius being noted at this point) or the *Loukios* who with Paul greets the Romans from Corinth in Rom 16:21 (and is called his cousin) (Reicke, *Luke,* pp. 10-24).

Albright, "Retrospect," pp. 34-35, has pointed out that this Roman freedman's name is not from *Lucius-Loukios* but is the "transcription of Aramaic *Luga* (like *Marga* for *Marcus-Markos*)." Reicke, *Luke,* p. 12, had noted how "Aramaic names like Kephas influenced the ending of Lukas and similar names," and Albright has perceived correctly that the name actually was Aramaic and thus only formally and apparently a hypocoristicon in *-as* (BDF §125). Thus the *Loukas* of Second Timothy and Colossians-Philemon is a Semite, though not necessarily a Jewish Semite. He might have been rather a "God-fearer" who (in the area of Syrian Antioch) came into contact with the earliest Christian preaching in that city and passed from paganism into Chrisianity. The Muratorianum has been conjectured to say that Paul took Luke along *quasi itineris studiosum* (i.e. as a man who liked to travel), though the text actually reads *quasi ut iuris studiosum,* i.e. with legal training (cf. Spicq, *EP,* p. 813; Fitzmyer, AB *Lk,* p. 37).

*Pick up Mark and bring him along with you, for he can be helpful to me in my ministry.* With *Markon analabōn age meta seautou,* the reason for the extended list of departures becomes quite clear. Timothy is indeed to come quickly (v. 9), but not just because Paul is lonely. He is to come to help man a decimated staff, and he is to bring another man with him for that same service, *estin gar moi euchrēstos eis diakonian.* Spicq, *EP,* p. 813, has noted that the aorist imperative *age* may imply that Mark is to be picked up along the way, at an unspecified point. Thus it is implied that he is not in Ephesus(?) with Timothy, but that the latter does know where to find him.

Who is this Mark *(Markon)?* It is a name found seven times otherwise in the NT, twice in the Paulines. In Col 4:10 he is numbered among the Jewish Christians and called "nephew" (cousin: Lohse, *Col,* p. 172 n. 21, and BAGD *s.v.*) of Barnabas. In Philem 24 he is listed along with Aristarchus, Demas, and Luke as one of Paul's *synergoi* (cf. Col 4:11). It seems to be of Mark that Col 4:10 says, "Concerning whom *(hou)* you have received instructions *(entolas)* if he comes *(ean elthēi)* to you, receive him." Thus the text of Second Timothy here would presume that Mark did indeed go to Asia Minor and that (years later?) he still remained in the neighborhood of Ephesus (Colossae is about a hundred miles to the east).

Acts 12:12, 25; 15:37, 39 knows a "John called Mark," son of Mary (a widow?) and perhaps a sister(-in-law) of Barnabas, to whose household Simon Peter was well known. John Mark apparently had a failure of nerve on the first Pauline mission (Acts 13:13) that led to his uncle(?) Barnabas's separating from

Paul and resuming with his nephew the mission to Cyprus. Years later he is again with Paul in the first Roman captivity (Colossians, Philemon), and as the apostle's life ends he can join this man's name to that of his beloved Timothy as one he wants with him. The one other NT occurrence of the name Mark is in 1 Pet 5:13, where he is (remembered as) with Peter "in Babylon." Haenchen, *Acts,* p. 474 n. 1, cautions about identifying all these as one person. The second Christian century, of course, prefixed his name to the second Gospel (as it put Luke's on the third). Papias's much controverted testimony means at least that much. The name Mark is otherwise unattested in the LXX or the Ap. Frs. If Albright's remark above holds, the name may be immediately from the Aramaic *Marga,* which would in turn have taken up the Latin *Marcus.* It ought to be recalled, however, that Acts is quite explicit about his having both a Semitic name (John) and a Hellenistic (Roman) one, and one ought to attach no more significance to the different spelling than one would to an Italian adding a final *-ah* to the pronunciation of an English term ending in a consonant.

The reason *(gar)* for Mark's accompanying Timothy is his being "helpful *(euchrēstos)*" to the apostle (*moi,* dative of advantage) *eis diakonian.* In this phrase the preposition *eis* has, according to BAGD *s.v.,* p. 230, §5, the sense "with respect" or "with reference" to and should be compared not only with the *eis* in 2 Tim 2:21 but also with *eutheton eis* . . . of Luke 14:35 and the *eis ouden heteron ēukairoun* of Acts 17:21. The Pauline and other uses cited there are also to be noted (e.g., Col 1:12).

The *diakonia* here is certainly to be considered part of the apostolic *diakonia* that the risen Jesus entrusted to Paul and that he shares with his colleagues. Thus personal service to the apostle is a service to the community that Paul guides. Mark not only *serves* him; he also shares in the *diakonia* that the Lord has given Paul. The precise reasons for Mark's usefulness are not further specified, though one recalls how Paul speaks of the convert slave Onesimus, *emoi euchrēston* (v. 11), whom he would like to have with him "that he might serve *(diakonēi)* me on your behalf during my imprisonment for the gospel" (v. 13).

12. *I have appointed Tychicus to go to Ephesus.* Since the PE are of a piece and to be read together as they now stand, it is altogether probable that the reader is meant to infer that Timothy himself was still there in Ephesus (1 Tim 1:3, *pace* D-C; note also the course of the journey presupposed in the following verse).

*Apesteila* is an "epistolary aorist," i.e. the action occurred at a past point in time from the view of the recipient of the letter. In other words, Paul is sending Tychicus to Ephesus, obviously to carry this note (cf. his previous mission to Colossae [Col. 4:7-8] and to Ephesus [Eph 6:20-21]), and the identification is meant to corroborate its authenticity and to validate Tychicus's departure from

Paul, since the shadow of Demas lies over this note (cf. the more casual way in which Zenas and Apollos are introduced in Titus 3:13 as the persons bearing the dispatch). The name Tychicus (and almost certainly the same person is intended) occurred also in the conclusion of Titus (3:12), where Paul was still undecided whether to send *(pempsō)* him to Crete to replace Titus, just as here he appears to be meant as Timothy's replacement, a task for which his "Asian" origin (Acts 20:4) would particularly fit him.

There are only three other uses of the verb *apostellein* in the Paulines, but all are very significant: Rom 10:15 ("How shall men proclaim the gospel if they are not sent"); 1 Cor 1:17 ("For Christ did not send me to baptize"); and 2 Cor 12:17 ("Did I take advantage of you through any of those I have sent to you?"). Out of the divine sending telescopes the sending of Paul, and from his sending comes that of these co-worker–emissaries, Titus in Second Corinthians and Tychicus here in the PE. For the Lukan writings this verb is synonymous with *pempein* (Luke-Acts account for twenty-one of the seventy-nine total NT uses of this verb [other Paulines, fourteen]), whose various forms are also Lukan favorites. Where a distinction can be made in the sense of these verbs in the NT, *pempein* stresses "the sending as such" whereas *apostellein* implies "the commission linked with" the action of sending. Rengstorf, *TDNT* 1.406, noted of the NT generally that this verb has a theological penumbra as it signifies "to send for the service in the kingdom of God with full authority (grounded in God)."

In his survey of the 700 LXX uses of *apostellein,* Rengstorf (pp. 400-402) has noted that this verb "is a technical term for the sending of a messenger with a special task" (cf. LXX Gen 8:7, 8; 31:4; 41:8, 14, etc.). The term stresses the deliberate authoritative will of the sender rather than the willingness of the one dispatched. The one sending has a plan/purpose; the one sent exists only to implement that purpose (thus Noah dispatching the birds from the ark, cited above).

Of the twenty-five occurrences of *šlḥ* in the Qumran concordances, 1QS 7.16-17, 25: Dupont-Sommer, *EWQ,* pp. 89-90, signifies an official expulsion from the community (also 8.22 and CD 20.3). In CD 4.13: Dupont-Sommer, *EWQ,* p. 128, it is used of Belial's being "unleashed *(mšwlḥ)*"; CD 11.18-19: Dupont-Sommer, *EWQ,* p. 153, of employing an unclean messenger to send an offering to the altar. 1QM 17.6: Dupont-Sommer, *EWQ,* p. 194, says of God, "He will send *(wyšlḥ)* final succour by the power of the great Angel to the lot whom he has [re]deemed . . ." (cf. Yadin, *War,* p. 340). 1QH 8.7, 10: Dupont-Sommer, *EWQ,* pp. 226-227, uses the verb in its allegory of trees (not) sending out shoots. 4QpHos$^{b}$ 2.4-5: Dupont-Sommer, *EWQ,* p. 277, writes, "They cast behind their backs [cf. Isa 38:17] those whom he had sent *(šlḥ)* to them, his servants, the prophets." 4QpPs 37; 4.9: Gaster, *DSS,* p. 329, speaks of "the Law *(htwrh)* which God has transmitted *(šlḥ)* to him" (i.e. to the righteous). 4*QdibHam* 3.13: Gaster, *DSS*, pp. 274-275, writes of "thy servants the prophets whom thou didst send to [procla]im unto us the evil which was to befall us in latter times," and in 6.8: Gaster, *DSS*, p. 277, "Thou who hast sent our enemies against us hast thyself given us courage." These texts tend to verify Rengstorf's observation on the tendency for *šlḥ* to be used of the divine authoritative sending (*TDNT* 1.402).

In the Ap. Frs. the sense here in 2 Tim 4:12 is vividly corroborated in *1 Clem.* 65.1 where Claudius Ephebus, Valerius Vite, and Fortunatus have been the *apestalmenous*, "the messengers," of the Roman church to the troubled Corinthian community, carrying this letter in which they are here identified. Ign. *Smyrn.* 12.1 sends a greeting from the church at Troas (cf. 2 Tim 4:13), "Whence I am writing *(graphō)* to you by Bourros, whom you . . . sent *(apesteilate)* with me (*met' emou* [cf. the phrase in 2 Tim 4:11]) . . . he is a pattern of God's ministry *(diakonias)*." The remaining uses in *Barnabas* (3.3; 14.9) and Hermas (perhaps eight times), though they bear out the above observations on authoritative (divine) commissioning, are less notable.

13. *When you come, bring along that cape which I left behind in Troas at Carpus's home.* The unexpressed link between this sentence and the preceding is that after you, Timothy, have read this note and Tychicus has taken your place in the Ephesian (?) congregation, you will proceed as soon as possible (cf. v. 21, "before winter" has closed the routes for navigation, around November 11) for Rome. The writer visualizes the route Timothy will follow (familiar from Acts too) as taking him by sea, winding along the coast of Asia Minor, up to Troas (150 miles as the crow flies from Ephesus; rather longer by boat; cf. the four [six] days from Troas to Miletus in Acts 20:13-16). Thus he writes, "When coming bring the cloak *(ton phailonēn . . . erchomenos phere)* which I left behind (*hōn apelipon* [see Titus 1:5]) in Troas *(en Trōiadi)* with Carpos *(para Karpōi)*. . . ."

In the phrase *ton phailonēn*, "the cloak," the definite article indicates that it is one that Timothy will recognize as Paul's. See Spicq, "Pèlerine," pp. 389-417, who has assembled an inventory of the ancient documents on cloaks (and other clothing) as well as the requests for the same. One has the impression after reading the references that there was a never-ending traffic in overcoats across the whole *orbis terrarum*.

The color of Paul's overcoat is beyond recall, though one of the more common overcoat colors in the ancient world seems to have been red in various shades (Spicq, "Pèlerine," p. 391 n. 8, on the *byrron:* p. 394 n. 14). The teaching of the PE has not ignored clothing (cf. 1 Tim 2:9; 6:8), and Acts 20:33 has Paul claim that he has not coveted anyone's gold, silver, or garment *(himatismou)*. It is quite conceivable that Paul had made this garment himself (Spicq, p. 400

n. 33). Even if he bought it for ten drachmas (cf. Spicq, p. 412 n. 65, for OxyP 4.736.4), that would represent around ten days' wages. These coats were made out of very heavy material (wool, sheepskin, goat hair) and were able to shed water. Thus they served not only to cover one's limbs but also to protect from the cold and even for a sleeping bag (Spicq, p. 395 n. 19). The poor man or the man of modest means had only one such garment; thus the careful, human legislation of Exod 22:26-27; Deut 24:13 and the point of the address to the soldier in Menander's *Sikyonios,* "Stratophanes, once you had one slave only and a plain little cloak *(chlamydion),*" K. 442; Loeb, LCL, 436-437 (Sandbach, *Menandri,* p. 285, §3).

The illustrations in *DACL* III (1), 365 (§2475), are particularly notable since they emphasize not only that this traveler's cape was particularly linked with the messengers of the ancient world but also that the Roman messenger of the gods, Mercury, was imagined in such garb (recall that Paul was called Hermes at Lystra "because he was the chief speaker" [Acts 14:12], and one might suggest also because he was clad in the traveler's cloak). Epictetus 4.8.34 speaks of those who affect philosophy by letting their hair grow long, putting on a rough cloak *(tribōna),* "and if he sees somebody in an overcoat *(en phainolēi)* he quarrels with him." See Sherwin-White, *RSRL,* who, after noting the sort of certificates that proved Roman citizenship ("small wooden diptychs . . . normally kept in the family archives," p. 149), makes some observations on the styles of garments that a Roman citizen might wear (toga, pallium, etc.) and notes that the *paenula* left in "Troas, a citizen colony, might be relevant" (p. 150).

This traveler's cape is now firmly identified in terms of where the apostle left it, *hon apelipon.* In the PE this verb was used of Paul's leaving Titus on Crete in Titus 1:5 and will be used again of his having left the ailing Trophimus in Miletus in 2 Tim 4:20 below, in each instance to signify a deliberate (though not necessarily pleasant) decision. In this light one presumes that it was no accident that this garment was left behind. If the leaving of the cloak was indeed deliberate, one could infer either that the departure was hurried and thus the cloak was left for the same reason that Trophimus was left at Miletus — there was not time to take it, as there was no time to await the latter's recovery — or that the cloak had been left in the early summer with the intention of his picking it up on another trip through that area.

The city where it was left is Troas, *en Trōiadi,* a city mentioned four times by Luke (Acts 16:8, 11; 20:5-6) and once in the other Paulines (2 Cor 2:12). This was a regular port of call on the main shipping lane along the west coast of Asia Minor and into Europe (thus Paul's call into the European mission was remembered as occurring in this city, where Luke also joined his entourage [?], and from here they sailed via Samothrace into Neapolis [Acts 16:11]). Second Corinthians 2:12 has Paul's own notice of a later stop there (sometime during his Ephesian mission) when he "preached the gospel of Christ" and "a door was opened for me in the Lord." In any event, when Paul (and Luke?) were on their trip down from Macedonia, after Passover in the spring of 58 C.E., they stayed a full week with a zealous congregation. At that time Paul left Troas on foot to walk about twenty miles south-southeast to the port of Assos while the boat took the longer and somewhat rougher trip around Cape Lectum (was he still foiling his persecutors by changing plans without notice?).

Troas, once Sigia but after c. 300 B.C.E. Alexandria Troas (see Magie, *Roman Rule, s.v.* index), was about ten miles south of ancient Troy and, because of the fabled link of Roman and Trojan, a tourist center as well as an important port. Suetonius recalls that Julius Caesar thought of moving the capital there (J. Caesar §79), and Augustus put a Roman colony in the city, "one of the three colonies on the long coast of the province of Asia" (Sherwin-White, *RSRL*, p. 176, who also notes that such colonies are rather rare and that Paul is remembered as visiting them with relative frequency; cf. on Pisidian Antioch, Lystra above). The aqueduct from the foothills of Mount Ida was built soon after 100 C.E. City walls, six miles in length, protected a community with baths, a theater, etc. (F. V. Filson, *IDB* 4.712-713).

If the name Carpus is in fact Latin (see Notes above), then one would infer (as in the example from the coin cited above) that this was the cognomen (or third Roman name). The individual would probably have been a (Roman?) convert from paganism. If indeed it was at the sudden arrest of Paul by the Roman police-authorities that the cloak and books were left, it is quite credible that the prisoner would have been allowed to deposit his bulkier possessions with a fellow Roman citizen. If this occurred in 66-67 C.E., after the outbreak in May 66 of the Palestinian rebellion, one can understand why papers and possessions would not be left with a fellow *Jewish* Christian, whom a Roman would suspect of sedition *ipso facto.*

*and bring the books, too, particularly the notebooks.* Far more than by the traveling cloak, commentators have been tantalized by the concomitant request, "(when you come, bring that cape . . .) and the books *(kai ta biblia)*, particularly the notebooks *(malista tas membranas)*." The proximity of the *paenula* to Paul's library has led some to interpret the *phailonēs* itself as a wrapper or covering for the manuscripts (cf. Martial, *Epigrams* 14.84; Spicq, "Pèlerine," p. 389 n. 2, points out, however, that the term in such a case would be *sakkos;* cf. G. Stählin, *TDNT* 7.58).

See the Notes above for a discussion on *ta biblia*. Schrenk, *TDNT* 1.615, 617, has noted how *biblos* and *biblion* can designate an epistle, citing LXX 2 Kgdms 11:14; 3 Kgdms 20:8; 4 Kgdms 10:1; Jer 36:1, for the latter. It is instructive to note that the seven letters of Rev 1:11 go *eis biblion,* i.e. into a single scroll, thus indicating that the letters are to be *together* (not as seven separate letter scrolls to as many congregations). The PE would be a similar composition of three letters in one book. Still when Paul, the Jew and rabbi, asks for *ta biblia,* one would infer that the phrase referred above all to the rolls (literally "volumes") of papyrus containing the Greek and/or Hebrew texts of the books sacred to Judaism.

The next phrase, *malista tas membranas,* literally "especially the parchments," introduces a distinction that permits one to see that *ta biblia* is being used generically and thus not only of papyrus rolls but also of volumes (and perhaps notebooks) written on the leather skins of animals, and these latter particularly are the object of the apostle's solicitude (cf. the use of *malista* above in 1 Tim 4:10; 5:8, 17). There is no other mention of *membrana* in the NT, LXX, or Ap. Frs., and the term itself is here transliterated from the Latin *membrana* (MM *s.v.* and the citation of Theodoret in D-C). Harrison, *Paulines,* p. 132, notes (with LSJ *s.v.*) two other late Greek uses: the Pergamum historian Charax 14 (second–third century C.E. or early Byzantine; cf. Roberts, *Codex,* p. 174 n. 4) and OxyP 2156.9 (fourth–fifth century C.E.).

There is no scarcity of Latin users of the term, however. The Romans seem to have used *membrana* in the singular for parchment (i.e. *pergamena,* the writing material fashioned especially at the city of Pergamum for its great library; just as the Greeks named papyrus for the city of *Byblos,* they named skins for writing for Pergamum, in Mysia in Asia Minor, a hundred miles overland from Troas [see Pliny, *NH* 13.21.70]). Latin also took up the term in the phrase *ta membrana Pergamēna* (as quoted by Lydus [sixth century C.E.], *de Mesibus* 1.28 *ap.* LSJ) from Catullus 22.6-8 through Horace, *Satires* 2.3.2; *Ars Poetica* 389; Juvenal 7.23; Martial 1.2.3 (and see Roberts and Skeat, *Birth,* pp. 24-25); and Gaius, *Inst.* 2.77 (all except the first in Spicq, who cites the last on p. 183 n. 1). See also Pliny, *NH* 7.21.21, and Quintilian 10.3.31.

The word is often used of the writing material for a draft copy, a working copy of a composition, as distinct from its public edition (as in Horace, *Ars* 389-390); see Roberts and Skeat, *Birth,* p. 20, who observe that the way in which Latin normally employs the plural *membranae* would indicate that it was the word for a notebook *(codex)* made of parchment leaves and not for a roll at all (only Pliny, *NH* 13.21.70, cited already, certainly specifies a roll in classical Latin; only Jerome, *In Ex* 47.21, thus far in Christian Latin). It was in precisely this period that in Rome, at any rate, some literary works were published *in membranis* or *in pugillaribus membraneis* (see Roberts and Skeat, *Birth,* p. 25). Martial 2.1 is at pains to show the convenience that such little books offer for the traveler (though he never calls them *codices;* Roberts and Skeat, *Birth,* p. 25 n. 3). From the way in which *membrana(e)* was used, one would infer it was cheaper than papyrus in the first Christian century (Roberts, *Codex,* p. 179). Cf.

Pliny the Younger, *Epis.* 8.15.2, on reusing pages because his funds are low (probably a joke!); Cicero, *Atticus* 5.4.4, implies that papyrus *(chartam)* was dear and at times hard to come by.

Thus when Paul here requests, literally "the rolls and especially the *membranas*," he would mean the expensive papyrus rolls containing the Jewish Scriptures, and perhaps parchment (or leather) rolls containing certain books (e.g., the Torah or an Isaiah, as 1QIs[a]), but more probably the parchment notebooks containing "unpublished" materials, collections of Jesus' *logia* (not only sayings but deeds; cf. the way Mark is described by Papias and note that Mark is to join the entourage *with Luke* at this point); scriptural *testimonia;* even the draft copies (cf. Horace, *Ars*) from which the final rolls of his epistles had been transcribed (cf. Suetonius, *Julius* 56.6, on Caesar's sending his letters in this form); perhaps the rough copies and drafts of preaching, teaching, and epistolary materials. If the deposit of these materials was with Carpus because of his arrest, then it is less likely that "personal" papers were left behind that would be needed in Roman legal processes. Considering the hypothesis that Luke is the apostle's amanuensis at this point (and has apparently accompanied him since his arrest), it is quite credible that some of the rolls and notebooks belonged to him too. Roberts, *Codex,* pp. 184-185, has noted the number of technical and *medical* compositions of pagan provenance that have survived in the codex form from the second Christian century, relatively large in proportion to the number of codices that were devoted to secular compositions.

14. *There in Troas, Alexander, the coppersmith, brought many false charges against me.* The occupation of the coppersmith was not an unusual one in the ancient Hellenistic world; it would have posed for a Jew or a Christian the problem of refusing to fashion idols from that metal (Rev 9:20). It was the pagan silversmiths *(argyrokopoi),* led by Demetrius, who fomented the Ephesian riot against the Pauline entourage around 57 C.E. (Acts 19:23-41: in v. 25 "workmen of like occupation," *tous peri ta toiauta ergatas;* in v. 38 they are *technitai*). Thus it is conceivable that this identification of "Alexander" is meant to suggest a pagan enemy of the apostle who was somehow threatened by his preaching. If this dispatch did originate in 66-67 C.E., it is quite possible that Paul was caught in the backlash against Judaism through a pagan's denunciation of one who taught that no image of God could be fashioned. Then his adherence to the Christian "way" could have further complicated the matter as judicial procedures progressed.

In any case, this Alexander the coppersmith witnessed to many evil things in Paul's regard. The legal connotation of *enedeixato* has appeared earlier in the PE, in the parenesis on the the service of Christian slaves in Titus 2:10. Thus when the apostle thinks of Timothy's journey, of Troas and of Carpus's home, he thinks of the man who at that point charged him (note the aorist) with many evils *(polla moi kaka).* The dative is, like that in verse 16 *infra,* one of (dis)/advantage. *Kaka* was used as adjective in the quotation of Titus 1:12, and it was used nominally in the quasi-proverbial citation of 1 Tim 6:10 where "the love of money" is "the root that lies under all *(pantōn)* evils." Perhaps an economic motive provoked this coppersmith to denounce the apostle. In any case, the use of *kaka* is in the Lukan tradition of Acts 9:13 (cf. 14-16) with its reference to the (false) charges brought against Jesus' followers and their planned arrest.

*(The Lord will give him the recompense that corresponds to his deeds.)* The memory of Alexander brings a parenthetical observation, in a quite Semitic word order, before the warning of verse 15. The reference is surely to the Lord Christ coming in final judgment (cf. the *apodōsei moi ho kyrios,* "the Lord will recompense me," of 4:8 *supra*) and a judgment on the actual deeds of individual persons in their own histories (cf. above on *ou kata ta erga hēmōn,* "did not correspond to our deeds," in 2 Tim 1:9). Justification does not come "according to works"; judgment does. For the use of *kata ta erga k.t.l.* note in the Paulines, Rom 2:6, of God *hos apodōsei hekastōi kata ta erga autou,* "he will recompense each one according to his work"; 2 Cor 11:15, "Their end [i.e. that of the false apostles] will correspond to their deeds *(estai kata ta erga autōn)*"; as well as in 1 Pet 1:17 of God the Father "who judges each one impartially according to his deeds" *(krinonta kata to hekastou ergon,* the only NT use of the singular in this phrase; cf. also the impressive cluster of occurrences in Rev 2:23; 18:6; 20:12-13). The only use in the Gospels is at Matt 23:3. The passage in Romans is particularly notable since such close verbal correspondence between the PE and one of the *Hauptbriefe* is quite unusual. The passage of Romans is a shade closer to the LXX, and LXX Ps 61 probably stands independently behind each passage rather than Second Timothy's taking up Romans. In any event, the apocalyptic usage of the NT has given an indelible color to this whole phrase. The divine reward or punishment is confidently predicted and explicitly taken out of human hands. For all the uses of *erga* in the Ap. Frs., the phrase *kata ta erga (ergon)* occurs only in *1 Clem.* 34.3, citing LXX Ps 61:13; and *2 Clem.* 17.4 (cf. 11.6). In both places the setting is that of the last judgment and the language is that of apocalyptic.

15. *Watch out for him yourself now, because his defiance of our words was frenzied.* After the parenthesis, in a relative connective clause that is "more Latin than Greek" (BDF §458), Timothy is warned. The instruction surely seems to imply that Timothy is liable to meet the man when he comes to Troas, not that he is already a threatening element in the community (Ephesus) where this letter is to be delivered. Indeed, the warning seems quite otiose if that is the case. Rather, Timothy, when he passes through Troas and picks up Paul's things at Carpus's home, is to keep himself from (note the middle imperative) the local coppersmith.

The commentary on 2 Tim 3:8 could have been written as a commentary on this passage if Alexander is in fact to be classed with the Hymenaeus and Philetus of 2:17 as still another example of the (Jewish?) Christian opposition to the Pauline preaching. The opposition was on a given occasion (second aorist); it was vehement *(lian);* it was "to *our* words," i.e. to the Christian preaching (on *logoi* see 1 Tim 4:6; 6:3; and 2 Tim 1:13) by Paul and his *synergoi* (cf. 2 Cor 1:19) and not simply to Paul personally or for some other-than-religious activity of the apostle. *Hēmeteros* (an emphatic adjective: Spicq) occurred nominally in Titus 3:14 to mean "our own people" (i.e. perhaps those converted from Judaism and paganism by Paul, or those who were Jewish Christians already when Paul arrived and welcomed the apostle and his converts), and the usage here in Second Timothy as in Rom 15:4 could accordingly mean "our" in the sense of the (Pauline) Christian congregation (cf. "our" as identifying with Judaism in Acts 24:6 [*s.v.l.*]; 26:5) and its public teaching.

If this is the sense here in Second Timothy, the apostle is indicating that Alexander's denunciation and preferring charges arose out of a highly charged public confrontation between the apostle, his co-workers, and the Christians of Troas with this coppersmith. Spicq would understand this of the actual legal deposition against Paul. That does not settle the question of Alexander's own religious persuasion. He could have denounced Paul as a pagan or even as a Jew. He could have been a convert from either paganism or Judaism who went sour and turned against his former confreres and mentors. In any case, he went for the top, rightly perceiving that Paul was the visible leader galvanizing this whole movement into life.

## V.B. Paul at Law (4:16-18)

*4 16At my first appearance in court no one was on my side; instead, all left me helpless. (May it not be held against them!) 17Still the Lord stood by me and put his strength in me, so that through me the proclamation would be carried out fully, or, in other words, so that all the pagans would listen to it, and I was delivered "from the lion's mouth." 18The Lord will deliver me from every one of these vicious attacks and he will save me for his kingdom, in heaven. To him, the glory for all eternity. Amen.*

### ♦ NOTES

4:16. *At my first appearance in court no one was on my side; instead, all left me helpless.* Lit. "In my first defense *(en tēi prōtēi mou apologiai)* no one (*oudeis* [the last of seven uses in the PE; see esp. 1 Tim 6:16; 2 Tim 2:4]) stood by me *(moi paregeneto).*" On *prōtos* see its previous uses in 1 Tim 1:15-16; 2:13; 5:12. The sense can be comparative in Hellenistic Greek (i.e. earlier *or* former of the two) or superlative (i.e. the first of a series). On the NT use of *apologia* see Comment below.

The LXX uses *apologia* only in Wis 6:10 of the "defense" that even kings have to present before God's tribunal (cf. also LXX Jer 20:12 for *apologēma* and LXX Jer 12:1; 38:6; 2 Macc 13:26 for the verb). The terminology is not documented in the Ap. Frs., though the verb does occur in *Mart. Pol.* 10.2, where Polycarp refuses the invitation of the proconsul to present his defense *(apologeisthai)* to the crowd. More revealing is the title of the Bodmer Papyrus of the Acts of Phileas (c. 300 C.E.) that reads *apologia Ph[i]leou episkopou Thmoueōs* (col. 1, line 1). The text (col. 1, line 5; Musurillo, 328-329) records, "Now at the time of his first defense *(en men tēi protēi apologeiai)* . . . he was cast into prison." It goes on to mention his third and fourth and finally to detail his fifth appearance before the Roman court. Spicq cites also the novelistic Acts of the pagan martyrs (*Acta Alexandrinorum* 4.2.1) and Philostratus, *Life of Apollonius of Tyana* (Loeb references to use of *apologia/-eisthai* in Munck, *PSM,* p. 329 n. 3). Cf. the use in Menander, *Sam.* 334 (Sandbach): "As it is, in my eyes now he's cleared himself *(apolelogētai),* for when this marriage scheme was broached, he eagerly gave ear." Cf. Munck, *PSM,* pp. 327-329.

This is the only use of *paraginesthai* in the PE. Of the thirty-five other NT uses, one is in the Paulines (1 Cor 16:3 = "arrive publicly") and twenty-eight (eight/twenty) are in Luke-Acts (cf., e.g., Acts 10:33; 18:27; 23:16; 24:17, which have the connotation of "coming to the aid" or "to help" near the surface). Spicq has noted the suggestion of coming to exercise a public function. MM *s.v.,* p. 481, are insistent that the nuance of come/arrive *to help* is here in Second Timothy to be found only in the dative of advantage, *moi,* which here alone in the NT follows *paraginesthai.* In the many LXX uses of this verb it seems never to have been followed by a dative, though the usage was classical enough; LSJ cite *Odyssey* 17.173 of the herald who was present (to help) at the banquet (Plato, *Republic* 329b). BAGD cites *Republic* 368b; and Aeschylus, *Eumenides* 319, "as upright witnesses for the slain *(thanousin)* do we present ourselves *(paragignomenai),*" may be especially noted.

Of the four uses of *paraginesthai* in the Ap. Frs., none actually takes the dative, though Ign. *Trall.* 1.1 comes close to it (the other uses are *1 Clem.* 12.6; Ign. *Rom.* 6.2; Hermas, *Sim.* 9.5.7).

The verb *egkatelipon* was analyzed above when it was used of the desertion of Demas in 2 Tim 4:10.

*(May it not be held against them!)* The NT has 40 uses of the verb *logizesthai;* the PE, only this one. In the other Paulines there are 33 uses of

*logizesthai,* but only 2 in the Lukan corpus (Luke 22:37, the verb of LXX Isa 53:12; cf. Heidland, *TDNT* 4.287 n. 12; and Acts 19:27). In the other Gospels, only John 11:50 uses the term.

Heidland, *TDNT* 4.284-292, has noted the basic senses of classical Greek usage, to add up/evaluate (keep track of) or to deliberate/conclude (cf. Menander, *Sam.* 4: Sandbach, p. 231). There are 123 uses of this verb in the LXX, almost always for the Hebrew *ḥšb* (Heidland, *TDNT* 4.284), and into the Greek usage via the Hebrew came not only the suggestion of subjective emotional thought but also "to count something personally to someone as. . . ." LXX Ps 31:2 can thus call the man happy *hou (al. lect, hōi) ou mē logisētai Kyrios hamartian,* "for whom the Lord imputes no sin" (trans. WCW), a passage that Paul took up in Rom 4:8 (where there are 10 other uses of this verb). First Corinthians 13:5, *hē agapē . . . ou logizetai to kakon,* probably ought to be translated, "Charity does not keep track of evil" (cf. Spicq, *Agape,* E.T., 2.156-157; Heidland, p. 289, notes — and probably overstresses — that this practical side of *logizesthai* tended to atrophy in Greek but to flourish in Hebrew). LXX Isa 40:17 uses this verb in rendering "All the nations are as nothing before him, they are accounted *(elogisthēsan)* by him as less than nothing ([LXX], *eis outhen*) and emptiness." LXX 2 Kgdms 19:19 has Shimei, who had reviled David, say, "Let not my lord hold me guilty *(mē dē logisasthō* [A. B. *dialog.*] *ho kyrios mou anomian)* or remember how your servant did wrong on the day my lord the king left Jerusalem; let not the king bear it in mind." LXX Job 31:28 has "and let this be counted against me as the greatest iniquity" (*kai touto moi ara anomia hē megistē logistheiē;* no corresponding Hebrew; trans. WCW). Cf. also LXX Lev 7:8 (MT 18) of a sacrifice "not to be credited *(ou logisthēsetai autōi)*" to a man and 17:4 of the blood guilt incurred *(logisthēsetai tōi anthrōpōi ekeinōi haima)* by the one who slaughters an animal and does not present it to the Lord.

There are thirty uses of *ḥšb* in the Qumran texts, including such fragmentary restorations as 1QpHab 1.9. There this verb is used in citing Isa 40:17 (4QdibHam 3.2-3) to describe the small intrinsic worth of moral man (cf. 1QS 11.21; 1QH 3.24; 4.8-9, 23 [cf. 3.6]; 18.26) and also to describe being reckoned (or not counted) as a member of this elect congregation (e.g., 1QS 3.1; 5.11, 17-18; CD 19.35). It also means to devise or contrive, etc. There seems to be no example in the Qumran texts of the PE notion of forgiving.

In the Ap. Frs., *First Clement* uses this verb five of six times in citing the Sacred Scripture: 10.6 = LXX Gen 15:6; 16:3-4, 13 = LXX Isa 53:3-4, 12; 50:6 = LXX Ps 31:2 (all evidently favored by Paul, James, not Luke in the NT). It is, significantly, in the great concluding prayer that the author takes up the psalmist's theme again, "reckon not every sin *(mē logisēi pasan hamartian)* of your servants and handmaids but cleanse us . . ." (60.2). Ign. *Trall.* 3.2 uses the verb in the sense "I think," as does *Barn.* 1.5. Of the three occurrences in Hermas, *Sim.* 8.9.3 speaks of those who "were reckoned with the heathen."

The use of the optative in the prayer ought not to be discounted here (cf. J. K. Elliott, *Greek Text,* p. 167) but taken at full value as one compares it with the 2 Tim 2:25; see above for further references.

17. *Still the Lord stood by me.* Lit. "the Lord *(ho kyrios),* however *(de),* was present with me *(moi parestē).*" On *paristanai,* cf. at 2 Tim 2:15 above for its transitive uses, where the forensic as well as cultic connotations of the term are noted. The intransitive usage is particularly characteristic of Luke (B. Reicke, *TDNT* 5.839, cites Luke 19:24 as well as Acts 1:10; 4:10, 26 [in a hostile sense, citing LXX Ps 2:2]; 9:39; 23:2, 4; 27:23-24 [of the appearance of an angel to Paul in the night and then of his own appearance before Caesar]). The intransitive usage here in 2 Tim 4:17 is evidently more Lukan (who uses both transitive and intransitive senses) than Pauline, who uses the intransitive form relatively less (two of fourteen times), but it does occur in Rom 14:10 and 16:2 (which is especially close to the sense here in Second Timothy).

For the LXX sense of "serving, helping, being at someone's disposal to save," see Bertram, *TDNT* 5.838-839. Particularly notable are the passages where this verb has God as its subject; thus the triumphant final affirmation of LXX Ps 108:31, "For (the Lord) stands at the right hand of the needy man *(parestē ek dexiōn penētos),* to save him from those who condemn him to death." In Wis 10:11 (cf. 12 on the contest), it is God as Wisdom who, "When his [i.e. Jacob's] oppressors were covetous, stood by him *(auton parestē)* and made him rich" (cf. Luke 21:15 where the persecuted will receive "a mouth and wisdom" from Jesus when they go on trial). In LXX Exod 34:5, "And the Lord descended in the cloud and stood with him (*kai parestē autōi* [i.e. with Moses]) there."

A striking passage in *Mart. Pol.* 2.2 ascribes the heroic silence of some martyrs under torture to the fact "that the Lord was standing by *(hoti parestōs ho Kyrios)* and talking with them."

*put his strength in me.* Lit. "he empowered me *(enedynamōsen me).*" *Endynamoō* occurred above in 1 Tim 1:12; 2 Tim 2:1 (see Notes on 1 Tim 1:12 for background).

*so that through me the proclamation would be carried out fully, or, in other words, so that all the pagans would listen to it, and I was delivered "from the lion's mouth."* A compound clause complements the two verbs of the main clause: "so that through me *(di' emou)* the proclamation *(to kērygma)* might reach fulfillment *(plērophorēthēi)* and all the pagans *(panta ta ethnē)* might hear *(akousōsin)*" and he strengthened me so that "I was delivered *(errysthēn)* from the lion's mouth *(ek stomatos leontos).*" This is the last use of the preposition *dia* in the PE, and the only use with the personal pronoun, though cf. *par' emou* in 2 Tim 2:2.

See Notes at 1 Tim 2:7 for the analysis of *kērygma* and *kēryssein;* cf. also 2 Tim 1:11. Note the "Semitic passive" of *plērophorēthēi* here; the verb has been analyzed at 4:5 *supra.*

The consummation of the proclamation is actually defined (*kai epexegeticum:* Spicq) as "all the nations *(panta ta ethnē)* having heard *(akousōsin).*" On "all the nations," note the previous analysis in 1 Tim 2:7 and 3:16. J. K. Elliott, *Greek Text,* p. 169, has called attention to the Semitic word order of *kai akousōsin k.t.l.* as well as the plural verb (with the neuter plural subject, as if Latin *gentes* had been the subject). *Akouein* was analyzed above at 1 Tim 4:16 and recurred in 2 Tim 1:13; 2:2, 14.

*and I was delivered "from the lion's mouth."* The parallels to this phrase from 1 Macc 2:60 (about Daniel) and 1QH 5.13 have been noted on 2 Tim 3:11 above. Mansoor, *Hymns,* pp. 133-134, does not refer to First Maccabees or Daniel, but he notes Ps 64:4 in connection with the further observation of the hymnist that these lions "sharpened their tongue as a sword." Gaster, *DSS,* p. 243 nn. 9-10, calls attention to Nah 2:12 for the lion's den and to Pss 120:4 (RSV 3-4); 140:4 (RSV 3). 1QH 5.8-19 declares of God, "You have delivered the soul of the poor one like a hu[nter snatching] the prey from the mouth of the lions *(mkḥ 'rywt)*" (trans. Dupont-Sommer [modified], *EWQ,* p. 216). "Mouth of the (young) lion(s)" occurs in 1QH 5.9: Dupont-Sommer, *EWQ,* p. 215: "You (O God) have closed up the mouth of the young lions." Though *kpyr* occurs four times elsewhere in 4QpHos[a] 1 and 4QpNah 5-6, 9, it is not used with *py.*

The noun *stoma* occurs only here in the PE. There are 77 other NT uses, 12 in the other Paulines, 21 (9/12) in Luke-Acts. Paul does not use the term figuratively otherwise than here in the PE, but figurative uses do occur in Luke 21:15, 24. K. Weiss, *TDNT* 7.692-701, has surveys of the secular and LXX usage (461 times).

The Ap. Frs. often employ *stoma,* particularly *First* and *Second Clement,* the former usually in citing the LXX. There is no use of the phrase "from the lion's mouth," and there is only one passage somewhat parallel to the concept here in the PE, *scil.* Hermas, *Vis.* 4.2.4, of the Lord's angel "who is over the beast 'and shut his mouth' [Dan 6:22; cf. Heb 11:33] that he should not hurt you."

*Leōn* occurs only here in the PE out of its nine NT uses, six of which are in Revelation. Elsewhere in the NT it occurs only in 1 Pet 5:8 (of the devil) and in Heb 11:33 of prophets "who stopped *(ephraxan)* lions' mouths *(stomata leontōn).*" The locusts of Rev 9:8 have "teeth like lions' teeth *(hoi odontes . . . hos leontōn),*" and in 13:2 the beast rising from the sea has "its mouth like a lion's mouth *(hōs stoma leontos)*" (cf. Dan 7:4).

Of the Ap. Frs. only Clement writes of the lion, in *1 Clem.* 35.11 (= a

Western insertion into LXX Ps 49:22 from LXX Pss 7:3 and 45:6 of Daniel "cast into the lions' den"). The phrase of PE and of LXX does not appear.

The phrase does not occur in the Milik Enoch fragments, but *Aḥikar* 2.59 (Syr) has "Visit the poor in his affliction and speak of him in the presence of the ruler and do one's diligence to save him from the lion" (Arabic: lion's mouth); Charles, *AP* 2.719, 736.

18. *will deliver.* On the verb *rhysetai* see 2 Tim 3:11 above.

*from every one of these vicious attacks.* Lit. "from every evil act *(apo pantos ergou ponērou).*" On *(pan) ergon* in the PE see Titus 1:16 etc.; on *ponēros,* 1 Tim 6:4 and 2 Tim 3:13. *Apo* has occurred a dozen times in the PE, with 6 before this in Second Timothy (1:2, 3; 2:19, 21; 3:15; and 4:4). Of its 645 NT uses, 95 are in the rest of the Paulines, 241 in Luke-Acts (127/114). Spicq reads it as suggesting a distancing from proximate peril.

In his survey of the LXX use of *ponēros,* Harder, *TDNT* 6.551, notes its use with *ergon* in 1 Esd 8:86 (*dia ta erga hēmōn ta ponēra,* "All that has happened to us has come about *because of our evil deeds* and our great sins"). This looks like the only use in the LXX as well as its standing antithesis to *kalon* (thus the visibly evil and repellent contrasted with the visibly good and attractive). Lohse, *Col,* p. 64 n. 12, has noted the use of the plural in *T. Asher* 6.5: de Jonge 66, where *erga ponēra,* "evil deeds," are parallel to *epithymiai,* "desires," and derive from service *hypo tou ponērou pneumatos,* "under the evil spirit."

In the Ap. Frs. it is only in Hermas that *erga ponēra* are mentioned, and the use of the phrase in the singular occurs in *Vis.* 1.2.4; *Man.* 4.1.2 (cf. Harder, p. 557 n. 74 also).

*and he will save me for his kingdom, in heaven.* Lit. "and he will save [me] *(sōsei)* unto *(eis)* his heavenly kingdom (or his kingdom, the heavenly one: *tēn basileian autou tēn epouranion*). . . ." Of the 106 uses of *sōizein,* "to save," in the NT, 7 occur in the PE; the verb is used in the other Pauline 22 times, and in Luke-Acts 30 times (17/13). W. Foerster, *TDNT* 7.994, has noted the novelty of the articulation of the thought here (on *eis,* cf. A. Oepke, *TDNT* 2.424, and Col 1:13: "He has delivered us [*errysato*] from the dominion of darkness and transferred us [*metestēsen*] to the kingdom [*eis tēn basileian*] of his beloved Son . . ."). On *basileia* and *epouranios* see the analysis at 2 Tim 4:1 above.

*To him, the glory for all eternity. Amen.* Lit. "To whom (is) the glory *(hōi hē doxa)* for the ages of ages *(eis tous aiōnas tōn aiōnōn).* Amen *(amēn).*" The final doxology is directed to the risen Jesus, the *Kyrios,* as is the thanksgiving of 1 Tim 1:12 (but not the doxology of that prayer). On *doxa* see Titus 2:13; 1 Tim 1:11, 17 (doxology); 3:16; and 2 Tim 2:10. On *eis tous aiōnas tōn aiōnōn. Amēn,* see the commentary on the identical phrase in the doxology of 1 Tim 1:17.

## ♦ COMMENT

It is difficult to decide whether a new paragraph begins at this point. However, the imperatives directed to Timothy with their intervening explanations (vv. 9-15) now give way to three verses of news and prayers with the third person predominating, which are then followed by four verses (19-22) of imperatives with interlarded observations that constitute the concluding greetings of this note and of the PE as well as First and Second Timothy. All seven verses appear to be bound together by the often-repeated *r* sound (twenty-one times, and *ph* four times), which gives a kind of staccato intensity to the whole conclusion.

4:16. *At my first appearance in court no one was on my side; instead, all left me helpless.* What is an *apologia?* What is "the first defense" (note the article) being described here? The noun has not been used before in the PE. There are seven other NT uses (including 1 Pet 3:15), of which four are in the Paulines: 1 Cor 9:3 and 2 Cor 7:11 use the legal figure of a defense in a formal trial though there is actually no such process occurring; in Phil 1:7, 16, however, the imprisonment of the apostle issues in "the defense and confirmation of the gospel *(en tēi apologiai kai bebaiōsei tou euaggeliou).*" Indeed, he lies in prison "for defense of the gospel *(eis apologian tou euaggeliou).*" Even here the legal process that is actually going on is seen as a reflex of the only *apologia* that really concerns Paul, the vindication of the good news that he has been commissioned to bring. See Munck, *PSM,* pp. 322-325, for the way in which Phil 1:15-17 depicts the Roman church divided vis-à-vis Paul, "the captured eagle" (p. 325). In the Paulines the cognate *apologeisthai* occurs in Rom 2:15 of the trial that goes on in a man's conscience as he accuses and excuses himself, and in 2 Cor 12:19 of Paul's defending himself with the Corinthians.

It is in Acts 22:1 and 25:16 that Luke uses *apologia,* first on Paul's lips as he begins his "defense" before the rioting mob in Jerusalem (cf. the use of the verb by the Jew Alexander before the Ephesian mob, in Acts 19:33) and then on the lips of Festus as he describes the Roman practice *(ethos)* of giving an accused man a chance to defend himself *(topon apologias)* face-to-face with his accusers, a confrontation that took place the day after Festus acquainted Paul's opponents with the procedure that would be followed (thus Acts 25:2-8). In Acts 25:8 Luke uses the cognate verb, writing, "Paul said in his defense that *(tou Paulou apologoumenou hoti)* . . . ," with a brief summary of the case he made before Festus for his innocence. The same verb (which occurs eight times in Luke-Acts) is then used three times over in Acts 26:1-2, 24, of Paul's speech defending himself before Agrippa (and Festus). In Acts 24:10 the same verb had been used to describe Paul's formal defense against his accusers in the presence of the previous governor, Felix. The uses of the verb in the Third Gospel (Luke 12:11; 21:14) are also of the defense that believers will have to give in formal trials before Jewish and Roman authorities ("synagogues . . . kings . . . governors"). Thus in Luke-Acts (unlike the Pauline usage of Romans and Second Corinthians) this cluster of terms always refers to some kind of public, formal speech, almost always in a strictly juridical process. Paul's *apologiai* in Acts are: (1) before the crowd when he was rescued from lynching (public though not a trial); (2) before Felix (legal); (3) before Festus (legal); and (4) finally before Agrippa and Festus (public, before a Jewish "king" and pagan governor but not a strictly legal procedure). For the way in which this part of Acts fits into what is known of Roman legal processes in the first Christian century, see Sherwin-White, *RSRL*, pp. 48-70.

If the author of the PE knew Acts (and especially if the same author wrote Acts and 2 Tim 4:16), then "the first defense" could well refer to the scene and speech *(apologias)* of Acts 22:1. Or, if the term is to be taken of a strictly legal confrontation, then what of Acts 24:10 *(apologoumai)*-21? In either instance Paul is utterly alone and abandoned (cf. *infra*), for only in Acts 24:23 does Felix allow Paul's friends to come to him. In either case, *prōtos* would refer to the first in a series of four "apologies" described in Acts, or the former of two legal confrontations with Paul's accusers. Note the similar flashback to sufferings recorded only in Acts and in 2 Tim 3:11.

If the reference is not to the narrative of Acts, then it may be to the first defense that occurred in Rome, before Caesar, after the two-year period with which the narrative of Acts concludes. In that case, a thumbnail sketch is here provided of the Pauline career after the narrative of Acts. How long after? That is the insoluble question. The reference could be to a vindication that ended in the apostle's release, further missionary journeys, and (after some years) another arrest and imprisonment of which we are meant to catch a glimpse throughout 2 Tim 4. It could also refer to an *apologia* immediately after the two years in Rome that was a success by the apostle's standards but, humanly and legally speaking, a disaster. In that case the historical data transmitted in Titus and First Timothy must be fit into the "interstices" of the Pauline career before the spring of 58 C.E. (*pace* Lestapis, Harrison, et al.). It could also refer to the beginning of a legal process that started after the second arrest and imprisonment of Paul.

Some (D-C, Kelly, et al. cited by Spicq) have interpreted the *prōtē apologia* here as the counterpart of the opposition of Alexander in the preceding verse and have inferred that this verse refers to a recent happening. The link between the two is not that evident, for a new paragraph does seem to start here, and the description of a different (though not necessarily unrelated) situation.

Some have explained "the first defense" here in Second Timothy in terms of the *prima actio* of the Roman court, an informational procedure that could issue in a *non liquet* (not enough evidence to proceed to trial) or in an *amplius* that led to the *secunda actio.* Some time could intervene between the *actiones.* In that case Paul had given his *apologia (defensio)* within the *prima actio;* this had issued in *amplius,* and the present writing takes place as he awaits the *secunda actio.* Whether that *prima actio* had taken place as much as four years before in Caesarea and 2 Tim 4:16 is conceived of as coming from some time (early or late) within the two years of Paul's Roman imprisonment, or whether one is to presume an otherwise unrecorded *prima actio* on the Roman scene in that same two years, at the end of it, or sometime later, is the problem.

Can the charges against the apostle be recovered? If so, do they shed any light on precisely when the *prōtē apologia* occurred? Munck, *PSM,* p. 316, and especially Sherwin-White, *RSRL,* pp. 49-52, agree that two can be retrieved from Acts, *scil.* that Paul took pagans beyond the Court of the Gentiles in the Jerusalem temple area, and second, that his teaching fomented sedition throughout the Jewish Diaspora that would involve an offense against the emperor as responsible ultimately for preserving the *pax Romana.* The first was presumably a capital offense for the accessory as well as the principal. The latter could certainly be capital. Both required witnesses and evidence, which had apparently evaporated in the course of the Caesarean imprisonment, to the extent that, according to Acts 26:31-32, Paul could have been acquitted on the spot except that he appealed to Caesar rather than become a doomed pawn of Festus in the Palestinian political game (cf. Sherwin-White, pp. 52-53, 65-67). Thus far there is nothing to prevent one's seeing an allusion to this situation in 2 Tim 4:16-18. But why then is the speaker of Second Timothy so pessimistic about the situation in which he now finds himself, if the situation is indeed within the mild, two-year Roman imprisonment described at the conclusion of Acts? Sherwin-White, pp. 112-117, has shown that the automatic dismissal of a case on the nonappearance of accusers after two years (Cadbury et al.) is a phantom. There was no such rule of Roman law in the first Christian century.

The actual facts at our disposal are that Paul did arrive in Rome and that at the end of two years the trial before the imperial court had not yet occurred. It is legitimate to infer that this delay was due to the failure of the accusers to appear with their evidence. There is no reason to infer that the case was *ipso facto* dismissed and "no necessity to construe Acts to mean that he was released at all" (Sherwin-White, pp. 118-119). Paul *could* have simply had his case dismissed by the imperial court as it cleared its crowded docket, but Acts provides no evidence for "a merely casual release" due to Nero's whimsical clemency. See also Haenchen's rejection of the "*biennium*" theory, *Acts,* pp. 724-726 (n. 3).

But there are other possibilities: The trial took place and Paul was then either condemned or acquitted. If the former, then this passage in the PE refers to a *prōtē apologia* in that first Roman imprisonment that made the outcome of the *secunda actio* far more precarious. If the latter, then Paul is looking back over several years to his previous successful deliverance and taking courage from it, or he is taking what little comfort he can from the *prima actio* after a second arrest and imprisonment, again on a capital charge but this one in circumstances that make it much more likely to stick.

The negative observation is next antithetically *(alla)* reinforced by the *pantes* (parallel to *oudeis* above) *me egkatelipon.* Here the sense of *egkatelipon* is the same as when it was used of the desertion of Demas in 2 Tim 4:10, "all left me helpless." Lestapis, *L'Énigme,* has argued for a reference here to the Jerusalem riot and/or the following *prōtē apologia* in Caesarea. In his hypothesis Timothy had not been in Palestine. Rather more probably he had accompanied Paul there, but there is no more improbability of a rehearsal of that here (*pace* D-C) than the previous reminder of the trials in Pisidian Antioch, Iconium, and Lystra (2 Tim 3:10-11) with which he was also well acquainted. If this is the reference, then the appeal to a history well known to both is being made the basis for the glimmer of hope in verse 18. See below on verse 17 also for its possible reference to Acts 23:11.

Still one must admit that the tone of this note suggests that it is giving Timothy news of what he had not yet heard, at least in any authentic way. In that case the reference is to the failure of anyone to vouch for Paul on his appearance before the imperial court "in my first defense." Against this possibility seems to be the fact that at least Luke and Tychicus (if not Demas, Crescens, and Titus) of his own entourage were still with him at this point in Rome (and both men had accompanied Paul to Palestine and could thus witness to Paul's innocence in that debacle; cf. Acts 20:4-5; 21:1; etc.). It is not so surprising that members of the Roman church (cf. v. 21 *infra*) could witness to nothing about an incident over four years past and 1,500 miles away.

How do we account for such abandonment on the part of a Tychicus or a Luke? Does this mean that the charges against Paul at this point really do not go back to the Jerusalem riot and the Caesarean defense? Or that none of his entourage at the moment had been with him when Alexander the coppersmith successfully delated the apostle and caused his arrest on a quite distinct matter? Or was perhaps Demas one who had been with him and who decided to vanish when the moment came for public witness to the apostle (the repetition of *egkataleipen/-on* is suggestive). The plural here in verse 16 indicates that there had been others, perhaps the pair mentioned in 2 Tim 1:15, who probably had split off rather earlier than Demas. In any case the *pantes* here in 2 Tim 4:16 reminds one of the similar *pantes* of 2:15 above. Moreover, for all the rhetorical poignancy of the language, it still seems most probable that the reference is not actually to all colleagues and co-workers (including Luke, 4:11) but to all who could and should bear witness to the apostle's innocence against Alexander's charges. If these inferences are correct, then this letter is indeed describing an arrest, an imprisonment, a trial that are completely distinct from those described in the closing chapters of Acts. The PE as a correspondence close with a Pauline imprisonment, as does the narrative of Acts.

*(May it not be held against them!)* As the recollection of Alexander and the arrest was accompanied by a parenthetical prayer (v. 14), so now the recollection of the abandonment is accompanied by a parenthetical prayer, *mē autois logistheiē* (note the reminiscence of *apologia*). *First Clement* comes close to the letter and the spirit of this little prayer in 2 Tim 4:16. It is, in its conceptualization, however, thoroughly Lukan, as Luke 23:34 and Acts 7:60 *(mē stēsēis autois tautēn tēn hamartian)* illustrate, and, in the hypothesis proposed for Luke-Acts-PE, seems to be the "last words" that Luke favors.

17. *Still the Lord stood by me and put his strength in me.* Against the human abandonment there stands in contrast *(de)*, "the Lord *(ho kyrios)*, however *(de)*, was present with me *(moi parestē)* and he empowered me *(enedynamōsen me)*. . . ." The chiastic arrangement of pronoun-verb-pronoun ought to be noted. The Lord, as seen at every turn in the PE, is the risen Jesus.

As *moi parestē* here in Second Timothy was antithetical with the preceding *oudeis moi paregeneto,* so now *enedynamōsen me* contrasts with *me egkatelipon. Endynamoō,* as previously at 1 Tim 1:12 and 2 Tim 2:1, understands the risen Jesus as having — at a given time (aorist) in this instance — "empowered" his disciple and given him help when human witnesses left him helpless. The concept of personal support, in this passage of the PE, has been stressed by W. Grundmann, *TDNT* 2.313.

What could have been the occasion of such an intervention by the risen Lord in the life of Paul, whose apostolate began with an encounter with the risen Jesus (Acts 9:5 and cf. on 1 Tim 1:12 *supra*)? Acts narrates regularly interventions by the Spirit, and the Spirit of Jesus, in the Pauline apostolate (cf. Acts 13:2; 16:7; 20:23; 21:11) as well as visions granted to Paul of other persons, including angels (Acts 9:12; 16:9; 27:23), and of the Lord Jesus himself (22:17-21 of the temple vision in Jerusalem on his return from Damascus after his conversion; 23:11, after the temple riot and arrest in 58 C.E.: "The following night the Lord stood by him [*epistas autōi*] and said, 'Take courage, for as you have testified about me in Jerusalem, so you must bear witness also at Rome'"). The last citation has particularly suggested to some (e.g., Lestapis) that the incidents described in these verses are in fact part of the history narrated in Acts 21:27 through 23:11. The coincidence of circumstances is in fact striking, for the narrative of Acts has depicted Paul as utterly abandoned and alone before the Roman Tribune, the mob, and the Jewish Council. The vision of the risen Jesus then occurs just before the assassination plot has been launched as a backup for the failure of the lynching and the legal process (cf. *infra* on the "lion's mouth"). Yet it must be conceded that, considering the way in which Acts has repeated these interventions of the risen Lord in the apostle's life, the reference here is to still another (a third) such experience of the apostle in what was to be the final, fatal attack on his life and one that presupposes a second imprisonment.

*so that through me the proclamation would be carried out fully, or, in other words, so that all the pagans would listen to it.* The Lord's intervention has as its purpose *(hina)* more than personal care for his chosen vessel. Now as this correspondence closes (and in our hypothesis the whole vast narrative of Luke-Acts as well), it is through the Pauline apostolate that this divinely willed mission will reach its consummation or full complement. *To kērygma* appeared as this correspondence opened in the great description of the Pauline ministry that prefaced Titus 1:3, and the cognate *kēryx* designates only Paul in the PE. The verb *kēryssein* occurred in 1 Tim 3:16; 2 Tim 4:2, also of the apostolic preaching to those who had not yet believed. Again the terminology will bear the interpretation of Lestapis, who refers this part of the clause to the Lord's promise to Paul in Acts 23:11 of bearing witness in Rome. Yet it could just as easily refer to the witness borne in a final Roman imprisonment and trial.

To what does this "hearing" by the pagans refer? Again it is notable that the visions of the risen Jesus recalled in Acts 22:17-21 and 23:11 are in connection with Paul's mission to the distant pagans and Rome. One could take the hearings before Felix and Festus as a witness to Roman pagans who were at least ready to listen to the proclamation (Acts 24:22-23; 25:19-20). Yet it is more natural to take the phrase of a witness at a trial in Rome itself either immediately after the present conclusion of Acts or after a second arrest and imprisonment. If the latter, then the *panta ta ethnē* may be intended to imply an actual voyage to Spain and the limits of the Roman world.

It appears beyond dispute, however, that a witness to *all* the pagans somehow involves a public witness in Rome and a kind of witness not yet given in that city, for obviously a Roman church consisting of not only Jewish Christians but also pagan converts was already for some time conspicuously in existence and so influential that it had evoked Paul's greatest epistle five years and more previously. Philippians 1:12-18 seems also to refer to Paul's witness in Rome as a prisoner. There is little doubt that Acts conceived this witness in terms of Paul's appeal to Caesar that would issue in his standing before Caesar (cf. Acts 27:24). Yet obviously Acts never says that it happened. Does that mean that the PE, and specifically 2 Tim 4:16-18, are a description of the conclusion of the first Roman imprisonment and of the special and supreme witness that the risen Lord willed that his apostle to the pagans give to all the nations? (See Spicq *in loc.*) Or does it mean that that first Roman imprisonment aborted and that the apostle actually carried the proclamation to "all the pagans" to the limits of the *orbis terrarum* and then went to death? It is as if the trial of Jesus had been appealed in Paul to the ultimate worldly tribunal and with Paul, as with his master, though his judges consider him innocent, the death sentence must be imposed.

*and I was delivered "from the lion's mouth."* This last phrase takes up a verb that appeared in 2 Tim 3:11 and that will begin the next verse here. It introduces an atmosphere of prayer that will continue through the *Amēn* of verse 18. Notable for understanding the phrase here in the PE is the profane use for the edge or point of the sword where *stoma* denotes the blade, piercing and tearing, as do the jaws of an animal (Weiss, *TDNT* 7.692-693; cf. LXX Gen 34:26 for OT and Luke 21:24 and Heb 11:34 for NT examples). In the LXX note particularly Ps 21:21 (Rahlfs 22), "Save me from the lion's mouth *(sōson me ek stomatos leontos)*," and cf. LXX Job 36:16 *ek stomatos echthrou.*

The only recurrence of *stoma leontos* in the NT is in an apocalyptic image for the first beast that precedes the beast who represents Nero (cf. Rev 13:18). W. Michaelis, *TDNT* 4.251-253, has noted the popularity of the lion image not only in literature but also in the art of both the Greek world and the Near East (p. 251), where it often suggests both power and courage. Of the roughly 150 LXX uses of *leōn,* it is notable in connection with this passage of the PE that a veritable pride of lion images were on the Solomonic throne and its dais (LXX 3 Kgdms 10:19-20) as well as on the bronze stands for the temple (LXX 3 Kgdms 7:29, 36; cf. Ezek 41:19), not to mention the partially leonine form of the cherubim around the ark (cf. LXX 3 Kgdms 6:23-28).

In the LXX the actual dead lion of Judg 14:8-9 has bees and honey deposited in its mouth, and Samson takes the honey, *apo stomatos tou leontos,* and fashions his impossible riddle. In LXX Amos 3:12, "As the shepherd rescues *(ekspasēi)* from the mouth of the lion *(ek stomatos tou leontos)*" a few scraps of his prey, so will it be with conquered Israel. Theod. Dan 6:20 (Rahlfs 21) has the king cry out, asking if Daniel's God can *exelesthai se ek stomatos tōn leontōn.* With the passages of Psalms and First Maccabees already cited, these are all the LXX passages that refer to "the lion's mouth." The phrase was scarcely stereotyped.

When it does occur, however, it is usually in a context dealing with one in authority with even royal power, and evidently the Daniel episode fixed itself in the imagination of later Judaism, including apocalyptic. Thus Michaelis, *TDNT* 4.253, is correct in hearing an OT resonance in this passage of the PE, but that still leaves open the question of to whom this image applies in 2 Tim 4:17. The prayer language is surely that of the Psalm of the Passion (Ps 21), but it grounds future confidence (v. 18) in an actual past deliverance (aorist) "from the lion's mouth." The reference could be to the deliverance from the Jewish plot and ambush of Acts 23:12-32 (cf. 3:11 *supra* of the Jewish persecutions, and Lestapis). But the reference could also be to the deliverance from the imperial power of Rome (cf. of Tiberius, *tethnēken ho leōn,* "the lion is dead": Josephus, *Ant.* 18.228) and Paul's release after his first imprisonment.

Somehow the singular (cf. the plural of 3:11 *supra,* but surely the metaphor is not to be pressed) and the definitive character of the rescue lead one to infer that the escape was rather more than getting into security quarters in prison. It was an escape not only from death but from the power of death, from the one who could inflict it; cf. LXX Esther 4:17$^{s}$. Perhaps we have here a sketch of the course from arrest in Jerusalem to final acquittal in Rome, or, more probably, a sketch of the Roman trial itself that ended in Paul's release. What had occurred before could happen again.

18. *The Lord will deliver me from every one of these vicious attacks and he will save me for his kingdom, in heaven. To him, the glory for all eternity. Amen.* With the hope that what had occurred before could happen again comes the hopeful, *rhysetai me ho kyrios,* "The Lord will rescue me . . . ," with the prediction of future deliverance by the risen Jesus grounded on the one that had taken place. Here the *rhysetai* is parallel to the following *sōsei* as the *apo . . .* phrase parallels antithetically the following *eis. . . .* Here the deliverance is *apo pantos ergou ponērou,* the only instance in the PE where this particle governs *ergon,* as it is the only instance in this correspondence where *ponēron* modifies this word.

In the NT *pan ergon ponēron* occurs only here in the PE, but the phrase does occur in the plural in Col 1:21 (Lohse, *Col,* pp. 63-64). Otherwise in the NT it is found, always in the plural, in the Johannine corpus (John 3:19; 7:7; 1 John 3:12; 2 John 11). The use of *pan* here in the PE makes the phrase conceptually equivalent to these uses. G. Bertram, *TDNT* 2.645, observes here a judgment on all human work as vain and sinful, but *nimis probat.* Closer to the mark is G. Harder, *TDNT* 6.557, who observes that in this passage of the PE the *ergon ponēron* is precisely that work or act which the pagan or unbeliever (cf. 2 Tim 3:13) directs against the divine messenger, in this case the "legal" accusations against the apostle. The reference is not to the devil as such or his direct attack (Harder, p. 561), but to an attack from external forces nonetheless.

The risen Lord will rescue his apostle from every wicked charge in this existence. The complement and parallel to this deliverance is, *and he will save me for his kingdom, in heaven.* Usually *sōizein* denotes the eschatological salvation itself; here rather it denotes the rescue *(rhysetai)* in this existence from the point of view of the gift granted in contrast to the evil avoided. Thus, however he accomplishes it, the Lord will be granting a salvation that must lead into another existence with him (see Excursus V, "The PE on Salvation," in AB *Titus*). The rescue to come will be part of the movement into another order where safety is definitive and beyond threat.

As the previous clause in verse 18 was reminiscent of the conclusion of the Lord's Prayer in its Matthean form, so here the mention of the kingdom, in heaven, recalls the opening of that prayer. The language and concepts of this whole section are at every turn influenced by the prayer life of the primitive church and not least by LXX Ps 21.

## V.C. Pauline Greetings to Ephesus (4:19-21a)

*4 [19]Greet Prisca and Aquila and the family of Onesiphorus. [20]Erastus stayed on in Corinth. I had to leave Trophimus behind in Miletus when he fell ill. [21a]Do your best to come here before winter.*

### ♦ NOTES

4:19. *Greet Prisca and Aquila.* Regarding *aspasai:* of the other fifty-five uses of the verb in the NT, most appear in epistolary formulas for greeting. Therefore, the verb is used in the rest of the Paulines thirty-six times, twenty-one of these being in Rom 16 (however, perhaps for literary reasons, there are no appearances in Galatians, Ephesians, or Second Thessalonians). Included in the greeting were words of appreciation or welcome, but also the kiss on the cheek and the amicable embrace frequently seen in the Mediterranean world to this day (see Rom 16:16; 1 Cor 16:20; 2 Cor 13:12; 1 Thess 5:26; it can be presumed, perhaps, in Luke 1:40; 10:4; Acts 18:22; 20:1; 21:7, 19; 25:13).

Both personal names are quite Latin. Aquila ("eagle") is found in the papyri (Preisigke, *Namenbuch,* p. 16) but only the masculine *Priskos* ("venerable," though *Priskilla* is documented: Preisigke, p. 345). There seems to be a Priscus (in Greek) in *CII* 196 (from Via Appia) and an Aquilina (*CII* 389, from Via Portuensis). The Ap. Frs. contain neither name, nor does the LXX.

20. *stayed.* On the verb *menein* see above on 1 Tim 2:15; 2 Tim 2:13; 3:14, but only here in the PE in a physical sense. But note also *prosmeinai en Ephesōi* in 1 Tim 1:3. It is Lukan literature in the NT that normally uses *menein en* of staying "in a house" (Luke 8:27; 10:7; 19:5), a ship (Acts 27:31), or a city (Acts 9:43; 20:5, 15). Only John 7:9 (in Galilee); 8:35 (in the house) seem to use the phrase of physical place otherwise.

*I had to leave Trophimus behind in Miletus when he fell ill.* Lit. "I, however, left *(apelipon) Trophimos* behind ill *(asthenounta)* in Miletus." On *apelipon* see Titus 1:5 and above on 2 Tim 4:13.

The name *Trophimus* is a Greek one (meaning "nourishing" — cf. the English name Foster — and thus also "nursling," the young heir; cf. Menander, *Epitr.* 160: L 44-45 and 531K, 1, 16; or foster child: MM, LSJ *s.v.*) and has been well documented in inscriptions and papyri (BAGD *s.v.;* MM; Preisigke, *Namenbuch,* p. 446; Spicq), particularly from Asia Minor (Spicq). The name does not occur in the LXX, but both a masculine and feminine form (father and daughter) are in *CII* 169 (Appian Way). It does not occur in the Ap. Frs. In the light of Acts 21:29 he must have been a convert from paganism.

The verb *asthenein* occurs only here in the PE and thirty-two times elsewhere in the NT (but note the noun *astheneia* in 1 Tim 5:23, of Timothy's own stomach troubles). There are, as is seen above at 1 Tim 5:23, fifteen other uses in the Paulines (usually of "weakness" of conscience), but Phil 2:26-27 uses the verb of the nearly fatal *(paraplēsion thanatou)* illness of Epaphroditus, and apparently 2 Cor 12:10 includes Paul's own illnesses. There are only four uses of this verb in Luke-Acts (one/three), all except Acts 20:35 (in Miletus!) certainly of physical illness, even a fatal one (Acts 9:37). With Trophimus here, as with Timothy in 1 Tim 5:23, there has been no gift of physical healing granted through the apostle's intercession (cf. A. Oepke, *TDNT* 3.214). G. Stählin, *TDNT* 1.490-493, has little on purely physical illness, but he does note the *pneuma . . . astheneias* of Luke 13:11 that reminds one that Timothy had received with Paul the precise opposite, a *pneuma . . . dynameōs* from God (2 Tim 1:7).

In the LXX there are only six uses of *astheneia* (cf. esp. 2 Macc 9:21-22 of Antiochus's final illness), but the verb is used about sixty-four times (plus six in Theod. Dan 11), translating most often the Hebrew *kšl* (to stumble, stagger, totter). Examples certainly referring to physical illness as such are hard to come by. The same seems to be true of the twenty-two uses of the adjective *asthenēs.*

In the Ap. Frs., *1 Clem.* 59.4 prays, "Heal the sick *(tous astheneis iasai),* raise up the weak *(exanastēson tous asthenountas),*" and *2 Clem.* 17.2 uses the verb of those who are morally weak. Otherwise *First Clement* uses the noun (36.1) and the adjective (four times), but not of physical illness. Polycarp, *Phil.* 6.1; 7.2, also does not use the adjective of illness as such, nor does *Barn.* 16.7.

MM *s.v.* notes that the verb is frequent in the papyri. Especially poignant is the *asthenō* "between some household details and concluding salutations in an undated letter."

21a. *before winter.* In the phrase *before winter (pro cheimōnos), pro* is used in the temporal sense that has occurred in the PE at Titus 1:2 and 2 Tim 1:9. This is the only way in which this particle is employed in the PE (in Luke-Acts fourteen times [seven/seven], and Paul nine times outside the PE, as well as elsewhere in the total of forty-seven NT uses; it has other senses as well).

The noun *cheimōn* occurs six times in the NT, and only here in the Paulines. Acts 27:20 (cf. 27:12, 18) employs the noun of a winter storm in the context of Mediterranean travel. In Mark 13:18 = Matt 24:20 the reference is to "flight in the winter," i.e. during the storms of the rainy season (cf. Matt 16:3; John 10:22), which made the *mare clausum* from November 11 to March 10 for ancient navigators. Cf. Horace, *Odes* 1.3.9-16, "Oak and triple bronze must have girt the breast of him who first committed his frail bark to the angry sea, and who feared not the furious south-west wind battling with the blasts of the north, nor the gloomy Hyades, nor the rage of Notus, than whom there is no mightier Master of the Adriatic, whether he choose to raise or calm the waves." Cf. *Odes* 3.3.4-5 on the determined, just man who fears not *Auster/dux inquieti turbidus Hadriae,* "Auster, the stormy master of the Adriatic."

The six LXX uses are at 1 Esd 9:6; 2 Esd 10:9; Job 37:6; Cant 2:11; Sir 21:8; 4 Macc 15:32 (metaphorical). Winds, rain, and cold are constituents of the season.

In the Ap. Frs. one must wait until Hermas, *Sim.* 3.2-3 and 4.2, for the noun, which is used metaphorically of the conditions that this world and the next afford for the righteous and sinners. However, note the cognates *cheimazein,* in Ign. *Pol.* 2.3 of the storm-tossed man seeking a harbor, and *cheimerinos* in *1 Clem.* 20.9 of the season between autumn and spring.

## ♦ COMMENT

4:19. *Greet Prisca and Aquila and the family of Onesiphorus.* After the closing prophetic prayer to and praise of Christ, in a postscript, the final greetings and injunctions have been added to this letter and *ipso facto* to the whole correspondence. "Greet *(aspasai)* Prisca and Aquila and the household *(ton . . . oikon)* of Onesiphorus." The verb *aspazomai* occurred above in the conclusion of Titus, there first in the present indicative and then in the aorist imperative, just as here in the reverse order (the present indicative is used in v. 21). The attachment of greetings to letters with this verb as a technical term seems to have become progressively more common in the Hellenistic age, and it is particularly characteristic of the Pauline correspondence.

In connection with "the household of Onesiphorus" that receives Paul's greeting at the end of this verse (see commentary on 2 Tim 1:16), note that Ignatius, too, greets households (*Smyrn.* 13.1), including one by name, *ton oikon Taouias (Smyrn.* 13.2, a lady, perhaps a widow who took care of a household of widows; cf. 13.1, *tas parthenous tas legomenas chēras).* MSS 181.460 have inserted the names of "Lectra his wife" and Simmias and Zeno (children) into the text from the Acts of Paul (Hennecke and Schneemelcher, *NT Apoc.* 2.353). One may well have here a greeting to a house church in which a community of widows was assembled and that was presided over by a widow (cf. 1 Tim 5:16).

The first persons to be greeted are a woman and a man, *Priskan kai Akylan,* presumably wife and husband, whose names appear only here in the PE; they are among the recipients of the greetings of Rom 16:3-4 (where they are fellow workers, *synergoi,* of Paul who have "risked their necks" for his sake), and they send greetings (as *Akylas kai Priska* along with "the church in their house," *kat' oikon autōn*) from Ephesus in 1 Cor 16:19. The same pair almost certainly appear again in Acts 18:2, 18, 26, but there the name of the wife is the diminutive, *Priskilla.* Acts remembers them as Jews (Aquila from Pontus), tentmakers (i.e. leatherworkers), expelled from Rome (as Jewish Christians) in the reign of Claudius and encountering Paul for the first time when the apostle came to Corinth about 51 C.E. When the apostle left for Ephesus, they accompanied him (Acts 18:18-19) and later helped to update the eloquent and learned Apollos (Acts 18:26). In both the latter passages Priscilla's name leads off the pair (as particularly active? cf. Haenchen, *Acts,* p. 550 n. 11; or was her Roman family of note? Spicq, *EP,* p. 822). If Rom 16 refers to persons residing in Rome about 57 C.E., then they had returned there in the meantime. If Rom 16 is actually addressed to the Ephesian congregation, then they stayed on, still furnishing a house church (of Jewish Christians). Second Timothy 4:19 apparently conceives of them as back in Ephesus again (or as never having left). If they continued to have a house church there, it may be significant that this team of Jewish Christians is named first.

20. *Erastus stayed on in Corinth.* "*Erastos* stayed on *(emeinen)* in Corinth." Whereas no city is actually mentioned in the previous verse, the mention of Corinth and Miletus here (not to mention Rome and Thessalonika above) seems to indicate that Ephesus is indeed the place to which the greetings and this note are being dispatched. In any case this letter is not going to the cities mentioned in this verse, and the little bits of news are perhaps meant delicately to imply that Timothy is to inquire after and greet the persons mentioned on his forthcoming trip to Paul's side, even though bringing news of Trophimus would make his journey several days longer (presuming that he would go down from Ephesus to Miletus and then sail by landfall for Troas, cross the Aegean, and go on to Corinth. The reverse order of this route was followed by Timothy along with the delegates carrying the collection for Jerusalem in Acts 20:4-5, 13-15).

Corinth would be the first stop on the shortest route from Ephesus to Rome, and, even with the longer route, the house of Carpus in Troas has already been mentioned. Accordingly the apostle, thinking of Corinth, reminds Timothy (or perhaps informs him) that Erastus stayed there. The implication is that up to that point he was accompanying the apostle, and one would normally (though not necessarily) infer that Paul had been passing through that city when Erastus, on his own initiative, decided to stay on there (contrast the *Trophimon de apelipon* where Paul's initiative is stressed).

Corinth is mentioned only here in the PE, but the city is named only three times otherwise in the Paulines (1 Cor 1:2; 2 Cor 1:1, 23; cf. 6:11 for the adjective), and otherwise in the NT only in Acts 18:1, 27 *(lect. dub.);* cf. 18:8 for the adjective. The Greek city, totally destroyed by the Romans in 146 B.C.E., was rebuilt and resettled by the Romans beginning with Julius Caesar. Its eastern and western ports and its commanding position on the isthmus separating the Peloponnesus from Attica brought it great wealth. Its immorality was, even among the Greeks, proverbial. Its Christian community was as continually refractory, divided, and troublesome as any in the first century. In this city Erastus stayed. In the conclusion of Romans (16:23), an "Erastus, the city manager [D-C "acountant"] (*ho oikonomos* [cf. Titus 1:7: *tēs poleōs*])," sends on greetings, and Haenchen, *Acts*, p. 569, considers him the one referred to here in 2 Tim 4:20. Thus in the mid-fifties of the first century this man (whether slave or freedman) was a Christian, and his Greek name (not in *CII* or Preisigke; Chantraine, *DELG*, "lovable") as well as his municipal (even Roman administrative) function in Corinth would favor his Gentile origin. The name was often given to a slave (Spicq, *EP*, p. 822, with references to J. and L. Robert). Particularly notable have been the discoveries in 1928-1929 and then in 1947 of three parts of an inscription naming the donor of the pavement near the Corinthian theater:

*[praenomen nomen] ERASTUS PRO AEDILITATE*
*S[.] P[.] STRAVIT*

"... Eratus in return for his aedileship laid (the pavement) at his own expense," J. H. Kent, *Corinth* viii.3. #232 (*op cit.* Spicq, *EP*, p. 822). Both Kent and Spicq have observed that the Neronian date, the name (otherwise not found in Corinthian inscriptions), the aedileship as designating a municipal office, all point to this man's being the same as the person mentioned in Rom 16 (and here in the PE). Cadbury, "Erastus of Corinth," pp. 42-58, even though he wrote long before the fuller text was available, is still to be consulted. He has abstracted P. Landvogt's dissertation (p. 47 n. 8) for all the inscriptional evidence on *oikonomos*, and he proposes that *ho oikonomos tēs poleōs* of Rom 16:23 is the equivalent of *arcarius* (cf. Vg) *rei publicae*. The editor of the inscription has no doubt that the *cognomen-nomen* of Erastus were on a (still lost) slab to the left and that possibly the *cognomen* was abbreviated (e.g., "*M.*"), leaving five or six letters for the *nomen*. Since this would imply no tribal or patronymic abbreviation, one would infer that this Erastus was a freedman who had amassed some wealth and political influence in Corinth.

Harrison, *Paulines*, pp. 100-105 (whose observations must be qualified in the light of the recovery of the fuller text), submits that Erastus became aedile after a long career as one of the town clerks in charge of public works (roads, buildings) in the absence of a regular appointee, and that he celebrated the honor, after long years of service as one of the public accountants, by giving the new paving. But Acts 19:22 also mentions an Erastus who, along with Timothy, was one of Paul's helpers *(diakonountōn)* in Ephesus and whom he sent on with Timothy to Macedonia, whither Paul followed (Acts 20:1).

That tantalizing glimpse of a Christian named Erastus who was with Timothy as part of the Pauline entourage in Ephesus and who must have been at least a freedman since he could travel at Paul's behest is not enough to fix his identity with the Erastus mentioned in Romans and Second Timothy. His presence with Paul (if he is the same person) could have been only occasional, unless his rise to *oikonomos tēs poleōs* within months of his arrival in Corinth (after living in Ephesus and traveling through Macedonia) was meteoric. That occasional presence would fit into his having been with Paul at the time of the second arrest (he was not among those who accompanied the collection to Jerusalem), perhaps in Troas. From there he went with the apostle to Corinth (perhaps keeping his distance) and then stayed on *(emeinen)* in the city, where he still had a responsible position. In any event, there is not the slightest hint of censure here in Paul's language. Timothy is simply informed of whom he can expect to meet en route.

*I had to leave Trophimus behind in Miletus when he fell ill.* In contrast to Erastus's own decision *(de)*, Paul himself left Trophimus behind *(apelipon)* sick *(asthenounta)* in the city of Miletus. That city is otherwise mentioned in the NT only in Acts 20:15, 17, where it is the scene of Paul's farewell to the Ephesian Christian leaders as he went to Jerusalem in the spring of 58 C.E. This great port on the Meander River, a planned city with magnificent public buildings, squares, colonnades, a theater for 15,000, is thirty-two miles as the crow flies south of Ephesus, but the land route requires at least two days (cf. Haenchen, *Acts*, p. 590). That is the only time that Paul is recalled as having visited the city, and then he did so only because he did not want to lose time by visiting Ephesus; moreover, not only Timothy but "the Asians, Tychicus and Trophimus" were then with him too.

However, there is no credible way for him to leave Trophimus behind sick on that occasion (as, e.g., Harrison has attempted), since Acts 21:29 notes that the Asian Jews had seen "Trophimus the Ephesian" in Jerusalem with Paul. Indeed, with these two references in Acts, there are no further NT references to Trophimus until 2 Tim 4:20 has Paul leave him behind sick in Miletus. He had evidently been part of the apostle's entourage on a return to that city, but not necessarily with Erastus. If the arrest took place in Troas, and the journey to Rome via Corinth began from that city, then Trophimus had been left behind previous to the voyage up to Troas.

Paul's leaving him behind reads like a deliberate decision, though one can only surmise why. There must have been a certain urgency in the journey itself. The illness must have been serious enough to make delay unthinkable, yet by no means so serious as to turn departure into abandonment of a dying man.

The mention of him here certainly indicates Paul's solicitude and is at least a hint that Timothy ought to bring information about Trophimus's recovery if not actually pay him a visit en route.

21a. *Do your best to come here before winter.* Literally, "Make every effort to come *(spoudason . . . elthein)* before winter *(pro cheimōnos).*" The verbs were used in 4:9 (see above for references). This sentence should almost certainly be read with the material from verse 9 on, with which it forms parentheses around this whole section. The closing note is perhaps somewhat more patient in tone than the opening, though it also may veil a hint to Timothy not to be late in starting lest his own health and life be endangered and lest Paul himself be no longer on earth when he finally does arrive (Spicq). In any event, read this sentence with what precedes, not with what follows as the verse division disposes one to do. As Titus 3:12 drew to a close with the mention of winter *(paracheimasai),* so now does the correspondence with Timothy.

## V.D. Roman Greetings (4:21b)

*4 21b Eubulus sends along greetings to you, Timothy, as do Pudens and Linus and Claudia and all our brothers.*

## ♦ NOTES

4:21b. *Eubulus sends along greetings to you, Timothy.* Lit. "Eubulus greets you *(aspazetai se).*" See above on 4:19.

*all.* On the textual problem with *pantes,* see J. K. Elliott, *Greek Text,* p. 172.

## ♦ COMMENT

4:21b. *Eubulus sends along greetings to you, Timothy, as do Pudens and Linus and Claudia and all our brothers.* With *aspazetai se,* the note returns to the greeting theme of verse 19, but whereas the previous greetings were those that Timothy was to give to others, in this new paragraph it is the greetings that four persons and the group of which they are part are giving to Timothy, who is accordingly presumed to be known to at least these four (from the time of the first imprisonment in Rome?). The polysyndetic form gives a certain solemnity to the list that begins with the names of three men (Eubulus, Pudens, Linus) and ends with "Claudia and all our brothers *(hoi adelphoi pantes).*" "The brothers" here does not designate the physical relationship (as in 1 Tim 5:1) but the "family" of believers (as in 1 Tim 4:6 and 6:2), the household of the faithful in the place from which the apostle writes. The emphasis, without qualification (contrast Titus 3:15 perhaps), upon the whole congregation *(pantes)* is a reassuring note considering the abandonment noted in 4:10, 16. In the light of 2 Tim 1:17 one would infer that "all our brothers" are the members of the Roman church (again, as is noted above, distinct from Paul's own entourage as well as from other congregations).

The names that are actually adduced at this point, Eubulus, Pudens, Linus, Claudia, never occur elsewhere in the NT, the LXX, or the Ap. Frs. (though the masculine *Klaudios Ephēbos,* one of the Roman delegates to Corinth, is found in *1 Clem.* 65.1; Lightfoot, *AF* 2.187, suggests a link with the former imperial household, i.e. of the Claudian *gens,* whether as slaves, freedmen, or higher officials; cf. *infra* for *CII*). Are these representing the four "orders" (cf. Tertullian) in the Roman church, presbyter-bishop-deacon-widow, and/or are they the "four witnesses" to a Roman will (see *Select Papyri* LCL 1.238, 248, 252, 254)?

*Eubulus* leads off the list, presumably as the one who is most important or has precedence when this note is being written. The name is the only pure Greek one in this list and means "discreet, well-advised, prudent" (LSJ, p. 707) or "(man of) good counsel" or "man of prudence" (cf. the English "Prudence"). It is not in *CII,* nor in Josephus, nor in MM, but Preisigke, *Namenbuch,* p. 110, has several entries. Though the term was an epithet for the pagan gods (Zeus, Dionysus, Pluto; see LSJ *in loc.*) and no form of the common adjective occurs in the LXX, Josephus (has the noun three times), and there is only one nominal use in Philo (*Mig. Abr.* 219; he has the cognate noun ten times), that infrequency does not mean that Jews abhorred the name in this period. However, onomastically speaking, the probabilities lie with a convert from paganism bearing the name Eubulus. Spicq has noted that there is not a trace of the name, however, in even the later apocryphal legends (not in *Acta Timothei*!). It is ironic that the leading name in a list of personalities in the Roman church, purporting to come from the sixties of the first century, has not spawned a single legend nor crept into a single episcopal catalogue.

*Poudēs* (= Latin, *Pudens,* "modest, chaste") (cf. *Pudens, lect. var.* in Theod. Mops.) is, like Claudia, a Latin name and has spawned legends in later Christian literature. The name of this man becomes that of the husband of Claudia *(infra).* The papyri do witness to this name in Greek (*Poudēs/Poudens* in Preisigke, *Namenbuch,* p. 341), but it is not in *CII.* Josephus tells the tale of a Roman soldier named *Poudēs* who perished in single combat with a certain Jonathan in the last days of the great Jewish revolt (*War* 6.172). The name was common enough, however, and even such coincidence as an Aulus Pudens marrying a Claudia Peregrina in 88 C.E. (Martial, *Epigr.* 4.13; 11.53; and Spicq), and the couple named Pudens and Claudia in *CII* 6.15066 *ap.* MM, p. 345, witness to the popularity of the names rather than even a probable identification of the persons in this verse. On *Const. Apost.* 7.46.17-19 see *infra* on Claudia.

The name *Linos* (= Greek, a mythical minstrel, perhaps from *linon,* "flax") is common enough in classical documents (see LSJ *s.v.*), and in popular documents is found at least once (Preisigke, *Namenbuch,* p. 197), not to mention the inscriptions cited by D-C, p. 125 n. 5. Among the Romans it never occurs in Livy, but see Virgil, *Eclogues* 4.56-57; Propertius 2.13a.8; Martial 9.86.4, and many others; see D-C, p. 125 n. 4. It could be the name of a slave or freedman.

According to Irenaeus, *Adversus haereses* 3.3.3, *PG* 7.849 (the Greek of which is found in Eusebius, *Church History* 5.6.1), "The blessed apostles Peter and Paul, then, having founded and built up the church, committed into the hands of *(enecheirisan)* Linus *(Linōi)* the ministry of the episcopate *(tēn tēs episkopēs leitourgian).* Of this Linus Paul makes mention in the epistles (*en tais . . . epistolais* [note that Irenaeus read the pair of letters as if they were a unit here]) to Timothy: to him succeeded Anacletus *(Anegklētos)*" (*Ante-Nicene Fathers* 1.416 and of Eusebius); cf. also Eusebius, *Church History* 3.4.8: "Linus, who is mentioned in the second Epistle to Timothy as present with him [Paul], has already been declared [*Church History* 3.2] to have been the first after Peter to be appointed to the episcopate of the church of Romans *(tēs Rhōmaiōn ekklēsias tēn episkopēn).*" Bevenot, "Clement of Rome," pp. 98-107, has interpreted the Irenaean text as describing a "team episcopate" of Linus and Anacletus (*Anegklēton:* Eusebius, *Church History* 3.15) which was later (after 100 C.E.) ironed out into a regular list. D. F. Wright "Clement," pp. 144-154, has taken issue with Bevenot's interpretation of Irenaeus's text. Perhaps this list in Second Timothy is in Bevenot's favor, indicating that the leadership in the Roman congregation was invested at this date (and in the lifetime of Paul) in a small board, which included Claudia (on which cf. *infra*).

The last name in the list is that of a woman and is indisputably Latin, Claudia (Catullus's Clodia has an alternate form of a praenomen derived from the name of two illustrious Roman *gentes,* one patrician, one plebeian, to whom the emperor Claudius had belonged). The term could derive from the Latin *claudere,* "to close, shut, hem in," or from *claudēre,* "to limp." The latter term had no perfect passive participle. Note that Livy 2.16.5 gives the original name of Appius Claudius as Attius Clausus (cf. Virgil, *Aeneid* 7.706-709: *Clausus . . . Claudia nunc a quo . . . gens,* "Clausus . . . from whom the Claudian tribe is spread"). On the other hand, Meillet, *DELL,* p. 126, proposes *"sans doute Claudius, Clodius"* as from *claudus,* "lame" (Spicq agrees).

Not only was the male a popular name among pagans, free or slave, of the first century, especially in Italy, and the female the most popular of names for women (Lightfoot, *AF* 1.1.79), but of the names here in Second Timothy none is found more often in *CII* for both men and women, in both Latin and Greek (thus 461, Via Portuensis [cf. p. 37]; 556 [cf. p. 44 in connection with this] and 561, both from the Naples area; and in Greek, 37, 130 [?], 319 [all from Roman area], 538 [Porto, but with Roman affinities], 694 [the Stobi synagogue], as well as the *Kla[u]dia Prima* of 366 [Via Portuensis]).

Thus this lady, certainly Christian, could be of Jewish or pagan origin; slave or free; single, married (and husband not mentioned or the wife of the preceding Linus or Pudens or Eubulus), or a widow (note that Hermas, *Vis.* 2.4.3, couples the name of Clement with an otherwise unknown *Graptē,* who has some care over widows and orphans). All of these possibilities tantalized the writers of early Christian romances and later exegetes. In *Const. Apost.* 7.46.6 (F. X. Funk, *Constitutiones,* p. 452), the list of the first bishops in the great sees has *tēs de Rhōmaiōn ekklēsias Linos men ho Klaudias prōtos hypo Paulou . . . kecheirotonētai,* "of the Church of Rome, Linus the son of Claudia was the first, ordained by Paul." Here Claudia is apparently the mother of Linus (Lightfoot, *AF* 1.1.76 n. 2); some more recent interpreters have made her the husband of Pudens (cf. the references above and see the critique of Lightfoot, 1.1.76-79).

## VI. FINAL PRAYERS (4:22)

*4 [22]The Lord be with your spirit, Timothy. Grace be with you all.*

### ♦ NOTES

4:22. *The Lord be with your spirit, Timothy. Grace be with you all.* Lit. "The Lord *(ho kyrios)* [be/is] with your spirit (*meta tou pneumatos sou* [note the sg.]). Grace *(hē charis)* [is/be] with you (*meth' hymōn* [note the pl.])." On the formal structure of the closing benediction see Mullins, "Bendiction," pp. 59-64. In the NT the form of a closing blessing regularly consists of three parts: the designation of what is prayed for; the divine source of such a blessing; and the recipient. The closing blessings of the PE contain the first of these, using *hē charis,* and the last, employing the plural address in the phrase *meth' humōn.* Although the second component, the divine source, is never specified in the PE's closing blessings, God the Father and Christ Jesus our savior (or our Lord) are always referred to in the opening blessings of these letters as the source of the blessings being prayed for. The mention of "grace" here is typical of the Pauline closing;

except for Hebrews, the other NT letters opt for *eirēnē,* "peace" (if they have anything at all), rather than *charis* in their concluding blessings.

The Ap. Frs. do not use this briefest of blessings to conclude their letters, though one might compare Ign. *Smyrn.* 13.2, *errōsthe en chariti theou,* "Farewell in the grace of God," and Ign. *Pol.* 8.2, who says of Polycarp and his messenger, "Grace will be with him through all and Polycarp too *(estai* [note future indicative] *hē charis met' autou . . .).*" One of the copyists of *Mart. Pol.* 22.2 closes with *hē charis meta pantōn.*

For a brief survey of the longer closing blessings see W. Grundmann, *TDNT* 7.778. He is also in agreement with Unnik's essay cited below and notes with him how these blessings and the concepts they implied spawned the *Dominus vobiscum — et cum spiritu tuo* dialogue that introduced the eucharistic prayer of the Roman liturgy as early as 200 C.E. (Unnik, *Sparsa,* pp. 380-381).

As for reading *meta sou,* "with you" (sg.), as this letter concludes, in place of *meth' hymōn,* "with you" (pl.), see J. K. Elliott, *Greek Text,* p. 172, who prefers to follow many minuscules and ancient versions in the second person singular, but certainly B. Metzger's explanation (*TCGNT,* p. 651) carries the day for the text as it stands in S*. A. C. G. 33. 81. 1881.

See B. Metzger, *TCGNT,* pp. 651-652, for the subscriptions. Note also the Western reading (D*. L. it) for the conclusion of this letter: *errōs'* (as in secular Hellenistic correspondence) *en eirēnēi* (the Jewish *šalōm*). Though the term *rhōnnymai,* "Farewell," is not found in the NT epistolary, it does occur without the additional phrase noted here at the end of the letter cited in Acts 15:29 and as a variant concluding the dispatch cited in Acts 23:30.

## ♦ COMMENT

4:22. *The Lord be with your spirit, Timothy. Grace be with you all.* The final sentences of this correspondence are a pair of telegraphic blessings, the former for Timothy, the latter for the church in whose midst he is. The "closing type" as well as the opening type have three fundamental elements: "*wish, divine source,* and *recipient*" with "one optional element . . . *the addressee*" (Mullins, "Benediction," p. 60). The LXX already arranges these elements in different orders, apparently for stylistic reasons, and the order here in 2 Tim 4:22, "divine source/wish/recipient," is the first of three types that Mullins has isolated in the LXX, though the verb for the wish is not explicit here in the PE. With Mullins, one notes that it is unnecessary to go further than the LXX as a source for the language and the form of these epistolary blessings. Of course that same LXX was read in the synagogue and furnished the terminology and model for blessings there too. Since these letters were read "in service," there is no call for surprise at the liturgical style of their closing.

"The Lord" is, as usual in the PE, the risen Jesus (see B. Metzger, *TCGNT,* p. 650, on the reading). Since the verb is not expressed in either of these sentences, one can take the blessings either as prophetic declarations, with all the certainty that that implies, or as subjunctive (or even optative) wishes that flow from the apostle's intercession for his co-worker and this church in which he labors. Unnik, *Sparsa,* pp. 270-305, has suggested (pp. 272-273, 281, 283-284, 292) that the indicative is to be preferred here, but a case still could be made for the subjunctive/optative (cf. the examples on p. 283).

What does it mean, in the biblical tradition, to declare or pray that the Lord is/may be with someone (cf. Unnik, *Sparsa,* pp. 376-380)? It is an assurance or prayer that a divine dynamic has entered or will enter a person's heart and visible life, a dynamic that has several aspects (protection, alliance, guidance to success, reassurance, encouragement, demanding obedience — pp. 376-377). Usually it is individuals who are so assured, and usually they are *"specially endowed with the Spirit of God"* (p. 382; italics by Unnik); they are pneumatics, charismatics, with a special work or task. Unnik, p. 381, has noted that the Pauline parallel phrases "the grace of our Lord Jesus Christ (be/is) with your [pl.] spirit" (Gal 6:18; in Phil 4:23 and Philem 25 without *our*) and simply "The grace of our Lord Jesus Christ is with you all" (Rom 16:24, cf. 20; 1 Cor 16:3; 2 Cor 13:13; etc.) have sometimes been taken to mean that *pneuma* was simply equivalent to the personal pronoun (thus, e.g., Schweizer, *TDNT* 6.435). But that is not the case. The *pneuma* stresses that these are believers endowed with the gift of the Spirit. Accordingly, it is possible that the blessing here for Timothy emphasizes that special charism by which he shared in the Pauline ministry and the apostolic witness to the risen Lord (cf. 2 Tim 1:6-7 and 1 Tim 4:14), a task for which he needed reassurance, courage, and protection.

W. Grundmann, *TDNT* 7.777-778, has noted that these Pauline blessing formulae (which resemble the Solomonic prayer formula associated with dedicating the temple = LXX 3 Kgdms 8:27) are still rather fluid in the epistolary, though *meta* with the genitive is invariable. The Lord, or God, or grace is to be with the recipients of the letters. "In place of God we find his gift, especially his grace. This means God himself is present in his gift. In his *gift* he gives himself" (p. 778).

In the Ap. Frs. the formula of final blessing is as little fixed as in the NT. *First* and *Second Clement* do not mention the Spirit in closing. Ign. *Magn.* 15.1 writes, "Farewell in godly concord and may you possess *(ktēmenoi)* a spirit that knows no division *(adiakriton pneuma),* for this is *(hos estin)* Jesus Christ"; his other closing references to the Spirit (*Trall.* 13.3; *Phld.* 11.2; *Smyrn.* 13.2) are even more distant. It is *Barn.* 21.9 who closes with the most notable parallel to

2 Tim 4:22, when he writes, *ho kyrios tēs doxēs kai pasēs charitos meta tou pneumatos hymōn,* "The Lord of glory and of all grace be with your spirit."

Thus in this final prayer of 2 Tim 4:22 the apostle intercedes with the risen Jesus to energize and support that gift of the Spirit which God has bestowed on Timothy. This reference to the Spirit ought not to be dismissed too quickly because it is in a formula. The formula was as yet by no means set, much less stereotyped, and the reference to the Spirit is really quite indistinguishable from that in the other Pauline blessings cited above.

The final prayer here occurred in identical form (and with the same textual problem) in 1 Tim 6:21 and in Titus 3:15 with the addition of *pantōn.* Whereas "the Lord" is to be with Timothy in his ministry, here *hē charis,* "grace," is to be with those ("you" pl.) who listen to this letter.

# Index of Modern Names

# Index of Scripture References

## 1 Corinthians

## Colossians



## 1 Thessalonians

## 2 Timothy

**Titus**

# Index of Ancient Sources

PSEUDEPIGRAPHA

## EARLY CHRISTIAN

GRECO-ROMAN